The Supreme Court in American Society

Equal Justice Under law

Edited with an introduction by

Kermit L. Hall

North Carolina State University

GARLAND PUBLISHING, INC.

A MEMBER OF THE TAYLOR & FRANCIS GROUP

New York & London

Published in 2001 by
Garland Publishing, Inc.
29 West 35th Street
New York, NY 10001

Published in Great Britain by
Garland Publishing, Inc.
11 New Fetter Lane
London EC4 4EE

Garland is an imprint of the Taylor & Francis Group

10 9 8 7 6 5 4 3 2 1

The Library of Congress Cataloging-in-Publication Data

The Supreme Court in American Society : equal justice under law / edited with an introduction by Kermit L. Hall.
p. cm.
ISBN 0-8153-3757-4 (alk. paper)
1. Constitutional law—United States. 2. Constitutional history—United States. 3. United States. Supreme Court—History. I. Hall, Kermit.

KF4550.
S84 2000
347.73'262—dc21 00-062241

Printed on acid-free, 250-year-life paper
Manufactured in the United States of America

Contents

Introduction

The inscription carved above the entrance to the Supreme Court of the United States is elegant in its brevity and powerful in its directness: "Equal Justice Under Law." No other words have been more regularly connected to the work of the nation's — indeed, one of he world's — most important judicial tribunal. Because the Court is the highest tribunal for all cases and controversies arising under the Constitution, laws, and treaties of the United States, it functions as the pre-eminent guardian and interpreter of the nation's basic law. There was nothing, of course, in the early history of the Court that guaranteed that it would do just that. The justices in their first decade of operation disposed of only a handful of cases, yet from the outset they understood that for the rule of law to succeed the power of the Court had to expand. During the subsequent two centuries the Court's influence mushroomed; it became not only the authoritative interpreter of the Constitution but the most important institution in defining separation of powers, federalism, and the rule of law, concepts at the heart of the American constitutional order.

Chief Justice Charles Evans Hughes once declared that the Court is "distinctly American in concept and function." Few other courts in the world have the same scope of power to interpret their national constitutions; none has done so for anything approaching the more than two centuries the Supreme Court has been hearing and deciding cases. During its history, moreover, the story of the Court has been more than the sum of either the cases it has decided or the justices that have decided them. Its story has been that of the country as a whole, in war and peace, in prosperity and depression, in harmony and discord. As Alexis de Tocqueville observed in *Democracy in America*, "I am unaware that any nation on the globe has hitherto organized a judicial power in the same manner as the Americans. . . . A more imposing judicial power was never constituted by any people." That power, as Tocqueville well understood, has given the justices a unique role in American life, one that combines elements of law and politics. "Scarcely any political question," Tocqueville wrote, "arises in the United States that is not revolved, sooner or later, into a judicial question."

Through the decisions of the Supreme Court, law has become a complement to political discourse. We appropriately think of the high court as a legal institution, but it is, in truth, a hybrid in which economics, cultural and social values, and political interests converge to produce what we call our constitutional law. The Court, as a legal entity, speaks through the law but its decisions are shaped by and at the same time shape the social order of which it is part. All of which is to say that, in the end, the high court is a human institution, a place where justices make decisions by applying legal precedent, logic, and a respect for the Constitution as informed by the principal of "Equal Justice Under Law." That the Court has at times, such as the struggle over slavery in the 1850s, not fully grasped all of the implications of those words does not, in the end, diminish the importance of the Court. Instead, it reminds us that no other institution in American life takes as its goal such a lofty aspiration. Given the assumptions of our constitutional system, that there is something like justice and freedom for all, the Court's operation is unthinkable without having the concept of the rule of law embedded in it.

The essays collected in this volume represent some of the best writing done about the history, political dynamics, and legal development of the Supreme Court. They remind us that interest in the Court as not just a legal but a political and cultural entity has been prodigious. No other court has attracted anything approaching the scholarly attention showered on the so-called "Marble Palace" in Washington, D.C. Biographers, such as Bernard Schwartz and G. Edward White, remind us that talent on the high bench has made a difference in the growth of judicial power and in adjusting the Constitution to fit emerging social realities. The historian William E. Leuchtenburg notes the powerful connection among the Great Depression, changing ideas about judicial review and judicial power, and the judicial selection process in assessing President Franklin D. Roosevelt's unsuccessful attempt to remake the high court in his image. At the same time, political scientists Henry J. Abraham and Paul J. Weber explain that the path to the bench has often been a difficult and unpredictable one, simply because fate and politics invariably mix in unusual ways.

Another group of essays deals with the social controversies that have reached the Court and the ways in which the justices attempted to deal with them and the results of their so doing. John Hart Ely analyzes the controversial abortion case of *Roe* v. *Wade* (1973); Randall Kennedy provocatively assesses the ways in which the justices have treated the death penalty; Michael McConnell reminds us the ways in which historical understandings about religion have shaped the Court's attitudes toward its place in the constitutional order; Robert C. Post offers a keen insight into the ways in which the justices have attempted to deal with sexual harassment, racism, and speech, among the most controversial matters to reach the high bench; and Judge J. Harvie Wilkinson argues that equal protection of the law does not translate into guaranteed social equality through the Constitution.

Yet another group of essays assess the particularly crucial role played by the justices in adjusting American democracy to the relentless pace of social and economic change. Michael Les Benedict, Loren P. Beth, and John R. Schmidhauser, for example, provide critical insight into the impact of the high court's treatment of federalism and the scope of civil rights and civil liberties. Jesse Choper, Archibald Cox, Robert Dahl, Ralph Lerner, Alpheus T. Mason, and Christopher Wolfe take aim at this matter in other ways. They seek to explain the ways in which the exercise of judicial power through an unelected Supreme Court contributes to the vitality of a popularly based form of representative democracy. The themes of federalism, civil liberties and civil rights, and the role of the justices as teachers through their opinions are particularly well represented in this collection of materials.

No single collection of essays can cover the work of the high court conclusively. The institution has too much historical depth, too much constitutional and political currency, and too much impact on American life to be neatly summarized between the covers of a single volume. Still, the essays in this volume serve as a powerful reminder of how important the Court has been in American life, how central a role it has played in interpreting the rule of law against a constantly evolving social order, and how much it has mirrored the controversies, debates, and political struggles of American history. The essays also generally echo the theme that the power of the Court is latent; it must be tapped by skillful lawyers capable of turning social controversies into meaningful constitutional disputes.

Finally, these essays remind us that substantial differences continue to exist, as they have since the beginning of the nation, about how to interpret the original constitutional debates in the summer of 1787 in Philadelphia and the subsequent discussions surrounding the adoption of the Bill of Rights, the Civil War amendments, and Progressive-era constitutional reforms. Since its inception, the question has always been whether the Court, in view of the changing understandings among Americans about equality and liberty, has an obligation to ensure that its decisions resonate with yesterday, today, tomorrow, or all three. By and large, these essays conclude that the justices, quite apart from issues of political theory, are more often than not put in the position of having to address controversial political and social issues that the political branches find too troubling. In that context, Tocqueville's insight that "[s]carcely any political question arises in the United States that is not revolved, sooner or later, into a judicial question," continues to echo down the halls of history.

The Supreme Court
In American Society

"A bench happily filled:" Some historical reflections on the

Politics and "balancing representation" may play a major role in the selection of Supreme Court justices, but the quality of those appointed has been consistently high.

A total of only 102 individuals have served to date on the Supreme Court of the United States, evincing an average longevity exceeded only by symphony orchestra conductors. I cannot speak to the latter, but what of the former's quantifiable characteristics?[1] The 101 men and the one woman were nominated by 35 presidents, with three—W. H. Harrison, Taylor, and Carter—having no opportunity to choose anyone at all, and one, Andrew Johnson, seeing his efforts frustrated by a hostile Senate. Not counting a mere refusal to act on nominations—of which there were several—that constitutional partner in the appointment process has so far formally rejected 26 presidential nominations to the Court, all but four of these (namely, lower federal court judges Parker, Haynsworth, and Carswell, and the aborted promotion of Justice Fortas to Chief Justice) coming in the nineteenth century.

The total rejection figure comprises a remarkable but contemporary unthinkable 23 per cent! Why were so many rejected by the Senate? Among the reasons, seven seem to be most compelling:

- Opposition to the nominating President, not necessarily the nominee—e.g., President John Quincy Adams' nomination of sometime United States Senator from Kentucky, John J. Crittenden, in 1828.
- The nominee's involvement with a visible or contentious issue of public policy—e.g., President George Washington's nomination of South Carolina's then Chief Justice, John Rutledge, as Chief Justice of the United States in 1795, because of the outspoken nominee's vigorous opposition to the Jay Treaty of 1794.
- Senatorial opposition to the record of the incumbent Court which the nominee seemed to support—e.g., President Ulysses S. Grant's selection of his own Attorney General, Ebenezer R. Hoar, in 1870.
- Senatorial courtesy, closely linked to the presumed consultative nominating process—e.g., President Grover Cleveland's choices of William B. Hornblower and Wheeler S. Peck-

This article was adapted from the "Annual Lecture" presented to The Supreme Court Historical Society on April 30, 1982 in the restored Supreme Court Chamber in the U.S. Capitol.

1. The following statistical information is taken from Abraham, JUSTICES AND PRESIDENTS: A POLITICAL HISTORY OF APPOINTMENTS TO THE SUPREME COURT, esp. Chs. 2 and 3 (New York: Oxford University Press, 1974 and Penguin Press, 1975).

Supreme Court appointment process

by Henry Abraham

ham in 1893 and 1894, respectively, both ardently opposed by their fellow New Yorker, Democratic Senator David B. Hill.

• A perceived "political unreliability" of the nominee—e.g., another unsuccessful Grant nomination, this one of his one-time Attorney General Caleb Cushing, to the Chief Justiceship in 1874.

• An alleged lack of qualification or limited ability on the nominee's part—e.g., President James Madison's selection of Connecticut attorney and ex-United States Collector of Customs, Alexander Wolcott, in 1811.

• Powerful opposition to an otherwise patently qualified nominee by special issue interest or pressure groups—e.g., President Herbert Hoover's attempted promotion of United States District Court Judge John R. Parker of North Carolina in 1930.

Not at all infrequently, more than one of these seven reasons has combined to bring about an individual's rejection. The unenviable record of having more nominees rejected than any other President (five) is held by John Tyler.

The successful appointees

The 102 successful lawyer-appointees have come from 10 major professional sub-groups, with 22 each from three of these, i.e., the lower federal judiciary, the state judiciary, and from diverse posts in the federal executive/administrative branch. Upon ascending to the high bench they resided in 31 different states, headed by 15 from New York, nine from Ohio, eight from Massachusetts, and seven from Virginia; 10 states have sent one; 19 none at all. The latter fact of political life prompted Republican Senator William ("Wild Bill") Langer of North Dakota, then a senior member of the Senate's Committee on the Judiciary, to commence in 1953 a campaign of opposition to any and all presidential nominees to the Court until his home state received a Supreme Court nomination. He went to his grave in 1959, his wish still unrealized—as it is to this day.

The acknowledged religious preferences of the 102 individual jurists fall into 12 different groups, the only ones in "double-digit-figures" being 27 Episcopalians, 25 avowedly unspecified Protestants, and 17 Presbyterians; there have been six Roman Catholics, five Jews, and the balance have been specified other Protestant adherents. Five professed political party designations characterize the successful nominees, including one Whig, one Independent, 12 Federalists, 40 Republicans, and 48 Democrats—hence, it is difficult to categorize an overwhelming partisan flavor to the bench.

Such a flavor unmistakably, however, has informed the selection of nominees in terms of their political affiliation in concord with that of the nominating president: the lowest partisan percentage to date—and now necessarily counting *all* federal judges—having been earned by President Ford (81.2 per cent Republican), the highest by President Washington (100 per cent Federalist). The lowest partisan-correlation nomination percentage in this century for all federal judges is still President Ford's aforementioned 81.2 (President Taft's 82.2 being a close second), the highest that by the sole Ph.D. in political science so far to occupy the White House, Woodrow Wilson, who amassed a near perfect 98.6 per cent score of Democratic appointees. More or less tied for the second highest correlative slot are presidents Carter and Harding, with 97.8 Democratic and 97.7 Republican identifications, respectively.

Indubitably the profile and statistics just cited point to a broad-gauged commitment to a "representative" philosophy for judicial appointments. Whether that is wise may be put aside for the moment in favor of an examination of the intention of the Founding Fathers on that always so lively controversial issue. The conclusion is as crystal clear as it is inevitable that "representativeness" was not even considered, let alone advocated. Merit was the sole criterion on the mind of the delegates, "representativeness" being reserved to the legislature.

Methodology, not qualifications

Monday, May 14, 1787, was the date agreed upon for the opening of the Federal Constitutional Convention in the Old Independence Hall, called the State House, down on Fifth and Chestnut Streets in Philadelphia. But since only two states—Virginia and Pennsylvania—were represented on that historic day, the Convention was compelled to adjourn for lack of a quorum. This procedure continued daily, until Friday, May 25, at last saw the requisite majority of the 13 constituent states in their seats. Some five months later, on Tuesday, September 17, 1787, the Convention adjourned, having signed the historic document, the nascent Constitution of the United States, on the preceding day, highlighted by Dr. Franklin's magnificent closing address to the assemblage (which was read for him by his fellow-Pennsylvanian, James Wilson). As the most authoritative accounts, records, and interpretations of the events of that historic period demonstrate reliably—for example, James Madison's *Notes of Debates in the Federal Convention of 1787*[2]; *The Federalist*[3]; Charles Warren's *The Making of the Constitution*[4]; and Joseph P. Harris' *The Advice and Consent of the Senate*[5]—while the question of the methodology to be employed for judicial appointments was subjected to intensive floor debate during 12 days in June, July, August and September, *criteria* for such appointments were neither debated nor did they appear to loom as a matter of either significance or puzzlement.

Those few delegates who vocalized the issue of *criteria* at all did so by assuming *viva voce* and *sub silentio* that *merit*, as opposed to favoritism, should, and indeed would, govern naturally. The central issue *cum* controversy concerned the degree of power to be vested in the executive and/or the degree of legislative participation. The provision finally agreed upon as a result of debates on September 6, 7 and 15, represented a compromise between those who, like Benjamin Franklin, James Madison, and John Rutledge, feared "monarchical" tendencies in strong solo executive prerogatives on the issue and called for a potent legislative role; and those who, like James Wilson, Alexander Hamilton, and Gouverneur Morris favored broadly independent executive appointive powers. It was the

2. Madison, NOTES OF DEBATES IN THE FEDERAL CONVENTION OF 1787; Introduction by Adrienne Koch (Athens, Ohio: Ohio University Press, 1966).

3. Lodge (ed.), THE FEDERALIST (New York: G. P. Putnam's Sons, 1888).

4. Warren, THE MAKING OF THE CONSTITUTION (Boston: Little, Brown and Company, 1937).

5. Harris, THE ADVICE AND CONSENT OF THE SENATE (Berkeley and Los Angeles: University of California Press, 1953).

latter group that did most of the compromising, resulting in the largely James Madison-fashioned ultimate adoption of Article II, Section 2, as we know that provision today.[6]

If it may be validly considered as having been raised at all, the issue of judicial qualifications was addressed, however briefly, on June 5 by Doctor Franklin in pointing to the Scottish mode of appointment "in which the nomination proceeded from the lawyers, who always selected the ablest of the profession in order to get rid of him, and share his practice among themselves."[7] If any concern about qualifications was subsequently expressed by delegates, it came all but inevitably in connection with the controversy over the role of the participatory political branch, ultimately the agreed-upon Senatorial one, about which James Madison, for one, notwithstanding his support of the legislative input, raised questions of "partiality." Delegates simply assumed, perhaps a mite naively, albeit quite understandably, that those selected as federal jurists would be chosen on the basis of merit. Period.

It is thus clear—with convenient 20/20 hindsight—that the Founding Fathers did not foresee the role political parties would soon come to play in the appointment process. Only John Adams among the notable contemporary statesmen—and he, of course, was not a member of the Constitutional Convention—visualized clearly the future rise of political parties and, as Harris put it well, "that partisan considerations rather than the fitness of nominees would often be the controlling consideration of the Senate in passing on nominations."[8]

Merit over politics

Little attention was given to the matter of judicial appointments in the debates surrounding the ensuing state ratifying conventions. It was assumed as a matter of course that merit would govern. Alexander Hamilton did address the appointment power in *The Federalist, Nos. 66, 72, 76,* and 77, which render patently evident that even that supreme political cognoscenti verily championed merit. Thus, in his *No. 66* he expressed full confidence that the Senate, whatever its stance on a particular nominee might be, would be guided by a candidate's *merit.*[9] In his famed *No. 76*, in which he so trenchantly and approbatively elucidated the judicial function, he lauded the Senate's putative role as "an excellent check upon a spirit of favoritism in the President... [one that] would tend greatly to prevent the appointment of unfit characters from State prejudice, from family connection, from personal attachment, or from a view of popularity"[10]

The Founding Fathers assumed that merit would govern judicial appointments.

And his *No. 77* assumed without self-doubt—and, of course, quite erroneously—that individual senators would not exert influence on presidential nominations. For he, too, quite unlike Adams, failed to foresee the influence that political parties would exert on appointments; the leverage they would provide thereby to an assertive chief executive; and the prominent role senators would soon play in dictating nominations.[11] In sum, and notwithstanding Hamilton's interest and concerns, the debates in the state constitutional conventions paid but passing heed, if any, to the appointive arrangements, in general, and judicial ones, in particular. Engaged by issues of far more moment to them in their crucial decision whether or not to ratify the handiwork of the Founding

6. Madison, *supra* n. 2, at 67-68; 112-113; 314-317; 343-46; 517; 527; 575.
7. *Id.*, at 67-68.
8. Harris, *supra* n. 5, at 28-30; 34.
9. The Federalist, supra n. 3, at 416-17.
10. *Id.*, at 474-75.
11. *Id.*, at 476-80.

Fathers, they assumed that those appointed to the bench would be qualified. Merit was assumed; "representativeness" did not even surface as an academic question.

Representativeness as an issue

Yet if it was not an issue then, it has assuredly become one—and increasingly so in modern mold. Indeed, it has become a demonstrable fact of the life of government and politics that so-called "equitable considerations" in the selection and nominations to the bench are not only omnipresent, but arguably omnipotent, in the decisional processes leading to selection, nomination, and appointment. And whereas initially these commitments were perhaps confined largely to the components of political persuasion and geography, the passing parade of the century in which we live has witnessed the insistent adoption and adaption of such additional expectations and requirements as contemporarily inform the "representation" of race, gender, religion, and perhaps even age. Whatever the Framer's ascertainable intentions may have been, the notion of the entitlement to a "peer model" has become all but pervasive in judicial staffing today.

If, as the great Holmes insisted so warmly, a page of history is truly worth more than a volume of logic, one might have little difficulty in arriving at history's verdict on the conundrum of "representativeness" in the appointment process. The past, however, is prologue as well as history. It may thus be argued with some cogency that the "equitable components enumerated above operate currently in a setting of our democratic polity that is naturally quite at variance with that of the late eighteenth century—in moral, in philosophical, and in political terms. It is a setting that would be demonstrably puzzling or foreign to the Founding Fathers, whose fledgling Republic enjoyed a degree of homogeneity never again to be equalled in this land's ensuing history. Nonetheless, even granting the imperatives of the polity's dramatic transformation, one may well still pose the troubling question that underlies these painful ruminations: Is the nation, is the citizenry, served better, served more appropriately, if "representativeness" is rendered a prolegomenum for judicial selection, nomination, and appointment?

The attempted answer has evoked lively, often bitter, debate for close to half-a-century now, reaching a crescendo during the past generation. [My 91-year old friend, Dumas Malone, tells me that Mr. Jefferson's definition of "generation" encompassed 20 years. Needless to say that I would never challenge my old teacher—and assuredly not on matters Jeffersonian!] I suspect that the verdict is in: if something can be "more or less" *res judicata*, it is obvious that the political branches have embraced "representativeness." That the pages of history demonstrate beyond any shadow of a doubt that the Founding Fathers did not ponder the issue does not necessarily determine its wisdom or desirability. But it is on those frontiers that an opinion opting for the sole criterion of *merit* as *the* irreducible imperative basic threshold requirement may be respectfully submitted, joined to the plea *cum* conviction that any "plus" considerations in behalf of "representativeness" must be wholly dependent upon the demonstrable presence of merit at the threshold.

The concept of merit

The concept, the phenomenon, of merit unfortunately defies universal definition; it is neither axiom nor theorem. It may even lie entirely in the eye and mind of the beholder—but it need not do so. It is possible to suggest a merit model, and I should like to suggest one—eschewing any claim to originality. A sextet, the model comprises the following self-evident components (in no particular order of significance):

One: demonstrated judicial temperament.
Two: professional expertise and competence.
Three: absolute personal as well as professional integrity.
Four: an able, agile, lucid mind.
Five: appropriate professional educational background or training.
Six: the ability to communicate clearly, both orally and in writing, especially the latter.

Not only are these attainable components, but the history of our Supreme Court has demonstrated their presence amply. If the Holmesian tongue-in-cheek aphorism that the job of a jurist requires a "combination of

The notion of entitlement to a "peer model" has become all but pervasive in judicial selection.

Justinian, Jesus Christ, and John Marshall"[12] may not always have been attainable—it is apposite to note that with one possible exception even that trio may not have been perfect! If political party affiliation has almost always played a role—well, there are but nine positions on the highest bench, and there are unquestionably just as many qualified Republicans as there are qualified Democrats, and as many qualified Democrats as there are qualified Republicans. Nor is there any gainsaying a nominator's resolve to select a nominee with whom he is ideologically and jurisprudentially comfortable. You would, and I would, act similarly, always assuming the presence of threshold merit.

At any rate, as president after president has found out, without any particular degree of amusement, if there is anything certain about his nominees' on-bench performance in jurisprudential terms, it is that it is hardly predictable with accuracy, let alone certainty—which, to a very considerable degree, is a comforting fact of the judicial process. "You shoot an arrow into a far-distant future," wrote Alexander M. Bickel not long before his untimely death, "when you appoint a justice and not the man himself can tell you what he will think about some of the problems he will face."[13]

That is, of course, why such wise politicans as that All-American boy President Theodore Roosevelt, in a famed exchange with Connecticut's United States Senator Henry Cabot Lodge regarding the potential candidacy of Democrat Horace H. Lurton in 1906, wrote his objecting fellow-Republican that "the nominal politics of the man has nothing to do with his actions on the bench. His *real* politics are all important..." And T.R. lauded Lurton's position on sundry policies "in which you and I believe."[14] Lodge concurred in substance, but replied that he saw no reason "why Republicans cannot be found who hold these opinions as well as Democrats."[15] And he urged the appointment of the incumbent Attorney General, William H. Moody, whom T. R. then sent to the Court.

Interestingly, but three years later Lurton was appointed by Roosevelt's successor, William Howard Taft—and precisely because of those "real politics" with which Taft was comfortable. Incidentally, it was Taft, our only president to date who would also serve as Chief Justice of the United States, who appointed the largest number of "other Party" members—three of his six—to the Supreme Court. How Chief Justice Taft loved his post—infinitely more so than being president! He regarded his chief justiceship as "...next to my wife and children... the nearest thing to my heart in life."[16] When President Harding nominated him in 1921, Taft exulted: "I love judges and I love courts. They are my ideals on earth of what we shall meet afterward in Heaven under a just God."[17] When fatal illness truncated his career nine years later, he formally resigned in tears on February 3, 1930. On his bedside table lay a touching message from his eight colleagues: "We call you Chief Justice still, for we cannot quickly give up the title by which we have known you for all these later years and which you have made so dear to us."[18]

Yet the moving finger of time wrote rapidly: within five hours of Taft's resignation, President Hoover would nominate—with Taft's advance blessings—another giant to

12. As quoted by Judge Irving R. Kaufman, *Charting a Judicial Pedigree*, The New York Times, January 24, 1981, p. 23.
13. Time Magazine, May 23, 1969, p. 24.
14. Abraham, *supra* n. 1, at 276, fn. 7.
15. *Id.*, at 229.
16. *Id.*, at 174.
17. *Id.*, at 175.
18. *Id.*, at 187.

the center chair: ex-Associate Justice of the Supreme Court, ex-Governor of New York, one time (and almost successful) candidate for the presidency, and ex-Secretary of State, Charles Evans Hughes. Yet, notwithstanding the selectee's indubitably outstanding qualifications for the post, 26 senators voted against his confirmation and 18 abstained—whereas but four had cast "nay" votes against his predecessor. Like his predecessor, he would grace the institution that Madison had so devoutly prayed to become "happily filled."

Reasons for selection

While there has been a trickle-increase in biographical studies of Supreme Court Justices, my recent involvement in researching just what has been done must render the regrettable judgment of "not nearly enough." There are many good reasons that account for that fact, among them the delicate and difficult problem of the existence and availability of the papers of justices, plus the dearth of biographical craftsmen of the stature of Alpheus Thomas Mason. Yet there are enough data to permit an annotated catalogue of the major ascertainable decisional reasons or motivations for the presidential selection of members of the bench. In rendering such judgments, one must acknowledge concurrently that only the president really knows why he either selected a nominee to the Court or gave the nod to others, in effect, to select for him.

History does demonstrate, however, that an identifiable quartet of such reasons or motivations has governed the selection process—a quartet that, were I a quantifyer or "behavioralist," might well lend itself to at least a measure of statistical proof. The quartet of criteria are: (1) objective merit; (2) personal and political friendship; (3) balancing "representation" on the Court; and (4) "real" political and ideological compatibility. Obviously, more than one of these factors was present in most of the nominations and in some all four were. Yet it is not impossible to point to one as the overriding one. My necessarily few examples endeavor to do so while minding the Jeffersonian-Malonian generational definition by doubling it and thus utilizing only illustrations that inform appointments more than 40 years ago—in any event, none made by any president after the one who had more opportunities than any other save George Washington, namely Franklin Delano Roosevelt.

1. Objective merit

A classic example of presidential selection based purely on the first category, objective merit, *qua* merit, is that of Democrat Benjamin Nathan Cardozo by Republican Herbert Hoover to succeed Justice Holmes early in 1932. The two were neither personal nor professional friends: they were hardly, not even arguably, politically or ideologically compatible; and there was no question of "balancing representation." If anything, as Hoover would soon make clear, his reluctance to appoint the long-time, great New York appellate jurist was at least partly due to the fact that two other distinguished New Yorkers already were ornaments of the bench, namely Justices Stone and Hughes, and Cardozo's religious faith—he was a Sephardic Jew—was "represented" by Justice Brandeis. Yet if ever a nomination was forced upon a president by all but unanimous public and private acclaim, this was it.

On January 15, 1932, Oliver Wendell Holmes, Jr., now almost 91 but still alert and cheerful, had bowed to old age and precarious health and resigned. More than three decades of an incredibly productive and towering judicial career thus came to an end. How to replace the "judicial philosopher of the age"? Hoover, striking out on his own, let it be known that he would like to see a "non-controversial western Republican" as the Old Yankee's successor. But almost at once the chairman of the Senate's Judiciary Committee, George W. Norris, made it plain to the President that he and his fellow committeemen, largely Democrats and Progressive Republicans, would insist on a judicial liberal in the Holmes mold.

Others were rather more specific: the entire faculty of the Law School of the University of Chicago urged Hoover to nominate Benjamin Nathan Cardozo, Chief Judge of the New York Court of Appeals—a man widely regarded as one of America's most brilliant jurists, one who might already have been on

PHOTO: SUPREME COURT HISTORICAL SOCIETY
ENGRAVING: U.S. BUREAU OF THE MINT

President Herbert Hoover's appointment of Benjamin Cardozo to the Supreme Court was based solely on merit.

the U.S. Supreme Court had it not been for Chief Justice Taft's sustained opposition to him during the 1920s. The deans of the schools of law of Harvard, Yale, and Columbia universities joined in a similar strongly worded plea. Labor as well as business leaders, liberals as well as conservatives, advocates of judicial self-restraint as well as judicial activists, all participated in a uniquely unified appeal on behalf of a candidate to the Court—so strong an impression had Cardozo made, so splendid a record had he achieved during his 18 years as associate judge and chief judge on New York's highest tribunal, then probably the country's busiest and most distinguished appellate state court.

The president could hardly have been unaware of the clamor for Cardozo's nomination! The now 62-year-old bachelor had not only made his mark as a jurist, but his stylistically beautiful and scholarly publications, such as the still-seminal *The Nature of the Judicial Process*,[19] had won him universal praise. His lucid, cogent opinions, his realistic approach to law and democratic society, his love of his land and its Constitution stamped him as Holmes' logical successor. But Hoover continued to demur; he really did not want to appoint a man, no matter how superbly and uniquely qualified he might be, from a state that already had two eminent such "representatives" whom, incidentally, he had sent there himself—and whose religion would assuredly cause Justice McReynolds to act up again (it did). No, Herbert Hoover would look elsewhere, even though Justice Stone had told him he would be willing to resign from the Court so that the nation might have Cardozo.[20]

Now, however, the powerful chairman of the Senate Foreign Relations Committee, Republican William E. Borah of Idaho, whose support Hoover needed on other fronts, became involved and loudly and repeatedly called for Cardozo's designation. No particular friend of Easterners, especially New Yorkers, Borah, like Norris, recognized Cardozo's rare merit. Twenty-four hours before Hoover

19. Cardozo, The Nature of the Judicial Process (New Haven: Yale University Press, 1921).

20. Mason, Harlan Fiske Stone: Pillar of the Law 336 (New York: Viking Press, 1956).

had indicated he would announce his candidate publicly, he called for Borah.

In an often-told, dramatic confrontation between two proud men, the President, after discussing the vacancy generally, suddenly handed Borah a list on which he had ranked those individuals he was considering for the nomination in descending order of preference. The name at the bottom was that of Benjamin N. Cardozo. Borah glanced at it and replied: "Your list is all right, but you handed it to me upside down." Hoover protested at first: there was the geographical question to be considered and he had to take "religious or sectarian repercussions" into account. Senator Borah sharply retorted that "Cardozo belongs as much to Idaho as to New York" and that "geography should no more bar the judge than the presence of two Virginians—John Blair and Bushrod Washington—should have kept President Adams from naming John Marshall to be Chief Justice." And, he added sternly, "anyone who raises the question of race (sic) is unfit to advise you concerning so important a matter."[21]

Hoover at last bowed to what he now regarded as the inevitable. His memoirs simply state: "... On February 15, 1932... I nominated Chief Justice Benjamin N. Cardozo of the New York Court of Appeals, a Democrat. The appointment met with Senate approval."[22] Indeed it did, instantly and unanimously, and without discussion or roll call when the nomination reached the floor of the Senate a few days later. In finally appointing Cardozo, commented Zechariah Chafee, "Hoover ignored geography and made history."[23]

Cardozo's brethren on the Court were delighted: "Hope you come soon," Stone wrote him on the very day of his official nomination. "We have been saving up some interesting cases for you."[24] Accurately *The New York Times* commented that "seldom, if ever, in the history of the Court has an appointment been so universally commended."[25] But fate would allow Cardozo a scant six years on the high bench—during which he penned more than 100 expertly crafted, stylistically beautiful opinions, including the 1937 *Social Security Cases*[26] and, of course, the seminal *Palko v. Connecticut*.[27]

Cardozo's friend and fellow judicial stylist and craftsman, Learned Hand, movingly eulogized the gentle spirit shortly after his death in 1938, concluding:

> In this America of ours when the passion for publicity is a disease, and where swarms of foolish, tawdry moths dash with rapture into its consuming fire, it was a rare good fortune that brought to such eminence a man so reserved, so unassuming, so retiring, so gracious to high and low, and so serene. He is gone, and while the west is still lighted with his radiance, it is well for us to pause and take count of our own coarser selves. He had a lesson to teach us if we care to stop and learn; a lesson at variance of most that we practice, and much that we profess.[28]

2. Personal and political friendship

Examples that point to personal and political friendship as the overriding causation for presidential choice are legion—although in most instances other considerations loomed as contributory, if perhaps either as buttressing or subsidiary reasons. One of the several illustrations that quickly come to mind, and that unquestionably were characterized by the threshold presence of merit, is President Andrew Jackson's selection—or, more accurately, selections—of Roger Brooke Taney upon the resignation from the Court of the octogenarian Justice Gabriel Duval of Maryland.

The worst apprehensions of contemporary Whigs and Calhounians were promptly confirmed when Jackson nominated his close friend, long-time loyal adviser and supporter, to the seat. Taney, now 58, had successfully navigated the political shoals from the localism of Maryland politics to national prominence, having served as chairman of the Jackson Central Committee of Maryland in 1828, as Jackson's attorney general and, on a recess

21. Johnson, Borah of Idaho 452 (New York: Longmans, Green & Co., 1936).

22. Hoover, The Memoirs of Herbert Hoover: The Cabinet and the President, 1920-1933, Vol. II, 269 (New York: The Macmillan Co., 1952).

23. Chafee, *Mr. Justice Cardozo*, Harper's Magazine, June 1932, p. 34.

24. Mason, *supra* n. 20, at 337.

25. The New York Times, February 15, 1932, p. 1.

26. Steward Machine Co. v. Davis, 301 U.S. 548, and Helvering v. Davis, 301 U.S. 619.

27. 302 U.S. 319 (1937).

28. As requoted in *The Talk of the Town*, The New Yorker, April 4, 1970, p. 33.

PHOTO: SUPREME COURT HISTORICAL SOCIETY
ENGRAVING: U.S. BUREAU OF THE MINT

Roger Brooke Taney was appointed a Supreme Court justice by his close friend President Andrew Jackson.

appointment, as secretary of the treasury after the Cabinet reorganization of 1832.

It was in the latter post that Taney had incurred the undying enmity of the Whig-Calhounian political axis: he had fully approved of and complied with Jackson's order that all government deposits be removed from the Bank of the United States—the major controversy of the time. The enraged opposition struck back at Jackson and Taney by rejecting the latter's formal appointment as secretary of the treasury, thus forcing him to resign. Jackson vowed revenge, and in a letter to Taney that left little doubt that his political opponents had not heard the last of the matter, he wrote: "For the prompt and disinterested aid thus afforded me, at the risk of personal sacrifice which were then probable and which has now been realized, I feel that I owe you a debt of gratitude and regard which I have not the power to discharge...."[29] Duval's resignation gave Jackson his first opportunity to discharge that debt of gratitude. The Senate thwarted him by "postponing" the nomination on the last day of its session—but not before it had voted to do away with the vacant seat entirely, a manuever that failed of enactment, however, in the House of Representatives.

Enraged, Jackson refused to make another nomination and resolved to try Taney again. Fate played into his hands. On July 6, 1835, after almost 35 years on the bench, Mr. Chief Justice John Marshall died in Philadelphia. Jackson now had two vacancies to fill. That one of them would go to Taney was a foregone conclusion. But the President bided his time; he appeared to be considering a host of candidates for both the associate and chief justice vacancies. All attention focused on his choice for chief justice, of course. A strong possibility was the brilliant Justice James Story, but Jackson was not about to promote the man whose record out-Marshalled Marshall. There was wide advocacy of Daniel Webster, but he, too, personified the old Federalist team. A good many urged the promotion of John McLean, but he had already incurred the displeasure of the president and most Democrats by his iconoclastic behavior on the Court. Jackson kept his counsel until

29. Taylor, ROGER BROOKE TANEY 233 (Baltimore: John Murphy and Co., 1872).

the end of December and then proposed Maryland's Taney to succeed John Marshall of Virginia and Philip P. Barbour of Virginia to succeed Gabriel Duval of Maryland. Even-steven geographically—and, "Senate of the United States, here we go again," Jackson might well have chuckled.

"Judge Story thinks the Supreme Court is gone, and I think so too," Daniel Webster had written on hearing of Taney's selection.[30] The remarkable chief justiceship of Taney would prove both men wrong, indeed. But first Jackson's favorite nominee would have to run the gauntlet of a hostile and powerful group of senators. For close to three months the battle raged in the upper house, but when the vote finally came it was not nearly so close as the bitter debates had led the country to believe. Taney won the nomination by a 14-vote margin, 29-15, opposed to the last by such powerful and influential Senate leaders as Calhoun, Clay, and Webster, who later would come to respect the superb performance of the man they had so ardently opposed.

Taney, whom history and the experts have justly accorded the mark of greatness, was resolved to enhance the role of the states as governmental and philosophical entities. But shrewd political tactician and skillful leader that he was, Taney knew how to exercise judicial self-restraint. Not a devotee of overt manifestations of power, he guided his Court along pathways of conciliation and compromise virtually devoid of dogmatism and ploys. Thus, not only were the Court's actions accepted by the majority of political leaders of the time, but its position as the logical ultimate, and fair-minded, arbiter of the Constitution was fully secured as well. Far from assaulting the Marshall-built fortress of judicial power, the Taney Court secured it and did so with all but general approbation.

Even the *Dred Scott* decision,[31] monumental aberration though it was, could not destroy the institution that Taney and Marshall had fashioned. It is a pity that Taney is so often remembered by that case rather than by his supreme accomplishments in achieving governmental concord and constitutional understanding. On October 12, 1864, he died at 87, having served in the center chair for three decades. Alone, tired, and disillusioned, when the end came, he did not recognize how much he had meant to his government and his people. Together, he and Marshall had presided over the Court for 65 years!

3. Balancing representation

Although demonstrated professional merit was indubitably present, a case of presidential choice committed patently to what I have categorized as the balancing of "representation," and in this instance that of *geography*, was F.D.R.'s early 1943 selection of Wiley Blount Rutledge of Iowa. Roosevelt had appointed eight justices in less than four years between 1937 and 1941. Barring unforeseeable illness or resignations, that certainly would presumably be the end of the line. Yet in October 1942 came Justice Byrne's resignation from the Court and the ninth vacancy! This time there was no obvious successor, no obvious political debt to be paid. Such major New Deal supporters as Messrs. Black, Reed, Frankfurter, Douglas, Murphy, Jackson, and Byrnes had been sent to the Court; others, such as Attorney General Francis Biddle, were not interested. At last F.D.R. might indulge his repeatedly expressed desire to nominate someone from west of the Mississippi.

There was no rush as far as he was concerned, and he asked Biddle to look around carefully for a likely candidate. The ultimate nominee, pressed on the Administration by Biddle as well as by such allies as Senator Norris of Nebraska, Justices Murphy and Douglas—Frankfurter and Stone still asked for Learned Hand—and particularly by the influential *Des Moines Register* and *Chicago Sun* journalist Irving Brant, was perhaps a rather "marginal" Westerner, but with identifiable claims to that region: 49-year-old Judge Wiley Rutledge of the United States Court of Appeals for the District of Columbia. Rutledge would be the only Roosevelt appointee with federal judicial experience (four years) and one of only three with any judicial background—the other two being

30. Warren, The Supreme Court in United States History, Vol. II, 10 (Boston: Little, Brown and Company, 1926).

31. Dred Scott v. Sandford, 19 Howard 393 (1857).

PHOTO: SUPREME COURT HISTORICAL SOCIETY
ENGRAVING: U.S. BUREAU OF THE MINT

The selection of Wiley Rutledge for the Supreme Court fulfilled President Franklin Roosevelt's desire to nominate someone from the west.

Black and Murphy. F.D.R. was not personally acquainted with Rutledge, but after chatting with him at the White House, and being assured by Biddle that the candidate was a bona fide libertarian, an early and solid New Dealer who ardently championed the Court-packing plan, and a judge whose opinions demonstrated a solid commitment to the presidential philosophy, he nominated him in February 1943. "Wiley, you have geography," F.D.R. beamed at his happy selectee.[32] Confirmation came readily without a formal roll call by the Senate.

Born in Kentucky, brought up there and in North Carolina and Tennessee, schooled in Tennessee and Wisconsin, Rutledge had taught and worked in the public school systems in Colorado, Indiana, and New Mexico before becoming professor of law at the University of Colorado, professor of law and dean at Washington University in St. Louis, and dean at the University of Iowa's School of Law. Once he attained the bench, Rutledge—who genuinely loved people of all walks of life—demonstrated his libertarian commitments. Indeed, his score in behalf of individual claims against alleged violations by government was higher than any of his colleagues (followed closely by Murphy's). Thus it was Rutledge who joined Murphy's broad-gauged extensions of civil liberty safeguards beyond the Constitution's verbiage when he concurred in the latter's famed dissenting opinion in *Adamson v. California* in 1947.[33]

During his scant six and a half years on the bench Rutledge's scholarship, his mastery of law, his articulate explication of difficult issues, and his prodigious workmanship combined to establish him as an all but universally respected jurist. He left a proud record, highlighted by some celebrated dissenting opinions, such as those for *In re Yamashita*[34] and *Everson v. Board of Education of Ewing Township*.[35] The former decision upheld, 7-2, Japanese General Tomoyuki Yamashita's summary military commission conviction for violating the rules of war. The latter sanctioned, 5-4, state-subsidized transportation of

32. As quoted by David Fellman (letter to author, August 13, 1974).
33. 332 U.S. 46.
34. 327 US. 1 (1946).
35. 330 U.S. 1 (1947).

President Warren G. Harding appointed his close political ally George Sutherland to the Supreme Court in 1922.

PHOTO: SUPREME COURT HISTORICAL SOCIETY
ENGRAVING: U.S. BUREAU OF THE MINT

parochial as well as public school students. Rutledge regarded these opinions as his best. Thus he admonished the Chief Justice Stone-led majority in *Yamashita* that it "is not in our tradition for anyone to be charged with crime which is defined after his conduct, alleged to be criminal, has taken place; or in language not sufficient to inform him of the nature of the offense or to enable him to make defense. Mass guilt we do not impute to individuals. . . .[36] And, in *Everson*, before appending Madison's "Memorial and Remonstrance Against Religious Assessment," Rutledge warned the Justice Black-authored majority:

> Like St. Paul's freedom, religious liberty with a great price must be bought. And for those who exercise it most fully, by insisting upon religious education for their children mixed with secular by the terms of our Constitution the price is greater than for others."[37]

When he succumbed to a cerebral hemmorhage at 55 while vacationing in Maine in September, 1949, an era had come to an end. Justice Rutledge—for whom Justice John Paul Stevens would clerk in 1947-48—had been the last of the nine Roosevelt appointees.

4. Political/ideological compatibility

The last of my suggested quartet of historically demonstrable major motivations in the presidential selection process of future justices of the Supreme Court is that of "real" political and ideological compatibility. My chosen example again points to the salutary fact that, notwithstanding the identifiable commitment to one or more of the quartet, threshold merit is prolegomenum or accompanist. Thus, it was patently true, too, of President Harding's Chief Justice Taft-inspired selection of George Sutherland of Utah in 1922.

That September 4, Justice John Hessin Clarke of Ohio had resigned after less than six years of service. The following day the president nominated the then 60-year-old Sutherland, and the Senate confirmed its two-term ex-fellow senator on the very same day, thereby establishing a speed record in the appointment process. Seldom in the history of the Court had, or indeed has, a successor-candidate been so universally obvious: a close per-

36. 327 U.S. 1 (1946), at 43.
37. 330 U.S. 1 (1947), at 59.

sonal and political ally of the president, Sutherland was insistently and enthusiastically backed by Taft, who earlier had written to the nominee: "I look forward to having you on the bench with me. I know, as you do, that the president intends to put you there."[38] Sutherland was the first (and to date the only) Supreme Court justice from Utah and one of the very few of foreign birth (England) to reach the Court.

Sutherland came to it with a wealth of legal and governmental experience: a leading expert in constitutional law and an active member of the Utah and U.S. Supreme Court bars for many years, he had served in the Utah Senate and the U.S. House of Representatives as well as the U.S. Senate. His friendship with Harding began when the two served together in the upper house, the association culminating in the role of brain truster to the president. He could have had any position in the Harding Administration he desired; but he preferred to accept spot and trouble-shooting assignments in Washington and abroad—in frank anticipation of a vacancy on the Court.

Once he attained the high tribunal, George Sutherland demonstrated that the evaluation of his supporters had been entirely correct: he not only proved himself to be the judicial conservative everyone knew him to be, but he soon became the lucid and articulate spokesman for the Court's so-called Darwin-Spencer wing (also consisting of his colleagues Van Devanter, McReynolds, and Butler). The jurist whom his biographer characterized aptly as "A Man Against the State"[39] spent 16 years on the Court as the personification of those against whom Holmes had railed in his anguished *Lochner* dissent, exclaiming that "The Fourteenth Amendment does not enact Mr. Herbert Spencer's Social Statics."[40] Yet to Sutherland, the Fourteenth Amendment meant "keep-your-hands-off, government!" and in the libertarian as well as the proprietarian sense. Thus it was he who in 1932 wrote the 7-2 majority opinion in the landmark "Scottsboro Case," *Powell v. Alabama*,[41] which became the bellwether in the gradually developing application of procedural safeguards in the Bill of Rights to the states by way of interpretation of the due process of law clause of the Fourteenth Amendment.

As the intellectual leader of the so-called "Four Horsemen" and their allies, Sutherland proved himself a worthy successor of the Field-Brewer-Peckham wing of the Fuller Court era. In the 1930s he became the scourge of the New Deal, heading a majority that struck down more than a dozen pieces of domestic legislation fundamental to the New Deal in 1935-36.[42] Yet he was not blindly opposed to the exercise of governmental power, particularly in the realm of foreign relations. One of the most significant opinions in support of Presidential authority, *United States v. Curtiss-Wright Export Corporation*, was from his pen. It is only just that no matter how many of them have disapproved of his philosophical imperatives, leading students of the Court have never hesitated to accord him the high regard and rating history has so deservedly bestowed upon him.

■ ■ ■

The four illustrations selected almost at random, as well as the numerous others alluded to with affection and admiration throughout these reflections, testify to the rich mine of giants that have served so remarkably well on the Court in its now almost two centuries of life. They provide proof positive of promises fulfilled and achievements rendered. Indeed, notwithstanding the often tiresome, and not infrequently self-serving—albeit exasperating—sniping that has characterized the Court's existence, sniping that has regrettably, although not surprisingly, emanated most loudly from prestigious centers of learning located near bodies of water on both the East and West Coasts, it has, I submit with conviction, truly been, in James Madison's words, a "bench happily filled." His wish *cum* plea, expressed in 1787, has stood the test of time admirably. ☐

HENRY ABRAHAM is James Hart Professor of Government and Foreign Affairs at the University of Virginia.

---

38. Paschal, MR. JUSTICE SUTHERLAND: A MAN AGAINST THE STATE 113 (Princeton: Princeton University Press, 1951).
39. *Id.* (The biography's subtitle.)
40. Lochner v. New York, 198 U.S. 45 (1905), at 74.
41. 287 U.S. 45.
42. *See* Abraham, *supra* n. 1, at Ch. 7, fn. 60.

MICHAEL LES BENEDICT

PRESERVING FEDERALISM: RECONSTRUCTION AND THE WAITE COURT

I. National Sovereignty, State Rights, and State Sovereignty

It has become a commonplace of American history that the Chase and Waite Courts subverted Congress's post–Civil War Reconstruction legislation. A typical reading is that the Court engaged in a "judicial counterrevolution," a "judicially-directed perversion of what the abolitionists tried to write into the Constitution," the most "striking instance in American constitutional history of outright judicial disregard for congressional intent."[1] Historians and legal scholars, in recognition that the postwar constitutional amendments were designed to write an antislavery theory of American rights into the Constitution, have damned the Court, essentially for two reasons. First, because the Court was so restrictive in its construction of the Fourteenth Amendment's Privileges and Immunities Clause. Second, because the Court gutted Republican efforts to make the national government the guarantor of citizens' rights. The vehicle for this subversion, it is charged, was the doctrine of "State

Michael Les Benedict is Associate Professor of History, Ohio State University.

[1] Gressman, *The Unhappy History of Civil Rights Legislation*, 50 Mich. L. Rev. 1323, 1339 (1952); Pritchett, The American Constitution 712 (2d ed. 1968).

action."[2] While this criticism has flourished since the 1930s, John Mabry Matthews and Charles Warren had earlier described the same judicial misbehavior, except that, on the whole, Matthews and Warren approved of it.[3]

No feat of revisionism can turn the Waite Court of the 1870s and 1880s into a firm and unflinching defender of black peoples' rights. But the fact is that the modern criticism distorts our constitutional history. It fails to distinguish the position of the Waite Court from its successors, accepting, for instance, the reactionary decisions of the Fuller Court in civil rights cases as logical extensions of Waite Court doctrines, which they were not. Moreover, the modern criticism proceeds from the assumptions of a constitutional theory of nationalism that is indigenous to our age, presumes that Reconstruction legislation proceeded upon the same theory, and judges the Supreme Court's nationalism against that standard. Historians of Reconstruction, however, are beginning to realize that Civil War–era Republicans adhered to a concept of nationalism far less expansive than what has since emerged. They fought for the Union they had known and loved, a Union in which the authority of the national government was balanced against the rights of the States. And they fought for freedom. After victory they wanted to make the rights inherent in that freedom secure, but they wanted to secure them within the old federal framework. As southern whites contested every inch of freedom's advance, it became ever more apparent that the Republicans' commitments both to federalism and

---

[2] Beth, The Development of the American Constitution, 1877–1917 191–99 (1971); Blaustein & Zangrado, Civil Rights and the Negro: A Documentary History 246–69 (1968); 2 Boudin, Government by Judiciary 94–150 (1932); Franklin, From Slavery to Freedom 331–32 (3d ed. 1967); Harris, The Quest for Equality 58, 82–91 (1960); Kelly & Harbison, The American Constitution 462–65 (5th ed. 1976); Kluger, Simple Justice 62–65 (1976); Logan, The Betrayal of the Negro 105–24 (1965); Magrath, Morrison R. Waite 130–49 (1963); Miller, The Petitioners 85–164 (1966); Mitchell & Mitchell, The Biography of the Constitution 304–10 (2d ed. 1975); Rodell, Nine Men 165–67 (1955); Boudin, *Truth and Fiction about the Fourteenth Amendment*, 16 N.Y.U. L. Rev. 19 (1938); Note, *Section 1983 and Federalism*, 90 Harv. L. Rev. 1133 (1977); Gaffnev, *History and Legal Interpretation—Early Distortion of the Fourteenth Amendment by the Gilded Age Court*, 25 Cath. U. L. Rev. 207, 236–47 (1972); Graham, *Our "Declaratory" Fourteenth Amendment*, in Graham, Everyman's Constitution 295 (1968); Kinoy, *The Constitutional Right of Negro Freedom*, 21 Rutgers L. Rev. 387 (1967); Woodson, *Fifty Years of Negro Citizenship as Qualified by the United States Supreme Court*, 6 J. Negro Hist. 1 (1921).

[3] Matthews, Legislative and Judicial History of the Fifteenth Amendment 97–126 (1909); 2 Warren, The Supreme Court in United States History 533–48, 600–18 (rev. ed. 1926).

to security of rights were in conflict, and they were forced to make an agonizing choice between them. The Supreme Court under Chase and Waite was faced with the same dilemma. Responding to it, the Justices did not bow to racism, betray nationalism, and revive discredited theories of federalism. They made the same effort as did the Republicans to preserve the balance of the old federal system, to protect the States' rights which had been an implicit element of nationalism as it had been understood for fifty years, and at the same time to recognize in Congress enough power to protect civil rights. In the process they reached surprisingly liberal conclusions about congressional power under the postwar Amendments, given the dominant ideas of federalism which provided the context in which they operated.

The essential difference between modern constitutional nationalism and that prevalent at the time of the Civil War was the latter's acceptance of the notion that there was a reserved area of State jurisdiction beyond the competence of national authority. Modern constitutional doctrine reflects the Supreme Court's conclusions in *United States v. Darby*—the deathblow to "dual federalism"—that the jurisdiction of the State governments is defined by that of the national, that the Tenth Amendment "states but a truism that all is retained which has not been surrendered."[4]

The focus of our attention has shifted dramatically from where it was when Americans went to war in 1861. The earlier era was State centered. In practical terms this was reflected in the small effect of national government on Americans' daily lives. From birth to death the only federal officials most Americans were likely to see in peacetime were their postmaster and a pension agent. Both were local men appointed for political services rendered in their own communities.[5] In political terms it was reflected in the continued domination from the 1830s to the eve of war of a political party founded upon a narrow conception of national power. And in legal-constitutional terms it was reflected in the acceptance, even among those who favored energetic national government, of the principles of what Edward S. Corwin identified as "dual federalism."

The basic doctrine of dual federalism—what we identify today as

---

[4] 312 U.S. 100, 124 (1941). See Corwin, *The Passing of Dual Federalism*, 36 Va. L. Rev. 1 (1950); Note, *supra* note 2, 90 Harv. L. Rev. at 1156–90.

[5] Hyman, A More Perfect Union 7–14 (1973); Paludan, A Covenant with Death 11–20 (1975).

"States' rights"—was, in Corwin's words, that "the coexistence of the states and their power is of itself a limitation upon the national power."[6] As originally fashioned by Andrew Jackson, other Democratic statesmen and politicians, and the Taney Court from principles articulated by Jefferson and Madison, it proceeded upon the assumption that the States had been sovereign before the ratification of the Constitution; that the Union was an indissoluble compact in which some sovereign jurisdiction was taken from the States and delegated to the national government; that the States retained sovereign jurisdiction in other areas and were therefore the equals of the national government in the federal system; that each of these governments had a complete, independent structure with which to exercise its powers and could not require the other to administer its laws; that the powers of each government were completely distinct and independent with each supreme in its own sphere; that the Tenth Amendment confirmed this structure and guaranteed that national powers would not be interpreted in such a way as to subvert the reserved sovereign jurisdiction of the States; and that the Supreme Court was the umpire of the federal system with the duty to protect the sovereignty of each government from encroachment by the other.[7] (Corwin did not coin the phrase "dual federalism" until the 1930s. Earlier he referred to a "moderate states rights" doctrine, to distinguish it from Calhounite "state sovereignty.")[8] Those who advocated broad expansion of the national role from the Progressive to the New Deal eras—especially Corwin himself—argued that this doctrine of dual federalism had subverted the nationalistic principles expounded by the Marshall Court. But in reality, most Americans had accepted dual federalism as implicit in those principles.

For most pre–Civil War nationalists, the crucial determinant of the constitutionality of national legislation was its purpose. Early nationalists like Marshall and Hamilton were determined to prevent

[6] Corwin, *The Power of Congress to Prohibit Commerce*, 18 CORN. L. Q. 477, 482 (1933).

[7] See CORWIN, THE COMMERCE POWER VERSUS STATES RIGHTS (1936); CORWIN, NATIONAL SUPREMACY: THE TREATY POWER V. STATE POWER (1913); Corwin, note 4 *supra;* Corwin, note 6 *supra.*

[8] For a good statement of dual federalist principles, see Schroth, Dual Federalism in Constitutional Law 376–80 (1941) (unpublished Ph.D. dissertation, Princeton University). Schroth, like his mentor Corwin, frequently confuses "dual federalism" with "state sovereignty."

an exaggerated commitment to State jurisdiction from inhibiting the national government from exercising its authority effectively. They stressed the sovereign authority of the national government to fulfill the purposes for which it was created. While they did not articulate the limits upon national jurisdiction very clearly, those limits were plainly there. "Let the end be legitimate, let it be within the scope of the constituton, and all means which are appropriate, which are plainly adapted to that end . . . are constitutional,"[9] wrote Marshall in his most celebrated enunciation of nationalist constitutional theory. This is something quite different from the modern gloss which has sustained a national police power and which might be stated, "Let the means be legitimate, let them be within the scope of the constitution, and all ends which are achieved by those means are constitutional." Although Marshall condoned the framing of legislation to carry out mandated objectives in such a way as to promote more general goals, it is plain that the constitutionality of such legislation depended "on their being the natural, direct, and appropriate means, or the known and usual means, for the execution of the given power."[10] Over and over again in his opinions and his extrajudicial defenses of them, Marshall defined the powers of the national government in terms of their purpose, deducing their constitutionality from the postulate that "in America, the powers of sovereignty are divided between the government of the Union, and those of the states. They are each sovereign with respect to the objects committed to it, and neither sovereign with respect to the objects committed to the other."[11] Although Marshall and his colleagues stressed the national sovereignty aspect of these principles to sustain national legislation against attacks based on State sovereignty, he left no doubt that the sword could cut both ways. In *McCulloch v. Maryland*, Marshall stated plainly: "Should congress under the pretext of executing its powers, pass laws for the accomplishment of objects, not entrusted to the government, it would become the painful duty of this tribunal . . . to say that such an act was not the law of the land."[12] Legal scholars have recognized re-

---

[9] McCulloch v. Maryland, 4 Wheat. 316, 421 (1819).

[10] GUNTHER, ED., JOHN MARSHALL'S DEFENSE OF MCCULLOCH V. MARYLAND 186 (1969).

[11] 4 Wheat. at 410.

[12] *Id.* at 423.

cently that the divergence between the Marshall and Taney Courts on matters of federalism has been exaggerated, but they have emphasized primarily the Court's continued commitment to national supremacy.[13] The foregoing suggests that the Taney Court's concern for the integrity of State jurisdiction was also implicit in the decisions of its predecessor. Although it is unclear whether Marshall would have accepted all the doctrines of dual federalism, and it is certain that Story rejected most of them, most Americans did not recognize in them any fundamental inconsistency with nationalist principles.[14] Even while disagreeing vigorously with strict constructionists over where the line between national and State jurisdiction lay, a nationalist like Edward Everett agreed that there was "a wise and happy partition of powers between the national and state governments, in virtue of which the national government is relieved from all odium of administration."[15] Webster too admitted the necessity for keeping "the general government and the State government each in its proper sphere."[16] It was that consideration which

---

[13] BAXTER, THE STEAMSHIP MONOPOLY: GIBBONS V. OGDEN, 1824 117–18 (1972); FRANKFURTER, THE COMMERCE CLAUSE UNDER MARSHALL, TANEY AND WAITE 46–73 (1937); Garvey, *The Constitutional Revolution of 1837 and the Myth of Marshall's Monolith*, 18 W. POL. Q. 27 (1965); KELLY & HARBISON, note 2 *supra*, at 282, 331; SCHMIDHAUSER, SUPREME COURT AS FINAL ARBITER IN FEDERAL-STATE RELATIONS, 1789–1937 50–79 (1958); SCHWARTZ, FROM CONFEDERATION TO NATION 7, 26–28, 33–37 (1973).

[14] Marshall surely would have disagreed with the Taney Court *dicta* in various Commerce Clause cases that inspection laws, immigration regulations, and the like were, by definition, exercises of police power and, therefore, not subject to congressional commerce regulation. See Gibbons v. Ogden, 9 Wheat. 1 (1824), and Willson v. Blackbird Marsh Creek Co. 2 Pet. 245 (1829), and compare New York v. Miln, 11 Pet. 102 (1837); BALDWIN, A GENERAL VIEW OF THE ORIGIN AND NATURE OF THE CONSTITUTION AND GOVERNMENT OF THE UNITED STATES 181–97 (1837); *The License Cases*, 5 How. 504 (1847); *The Passenger Cases*, 7 How. 283 (1845); and Groves v. Slaughter, 15 Pet. 449 (1841).

Marshall did take a distinctly dual federalist view of Congress's taxing power, when he announced that "Congress is not empowered to tax for those purposes which are in the exclusive province of the states." *Gibbons*, 19 Wheat. at 199; GUNTHER, note 8 *supra*, at 100.

Story was consistent in his rejection of dual federalism. STORY, COMMENTARIES ON THE CONSTITUTION OF THE UNITED STATES §§ 1063–66, §§ 1254–1322, §§ 955–89, §§ 1072–89 (1833). But see Prigg v. Pennsylvania, 16 Pet. 539 (1842). Story believed that "new men and new opinions have succeeded" the nationalistic ones that he and Marshall shared, and he contemplated resigning his place on the Taney Court. 2 STORY, ED., LIFE AND LETTERS OF JOSEPH STORY 527–29 (1851).

Gerald Gunther has indicated that there were limits to Marshall's nationalism, GUNTHER, note 10 *supra*, at 19–21. William H. Hatcher noted, but could not explain, a weakening in the Marshall Court's nationalism in its later years. Hatcher, *John Marshall and States' Rights*, 3 S.Q. 207 (1965).

[15] Quoted in PALUDAN, note 5 *supra*, at 14–15.

[16] WEBSTER, THE GREAT SPEECHES AND ORATIONS OF DANIEL WEBSTER 272 (Whipple ed. 1889).

led him to urge adherence to a strict conceptual differentiation between national regulations of interstate commerce and state police powers affecting commerce, such as inspection and quarantine laws; toll-road, ferry, and bridge regulations; and restrictions on black immigration. "If all these be regulations of commerce," he warned, "does it not admit the power of Congress . . . upon all these minor objects of legislation, . . . acknowledg[ing] the right of Congress over a vast scope of internal legislation, which no one has heretofore supposed to be within its powers" and subjecting "all State legislation over such subjects . . . to the superior power of Congress, a consequence which no one would admit for a moment."[17] Thus, on the eve of Civil War, even the Republican party, the political heir to the nationalist sentiments of the Federalists and Whigs, acknowledged the obligation to preserve "the rights of the States . . . inviolate . . . , and especially the right of each State to order and control its own domestic institutions . . . exclusively, 'rights' essential to that balance of power on which the perfection and endurance of our political fabric depends."[18]

It was not the doctrine of dual federalism, or "State rights," that threatened to disrupt the Union in 1861, but rather that of "State sovereignty." While this theory of federalism involved many principles similar to those expressed by dual federalists with the strictest notions of national power, permitting legal and especially political cooperation of adherents of the two theories within the Democratic party, it differed on the crucial question of where authority lay to define constitutional powers. Even the most extreme dual federalist acknowledged the Supreme Court as the ultimate arbiter of the federal system. State sovereignty exponents, convinced that sovereignty was indivisible and therefore that the Union was merely a league of sovereign states, insisted that the people of the individual

[17] Like most Americans in an age of inactive government, Webster did not recognize the inconsistency between such statements and his Storyesque argument in defense of the protective tariff that there could be no inquiry into the motive with which Congress levied duties and imposts once the power was conceded. He may have been blinded to the implications of such an argument because he, like Story, believed protection of domestic industry to be within the acknowledged scope of foreign commerce power and not an indirect benefit of that power. See *id.* at 321.

[18] The phrasing comes from resolutions two and four of the Republican national platform of 1860. Porter & Johnson, National Party Platforms, 1840–1956 32 (1956). For similar descriptions of pre–Civil War legal theory in regard to federalism, see Bennett, American Theories of Federalism 168–69 (1964); Note, *supra* note 2, 90 Harv. L. Rev. at 1138–41.

States had the ultimate right to define the boundaries of the federalism.[19] Moreover, by the 1850s southern adherents of State sovereignty were challenging other fundamental tenets of dual federalism, insisting that as an agent of sovereign states the national government was obligated to use its power to promote the interests of all of them and never to oppose the interests of any of them. Thus, they challenged the cherished notion of their closest allies that the national and State spheres were distinct and independent.[20] When applied to the national government's power to govern United States territories, the conflict disrupted the Democratic party. When State sovereignty doctrines were expressed in the form of nullification and secession, the fundamental differences with even the most anti-national-power dual federalists became apparent, as northern Democrats rallied to the flag. In terms of constitutional theory, the Civil War was fought between the concepts of State sovereignty and what we would now identify as State rights.

Historians have accurately perceived in the legislation of the Civil War years an application of constitutional nationalism much more similar to our own than what had gone before—a "Blueprint for Modern America," as one termed it.[21] Even as they fought to maintain national supremacy, northerners divided on whether the very existence of sovereign States imposed some limitation upon the jurisdiction of the national government. Under the pressure of war, Republicans seemed to repudiate the idea, justifying confiscation, emancipation, construction and operation of railroads and telegraphs, and supervision and care of large populations as "necessary and proper" uses of the war power. At the same time they took a modern view of the taxing and spending power, repudiating dual federalist limitations upon it, and reconfirmed interpretations of national authority over interstate and foreign commerce that justified protective tariffs and national support for internal improvements. Traditionalists, mostly Democrats but also conservative ex-

---

[19] BAUER, COMMENTARIES ON THE CONSTRUCTION, 1790–1860 (1952); BENNETT, note 18 *supra*, at 108–59; 4 BEVERIDGE, THE LIFE OF JOHN MARSHALL 309–96 (1919); CARPENTER, THE SOUTH AS A CONSCIOUS MINORITY, 1789–1861 (1930); HAINES, THE AMERICAN DOCTRINE OF JUDICIAL SUPREMACY 285–344 (1959); MUDGE, THE SOCIAL PHILOSOPHY OF JOHN TAYLOR OF CAROLINE 60–76, 133–44 (1939); SPAIN, *The Political Thought of John C. Calhoun* (1968); Note, *Judge Spencer Roane of Virginia: Champion of States' Rights—Foe of John Marshall*, 66 HARV. L. REV. 1242 (1953).

[20] Bestor, *State Sovereignty and Slavery: A Reinterpretation of Proslavery Constitutional Doctrine, 1846–1860*, 54 J. ILL. H. SOC'Y 1 (1961).

[21] CURRY, BLUEPRINT FOR MODERN AMERICA (1968).

Whigs and Republicans, responded with a barrage of denunciation in the press, Congress, political oratory, legal arguments and court opinions, and treatises on constitutional law.[22]

Even as they set precedents for modern nationalism, however, Republicans could not shake off their commitment to older notions of federalism. Republican reliance upon a broad interpretation of national war powers to sustain their legislation enabled them to isolate the peacetime restrictions from wartime experience. When the war ended Republican leaders urged: "During the prevalence of the war we drew to ourselves here as the Federal Government authority which had been considered doubtful by all and denied by many of the statesmen of this country. That time . . . has ceased and ought to cease. Let us go back to the original condition of things, and allow the States to take care of themselves."[23]

This commitment to State rights within the federal system seriously compromised Republican efforts to establish full freedom and equality for the newly freed slaves. Historians now recognize that every Reconstruction-era effort to protect the rights of citizens was tempered by the fundamental conviction that federalism required that the day-to-day protection of the citizen had to remain the duty of the States.[24] Direct national control of the South and early super-

[22] See HYMAN, note 5 *supra* at 156–70, 207–62; RANDALL, CONSTITUTIONAL PROBLEMS UNDER LINCOLN (1951); PALUDAN, note 5 *supra* at 109–69; BURGESS, THE CIVIL WAR AND THE CONSTITUTION, 1859–1865 (1901); SILBEY, A RESPECTABLE MINORITY 62–88 (1977). Democrats invited the cooperation of all opponents of Republican policies during the war and after, often denominating themselves Conservatives, announcing "that the aim and object of the Democratic party is to preserve the Federal Union and the rights of the States unimpaired." PORTER & JOHNSON, note 18 *supra*, at 34; SILBEY, *supra*, at 138 and *passim*.

[23] CONG. GLOBE, 39th Cong., 1st Sess., 2446 (1866). These remarks were made by James W. Grimes, one of the most important Republican Senators and a member of the Joint Committee on Reconstruction, which framed the Fourteenth Amendment, in the course of opposing a bill that would have established a national quarantine during the cholera epidemic of 1866—a clear exercise of a national "police" power under the authority of the Commerce Clause. The bill failed, with Republicans dividing and Democrats almost unanimously opposed. See Benedict, *Contagion and the Constitution: Quarantine Agitation from 1859 to 1866*, 25 J. H. MED. & ALLIED SCI. 177 (1970). See also the similar remarks of Fessenden, the chairman of the Joint Committee on Reconstruction, CONG. GLOBE, 39th Cong., 1st Sess., 27–28 (1866); PALUDAN, note 5 *supra*, at 28–48; Benedict, *Preserving the Constitution: The Conservative Basis of Radical Reconstruction*, 61 J. AM. H. 65 (1974) [hereinafter *Preserving the Constitution*.]

[24] BELZ, A NEW BIRTH OF FREEDOM 113–37, 157–82 (1976); *Preserving the Constitution*; HYMAN, note 5 *supra*, at 282–306, 414–542; KELLER, AFFAIRS OF STATE 37–73 (1977); Kelly, *Comment on H. M. Hyman's Paper*, in HYMAN, NEW FRONTIERS OF THE AMERICAN RECONSTRUCTION 40 (1966); PALUDAN, note 5 *supra;* Note, note 2 *supra*, 90 HARV. L. REV. at 1141–47.

vision of the transition from slave to free labor were considered temporary and justified on grounds expressly contrived to avoid setting precedents dangerous to the future balance of federalism.[25] As to the permanent protections for Americans' rights, despite arguments to the contrary by those modern legal scholars who write in the tradition of a new nationalism, all the evidence of the congressional discussions, the ratification debates, and the public controversy indicates that Republicans intended the States to retain primary jurisdiction over citizen's rights. They attempted to write into the Constitution an obligation that antislavery theorists already believed incumbent on the States: the requirement that they protect all citizens equally in fundamental human rights. They did not intend the national government to replace the States in fulfilling that obligation. Throughout the early years of Reconstruction, the focus of Republican concern was active State discrimination against blacks in basic rights. Republicans stressed over and over again that if the States simply performed their constitutional obligations to protect citizens equally in basic rights, the Reconstruction legislation and Amendments would work no substantial change in the federal system.[26]

---

[25] *Preserving the Constitution.*

[26] See, *e.g.*, Cong. Globe, 39th Cong., 1st Sess., 1785 (1866) (Sen. Stewart); *id.* at 476, 600 (Sen. Trumbull); Letter from Ohio Governor Jacob D. Cox to Andrew Johnson (March 22, 1866); Schurz, *The Logical Results of the War*, in 1 Speeches, Correspondence, and Political Papers of Carl Schurz 377 (F. Bancroft, ed. 1913). For a clear indication of how State-centered Republicans understood the Fourteenth Amendment to be, see Fairman, *Does the Fourteenth Amendment Incorporate the Bill of Rights? The Original Understanding*, 2 Stan. L. Rev. 5, especially 41–134 (1949). The evidence is all the more persuasive because Fairman was dealing with a different question—the scode of rights protected, not which government was to do the protecting. See also *Preserving the Constitution, passim.*

An excellent insight into the framers' early interpretation of the national government's power to enforce the provisions of the Fourteenth Amendment is revealed by Representative John A. Bingham, explaining the meaning of the original version, worded to give Congress direct, positive power to make laws necessary and proper to protect the civil rights. Insisting that State officials were obligated to protect the rights enumerated in the Bill of Rights, he argued: "The question is, simply, whether you will give by this amendment to the people of the United States the power, by legislative enactment, to punish officials of States for violations of the oaths enjoined upon them by their Constitution? That is the question, and the whole question. The adoption of the proposed amendment will take from the States no rights that belong to the States. They elect their Legislatures; they enact their laws for the punishment of crimes against life, liberty, and property; but in the event of the adoption of this amendment, if they conspire together to enact laws refusing equal protection to life, liberty, or property, the Congress is thereby vested with powers to hold them to answer before the bar of the national courts for the violation of their oaths and of the rights of their fellow-men." Cong. Globe, 39th

Since Americans believed that the main purpose of government was to protect citizens against wrongs perpetrated by others, Republicans believed that by banning State discrimination they were guaranteeing positive protection to freed slaves. "The presumption was that these States would be obedient to the Constitution and the laws," James G. Blaine remembered.[27] "But for this presumption, legislation would be but idle play, and a government of laws would degenerate at once into a government of force. In enacting the Reconstruction laws, Congress proceeded upon the basis of faith in Republican government."[28] Had southerners only fulfilled this naive expectation, the sanguine prophecy made by Ohio's conservative Republican Governor Jacob Dolson Cox might have come true: "If the Southern people will . . . do right themselves, by legislation of their own which shall break down distinctions between classes . . ., the law itself would become of little practical moment . . . and a very short time would make it a practically dead letter."[29]

Cong., 1st Sess. 1090 (1866). The wording of the proposed amendment at this time was: "That Congress shall have power to make all laws which shall be necessary and proper to secure to the citizens of each State all the privileges and immunities of citizens in the several States, and to all persons in the several States equal protection in the rights of life, liberty, and property." *Id.* at 1033–34. Thus, with an amendment apparently worded to give Congress the broadest possible range of powers, its author intended it to operate upon State laws and State officials, not to authorize Congress to establish a general criminal code.

[27] 2 Blaine, Twenty Years of Congress 466 (1886).

[28] *Ibid.* The Lockean conviction that "the great and chief end of . . . men uniting into commonwealths and putting themselves under government, is the preservation of their property," by which is meant the individual's "life, liberty and estate," was an axiom of American constitutional thought, enshrined in the Declaration of Independence's avowal that all men were endowed "with certain unalienable Rights" and "[t]hat to secure these rights Governments are instituted among men." See Locke, Two Treatises on Government 163–84 (Cook ed. 1947). See also The Federalist 35 (Rossiter ed. 1961); Wilson, The Works of James Wilson 171–72 (McCloskey ed. 1967); Chipman, Principles of Government 55–56 (1833); 1 Lieber, Manual of Political Ethics 156–57 (Woolsey ed. 1890) (Joseph Story called this work "the fullest and most correct development of the theory of what constitutes the States that I have ever seen." *Id.* at 3.), 1 Leggett, A Collection of the Political Writings of William Leggett 162 (Sedgwick ed. 1840); Mulford, The Nation: The Foundations of Civil Order and Political Life in the United States 285–88 (1870); Rawle, A View of the Constitution of the United States of America 89, 92 (2d ed. 1829); Wedgewood, The Government and Laws of the United States 66–68 (1867); Young, The Citizen's Manual of Government and Law 17–21 (rev. ed. 1858). Justice Bushrod Washington had placed "protection by the government" at the very head of the list of citizens' privileges and immunities in his celebrated opinion in Corfield v. Coryell, 6 Fed. Cas. 546, 551 (# 3,230) (C.C.E.D. Pa. 1823).

[29] Letter from Jacob D. Cox to Andrew Johnson (March 22, 1866).

It was not until the Ku Klux Klan violence of 1868 through 1872 that Republicans began to recognize that superficially equal laws did not guarantee full protection of rights. As early as 1870 they began to pass laws making it a crime punishable in national courts for individuals to infringe upon citizens' right to vote whether or not they acted under State authority,[30] despite the fact that the Fifteenth Amendment was worded as a prohibition upon States just as the Fourteenth Amendment was.

By 1871, when they passed the so-called Ku Klux Klan Act, Republicans had developed a carefully reasoned constitutional argument that State failure to protect rights guaranteed by the Fourteenth and Fifteenth Amendments amounted to such State action as justified congressional intervention. And that intervention could take the form of positive congressional enactments to punish individual wrongdoers.[31] Even this interpretation, however, stressing as it did the States' primary jurisdiction over crimes, put a tremendous strain upon Republicans. It seemed to encroach upon the heart of State jurisdiction. Key leaders, like Lyman Trumbull, the author of most of the Reconstruction legislation of the 1860s, abandoned the party over the issue. Even as he pressed for direct national punishment of ordinary crimes where States failed to act, John A. Bingham, the chief author of the Fourteenth Amendment, exclaimed, "God forbid . . . that by so legislating we would strike down the rights of the State . . . . I believe our dual system of government essential to our national existence."[32] No one who reads the debates over the Ku Klux Klan Act can fail to be impressed with the effort Republicans made to reconcile their desire to afford protection to citizens in the South with the contours of the federal system they wanted to preserve, one with "a clear and well defined line between the powers of the General Government and the powers of the States."[33]

---

[30] Enforcement Act of 1870, 16 Stat. 140 (1870).

[31] Avins, *The Ku Klux Klan Act of 1871: Some Reflected Light on State Action and the Fourteenth Amendment*, 11 St. Louis U.L.J. 331 (1967); Harris, note 2 *supra*, at 41–53. An excellent summary of the development of the arguments may be found in the reader's guide section of Avins, The Reconstruction Amendments' Debates: The Legislative and Contemporary Debates in Congress on the 13th, 14th, and 15th Amendments xx–xxiv (1967).

[32] Cong. Globe, 42d Cong., 1st Sess., app. 84 (1871).

[33] Representative Charles Williard, *id.* at app. 187; Lionel A. Sheldon, *id.* at 368–69; Jesse H. Moore, *id.* at app. 112; John B. Hawley, *id.* at 382; Garfield, *id.* at app. 150–53;

The suspension of the privilege of the writ of *habeas corpus* in South Carolina in 1872, the direct interference of the national government to settle disputed elections results in the South in 1872–73 and 1874–75, and especially the 1875 purge of Democrats from contested seats in the Louisiana State legislature at the point of federal bayonets made it ever more difficult to reconcile protection of rights in the South with the federal system Americans wanted to preserve. An old abolitionist expressed the simple but tragic truth when he wrote as Republicans gave up the struggle: "We never contemplated when we took the freed blacks under the protection of the North that the work was to be for an unlimited time. We hoped that if for a few years we lent them a helping hand, self interest, if not a sense of right, would prompt the Southern whites to do their duty by them."[34]

Americans' desire to preserve the old balance of federalism was reflected in the post–Civil War writings of legal scholars and political philosophers. Before the war, exaggerated notions of State rights enervated the national government and finally almost destroyed it, the respected jurist Isaac F. Redfield wrote in 1867: "The great danger now will be that things will rush in the opposite direction, and the central authority from being limited and straitened in all its powers and functions, . . . will be in danger of absorbing all the important functions of governmental administration."[35] The most important legal thinker of the post–Civil War era, Michigan Judge Thomas M. Cooley, echoed him: "The proper boundary between national and state powers . . . has been found so satisfactory that we have willingly endured a war in its defence. The cost of that war has been in vain if at its conclusion we propose to treat that boundary as a shadow line which none need regard."[36] The Civil War killed State sovereignty, and the postwar era saw the growing influence of the "organic theory" of American nationalism posited most influentially before the war by Francis

Burton H. Cook, *id.* at 485–86; Horatio C. Burchard *id.* at app. 313–15; Note, note 2 *supra*, 90 HARV. L. REV. at 1156.

[34] Letter from Francis Cope to Laura Towne (November 19, 1877), reprinted in ROSE, REHEARSAL FOR RECONSTRUCTION 403–04 (1964).

[35] Redfield, *The Proper Limits between State and National Legislation and Jurisdiction*, 15 AM. L. REG. 193, 197 (1867).

[36] Cooley, *The Legal Aspects of the Louisiana Case*, 1 S.L. REV. (n.s.) 18, 42 (1875).

Lieber. These nationalists asserted that American nationality predated the Constitution. They argued that the Constitution emanated from an entire people rather than from States or even the people of the States. But their conclusion also sustained the doctrines of dual federalism. The people of the United States created both State and national governments. "The two together constitute the government of the United States," explained Orestes A. Brownson: "The powers of each are equally sovereign . . . . In their respective spheres neither yields to the other. In relation to the matters within its jurisdiction, each government is independent and supreme in regard of the other."[37] Another influential nationalist legal scholar put it more succinctly: "Within their respective spheres, these two classes of governments are as independent as though they represented different nations."[38] As a recent investigator has observed, "The nationalist commentators of the post–Civil War era were able to reconcile their uncompromising hostility to the Confederacy . . . with an ardent advocacy of their own particular version of state rights. Indeed, it seemed at times that their nationalism consisted almost solely in their attacks upon the doctrines of nullification and secession."[39] No wonder, then, that as he left Faneuil Hall after

---

[37] BROWNSON, THE AMERICAN REPUBLIC, ITS CONSTITUTION, TENDENCIES AND DESTINY 234, 256 (1865).

[38] Pomeroy, *The Force Bill*, 12 THE NATION 268, 269 (1871).

[39] Larsen, *Nationalism and States' Rights in Commentaries on the Constitution after the Civil War*, 3 AM. J.L. HIST. 360, 366 (1959). For a similar conclusion, see PALUDAN, note 5 *supra*, at 219–73; and McCurdy, *Legal Institutions, Constitutional Theory, and the Tragedy of Reconstruction*, 4 REV. AM. HIST. 203 (1976). Walter H. Bennett concluded that postwar constitutional theory elevated the United States to the plane of sovereign equality with the States. BENNETT, note 18 *supra*, at 179–81. For what might be called "state rights nationalism," see BROWNSON, note 37 *supra;* POMEROY, AN INTRODUCTION TO THE CONSTITUTIONAL LAW OF THE UNITED STATES (1870), and Pomeroy, *The Supreme Court and Its Theory of Nationality*, 12 THE NATION 445 (1871); HARE, AMERICAN CONSTITUTIONAL LAW (1889); HURD, THE THEORY OF OUR NATIONAL EXISTENCE, AS SHOWN BY THE GOVERNMENT OF THE UNITED STATES SINCE 1861 (1881). Cooley was one of the few nationalist constitutional commentators to adhere to the notion that the people of the individual states had created the Union, but his acceptance of national supremacy was as thorough as that of other analysts. COOLEY, A TREATISE ON CONSTITUTIONAL LIMITATIONS (2d ed. 1871); Cooley, *The Guarantee of Order and Republican Government in the United States*, 2 INT'L REV. 57 (1875).

With the works of these legal scholars, compare the analysis of Timothy Farrar, a Civil War nationalist with ideas more similar to our own. According to Farrar, the States derived their power not from preexisting sovereignty but from the Constitution. Since the national government determines whether a subject is under national or state jurisdiction, it is the United States which is sovereign and not the State government. Like modern constitutional nationalists, Farrar scouted the notion of implied limitations upon

Charles Sumner delivered his intensely nationalistic lecture, *Are We a Nation?* Sumner's senatorial colleague, Henry Wilson, grumbled, "The States are something still."[40]

II. The Court, the Amendments, and Federalism

It was this State-centered nationalism, held in common with different degrees of commitment (especially when compared to the necessity to protect freedmen's rights) by Democrats and Republicans, politicians and jurists, that the Supreme Court articulated in the years following the Civil War. Both the States and the United States held equal places in our scheme of government, each with independent authority within its sphere of jurisdiction—"an indestructible Union, composed of indestructible States," as the Court expressed it in one of its most memorable phrases.[41] And the Constitution imposed just as great a duty to protect and maintain the integrity of the State governments as the national government. "The Supreme Court has thus . . . placed the nation and the States upon the same footing," nationalist constitutional commentator John Norton Pomeroy wrote happily. "As we have in this theory the greatest security for the nation, we have also the greatest security for the several States."[42]

The consequence of such concern for the integrity of State as well as national jurisdiction was the continued adherence to the doctrines of dual federalism. As early as 1864 Republican State courts in Indiana, Wisconsin, and Michigan were applying dual federalist glosses to the doctrines enunciated by Marshall in *McCulloch v. Maryland*, holding unconstitutional provisions of the federal internal revenue code levying stamp taxes upon State court

national power arising from preexisting State sovereignty. "All state rights and powers must be carved out of what the people of the United States have left after having delegated the powers of the Constitution [to the national government]. . . . They have given no right to anybody, to come in competition with their own supreme law, or any power lawfully exercised under it." Farrar, *State Rights*, 21 New Englander 695, 723 (1862).

[40] 4 Pierce, Memoir and Letters of Charles Sumner 335 (1893).

[41] Texas v. White, 7 Wall. 700, 725 (1868). For a full appreciation of the state-centeredness of the Supreme Court doctrine expressed in this case, read Lane Cty. v. Oregon, 7 Wall. 71 (1868), decided at the same Term and in conjunction with it.

[42] Pomeroy, note 39 *supra*, at 445. Chase wrote Pomeroy that the opinion reflected many of Pomeroy's ideas. Pomeroy, note 39 *supra*, at 521n.

writs, State tax deeds, or surety bonds required of State officers,[43] despite the fact that the Constitution limits the national taxing power only by requiring that taxes be levied directly and for common defense, payment of debts, or the national welfare. With Cooley and future Republican Senator Isaac Christiancy concurring, Michigan Supreme Court Justice James V. Campbell justified such rulings in sweeping dual federalist language: "Our whole system is based upon the principle that local affairs must be administered by state authority. . . . The same supreme power which established the departments of the general government, determined that the local governments should also exist for their own purposes. . . . Each of these several agencies is confined to its own sphere, and all are . . . independent of other agencies, except as thereby made dependent. There is nothing in the constitution which can be made to admit of any interference by Congress with the secure existence of any State authority within its lawful bounds. And any such interference by the indirect means of taxation, is quite as much beyond the bounds of the national legislature, as if the interference were direct and extreme."[44]

Cooley endorsed this principle of State immunity from taxation in his *Constitutional Limitations*.[45] Four different United States Attorneys General expressed similar opinions between 1867 and 1871.[46] And the Supreme Court concurred in *Collector v. Day* in 1871[47] and *United States v. R.R. Co.* in 1873.[48] Even while affirming Congress's power to tax State-chartered banks out of existence in one of the most nationalistic decisions of the nineteenth century, the Court agreed that "there are . . . certain virtual limitations [upon the taxing power] arising from the principles of the Constitution itself. . . . It would undoubtedly be an abuse of the power . . . if exercised for

---

[43] Warren v. Paul, 22 Ind. 279 (1864); Jones v. Estate of Keep, 19 Wis. 369 (1865); Sayles v. Davis, 22 Wis. 217 (1867); Fifield v. Close, 15 Mich. 505 (1867); State ex rel. Lakey v. Garton, 32 Ind. 1 (1869).

[44] Fifield v. Close, 15 Mich. at 509.

[45] COOLEY, note 39 *supra*, at 482–83.

[46] The Attorneys General did not hold provisions of the internal revenue laws unconstitutional, but opined that Congress could not have intended to include States and municipalities among taxable corporate bodies because of the principle involved. 12 OP. ATT'Y GEN. 277 (1867); 12 OP. ATT'Y GEN. 376 (1868); 13 OP. ATT'Y GEN. 67 (1869); 13 OP. ATT'Y GEN. 439 (1871).

[47] 11 Wall. 113 (1871).

[48] 17 Wall. 322 (1873).

ends inconsistent with the limited grants of power in the Constitution."[49] Thus the Court rejected Story's views and took the same position that would overturn the Agricultural Adjustment Act some sixty-five years later.[50]

The Justices also displayed a disposition to sustain State police regulations in the 1870s and 1880s. Quick to overturn State interferences with foreign or interstate commerce for the mere purpose of raising revenue and interferences with the free travel of United States citizens,[51] the majority put safety, moral, and health regulations under much milder scrutiny. The Court denied that the "original package rule" of *Brown v. Maryland*[52] meant that the national commerce power superseded State prohibition laws or that national licensing of lottery-ticket or liquor sales to raise money displaced State bans on such sales.[53] It held that States could ban corporations chartered in other States from doing business within their boundaries and that businesses engaged in interstate commerce could be charged more for licenses than those whose business was limited to States or municipalities.[54] The Court sustained broad State taxing authority against charges that State and municipal levies inhibited interstate or foreign commerce.[55] It protected States' power to tax dividends on national bank shares.[56] It followed the precedent of *Willson v. Blackbird Creek Marsh Co.*[57] rather than the *Wheeling*

[49] Veazie Bank v. Fenno, 8 Wall. 533 (1870). Although the Court held that it could not question the reasonableness of the exercise of legislative power where it is expressly granted, it also relied heavily upon Congress's power to regulate the currency as justification for the tax. The Court was plainly uncomfortable with the implications of the broader argument.

[50] United States v. Butler, 297 U.S. 1 (1936). See also the dual federalist dicta pervading Justice Field's rejection of State court power to enforce writs of habeas corpus on behalf of those claimed to be held by national authority. *Tarble's Case*, 13 Wall. 397, especially at 406–08 (1872).

[51] E.g., Crandall v. Nevada, 6 Wall. 35 (1867); Ward v. Maryland, 12 Wall. 163 (1871); *Case of the State Freight Tax*, 15 Wall. 232 (1873); Henderson v. Mayor of New York, 92 U.S. 259 (1875).

[52] 12 Wheat. 419 (1827).

[53] McGuire v. Commonwealth, 3 Wall. 387 (1866); Pervear v. The Commonwealth, 5 Wall. 475 (1867). See also *The License Tax Cases*, 5 Wall. 462 (1867).

[54] Paul v. Virginia, 8 Wall. 168 (1869); Osborne v. Mobile, 16 Wall. 479 (1873).

[55] Waring v. The Mayor, 8 Wall. 110 (1869); Woodruff v. Parham, 8 Wall. 123 (1869); *Cases of the State Tax on Ry. Gross Receipts*, 15 Wall. 284 (1873).

[56] Van Allen v. Assessors, 3 Wall. 573 (1866); National Bank v. Commonwealth, 9 Wall. 353 (1870).

[57] 2 Pet. 245 (1829).

Bridge case[58] to sustain the State's authority to charter the building of railroad bridges across tidal waters.[59] And, in a forerunner to the *Granger Cases*,[60] the Justices ruled that State requirements that railroads set and post rates once a year, punishing those who levied charges in excess of the stated tariff, were legitimate exercises of the police power rather than commerce regulations.[61]

Constitutional historians recognize that the majority of the Justices adopted a similarly restrained view of the Due Process Clause of the Fourteenth Amendment in the early years of its construction. Despite persistent efforts to set it up as the protector of "vested rights" against legislative infringement, they refused to enforce the Clause as a restraint upon the substance of laws.[62] As late as 1889, Charles A. Kent instructed a college audience, "Many as are the suits in which its jurisdiction rests on the allegation of such a conflict, in perhaps no case has the judgment of the State court been reversed on this ground."[63]

The Supreme Court's construction of the legislation and constitutional amendments of the Reconstruction era must be understood within the context of this State-centered nationalism. For if Republican legislators ultimately came to see that their desire to protect

---

[58] Pennsylvania v. Wheeling & Belmont Bridge Co., 13 How. 518 (1851).

[59] Gilman v. Philadelphia, 3 Wall. 713 (1866).

[60] 94 U.S. 113 (1877).

[61] R.R. Co. v. Fuller, 17 Wall. 560 (1873).

[62] The most famous in this line of decisions were the *Granger Cases*, Munn v. Illinois and its sister cases, 94 U.S. 113 (1877). In 1878 a frustrated Justice Miller noted the number of due process cases being filed despite the Court's consistent rebuffs, complaining, "There is here abundant evidence that there exists some strange misconception of the scope of this provision, as found in the Fourteenth Amendment."Davidson v. New Orleans, 96 U.S. 97, 104 (1878). The complaint was repeated by—of all people—Justice Field in Missouri Pac. Ry. v. Humes, 115 U.S. 512, 519–20 (1885). See KELLY & HARBISON, note 2 *supra*, at 468–88, although with hindsight the authors stress how doctrines of "substantive due process" slowly developed rather than how long that development took. See also FAIRMAN, MR. JUSTICE MILLER AND THE SUPREME COURT, 1862–1890 179–206 (1939); MAGRATH, note 2 *supra*, at 173–203.

For the relationship of the doctrine of "vested rights"—the idea that there were strict limitations upon legislative power over property rights—and "substantive due process," see Corwin, *The Doctrine of Due Process of Law Before the Civil War*, 24 HARV. L. REV. 366, 460 (1911); Corwin, *The Basic Doctrine of American Constitutional Law*, 12 *Mich.* L. REV. 247 (1914).

[63] Kent, *Constitutional Development in the United States, as Influenced by Decisions of the Supreme Court since 1864*, in COOLEY, HITCHCOCK, BIDDLE, KENT, & CHAMBERLAIN, CONSTITUTIONAL HISTORY OF THE UNITED STATES AS SEEN IN THE DEVELOPMENT OF AMERICAN LAW 232 (1889).

rights was at war with their desire to preserve federalism, the Court had to face that dilemma even earlier, and in its starkest aspect, in the *Slaughter-House Cases* of 1873.[64]

The *Slaughter-House Cases* brought into focus the Fourteenth Amendment's potential for revolutionary change in American federalism in a way the black-rights-oriented legislation of Congress simply had not. The doctrines the lawyers for the New Orleans butchers advocated were aimed at more than the Crescent City Live-Stock and Slaughter-House Company's "monopoly" (which was in reality no monopoly at all). Their arguments attacked State legislation regulating the State lottery, municipal gas supply, levee repair, funding of the State debt, "prodigal expenditures and jobs innumerable."[65] The Fourteenth Amendment was designed to protect individuals from State invasion of all citizens' fundamental rights and immunities, broadly construed, they insisted. Assume a narrower purpose and "the State may deny individual rights and liberties, and claim to perform all the offices and duties of society, and under the names of socialism, communism, and other specious pretences, control all the revenues and labor of the State."[66] The argument for broad protection for citizens' privileges and immunities under the Fourteenth Amendment was no effort to secure the rights of black Americans. It was an invitation to the Court to write the "vested rights" doctrine into the Constitution through the Privileges and Immunities Clause in 1873 as they would write it into the Due Process Clause twenty years later. Defendant's counsel saw this clearly: "The result of the argument against the validity of this charter must . . . be this: that the 14th amendment does not prohibit State legislatures from passing acts of municipal legislation which abridge the privileges and immunities of citizens, provided such acts appear to be reasonable, but does prohibit the passing of acts which appear to be unreasonable; that it is for this court to determine whether such acts are reasonable or unreasonable."[67]

---

[64] 16 Wall. 36 (1873).

[65] Argument for Plaintiff, *Slaughter-House Cases*, 21 L. Ed. at 395–99.

[66] Brief for Plaintiff upon Reargument, *Slaughter-House Cases*, 83 U.S. (16 Wall.) 36 (1873), in 6 Kurland & Casper (eds.), Landmark Briefs and Arguments of the Supreme Court of the United States: Constitutional Law 639, 669 (1975) [hereinafter Landmark Briefs].

[67] Brief for the Defendants, 6 Landmark Briefs at 587, 601.

Moreover, this proposition was being posited in an era of active congressional civil rights legislation, long before the Supreme Court became the most active protector of rights among the branches of the national government. Although the butchers' lawyers avoided the issue, there was no convincing reason why Congress should not accept the same invitation so temptingly offered the Justices. Even proponents of the broad view worried about such a revolution in the federal system. John Norton Pomeroy tried to demonstrate that the rights secured by the Privileges and Immunities Clause could be enforced only by the judiciary, but he was not very convincing. What was convincing was the terrible consequence he predicted from such an assumption of jurisdiction by Congress: "If the Democratic party should come to power, it is certainly within the range of possibilities that it should endeavor to uphold and sustain the liquor interest by Congressional legislation directed against State prohibitory and license laws. . . . [T]he State laws could be declared void; the States enacting and sustaining them could be described as 'abridging the privileges and immunities of citizens of the United States' . . . " Likewise, Congress could protect privileges and immunities by nullifying Sabbath laws or restrictions against church endowments.[68]

It is in light of the commitment of Americans generally to the idea that the States had a reserved area of jurisdiction that the query in Justice Miller's majority opinion must be read: "Was it the purpose of the fourteenth amendment . . . to transfer the security and protection of all the civil rights [broadly defined] . . . from the States to the Federal Government? . . . [W]as it intended to bring within the power of Congress the entire domain of civil rights heretofore belonging exclusively to the States?"[69] If so, "Congress . . . may pass laws . . . limiting and restricting the exercise of legislative power by the States, in their most ordinary and usual functions," and the Supreme Court would be "constitute[d] a perpetual censor upon all legislation of the States, on the civil rights of their own

[68] Pomeroy, *Political Precedents*, 12 THE NATION 300, 301 (1871); Pomeroy, *Police Duty*, 12 *id.* at 284–85; Pomeroy, *The Rights of Citizens*, 12 *id.* at 335–36. In his dissenting opinion in *Slaughter-House*, Bradley insisted that the Amendment would virtually be self-executing, but did not echo Pomeroy's strictures against congressional authority. 16 Wall. at 123–24.

[69] 16 Wall. at 77.

citizens, with authority to nullify such as it did not approve as consistent with those rights."[70]

Given such possibilities, it is not surprising that the majority of the Justices sought to avoid what seemed to many the obvious meaning of the Fourteenth Amendment's Privileges and Immunities Clause. And given the doctrines of dual federalism that the Court had already endorsed in *Collector v. Day*, it is not surprising that they found the way out in the notion that Americans held privileges and immunities as citizens of the United States different from those they held as citizens of the individual States.

Constitutional historians have severely criticized the *Slaughter-House* decision for nullifying the plain meaning of the Fourteenth Amendment's Privileges and Immunities Clause as defined by its framers.[71] As early as 1879, a critic wondered what fiery old Thaddeus Stevens's reaction would have been if told that all he had intended to secure through that clause were the rights of ex-slaves to protection on the high seas, to travel freely between States, or to petition the government.[72] There can be no doubt that the point was well made. Whatever Republicans intended "privileges and immunities of citizens of the United States" to mean, it was more than that. But Stevens would have been just as incredulous to learn that he had given Congress or the Supreme Court the power to nullify Louisiana's regulations of slaughterhouses, and that is the nub of the conundrum the Court faced. As the *American Law Review* understood, the problem in construing the Amendment's provisions was to "apply their letter . . . to new states of fact not contemplated by Congress nor the legislatures that made them."[73]

Critics of the *Slaughter-House Cases* argue that the Court majority ignored the well-known intent of the Fourteenth Amendment and that Miller's eloquent articulation of its "one pervading purpose," to secure full liberty to blacks, was merely "a strategic ob-

[70] *Id.* at 78.

[71] KELLY & HARBISON, note 2 *supra*, at 476; Beth, *The Slaughter-House Cases Revisited*, 23 LA. L. REV. 487 (1963); Graham, *Our "Declaratory" Fourteenth Amendment*, in GRAHAM, EVERYMAN'S CONSTITUTION, note 2 *supra*, at 319–35; MILLER, note 2 *supra*, at 102–69; 4 BOUDIN, note 2 *supra*, at 94–150.

[72] Royall, *The Fourteenth Amendment: The Slaughter-House Cases*, 4 S.L. REV. (n.s.) 558, 576n (1878).

[73] Note, 8 AM. L. REV. 732 (1873).

fuscation of the issues."[74] But it was those who contended for the broad interpretation of privileges and immunities who had to concede they were innovating. "It is possible that those who framed the article were not themselves aware of the far reaching character of its terms," Justice Bradley admitted in his circuit court decision sustaining the butchers.[75] "Yet, if the amendment, as framed and expressed, does in fact bear a broader meaning, and does extend its protecting shield over those who were never thought of when it was conceived and put in form . . . , it must be presumed that the American people, in giving it their imprimatur, understood what they were doing."[76] The butchers' Democratic counsel insisted they were compelled on principle to "assume" a broader meaning for the Amendment than the merely "partisan" one that might be attributed to it.[77] It was the Court majority and the defendant's lawyers, on the other hand, who argued, "So far as can be judged by the public debate upon the subject, it was certainly never intended or contemplated that this Amendment should receive such a construction." "Have Congress and the whole nation been deceived?" they asked. "Have they done what they did not intend to do?"[78]

In virtually eliminating the Privileges and Immunities Clause as a source of national power to protect citizens' rights, Miller and the lawyers for the Slaughter-House "monopoly" insisted that they intended no subversion of black men's liberty. As noted, Miller was eloquent upon the "one pervading purpose" of the Amendment to protect black rights, and several of the "monopoly's" lawyers were active radical Republicans.[79] Their conviction that the well-known

---

[74] Beth, note 71 *supra*, at 501.

[75] *Live-Stock Dealers and Butcher's Ass'n v. Crescent City Live-Stock Landing and Slaughter-House Co.*, 15 Fed. Cas. 649, 652 (# 8,408) (C.C.D. La. 1870).

[76] *Ibid.*

[77] Note 66 *supra*, at 657, 668.

[78] Argument for the Defendant, 21 L. Ed. 399, at 401 (1873); Brief for Defendant, Slaughter-House Cases, in 6 Landmark Briefs at 603–04; Brief for Defendant on Reargument, *id.* at 726–27; 16 Wall. at 67–72.

[79] 16 Wall. at 71. Among defendant's counsel were Thomas J. Durant, a Louisiana radical who had pressed for black suffrage as early as 1864, and Matthew Hale Carpenter, Republican Senator and floor manager of the Civil Rights Act of 1875. Miller himself, a conservative Republican, was impelled to support congressional Reconstruction legislation by southern subversion of freedmen's liberty after the war. Fairman, note 62 *supra*, at 189–93.

purpose of the Amendment "was to secure all citizens and persons the same rights as white citizens and persons"[80] suggests that they placed primary reliance upon its Equal Protection Clause.[81] That ultimately proved to be a weak reed, but there is no reason to believe that a broader definition of the Privileges and Immunities Clause would have provided any stronger support for black rights. The real obstacle to protection for those rights was the Court's insistence that they were protected only against State infringement and not against individual violence. The Privileges and Immunities Clause was subject to the same limitation, and those who sustained a broad view of it made clear that they interpreted it the same way.[82]

Moreover, those who advocated a broad interpretation of privileges and immunities intended to leave their definition to the vagaries of the judiciary, just as "due process of law" would be subject to judicial construction decades later. The implications are obvious in the result of *Bradwell v. Illinois*,[83] decided only the next day. In that case three of the four Justices who advocated the broader view of privileges and immunities in Slaughter-House concluded that a regulation barring women from practicing law was a "reasonable" exercise of the State police power. It was consistent with "the divine law of the Creator," which made woman's "paramount destiny and mission . . . to fulfill the noble and benign offices of wife and mother."[84] The same "divine law" could be—and would be—cited to ordain "reasonable" regulations of the privileges and immunities of freedmen.[85]

Just as the almost universal desire of Americans to preserve the basics of the federal system impelled the Justices to avoid the revolutionary potential of the Privileges and Immunities Clause of the

---

80 Argument for the Defendant, 21 L. Ed. at 402.

81 See also Miller's discussion of that Clause. 16 Wall. at 81.

82 *Id.* at 83*ff*.

83 16 Wall. 130 (1873).

84 *Id.* at 141.

85 In 1880 and 1881 Justices Field and Clifford would deny that the right to sit upon a jury was included even within the broad category of privileges and immunities of citizens of the States. Ex parte Virginia, 100 U.S. 339, 365-66 (1880); Neal v. Delaware, 103 U.S. 370, 406 (1881).

Fourteenth Amendment, it led them to adopt the doctrine of "State action." As early as 1872 they had demonstrated their concern that a broad interpretation of Reconstruction-era legislation might subvert the reserved area of State jurisdiction. In *Blyew v. United States*[86] they had considered the Civil Rights Act's removal provisions, which permitted transfer of cases from State to national courts when they "affected" a person whose rights as defined by the Act were denied. The victim of a crime was not a party legally "affected" in the culprit's prosecution, the Court ruled, nor were witnesses who could not testify in the case because of their color. Once again the Court's opinion reflected the concern for State authority that pervaded its pre-Reconstruction cases: "It will not be thought that Congress intended to give to the District and Circuit Courts jurisdiction over all causes both civil and criminal . . . . And yet if all those who may be called as witnesses in a case, were intended to be described in the class of persons affected by it . . . , there is no cause either civil or criminal of which those courts may not take jurisdiction . . . [because] such an allegation might always be made."[87]

In case after case in the 1870s and 1880s the Justices construed the Reconstruction Amendments and legislation in light of these considerations. The practical results in individual cases still shock the researcher—the release of Blyew and his confederate, who butchered an innocent black woman in paranoid expectation of a race war; the freeing of the Colfax rioters, who had massacred defenseless, fleeing blacks.[88] One cannot help but suspect that had the Court been more sensitive to blacks' rights, they would have found the grounds upon which to do justice. But that does not mean that the Justices were motivated by the desire to cement the Union with the blood of the Negro, as some scholars have alleged.[89] It was the duty of the States, not Congress, to punish such outrages, they insisted. To hold otherwise "would be to clothe congress with power to

---

[86] 13 Wall. 581 (1872).

[87] *Id.* at 592.

[88] United States v. Cruikshank, 92 U.S. 542 (1876). United States v. Harris, 106 U.S. 629 (1883), also involved southern white rioters.

[89] MAGRATH, note 2 *supra*, at 136–49; Scott, *Justice Bradley's Evolving Concept of the Fourteenth Amendment from the Slaughter-House Cases to the Civil Rights Cases*, 25 RUTGERS L. REV. 552, 564–69 (1971); Kinoy, note 2 *supra*, at 396–97.

pass laws for the general preservation of social order in every state."[90]

When one assesses the Supreme Court's decisions within the context of the doctrines of dual federalism accepted by most Americans in the nineteenth century, however, what is remarkable is the degree to which the Court sustained national authority to protect rights rather than the degree to which they restricted it. In fact, although the Justices found fault with indictments and ruled Reconstruction legislation unconstitutional for excessive breadth, they made clear that with the exception of a few of the *Civil Rights Cases*,[91] every single prosecution brought before them could have been sustained by an appropriate national law. In the very decisions that released southern defendants as well as in those that affirmed their convictions, the Court rejected nearly all the arguments against national enforcement of rights put forward by its opponents. The Justices adhered to the doctrine of "state action" under the Fourteenth Amendment—the crucial element in the maintenance of the federal system they believed in. They repudiated every other restriction.

In Congress, in political platforms, campaign literature and oratory, and finally in legal briefs, arguments, and opinions, opponents of Reconstruction legislation developed a catalogue of limitations upon national authority to protect civil and political rights that truly would have nullified the constitutional amendments had it been accepted, and caused incalculable embarrassment to modern federal civil rights protection, much of which is still based upon the Reconstruction-era laws.

They insisted that the Thirteenth Amendment itself did no more than abolish the institution of slavery. Legislation authorized by its enforcement provision could reach nothing more than peonage and coolyism. Thus if the Fourteenth Amendment had not been passed, the Civil Rights Act of 1866 would have been unconstitutional.[92] If the Thirteenth Amendment did not give Congress power to pro-

---

[90] Bradley in United States v. Cruikshank, 25 Fed. Cas. 707, 710 (# 14,897) (C.C.D. La. 1874).

[91] 109 U.S. 3 (1883).

[92] E.g., CONG. GLOBE, 39th Cong., 1st Sess., 623 (1866) (Rep. Kerr); *id.* at 628 (Rep. Marshall); *id.* at 499 (Sen. Cowan); *id.* at 1156 (Rep. Thornton); *id.* at 476 (Sen. Saulsbury); Bowlin v. Kentucky, 65 Ky. 5 (1867); People v. Brady, 40 Cal. 198 (1870).

tect rights, the Fourteenth and Fifteenth Amendments did little more, according to the conservative argument. Not only were the prohibitions of the Fourteenth and Fifteenth Amendments aimed only at States, they were aimed at States only in their corporate capacities. Thus, they operated directly upon offending State laws, rendering them immediately null and void, but could not authorize criminal or civil action against State officers who carried out those laws. In a federal system in which State and nation were equally sovereign, neither government could impose duties on the officers of the other.[93] And that was even more certainly true if the officer's act was not sanctioned by State law or was in actual contravention of it.[94] Moreover, it was a plain violation of the Constitution to make the same act both a State and a national crime, so no offense against a State law could be prosecuted by the national government merely by giving it another name.[95]

All these positions were grounded in the notion of State independence from national impositions that the Supreme Court itself had recognized in *Collector v. Day* and *United States v. R.R. Co.* But the commitment to maintaining the State's primary jurisdiction over protection of rights against individual infringement, embodied in the State action doctrine, led inexorably to an even more extreme conclusion—that despite provisions directly affirming congressional power to enforce the Amendments by appropriate legislation, Congress had no more power to enforce Fourteenth and Fifteenth Amendment prohibitions than it had to enforce the Constitution's Obligation of Contracts or Ex Post Facto Clauses. In quintessential dual federalist argument against the constitutionality of the 1871 Enforcements Acts, Justice Field's brother, David Dudley Field,

---

[93] CONG. GLOBE, 41st Cong., 2d Sess., 3667, appendix, 422 (1870) (Sen. Fowler); *id.* 42d Cong., 1st Sess., app. 231 (1871) (Sen. Blair); *id.* at appendix, 217 (Sen. Thurman formerly chief justice of the Ohio Supreme Court); Brief for Petitioner, Ex parte Virginia, 8 LANDMARK BRIEFS 113–24; Brief for Defendants, United States v. Cruikshank, 7 *id.* at 340; Biddle, *Indictment of Judge Coles*, 6 S.L. REV. (n.s.) 206, 216–20 (1880); Justices Field and Clifford, dissenting in Ex parte Virginia, 100 U.S. at 349–70, and in Ex parte Clarke, 100 U.S. 399, 404–22 (1880). The argument was also made, apparently, by defense counsel in United States v. Given, 25 Fed. Cas. 1329 (# 15,211 C.C.D. Del. 1873). It is implicit in Bowlin v. Kentucky, 65 Ky. 5, 7–14 (1867) (Williams, J. concurring), and State v. Rash, 1 Houston's Crim. Rep. 271 (Del. 1867).

[94] CONG. GLOBE, 41st Cong., 2d Sess., 472–73 (1870) (Sen. Casserly); United States v. Jackson, 26 Fed. Cas. 563 (# 15,459) (C.C.D. Cal. 1874).

[95] CONG. GLOBE, 41st Cong., 2d Sess., 3674 (1870) (Sen. Thurman); *id.*, 42d Cong., 1st Sess., 572 (1871) (Sen. Stockton).

established the underpinnings of such a position: "Congress . . . is judge of the means to be chosen for attaining a desired end, only in this sense, that it must choose *appropriate* means . . . such as are not *expressly or by implication prohibited*. . . . There are many limitations upon the choice of means beyond those which are expressed. They are implied from the nature of the government. . . . The right to declare an act invalid, because incompatible with the Constitution, applies with the same effect where the incompatibility relates to the implied, as where it relates to the express limitations of the Constitution."[96] With every justification Field was able to cite *Collector v. Day* as authority for this argument—"The case itself is the strongest possible example of an implied limitation upon the powers of Congress. Its power to tax is apparently unlimited, and it had passed an act, by the terms of which the salary of a State judge was liable to taxation, but this court pronounced the act unconstitutional, because, in the exercise of an express power, Congress had transgressed the implied limitations."[97] Given the nature of the American federal system, what could Congress do, then, if a State violated the Fourteenth or Fifteenth Amendments? The conclusion Field offered echoed the position Democrats had taken since the introduction of enforcement legislation: "The answer must be, Congress may do nothing whatever, beyond providing judicial remedies in federal courts for parties aggrieved by deprivation of their rights. Beyond this there is no alternative between doing nothing or doing everything, between leaving the States alone or destroying them altogether. Congress cannot do everything, because that would be the annihilation of the States; therefore it can do nothing, beyond providing the judicial remedies here indicated. . . . [A]n act of a State in violation of the prohibitions of the amendments would be a nullity. . . . Congress, being authorized to enforce the prohibitions by appropriate legislation, the natural, the true, and the only constitutional mode of enforcement, is by the judicial remedies to establish and enforce the nullity."[98]

---

[96] 7 LANDMARK BRIEFS 430–31. Cooley referred to similar "implied restrictions" upon congressional power, in COOLEY, THE GENERAL PRINCIPLES OF CONSTITUTIONAL LAW IN THE UNITED STATES OF AMERICA 97 (1880).

[97] 7 LANDMARK BRIEFS 432–33.

[98] *Id.* at 441–43. See also Thurman's closely reasoned argument against the constitutionality of the 1871 Enforcement Act. CONG. GLOBE, 42d Cong., 1st Sess., 216, 221–22 (1871), an elaboration of a notion he expressed earlier in opposition to the 1870 En-

Justices Field and Clifford accepted David Dudley Field's argument, going further and finding unconstitutional even the judicial remedy embodied in the 1866 Civil Rights Act's removal provisions. Unconstitutional State laws must be reversed upon appeal to the Supreme Court from State tribunals, they insisted. This "gives to the Federal courts the ultimate decision of Federal questions without infringing upon the dignity and independence of the State courts. By it harmony between them is secured [and] the rights of both Federal and State governments maintained."[99]

The majority of the Justices, however, rejected every one of these arguments. In the process they construed the Amendments in a fashion surprisingly similar to the Court's interpretations of the past twenty years.

First, the Justices never rejected absolutely and without cavil Republican legislators' contentions that Congress might protect rights directly when they were violated by individuals in consequence of State inaction rather than action. Justices Strong and Woods, on the contrary, sustained the Republican position in circuit court decisions shortly after the passage of the 1870 and 1871 Enforcement Acts.[100] In his two seminal Reconstruction-law opinions, the circuit court decision in *United States v. Cruikshank*[101] and the Supreme Court decision in the *Civil Rights Cases*,[102] Justice Bradley spoke, not only in terms of States' primary jurisdiction over private infringement of individual rights, but of the duty of States to protect persons against such infringements and the presumption that they were fulfilling that duty in the absence of allegations to the contrary. Woods expressed a similar presumption when he spoke for the Court in *United States v. Harris*, holding unconstitutional a portion of the 1871 Enforcement Act.[103] In a

forcement Act. *Id.*, 41st Cong., 2d Sess., 3664 (1870). See Senator Davis's similar argument, *id.* at 3667; *id.* 42d Cong., 1st Sess., appendix, 49 (1871) (Rep. Kerr).

[99] Virginia v. Rives, 100 U.S. 313, 324–28, 338 (1880); Ex parte Virginia, 100 U.S. 339, 349–70 (1880).

[100] United States v. Given, 25 Fed. Cas. 1324 (# 15,210) (C.C.D. Del. 1873); United States v. Hall, 26 Fed. Cas. 79 (# 15,282 C.C.D. Ala. 1871). Woods had not yet been appointed to the Supreme Court when he delivered his opinion. See also the opinion of Judge Bradford in United States v. Given, 25 Fed. Cas. 1328 (# 15,211) (C.C.D. Del. 1873), which put the "state inaction" argument even more forcefully than did Strong.

[101] 25 Fed. Cas. 707, 710, 714 (# 14,897) (C.C.D. La. 1874).

[102] 109 U.S. 3, 14 (1883).

[103] 106 U.S. 629, 639 (1883).

thorough study of the Court's Reconstruction Amendment opinions, Laurent B. Frantz has made about as strong an argument as possible that such language meant that the Court would have sustained direct congressional protection of civil rights upon demonstration of State dereliction,[104] and he may be right, although there is much to suggest he is not.

A jurist's conviction that the Fourteenth Amendment restated the State's positive duty to provide full protection of the laws did not necessarily mean that he believed Congress could remedy its failure to fulfill it. The nationalist constitutional commentator Pomeroy, who did share this conviction, denied that State dereliction activated national authority. "If the good and valid laws which legislatures have enacted are not fully administered, there is no legal remedy to be obtained . . . from Congress . . . ; redress must be found alone in a change of officers through the ordinary processes of election and appointment," he insisted.[105] While the Court never repudiated the notion in words as direct as David Dudley Field's—"State inaction . . . is no cause for federal action"[106]—neither did it repeat Woods's dictum from his days as district judge that "denying includes inaction as well as action, . . . the omission to protect, as well as the omission to pass laws for protection."[107] It would have been easy to do either.

The Court did, however, reject totally the contention that the Fourteenth Amendment referred to the action of States only in their corporate capacities. As early as 1870 federal judges were sustaining prosecutions of State officers for failures to administer State laws equally, whether or not the laws were discriminatory on their face.[108] In circuit court in 1873 Justice Strong upheld the conviction of a tax collector who refused to accept a black man's tender of taxes required to vote under State law.[109] Seven years later he delivered the Court's opinion that even State judges were liable to con-

---

[104] Frantz, *Congressional Power to Enforce the Fourteenth Amendment against Private Acts*, 73 YALE L. J. 1353 (1964).

[105] Pomeroy, *Rights of Citizens*, note 68 *supra*, at 335.

[106] Note 98 *supra*, at 437.

[107] United States v. Hall, 26 Fed. Cas. 79, 81 (# 15282) (C.C.D. Ala. 1871).

[108] McKay v. Campbell, 16 Fed. Cas. 157 (# 8,839) (D.C.D. Ore. 1870); United States v. Petersburg Judges of Election, 27 Fed. Cas. 506 (# 16,036) (C.C.E.D. Va. 1874).

[109] United States v. Given, 25 Fed. Cas. 1324 (# 15,210) (C.C.D. Del. 1873).

viction for carrying out unfairly nonjudicial functions imposed by superficially equal State laws.[110] Moreover, in a cognate case, Strong made clear that even if a State officer deprived a person of a right in direct contravention of State law, such a violation would both make him "liable to punishment at the instance of the State and under the laws of the United States."[111] At the same time the Court upheld congressional laws aimed directly at State officers' interference with voting rights at federal elections.[112]

While we might take such decisions for granted today, within the context of nineteenth-century federalism these were bold rulings indeed. (In fact, from around 1900 until *United States v. Classic* in 1941[113] the federal courts refused to sustain prosecutions or suits against State officers for civil rights violations that apparently violated State as well as national laws.[114]) The laws the Court thus sustained asserted "a power inconsistent with, and destructive of, the independence of the States," Field and Clifford insisted in dissent.[115] "The right to control their own officers, to prescribe the duties they shall perform, without the supervision or interference of any other state authority . . . is essential to that independence."[116]

In response Strong and Bradley, speaking for the majority in different cases, went to the verge of repudiating the entire notion of dual sovereignty. In language that the Roosevelt Court would echo sixty years later, Strong rejected the idea of "implied limitations" on congressional authority. "The prohibitions of the Fourteenth Amendment are directed to the States," he answered, "and they are to a degree restrictions of State power. It is these which Congress is empowered to enforce, and to enforce against State action, however put forth. . . . Such enforcement is no invasion of State sovereignty. No law can be, which the people of the United States have, by the Constitution of the United States, empowered Congress to enact."[117]

---

[110] Ex parte Virginia, 100 U.S. 339 (1880).

[111] Virginia v. Rives, 100 U.S. 313, at 321 (1880).

[112] Ex parte Siebold, 100 U.S. 371 (1880); Ex parte Clarke, 100 U.S. 399 (1880).

[113] 313 U.S. 299 (1941).

[114] Note, note 2 *supra*, 90 HARV. L. REV. at 1160–61n, 1167–69.

[115] 100 U.S. at 409.

[116] *Ibid.*

[117] Ex parte Virginia, 100 U.S. 339, 346 (1880).

Such language rebuffed the argument that Congress was limited to providing judicial remedies for State violations of the constitutional amendments. "It seems often overlooked that a National Constitution has been adopted in this country, establishing a real government therein, operating upon persons and territory and things," Bradley observed in rebutting the narrow view of national power.[118] At the same time he attacked the sentiment that lay at the foundation of dual federalism, confronting the "mistaken notions with regard to the relations which subsist between the State and national Governments."[119] The national government "is, or should be, as dear to every American citizen as his State Government is," he insisted.[120] "[I]f we allow ourselves to regard it as a hostile organization, opposed to the proper sovereignty and dignity of the State Governments, we shall continue to be vexed with difficulties as to its jurisdiction and authority. . . . Both are essential to the preservation of our liberties and the perpetuity of our institutions. But, in endeavoring to vindicate the one, we should not allow our zeal to nullify or impair the other."[121] With justification, Field perceived in such reasoning "a new departure."[122] In the less restrained world of journalism, the editor of a newspaper established in 1880 to boost Field's presidential ambitions, exploded, "They are revolution. They are a complete overthrow of our institutions."[123]

Even more enlightening is the reasoning by which the Supreme Court tried to sustain national authority to protect individual rights directly without permitting precedents that might later destroy the established lines between State and national power. The Justices did this through doctrines first propounded by Bradley in his circuit court opinion in *Cruikshank*.[124] In that prosecution the United States district attorney for Louisiana, James Beckwith, sought the convictions of the Grant Parish rioters under section six of the Enforcement Act of 1870, which made it illegal for two or more people to

[118] Ex parte Siebold, 100 U.S. 371, 393–94 (1880).

[119] *Ibid.*

[120] *Ibid.*

[121] *Ibid.*

[122] Ex parte Clarke, 100 U.S. 399, 414 (1880).

[123] *Richmond Daily Commonwealth*, March 5, 1880.

[124] 25 Fed. Cas. 707 (# 14,897) (C.C.D. La. 1874).

injure or threaten any citizen "with intent to prevent or hinder his free exercise and enjoyment of any right or privilege granted or secured to him" by the United States Constitution or laws. The indictment alleged several counts of murder with the intent to deprive the victims of various rights secured by the Constitution—to bear arms, to assemble peaceably, to equal protection of the laws, to enjoyment of life and liberty unless deprived of them by due process of law, to rights secured by the State and national constitutions because of their color, the right to vote, and all the privileges and immunities of citizens of the United States.

The defendants' lawyers attacked the constitutionality of the law itself, insisting it usurped the States' jurisdiction over individual crimes. Bradley agreed that the Fourteenth Amendment prohibited State action only and that protection of rights was primarily the duty of the States. Any other holding "would be to clothe congress with power to pass laws for the general preservation of social order in every state."[125] Yet despite these strictures, he upheld the law as an exercise of congressional power, not under the Fourteenth Amendment, but under the Thirteenth and Fifteenth.

The Thirteenth Amendment, Bradley asserted, involved more than the mere nullification of the formal institution of slavery. It implied the vesting of the positive rights of freedom. Therefore it authorized Congress "to make it a penal offense to conspire to deprive a person of, or hinder him in, the exercise and enjoyment of the rights and privileges conferred by the 13th amendment and the laws thus passed in pursuance thereof."[126] So not only was Congress freed of the "State action" limitation by Bradley's construction, but the "rights and privileges" protected by the Enforcement Act were those of citizenship in general, not the limited ones the Supreme Court perceived incident to United States citizenship in *Slaughter-House*. Still committed to preserving the basic demarcations of the federal system, Bradley carefully defined the power he was conceding: Congress could punish directly only those offenses perpetrated to deprive persons of rights because of race, color, or previous condition of servitude, not offenses motivated by ordinary malice or greed. As an example, he cited the case where a freedman sought to lease and cultivate a farm but was prevented from doing

[125] *Id.* at 710–11.

[126] *Id.* at 711.

so on account of his color by whites. "It cannot be doubted that this would be a case within the power of Congress to remedy and redress. It would be a case of interference with that person's exercise of his rights as a citizen because of his race."[127] If, however, the same offense were motivated by other considerations, "without any design to interfere with his rights of citizenship or equality before the laws, as being a person of a different race or color . . . , it would be an ordinary crime, punishable by the state law only."[128] Thus, in 1875, Bradley construed the Thirteenth Amendment in a manner not revived by the Twentieth-Century Supreme Court until it decided *Jones v. Mayer* in 1968.[129]

Bradley went even further, concluding that the "rights and privileges" directly protected by the Enforcement Act included voting rights. Since the Amendment simply states that the citizen's right to vote "shall not be denied or abridged by the United States or any State" on account of race or previous condition, Bradley was interpreting away what seems to be another State action limitation. Despite its unusual formulation, Bradley asserted, the Fifteenth Amendment "confers a right not to be excluded from voting by reason of race, color, or previous condition of servitude."[130] In essence it was "a constitutional extension of the civil rights bill, conferring upon the emancipated slave . . . another specific right" of citizenship.[131] Just as in the case of Thirteenth Amendment rights, "Congress has the power directly to enforce the right and punish individuals for its violation,"[132] no matter what the State does in the premises. "There is no essential incongruity in the coexistence of concurrent laws, state and federal, for the punishment of the same unlawful acts."[133]

But once again, Bradley carefully defined Congress's jurisdiction. The "right and privilege" protected by the Enforcement Act was the right not to be deprived of the power to vote because of color.

---

[127] *Id.* at 712.

[128] *Ibid.*

[129] 392 U.S. 409 (1968). See Casper, *Jones v. Mayer: Clio, Bemused and Confused Muse*, 1968 SUPREME COURT REVIEW 89.

[130] United States v. Cruikshank, 25 Fed. Cas. 707, 712 (# 14.897) (C.C.D. La. 1874).

[131] *Ibid.*

[132] *Id.* at 713.

[133] *Ibid.*

Congress did not acquire general power to regulate voting from the Fifteenth Amendment.[134]

Having defined Congress's powers in such a way as to sustain broad authority to protect rights, Bradley found the individual counts of the indictment wanting. Some claimed an intent to violate rights not guaranteed or secured by the Constitution; others were too vague. But the biggest obstacle was the very ground upon which Bradley had protected national power. Under his construction, the Colfax rioters must have intended to violate their victims' rights on account of their color or previous condition of servitude in order to be convicted. Because Beckwith had failed to allege that motivation, convictions were reversed on counts that otherwise would have been sustained. "Perhaps such a design may be inferred from the allegation that the persons injured were of the African race . . . . But it ought not to have been left to inference; it should have been alleged."[135] Throughout his discussion of the individual counts, Bradley—having conceded so much to Congress—seemed intent on assuring that the counts of the Colfax rioters' indictment transgress by not one inch over what he had reserved to the States.[136]

The Court endorsed Bradley's expansive view of congressional authority to enforce the Fifteenth Amendment against individual infringements of the rights to vote in both *United States v. Reese*[137] and *United States v. Cruikshank*,[138] agreeing that Congress could punish private offenses against citizens' voting rights so long as they were motivated by race or previous condition of servitude. In *Reese*, the Court ruled unconstitutional two provisions of the 1870 Enforcement Act. One punished State officials who at any election refused to accept ballots from voters who had been denied the opportunity to meet voting qualifications by others on account of their race. The other punished anyone who tried to interfere with any citizen's effort to meet voting qualifications. Although the second provision posited no State action, the Court did not rule it unconstitutional on those grounds. Nor did the Justices accept the argument that Congress could impose no duties on officers of the

---

[134] *Id.* at 714.

[135] *Id.* at 715.

[136] *Ibid.*

[137] 92 U.S. 214 (1876).

[138] 92 U.S. 542 (1876).

"independent" State sovereignties. Still less did they accept David Dudley Field's argument, made on behalf of Cruikshank, that Congress could do no more than provide judicial remedies. Instead, Waite took the position which Bradley had developed in his *Cruikshank* circuit court opinion. Although the citizen's right to vote does not emanate from the national government and the government therefore has no general power over it, the Amendment "has invested citizens with a new constitutional right which is in the protecting power of Congress. The right is exemption in the exercise of the elective franchise on account of race, color, or previous condition of servitude."[139] The two Enforcement Act provisions were unconstitutional, not because of any State action requirements, but because they did not require the allegation that offenses be motivated by the race or previous condition of the victims. It was true that the indictments themselves alleged the requisite motivation. But that could not cure the defect. The statute covered offenses both within and without congressional jurisdiction. Like Bradley, having conceded Congress direct power in an area at the heart of State jurisdiction, the Court was unwilling to concede one inch more. Reese and his codefendants were released, not because Congress lacked authority to punish them, but because it "ha[d] not as yet provided by 'appropriate legislation' for the punishment of the offense."[140]

In *Cruikshank*,[141] Waite once more followed Bradley's construction of the Fifteenth Amendment, holding invalid the counts of the indictment alleging intent to deprive voting rights for failure to allege racial motivation, rather than for lack of State action. Waite again sustained Congress's power to protect voting rights against racially motivated private assaults two years later, while trying the Ellenton, South Carolina, rioters on circuit.[142] And Justice Woods reaffirmed the Bradley construction in 1883 in *United States v. Harris*,[143] while holding a provision of the 1871 Enforcement Act unconstitutional because it did not require racial motivation for the offense against voting rights that it punished. As in

[139] United States v. Reese, 92 U.S. 214, 218 (1876).

[140] *Id.* at 221.

[141] United States v. Cruikshank, 92 U.S. 542 (1876).

[142] United States v. Butler, 25 Fed. Cas. 213 (No. 14,700) (C.C.D.S.C. 1877).

[143] 106 U.S. 629 (1883).

Reese, the fact that such motivation was alleged in the indictment and proved could not rescue the Act itself. Once again, the offenders would have been liable to conviction for the same acts under a properly drawn statute.

The Court went further in sustaining congressional power to protect voting rights. In his *Reese* opinion, Waite expressly limited to local and State elections his argument that States retained general authority over voting, implying broader congressional power over federal elections.[144] As in the Ellenton riot case he tried on circuit in 1878, he ruled that in federal elections Congress had plenary power to protect the rights of all voters against individual interference whether motivated by racial hostility or not.[145] And the entire Court took the same view in the 1880s,[146] sustaining convictions of white voting officials and rioters for precisely the same acts alleged in *Reese* and *Cruikshank*.[147] Thus the Waite Court established Congress's power to protect voting rights against private infringement in State and local elections in any case where the offense was racially motivated, and on any grounds whatever in federal elections.

It is not clear whether the whole Court immediately accepted Bradley's recognition of broad congressional power to enforce the Thirteenth Amendment. Bradley's colleagues certainly did not reject it when his *Cruikshank* opinion came before them a year later.[148] Waite's majority opinion sustaining Bradley's circuit court judgment is unclear on the grounds on which the Justices upheld the constitutionality of the Enforcement Act provisions before them. Waite, however, followed Bradley's analysis of the specific counts closely, and Bradley did not write a separate opinion, suggesting that he saw nothing inconsistent between Waite's views and his own. In *United States v. Harris*,[149] where a lynch mob was accused of killing their victims with intent to deny their right to equal protection of the laws, Justice Woods tested the provisions of the Enforcement Act against Congress's power to protect rights di-

[144] 92 U.S. at 216, 218.

[145] United States v. Butler, 25 Fed. Cas. 213 (No. 14,700) (C.C.D.S.C. 1877).

[146] Ex parte Siebold, 100 U.S. 371 (1880); Ex parte Clarke, 100 U.S. 399 (1880); Ex parte Yarbrough, 110 U.S. 651 (1884).

[147] United States v. Reese, 92 U.S. 214 (1875); United States v. Cruikshank, 92 U.S. 542 (1876).

[148] United States v. Cruikshank, 92 U.S. 542 (1876).

[149] 106 U.S. 629 (1883).

rectly under the Thirteenth Amendment, but without committing the whole Court to Bradley's views. "Even if the Amendment is held to be directed against the action of private individuals," he wrote, "the law under consideration covers cases both within and without the provisions of the Amendment" because it does not require racial motivation for the offense. Therefore, under the rule of construction enunciated in *Reese*, the law fell.[150]

But if the Court did not endorse Bradley's views unequivocally in *Cruikshank* or *Reese*, it certainly acquiesced in them when he wrote the opinion striking down the Civil Rights Act of 1875. In the famous (or perhaps infamous) *Civil Rights Cases*,[151] Bradley tested the law against both the Fourteenth and the Thirteenth Amendments. Rejecting arguments that the businesses and institutions covered by the act were quasi-state agencies, he held the law unwarranted by the Fourteenth Amendment on State action grounds.[152] But when it came to treating the Thirteenth Amendment, Bradley took advantage of the opportunity to write his expansive views of that Amendment—the heritage of the antislavery legal argument—squarely into the Court's opinion. "It is true, that . . . the Thirteenth Amendment may be regarded as nullifying all State laws which establish or uphold slavery. But it has a reflex character also, establishing and decreeing universal civil and political freedom throughout the United States; and it is assumed, [by those upholding the law,] that the power vested in Congress to enforce the article by appropriate legislation, clothes Congress with power to pass all laws necessary and proper for abolishing all badges and incidents of slavery in the United States."[153] Bradley conceded

[150] 106 U.S. at 640–41. Woods added that this particular offense—acting with intent to deprive persons of equal protection of the laws—could not be punished under Thirteenth Amendment authority in any case, even if the law required racial motivation. Since only governments can pass laws, he wrote, denial of their protection by individuals could be accomplished only by violating a law. "[I]f, therefore, we hold that [the law] . . . is warranted by the Thirteenth Amendment, we should . . . accord to Congress the power to punish every crime by which the right of any person to life, property, or reputation is invaded." *Id.* at 643. This is a troubling *dictum*, directly counter to Bradley's *dictum* in the circuit court *Cruikshank* opinion, 25 Fed. Cas. at 715, implying that a count alleging such an offense, if racially motivated, could be sustained if its specifications were made clear. For example, Bradley's *dictum* would sustain, and Woods's would condemn, a national antilynching law.

[151] 109 U.S. 3 (1883).

[152] *Id.* at 8–19.

[153] *Id.* at 20.

the truth of the assumption,[154] but then rejected the proposition that denial of equal accommodations and privileges was an incident of slavery.[155]

Bradley's problem was that his own interpretation of the Thirteenth Amendment threatened to justify national punishment of any private invasion of a citizen's rights where race was the motive, to sustain a national criminal code protecting blacks against ordinary crimes against life and property. He apparently felt impelled to draw the line somewhere. In his cruel sentence—"When a man has emerged from slavery, . . . there must be some stage in the progress of his elevation when he takes the rank of a mere citizen, and ceases to be the special favorite of the laws, and when his rights as a . . . man, are to be protected in the ordinary modes by which other men's rights are protected"[156]—Bradley, it would seem, was referring to stages of law, not time. Direct national legislation protecting basic rights inherent in freedom was legitimate; legislation protecting more elevated rights was not. Moreover, Bradley believed that State courts had held the common law to require equal access for all citizens to inns and public conveyances. Any change in that requirement would have to be made by statute. He implied that if such statute caused an unjust discrimination, it would violate the Fourteenth Amendment.[157] And he carefully avoided any suggestion that Congress lacked authority to pass a similar law restricted in its application to interstate conveyances and United States territory and the District of Columbia.[158]

A recent analyst has stated aptly that "both the majority position in the *Civil Rights Cases* and the Harlan dissent . . . were fashioned by Joseph Bradley."[159] Like Bradley, Harlan rejected the *Slaughter-House Cases*' narrow conception of congressional authority under the Fourteenth Amendment to protect rights of citizenship.[160] But

[154] *Id.* at 20–21, 23.

[155] *Id.* at 23–25.

[156] *Id.* at 25.

[157] *Ibid.*

[158] *Id.* at 19.

[159] Scott, note 89 *supra*, at 564.

[160] Harlan went about it a different way. Instead of rejecting the Court's differentiation between rights of United States citizens and rights of State citizens, Harlan argued that Congress had power to protect rights under the first clause of the Amendment defining citizenship. 109 U.S. at 46–48.

that was a lost cause. Harlan's dissent challenged Bradley most powerfully by accepting Bradley's own views of the Thirteenth Amendment. "The Thirteenth Amendment, it is conceded, did something more than to prohibit slavery as an *institution*, resting upon distinctions of race, and shielded by positive law," Harlan wrote.[161] "My brethren admit that it established and decreed universal *civil freedom*. . . . They admit . . . that there are burdens and disabilities, the necessary incidents of slavery, which constitute its substance and visible form; that Congress, by the [Civil Rights] Act of 1866, passed in view of the Thirteenth Amendment, . . . undertook to remove certain burdens and disabilities . . . and secure to all citizens of every race and color . . . those fundamental rights which are the essence of civil freedom . . . ; that under the 13th Amendment . . . legislation, so far as necessary and proper to eradicate all forms and incidents of slavery and involuntary servitude may be direct and primary, operating upon the acts of individuals, whether sanctioned by state legislation or not."[162] Harlan recognized what most scholars have not; to reverse Bradley's judgment it was not necessary to challenge his construction of the constitutional amendments. It was merely necessary to challenge his definition of the "incidents" of slavery.[163]

In sum, then, the Supreme Court's construction of congressional power under the constitutional amendments hardly subverted Republican intent. Committed, as were nearly all Americans of the time, to maintaining the State's primary jurisdiction over criminal offenses, endorsing the basic concepts of dual federalism, the Court still managed to sustain Congress's power to protect directly citizens' fundamental civil and political rights. That Congress did not take advantage of that opportunity reflected the fact that other issues had become more important to a majority of Americans than protection of civil rights. One should not forget, however, that the first time Republicans regained control over all three branches of

---

[161] *Id.* at 34.

[162] *Id.* at 35–36.

[163] Citing *Reese* and *Cruikshank*, Harlan pointed to the Court's own recognition, based upon the theories Bradley articulated in his circuit court *Cruikshank* opinion, that emancipation had created a national privilege not to be deprived of rights on account of color—that racial discrimination was the most fundamental "incident" of slavery. "If, then, exemption from discrimination in respect of civil rights, is a new constitutional right, . . . why may not the nation . . . protect and enforce that right?" he asked. *Id.* at 50.

the national government after 1874, they attempted to pass a law to protect voting rights according to the guidelines set by the Waite Court. It was draconian enough to be called the Force Act of 1890—the direct heir of the Force Act of 1871.[164]

Nearly all of the Waite Court's assertions of broad congressional power under the Thirteenth and Fifteenth Amendments were *dicta*. It was this that permitted the Fuller Court to ignore them in later years. One need only compare the Court's opinion in *Williams v. Mississippi*[165] with Strong's language in *Strauder* and *Ex parte Virginia* to recognize the magnitude of the change.[166] In *James v. Bowman*,[167] the Fuller Court ignored the Waite Court's *dicta* and held the Fifteenth Amendment subject to the same State action limitations as the Fourteenth. In doing so, the Justices overturned a district court decision to the contrary[168] which had been based squarely upon the *dicta* in *Cruikshank*, *Reese*, and *Harris*. The Court merely announced that the Fifteenth Amendment incorporated the same limitations as the Fourteenth and then cited the Waite Court's Fourteenth Amendment opinions as authority. In *Barney v. City of New York*,[169] it held that offenses of State officers in violation of State law could not constitute State action. And in a series of cases it refused to provide relief to blacks disenfranchised under the new southern constitutions of the 1890s and early 1900s.[170] Once again, one need only compare the Fuller Court's language with that of the Waite Court in *Ex parte Yarbrough* to appreciate the difference in the attitudes of the Justices.

Of course neither black Americans nor radical Republicans felt

---

[164] HIRSHON, FAREWELL TO THE BLOODY SHIRT 200–33 (1962).

[165] 170 U.S. 213 (1898).

[166] In this case the Fuller Court ignored the obvious discrimination in the administration of Mississippi's new voting laws of the 1890s, accepting the State's argument that they purged from the voting rolls persons with certain "characteristics," not persons of a certain race. Thus all-white juries chosen from the purged voting lists did not violate the Constitution.

[167] 190 U.S. 127 (1903).

[168] United States v. Lackey, 99 Fed. 952 (D.C.D. Ky. 1900).

[169] 193 U.S. 430 (1904). It is not clear that the Court intended to preclude national authority in all such circumstances in this property-rights case, but it was so interpreted. See Note, note 2 *supra*, 90 HARV. L. REV. at 1160–61n.

[170] Mills v. Green, 159 U.S. 651 (1895); Giles v. Harris, 189 U.S. 475 (1903); Jones v. Montague, 194 U.S. 147 (1904); Selden v. Montague, 194 U.S. 153 (1904); Giles v. Teasley, 193 U.S. 146 (1904).

much like thanking the Waite Court for sustaining congressional power while they released southern killers and election riggers. Democrats and "liberal" or "Mugwump" Republicans demanding sectional reconciliation at the price of black rights praised Court decisions that protected "State rights" by releasing undoubted criminals upon technicalities of statutory construction. It was in their interests politically to ignore the fact that these decisions were based on technicalities, that beneath the surface most of Congress's power to protect rights remained unimpaired. But when one steps back from the immediate political circumstances of the decisions, when one assesses them in light of contemporary doctrines of federalism rather than our own, one reaches a more balanced conclusion. No one can accuse the Justices of the Waite Court of wearing their hearts upon the sleeves of their robes, but they left a heritage of sanctioned congressional power over civil rights that was ignored by their immediate successors and only recently resurrected, without credit to them, by the new abolitionists of the mid-twentieth century.

CIVIL LIBERTIES AND THE AMERICAN SUPREME COURT

LOREN P. BETH[1]
University of Leicester

JUDICIAL review is an American invention, even if it is no longer uniquely an American practice. It is an invention which British observers have often regarded as unnecessary or even pernicious. But many British scholars, like Lord Bryce, Henry Sidgwick, Professor Wheare, and even Professor Brogan at times, have seen in it an institution which while perhaps not suited to the British political mind, is not only suitable but possibly even essential in the American system. Together with federalism it is the most distinctive (and some would add, the most significant) American contribution to the art and science of government

Nevertheless, judicial review has often been criticized both in principle and in application by the Americans themselves, and there are even judges on the Supreme Court bench who have at times expressed implicitly some regret that such an institution has been fastened barnacle-like to the American ship of state. The criticisms are perhaps too well known to need restatement here. On the contrary, it is the purpose of this paper to attempt a defence of judicial review: a task which no American liberal would have essayed twenty years ago and which is even today to some extent an uncongenial enterprise. I am concerned with what is nowadays (in America) a rather conservative position: the view that the Constitution is a body of limitations upon the proper actions of government—limitations which in the American experience we cannot entirely trust our governments to observe. Indeed, it is possible that the trials through which the world has gone in the past fifty years indicate that a well-established and popularly accepted system of judicial review is a desirable part of the institutions of any country which uses a democratic written constitution as the basis of its politics.

It is unfortunate that the Supreme Court has itself made the use of the constitutionalist approach difficult by frequently going beyond the proper limits of judicial review. During the period in which both federal and state

[1] Senior Fulbright Lecturer in Politics, University of Leicester; Professor of Government, University of Massachusetts.

Political Studies, Vol. VI, No. 2 (1958, 134–146).

laws were most frequently invalidated by the Court, the reasons given were almost always based on some imagined economic doctrine which, search as one will, one cannot find in the words of the Constitution or even in its spirit. The application of this doctrine of *laissez-faire* during the years from 1870 to 1937 involved the inversion of the Constitution. Instead of enforcing the limitations contained therein, the Court found implied limits on the powers granted. As often as not it refused to enforce the proper limitations while at the same time dreaming up its own.

Against such perversions of judicial review liberals like Justice Brandeis, and later Franklin Roosevelt and Felix Frankfurter, reacted strongly. At times they reacted not only against the perversion but against the institution itself, assaulting, as it were, not only the King but the Crown: Both the perversion and the consequent reaction culminated in the New Deal period, during which the Court regularly frustrated New Deal aims by failing to find in the Constitution's grants of power to the federal government any power to do those things which the New Dealers felt were both necessary and constitutional.

During most of the same period (1870–1937) the Supreme Court was just as resolutely refusing to protect citizens against governmental actions infringing their civil rights and liberties. It completely failed to protect negroes in the exercise of their newly won rights as citizens after the Civil War. At the same time it denied court protection to various assorted socialists, anarchists, and persons denied fair trials in state courts. It was not until the 1930's that the Supreme Court began to take an affirmative interest in such matters.

The watershed of 1937 brought a pronounced change in the Court—a change which has been reflected in the issues which have come before it. The 'switch in time that saved nine' performed by the judges in that year meant, fundamentally, that the Court was no longer prepared to read grants of power as if they were limitations on power: it was instead ready to allow both federal and state governments relatively free hands to deal with economic questions. This shift made the litigation of cases involving the constitutionality of economic legislation unprofitable for the business interests, and there is comparatively little such litigation today. Neither federalism nor substantive due process has been used to limit the reach of governmental economic regulation since 1937.

At the same time the fears of conservatives that the New Deal was socialistic or even communistic combined with the war and its cold war legacy to produce a rash of state and federal laws imposing new limits on the private freedoms of American citizens; and an awakening public conscience demanded that the negro be assured his rights as a first-class citizen. Whatever one's conclusions as to decisions in particular cases, no one can rightly say that the Supreme Court has not given its careful attention to these new types of cases, which have in fact become the major proportion of cases involving the constitutionality of state and federal laws.

This significant shift in emphasis was not achieved without a good deal of soul-searching among liberals both on and off the Court. After all, it was the liberals who had been most prominent in attacking the uses to which judicial review had been put during the preceding half-century; and while most of them did not go to the extreme of denying the existence of the power of review, yet like Justice Frankfurter they felt that it was the duty of judges to be passivists in the political struggle. They wished to be absolutely sure that they were not substituting their own judgements of wise policy—in the guise of constitutional law—for the decisions of the 'political' branches of the government. But it seemed logical to them that if judges cannot be activists in economic cases, such as those which confronted the courts in the twenties and thirties, they cannot be activists in any field; and if government should be allowed a free hand to deal with economic problems, so it should also in all other problems. And thus even judges who believed strongly in civil liberties and wished to try to preserve them, felt a certain ambivalence in their attempts to do so. The situation has been well summarized by Professor Earl Latham in the following words:

> . . . [T]he abdication of social and economic policy to legislative majorities has seriously handicapped the effort to retain decisive judicial control in the field of civil liberty. We are all familiar with the ambivalent approach of the judges in the cases involving social and economic legislation and those involving civil liberties. In the first the Court assumes that the statutes are constitutional, and the principal question is whether the federal statute has priority over the state or whether unused federal power is threatened in any way by state enactments. In the second, the statute is assumed to be unconstitutional and something like a doctrine of emergency power to act has been worked out. But why should judges defer to the majority desire for social and economic legislation and resist the majority desire for legislation that curbs activities thought by the judges to be within the domain of civil liberties? The judges have so far failed to work out a satisfactory rationale for the ambivalent approach; much of their confusion and consternation with each other stems from this failure.[1]

This problem, it should be emphasized, has faced American liberals rather than conservatives. Conservatives had never been especially opposed to judicial review in economic cases, since they could use it to protect their own positions. And many of them were afraid of the New Deal and its 'socialistic drift' so that they were not concerned by the possible diminution of civil liberty: many of them were, in fact, leading McCarthyists. Liberals,

[1] Earl Latham, 'The Supreme Court and the Supreme People', *Journal of Politics*, May 1954, pp. 207–35.

on the other hand, believed in the welfare state—a belief which necessitated a broad reading of the constitutional grants of power to the federal government, and a tolerant hands off attitude by the courts. But they also had a strong emotional attachment to the traditional liberal values contained in the Bill of Rights. So the very men who in the thirties had called for a relatively unlimited legislative power in the hands of Congress and the states, now were in the strange position of asking the courts to place distinct limits on these powers.

Professor Latham, however, exaggerates the difficulty of this liberal dilemma. There are, in fact, at least two ways of justifying the liberal position. One is to state frankly the belief that civil liberties are so important to human beings and (more significant) to the maintenance of a democratic system of politics, that their infringement cannot be countenanced without a clear showing of governmental necessity. Such an argument would presumably make use of John Milton and J. S. Mill; it has been ably developed on the U.S. Supreme Court bench by Justice Hugo Black. However, it suffers in use by a court by the fact that it is not a constitutional argument except in a tenuous sense. It is, in other words, a tenable position only for the liberal who is not at the same time a judge wielding the power of judicial review, which must by definition be used only with reference to constitutional provisions.

The second justification is at the same time more obvious and more in keeping with proper canons of constitutional construction. It involves a close look at the American Constitution in the light of what a constitution *is*, and also of what this particular constitution *says*. It thus involves both a concept of constitutionalism and a principle of constitutional interpretation.

Constitutionalism can be used in various ways; Locke used it to justify a revolution, Burke to oppose one. The Americans, however, have always been better followers of Locke than of Burke, and they justified their own revolt against English authority in terms largely drawn from Lockian doctrine, as the words of the Declaration of Independence indicate:

> We hold these truths to be self-evident, That all men are created equal, that they are endowed by their creator with certain inalienable rights; that among these are life, liberty & the pursuit of happiness; that to secure these rights governments are instituted among men, deriving their just powers from the consent of the governed; that whenever any form of government becomes destructive of these ends, it is the right of the people to alter or abolish it, and to institute new government, laying its foundation on such principles and organizing its powers in such form, as to them shall seem most likely to effect their safety and happiness.

And,

> . . . [W]hen a long train of abuses & usurpations pursuing invariably the same

object evinces a design to reduce them under absolute despotism, it is their right, it is their duty to throw off such government and to provide new guards for their future security.

The idea of popular consent expressed in these passages is not of present concern; instead the interest lies in the plain assumption that there are limits to governmental power, for the word 'usurpation' can have no other meaning. Constitutionalism in itself provides no remedy for usurpation, since the right of revolution is not an integral part of constitutional theory. But it does include the simple idea that the usurpation of powers is a moral wrong for which *some* remedy should be found. Revolution, however, as Jefferson states elsewhere in the Declaration, is not a thing to be undertaken lightly or frequently; it is so drastic a remedy that it must be reserved for drastic usurpations. Yet what checks short of revolution are possible? One, obvious in the light of American history, is the use of a legal check such as judicial review provides.

Judicial review is, perhaps, as implicit in the British Constitution as in the American (Chrimes, for instance, points out that there is no legal provision binding English judges to apply Parliamentary acts);[1] but because of the lack of a written statement of limitations which courts could apply it cannot be made explicit: thus the doctrine of parliamentary supremacy (in which, it seems, few Britishers really believe, for it includes the possibility of acts which they cannot conceive as being proper). With a written constitution—more especially one which does contain explicit prohibitions on the use of government power—judicial review is a logical development. (Unless, indeed, the constitution itself denies the power of review to the courts, as does the Swiss constitution when it states that the legislature shall be supreme.) However, Professor McIlwain in his various works has gone so thoroughly into the concept of constitutionalism that it seems profitless to repeat it here. To those who are familiar with the American Constitution it will be obvious that if constitutionalism does include this idea of limitations on government the American document is probably the world's first written charter which makes a clear attempt to put the doctrine into practice. The Bill of Rights, and the various other specific prohibitions scattered through the Constitution, are the American statement of the proper limits to government action. Most of these provisions are what are popularly called 'civil' rights and liberties. The freedoms of the mind contained in the First Amendment are the most obvious, but the attempts to limit courts and police in their dealings with citizens are perhaps as important.

If it follows the tradition of constitutionalism, then, a written constitu-

[1] S. B. Chrimes, *English Constitutional History*, p. 6.

tion must contain such limitations; and it must be expected that the government will observe the defined limits, unless one is to regard their statement as mere verbiage. How they are to be maintained in the face of an unwilling government is another question; the American political system regards the courts as the proper agency for so doing, and considering the common law tradition of the United States this is certainly not an illogical development.

One can always clinch an argument in the United States by referring to the doctrines of Madison and Jefferson, the one as 'the father of the Constitution' and the other as patron saint of both political parties. And oddly enough, though both men have been famous as opponents of judicial review, it seems almost certain that they would have agreed with the general tenor of the foregoing analysis. Both men are on record as having made very similar statements in reference to the Bill of Rights, which taken together with their general attitudes on judicial review indicate that they believed that constitutional limitations are more than mere hortatory symbols, and that the courts could properly enforce them through legal channels. Jefferson, for instance, wrote:

> In the arguments in favor of a declaration of rights, you omit one which has great weight with me, the legal check which it puts into the hands of the judiciary. This is a body, which if rendered independent and kept strictly to their own department merits great confidence for their learning and integrity. In fact what degree of confidence would be too much for a body composed of such men as Wythe, Blair and Pendleton? On characters like these the *civium ardor prava jubentium* would make no impression.[1]

Madison likewise, in arguing before Congress for the adoption of the Bill of Rights, remarked that the 'independent tribunals of justice would become [its] special guardians. The federal courts would be an impenetrable bulwark against every assumption of power.'[2]

Complementing the argument that constitutionalism justifies, if it does not indeed require, judicial review in cases where violations of constitutional limitations are charged, are two logical and relevant rules of constitutional interpretation. One is the mere fact that in construing a constitution one is always obliged to pay more attention to what is said than to what may be implied although left unsaid. In justifying judicial activism in civil liberties as against restraint in economic cases this rule of construction has great utility, for while the Constitution is quite specific in denying government the power to infringe freedom of speech or religion, or to deprive

[1] Jefferson to Madison, 15 Mar. 1789. Reprinted in *Basic Writings of Thomas Jefferson*, ed. Philip S. Foner, p. 577.
[2] Quoted in Irving Brant, *James Madison, Father of the Constitution 1787–1800*, pp. 266–7.

persons of the essential elements of a fair trial, it has surprisingly little to say (either affirmatively or negatively) about the proper role of government in the economy. While it is true that the Constitution-makers were firm believers in the institution of private property and were indeed writing the document partly as a means of protecting their own holdings of that precious commodity, the fact remains that they left the protection of property primarily to the working out of the institutional arrangements they were creating. The federal system and the bicameral legislature were particularly designed for this purpose. There is no provision of the Constitution which can be said to institute a Constitutional system of *laissez-faire* economics. There are only three important economic prohibitions contained in the Constitution: the clause which prohibits state governments from 'impairing the obligation of contracts', the Fifth Amendment provision requiring the federal government to give 'just compensation' for the taking of private property for public use, and the clauses of the Fifth and Fourteenth Amendments which prohibit federal and state governments from depriving any person of property 'without due process of law'. Only by highly ingenious and dubious implied constructions can any of these, or all of them together, be taken to limit seriously the power of authority to regulate business or the economy in general.

This is doubtless what Chief Justice Stone had in mind when he accomplished what Professor Latham regards as the 'ambivalent' feat of believing in judicial restraint and judicial activism at the same time. Stone is well known for his comment in one of the New Deal cases that the only check upon the power of the Supreme Court is its own 'sense of self-restraint'.[1] But a few years later, when the issue was not the regulation of agriculture but the requirement of a flag salute as against religious scruples, he wrote:

> The very fact that we have constitutional guarantees of civil liberties and the specificity of their command where freedom of speech and of religion are concerned require some accommodation of the powers which government normally exercises, when no question of civil liberty is involved, to the constitutional demand that these liberties be protected against the action of government itself.[2]

It is, then, the difference between a specific prohibition and one which is at best implied which is crucial. No court can rightly invent prohibitions; but it has a duty to apply those which exist.

A second rule of constitutional construction, flowing from the above, requires that affirmative grants of governmental power in a constitution ought to be broadly construed so as to give the government the maximum

[1] *U.S.* v. *Butler*, 297 U.S. 1 (dissenting opinion).
[2] *Minersville School District* v. *Gobitis*, 310 U.S. 586 (dissenting opinion).

ability to deal with the unforeseen problems which will undoubtedly arise after the document is adopted; but on the other hand, the negative parts of a constitution—those explicitly denying power to government—should be strictly construed in order to provide a working system of effective limits to the actions of officialdom. This has as its base the distinction used by Professor McIlwain between *gubernaculum*, in which the King's authority was 'regal and unlimited', and *jurisdictio*, in which he was 'governed by law'. In the area of power (prerogative) we should depend on the political responsibility of the government to the governed, maintained through the representative system; but in the area of limitation we should maintain legal limits to arbitrary power.[1]

Some such distinction seems essential to the maintenance of a political system depending on a written constitution. What happens without it is sadly illustrated by the history of constitutionalism in countries in which the principle has not been observed. When put to the test of governmental authority which was strong and arbitrary the constitutions of European nations have always failed. It is my thesis that a working power of judicial review, using some such canon of construction as here outlined, might have helped to prevent the misdeeds of Hitler and the unfortunate failure of successive French constitutions. This statement is made with distinct reservations due to the knowledge of the differences between European and American society, yet it seems of some importance anyway.

The distinction between affirmative and negative provisions has a utilitarian as well as a constitutional justification. It has often been pointed out that the longevity of the American Constitution is due at least partially to the kind of broad interpretation of its affirmative clauses to which I have alluded above. Only such interpretation has kept the Constitution modern, and allowed government to adapt to the drastic changes in society brought about by the Industrial Revolution. The rule of constitutions is: adapt or die. And there is nothing in the Constitution which prevents such adaptation, provided only that the efficient parts of the document are read in accordance with their purpose and spirit, which are to provide effective government capable of meeting the needs and desires of the people. It was a major count against the Supreme Court in the years 1870 to 1937 that it did not keep this in mind.

It is otherwise with the civil liberties which the constitutional fathers thought so important. For there is little evidence that the existence of these liberties is any less significant to social life today than it was in 1790. Indeed, the rise of modern democracy has perhaps rendered free speech even more important, since one cannot conceive how a democracy could operate without a very broad area of freedom of the mind. Indeed, it is the

[1] C. H. McIlwain, *Constitutionalism, Ancient and Modern*, pp. 78–79, 146, and *passim*.

lack of this freedom which makes us so sure that Soviet Russia is no democracy. For this reason western democracy is also limited (or constitutional): 'we the people' dare not even trust ourselves with the maintenance of our precious freedom. Anyone who looks at American history with a clear eye will be aware, I think, that the American people (at least) are not a sure repository of freedom. We are too close to McCarthyism and the various laws restricting negro rights to blind ourselves to this fact. Constitutional limitations, then, were included in the Constitution for a purpose; they are still there today, and the presumption is that they remain because they still have that purpose.

The role of courts, however, is not merely that of a policeman. It is not only the job of holding the line against 'the never-ending audacity' of the public official. For not all officials are audacious; many, indeed, believe in civil liberties as deeply as do the judges. But it is not only the case that constitutional limitations are not self-enforcing, but also that their meaning is not self-evident. Especially is this true over a period of time which has seen the development of such new and radically different modes of communication. What does the phrase 'freedom of speech' mean as applied to the problem of wire-tapping? The answer is anything but self-evident; and I would not be happy to have it provided by the FBI or the New York City police. Nor would I wish to leave to a Congressional committee chairman the decision as to how far the right against self-incrimination goes. The courts are important not only (perhaps not mainly) to *apply* constitutional limitations, but to decide what they mean in actual cases. Here is the crucial problem of recent Court history. For no Justice, not even Frankfurter, has refused to admit that the courts should use judicial review in civil liberties cases; instead, the argument has concerned the proper methods of interpretation. The Frankfurter approach believes in allowing to government all reasonable scope for action (in much the same way as this is now allowed in reference to the power-granting sections of the Constitution). The approach taken by Justices Black and Douglas, on the contrary, insists that civil liberties cases require an assumption that a law interfering with civil liberties (even tangentially) is *prima facie* invalid unless the government can prove to the judges that there is a real and important necessity for the action. Fundamentally Justice Frankfurter is on the side of government: he believes that the government has relatively unrestricted power in the civil liberties field provided only that its use of the power is reasonable. The Black–Douglas view is that government has no power in these fields unless there is a compelling justification. For instance, it may be said that the case for the ordinary law of civil libel is so strong as to render such laws legitimate despite the Black–Douglas presumption of invalidity. But a criminal libel law protecting a whole race or religious group cannot be thus legitimized, since it partially closes off public discussion of problems of great and valid public interest.

It would not be proper to complete this analysis without mention of the real difficulties standing in the way of using the methods here outlined. In the first place, it must be admitted that the type of case presented to the courts in civil liberties are very difficult of decision. If it be true, as Justice Holmes wrote, that 'hard cases make bad law', we should not expect that the issues can be solved merely by the application of a formula. It does no good, Justice Frankfurter has said, to apply a standard if it 'merely expresses a complicated process of constitutional adjudication by a deceptive formula'.[1] Certainly this is so if the deception is a self-deception in which the judges believe problems can be solved by reference to a philosopher's stone. Frankfurter fears that formulas and methods may become substitutes for thought.

Acknowledging this possibility, it still remains true that a judge cannot help but approach constitutional cases from some kind of a frame of reference. So long as he does not delude himself by using the frame uncritically to decide all the cases he can cram into it—so long as he exercises due care to probe carefully the actual circumstances of each case, and the actual alternatives open to the court—he surely cannot be criticized for using some set of assumptions as to the nature of the Constitution and as to the proper functions of the courts in relation to it.

But make no mistake: these are difficult cases. They often involve clashes between two or more values which are nearly equally cherished both in Constitution and public ideology. It is not easy to decide between the right of free comment and the protection of almost defenceless minorities, especially when (as in the *Beauharnais* case) the free comment is both irresponsible and scurrilous. Nor is it easy to decide whether the right of the free publication of religious views should supersede the privacy of the home—the question presented by some of the Jehovah's Witness cases. Such issues are not resolved through the automatic operation of a rule of presumptive validity or invalidity. There is no substitute for thought.

A second difficulty arises from the difficulty of maintaining what may be regarded as a rather artificial separation between economic and 'civil' rights. Many political thinkers at least since Harrington have felt that the two cannot be separated; it is not difficult to find statements of the idea that freedom is indivisible, and that the loss of economic freedom necessarily entails the eventual loss of civil freedom as well. This doubt cannot be removed here; but it can at least be observed that judges in America are not called upon to be political philosophers beyond the needs of construing particular clauses of the Constitution. It is not up to them to deal

[1] *Kovacs* v. *Cooper*, 336 U.S. 77 (concurring opinion).

with such difficulties in their judicial capacities, for they are confined to the words of the Constitution (broad as those words often are).

We have already seen that the framers of the Constitution do, for the most part, treat economic and civil liberty as separable, and that they were attempting to build the protection of economic rights into the very structure of the political system rather than entrusting it to the vagaries of ambiguous phrases on a scrap of paper. And except as amendments may have modified it, the protection of economic liberty is the same today as it was in 1789: the system of representation, of separation of powers, of checks and balances, and of federalism. These are all operable parts of the contemporary Constitution. The Constitution, then, does make a distinction between civil and economic rights, and the courts must take the Constitution as they find it.

The most important obstacle to effective judicial protection of civil liberties comes from the nature of the courts themselves. It has often been pointed out that the Supreme Court has no power to enforce its own decisions; that its effectiveness is based largely on the respect and prestige it enjoys; and that decisions which are too unpopular may not be observed, which would make uncertain the effectiveness of future rulings. This feeling has been epitomized in Mr. Dooley's famous statement that 'Th' Supreem Coort follows th' iliction returns', and in the equally well-known remark that 'the Court protects liberty least when it needs it most'. And no less a spokesman than the late Justice Jackson could find 'no modern instance in which any judiciary has saved a whole people from the great currents of intolerance, passion, usurpation and tyranny which have threatened liberty and free institutions'.[1]

Even if this be true there would seem to be at least three significant functions left for the courts. They may, first, act as delaying agencies. It is noteworthy that periods of popular pressure for the suppression of liberties are usually short-lived. The mood is fickle; yet laws passed during periods of public hysteria may remain on the statute books permanently, so that a slow erosion of liberty may occur without anyone wanting it or indeed even knowing it. But since the wheels of justice turn exceeding slow, it is quite possible that a court decision may come after the original impetus behind a law has spent itself. The Smith Act of 1940, for instance, was not adjudicated until very recently. The point is merely that by the time courts finally rule on a law's validity, the public mood may already have changed, so that a judicial invalidation may be perfectly acceptable to the general public. Even if public opinion is unchanged the force of the court's decision may lead to a constructive rethinking of the situation. One might like to see the courts do their duty regardless of consequences, but perhaps this is too much to expect of men who are well aware that

[1] Robert H. Jackson, *The Supreme Court in the American System of Government*, p. 80.

their power depends on the degree to which their actions are acquiesced in by the people. There is, in any case, little danger that courts will prevent government from taking necessary preventive action: the Japanese exclusion cases of the Second World War show that the probability is rather that judges will bow too readily to the claim of 'reason of state'.

A second valuable feature of judicial review is based on the contrast between ideal and reality. If we regard, as I think we may, the Bill of Rights as an authoritative statement of the highest political ideals of American society, and yet realize that nations, like individuals, seldom achieve their ideals, we may regard the Supreme Court as a national conscience. It may hold the 'immanent component' of American ideals before us, recalling those things which we have failed to make articulate in our national life. One of America's greatest jurists, Justice Cardozo, has put this into words:

> ... The great ideals of liberty and equality are preserved against the assaults of opportunism, the expediency of the passing hour, the erosion of small encroachments, the scorn and derision of those who have no patience with general principles, by enshrining them in constitutions and consecrating to the task of their protection a body of defenders. By conscious or subconscious influence, the presence of this restraining power, aloof in the background, but none the less always in reserve, tends to stabilize and rationalize the legislative judgement, to infuse it with the glow of principle, to hold the standard aloft and visible for those who must run the race and keep the faith. . . . Great maxims, if they may be violated with impunity, are honored often with lip-service, which passes easily into irreverence. The restraining power of the judiciary does not manifest its chief worth in the few cases in which the legislature has gone beyond the lines that mark the limits of discretion. Rather we shall find its chief worth in making audible the ideals that might otherwise be silenced, in giving them continuity of life and expression, in guiding and directing choice within the limits where choice ranges. . . .[1]

Finally, the Supreme Court in exercising its power of review is acting as an educational agency in much the same way as the debates in the House of Commons or the report of a Royal Commission may do in England. It is not, I think, sufficiently recognized by foreign observers that such materials as legislative debates do not have, in America, in any degree the amount of public attention focused upon them that exists in England. It is particularly true of the state legislatures, but even of Congress itself, that most of what goes on is completely unknown to all save a few specialists. Once in a while a Congressional investigation, like the recent one into the affairs of the labour unions, may perform something of this function. But American legislatures are primarily law-making bodies, not arenas of public debate; and even in the debate that does take place there, some

[1] Benjamin A. Cardozo, *The Nature of the Judicial Process*, pp. 92–94.

important subjects are practically foreclosed because the make-up of the legislature is such that they can gain no hearing. The prime contemporary instance of this sort has been the set of court decisions regarding negro rights, for here was something that only the Supreme Court could do. No southern legislature would willingly have broached the matter, while Congress is constitutionally barred from legislating on it. The Court's opinions and decisions sparked, for good or ill, a great public self-searching of the conscience. I believe this could have been done in no other way. For when the Supreme Court speaks on an important constitutional issue (which is also inevitably a great political issue) the nation listens. It is not perhaps of primary importance that the Court be right; what is important is that it speak. It is one of the essential elements in a great national forum. Public discussion would be the poorer without it, dissenting opinions and all.

On The Warren Court and Judicial Review*

JESSE H. CHOPER**

I. Introduction

Consensus among its "constituents" has not been one of the identifiable products of the United States Supreme Court since the October Term 1953. If there is any non-controversial statement that may be voiced about the Supreme Court under the stewardship of Chief Justice Earl Warren it is that the Court has not been wanting in either critics or criticism.

It is not my intention to respond to the massive volume of uninformed, unthinking, unbridled, largely undocumented, and generally unsound carping and baiting that has been placed, mainly by irresponsible and legally ignorant attackers, under the heading of "criticism." "Venom," I think, would be a singularly more appropriate term for this commentary. As illustrations, one might point to the statement of the late Senator Harry Byrd of Virginia branding the present Chief Justice as one "who has done and is doing more to destroy the form of government we have in this country than has any Chief Justice in the history of the United States,"[1] or the charge of the then president of the National Association of District Attorneys that the Supreme Court is "destroying the nation."[2]

Not only am I unwilling to dignify such intemperate tirades by responding to them but, to you who are legally literate, I deem it wholly unnecessary to do so. It is enough to say that such vindictive assaults have not been confined

---

* Delivered as the second annual summer University Lecture, Catholic University, July 26, 1967.

** Professor of Law, University of California, Berkeley. B.S., Wilkes, 1957; LL.B., University of Pennsylvania, 1960; D. Hu. L. (hon.), Wilkes, 1967. The author wishes to express appreciation to Professors Yale Kamisar, Frank Goodman, and Philip Johnson for their helpful comments on a draft of this paper.

1. 103 CONG. REC. 10675 (1957). See many of the columns by Mr. David Lawrence in the U.S. News & World Rep., *e.g.*, Mar. 7, 1958, at 108; Nov. 8, 1957, at 136; May 25, 1964, at 120.
2. Boston Globe, July 14, 1964, at 1, 26.

to Chief Justice Earl Warren, to the present Supreme Court, or even to the twentieth century. John Marshall was subjected to similar abuse, as was Roger B. Taney. In May of 1861, the New York Times described the latter Chief Justice as "too feeble to wield the sword against the Constitution, too old and palsied and weak to march in the ranks of rebellion and fight against the Union, he uses the powers of his office to serve the cause of traitors."[3] And the examples could be multiplied.

But it would be inaccurate to lump all of the critics of the Warren Court with the late Senator Byrd or to characterize all of the criticism as wholly irresponsible. Self-serving office seekers and hot-headed extremists have not been the only groups dissatisfied with the work of the Court. Forceful challenge has also come from legal scholars and other students of constitutional adjudication.

II. The Voice of the Critics

In the vanguard of this latter group, Professor Philip B. Kurland recently wrote that during the "fateful decade" between 1954 and 1964, "a period almost coincidental . . . with the presence on the Court of Mr. Chief Justice Warren . . . the Justices have wrought more fundamental changes in the political and legal structure of the United States than during any similar span of time since the Marshall Court had the unique opportunity to express itself on a *tabula rasa*."[4] And, just a few months ago, Professor Kurland evidenced no reluctance to extend his charge through the three years following 1964.[5]

What of his assertion? First, it would be foolhardy to deny that the Warren Court has rendered an impressive number of significant decisions—not just a few breaking new ground or reversing doctrines thought to be inconsistent with developing societal values and emerging human demands under a "living" constitution, a document constructed to assure flexibility in the administration of government for centuries, as well as continuity.[6] (It is well to recall that it is the Constitution, not the Internal Revenue Code, that the Court is expounding. The insight of Chief Justice Marshall, ". . . that it is a constitution we are expounding,"[7] although not subject to easy, explicit or concise explanation, was referred to by Mr. Justice Frankfurter as "the single most important utterance in the literature of constitutional law—most important because most comprehensive and comprehending."[8]) One need only

3. Quoted in 2 C. Warren, The Supreme Court in United States History 370 (1926).

4. Kurland, *Foreword: "Equal in Origin and Equal in Title to the Legislative and Executive Branches of the Government,"* 78 Harv. L. Rev. 143-44 (1964).

5. *See* Kurland, *The Supreme Court Today*, 3 Trial, April-May 1967, at 12.

6. *See* Rostow, *The Supreme Court and the People's Will*, 33 Notre Dame Law. 573, 579 (1958).

7. McCulloch v. Maryland, 17 U.S. (4 Wheat.) 415, 422 (1819).

8. Frankfurter, *John Marshall and the Judicial Function*, 69 Harv. L. Rev. 217, 219 (1955). *But see* L. Hand, The Bill of Rights 65-66 (1958).

mention such cases as *Brown v. Board of Education,*[9] *Baker v. Carr*[10] and *Reynolds v. Sims,*[11] *Engel v. Vitale*[12] and *School District v. Schempp,*[13] *Mapp v. Ohio*[14] and *Miranda v. Arizona,*[15] *New York Times Co. v. Sullivan,*[16] and *Katzenbach v. Morgan*[17] to acknowledge the pace of the Warren Court.

III. The Vinson and Stone Courts

But what of the past? Are Supreme Court judgments that overrule precedents no longer considered worthy and sound or that have highly significant national impact a novel exercise of the Warren Court?

Examination of the work of the Stone Court and of the Vinson Court, of the twelve years preceding the appointment of Chief Justice Warren, reveals that a charge similar to that of Professor Kurland's might well have also been propounded in 1953. Again, mention of only a handful of decisions indicates that those Supreme Courts were not so far behind the Warren Court as some would have us believe in such matters as innovation in the political and legal arena and in reconsideration of precedent.

In *Dennis v. United States,*[18] described at the time as "by all odds the most important and far-reaching of the recent civil rights cases,"[19] the Vinson Court clearly reformulated, if not eviscerated,[20] the Holmes-Brandeis "clear and present danger" test[21] which had seemed to have evolved as the governing rule for decision.[22] In *Korematsu v. United States,*[23] the Stone Court upheld the Japanese exclusion order, a decision then characterized as "the worst blow our liberties have sustained in many years."[24] In *Shelley v. Kraemer,*[25] the Vinson Court announced an enigmatic interpretation of the fourteenth amendment's "state action" element, potentially imposing con-

9. 347 U.S. 483 (1954).
10. 369 U.S. 186 (1962).
11. 377 U.S. 533 (1964).
12. 370 U.S. 421 (1962).
13. 374 U.S. 203 (1963).
14. 367 U.S. 643 (1961).
15. 384 U.S. 436 (1966).
16. 376 U.S. 254 (1964).
17. 384 U.S. 641 (1966).
18. 341 U.S. 494 (1951).
19. Rostow, *The Democratic Character of Judicial Review*, 66 HARV. L. REV. 193, 222 (1952).
20. *See id.* at 217-23; Gorfinkel & Mack, *Dennis v. United States and the Clear and Present Danger Rule,* 39 CALIF. L. REV. 475 (1951); Nathanson, *The Communist Trial and the Clear-and-Present-Danger Test,* 63 HARV. L. REV. 1167 (1950). For general discussion, *see* W. LOCKHART, Y. KAMISAR & J. CHOPER, CONSTITUTIONAL LAW: CASES—COMMENTS—QUESTIONS 812-17 (2d ed. 1967).
21. *See* Gitlow v. New York, 268 U.S. 652 (1925) (dissenting opinion); Whitney v. California, 274 U.S. 357 (1927) (concurring opinion).
22. Dennis v. United States, *supra* note 18, at 507.
23. 323 U.S. 214 (1944).
24. Rostow, *The Japanese American Cases—A Disaster,* 54 YALE L.J. 489, 490 (1945).
25. 334 U.S. 1 (1948).

stitutional review by the courts of virtually all commonplace transactions,[26] and whose meaning and scope still baffles many of those who deal with the case.[27] In *United States v. South-Eastern Underwriters Association*,[28] the Stone Court negated a 75-year precedent[29] when it held that insurance was commerce within the purview of congressional regulation. In *Illinois* ex rel. *McCollum v. Board of Education*,[30] the Vinson Court, then scorned as "eager crusaders,"[31] for the first time, 80 years after the adoption of the fourteenth amendment, held that the first amendment's "establishment clause" invalidated a state-sponsored program, in this case, released time for religious instruction, prompting Mr. Justice Jackson to charge that the Court had become "a super board of education for every school district in the nation."[32] In *Smith v. Allwright*,[33] the Stone Court ruled that a primary election, held not by the state but by a political party, was subject to the prohibitions of the fifteenth amendment, overruling a decision[34] not yet ten years old, and provoking Mr. Justice Roberts to charge that the Court, having overruled three cases that term, had become "the breeder of fresh doubt and confusion in the public mind as to the stability of our institutions."[35] And the examples could be multiplied.

The point, of course, is not that the Warren Court has faithfully adhered to the dictates of its predecessors, or that it has gingerly avoided moving into areas of political and legal controversy; rather, it is that the charges brought against the Warren Court for ignoring precedent, advancing novel doctrine, and sponsoring broad redistributions of power in the federal system are not unlike charges that could have been made—and *have* been made—against every Supreme Court in the nation's history.

We have briefly examined the twelve-year period of the Stone and Vinson Courts that immediately preceded the Warren Court's birth. Perhaps recitation of the cases selected from that period falls short of persuading you that the Warren Court is not a wholly different animal. Perhaps the pace of the Warren Court has been more rapid, its impact wider. But I suspect that stu-

26. *See* commentary discussed in W. Lockhart, Y. Kamisar & J. Choper, *supra* note 20, at 1309-14.

27. *Ibid. See also* Bell v. Maryland, 378 U.S. 226 (1964) (opinions of Douglas, J. and Black, J.).

28. 322 U.S. 533 (1944).

29. Paul v. Virginia, 75 U.S. (8 Wall.) 168 (1868).

30. 333 U.S. 203 (1948).

31. Corwin, *The Supreme Court as National School Board*, 14 Law & Contemp. Prob. 3, 14 (1949).

32. Illinois *ex rel.* McCollum v. Board of Educ., *supra* note 30, at 237. Elsewhere, I have argued for approval of *McCollum*, as well as the *Regent's Prayer* and *Bible-Reading* cases cited *supra* notes 12, 13. Choper, *Religion in the Public Schools: A Proposed Constitutional Standard*, 47 Minn. L. Rev. 329 (1963).

33. 321 U.S. 649 (1944).

34. Grovey v. Townsend, 295 U.S. 45 (1935).

35. Smith v. Allwright, *supra* note 33, at 670.

dents of human psychology, if not students of law, would tell us that the heat of the moment colors our judgments and magnifies current events, and that the passage of time produces a strong tendency to accept past momentous events as being quite ordinary.

I further suspect that Supreme Court historians will not judge the twelve years of the Stone and Vinson Courts as being especially eventful. But despite this perspective of the mid-1960's on the tenure of those Courts, Professor Alexander H. Pekelis could write in 1950:

> The charges that one finds most clearly formulated in the present offensive against the Court can be summarized as follows:
>
> * * *
>
> 2. The Court systematically disregards its own precedents....
> 3. The Court fails to confine itself to the interpretation of the law as it is. In the words of a New York Times editorial, "The majority of the new appointees came to the Court . . . apparently under the theory that their function was not so much to know and apply the law as it stands, or in case of doubt to interpret it objectively, but to apply a new 'social philosophy' in their decisions. The inevitable effect of such an approach could only be to create uncertainty regarding the law and turn the Supreme Court, in effect, into a third legislative house."[36]

Much the same is now being said of the Warren Court, but the attitude is that the present Court is acting markedly different than any Court before it. Yet Professor Pekelis wrote seventeen years ago of a different Court that many now consider to rank low on the "activist" scale. I suspect that it will be said again of future Courts. Surely it could be said with justice of past Supreme Courts.

IV. The Distant Past

In 1803, the Marshall Court decided *Marbury v. Madison*,[37] holding that the Supreme Court has the power to declare an act of a coordinate branch of the government unconstitutional. Thus, there was the establishment of the power of judicial review. It is surely fair to say that this most historic and momentous Supreme Court ruling was clearly not preordained. Professor Alexander M. Bickel has impellingly demonstrated that the text of the Constitution provides no explicit or even firm support for Chief Justice Marshall's assumption of authority for the judiciary, at least in respect to invalidating acts of Congress and the President.[38] And it is by no means

36. A. Pekelis, Law and Social Action 195 (1950).
37. 5 U.S. (1 Cranch) 137 (1803).
38. A. Bickel, The Least Dangerous Branch 3-14 (1962). *But see* Wechsler, *Foreword: Toward Neutral Principles of Constitutional Law*, 73 Harv. L. Rev. 1, 3-5 (1959).

generally agreed that the Framers intended to vest the Supreme Court with such an extensive and final command.[39]

The critics of the Warren Court charge it with "the enhancement of judicial dominion at the expense of the power of other branches of government, national as well as state."[40] If this be accurate, it may be confidently said that no Supreme Court opinion in history better fulfills that characterization than does *Marbury v. Madison*.[41]

But *Marbury*, a decision to which we shall return, does not stand as the sole or even necessarily the most poignant example of the great Supreme Court judgments in history that would fall under the analysis of those who criticize the Warren Court.

Article I, section 8 of the Constitution provides that "The Congress shall have Power . . . To regulate Commerce with foreign Nations, and among the several States. . . ." The desperate need of the national legislature for this dominion was evidenced by the fact that matters of finance, commerce and business motivated the call of the Constitutional Convention in Philadelphia in 1787.[42] Under the Articles of Confederation, the infant nation was beset

39. *Compare* L. HAND, THE BILL OF RIGHTS 28 (1958); M. COHEN, THE FAITH OF A LIBERAL 184 (1946) *with* H. HART & H. WECHSLER, THE FEDERAL COURTS AND THE FEDERAL SYSTEM 14-18 (1953); Rostow, *The Democratic Character of Judicial Review*, 66 HARV. L. REV. 193, 195-96, 198-99 (1952). *See generally* L. POLLAK, THE CONSTITUTION AND THE SUPREME COURT 75-84, 91-96, 156-58 (1966).

40. Kurland, *supra* note 4, at 144.

41. *Supra* note 37. Professor Kurland, and others, also find as an "element that courses through the opinions of the [Warren] Court . . . the absence of workmanlike product, the absence of right quality." Kurland, *supra* note 4, at 144-45. We are told of "opinions that do not opine." Again, if this be accurate, it may confidently be said, as Professor Norman Redlich has ably shown, that no Supreme Court opinion in history better fulfills that characterization than *Marbury v. Madison*. Redlich, *The Supreme Court—1833 Term—Foreword: The Constitution—"A Rule for the Government of Courts, as Well as of the Legislature,"* 40 N.Y.U.L. REV. 1, 3-5 (1965).

Nor, on this count, does *Marbury* stand alone. As Professor Charles Alan Wright has recently asked:

> What Court in the past achieved a higher level of professional craftsmanship than the present Court? The great opinions of Chief Justice Marshall surely fail the test. Marshall discusses issues not properly before him, he flirts with provocative ideas and then puts them to one side, he resorts to esoteric statutory construction to avoid deciding constitutional questions, and he announces important conclusions without any reasoning to support them. Has any later Court done better?

Wright, *The Supreme Court Today*, 3 TRIAL, April-May 1967, at 10-11.

Many of the turgid opinions of Mr. Justice Holmes can be similarly criticized, *e.g.*, the landmark Holmes and Brandeis opinions articulating the "clear and present danger" test, *see* cases cited *supra* note 20; Schenck v. United States, 249 U.S. 47 (1919); Abrams v. United States, 250 U.S. 616 (1919) (dissenting opinion), which leave the most difficult and provocative questions unanswered. And the examples could be multiplied. *See, e.g.*, the opinion of Mr. Justice Frankfurter in Lane v. Wilson, 307 U.S. 268 (1939), whose implications are explored in W. LOCKHART, Y. KAMISAR & J. CHOPER, *supra* note 20, at 1208-10. *See also* Wright, *id.* at 11, regarding Mr. Justice Frankfurter.

42. 1 A. BEVERIDGE, THE LIFE OF JOHN MARSHALL 310 (1916); C. SWISHER, AMERICAN CONSTITUTIONAL DEVELOPMENT 25-27 (2d ed. 1954); Stern, *That Commerce Which Concerns More States Than One*, 47 HARV. L. REV. 1335, 1337 (1934).

with severe economic problems. Protectionist-minded states established discriminatory and burdensome artificial trade barriers against their sister states as well as against foreign nations.[43] Other countries preyed on the newly established industries in the states by refusing to deal with them on reasonable terms.[44] The individual states were incompetent to cope with these problems of commerce,[45] and, under the Articles of Confederation, Congress was equally powerless.

Thus, in brief, the great purpose of the commerce clause was to enable Congress to facilitate interstate trade, to promote development of national industries and markets and, generally, to encourage economic growth. Yet, in *Champion v. Ames*,[46] the famous *Lottery Case*, the Fuller Court (although Mr. Chief Justice Fuller, joined by three of his brethren, dissented) held that the commerce clause authorized Congress to *prohibit* the transportation in interstate commerce of articles intrinsically harmless—a decision whose principle has lead "to the conclusion that Congress may arbitrarily exclude from commerce among the states any article, commodity, or thing, of whatever kind or nature, or however useful or valuable, which it may choose, no matter with what motive. . . ."[47] Thus, despite the purposes of the commerce clause, the Fuller Court upheld Congressional power to hinder interstate trade and, effectively, to destroy those national industries and markets that it wished.

We are told that a major theme of the Warren Court "has been the effective subordination, if not destruction, of the federal system."[48] If this be accurate, I suggest that much of the job had been done at least a half century before. And it was nearly 100 years before the *Lottery Case* that Thomas Jefferson said of the Marshall Court that it was "the subtle corps of sappers and miners constantly working underground to undermine the foundations of our confederated fabric."[49]

You will recall that the commerce clause concerns a grant of power to Congress. It is found in article I of the Constitution, which deals with the Legislative power. The commerce clause makes no mention, directly or indirectly, of the Judiciary, whose constitutional power is described in article III. Yet in 1851, the Taney Court, in *Cooley v. Board of Wardens*,[50] found that, in the absence of relevant federal legislation, the federal judiciary itself has the power to strike down state regulations of interstate commerce. Yet, it is the Warren Court that is charged today by some of its lettered observers with

43. A. BEVERIDGE, *supra* note 42, at 310-12.
44. C. SWISHER, *supra* note 42, at 25.
45. Stern, *supra* note 42, at 1337-41.
46. 188 U.S. 321 (1903).
47. *Id.* at 362. *See* United States v. Darby, 312 U.S. 100 (1941).
48. Kurland, *supra* note 4, at 144.
49. 15 WRITINGS OF THOMAS JEFFERSON 297 (1904).
50. 53 U.S. (12 How.) 299 (1851).

enhancing "judicial dominion at the expense of the power of other branches of government, national as well as state,"[51] and with "the effective subordination, if not destruction, of the federal system."[52] The implication is that this could never be said before. But it was of the Taney Court that the New York Tribune asserted, "Of all the tyrannies that afflict mankind, that of the Judiciary is the most insidious, the most intolerable, the most dangerous."[53]

In evaluating charges made against the Warren Court from the perspective of Supreme Court rulings many decades earlier, I have not referred to decisions that have, for one reason or another, fallen into disrepute—decisions such as *Lochner v. New York*,[54] *Dred Scott v. Sandford*,[55] *Pollock v. Farmers' Loan & Trust Co.*,[56] or the broad federal immunity doctrine in *McCulloch v. Maryland*.[57] This would be too easy. Rather, we have seen that some of the grand landmarks in the judicial history of the United States, decisions that have preserved and enriched the Union, easily and perhaps more accurately lend themselves to the very indictments brought against the work of the Warren Court. Today, we accept and applaud these great decisions of the past. I suggest that in not too many years, the momentous decisions of the Warren Court, highly controversial and roundly criticized when rendered, will similarly be accepted and applauded. The fact of the matter is that this is already true of many, such as *Brown v. Board of Education*[58] and *Gideon v. Wainwright*,[59] and is increasingly becoming true of a number of others, such as the *Reapportionment Cases*[60] and the *School Prayer Cases*.[61] The passage of time and appreciation of the resulting operation of the decisions seem to soothe the fears of the critics.[62]

51. Kurland, *supra* note 4, at 144.
52. *Ibid.*
53. C. WARREN, *supra* note 3.
54. 198 U.S. 45 (1905).
55. 60 U.S. (19 How.) 393 (1857).
56. 157 U.S. 429 (1895).
57. *Supra* note 7.
58. *Supra* note 9.
59. 372 U.S. 335 (1963).
60. *Supra* notes 10, 11.
61. *Supra* notes 12, 13.
62. As Dean Erwin Griswold expressed it recently:

> We take pride in the administration of justice in this country and rightly so. But it has not always been on the level that it has reached now, and we should hardly be surprised if the present level is not the final one. In each instance, as the level has been raised, those who were currently administering justice have been troubled. It is not easy to accept new things, especially when the impetus comes from elsewhere. . . . Throughout history the judges who have been known as great judges have been innovators. . . . Often, there was much grumbling at the time; but in the perspective of history it becomes clear that they have helped to bring our law up to new levels. These are levels of which we soon become proud once we become accustomed to them, and the newness of the new standard wears off.

Griswold, *The Long View*, 51 A.B.A.J. 1017, 1018 (1965).

Miranda v. Arizona, 384 U.S. 436 (1966), bears a substantial brunt of most recent criticism, the charge generally being that its obligation on the police to inform the accused,

V. The Theme of Equality

To this point, we have examined two of the "three dominant movements"[63] that Professor Kurland critically finds characteristic of the Warren Court—"the enhancement of judicial dominion"[64] and "the effective subordination . . . of the federal system."[65] But it is the other "theme"—"the rise of egalitarianism"—that he tells us "contains the most novelty."[66] Here he appears

during custodial interrogation, of his right to silence and to counsel will severely damage law enforcement; that the rule will "markedly decrease the number of confessions," 384 U.S. at 516 (Harlan, J., dissenting), and "measurably weaken the ability of the criminal law to perform," 384 U.S. at 541 (White, J., dissenting).

It is noteworthy that, in the decision's first year of operation, at least some of the nation's most prominent law enforcement officers have not found this to be true at all. See the statements of Attorney General Ramsey Clark, N.Y. Times, May 1, 1967, at 54, col. 3; and District Attorney of Los Angeles County Evelle Younger, 5 AM. CRIM. L.Q. 32 (1966). But, apart from this, perhaps it is true that *Miranda* will, at least in the short run, result in a reduced number of confessions and an increased number of failures to convict. If so, this will be due, in many cases, to the fact, as stated by one public official, that too many law enforcement officers "really know very little about scientific criminal investigation—I doubt that some can even take fingerprints properly—but they often become tremendously effective interrogators." Quoted in Kamisar & Choper, *The Right to Counsel in Minnesota: Some Field Findings and Legal-Policy Observations*, 48 MINN. L. REV. 1, 52 (1963). Or to the fact, as stated by a former prosecutor, that "the weakest part of police work is their insufficient use of surveillance and interviewing before they 'pop the arrest.'" *Id.* at 48 n.202. Compare the record in areas where improvements in the quality, training, and facilities of law enforcement officers have been undertaken. See the statement of then U.S. Attorney for the District of Columbia, Oliver Gasch, in the Washington Post, March 26, 1960, § D, at 1.

Perhaps as suggested by Judge Henry J. Friendly, we do not "truly *know* that, as asserted in *Escobedo*, 378 U.S. at 488-89 (footnotes omitted), 'a system of criminal law enforcement which comes to depend on the "confession" will, in the long run, be less reliable and more subject to abuses than a system which depends on extrinsic evidence independently secured through skillful investigation,'" Friendly, *The Bill of Rights as a Code of Criminal Procedure*, 53 CALIF. L. REV. 929, 955 n.138 (1965). But I think that we may be confident that the Warren Court's *Miranda* decision will, in the not distant future, be commended as a material motivator of greatly improved law enforcement techniques throughout the country, as has, for example, the Hughes Court's decision in Brown v. Mississippi, 297 U.S. 278 (1936), outlawing the "third-degree"—a decision, concededly involving police conduct of a vastly different nature, that also decreased the number of confessions and convictions.

If law enforcement's failure forcefully to advance its detection proficiency were to deter the Court from recognizing and enforcing vital constitutional protections of those accused of crime, this would truly be "treating the sore by encouraging the infection." Rothblatt & Rothblatt, *Police Interrogation: The Right to Counsel and to Prompt Arraignment*, 27 BROOKLYN L. REV. 24, 68 (1960). And, although pragmatic considerations certainly must play a role in all constitutional adjudication, surely it is too late in the day to argue that highly important rights must be submerged because their vindication will result in some crimes not being solved. *See* Weisberg, *Police Interrogation of Arrested Persons: A Skeptical View*, in POLICE POWER AND INDIVIDUAL FREEDOM 171-72 (Sowle ed. 1962); *cf.* Schwartz, *On Current Proposals To Legalize Wire Tapping*, 103 U. PA. L. REV. 157 (1954). *Miranda* has yet to be accorded the benefits of time. I feel not overly optimistic in believing that its greatest impact will be not so much in protection of the accused, but in protection of the public through invigorated law enforcement and crime prevention long overdue.

63. Kurland, *Foreword: "Equal in Origin and Equal in Title to the Legislative and Executive Branches of the Government,"* 78 HARV. L. REV. 143, 144 (1964).

64. *See* text at notes 40 and 51 *supra.*

65. *See* text at notes 48 and 52 *supra.*

66. Kurland, *supra* note 63, at 144.

to be most disapproving, writing that the present Court has "sponsored [an] egalitarian revolution in judicial doctrine,"[67] while pointing to Mr. Justice Holmes' dictum of 40 years ago "that the equal protection clause was 'the usual last resort of constitutional arguments.' "[68] He describes "a good deal of the product of the Warren Court in its search for equality" as "a work of 'jejune logomachy.' "[69]

Again, the basic charge need not be seriously disputed. More moderate[70] commentators have recognized the "heightened concern for equality before the law"[71] of the Warren Court.

Contrary to the plaint of the hostile critics, I suggest that the Court's recent turn to egalitarianism is a salutary movement, quite properly fulfilling its role in a democratic society. For, as those who have carefully examined the complexities of our form of government observe, equality is an essential part of democracy;[72] "our type of civilization depends on 'equal justice under law.' "[73] Indeed, "the premise of democracy is egalitarian."[74]

Before turning more generally to a discussion of the role of the Supreme Court in a democratic society, some examination of the Warren Court's employment of the equal protection clause is warranted. Little need now be said in defense of the Warren Court's first great effort in this connection—its condemnation of all state-imposed racial segregation,[75] thus overturning the Fuller Court's decision in *Plessy v. Ferguson.*[76] It should suffice to note that the earliest decisions interpreting the equal protection clause, those of the Chase and Waite Courts,[77] as well as the overwhelming judgment of students of constitutional law,[78] confirm that it was the Fuller Court and not the War-

67. *Ibid.*

68. *Ibid.*, quoting from Buck v. Bell, 274 U.S. 200, 208 (1927), the Virginia sterilization case, where, one might note parenthetically, the great Justice also noted that "three generations of imbeciles are enough."

69. Kurland, *The Supreme Court Today*, 3 TRIAL, April-May 1967, at 12, 13.

70. *See id.* at 12, for Professor Kurland's description of Professor Paul Freund as "the epitome of Judge Learned Hand's spirit of moderation."

71. Freund, *The Supreme Court Today*, 3 TRIAL, April-May 1967, at 11. *See also* Wright, *The Supreme Court Today*, 3 TRIAL, April-May 1967, at 10.

72. *See* H. MAYO, AN INTRODUCTION TO DEMOCRATIC THEORY 62-64 (1960).

73. Vanderbilt, *The New Federal Criminal Rules*, 51 YALE L.J. 719, 722 (1942).

74. A. BICKEL, THE LEAST DANGEROUS BRANCH 28 (1962). Even Professor Kurland, at an earlier date, has noted that equality is one of the "fundamental objectives of our legal structure . . . ." Kurland, *Of Church and State and the Supreme Court*, 29 U. CHI. L. REV. 1, 96 (1961).

75. For a listing and description of cases, after Brown v. Board of Education, *supra* note 9, holding racial segregation invalid in numerous areas, *see* W. LOCKHART, Y. KAMISAR & J. CHOPER, CONSTITUTIONAL LAW: CASES—COMMENTS—QUESTIONS 1228 (2d ed. 1967).

76. 163 U.S. 537 (1896).

77. Slaughter-House Cases, 83 U.S. (16 Wall.) 36, 71-72 (1873); Strauder v. West Virginia, 100 U.S. 303, 306-08 (1880).

78. *See Brief for the Committee of [almost 200] Law Teachers Against Segregation in Legal Education*, reprinted as *Segregation and the Equal Protection Clause*, 34 MINN. L. REV. 289, 291-92 (1950).

ren Court that was unfaithful to the fourteenth amendment's command of equality.

A. Reapportionment

The 1964 *Reapportionment Cases*,[79] holding that "as a basic constitutional standard, the equal protection clause requires that the seats in both houses of a bicameral state legislature must be apportioned on a population basis,"[80] the other of the Warren Court's grave equal protection judgments, also merits comment. Concededly, the subject matter of these cases, unlike the "hardships being visited on the colored race," was not the "immediate preoccupation"[81] of those who produced the equal protection mandate. But it was equally apparent that the relevant constitutional language "deals not only with racial discrimination, but also with discrimination whether or not based on color."[82] Thus, it was open to the Court, in the "tradition of a broadly worded organic law . . . necessarily intended for permanence,"[83] to treat the matter of legislative apportionment within the confines of the equal protection clause.[84]

As to the constitutional standard adopted, it must be perceived that in the *Reapportionment Cases* the Court "recognized as constitutional rights . . . 'the democratic ideals of equality and majority rule.' "[85] The Court, cogently fulfilling its role in a democratic society, ruled for the majority of citizens and voters in the nation, mostly living in urban areas, whose political influence was being seriously diluted by state legislatures dominated by minority rural interests. On the question of the standard adopted, I believe it is adequate here to point out, as Professor Carl A. Auerbach has thoroughly and admirably demonstrated, that "no reason consistent with the democratic ideals . . . has been advanced for not effectuating"[86] the Court's "one man—one vote" principle; that it is

79. Reynolds v. Sims, 377 U.S. 533 (1964).
80. *Id.* at 568.
81. Bickel, *The Original Understanding and the Segregation Decision*, 69 HARV. L. REV. 1, 60 (1955).
82. *Id.* at 60.
83. *Id.* at 59.
84. *With* Mr. Justice Harlan's contention that "the history of the adoption of the Fourteenth Amendment provides conclusive evidence that neither those who proposed nor those who ratified the Amendment believed that the Equal Protection Clause limited the power of the States to apportion their legislatures as they saw fit," *supra* note 79, at 595, *compare* Van Alstyne, *The Fourteenth Amendment, The "Right" to Vote, and the Understanding of the Thirty-Ninth Congress*, 1965 SUP. CT. REV. 33; Goldberg, *Mr. Justice Harlan, The Uses of History, and the Congressional Globe*, 15 J. PUB. L. 181 (1966). *See also* Auerbach, *The Reapportionment Cases: One Person, One Vote—One Vote, One Value*, 1964 SUP. CT. REV. 1, 77-78; R. MCKAY, REAPPORTIONMENT: THE LAW AND POLITICS OF EQUAL REPRESENTATION 144-45 (1965).
85. Auerbach, *id.* at 66.
86. *Id.* at 67.

> paradoxical for the advocates of judicial self-limitation to criticize the Court for helping to make the majority rule effective, because the case for self-restraint rests on the assumption that the Court is reviewing the legislative acts of representatives who are put in office and can be turned out of office by a majority of the people.[87]

But the Court also ruled in the 1964 *Reapportionment Cases* that a system of legislative malapportionment is violative of equal protection even if the product of a state initiative procedure and even if adopted "by a vote of a majority of a State's electorate."[88] Is this consistent with the Court's basic concern under the equal protection guarantee for "democratic ideals"?

It must first be asked, what would such a "majority of a State's electorate" consist of? Suppose that the "majority" of the state's citizens who voted to under-represent, say, the numerically superior urban population, consisted of a high percentage of the rural voters plus a minority of the urban voters. In this instance, the Court's rule is persuasive: surely, the constitutional right of the majority established by the Court should not be swept away by a combined vote of (a) the rural minority and (b) a minority of the urban majority.

But suppose that the "majority" creating the malapportionment included a majority of those that would be under-represented by the apportionment scheme? Of course, it is highly unlikely that the majority could be found to have voted contrary to their seeming interest, especially when we are confronted with the tremendous complexities involved in identifying which "interest" is represented by which "majority."[89] Perhaps this alone justifies the Court's rule. But, although unlikely, it is conceivable. For example, a majority of urban voters might seek to establish rural over-representation, despite the fact that this would be generally disadvantageous to them, in the belief that a rural-dominated legislature would be less favorably disposed toward affording Negroes equal opportunity.

The Court's rule forbids this, reasoning that the "constitutional rights [of an urban citizen who does not want rural over-representation] can hardly be infringed simply because a majority of the people choose that it be."[90] If the right of an urban citizen "to cast an equally weighted vote,"[91] is an *individual* right, in the same sense as the right of a Negro child to an education free from state-imposed racial segregation, surely the Court's position is unassailable, since a plan of racially segregated education, even if enacted by a referendum with the vote of a majority of both racial groups, would clearly vio-

87. *Id.* at 2.
88. Lucas v. Colorado Gen. Assembly, 377 U.S. 713, 736 (1964).
89. *See* Auerbach, *supra* note 84, at 55-56; W. Lockhart, Y. Kamisar & J. Choper, *supra* note 75, at 1394 *n.b.*
90. Lucas v. Colorado Gen. Assembly, *supra* note 88, at 736-37.
91. *Id.* at 736.

late equal protection. But it is not clear that the rights are the same. The Negro child's right may be vindicated effectively by ordering that *he* be assigned to an integrated school. The urban voter's right may only be vindicated effectively by ordering that *all* urban voters "cast an equally weighted vote." In our hypothetical, a majority of all urban voters have elected *not* to cast an equally weighted vote. While it may convincingly be said that urban citizens, challenging urban under-representation enacted not by a referendum but by a rural-dominated legislature, "seek relief in order to protect or vindicate an interest of their own, and of those similarly situated,"[92] the point is considerably more difficult if a truly free-willed referendum of the kind described above has been held.

This is not to contend that the Court's rule fails. It gains support by reference to other areas of constitutional law in which effectuation of constitutional rights is not hindered by the majority's willingness to waive these rights for themselves. For example, if a referendum were to authorize a state appropriation to construct a Methodist church building, the fact that a majority of non-Methodists had voted approval would not seem to bar an injunction against *any* state payment pursuant thereto as violative of the first amendment's establishment clause made applicable to the states by the fourteenth amendment. Perhaps the constitutional right recognized by the Warren Court in the *Reapportionment Cases* is similar to the right against laws respecting an establishment of religion.

The important point is that despite all the criticism generated by the *Reapportionment Cases,* virtually no analysis is found of this delicate, narrow problem.[93] Here, I suggest, a most useful service could be performed by those who challenge this aspect of the work of the Warren Court.

B. Choice of Grounds for Decision

Finally, in respect to what may well be considered a wholesome use by the Warren Court of the doctrine of equality, it should be noted that, in many contexts, the Court's choice of the equal protection clause is effective in fulfilling the Court's obligations, yet moderate, in that it skillfully permits a measure of free play in the federal system. As Mr. Justice Jackson explained, when the Court invalidates state action as being violative of equal protection, frequently it

> does not disable any governmental body from dealing with the subject at hand. It merely means that the prohibition or regulation must have a broader impact. . . .
>
> The framers of the Constitution knew . . . that there is no more effective practical guaranty against arbitrary and unreasonable gov-

92. Baker v. Carr, *supra* note 10, at 207.
93. *But cf.* Neal, *Baker v. Carr, Politics in Search of Law,* 1962 SUP. CT. REV. 252, 271-74.

> ernment than to require that the principles of law which officials would impose upon a minority must be imposed generally. Conversely, nothing opens the door to arbitrary action so effectively as to allow those officials to pick and choose only a few to whom they will apply legislation and thus to escape the political retribution that might be visited upon them if larger numbers were affected. Courts can take no better measure to assure that laws will be just than to require that laws be equal in operation.[94]

Only infrequently have past Courts efficiently utilized this device. The most noteworthy example, keenly illustrating Mr. Justice Jackson's rationale, is the 1942 decision in *Skinner v. Oklahoma*,[95] in which the Stone Court struck down the state's Habitual Criminal Sterilization Act, not on the ground that the state was without power to sterilize, but rather because the statute's impact was too narrow, including larcenists but not embezzlers. If Oklahoma wished to sterilize, to deny the basic right of procreation, it must do so on a broader basis. The choice was left to the state.

The two great equal protection decisions of the Warren Court that we have examined have not left a truly effective choice to the state. Rather, the *Segregation Cases* and the *Reapportionment Cases,* as a practical matter, clearly applied substantive requirements that cried out for imposition, leaving little room for flexibility.[96] But in confronting other sensitive issues, especially in the past several years, the Warren Court has entered the area restrainedly through the use of the equal protection clause. Thus, in *Baxstrom v. Herold*,[97] the Court avoided deciding the increasingly pressing question of whether a mental commitment must be preceded by a fair judicial hearing with a jury. Rather, the Court was able to hold that New York could not differentiate, for these purposes, between those it considered "civilly insane" and those it considered "criminally insane." Referring to such a hearing as a "matter affecting . . . fundamental rights,"[98] the Court declined to hold that due process inflexibly requires it, but rather forced New York to decide whether, as a political matter, it should withdraw the opportunity for such a hearing to those who already were beneficiaries of it under existing state legislation.[99]

Although this moderate equal protection approach is not without its critics who wish the Court to do more,[100] its use, when appropriate, judiciously fulfills the Court's role in the political framework. Thus, in *Griffin v. Illi-*

94. Railway Express Agency v. New York, 336 U.S. 106, 112-13 (1949) (concurring opinion).
95. 316 U.S. 535 (1942).
96. *See also* Harper v. Virginia Bd. of Elections, 383 U.S. 663 (1966).
97. 383 U.S. 107 (1966).
98. *Id.* at 113.
99. *See also* Rinaldi v. Yeager, 384 U.S. 305 (1966).
100. *See* Foote, *The Proper Role of the United States Supreme Court in Civil Liberties Cases*, 10 WAYNE L. REV. 457, 471-72 (1964).

nois,[101] the Warren Court continued to rest with the states the responsibility for deciding whether they shall "provide appellate courts or a right to appellate review at all."[102] Nevertheless, the Court *held* that if a state chooses to provide appellate review, a matter genuinely affecting "fundamental rights," the "equality demanded by the Fourteenth Amendment"[103] requires that it do not "do so in a way that discriminates against some convicted defendants on account of their poverty."[104]

The "rise of egalitarianism"[105] is conceded, but it is to be commended. In fact, perhaps its rise may not have been extensive enough. Perhaps the decision in *Griswold v. Connecticut,*[106] invalidating the Connecticut anticontraceptive law, might better have been grounded in equal protection rather than in the substantive "peripheries," "penumbras," and "emanations" "created by several fundamental constitutional guarantees,"[107] or in "the language and history of the Ninth Amendment,"[108] or in the seemingly discredited doctrine of substantive due process.[109] The fact appears to be that, in Connecticut, those informed persons who could afford to consult private physicians within or without the state had no difficulty obtaining advice about contraception; that the law was enforced effectively only against birth control clinics which, in the main, aided those "without either adequate knowledge or resources to obtain private counseling."[110]

Had the Court held that the operative discrimination of the law in this "fundamental" area of privacy, requiring "strict scrutiny,"[111] violated equal protection, it could have immunized itself from Mr. Justice Black's charge of engaging in "natural law due process philosophy."[112] Also, Connecticut would have been faced with the choice of abandoning its "uncommonly silly law"[113] or applying it generally, rather than upon a politically weak minority—a choice, but one providing an "effective practical guaranty against arbitrary and unreasonable government."[114]

Even *Miranda v. Arizona*[115] might have lent itself to the "egalitarian revolution."[116] Could the Court thus have reserved the question of whether the

101. 351 U.S. 12 (1956).
102. *Id.* at 18. *See* McKane v. Durston, 153 U.S. 684 (1894).
103. Douglas v. California, 372 U.S. 353, 358 (1963).
104. Griffin v. Illinois, *supra* note 101, at 18.
105. *See* text at note 66 *supra.*
106. 381 U.S. 479 (1965).
107. *Id.* at 485.
108. *Id.* at 487 (Goldberg, J., concurring).
109. *Id.* at 499, 502 (Harlan and White, JJ., concurring).
110. *Id.* at 503 (White, J., concurring).
111. *Id.* at 504 (White, J., concurring).
112. *Id.* at 515 (Black, J., dissenting).
113. *Id.* at 527 (Stewart, J., dissenting).
114. *See* text at note 94 *supra.*
115. *Supra* note 62.
116. *See* text at note 67 *supra.*

privilege against self-incrimination extends to custodial police interrogation[117] and proceeded instead under the precept of "equal justice"?[118] As Judge J. Skelly Wright reports: "The representative of organized crime, when arrested . . . has his lawyer meet him at the precinct station. . . . The same is true of the white collar offender—the influence peddler, the income tax and antitrust violators."[119] Could not the Court have held that the "equality demanded by the Fourteenth Amendment"[120] requires no less for the impecunious and unaware during his period of interrogation, "the most critical period of his ordeal"?[121] While some states undoubtedly would respond by denying counsel to all at this time, some would likely provide it to all rather than forbid it across the board,[122] thus providing a factual record of the effect of providing counsel immediately after arrest. Would this judicial approach not have blunted the complaint of Mr. Justice Harlan, and many others, if the Court were later to extend the privilege against self-incrimination, that the Court did not "have the vast advantage of empirical data and comprehensive study"?[123] Of course, without the Court's impetus,

117. *See generally* Kamisar, *A Dissent from the Miranda Dissents: Some Comments on the "New" Fifth Amendment and the Old "Voluntariness" Test*, 65 MICH. L. REV. 59, 64 (1966).

118. Griffin v. Illinois, 351 U.S. 12, 19 (1956).

119. Wright, *The Supreme Court Today*, 3 TRIAL, April-May 1967, at 14, 16. *See also*, W. BEANEY, THE RIGHT TO COUNSEL IN AMERICAN COURTS 207 (1955): "[I]t is not uncommon in some cities for a 'mouthpiece' to appear at precinct headquarters before [a "professional criminal" or "syndicate representative"] is brought in. The undefended criminals, for the most part, are perpetrators of amateur crime . . . or they are first or youthful offenders." And Professor Wayne LaFave, in his recently published study of police practices in the late 1950's, noted, W. LAFAVE, ARREST 393-94 (1965):

> [R]etained counsel often do enter a case shortly after arrest and immediately confer with their clients or are present when the case reaches the district attorney's office. In Milwaukee, they may actually sit in on the police interrogation. Indigent suspects are not afforded counsel at these early stages.

Along the same lines, a recent New York City Bar report disclosed that

> . . . when an employee [of a policy game or other organized criminal activity] is apprehended and brought before the Judge, there appears at his side a bondsman and an attorney, both unknown and unbidden, by the defendant at least. . . . [F]requently collectors are back on the street taking bets again a few hours after being arrested. . . .

Quoted in D. FREED & P. WALD, BAIL IN THE UNITED STATES: 1964, at 35 (1964).

120. *See supra* note 103.

121. Crooker v. California, 357 U.S. 433, 444 (1958) (dissenting opinion). *See generally* Kamisar & Choper, *supra* note 62, at 55-61.

122. *See* Kamisar, *Equal Justice in the Gatehouses and Mansions of American Criminal Procedure*, in CRIMINAL JUSTICE IN OUR TIME 69 (Howard ed. 1965):

> There is no more effective practical guaranty against arbitrary and unreasonable government then to require that the poor and the stupid and the ignorant be subjected to police interrogation in no greater measure than the rich and the bright and the educated; that the protections extended to the favored few be imposed generally. Conversely, nothing opens the door to arbitrary action so effectively as to allow officials to pick and choose only the less fortunate and the less endowed to be the subjects of secret and persistent police interrogation and thus to escape the political retribution that might be visited upon them if all segments of society were so affected.

123. Miranda v. Arizona, 384 U.S. 436, 524 (dissenting opinion).

I am confident that little "experimentation"[124] would occur, because the states, acting without the Court's prodding, have not been noted for experimenting by expanding the rights of the accused. Rather, the experience has been quite the reverse.[125]

VI. Judicial Review in a Democracy

We turn then, finally, to a broader appraisal of the work of the Warren Court in light of the peculiar position that the United States Supreme Court—a group of nine men, with lifetime appointments, "hedged about by an unusually intricate impeachment process and an absolute guaranty against diminution of compensation"[126]—occupies in a democratic society.

A. Discussion of Theory

It is not my purpose to enter debate on the question of defining precisely what is "democracy." But I hope that you will accept—at least as a general, working definition—one put together recently by Professor Clifton McCleskey: "[A] democratic political system is one in which public policies are made, on a majority basis, by representatives subject to effective popular control at periodic elections which are conducted on the principle of political equality and under conditions of political freedom."[127]

I think you will agree, as earlier noted, that, if anything, the Warren Court's reapportionment decisions[128] promote democratic *values* as so defined. But I think you will further agree that it is not easy to classify the Supreme Court of the United States as established by the Constitution as a democratic *institution.* Mr. Justice Frankfurter wrote that the Court's

124. *Ibid.*

125. Consider the oral argument of Assistant Attorney General of Alabama, George Mentz, appearing as amicus curiae for Florida, in the *Gideon* case. As described by Anthony Lewis in GIDEON'S TRUMPET 179-80 (1964), the following exchanges occurred:

Justice Harlan: "Supposing *Betts* is not overruled. How many years is it going to take Alabama to pass a law like New York and the other states?"
Mentz: "I don't know, but there is a growing feeling in the trial courts that something should be done."

* * *

Justice Harlan: "Supposing you had a choice—as you see it, representing the state—of maintaining *Betts* on the books and then having a succession of cases come to this Court every one of which was reversed by finding special circumstances [of prejudice, because of the absence of counsel], so that everyone would know we were only paying lip service to *Betts*, or of overruling it."
Mentz: "We would rather see them decided case by case."
Justice Harlan: "Even though you know how all of them will come out."
Mentz: "Hope springs eternal." [laughter in the courtroom.]

126. McGowan, *The Supreme Court in the American Constitutional System*, 33 NOTRE DAME LAW. 527, 539 (1958).

127. McCleskey, *Judicial Review in a Democracy: A Dissenting Opinion*, 3 HOUSTON L. REV. 354, 357 (1966).

128. *See* text at notes 85 and 86 *supra.*

powers are "inherently oligarchic";[129] Mr. Justice Brandeis, we are told, was not "wholly without question as to the efficacy and propriety of judicial power in a democratic system."[130] If you refuse to accept the contention that the Court is an antidemocratic institution (although, surely, carefully limited in the exercise of power),[131] then you must agree that it is at least "antimajoritarian,"[132] for even the rarely used control of constitutional amendment does not satisfy the wishes of a simple majority.

It is not my position that the presence of the Court in our political scheme makes our society undemocratic,[133] but with regard to the Court's exercise of the power of judicial review, established in 1803 in *Marbury v. Madison*,[134] it may truly be said "that when the Supreme Court declares unconstitutional a legislative act or the action of an elected executive, it thwarts the will of representatives of the actual people of the here and now; it exercises control, not in behalf of the prevailing majority but against it";[135] "that judicial review is a deviant institution in the American democracy."[136]

This, of course, is by no means to say that the Supreme Court and the doctrine of judicial review do not occupy a meaningful, justifiable, and desirable status in our governmental system. It is merely to state certain premises.

Whether the power of the Supreme Court "to outlaw as unconstitutional acts of elected officials or of officers controlled by elected officials"[137] was intended by the Framers or granted by the Constitution is no longer the real issue. Rather, as Dean Eugene V. Rostow has put it, the power of judicial review "has been exercised by the Court from the beginning. . . . And it stands now, whatever the Founding Fathers may in fact have meant, as an integral feature of the living constitution, long since established as a working part of the democratic political life of the nation."[138] "The weight of . . . history is evidence that the people do expect the courts to interpret, declare, adapt and apply these constitutional provisions, as one of their main protections against the possibility of abuse by Presidents and legislatures."[139]

The meaningful and critical issue *now* is how should this power of judicial

129. AFL v. American Sash & Door Co., 335 U.S. 538, 555 (1949) (concurring opinion).

130. Jaffe, *Was Brandeis an Activist? The Search for Intermediate Premises*, 80 HARV. L. REV. 986, 989 (1967).

131. *See* Rostow, *The Democratic Character of Judicial Review*, 66 HARV. L. REV. 193, 198 (1952).

132. *See generally* McCleskey, *supra* note 127.

133. *See* Rostow, *supra* note 131, at 199-200.

134. *See* text following note 37 *supra*.

135. A. BICKEL, THE LEAST DANGEROUS BRANCH 16-17 (1962).

136. *Id.* at 18.

137. Rostow, *supra* note 131, at 193.

138. Rostow, *The Supreme Court and the People's Will*, 33 NOTRE DAME LAW. 573, 576 (1958).

139. *Id.* at 590.

review be exercised? By what standard?[140] By a Court that is "activist" or "restrained"? In meeting these and related issues, a justifying rationale for the role of the Supreme Court and judicial review in a democratic society becomes highly relevant.

Defenders and explicators of judicial review have not been lacking. Lord Bryce thought of the Court as "the conscience of the people, who have resolved to restrain themselves from hasty or unjust action by placing their representatives under the restriction of a permanent law."[141] Dean Rostow feels that "[t]he discussion of problems and the declaration of broad principles by the Courts is a vital element in the community experience through which American policy is made. The Supreme Court is, among other things, an educational body, and the Justices are inevitably teachers in a vital national seminar."[142] Professor Bickel submits that the Court performs the task, for which "elected institutions are ill fitted," of supporting and maintaining "enduring general values."[143] Professor Charles L. Black contends that "judicial review is the people's institutionalized means of self-control."[144] "[I]t can be justified as something that fulfills popular desire."[145]

But further theory may be advanced. Granting that the Supreme Court is a "deviant institution in the American democracy,"[146] it must also be recognized that, in an important sense, the Constitution itself is similarly antimajoritarian or, if you will, antidemocratic, at least in a limited fashion. Its provisions set the boundaries of each federal department's power vis-à-vis that of the others, of federal power vis-à-vis that of the states, of governmental power vis-à-vis that of the individual. The Constitution commands that these powers may not be exceeded by simple majority will; that a special marshalling of the people's forces is required to alter the boundaries, *i.e.*, to amend the Constitution. Our written Constitution establishes certain "enduring general values,"[147] ultimately subject to democratic modification, but only if the "buffer zone" of the amending process is crossed. This "buffer zone"—the difficult requirement of action by majorities of two-thirds and three-fourths[148]—protects these enduring values against hasty, ill-considered, emotion-ridden action and demands sober, deliberative, reflective consideration.

The perplexing questions here are: *When* is the Constitution violated?

140. *Cf.* Thayer, *The Origin and Scope of the American Doctrine of Constitutional Law*, 7 HARV. L. REV. 129 (1893).
141. I. BRYCE, THE AMERICAN COMMONWEALTH 273 (1913).
142. Rostow, *supra* note 131, at 208.
143. A. BICKEL, *supra* note 135, at 27.
144. C. BLACK, THE PEOPLE AND THE COURT 107 (1960).
145. *Id.* at 117.
146. A. BICKEL, *supra* note 135, at 18.
147. A. BICKEL, *supra* note 135, at 27.
148. U.S. CONST. art. V.

What body of government should decide? *Marbury v. Madison* assigned the task to the Court. And again the question: by what standard should the Court decide?

In exploring this ultimately crucial problem, it seems to me that we must distinguish between two different types of constitutional issues. One is whether authority over the subject matter of federal action has been "delegated" by the Constitution to the national government or whether it has been "reserved to the States."[149] For example, under its delegated powers, is Congress authorized to regulate agricultural production,[150] to tax gambling,[151] to forbid racial discrimination by motels serving interstate travelers,[152] to prohibit states from denying the right to vote to those who are not literate in English?[153] Or are these matters beyond the federal realm and thus reserved to the respective states? Put succinctly, do these federal actions violate "states' rights"?

The other general issue that arises[154] is whether a particular exercise of governmental power, national or state, infringes individual rights guaranteed by the Constitution. Without exhausting the list of these individual rights afforded constitutional protection or, in any way, attempting to define their substantive content, one need only refer, as examples, to the original Constitution's prohibitions of bills of attainder and ex post facto laws,[155] to the first eight amendments (popularly known as the Bill of Rights), to the fourteenth amendment's guarantees of due process and equal protection.

It seems to me that if the constitutional issue is one only of states' rights, the role of the Supreme Court, in determining whether the national government has unconstitutionally invaded the domain of the states, should be severely limited. The justification for *judicial* review in this instance, for the final constitutional word to be spoken by a "deviant institution"[156] in a democracy, is weak. The states, whose constitutional rights are allegedly being assaulted, are well represented in the councils of national government (especially the Congress) and are in a peculiarly strong position to protect themselves against national encroachment.[157] Here, the political process may generally be depended upon to produce a fair judgment. If a majority of the states' representatives (and I believe this is a wholly accurate description of

149. U.S. CONST. amend. X.
150. *See* United States v. Butler, 297 U.S. 1 (1936); Wickard v. Filburn, 317 U.S. 111 (1942).
151. *See* United States v. Kahriger, 345 U.S. 22 (1953).
152. *See* Heart of Atlanta Motel, Inc. v. United States, 379 U.S. 241 (1964).
153. *See* Katzenbach v. Morgan, 384 U.S. 641 (1966).
154. The matter of division of power among the federal departments is beyond the specific scope of the discussion.
155. U.S. CONST. art. I, § 10.
156. A. BICKEL, *supra* note 135, at 18.
157. *See* Dowling, *The Methods of Mr. Justice Stone in Constitutional Cases*, 41 COLUM. L. REV. 1160, 1173 (1941).

members of Congress) determine that federal power has not been exceeded, then the Court should overturn the decision, if at all, only if it is so clearly in error as not to be "open to rational question."[158]

But if the issue is one of alleged governmental infringement of individual rights protected by the Constitution, it seems to me that the Court's role should be quite different. These constitutional guarantees—such as the freedoms of speech and religion, the constitutional rights of those accused of crime, the right to be free from certain racial discrimination—are generally rights of "politically impotent minorities."[159] By definition, the processes of democracy bode poorly for the security of such rights.[160] Rather, such rights are frequently endangered by popular majorities.[161] Thus, the task of guarding these constitutionally prescribed liberties sensibly falls upon a body that is not politically responsible, that is not beholden to the grace of excited majoritarianism—the United States Supreme Court. Herein lies the great justification for the power of judicial review, the wisdom of *Marbury v. Madison*. In this area, the Court, if it is properly to fulfill its place in American democratic society, must act more forcefully[162]—perhaps "by creating a presumption against the validity of the contested action,"[163] perhaps "by more

158. Thayer, *supra* note 140, at 141. Some limited degree of judicial supervision in this area may be justified if the confinement of federal power to that specified in the Constitution is seen as having a purpose beyond the protection of "states' rights", *i.e.*, if a secondary or indirect purpose of providing that the central government be one of limited powers is the protection of the individual against the potential abuses of an all-powerful national government.

159. Rostow, *supra* note 131, at 202.

160. Consider the remarks of former Senator Kenneth Keating, *Harvard Legal Aid Bureau* Annual Banquet, Feb. 18, 1965, at 18-20:

> I think it is probably fair to say the indigent persons generally, but especially those who are alleged to be not among the law-abiding, are at the tender mercies of all the rest of us, especially those who sit in the Halls of Congress. We are all aware of the weighty influence wielded, for example, by the organized *medical* profession and the organized *bar* upon legislation in Congress. It has become commonplace to speak of the "A.M.A. Lobby" or, in the education field, the "N.E.A. Lobby." But there is no lobby of the A.C.D.A., The American Criminal Defendant's Association. . . .
>
> Fortunately, there are groups such as the American Civil Liberties Union and the NAACP which take a strong interest in the administration of the criminal law as it affects the disadvantaged defendant. But their voice in the legislative process is diluted by the fact that the clientele group for which they purport to speak normally exercises little political power, and, in fact, those in the group who have been convicted of felony have been by law politically sterilized. . . . This is the key explanation of why the recognition of the rights of indigents has been largely confined to the judicial process. And it is one of the great ironies of American life, and always has been, that the Congress and State legislatures will be critical of judicial law-making particularly in the administration of criminal justice, while failing to recognize that the courts cannot but respond firmly to social necessity when the legislative branch abdicates responsibilities for constructive action.

161. *See* C. Black, *supra* note 144, at 103-04.

162. *Contra*, L. Hand, The Bill of Rights 66-67 (1958).

163. Dowling, *supra* note 157, at 1176.

closely scrutinizing the methods employed and the objectives to which they lead."[164]

B. The Warren Court's Role

The Warren Court has admirably fulfilled this critical role. It has courageously spoken in behalf of individual rights and these decisions have produced the bulk of the attack against it. It was for the Warren Court to sustain the promise of the equal protection clause in *Brown v. Board of Education,* for "neither the Presidency nor the Congress, nor the states acted to protect the rights of Negro citizens."[165] Nor, unfortunately, as a realistic matter, should we have expected political protection for the racial minority. It was for the Warren Court to insure a fair and effective political process and "to fill a vacuum created by the paralysis of the legislative branches of our governments"[166] in the *Reapportionment Cases,* for it was clear " that those elected officials, who held their offices by reason of a rotten borough system, could not be expected to vote for its abolition."[167] It was for the Warren Court to assure the rights of citizens to be free from unreasonable searches and seizures in *Mapp v. Ohio,*[168] for it was plain that the political process was inadequate; twelve years had passed since the states had been told that such action violated the Constitution, yet more than half of them continued to admit into evidence the fruit of the violation.[169] It was for the Warren Court to defend the right of free speech[170] against overly broad governmental attacks on communism and "disloyalty," because unlike such countries as France or Italy, communism here is an impotent domestic political force.[171] And the examples could be multiplied.

Likewise, in cases involving states' rights, the Warren Court has acted with suitable restraint. And it has been the refusal of past Supreme Courts to do so that has frustrated efforts to combat frightful national crises such as the Great Depression.[172] In sustaining congressional power under the commerce

164. *Ibid.*
165. Wright, *supra* note 119, at 15.
166. *Id.* at 16.
167. *Ibid.*
168. 367 U.S. 643 (1961).
169. *Id.* at 680 (dissenting opinion). Perhaps the best evidence of the need for an exclusionary rule to assure the fourth amendment guaranty was the reaction of a number of law enforcement officers to the rule's imposition. *See* Kamisar, *The Tactics of Police-Prosecution Oriented Critics of the Courts,* 49 CORNELL L.Q. 436, 440 (1964):

> [M]any in [state] law enforcement reacted to the adoption of the exclusionary rule as if the guarantees against unreasonable search and seizure *had just been written!* They talked as if and acted as if the exclusionary rule *were* the guaranty against unreasonable search and seizure. What disturbed them so much was that the courts were now operating on the same premise.

170. *See, e.g.,* Elfbrandt v. Russell, 384 U.S. 11 (1966); Keyishian v. Board of Regents, 385 U.S. 589 (1967); DeGregory v. Attorney General, 383 U.S. 825 (1966).
171. *See* Rostow, *supra* note 131, at 203.
172. *See, e.g.,* Schecter Poultry Corp. v. United States, 295 U.S. 495 (1935); Carter v. Carter

clause to enact provisions of the Civil Rights Act of 1964, in *Heart of Atlanta Motel, Inc. v. United States*[173] and *Katzenbach v. McClung*,[174] the Warren Court adhered to an established tradition of granting a strong presumption to an exercise of national control over the economy.[175] But, in sustaining congressional power under the enforcement clauses of the fourteenth and fifteenth amendments to enact provisions of the Voting Rights Act of 1965, in *South Carolina v. Katzenbach*[176] and *Katzenbach v. Morgan*,[177] the Warren Court seemingly adopted a newer theme, granting virtually unlimited power "for a vast expansion of congressional legislation promoting human rights."[178] And, in my view, this is as it should be. For the basic issue involved under section 5 of the fourteenth amendment and section 2 of the fifteenth amendment is the same as that under the commerce clause: whether Congress has exceeded its powers and encroached on an area reserved to the states. Given the political influence possessed by the states in Congress, the constitutional issue should virtually always be resolved there.

VII. Conclusion

The Supreme Court of the United States need not be, nor is it, "the conscience of the people."[179] Nor, for that matter, need it be, nor is it, a "one-man band,"[180] that department of government to cure all social and political ills in the country. One need not approve nor agree with every judgment that the Court has made. I certainly do not. I do believe that the strongest indictment of the Warren Court is that it has zealously—perhaps, in some cases, even overzealously—guarded the asserted constitutional rights of those whose only effective forum for expression of those rights has been the Court itself. For example, those disenfranchised Negroes, particularly in some parts of the South, who could not obtain any help from legislatures where they were not represented and those partially disenfranchised citizens in urban centers throughout the country to whom rural dominated legislatures turned their backs. To the charge of protecting the rights of groups such as these, a plea

---

Coal Co., 298 U.S. 238 (1936); United States v. Butler, 297 U.S. 1 (1936); Railroad Retirement Bd. v. Alton R.R., 295 U.S. 330 (1935); Louisville Joint Stock Land Bank v. Radford, 295 U.S. 555 (1935); Ashton v. Cameron County Dist., 298 U.S. 513 (1936).

173. 379 U.S. 241 (1964).

174. 379 U.S. 294 (1964).

175. *See, e.g.*, Gibbons v. Ogden, 22 U.S. (9 Wheat.) 1 (1824); United States v. Darby, 312 U.S. 100 (1941).

176. 383 U.S. 301 (1966).

177. 384 U.S. 641 (1966).

178. Cox, *Foreword: Constitutional Adjudication and the Promotion of Human Rights*, 80 HARV. L. REV. 91, 107 (1966).

179. *See* text at note 141 *supra*.

180. Kurland, *Foreword: "Equal in Origin and Equal in Title to the Legislative and Executive Branches of the Government,"* 78 HARV. L. REV. 143, 176 (1964).

of guilty may well be advised. But for what more important function was the Supreme Court created? Remove this avenue for protection of the constitutional rights of the individual and, I suggest, the fight, inherently incapable of being waged in the legislative halls, has only one remaining battleground. That is the streets. The alternatives to careful judicial review are either disobedience of the law (which could not be changed otherwise) or complacent acceptance (for attempts to sear the consciences of those in power have been notable failures). Both alternatives—violence and decadence—are intolerable. The Warren Court today fulfills the central justification of *Marbury v. Madison*—concern for those about whom the other branches and divisions of government often will not be concerned.

THE ROLE OF THE SUPREME COURT IN AMERICAN SOCIETY

ARCHIBALD COX*

One hundred and thirty years have done nothing to diminish the truth of De Tocqueville's observations upon the pervasiveness of law in American society[1] but, if we are a people ruled by law and lawyers, we are also the freest people the world has ever known. The coincidence of these two facts is not mere happenstance. We are free because we have subjected ourselves to the rule of law.

The reason is this. Men can be lifted from savagery to a form of civilization solely through the pacification achieved by concentrating power in the hands of the State, but neither mere pacification nor the concentration of power will secure individual liberty and opportunities for each generation to remake society, if it can, without a violent revolution. To achieve those goals even the power of the government must be restrained and ways must be found by which men can live together not by power, be it physical, economic, or in some cases even political, but by what reason shows is just. There can be neither liberty nor opportunity for peaceful changes without a substitute for power.

Our substitute is the rule of law. Our constitutionalism is founded upon seven or eight centuries of continuous concern for the institutions and aspirations—for the processes, standards, ideals and sense of right and justice—that make for a free and civilized society achieved with a minimum of force and a maximum of reason. The germ of the idea that law was the bulwark of the individual against the sovereign was expressed in Magna Carta and restated by Bracton: *"Nonsub homine sub Deo et lege."* Lord Coke revitalized the principle when he told King James that the King might find ten new judges who would subordinate their decisions to the royal prerogative but never ten lawyers. Through our own Bill of Rights even the people, the ultimate rulers in the United States, have voluntarily subjected themselves to the restraint of law, and we have created courts to help us observe the law's prohibitions. Ours is a free society because the law binds all men equally, the governors as well as the governed, the judges as well as the litigants.

It is the capacity to command free assent that makes law a substitute for power. The force of legitimacy—and conversely the habit of voluntary compliance—is the foundation of the law's civil-

* Williston Professor of Law, Harvard Law School. Solicitor General of the United States, 1961-65. B.A., Harvard, 1934, LL.B., Harvard, 1937.

[1] DE TOCQUEVILLE, DEMOCRACY IN AMERICA 272-280 (Alfred A. Knopf, Inc. 1945).

izing and liberalizing influence. There appears to be no alternative short of the millennium.

Both the pervasiveness of law in American society and the dependency of law upon consent are epitomized in the role of the Supreme Court of the United States. As De Tocqueville observed, "Scarcely any political question arises in the United States that is not resolved, sooner or later, into a judicial question,"[2] and it is to the Supreme Court that those political questions ultimately come. Part of the Supreme Court's docket is unusual only in its difficulty but the other part—much the more important part—is utterly unlike the usual flow of litigation through the State and lower federal courts. Many of the cases would never come before the judiciary in any other country. Where else would you find a court charged with deciding whether prayers should be said or the Bible read at the start of the day in the schoolhouse;[3] whether Negroes are entitled to equal public accommodations;[4] or how the seats should be apportioned in a State legislature.[5] Another example is the litigation over the apportionment of the waters of the Colorado River, which might well determine the relative opportunities for agricultural and industrial development in Arizona and California.[6] In the United States, as nowhere else in the world, we have developed the extraordinary habit of casting critical aspects of social, economic, political and even philosophical questions into the form of actions at law and suits in equity so that the courts may participate in their disposition.

Each decade produces its own example of constitutional litigation resulting from the problems and divisions in contemporary society. Since our era is dominated by the coming of age, politically and economically, of the people of Asia and Africa, many of today's great constitutional issues grow out of the problems of race relations: the school desegregation cases,[7] the sit-in litigation[8] and the various challenges to the constitutionality of the Civil Rights Act.[9] You will think of many other examples of the Court's concern with

[2] *Id.* at 280.
[3] Engel v. Vitale, 370 U.S. 421 (1962); Abington School District v. Schempp, 374 U.S. 203 (1963).
[4] Bell v. Maryland, 378 U.S. 226 (1964).
[5] Baker v. Carr, 369 U.S. 186 (1962); Reynolds v. Sims, 377 U.S. 533 (1964).
[6] Arizona v. California, 373 U.S. 546 (1963).
[7] Brown v. Board of Education, 347 U.S. 483 (1954); Goss v. Board of Education, 373 U.S. 683 (1963); Griffin v. County School Board, 377 U.S. 218 (1964).
[8] *E.g.* Garner v. Louisiana, 368 U.S. 157 (1961); Peterson v. Greenville, 373 U.S. 244 (1963); Lombard v. Louisiana, 373 U.S. 267 (1963); Bell v. Maryland, 378 U.S. 226 (1964); Hamm v. City of Rock Hill, 379 U.S. 306 (1964).
[9] United States v. Raines, 362 U.S. 17 (1960); Alabama v. United States, 371 U.S. 37 (1965); Heart of Atlanta Motel v. United States, 379 U.S. 241 (1964); Katzenbach v. McClung, 379 U.S. 294 (1964); South Carolina v. Katzenbach, 383 U.S. 301 (1966).

the deep-running tensions in our national life. The reapportionment cases beginning with *Baker v. Carr*[10] emerged from the contest between rural and urban or suburban voters. Others result from the conflict between ideals of individual liberty and pressures for conformity at times when our national security seems threatened.[11] In any age of increasing regulatory measures a large part of the Court's work involves the protection of the individual against thoughtless, inept and occasionally oppressive government officials.

Individuals bring these cases. Lawyers remember them by their names. But the issues transcend and the rulings long survive the individuals' quarrels. Often they are questions upon which the country appears deeply divided. They arouse intense emotions. Their resolution writes our history. Yet we leave them, at least partly and often finally, to the Court.

The unique nature of the Court's work, more than any other characteristic, places its stamp upon the institution, creates the Court's own peculiar problems, and shapes its role in our national life.

Thus, it is the special quality of the issues that does most to explain the sharp divisions within the Court. Such disagreements and five-to-four or six-to-three decisions are not merely unavoidable but desirable. Unanimity could be achieved only by appointing to the Court nine justices with the same cast of mind and the same set of experiences. Then we would have unanimous decisions and a clear-cut line of authority, all one way or all the other. That might seem desirable to those who are convinced that they know all the right answers to all the questions—might seem desirable if the Court's unanimous answers were the same as theirs. In truth, the community's most fundamental and divisive issues should not be decided overnight nor should they be decided in clean-cut fashion, all one way or all the other, until time and events have matured the analysis. One makes safer and quicker progress through an unfamiliar swamp by proceeding from hummock to hummock and island to island sometimes taking one step back for every two steps forward or even one step forward and two steps back.

It is the character of the Court's business which catches it up in public debate and makes individual justices the subjects of bitter criticism. This is nothing new. John Marshall was reviled in terms more virulent than even the present Chief Justice. Proper criticism is not to be regretted, whether it comes from laymen or lawyers.

[10] 369 U.S. 186 (1962).

[11] *E.g.* Watkins v. United States, 354 U.S. 178 (1957); Barenblatt v. United States, 360 U.S. 109 (1959); Yellin v. United States, 374 U.S. 109 (1963); Communist Party v. Subversive Activities' Control Board, 367 U.S. 1 (1961); Albertson v. Subversive Activities' Control Board, 382 U.S. 70 (1965).

It is essential, because the public questions which the Court faces are pressing and divisive, that they should be publicly debated each step at a time while the Court is pragmatically evolving new principles. The ultimate resolution of questions so fundamental to the whole community as to be constitutional must be based in a common consensus of opinion.

The nature of the Court's business also shapes the process of reaching decisions. We refer constitutional issues to the Court not for the opinion of a Council of Wise Men as to what is good or just or wise but for a decision according to law. Charles Evans Hughes, in a series of lectures delivered after his service as an Associate Justice but before he became Chief Justice of the United States, remarked that:

> The success of the work of the Supreme Court . . . has been due largely to the deliberate determination of the Court to confine itself to its judicial task.[12]

Yet the very fact that its decisions involve some of our most fundamental public issues inescapably requires the Court to consider the social, economic and policy consequences of its decisions. One might as well ask the sun to stand still as expect the Court to rule upon the constitutionality of the Voting Rights Act of 1965 without considering the effect of the decision upon the civil rights movement and confidence in our political system. Surely this is proper. Law, like other aspects of government, is a human institution designed to meet men's needs. The civil rights movement tests our capacity to accomplish within the framework of domestic government and the rule of law the revolutionary changes required for rudimentary human justice. Three continents are watching us while they choose whether to nurture or reject the ways of democratic constitutionalism and legality. Similarly, the school desegregation cases, the "sit-in" litigation, and the challenges to constitutionality of the several civil rights acts could not have been decided wisely nor can the Court's work be understood without recognizing that it is called upon to preside over parts of a social and political upheaval.

Thus, the constitutional litigation presents a dilemma: it requires the Supreme Court to be more judicial than other governmental bodies yet more political (*i.e.*, concerned with policy) than other courts.

I shall return to this dilemma a little later but first it seems appropriate, having canvassed the unique character of the Supreme Court's business, to ask why we refer such questions to the courts. In De Tocqueville's words, why is it that scarcely any political

[12] HUGHES, THE SUPREME COURT OF THE UNITED STATES 40-41 (1963).

question arises that we do not resolve, sooner or later, into a judicial question? The ultimate answer is the faith in law to which I have already adverted. The immediate answers are the duties put upon the Court.

I

One special charge of the Court is responsibility for the framework of our government. The Founding Fathers believed that the organization of any government would powerfully affect its substantive policies, and therefore they carefully divided the sum of all sovereign power between the Nation and the States; and then divided it again, in the national sphere, between three coordinate branches. A century later Lord Acton idealized the choice:

> If the distribution of power among the several parts of the State is the most efficient restraint on monarchy, the distribution of power among several States is the best check upon democracy. By multiplying centers of government and discussion it promotes the diffusion of political knowledge and the maintenance of healthy and independent opinion. It is the protectorate of minorities and the consecration of self-government.[13]

Through the genius of John Marshall the Court became the guardian and umpire of this extraordinarily complicated framework. For a century, perhaps even a century and a half, the dominant aspect of its work was mediating between States and Nation, dividing between them the sum of all governmental power and keeping the whole in that balance best suited to the long-term needs of the community. The process is infinitely complex for it deals not only with the respective powers of the State and federal governments to regulate and the States' power to tax but also with the interrelationships between separate State and federal courts each charged with applying its own set of laws and also the laws of the other sovereign.

Since the beginning the trend has been toward the nationalization of governmental power. I do not mean to suggest that the constitutional principle has changed from that stated by Marshall in *Gibbons v. Ogden:*

> The genius and character of the whole government seem to be, that its action is to be applied to all the external concerns of the nation, and to those internal concerns which affect the States generally; but not to those which are completely within a particular State, which do not affect other States, and with which it is not necessary to interfere, for the pur-

[13] Acton, *The History of Freedom in Antiquity, in* ESSAYS ON FREEDOM AND POWER, p. 72 (Meridian Books, 1957).

pose of executing some of the general powers of the government.[14]

It is the facts that have altered. Economic as well as scientific and technological revolutions have made the economy so interdependent and the interrelation so plainly apparent that there are few internal concerns—almost none of a commercial or business character—which do not, in Marshall's words, so "affect the states generally" as to be within the power of Congress. The issue today is seldom what has Congress *power* to regulate; it is what degree of central regulation is it wise to impose, bearing in mind the effects of the centralization of regulatory authority. The growth of national markets and an integrated economy has shifted the ultimate responsibility for the balance of the federal system from the courts to the Congress.

The pressure toward national determination has also been felt in the area of voting and here, to a degree, the question is still constitutional. Establishing voter qualifications has always been a State function, not only by continuous tradition but also by the plain implication of the constitutional provision stipulating that qualifications of voters in federal elections shall be those required of the electors for the most numerous branch of each State legislature.[15] The Fifteenth Amendment qualified the State's prerogative to the extent of prohibiting abridgment of the right of citizens to vote on account of race or color, but history makes it plain that Congress assumed that this provision would leave States free to establish literacy tests for voting. The Voting Rights Act of 1965 abolishes all State literacy tests, however administered in the future, where there is evidence of past discriminatory administration, as a means of enforcing the Fifteenth Amendment.[16] This legislation, so long as the danger of racial discrimination exists, will make a profound change in the distribution of State and national power, and I suspect that its nationalizing influence upon the federal system will be felt long after the occasion for the exercise of the power has departed.

The constitutionality of the Voting Rights Act has not yet been decided.[17] Section 2 of the Fifteenth Amendment gives Congress power—

> to enforce this article by appropriate legislation.

---

[14] 22 U.S. (9 Wheat.) 1 (1824).

[15] U.S. Const. art. I, §2.

[16] Section 4(a), P.L. 89-110, 79 Stat. 437 (1965).

[17] The constitutionality of the Act was sustained on March 7, 1966. South Carolina v. Katzenbach, 383 U.S. 301 (1966). The text of this lecture, which was delivered prior to the decision, has been left unchanged.

In the case now pending before the Supreme Court, South Carolina pitched much of her case upon the argument that appropriate legislation "to enforce" the prohibition is confined to dealing with actual violations and does not include the enactment of regulatory laws reducing the danger of violations. The Attorney General joined issue, arguing upon precedent and analogy to the congressional powers under Article I that the power to enact appropriate legislation for the prevention of discrimination in voting includes all measures which Congress could reasonably deem related to that objective.

Having participated in drafting the Voting Rights Act and the argument in support of its constitutionality, my view of the case is hardly neutral, but it may be permissible to repeat that the issue thus joined reveals the dilemma which the Court faces in passing the final word upon questions of enormous practical and political consequence. The Court cannot ignore the practical consequences of its action. At the same time its constitutional function, defined by history as well as the implications of the document, is to decide whether the exercise of such national power disturbs the frame of government erected in 1789 as modified by the Fourteenth and Fifteenth Amendments. The performance of that function is of inestimable political importance if, as the founders believed, the frame of government influences substantive policies. Another judgment upon the wisdom of the policy embodied in a statute is no substitute for the voice of the organ of government charged with the long-run allocation of power. Somehow the Court must avoid both horns of this dilemma.

II

To the Supreme Court we have also committed a special and ultimate responsibility for the relationship between the individual and the State. In the debate upon the first ten amendments Madison explained:

> If they are incorporated into the Constitution, independent tribunals of justice will consider themselves in a peculiar manner the guardian of those rights; they will be an impenetrable bulwark against every assumption of power in the Legislative or the Executive; they will be naturally led to resist every encroachment upon rights expressly stipulated for in the Constitution by the declaration of rights.[18]

The flowering of this judicial function was reserved for an age in which the increasing interdependence and complexity of all parts of human society enormously multiplied and magnified governmental activity. As late as 1922 the Court declared, "neither the

[18] 1 Annals of Congress, 1st Cong., 1st and 2nd Sess., 439.

Fourteenth Amendment nor any other provision of the Constitution of the United States imposes upon the States any restrictions about freedom of speech" (*Prudential Ins. Co. v. Cheek,* 259 U.S. 530, 543). Today, less than half a century later, a major part of the constitutional litigation is concerned with imposing restrictions upon what States may do about both freedom of speech and freedom of association. This increase in civil liberties' litigation has paralleled the growth of governmental activity for at least two reasons: (1) the enormous growth of public regulation proliferates the occasions on which government collides with personal liberty; (2) the very intervention of government into more and more aspects of our daily lives makes us more conscious of the necessity of marking off a private spiritual area into which government should be forbidden to enter.

The task of protecting the individual against the aggressions of government, which under our system usually means aggressions willed by representatives of a majority of the people, often conflicts with the Court's special duty of maintaining the frame of government, which includes the separation of legislative and judicial power. Judicial review calls upon the Court to go over the very social, political and economic questions committed to the Congress and State legislatures, yet it can scarcely do so without usurping in some degree the legislative function of weighing and balancing competing interests. Here is a third basic dilemma in constitutional adjudication.

The point can be illustrated by an example based upon last Term's litigation over the restrictions on travel to Castro's Cuba.[19] If a statutory ban were proposed, a legislator would have to consider the effect of inability to protect our citizens traveling in those areas upon the protection afforded elsewhere, the risk that attacks upon U. S. citizens in Cuba would embroil us in diplomatic difficulties or even war, the pressure upon the Castro regime of suspending intercourse, and the relation between the prohibition and inter-American efforts to prevent Castro from exporting sedition and revolution to other Latin American countries. Against such considerations the legislator would weigh the cost in terms of individual liberty of suspending freedom of travel and the effects, both here and in Communist countries, of erecting a wall against the exchange of ideas. The breadth of the proposed ban might affect one's thinking.

If majorities in Congress and the President struck the balance

[19] Zemel v. Rusk, 381 U.S. 1 (1965). The example used in the text differs significantly from the actual case which involved executive power to withhold passports for Cuba under existing legislation.

in favor of the statutory prohibition and its constitutionality were challenged, how could the Court decide the case at all and still avoid substituting its judgment for that of Congress?

There is no satisfactory answer to this question. One approach is to ask whether the Bill of Rights specifically secures freedom to travel abroad and to uphold any legislation that does not curtail a right specifically mentioned in the Constitution upon the ground that a legislature is not restricted by the due process clause except as it incorporates specific constitutional guarantees.[20] There is no explicit guarantee of freedom to travel in the Constitution.

Alternatively, one might contend that travel abroad is necessary to secure information about social, economic and political conditions and such knowledge is indispensable to free discussion in political debate or simply in expanding human knowledge, thus bringing liberty of travel within the constitutional guaranty of freedom of speech.[21] On this predicate it could be argued that since the First Amendment provides that Congress shall make *no law* restricting freedom of speech, it can make no law restricting freedom of travel.

The Court appears to have rejected these approaches in favor of the view that the liberty guaranteed by the Fifth Amendment includes a right to travel but the liberty is not absolute.[22] It would seem quite plain, for example, that travel to an area ravaged by famine, flood or disease can be restricted in the interest of health and public order. Applied to our hypothetical restriction upon travel to Cuba, this approach seemingly requires the Court to go over the very same ground covered in the legislature and thus to review its judgment. How can the Court determine whether the legislative restriction violates due process without evaluating both the right and the need for curtailment? If the Court does that, is it not usurping the function of the Congress and violating the separation of powers? If it fails to do that, is it not abdicating the function of enforcing constitutional restrictions?

The conventional escape from this dilemma is to say that the conclusions of Congress will stand unless they are so wrong, upon any state of facts that might rationally be supposed to exist, as to be irrational, arbitrary or capricious, fundamentally unfair or shocking to the conscience of a free people. The formula has substance to command it but the difference between saying that an important law is foolish and saying that it is arbitrary or violates fundamental

[20] Compare Justices Black and Stewart dissenting in Griswold v. Connecticut, 381 U.S. 479, 507-531 (1965).

[21] Zemel v. Rusk, 381 U.S. 1, 25-26 (1965) (dissenting opinion of Justice Douglas).

[22] Zemel v. Rusk, 381 U.S. 1, 13-17 (1965).

rights lies chiefly in the strength of the speaker's conviction. Any weighing and balancing of the very same interests appraised by the legislature inescapably evokes personal judgments upon the relative importance of imponderable elements.

Whatever the answer to these questions the Court's responsibility for the framework of government does less to check the Court's reviewing of laws affecting personal liberty than its scrutiny of statutes regulating business and economic practices. This position has strong roots in constitutional history. The Bill of Rights is the chief express constitutional limitation upon legislative power. It is concerned not with the physical safety of society, jobs or economic activity and security—the bricks and mortar of the community—but with the realm of the spirit. The Framers dreamed that if their hopes for civil liberty were codified, man's energies of mind and spirit, released from fear, would flourish. They also knew that society's respect for the freedom of a man to grow and choose the best he can discern must be founded upon the protection of privacy and just and humane criminal procedure. Regulation of economic activity and the use of property would seem to belong in a different area of discourse, even though the dividing line is blurred by the use of speech for the economic purposes of management and labor.[23] There is force, too, in Chief Justice Stone's suggestion that the nature of representative government requires more exacting scrutiny of legislation which restricts those political processes which can ordinarily be expected to bring about the repeal of undesirable legislation, or which is directed at minorities whose condition is so peculiar as to escape political resolution.[24]

III

Until recently the Court's responsibility for the relationship between the individual and the government centered upon protection against a hostile government. Today that responsibility extends, I think, to a second aspect of the relation—the affirmative obligations of the government to its citizens. The difference is between warding off legislative attacks upon civil liberties and securing civil rights. The impetus came from the demand for racial equality which is so profoundly influencing other aspects of our fundamental law. Already the negative side of constitutionalism is beginning to be matched by an affirmation of the State's duty to advance fundamental human rights. This new development greatly complicates the role of the Court.

---

[23] Compare Thornhill v. Alabama, 310 U.S. 88 (1940) with such later cases as Teamsters Union v. Vogt, Inc., 354 U.S. 284 (1957). See also NLRB v. Virginia Electric & Power Co., 314 U.S. 469 (1941).

[24] United States v. Carolene Products Co., 304 U.S. 144, 152, note 4 (1938).

The roots of the development go back to the post-Civil War Reconstruction. The original Bill of Rights had two important limitations. *First,* it applied only to the federal government. The relations between a State government and the individual were left entirely to local determination.[25] *Second,* the Bill of Rights was negative. My colleague Mark De Wolfe Howe points out that it should have been called a schedule of immunities because it was essentially a "no trespassing sign marking off a world of the spirit where government would have no jurisdiction."

The adoption of the Civil War Amendments removed both limitations. When the Fourteenth Amendment provided that no State should deprive any person of life, liberty or property without due process of law, it made the Bill of Right's guarantee of civil liberty, privacy and fair criminal procedure at least partly applicable to State governments. With that step the national government pledged itself to make the guarantees effective. The pledge affirms a governmental role in securing liberty, and the whole truth can no longer be expressed in a metaphoric reference to the privilege of being let alone and a lack of governmental jurisdiction.

Indeed, the Fourteenth and Fifteenth Amendments, despite their generally negative language, carry unmistakable overtones of individual's claims on government—of civil rights, and not merely civil liberties—so fundamental as to require expression in the Constitution. Shortly after the enactment of the Fifteenth Amendment, in *United States v. Cruikshank,*[26] Mr. Justice Bradley, while sitting on circuit, pointed out that the Fifteenth Amendment:

> confers a positive right which did not exist before. The language is peculiar. It is composed of two negatives. The right shall not be denied. That is, the right shall be enjoyed. . . .[27]

Much the same appears true of the equal protection clause of the Fourteenth Amendment. Abstractly a State can avoid violations by granting no one the protection of its laws, but in truth the prohibition against discrimination carries an obligation to extend the laws and other State benefits equally to all races. The school desegregation cases are the plainest illustrations. *Brown v. Board of Education*[28] contemplated the extension of unsegregated public education to Negroes, not the closing of all public schools, and while no cases are squarely in point it is noticeable that attempts to evade affirmatively fulfilling the duty by such measures as closing the

[25] Barron v. Baltimore, 32 U.S. (7 Pet.) 243 (1833).
[26] 25 Fed. Cas. 707 (1875), aff'd 92 U.S. 542 (1876).
[27] *Id.* at 712.
[28] 347 U.S. 483 (1954).

schools in a county subject to a judicial order to desegregate,[29] or by contracting out the operation of public facilities,[30] or by resigning as municipal trustee of a public park,[31] have all been unsuccessful.

The idea that the State has affirmative obligations to its citizens which attain constitutional magnitude is far more congenial to our age than to that which followed the adoption of the Fourteenth Amendment. Contemporary political theory acknowledges the duty of government to provide jobs, social security and medical care as well as widespread regulatory protection of various classes. Its constitutional affirmations begin with racial equality but, since the words are not limited to race, they may as logically be read to affirm constitutional rights to equality despite other differences in station or inheritance. Once loosed, equalitarianism is not easily cabined. Equality of all kinds is becoming an increasingly important theme in our constitutional law. In the legislative reapportionment cases the complainants were asserting the States' duty not merely to leave them alone but to give each citizen an equal voice in government regardless of any other consideration.[32] In the poll tax cases now before the Supreme Court it is argued that the opportunity to vote must be made available to rich and poor upon equal terms and, since a poll tax of $2 or $3 is more difficult for the poor to pay than the rich, the tax is unconstitutional.[33] Similarly, the idea that the State sometimes has a duty to eliminate inequalities of wealth seems to lie behind the decisions requiring it to supply indigents with counsel and transcripts of the evidence in criminal cases.[34] How far the idea will spread is beyond my powers of prediction.

The shift in emphasis from constitutional restrictions upon State regulation to constitutional enforcement of a State's affirmative obligations introduces major new difficulties into constitutional adjudication which I can best introduce by referring to the efforts to desegregate a wide variety of establishments and institutions ranging from restaurants through charities to public works.

---

[29] Griffin v. County School Board, 377 U.S. 218 (1964).
[30] Muir v. Louisville Park Theatrical Association, 347 U.S. 971 (1954) vacating and remanding 202 F.2d 275 (6th Cir. 1953); Aaron v. Cooper, 261 F.2d 97 (8th Cir. 1958); City of Greensboro v. Simkins, 246 F.2d 425 (4th Cir. 1957); Tate v. Department of Conservation & Development, 133 F.Supp. 53 (E.D.Va. 1955), aff'd 231 F.2d 615 (4th Cir. 1956), certiorari denied, 352 U.S. 838 (1956).
[31] Evans v. Newton, 382 U.S. 296 (1966).
[32] *E.g.* Baker v. Carr, 369 U.S. 186 (1962); Reynolds v. Sims, 377 U.S. 533 (1964).
[33] Harper v. Virginia State Board of Elections, 383 U.S. 663 (1966).
[34] Griffin v. Illinois, 351 U.S. 12 (1956); Draper v. Washington, 372 U.S. 487 (1963); Douglas v. California, 372 U.S. 353 (1963).

Consider first the "sit-in" cases as they arose in 1961-64 before the enactment of the federal equal public accommodations law.[35] Many stores and restaurants refused to serve Negroes or else required them to use segregated facilities. Young Negroes protesting this indignity went quietly to lunch counters, sat down and requested service. When service was refused, they refused to leave. Later they were arrested and convicted of criminal trespass or some similar offense under State law. The demonstrators contended that the convictions violated the Fourteenth Amendment's command that *no State* shall deny any person the equal protection of its laws. There was a denial of equality by the States, they said, because State officials made the arrests and State courts sentenced them to fines or imprisonment. The answer for the prosecution was that a State does not deny equal protection of its laws when it simply enforces the right of any owner of private property to determine whom he will invite upon his premises and whom he will exclude as trespassers. In such cases, it could truthfully be said, the State law is color blind in fact as well as theory. The State punishes anyone whom the owner wishes to exclude from his property. Any discrimination is individual, not governmental.

One agonizing difficulty in these cases, as many saw them, grew out of the sharp conflict between sound policy and good law—between the right as it might be determined by a council of wise men and the decision suitable for the judgment of a court. Racial discrimination in places of public accommodation ought to be abolished. A decision sustaining the convictions of the sit-in demonstrators seemed likely to injure the entire civil rights movement and would surely have impaired the Negroes' confidence in the integrity and human justice of our legal system. On the other hand, an essential characteristic of a decision according to law is that it be rooted in a continuous community of principle found in the words of the constitution, judicial precedents, constitutional practice and like sources of law. Here constitutional tradition seemed to be on the side of the prosecution not because it favored racial discrimination but because a private citizen's discrimination had never been treated as the action of a State and, according to accepted notions, the Fourteenth Amendment does not apply to individuals. Constitutional decisions, moreover, ought to be upon grounds that will stand generalization. Few would challenge the propriety of eradicating discrimination in places of public accommodation but the chief constitutional principle invoked in support of that conclusion would not stand generalization. To hold that a private decision becomes

---

[35] See cases cited at n. 8 *supra*.

State action for the purposes of the Fourteenth Amendment whenever the citizen resorts to law to support his personal choice would obliterate any distinction between private and official action and submit both to constitutional restrictions theretofore applied only to officials. For a civilized community, freedom of private choice depends upon legal sanctions against aggression. Thus, the sit-in cases put the Court in a dilemma: the answer to the question, "what result would be best for the country today," clashed with the answer to the question, "policy aside, which decision is according to law."

One may deny the existence of the dilemma by insisting that the Court should concern itself with law and leave policy to legislative bodies. Such a course has more to commend it when the Court is dealing with the declaration and enforcement of the government's affirmative obligations to citizens than it has when the court is concerned with the constitutionality of legislative action restricting personal liberty. In the former case the legislature can fill the gap left open by the Court. Nevertheless, I would argue that rigid adherence to such a formula in all cases takes too narrow a view of both the function of law and the role of the Court. Law must grow and change in response to the needs of the community. The Court's influence goes far beyond the formal limits of its decrees. Had the Court denied the constitutional claims of the sit-in demonstrators, a lawyer might accurately have said that the decision had nothing to do with morality or policy but represented only the limited function of a constitutional court. To the layman and legislator, however, the Court's decree would undeniably have legitimatized the convictions and even the racial discrimination that lay behind them. The force of legality would have influenced both the national consciousness and the debate upon legislative solutions. In short, whatever the legal conception, affirmation of the convictions would have aided the advocates of segregation.

The sit-in cases also illustrate a second characteristic of litigation to enforce affirmative constitutional rights. The issue is less likely to lie between the government and the individual than when one deals with restrictions upon official action. The civil rights claimed by one group are likely to conflict with the civil liberties claimed by another—requiring the Court to strike a delicate balance.

This necessity was involved in the sit-in cases although one sees it more sharply in later cases seeking to apply the Fourteenth Amendment to parks, hospitals and educational institutions founded by private charity. In each instance the formal legal question is whether there was "State action" for the purposes of the Fourteenth Amendment but each extension of that concept in the interest of equality involves some surrender of individual freedom of choice and some sacrifice of the opportunities for a varied and diverse society. One may deplore the individual's choice but freedom to decide means freedom to be foolish as well as wise, to be wrong as well as right; indeed, the chief justification for freedom may be that it calls upon man to exercise his noblest quality—the power of choice between good and evil. Furthermore, any constitutional rule defining State action might well require generalization beyond the problems of race where the choice is so easy. Legislation striking the balances and drawing the necessary lines through the processes of representative government can be more pragmatic, can make compromises and adjustments and may therefore provide more acceptable solutions than adjudication by a court.

A third point also proved vexing: how much of the burden of leadership in the field of civil rights should the Supreme Court carry. Constitutional government operates by consent of the governed. Court decrees, unlike statutes, draw no power from the participation of the people. Their power to command consent comes partly from the belief that judicial decisions are based upon principles which bind the judges as well as the litigants. In the sit-in cases it was highly uncertain whether a Court decision sustaining the claim that the Fourteenth Amendment itself required the desegregation of lunch counters and restaurants without the need for legislative action could possibly command the degree of voluntary acceptance necessary to make the prohibition against discrimination effective. The response to the school desegregation decisions suggested a negative answer. In retrospect, moreover, it seems clear that the public accommodations sections of the Civil Rights Act of 1964, after the Supreme Court decision upholding their constitutionality,[36] commanded wider and deeper acceptance in all parts of the country than would ever have been accorded a Supreme Court ruling. Similarly, the Supreme Court decision that the equal protection clause forbids segregation in public education became more deeply imbeded in our constitutionalism after it received legislative approval in the enactment of Title VI of the Civil Rights Act of 1964.

This is not to say that, if the Supreme Court had reached the ultimate constitutional issue, it should have decided the sit-in cases against the demonstrators.[37] Happily, fate decreed that each of the

[36] Heart of Atlanta Motel Inc. v. United States, 379 U.S. 241 (1964); Katzenbach v. McClung, 379 U.S. 394 (1964).

[37] The United States, while the author was Solicitor General, consistently urged reversal of sit-in convictions upon grounds not reaching the ultimate constitutional question and, when it seemed inescapable, argued that the history of State support for segregation plus arrest and prosecution was sufficient State involvement to violate the Fourteenth Amendment. See Supplemental

cases could be decided in favor of the sit-in demonstrators upon very narrow grounds not inconsistent with prior law and not unacceptable as generalized rules for the future. And Congress acted before the ultimate issue was inescapably before the Court.

Nor do I mean to say that the considerations mentioned counsel a less active judicial role than the Court has assumed in affirming the duties of constitutional government to the individual. They raise problems not found in protecting civil liberties against legislative and judicial aggression. The need for judicial solutions is less because the enforcement of rights may be undertaken by the executive and legislative branches. But even here there are forces pulling in the opposite direction. The Court's role in our national life gives its rulings an influence broader, stronger and more enduring than the command of its mandate—an influence which also requires stress not upon inherited rules but upon what is right and just and wise. The Court's intellectual contributions to the process of self-government help to shape our national understanding of ourselves. Especially in the field of civil liberties, my colleague Paul Freund reminds us, where the British would call upon Milton and Mill, we evoke the words of Holmes, Brandeis and Hughes.[38] Often the opinion of the Court is the voice of the spirit telling us what we are by reminding us what we can be, leading us to guide ourselves not by our conduct but our aspirations.

During the oral argument in *Baker v. Carr*,[39] Mr. Justice Frankfurter referred to the limited power of the Court in comparison with other branches of government and asked whether the discouraging record of noncompliance with the school desegregation ruling in *Brown v. Board of Education* was not a complete answer to those who thought the Court should enter the field of legislative apportionment where resistance to its decree might be many times greater. Unhappily, the argument drifted into a relatively minor colloquy over whether the resistance would be greater or less. A better answer would have been that the *Brown* decision had an importance, and a contrary ruling would have been a tragedy, not to be measured by the practical test of immediate enforcement. The *Brown* decision lighted a beacon of hope for the Negro and restated the spirit of America at a time when other governmental voices were muted. It has taken the support of the legislative branch and will require still more vigorous executive action to make the constitutional principle a reality but surely no one supposes that those

---

Brief for the United States in Griffin v. Maryland and companion cases, Nos. 6, 9, 10, 12 and 60, October Term 1963.

[38] Freund THE SUPREME COURT OF THE UNITED STATES 89 (Meridian Books 1961).

[39] 369 U.S. 186 (1962).

would have been forthcoming during the 1960's but for the "non-judicial power of the Court."

Baker v. Carr, the initial reapportionment case, epitomized the dilemma. Although I failed to perceive the difference at the time, it seems plain now that the issue related not to official aggression against personal liberty but to the share to be given to the citizen in democratic government. The enormous difficulty of finding standards for ruling upon questions of legislative apportionment, the risk of divisive controversy, the lack of precedent, the long history of congressional inaction and the uncertainty concerning the courts' ability to force reapportionment upon truly recalcitrant legislatures all counselled judicial abnegation. Yet against all this there weighed the stark fact that unless the Court intervened, the evil of malapportionment would continue. There was no other remedy. However the Court dressed its decision in the language of jurisdiction, its refusal to act would have the effect of legitimizing the evil. The Court could not do everything but it could do something, and there was reason to hope that the moral force of its decision plus its feeble sanctions and the weight of legitimacy placed on the side of reform might command a sufficient measure of assent to make the ruling effective. Events have proved (far beyond the expectations of counsel) the power of the Court to bespeak a national consensus.

IV

It is sometimes said that the Supreme Court has been too free in recent years in overturning precedent and that it exaggerates the judge's freedom and gives too little heed to the values of certainty, continuity and stability. Judged by an older past, the pace of new departures is swift indeed, but I wonder whether the critics give enough attention to the concurrence of forces today making for rapid changes in the law.

There is scarcely need to mention the revolutionary social and economic conditions: the growth of the population; the freeing of most men, in the United States at least, from the age-old necessity of spending nearly all their time and energy providing food, clothes and shelter for themselves and their dependents; the scientific and the consequent technological revolution; and the civil rights movement. Such rapid changes, reaching the roots of society, require pervasive changes in the law just as the change in the national economy required reinterpretation of the rules defining the power of Congress to regulate interstate commerce.

Revolutionary developments in other fields, I suspect, also influence the intellectual atmosphere in which the judges work. When the physical scientists are demolishing the old laws of physics and chemistry and the social scientists are giving us new insights into the nature of man, the judge is not unnaturally impelled to examine pretty closely the rules that he has always followed. Sometimes the relation is one of direct cause and effect. All the ferment in criminal law—the area in which the changes in constitutional decisions are most frequent and most controversial—stems partly from the deeper inquiries of social scientists into freedom of the will, the causes of crime and the effects of punishment.

What the Supreme Court does in making new law through constitutional adjudication is also related to the action or inaction of other branches of the government. It would have been best, no doubt, for the Congress to have taken the initiative in compelling school desegregation, but legislative action was blocked by the power of the Southern Congressmen and the filibuster. The Executive theoretically could have given more leadership. As a practical matter, however, the task of initiating steps to realize a national ideal fell to the Court; either it must act or nothing would be done. Again, it would have been better if the States had themselves reformed their criminal procedure by providing counsel for all indigent defendants at public expense, but the simple fact is that a minority of States failed to act despite a long period of warning. The reapportionment cases are another illustration. In *Baker v. Carr*, the case in which the Supreme Court first intervened, the Tennessee legislature, elected by only a small minority of the people, had been violating even Tennessee's own constitution for sixty years. So far as one could tell from the record, there had to be either a constitutional remedy in the Supreme Court or nothing would be done.

Mr. Justice Frankfurter often warned that proof of a wrong was not alone enough to justify judicial, still less, constitutional intervention.[40] Ideally he was correct. Not all the business of government is constitutional law. Most wrongs must find their remedies in other forums. The federal judicial branch ought not to enlarge its own jurisdiction because Congress and State governments have failed to solve the problems confided to them. The remedy is to reform the delinquents. But government is more pragmatic than ideal. In a practical world there is, and I suspect has to be, a good deal of play in the joints. If one arm of government cannot or will not solve an insistent problem, the pressure falls upon another. I suspect that a careful study would reveal that the Supreme Court today is most "activist" in the areas of the law where political processes have been inadequate, because the problem was neglected by politicians.

[40] *E.g.* Baker v. Carr, 369 U.S. 186, 269-270 (1962) (dissenting opinion).

Only history will know whether the present court has avoided both horns of the dilemma that lie at the bottom of its work. Today the question is open to debate. For myself, I am confident that historians will write that the trend of Supreme Court decisions during the 1950's and 1960's was in keeping with the main-stream of American history—a bit progressive but also moderate, a bit humane but not sentimental, a bit idealistic but seldom doctrinaire, and in the long run essentially pragmatic—in short, in keeping with the true genius of our institutions.

But perhaps I am prejudiced. One who has sat in the Supreme Court almost daily awaiting oral argument or the delivery of opinions acquires both admiration and affection for the Court and for all the justices. The problems with which they deal are so difficult, the number and variety of cases are so overwhelming, the implications are so far-reaching, that one sits humbled by the demands upon them. That the institution of constitutional adjudication works so well on the whole is testimony not only to the genius of the institution but to the wisdom and courage of the individual justices.

Role of the Supreme Court Symposium, No. 1

DECISION-MAKING IN A DEMOCRACY: THE SUPREME COURT AS A NATIONAL POLICY-MAKER

Robert A. Dahl*

To consider the Supreme Court of the United States strictly as a legal institution is to underestimate its significance in the American political system. For it is also a political institution, an institution, that is to say, for arriving at decisions on controversial questions of national policy. As a political institution, the Court is highly unusual, not least because Americans are not quite willing to accept the fact that it *is* a political institution and not quite capable of denying it; so that frequently we take both positions at once. This is confusing to foreigners, amusing to logicians, and rewarding to ordinary Americans who thus manage to retain the best of both worlds.

I

A policy decision might be defined as an effective choice among alternatives about which there is, at least initially, some uncertainty. This uncertainty may arise because of inadequate information as to (a) the alternatives that are thought to be "open"; (b) the consequences that will probably ensue from choosing a given alternative; (c) the level of probability that these consequences will actually ensue; and (d) the relative value of the different alternatives, that is, an ordering of the alternatives from most preferable to least preferable, given the expected consequences and the expected probability of the consequences actually occurring. An *effective* choice is a selection of the most preferable alternative accompanied by measures to insure that the alternative selected will be acted upon.

No one, I imagine, will quarrel with the proposition that the Supreme Court, or indeed any court, must make and does make policy decisions in this sense. But such a proposition is not really useful to the question before us. What is critical is the extent to which a court can and does make policy decisions by going outside established "legal" criteria found in precedent,

* Eugene Meyer Professor of Political Science, Yale University; author, A Preface to Democratic Theory (1956) and other works.

statute, and constitution. Now in this respect the Supreme Court occupies a most peculiar position, for it is an essential characteristic of the institution that from time to time its members decide cases where legal criteria are not in any realistic sense adequate to the task. A distinguished associate justice of the present Court has recently described the business of the Supreme Court in these words:

> It is essentially accurate to say that the Court's preoccupation today is with the application of rather fundamental aspirations and what Judge Learned Hand calls "moods," embodied in provisions like the due process clauses, which were designed not to be precise and positive directions for rules of action. The judicial process in applying them involves a judgment . . . . that is, on the views of the direct representatives of the people in meeting the needs of society, on the views of Presidents and Governors, and by their construction of the will of legislatures the Court breathes life, feeble or strong, into the inert pages of the Constitution and the statute books.[1]

Very often, then, the cases before the Court involve alternatives about which there is severe disagreement in the society, as in the case of segregation or economic regulation; that is, the setting of the case is "political." Moreover, they are usually cases where competent students of constitutional law, including the learned justices of the Supreme Court themselves, disagree; where the words of the Constitution are general, vague, ambiguous, or not clearly applicable; where precedent may be found on both sides; and where experts differ in predicting the consequences of the various alternatives or the degree of probability that the possible consequences will actually ensue. Typically, in other words, although there may be considerable agreement as to the alternatives thought to be open [(a)], there is very serious disagreement as to questions of fact bearing on consequences and probabilities [(b) and (c)], and as to questions of value, or the way in which different alternatives are to be ordered according to criteria establishing relative preferability [(d)].

If the Court were assumed to be a "political" institution, no particular problems would arise, for it would be taken for granted that the members of the Court would resolve questions of fact and value by introducing assumptions derived from their own predispositions or those of influential clienteles and constituents. But, since much of the legitimacy of the Court's decisions rests upon the fiction that it is not a political institution but exclusively a legal one, to accept the Court as a political institution would solve one set of problems at the price of creating another. Nonetheless, if it is true that

1 Frankfurter, The Supreme Court in the Mirror of Justices, 105 U. of Pa. L. Rev. 781, 793 (1957).

the nature of the cases arriving before the Court is sometimes of the kind I have described, then the Court cannot act strictly as a legal institution. It must, that is to say, choose among controversial alternatives of public policy by appealing to at least some criteria of acceptability on questions of fact and value that cannot be found in or deduced from precedent, statute, and Constitution. It is in this sense that the Court is a national policy-maker, and it is this role that gives rise to the problem of the Court's existence in a political system ordinarily held to be democratic.

Now I take it that except for differences in emphasis and presentation, what I have said so far is today widely accepted by almost all American political scientists and by most lawyers. To anyone who believes that the Court is not, in at least some of its activities, a policy-making institution, the discussion that follows may seem irrelevant. But to anyone who holds that at least one role of the Court is as a policy-making institution in cases where strictly legal criteria are inadequate, then a serious and much debated question arises, to wit: Who gets what and why? Or in less elegant language: What groups are benefited or handicapped by the Court and how does the allocation by the Court of these rewards and penalties fit into our presumably democratic political system?

II

In determining and appraising the role of the Court, two different and conflicting criteria are sometimes employed. These are the majority criterion and the criterion of Right or Justice.

Every policy dispute can be tested, at least in principle, by the majority criterion, because (again: in principle) the dispute can be analyzed according to the numbers of people for and against the various alternatives at issue, and therefore according to the proportions of the citizens or eligible members who are for and against the alternatives. Logically speaking, except for a trivial case, every conflict within a given society must be a dispute between a majority of those eligible to participate and a minority or minorities; or else it must be a dispute between or among minorities only.[2] Within certain limits, both possibilities are independent of the number of policy alternatives at issue, and since the argument is not significantly affected by the number of alternatives, it is convenient to assume that each policy dispute represents only two alternatives.[3]

---

2 Provided that the total membership of the society is an even number, it is technically possible for a dispute to occur that divides the membership into two equal parts, neither of which can be said to be either a majority or minority of the total membership. But even in the instances where the number of members is even (which should occur on the average only half the time), the probability of an exactly even split, in any group of more than a few thousand people, is so small that it may be ignored.

3 Suppose the number of citizens, or members eligible to participate in collective decisions, is *n*. Let each member indicate his "most preferred alternative." Then it is obvious that

If everyone prefers one of two alternatives, then no significant problem arises. But a case will hardly come before the Supreme Court unless at least one person prefers an alternative that is opposed by another person. Strictly speaking, then, no matter how the Court acts in determining the legality or constitutionality of one alternative or the other, the outcome of the Court's decision must either (1) accord with the preferences of a minority of citizens and run counter to the preferences of a majority; (2) accord with the preferences of a majority and run counter to the preferences of a minority; or (3) accord with the preferences of one minority and run counter to the preferences of another minority, the rest being indifferent.

In a democratic system with a more or less representative legislature, it is unnecessary to maintain a special court to secure the second class of outcomes. A case might be made out that the Court protects the rights of national majorities against local interests in federal questions, but so far as I am aware, the role of the Court as a policy-maker is not usually defended in this fashion; in what follows, therefore, I propose to pass over the ticklish question of federalism and deal only with "national" majorities and minorities. The third kind of outcome, although relevant according to other criteria, is hardly relevant to the majority criterion, and may also be passed over for the moment.

One influential view of the Court, however, is that it stands in some special way as a protection of minorities against tyranny by majorities. In the course of its 167 years, in seventy-eight cases, the Court has struck down eighty-six different provisions of federal law as unconstitutional,[4] and by interpretation it has modified a good many more. It might be argued, then, that in all or in a very large number of these cases the Court was, in fact,

---

the maximum number of most preferred alternatives is n. It is equally obvious that if the number of most preferred alternatives is more than or equal to $n/2$, then no majority is possible. But for all practical purposes those formal limitations can be ignored, for we are dealing with a large society where the number of alternatives at issue before the Supreme Court is invariably quite small. If the number of alternatives is greater than two, it is theoretically possible for preferences to be distributed so that no outcome is consistent with the majority criterion, even where all members can rank all the alternatives and where there is perfect information as to their preferences; but this difficulty does not bear on the subsequent discussion, and it is disregarded. For an examination of this problem, consult Arrow, Social Choice and Individual Values (1951).

4 Actually, the matter is somewhat ambiguous. There appear to have been seventy-eight cases in which the Court has held provisions of federal law unconstitutional. Sixty-four different acts in the technical sense have been construed, and eighty-six different provisions in law have been in some respects invalidated. I rely here on the figures and the table given in Library of Congress, Legislative Reference Service, Provisions of Federal Law Held Unconstitutional By the Supreme Court of the United States 95, 141-47 (1936), to which I have added United States v. Lovett, 328 U.S. 303 (1946), and United States ex rel. Toth v. Quarles, 350 U.S. 11 (1955). There are some minor discrepancies in totals (not attributable to the differences in publication dates) between this volume and Acts of Congress Held Unconstitutional in Whole or in Part by the Supreme Court of the United States, in Library of Congress, Legislative Reference Service, The Constitution of the United States of America, Analysis and Interpretation (Corwin ed., 1953). The difference is a result of classification. The latter document lists seventy-three acts held unconstitutional (to which Toth v. Quarles, supra, should be added) but different sections of the same act are sometimes counted separately.

defending the rights of some minority against a "tyrannical" majority. There are, however, some exceedingly serious difficulties with this interpretation of the Court's activities.

III

One problem, which is essentially ideological in character, is the difficulty of reconciling such an interpretation with the existence of a democratic polity, for it is not at all difficult to show by appeals to authorities as various and imposing as Aristotle, Locke, Rousseau, Jefferson, and Lincoln that the term democracy means, among other things, that the power to rule resides in popular majorities and their representatives. Moreover, from entirely reasonable and traditional definitions of popular sovereignty and political equality, the principle of majority rule can be shown to follow by logical necessity.[5] Thus to affirm that the Court supports minority preferences against majorities is to deny that popular sovereignty and political equality, at least in the traditional sense, exist in the United States; and to affirm that the Court *ought* to act in this way is to deny that popular sovereignty and political equality *ought* to prevail in this country. In a country that glories in its democratic tradition, this is not a happy state of affairs for the Court's defenders; and it is no wonder that a great deal of effort has gone into the enterprise of proving that, even if the Court consistently defends minorities against majorities, nonetheless it is a thoroughly "democratic" institution. But no amount of tampering with democratic theory can conceal the fact that a system in which the policy preferences of minorities prevail over majorities is at odds with the traditional criteria for distinguishing a democracy from other political systems.[6]

Fortunately, however, we do not need to traverse this well-worn ground; for the view of the Court as a protector of the liberties of minorities against the tyranny of majorities is beset with other difficulties that are not so much ideological as matters of fact and logic. If one wishes to be at all rigorous about the question, it is probably impossible to demonstrate that any particular Court decisions have or have not been at odds with the preferences of a "national majority." It is clear that unless one makes *some* assumptions as to the kind of evidence one will require for the existence of a set of minority and majority preferences in the general population, the view under consideration is incapable of being proved at all. In any strict sense, no adequate evidence exists, for scientific opinion polls are of relatively recent origin, and national elections are little more than an indication of the first preferences of a number of citizens—in the United States the number ranges between about

[5] Dahl, A Preface to Democratic Theory, c. 2 (1956).
[6] Compare Commager, Majority Rule and Minority Rights (1943).

forty and sixty per cent of the adult population—for certain candidates for public office. I do not mean to say that there is no relation between preferences among candidates and preferences among alternative public policies, but the connection is a highly tenuous one, and on the basis of an election it is almost never possible to adduce whether a majority does or does not support one of two or more policy alternatives about which members of the political elite are divided. For the greater part of the Court's history, then, there is simply no way of establishing with any high degree of confidence whether a given alternative was or was not supported by a majority or a minority of adults or even of voters.

In the absence of relatively direct information, we are thrown back on indirect tests. The eighty-six provisions of federal law that have been declared unconstitutional were, of course, initially passed by majorities of those voting in the Senate and in the House. They also had the president's formal approval. We could, therefore, speak of a majority of those voting in the House and Senate, together with the president, as a "lawmaking majority." It is not easy to determine whether any such constellation of forces within the political elites actually coincides with the preferences of a majority of American adults or even with the preferences of a majority of that half of the adult population which, on the average, votes in congressional elections. Such evidence as we have from opinion polls suggests that Congress is not markedly out of line with public opinion, or at any rate with such public opinion as there is after one discards the answers of people who fall into the category, often large, labelled "no response" or "don't know." If we may, on these somewhat uncertain grounds, take a "lawmaking majority" as equivalent to a "national majority," then it is possible to test the hypothesis that the Supreme Court is shield and buckler for minorities against national majorities.

Under any reasonable assumptions about the nature of the political process, it would appear to be somewhat naive to assume that the Supreme Court either would or could play the role of Galahad. Over the whole history of the Court, on the average one new justice has been appointed every twenty-two months. Thus a president can expect to appoint about two new justices during one term of office; and if this were not enough to tip the balance on a normally divided Court, he is almost certain to succeed in two terms. Thus, Hoover had three appointments; Roosevelt, nine; Truman, four; and Eisenhower, so far, has had four. Presidents are not famous for appointing justices hostile to their own views on public policy nor could they expect to secure confirmation of a man whose stance on key questions was flagrantly at odds with that of the dominant majority in the Senate. Justices are typically men who, prior to appointment, have engaged in public life and have committed themselves publicly on the great questions of the day. As Mr. Justice Frankfurter has recently reminded us, a surprisingly large proportion of the justices, particularly of the great justices who have left their stamp upon the decisions of the Court, have had little or no prior judicial experience.[7] Nor have the justices—certainly not the great justices—been timid men with a passion for anonymity. Indeed, it is not too much to say that if justices were appointed primarily for their "judicial" qualities without regard to their basic attitudes on fundamental questions of public policy, the Court could not play the influential role in the American political system that it does in reality play.

The fact is, then, that the policy views dominant on the Court are never for long out of line with the policy views dominant among the lawmaking majorities of the United States. Consequently it would be most unrealistic to suppose that the Court would, for more than a few years at most, stand against any major alternatives sought by a lawmaking majority. The judicial agonies of the New Deal will, of course, quickly come to mind; but Mr. Roosevelt's difficulties with the Court were truly exceptional. Generalizing over the whole history of the Court, the chances are about one out of five that a president will make one appointment to the Court in less than a year, better than one out of two that he will make one within two years, and three out of four that he will make one within three years. Mr. Roosevelt had unusually bad luck: he had to wait four years for his first appointment; the odds against this long an interval are four to one. With average luck, the battle with the Court would never have occurred; even as it was, although

TABLE 1

The Interval Between Appointments to the Supreme Court.

Interval in Years	Per Cent of Total Appointments	Cumulative Per Cent
Less than 1	21	21
1	34	55
2	18	73
3	9	82
4	8	90
5	7	97
6	2	99
—	—	—
12	1	100
Total	100	100

Note: The table excludes the six appointments made in 1789. Except for the four most recent appointments, it is based on data in the Encyclopedia of American History 461-62 (Morris ed., 1953). It may be slightly inaccurate because the source shows only the year of appointment, not the month. The twelve-year interval was from 1811 to 1823.

7 Frankfurter, op. cit. supra note 1, at 782-84.

the "court-packing" proposal did formally fail, by the end of his second term Mr. Roosevelt had appointed five new justices and by 1941 Mr. Justice Roberts was the only remaining holdover from the Hoover era.

It is to be expected, then, that the Court is least likely to be successful in blocking a determined and persistent lawmaking majority on a major policy and most likely to succeed against a "weak" majority; e.g., a dead one, a transient one, a fragile one, or one weakly united upon a policy of subordinate importance.

IV

An examination of the cases in which the Court has held federal legislation unconstitutional confirms, on the whole, our expectations. Over the whole history of the Court, about half the decisions have been rendered more than four years after the legislation was passed.

TABLE 2

Percentage of Cases Held Unconstitutional Arranged by Time Intervals Between Legislation and Decision.

Number of Years	New Deal Legislation %	Other %	All Legislation %
2 or Less	92	19	30
3 - 4	8	19	18
5 - 8	0	28	24
9 - 12	0	13	11
13 - 16	0	8	6
17 - 20	0	1	1
21 or More	0	12	10
Total	100	100	100

Of the twenty-four laws held unconstitutional within two years, eleven were measures enacted in the early years of the New Deal. Indeed, New Deal measures comprise nearly a third of all the legislation that has ever been declared unconstitutional within four years after enactment.

TABLE 3

Cases Holding Legislation Unconstitutional Within Four Years After Enactment.

Interval in Years	New Deal No.	New Deal %	Other No.	Other %	Total No.	Total %
2 or Less	11	29	13	34	24	63
3 to 4	1	3	13	34	14	37
Total	12	32	26	68	38	100

It is illuminating to examine the cases where the Court has acted on legislation within four years after enactment—where the presumption is, that is to say, that the lawmaking majority is not necessarily a dead one. Of the twelve New Deal cases, two were, from a policy point of view, trivial; and two, although perhaps not trivial, were of minor importance to the New Deal program.[8] A fifth[9] involved the NRA, which was to expire within three weeks of the decision. Insofar as the unconstitutional provisions allowed "codes of fair competition" to be established by industrial groups, it is fair to say that President Roosevelt and his advisers were relieved by the Court's decision of a policy they had come to find increasingly embarrassing. In view of the tenacity with which Mr. Roosevelt held to his major program, there can hardly be any doubt that had he wanted to pursue the major policy objective involved in the NRA codes, as he did, for example, with the labor provisions, he would not have been stopped by the Court's special theory of the Constitution. As to the seven other cases,[10] it is entirely correct to say, I think, that whatever some of the eminent justices might have thought during their fleeting moments of glory, they did not succeed in interposing a barrier to the achievement of the objectives of the legislation; and in a few years most of the constitutional interpretation on which the decisions rested had been unceremoniously swept under the rug.

The remainder of the thirty-eight cases where the Court has declared legislation unconstitutional within four years of enactment tend to fall into two rather distinct groups: those involving legislation that could reasonably be regarded as important *from the point of view of the lawmaking majority* and those involving minor legislation. Although the one category merges into the other, so that some legislation must be classified rather arbitrarily, probably there will be little disagreement with classifying the specific legislative provisions involved in eleven cases as essentially minor from the point of view of the lawmaking majority (however important they may have been as constitutional interpretations).[11] The specific legislative provisions in-

8 Booth v. United States, 291 U.S. 339 (1934), involved a reduction in the pay of retired judges. Lynch v. United States, 292 U.S. 571 (1934), repealed laws granting to veterans rights to yearly renewable term insurance; there were only twenty-nine policies outstanding in 1932. Hopkins Federal Savings & Loan Ass'n v. Cleary, 296 U.S. 315 (1935), granted permission to state building and loan associations to convert to federal ones on a vote of fifty-one per cent or more of votes cast at a legal meeting. Ashton v. Cameron County Water Improvement District, 298 U.S. 513 (1936), permitting municipalities to petition federal courts for bankruptcy proceedings.

9 Schechter Poultry Corp. v. United States, 295 U.S. 495 (1935).

10 United States v. Butler, 297 U.S. 1 (1936); Perry v. United States, 294 U.S. 330 (1935); Panama Refining Co. v. Ryan, 293 U.S. 388 (1935); Railroad Retirement Board v. Alton R. Co., 295 U.S. 330 (1935); Louisville Joint Stock Land Bank v. Radford, 295 U.S. 555 (1935); Rickert Rice Mills v. Fontenot, 297 U.S. 110 (1936); Carter v. Carter Coal Co., 298 U.S. 238 (1936).

11 United States v. Dewitt, 9 Wall. (U.S.) 41 (1870); Gordon v. United States, 2 Wall. (U.S.) 561 (1865); Monongahela Navigation Co. v. United States, 148 U.S. 312 (1893); Wong Wing v. United States, 163 U.S. 228 (1896); Fairbank v. United States, 181 U.S. 283 (1901); Rassmussen v. United States, 197 U.S. 516 (1905); Muskrat v. United States, 219

volved in the remaining fifteen cases are by no means of uniform importance, but with one or two possible exceptions it seems reasonable to classify them as major policy issues from the point of view of the lawmaking majority.[12] We would expect that cases involving major legislative policy would be propelled to the Court much more rapidly than cases involving minor policy, and, as the table below shows, this is in fact what happens.

TABLE 4

Number of Cases Involving Legislative Policy Other than Those Arising Under New Deal Legislation Holding Legislation Unconstitutional Within Four Years After Enactment.

Interval in Years	Major Policy	Minor Policy	Total
2 or Less	11	2	13
3 to 4	4	9	13
Total	15	11	26

Thus a lawmaking majority with major policy objectives in mind usually has an opportunity to seek for ways of overcoming the Court's veto. It is an interesting and highly significant fact that Congress and the president do generally succeed in overcoming a hostile Court on major policy issues.

TABLE 5

Type of Congressional Action Following Supreme Court Decisions Holding Legislation Unconstitutional Within Four Years After Enactment (Other than New Deal Legislation).

Congressional Action	Major Policy	Minor Policy	Total
Reverses Court's Policy	10[a]	2[d]	12
Changes Own Policy	2[b]	0	2
None	0	8[e]	8
Unclear	3[c]	1[f]	4
Total	15	11	26

Note: For the cases in each category, see footnote 13.

U.S. 346 (1911); Choate v. Trapp, 224 U.S. 665 (1912); Evans v. Gore, 253 U.S. 245 (1920); Untermyer v. Anderson, 276 U.S. 440 (1928); United States v. Lovett, 328 U.S. 303 (1946). Note that although the specific legislative provisions held unconstitutional may have been minor, the basic legislation may have been of major policy importance.

12 Ex parte Garland, 4 Wall. (U.S.) 333 (1867); United States v. Klein, 13 Wall. (U.S.) 128 (1872); Pollock v. Farmers' Loan & Trust Co., 157 U.S. 429 (1895), rehearing granted 158 U.S. 601 (1895); Employers' Liability Cases, 207 U.S. 463 (1908); Keller v. United States, 213 U.S. 138 (1909); Hammer v. Dagenhart, 247 U.S. 251 (1918); Eisner v. Macomber, 252 U.S. 189 (1920); Knickerbocker Ice Co. v. Stewart, 253 U.S. 149 (1920); United States v. Cohen Grocery Co., 255 U.S. 81 (1921); Weeds, Inc. v. United States, 255 U.S. 109

It is particularly instructive to examine the cases involving major policy. In two cases involving punitive legislation enacted by Radical Republican Congresses against supporters of the Confederacy during the Civil War, the Court faced a rapidly crumbling majority whose death knell as an effective national force was sounded with the election of 1876.[14] Three cases are difficult to classify and I have labelled them "unclear." Of these, two were decisions made in 1921 involving a 1919 amendment to the Lever Act to control prices.[15] The legislation was important, and the provision in question was clearly struck down, but the Lever Act terminated three days after the decision and Congress did not return to the subject of price control until World War II, when it experienced no constitutional difficulties arising from these cases (which were primarily concerned with the lack of an ascertainable standard of guilt). The third case in this category successfully eliminated stock dividends from the scope of the Sixteenth Amendment, although a year later Congress enacted legislation taxing the actual income from such stock.[16]

The remaining ten cases were ultimately followed by a reversal of the actual policy results of the Court's action, although not necessarily of the specific constitutional interpretation. In four cases,[17] the policy consequences of the Court's decision were overcome in less than a year. The other six required a long struggle. Workmen's compensation for longshoremen and harbor workers was invalidated by the Court in 1920;[18] in 1922 Congress passed a new law which was, in its turn, knocked down by the Court in 1924;[19] in 1927 Congress passed a third law, which was finally upheld in

---

(1921); Bailey v. Drexel Furniture Co., 259 U.S. 20 (1922); Hill v. Wallace, 259 U.S. 44 (1922); Washington v. Dawson & Co., 264 U.S. 219 (1924); Trusler v. Crooks, 269 U.S. 475 (1926).

13a Pollock v. Farmers' Loan & Trust Co., 157 U.S. 429 (1895); Employers' Liability Cases, 207 U.S. 463 (1908); Keller v. United States, 213 U.S. 138 (1909); Hammer v. Dagenhart, 247 U.S. 251 (1918); Bailey v. Drexel Furniture Co., 259 U.S. 20 (1922); Trusler v. Crooks, 269 U.S. 475 (1926); Hill v. Wallace, 259 U.S. 44 (1922); Knickerbocker Ice Co. v. Stewart, 253 U.S. 149 (1920); Washington v. Dawson & Co., 264 U.S. 219 (1924).

b Ex parte Garland, 4 Wall. (U.S.) 333 (1867); United States v. Klein, 13 Wall. (U.S.) 128 (1872).

c United States v. Cohen Grocery Co., 255 U.S. 81 (1921); Weeds, Inc. v. United States, 255 U.S. 109 (1921); Eisner v. Macomber, 252 U.S. 189 (1920).

d Gordon v. United States, 2 Wall. (U.S.) 561 (1865); Evans v. Gore, 253 U.S. 245 (1920).

e United States v. Dewitt, 9 Wall. (U.S.) 41 (1870); Monongahela Navigation Co. v. United States, 148 U.S. 312 (1893); Wong Wing v. United States, 163 U.S. 228 (1896); Fairbank v. United States, 181 U.S. 283 (1901); Rassmussen v. United States, 197 U.S. 516 (1905); Muskrat v. United States, 219 U.S. 346 (1911); Choate v. Trapp, 224 U.S. 665 (1912); United States v. Lovett, 328 U.S. 303 (1946).

f Untermyer v. Anderson, 276 U.S. 440 (1928).

14 Ex parte Garland, 4 Wall. (U.S.) 333 (1867); United States v. Klein, 13 Wall. (U.S.) 128 (1872).

15 United States v. Cohen Grocery Co., 255 U.S. 81 (1921); Weeds, Inc. v. United States, 255 U.S. 109 (1921).

16 Eisner v. Macomber, 252 U.S. 189 (1920).

17 Employers' Liability Cases, 207 U.S. 463 (1908); Keller v. United States, 213 U.S. 138 (1909); Trusler v. Crooks, 269 U.S. 475 (1926); Hill v. Wallace, 259 U.S. 44 (1922).

18 Knickerbocker Ice Co. v. Stewart, 253 U.S. 149 (1920).

19 Washington v. Dawson & Co., 264 U.S. 219 (1924).

1932.[20] The notorious income tax cases[21] of 1895 were first somewhat narrowed by the Court itself;[22] the Sixteenth Amendment was recommended by President Taft in 1909 and was ratified in 1913, some eighteen years after the Court's decisions. The two child labor cases represent the most effective battle ever waged by the Court against legislative policy-makers. The original legislation outlawing child labor, based on the commerce clause, was passed in 1916 as a part of Wilson's New Freedom. Like Roosevelt later, Wilson was somewhat unlucky in his Supreme Court appointments; he made only three appointments during his eight years, and one of these was wasted, from a policy point of view, on McReynolds. Had McReynolds voted "right," the subsequent struggle over the problem of child labor need not have occurred, for the decision in 1918 was by a Court divided five to four, McReynolds voting with the majority.[23] Congress moved at once to circumvent the decision by means of the tax power, but in 1922 the Court blocked that approach.[24] In 1924 Congress returned to the engagement with a constitutional amendment that was rapidly endorsed by a number of state legislatures before it began to meet so much resistance in the states remaining that the enterprise miscarried. In 1938, under a second reformist president, new legislation was passed, twenty-two years after the first; this a chastened Court accepted in 1941,[25] and thereby brought to an end a battle that had lasted a full quarter-century.

The entire record of the duel between the Court and the lawmaking majority, in cases where the Court has held legislation unconstitutional within four years after enactment, is summarized in Table 6.

TABLE 6

Type of Congressional Action After Supreme Court Decisions Holding Legislation Unconstitutional Within Four Years After Enactment (Including New Deal Legislation).

Congressional Action	Major Policy	Minor Policy	Total
Reverses Court's Policy	17	2	19
None	0	12	12
Other	6*	1	7
Total	23	15	38

* In addition to the actions in Table 5 under "Changes Own Policy" and "Unclear," this figure includes the NRA legislation affected by the *Schechter Poultry* case.

20 Crowell v. Benson, 285 U.S. 22 (1932).
21 Pollock v. Farmers' Loan & Trust Co., 157 U.S. 429 (1895).
22 Nicol v. Ames, 173 U.S. 509 (1899); Knowlton v. Moore, 178 U.S. 41 (1900); Patton v. Brady, 184 U.S. 608 (1902); Flint v. Stone Tracy Co., 220 U.S. 107 (1911).
23 Hammer v. Dagenhart, 247 U.S. 251 (1918).
24 Bailey v. Drexel Furniture Co., 259 U.S. 20 (1922).
25 United States v. Darby, 312 U.S. 100 (1941).

Thus the application of the majority criterion seems to show the following: First, if the Court did in fact uphold minorities against national majorities, as both its supporters and critics often seem to believe, it would be an extremely anomalous institution from a democratic point of view. Second, the elaborate "democratic" rationalizations of the Court's defenders and the hostility of its "democratic" critics are largely irrelevant, for lawmaking majorities generally have had their way. Third, although the Court seems never to have succeeded in holding out indefinitely, in a very small number of important cases it has delayed the application of policy up to as much as twenty-five years.

V

How can we appraise decisions of the third kind just mentioned? Earlier I referred to the criterion of Right or Justice as a norm sometimes invoked to describe the role of the Court. In accordance with this norm, it might be argued that the most important policy function of the Court is to protect rights that are in some sense basic or fundamental. Thus (the argument might run) in a country where basic rights are, on the whole, respected, one should not expect more than a small number of cases where the Court has had to plant itself firmly against a lawmaking majority. But majorities may, on rare occasions, become "tyrannical"; and when they do, the Court intervenes; and although the constitutional issue may, strictly speaking, be technically open, the Constitution assumes an underlying fundamental body of rights and liberties which the Court guarantees by its decisions.

Here again, however, even without examining the actual cases, it would appear, on political grounds, somewhat unrealistic to suppose that a Court whose members are recruited in the fashion of Supreme Court justices would long hold to norms of Right or Justice substantially at odds with the rest of the political elite. Moreover, in an earlier day it was perhaps easier to believe that certain rights are so natural and self-evident that their fundamental validity is as much a matter of definite knowledge, at least to all reasonable creatures, as the color of a ripe apple. To say that this view is unlikely to find many articulate defenders today is, of course, not to disprove it; it is rather to suggest that we do not need to elaborate the case against it in this essay.

In any event the best rebuttal to the view of the Court suggested above will be found in the record of the Court's decisions. Surely the six cases referred to a moment ago, where the policy consequences of the Court's decisions were overcome only after long battles, will not appeal to many contemporary minds as evidence for the proposition under examination. A natural right to employ child labor in mills and mines? To be free of income taxes by the federal government? To employ longshoremen and harbor workers without the protection of workmen's compensation? The Court itself did not rely upon such arguments in these cases, and it would be no credit to their opinions to reconstruct them along such lines.

So far, however, our evidence has been drawn from cases in which the Court has held legislation unconstitutional within four years after enactment. What of the other forty cases? Do we have evidence in these that the Court has protected fundamental or natural rights and liberties against the dead hand of some past tyranny by the lawmakers? The evidence is not impressive. In the entire history of the Court there is not one case arising under the First Amendment in which the Court has held federal legislation unconstitutional. If we turn from these fundamental liberties of religion, speech, press and assembly, we do find a handful of cases—something less than ten—arising under Amendments Four to Seven in which the Court has declared acts unconstitutional that might properly be regarded as involving rather basic liberties.[26] An inspection of these cases leaves the impression that, in all of them, the lawmakers and the Court were not very far apart; moreover, it is doubtful that the fundamental conditions of liberty in this country have been altered by more than a hair's breadth as a result of these decisions. However, let us give the Court its due; it is little enough.

Over against these decisions we must put the fifteen or so cases in which the Court used the protections of the Fifth, Thirteenth, Fourteenth and Fifteenth Amendments to preserve the rights and liberties of a relatively privileged group at the expense of the rights and liberties of a submerged group: chiefly slaveholders at the expense of slaves,[27] white people at the expense of colored people,[28] and property holders at the expense of wage earners and other groups.[29] These cases, unlike the relatively innocuous ones of the preceding set, all involved liberties of genuinely fundamental importance, where an opposite policy would have meant thoroughly basic shifts in the distribution of rights, liberties, and opportunities in the United States—

---

26 The candidates for this category would appear to be Boyd v. United States, 116 U.S. 616 (1886); Rassmussen v. United States, 197 U.S. 516 (1905); Wong Wing v. United States, 163 U.S. 228 (1896); United States v. Moreland, 258 U.S. 433 (1922); Kirby v. United States, 174 U.S. 47 (1899); United States v. Cohen Grocery Co., 255 U.S. 81 (1921); Weeds, Inc. v. United States, 255 U.S. 109 (1921); Justices of the Supreme Court v. United States ex rel. Murray, 9 Wall. (U.S.) 274 (1870); United States ex rel. Toth v. Quarles, 350 U.S. 11 (1955).

27 Dred Scott v. Sandford, 19 How. (U.S.) 393 (1857).

28 United States v. Reese, 92 U.S. 214 (1876); United States v. Harris, 106 U.S. 629 (1883); United States v. Stanley (Civil Rights Cases), 109 U.S. 3 (1883); Baldwin v. Franks, 120 U.S. 678 (1887); James v. Bowman, 190 U.S. 127 (1903); Hodges v. United States, 203 U.S. 1 (1906); Butts v. Merchants & Miners Transportation Co., 230 U.S. 126 (1913).

29 Monongahela Navigation Co. v. United States, 148 U.S. 312 (1893); Adair v. United States, 208 U.S. 161 (1908); Adkins v. Children's Hospital, 261 U.S. 525 (1923); Nichols v. Coolidge, 274 U.S. 531 (1927); Untermyer v. Anderson, 276 U.S. 440 (1928); Heiner v. Donnan, 285 U.S. 312 (1932); Louisville Joint Stock Land Bank v. Radford, 295 U.S. 555 (1935).

where, moreover, the policies sustained by the Court's action have since been repudiated in every civilized nation of the Western world, including our own. Yet, if our earlier argument is correct, it is futile—precisely because the basic distribution of privilege *was* at issue—to suppose that the Court could have possibly acted much differently in these areas of policy from the way in which it did in fact act.

VI

Thus the role of the Court as a policy-making institution is not simple; and it is an error to suppose that its functions can be either described or appraised by means of simple concepts drawn from democratic or moral theory. It is possible, nonetheless, to derive a few general conclusions about the Court's role as a policy-making institution.

National politics in the United States, as in other stable democracies, is dominated by relatively cohesive alliances that endure for long periods of time. One recalls the Jeffersonian alliance, the Jacksonian, the extraordinarily long-lived Republican dominance of the post-Civil War years, and the New Deal alliance shaped by Franklin Roosevelt. Each is marked by a break with past policies, a period of intense struggle, followed by consolidation, and finally decay and disintegration of the alliance.

Except for short-lived transitional periods when the old alliance is disintegrating and the new one is struggling to take control of political institutions, the Supreme Court is inevitably a part of the dominant national alliance. As an element in the political leadership of the dominant alliance, the Court of course supports the major policies of the alliance. By itself, the Court is almost powerless to affect the course of national policy. In the absence of substantial agreement within the alliance, an attempt by the Court to make national policy is likely to lead to disaster, as the *Dred Scott* decision and the early New Deal cases demonstrate. Conceivably, the cases of the last three decades involving the freedom of Negroes, culminating in the now famous decision on school integration, are exceptions to this generalization; I shall have more to say about them in a moment.

The Supreme Court is not, however, simply an *agent* of the alliance. It is an essential part of the political leadership and possesses some bases of power of its own, the most important of which is the unique legitimacy attributed to its interpretations of the Constitution. This legitimacy the Court jeopardizes if it flagrantly opposes the major policies of the dominant alliance; such a course of action, as we have seen, is one in which the Court will not normally be tempted to engage.

It follows that within the somewhat narrow limits set by the basic policy goals of the dominant alliance, the Court *can* make national policy. Its discretion, then, is not unlike that of a powerful committee chairman in Congress who cannot, generally speaking, nullify the basic policies substantially agreed on by the rest of the dominant leadership, but who can, within these limits, often determine important questions of timing, effectiveness, and subordinate policy. Thus the Court is least effective against a current lawmaking majority—and evidently least inclined to act. It is most effective when it sets the bounds of policy for officials, agencies, state governments or even regions, a task that has come to occupy a very large part of the Court's business.[30]

Few of the Court's policy decisions can be interpreted sensibly in terms of a "majority" versus a "minority." In this respect the Court is no different from the rest of the political leadership. Generally speaking, policy at the national level is the outcome of conflict, bargaining, and agreement among minorities; the process is neither minority rule nor majority rule but what might better be called *minorities* rule, where one aggregation of minorities achieves policies opposed by another aggregation.

The main objective of presidential leadership is to build a stable and dominant aggregation of minorities with a high probability of winning the presidency and one or both houses of Congress. The main task of the Court is to confer legitimacy on the fundamental policies of the successful coalition. There are times when the coalition is unstable with respect to certain key policies; at very great risk to its legitimacy powers, the Court can intervene in such cases and may even succeed in establishing policy. Probably in such cases it can succeed only if its action conforms to and reinforces a widespread set of explicit or implicit norms held by the political leadership; norms which are not strong enough or are not distributed in such a way as to insure the existence of an effective lawmaking majority but are, nonetheless, sufficiently powerful to prevent any successful attack on the legitimacy powers of the Court. This is probably the explanation for the relatively successful work of the Court in enlarging the freedom of Negroes to vote during the past three decades and in its famous school integration decisions.[31]

Yet the Court is more than this. Considered as a political system, democ-

---

30 "Constitutional law and cases with constitutional undertones are of course still very important, with almost one-fourth of the cases in which written opinions were filed [in the two most recent terms] involving such questions. Review of administrative action . . . constitutes the largest category of the Court's work, comprising one-third of the total cases decided on the merits. The remaining . . . categories of litigation . . . all involve largely public law questions." Frankfurter, op. cit. supra note 1, at 793.

31 Rice v. Elmore, 165 F.2d 387 (C.A. 4th, 1947), cert. denied 333 U.S. 875 (1948); United States v. Classic, 313 U.S. 299 (1941); Smith v. Allwright, 321 U.S. 649 (1944); Grovey v. Townsend, 295 U.S. 45 (1935); Brown v. Board of Education, 347 U.S. 483 (1954); Bolling v. Sharpe, 347 U.S. 497 (1954).

racy is a set of basic procedures for arriving at decisions. The operation of these procedures presupposes the existence of certain rights, obligations, liberties and restraints; in short, certain patterns of behavior. The existence of these patterns of behavior in turn presupposes widespread agreement (particularly among the politically active and influential segments of the population) on the validity and propriety of the behavior. Although its record is by no means lacking in serious blemishes, at its best the Court operates to confer legitimacy, not simply on the particular and parochial policies of the dominant political alliance, but upon the basic patterns of behavior required for the operation of a democracy.

The Wages of Crying Wolf: A Comment on *Roe* v. *Wade**

John Hart Ely**

> The interests of the mother and the fetus are opposed. On which side should the State throw its weight? The issue is volatile; and it is resolved by the moral code which an individual has.[1]

In *Roe v. Wade*,[2] decided January 22, 1973, the Supreme Court—Justice Blackmun speaking for everyone but Justices White and Rehnquist[3]—held unconstitutional Texas's (and virtually every other state's[4]) criminal abortion statute. The broad outlines of its argument are not difficult to make out:

1. The right to privacy, though not explicitly mentioned in the Constitution, is protected by the Due Process Clause of the Fourteenth Amendment.[5]

2. This right "is broad enough to encompass a woman's decision whether or not to terminate her pregnancy."[6]

3. This right to an abortion is "fundamental" and can therefore be regulated only on the basis of a "compelling" state interest.[7]

4. The state does have two "important and legitimate" interests here,[8] the first in protecting maternal health, the second in protecting the life (or potential life[9]) of the fetus.[10] But neither can be counted "compelling" throughout the entire pregnancy: Each matures with the unborn child.

These interests are separate and distinct. Each grows in substan-

** Professor of Law, Yale Law School.
1. United States v. Vuitch, 402 U.S. 62, 80 (1971) (Douglas, J., dissenting in part).
2. 93 S. Ct. 705 (1973).
3. Were the dissents adequate, this comment would be unnecessary. But each is so brief as to signal no particular conviction that *Roe* represents an important, or unusually dangerous, constitutional development.
4. *See* 93 S. Ct. at 709-10 n.2. *See also* Doe v. Bolton, 93 S. Ct. 739, 742 (1973).
5. *Id.* at 727. *But cf.* note 58 *infra*.
6. 93 S. Ct. at 727.
7. *Id.* at 728.
8. *Id.* at 731.
9. The Court indicates that the constitutional issue is not to be solved by attempting to answer "the difficult question of when life begins." *Id.* at 730. *See also id.* at 725. *But see* pp. 925-26 *infra*.
10. The suggestion that the interest in protecting prenatal life should not be considered because the original legislative history of most laws restricting abortion concerned itself with maternal health, *see* 93 S. Ct. at 725-26, is rightly rejected—by clear implication in *Roe* and rather explicitly in *Doe*. *Id.* at 747.

tiality as the woman approaches term and, at a point during pregnancy, each becomes "compelling."[11]

5. During the first trimester of pregnancy, neither interest is sufficiently compelling to justify any interference with the decision of the woman and her physician. Appellants have referred the Court to medical data indicating that mortality rates for women undergoing early abortions, where abortion is legal, "appear to be as low as or lower than the rates for normal childbirth."[12] Thus the state's interest in protecting maternal health is not compelling during the first trimester. Since the interest in protecting the fetus is not yet compelling either,[13] during the first trimester the state can neither prohibit an abortion nor regulate the conditions under which one is performed.[14]

6. As we move into the second trimester, the interest in protecting the fetus remains less than compelling, and the decision to have an abortion thus continues to control. However, at this point the health risks of abortion begin to exceed those of childbirth. "It follows that, from and after this point, a State may regulate the abortion procedure to the extent that the regulation reasonably relates to the preservation and protection of maternal health."[15] Abortion may not be prohibited during the second trimester, however.[16]

7. At the point at which the fetus becomes viable[17] the interest in protecting it becomes compelling,[18] and therefore from that point on the state can prohibit abortions *except*—and this limitation is also apparently a constitutional command, though it receives no justification in the opinion—when they are necessary to protect maternal life or health.[19]

11. *Id.* at 731.
12. *Id.* at 725. *But cf.* note 117 *infra.*
13. *See* pp. 925-26 *infra.*
14. *See* 93 S. Ct. at 732. *But see* note 117 *infra.*
15. 93 S. Ct. at 732. *But see* note 117 *infra.*
16. 93 S. Ct. at 732.
17. This, the Court tells us, is somewhere between the twenty-fourth and twenty-eighth weeks. *Id.* at 730. *But cf.* p. 924 *infra.*
18. *See* p. 924 *infra.*
19. 93 S. Ct. at 732. (Thus the statutes of most states must be unconstitutional *even as applied to the final trimester,* since they permit abortion only for the purpose of saving the mother's life. *See id.* at 709.) This holding—that even after viability the mother's life *or health* (which presumably is to be defined very broadly indeed, so as to include what many might regard as the mother's convenience, *see* 93 S. Ct. at 755 (Burger, C.J., concurring)); United States v. Vuitch, 402 U.S. 62 (1971), must, as a matter of constitutional law, take precedence over what the Court seems prepared to grant at this point has become the fetus's *life, see* p. 924 *infra*—seems to me at least as controversial as its holding respecting the period prior to viability. (Typically, of course, one is not privileged even statutorily, let alone constitutionally, to take another's life in order to save his own life, much less his health.) Since, however, the Court does not see fit to defend this aspect of its decision at all, there is not a great deal that can be said by way of criticism.

I

A number of fairly standard criticisms can be made of *Roe*. A plausible narrower basis of decision, that of vagueness, is brushed aside in the rush toward broader ground.[20] The opinion strikes the reader initially as a sort of guidebook, addressing questions not before the Court and drawing lines with an apparent precision one generally associates with a commissioner's regulations.[21] On closer examination, however, the precision proves largely illusory. Confusing signals are emitted, particularly with respect to the nature of the doctor's responsibilities[22] and the permissible scope of health regulations after the first trimester.[23] The Court seems, moreover, to get carried away on the subject of remedies: Even assuming the case can be made for an unusually protected constitutional right to an abortion, it hardly seems necessary to have banned during the first trimester *all* state regulation of the conditions under which abortions can be performed.[24]

By terming such criticisms "standard," I do not mean to suggest they are unimportant, for they are not. But if they were all that was wrong with *Roe,* it would not merit special comment.[25]

20. The Court's theory seems to be that narrow grounds need not be considered when there is a broad one that will do the trick: "This conclusion makes it unnecessary for us to consider the additional challenge to the Texas statute asserted on grounds of vagueness." 93 S. Ct. at 732. *Compare id.* at 710 n.3, 710-11; Doe v. Bolton, 93 S. Ct. at 747; Roe v. Wade, 314 F. Supp. 1217, 1223 (N.D. Tex. 1970); cases cited 93 S. Ct. at 727; and United States v. Vuitch, 402 U.S. 62 (1971), bearing in mind that the Supreme Court lacks jurisdiction to "construe" a state statute so as to save it from the vice of vagueness.

21. *See also* Doe v. Bolton, 93 S. Ct. 739 (1973).

22. Apparently doctors are expected, or at least can be required despite the decisions, to exercise their best "medical" or "clinical" judgment (and presumably can be prosecuted if they perform abortions conflicting with that judgment). 93 S. Ct. at 747, 751. *But cf.* United States v. Vuitch, 402 U.S. 62, 97 (Stewart, J., dissenting in part). But if it is unconstitutional to limit the justifications for an abortion to considerations of maternal life and health, what kind of "medical" judgment does the Court have in mind? *See* Stone, *Abortion and the Supreme Court,* MODERN MEDICINE (forthcoming 1973): "[T]here are no clear medical indications for abortion in the vast majority of cases. Where there are no indications, there is no room for clinical judgment."

23. *Compare* 93 S. Ct. at 732 *with id.* at 748-51. An additional element of confusion may have been injected by Justice Douglas's indication in his concurrence that "quickening" is the point at which the interest in protecting the fetus becomes compelling. *Id.* at 759. *But see id.* at 730, where the Court distinguishes quickening from viability and holds the latter to be the crucial point. *See also id.* at 732; p. 924 *infra.*

24. The state *can* require that the abortion be performed by a doctor, but that is all. *But see* note 117 *infra.* Even after the first trimester, the limits on state regulation of the conditions under which an abortion can be performed are extremely stringent. *See* Doe v. Bolton, 93 S. Ct. 739 (1973).

25. With respect to the capital punishment litigation too, the Court rejected a narrow ground of invalidation one term only to come back with a *coup de main* the next. *Compare* McGautha v. California, 402 U.S. 183 (1971) *with* Furman v. Georgia, 408 U.S. 238 (1972). Miranda v. Arizona, 384 U.S. 436 (1966), has something of a "guidebook" quality about it. *See* Dershowitz & Ely, Harris v. New York: *Some Anxious Observations on the Candor and Logic of the Emerging Nixon Majority,* 80 YALE L.J. 1198, 1210 (1971). United States v. Wade, 388 U.S. 218 (1967), to take but one example, has always struck

II

Let us not underestimate what is at stake: Having an unwanted child can go a long way toward ruining a woman's life.[26] And at bottom *Roe* signals the Court's judgment that this result cannot be justified by any good that anti-abortion legislation accomplishes. This surely is an understandable conclusion—indeed it is one with which I agree[27]—but ordinarily the Court claims no mandate to second-guess legislative balances, at least not when the Constitution has designated neither of the values in conflict as entitled to special protection.[28] But even assuming it would be a good idea for the Court to assume this function, *Roe* seems a curious place to have begun. Laws prohibiting the use of "soft" drugs or, even more obviously, homosexual acts between consenting adults can stunt "the preferred life styles"[29] of those against whom enforcement is threatened in very serious ways. It is clear such acts harm no one besides the participants, and indeed the case that the participants are harmed is a rather shaky one.[30] Yet such laws survive,[31] on the theory that there exists a societal consensus that the behavior involved is revolting or at any rate immoral.[32] Of course the consensus is not universal but it is sufficient, and this is what is counted

me as a case where the Court, starting from the entirely valid realization that trials cannot be fair if lineups are not, went a bit far in limiting the appropriate remedies. And of course many opinions have emitted confusing signals respecting what is henceforth permissible. *See, e.g.*, pp. 929-30 *infra.*

26. The child may not fare so well either. Of course the Court requires of the mother neither sort of showing, though it may be hoping the doctors will do so. *But cf.* note 22 *supra.*

It is also probably the case, although this is the sort of issue where reliable statistics and comparisons are largely unobtainable, that a number of women have died from illegal abortions who would have lived had they been able to secure legal abortions. It is a strange argument for the unconstitutionality of a law that those who evade it suffer, but it is one that must nevertheless be weighed in the balance as a cost of anti-abortion legislation. The Court does not mention it, however; and given the severe restrictions it places on state regulation of the conditions under which an abortion can be performed, it apparently did not appreciably inform its judgment.

27. *See* pp. 926-27 *infra.*

28. *See* pp. 926-37 *infra.* Even where the Constitution does single out one of the values for special protection, the Court has shown an increasing tendency to avoid balancing, or at least to talk as though it were. *See* Brandenburg v. Ohio, 395 U.S. 444 (1969). *See also* United States v. Robel, 389 U.S. 258, 268 n.20 (1967); *but see* Note, *Less Drastic Means and the First Amendment,* 78 YALE L.J. 464, 467-68 (1969). *See also* United States v. O'Brien, 391 U.S. 367, 376-77 (1968); *but cf.* Ely, *Legislative and Administrative Motivation in Constitutional Law,* 79 YALE L.J. 1205, 1340-41 (1970).

29. 93 S. Ct. at 759 (Douglas, J., concurring).

30. The claim that the participants are injuring their health seems at least as plausible respecting abortion. *Cf.* note 117 *infra.* To the extent that the use of soft drugs and homosexual activities interfere with the lives of those other than the participants, those interferences can be dealt with discretely.

31. *Cf.* Poe v. Ullman, 367 U.S. 497, 551-53 (1961), (Harlan, J., dissenting), *quoted* in part in Griswold v. Connecticut, 381 U.S. 479, 499 (1965) (Goldberg, J., concurring), distinguishing laws proscribing homosexual acts (even those performed in the home) as not involving the "right" at stake in those cases.

32. *See, e.g.,* Poe v. Ullman, 367 U.S. 497, 545-46 (Harlan, J., dissenting).

crucial, to get the laws passed and keep them on the books. Whether anti-abortion legislation cramps the life style of an unwilling mother more significantly than anti-homosexuality legislation cramps the life style of a homosexual is a close question. But even granting that it does, the *other* side of the balance looks very different. For there is more than simple societal revulsion to support legislation restricting abortion:[33] Abortion ends (or if it makes a difference, prevents) the life of a human being other than the one making the choice.

The Court's response here is simply not adequate. It agrees, indeed it holds, that after the point of viability (a concept it fails to note will become even less clear than it is now as the technology of birth continues to develop[34]) the interest in protecting the fetus is compelling.[35] Exactly why that is the magic moment is not made clear: Viability, as the Court defines it,[36] is achieved some six to twelve weeks after quickening.[37] (Quickening is the point at which the fetus begins discernibly to move independently of the mother[38] and the point that has historically been deemed crucial—to the extent *any* point between conception and birth has been focused on.[39]) But no, it is *viability* that is constitutionally critical: the Court's defense seems to mistake a definition for a syllogism.

> With respect to the State's important and legitimate interest in potential life, the "compelling" point is at viability. This is so because the fetus then presumably has the capacity of meaningful life outside the mother's womb.[40]

With regard to why the state cannot consider this "important and legitimate interest" prior to viability, the opinion is even less satis-

33. Nor is the Court's conclusion that early abortion does not present serious physical risk to the woman involved shared by all doctors. *Cf.* note 117 *infra*.
34. It defines viability so as not to exclude the possibility of artificial support, 93 S. Ct. at 730, and later indicates its awareness of the continuing development of artificial wombs. *Id.* at 731. It gives no sign of having considered the implications of that combination for the trimester program the Constitution is held to mandate, however.
35. Albeit not so compelling that a state is permitted to honor it at the expense of the mother's health. *See* note 19 *supra*.
36. Note 17 *supra*.
37. *See* 93 S. Ct. at 716.
38. *Id.*
39. *Id.* at 716-20.
40. *Id.* at 732. *See also id.* at 730:

> Physicians and their scientific colleagues have regarded [quickening] with less interest and have tended to focus either upon conception or upon live birth or upon the interim point at which the fetus becomes "viable," . . . .

The relevance of this observation is not explained. It is, moreover, of questionable validity:

> This line is drawn beyond quickening, beyond the point where any religion has assumed that life begins, beyond the time when abortion is a simple procedure, and beyond the point when most physicians and nurses will feel the procedure is victimless. It is also beyond the point which would have satisfied many who, like myself, were long term supporters of the right to abortion.

Stone, *supra* note 22.

factory. The discussion begins sensibly enough: The interest asserted is not necessarily tied to the question whether the fetus is "alive," for whether or not one calls it a living being, it is an entity with the potential for (and indeed the likelihood of) life.[41] But all of arguable relevance that follows[42] are arguments that fetuses (a) are not recognized as "persons in the whole sense" by legal doctrine generally[43] and (b) are not "persons" protected by the Fourteenth Amendment.[44]

To the extent they are not entirely inconclusive, the bodies of doctrine to which the Court adverts respecting the protection of fetuses under general legal doctrine tend to undercut rather than support its conclusion.[45] And the argument that fetuses (unlike, say, corporations) are not "persons" under the Fourteenth Amendment fares little better. The Court notes that most constitutional clauses using the word "persons"—such as the one outlining the qualifications for the Presidency—appear to have been drafted with postnatal beings in mind. (It might have added that most of them were plainly drafted with

41. Logically, of course, a legitimate state interest in this area need not stand or fall on acceptance of the belief that life begins at conception or at some other point prior to live birth. In assessing the State's interest, recognition may be given to the less rigid claim that as long as at least *potential* life is involved, the State may assert interests beyond the protection of the pregnant woman alone.

93 S. Ct. at 725. *See also id.* at 730:

> We need not resolve the difficult question of when life begins. When those trained in the respective disciplines of medicine, philosophy, and theology are unable to arrive at any consensus, the judiciary, at this point [sic] in the development of man's knowledge, is not in a position to speculate as to the answer.

The Texas statute, like those of many states, had declared fetuses to be living beings. *See id.* at 709 n.1, 710 n.3; *cf. id.* at 721, 723 n.40, 729 n.55.

42. The opinion does contain a lengthy survey of "historical attitudes" toward abortion, culminating in a discussion of the positions of the American Medical Association, the American Public Health Association, and the American Bar Association. *Id.* at 715-24. (The discussion's high point is probably reached where the Court explains away the Hippocratic Oath's prohibition of abortion on the grounds that Hippocrates was a Pythagorean, and Pythagoreans were a minority. *Id.* at 715-16.) The Court does not seem entirely clear as to what this discussion has to do with the legal argument, *id.* at 709, 715, and the reader is left in much the same quandary. It surely does not seem to support the Court's position, unless a record of serious historical and contemporary dispute is somehow thought to generate a constitutional mandate.

43. *Id.* at 731.

44. *Id.* at 728-30.

45. [T]he traditional rule of tort law had denied recovery for prenatal injuries even though the child was born alive. That rule has been changed in almost every jurisdiction. In most States recovery is said to be permitted only if the fetus was viable, or at least quick, when the injuries were sustained, though few courts have squarely so held. In a recent development, generally opposed by the commentators, some States permit the parents of a stillborn child to maintain an action for wrongful death because of prenatal injuries. Such an action, however, would appear to be one to vindicate the parents' interest and is thus consistent with the view that the fetus, at most, represents only the potentiality of life. Similarly, unborn children have been recognized as acquiring rights or interests by way of inheritance or other devolution of property, and have been represented by guardians *ad litem*. Perfection of the interests involved, again, has generally been contingent upon live birth. In short, the unborn have never been recognized in the law as persons in the whole sense.

Id. at 731 (footnotes omitted). *See also, e.g.,* W. PROSSER, HANDBOOK OF THE LAW OF TORTS 355 (3d ed. 1964).

adults in mind, but I suppose that wouldn't have helped.) In addition, "the appellee conceded on reargument that no case can be cited that holds that a fetus is a person within the meaning of the Fourteenth Amendment."[46] (The other legal contexts in which the question could have arisen are not enumerated.)

The canons of construction employed here are perhaps most intriguing when they are contrasted with those invoked to derive the constitutional right to an abortion.[47] But in any event, the argument that fetuses lack constitutional rights is simply irrelevant. For it has never been held or even asserted that the state interest needed to justify forcing a person to refrain from an activity, *whether or not that activity is constitutionally protected,* must implicate either the life or the constitutional rights of another person.[48] Dogs are not "persons in the whole sense" nor have they constitutional rights, but that does not mean the state cannot prohibit killing them: It does not even mean the state cannot prohibit killing them in the exercise of the First Amendment right of political protest. Come to think of it, draft cards aren't persons either.[49]

Thus even assuming the Court ought generally to get into the business of second-guessing legislative balances, it has picked a strange case with which to begin. Its purported evaluation of the balance that produced anti-abortion legislation simply does not meet the issue: That the life plans of the mother must, not simply may, prevail over the state's desire to protect the fetus simply does not follow from the judgment that the fetus is not a person. Beyond all that, however, the Court has no business getting into that business.

III

Were I a legislator I would vote for a statute very much like the one the Court ends up drafting.[50] I hope this reaction reflects more

46. *Id.* at 728-29 (footnote omitted).
47. *See* pp. 928-33 *infra.*
48. Indeed it is difficult to think of a single instance where the justification given for upholding a governmental limitation of a protected right has involved the constitutional rights of others. A "free press-fair trial" situation might provide the basis for such an order, but thus far the Court has refused to approve one. *See* Ely, *Trial by Newspaper & Its Cures,* ENCOUNTER, March 1967, at 80-92.

In the Court's defense it should be noted that it errs in the other direction as well, by suggesting that if a fetus *were* a person protected by the Fourteenth Amendment, it would necessarily follow that appellants would lose. 93 S. Ct. at 728. Yet in fact all that would thereby be established is that one right granted special protection by the Fourteenth Amendment was in conflict with what the Court felt was another; it would not tell us which must prevail.

49. *See* United States v. O'Brien, 391 U.S. 367, 376-77 (1968). And if you don't like that example, substitute post offices for draft cards.
50. I would, however, omit the serious restrictions the Court puts on state health regulation of the conditions under which an abortion can be performed, and give

than the psychological phenomenon that keeps bombardiers sane—the fact that it is somehow easier to "terminate" those you cannot see—and am inclined to think it does: that the mother, unlike the unborn child, has begun to imagine a future for herself strikes me as morally quite significant. But God knows I'm not *happy* with that resolution. Abortion is too much like infanticide on the one hand, and too much like contraception on the other, to leave one comfortable with any answer; and the moral issue it poses is as fiendish as any philosopher's hypothetical.[51]

Of course, the Court often resolves difficult moral questions, and difficult questions yield controversial answers. I doubt, for example, that most people would agree that letting a drug peddler go unapprehended is morally preferable to letting the police kick down his door without probable cause. The difference, of course, is that the Constitution, which legitimates and theoretically controls judicial intervention, has some rather pointed things to say about this choice. There will of course be difficult questions about the applicability of its language to specific facts, but at least the document's special concern with one of the values in conflict is manifest. It simply says nothing, clear or fuzzy, about abortion.[52]

The matter cannot end there, however. The Burger Court, like the Warren Court before it, has been especially solicitous of the right to travel from state to state, demanding a compelling state interest if it is to be inhibited.[53] Yet nowhere in the Constitution is such a right mentioned. It is, however, as clear as such things can be that this right was one the framers intended to protect, most specifically[54] by the Privileges and Immunities Clause of Article IV.[55] The right is, moreover, plausibly inferable from the system of government, and the citizen's role therein, contemplated by the Constitution.[56] The Court

serious thought—though the practical difference here is not likely to be great—to placing the critical line at quickening rather than viability. *See* note 40 *supra*.

51. Some of us who fought for the right to abortion did so with a divided spirit. We have always felt that the decision to abort was a human tragedy to be accepted only because an unwanted pregnancy was even more tragic.

Stone, *supra* note 22.

52. Of course the opportunity to have an abortion should be considered part of the "liberty" protected by the Fourteenth Amendment. *See* p. 935 *infra*.

53. *See, e.g.*, Dunn v. Blumstein, 405 U.S. 330 (1972); Shapiro v. Thompson, 394 U.S. 618 (1969).

54. *See also* Edwards v. California, 314 U.S. 160 (1941).

55. *See* United States v. Wheeler, 254 U.S. 281, 294 (1920); Slaughterhouse Cases, 83 U.S. (16 Wall.) 36, 75 (1872); U.S. Arts. Confed. art. IV; 3 M. Farrand, The Records of the Federal Convention of 1787, at 112 (1911); *cf.* The Federalist, No. 42, at 307 (Wright ed. 1961).

56. *See* Crandall v. Nevada, 73 U.S. (6 Wall.) 35 (1867); C. Black, Structure and Relationship in Constitutional Law (1969). The Court seems to regard the opportunity to travel *outside* the United States as merely an aspect of the "liberty" that under the Fifth and Fourteenth Amendments cannot be denied without due process. *See* Zemel v. Rusk, 381 U.S. 1, 14 (1965). *Cf.* p. 935 *infra*.

in *Roe* suggests an inference of neither sort—from the intent of the framers,[57] or from the governmental system contemplated by the Constitution—in support of the constitutional right to an abortion.

What the Court does assert is that there is a general right of privacy granted special protection—that is, protection above and beyond the baseline requirement of "rationality"—by the Fourteenth Amendment,[58] and that that right "is broad enough to encompass" the right to an abortion. The general right of privacy is inferred, as it was in *Griswold v. Connecticut,*[59] from various provisions of the Bill of Rights manifesting a concern with privacy, notably the Fourth Amendment's guarantee against unreasonable searches, the Fifth Amendment's privilege against self-incrimination, and the right, inferred from the First Amendment, to keep one's political associations secret.[60]

One possible response is that all this proves is that the things explicitly mentioned are forbidden, if indeed it does not actually demonstrate a disposition *not* to enshrine anything that might be called a general right of privacy.[61] In fact the Court takes this view when it suits its purposes. (On the *same day* it decided *Roe,* the Court held that a showing of reasonableness was not needed to force someone to provide a grand jury with a voice exemplar, reasoning that the Fifth Amendment was not implicated because the evidence was not "testi-

57. Abortions had, of course, been performed, and intermittently proscribed, for centuries prior to the framing of the Constitution. That alone, however, need not be dispositive. *See* p. 929 *infra* & note 97 *infra.*

58. The Court does not seem entirely certain about which provision protects the right to privacy and its included right to an abortion.

> Appellant would discover this right in the concept of personal "liberty" embodied in the Fourteenth Amendment's Due Process Clause; or in personal, marital, familial, and sexual privacy said to be protected by the Bill of Rights or its penumbras . . . or among those rights reserved to the people by the Ninth Amendment . . . .

93 S. Ct. at 715.

> This right of privacy, whether it be founded in the Fourteenth Amendment's concept of personal liberty and restrictions upon state action, as we feel it is, or, as the District Court determined, in the Ninth Amendment's reservation of rights to the people, is broad enough to encompass a woman's decision whether or not to terminate her pregnancy.

Id. at 727. This inability to pigeonhole confidently the right involved is not important in and of itself. It might, however, have alerted the Court to what *is* an important question: whether the Constitution speaks to the matter at all.

59. 381 U.S. 479 (1965).

60. *See* NAACP v. Alabama, 357 U.S. 449 (1958), relied on in *Griswold,* 381 U.S. at 483. The *Roe* Court's reference to Justice Goldberg's concurrence in *Griswold* for the proposition that "the roots of" the right of privacy can be found in the Ninth Amendment, 93 S. Ct. at 726, misconceives the use the earlier opinion made of that Amendment. *See* 381 U.S. at 492-93. A reference to "the penumbras of the Bill of Rights," 93 S. Ct. at 726, can have no content independent of a description of some general value or values inferable from the provisions involved (and therefore assignable to their penumbras). *See* San Antonio Independent School Dist. v. Rodriguez, 41 U.S.L.W. 4407, 4438 (U.S. March 21, 1973) (Marshall, J., dissenting); pp. 929-30 *infra.*

61. *See* Katz v. United States, 389 U.S. 347, 364 (1967) (Black, J., dissenting); Griswold v. Connecticut, 381 U.S. 479, 529 (Stewart, J., dissenting).

monial" and that the Fourth Amendment did not apply because there was no "seizure."[62]) But this approach is unduly crabbed. Surely the Court is entitled, indeed I think it is obligated, to seek out the sorts of evils the framers meant to combat and to move against their twentieth century counterparts.[63]

Thus it seems to me entirely proper to infer a general right of privacy, *so long as some care is taken in defining the sort of right the inference will support.* Those aspects of the First, Fourth and Fifth Amendments to which the Court refers all limit the ways in which, and the circumstances under which, the government can go about gathering information about a person he would rather it did not have.[64] *Katz v. United States,*[65] limiting governmental tapping of telephones, may not involve what the framers would have called a "search," but it plainly involves this general concern with privacy.[66] *Griswold* is a long step, even a leap, beyond this, but at least the connection is discernible. Had it been a case that purported to discover in the Constitution a "right to contraception," it would have been *Roe*'s strongest precedent.[67] But the Court in *Roe* gives no evidence of so regarding it,[68] and rightly not.[69] Commentators tend to forget, though the Court

62. United States v. Dionisio, 93 S. Ct. 764 (1973). *See also* United States v. Mara, 93 S. Ct. 774 (1973) (handwriting exemplars), also decided the same day as *Roe,* and Couch v. United States, 93 S. Ct. 611 (1973) (finding no privacy interest in records a taxpayer had turned over to her accountant) decided thirteen days earlier.

63. [T]he proper scope of [a constitutional provision], and its relevance to contemporary problems, must ultimately be sought by attempting to discern the reasons for its inclusion in the Constitution, and the evils it was designed to eliminate.
United States v. Brown, 381 U.S. 437, 442 (1965). *See also* Weems v. United States, 217 U.S. 349, 373 (1910); Reich, *Mr. Justice Black and the Living Constitution,* 76 Harv. L. Rev. 673 (1963); Note, *The Bounds of Legislative Specification: A Suggested Approach to the Bill of Attainder Clause,* 72 Yale L.J. 330 (1962).

64. *Cf.* Fried, *Privacy,* 77 Yale L.J. 475 (1968). The Third Amendment, mentioned in *Griswold* though not in *Roe,* surely has this aspect to it as well, though it probably grew in even larger measure out of a general concern with the pervasiveness of military power.

65. 389 U.S. 347 (1967).

66. *Cf.* Schmerber v. California, 384 U.S. 757 (1966).

67. Contraception and at least early abortion obviously have much in common. *See* Stone, *supra* note 22.

68. The *Roe* opinion does not rely on the obvious contraception-abortion comparison and indeed gives no sign that it finds *Griswold* stronger precedent than a number of other cases. *See* 93 S. Ct. at 726-27; note 79 *infra.* In fact it seems to go out of its way to characterize *Griswold* and Eisenstadt v. Baird, 405 U.S. 438 (1972), as cases concerned with the privacy of the bedroom. *See* 93 S. Ct. at 730; note 79 *infra.* It is true that in *Eisenstadt* the Court at one point characterized *Griswold* as protecting the "decision whether to bear and beget a child," 405 U.S. at 453, but it also, mysteriously in light of that characterization, pointedly refused to decide whether the earlier case extended beyond use, to the distribution of contraceptives. *Id.* at 452-53. Nor is there any possibility the refusal to extend *Griswold* in this way was ill-considered; such an extension would have obviated the *Eisenstadt* Court's obviously strained performance respecting the Equal Protection Clause.

69. Admittedly the *Griswold* opinion is vague and openended, but the language quoted in the text at note 72 *infra* seems plainly inconsistent with the view that it is a case not about likely invasions of the privacy of the bedroom but rather directly enshrining a right to contraception.

plainly has not,[70] that the Court in *Griswold* stressed that it was invalidating only that portion of the Connecticut law that proscribed the *use,* as opposed to the manufacture, sale, or other distribution of contraceptives. That distinction (which would be silly were the right to contraception being constitutionally enshrined) makes sense if the case is rationalized on the ground that the section of the law whose constitutionality was in issue was such that *its enforcement would have been virtually impossible without* the most outrageous sort of governmental prying into the privacy of the home.[71] And this, indeed, is the theory on which the Court appeared rather explicitly to settle:

> The present case, then, concerns a relationship lying within the zone of privacy created by several fundamental constitutional guarantees. And it concerns a law which, in forbidding the *use* of contraceptives rather than regulating their manufacture or sale, seeks to achieve its goals by means having a maximum destructive impact upon that relationship. Such a law cannot stand in light of the familiar principle, so often applied by this Court, that "a governmental purpose to control or prevent activities constitutionally subject to state regulation may not be achieved by means which sweep unnecessarily broadly and thereby invade the area of protected freedoms." *NAACP v. Alabama,* 377 U.S. 288, 307. Would we allow the police to search the sacred precincts of marital bedrooms for telltale signs of the use of contraceptives? The very idea is repulsive to the notions of privacy surrounding the marriage relationship.[72]

Thus even assuming (as the Court surely seemed to) that a state can constitutionally seek to minimize or eliminate the circulation and use of contraceptives, Connecticut had acted unconstitutionally by selecting a means, that is a direct ban on use, that would generate intolerably intrusive modes of data-gathering.[73] No such rationalization is attempted by the Court in *Roe*—and understandably not, for whatever else may be involved, it is not a case about governmental snooping.[74]

70. *See* Eisenstadt v. Baird, 405 U.S. 438, 443 (1972). *Cf.* 93 S. Ct. at 730; note 79 *infra.*

71. Stanley v. Georgia, 394 U.S. 557 (1969), cited by the Court in *Roe,* might also be rationalized on such a theory, *cf. id.* at 565, though it reads more like a "pure" First Amendment case concerned with governmental attempts at thought control.

72. 381 U.S. at 485-86 (emphasis in original).

73. *See also* Poe v. Ullman, 367 U.S. 497, 548-49, 553-54 (1961) (Harlan, J., dissenting). That the Court in *Griswold* saw fit to quote Boyd v. United States, 116 U.S. 616, 630 (1886), is also significant. *See* 381 U.S. at 484-85 n.*. *See also* United States v. Grunewald, 233 F.2d 556, 581-82 (2d Cir. 1956) (Frank, J., dissenting).

The theory suggested in Poe v. Ullman, *supra,* at 551-52 (Harlan, J., dissenting), extending heightened protection to activities (though it turns out to be *some* activities, note 31 *supra)* customarily performed in the home, is also inapplicable to *Roe.*

74. Of course in individual cases the government might seek to enforce legislation restricting abortion, as indeed it might seek to enforce any law, in ways that violate the

The Court reports that some amici curiae argued for an unlimited right to do as one wishes with one's body. This theory holds, for me at any rate, much appeal. However, there would have been serious problems with its invocation in this case. In the first place, more than the mother's own body is involved in a decision to have an abortion; a fetus may not be a "person in the whole sense," but it is certainly not nothing.[75] Second, it is difficult to find a basis for thinking that the theory was meant to be given constitutional sanction: Surely it is no part of the "privacy" interest the Bill of Rights suggests.[76]

> [I]t is not clear to us that the claim . . . that one has an unlimited right to do with one's body as one pleases bears a close relationship to the right of privacy . . . .[77]

Unfortunately, having thus rejected the amici's attempt to define the bounds of the general constitutional right of which the right to an abortion is a part,[78] on the theory that the general right described has little to do with privacy, the Court provides neither an alternative definition[79] nor an account of why *it* thinks privacy is involved. It

Fourth Amendment or otherwise intrude upon the general privacy interest the Bill of Rights suggests. The Court does not suggest, however, that the laws at issue in *Roe* are in any sense unusually calculated to generate such intrusions.

75. *See* pp. 925-26 *supra*.

76. *See* pp. 929-30 *supra*.

77. 93 S. Ct. at 727.

78. The Court's rejection of the "non-paternalism" argument is of course underlined by the health regulations it is prepared to allow during the second trimester, *before* the interest in protecting the fetus is cognizable. *See* p. 921 *supra*.

79. The Court does assert that

> only personal rights that can be deemed "fundamental" or "implicit in the concept of ordered liberty," Palko v. Connecticut, 302 U.S. 319, 325 (1937), are included in this guarantee of personal privacy. They also make it clear that the right has some extension to activities relating to marriage, Loving v. Virginia, 388 U.S. 1, 12 (1967), procreation, Skinner v. Oklahoma, 316 U.S. 535, 541-42 (1942), contraception, Eisenstadt v. Baird, 405 U.S. 438, 453-54 (1972); *id.* at 460, 463-65 (White, J., concurring), family relationships, Prince v. Massachusetts, 321 U.S. 158, 166 (1944), and child rearing and education, Pierce v. Society of Sisters, 268 U.S. 510, 535 (1925), Meyer v. Nebraska, [262 U.S. 390, 399 (1923)].

93 S. Ct. at 726-27. The *Palko* test was stated and has heretofore been taken as a definition (of questionable contemporary vitality) of due process generally, not of privacy. *Loving* was a case involving explicit racial discrimination and therefore decidable (and decided) by a rather straightforward application of the Equal Protection Clause. *See* Ely, *supra* note 28, at 1230. And while the *Loving* Court did, inexplicably, append a reference to due process, it did not mention privacy. *Skinner* invalidated the Oklahoma criminal sterilization act's distinction between larcenists and embezzlers. Although it too did not allude to privacy, it did suggest it was applying a higher equal protection standard than usual. Why it did so is unclear. "Faced with the possibility of a finding of cruel and unusual punishment and the virtual certainty of invalidation under the clause proscribing *ex post facto* laws, the state declined to argue the case on the theory that the . . . Act was a penal statute, and therefore tried to justify the distinction in 'regulatory' terms." Ely, *supra*, at 1235 n.101. That being so, the state was unable to come up with even a plausible justification for the distinction. *Eisenstadt* was a case applying "traditional" equal protection standards, albeit in a less than satisfactory way. *See* Note, *Legislative Purpose, Rationality, and Equal Protection,* 82 YALE L.J. 123 (1972). The

simply announces that the right to privacy "is broad enough to encompass a woman's decision whether or not to terminate her pregnancy." Apparently this conclusion is thought to derive from the passage that immediately follows it:

> The detriment that the State would impose upon the pregnant woman by denying this choice altogether is apparent. Specific and direct harm medically diagnosable even in early pregnancy may be involved. Maternity, or additional offspring, may force upon the woman a distressful life and future. Psychological harm may be imminent. Mental and physical health may be taxed by child care. There is also the distress, for all concerned, associated with the unwanted child, and there is the problem of bringing a child into a family already unable, psychologically and otherwise, to care for it. In other cases, as in this one, the additional difficulties and continuing stigma of unwed motherhood may be involved.[80]

All of this is true and ought to be taken very seriously. But it has nothing to do with privacy in the Bill of Rights sense or any other the Constitution suggests.[81] I suppose there is nothing to prevent one from using the word "privacy" to mean the freedom to live one's life without governmental interference. But the Court obviously does not so use the term.[82] Nor could it, for such a right is at stake in *every* case. Our

passage cited by the Court in *Roe* reiterated *Griswold*'s conclusion that privacy interests are threatened by a ban on the use of contraceptives, but declined to decide whether its rationale should be extended to restrictions on distribution. *See* p. 930 *supra*. *Prince* upheld the application of a child labor law to Jehovah's Witness children distributing religious literature. It did, however, reiterate the conclusion of *Pierce* and *Meyer* that family relationships are entitled to special protection. Those two cases are products of "the *Lochner* era," *see* pp. 937-43 *infra*. The vitality of the theory on which they rested has been questioned, Epperson v. Arkansas, 393 U.S. 97, 105-06 (1968), and the Court has attempted to recast them as First Amendment cases. Griswold v. Connecticut, 381 U.S. 479, 482 (1965); *cf.* Poe v. Ullman, 367 U.S. 497, 533-34 (1961) (Harlan, J., dissenting). Even reading the cases cited "for all that they are worth," it is difficult to isolate the "privacy" factor (or any other factor that seems constitutionally relevant) that unites them with each other and with *Roe*. So the Court seems to admit by indicating that privacy has "some extension" to the activities involved, and so it seems later to grant even more explicitly.

> The pregnant woman cannot be isolated in her privacy. She carries an embryo and, later, a fetus. . . . The situation therefore is inherently different from marital intimacy, or bedroom possession of obscene material, or marriage, or procreation, or education, with which *Eisenstadt, Griswold, Stanley, Loving, Skinner, Pierce,* and *Meyer* were respectively concerned.

93 S. Ct. at 730.

80. 93 S. Ct. at 727. *See also id.* at 757 (Douglas, J., concurring).

81. It might be noted that most of the factors enumerated also apply to the inconvenience of having an unwanted two-year-old, or a senile parent, around. Would the Court find the constitutional right of privacy invaded in those situations too? I find it hard to believe it would; even if it did, of course, it would not find a constitutional right to "terminate" the annoyance—presumably because "real" persons are now involved. *But cf.* p. 926 *supra* & note 48 *supra*. But what about ways of removing the annoyance that do not involve "termination"? Can they really be matters of constitutional entitlement?

82. *But cf.* 93 S. Ct. at 758-59 (Douglas, J., concurring).

life styles are constantly limited, often seriously, by governmental regulation; and while many of us would prefer less direction, granting that desire the status of a preferred constitutional right would yield a system of "government" virtually unrecognizable to us and only slightly more recognizable to our forefathers.[83] The Court's observations concerning the serious, life-shaping costs of having a child prove what might to the thoughtless have seemed unprovable: That even though a human life, or a potential human life, hangs in the balance, the moral dilemma abortion poses is so difficult as to be heartbreaking. What they fail to do is even begin to resolve that dilemma so far as our governmental system is concerned by associating either side of the balance with a value inferable from the Constitution.

But perhaps the inquiry should not end even there. In his famous *Carolene Products* footnote, Justice Stone suggested that the interests to which the Court can responsibly give extraordinary constitutional protection include not only those expressed in the Constitution but also those that are unlikely to receive adequate consideration in the political process, specifically the interests of "discrete and insular minorities" unable to form effective political alliances.[84] There can be little doubt that such considerations have influenced the direction, if only occasionally the rhetoric, of the recent Courts. My repeated efforts to convince my students that sex should be treated as a "suspect classification" have convinced me it is no easy matter to state such considerations in a "principled" way. But passing that problem, *Roe* is not an appropriate case for their invocation.

Compared with men, very few women sit in our legislatures, a fact I believe should bear some relevance—even without an Equal Rights Amendment—to the appropriate standard of review for legislation that favors men over women.[85] But *no* fetuses sit in our legislatures. Of

83. *Cf.* Katz v. United States, 389 U.S. 347, 350-51 (1967).

84. United States v. Carolene Products Co., 304 U.S. 144, 152 n.4 (1938).

85. This is not the place for a full treatment of the subject, but the general idea is this: Classifications by sex, like classifications by race, differ from the usual classification—to which the traditional "reasonable generalization" standard is properly applied—in that they rest on "we-they" generalizations as opposed to a "they-they" generalization. Take a familiar example of the usual approach, Williamson v. Lee Optical Co., 348 U.S. 483 (1955). Of course few legislators are opticians. But few are optometrists either. Thus while a decision to distinguish opticians from optometrists will incorporate a stereotypical comparison of two classes of people, it is a comparison of two "they" stereotypes, *viz.* "They [opticians] are generally inferior to or not so well qualified as *they* [optometrists] are in the following respect(s), which we find sufficient to justify the classification: . . . ." However, legislators traditionally have not only not been black (or female); they have been white (and male). A decision to distinguish blacks from whites (or women from men) will therefore have its roots in a comparison between a "we" stereotype and a "they" stereotype, *viz.* "They [blacks or women] are generally inferior to or not so well qualified as *we* [whites or men] are in the following respect(s), which we find sufficient to justify the classification: . . . ."

course they have their champions, but so have women. The two interests have clashed repeatedly in the political arena, and had continued to do so up to the date of the opinion, generating quite a wide variety of accommodations.[86] By the Court's lights virtually all of the legislative accommodations had unduly favored fetuses; by its definition of victory, women had lost. Yet in every legislative balance one of the competing interests loses to some extent; indeed usually, as here, they both do. On some occasions the Constitution throws its weight on the side of one of them, indicating the balance must be restruck. And on others—and this is Justice Stone's suggestion—it is at least arguable that, constitutional directive or not, the Court should throw *its* weight on the side of a minority demanding in court more than it was able to achieve politically. But even assuming this suggestion can be given principled content, it was clearly intended and should be reserved for those interests which, *as compared with the interests to which they have been subordinated,* constitute minorities unusually incapable of protecting themselves.[87] Compared with men, women may constitute

The choice between classifying on the basis of a comparative generalization and attempting to come up with a more discriminating formula always involves balancing the increase in fairness which greater individualization will produce against the added costs it will entail. It is no startling psychological insight, however, that most of us are delighted to hear and prone to accept comparative characterizations of groups that suggest that the groups to which *we* belong are in some way superior to others. (I would be inclined to exclude most situations where the "we's" used to be "they's," *cf.* Ferguson v. Skrupa, 372 U.S. 726 (1963), and would therefore agree that the unchangeability of the distinguishing characteristic is indeed relevant, though it is only part of the story.) The danger is therefore greater in we-they situations that we will overestimate the validity of the proposed stereotypical classification by seizing upon the positive myths about our own class and the negative myths about theirs—or indeed the realities respecting some or most members of the two classes—and too readily assuming that virtually the entire membership of the two classes fit the stereotypes and therefore that not many of "them" will be unfairly deprived, nor many of "us" unfairly benefitted, by the proposed classification. In short, I trust your generalizations about the differences between my gang and Wilfred's more than I do your generalizations about the differences between my gang and yours.

Of course most judges, like most legislators, are white males, and there is no particular reason to suppose they are any more immune to the conscious and unconscious temptations that inhere in we-they generalizations. Obviously the factors mentioned can distort the evaluation of a classification fully as much as they can distort its formation. But all this is only to suggest that the Court has chosen the right course in reviewing classifications it has decided are suspicious—a course not of restriking or second-guessing the legislative cost-benefit balance but rather of demanding a congruence between the classification and its goal as perfect as practicable. When in a given situation you can't be trusted to generalize and I can't be trusted to generalize, the answer is not to generalize—so long as a bearable alternative exists. And here, the Court has recognized, one does—the alternative of forcing the system to absorb the additional cost that case by case determinations of qualification will entail. Legislatures incur this cost voluntarily in a great many situations, and courts have on other occasions forced them to do so where constitutionally protected interests will be threatened by an imperfectly fitting classification. The unusual dangers of distortion that inhere in a we-they process of comparative generalization, the Court seems to have been telling us in the racial classification cases, also demand that we bear the increased cost of individual justice.

86. *See* 93 S. Ct. at 708-10, 720, 723-24, 742-43, 752-55.

87. If the mere fact that the classification in issue disadvantages a minority whose viewpoint was not appreciated by a majority of the legislature that enacted it were sufficient to render it suspect, *all* classifications would be suspect.

such a "minority"; compared with the unborn, they do not.[88] I'm not sure I'd know a discrete and insular minority if I saw one, but confronted with a multiple choice question requiring me to designate (a) women or (b) fetuses as one, I'd expect no credit for the former answer.[89]

Of course a woman's freedom to choose an abortion is part of the "liberty" the Fourteenth Amendment says shall not be denied without due process of law, as indeed is anyone's freedom to do what he wants. But "due process" generally guarantees only that the inhibition be procedurally fair and that it have some "rational" connection—though plausible is probably a better word[90]—with a permissible governmental goal.[91] What is unusual about *Roe* is that the liberty involved is accorded a far more stringent protection, so stringent that a desire to preserve the fetus's existence is unable to overcome it—a protection more stringent, I think it fair to say, than that the present Court accords the freedom of the press explicitly guaranteed by the First Amendment.[92] What is frightening about *Roe* is that this super-protected right is not inferable from the language of the Constitution,

88. Even if the case could be made that abortion is an issue that pits the interests of men against those of women, that alone would not bring it within a theory that renders suspect classifications based on generalizations about the characteristics of men and women. And even if there were some way to expand the theory (and I confess I cannot see what judicial remedy would be appropriate were the theory so expanded, *but see* note 85 *supra*, third paragraph) to cover all "interests of men versus interests of women" situations, it will take some proving to establish that this is one:

> [D]ecisions in society are made by those who have power and not by those who have rights. Husbands and boy friends may in the end wield the power and make the abortion decision. Many women may be forced to have abortions not because it is their right, but because they are forced by egocentric men to submit to this procedure to avoid an unwanted inconvenience to men.

Stone, *supra* note 22.

89. It might be suggested that legislation restricting abortion had been kept on the books by the efforts of an intense minority and did not represent the will of most legislative majorities. Though I am aware of no basis for inferring this is any truer here than it is with respect to other sorts of legislation, *see also* note 86 *supra*, it is the sort of claim that is hard to disprove. (The phenomenon described at pp. 946-47 *infra*, one of relief that the issue has been taken out of the political arena, is a very different matter.) In any event it is not the Court's job to repeal such legislation. In the first place there is nothing unusual, and I was not aware there was anything wrong, with an intense minority's compromising on issues about which it feels less strongly in order to garner support on those it cares most about. Moreover, precisely because the claims involved are difficult to evaluate, I would not want to entrust to the judiciary authority to guess about them—certainly not under the guise of enforcing the Constitution. Leaving aside the arguable case of a law that has been neither legislatively considered *nor enforced* for decades, *see* A. BICKEL, THE LEAST DANGEROUS BRANCH 143-56 (1962), the Court should rest its declaration of unconstitutionality, if any, on more than a guess about how widespread and intense the support for the law "really" is.

90. The claimed connection is often empirical, causal or normative. About all that does *not* seem to become involved is formal logic. *See* p. 941 *infra;* Ely, *supra* note 28, at 1237-49.

91. Even this statement of the demands of "substantive due process" is too strong for many Justices and commentators, who deny that any such doctrine should exist. *See, e.g.*, pp. 937-38 *infra*.

92. *See* Branzburg v. Hayes, 408 U.S. 665 (1972).

the framers' thinking respecting the specific problem in issue, any general value derivable from the provisions they included,[93] or the nation's governmental structure. Nor is it explainable in terms of the unusual political impotence of the group judicially protected vis-à-vis the interest that legislatively prevailed over it.[94] And that, I believe—the predictable[95] early reaction to *Roe* notwithstanding ("more of the same Warren-type activism"[96])—is a charge that can responsibly be leveled at no other decision of the past twenty years.[97] At times the

93. *See* pp. 928-33 *supra*. Necessarily, a claim of this sort can never be established beyond doubt; one can only proceed by examining the claims of those values he thinks, or others have suggested, are traceable to the Constitution. It is always possible, however, that someone will develop a general theory of entitlements that encompasses a given case and plausibly demonstrate its constitutional connections. It is also possible that had the constitutional right to an abortion been developed as constitutional doctrines usually are—that is incrementally, rather than by the quantum jump of *Roe*—the connection of the first step with the Constitution, and that of each succeeding step with its predecessor, would have seemed more plausible. I cannot bring myself to believe, however, that any amount of gradualism could serve to make anything approaching the entire inference convincing.

94. The thing about permitting disparity among state laws regulating abortion that *I* find most troubling is not mentioned by the Court, and that is that some people can afford the fare to a neighboring state and others cannot. Of course this situation prevails with respect to divorce and a host of other sorts of laws as well. I wish someone could develop a theory that would enable the Court to take account of this concern without implying a complete obliteration of the federal system that is so obviously at the heart of the Constitution's plan. I have not been able to do so. *See* note 87 *supra*.

95. *See* pp. 943-45 *infra*.

96. *See, e.g., Abortion,* THE NEW REPUBLIC, Feb. 10, 1973, at 9; Stone, *supra* note 22.

97. Of course one can disagree with the lengths to which the inferences have been taken; my point is that the prior decisions, including those that have drawn the most fire, at least started from a value singled out by, or fairly inferable from, the Constitution as entitled to special protection. Whatever one may think of the code of conduct laid down in Miranda v. Arizona, 384 U.S. 436 (1966), the Constitution does talk about the right to counsel and the privilege against self-incrimination. Whatever one may think of the strictness of the scrutiny exercised in Furman v. Georgia, 408 U.S. 238 (1972), the Eighth Amendment surely does indicate in a general way that punishments are to be scrutinized for erratic imposition ("unusual") and severity disproportionate to any good they can be expected to accomplish ("cruel").

Note that the claim in the text has to do with the capacity of the earlier decisions to be *rationalized* in terms of some value highlighted by the Constitution, not with the skill with which they were in fact rendered. It is now pretty generally recognized, for example, that the various "wealth discrimination" cases could better have been defended in terms of the constitutional attention paid explicitly or implicitly to the "goods" whose distribution was in issue—the right to vote and the assurance of fair judicial procedures. *See, e.g.,* Michelman, *Foreword: On Protecting the Poor Through the Fourteenth Amendment,* 83 HARV. L. REV. 7 (1969). Reynolds v. Sims, 377 U.S. 533 (1964), is a badly articulated opinion. Its only response to the argument made by Justice Stewart—that since an equal protection claim was involved, a rational defense of a disparity among the "weights" of votes should suffice—was simply to announce that the goals Justice Stewart had in mind were off limits. *See* Ely, *supra* note 28, at 1226-27. But even Justice Stewart could not take the equal protection mold too seriously, for he added he would not approve a plan that permitted "the systematic frustration of the will of a majority of the electorate of the State." Lucas v. Colorado Gen. Assembly, 377 U.S. 713, 753-54 (1964) (footnote omitted). Such a plan, however, could be quite "rational" in terms of the sort of goals Justice Stewart had in mind, goals that in other contexts would count as legitimate. Obviously Justice Stewart was moved to some extent by the notion that a system whereby a minority could perpetuate its control of the government was out of accord with the system of government envisioned by the framers. *See also* Kramer v. Union Free School District No. 15, 395 U.S. 621, 628 (1969) (Warren, C.J., for the Court). This was what moved the Court too, though much further. And though the Court did

inferences the Court has drawn from the values the Constitution marks for special protection have been controversial, even shaky, but never before has its sense of an obligation to draw one been so obviously lacking.

IV

Not in the last thirty-five years at any rate. For, as the received learning has it, this sort of thing did happen before, repeatedly. From its 1905 decision in *Lochner v. New York*[98] into the 1930's the Court, frequently though not always under the rubric of "liberty of contract," employed the Due Process Clauses of the Fourteenth and Fifth Amendments to invalidate a good deal of legislation. According to the dissenters at the time and virtually all the commentators since, the Court had simply manufactured a constitutional right out of whole cloth and used it to superimpose its own view of wise social policy on those of the legislatures. So indeed the Court itself came to see the matter, and its reaction was complete:

> There was a time when the Due Process Clause was used by this Court to strike down laws which were thought unreasonable, that is, unwise or incompatible with some particular economic or social philosophy. In this manner the Due Process Clause was used, for example, to nullify laws prescribing maximum hours for work in bakeries, *Lochner v. New York,* 198 U.S. 45 (1905), outlawing

not give the reason, there is one: a fear that by attempting to apply Justice Stewart's "in between" standard it would become embroiled in unseemly "political" inquiries into the power alignments prevalent in the various states. *See* Deutsch, *Neutrality, Legitimacy, and the Supreme Court: Some Intersections Between Law and Political Science,* 20 STAN. L. REV. 169, 246-47 (1968); *cf.* note 89 *supra; but cf.* Mahan v. Howell, 41 U.S.L.W. 4277 (U.S. Feb. 20, 1973). Though the point is surely debatable, the impulse is understandable, and the fight in *Reynolds,* like that in *Miranda,* turns out to be not so much over the underlying values as over the need for a "clean" prophylactic rule that will keep the courts out of messy factual disputes.

In his concurrence in *Roe,* Justice Stewart lists ten cases to prove that "the Due Process Clause of the Fourteenth Amendment covers more than those freedoms explicitly named in the Bill of Rights." 93 S. Ct. at 734. His point is obviously that the freedoms involved were given protection above and beyond the ordinary demand for a "rational" defense and therefore *Roe* is just more of the same. It is not. Schware v. Bd. of Bar Examiners, 353 U.S. 232 (1957); Aptheker v. Secretary of State, 378 U.S. 500 (1964); and Kent v. Dulles, 357 U.S. 116 (1958), are all obviously rationalizable as First Amendment cases and indeed have since been so rationalized. Concerning *Schware,* see Griswold v. Connecticut, 381 U.S. 479, 483 (1965); *cf.* United States v. Brown, 381 U.S. 437, 456 (1965). As to *Aptheker* and *Kent,* see Zemel v. Rusk, 381 U.S. 1, 16 (1965); United States v. Brown, 381 U.S. at 456. Concerning Pierce v. Society of Sisters and Meyer v. Nebraska, see note 79 *supra.* As to Shapiro v. Thompson, 394 U.S. 618 (1969), and United States v. Guest, 383 U.S. 745 (1966), see p. 927 *supra.* With respect to Carrington v. Rash, 380 U.S. 89 (1965), see the preceding paragraph of this footnote and C. BLACK, *supra* note 56. Concerning Bolling v. Sharpe, 347 U.S. 497 (1954), see note 79 *supra; but cf.* Linde, *Judges, Critics, and the Realist Tradition,* 82 YALE L.J. 227, 233-35 (1972). And *compare* Truax v. Raich, 239 U.S. 33 (1915), *with* Graham v. Richardson, 403 U.S. 365 (1971), *and* note 85 *supra.*

98. 198 U.S. 45 (1905).

> "yellow dog" contracts, *Coppage v. Kansas,* 236 U.S. 1 (1915), setting minimum wages for women, *Adkins v. Children's Hospital,* 261 U.S. 525 (1923), and fixing the weight of loaves of bread, *Jay Burns Baking Co. v. Bryan,* 264 U.S. 504 (1924). This intrusion by the judiciary into the realm of legislative value judgments was strongly objected to at the time . . . . Mr. Justice Holmes said,
>
> > "I think the proper course is to recognize that a state legislature can do whatever it sees fit to do unless it is restrained by some express prohibition in the Constitution of the United States or of the State, and that Courts should be careful not to extend such prohibitions beyond their obvious meaning by reading into them conceptions of public policy that the particular Court may happen to entertain."
>
> . . . The doctrine that prevailed in *Lochner, Coppage, Adkins, Burns,* and like cases—that due process authorizes courts to hold laws unconstitutional when they believe the legislature has acted unwisely—has long since been discarded. We have returned to the original constitutional proposition that courts do not substitute their social and economic beliefs for the judgment of legislative bodies, who are elected to pass laws.[99]

It may be objected that *Lochner et al.* protected the "economic rights" of businessmen whereas *Roe* protects a "human right." It should be noted, however, that not all of the *Lochner* series involved economic regulation;[100] that even those that did resist the "big business" stereotype with which the commentators tend to associate them; and that in some of them the employer's "liberty of contract" claim was joined by the employee, who knew that if he had to be employed on the terms set by the law in question, he could not be employed at all.[101] This is a predicament that is economic to be sure, but is not without its "human" dimension. Similarly "human" seems the predicament of the appellees in the 1970 case of *Dandridge v. Williams,*[102] who challenged the Maryland Welfare Department's practice of limiting AFDC grants to $250 regardless of family size or need. Yet in language that remains among its favored points of reference,[103] the

99. Ferguson v. Skrupa, 372 U.S. 726, 729-30 (1963) (footnotes omitted). *See also* Lincoln Federal Labor Union v. Northwestern Iron & Metal Co., 335 U.S. 525, 533-37 (1949).

100. *See* Pierce v. Society of Sisters, 268 U.S. 510 (1925); Meyer v. Nebraska, 262 U.S. 390 (1923).

101. *E.g.,* Adkins v. Children's Hospital, 261 U.S. 525, 542-43 (1923). *See also* Adair v. United States, 208 U.S. 161, 172-73 (1908). *Cf.* Hammer v. Dagenhart, 247 U.S. 251 (1918).

102. 397 U.S. 471 (1970).

103. *See, e.g.,* San Antonio Independent School Dist. v. Rodriguez, 41 U.S.L.W. 4407, 4417 (U.S. March 21, 1973); Ortwein v. Schwab, 41 U.S.L.W. 3473, 3474 (U.S. March 5, 1973); United States v. Kras, 93 S. Ct. 631, 638 (1973).

Court, speaking through Justice Stewart,[104] dismissed the complaint as "social and economic" and therefore essentially Lochneresque.

> [W]e deal with state regulation in the social and economic field, not affecting freedoms guaranteed by the Bill of Rights. . . . For this Court to approve the invalidation of state economic or social regulation as "overreaching" would be far too reminiscent of an era when the Court thought the Fourteenth Amendment gave it power to strike down state laws "because they may be unwise, improvident, or out of harmony with a particular school of thought." . . . That era long ago passed into history. . . .
>
> To be sure, the cases cited . . . have in the main involved state regulation of business or industry. The administration of public welfare assistance, by contrast, involves the most basic economic needs of impoverished human beings. We recognize the dramatically real factual difference between the cited cases and this one, but we can find no basis for applying a different constitutional standard. . . . It is a standard . . . that is true to the principle that the Fourteenth Amendment gives the federal courts no power to impose upon the States their views of wise economic or social policy.[105]

It may be, however—at least it is not the sort of claim one can disprove—that the "right to an abortion," or noneconomic rights generally, accord more closely with "this generation's idealization of America"[106] than the "rights" asserted in either *Lochner* or *Dandridge*. But that attitude, of course, is *precisely* the point of the *Lochner* philosophy, which would grant unusual protection to those "rights" that somehow *seem* most pressing, regardless of whether the Constitution suggests any special solicitude for them. The Constitution has little to say about contract,[107] less about abortion, and those who would speculate about which the framers would have been more likely to protect may not be pleased with the answer. The Court continues to disavow the philosophy of *Lochner*.[108] Yet as Justice Stewart's concurrence admits, it is impossible candidly to regard *Roe* as the product of anything else.[109]

104. *But cf.* note 109 *infra*.

105. 397 U.S. at 484-86.

106. Karst & Horowitz, Reitman v. Mulkey: *A Telephase of Substantive Equal Protection,* 1967 SUP. CT. REV. 39, 57-58; *cf.* 2 L. POLLAK, THE CONSTITUTION AND THE SUPREME COURT: A DOCUMENTARY HISTORY 266-67 (1966).

107. *But see* U.S. CONST. art. I, § 10; Calder v. Bull, 3 U.S. (3 Dall.) 386 (1798).

108. *See* note 103 *supra*.

109. 93 S. Ct. at 734. The only "*Lochner* era" cases Justice Stewart cites are *Meyer* and *Pierce*. It therefore may be he intends to pursue some sort of "economic-noneconomic" line in selecting rights entitled to special protection. *But see* text at note 105 *supra*. The general philosophy of constitutional adjudication, however, is the same. *See* text at notes 106-07 *supra*. Justice Stewart rather clearly intends his *Roe* opinion as a repudiation

That alone should be enough to damn it. Criticism of the *Lochner* philosophy has been virtually universal and will not be rehearsed here. I would, however, like to suggest briefly that although *Lochner* and *Roe* are twins to be sure, they are not identical. While I would hesitate to argue that one is more defensible than the other in terms of judicial style, there *are* differences in that regard that suggest *Roe* may turn out to be the more dangerous precedent.

All the "superimposition of the Court's own value choices" talk is, of course, the characterization of others and not the language of *Lochner* or its progeny. Indeed, those cases did not argue that "liberty of contract" was a preferred constitutional freedom, but rather represented it as merely one among the numerous aspects of "liberty" the Fourteenth Amendment protects, therefore requiring of its inhibitors a "rational" defense.

> In our opinion that section . . . is an invasion of the personal liberty, as well as of the right of property, guaranteed by that Amendment. Such liberty and right embraces the right to make contracts for the purchase of the labor of others and equally the right to make contracts for the sale of one's own labor; each right, however, being subject to the fundamental condition that no contract, whatever its subject matter, can be sustained which the law, upon reasonable grounds, forbids as inconsistent with the public interests or as hurtful to the public order or as detrimental to the common good.[110]

> Undoubtedly, the police power of the State may be exerted to protect purchasers from imposition by sale of short weight loaves. . . . Constitutional protection having been invoked, it is the duty of the court to determine whether the challenged provision has reasonable relation to the protection of purchasers of bread against fraud by short weights and really tends to accomplish the purpose for which it was enacted.[111]

of his *Griswold* dissent, and not simply as an acquiescence in what the Court did in the earlier case. *See* 93 S. Ct. at 735.

Having established to his present satisfaction that the Due Process Clause extends unusual substantive protection to interests the Constitution nowhere marks as special, *but see* note 97 *supra*, he provides no further assistance respecting the difficult questions before the Court, but rather defers to the Court's "thorough demonstration" that the interests in protecting the mother and preserving the fetus cannot support the legislation involved. *But see* pp. 922-26 *supra*.

110. Adair v. United States, 208 U.S. 161, 172 (1908). *See also id.* at 174.

111. Jay Burns Baking Co. v. Bryan, 264 U.S. 504, 513 (1924). *See also id.* at 517; Meyer v. Nebraska, 262 U.S. 390, 399-400, 403 (1923); Adkins v. Children's Hospital, 261 U.S. 525, 529 (1923); Coppage v. Kansas, 236 U.S. 1, 14 (1915); Lochner v. New York, 198 U.S. 45, 53, 54, 56, 57 (1905); *id.* at 68 (Harlan, J., dissenting).

Thus the test *Lochner* and its progeny purported to apply is that which would theoretically control the same questions today: whether a plausible argument can be made that the legislative action furthers some permissible governmental goal.[112] The trouble, of course, is they misapplied it. *Roe,* on the other hand, is quite explicit that the right to an abortion is a "fundamental" one, requiring not merely a "rational" defense for its inhibition but rather a "compelling" one.

A second difference between *Lochner et al.* and *Roe* has to do with the nature of the legislative judgments being second-guessed. In the main, the "refutations" tendered by the *Lochner* series were of two sorts. The first took the form of declarations that the goals in terms of which the legislatures' actions were defended were impermissible. Thus, for example, the equalization of unequal bargaining power and the strengthening of the labor movement are simply ends the legislature had no business pursuing, and consequently its actions cannot thereby be justified.[113] The second form of "refutation" took the form not of denying the legitimacy of the goal relied on but rather of denying the plausibility of the legislature's empirical judgment that its action would *promote* that goal.

> In our judgment it is not possible in fact to discover the connection between the number of hours a baker may work in the bakery and the healthful quality of the bread made by the workman.[114]

> There is no evidence in support of the thought that purchasers have been or are likely to be induced to take a nine and a half or a ten ounce loaf for a pound (16 ounce) loaf, or an eighteen and a half or a 19 ounce loaf for a pound and a half (24 ounce) loaf; and it is contrary to common experience and unreasonable to assume that there could be any danger of such deception.[115]

The *Roe* opinion's "refutation" of the legislative judgment that anti-abortion statutes can be justified in terms of the protection of the fetus takes neither of these forms. The Court grants that protecting the fetus is an "important and legitimate" governmental goal,[116] and of course

112. *But cf.* note 91 *supra.*
113. Coppage v. Kansas, 236 U.S. 1, 16-17, 17-18 (1915). *See also* Meyer v. Nebraska, 262 U.S. 390, 403 (1923); Adair v. United States, 208 U.S. 161, 174-75 (1908); Lochner v. New York, 198 U.S. 45, 57-58 (1905).
114. Lochner v. New York, 198 U.S. 45, 62 (1905). *See also id.* at 57, 58, 59, 64.
115. Jay Burns Baking Co. v. Bryan, 264 U.S. 504, 517 (1924). *See also* Coppage v. Kansas, 236 U.S. 1, 15-16 (1915).
116. Note 8 *supra.*

it does not deny that restricting abortion promotes it.[117] What it does, instead, is simply announce that that goal is not important enough to sustain the restriction. There is little doubt that judgments of this sort were involved in *Lochner et al.*,[118] but what the Court *said* in those cases was not that the legislature had incorrectly balanced two legitimate but competing goals, but rather that the goal it had favored was impermissible or the legislation involved did not really promote it.[119]

Perhaps this is merely a rhetorical difference, but it could prove to be important. *Lochner et al.* were thoroughly disreputable decisions, but at least they did us the favor of sowing the seeds of their own destruction. To say that the equalization of bargaining power or the fostering of the labor movement is a goal outside the ambit of a "police power" broad enough to forbid all contracts the state legislature can reasonably regard "as inconsistent with the public interests or as hurtful to the public order or as detrimental to the common good"[120] is to say something that is, in a word, wrong.[121] And it is just as obvi-

117. The *Lochner* approach to factual claims is, however, suggested by the Court's ready acceptance—by way of nullifying the state's health interest during the first trimester —of the data adduced by appellants and certain *amici* to the effect that abortions performed during the first trimester are safer than childbirth. 93 S. Ct. at 725. This is not in fact agreed to by all doctors—the data are of course severely limited—and the Court's view of the matter is plainly not the only one that is "rational" under the usual standards. *See* San Antonio Independent School Dist. v. Rodriguez, 41 U.S.L.W. 4407, 4420 (U.S. March 21, 1973); Eisenstadt v. Baird, 405 U.S. 438, 470 (1972) (Burger, C.J., dissenting):

> The actual hazards of introducing a particular foreign substance into the human body are frequently controverted, and I cannot believe the unanimity of expert opinion is a prerequisite to a State's exercise of its police power, no matter what the subject matter of the regulation. Even assuming no present dispute among medical authorities, we cannot ignore that it has become commonplace for a drug or food additive to be universally regarded as harmless on one day and to be condemned as perilous the next. It is inappropriate for this Court to overrule a legislative classification by relying on the present consensus among leading authorities. The commands of the Constitution cannot fluctuate with the shifting tides of scientific opinion.

I suppose the Court's defense of its unusual reaction to the scientific data would be that the case is unusual, in that it involves a "fundamental" interest. It should be noted, however, that even a sure sense that abortion during the first trimester is safer than childbirth would serve only to blunt a state's claim that it is, for reasons relating to maternal health, entitled to *proscribe* abortion; it would not support the inference the Court draws, that *regulations designed to make the abortion procedure safer* during the first trimester are impermissible. *See* 93 S. Ct. at 732.

118. *Cf.* Meyer v. Nebraska, 262 U.S. 390 (1923); Adkins v. Children's Hospital, 261 U.S. 525, 546 (1923), Lochner v. New York, 198 U.S. 45, 53-54, 57 (1905).

119. And even those cases that interlaced such claims with indications of a balancing test, *see* note 118 *supra*, sowed the seeds of their own reversal. *See* text at notes 120-21 *infra*. A claim that X weighs more than Y will have little persuasive or precedential value if it is bracketed with an indefensible assertion that Y is nothing.

120. Adair v. United States, 208 U.S. 161, 172 (1908), quoted more fully at p. 932 *supra*. *See also, e.g.*, Lochner v. New York, 198 U.S. 45, 54 (1905).

121. Wrong, that is, if one assigns to the words anything resembling their ordinary meanings. *See, e.g.*, Daniel v. Family Insurance Co., 336 U.S. 220, 224 (1949). One can of course argue that states should also have governments of few and defined powers, that they should not be vested with broad authority to go after whatever they regard as evils. But the Federal Constitution imposes no such restraint, and according to the test accepted even at the time of *Lochner* such authority, at least as a matter of federal constitutional law, does exist.

ously wrong to declare, for example, that restrictions on long working hours cannot reasonably be said to promote health and safety.[122] *Roe's* "refutation" of the legislative judgment, on the other, is *not* obviously wrong, for the substitution of one nonrational judgment for another concerning the relative importance of a mother's opportunity to live the life she has planned and a fetus's opportunity to live at all, can be labeled neither wrong nor right. The problem with *Roe* is not so much that it bungles the question it sets itself,[123] but rather that it sets itself a question the Constitution has not made the Court's business. It *looks* different from *Lochner*—it has the shape if not the substance of a judgment that is very much the Court's business, one vindicating an interest the Constitution marks as special—and it is for that reason perhaps more dangerous. Of course in a sense it is more candid than *Lochner*.[124] But the employment of a higher standard of judicial review, no matter how candid the recognition that it is indeed higher, loses some of its admirability when it is accompanied by neither a coherent account of why such a standard is appropriate nor any indication of why it has not been satisfied.

V

I do wish "Wolf!" hadn't been cried so often. When I suggest to my students that *Roe* lacks even colorable support in the constitutional text, history, or any other appropriate source of constitutional doctrine, they tell me they've heard all that before. When I point out they haven't heard it before from *me*, I can't really blame them for smiling.

But at least crying "Wolf!" doesn't influence the wolves; crying "Lochner!" may. Of course the Warren Court was aggressive in enforcing its ideals of liberty and equality. *But by and large, it attempted to defend its decisions in terms of inferences from values the Constitution marks as special.*[125] Its inferences were often controversial, but just as

122. It is possible, of course, that I am here time-bound, and that the wrongness of *Lochner et al.* is obvious only because a half century of commentary has made it so. While I cannot rebut this, I am inclined to doubt it. In those decisions the Court stated the applicable tests in language much the same as would be used today—language the dissents cogently demonstrated could not be reconciled with the results. That views with which one disagrees can be reasonable nonetheless was a concept hardly new to lawyers even in 1900.

123. *But compare* 93 S. Ct. at 732 *with* Doe v. Bolton, 93 S. Ct. 739 (1973). *See also* pp. 922-26 *supra.*

124. With respect to the Equal Protection Clause, by way of contrast, the Court has taken to claiming it is simply applying the traditional rationality standard, whether it is or not. For a more optimistic view of the development, *see* Gunther, *Foreword: In Search of Evolving Doctrine on a Changing Court: A Model for a Newer Equal Protection,* 86 HARV. L. REV. 1 (1972).

125. *See* note 97 *supra.* The "footnote 4" argument suggested in note 85 *supra* responds not so much to any clear constitutional concern with equality for women (*but*

often our profession's prominent criticism deigned not to address them on their terms and contented itself with assertions that the Court was indulging in sheer acts of will, ramming its personal preferences down the country's throat—that it was, in a word, Lochnering. One possible judicial response to this style of criticism would be to conclude that one might as well be hanged for a sheep as a goat: So long as you're going to be told, no matter what you say, that all you do is Lochner, you might as well Lochner. Another, perhaps more likely in a new appointee, might be to reason that since Lochnering has so long been standard procedure, "just one more" (in a good cause, of course) can hardly matter. Actual reactions, of course, are not likely to be this self-conscious, but the critical style of offhand dismissal may have taken its toll nonetheless.

Of course the Court has been aware that criticism of much that it has done has been widespread in academic as well as popular circles. But when it looks to the past decade's most prominent academic criticism, it will often find little there to distinguish it from the popular. Disagreements with the chain of inference by which the Court got from the Constitution to its result, if mentioned at all, have tended to be announced in the most conclusory terms, and the impression has often been left that the real quarrel of the Academy, like that of the laity, is with the results the Court has been reaching and perhaps with judicial "activism" in general.[126] Naturally the Court is sensitive to criticism of this sort, but these are issues on which it will, when push comes to shove, trust its own judgment. (And it has no reason not to: Law professors do not agree on what results are "good," and even if they did, there is no reason to assume their judgment is any better on *that* issue than the Court's.) And academic criticism of the sort that might (because it should) have some effect—criticism suggesting misperceptions in the Court's reading of the value structure set forth in the document from which it derives its authority, or unjustifiable inferences it has drawn from that value structure—has seemed

see U.S. Const. amend. XIX) as to the unavoidable obligation to give "principled" content to the facially inscrutable Equal Protection Clause. *See* pp. 948-49 *infra*. Virtually everyone agrees that classifications by race were intended to be and should be tested by a higher than usual standard, and that at least some others—though the nature and length of the list are seriously disputed—are sufficiently "racelike" to merit comparable treatment. *See, e.g.*, Graham v. Richardson, 403 U.S. 365 (1971). The problem thus becomes one of identifying those features of racial classifications that validly compel the deviation from the usual standard, and in turn those classifications that share those features.

126. *See, e.g.*, Kurland, *Foreword: "Equal in Origin and Equal in Title to the Legislative and Executive Branches of Government*, 78 Harv. L. Rev. 143, 144-45, 149, 163, 175 (1964).

for a time somehow out of fashion, the voguish course being simply to dismiss the process by which a disfavored result was reached as Lochnering pure and simple. But if the critics cannot trouble themselves with such details, it is difficult to expect the Court to worry much about them either.

This tendency of commentators to substitute snappy dismissal for careful evaluation of the Court's constitutional inferences—and of course it is simply a tendency, never universally shared and hopefully on the wane—may include among its causes simple laziness, boredom and a natural reluctance to get out of step with the high-steppers. But in part it has also reflected a considered rejection of the view of constitutional adjudication from which my remarks have proceeded. There is a powerful body of opinion that would dismiss the call for substantive criticism—and its underlying assumption that some constitutional inferences are responsible while others are not—as naive. For, the theory goes, except as to the most trivial and least controversial questions (such as the length of a Senator's term), the Constitution speaks in the vaguest and most general terms;[127] the most its clauses can provide are "more or less suitable pegs on which judicial policy choices are hung."[128] Thus anyone who suggests the Constitution can provide significant guidance for today's difficult questions either deludes himself or seeks to delude the Court. Essentially all the Court *can* do is honor the value preferences it sees fit, and it should be graded according to the judgment and skill with which it does so.[129]

One version of this view appears to be held by President Nixon. It is true that in announcing the appointment of Justices Powell and Rehnquist, he described a "judicial conservative"—his kind of Justice —as one who does not "twist or bend the Constitution in order to perpetuate his personal political and social views."[130] But the example he then gave bore witness that he was not so "naive" after all.

> As a judicial conservative, I believe some court decisions have gone too far in the past in weakening the peace forces as against the criminal forces in our society. . . . [T]he peace forces must

127. *See, e.g.*, A. Bickel, *supra* note 89, at 84-92; A. Bickel, The Supreme Court and the Idea of Progress 177 (1970); Mendelson, *On the Meaning of the First Amendment: Absolutes in the Balance*, 50 Calif. L. Rev. 821 (1962).

128. Linde, *supra* note 97, at 254.

129. The Court will continue to play the role of the omniscient and strive toward omnipotence. And the law reviews will continue to play the game of evaluating the Court's work in light of the fictions of the law, legal reasoning, and legal history rather than deal with the realities of politics and statesmanship.

Kurland, *supra* note 126, at 175.

130. 7 Weekly Comp. of Presidential Documents 1431 (Oct. 25, 1971).

not be denied the legal tools they need to protect the innocent from criminal elements.[131]

That this sort of invitation, to get in there and Lochner for the right goals, can contribute to opinions like *Roe* is obvious. In terms of process, it is just what the President ordered.

The academic version of this general view is considerably more subtle. It agrees that the Court will find little help in the Constitution and therefore has no real choice other than to decide for itself which value preferences to honor, but denies that it should necessarily opt for the preferences favored by the Justices themselves or the President who appointed them. To the extent "progress" is to concern the Justices at all, it should be defined not in terms of what they would like it to be but rather in terms of their best estimate of what over time the American people will make it[132]—that is, they should seek "durable" decisions.[133] This, however, is no easy task, and the goals that receive practically all the critics' attention, and presumably are supposed to receive practically all the Court's, are its own institutional survival and effectiveness.[134]

Whatever the other merits or demerits of this sort of criticism, it plainly is not what it is meant to be—an effective argument for judicial self-restraint. For a Governor Warren or a Senator Black will rightly see no reason to defer to law professors on the probable direction of progress; even less do they need the Academy's advice on what is politically feasible; and they know that despite the Court's history of frequent immersion in hot water,[135] its "institutional position" has been getting stronger for 200 years.

Roe is a case in point. Certainly, many will view it as social progress. (Surely that is the Court's view, and indeed the legislatures had been moving perceptibly, albeit too slowly for many of us, toward relaxing

131. *Id.* at 1432.

132. *See generally* A. Bickel, The Supreme Court and the Idea of Progress (1970). Professor Bickel's thought is of course much richer than it is here reported. But the catchier aspects of a person's work have a tendency to develop a life of their own and on occasion to function, particularly in the thinking of others and perhaps to an extent even in the author's own, without the background against which they were originally presented. *Cf.* note 138 *infra.*

133. *See* Hart, *Foreword: The Time Chart of the Justices,* 73 Harv. L. Rev. 84, 99 (1959). *See also* A. Bickel, *supra* note 127, at 99; Kurland, *Earl Warren, the "Warren Court," and the Warren Myths,* 67 Mich. L. Rev. 353, 357 (1968). *Cf.* Karst, *Invidious Discrimination: Justice Douglas and the Return of the "Natural-Law—Due-Process" Formula,* 16 U.C.L.A.L. Rev. 716, 746-48 (1969); Karst & Horowitz, *supra* note 106, at 79.

134. *E.g.,* A. Bickel, *supra* note 127, at 95; Kurland, *Toward a Political Supreme Court,* 32 U. Chi. L. Rev. 19, 20, 22 (1969).

135. *See generally* W. Murphy, Congress and the Court (1962); C. Warren, The Supreme Court in United States History (rev. ed. 1932).

their anti-abortion legislation.)[136] And it is difficult to see how it will weaken the Court's position. Fears of official disobedience are obviously groundless when it is a criminal statute that has been invalidated.[137] To the public the *Roe* decision must look very much like the New York Legislature's recent liberalization of its abortion law.[138] Even in the unlikely event someone should catch the public's ear long enough to charge that the wrong institution did the repealing, they have heard that "legalism" before without taking to the streets. Nor are the political branches, and this of course is what really counts, likely to take up the cry very strenuously: The sighs of relief as this particular albatross was cut from the legislative and executive necks seemed to me audible. Perhaps I heard wrong—I live in the Northeast, indeed not so very far from Hyannis Port. It is even possible that a constitutional amendment will emerge, though that too has happened before without serious impairment of the Position of the Institution. But I doubt one will: *Roe v. Wade* seems like a durable decision.

It is, nevertheless, a very bad decision. Not because it will perceptibly weaken the Court—it won't; and not because it conflicts with either my idea of progress[139] or what the evidence suggests is society's[140]—it doesn't. It is bad because it is bad constitutional law, or rather because it is *not* constitutional law and gives almost no sense of an obligation to try to be.[141]

136. In the past several years, however, a trend toward liberalization of abortion statutes has resulted in adoption, by about one-third of the States, of less stringent laws, most of them patterned after the ALI Model Penal Code . . . .

93 S. Ct. at 720.

By the end of 1970, four other States had repealed criminal penalties for abortions performed in early pregnancy by a licensed physician, subject to stated procedural and health requirements. Alaska Stat. § 11.15.060 (1970); Hawaii Rev. Stat. § 453-16 (Supp. 1971); N.Y. Penal Code § 125.05 (McKinney Supp. 1972-1973); Wash. Rev. Code §§ 9.02.060 to 9.02.080 (Supp. 1972) . . . .

Id. at 720 n.37.

137. As opposed to the invalidation of a police practice. *Cf.* Miranda v. Arizona, 384 U.S. 436 (1966). *See also, e.g.,* Engel v. Vitale, 370 U.S. 421 (1962).

138. Even the headline in *The New York Times* announced: "High Court Rules Abortions Legal [sic] the First 3 Months." N.Y. Times, January 23, 1973, p. 1, cols. 1-8.

139. *See* pp. 926-27 *supra.* Of course there are some possible uses of the decision that scare me, particularly when it is considered in conjunction (a) with some of this Court's motions relating to a mother's "waiver" of AFDC assistance, *see* Wyman v. James, 400 U.S. 309 (1971), and (b) with Buck v. Bell, 274 U.S. 200 (1927), which was indeed relied on by the Court in *Roe,* 93 S. Ct. at 727, and cited without apparent disapproval in Justice Douglas's concurrence, *id.* at 759. But those are quite different cases I'm conjuring up.

140. *See* note 136 *supra. But cf. Abortion,* THE NEW REPUBLIC, Feb. 10, 1973, at 9:

[I]f the Court's guess concerning the probable and desirable direction of progress is wrong, it will nevertheless have been imposed on all 50 states, and imposed permanently, unless the Court itself should in the future change its mind. Normal legislation, enacted by legislatures rather than judges, is happily not so rigid, and not so presumptuous in its claims to universality and permanence.

141. In judicial review, the line between the "juridical" and the "legislative" mode does not run between "strict constructionists" and competing theorists of constitu-

I am aware the Court cannot simply "lay the Article of the Constitution which is invoked beside the statute which is challenged and . . . decide whether the latter squares with the former."[142] That is precisely the reason commentators are needed.

> [P]recisely because it is the Constitution alone which warrants judicial interference in sovereign operations of the State, the basis of judgment as to the Constitutionality of state action must be a rational one, approaching the text which is the only commission for our power not in a literalistic way, as if we had a tax statute before us, but as the basic charter of our society, setting out in spare but meaningful terms the principles of government.[143]

> No matter how imprecise in application to specific modern fact situations, the constitutional guarantees do provide a direction, a goal, an ideal citizen-government relationship. They rule out many alternative directions, goals, and ideals.[144]

And they fail to support the ruling out of others.

Of course that only begins the inquiry. Identification and definition of the values with which the Constitution is concerned will often fall short of indicating with anything resembling clarity the deference to be given those values when they conflict with others society finds important. (Though even here the process is sometimes more helpful than the commentators would allow.) Nor is it often likely to generate, fullblown, the "neutral" principle that will avoid embarrassment in future cases.[145] But though the identification of a constitutional connection is only the beginning of analysis, it is a necessary beginning. The point that often gets lost in the commentary, and obviously got

> tional interpretation. Rather, it divides constructionists and non-constructionists, those who do and those who do not see judicial review as a task of construing the living meaning of past political decisions—a division in which the alternating libertarianism and conservatism of the late Justices Black and Harlan were on the same side.

Linde, *supra* note 97, at 254-55 (footnote omitted).

142. United States v. Butler, 297 U.S. 1, 62 (1936).

143. Poe v. Ullman, 367 U.S. 497, 539-40 (1961) (Harlan, J., dissenting).

144. Wright, *Professor Bickel, The Scholarly Tradition, and the Supreme Court,* 84 HARV. L. REV. 769, 785 (1971) (footnote omitted).

145. *See generally* Ely, *supra* note 28.

> Starting from a clearly unconstitutional course of action—and I have trouble seeing the unconstitutionality of a tax exemption for only Caucasian children as a controversial assumption—and attempting to explain why it is unconstitutional in terms of a theory capable of acceptable and consistent application to other areas, is a perfectly sensible way of developing constitutional doctrine.

Id. at 1262. I might have made (even more) explicit that the action around which the search for the "principled" approach is to be centered should be one—and, to paraphrase myself, I have trouble seeing the example I chose as controversial in this regard—whose impermissibility is established by values traceable to the Constitution.

lost in *Roe,* is that *before* the Court can get to the "balancing" stage, *before* it can worry about the next case and the case after that (or even about its institutional position) it is under an obligation to trace its premises to the charter from which it derives its authority. A neutral and durable principle may be a thing of beauty and a joy forever. But if it lacks connection with any value the Constitution marks as special, it is not a constitutional principle and the Court has no business imposing it.[146] I hope that will seem obvious to the point of banality. Yet those of us to whom it does seem obvious have seldom troubled to say so.[147] And because we have not, we must share in the blame for this decision.

146. *But see, e.g.,* Hart, *supra* note 133, at 99, *quoted* in part in Bickel, *Foreword: The Passive Virtues,* 75 HARV. L. REV. 40, 41 (1961):

> [T]he Court is predestined . . . to be a voice of reason, charged with the creative function of discerning afresh and of articulating and developing impersonal and durable principles . . . .

But discerning constitutional principles afresh is one thing; developing them, no matter how neutral and durable, is quite another. An institution charged with looking after a set of values the rest of us have entrusted to it is significantly different from one with authority to amend the set.

147. *But see, e.g.,* Linde, *supra* note 97. *Cf.* Bork, *Neutral Principles and Some First Amendment Problems,* 47 IND. L.J. 1, 6-11 (1971), espousing the general view of constitutional adjudication espoused here, but characterizing *Griswold* as a typical Warren Court product, *id.* at 7, in order to buttress the more general claim—equally unfair in my view—that one cannot accept that general view and at the same time generally approve the work of that Court. *Id.* at 6. *See* Griswold v. Connecticut, 381 U.S. 479, 527 n.23 (1965) (Black, J., dissenting).

MCCLESKEY V. KEMP: RACE, CAPITAL PUNISHMENT, AND THE SUPREME COURT

*Randall L. Kennedy**

IN 1978, Warren McCleskey, a young black man, was convicted in Fulton County, Georgia, of robbing a furniture store and killing Frank Schlatt, a white police officer. A jury composed of eleven whites and one black sentenced McCleskey to life imprisonment for the robbery and death for the murder.[1] His subsequent appeals followed the normal, dreary route of post-conviction proceedings in capital cases.[2] When McCleskey sought habeas corpus relief from the federal district court, however, his conventional struggle against execution was transformed into an extraordinary challenge to the entire system of capital punishment in Georgia. Supported by the most comprehensive statistical analysis ever done on the racial demographics of capital sentencing in a single state,[3] McCleskey argued that his sentence should be nullified because, among other things, there existed a constitutionally impermissible risk that both his race and that of his victim played a significant role in the decision to sentence him to death. His arguments were rejected at every level of the federal judiciary.[4] Even though the Supreme Court assumed the validity of statistics indicating that murderers of whites are four times more likely to be sentenced to death than murderers of blacks, it nonetheless held against the petitioner.

The Court's decision in *McCleskey v. Kemp*[5] was immediately beset by sharp criticism and, in some instances, outright denunciation. Anthony Lewis charged that the Court had "effectively condoned the expression of racism in a profound aspect of our law."[6] Hugo

---

* Assistant Professor of Law, Harvard Law School. I would like to thank the many individuals who have aided me in writing this article. Among those who have been particularly helpful are Hugo Bedau, Derrick Bell, John Boger, Robert Burt, Richard Fallon, William Fisher, Owen Fiss, Samuel Gross, Yale Kamisar, John Kaplan, Duncan Kennedy, Dan Meltzer, Frank Michelman, Martha Minow, Charles Nesson, Charles Ogletree, David Shapiro, Kathleen Sullivan, Cass Sunstein, Don Trautman, Lloyd Weinreb, and David Wilkins. I would also like to thank the Yale Law School Legal Theory Workshop for enabling me to present an earlier version of this Article. The criticisms voiced on that occasion were extremely useful.

[1] *See* McCleskey v. Zant, 580 F. Supp. 338, 345–46, 369 (N.D. Ga. 1984).

[2] *See* McCleskey v. Kemp, 107 S. Ct. 1756, 1763 (1987) (describing McCleskey's petition for a new trial, mandatory appeal to the state supreme court, and application for state habeas corpus relief).

[3] *See infra* pp. 1396–1400.

[4] *See* McCleskey v. Kemp, 107 S. Ct. 1756 (1987); McCleskey v. Kemp, 753 F.2d 877 (11th Cir. 1985) (en banc); McCleskey v. Zant, 580 F. Supp. 338 (N.D. Ga. 1984).

[5] 107 S. Ct. 1756 (1987).

[6] *See* Lewis, *Bowing to Racism*, N.Y. Times, Apr. 28, 1987, at A31, col. 1; *see also Discrimination in Death? Yes, 5–4*, N.Y. Times, Apr. 24, 1987, at A30, col. 1; *Killers of Whites, Killers of Blacks*, N.Y. Times, Oct. 16, 1986, at A38, col. 1.

Bedau[7] likened the decision to such notorious holdings as *Dred Scott v. Sandford*,[8] *Plessy v. Ferguson*,[9] and *Korematsu v. United States*.[10] The *Harvard Law Review* described the *McCleskey* decision as "logically unsound, morally reprehensible, and legally unsupportable."[11]

I, too, believe that both the Court's ruling and the way it was articulated are grievously flawed. Professor Bedau does not exaggerate when he compares *McCleskey* to *Plessy* and *Korematsu*. As in those prior disasters of judicial decisionmaking, the majority in *McCleskey* repressed the truth and validated racially oppressive official conduct. In the same way, however, that those earlier cases posed difficult choices to the Justices, so too is *McCleskey* a hard case. I shall argue that the Court's opinion, albeit detestable, was hardly deviant; that more than moral callousness informed the Court's analysis; and that the issues the case implicates, particularly with respect to remedy, are genuinely troublesome.

Although *McCleskey* raises a host of constitutional concerns,[12] I shall focus almost exclusively on the equal protection aspect of the

---

[7] *See* Bedau, *Someday* McCleskey *Will Be Death Penalty's* Dred Scott, L.A. Times, May 1, 1987, § 2, at 5, col. 1.

[8] 60 U.S. (19 How.) 393 (1857).

[9] 163 U.S. 537 (1896).

[10] 323 U.S. 214 (1944).

[11] *The Supreme Court, 1986 Term — Leading Cases*, 101 HARV. L. REV. 119, 158 (1987); *see also* Note, *Social Science Statistics in the Courtroom: The Debate Resurfaces in* McCleskey v. Kemp, 62 NOTRE DAME L. REV. 688, 689 (1987) (criticizing the *McCleskey* Court for narrowing the applicability of social science statistics in death penalty trials and appeals); Bienen, *Of Race, Crime and Punishment*, N.Y. Times, June 21, 1987, at A22, col. 1 (criticizing the standard of proof required by the *McCleskey* Court); Tubak, *New Decisions Ratify Unfair Death Penalty*, Legal Times, May 4, 1987, at 18, col. 1 (arguing that *McCleskey* represents a break with precedent).

The harsh criticism directed at the Supreme Court's decision is, to a large extent, a reprise of the excoriating commentary that greeted the lower courts' handling of the case. *See, e.g.*, W. WHITE, THE DEATH PENALTY IN THE EIGHTIES: AN EXAMINATION OF THE MODERN SYSTEM OF CAPITAL PUNISHMENT 129–35 (1987) (arguing that the court of appeals repressed the ugly reality of racially patterned sentencing decisions); Gross, *Race and Death: The Judicial Evaluation of Evidence of Discrimination in Capital Sentencing*, 18 U.C. DAVIS L. REV. 1275 (1985) (same); Berger, Book Review, 87 COLUM. L. REV. 1301, 1310 (1987) (reviewing W. WHITE, *supra*) (stating that the court of appeals imposed a "crippling and wholly unprecedented burden of proof"); Comment, McCleskey v. Kemp: *Constitutional Tolerance for Racially Disparate Capital Sentencing*, 41 U. MIAMI L. REV. 295 (1986) (arguing that the courts' response to McCleskey's allegations were "disingenuous" and "constitutionally intolerable").

There are, of course, those who defend the Supreme Court's decision. *See, e.g.*, Scheidegger, *Capital Punishment in 1987: The Puzzle Nears Completion*, 15 W. STATE U.L. REV. 95, 121–25 (1987). Daniel Popeo, the head of the Washington Legal Foundation, is reported to have expressed elation over the decision and to have said that if the Court had ruled in favor of McCleskey, "sociologists and statisticians would have become more important than judges and juries." *See* L.A. Times, Apr. 23, 1987, at 1, col. 5.

[12] In addition to alleging violations of the equal protection clause of the fourteenth amendment, McCleskey also claimed that the state had infringed upon his eighth amendment rights.

case. More specifically, I shall elaborate a claim that has largely been ignored: the right of black victims or potential victims of murder to a response on the part of the state that is equally as vigorous as that which follows the murder of whites. McCleskey asserted two very different equal protection theories. The first, a theory of race-of-the-defendant discrimination, maintains that sentencing in Georgia is improperly influenced by the race of the defendant; the second, a theory of race-of-the-victim discrimination, maintains that sentencing is improperly influenced by the race of the victim. It now appears that even on the basis of the very studies on which McCleskey relied, there existed no statewide, statistically significant evidence to support his allegation of race-of-the-defendant discrimination.[13] In this Arti-

---

See McCleskey v. Kemp, 107 S. Ct. 1756, 1770–78 (1987) (rejecting eighth amendment claims); *id.* at 1783–93 (Brennan, J., dissenting) (finding a violation under the eighth amendment). He raised a wide variety of other claims as well. Among those receiving no judicial support were the following: (1) the trial judge's jury instructions deprived him of due process by relieving the prosecution of proving beyond a reasonable doubt every essential element of the crime for which he was convicted, *see* McCleskey v. Zant, 580 F. Supp. 338, 384–87; (2) the prosecutor improperly referred to the appellate process during his arguments to the jury at the sentencing phase of the trial, *see id.* at 387–88; (3) the trial court denied him due process by refusing him funds to obtain an expert to impeach the testimony of the state's ballistics expert, *see id.* at 388–89; (4) the trial judge improperly instructed the jury regarding the use of evidence implicating McCleskey in other crimes, *see id.* at 389; (5) at the sentencing phase, the trial judge improperly provided the jury with unlimited access to all the evidence presented at the trial, including evidence of nonstatutory aggravating offenses, *see id.* at 390–91; (6) the trial judge improperly admitted into evidence facts concerning prior crimes, including two armed robberies for which he had not been indicted, *see id.* at 391–93; (7) the petitioner was subjected to an improperly suggestive lineup, *see id.* at 393–94; (8) the trial judge improperly admitted into evidence statements that were not freely given, *see id.* at 394–95; (9) the jury was improperly selected because of the exclusion of two prospective jurors on the basis of their opposition to the death penalty, *see id.* at 395–96; (10) the death penalty fails to serve any rational interest, *see id.* at 396; (11) prior to trial, petitioner was improperly denied exculpatory evidence in the possession of the prosecutor, *see id.* at 396–97; (12) there was insufficient evidence produced at trial to support petitioner's conviction for murder, *see id.* at 397–98; and (13) petitioner was denied effective assistance of counsel, *see id.* at 398–402.

The district court, however, did vacate McCleskey's murder conviction on the grounds that the state had wrongly failed to reveal that police officials had promised to intercede with federal authorities on behalf of a key prosecution witness who was himself facing criminal charges. *See* 580 F. Supp. at 380–84. This aspect of the district court's ruling was later reversed by the court of appeals, which ruled that the prosecution had not really "promised" anything of substantial value to the prosecution witness at issue and that, even if an illicit promise had been offered, it constituted harmless error. *See* McCleskey v. Kemp, 753 F.2d at 882–85. Recently, the district court again granted habeas corpus relief, this time on the grounds that police officials intentionally placed the witness whom they aided next to McCleskey's cell for the purpose of eliciting incriminating evidence. *See* McCleskey v. Kemp, No. C87-1517A (N.D. Ga. Dec. 23, 1987).

[13] McCleskey's claim of race-of-the-defendant discrimination was clearly subordinated to his claim of race-of-the-victim discrimination. *See* Transcript of Oral Argument at 16, McCleskey v. Kemp, 107 S. Ct. 1756 (1987) (No. 84-6811) ("[R]ace of defendant discrimination exists . . . but it's not as pervasive. It really is more of a subdivision of the cases in Georgia. But the

cle, therefore, I shall largely disregard the race-of-the-defendant theory. A different problem is posed by the race-of-the-victim theory that McCleskey asserts. He claims that race-of-the-victim discrimination deprived him of rights protected by the equal protection clause by increasing the likelihood that he would be sentenced to death. He emphasizes the unfairness that race-of-the-victim discrimination visits upon those who happen to murder whites. I emphasize, by contrast, the unfairness that race-of-the-victim discrimination visits upon the black community by denying it equal treatment with respect to those who kill its members. McCleskey's theory is defendent-oriented while mine is community-oriented. Although there is considerable congruence between the two, their points of departure and remedial destinations are different.

Many observers have contended — correctly, I think — that Georgia's race-of-the-victim disparities indicate a devaluation of black victims: put bluntly, officials in Georgia "place[] a higher value on the lives of whites than blacks."[14] Typically, however, analyses of

---

race of victim discrimination . . . is statewide, and in all the cases."). McCleskey asserted in his briefs, as in oral argument, that race-of-the-defendant discrimination did play a substantial role in capital sentencing in Georgia, albeit one of lesser importance than race-of-the-victim discrimination. *See, e.g.*, Brief for Petitioner at 35, *McCleskey* (No. 84-6811) (asserting that "the race of the defendant — especially when the defendant is black and the victim white — influences Georgia's capital sentencing process"). Yet in articles published after McCleskey's suit for *habeas* relief, his own experts discounted the significance of race-of-the-defendant discrimination. Viewing the evidence on a statewide basis, they found "neither strong nor consistent" evidence of discrimination directed against black defendants because of their race. *See* Baldus, Woodworth & Pulaski, *Arbitrariness and Discrimination in the Administration of the Death Penalty: A Challenge to State Supreme Courts*, 15 STETSON L. REV. 133, 158 (1986) [hereinafter Baldus, *Arbitrariness and Discrimination*]; Baldus, Woodworth & Pulaski, *Monitoring and Evaluating Contemporary Death Sentencing Systems: Lessons From Georgia*, 18 U.C. DAVIS L. REV. 1375, 1404 (1985) [hereinafter Baldus, *Lessons from Georgia*]; *accord* Bennet, *Some Distribution Patterns for the Georgia Death Sentence*, 18 U.C. DAVIS L. REV. 1327, 1349 (1985).

When Professor Baldus and his colleagues disaggregated the data and examined separately urban and rural areas, they found that "in rural areas black defendants with white victims still received somewhat more severe treatment." Baldus, *Arbitrariness and Discrimination*, *supra*, at 1404. They observed, however, that these differences were not statistically significant. *See id.* They found, moreover, that in urban areas, such as the one in which McCleskey was tried and sentenced, race-of-the-defendant disparities tended to run against *white* defendants. *See id.* at 1406. In the end, they concluded that "the discrimination against black defendants in rural areas and the discrimination against white defendants in urban areas cancelled each other out" on a statewide basis. *Id.* The absence of statistically significant evidence of race-of-the-defendant discrimination in one study covering one jurisdiction with respect to capital sentencing does not mean, of course, that there exists no bias in the sentencing of black defendants. For a discussion of studies indicating widespread presence of race-of-the-defendant discrimination, see *Developments in the Law — Race and the Criminal Process*, 101 HARV. L. REV. 1472, 1525–28 (1988).

[14] *The Supreme Court, 1986 Term — Leading Cases*, *supra* note 11, at 158; *see also* McCleskey v. Kemp, 753 F.2d at 920 (Clark, J., dissenting in part and concurring in part) (arguing that

McCleskey have failed to explore the implications of the undervaluation thesis. Doing so reveals the disturbing irony that diminishing race-of-the-victim disparities while maintaining capital punishment might actually lead to the execution of more black defendants.[15] In Georgia, as elsewhere, most killers of blacks are other blacks. Thus, if killers of blacks are sentenced to death with the same frequency as similarly situated killers of whites, the number of blacks sentenced to death may well increase.[16] A second aspect of this irony involves a conflict of interest within the black community: the community as a

---

the Baldus statistics indicate that in Georgia's death penalty system "the life of a white is dearer, the life of a black cheaper"); W. WHITE, *supra* note 11, at 135 (stating that the Baldus statistics indicate that "society places a higher value on a white life than on a black one"); Bruck, *Decisions of Death*, NEW REPUBLIC, Dec. 12, 1983, at 24 ("Not even the most elaborate jury instructions will ever ensure that an all white jury will weigh a black life as heavily as a white life."); Zeisel, *Race Bias in the Administration of the Death Penalty: The Florida Experience*, 95 HARV. L. REV. 456, 467 (1981).

[15] This point has received strikingly little attention. At oral argument it became clear that several Justices were aware of it and its troubling implications. One mused out loud: "It's such a curious case, because what's the remedy? Is it to execute more people?" *See* Transcript of Oral Argument at 17, *McCleskey* (No. 84-6811). At another point, the same or perhaps another Justice commented: "[T]he claim being made here is a curious one, in the sense that in many death penalty cases, what the defendant comes forward asking for is more opportunities for the exercise of mercy, and to allow juries, for whatever reason, not to impose the death penalty. And yet [the petitioner] come[s] forward with a claim that says, in effect . . . the death penalty is not being imposed on enough people." *Id.* at 27. Nowhere in the Justices' opinions, however, is this issue elaborated upon. *See also* Lempert, *Capital Punishment in the '80s: Reflections on the Symposium*, 74 J. CRIM. L. & CRIMINOLOGY 1101, 1111 (1983) ("If prosecutors seek to resolve those racial disparities that turn on the victim's race by consciously surpressing this factor in deciding whether to seek death, the overwhelming number of those who suffer for it will be blacks.").

[16] In Georgia, between 1974 and 1979, there were 1438 cases of black-on-black homicide that resulted in sentencing. By contrast, there were 228 black-on-white homicides. *McCleskey*, 753 F.2d at 920 (Clark, J., dissenting in part and concurring in part). The Georgia experience is by no means atypical. "[B]lack Americans are twice as likely as whites to be robbed or raped, and stand a four times greater chance of being murdered, mainly by other blacks . . . . Murders of blacks by other blacks have become so commonplace that homicide is now the chief cause of death among black youths." Hacker, *Black Crime, White Racism*, N.Y. REV. BOOKS, Mar. 3, 1988, at 36; *see also* Sargent, *The Curse of Blacks Killing Blacks*, Wash. Post, Mar. 2, 1986, at C1, col. 1 ("Currently, about 95 percent of murdered black males between 15 and 34 are killed by other young black males . . . . These men who call each other 'brother' are killing each other faster than any disease, including AIDS, cancer, sickle cell anemia and high blood pressure. Murder is the leading cause of death of young black males.").

It should be noted, however, that according to McCleskey's expert witnesses, in the absence of race-of-the-victim bias, the number of black defendants sentenced to death in Georgia would increase only marginally. This conclusion is based on the belief that in the absence of race-of-the-victim bias, some black killers of whites would be spared capital punishment while a slightly larger number of black killers who had killed black victims would be added to death row. *See* Petitioner's Exhibit DB100 — A Comparison of the Distribution of Death Row Defendants by Defendant/Victim Racial Characteristics Actually Observed in Georgia and the Distribution Expected in an Even Handed Charging and Sentencing System, *McCleskey*, 107 S. Ct. 1756 (1987) (No. 84-6811).

whole is disadvantaged by the relative leniency extended to killers of blacks, but black (as well as white) criminals who murder Negroes *benefit* from the undervaluation of black victims. Remedying that bias along certain lines might move some black criminals closer to the gas chamber. There has been little discussion, however, of such remedies. This is due in large part to the fact that many of the leading advocates for racial justice are also death penalty abolitionists. The distinction between racial justice questions in capital cases and questions involving other interests has thus been blurred.[17] Outrage at the racial inequality alleged in *McCleskey* has figured prominently in criticisms of Georgia's death penalty system and the Supreme Court's affirmation of it. Abolitionist sentiments, however, have determined the response of those outraged by racial patterns in capital sentencing.[18]

---

[17] Justices Brennan and Marshall, the two most outspoken champions of racial justice on the Supreme Court, are also the two Justices who, as a matter of principle, reject the imposition of the death penalty in all circumstances. *See* Gregg v. Georgia, 428 U.S. 153, 227–31 (1976) (Brennan, J., dissenting) (arguing that the death penalty is in all circumstances forbidden by the eighth and fourteenth amendments); *id.* at 231–41 (Marshall, J., dissenting) (same). The Legal Defense and Educational Fund (LDF) of the National Association for the Advancement of Colored People (NAACP), the country's single most important organization devoted to racial justice issues, is also the leading organization in the litigation campaign against the death penalty. As Hugo Bedau observes, "[i]f one group has to be identified as chiefly responsible for the progress since the 1960's toward abolition of the death penalty in the United States, it would be the LDF." H. BEDAU, DEATH IS DIFFERENT: STUDIES IN THE MORALITY, LAW, AND POLITICS OF CAPITAL PUNISHMENT 136 (1987). Fittingly, the attorneys who represented Warren McCleskey before the Supreme Court are LDF attorneys.

The symbiotic relationship between advocacy for racial justice and advocacy for abolition is rooted in the historical fact that much of the litigation to reform administration of capital punishment stems from attempts to rescue black defendants victimized by racist law enforcement officials. The campaign to save a Negro sentenced to death for defending his family, and killing a policeman in the process, is what led the NAACP to create a legal department. *See* C. KELLOGG, 1 NAACP: A HISTORY OF THE NATIONAL ASSOCIATION FOR THE ADVANCEMENT OF COLORED PEOPLE, 1909–1920, at 57–61 (1967) (describing the NAACP's role in Franklin v. South Carolina, 218 U.S. 161 (1910)). For other important capital cases involving race relations themes see, for example, Turner v. Murray, 476 U.S. 28 (1986) (entitling a defendant in a capital case to inquire into whether race would affect the judgment of potential jurors); Brown v. Mississippi, 297 U.S. 278 (1936) (reversing a conviction because the Negro defendant's confession was elicted by beating); Norris v. Alabama, 294 U.S. 587 (1935) (reversing a conviction because of racial exclusion in composition of grand and petit juries); and Powell v. Alabama, 287 U.S. 45 (1932) (reversing a conviction of Negro defendants because of the absence of assistance of counsel).

[18] *Cf.* Muller, *The Legal Defense Fund's Capital Punishment Campaign: The Distorting Influence of Death*, 4 YALE L. & POL'Y REV. 158, 181 (1985):

> [The enlistment of the LDF in the campaign to abolish capital punishment] distorted [its] traditional focus on the treatment of the black American. Although the Fund's involvement at first stressed traditional issues of racial discrimination, non-racial formulations soon crept into the campaign's arsenal . . . . [It became difficult] to determine whether, at very bottom, it was the mere presence of racism in the capital process, or the ominous possibility of death at the end of that process, which was truly propelling the campaign.

My critique of *McCleskey v. Kemp* does not proceed from abolitionist premises. Rather, it seeks to delineate a response to race-of-the-victim disparities that vindicates the claims of racial justice — with or without capital punishment. I am more concerned with the plight of black communities whose welfare is slighted by criminal justice systems that respond more forcefully to the killing of whites than the killing of blacks than I am concerned with the plight of convicted murderers, black or white. McCleskey understandably portrayed the case in a defendent-oriented fashion. I portray the case, by contrast, in a community-oriented fashion. I conceptualize *McCleskey* as an instance of racial inequality in the provision of public goods.[19] Whereas other cases have involved the racially unequal provision of street lights, sidewalks, and sewers, *McCleskey* involves racial inequality in the provision of a peculiar sort of public good — capital sentencing.[20]

In Part I, I present the essential background of the case, setting forth the basic findings of the statistical study on which McCleskey relied and the judicial response to it. In Part II, I argue that precedent offers considerable support for the way in which the Court handled the case. In Part III, I offer a critique of the *McCleskey* decision that focuses upon lapses in the Court's argumentation and deficiencies in its constitutional doctrine of purposeful discrimination. In Part IV, I posit the basis on which the Court should have declared a constitutional violation. I note that conventional standing doctrine and the Court's doctrine of purposeful discrimination pose important obstacles to the practical implementation of the theory I propose. Still I argue that even in the absence of discriminatory purpose, the unjustified racial disparities that characterize capital sentencing in Georgia should be viewed as giving rise to a constitutional violation: the failure of Georgia to provide to its black residents the equal protection of the

---

[19] For examples of equal protection challenges to the provision of public services by municipalities, see Dowdell v. Apopka, 698 F.2d 1181 (11th Cir. 1983), and Hawkins v. Town of Shaw, 461 F.2d 1171 (5th Cir. 1972) (en banc) (per curiam). *See generally* C. HAAR & D. FESSLER, THE WRONG SIDE OF THE TRACKS 27–54 (1986); Ratner, *Inter-Neighborhood Denials of Equal Protection in the Provision of Municipal Services*, 4 HARV. C.R.-C.L. L. REV. 1 (1968); Comment, *The Evolution of Equal Protection: Education, Municipal Services, and Wealth*, 7 HARV. C.R.-C.L. L. REV. 103 (1972).

[20] That a large sector of the population views capital punishment as a valuable public policy is beyond dispute. Thirty-seven states currently authorize capital punishment, and thirty-three have actually carried out death sentences since 1976. *See McCleskey*, 107 S. Ct. at 1771 n.23. On the other hand, death penalty abolitionists have argued movingly that capital punishment is wrong in principle and vicious in practice inasmuch as its administration reflects the pervasive racial and economic injustices of American society. *See, e.g.*, H. BEDAU, *supra* note 17; C. BLACK, JR., CAPITAL PUNISHMENT: THE INEVITABILITY OF CAPRICE AND MISTAKE 94–102 (2d ed. 1981). Although I concede the powers of these arguments, I am not an abolitionist. In my view, considerations of deterrence and retribution sometimes justify condemning criminals to death.

laws. In Part V, I turn to the problem of remedy and show that all of the available alternatives are disturbingly inadequate. I conclude by arguing that race-of-the-victim sentencing disparities are but one manifestation of a peculiar type of racial oppression — oppression without animus — and, further, that race-based devaluations of human life constitute simply one instance of a universal phenomenon: the propensity for persons to empathize more fully with those with whom they can identify.

I. *McCleskey* and The Judicial Response to Statistical Evidence of Racial Disparities in Capital Sentencing

Writing in 1940, Charles Mangum, Jr. complained that "[i]n the matter of the comparative sentences imposed upon members of the two races, white and colored, there seems to be a startling lack of reliable statistical information."[21] He suggested that "it should occasion no great surprise [if data indicated], especially in interracial homicide and sex crimes, a decided tendency toward a longer or more severe sentence where the victim was white and a lighter punishment where the victim was colored."[22] But he refrained from alleging the actual existence of racially selective sentencing practices because "[m]ost of the instances which have been unearthed in an effort to prove that such unfairness really exists are so complicated by the presence of other social phenomena as to be practically useless in an attempt to show that the injustice was due to racial distinction alone."[23]

Soon thereafter, Guy B. Johnson, a pioneer in the sociology of sentencing, offered the following hypothesis:

> If caste values and attitudes mean anything at all, they mean that offenses by or against Negroes will be defined not so much in terms of their intrinsic seriousness as in terms of their importance in the eyes of the dominant group. Obviously the murder of a white person by a Negro and the murder of a Negro by a Negro are not at all the same kind of murder from the standpoint of the upper caste's scale of values . . . . Instead of two categories of offenders, Negro and white, we really need four offender-victim categories, and they would probably rank in seriousness from high to low as follows: (1) Negro versus white, (2) white versus white, (3) Negro versus Negro, (4) white versus Negro . . . . [If] our hypothesis is correct, the differentials which we have suggested should show up in mass statistics based on offender-victim categories.[24]

---

[21] C. Mangum, The Legal Status of the Negro 368 (1940).

[22] *Id.* at 368–70.

[23] *Id.* at 368.

[24] Johnson, *The Negro and Crime*, 217 Annals 93, 98 (1941).

Since the publication of Johnson's essay, scholars in various disciplines have produced a steady flow of empirical research on race and capital sentencing.[25] One feature common to almost all of them is a finding of striking disparities in sentencing that correlate with the race of the victim.[26] Researchers have concluded repeatedly that defendants who kill whites are more likely to be sentenced to death than defendants who kill blacks.[27]

McCleskey largely predicated his claim of race-of-the-victim discrimination on the oral testimony and written presentations of David C. Baldus, George Woodworth, and Charles A. Pulaski, Jr., the authors of the most comprehensive analysis to date of racial influences in capital sentencing in a single state.[28] The Baldus study data was

---

[25] For commentary on this research, see W. BOWERS, G. PIERCE & J. MCDEVITT, LEGAL HOMICIDE 67–102 (1984); S. DIKE, CAPITAL PUNISHMENT IN THE UNITED STATES 30–51 (1982); Gross & Mauro, *Patterns of Death: An Analysis of Racial Disparities in Capital Sentencing and Homicide Victimization*, 37 STAN. L. REV. 27, 38–49 (1984); and Kleck, *Racial Discrimination in Criminal Sentencing: A Critical Evaluation of the Evidence with Additional Evidence on the Death Penalty*, 46 AM. SOC. REV. 783 (1981).

[26] One exception is a study conducted by the *Stanford Law Review* in 1969 which found that neither the race of the defendant nor the race of the victim was associated with patterns of capital sentencing in California between 1958 and 1966. *See A Study of the California Penalty Jury in First-Degree Murder Cases*, 21 STAN. L. REV. 1297, 1421 (1967). The contrast between the *Stanford Law Review* study and most of the other research on capital sentencing may reflect real differences in the jurisdictions examined or methodological deficiencies in the Stanford study, which might have obscured racial influences upon capital sentencing in California. *See* Gross & Mauro, *supra* note 25, at 41 n.55.

[27] *See, e.g.*, W. BOWERS, G. PIERCE & J. MCDEVITT, *supra* note 25, at 193 (covering sentencing patterns in Florida, Georgia, Ohio, and Texas from the effective date of each state's post-*Furman* capital sentencing statute until 1978); Garfinkel, *Research Note on Inter- and Intra-Racial Homicides*, 27 SOC. FORCES 369 (1949) (studying ten counties in North Carolina between 1930 and 1940); Gross & Mauro, *supra* note 25 (examining racial patterns in capital sentencing in Arkansas, Florida, Georgia, Illinois, Mississippi, North Carolina, Oklahoma, and Virginia between 1976 and 1980); Radelet, *Racial Characteristics and the Imposition of the Death Penalty*, 46 AM. SOC. REV. 918 (1981) (studying 20 counties in Florida between 1976 and 1977); Riedel, *Discrimination in the Imposition of the Death Penalty: A Comparison of the Characteristics of Offenders Sentenced Pre-*Furman *and Post-*Furman, 49 TEMP. L.Q. 261 (1976) (finding continued disproportionate death sentencing of nonwhites after the *Furman* decision); Zeisel, *supra* note 14, at 466–68; Zimring, Eigen & O'Malley, *Punishing Homicide in Philadelphia: Perspectives on the Death Penalty*, 43 U. CHI. L. REV. 227 (1976) (reporting homicides in Philadelphia during a portion of 1970); Note, *Discrimination and Arbitrariness in Capital Punishment: An Analysis of Post-*Furman *Murder Cases in Dade County, Florida, 1973–1976*, 33 STAN. L. REV. 75 (1980). Even William Wilbanks, who generally derides allegations that criminal laws are enforced in a racially discriminatory fashion, believes that in the context of capital punishment the race of the victim consistently influences sentencing decisions. *See* W. WILBANKS, THE MYTH OF A RACIST CRIMINAL JUSTICE SYSTEM 120 (1987).

[28] For judicial descriptions of the Baldus study, see McCleskey v. Kemp, 107 S. Ct. at 1763–65; McCleskey v. Kemp, 753 F.2d at 887; and McCleskey v. Zant, 580 F. Supp. at 352–79. For a view of the Baldus study from the perspective of McCleskey's attorneys, see Petitioner's Post-Hearing Memorandum in Support of His Claims of Arbitrariness and Racial Discrimination, at 3–41, 54–56, McCleskey v. Zant, 580 F. Supp. 338 (N.D. Ga. 1984) (No. C81-2434A)

derived from records involving the disposition of over 2000 murder cases between 1973 and 1979.[29] The Georgia Department of Pardons and Paroles and other state agencies provided the Baldus study researchers with police reports, parole board records, prison files, and other items that evidenced the process by which state authorities handled criminal homicides.[30]

Two aspects of the Baldus study are particularly relevant to an understanding of the legal arguments that surround it. First, Baldus noted that among the variables that plausibly might influence capital sentencing, the race of the victim emerged as a consistent and powerful factor. Initially, simple correlations suggested the importance of this variable. Without attempting to control for the possible effects of competing variables, Baldus found that perpetrators in white-victim cases were eleven times more likely to be condemned to death than perpetrators in black-victim cases.[31] Professor Baldus and his associates subjected this and similarly striking correlations to extensive statistical analysis to test whether the seemingly racial nature of this disparity was explainable in terms of hidden factors confounded with race. He eventually took into account some 230 non-racial variables that might have influenced the pattern of sentencing. He concluded that even after accounting for every non-racial variable that might plausibly have mattered, the race of the victim continued to have a statistically significant correlation with the imposition of capital sentences.[32] Applying a statistical model that included the thirty-nine

---

[hereinafter Petitioner's Post-Hearing Memorandum]; and Brief for Petitioner, McCleskey v. Kemp, 107 S. Ct. 1756 (1987) (No. 84-6811). For a defense of the Baldus study by its authors, see D. BALDUS, G. WOODWORTH & C. PULASKI, *MCCLESKEY V. ZANT* AND *MCCLESKEY V. KEMP*: A METHODOLOGICAL CRITIQUE (forthcoming supplement to D. BALDUS & J. COLE, STATISTICAL PROOF OF DISCRIMINATION (1980)) [hereinafter A METHODOLOGICAL CRITIQUE]. For published research by Professor Baldus and his associates related to the testimony they offered on behalf of McCleskey, see Baldus, Pulaski & Woodworth, *Comparative Review of Death Sentences: An Empirical Study of the Georgia Experience*, 74 J. CRIM. L. & CRIMINOLOGY 661 (1983); Baldus, Pulaski, Woodworth & Kyle, *Identifying Comparatively Excessive Sentences of Death: A Quantitative Approach*, 33 STAN. L. REV. 1 (1980); Baldus, *Arbitrariness and Discrimination*, cited above in note 13, at 133; and Baldus, *Lessons From Georgia*, cited above in note 13, at 1375.

29 *See* Brief for Petitioner at 11, McCleskey v. Kemp, 107 S. Ct. 1756 (1987) (No. 84-6811).

30 Professor Baldus and his associates created the data base upon which their study is grounded with the assistance of student researchers who coded detailed questionnaires. One questionnaire was about 120 pages long with blanks for the entry of some 500 variables. Another was 42 pages long with blanks for the entry of about 595 variables. *See* McCleskey v. Zant, 580 F. Supp. at 354–57.

31 *See* 107 S. Ct. at 1763. Another unadjusted correlation discovered by Baldus and noted by the Supreme Court is the fact that prosecutors sought the death penalty in 70% of the cases involving black defendants and white victims, 32% of the cases involving white defendants and white victims, 19% of the cases involving white defendants and black victims, and 15% of the cases involving black defendants and black victims. *See id.*

32 *See id.* at 1764 & n.5.

non-racial variables believed most likely to play a role in capital punishment in Georgia, the Baldus study indicated that the odds of being condemned to death were 4.3 times greater for defendants who killed whites than for defendants who killed blacks,[33] a variable nearly as influential as a prior conviction for armed robbery, rape, or even murder.[34]

Second, Baldus concluded that racial disparities in capital sentencing are most dramatic in that category containing neither the most aggravated nor the least aggravated homicides. Racial disparities are greatest, he argued, in the middle-range of aggravated homicides.[35] In the most aggravated cases, decisionmakers typically impose the death sentence regardless of racial variables, and in the least aggravated cases decisionmakers typically spare the defendant regardless of racial variables. In the middle range of aggravation, however, where a decision could go either way, the influence of racial variables emerges most powerfully. This hypothesis is particularly relevant to McCleskey because, in Baldus' view, his crime was situated in the middle-range of aggravated homicide.[36]

After an evidentiary hearing, District Judge J. Owen Forrester rejected McCleskey's race discrimination claim primarily on the ground that the Baldus study did not represent "good statistical methodology."[37] He objected to what he viewed as significant omissions, errors, and inconsistencies in Baldus' data base and inadequacies in the design of Baldus' statistical models.[38] Judge Forrester's findings have been rendered largely moot because the court of appeals and the Supreme Court resolved the case without reviewing them; the appellate courts assumed arguendo that the Baldus study was valid.[39] As a legal matter, this assumption has no substantive meaning; it merely facilitated the dispostion of the case. There is much, however, that indicates that the district court was clearly erroneous.[40] First, the

---

33 *See id.* at 1800 n.9 (Blackmun, J., dissenting).

34 Professor Baldus concluded that murdering a white victim increases one's odds of being sentenced to death by a factor of 4.3, while a prior conviction for armed robbery, rape, or murder increases one's odds of being sentenced to death by a factor of 4.9. *See id.* at 1800 n.10.

35 *See McCleskey*, 107 S. Ct. at 1764 n.5.

36 *See id.* at 1764 n.5. According to Professor Baldus' colleague, Dr. George Woodworth, "'[A]t Mr. McCleskey's level of aggravation the average white victim case has approximately a twenty [20] percentage point higher risk of receiving the death sentence than a similarly situated black victim case.'" Brief for Petitioner at 85, McCleskey v. Kemp, 107 S. Ct. 1756 (1987) (No. 84-6811) (quoting Federal Trial Transcript at 1740, McCleskey v. Zant, 580 F. Supp. 338 (N.D. Ga. 1984)).

37 580 F. Supp. at 379.

38 *See id.* at 352–80.

39 *See* 107 S. Ct. at 1776 & n.7; 753 F.2d at 898.

40 Ironically, there now exists far more detailed and systematic evidence that states administer the death penalty arbitrarily and discriminatorily than there existed in 1972, when the Court

methodology of the Baldus study received high praise from many of the most distinguished researchers who have investigated the application of statistics to legal problems. Professor Richard Berk, a member of the National Academy of Sciences' Committee on Sentencing Research, testified that the Baldus study has "'very high credibility'" and "'is far and away the most complete and thorough analysis of sentencing that[has] ever been done.'"[41] Similarly, several leading scholars in the field have collectively affirmed that the Baldus inves-

---

invalidated all then-existing state statutes authorizing capital punishment. *See* S. GROSS & R. MAURO, DEATH & DISCRIMINATION: RACIAL DISPARITIES IN CAPITAL SENTENCING (forthcoming 1988); *see also infra* pp. 1410–11 (contrasting the perfectionist rigor that the Justices demand in certain contexts with their willingness in others to rule on the basis of naked intuition).

We should beware, however, of falling victim to scientistic illusions that prevent us from acknowledging the reality of a given phenomenom unless we can definitively "prove" its existence. *See* C. BLACK, *supra* note 20, at 101–02 & n.2 (suggesting that studies detailing racial patterns in capital sentencing, although valuable, simply confirm what Americans should already know about the way in which their society operates with respect to racial matters); Black, *The Lawfulness of the Segregation Decisions*, 69 YALE L.J. 421, 427 (1960) (eschewing metaphysical sociology for sociology rooted in history and common knowledge).

At the same time, it is important to acknowledge the unavoidably "political" nature of *all* academic analyses of social practices, particularly those that are controversial. In considering the politics of the Baldus study, two considerations are especially relevant. First, although Baldus was permitted to publish whatever he concluded from his investigation, it should be noted that his study was partially financed by funds either provided by or distributed by the NAACP Legal Defense Fund — McCleskey's lawyers. *See* Petitioner's Post-Hearing Memorandum, *supra* note 28, at 7–8, 13–14. Moreover, Baldus and his colleagues state that after a certain point in their analysis they began to conduct their research with litigation in mind. *See* A METHODOLOGICAL CRITIQUE, *supra* note 28, at 9–10. The connection between the LDF and the Baldus researchers caught the attention of at least one Justice. *See* Transcript of Oral Argument at 12–14, *McCleskey* (No. 84-6811). Second, while it is true that leading academic experts in the application of statistics to legal issues have praised the Baldus study, *see infra* pp. 1399–1400, it is also true that the elite cadre of legal academics and social scientists is tilted strongly against the death penalty. *See* H. BEDAU, supra note 17, at 141–45 (observing that "without the enterprise of social scientists who favor abolition and the support of private foundations, the empirical basis on which the death penalty has been examined . . . would not have existed").

These comments should not be viewed as impugning the value of the Baldus study. They suggest that one should simultaneously recognize that the Baldus study emerges from the anti-death penalty wing of the academic community *and* that it reports reliable findings about racial patterns in capital sentencing in Georgia. On the theoretical concerns that prompt these remarks, see generally A. GOULDNER, THE COMING CRISIS OF WESTERN SOCIOLOGY (1970); T. KUHN, THE STRUCTURE OF SCIENTIFIC REVOLUTIONS (2d ed. 1970); and K. MANNHEIM, IDEOLOGY AND UTOPIA: AN INTRODUCTION TO THE SOCIOLOGY OF KNOWLEDGE (1936). *Cf.* Yudolf, *School Desegregation: Legal Realism, Research and Elaboration, and Social Science Research in the Supreme Court*, LAW & CONTEMP. PROBS., Autumn 1978, at 57 (suggesting that widespread embrace of methodologically unsound studies by liberal scientists bent on attacking segregation might subsequently have chilled the willingness of courts to rely on social scientific expertise in the resolution of public problems).

[41] Brief for Petitioner at 67, McCleskey v. Kemp, 107 S. Ct. 1756 (1987) (No. 84-6811) (quoting Federal Trial Transcript at 1740, McCleskey v. Zant, 580 F. Supp. 338 (N.D. Ga. 1984)).

tigations "are among the best empirical studies on criminal sentencing ever conducted."[42] Second, the Baldus study is consistent with conclusions reached by a solid body of prior research.[43] Moreover, specialists in applied statistics have raised disturbing questions regarding the basic competence of Judge Forrester's analysis.[44] But even beyond the technical deficiencies noted by experts, Judge Forrester displayed a glaringly obvious hostility in his evaluation of the Baldus study — a hostility detectable simply by the application of common sense. Nothing better illustrates this point than Judge Forrester's conclusion that the data base of the Baldus study was irredeemably flawed because the questionnaires used to collect information "could not capture every nuance of every case."[45] First, as Judge Johnson noted in dissent at the court of appeals, Judge Forrester neglected to specify the significance of the omissions he deemed so important.[46] Second, and more fundamentally, Judge Forrester's objection is premised upon a wildly perfectionist standard that is impossible to satisfy. "By insisting on a standard of 'absolute knowledge' about every single case, [Judge Forrester] implicitly rejected the value of all applied statistical analysis."[47]

A sharply divided court of appeals assumed the validity of the Baldus study, but nevertheless affirmed the district court's race discrimination holding on the grounds that the statistical disparities and supplemental evidence failed to prove a constitutional violation.[48] The court of appeals declared that in order to succeed, McCleskey would have had to produce evidence indicating that *his* sentence was the product of race-dependent decisionmaking.[49] But the Baldus study "only" showed "that in a group involving blacks and whites, all

---

42 Brief *Amici Curiae* for Dr. Franklin M. Fisher, Dr. Richard O. Lempert, Dr. Peter W. Sperlich, Dr. Marvin E. Wolfgang, Professor Hans Zeisel & Professor Franklin E. Zimring in Support of Petitioner Warren McCleskey at 3, *McCleskey* (No. 84-6811) [hereinafter Brief *Amici Curiae* for Dr. Fisher].

43 *See supra* notes 21–27 and accompanying text.

44 *See* Brief *Amici Curiae* for Dr. Fisher, *supra* note 42, at 3 (stating that Judge Forrester's critique of the Baldus study was "uninformed and indefensible"); *see also* Gross & Mauro, *supra* note 25, at 91–92. Arguing that several of Judge Forrester's forays into statistical methodology were "ill-informed and wrong," Professors Gross and Mauro highlight five instances in which the judge's assertions are contradicted by academic authorities. *Id.*

45 580 F. Supp. at 356. More recently, Judge Forrester revealed contempt for the Baldus study by writing that the racial disparities it found were produced by "arbitrarily structured little rinky-dink regressions that accounted for only a few variables. . . . They prove nothing other than the truth of the adage that anything may be proved by statistics." McCleskey v. Kemp, No. C87-1517A, at 12 (N.D. Ga. Dec. 23, 1987) (order granting relief to McCleskey on other grounds).

46 *See* 753 F.2d at 914–17 (Johnson, J., dissenting).

47 *See* Brief *Amici Curiae* for Dr. Fisher, *supra* note 42, at 23.

48 *See McCleskey*, 753 F.2d at 899.

49 *See id.* at 895–900.

of whose cases are virtually the same, there would be . . . more murderers of whites receiving the death penalty than murderers of blacks."[50] The court conceded that the statistics demonstrate that "there is a race-of-the-victim relationship with the imposition of the death sentence discernible in enough cases to be statistically significant in the system as a whole."[51] It concluded, however, that "[n]o single petitioner could, on the basis of these statistics alone, establish that he received the death sentence because, and only because, his victim was white."[52]

Justice Powell's opinion for the Supreme Court largely followed the court of appeals' equal protection analysis. Like their colleagues below, the Justices also assumed, arguendo, the validity of the Baldus study.[53] Similarly, they insisted that the constitutionality of McCleskey's sentence must be determined by asking whether officials in his case purposefully discriminated on the basis of race.[54] The Court concluded that no such inference could be drawn from the Baldus statistics.[55] Justice Powell noted that in some contexts a "'stark'" pattern of statistical disparities may create a prima facie case which shifts onto the state the burden of rebutting the allegation of racial discrimination.[56] He observed, however, that in the context of capital sentencing, where discretion has been deemed a constitutional requirement, the Court "would demand exceptionally clear proof before [inferring] that the discretion has been abused."[57] In the majority's view, the correlations revealed by the Baldus study did not meet that standard.

Justice Powell also noted reasons of policy that informed the Court's decision. First, he observed with alarm that "McCleskey's claim, taken to its logical conclusion, throws into serious question the principles that underlie our entire criminal justice system," because, if accepted, the Court "could soon be faced with similar claims to other types of penalty" from members of other groups alleging bias.[58] Second, he invoked considerations of judicial competence and judicial

---

[50] *Id.* at 895.

[51] *Id.* at 897.

[52] *Id.* at 896; *see also id.* at 897 ("The magnitude [of the statistics] cannot be called determinative in any given case.").

[53] *See* McCleskey v. Kemp, 107 S. Ct. at 1766 & n.7.

[54] The Court also held that McCleskey had failed to prove that the state as a whole acted with a discriminatory purpose in enacting and maintaining capital punishment. *See id.* at 1769–70. It should be noted, however, that McCleskey never asserted the proposition the Court rejects.

[55] *See* id. at 1769.

[56] *Id.* at 1767 & n.12 (quoting Village of Arlington Heights v. Metropolitan Hous. Dev. Corp., 429 U.S. 252, 266 (1977)).

[57] *Id.* at 1769.

[58] *Id.* at 1779.

restraint as reasons for avoiding intervention. "McCleskey's arguments," he declared, "are best presented to legislative bodies. . . . It is the legislatures, the elected representatives of the people, that are 'constituted to respond to the will and consequently the moral values of the people.'"[59]

II. *McCleskey* and Precedent — The Temptations of Sentimentality

The first point to establish in coming to grips with *McCleskey* is that the rejection of McCleskey's claims by all levels of the federal judiciary should come as no surprise. Some critics of the Supreme Court's ruling portray it as a betrayal of the Court's grand traditions. For instance, Justice Blackmun maintained in dissent that he was "disappointed with the Court's action . . . because of its departure from . . . well-developed constitutional jurisprudence."[60] This description, however, ignores important aspects of the Court's traditional response to allegations of racial discrimination in the administration of criminal justice. Existing doctrine would not have made a contrary result implausible; had there been the will, available precedent could have lit the way.[61] The point is that the decision rendered, albeit lamentable, was well within the ambit of expectations reasonably derived from prior rulings.

Critics of *McCleskey* must face the fact that, as far as reported cases disclose, *no defendant in state or federal court has ever successfully challenged his punishment on grounds of racial discrimination in sentencing.*[62] This unbroken line of judicial rejection has received

[59] *Id.* at 1781 (quoting Furman v. Georgia, 408 U.S. 238, 383 (1972) (Burger, C.J., dissenting)).

[60] *Id.* at 1794 (Blackmun, J., dissenting); *see also supra* notes 6, 7, 11.

[61] *See infra* pp. 1425–29.

[62] For useful discussions of the ways in which courts have nullified equal protection challenges to criminal law enforcement, see Cardinale & Feldman, *The Federal Courts and the Right to Nondiscriminatory Administration of the Criminal Law: A Critical View*, 29 SYRACUSE L. REV. 659 (1978); Goldstein, *Police Discretion Not to Invoke the Criminal Process: Low Visibility Decisions in the Administration of Justice*, 69 YALE L.J. 543, 573–80 (1960); Reiss, *Prosecutorial Intent in Constitutional Criminal Procedure*, 135 U. PA. L. REV. 1365 (1987); Tieger, *Police Discretion and Discriminatory Enforcement*, 1971 DUKE L.J. 717, 724–43; Comment, *The Right to Nondiscriminatory Enforcement of State Penal Laws*, 61 COLUM. L. REV. 1103 (1961); and Note, *Discriminatory Law Enforcement and Equal Protection from the Law*, 59 YALE L.J. 354 (1950).

Two decisions separated by half a century but united by a similar resistance to allegations of racial discrimination in the enforcement of criminal law are Ah Sin v. Wittman, 198 U.S. 500 (1905), and Butler v. Cooper, 554 F.2d 645 (4th Cir. 1977). In *Ah Sin* the petitioner sought relief from conviction for violating a gambling statute on the grounds that only Chinese were prosecuted for such infractions. *See* 198 U.S. at 506–07. The Court rejected the petitioner's claim because he had failed to produce evidence indicating that others had violated the law.

its most emphatic elaboration in decisions turning aside challenges to capital punishment.[63] Had the Court ruled differently in *McCleskey* it would not have been in step with judicial tradition; to the contrary, it would have been making an unprecedented step forward.

A variety of factors explain the staunch resistance of courts to challenges of sentencing on grounds of racial discrimination. Perhaps the most important is the reluctance of judges to interfere with punishment for criminal acts because of flaws having no bearing upon an individual's personal culpability; Warren McCleskey and similarly situated petitioners are, after all, convicted murderers. That reluctance is reflected in a wide range of doctrines including harmless error[64] and restrictions on the availability of federal habeas corpus relief.[65]

"No latitude of intention should be indulged in a case like this," Justice Joseph McKenna declared for the Court. *Id.* at 508. "[T]here should be certainty to every intent. . . . This is a matter of proof, and no fact should be omitted to make it out completely." *Id.*

Butler involved an allegation of racially discriminatory enforcement of liquor laws in Portsmouth, Virginia. *See* 544 F.2d at 646. The plaintiffs showed that while only one-third of the city's population was black, Negroes accounted for 84% of the persons arrested for violating liquor laws during one 20-month period and that in some months blacks accounted for almost 100% of those arrested. *See id.* at 649 (Butzner, J., dissenting). The Court of Appeals for the Fourth Circuit, in the face of a strong dissent, affirmed the district court's grant of summary judgment to the defendant, holding that the statistics noted did not even raise a genuine issue of material fact as to whether the police had engaged in purposeful discrimination. *See Butler*, 544 F.2d at 648.

63 *See, e.g.*, Sullivan v. Wainwright, 464 U.S. 109 (1984) (denying application for stay of execution for a petitioner raising a claim of racial discrimination in application of capital punishment); Smith v. Kemp, 464 U.S. 1032 (1983) (same); Prejean v. Blackburn, 743 F.2d 1091, 1099–102 (5th Cir. 1984), *modified*, 765 F.2d 482, 486–87 (5th Cir. 1985); Shaw v. Martin, 733 F.2d 304, 311–14 (4th Cir. 1983), *cert. denied*, 469 U.S. 1067 (1984); Smith v. Balkcom, 660 F.2d 573, 584–85 (5th Cir. 1981), *modified*, 671 F.2d 858, 859–60 (5th Cir.), *cert. denied*, 459 U.S. 882 (1982); Spinkellink v. Wainwright, 578 F.2d 582, 612–16 (5th Cir. 1978), *cert. denied*, 440 U.S. 976 (1979); Maxwell v. Bishop, 398 F.2d 138, 141–48 (8th Cir. 1968) (opinion of Blackmun, J.), *vacated and remanded on other grounds*, 398 U.S. 262 (1970).

Clear and strong evidence of racial discrimination in capital sentencing for rape made the death penalty a target of the civil rights bar. *See* M. MELTSNER, CRUEL AND UNUSUAL: THE SUPREME COURT AND CAPITAL PUNISHMENT 73–105 (1973) (discussing efforts undertaken during the 1960's and early 1970's); *see also* Wolfgang & Riedel, *Racial Discrimination, Rape, and the Death Penalty*, in THE DEATH PENALTY IN AMERICA 194 (H. Bedau ed. 1982); Dorin, *Two Different Worlds: Criminologists, Justices and Racial Discrimination in the Imposition of Capital Punishment in Rape Cases*, 72 J. CRIM. L. & CRIMINOLOGY 1667, 1667–68 (1981). However, when the Supreme Court finally invalidated the death penalty as a punishment for rape in Coker v. Georgia, 433 U.S. 584 (1977), it made no mention of race discrimination.

64 *See, e.g.*, Harrington v. California, 395 U.S. 250, 254 (1969) (affirming conviction where "overwhelming" evidence rendered harmless a confrontation clause violation); Field, *Assessing the Harmlessness of Federal Constitutional Error — A Process in Need of a Rationale*, 125 U. PA. L. REV. 15 (1976) (attempting to formulate precise and narrow rules in the harmless error area).

65 *See, e.g.*, Stone v. Powell, 428 U.S. 465, 490 (1976) (excluding state prisoners from federal habeus corpus relief based on alleged fourth amendment violations because, among other considerations, a "windfall afforded a guilty defendant" by application of the exclusionary rule

The strength of this reluctance, moreover, appears to grow in direct proportion to the seriousness of the crime involved.[66] In certain contexts, courts do nullify convictions on grounds having nothing to do with guilt or innocence; violations of the fourth amendment provide the most troubling instances of this response.[67] Judges have admitted, however, that the social cost of providing such relief has decreased their willingness to "reward" criminal defendants for bringing to light unconstitutional acts by officials in the criminal justice system.[68]

In the race relations context, the most significant obstacle to federal judicial interference with sentencing decisions is the Supreme Court's doctrine of purposeful discrimination. The Court insists that only "purposeful" discrimination violates the equal protection clause.[69] For the past decade the Court has conceptualized discriminatory purpose in an increasingly narrow fashion. It has largely rejected arguments that discriminatory purpose can be inferred from the predictable consequences of an action or even from an awareness that a given course of action will impose an adverse and reasonably avoidable burden upon a historically oppressed group.[70] Rather the Court has maintained that a finding of discriminatory purpose must be predicated

---

would be contrary to the idea of proportionality); Friendly, *Is Innocence Irrelevent? Collateral Attack on Criminal Judgments*, 38 U. CHI. L. REV. 142 (1970) (advocating the restriction of *habeas* petitions to those that raise questions about the correctness of guilty verdicts).

[66] *See, e.g.*, State v. Bolt, 142 Ariz. 260, 270–72, 689 P.2d 519, 529–31 (1984) (Cameron, J., concurring) (advocating a balancing approach that would prevent the exclusionary rule from being applied in cases where the societal cost of invoking the rule exceeds the societal benefits); Kaplan, *The Limits of the Exclusionary Rule*, 26 STAN. L. REV. 1027, 1046–49 (1974) (arguing that the exclusionary rule should not be applied in "serious" cases where police departments have taken institutional measures to conform police behavior to the fourth amendment). For a critical analysis repudiating suggestions that the seriousness of offenses be taken into account in determining whether to provide relief under the exclusionary rule, see Kamisar, *"Comparative Reprehensibility" and the Fourth Amendment Exclusionary Rule*, 86 MICH. L. REV. 1, 19–32 (1987).

[67] *See, e.g.*, Coolidge v. New Hampshire, 403 U.S. 443, 472–73 (1971) (overturning a murder conviction secured with illegally obtained evidence); Davis v. Mississippi, 394 U.S. 721, 727–28 (1969) (overturning a rape conviction secured with illegally obtained evidence); Bumper v. North Carolina, 391 U.S. 543, 552–54 (1968) (same).

[68] *See, e.g.*, United States v. Leon, 468 U.S. 897, 907–09 (1984) (establishing a good faith exception to the exclusionary rule largely because of the social costs of excluding relevant evidence). For an illuminating analysis of the criminal defendant as private attorney general, see Meltzer, *Deterring Constitutional Violations by Law Enforcement Officials: Plaintiffs and Defendants as Private Attorneys General*, 88 COLUM. L. REV. 247, 248–78 (1988).

[69] *See, e.g.*, *McCleskey*, 107 S. Ct. at 1770; Washington v. Davis, 426 U.S. 229 (1976).

[70] *See* Personnel Adm'r of Mass. v. Feeney, 442 U.S. 256, 274–75 (1979) (upholding governmental preferences for veterans against a sex discrimination challenge); Village of Arlington Heights v. Metropolitan Hous. Dev. Corp., 429 U.S. 252, 264–71 (1977) (upholding a rezoning decision against a racial discrimination claim lacking proof of discriminatory intent); *Davis*, 426 U.S. at 246 (upholding the use of a civil service exam despite its racially disproportionate impact). *See generally* Binion, *"Intent" and Equal Protection: A Reconsideration*, 1983 SUP. CT. REV. 397, 447–56 (advocating strict scrutiny without an intent requirement).

upon a showing that the decisionmaker "selected or reaffirmed a particular course of action at least in part 'because of' and not merely 'in spite of' its adverse effects upon an identifiable group."[71] The Justices have demanded proof, in other words, that officials were "out to get" a person or group on account of race. The Court has thus forced equal protection claims to assume the form of allegations of selective prosecution. Typically, such allegations are difficult to prove. Officials now rarely express their prejudices openly, even when they seek self-consciously to harm a person or group on the basis of race.[72] And the doctrine of purposeful discrimination insulates entirely many of the unconscious ways in which prejudiced social values give rise to differential treatment on the basis of race.[73]

Although the Court has imposed particularly stringent evidentiary standards in racial discrimination cases, it has demonstrated a willingness to infer discriminatory purpose from extraordinary disparities in certain circumstances. In *Yick Wo v. Hopkins*,[74] the Court granted habeas corpus relief to a Chinese man jailed for violating an ordinance that had been administered in such a way that all but one white applicant had received a permit to operate laundries while each of more than 200 Chinese applicants had been rejected.[75] Similarly, in *Gomillion v. Lightfoot*,[76] the Court invalidated an electoral redistricting in Tuskegee, Alabama that excluded from the city 395 of 400 black voters without excluding a single white voter.[77] Arguably, the statistics presented in *McCleskey* are sufficiently stark to qualify the case for res ipsa loquitur status on the *Yick Wo* or *Gomillion* model.

The Court, however, has rejected the claims of other petitioners that relied overwhelmingly on evidence of disproportionate effects to trigger a prima facie finding of discriminatory intent. In *National Educational Association v. South Carolina*,[78] the Court upheld the state's use of an examination for public school teachers even though it disqualified 83% of black applicants but only 17.5% of white ap-

---

[71] *Feeney*, 442 U.S. at 279.

[72] Ironically, in past eras, when white officials did openly express their purpose to single out and burden blacks on the basis of race, the Supreme Court declared legislative purpose immaterial as a constitutional concern. The Mississippi Supreme Court candidly admitted, for instance, that those who amended that state's constitution in 1890 "swept the field of expedients, to obstruct the exercise of suffrage by the negro race." Williams v. Mississippi, 170 U.S. 213, 222 (1898) (quoting Ratcliff v. Beale, 20 So. 865 (Miss. 1896)). The United States Supreme Court concluded, however, that "nothing tangible can be deduced from this." 170 U.S. at at 222.

[73] *See generally* Lawrence, *The Id, the Ego, and Equal Protection: Reckoning With Unconscious Racism*, 39 STAN. L. REV. 317 (1987).

[74] 118 U.S. 356 (1885).

[75] *See id.* at 361–63.

[76] 364 U.S. 339 (1960).

[77] *See id.* at 341, 347–48.

[78] 434 U.S. 1026 (1978) (mem.).

plicants, had not been certified as job-related, was not intended by its authors to be used for the function to which South Carolina officials applied it, and was applied in a state with a long history of racial mistreatment of blacks in general and black teachers in particular.[79] Similarly, in *City of Mobile v. Bolden*,[80] the Court upheld an at-large voting scheme in Mobile, Alabama, even though the plaintiff proved that it had had the effect of preventing the election of any black candidates to the three-seat city commission for nearly seventy years in a city in which Negroes comprised approximately 35% of the population.[81]

McCleskey is in line with these latter decisions. No "smoking gun" was produced. Moreover, McCleskey's race-of-the-victim claim does not comfortably fit the doctrinal mold the Court has fashioned to protect persons or groups from officials who intend to harm them. There have been eras in the nation's history when states, as a matter of official policy, treated the murder of blacks less seriously than the murder of whites.[82] That, however, is not the type of conduct at issue in *McCleskey*. At issue is the legal significance of discrete, isolated decisions that are susceptible to a non-racial explanation when considered individually, but reveal a pattern clearly shaped by racial sentiment when considered en masse. McCleskey sought to bring one such pattern, delineated by race-of-the-victim statistics, within the boundaries of the Court's conception of purposeful discrimination. With some judicial solicitude this task could have been accomplished. Doing so, however, would have required the Justices to make a special effort, while declining to do so was relatively easy: the latter course simply meant following an established line of substantive, evidentiary, and procedural precepts.

A different issue is raised by critics who charge that *McCleskey* defies the longstanding view that allegations of unfairness with respect to the death penalty are entitled to special judicial solicitude.[83] Justice Blackmun complained, for example, that the *McCleskey* Court gave

---

[79] *See id.* at 1026–27 (White, J., dissenting).

[80] 446 U.S. 55 (1980).

[81] *See id.* at 58–59, 68–74.

[82] *See infra* pp. 1411–12.

[83] For examples of this special solicitude, see Reid v. Covert, 354 U.S. 1, 77 (1957) (Harlan, J., concurring) ("So far as capital cases are concerned, I think they stand on quite a different footing than other offenses. In such cases the law is especially sensitive to demands for . . . procedural fairness."); and Stein v. New York, 346 U.S. 156, 196 (1953) ("When the penalty is death, we, like state court judges, are tempted to strain the evidence and even, in close cases, the law in order to give a doubtfully condemned man another chance."). *See also* Hamilton v. Alabama, 368 U.S. 52, 55 (1961); Williams v. Georgia, 349 U.S. 375, 391 (1955); Andres v. United States, 333 U.S. 740, 752 (1948); Powell v. Alabama, 287 U.S. 45, 71–72 (1932); Diaz v. United States, 223 U.S. 442, 455 (1912).

"a new meaning" to the notion that "death is different" by applying lesser rather than greater scrutiny to the state's decisionmaking process in the capital punishment context.[84] But in cases prior to *McCleskey*, the Court had sufficiently ignored or minimized the "death is different" idea to raise strong doubts regarding its continuing significance as an aspect of the Court's death penalty jurisprudence.[85] After all, the Court had already applied the rules of procedural forfeiture[86] and harmless error[87] to capital cases and had already ruled that it may be appropriate for federal appellate courts to establish special summary procedures to prevent delays in the carrying out of executions.[88] True, most of the Justices have acknowledged that death is different when compared to other punishments. Before *McCleskey*, however, the majority of them also clearly had demonstrated a decreased willingness to believe that this difference matters very much.[89]

As a capital sentencing case, *McCleskey* occupies a particularly sensitive place at the intersection of criminal and race relations law. Allegations involving unfairness with respect to both race relations[90] and the death penalty[91] have widely been viewed as claims that deserve special sensitivity from the courts. But *McCleskey* highlights the extent to which these conventional generalizations misdescribe the actual course of Supreme Court decisionmaking in the era of the Burger and Rehnquist Courts. Particularly with respect to the constitutional law of race relations, the Court is far less supportive of complainants than conventional wisdom counsels: whereas proof of illicit purpose is not essential to a variety of other constitutional

---

84 *McCleskey*, 107 S. Ct. at 1796 (Blackmun, J., dissenting).

85 *See generally* Amsterdam, *In Favorem Mortis: The Supreme Court and Capital Punishment*, HUM. RTS., Winter 1987, at 14.

86 *See* Smith v. Murray, 106 S. Ct. 2661, 2668–69 (1986) (rejecting "the suggestion that there is anything 'fundamentally unfair' about enforcing procedural default rules in cases devoid of any substantial claim that the alleged error undermined the accuracy of the guilt or sentencing determination").

87 *See* Skipper v. South Carolina, 476 U.S. 1, 6–10 (1986); Note, *Deadly Mistakes: Harmless Error in Capital Sentencing*, 54 U. CHI. L. REV. 740, 749 (1987) (noting that "the Court has never distinguished capital sentencing from other types of cases when deciding whether to apply harmless error rules").

88 *See* Barefoot v. Estelle, 463 U.S. 880, 889 (1983).

89 *See* Amsterdam, *supra* note 85.

90 For instance, all governmental classifications that refer to race are subject to heightened judicial scrutiny. *See, e.g.*, Wygant v. Jackson Bd. of Educ., 476 U.S. 267, 274 (1986) (plurality opinion) (arguing that any expressly racial preference, inluding those favoring historically oppressed groups, must be subjected to "'a most searching examination'" (quoting Fullilove v. Klutznick, 448 U.S. 448, 491 (1980))); Palmore v. Sidoti, 466 U.S. 429, 432 (1984) (arguing that racial classifications are subject to "the most exacting scrutiny"); Korematsu v. United States, 323 U.S. 214, 216 (1944) (stating that "all legal restrictions which curtail the civil rights of a single racial group are immediately suspect").

91 *See supra* note 83.

claims,[92] it has been deemed the *sine qua non* of an equal protection challenge.

The previous discussion has served to rebut sentimental claims that *McCleskey* constitutes a marked departure from past Supreme Court practice. If the decision disappoints, it does so on some basis other than recent precedent, for the majority cannot rightly be accused of having promulgated a startling ruling. To the contrary, *McCleskey* was all too predictable.

III. *McCLESKEY* AND FAILURE IN JUDICIAL CRAFT AND SUBSTANCE

There are, however, other lines along which *McCleskey* can legitimately be criticized. My critique proceeds along two. The first discusses *McCleskey* in terms of judicial craft. I maintain that apart from its substantive demerits, the opinion is poorly argued, revealing disturbing features of the Court's perception of its powers and responsibilities. The second questions whether the *McCleskey* Court's equal protection doctrine effectively addresses the type of racial oppression that the Baldus statistics describe. I argue that its doctrine is woefully inadequate.

A. McCleskey *and Problems of Judicial Craft*

In the same way that the fight against bad English is far from frivolous, so too is the fight against bad judicial opinions far from insignificant. Just as "the slovenliness of our language makes it easier for us to have foolish thoughts,"[93] so too does slovenly judicial analysis facilitate misunderstandings about the mechanics and objects of judicial power. The candid, careful making of distinctions resides at the heart of judging. Line drawing is, as Professor Henkin has ob-

---

[92] Under the first amendment and even without any allegation of illicit purpose, the Court has invalidated the application of laws having an adverse impact on freedom of expression or freedom of religion. *See, e.g.*, *In re* Primus, 436 U.S. 412 (1978); Wisconsin v. Yoder, 406 U.S. 205 (1972); Sherbert v. Verner, 374 U.S. 398 (1963). Similarly, under the sixth amendment and even without any allegation of illicit purpose, the Court has invalidated convictions in which the defendant did not enjoy the assistance of counsel. *See, e.g.*, Argersinger v. Hamlin, 407 U.S. 25 (1972); Gideon v. Wainwright, 372 U.S. 335 (1963); Powell v. Alabama, 287 U.S. 45 (1932). For commentary elaborating upon the Court's restrictive interpretation of the equal protection clause, particularly in the race relations context, see Binion, cited above in note 70, at 416–20; Eisenberg, *Disproportionate Impact and Illicit Motive: Theories of Constitutional Adjudication*, 52 N.Y.U. L. REV. 36, 165–66 (1977); and Perry, *The Disproportionate Impact Theory of Racial Discrimination*, 125 U. PA. L. REV. 540, 556 (1977).

[93] G. ORWELL, *Politics and the English Language*, in A COLLECTION OF ESSAYS 162 (Anchor Books ed. 1954).

served, "the symbol of rationality in the judicial process."[94] The line drawing in *McCleskey*, however, is gracelessly executed. The Court's opinion evinces an awareness of the variability of the point at which it may choose to infer discrimination from a given set of facts. The Justices demanded, for instance, that McCleskey's evidentiary showing be *especially* convincing because he was challenging discretionary decisions "at the heart of the State's criminal justice system."[95] Yet the opinion fails even to address the obvious counterargument that it is precisely because the challenged conduct arises in a criminal justice setting that the Court should be *more*, not less, sensitive to any hint of racial inequality. After all, the Court itself has noted that while racial discrimination is "odious in all respects," it "is especially pernicious in the administration of justice."[96]

Invoking the judicial analogue to the domino theory, Justice Powell proceeded to suggest that a victory for McCleskey's challenge to capital sentencing would set the stage for equal protection challenges to *all* criminal punishments by *all* disadvantaged groups. In detailing the potential costs of judicial intervention, however, the Court barely considered boundaries of containment which, if adopted, could minimize the expense feared. The Court's opinion says virtually nothing, for instance, in response to the dissenters' charge that the majority completely disregarded the "death is different" distinction. There are, as I have noted, several prior cases indicating the limited extent to which that distinction makes a significant difference to the Court.[97] Still, the majority's silence is — or should be — embarrassing, particularly in light of *Booth v. Maryland*,[98] another case authored by Justice Powell, which was decided just three weeks after *McCleskey*. *Booth* invalidated a state statute that allowed victim impact statements to be introduced in capital cases. The Court, however, carefully reserved the question of their admissibility in other settings, thereby recognizing the distinction between capital and noncapital contexts.

The *McCleskey* opinion does acknowledge race as a possible limiting boundary. But the Court ultimately rejected it because of apprehension that the boundary would fail to prevent members of other groups — "even" women[99] — from launching equal protection challenges to criminal punishments. To help justify closing the door on blacks, the paradigmatic "out-group" in our political culture, the Court argued that no "logical" reason exists for distinguishing racial or gen-

---

94 Henkin, *The Supreme Court, 1967 Term — Foreword: On Drawing Lines*, 82 HARV. L. REV. 63, 64 (1968).

95 *McCleskey*, 107 S. Ct. at 1769.

96 Rose v. Mitchell, 443 U.S. 545, 555 (1979).

97 *See supra* notes 84–89.

98 107 S. Ct. 2529 (1987).

99 *McCleskey*, 107 S. Ct. at 1779–80.

der bias from any other sort of invidious bias — a bias, for instance, against facial unattractiveness.[100] The life of the law, however, is not logic but experience.[101] And experience teaches that in the United States racial prejudice — particularly that which is anti-black — displays an intensity and persistence that is distinguishable from all other biases.[102] Moreover, there exists textual warrant in the Constitution for distinguishing racial and, to a lesser extent, gender bias from other sorts of prejudice.[103]

The Court's response to McCleskey's allegations contrasts sharply with its response to attacks on the administration of capital sentencing in other contexts. In *Woodson v. North Carolina*,[104] one of the justifications noted for invalidating mandatory death sentences was that juries would choose to free certain defendants, regardless of guilt, rather than consign them automatically to death. Part of the empirical basis of the plurality opinion that Justice Powell joined was anecdotal: "Nineteenth century journalists, statesmen, and jurists repeatedly observed that jurors were often deterred from convicting palpably guilty men of first degree murder under mandatory statutes."[105] Another part consisted of decisions by Congress and most states to authorize discretionary jury sentencing.[106] Although these data lend some support to the Court's hypothesis, the evidence fails to come close to satisfying the heavy burden of persuasion the Court imposed in *McCleskey*. To buttress its position that mandatory sentences offend "contemporary standards of decency,"[107] the *Woodson* plurality noted dicta from prior opinions, studies indicating that juries armed with discretion condemn to death only a relatively small percentage of people, and polls showing that many people generally supportive of capital punishment nonetheless want it imposed on a discretionary rather than a mandatory basis.[108] Here again, the softness of the evidence is striking when compared to McCleskey's statistics and corroborative historical data.

Similarly, in *Booth* the Court concluded that:

---

[100] *See id.*

[101] *See* O.W. HOLMES, THE COMMON LAW 1 (1881).

[102] *But cf.* Regents of the Univ. of Cal. v. Bakke, 438 U.S. 265, 295 (1978) (opinion of Powell, J.) ("[T]he white 'majority' itself is composed of various minority groups, most of which can lay claim to a history of prior discrimination at the hands of the State and private individuals.").

[103] *See* U.S. CONST. amends. XV, XIX; *see also McCleskey*, 107 S. Ct. at 1792 (Brennan, J., dissenting) ("Race is a consideration whose influence is expressly constitutionally proscribed.").

[104] 428 U.S. 280 (1976) (plurality opinion).

[105] *Id.* at 293.

[106] *See id.* at 293–95 & n.30.

[107] *Id.* at 294–95.

[108] *See id.* at 295–99 & n.34.

> Allowing the jury to rely on a [victim impact statement] . . . could result in imposing the death sentence because of factors about which the defendant was unaware [for example, the existence and characteristics of the victim's family], and that were irrelevant to the decision to kill. The evidence thus could divert the jury's attention away from the defendant's background and record, and the circumstances of the crime.[109]

This statement was appropriately couched as a conditional proposition, for the Court could point to no direct indications that these dangers had, in fact, materialized. Nor did the Court attempt to base its estimation of risk on any basis other than common sense and intuition.[110] The *McCleskey* Court stated that proof of racial selectivity would have to be "exceptionally clear," because the petitioner called into question the exercise of discretion essential to the criminal justice process.[111] Yet, without referring to any empirical verification whatsoever, the *Booth* Court held in favor of the petitioner even though he, like McCleskey, called into question the administration of juror discretion.

Deficient argumentation also characterizes the Court's handling of McCleskey's historical evidence. Prior to the Civil War, Georgia, like most slave states, enacted laws that expressly demanded racially discriminatory criminal punishments keyed to the race of both perpetrators and victims. For instance, conviction for raping a white woman carried a prison sentence of two to twenty years for a white man, while the same offense carried a mandatory death sentence for a Negro.[112] At the same time, the rape of a black woman by either a black man or a white man carried the far less imposing sentence of "fine and imprisonment, at the discretion of the Court."[113] Different standards also applied to homicide, with the most severe penalty reserved, of course, for black-on-white killings.[114] In the aftermath of slavery, Southern officials continued to administer the death penalty, and indeed the entire apparatus of the criminal law, in a patently racist fashion.[115] Racist administration of criminal law did not wither

---

109 Booth v. Maryland, 107 S. Ct. 2529, 2534 (1987).

110 The lack of any empirical evidence was pointed out by the dissenters. *See id.* at 2541 n.3 (White, J., dissenting). Common sense and intuition are valuable sources of judgment. The point here is to note the inconsistency with which the Court repairs to these resources.

111 107 S. Ct. at 1769.

112 *See id.* at 1786 (Brennan, J., dissenting) (citing GA. PENAL CODE pt. 4, tit. 1, div. 4, § 4704 (1861)).

113 *Id.* (citing GA. PENAL CODE pt. 4, tit. 1, div. 4, § 4249 (1861)).

114 *See id.* at 1786–87.

115 "[T]he legislative history of the Fourteenth Amendment reminds us that discriminatory enforcement of States' criminal laws was a matter of great concern for the drafters." *Id.* at 1795. (Blackmun, J., dissenting). Professor Leon Litwack observes that "[t]he double standard

away; it persisted. In 1972, when the Court struck down the Georgia capital sentencing statute in *Furman v. Georgia*,[116] a number of Justices acknowledged the existence of credible evidence indicating that race had continued to serve as a basis for inflicting the death sentence.[117] Moreover, if one views capital punishment in Georgia in light of experience derived from other contemporaneous aspects of the state's criminal justice system, the historical argument in favor of McCleskey's contention gains even more force.[118]

The Court, however, curtly dismissed McCleskey's reference to historical context:

> [McCleskey's "historical evidence"] focuses on Georgia laws in force during and just after the Civil War. Of course, the "historical background of the decision is one evidentiary source" for proof of intentional discrimination. But unless historical evidence is reasonably contemporaneous with the challenged decision, it has little probative value. Although the history of racial discrimination in this country is undeniable, we cannot accept official actions taken long ago as evidence of current intent.[119]

The Court's comment, however, misrepresents McCleskey's evidence and argument. McCleskey did not call attention solely to laws in force "during and just after the Civil War." Rather, he focused on the *continuity* of formal and informal racial discrimination in Georgia's criminal justice system from the slavery era to the present moment. That background illuminates the statistical data that comprised the core of McCleskey's case. As Justice Brennan rightly observed, it is "unrealistic to ignore the influence of history in assessing the plau-

---

of white justice was nowhere clearer . . . than in the disparate punishments meted out to whites and blacks convicted of similar crimes." He quotes a Freedmen's Bureau officer in Georgia who doubted that whites would easily be persuaded of the moral equality of black and white victims of violence: "The best men in the State admit that no jury would convict a white man for killing a freedman, or fail to hang a negro who had killed a white man in self-defence [sic]." L. LITWACK, BEEN IN THE STORM SO LONG: THE AFTERMATH OF SLAVERY 285–86 (1979).

[116] 408 U.S. 238 (1972).

[117] *See id.* at 256–57 (Douglas, J., concurring); *id.* at 310 (Stewart, J., concurring); *id.* at 364 (Marshall, J., concurring).

[118] An egregious example of contemporary racism in Georgia's criminal justice system is displayed by Amadeo v. Kemp, 816 F.2d 1502, *reh'g denied*, 822 F.2d 65 (11th Cir. 1987), *cert. granted*, 108 S. Ct. 257 (1987). In that case, a prisoner has sought federal habeas corpus relief with new evidence indicating that in the county where he was convicted, the prosecutor advised the local jury commission to compile jury lists that would underrepresent blacks by a percentage just small enough to avoid challenges that could successfully be asserted on the basis solely of statistical evidence. *See* id. at 1506–07.

[119] 107 S. Ct. at 1770 n.20 (citations omitted). In the district court, Judge Forrester reacted more strongly, charging that McCleskey's historical references typified "stereotypical prejudice against Southern jurisdictions." McCleskey v. Zant, 580 F. Supp. at 368 n.50.

sible implications of [the statistical] evidence."[120] The Court's suggestion that the legacy of Georgia's history shines no light on the Baldus statistics offends common sense; it makes one laugh — and cry.[121]

B. McCleskey, *Candor, and the Concept of Purposeful Discrimination*

One of the most interesting features of the Court's *McCleskey* opinion is its oscillation between candor and obfuscation.[122] In the end, the Court chose self-consciously to prefer the evils revealed by the Baldus studies to those that they believed would be set loose by ruling differently. The Court's opinion on this score is refreshingly candid. It admitted that legal concepts often viewed as autonomous, independent variables in fact consist of manipulable, dependent variables. Hence, the Court's opinion forthrightly declared that the amount of evidence the Justices require in order to "find"[123] purposeful discrimination depends upon their assessment of the government practice being challenged. Because the majority deemed discretion in capital sentencing to be "essential," it demanded "exceptionally clear" proof before they would infer intentional discrimination on the basis of race.[124] The Court also noted that its decision was affected by apprehensions regarding the generative power of the petitioner's claim. "[I]f we accepted McCleskey's claim," Justice Powell worriedly observed, "we could soon be faced with similar claims [from members of other groups] as to other types of penalty."[125]

Justices Brennan and Blackmun both rebuked the Court for its hesitance to find a violation of the equal protection clause because of unease over remedial costs. The Court's rationale, Justice Brennan

---

120 107 S. Ct. at 1788 (Brennan, J., dissenting); *see also id.* at 1786 ("Georgia's legacy of a race-conscious criminal justice system . . . indicate[s] that McCleskey's claim is not a fanciful product of mere statistical artiface.").

121 *Cf.* Black, *The Lawfulness of the Segregation Decisions*, 69 YALE L.J. 421, 424 (1960) (reserving the right to exercise "one of the sovereign prerogatives of philosophers" — that of laughter — at the suggestion that a segregation system designed to confine one race to an inferior station might represent equality).

122 For an insightful discussion of the place of candor in judging, see Shapiro, *In Defense of Judicial Candor*, 100 HARV. L. REV. 731 (1987).

123 In their classic article, Lon Fuller and William Perdue, Jr., observed that "the things which the law of damages purports to 'measure' and 'determine' . . . are in considerable part its own creations," and that the process of "[measuring and determining] them is really a part of the process of creating them." Fuller & Perdue, *The Reliance Interest in Contract Damages*, 46 YALE L.J. 52 (1936). The same holds true for "finding" racial discrimination, which does not exist as a predetermined thing, but is called into existence as a legally cognizable phenomenon by being found. The process of finding racial discrimination is part of the process of creating it as a social problem requiring a remedy.

124 *McCleskey*, 107 S. Ct. at 1769.

125 *Id.* at 1779.

acidly observed, "seems to suggest a fear of too much justice."[126] Similarly, Justice Blackmun described this element of the Court's opinion as possibly its "most disturbing aspect."[127]

The dissenters' critique is well taken but far too limited. For one thing, they refrained from repudiating the primary manifestation of the attitude they reject, the central conceptual device with which the Court rationalizes *McCleskey* — the doctrine that a finding of purposeful discrimination is necessary to assert successfully an equal protection claim. That doctrine itself was born of a fear of too much justice. When the Court announced in *Washington v. Davis*[128] that discriminatory purpose constituted the *sine qua non* of equal protection claims, it stated as an important justification the need to limit the intrusiveness of federal judicial remedies.[129] Apprehensions over perceived remedial costs have prompted the Court increasingly to narrow the definition of violations.[130] The Justices have made the violations they are willing to recognize dependent upon the remedies they are willing to provide.[131] They have tailored declarations of

---

[126] *Id.* at 1791 (Brennan, J., dissenting).

[127] *Id.* at 1805 (Blackmun, J., dissenting).

[128] 426 U.S. 229 (1976).

[129] *See id.* at 248 (suggesting that an alternative ruling "would be far reaching and would raise serious questions about, and perhaps invalidate, a whole range of tax, welfare, public service, and licensing statutes"); *see also* L. TRIBE, AMERICAN CONSTITUTIONAL LAW § 16-20 (2d ed. 1988) ("The Problem of Discriminatory Purpose: When Reservations About Remedies Masquerade as Questions About the Existence of Constitutional Violations"); Binion, *supra* note 70, at 406–08 ("Significant support for the intent rule stems from concern about potentially far-reaching judicial remedies."); Sellers, *The Impact of Intent on Equal Protection Jurisprudence*, 84 DICK. L. REV. 363, 387 (1980) ("By its use of the intent rule, the Supreme Court has essentially provided that a finding of a violation of the equal protection clause turns on the manageability and burdensomeness of the remedies that would be fashioned to redress the wrong.").

[130] *See* City of Mobile v. Bolden, 446 U.S. 55 (1980); Personnel Adm'r of Mass. v. Feeney, 442 U.S. 256 (1979); Village of Arlington Heights v. Metropolitan Hous. Dev. Corp., 429 U.S. 252 (1977). Writing in 1983, Professor Binion observed that the Court had erected "a progressively more impenetrable barrier of 'intent'" insulating defendants from equal protection challenges. *See* Binion, *supra* note 70, at 397. No decision since 1983 requires any modification of her observation.

[131] This strategy played an important role in several crucial cases in the early 1970's that effected the constitutional retrenchment in which we are currently stuck. *See* Milliken v. Bradley, 418 U.S. 717 (1974); San Antonio Indep. School Dist. v. Rodriguez, 411 U.S. 1 (1973). In *Milliken*, for instance, the Supreme Court drastically reduced the scope of the equal protection clause in the context of public schooling despite a violation found and affirmed by the courts below. The Court's discussion of the scope of the clause was dominated, however, by expressions of apprehension over remedial costs. *See Milliken*, 418 U.S. at 742–44. The remedy imposed by the lower courts would require, the Court observed, "consolidation of 54 independent school districts historically administered as separate units into a vast new super school district . . . . Entirely apart from the logistical and other serious problems attending large-scale transportation of students, the consolidation would give rise to an array of other problems in financing and operating this new school system." *Id.* at 743. The Court narrowed the scope of the violation

rights to fit their perceptions of acceptable remedies. Unpersuaded in *McCleskey* that an acceptable solution could be found, the Court obviated the remedial question simply by declining to find a constitutional problem.[132]

Defining violations of rights on the basis of concern over remedies is an approach to constitutional decisionmaking ridden with pernicious vices.[133] It leads the Justices to obscure — for themselves and society as a whole — the reality they purportedly address. Mesmerized by what they thought they would have to do if they declared a violation in *McCleskey*, the Justices in the majority paid distressingly little attention to the factual predicate of McCleskey's allegation.[134] The Court was confronted by the most extensive study of capital sentencing in American history, a study that presented patterns of racial disparity that are undeniably suspicious, regardless of one's eventual judgment as to the legal status of McCleskey's claim. Yet, in the face of this evidence, the Court stated blandly that "[a]t most [the study] indicates a discrepancy that appears to correlate with race"[135] — a statement as correct and as vacuous as one declaring, say, that "at most studies on lung cancer indicate a discrepancy that appears to correlate with smoking." Paralyzed by fear that seeing would entail doing, the Justices inflicted upon themselves a myopia reminiscent of the one that

---

found by the lower courts and in so doing reduced the attendant scope of the remedy. The Court never explicitly stated that its decision was based on remedial considerations. Scholars of widely divergent views, however, agree that fears generated by the perceived consequences of lower courts' remedies drove the Supreme Court to limit the ambit of the right in question. From right to left, see J. WILKINSON, FROM BROWN TO BAKKE 223–29 (1979); Fiss, *The Supreme Court, 1978 Term — Foreword: The Forms of Justice*, 93 HARV. L. REV. 1, 47 (1979); Note, *Judicial Right Declaration and Entrenched Discrimination*, 94 YALE L.J. 1741, 1750–56 (1985) (authored by Gene Sperling) [hereinafter Note, *Judicial Right Declaration*]; Note, *Making the Violation Fit the Remedy: The Intent Standard and Equal Protection Law*, 92 YALE L.J. 328 (1982); and Freeman, *Legitimizing Racial Discrimination Through Antidiscrimination Law: A Critical Review of Supreme Court Doctrine*, 62 MINN. L. REV. 1049, 1107–11 (1978). Gene Sperling correctly observes that Justice Powell's opinions are typically "the most susceptible to the claim that remedial concerns are affecting both the scope and the findings of constitutional violations." Note, *Judicial Right Declaration*, *supra*, at 1754–55 n.76.

[132] In the oral argument before the Court, Justices adverted on several occassions to the remedial difficulties posed by the case. *See* Transcript of Oral Argument at 17, 27, 29, *McCleskey* (No. 84-6811) (noting remedial problems that might be posed by ruling in favor of McCleskey); *see also supra* pp. 1401–02.

[133] For useful commentaries on the relationship between judicial declaration of rights and remedies, see generally L. TRIBE, cited above in note 129, at 1512–13; Chayes, *The Role of the Judge in Public Law Litigation*, 89 HARV. L. REV. 1281 (1976); Fiss, cited above in note 131; Fletcher, *The Discretionary Constitution: Institutional Remedies and Judicial Legitimacy*, 91 YALE L.J. 635 (1982); Gewirtz, *Remedies and Resistance*, 92 YALE L.J. 587 (1983); and Note, *Judicial Right Declaration*, cited above in note 131.

[134] *Cf.* S. GROSS & R. MAURO, *supra* note 40, ch. 10 (arguing that a striking feature of *McCleskey* is the "evaporation of the factual question with which the case began: Does the Baldus study demonstrate race discrimination in capital sentencing in Georgia?").

[135] *McCleskey*, 107 S. Ct. at 1777.

afflicted the Court during the reign of *Plessy v. Ferguson.*[136] Nothing better illustrates the Court's resolute unwillingness to face facts than its statement that it would "decline to assume that what is unexplained is invidious."[137] The petitioner, of course, was not asking the Court to make any such assumption. Rather, he offered into evidence a comprehensive study showing that certain patterns in capital sentencing cannot plausibly be explained by any variable other than race. The prisoner of unshakeable assumptions in this case was not McCleskey, but the Court itself.

An important consequence of the Court's whitewashing of disturbing realities is that it conveys the wrong message to other officials who could potentially provide alternative remedial responses. The Court itself suggested that McCleskey should have taken his complaint to legislative bodies, not the federal courts.[138] But by allowing concerns over remedy to determine its assessment of the social reality at issue, the Court's opinion miseducates the executives, legislators, constituents, and other possible participants in the controversy. By suggesting that there exists no real racial problem in Georgia's administration of the death penalty, the Court makes discussion of any remedy far more difficult: in the wake of *McCleskey*, those seeking reform must attempt to change a popular but unfairly administered institution on the basis, in part, of racial disparities the Supreme Court of the United States appears to have found completely untroubling.[139]

In dissent, Justice Brennan insinuated that the *McCleskey* decision reflected the majority's own racial biases when he remarked that the

---

[136] 163 U.S. 537 (1896). The New York Times put the point nicely:

> For the Court to ignore the obvious evokes the infamous 1896 Plessy v. Ferguson decision. 'Separate but equal' is discriminatory only if blacks choose to see it that way, the Court said then. What the Court says now, in the face of telling evidence that the victim's race is often decisive in capital cases, is, well that's just a theory.

Discrimination in Death? Yes 5–4, N.Y. Times, Apr. 24, 1987, at A30, col. 1. What Professor Gross says about the court of appeals applies as well to the Supreme Court: "The world is not as the Court would have it. . . . [T]he Court seems to have been bound and determined to conclude that there is no evidence of racial discrimination in capital sentencing in Georgia." Gross, *supra* note 11, at 1321–22.

[137] 107 S. Ct. at 1778.

[138] *Id.* at 1781.

[139] Professor Tribe comments that the *McCleskey* decision "arguably left room for Congress, exercising its enforcement power under § 5 of the fourteenth amendment, to regulate state death penalty procedures that, whether intentionally or not, whether consciously or unconsciously, discriminate against the black murderers of white victims and against the black victims of white murderers." *See* L. TRIBE, *supra* note 129, at 1514 n.97. Representative Conyers has introduced a bill that seeks to address the type of racial disparity that arose in *McCleskey*. *See* H.R. 4442, 100th Cong., 2d Sess., 134 CONG. REC. E1174 (daily ed. April 21, 1988). But obtaining congressional action regulating capital sentencing — an implausible scenario at best, given the popularity of the death penalty and predictable opposition on federalism grounds — was rendered even more difficult by the Court's apparent lack of concern over the disparities revealed by the Baldus statistics.

Court had fallen victim to the tempting illusion "that minorities on death row share a fate in no way connected to our own."[140] One implication of his observation is that the Court's decision reflected a variant of precisely what McCleskey accused Georgia's officials of exhibiting: racially selective patterns of emotional response. There is considerable intuitive appeal to this explanation: given the pervasiveness and power of racial sentiments, it stands to reason that Justices no less than other citizens are influenced by them.[141]

Moreover, the manner in which the *McCleskey* majority articulated and defended its decision shows an egregious disregard for the sensibilities of black Americans.[142] When it has addressed even the most

---

[140] *See* 107 S. Ct. at 1794 (Brennan, J., dissenting); *cf.* Maher v. Roe, 432 U.S. 464, 483 (1977) (Brennan, J., dissenting) (accusing the Court, in its decision upholding a state's anti-abortion funding policy, of displaying "a distressing insensitivity to the plight of impoverished pregnant women").

[141] Far too little systematic attention has been focused upon the influence of political, racial, moral, and idiosyncratic factors in judicial decisionmaking. Consider, for instance, the importance of Chief Justice Burger's sympathy and admiration for the Amish in Wisconsin v. Yoder, 406 U.S. 205, 212–13 (1972), which prohibited enforcement of a compulsory school-attendance law against the "law-abiding" and "self-sufficient" Amish. This is, of course, an old complaint. *See, e.g.*, Brest, *Who Decides?*, 58 S. CAL. L. REV. 661 (1985); Cohen, *Transcendental Nonsense and the Functional Approach*, 35 COLUM. L. REV. 809, 845 (1935) ("We are still in the stage of guesswork and accidentally collected information, when it comes to formulating the social forces which mold the course of judicial decision.").

There is some useful literature on the racial sentiments of jurists in the past. *See, e.g.*, Glennon, *Justice Henry Billings Brown: Values in Tension*, 44 U. COLO. L. REV. 553, 600 (1973); Rogat, *Mr. Justice Holmes: A Dissenting Opinion*, 15 STAN. L. REV. 254, 255 (1963); Westin, *John Marshall Harlan and the Constitutional Rights of Negroes: The Transformation of a Southerner*, 66 YALE L.J. 637 (1957). There is little systematic analysis of the racial sentiments of sitting jurists and the extent to which these sentiments affect their judicial performance. Scholarly inquiry into this subject would probably be viewed with distaste by many legal academics. *Cf.* Cohen, *supra*, at 846 (suggesting that a systematic study of personal, political, and moral predilections of judges would be considered "disrespectable"). For preliminary ventures into this difficult terrain, see D. BELL, RACE, RACISM AND AMERICAN LAW 39–44 (2d. ed. 1980); Lawrence, cited above in note 73, at 380 (1987) ("Judges are not immune from our culture's racism."); and Steel, *Nine Men in Black Who Think White*, N.Y. Times, Oct. 13, 1968, § 6 (Magazine), at 56.

[142] Perhaps it is worth noting that the only two black judges who reviewed *McCleskey* — Judge Hatchett at the court of appeals and Justice Marshall at the Supreme Court — both ruled in McCleskey's favor. Judge Hatchett dissented in a laconic opinion. *See McCleskey*, 753 F.2d at 918–19 (Hatchett, C.J., dissenting in part and concurring in part). Justice Marshall was the only dissenter in the Supreme Court who did not write an opinion. His stony silence was unusual, as he typically expresses himself in race or capital cases of this magnitude. *See, e.g.*, Regents of the Univ. of Cal. v. Bakke, 438 U.S. 265, 387–402 (1978) (Marshall, J., concurring in the judgment in part and dissenting in part); Gregg v. Georgia, 428 U.S. 153, 231–41 (1976) (Marshall, J., dissenting). Although Justice Marshall has not indicated publicly what lay behind his decision to forgo writing an opinion, one speculative reading of his silence is that he sought to use this break with his own traditional practice to convey the extremity of his sense of alienation from the Court. Perhaps in his view the Court had issued an opinion beneath discussion.

blatant manifestations of white racism, the Court has been careful to avoid hurting the feelings of whites. For instance, when it finally invalidated de jure segregation, the Court refrained from stating fully and explicitly the purpose that segregation was meant to serve or the injuries that it imposed so destructively. Chief Justice Warren informed his colleagues that the opinion in *Brown v. Board of Education*[143] should be "non-rhetorical, unemotional and, above all, non-accusatory."[144] By contrast, in *McCleskey*, there is no hint of solicitude for the feelings of Afro-Americans. The Court made no attempt to assuage the inevitable anger and anxiety that the decision would generate within the black community. The rhetoric of the opinion displays a complacency disturbingly reminiscent of the Court's race relations opinions around the turn of the century.[145] As Professor Carter has observed, the Court's response to the Baldus statistics "was a labored 'So what?'"[146]

The Court's lack of concern for the feelings of blacks may be related to its very keen concern for the sensitivities of those — mainly whites — subject to being labeled "racist." One of the great achievements of social reform in American history has involved the stigmatization of overt racial prejudice. But this triumph in principle has produced an unforseen consequence in application: it is precisely the sense that racial discrimination is a terrible evil that inhibits the Justices from "finding" it in all but the clearest circumstances. Perhaps they assume that conduct so horrible must be plainly observable. Or perhaps their sense of the shamefulness of racism is so intense that they find it difficult to burden an official or agency with the moral opprobrium that the "racist" label connotes without absolutely positive proof of culpability.

One example of the paradoxical consequence of stigmatizing racism is illustrated by Justice Powell's reaction to the claim asserted in *Turner v. Murray*.[147] In *Turner*, the Court held that, in capital cases arising from interracial crimes, defendants are entitled to question jurors on the issue of racial bias. Justice Powell dissented vociferously, arguing that such a rule amounts to "a singularly unwise and unjus-

---

[143] 347 U.S. 483 (1954).

[144] *See* Burt, *Disorder in the Court: The Death Penalty and the Constitution*, 85 MICH. L. REV. 1741, 1762 n.107 (1987) (quoting Chief Justice Warren, Memorandum to Members of the Court (May 7, 1954), *quoted in* D. O'BRIEN, STORM CENTER: THE SUPREME COURT AND AMERICAN POLITICS 281 (1986)); *see also* Hutchinson, *Unanimity and Desegregation: Decision-making in the Supreme Court, 1948–1958*, 68 GEO. L.J. 1, 10–12 (1979) (discussing disagreements among the Justices over the tone appropriate for announcing the invalidation of racist policies).

[145] *See, e.g.*, Franklin v. South Carolina, 218 U.S. 161 (1910) (rejecting an equal protection challenge to racial disparities in jury selection); Thomas v. Texas, 212 U.S. 278 (1909) (same); Murray v. Louisiana, 163 U.S. 101 (1896) (same).

[146] Carter, *When Victims Happen to Be Black*, 98 YALE L.J. (forthcoming 1988).

[147] 476 U.S. 28 (1986).

tified presumption that capital jurors harbor latent racial bias."[148] The Court made no such presumption, however; it simply held that defendants, in cases involving racial violence, are entitled to question jurors on the issue of racial bias if their attorneys choose to do so. But Justice Powell's anxiety about wrongful stigmatization was so great that he resisted a rule that even implied that *some* jurors *might* harbor latent racial prejudice. If such a high level of resistance was generated by the modest rule pronounced in *Turner*, one can more fully comprehend the resistance generated by a claim that, if accepted, would have stigmatized as racist an entire state's system of capital punishment.[149]

The main doctrinal manifestation of the Court's decisionmaking strategy is its theory of purposeful discrimination. The great failing of that theory is its hopeless inadequacy as a tool for responding to racial oppression in its subtle modern guises. By conditioning the availability of a remedy under the fourteenth amendment on proof that a decisionmaker purposefully set out to harm a person or group because of race, Justice Powell and his colleagues display minds trapped by visions of old conquests — the battles against de jure segregation[150] and overt, intentional discrimination in the administration of statutes making no mention of race.[151] They articulate a conception of discrimination that ignores the chameleonlike ability of prejudice to adapt unobtrusively to new surroundings and, further, to hide itself even from those firmly within its grip. They manifest views attuned only to the most blatant deprivations of the equal protection of the laws.

The Court's theory of purposeful discrimination leaves untouched deeper layers of racially oppressive official action. One consists of hurtful decisions taken not because decisionmakers have designs against blacks but because decisionmakers leave blacks out of their designs. This phenomenon is relevant to the equal protection problem in *McCleskey* insofar as one theory of race-of-the-victim sentencing disparities posits that prosecutors, mindful of election, focus their scarce resources in ways that will please the most politically powerful elements of their constituencies. To the extent that blacks are politically weak in a given jurisdiction and less committed than whites to

---

148 *Id.* at 53 (Powell, J., dissenting).

149 Justice Brennan acknowledged the problem of creating resistance to accurate depictions of reality when he noted, as a defensive measure, that his historical review of Georgia criminal law "is not intended as a bill of indictment." *McCleskey*, 107 S. Ct. at 1788 (Brennan, J., dissenting).

150 *See, e.g.*, Brown v. Board of Educ., 374 U.S. 483 (1954) (invalidating de jure segregation in public schooling).

151 *See, e.g.*, Louisiana v. United States, 380 U.S. 145 (1965) (invalidating voter qualification tests that, as applied, served to exclude blacks from the franchise on the basis of race).

capital punishment,[152] heightened attentiveness to white-victim homicide is simply a "natural" outcome of majoritarian politics.[153] A virtue of the purposeful discrimination doctrine is the deference it shows to majoritarian politics; a vice is the insufficient attention it pays to the racially oppressive consequences of political choices untainted by any conscious intent to harm blacks.

Another level of racially oppressive conduct that often operates undisturbed by the Court's doctrine of purposeful discrimination includes practices that emerge from "the unconscious failure to extend to [blacks] the same recognition of humanity, and hence the same sympathy and care, given as a matter of course to [whites]."[154] This phenomenon, too, is directly relevant to the *McCleskey* problem, for race-of-the-victim disparities in sentencing probably reflect racially selective empathy more than racially selective hostility. The white officials who dominate the administration of criminal justice in Georgia — prosecutors, jurors, and judges — may show relatively more leniency in black-victim crimes not because of anti-black prejudice but rather because they relate more fully to the suffering of white victims; black victims remain strangers while white victims can be imagined as family or friends. In a society that remains largely segregated socially, white officials are simply less likely to identify with black victims.[155] So long, however, as officials refrain from explicitly confessing the racial selectivity of their sympathies,[156] it is unlikely

[152] Perhaps because anti-black racial discrimination has historically attended the administration of capital punishment in racially mixed communities, a relatively large percentage of blacks favor abolishing the death penalty. *See* Lockhart v. McCree, 476 U.S. 162, 201 (1986) (Marshall, J., dissenting) (stating that "opposition to capital punishment is significantly more prevalent among blacks than among whites"); Grigsby v. Marby, 569 F. Supp. 1273, 1293–94 (E.D. Ark. 1983) (surveying studies finding that proportionally more blacks than whites oppose the death penalty), *aff'd*, 758 F.2d 226 (8th Cir.), *rev'd sub nom.* Lockhart v. McCree, 476 U.S. 162 (1986); Hovey v. Superior Ct., 28 Cal. 3d 1, 56, 168 Cal. Rptr. 128, 165, 616 P.2d 1301, 1338–39 (1980) (finding that the disparity in views between blacks and whites on the death penalty has been increasing); White, *The Constitutional Invalidity of Convictions Imposed by Death-Qualified Juries*, 58 CORNELL L. REV. 1176, 1186 (1973) (quoting a Harris Poll finding that opposition to the death penalty is more prevalent among blacks than whites — 52% to 33%).

[153] *See* Zeisel, *supra* note 14, at 466–67.

[154] Brest, *The Supreme Court, 1975 Term — Foreword: In Defense of the Antidiscrimination Principle*, 90 HARV. L. REV. 1, 7–8 (1976) (citations omitted).

[155] *See* Gross & Mauro, *supra* note 25, at 108 (discussing racially selective sympathies of white jurors); *see also* Lempert, *supra* note 15, at 1113–14 (suggesting that racially selective leniency is a function of empathy); *infra* notes 239–241 and accompanying text.

The invisibility of the Negro to white decisionmakers is an extreme version of the way in which racial lines have prevented interracial empathy. No one has explored this theme more deeply and articulately than Ralph Ellison, who opens his classic novel *Invisible Man* with the following statement by his black protagonist: "I am an invisible man. . . . I am invisible, understand, simply because people refuse to see me . . . . [My invisibility] occurs because of a peculiar disposition of the eyes of those with whom I come in contact." R. ELLISON, INVISIBLE MAN 1 (1948). The Baldus statistics chart, in part, the invisibility of black victims of homicide.

[156] *Cf.* Note, *Battered Women and the Equal Protection Clause: Will the Constitution Help*

that the doctrine of purposeful discrimination will ever facilitate judicial intervention against the sort of conduct delineated by the Baldus study. The problems that this doctrine is capable of addressing suitably — action that is purposeful and openly aimed at harming a given group — is simply too far afield from the problem highlighted by the Baldus statistics.

IV. An Alternative Approach to *McCleskey*

In the previous section I set forth various criticisms of the Court's *McCleskey* opinion. In this section, I propose an alternative way of approaching the case that is different from that posited by the Court or argued by McCleskey. First, I reconceptualize the equal protection claim at issue as one that asserts the rights of the black community to an equal share of death penalty services. Second, I address the issue of standing that would lurk beneath such an assertion. Third, I set forth the vision of equal protection that should be brought to bear upon an argument that the Baldus statistics evidence a violation of the right of black victims and potential victims of homicide to the equal protection of the law.

A. The Nature of the Race-of-the-Victim Claim

The primary evidence upon which Warren McCleskey relied were statistics indicating that murderers of whites are substantially more likely to be sentenced to death than are murderers of blacks. One can derive from this evidence a claim for relief based on the theory that it is unfair to subject those who happen to kill whites to a harsher punishment than those who happen to kill blacks. This is the argument McCleskey advanced. It is an argument against arbitrariness in punishment. It sounds in notions of due process. It is individualistic and defendant-centered. But one can also derive from the evidence a claim that it is wrong for the state to react less vigorously to the murder of blacks than to the murder of whites. This is an argument against racial oppression in the context of sentencing. It sounds in notions of racial justice. It is group-based[157] and community-centered.

Them When the Police Won't?, 95 YALE L.J. 788 (1986). Given society's relative insensitivity to issues of sexism, police officers often explicitly confess to maintaining a policy of nonarrest in cases of domestic violence, even when such a policy of sex discrimination denies women equal protection of the laws. *See id.* at 788 n.3. In light of society's heightened sensitivity to issues of racism, by contrast, it is unlikely that decisionmakers would openly confess to an analogous policy of race discrimination.

[157] I recognize that in speaking in terms of group rights I am taking sides in a controversial debate over the legitimacy of group rights as distinct from the more familiar conception of individual rights. *See, e.g.*, Fiss, *Groups and the Equal Protection Clause*, 5 PHIL. & PUB. AFF. 107 (1976); Garet, *Communality and Existence: The Rights of Groups*, 56 S. CAL. L. REV.

In *McCleskey*, neither the lawyers for the petitioner nor any of the Justices articulated a community-oriented reading of the race-of-the-victim evidence. The majority and the dissenters struggled over whether the Baldus statistics showed that the state subjected McCleskey to an impermissible risk of illicit official conduct. All were silent, however, about the meaning of those statistics for the community of black victims or potential victims. The defendant-centered paradigm never allowed the victimization of the black community to reach the surface of the debate.[158] Yet the state's response to the murder of members of that community is precisely what the race-of-the-victim statistics chart. Arguably what that chart shows is that blacks in Georgia are quite literally being denied the equal *protection* of the laws. That argument, though essentially ignored, is what should have lain at the center of *McCleskey*.

B. The Question of Standing

In *McCleskey*, the Supreme Court recognized the petitioner's standing to claim that he was discriminated against on the basis of his victim's race.[159] The Court never directly addressed whether he would be granted standing to litigate on behalf of black victims or potential victims because he did not seek to assert their rights. Had he done so, he might have encountered difficulty. As a general rule the federal courts allow litigants to assert only their own legal rights and not those of third parties. Hence, some courts have denied standing to defendants raising race-of-the-victim challenges. In *Britton v. Rogers*,[160] for instance, the Eighth Circuit denied standing to a convicted rapist in Arkansas who sought to challenge his punishment on the grounds that that state consistently imposed harsher sentences upon those convicted of raping white women than those convicted of raping black women. "It is the black women of Arkansas," the *Britton* Court observed, "who should be raising this claim, not [the defendant], a convicted rapist."[161] In *McCleskey*, however, there should exist no

1001 (1983); Marshall, *A Comment on the Nondiscrimination Principle in a "Nation of Minorities,"* 93 YALE L.J. 1006 (1984); Reynolds, *Individualism vs. Group Rights: The Legacy of* Brown, 93 YALE L.J. 995 (1984).

[158] *Cf.* Bell, *Serving Two Masters: Integration Ideals and Client Interests in School Desegregation Litigation*, 85 YALE L.J. 470 (1976) (noting the conflict between civil rights attorneys and members of black communities over the proper place of integration in educational policy); Bell, Bakke, *Minority Admissions, and the Usual Price of Racial Remedies*, 67 CALIF. L. REV. 3, 3–7 (1979) (arguing that important facets of Regents of the University of California v. Bakke, 438 U.S. 265 (1978), were overlooked or misperceived because of the absence of minority group participation in the litigation).

[159] *McCleskey*, 107 S. Ct. at 1766 n.8.

[160] 631 F.2d 572 (8th Cir. 1980).

[161] *Id.* at 577 n.3. The district court in *McCleskey* agreed with the *Britton* court's analysis but felt bound by the precedent governing the Eleventh Circuit to acknowledge McCleskey's standing. *See* McCleskey v. Zant, 580 F. Supp. at 347.

real problem with respect to third-party standing because the petitioner himself is affiliated with the group whose rights he would be seeking to vindicate; after all, the petitioner is a potential black victim of homicide.[162] A different issue is posed by rulings which suggest that the Court might deny standing to anyone seeking prospective relief for potential black victims of crime absent an allegation of an imminent threat of specific injury attributable to the challenged governmental practice.[163] There is no argument available that clearly removes the community-oriented race-of-the-victim theory from the doctrinal cul-de-sac created by this aspect of the Court's standing doctrine. It would be difficult for anyone in the class of black potential victims to claim persuasively that the state's sentencing practices caused him to be threatened by a definite and immediate risk of injury. And the Court appears unwilling to aggregate individual risks. Others have extensively criticized the restrictiveness of the Court's standing decisions.[164] The point here is simply that if conventional standing doctrine does frustrate efforts to raise a community-oriented, race-of-the-victim equal protection claim, that result should itself call into question the legitimacy of that doctrine. Nothing would represent a more intolerable denial of the equal protection of the laws than a situation in which, on a racial basis, the law enforcement apparatus of a state responded less vigorously to black victimization than white victimization. Yet standing doctrine in its current phase may discourage redress of that denial by any litigation strategy that would place at its core vindicating the rights of the black community.[165]

---

[162] The Court, however, might deny standing to a white defendant seeking to raise a claim on behalf of a black victims or potential victims of murder. In Hobby v. United States, 468 U.S. 339 (1983), the Court held against a white male defendant who challenged the alleged exclusion of blacks from the post of grand jury foreman. The Court distinguished this case from others in which black defendants asserted analogous claims of racial discrimination. According to one keen observer, "[t]his distinction casts doubt on the ability of white defendants to challenge on equal protection grounds the exclusion of blacks from grand juries." Meltzer, *supra* note 68, at 264.

[163] *See, e.g.*, Allen v. Wright, 468 U.S. 737 (1984); City of Los Angeles v. Lyons, 461 U.S. 95 (1983); Rizzo v. Goode, 423 U.S. 362 (1976); O'Shea v. Littleton, 414 U.S. 488 (1974); Linda R.S. v. Richard D., 410 U.S. 614 (1973); *see also* Tribe, *supra* note 129, at 123–24 (noting that "the interest in the just administration of the laws, including the interest in nondiscriminatory criminal enforcement, is presumptively deemed nonjusticiable even if invoked by persons with something beyond a generalized bystander's concern; only if the litigant is immediately affected as a target of enforcement can that presumption be overcome").

[164] *See, e.g.*, Chayes, *The Supreme Court, 1981 Term — Foreword: Public Law Litigation and the Burger Court*, 96 HARV. L. REV. 4, 8–26 (1982); Fallon, *Of Justiciability, Remedies, and Public Law Litigation: Notes on the Jurisprudence of* Lyons, 59 N.Y.U. L. REV. 1 (1984); Meltzer, *supra* note 68, at 295–311.

[165] In his *McCleskey* dissent, Justice Blackmun pointed out that one of the conditions giving rise to demands for enactment of the fourteenth amendment was the unwillingness of law enforcement officials in southern states to protect blacks and their white allies against criminal

C. The Nature of the Equal Protection Violation

The starting point of a community-oriented race-of-the-victim claim is the now uncontroversial proposition that blacks are entitled to the equal protection of the laws. This means that they are entitled to the same degree of respect and solicitude that the state provides to whites. The Supreme Court maintains, through its doctrine of purposeful discrimination, that this norm of racial equality is violated only when officials, without a compelling justification, purposefully discriminate on the basis of race.[166] This perspective on equal protection focuses on whether particular defendants have harmed particular complainants by actions undertaken with illicit motives. A better way to formulate the meaning of equal protection in the race-relations context is to focus upon the right of minorities to be free of racial subordination.[167] This perspective looks beyond the process producing inequality in the social relations of racially identifiable groups, to the objective indicia of inequality itself.

The antisubordination perspective on equal protection is preferable because it better addresses both the great historic wrong that gave rise to the Reconstruction amendments and the great contemporary injustice that, more than any other, continues to plague the American legal order: the racial subordination of the Negro. As noted above, the problem with the Court's perspective is that it is sensitive to only one mechanism of oppression: "the purposeful affirmative adoption or use of rules that disadvantage the target group."[168] Racial subordination, however, can be maintained without discrete, episodic, affirmative acts of purposeful discrimination. Indeed it can be more securely entrenched by habitual patterns of action and inaction that inflict harms upon blacks without any intentional design whatsoever.

The phenomenon of racial subordination without racial animus is exemplified by race-of-the-victim disparities in Georgia. There was a time when, as a matter of policy, the state directly devaluated the lives of blacks by making the murder of a Negro a less severely punished crime than the murder of a white.[169] Now, however, de-

---

violence in the aftermath of the Civil War. *See* 107 S. Ct. at 1795 & n.2 (Blackmun, J., dissenting).

[166] *See supra* notes 69–71 and accompanying text.

[167] *See* L. TRIBE, *supra* note 129, at 1514–21; Colker, *Anti-Subordination Above All: Sex, Race and Equal Protection*, 61 N.Y.U. L. REV. 1003 (1986); Dimond, *The Anti-Caste Principle — Toward a Constitutional Standard for Review of Race Cases*, 30 WAYNE L. REV. 1 (1983); Freeman, *supra* note 131, at 1049; Lawrence, *supra* note 73; Schnapper, *Perpetuation of Past Discrimination*, 96 HARV. L. REV. 828 (1983).

[168] L. TRIBE, *supra* note 129, at 1518.

[169] *See supra* p. 1411; *see also* Fede, *Legitimized Violent Slave Abuse in the American South, 1619–1865: A Case Study of Law and Social Change in Six Southern States*, 29 AM. J. LEGAL HIST. 93 (1985).

valuation is mainly indirect. Prosecutors, juries, and judges do not intentionally underenforce along racial lines the law governing capital punishment; instead, underenforcement emerges "naturally" from the underlying structure of the institutions, ideas, and sentiments that constitute Georgian society. The absence of discriminatory purpose marks an important milestone in the unfinished journey from slavery to freedom. But even without any intent to harm the black community, the legal authorities in Georgia do so when they repeatedly sentence killers of blacks less harshly than killers of whites for approximately similar crimes. One aspect of the harm is material. It consists of facilitating a spirit of lawlessness that preys upon black communities, a belief that one can, quite literally, get away with murder.[170] This assertion is admittedly speculative; there exists no decisive proof that underenforcement of capital sentencing in black-victim cases substantially affects crime rates against blacks. But to the extent that capital punishment has any deterrent force,[171] that force is undermined in a fashion particularly burdensome to black citizens by racially disparate leniency. Moreover, underenforcement of capital sentencing may reflect a wider pattern of conduct in which officials, without nonracial justification, respond less vigorously to the law enforcement needs of black communities than those of white communities.[172] Another aspect of the harm imposed by racially disparate leniency in capital sentencing is symbolic. The black community is stigmatized insofar as officials treat the murder of Negroes with less seriousness than the murder of whites. This difference in treatment signals that, in practice if not by conscious intention, blacks are assigned a lowlier place in the polity than members of other groups.[173]

Although the Court's conception of purposeful discrimination largely ignores important concerns underlying the antisubordination model of the equal protection clause, there exists a line of precedent sensitive to those concerns. As the *McCleskey* dissenters observed, in

---

[170] *See, e.g.*, Sargent, *supra* note 16, at C3, col. 6 (noting that violence against blacks is high in part because "black life sometimes carries a very cheap price").

[171] Whether or the extent to which capital punishment has any deterrent effect is a highly controversial topic. For useful overviews of the debate, see W. BERNS, FOR CAPITAL PUNISHMENT: CRIME AND THE MORALITY OF THE DEATH PENALTY 83–127 (1979); W. BOWERS, G. PIERCE & J. MCDEVITT, cited above in note 25, at 271–336; S. DIKE, cited above in note 25, at 30–43; and THE DEATH PENALTY IN AMERICA 95–185 (H. Bedau 3d ed. 1983).

[172] *See, e.g.*, Ratner, *supra* note 19, at 8–10 (noting studies detailing ways in which police have provided inferior law enforcement services to black neighborhoods).

[173] *Cf.* Bentele, *The Death Penalty in Georgia: Still Arbitrary*, 62 WASH. U.L.Q. 573, 619 (1985) (noting prosecutors' decision to decline asking for the death penalty in two cases in which the victims were a drug dealer and a suspected homosexual because of apprehension that the victims' low standing in the community would dissuade any jury from sentencing their assailants to death).

cases involving challenges to the exercise of discretion by jury commissioners, the Court has shown itself willing to shift the burden of explanation to the state when presented with evidence indicating significant discrepancies between the percentage of the population of eligible racial minorities in a given jurisdiction and the percentage of racial minorities selected for possible jury service.[174] This line of cases is by no means straight; viewed·closely, it reveals that every movement of the Court towards realistic appraisal of racial subordination is checked eventually by retrenchment.[175] Nonetheless, the overall tendency of the Court's decisions on the racial composition of juries has shown a salutary skepticism towards unexplained racial disparities.[176]

The rationale of these rulings consists principally of three ideas: (1) discretion is a type of power that is particularly susceptible to abuse, (2) abused discretion is particularly difficult to detect, and (3) when discretion is employed in a process that produces racial disparities that cannot be readily explained on a nonracial basis, the state should be called upon to give justification.[177] *Castaneda v.*

---

[174] *See McCleskey*, 107 S. Ct. at 1798–805 (Blackmun, J., dissenting); *see also* Note, *To Infer or Not to Infer a Discriminatory Purpose: Rethinking Equal Protection Doctrine*, 61 N.Y.U. L. REV. 334, 351–64 (1986) (discussing the "impact-inference" standard applied in Castaneda v. Partida, 430 U.S. 482 (1977)).

[175] *Compare* Arnold v. North Carolina, 376 U.S. 773 (1964) (finding discrimination based on the plaintiff's unrebutted prima facie evidence that only one black in twenty-four years had served on the county grand jury) *with* Swain v. Alabama, 380 U.S. 202, 222–26 (1965) (holding that the petitioner failed to make even a prima facie case of discrimination even though no black in the memory of living persons had *ever* sat on petit jury in the county at issue). *Compare* Norris v. Alabama, 294 U.S. 587 (1935) (finding discrimination after asserting the responsibility of federal courts to review state conclusions of law regarding federal rights) *with* Akins v. Texas, 325 U.S. 398, 406–07 (1945) (rejecting the allegation that officials had purposefully limited black participation on grand juries to one Negro per grand jury panel, even though one jury commissioner admitted that "[w]e had no intention of placing more than one negro on the panel"). *Compare* Neal v. Delaware, 103 U.S. 370, 393–96 (1880) (finding discrimination when the state admitted that no blacks had ever served on its juries) *with* Murray v. Louisiana, 163 U.S. 101 (1896) (failing to find even a prima facie case of discrimination, despite evidence that in a county in which blacks comprised at least one-fifth of the adult population, only two blacks were selected for a jury wheel containing 1,000 names).

[176] *See, e.g.*, Castaneda v. Partida, 430 U.S. 482 (1977) (finding that a 2 to 1 disparity between whites and Mexican-Americans selected for jury service triggered an inference of purposeful discrimination); Turner v. Fouche, 396 U.S. 346 (1970) (holding that a disparity of 1.6 to 1 between whites and blacks selected for grand jury service made out a prima facie case of purposeful discrimination); Whitus v. Georgia, 385 U.S. 545 (1967) (holding that a 3 to 1 disparity between whites and blacks selected for the grand jury venire triggered an inference of purposeful discrimination).

[177] Writing for the Court in *Castaneda*, Justice Blackmun observed:

> The idea behind the rule of exclusion is not at all complex. If a disparity is sufficiently large, then it is unlikely that it is due solely to chance or accident and, in the absence of evidence to the contrary, one must conclude that racial or other class-related factors entered into the selection process.

430 U.S. at 494 n.13 (citations omitted). By contrast, Justice Powell maintained in *McCleskey* that "[w]here the discretion that is fundamental to our criminal justice is involved, we decline

Partida[178] is exemplary. In *Castaneda*, the Court held that the defendant made out a prima facie case of unconstitutional racial discrimination in the selection of grand juries simply by showing (1) that the group to which he belonged — Mexican-Americans — is a distinct, recognizable group, (2) that the jury commissioners were granted considerable personal discretion in choosing grand jurors, and (3) that over an eleven-year period, only thirty-nine percent of those summoned to grand jury service were Mexican-American, although the county population was seventy-nine percent Mexican-American.[179]

The *McCleskey* Court distinguished *Castaneda* factually, arguing that the essential elements involved in evaluating a challenge to jury selection are "fundamentally different" from the corresponding elements that must be taken into account in evaluating a challenge to capital sentencing.[180] However, the arguments posited by the Court to establish this difference are unpersuasive.[181] The Court stated that each particular decision to impose a death sentence is made by a properly selected petit jury. But even if one assumes that juries have been selected properly, the question remains whether the jurors have shown racially selective sympathies in deciding whether to sentence individuals to death. Perhaps the Justices meant to suggest that the risks of such selectivity are significantly diminished in the presence of properly constituted juries. But this potential safeguard surely should not be allowed to overshadow the presence of suspicious statistical anomalies in sentencing results. Presumably the officials who select juries have assumed their places lawfully, yet this fact has not prevented the Court from using statistics to detect whether they have carried out their duties in a manner that violates the equal protection clause.[182]

The Court states, as another basis for distinction, that "[e]ach jury is unique in its composition."[183] But the uniqueness of the composition of each jury cannot be used as a satisfactory basis for distinction unless the Court would also be willing to forego statistical evidence in a situation in which jury commissioners were constantly changed,

---

to assume that what is unexplained is invidious." 107 S. Ct. at 1778. An indication that this contrast is explained by something other than differences between the type of discretion exercised is that in *McCleskey*, Justice Powell echoes essentially the same message he voiced in dissent in *Castaneda*. *See* 430 U.S. at 508 (Powell, J., dissenting).

[178] 430 U.S. 482 (1977).

[179] *See id.* at 494–97.

[180] *See* 107 S. Ct. at 1767.

[181] For Justice Blackmun's criticism of Justice Powell on this point, see 107 S. Ct. at 1803–04 (Blackmun, J., dissenting).

[182] *See supra* note 176. *See generally* Finkelstein, *The Application of Statistical Decision Theory to the Jury Discrimination Cases*, 80 HARV. L. REV. 338 (1966) (arguing that statistical decision theory must be used rationally to apply legal principles concerning discriminatory jury selection).

[183] 107 S. Ct. at 1767.

so that each selection decision emanated from a unique collection of persons. Although statistics keyed to the results of decisions generated by groups cannot isolate with particularity the source of prejudiced action, that limitation applies to jury commissions, as well as any other bureaucracy.

The Court maintained that the capital sentencing decision that emanates from a jury is fundamentally different because it "rest[s] on consideration of innumerable factors" that vary according to the perpetrator and his offense.[184] But in many states jury commissioners are empowered with discretion to select persons according to such subjective criteria as uprightness, moral character, and sound judgment.[185] The Court contended that "[t]hese considerations are uniform for all potential jurors, and [that] although some factors may be said to be subjective, they are limited and, to a great degree, objectively verifiable."[186] But this comment simply indicates the extent to which the Justices were willing to stand on rhetorical stilts. For on at least some occasions — those in which the Court tries to portray capital punishment as something other than a creature of caprice — the Justices have suggested that jurors in capital cases must also apply criteria that are uniform, subject to limits, and objectively verifiable. Indeed, the *McCleskey* Court approvingly described Georgia's capital sentencing scheme in approximately these terms just a few pages after it sought to distinguish capital sentencing: "'[W]hile some jury discretion still exists,'" the Court noted when the spectre of statistics no longer loomed, "'"the discretion to be exercised is controlled by clear and objective standards so as to produce non-discriminatory application."'"[187]

The Court did identify a substantial distinction when it noted that jury discrimination cases typically involve fewer actors than those implicated in *McCleskey*. Jury discrimination cases generally focus upon the actions of a discrete group of officials in a particular county. McCleskey's complaint, by contrast, called into question the conduct of countless police, prosecutors, judges, and juries — the entire criminal justice apparatus of the state. The implications that should be drawn from this distinction, however, are the opposite of those drawn by the Court. The Court maintained that the variety of actors and complexity of actions that together created the patterns of sentencing

---

[184] *Id.*

[185] *See* Carter v. Jury Comm'n, 396 U.S. 320, 331–37 & nn.31–33 (1970) (upholding a state law requiring jury commissioners to select persons for jury service who were "'generally reputed to be honest and intelligent and . . . esteemed in the community for their integrity, good character and sound judgement'" (quoting ALA. CODE tit. 30, § 21 (Supp. 1967))).

[186] 107 S. Ct. at 1768 n.14.

[187] *Id.* at 1772 (quoting Gregg v. Georgia, 428 U.S. 153, 197–98 (1976) (quoting Coley v. State, 231 Ga. 829, 834, 204 S.E.2d 612, 615 (1974))).

at issue in *McCleskey* justified imposing a heightened evidentiary standard to prove discrimination.[188] But these very factors warrant *lowering* the evidentiary requirements: the greater difficulty of penetrating the "mind" of the capital sentencing apparatus should make the courts more, rather than less, willing to rely upon objective statistical evidence.

A final reason the Court asserted for imposing a more restrictive evidentiary standard is that the exercise of discretion by capital sentencing juries is constitutionally required.[189] But the constitutional status of juror discretion does not negate the proposition, affirmed by the Court, that discretionary decisions are particularly vulnerable to racially selective responses.[190] That enhanced vulnerability, coupled with the weightiness of the matter at stake — the state's response to homicide — would seem to counsel in favor of more, rather than less, judicial respect for the evidence McCleskey offered. What his evidence shows are disparities that are not only larger than those at issue in *Castaneda*, but are more precisely linked to race as distinct from some other variable.[191] In the absence of a persuasive rebuttal by the state, these disparities, in conjunction with the somber lessons of history, should have led to a declaration that Georgia's administration of the death penalty violates the right of its black citizens to the equal *protection* of the laws.

V. The Problem of Remedy

From a racial justice perspective that seeks to vindicate the rightful claims of the black community, a proper response to race-of-the-victim disparities entails evaluating a broad spectrum of remedial alternatives — from abolition of capital punishment on one extreme to its widened

---

[188] *See id.* at 1768.

[189] *See id.* at 1769 (arguing that "discretion is essential to the criminal justice process").

[190] *See* Turner v. Murray, 476 U.S. 28, 36 n.8 (1986) (noting that entrusting discretion to a jury at a capital sentencing hearing gives greater opportunity for racial prejudice than does restricting the jury to factfinding).

[191] *Compare Castaneda*, 430 U.S. at 495 (stating that 79% of the population was Mexican-American but only 39% of the grand jurors were Hispanics, a disparity of 2 to 1) *with McCleskey*, 107 S. Ct. at 1764 (stating that 22% of the black defendants killing whites were executed but only 1% of the whites killing blacks were executed, a disparity of 11 to 1). The disparities at issue in *Castaneda* were not subjected to anything like the scrutiny that the Baldus study focused upon capital sentencing disparities in Georgia. *Compare Castaneda*, 430 U.S. at 492–96 (accepting disparities as sufficient to shift the burden of proof because they were greater than those presented in previous cases) *with McCleskey*, 107 S. Ct. at 1767–68 (concluding that statistical evidence provides less proof of particularized discrimination in the sentencing context than in the jury selection or employment contexts).

application on the other.[192] Given the Court's holding, it had no occasion to discuss the remedial question at length. The Court indicated rather clearly, however, that apprehensions over the remedial difficulties that might attend a ruling in favor of McCleskey did influence its analysis of the rights asserted.[193] Justice Brennan, joined by Justice Marshall, announced his familiar resolution: vacation of McCleskey's sentence, and all other death sentences. That proposal, however, rested not principally upon any equal protection claim but rather upon the Justice's long-standing belief that capital punishment is in all circumstances unconstitutional.[194]

Justice Stevens, joined by Justice Blackmun, proposed to limit the class of persons eligible for capital punishment to those who had committed only the worst type of homicides.[195] This proposal flowed from his belief that "[o]ne of the lessons of the Baldus study is that there exist certain categories of extremely serious crimes for which prosecutors consistently seek, and juries consistently impose, the death penalty without regard to the race of the victim."[196] He contended

---

[192] In devising relief, courts should provide incentives for persons to bring to the attention of the federal judiciary profound violations of federal constitutional norms. Hence, in responding to a meritorious claim, whether it be defendant-oriented or community-oriented, courts should be prepared to reduce a death sentence to a life sentence. This manner of proceeding does give a windfall to a convicted murderer — a far from insignificant cost. On the other hand, this cost is far less severe than the cost in other contexts in which courts have provided remedies that extend beyond redressing a right of the litigant himself, in order to affirm constitutional values and deter government misconduct in the future. The two most striking instances of remedial windfalls involve the application of the exclusionary rule for violations of the fourth amendment, *see, e.g.*, Coolidge v. New Hampshire, 403 U.S. 443, 473 (1971), and the overturning of convictions in cases in which minority defendants have been indicted by grand juries from which minorities had been systematically excluded, *see, e.g.*, Vasquez v. Hillery, 474 U.S. 254, 264 (1986). For an illuminating discussion of the usefulness, in certain contexts, of giving defendants more relief than they are individually entitled to, see Meltzer, cited above in note 68, at 267–78. To the extent that isolated windfalls help us to achieve the state of race relations to which we aspire, they are worth the costs they impose. Although this argument is predicated upon an empirical basis, there is no way of measuring precisely the costs and benefits of alternatives. My conclusion is intuitive. *Cf.* Meltzer, *supra* note 68, at 268 n.98 ("Solid empirical proof or disproof of the [exclusionary] rule's efficacy does not exist and is unlikely ever to be found.").

[193] *See* 107 S. Ct. at 1779–81; *see also supra* pp. 1413–15. Although there is considerable overlap between the remedial issues raised by the race-of-the-victim theory of discrimination McCleskey asserted and the theory I propose, there are also important differences. If one decides the case under the theory McCleskey asserted, the central remedial problem is what should be done with those sentenced to death under Georgia's system of capital punishment. If one decides the case under the theory I propose, the central remedial problem is what should be done to ensure that the black community receives an equally vigorous response from the states when its members are murdered.

[194] *See* 107 S. Ct. at 1781–82 (Brennan, J., dissenting).

[195] *See id.* at 1806 (Stevens, J., dissenting).

[196] *Id.* The "worst case only" solution is based upon the hypothesis that there exist three discernible subcategories of murder within the category that makes a defendant eligible for

that "[i]f Georgia were to narrow the class of death-eligible defendants to those categories, the danger of arbitrary and discriminatory imposition of the death penalty would be significantly decreased, if not eradicated."[197]

There are two main problems with Justice Stevens' proposal. First, Justice Stevens overestimated the institutional abilities of appellate courts to demarcate degrees of aggravation distinguishing one capital crime from another. His proposed remedy replicates the intractable line-drawing problems that have beset the Court's post-*Furman* approach to capital punishment jurisprudence. The one thing upon which death penalty deregulators and death penalty abolitionists agree is that "the task of selecting in some objective way those persons who should be condemned to die is one that remains beyond the capacities of the criminal justice system."[198] The notorious indeter-

---

capital punishment. The first category is comprised of murders so aggravated that those who commit them are consistently sentenced to death, regardless of the race of the victim. The second category is comprised of murders with enough mitigating circumstances that those who commit them are typically spared a death sentence. The third category is comprised of a middle tier of murders for which the circumstances produce far less consistent sentencing patterns. Officials feel most ambivalent with respect to this third category, thus providing an opening for racial bias to enter. To preclude, or at least minimize, the possibility of race-dependent capital sentencing, Justices Stevens and Blackmun suggested limiting capital punishment in Georgia only to those who have committed worst-case murders. *See id.* This remedy would appear to require no formal judicial intervention prior to conviction. After sentencing, however, the state appellate courts would be obliged to review each death sentence, commuting to life imprisonment all that could not properly be located in the worst-case category. *See* A METHODOLOGICAL CRITIQUE, *supra* note 28, at 44–48; Baldus, *Arbitrariness and Discrimination*, *supra* note 13, at 202–07.

[197] 107 S. Ct. at 1806 (Stevens, J., dissenting).

[198] Godfrey v. Georgia, 446 U.S. 420, 442 (1980) (Marshall, J., concurring). *Compare, e.g.*, Woodson v. North Carolina, 428 U.S. 280, 316 (1976) (Rehnquist, J., dissenting) (arguing that appellate review of death sentences will not afford meaningful protection against vagaries or biases set loose by jury discretion in sentencing) *with Godfrey*, 446 U.S. at 438–39 (Marshall, J., concurring) (arguing that appellate review of capital sentencing cannot assure "objectivity and evenhandedness"). For a prescient warning against attempts to inject due process within the anarchical domain of capital sentencing, see McGautha v. California, 402 U.S. 183, 204 (1971), in which Justice Harlan observed that "[t]o identify before the fact those characteristics of criminal homicides and their perpetrators which call for the death penalty, and to express these characteristics in language which can be fairly understood and applied by the sentencing authority, appear to be tasks which are beyond present human ability."

For a scathing abolitionist attack on the Court's attempts to rationalize capital sentencing, see C. BLACK, JR., cited above in note 20, at 111–56. But it is Professor Weisberg who provides the most rounded evaluation of the attempt to affirm legal formality within the death penalty context:

> Capital punishment is at once the best and worst subject for legal rules. The state's decision to kill is so serious, and the cost of error so high, that we feel impelled to discipline the human power of the death sentence with rational legal rules. Yet a judge or jury's decision is an intensely moral, subjective matter that seems to defy the designers of general formulas for legal decision.

Weisberg, *Deregulating Death*, 1983 SUP. CT. REV. 305, 308.

minacy involved in applying statutory aggravating circumstances in the penalty phase of a capital trial[199] or in applying proportionality review[200] to death sentences would be compounded by the requirement that appellate courts distinguish worst-case murders from those in the so-called middle range.

The futility of this task is suggested by the *McCleskey* case itself. According to Professor Baldus, the murder for which McCleskey was convicted should be located in the middle range. Yet the basis on which he makes this judgment is far from clear. It is difficult to discern either what he means by middle range — he notes that spectrums of criminality can be defined in various ways[201] — or the justifications for the weight he attached to the factors that led him to

---

[199] *See* Bentele, *supra* note 173, at 577–85 (arguing that requiring a jury to find aggravating circumstances before it can impose a death sentence does little in practice to guide discretion); Weisberg, *supra* note 198, at 328–35.

[200] The Georgia experience with proportionality review is instructive. The Georgia Supreme Court is directed by statute to review all cases in which a defendant is condemned to death and to determine whether the sentence "is excessive or disproportionate to the penalty imposed in similar cases, considering both the crime and the defendant." GA. CODE ANN. § 27-2537(c)(3) (1983). After careful study, however, several scholars have concluded that the Georgia Supreme Court has failed — and perhaps could do nothing but fail — to develop any coherent method to distinguish in a predictable way those defendants who deserve the death penalty from those who do not. *See* Bentele, *supra* note 173, at 591–608; Dix, *Appellate Review of the Decision to Impose Death*, 68 GEO. L.J. 97 (1979); Liebman, *Appellate Review of Death Sentences: A Critique of Proportionality Review*, 18 U.C. DAVIS L. REV. 1433, 1434, 1442–58 (1985).

In Godfrey v. Georgia, 446 U.S. 420 (1980), the Supreme Court reversed the Georgia Supreme Court's affirmation of a death sentence that had been given proportionality review. The plurality opinion declared that the state court must construe heinousness in such a way as to enable rational distinctions to be drawn among levels of depravity in murder. *See id.* at 428–33. Nonetheless, the Court itself disagreed over the heinousness of the crime at issue. According to Justice Stewart's plurality opinion, the crimes of the petitioner:

> cannot be said to have reflected a consciousness materially more 'depraved' than that of any person guilty of murder. His victims were killed instantaneously. They were members of his family who were causing him extreme emotional trauma. Shortly after the killings, he acknowledged his responsibility and the heinous nature of his crimes.

Id. at 433 (footnote omitted). Chief Justice Burger, on the other hand, described the case as follows:

> After murdering his wife and mother-in-law, petitioner informed the police that he had committed a 'hideous' crime. . . . [P]etitioner himself characterized his crime in terms equivalent to those employed in the Georgia statute. For my part, I prefer petioner's characterization of his conduct to the plurality's effort to excuse and rationalize that conduct as just another killing.

Id. at 442–43 (Burger, C.J., dissenting).

[201] *See* Baldus, *Arbitrariness and Discrimination*, *supra* note 13, at 175–78. Professor Baldus and his colleagues describe two ways to classify cases for the purpose of determining various ranges of culpability. One approach is termed a priori: "[T]he a priori approach endeavors to classify cases as similar on the basis of criteria which, from a legal or moral perspective, the court believes should govern the appropriate sentence." *Id.* at 176–77. A second approach is termed empirical: "In contrast to the a priori approach — which selects those factual characteristics on a normative basis — the empirical approach tries to employ those case characteristics that best explain statistically the observed sentencing results." *Id.* at 177.

place McCleskey's crime in the intermediate as opposed to the highest category of culpability. McCleskey's crime involved, after all, the murder of a policeman during a robbery by a recidivist who is said to have boasted of the killing.[202] In an article written outside the specific context of the *McCleskey* litigation, Professor Baldus and his associates ranked a crime that appears very similar to McCleskey's in the upper reaches of a category of murders just below the category they appear to view as the worst cases.[203] But it is unclear why that crime was deemed less aggravated than murders listed in the higher category.[204] Whatever the criteria used, various judges looking at the same data would surely rank the offenses differently. Given the irreducible degree of subjectivity that must adhere to any attempt to distinguish bad cases from "worst cases," there will exist an opening for the unavoidable corruption — the exercise of race-based empathy — that gave rise to the need for a remedy in the first place.

Second, from the point of view of those who view capital punishment as a valuable tool of public policy and who insist upon the equal provision of this tool to the black community, Justice Stevens' solution is misdirected or, at least, mistimed. It can be viewed as vindicating the right of the black community to equal treatment by levelling *downwards* the availability of a valuable public good *before* attempting to vindicate the claims of equality by levelling *upwards* the availability of that good. It may well be that the fourteenth amendment requires that, left with no alternative, judges must command equal deprivation

---

[202] *See* McCleskey v. Zant, 580 F. Supp. at 345–66. Critics of *McCleskey* should not forget that the man whose claim they support was himself a callous victimizer. It is an interesting commentary on the politics of the struggle over the death penalty that while Warren McCleskey has received tremendous attention and solicitude by molders of public opinion, his victim — Officer Frank Schlatt — appears to have become an invisible man whose name is generally omitted from discussions of the case.

[203] *See* Baldus, *Arbitrariness and Discrimination*, *supra* note 13, at 219. In the *McCleskey* litigation, Baldus spoke in terms of a tripartite division of capital crimes. In the article referred to above, he divided the capital cases into five categories in terms of increasing levels of culpability. It is unclear whether a crime located by Baldus in the upper reaches of Category IV would count as a worst case were the breakdown limited to the tripartite model. I shall assume that, to Baldus, no Category IV crimes warrant the label of worst-case offenses. This confusion is itself indicative of the problems that would attend attempts to put the Stevens-Baldus remedy into operation.

[204] After dividing homicides into five levels of seriousness, Professor Baldus and his associates ranked as an upper level Category IV crime a murder during the course of a robbery in which a policeman was shot by a man with four prior convictions, two of which were for non-violent offenses. *See id.* at 219 (case number 862). They ranked as a Category V — a worst case crime — a murder committed during the course of a robbery that the defendant and his coperpetrator were hired to perform. The defendant was apparently designated as the triggerman although the coperpetrator appears to have actually done the killing. The defendant had only one prior offense on his record and that was nonviolent. *See id.* at 221 (case number C82). Why is it clear that his offense should place him in the worst-case category, while that of the defendant described above should receive a less serious designation?

rather than acquiesce to the racially unequal provision of public services.[205] But in the context of *McCleskey*, plausible alternatives appear to exist that at least warrant discussion.

Another possible remedial response to race-of-the-victim disparities would be for the Court to retract its rejection of mandatory death sentences.[206] In 1972 the Court struck down all then-existing state death penalty statutes on the grounds that, by delegating unguided discretionary power to sentencing authorities, they provided insufficient protection against arbitrariness or discrimination.[207] Ten states responded by enacting statutes prescribing capital punishment as the mandatory sentence for the commission of certain crimes.[208] The Court invalidated these laws on the grounds that they were inconsistent with fundamental trends in social mores, encouraged juries to shape their verdicts to avoid the harshness of mandatory sentences, and failed to consider each defendant in a sufficiently individualized manner.[209] The Justices imposed a constitutional requirement that sentencers in capital trials be provided with discretion to extend mercy.[210] But it is precisely this power to grant leniency that opens the door to the problem in *McCleskey*. As Kenneth Culp Davis observes, "[t]he discretionary power to be lenient has a deceptive quality that is dangerous to justice. . . . [T]he power to be lenient is the power to discriminate."[211]

Whether and to what extent the Court's reversing its stand on mandatory capital sentencing would affect race-of-the-victim disparities is highly debatable. First, even if mandatory capital sentencing were allowed and implemented, there would remain the possibility that juries would continue to extend relatively more leniency to the killers of blacks, declining more frequently to convict such killers of crimes that trigger automatic death sentences. Second, and probably more importantly, the institutional actors who have the most to do with the prevalence and incidence of capital sentences are prosecutors,

---

205 *See supra* note 19.

206 At oral argument before the Supreme Court, one of the Justices asked McCleskey's counsel whether the Court should "move [capital sentencing] back toward less discretion?" The attorney's response was equivocal. *See* Transcript of Oral Argument at 28, *McCleskey* (No. 84-6811).

207 *See* Furman v. Georgia, 408 U.S. 238 (1972).

208 *See* W. LOCKHART, Y. KAMISAR, J. CHOPER & S. SHIFFRIN, CONSTITUTIONAL LAW 577 (6th ed. 1986).

209 *See* Roberts v. Louisiana, 428 U.S. 325 (1976); Woodson v. North Carolina, 428 U.S. 280 (1976).

210 Underlining its insistence that sentencing authorities must be allowed to extend mercy, the Court has held that sentencers must also be allowed to consider any mitigating evidence that a defendant seeks to introduce. *See* Eddings v. Oklahoma, 455 U.S. 104, 113–14 (1982); Lockett v. Ohio, 438 U.S. 586, 604 (1978).

211 K. DAVIS, DISCRETIONARY JUSTICE 170 (1969). *But cf.* Gregg v. Georgia, 428 U.S. 153, 199 (1976) (plurality opinion) ("Nothing in any of our cases suggests that the decision to afford an individual defendant mercy violates the Constitution.").

not jurors. Prosecutors decide, among other things, whether to charge a defendant with a capital crime or to accept a plea-bargain for a non-capital offense.[212] Researchers have found that prosecutors can be strongly influenced by the race of victims.[213] Some of the most striking disparities revealed by the Baldus study directly chart patterns of prosecutorial decisionmaking.[214] Yet mandatory sentencing schemes do little to address the problem of race-dependent leniency on the part of prosecutors. Mandatory sentencing provisions would limit, to some extent, the discretion of jurors in responding to choices framed by prosecutors, but such laws would do nothing to constrain the prior exercise of prosecutorial discretion.

Justice Blackmun in dissent noted that prosecutors in Georgia are governed by virtually no authoritative instructions regarding the way they should decide whom to charge with capital crimes.[215] He suggested that another possible remedy for racial disparities in capital sentencing would be the establishment of "guidelines" setting forth the appropriate bases for exercising prosecutorial discretion in homicide cases that potentially implicate capital punishment.[216] Justice Blackmun was silent, however, about the substantive content of the guidelines he had in mind. In light of the failure of statutory guidelines that supposedly channel juror discretion, it is difficult to imagine instructions to prosecutors that would compel, or even facilitate, the consistency that Justice Blackmun envisions.[217]

There exist other remedial possibilities. The Court could declare a constitutional violation but leave to state officials, at least in the first instance, the responsibility for formulating an affirmative remedy. Such a procedure would evince respect for the prerogatives of state authorities and might encourage them to apply their knowledge and creativity to improve local conditions.[218] There are many problems,

---

[212] On the power of prosecutors in Georgia's system of capital punishment, see Bentele, cited above in note 173, at 609–20. *See also* B. NAKELL & K. HARDY, THE ARBITRARINESS OF THE DEATH PENALTY 152–58 (1987); Foley & Powell, *The Discretion of Prosecutors, Judges, and Juries in Capital Cases*, CRIM. JUST. REV., Fall 1982, at 16. The influence of prosecutors in the context of capital cases is only the most dramatic instance of their extraordinary power in the administration of criminal justice as a whole. *See generally* Vorenberg, *Decent Restraint of Prosecutorial Power*, 94 HARV. L. REV. 1521 (1981); *Developments in the Law — Race and the Criminal Process*, 101 HARV. L. REV. 1472, 1520–57, 1588–95 (1988).

[213] *See* Jacoby & Paternoster, *Sentencing Disparity and Jury Packing: Further Challenges to the Death Penalty*, 73 J. CRIM. L. & CRIMINOLOGY 379 (1982); Paternoster, *Race of Victim and Location of Crime: The Decision to Seek the Death Penalty in South Carolina*, 74 J. CRIM. L. & CRIMINOLOGY 754 (1983); Radelet & Pierce, *Race and Prosecutorial Discretion in Homicide Cases*, 19 LAW & SOC'Y REV. 587 (1985).

[214] *See* 107 S. Ct. at 1800–02 (Blackmun, J., dissenting).

[215] *See id.* at 1800–02, 1805.

[216] *See id.* at 1805.

[217] *See supra* note 199.

[218] For useful studies detailing judicial strategies aimed at effectuating decrees, see LIMITS

of course, that may attend this response. Officials have often proven to be stubbornly recalcitrant.[219] But even if the Court were to find that no effective relief was possible, the Court's bare declaration that Georgia's sentencing practices violated constitutional norms would still be far better than the course actually taken by the Justices. First, even in the absence of an active remedy, announcing the violation of a right at least creates a basis for criticizing a given social practice.[220] Telling the truth is itself a partial remedy — an antidote to complacency and the mystification of pervasive social ills. Second, a declaration that a right has been violated can sometimes serve as a magnet around which to organize dissatisfaction; the very existence of such a pronouncement may catalyze, in unforeseen ways, the remedial capabilities of other sectors of the society.[221]

Finally, there remain other more far-reaching remedial possibilities: one might entail broadening the scope of capital sentencing, and a second entails abolishing capital punishment. The first of these remedial scenarios — the level-up solution — rests on the assumption that put to a choice, jurisdictions committed to capital punishment would opt to increase the level of capital sentencing for black-victim murders rather than abolish capital punishment or lower the level of capital sentencing for white-victim murders.[222] The proposal to level upwards the provision of capital sentencing would involve two steps: (1) allowing capital sentencing to proceed and (2) suspending executions of all persons sentenced to death until the state can show affirmatively that illicit racial disparities have been eliminated. This plan would encourage state officials to change the sentencing habits of prosecutors, juries, and judges because, unless they did so, the state would be precluded permanently from executing anyone.

OF JUSTICE: THE COURTS' ROLE IN SCHOOL DESEGREGATION (H. Kalodner & J. Fishman eds. 1978), and Special Project, *The Remedial Process in Institutional Reform Litigation*, 78 COLUM. L. REV. 784 (1978).

[219] *See* Gewirtz, *Remedies and Resistance*, 92 YALE L.J. 585, 608–28 (1983) (describing the history of resistance to school desegregation).

[220] *See* Fiss, *supra* note 131, at 52 (arguing that a right can exist without a remedy, in which case the right at least serves as a "standard for evaluating present social practice"). With characteristic eloquence, Frederick Douglass observed that even if the public accommodations provision of the Civil Rights Act of 1875 could not be enforced, it was still useful as "a banner on the outer wall of American liberty, a noble moral standard, uplifted for the education of the American people. . . . This law, though dead, did speak." *See* 4 P. FONER, THE LIFE AND WRITINGS OF FREDERICK DOUGLASS 401 (1955) (criticizing the Civil Rights Cases, 109 U.S. 3 (1883), in which the Supreme Court invalidated much of the Civil Rights Act).

[221] *See* Note, *Judicial Right Declaration*, *supra* note 131, at 1743–47 (discussing the ways in which the declaration of a right in *Brown v. Board of Education* supported the civil rights movement, which eventually effectuated the right the Court had recognized).

[222] *See infra* p. 1439. The "level-up"/"level-down" terminology is derived from Fleischman & McCorkle, *Level-Up Rather Than Level-Down: Toward a New Theory of Campaign Finance Reform*, 1 J.L. & POL. 211 (1984).

In judging the level-up solution to the *McCleskey* problem, we must determine whether, in the death penalty context, the legal system should accommodate costs that it is willing to bear in other contexts in which remedial race-conscious decisionmaking has been introduced. This determination must be made in the face of a familiar dilemma: "[o]fficial actions ought not disproportionately disadvantage minorities; yet active steps to avoid disproportionate impact are also offensive."[223] Some of the arguments against the formal recognition of race-consciousness in capital sentencing are the same as those made in debates over racial policy in other areas.[224] One is that using racial classifications to remedy racial oppression further entrenches race lines in our society.[225] The second is that racial classifications inescapably undermine the idea that persons should be evaluated solely on the basis of individual merit, as opposed to their ascribed affiliation with a particular group.[226] The latter argument takes on particular bite in the death penalty context where, in the eyes of many including a majority of the Justices, it is a moral and constitutional imperative for sentencing to be strictly tailored to the particular moral conduct and character of individual defendants.[227]

The idea of using race-conscious measures to reform the administration of capital punishment may seem bizarre at first blush. But that reaction is likely to be based in part upon an exaggerated perception of the extent to which notions of individualism currently infuse sentencing practices. Typically, sentencing responds not only to the moral deserts of individual defendants but also to utilitarian calculations regarding society's needs. Punishment is used by those pronouncing sentence upon convicted defendants to instruct an onlooking

---

[223] Eisenberg, *supra* note 92, at 42.

[224] The literature on this subject is enormous. For some of the articles I have found most useful, see Bell, cited above in note 158; Brest, cited above in note 154; Eisenberg, cited above in note 92; Ely, *The Constitutionality of Reverse Discrimination*, 41 U. CHI. L. REV. 723 (1974); Fiss, cited above in note 157; Kaplan, *Equal Justice in an Unequal World: Equality for the Negro — The Problem of Special Treatment*, 61 NW. U.L. REV. 363 (1966); Karst, *The Cost of Motive-Centered Inquiry*, 15 SAN DIEGO L. REV. 1163 (1978); Perry, cited above in note 92; Sullivan, *The Supreme Court, 1986 Term — Comment: Sins of Discrimination: Last Term's Affirmative Action Cases*, 100 HARV. L. REV. 78 (1986); Van Alstyne, *Rites of Passage: Race, the Supreme Court, and the Constitution*, 46 U. CHI. L. REV. 775 (1979); and Note, *The Constitutional Imperative of Proportional Representation*, 94 YALE L.J. 163 (1984).

[225] *See, e.g.*, Kaplan, *supra* note 224, at 374 (arguing that "any legal classification by race weakens the government as an educative force" promoting the idea that race should be an irrelevant consideration); Van Alstyne, *supra* note 224, at 809 (declaring that "one gets beyond racism by getting beyond it now: by a complete, resolute, and credible commitment *never* to tolerate in one's own life — or in the life or practices of one's government — the differential treatment of other human beings by race").

[226] *See, e.g.*, Reynolds, *supra* note 157, at 1003.

[227] *See, e.g.*, Roberts v. Louisiana, 428 U.S. 325 (1976) (invalidating a law prescribing mandatory death sentences); Woodson v. North Carolina, 428 U.S. 280 (1976) (same).

society.[228] Forcing state officials to alter their capital sentencing habits in order to vindicate the black community's right to equal treatment would thus be an additional but surely not an isolated derogation of individualism in our system of criminal punishment.[229]

Another problem with the level up alternative is that even those who favor, or at least tolerate, race-conscious remedies reach a point where they find that remedial costs are simply too severe to impose upon individuals who themselves played no direct part in inflicting the injury giving rise to litigation.[230] The Supreme Court, for instance, has drawn the line at employment layoffs.[231] Affirmative action for racial minorities that decreases the chances that white applicants will be hired is allowable, because the burden to be borne "is diffused to a considerable extent among society generally."[232] Affirmative action that results in the layoff of white workers, however, is deemed a burden that is "too intrusive" to accept.[233] Transposed to the death penalty context, the argument would run that sentencing individuals to death pursuant to a race-conscious plan to equalize the provision of death penalty services is simply too harsh a social tax to impose even upon convicted murderers who are, because of their own conduct, "eligible" for execution.

This argument rests heavily upon the death is different distinction. It loses considerable force, however, to the extent that one sees the death penalty as part of a continuum of punishments rather than a unique phenomenon occupying a wholly different moral plane. For those, like myself, who see the death penalty from the former perspective, it is not self-evident why — if race can and should be taken into account in redressing racial injustice in employment, housing, voting, and education — race cannot also be taken into account in reforming capital sentencing. Although race-conscious decisionmaking is problematic in a variety of important respects, it has received judicial sanction in each of the areas noted above because, ultimately,

---

228 *See, e.g.*, United States v. Bergman, 416 F. Supp. 496, 499 (S.D.N.Y. 1976) (basing a sentencing decision in part on considerations of general deterrence, "the effort to discourage similar wrongdoing by others through a reminder that the law's warnings are real").

229 Of course, the imposition of this remedy would not truly "force" states to embrace race-conscious measures; as an alternative, states could always choose to abolish capital punishment. *See infra* pp. 1439–40.

230 *See, e.g.*, Fallon & Weiler, Firefighters v. Stotts: *Conflicting Models of Racial Justice*, 1984 SUP. CT. REV. 1, 58–60 (arguing that although race-based preferential treatment is generally permissible, racial quotas that eviscerate seniority rights impose an excessive burden on displaced individuals).

231 *See* Wygant v. Jackson Bd. of Educ., 476 U.S. 267, 283 (1986) (invalidating a plan giving preferential protection against layoffs to some employees because of their race as an overly intrusive means of achieving racial equality).

232 *Id.* at 282.

233 *See id.* at 283. *But see id.* at 296 (Marshall, J., dissenting) ("I, too, believe that layoffs are unfair. But unfairness ought not to be confused with constitutional injury.").

the courts and other centers of public power acknowledge the truth of Justice Blackmun's observation that "[i]n order to get beyond racism, we must first take account of race."[234] It may turn out, as some fear, that race-conscious reform would simply degenerate into an expedient tokenism designed to save capital punishment. There is a real danger that defendants might be sentenced to death primarily to create "good" statistics.[235] On the other hand, suspending executions pending the eradication of unjustified race-of-the-victim disparities might help to encourage officials to take more seriously the security and suffering of black communities. Such a measure would symbolize an affirmative constitutional obligation to insure some rough measure of substantive racial equality in every sphere of American life — including sentencing. And despite risks that would have to be carefully monitored, a level-up remedy for race-of-the-victim disparities would be far preferable to the situation bequeathed to us by the *McCleskey* Court.

The judicial abolition of capital punishment in Georgia would address the problem of inequality by levelling downwards the provision of death penalty services. This response would fall far short of what abolitionists demand, for it would mean the permanent cessation of capital punishment in only a single state, would rest upon a claim of racial oppression that might not be sustainable in other jurisdictions, and would implicitly concede that states may legitimately execute the perpetrators of certain crimes absent unjustifiable racial disparities or some similar infirmity. But this solution would demonstrate the authenticity of the Court's admonition that capital punishment must be administered equally or not at all.[236] It would also signal

---

[234] *See* Regents of the Univ. of Cal. v. Bakke, 438 U.S. 265, 407 (1978) (opinion of Blackmun, J.).

[235] *See* Zeisel, *supra* note 14, at 464–66 (suggesting that Florida prosecutors requested the death penalty in certain black-victim homicides only as a token effort to improve the appearance of that state's death penalty statistics). *But see* W. WHITE, LIFE IN THE BALANCE: PROCEDURAL SAFEGUARDS IN CAPITAL CASES 7 (1984) (arguing that the change in prosecutors' conduct might have indicated that they were taking greater care to ensure that sentencing decisions were racially fair). There also exists the danger that prosecutors might resort to race-of-the-defendant discrimination to address race-of-the-victim disparities. One can imagine, for instance, a prosecutor discriminatorily requesting death sentences against black perpetrators of black-victim crimes in order to "improve" his black-victim statistics. It might seem unduly cynical to raise the possibility that officials would react in such a manner. Racist outrages of this sort do occur, however. *See, e.g., supra* note 118 (discussing Amadeo v. Kemp, 816 F.2d 1502, *reh'g denied*, 822 F.2d 65 (11th Cir.), *cert. granted*, 108 S. Ct. 257 (1987)). That reality supports increased judicial vigilance; it is not a reason to eschew considering new approaches to the problem of racially oppressive leniency in sentencing.

[236] *See* Eddings v. Oklahoma, 455 U.S. 104, 112 (1982); *see also McCleskey*, 107 S. Ct. at 1806 (Stevens, J., dissenting) ("If society were indeed forced to choose between a racially discriminatory death penalty (one that provides heightened protection against murder 'for whites only') and no death penalty at all, the choice mandated by the Constitution would be plain.").

powerfully a determination to prevent officials from privileging one racial group over another, even when they do so without racial animus. Abolition, however, is painful medicine to the extent that the death penalty constitutes — as most Americans believe that it does — a useful and highly valued public good. From the perspective of a proponent of capital punishment, abolition as a remedy for race-of-the-victim disparities is equivalent to reducing to darkness a town in which street lights have been provided on a racially unequal basis; the norm of equality is enforced but at the cost of a reduction in services to all.[237]

VI. Conclusion

There is, in the end, no entirely satisfying way to address from a community-oriented perspective the race-of-the-victim equal protection problem in *McCleskey*. Of the available alternatives, however, the Supreme Court chose the very worst: the pretense that no problem of constitutional magnitude even exists. That choice was particularly unfortunate because, in our political system, decisions rendered by the Justices of the Supreme Court have a very special moral meaning. The decisions of the other branches chart the lines of power but, in the eyes of many, the decisions of the Court chart the lines of legitimacy. That special authority to legitimate should be accompanied by special expectations and scrutiny. Thus, in evaluating the conduct of the officials implicated by *McCleskey*, those most deserving of censure are not the jurors and prosecutors situated in the intermediate ranks of the criminal justice system, but rather the Justices situated at the top of the pyramid. It is one thing for officials in Georgia to display racially selective leniency in charging and sentencing practices; it is different, far worse, and ultimately more corrosive for the Supreme Court, after full deliberation, to *legitimate* that conduct.[238]

---

[237] *See* Scheidegger, *supra* note 11, at 125 (applauding the *McCleskey* Court for upholding the notion that "equally devaluing the lives of white victims is not the answer" to the problem of devaluing the lives of black victims). The most outspoken critic of level-down equality in the death penalty context is Ernest van den Haag:

> If we grant that some (even all) murderers of blacks, or, some (even all) white and rich murderers, escape the death penalty, how does that reduce the guilt of murderers of whites, or of black and poor murderers, so that they should be spared execution too? Guilt is personal. No murderer becomes less guilty, or less deserving of punishment, because another murderer was punished leniently, or escaped punishment altogether. . . . A group of murderers does not become less deserving of punishment because another equally guilty group is not punished, or punished less.

van den Haag, *Refuting Reiman and Nathanson*, 14 Phil. & Pub. Aff. 165, 173–74 (1985).

[238] The argument here owes much to Rostow, *The Japanese American Cases — A Disaster*, 54 Yale L.J. 489 (1945) (criticizing Korematsu v. United States, 323 U.S. 214 (1944)). On the legitimating function of judicial review, see C. Black, The People and the Court: Judicial Review in a Democracy 56–86 (1960).

Although the *McCleskey* Court's performance can rightly be condemned, outrage should not be allowed to obscure the intractability of the underlying problem: *in Georgia's marketplace of emotion the lives of blacks simply count for less than the lives of whites*. This reality grows out of America's tragic history of race relations. But it is also a reality related to a wider, perhaps even universal problem. Thousands of people die every day, yet most of us grieve only for those few with whom we most identify: parents, children, siblings, spouses, friends. In a sense, we all devalue the rest of the world in relation to our own small circle of loved ones; hence Rousseau's charge that the preferences of friendship are "thefts" against humanity.[239] Typically when we speak in sorrow about those killed in war, we refer to the casualties on *our* side. When an airplane disaster occurs, local newspapers typically highlight only the lives of local victims. Ever since Acquired Immune Deficiency Syndrome (AIDS) emerged as a public health issue, members of so-called "high risk groups" have bitterly observed that less concern was initially invested in arresting the epidemic because of the devalued nature of those whom it primarily affected — homosexual men and intravenous drug abusers.[240]

---

[239] "We are justly punished for those exclusive attachments which make us blind and unjust, and limit our universe to the persons we love. All the preferences of friendship are thefts committed against the human race and the fatherland. Men are all our brothers, they should all be our friends." J. ROUSSEAU, 4 CORRESPONDENCE GENERALE 82 (1925), *quoted in* Levinson, *Testimonial Privileges and the Preferences of Friendship*, 1984 DUKE L.J. 631, 631.

[240] *See, e.g.*, R. SHILTS, AND THE BAND PLAYED ON: POLITICS, PEOPLE AND THE AIDS EPIDEMIC 101, 110, 143–45, 186–87 (1987) (contrasting the public response to AIDS with the public response to Legionnaires' disease); *id.* at 579–81 (contrasting the response to Rock Hudson's affliction with AIDS to the response to deaths of ordinary AIDS victims); *id.* at 510–13 (contrasting public indifference over the risk of homosexual transmission of AIDS with public panic over the risk of heterosexual transmission); A. FETTNER & W. CHECK, THE TRUTH ABOUT AIDS: EVOLUTION OF AN EPIDEMIC 196 (1984) ("Because those who are afflicted [with AIDS] are predominantly members of 'fringe' groups, the general population's perception of the disease is skewed by its perception of these groups.").

There is also a distinctly racial element to the incidence of the disease and the politics of response. AIDS afflicts a strikingly high number of blacks in relation to other groups:

> Whereas blacks account for only 11.5 percent of the U.S. population, black people represent 25 percent of reported AIDS cases overall, 51 percent of all women with AIDS, and 58 percent of all children with AIDS. Whereas fewer than 12 percent of white adults with AIDS are strictly heterosexual, 46 percent of black adults with AIDS fall into that category. . . . Aproximately 7.4 percent of white adults with AIDS reportedly used intravenous drugs; for black adults with AIDS, the comparable figure is 43 percent.

Greaves, *The Black Community*, in AIDS AND THE LAW: A GUIDE FOR THE PUBLIC 281 (H. Dalton, S. Barris & the Yale AIDS Law Project eds. 1987). Yet these facts were, for a time, largely ignored. Whether this indicates damnable insensitivity or a laudable desire to avoid racial scapegoating or perhaps both is a subject worthy of further inquiry. For an informative discussion of the race question in the AIDS epidemic, see Greaves, cited above. *See also* Shilts, *Interview*, Village Voice, Feb. 23, 1988, at 23, col. 1 ("What I fear is that, as white middle-class heterosexuals realize that they're not getting [AIDS] in large numbers, we could have the same problem that we had in the early 1980's, when AIDS was killing gay men, and nobody

The *McCleskey* statistics, in other words, do not represent something confined to race (because we all engage in differential valuations of human life according to clannish criteria — family, locality, nationality), nor even something that is wholly evil (that individuals feel greater identification with the victimization of members of a particular racial group bespeaks, after all, a certain sense of community).[241]

By recognizing the extent to which the *McCleskey* problem is related to a general problem of social relations, we can perhaps facilitate a more realistic discourse in which judges might more easily acknowledge the pervasive and constitutionally troubling existence of practices that reflect and reinforce racial devaluation. Destigmatizing the individual decisionmakers caught up in capital sentencing would encourage a recognition that the Baldus statistics reflect a broader problem of institutionalized racial inequality.[242] After all, statistical patterns analogous to those at issue in *McCleskey* are also revealed by analyses of employment, income, infant mortality, and other dimensions of social welfare.[243] To some, the very breadth of this

---

really cared about them. . . . [U]nfortunately, I think our society cares even less about black and Hispanic drug addicts and their partners.").

[241] The notion that racially selective empathy in the context of sentencing embodies sentiments that are not wholly evil may jar the sensibilities of some readers. But it is a point that needs to be considered if discussion of race relations is to be lifted above the confining moralism in which it is often encased. Professor Richard Lempert reflects this understanding when he suggests that the death penalty may be inescapably arbitrary and capricious:

> not for the worst of reasons but for the best. . . . Whites, who as judges, prosecutors and jurors dominate the death sentencing process, cannot help feeling more indignation upon learning that a white (like them) has been killed than they do when there is a black victim. . . . [Such reactions] are simply part of what it is to be human in a race-conscious society.

Lempert, *supra* note 15, at 1113–14.

[242] Professor Lawrence, for instance, describes racism in a way that destigmatizes individual decisionmakers and emphasizes the racially oppressive cultural matrix in which we are all caught. "Americans share a common historical and cultural heritage in which racism has played a dominant role. . . . [W]e are all racists." Lawrence, *supra* note 73, at 322; *see also* Karst, *supra* note 224, at 1165 (arguing that a motive-centered theory "forces litigants in a race case into name-calling on one side and self-righteousness on the other").

One difficulty with conceptualizing racist conduct as an ordinary feature of our social life, a flaw in our culture rather than an individual failing, is that it may erode the moral condemnation that now attaches to behavior that is authoritatively labelled as racially discriminatory. *See* Blumstein, *Defining and Proving Race Discrimination: Perspectives on the Purpose vs. Results Approach from the Voting Rights Act*, 69 VA. L. REV. 633, 644 n.55 (1983) ("[O]ne of the reasons we find racial discrimination to be opprobrious is that it reflects improper conduct. . . . [W]ithdrawing the element of responsibility from the finding deprives the concept of discrimination of much of its moral force.").

[243] Arguing that the judiciary has accomplished far less than some claim in terms of reforming race relations, Professor Allen Hutchinson notes that in the United States the percentage of blacks unemployed in 1984 was 17.2 while the corresponding percentage of whites was 7.2; that the percentage of black families below the poverty level was 32.4 while the corresponding percentage for white families was 9.7; that the chance that a black male will be murdered in a given year is 1 in 1539 while the corresponding figure for a white male is 1 in 9927; that the

problem suggests the appropriateness of a laissez-faire judicial policy that views wrongs of this magnitude as essentially nonjusticiable. In my view, however, the constitutional requirement of racial justice embedded in the Reconstruction amendments demands judicial intervention — even if it begins with no more than a candid announcement that existing conditions violate the norms of the equal protection clause.

---

ratio of male black children dying in their first year of life to male white children dying in their first year of life is 1.8 to 1. Hutchinson, *Book Review*, 96 YALE L.J. 637, 662–63 (1987). Justice Marshall emphasized similarly disturbing statistics in his *Bakke* dissent. *See* Regents of the Univ. of Cal. v. Bakke, 438 U.S. 265, 395 (1978) (Marshall, J., concurring in judgment in part and dissenting).

The Supreme Court in Periods of Critical Realignment

William Lasser
Clemson University

The Supreme Court played a major role in the process of critical realignment in all three periods studied (the 1850s, 1890s, 1930s). At a key moment in the developing realignment crisis, the Court was "captured" by its conservative wing and struck down an important piece of moderate legislation. By making centrist positions untenable, the Court facilitated the takeover of the major parties by their extremist factions. In two of the three periods, in turn, the Court found itself at the center of intense controversy and criticism.

The Supreme Court of the United States is a political as well as a legal institution, and is affected by the long-term and short-term trends in American politics. Over the long term, as Robert A. Dahl suggested, "the Supreme Court is inevitably a part of the dominant national alliance"; and the justices can be expected to reflect the political views of the leaders of that alliance. During periods of critical realignment, however, "when the old alliance is disintegrating and the new one is struggling to take control of political institutions," the Court's behavior is less certain (Dahl, 1957, p. 293). This paper is an attempt to provide what Richard Funston called for in 1975: "an extended, systematic, historical examination" of the Supreme Court in periods of critical realignment (Funston, 1975, p. 808).

I

Realignments are "fundamental shifts in the structure of the party system." They are marked by changes in voting behavior and in the "basic party attachments of the voting citizens." They result in "a change in the structure of the party conflict and hence the establishment of a new line of partisan cleavage on a different axis within the electorate" (Sundquist,

*This article represents a summary of the argument presented in my dissertation, "Crisis and the Court: Judicial Politics in Periods of Critical Realignment (Ph.D. Dissertation, Harvard University, 1983). An earlier version of this article was presented at the 5th meeting of the Southern Political Science Association, Birmingham, AL, 4 November 1983. I would like to thank James Q. Wilson, Harry N. Hirsch, Walter Dean Burnham, Richard Funston, and those who reviewed this article for the *Journal of Politics*.

1983, pp. 4-5, 14). Realignments that occur gradually, the result of processes that "operate inexorably, and almost imperceptibly, election after election," are known as secular realignments. Those that occur "sharply and decisively," involving "a change in the terms of the party conflict and the composition of the party coalitions," are known as critical realignments.

Critical realignments are "extraordinary upheavals in the flow of American electoral and policy history that occur under conditions of abnormal and general crisis" (Burnham, 1982, p. 10). They

> are marked by short, sharp reorganizations of the mass coalitional base of the major parties which occur at periodic intervals on the national level; are often preceded by major third-party revolts; . . . are closely associated with abnormal stress in the socioeconomic system; are marked by ideological polarizations and issue-distances between the major parties which are exceptionally large by normal standards; and have durable consequences as constituent acts which determine the outer boundaries of policy in general, though not necessarily of policies in detail (Burnham, 1970, p. 10).

Critical realignments, it is generally agreed, occurred in the 1850s, 1890s, and 1930s.[1]

Critical realignments are provoked by the sudden flare-up of a particularly important and divisive issue (or "cluster of related issues") that cuts across the existing lines of party cleavage. The emergence of a crosscutting issue does not by itself presage a critical realignment; in order to provoke a realignment, such an issue must come to be "of such paramount concern to some proportion of the voters that if it encounters resistance from the parties with which they are affiliated, it overrides all the considerations that form the basis of their attachment to the existing parties" (Sundquist, 1983, p. 35). At such time the issue can be considered a critical issue.

Critical issues are not new issues. Typically, they are old issues which suddenly become critical under the pressure of what Walter Dean Burnham calls "triggering events," such as the passage of the Kansas-Nebraska Act or the onset of the Great Depression. The period before a realignment, during which a crosscutting issue divides the electorate but does not provoke a critical realignment, can last several decades (the slavery issue, for example, divided the polity for well over four decades before the realignment of the 1850s actually began). During this so-called "prerealignment" period, groups form within each of the major parties at each pole of the potential realigning issue; alternatively, minor third parties may be formed to espouse the polar position on one or both sides.

[1] Scholars agree that the last critical realignment took place in the 1930s, and that since then the party system has been undergoing a long period of "dealignment." See Burnham, 1970; Beck, 1979; and Sundquist, 1983, for different viewpoints and a general discussion.

Meanwhile a large group within each party, along with the leadership, remains in the center.

Before an issue becomes a critical issue, party leaders have an incentive to suppress it and seek compromise and conciliation. Future critical issues are by definition issues on which members of each party, for the time being, agree to disagree. Party leaders hope to maintain that agreement. Some of the party leaders are concerned primarily with patronage and organization and are simply not policy oriented. Those politicians who are concerned with the substance of policy are oriented towards the issues of the last realignment rather than the ongoing one (Sundquist, 1983, p. 307). Thus both by interest and inclination the leaders of the major parties try to reach compromise solutions on crosscutting issues or hope they disappear altogether.

As long as the centrists remain in control of both major parties, no realignment can take place. However,

> if the new issue becomes increasingly dominant, the polar forces will grow at the expense of the centrists, and eventually the centrists in one or both major parties will be forced to take sides or will be overthrown. At that point, when one of the major parties comes under the control of a polar force and so moves to the polar position on the crosscutting issue, the realignment is precipitated (Sundquist, 1983, p. 36).

Although critical realignments develop over long periods of time, the pace of the realignment process seems to accelerate as one or both of the major parties is "captured" by the polar forces. Finally, a "critical election turns on the [critical] issue and the voters make their choice." After the critical election, "the party system has a new rationale, an old conflict has been displaced by a new one for a segment of the electorate, and that segment of the electorate has formed, or is in the process of forming, new party attachments on the basis of that rationale" (Sundquist, 1983, p. 37).

II

Several hypotheses have been advanced to explain the Supreme Court's behavior during periods of critical realignment. One, advanced by Richard Funston, postulates that

> over long periods of time, the Supreme Court reflects the will of the dominant political forces; however, during transitional periods, in which the Court is a holdover from the old coalition, the Court will be most likely to perform the counter-majoritarian function [of striking down national legislation] ascribed to it by traditional theory (Funston, 1975, p. 796; footnote omitted).

This hypothesis is based on the assumption that during transitional periods "the Court, by virtue of the life tenure of the justices, will be out of step with the political times" (Funston, 1975, p. 796). According to this argument, all the justices appointed by presidents of the old alliance will unite behind the policy views of the old alliance and be hostile to the policies of a new alliance. The classic example of such a scenario, it is argued, occurred in the New Deal period.

There is a problem with this hypothesis, however. Critical issues are, by definition, crosscutting issues. Since critical issues cut across the existing line of party cleavage and split the two major parties into competing factions, there is no "old regime" or "dominant party" position on the critical issue. Instead, both parties are divided over the critical issue.[2] If there is no old-regime position on the critical issue, the Supreme Court cannot be expected to unite behind such a position; instead, we can expect the justices of the Supreme Court to be deeply divided over the critical issue. Moreover, we would expect that division to be unrelated to old partisan loyalties.

The historical evidence supports this theory. The Court was divided over the critical issue in all three realignments between 1850 and 1940; in no case did it divide along party lines. Both the Marshall and early Taney Courts were deeply divided in cases with slavery overtones.[3] In the *Dred Scott* case itself, the Court divided 6-3 on the key question of the constitutionality of the Missouri Compromise. The six justices who voted to strike down the Missouri Compromise were all Democrats; those who voted not to invalidate that law included a Democrat (Nelson), a Whig (Curtis), and a Democrat-turned-Republican (McLean). (That all those in the majority were Democrats seems to reflect the fact that there was only one Whig on the Court at the time of the *Dred Scott* case.)[4] In the 1890s, the majority of five in the income tax case consisted of two Democrats and three Republicans; the minority consisted of two Democrats and two Republicans. In the 1930s, there were four anti-New Deal justices—two Democrats and two Republicans; three consistent supporters of the New Deal—two Democrats and one Republican; and two swing men, both Republicans.[5]

---

[2] In some historical party systems, moreover, it is impossible to speak of a "dominant party"; an example is the later stages of the third party system, in which Democratic and Republican strength was almost evenly divided.

[3] See, for example, *Groves* v. *Slaughter*, 15 Peters (40 U.S.) 449 (1841); *Prigg* v. *Pennsylvania*, 16 Peters (41 U..S.) 539 (1842); the *License* cases, 5 Howard (46 U.S.) 504 (1847); and the *Passenger* cases, 7 Howard (48 U.S.) 283 (1849). An excellent discussion of the Taney Court and the slavery issue appears in Hyman and Wiecek, 1982, pp. 78-114.

[4] The reason there was only one Whig on the Court in 1857 is that Democrats controlled the White House for twenty of the twenty-eight years between 1828 and 1856; the Whigs controlled the White House for only eight years, and Whig presidents made only two appointments to the Supreme Court. One of these two, moreover, was Samuel Nelson, a Democrat!

[5] The Democrats in the majority in the income tax case were Field and Fuller; the Republicans were Brewer, Gray, and Shiras. The Democrats in the minority were Jackson and

A related hypothesis suggests that "the Supreme Court will ordinarily side with the presidential wing of the [old dominant] party in shaping a strategy for dealing with" critical issues (Adamany, 1980, p. 248). This hypothesis is based on the explicit assumption that "justices named by succeeding presidents of the same party will usually share a coherent executive perspective on crucial national issues" (Adamany, 1980, p. 248). We have already seen, however, that the centrist leaders of the major parties typically seek to suppress crosscutting (and hence future critical) issues, and do not use them as tests of party loyalty. Thus, it is entirely possible for even succeeding presidents of the same party to have opposing views on such an issue, and, in any event, a president would not be likely to make his judicial appointments solely on the basis of the candidates' positions on an issue on which members of his own party have agreed to disagree. Furthermore, at any given time there may be a number of crosscutting issues. A president of the "old coalition" would be unable to predict that a particular issue would eventually become a critical issue, and so would have no reason to make judicial appointments with that issue in mind.

In none of the three realignment periods did the Court split along the lines of presidential appointment. The nine justices who participated in the *Dred Scott* case were appointed by six different presidents. The two most strongly pro-slavery justices, Taney and Wayne, were appointed by Andrew Jackson, who also appointed the most rabidly anti-slavery justice, John McLean. The other six justices were appointed by five different presidents in no apparent pattern. Benjamin Harrison appointed two of the justices who were in the majority in the income tax case (Brewer and Shiras), but he also appointed two of the minority justices (Harlan and Brown). Grover Cleveland appointed one justice on each side (Fuller and White). The Hughes Court consisted of three generally pro-New Deal justices (Cardozo, Brandeis, and Stone); four committed anti-New Deal justices (Van Devanter, Butler, McReynolds, and Sutherland); and two "swing" justices (Hughes and Roberts), whose votes varied. The liberal Cardozo was appointed by Hoover; Stone, also a consistent supporter of the New Deal, was appointed by Coolidge. On the other side, the conservative Justice McReynolds was appointed by the progressive Woodrow Wilson. Not a single one of the four justices who consistently opposed the New Deal was appointed by Hoover.

Occasionally, there are presidents whose Supreme Court appointees share similar judicial and political philosophies and stand as a bloc in cases

---

White; the Republicans were Harlan and Brown. Of the four anti-New Deal justices, Butler and McReynolds were Democrats, while Van Devanter and Sutherland were Republicans. Of the three liberals, Cardozo and Brandeis were Democrats, while Stone was a Republican. Hughes and Roberts were Republicans.

involving a critical issue. The best examples are William Howard Taft and Warren G. Harding, whose appointees were all conservatives on economic and property matters. In fact, Taft (whom Harding appointed to the Court) played a major role in advising Harding on his judicial appointments. Taft, however, was atypical in his desire to appoint a philosophically monolithic judiciary. Wilson, as noted above, appointed both Brandeis and McReynolds; Coolidge appointed Stone; and Hoover appointed Hughes, Roberts, and Cardozo. The evidence is quite clear that Hoover in particular did not choose his Supreme Court nominees on the basis of their views on economic issues that might come before the Court.[6]

III

The key to understanding the behavior of the Supreme Court during periods of critical realignment, as Paul A. Beck and David Adamany have suggested, is to examine the Court's role in the process of realignment itself (Beck, 1976; Adamany, 1980). Since "the Court is a political institution whose members are recruited with their political preferences and prejudices in mind" (Adamany, 1980), it seems likely that, during a realignment crisis, the justices' behavior will parallel that of other political actors.

Politicians, as we have seen, respond to crosscutting issues by straddling them or by moving to one extreme or the other. Each party is split thereby into three competing factions: moderates, and conservative and progressive extremists. As the crisis progresses, more and more politicians and voters in the center are driven to one pole or the other, and the stage is set for a critical election.

At all points in this process, the Supreme Court justices behave just like their political counterparts. In the stable phase before a realignment, the majority of the justices take a moderate position on the constitutional questions related to the future critical issue. That is, they uphold Congress's discretion to act as it wishes. At the same time, some justices express the extremist view that Congress does not have the constitutional authority to act. Unlike the party system, the Court is split not into three factions, but into two: a moderate group upholdng Congress's power to act, and a polar group espousing the view that Congress is prohibited from acting. In past realignment periods, there was no group on the Court corresponding to the progressive extremists in the political arena, since in the past the courts rarely if ever declared that Congress was constitutionally required to

[6] Hoover made his selections almost entirely on the basis of geographical representativeness. See Carmen, 1969, p. 649.

exercise its power to regulate in a given area.[7] Like the political parties, the Court for many years prior to the realignment crisis is controlled by its moderate center. When faced with the future critical issue in the form of a constitutional question, the moderate majority tends to uphold congressional discretion to act or to refrain from acting as it sees fit.[8]

During all three realignment periods, the Supreme Court moved away from its moderate course and struck down one or more laws related to the critical issue which moderates of both parties supported.[9] The law struck down in *Dred Scott* was the Missouri Compromise of 1820, which had been, as the name suggests, a compromise between southern proponents and northern opponents of slavery. By 1857, the principle behind the law was anathema to extremists on both sides. The income tax of 1894, though introduced by William Jennings Bryan, was supported by many moderate Republicans and Democrats. Even President Cleveland, while not explicitly endorsing the income tax, refused to speak out against it and even gave hints of support (Nevins, 1932, p. 667). The early New Deal legislation follows this pattern as well. The laws of the first New Deal (nullified in 1935 and 1936) were attacked by conservatives for over-regulating the economy and by progressives and radicals for being too friendly to business. Most moderates of both parties supported the first New Deal at least through the end of 1934.[10]

---

[7] In the modern era, of course, the federal courts quite frequently impose on Congress or the states positive requirements to act. Still, as late as 1943 Felix Frankfurter could write accurately that "a court can only strike down. It can only say 'This or that law is void.' " (*West Virginia v. Barnette*, 319 U.S. 624 (1943), p. 651).

[8] The Court has upheld congressional discretion in a variety of ways. It tried to avoid slavery issues altogether in the period before Dred Scott, making generally narrow and uncontroversial decisions in this area. It directly upheld the constitutionality of a federal income tax in several cases between 1796 and 1895, the most recent of which had been *Springer v. United States*, 102 U.S. 586 (1881). In the period between 1900 and 1935, the Court upheld broad federal powers in the economic regulation area, though it did strike down attempts to regulate child labor, abolish "yellow dog" contracts, and impose minimum wages. In general, "most of the important legislative measures that were really demanded by public opinion did . . . manage to survive the gauntlet of judicial review" (McCloskey, 1960, p. 151). The Court's deference to the political branches may stem from the majority's realization of the divisive character of the issues involved, or from their sensitivity to the limits of judicial power.

[9] The cases in which these laws were struck down are *Dred Scott v. Sandford*, 19 Howard (60 U.S.) 393 (1857); *Pollock v. Farmers' Loan and Trust Co.*, 157 U.S. 429 (1895); and, in the New Deal, *Panama City Refining v. Ryan*, 293 U.S. 388 (1934); *Railroad Retirement Board v. Alton*, 295 U.S. 330 (1935); *Schechter Bros. v. United States*, 295 U.S. 495 (1935); *United States v. Butler*, 297 U.S. 1 (1936); and *Carter v. Carter Coal Co.*, 298 U.S. 238 (1936).

[10] The *Literary Digest*, for example, wrote in October 1934 that the debate in the ongoing mid-term election campaign was "not between the New Deal and the Old, but between the New Deal and one newer still" (*Literary Digest*, 27 October 1934, p. 13). See generally Leuchtenberg, 1963, pp. 67-95, 115-117.

In declaring that Congress possessed no power to pass a key piece of compromise legislation dealing with the critical issue, the Court also made it clear in each realignment that the as yet unenacted programs demanded by the progressive extremists would also be unconstitutional. For example, the *Dred Scott* decision made it clear that the Republican Party's platform promise to ban slavery in all the federal territories would also be unconstitutional if enacted. The anti-New Deal decisions of mid-1935 also seemed to indicate that the more progressive legislation of the second New Deal would be unconstitutional as well. Thus, at one blow the platforms of the progressive extremists and of the moderate centrists were declared unconstitutional, and the platform of the conservative extremists was declared to be the law of the land. Conservatives won a victory in each case. Progressives could aim for a reversal by the Court, by whatever means. Moderates were left helplessly in the middle. The Court thus acted as a catalyst for the polarization of the party system around the critical issue, and helped to set the agenda for the upcoming critical election.

The Court's switch away from its moderate course occurred suddenly, as one or more justices moved from the Court's center to its conservative pole.[11] (In none of the three periods was the switch caused by the appointment of new justices to the Court.) The capture of the Court by its conservative wing came at a key point in each realignment period and had a clear and decisive political impact in each case. The *Dred Scott* decision came just after a presidential election in which the northern and southern wings of the Democratic Party had papered over their differences on the territorial question. The Court's decision, by explicitly declaring the southern position to be the law of the land, made it exceedingly difficult for the party to maintain its unity. The decision in the income tax cases came in the late spring of 1895, precisely at the moment when the silver craze took hold of the Democratic Party and conservatives were maneuvering to capture the Republican Party. The first anti-New Deal decisions came in early to mid-1935, just as opposition to Franklin D. Roosevelt peaked and the president deliberated over whether to follow the suggestions of his moderate or more progressive advisers.

---

[11] In many cases, the "switch" of individual justices can be dated to within months or even days. Justice Grier, for example, is known to have voted to avoid the political questions in the Dred Scott case on February 14, 1857; on February 23, only nine days later, Grier informed President Buchanan that he would vote with the southern majority to invalidate the Missouri Compromise. See Auchampaugh, 1926, pp. 231-240. In the income tax case, one justice (though scholars disagree as to which one) switched between the Court's first decision in April 1895 and its second and final decision a month later, in May (Paul, 1976, pp. 214-8). Finally, the original switch of Justice Roberts (from a pro-New Deal to an anti-New Deal position) occurred between February 1935, when he sided with the majority in upholding the Gold Clause Resolution, and May 1935, when he provided the fifth vote needed to invalidate the Railroad Retirement Act.

By declaring the extremist conservative platform to be the law of the land, the Court legitimated that position and delegitimated the progressive and moderate positions. The effect of the Court decision on the moderate position was particularly important, because the invalidation in advance of potential compromise positions made it easier for conservative extremists to capture one of the major parties. Conservative extremists could now reject all attempts at compromise—whether real or potential—as unconstitutional, thus weakening the moderates' hold on the party platform and leadership. This is precisely what happened to Stephen A. Douglas, whose moderate "popular sovereignty" platform was struck down along with the Republican platform in the *Dred Scott* case. Thereafter, southern conservatives were in no mood to accept Douglas's position. Their own views on congressional power over slavery in the territories had been confirmed by the United States Supreme Court and were now law. Similarly, the Court's decisions in 1895 and in 1935 endorsed conservative extremist positions. Conservatives insisted that their own views were not only politically desirable but also constitutionally required. And FDR's decision to push forward with the more progressive second New Deal came in the wake of the *Schechter* decision, which struck down the National Industrial Recovery Act.

In all three periods, the Court decisions accelerated the polarization of the party system and clearly shaped the agenda for the next presidential election, in which the two parties presented to the electorate a clear choice on the critical issue. Such were the elections of 1860, 1896, and 1936.[12] Once the electorate made its choice, the Court did not try to oppose the implementation of the policy goals implied by that choice in any of the three periods. Even in the New Deal case, the Court succumbed to the verdict of the people within six months of the election.[13]

---

[12] In the elections that preceded these three, significant shifts can be seen in the partisan preferences of the electorate. Republican strength in 1856, the first year the party contested a presidential election, was decidedly greater than that of the various anti-slavery parties in 1852 and before. The election of 1892 saw the entrance of the populists onto the political stage, and they captured over a million votes. And shifts towards the Democratic party in key states can be seen both in 1928 and 1932. Still, it was not until the elections of 1860, 1896, and 1936 that both parties took relatively extreme views on the critical issue. That is what makes these elections decisive.

[13] The Court was spurred on to its "switch in time that saved nine" by the introduction of FDR's "Court-packing" plan in February 1937. Evidence indicates, however, that Owen Roberts had switched to the liberal side as early as December 1936. In that month the Court upheld (albeit in a technical decision) a New York unemployment compensation statute, despite arguable similarities to the federal law struck down in the Railroad Retirement Case three years before. The vote was four to four, with Justice Stone—normally on the liberal side—not participating; thus it can be concluded that Roberts was on the liberal side. See Frankfurter, 1955.

There was nothing inevitable about the Supreme Court's involvement in these three realignment crises. By maintaining its moderate course, the Court could have avoided entering the political thicket in all three periods. In fact, the Court came very close to staying out of all three realignment crises, and would have done so if not for a last-minute switch by one or more of the justices from the moderate center to the conservative pole. In the heat of realignment politics, however, when the party system is polarizing around a critical issue, it seems to be very difficult for justices to remain above or outside the political fray. In fact, it is precisely during periods of critical realignment that the Court seems most political and ideological. Both the Taney Court and the New Deal Court suffered constant criticism that they were indulging in partisan or parochial politics.

In all three periods the Court became involved in the realignment after one or more justices switched from a moderate to an extremist position. All three times, moreover, the Court ended up at the conservative pole. How can the Court's conservatism be explained? It cannot be explained with reference to the natural conservatism of a legal system based on the principle of *stare decisis*. In two of the three cases the Court's decisions were a clear break with precedent; the *Dred Scott* case overrruled the Marshall Court's doctrine that Congress's authority over the territories was plenary, and the income tax case reversed the long-standing precedent that income taxes were not "direct" taxes under the Constitution and therefore did not have to be apportioned among the states. The Court's New Deal decisions were mixed in terms of their fidelity to precedent. Some, such as the delegation portions of the *Schechter* decision or the minimum wage decision in *New York v. Morehead* ex rel. *Tipaldo*, were clearly in line with existing precedent; others, such as the invalidation of the Agricultural Adjustment Act in *Butler v. United States*, in effect created new law where none had previously existed; still others, such as the Railroad Retirement case, seem utterly at odds with precedent. In most of the New Deal cases the Court faced two sets of conflicting precedents, and, typically, they chose to follow the more conservative set.

Instead, the Court's conservatism must be ascribed to the fact that one or more justices succumbed to pressure—direct or otherwise—to move to the conservative pole. In the *Dred Scott* case, for example, President Buchanan interceded with Justice Grier, asking him to concur with Taney's opinion of the Court. In the 1890s and 1930s, moderate justices such as Howell Jackson, Edward White, and Owen Roberts were subjected to pressures from the press, the public, and probably their fellow justices. The spring of 1895 produced what Arnold Paul has called a "crisis psychology" on the Court as well as in the country. In the spring of 1935, likewise, Justice

Roberts was the subject of intense speculation and controversy concerning his behavior.[14]

The forces at work on the Court that ultimately caused several of the justices to move to the conservative pole were the same forces that were at work in the polity at large. Men who previously had suppressed or compromised on a controversial issue for many decades suddenly found themselves under intense pressure to take sides; under the pressure of events and of an increasingly polarized public opinion, one or more of them abandoned their moderate positions in favor of more radical ones. Two good examples are John A. Campbell of Alabama, who sided with the majority in the *Dred Scott* case, and Owen J. Roberts, who became the fifth vote against the New Deal in May of 1935. Campbell, prior to his appointment to the Court, had been a moderate southerner who had freed his own slaves and who had spoken out in favor of limited reforms of the slave system. The disparity between his earlier private views on slavery and his public stance in *Dred Scott* prompted his biographer to speculate that Campbell "was partially proscribed from consistency and moderation by southern feelings. Certainly, the price of southern membership in the Union was rising, and perhaps Campbell was caught in the drift of southern expectations and pressure" (Friedman and Israel, 1969, p. 2:934). Roberts, who in 1934 was on the liberal side in two key state cases dealing with economic regulation and who voted to uphold the Gold Clause Resolution in February 1935, moved under pressure to the conservative side by May 1935, aligning himself with the Court's most conservative wing.

The Court's conservatism in each of the three periods depended on the somewhat fortuitous movement of moderate justices to the conservative pole. This shift to the right involved the Court in the developing realignment crisis. If these justices had not moved to the right, the Court would have remained above and outside the realignment process. There was no opportunity for the justices to catalyze the realignment by moving to the progressive pole, however, because there was no legal position equivalent to the political views of the progressive extremists.

---

[14] On the 1850s, see Auchampaugh, 1926. On the 1890s, see Paul, 1976, pp. 217-8. On the 1930s, see generally Leuchtenberg, 1963, pp. 143-6. The level of excitement over the gold clause cases was so high that the Court took the extremely unusual step of announcing on consecutive Saturdays that the decision would not be made the following Monday. The columnist T.R.B., of the *New Republic*, commented after the gold clause decision that "since they [the majority in the gold clause cases] were forced by circumstances and expediency into a clearly reluctant backing of the New Deal in the gold clause cases, the natural tendency of at least one or two of them will be to react in the other direction at the earliest opportunity" (March 6, 1935, p. 100). In May, T.R.B. noted that lawyers within the administration had come to the conclusion that "Mr. Justice Roberts is lost to the New Deal and his switch is regarded as the worst blow it [the administration] has had since its inauguration" (May 22, 1935, p. 46).

Although the Supreme Court's role in each of the three realignments studied follows a consistent pattern, the similarities among the three periods should not be allowed to obscure the differences. One obvious difference lies in the relationship between the legal issues facing the Court in a given realignment period and the political issues which lie at the heart of the realignment. In the 1850s and 1930s the legal issues were essentially identical to the critical issue; in the 1890s, the tax issue was only symbolically related to the critical issue, which involved monetary policy. This is one reason why the Court's role in the 1850s and 1930s is more dramatic than its role in the 1890s. This difference also helps to explain why the *Dred Scott* and New Deal decisions provoked intense negative responses from progressives (Republicans and liberal New Dealers, respectively), while the income tax decision produced relatively little public outcry.[15] Ante-bellum Republicans and liberal New Dealers found their political platforms declared unconstitutional by the Supreme Court, but the populists had lost only one small part of their program and, in any event, were moving at precisely the same time towards the monetary issue.

The timing of the Court's involvement in the realignment process also affects its role as a catalyst in the polarization of the party system. The *Dred Scott* decision, for example, came after the Republican Party had already moved to the progressive pole on the slavery extension issue and had replaced the Whigs as a major party. The New Deal decisions came before either party had been captured by polar extremists. Thus while the Court decision catalyzed only the movement toward the conservative pole in 1850, it catalyzed the movement toward both poles in the 1930s.[16]

The Supreme Court's role in critical realignments is not to shape "party policies as a majority coalition becomes unstable in response to emerging, crosscutting political issues," as David Adamany contends (Adamany, 1980, p. 257). Nor does the Court move in to "fill the power vacuum" left by the inability of the "popular branches of government . . . to synchronize their actions," as another scholar has speculated (Beck, 1979, p. 152). Rather, the moderate justices act just like the moderates in each of the two major political parties, first resisting the pressure to take sides on the critical

[15] Although the proximate critical issue in 1896 was the monetary question, this issue was symbolic of a deeper cultural and geographical split in the nation. Both sides attached symbolic importance to the income tax case, though—contrary to the common interpretation—the conservatives attached more significance to the case than the populist/progressives. See Jensen, 1971, and Lasser, 1983, pp. 151-62.

[16] The Court's first anti-New Deal decisions—along with its clear disapproval, expressed in dicta, of the Gold Clause Resolution of 1933—helped to crystallize opposition to Roosevelt in early 1935. Its invalidation of the National Industrial Recovery Act in May 1935 gave Roosevelt the final push he needed to abandon the "all-class alliance" and align himself with labor, as his most progressive advisers urged (Leuchtenberg, 1963, pp. 146-8; Lasser, 1983, pp. 208-211).

issue, then giving in and taking sides clearly and dramatically. When that happens, the Court can be captured by its conservative polar wing, and its decision or decisions on the critical issue can catalyze the further polarization of the party system, a polarization that is a prerequisite to realignment. The Court's role in the realignment process may place the justices at the center of a political firestorm. The Court's involvement may also provoke a constitutional crisis of the highest order. It is no coincidence that the two most serious crises in the Court's history grew out of the two most serious crises in the nation's history: the Civil War and the New Deal.

References

Adamany, David (1973). "Law and Society: Realigning Elections and the Supreme Court." *Wisconsin Law Review* 1973: 790-846.

_____ (1980). "The Supreme Court's Role in Critical Elections." In Bruce A. Campbell and Richard J. Trilling (eds.), *Realignment in American Politics*. Austin, TX: University of Texas Press.

Auchampaugh, Philip (1926). "James Buchanan, the Court, and the Dred Scott Case." *Tennessee Historical Magazine* 9: 231-240.

Beck, Paul Allen (1976). "Critical Elections and the Supreme Court: Putting the Cart After the Horse." *American Political Science Review* 70: 930-32.

_____ (1979). "The Electoral Cycle and Patterns of American Politics." *British Journal of Political Science* 9: 129-36.

Burnham, Walter Dean (1970). *Critical Elections and the Mainsprings of American Politics*. New York: W. W. Norton.

_____ (1982). *The Crisis of American Politics*. New York: Oxford University Press.

Canon, Bradley C., and S. Sidney Ulmer (1976). "The Supreme Court and Critical Elections: A Dissent." *American Political Science Review* 70: 1215-21.

Carmen, Ira H. (1969). "The President, Politics, and the Power of Appointment: Hoover's Nomination of Mr. Justice Cardozo." *Virginia Law Review* 55: 616-59.

Chayes, Abram (1970). "The Role of the Judge in Public Law Litigation." *Harvard Law Review* 89: 1281-1316.

Dahl, Robert A. (1957). "Decision-Making in a Democracy: The Supreme Court as a National Policy Maker." *Journal of Public Law* 6: 279-95.

Dunne, F. P. (1906). *Mr. Dooley's Opinions*. New York: Harper and Brothers.

Frankfurter, Felix (1955). "Mr. Justice Roberts." *University of Pennsylvania Law Review* 104: 311.

Friedman, Leon, and Fred L. Israel (1969). *The Justices of the United States Supreme Court 1789-1969: Their Lives and Major Opinions*. 5 vols. New York: Chelsea House Publishers.

Funston, Richard (1975). "The Supreme Court and Critical Elections." *American Political Science Review* 69: 795-811.

Hyman, Harold M., and William M. Wiecek (1982). *Equal Justice Under Law: Constitutional Development, 1835-1875*. New York: Harper and Row.

Jensen, Richard (1971). *The Winning of the Midwest: Social and Political Conflict, 1888-96*. Chicago: University of Chicago Press.

Lasser, William (1983). "Crisis and the Court: Judicial Politics in Periods of Critical Realignment." Ph.D. Dissertation, Harvard University.

Leuchtenberg, William E. (1963). *Franklin D. Roosevelt and the New Deal.* New York: Harper and Row.

McCloskey, Robert G. (1960). *The American Supreme Court.* Chicago: University of Chicago Press.

Nagel, Stuart S. (1965). "Court-Curbing Periods in American History." *Vanderbilt Law Review* 18: 925-44.

Nevins, Allan (1932). *Grover Cleveland: A Study in Courage.* New York: Dodd, Mead and Co.

Nichols, Roy F., and Philip S. Klein (1971). "The Election of 1856." In Arthur M. Schlesinger and Fred L. Israel (eds.), *History of American Presidential Elections.* 5 vols. New York: Chelsea House.

Paul, Arnold M. (1976). *Conservative Crisis and the Rule of Law.* Gloucester, MA: Peter Smith.

Sundquist, James L. (1983). *Dynamics of the Party System.* Washington: The Brookings Institution.

RALPH LERNER

THE SUPREME COURT AS REPUBLICAN SCHOOLMASTER

Students of judicial politics have long been mindful of the close connection between judicial power and public opinion. Tocqueville, for one, limned the character of the good judge in a democratic regime with a full awareness of the problem raised by that relation. Recognizing that no regime can safely avoid hard, politically unpopular decisions, Tocqueville was alert for ways in which such decisions might be made palatable to a modern democratic people, a benevolent people not given to self-denial:[1]

> The power of the Supreme Court Justices is immense, but it is power springing from opinion. They are all-powerful so long as the people consent to obey the law; they can do nothing when they scorn it. Now, of all powers, that of opinion is the hardest to use, for it is impossible to say exactly where its limits come. Often it is as dangerous to lag behind as to outstrip it.
>
> The federal judges therefore must not only be good citizens and men of education and integrity, qualities necessary for all magistrates, but must also be statesmen; they must know how to understand the spirit of the age, to confront those ob-

---

Ralph Lerner is Associate Professor of the Social Sciences, The College, The University of Chicago.

Author's acknowledgment: My thanks are due to Marvin Meyers (Brandeis University) and Herbert J. Storing (The University of Chicago) for their critical scrutiny of my argument. The research for this paper was supported in part by an Inland Steel Faculty Fellowship.

[1] TOCQUEVILLE, DEMOCRACY IN AMERICA 137 (Lawrence trans. 1966).

stacles that can be overcome, and to steer out of the current when the tide threatens to carry them away, and with them the sovereignty of the Union and obedience to its laws.

An adequate judiciary in a democratic regime must be at once upright and subtle. So Tocqueville maintained, and so too did many of the shapers and leaders of the early national judiciary. The consequence of so regarding the judge is to thrust him—and the whole machinery of justice—into the role of an educator, molder, or guardian of those manners, morals, and beliefs that sustain republican government. That Tocqueville, at any rate, viewed the legal profession as the saving element in a democracy by virtue of that profession's quasi-aristocratic habit of mind is notorious and requires no elaboration.[2] But it is not so obvious that the earliest generation of national judges consciously acted as statesmen-teachers, or that they were supposed to assume any such role.

In current discussions, we find an array of arguments, separately attractive yet at odds with one another, about the proper role of the modern judge. Some maintain that judges educate willy-nilly through example and that judicial decision-making is in some sense a model for other forms of political decision-making. According to this view, sensible judges, while mindful of the "contagious consequences" of the standards of their decisions upon civic habits, will eschew teaching or preaching as such, be it of principles or of policies, in the courtroom. Only "self-willed judges" would be guilty of such an offense.[3] Others maintain that such heterogeneous elements go into the selection and appointment of a judge that it takes a wholly unwarranted credulity to expect these men to be "thereby transmuted into something of a priesthood to whose ministrations, nurture, and wise discretion higher values and principles appropriate to a great nation have been, or prudently could be, committed."[4] Still others simply say, in effect, that courts have no decisive educative task, that in the last analysis the judiciary's efforts to instill and sustain "fundamental principles of equity and fair play" are either superfluous or unavailing.[5]

---

[2] *Id.* at 247–48, 252–54.

[3] Frankfurter, *John Marshall and the Judicial Function*, in SUTHERLAND, GOVERNMENT UNDER LAW 31 (1956).

[4] Brown, *Quis Custodiet Ipsos Custodes?—The School-Prayer Cases*, 1963 SUPREME COURT REVIEW 4.

[5] HAND, THE SPIRIT OF LIBERTY 164 (Dilliard ed., 3d ed. 1960).

A partial resolution of the difficulties raised by these differing views may be sought in the origins of the American national judiciary. That original understanding is to be reconstructed, not with a view to finding a ready-made model for the modern judge, but with the hope of seeing more clearly the political positions, opportunities, and dangers judges must be attentive to in a democratic regime. My concern is to recover and assess the evidence that the national judiciary from the very beginning acted as "teachers to the citizenry."[6] Beyond that, I shall examine the evidence that those who drafted the Constitution and thought most coherently about the place of the Supreme Court in the proposed government expected the Court to engage in high political education. Although the modes in which judges have responded may change, the problem to which they have responded persists. That problem—the proper connection between judicial power and public opinion—remains live and urgent, if mocking of final formulations.

I. The Use and Abuse of the Grand Jury Charge by Pre-Marshall Justices

The legislative history of Senate Bill 1 of the first session of the First Congress must, in many interesting particulars of motive and intention, remain hidden from us. The genesis of what was to be called the Judiciary Act of 1789 has been examined and re-examined, sometimes with great care,[7] but always with a number of questions unanswered and perhaps unanswerable. The secrecy in which the Senate then conducted its business and the heedless indifference with which Americans long treated their public records obscure the purposes Congress intended to serve by enacting

[6] This characterization of the courts is, more recently, that of Judge Charles E. Wyzanski, Jr. See his *Constitutionalism: Limitation and Affirmation*, in Sutherland, *supra* note 3, at 485–86, and his letter to Sen. Saltonstall, Jan. 12, 1959, reprinted in Murphy & Pritchett, Courts, Judges, and Politics 324–25 (1961). Especially apposite here is his *Comment*, in Sutherland, *supra*, at 493: "But we are told that we expect too much from the courts. And Judge Learned Hand, and if I understand him correctly, Mr. Justice Frankfurter, suggest to us that political virtue is habit. I suggest that Socrates was nearer right, and as extreme as it seems at first, 'virtue is knowledge.' And that universities and courts and like institutions engaged in spreading knowledge, in dealing *concretely* with cases, enhance political morality and do in fact preserve the state in its ultimate purpose."

[7] See, above all, Warren, *New Light on the History of the Federal Judiciary Act of 1789*, 37 Harv. L. Rev. 49 (1923).

the Judiciary Act. What broad political functions were the Justices of the highest court of the land expected to perform? We can give at best a probable answer. To what extent were the political and psychological premises underlying the national judicial establishment of a piece with those on which the other parts of the new government were founded? On such a fundamental question we are obliged to speak with no less caution. We are dealing with matters that not only admit of speculation, but fairly require it.

It is not only such large questions that are difficult to answer with confidence. Many narrower problems are equally beset with ambiguities and uncertainties. Consider the simple question: What led Congress to send members of the Supreme Court riding circuit over the length and breadth of the land? There may be parallels between the organization of the Circuit Courts and the English Assize system[8] or the colonial or state courts.[9] But earlier practice contained no precise analogy to the way in which members of the nation's highest court were brought directly into the milieu of local laws and usages, local lawyers and jurors. Members of the Supreme Court, sitting as Circuit Court judges, instructed grand juries and presided over trials while disposing of the considerable original jurisdiction vested in the Circuit Courts. It bespeaks some legislative purpose, not to say single-mindedness, to compel the disgruntled members of the highest national tribunal to perform tiring and hazardous circuit duties.[10] It is plausible, even likely, that nothing more lies behind this feature of the judicial system than a close-fisted Connecticut concern to get value for money. The early expectations for the Supreme Court's business, both original and appellate, suggested that ennui rather than exhaustion would be the Justices' probable occupational hazard. Jealous guardians of the public purse might very well have seen circuit-riding as a cure to

---

8 See 2 REGISTER OF DEBATES IN CONGRESS, 19th Cong., 1st Sess., Pt. I, col. 110.1 (Jan. 24, 1826) (Rep. Kerr); FRANKFURTER & LANDIS, THE BUSINESS OF THE SUPREME COURT 12–13 (1927); ARCHER, THE QUEEN'S COURTS 250–51 (1956).

9 POUND, ORGANIZATION OF COURTS 107 (1940); Letter of "A Democratic Federalist" (Oct. 23, 1787), reprinted in MCMASTER & STONE, PENNSYLVANIA AND THE FEDERAL CONSTITUTION 1787–1788 153 (1888). But see 2 REGISTER OF DEBATES IN CONGRESS, 19th Cong., 1st Sess., Pt. I, cols. 873–74 (Jan. 4, 1826) (Rep. Webster).

10 The story of complaints, recommendations, and responses is summarized, along with much relevant historical background, in FRANKFURTER & LANDIS, *supra* note 8, at 4–30. See also WHITE, THE FEDERALISTS 483–84 (1965); 1 WARREN, THE SUPREME COURT IN UNITED STATES HISTORY 85–90 (1923).

boredom and a way of serving both justice and economy, to neither's disadvantage.[11]

However onerous members of the Supreme Court felt their circuit duties to be, it cannot be said that they failed to take advantage of the opportunities thus presented. The Justices of the Federalist period sensed and were reminded of the novelty of giving substance to the Philadelphia Convention's founding act.[12] It is not farfetched to suspect that the Justices saw themselves as having a unique responsibility, beyond those shared by other courts in the system. They were all Federalists. They were not narrow professional lawyers, but revolutionary patriots and statesmen whose involvement in the founding and ratification controversies made it natural for them to think politically and to feel some proprietary relationship to the new order. The Justices were quick to see and seize the chance to proselytize for the new government and to inculcate habits and teachings most necessary in their view for the maintenance of self-government. (In so doing they left later interpreters with the problem of distinguishing a defense of the regime and of the Constitution from a defense of an administration and of a party.) The main vehicle for this instruction was the charge to the grand jury, with which the presiding judge formally opened the proceedings of a Circuit Court session.

The prevailing practice was for a judge to summarize for a newly empaneled grand jury the statutes and, in the state courts, the common law relevant to the performance of their duty. It was the grand jury's duty to return such indictments and presentments alleging violations of the laws as in its judgment were warranted by the evidence already known to it or presented to it. In the state courts it was common for the grand jury to present grievances about poor administration of the laws and the need for new laws, reaching down to matters of narrow local concern and great specificity:[13]

---

11 2 Register of Debates in Congress, 19th Cong., 1st Sess., Pt. I, col. 977 (Jan. 13, 1826) (Rep. Powell).

12 30 Writings of George Washington 424, 428 ("Bicentennial Ed." 1939).

13 Addison, Reports of Cases on the County Courts of the Fifth Circuit . . . of Pennsylvania, And Charges to Grand Juries of those County Courts [Part II] 75–76 (1800). For a British statement of the grand jury's censorial office, see Henry Fielding's charge to a grand jury at Westminster, June 29, 1749, reprinted in 13 Henley, Complete Works of Henry Fielding 218–19 (1903). See also 2 Radzinowicz, History of English Criminal Law 6–7 (1956).

> A kind of censorial authority is sometimes exercised by the grand jury. Viewing themselves not as the representatives, but as a respectable collection, of the people of the county, they consider it proper to express, in a public manner, their united sentiments of public inconveniences, improvements, or other transactions, measures, or things, of a general nature, and affecting the welfare of the county, or on which it is proper for their voice to be known; express praise or blame, according to their nature or tendency; and suggest or recommend the prosecution of public benefits, and redress of public gr[ie]vances. In this, they act not in their official capacity; nor is the exercise of this authority founded on any law. This authority is founded only on use, and a presumed public convenience; and, when exercised discreetly, it may be attended with good effects.

None of this was new or extraordinary. But out of the years of stress that preceded and led to the break with Britain, another kind of dialogue between judge and jurors matured. In a growing number of instances the judge came to regard himself as an exhorter and teacher, obliged at all times (but above all at moments of crisis), "boldly [to] declare the law to the people, and instruct them in their civil rights."[14] By 1785 John Dickinson could write to members of the Pennsylvania Supreme Court, about to go on circuit,[15]

> that besides the Terror of legal Penalties, all the Influence to be derived from your Characters, and the Dignity of your Stations, might be applied in disseminating the best Principles & setting forward the most effectual Regulations for the prevention of offences.
>
> You Gentlemen, well know how vain are Laws without Manners.

That the judges would respond to such instructions with differing degrees of avidity may safely be presumed. But for two reasons we can be quite certain that when they did undertake political education they did so with self-awareness.

The political charge was a deviation from the ordinary and rec-

---

[14] Grand jury charge of South Carolina Judge William Henry Drayton (Nov. 5 and 15, 1774), printed in 1 Force, American Archives cols. 599-601 (4th ser. 1837). If duties are derivative from rights, as Judge Drayton believed, the instruction in rights must precede the sense of obligation and the performance of duties.

[15] Letter of John Dickinson, President of the State of Pennsylvania, to the Chief Justice and other Judges of the Pennsylvania Supreme Court (Oct. 8, 1785), printed in 10 Hazard, Pennsylvania Archives 523-24 (1st ser. 1854).

ognized as such by the judges who used it. James Iredell, at the time a North Carolina judge, could cut short, after five pages, a sermon on natural rights and patriotism—itself a sort of prelude to a brief grand jury charge—by recalling that "the time, and even the occasion, [would] not properly permit" his elaborating on these themes.[16] Another North Carolina judge could surround a long and impassioned plea that "the love of our country rise superior to the turpid and base passion for gain" with unmistakable signs that he knew his political charge was not of a piece with his just-concluded statement of the law: "Gentlemen, give me leave now, before you retire to business, to address a few words to you in another character." "Gentlemen, you will, I hope, excuse my traveling out of the line of Business for which you have been summoned here at this time."[17] This self-consciousness when delivering political charges persisted. Indeed, this open self-consciousness was in later days often a sign of sensible use of the political charge. American oratory at large might have made this kind of speech familiar, but not to the extent of making it so habitual that the members of the new national judiciary could forget the customary bounds of judicial propriety, even while exceeding them.

Chief Justice John Jay defended himself by saying in the charge delivered on his first circuit: "These remarks may not appear very pertinent to the present occasion, and yet it will be readily admitted that occasions of promoting good-will, and good-temper, and the progress of useful truths among our fellow-citizens should not be omitted."[18] Similarly, a district judge could declare to a grand jury that "[t]o forbear to speak of this government on this occasion, (altho it may not be necessary to the business for which you are now assembled) might argue an insensibility towards it, which no citizen should ever feel." Having said this much, he was free to extol the new Constitution through contrast with the old and through hopeful anticipation of public prosperity.[19]

---

16 1 McRee, Life and Correspondence of James Iredell 387–88 (1857–58); see also *id.* at 386 (May 1, 1778).

17 Grand jury charge of Judge Samuel Ashe (June 11, 1778), reprinted in 13 Clark, State Records of North Carolina 443, 441, 444 (1896).

18 3 Johnston, Correspondence and Public Papers of John Jay 390 (1891) (April–May, 1790).

19 Grand jury charge of District Judge John Sitgreaves (Apr. 4, 1791), printed in Gazette of the United States (Philadelphia), May 4, 1791, p. 3, col. 1.

Consider also the remarks of Pennsylvania Judge Alexander Addison: "Perhaps

It was not only the novelty of the political charge that led the judges to signal their auditors (and themselves) of a departure from customary decorum. At least as powerful an inducement to judicial self-awareness and self-control were the uneven and fluctuating reactions to the practice by grand juries. If there were times when judge and jurors sang in beautiful harmony—now in outrage against the British, then in stirring defense of the revolutionary cause—there were other times when cacophony prevailed. The political charge could and did exacerbate political differences: most evidently before the Revolution when Loyalist judges chastised grand juries for failing to make presentments and indictments against libelers and tea-burners and other local revolutionaries, less dramatically after the Revolution when state judges' urgings of moderation in the treatment of Loyalists were received with little enthusiasm by grand jurors.[20] During the first decade of the national judiciary, the political charge was subjected yet again to the full cycle of popular applause and disdain. Toward the end of the period, one state judge could exhort a grand jury to steer clear of political presentments, "not [to] think of introducing politics into a court of justice which *cannot* or *ought not* to have anything to do with it," and to keep to the business of grand juries as defined by the state legislature.[21] By the end of the period, the publication of another state judge's collected grand jury charges required this kind of prefatory defense:[22]

---

these observations may be unkindly considered as impertinent deviations from my line of duty, and may be called insolent dictating, in matters which do not concern me. . . . Though no officer has a right to employ his official situation, to gratify his own private views; yet the officer, who confines himself to the strict duties of his station, seems to me to be less useful, than he who seizes those opportunities, which his station affords him, to do good actions, or communicate good advice." ADDISON, *supra* note 13, at 165–66 (Sept., 1795); *id.* at 187 (Sept., 1796). Addison's is a case where self-awareness was not always accompanied by self-restraint. For some results of his charges, see MILLER, CRISIS IN FREEDOM: THE ALIEN AND SEDITION ACTS 140 (1951).

20 For Thomas Hutchinson, C.J., see QUINCY, REPORTS OF CASES . . . OF THE PROVINCE OF MASSACHUSETTS BAY, BETWEEN 1761 AND 1772 262–70, 309 (1865). For Frederick Smyth, C.J., see Field, *Provincial Courts of New Jersey, with Sketches of the Bench and Bar*, in 3 COLLECTIONS OF THE NEW JERSEY HISTORICAL SOCIETY 175, 180–81 (1849). For postwar resentment, see YOUNGER, PEOPLE'S PANEL: THE GRAND JURY IN THE UNITED STATES, 1634–1941 41 (1963).

21 Grand jury charge of Virginia Judge Richard Parker (June, 1798), printed in Palladium (Frankfort, Ky.), Oct. 23, 1798, p. 2, col. 4.

22 ADDISON, *supra* note 13, at iii–iv.

> A stronger evidence of a disposition in some men, to monopolize the direction of public opinion, can hardly be given, than the harsh censures which have been propagated on what are called *Political Charges;* nor of the depravity of public opinion, than the approbation with which those censures have been received. While so many set themselves up as political instructors, and, in this capacity, with all the confidence, industry, and zeal of inspired missionaries, preach error and sedition; it would seem hard, if men whose education, habits, and experience, may have qualified them to think justly on public affairs, should be condemned to silence; or, while interposing their sentiments against the torrent of delusion, deny them the solemnity of a public station. I flatter myself, that such censures come not from the wisest and best part of the community. . . .

But by then the days of the political charge (and of Judge Addison's tenure) were numbered.

The reports of the manner in which these charges were delivered and received suggest a cross between a political sermon and a speech from the throne.[23] It would be a mistake, as the substance of the statements shows, to dismiss these charges as the merest Federalist propaganda, although one of their intended effects was to bolster Federalist theories and practices. Lumping all these charges and reducing them to simple apologetic would make it hard to discriminate between Chief Justice Jay's use and Justice Samuel Chase's abuse of the judicial charge. Some of these political sermons ought to be considered rather as carefully composed, self-conscious appeals to that portion of the population which was then politically influential—appeals to be good republicans coupled with some rules for being good republicans. Depending on the judge and the occasion, the political charges presented the full range from judicial elevation to intemperate special pleading. These appeals were often printed in the newspapers at the request of the grand jurors and then reprinted farther afield. The Justices knew that their audience extended beyond the confines of the courtroom. An occasion for a ceremonial pronouncement was seized, the pronouncement itself given a character both judicial and political—like, yet unlike, what a President might say—and a certain concep-

[23] Descriptions of these occasions are to be found in: MONAGHAN, JOHN JAY 314 (1935); 2 MCREE, *supra* note 16, at 435; VAN SANTVOORD, SKETCHES OF THE LIVES AND JUDICIAL SERVICES OF THE CHIEF-JUSTICES OF THE SUPREME COURT OF THE UNITED STATES 262–63 (1854); BROWN, LIFE OF OLIVER ELLSWORTH 245 (1905); FRANKFURTER & LANDIS, *supra* note 8, at 20; 1 WARREN, *supra* note 10, at 59 n. 1.

tion of the public good promoted through a calculated exhortation. Before one can judge the adequacy and fairness of the conception of the public good implicit in the exhortation, one has to see precisely what the judicial teaching was.

Chief Justice Jay, in his charge to grand juries repeated throughout the Eastern Circuit on the occasion of his first convening these courts in the spring of 1790, opened appropriately enough with the question to which the history of the United States was to provide the answer. In accents reminiscent of the initial paragraph of *Federalist No. 1*, the Chief Justice began:[24]

> Whether any people can long govern themselves in an equal, uniform, and orderly manner, is a question which the advocates for free government justly consider as being exceedingly important to the cause of liberty. This question, like others whose solution depends on facts, can only be determined by experience. It is a question on which many think some room for doubt still remains.

It had fallen—providentially fallen—to the Americans to have "more perfect opportunities of choosing, and more effectual means of establishing their own government, than any other nation has hitherto enjoyed."[25] The force and fraud that seem to have shaped constitutions and governments in most other times and places appear to have been frustrated, at least for the while. The sometimes painful experiences of establishing and correcting state governments "have operated as useful experiments, and conspired to promote our advancement in this interesting science."[26] Similarly, the future lessons of time and experience will be applied to improve this new national government as long as the people rely—and have reason to rely—on their own good sense.[27]

Other Supreme Court Justices, such as Iredell and Ellsworth, elaborated upon this theme. "The noble experiment" that the Americans had undertaken would test the limits of human nature as well as the cause of "a government of reason." "A higher degree of freedom [than that provided by the Constitution], consistent with any government at all, is not exerciseable by human nature." At

---

[24] 3 JOHNSTON, *supra* note 18, at 387 (April–May, 1790) (Jay).

[25] *Id.* at 388.

[26] *Ibid.*

[27] See also grand jury charges of district judges in New Hampshire and Maine printed in Columbian Centinel (Boston), July 31, 1790, p. 2, cols. 2–3 (John Sullivan), and Aug. 25, 1790, p. 1, cols. 2–3 (David Sewall).

the same time, "[n]o people . . . can rationally desire more than that they should themselves choose the government under which they are to live."[28] Jay cautioned his audience to temper their theory with some sober practice, just as Jefferson was to appeal to his fellow citizens not to abandon the experiment represented by "this government, the world's best hope," on the basis of some "theoretic and visionary fear."[29] "If, then, so much depends on our rightly improving the before-mentioned opportunities, if the most discerning and enlightened minds may be mistaken relative to theories unconfirmed by practice, if on such difficult questions men may differ in opinion and yet be patriots, and if the merits of our opinions can only be ascertained by experience, let us patiently abide the trial, and unite our endeavours to render it a fair and an impartial one."[30] It was in this mixed spirit of high hope and sober sense, equally removed from the doctrinaire and the cold legalism, that some Justices instructed the people in republicanism.

The foremost of the themes repeated and elaborated upon by the Justices was that of the close connection between self-restraint and true liberty. The Justices showed an awareness that the civil liberty of a people free to choose its governors cannot, for long, be restrained in a manner that is not generally accepted. No matter how well-born or high-toned they are, governors dependent on the popular franchise cannot expect simply to prescribe opinions and codes that will be authoritative. The more intelligent Justices recognized this from the outset and took such steps as they could to persuade men to adopt their opinions. While the courtroom circumstances in which the charges were delivered could have brought to mind ex cathedra pronouncement, the rhetoric actually employed shows that the Justices chose not to rest with appeals to their authority. They began, rather, by appealing to fairly narrow calculations of self-interest, broadening the range of considerations as the argument moved from self to nation to type of regime. "It cannot be too strongly impressed on the minds of us all how greatly our individual prosperity depends on our national prosperity, and how greatly our national prosperity depends on a well organized,

---

[28] 2 McRee, *supra* note 16, at 394 (May, 1793), 484 (May 23, 1796) (Iredell); Brown, *supra* note 23, at 247 (April, 1796) (Ellsworth).

[29] Jefferson, *First Inaugural Address*, in Koch & Peden, Life and Selected Writings of Thomas Jefferson 322–23 (1944).

[30] 3 Johnston, *supra* note 18, at 389–90 (April–May, 1790) (Jay).

vigorous government." Jay was quick to reassure his listeners that such a government is not "unfriendly to liberty—to that liberty which is really inestimable." And, having gone so far, he proceeded to define civil liberty as "an equal right to all the citizens to have, enjoy, and to do . . . whatever the equal and constitutional laws of the country admit to be consistent with the public good." It is true that Jay, like Iredell and Ellsworth, was prone to see a divine plan (or the tracks of one) in political affairs, but that was not the sole or main thrust of his argument. If an appeal was to be made to his contemporaries, it had to be to both "the duty and the interest . . . of all good citizens."[31] Once led to see the connection between their material well-being and law-abidingness, they would be less apt to be startled by false alarms. They would be better able to distinguish "[t]rue liberty" from the "unbounded liberty of the strongest man," or the "unlimited sway of a majority," or "[u]nlicensed indulgence to all the passions of men." "Let each man consider, that his liberty and his property cannot be secured without forming a common interest with all the other members of the society to which he belongs." The cultivation of this common interest, the adjustment as far as possible of "the common welfare of the whole jointly" to the welfare of the individuals and states forming the whole, are tasks to which "[m]oderation and good sense" are indispensable.[32]

These are hardly abstruse teachings; reasoning back from consequences, each man can draw the proper moral. "Perhaps in no country in the world have been within so few years exemplified such awful and important lessons."[33] These sentiments of Iredell at Boston were reaffirmed by Chief Justice Oliver Ellsworth at Savannah:[34]

---

[31] *Id.* at 394–95 (April–May, 1790). See also Pennsylvania Gazette (Philadelphia), Apr. 14, 1790, p. 3, col. 2 (Wilson), and Columbian Centinel (Boston), July 28, 1792, p. 1, col. 3 (Jay). Justice Wilson was especially insistent upon developing a kind of patriotism and law-abidingness that grew out of "rationally beloved" laws: "I mean not . . . to recommend to you an implicit and an undistinguishing approbation of the laws of your country. Admire; but admire with reason on your side." 3 WILSON, WORKS OF THE HONOURABLE JAMES WILSON 393 (1804) (May, 1791).

[32] 2 McREE, *supra* note 16, at 365–66 (Oct. 12, 1792); see also *id.* at 484 (May 23, 1796) (Iredell).

[33] *Id.* at 365 (Oct. 12, 1792).

[34] BROWN, *supra* note 23, at 246 (April, 1796) (Ellsworth).

> Institutions without respect, laws violated with impunity, are, to a Republic, the symptoms and the seed of death. . . . The national laws are the national ligatures and vehicles of life. Though they pervade a country as diversified in its habits as it is vast in extent, yet they give to the whole harmony of interest and unity of design. They are the means by which it pleases Heaven to make, of weak and discordant parts, one great people, and to bestow upon them unexampled prosperity, and so long as America shall continue to have one will, organically expressed and enforced, must she continue to rise in opulence and respect.

The recent history of American public affairs might well have contained important and even salutary lessons, but as can be seen here those lessons were subject to interpretations. That the cause of individual liberty required that a price be paid to a larger whole, and that genuine liberty was fundamentally dependent upon law-abidingness were propositions to which no thinking man could take exception. But thinking men could and did disagree about the environment most favorable to liberty. It was a frequent Antifederalist argument—and one with respectable theoretical credentials—that liberty was neither safe nor securable under a single government extending over so large and varied a country as this. More than one response was possible, and more than one was made. A comparison of Ellsworth's language with Jay's in *Federalist No. 2* reveals not that one response was more mythopoeic than the other but that the voice of the judge speaking as judge had a rhetoric of its own. To the contention that America was too extensive and heterogeneous to have one will (unless it were coerced by Janizaries), Jay, writing as Publius, replied by denying the significance and even the existence of barriers to union.[35] Ellsworth, in contrast, speaking as Chief Justice, turned the argument around. Far from being too vast to be bound together by good laws, this country would be held together precisely and above all by good laws. Not the ties of kinship, not the memories of common disasters and victories—important as these were—but the ligatures of national laws were most to be relied upon. It was for a judge, a teaching judge, to make this point and to create the occasions for reiterating it. Beneath the laws

[35] The Federalist, No. 2, p. 9 (Cooke ed., 1961). References to this edition are hereinafter cited simply as The Federalist. *Cf.* 1 Adams, History of the United States of America 1–11 (1889–92), for another view of Jay's providentially blessed land.

lay political preconditions; beyond the laws stretched political consequences. For a moment there merged the inclination and the opportunity to expound these matters to the citizenry.

Implicit and often explicit in the Supreme Court Justices' political charges was the advocacy of a certain kind of conduct, corresponding to a certain type of citizen: plain-spoken, self-possessed, manly in a quiet rather than gallus-tugging fashion; jealous of his rights, but aware of his duties and the self-esteem of others. It is arguable that the Justices were at least as concerned with sustaining an already existing type as with creating a model republican. The republic itself showed such moderation and presupposed it in its citizens. Jay observed that:[36]

> [G]overnment or laws which are calculated only on the virtues of mankind, always terminate in disorder and disappointment, while on the contrary, those which regard only their vices are generally marked by oppression and undue severity. Both should be considered with equal attention, or a just estimate of their influence and operation cannot be formed, nor a proper mean between the two extremes observed. It is pleasing to remark, that the national laws appear to have been mindful of both; for while they meet transgression with punishment, their mildness manifests much confidence in the reason and virtue of the people.

This confidence, however, was not to be taken for granted. Popular government, more than other forms, tries men's capacities for enduring disappointment gracefully. After being invited—indeed, obliged—to declare his views on the public business, the citizen of a republic is further obliged "cheerfully [to] submit" to constitutional majority determinations. This "deference of private sentiment to that of the public" is "the very basis of all republican governments."[37] The greater diffusion of political rights carries with it a need for a more broadly distributed sense of political responsibility, the quality of which is seen most clearly perhaps in the way in which public discussion is conducted. The freer the government the greater its dependence on popular confidence; and that confidence, to be worth anything, requires of each citizen that he exercise his right of public comment so "that he may neither be unwarily misled himself, nor unwarily mislead others." Such consider-

[36] Columbian Centinel (Boston), July 28, 1792, p. 1, col. 1 (Jay).

[37] 2 McRee, *supra* note 16, at 467 (Apr. 12, 1796), 507 (May 22, 1797) (Iredell).

ations—to say nothing for the moment of the special problem of those who deliberately deceive the public—point to "that salutary caution with which all public measures ought to be discussed." Nowhere is this more needed than in discussions of policy, "because nothing is more fallible than human judgment when it extends its views into a futurity." Diffidence, moderation, and a cautious weighing of inconveniences and advantages were in order: "Any other mode of considering great questions of public policy is idle and insignificant."[38] Above all, the enlightened citizen will remember in his deliberations that "things and not names ought to decide our judgments."[39]

There are lessons to be drawn from the past, lessons to be passed on to present and future generations. In this continuous process of extraction and transmission, many of the Justices saw their relations to the grand jury as central. Every nation, but especially "an extensive country,"[40] will have to learn to cope with men who, "impelled by avarice or ambition, or by both," are prepared to gratify their longings at the expense of the public good. Add to this peril the natural effects of partisanship upon even "the best men": "our wishes and partialities becoming inflamed by opposition, often cause indiscretions, and lead us to say and to do things that had better have been omitted."[41] Between these arts of the deceitful and the weaknesses of the honest, republics have come to ruin. For these old dangers, remedies—both old and new—are needed: government by representatives, a divided and balancing legislature, a vigorous executive. As fundamental as any of these are the qualities called for by Ellsworth: "vigilance, constant diligence, and fidelity for the execution of laws"—traits needed in any good republican, but especially in a republican grand juror.[42] And from the grand juror would go forth the law, both the knowledge of it and the spirit of it. "I offer no apology, gentlemen, for the nature or the length of this address," Justice James Wilson said in concluding a charge whose printed version could not easily have taken less than an hour to deliver. "In the situation, in which I have the honour to be

[38] *Id.* at 484–85 (May 23, 1796), 506–07 (May 22, 1797) (Iredell).

[39] Columbian Centinel (Boston), July 28, 1792, p. 1, col. 1 (Jay).

[40] 2 McRee, *supra* note 16, at 485 (May 23, 1796) (Iredell).

[41] Wharton, State Trials of the United States during the Administrations of Washington and Adams 57 (1849) (Jay).

[42] Brown, *supra* note 23, at 247 (April, 1796) (Ellsworth).

placed, I deem it my duty to embrace every proper opportunity of disseminating the knowledge of [the criminal code] far and speedily. Can this be done with more propriety than in an address to a grand jury . . . ?" And later: "Inform and practically convince every one within your respective spheres of action and intercourse, that, as excellent laws improve the virtue of the citizens, so the virtue of the citizens has a reciprocal and benign energy in heightening the excellence of the law."[43]

These admonitions and appeals ought not to be mistaken for simple declarations of the need for vigorous administration and good government. Some measure of popular self-restraint is indispensable for good government, while one of the surest effects of good administration is the way it secures the voluntary attachment of the people. If there can be no good government without some citizen virtue, there can be no highly developed sense of citizenship without good government.[44] The itinerant Justice, in this early stage of national life, improved the judicial occasion by drawing out the deeper implications of national law-enforcement for both liberty and union. When he did his work with finesse, the teaching judge was more than a scrupulous craftsman, if less than a philosopher-king, and quite other than the partisan. It is not hard to see that the task of political education would be complicated and even defeated once it fell to the hands of coarse judges and once harsher party conflicts emerged.

---

[43] 3 WILSON, *supra* note 31, at 392, 393 (May, 1791). See also WHARTON, *supra* note 41, at 62, where Wilson spoke of the useful lessons to be taught and learned in the courtroom so that "a practical knowledge and a just sense" of a free people's duties might be "diffused universally among the citizens."

This theme of the grand jurors' duty to instruct others "when you blend yourselves again among your neighbors" is well stated by Chief Justice William Henry Drayton of South Carolina in some of his charges to Charleston grand juries in 1776 and 1777. See NILES, PRINCIPLES AND ACTS OF THE REVOLUTION IN AMERICA 333, 347, 352 (1876). See also ADDISON, *supra* note 13, at 110 (Sept.. 1794).

That the grand jury's educational service as "a great channel of communication" between governors and governed is not unidirectional is shown by the expectation that the grand juries "may suggest public improvements, and the modes of removing public inconveniencies: They may expose to public inspection, or to public punishment, bad public men, and bad public measures." Pennsylvania Gazette (Philadelphia), Apr. 14, 1790, p. 2, col. 2 (Wilson).

[44] Consider *The Federalist's* explicit and implicit forecast that a more efficiently administered national government would lead the people to transfer their primary political attachments from the states to the new government. THE FEDERALIST, No. 3, p. 15; No. 17, pp. 106, 107; No. 27, pp. 171–74; No. 46, pp. 316–17; No. 68, pp. 460–61.

However salutary the lessons he has to convey, a sensible teacher will first pay heed to the context of his instruction. In the measure of care that the Justices took in considering those limits, we find a way of discriminating the use from the abuse of the judicial charge. By examining two of the instances where judicial pronouncements ran counter to strong popular and partisan opinion, we can get a sense of the strengths and weaknesses of this variety of judicial politics.

The conduct of foreign policy became a theme of judicial teaching in two ways. To the extent that the grand jury's duty to investigate suspected breaches of the laws of the United States touched upon treaties, the law of nations, and the like, it was beyond debate that the Justices should instruct the grand jury out of their superior judicial understanding of international law. This the Justices did. But not only this. Prompted by the occasion—and by the passions quickened by Washington's proclamation of neutrality of April 22, 1793—the Justices went on to pronounce some lessons in foreign policy. In their remarks they tried to steer a narrow course between an examination of the particulars that vexed domestic politics throughout most of the first decade of the new government and an overly vague statement of what constituted good manners in international conduct. Chief Justice Jay's grand jury charge at Richmond, delivered a month after Washington's proclamation, is a fair sample of the concerns for policy and professional duty that merged in the political charge.[45]

The grand theme running through Jay's charge is that the demands of duty and interest coincide, that neither individuals nor nation will find their genuine interests slighted when they act in an honorable fashion. The aptness of this theme is illustrated in various ways. Thus the old maxim, that one should use one's own property so as not to harm others, is generalized beyond the realm of property to comprehend men's liberty, power, "and other blessings of every kind." The very purpose of free government is to restrain men to act in accord with this maxim. It is precisely in a regime where all powers are derivative from the popular will that the need for strong government is most acute, for it is there that the number of rights to be

[45] There are two texts in print. The original draft is in 3 JOHNSTON, *supra* note 18, at 478–85 (May 22, 1793). The final version, which was delivered and then "printed by the government for the purpose of explaining abroad the position of the United States," appears in WHARTON, *supra* note 41, at 49–59.

protected and the difficulty in restraining men are greatest. It is above all in a free government that "the duty and interest of us all, that the laws be observed, and irresistibly executed" are clearest, for it is above all in such a government that the laws express the will, and secure the benefit, of the citizens as a whole:[46]

> He is not a good citizen who violates his contract with society; and when society execute their laws, they do no more than what is necessary to constrain individuals to perform that contract, on the due operation and observance of which the common good and welfare of the community depend; for the object of it is to secure to every man what belongs to him, as a member of the nation; and by increasing the common stock of property, to augment the value of his share in it.

In reviewing the laws of which the grand jurors ought to take cognizance, Jay was careful to instruct the jurors in the "general principles" that guided relations among the nations and, going beyond this, to argue that utility and justice coincided in recommending a policy of neutrality for the United States. The bulk of the charge is taken up with a discussion of the relevant laws, under the headings of treaties, law of nations, and Constitution and statutes. Treaties ought not to be mistaken for statutes: the unilateral discretion available for changing and repealing the latter does not apply to the former. The special standing that treaties enjoy as part of the supreme law of the land is a token of the practical restrictions upon each contracting power. There are maxims and principles of the law of nations that prescribe and define fidelity to treaties. Not who the parties are, but the fact of their mutual pledge, makes the obligation binding. Similarly, the law of nations imposes duties as well as rights upon the United States. In urging "a conduct friendly and impartial towards the belligerent powers," Washington's proclamation "is exactly consistent with and declaratory of the conduct enjoined by the law of nations." Its domestic consequences, restricting citizens and aliens alike from behaving in a manner that jeopardized that neutrality, are well supported by the law of nations. "The respect which every nation owes to itself imposes a duty on its government to cause all its laws to be respected and obeyed." Considerations of duty, interest, and disposition all support a policy of neutrality and bind the grand jurors to ferret

[46] WHARTON, *supra* note 41, at 49–52, 58–59. For the roots of this view of society as a contract for increase, see 2 LOCKE, TWO TREATISES OF GOVERNMENT §§ 41–42.

out those seeking to frustrate that policy. As though this would not suffice, Jay proceeded to defend the wisdom of the neutrality proclamation in terms going beyond the judge's or jurors' province strictly defined. It is not enough to "be faithful to all—kind to all—but let us also be just to ourselves." America now enjoyed peace, liberty, safety, and unparalleled prosperity. A policy of neutrality left her free to pursue her offices of humanity and benevolence—as well as her commerce—toward all the belligerents. An enlightened self-interest also dictated that Americans act with an awareness of the domestic causes that might lead the country into war. There was a possibility of war arising from the narrowly self-regarding actions of men who would "not hesitate to gratify [their] passions [of avarice or ambition or both] at the expense of the blood and tears even of those who are free from blame." Or war might equally arise out of the partisan indiscretions from which even the best men are not exempt. "Prudence directs us to look forward to such an event, and to endeavour not only to avert, but also to be prepared for it." The principal precaution is "union in sentiments and measures relative to national objects," the avoidance of parties that are partisans of one foreign power or another. There is, in short, a kind of conduct becoming a free people in peace and war:[47]

> But, if neither integrity nor prudence on our part should prove sufficient to shield us from war, we may then meet it with fortitude, and a firm dependence on the Divine protection; whenever it shall become impossible to preserve peace by avoiding offences, it will be our duty to refuse to purchase it by sacrifices and humiliations, unworthy of a free and magnanimous people, either to demand or submit to. The subject presented by the proclamation, appeared to me to be highly interesting, and I thought it useful to treat it with much plainness, as well as latitude. I was aware that I was treading on delicate ground; but as the path of my duty led over it, it was incumbent on me to proceed.

However one regards the law of nations—as rules for relations between states or (with Justice Wilson) as "the duties which a nation owes to itself"[48]—it is to be understood in the light of a few well-known facts. In Chief Justice Jay's words, "Nations are, in respect to each other, in the same situation as independent individuals in a state of nature." Having no common judge on earth, these nations

---

47 WHARTON, *supra* note 41, at 52–58 (Jay).

48 *Id.* at 62 (Wilson).

"have a perfect right to establish such governments and build such houses as they prefer, and their neighbors have no right to pull down either because not fashioned according to their ideas of perfection."[49] The indisputably superior merit and justice of the American form of government (and none of the Justices was shy about so judging it) ought to commend it to the world, but do not entail a general commission to remake the world after the American likeness. Nonintervention and self-determination seem, rather, to be the standing order. But if "strict impartiality" is the rule—"it is no less our interest than our duty to act accordingly"—it is a rule open to qualifications and, in any event, is not to be mistaken for indifference.[50] There are standards of conduct, standards of civility, to which nations, no less than individuals, ought to be held. Unless prior treaty commitments require it, Americans ought not to be partisans of one belligerent or the other. If the war is about objects in which America is not interested, she ought not to interfere except as a mediator and friend to peace.[51]

It also is to be borne in mind that in Wilson's formulation, there are certain self-regarding duties that neither states nor individuals properly can shirk. Predictably, "self-preservation is a primary duty." Beyond that is the duty to "love and to deserve an honest fame."[52] In the midst of the controversy over the neutrality proclamation, Jay could declare in a grand jury charge:[53]

> A just war is an evil, but it is not the greatest; oppression and disgrace are greater. War is not to be sought, but it is not to be fled from. Let us do exactly what is just and right, and then remain without fear, but not without care about the consequences.

Honest fame, a due regard for national dignity and character, all required a state of mind that would neither give nor brook insult and disgrace.

The Justices' international and domestic teachings were as one. They saw a need in each case to elevate self-interest into republican virtue, manly independence, self-respect, and patriotism. In the

---

49 3 JOHNSTON, *supra* note 18, at 481 (May 22, 1793).

50 *Id.* at 482.

51 *Ibid.* Nothing in Jay's charge runs counter to Hamilton's argument in Pacificus No. 4 (July 10, 1793), on the limits or inappropriateness of gratitude as a principle of international conduct.

52 WHARTON, *supra* note 41, at 62 (Wilson).

53 3 JOHNSTON, *supra* note 18, at 482 (Jay).

course of reciting the reasoning that in his judgment gave issue to the Washingtonian policy, the Chief Justice could not but be aware of the fact that the merits of that policy were a subject of bitter partisan dispute. Yet even here there was a lesson to be learned, a moral to be drawn. However heated the controversy and debatable the policy, as law of the land the proclamation bound judge and juror alike. The duty to enforce the law overbore individual scruples and misgivings. Outside the courtroom, in the political forum, "[a]s free citizens we have a right to think and speak our sentiments on this subject, in terms becoming freemen—that is, in terms explicit, plain, and decorous."[54] Within the courtroom, in the very act of performing an unpleasant duty, grand jurors would have occasion to learn the truth of "the excellent principle" that "the interests and the duties of men are inseparable."[55]

There seems to be general agreement that the use of the charge as a means of political education was the introduction of a new purpose to what originally had been "a mere abstract of crimes and punishments."[56] But not every such introduction is impudent meddling. What saves Jay's charges (and those like his) from the scorn justly directed toward hot-headed political preachments from the bench[57] is precisely the consciousness that he "was treading on deli-

[54] *Id.* at 485.

[55] Columbian Centinel (Boston), July 28, 1792, p. 1, col. 1 (Jay). A distinction was drawn by Jay in THE FEDERALIST, Nos. 3 and 4, between the "*real*" or "*just* causes of war" and the "*pretended*" causes. The latter are held to be disgraceful but no less natural for all that. It is not clear from *The Federalist*'s argument what, if any, bearing this distinction has on the conduct of foreign policy and providing for the common defense.

[56] LLOYD, TRIAL OF ALEXANDER ADDISON, ESQ. . . . ON AN IMPEACHMENT . . . 95 (1803) (A. J. Dallas). See also EVANS, REPORT OF THE TRIAL OF THE HON. SAMUEL CHASE . . . 243*–44* (1805) (R. G. Harper). The Samuel H. Smith–Thomas Lloyd transcription of the Chase impeachment is reprinted in DEBATES AND PROCEEDINGS IN THE CONGRESS OF THE UNITED STATES, 8th Cong., 2d Sess. (1805); there see cols. 557–58.

[57] Alexander J. Dallas' speech of Jan. 19, 1803, in the Pennsylvania impeachment of Judge Addison states the objection concisely: "Even in the judicial history of England . . . you will find it difficult to trace any instance to countenance the political declamations, the party invectives, which have, of late, become a sort of prelude to the commencement of every session of our courts of justice. . . . We entered our courts, not as to a scene of administrative law, but to a scene of political speculation; in which no precise object was presented to the mind; but instead of a definition of crimes and punishments, the attention was engaged by theoretical declamations, or the feelings were exasperated by the forensic denunciations; and every mind drew different conclusions from the display, having different prej-

cate ground." Jay enacted in the courtroom the very spirit and teaching he would inculcate in others. He knew, and acted and spoke as though he knew, that "on such difficult questions men may differ in opinion and yet be patriots."[58] It is one thing to declaim (like Ellsworth) against the evil effects of disorganization and impiety, showing that, "unhinged and imperious, the mind revolts at every institution which can preserve order, or protect right, while the heart, demoralized, becomes insensible to social and civil obligations."[59] But it is another, and more difficult, thing to avoid both the erroneous doctrine and the erroneous manner of "heated divines" and of "some enthusiastic politicians."[60]

The troubles of Justice Chase flowed from various causes, some of them peculiar to that able but intemperate man. The larger political controversies behind the impeachment are not my concern now. Nor do I mean to assert—what cannot be proved one way or the other—that more cautious charges could long have preserved the Federalist judiciary from the watchful hostility of the Jeffersonian administration and Congress.[61] Nonetheless, it is possible and even

---

udices and opinions, to indulge." LLOYD, *supra* note 56, at 95–96. (Parts of this speech, including the portions referred to here, are reprinted, with minor changes, in DALLAS, LIFE AND WRITINGS OF ALEXANDER JAMES DALLAS 79–87 (1871). See also 3 BEVERIDGE, LIFE OF JOHN MARSHALL, 46 n. 2 (1919).

58 WHARTON, *supra* note 41, at 58; 3 JOHNSTON, *supra* note 18, at 389–90 (April–May, 1790) (Jay).

59 2 FLANDERS, LIVES AND TIMES OF THE CHIEF JUSTICES OF THE SUPREME COURT OF THE UNITED STATES 192 (rev. ed. 1875) (Ellsworth).

60 2 MCREE, *supra* note 16, at 467 (Apr. 12, 1796) (Iredell).

61 It would be hard to maintain that the excesses Chase allowed himself in a political charge to a grand jury in circuit court at Baltimore, on May 2, 1803, would have sufficed by themselves to lead to his impeachment. Yet the character of that charge, when considered together with other repeated displays of judicial pique, was enough to form one of the articles of his impeachment by the House of Representatives; and in fact this eighth article was the one on which the greatest number of Senators (albeit a constitutionally insufficient number) voted "guilty." Indeed, Henry Adams goes so far as to say of this eighth article: "There lay the true cause of impeachment; yet this charge had been least pressed and least defended." 2 ADAMS, *supra* note 35, at 239. The proximate cause of the initiation of impeachment proceedings against Chase is traced by Adams to a letter from Jefferson to Rep. Joseph H. Nicholson (May 13, 1803) in which the President protests against Chase's Baltimore charge and urges his punishment. *Id.* at 149–50. For Republican objections to the impeachment of any judge for delivering political charges, see the letter of Nathaniel Macon, Speaker of the House of Representatives, to Nicholson (Aug. 6, 1803), in 3 JOHN P. BRANCH HISTORICAL PAPERS OF RANDOLPH-MACON COLLEGE 40–41 (June, 1909).

useful to try to detect that respect in which Chase's style in his political charges differed from Jay's.

Justice Chase's scandalizing charge[62] may be considered in its three parts: an exordium stating the problem and the speaker's credentials to speak to it; a critique of three accomplished or proposed changes in the laws; and finally, an analysis and rejection of the theoretical foundations of those changes in the laws. The political charge itself is seen as extra matter, the delivery of which was prompted by a concern for the welfare of the country.

> It is essentially necessary at all times, but more particularly at the present, that the public mind should be truly informed; and that our citizens should entertain correct principles of government, and fixed ideas of their social rights. It is a very easy task to deceive or mislead the great body of the people, by propagating plausible, but false doctrines; for the bulk of mankind are governed by their passions, and not by reason.

Chase saw his task as countering pleasant-sounding nonsense, even at the risk of saying things "repugnant to popular prejudice." Yet there is more than a consciousness of good intentions; he identified himself as a man of '76, an authentic long-time republican. The problem as it emerges in the charge is that a change is occurring in the ordinary understanding of representation and liberty; and that change is such, according to Chase, that the "fast approaching" result will be that "the people are *not free*, wh[a]tever may be their form of government."

Indicative of this evil end are the institutional changes condemned and deplored by Chase in the central part of his charge.

> You know, gentlemen, that our state and national institutions were framed to secure to every member of the society, equal liberty and equal rights; but the late alteration of the federal judiciary by the abolition of the offices of the sixteen circuit judges, and the recent change in our state [Maryland] constitution, by the establishing of universal suffrage, and the further alteration that is contemplated in our state judiciary (if adopted) will, in my judgment, take away all security for property and personal liberty. The independence of the national judiciary, is already shaken to its foundation, and the virtue of the people alone can restore it. The independence of the judges of this state will be entirely destroyed, if the bill

[62] The text is reproduced in EVANS, *supra* note 56, at App. pp. 60–62, and in DEBATES AND PROCEEDINGS, *supra* note 56, at cols. 673–76.

for the abolition of the two supreme courts should be ratified by the next general assembly. The change of the state constitution, by allowing universal suffrage, will, in my opinion, certainly and rapidly destroy all protection to property, and all security to personal liberty; and our republican constitution will sink into a mobocracy, the worst of all possible governments.

I can only lament, that the main pillar of our state constitution, has already been thrown down by the establishment of universal suffrage. By this shock alone, the whole building totters to its base, and will crumble into ruins, before many years elapse, unless it be restored to its original state. If the independency of your state judges, which your bill of rights wisely declares "to be essential to the impartial administration of justice, and the great security to the rights and liberties of the people," shall be taken away by the ratification of the bill passed for that purpose, it will precipitate the destruction of your whole state constitution; and there will be nothing left in it, worthy the care or support of freemen.

What is one to make of this prose? Let us grant that the Judiciary Act of 1802 threatened the independence of the national judiciary, though this is a proposition not easily supported by Chase's behavior here or by that of a unanimous Supreme Court less than ten weeks before in *Marbury v. Madison*,[63] or by the Court's acquiescence in *Stuart v. Laird*[64] in the re-establishment of the circuit-riding system prescribed by the Judiciary Act of 1789. Even granting this, though, what can be intended by the appeal to the virtue of the people? Could Chase have expected that those who had entrusted and re-entrusted their affairs to the Jeffersonians would throw the rascals out the next time around for their repeal of the Judiciary Act of 1801?[65] The attack on the extension of the Maryland suffrage to

[63] 1 Cranch 137 (1803). [64] 1 Cranch 299 (1803).

[65] Yet this was Justice Chase's hope. See his gloss on this text in EVANS, *supra* note 56, at App. p. 39, and in DEBATES AND PROCEEDINGS, *supra* note 56, at col. 148. In JOHN RANDOLPH 136 (1883), Henry Adams comments on this passage of the charge: "There was gross absurdity in the idea that the people who, by an immense majority, had decided to carry on their government in one way should be forced by one of their own servants to turn about and go in the opposite direction; and the indecorum was greater than the absurdity, for if Judge Chase or any other official held such doctrines, even though he were right, he was bound not to insult officially the people who employed him." There was absurdity enough, perhaps, without exaggerating the matter. Chase did not entertain the delusion that the people could "be forced" to adopt contrary principles, but he obviously acted as though he believed they had been persuaded out of one set of opinions and into

a population beyond those "who have property in, a common interest with, and an attachment to, the community" seems, if anything, even more futile than the attack on the Judiciary Act of 1802. By what stretch of a political imagination can the narrowing of a once-extended suffrage be envisioned through reinstituted property qualifications? To what majority is such an appeal addressed?

The practices Chase censured stem from bad opinions, and it was to those opinions, or rather to the theoretical underpinnings of those opinions, that he turned in the final part of his charge:

> The declarations, respecting the natural rights of man, which originated from the claim of the British parliament to make laws to bind America in all cases whatsoever; the publications, since that period, of visionary and theoretical writers, asserting that men, in a state of society, are entitled to exercise rights which they possessed in a state of nature; and the modern doctrines by our late reformers, that all men, in a state of society, are entitled to enjoy equal liberty and equal rights, have brought this mighty mischief upon us; and I fear that it will rapidly progress, until peace and order, freedom and property, shall be destroyed. Our people are taught as a political creed, that men, living under an established government, are nevertheless entitled to exercise certain rights which they possessed in a state of nature; and also, that every member of this government is entitled to enjoy an equality of liberty and rights.

The Justice's critique of these opinions would not seem strange to anyone who knew *Reflections on the Revolution in France*, yet Chase's attack, if similar to Burke's, is also more extreme than Burke's. An attack is mounted against a fallacious doctrine—but it is done in the name of a doctrine or from a doctrinal position. The critique displays an insufficient regard to what Burke held to be of central importance: circumstances.[66] To the assertion of the natural rights of man, Chase brought the counterassertion that there are no natural rights; nor, in his view, is there any state of nature. "I really consider a state of nature as a creature of the imagination only, al-

another set. Chase alone, among the Justices participating in *Stuart v. Laird*, 1 Cranch 299 (1803), called for resistance to the circuit-duty provisions of the Judiciary Act of 1802. See the discussion in 1 WARREN, *supra* note 10, at 269–72.

66 "Circumstances (which with some gentlemen pass for nothing) give in reality to every political principle its distinguishing colour and discriminating effect. The circumstances are what render every civil and political scheme beneficial or noxious to mankind." 2 BURKE, WORKS 282 (Bohn's British Classics ed. 1855).

though great names give a sanction to a contrary opinion." In this categorical denial, Chase went beyond Burke; and—what is more revealing—Chase was recklessly separating himself from such "Founding Federalists" as Jay and Wilson by rejecting one of the fundamentals of the Revolution.[67] To the views of those "visionary and theoretical writers" who argued that men could enjoy their natural rights in society, Chase replied with a denial that there could be any personal liberty and rights before, or outside of, society. All rights are social, conventional. And to the egalitarian doctrines of latter-day reformers, Chase replied in a fashion that can best be summarized by Burke's dictum: "In this partnership all men have equal rights; but not to equal things."[68]

What is most striking about Chase's grand jury charge, if compared with that of Jay, is not that his teaching was bizarre but that it was propounded immoderately. Jay was upholding the law and calling for obedience; Chase was attacking the laws and calling for resistance, repeal, and restoration. Although Chase's teaching perhaps resembled Jonathan Boucher's too much to suit contemporary tastes, it must be said that his general political position was sound Federalism.[69] Chase was not playing Sir Robert Filmer to nineteenth-century Americans, but his words give little sign that he appreciated how irrelevant his mode of teaching had been rendered by the change in opinions that he was deploring. In the eyes of Jefferson and his followers, the results of the election of 1800 were as momentous as the events of 1776. (More than a few Federalists agreed.) The principles of '76 were now triumphant, the last vestiges of monocratic power would be erased, and the promise of the great documents and pamphlets of the revolutionary struggle would be fulfilled. Yet if the election of 1800 was a political revolution, it was one secured by a margin of eight electoral votes. It was an election in which Maryland had split evenly and following which the state Federalist party retained significant strength. Chase, however,

[67] *Cf. id.* at 332, 334. Burke's views on this point are derived from 2 Locke, *supra* note 46, at §§ 128–30. The first published account of Chase's charge found its theorizing repulsive and could attack it for its "unjust reproaches cast upon . . . the fundamental and characteristic principles of the nation itself." National Intelligencer and Washington Advertiser (Washington), May 20, 1803, p. 3, col. 2.

[68] 2 Burke, *supra* note 66, at 332.

[69] In one respect, though, the position of Chase, a former Antifederalist turned Federalist, was more orthodox than that of his state party. A number of Maryland Federalists (especially the younger ones) backed suffrage reform.

showed no sign of acting on the premise that a more moderate political charge would be likely to receive a respectful hearing or have the desired effect. Instead, he mounted a frontal attack against Jeffersonian doctrine. That exhilarating teaching (however remote from Jeffersonian practice) had kindled the imaginations and aspirations of New England and Appalachia alike. In the face of widespread expectations that political life was to be restored, purified, raised to new heights, how could Chase have expected to move men with a categorical rejection of Jeffersonian doctrine and with an appeal of this sort?

> I cannot but remember the great and patriotic characters, by whom your state constitution was framed. I cannot but recollect that attempts were then made in favor of universal suffrage; and to render the judges dependent upon the legislature. You may believe, that the gentlemen who framed your constitution, possessed the full confidence of the people of Maryland, and that they were esteemed for their talents and patriotism, and for their public and private virtues. You must have heard that many of them held the highest civil and military stations, and that they, at every risk and danger, assisted to obtain and establish your independence. Their names are enrolled on the journals of the first Congress, and may be seen in the proceedings of the convention that framed our form of government. With great concern I observe, that the sons of some of these characters have united to pull down the beautiful fabric of wisdom and republicanism, that their fathers erected!

Chase, a leading framer of the Maryland constitution of 1776, found all the more rankling the participation of the sons (many of them young Federalists) in the undoing of their fathers' handiwork.[70] But his appeal from the new to the old Federalists fell upon deaf ears. Starting not from where his audience was, but from where (in his judgment) they ought to be, Chase made his argument out of exhortation, remonstrance, and appeal to venerable authority. His impatience with the errors of his audience deprived him of the ingratiating arts and courteous consideration that might have moved his audience to recognize some reasonableness in his position. Even more did his impatience deprive him of a recognition

---

[70] See Crowl, Maryland during and after the Revolution: A Political and Economic Study 31–32, 34 (1943); Fischer, Revolution of American Conservatism 162 (1965).

of the deeper calculations that would lead one of the most aristocratic of states to introduce the most democratic forms.[71] Taking arms, as he did, against a sea of troubles, Justice Chase would have drowned—had not his firm but prudent counsel adopted another style in addressing the Senate when it sat as a court of impeachments.

It is easy to see that Chase's excesses and subsequent impeachment would have effects that went beyond merely cooling intemperate judges. Both sides at his trial held to the tacit premise that the day of the political charge had passed. Even Chase's counsel felt obliged to say that using the grand jury charge as a vehicle for arguing against a public measure "may, perhaps, be ill-judged indiscreet or ill-timed. I am ready to admit that it is so: for I am one of those who have always thought, that political subjects ought never to be mentioned in courts of justice." The real issue, however, was criminality; and here the defense raised was that the political charge had become customary and that its use had been explicitly and implicitly approved. "From the time of judge Drayton to the time of judge Chase, it has been considered as innocent."[72] In Chase's own words:[73]

> It has been the practice in this country, ever since the beginning of the revolution, which separated us from Great Britain, for the judges to express from the bench, by way of charge to the grand jury, and to enforce to the utmost of their ability, such political opinions as they thought correct and useful. There have been instances in which the legislative bodies of this country, have recommended this practice of the judges; and it was adopted by the judges of the supreme court of the United States, as soon as the present judicial system was established.

[71] See the evidence of Maryland aristocrats' "exciting the favor of the people they associate with on no other occasion," in WILLIAMSON, AMERICAN SUFFRAGE FROM PROPERTY TO DEMOCRACY 1760–1860 140–46 (1960). A sufficient explanation of aristocratic acquiescence in suffrage reform is given in TOCQUEVILLE, *supra* note 1, at 52.

[72] EVANS, *supra* note 56, at 242*, 243*–44*; DEBATES AND PROCEEDINGS, *supra* note 56, at cols. 556, 557–58 (R. G. Harper). See notes 14 and 43 *supra* for references to William Henry Drayton.

[73] EVANS, *supra* note 56, at App. 37–38; DEBATES AND PROCEEDINGS, *supra* note 56, at col. 146.

If this was prescription, it was not old prescription. Nor was the appeal to practice a sufficient response to the allegation of impropriety. This was not a strong defense against an attack that could point to "a judge of the United States, passing judgment of condemnation on the laws which he was bound to conform to, and execute, and with the policy of which, in his judicial character, he had nothing to do."[74]

A comparison of Jay and Chase in their capacity as teaching judges supports the truth and aptness of Tocqueville's standard for measuring judicial behavior. In the passage quoted near the beginning of this article, Tocqueville stressed the need for judges who combined legal learning, civic rectitude, and political adroitness. The manner in which the judge performed his duties was of decisive importance. Jay tied his political teaching, however broadly stated, to the proper business of a grand jury—in this instance, enforcing the Neutrality Proclamation as declared national policy. He combined his character of a judge with his larger function. Chase, in contrast, appeared more nakedly as a partisan political advocate, and at that as an opponent of the laws of the land. His sense of the rightness of his intentions could not make up for the lack of prudence displayed in his exhortation.

It took high political finesse to use the grand jury charge as a means of political education. Abuse led to disuse, and disuse led to a kind of forgetfulness. Barely four decades after one Chief Justice could speak of not omitting occasions for promoting good will, good temper, and the progress of useful truths among the citizenry, another Chief Justice could opine confidently to a grand jury that "it would be a waste of time in the court to engage itself in discussing principles, and enlarging upon topics which are not to lead us to some practical result. . . . [N]ot a moment should be wasted in unnecessary forms."[75]

---

74 Debates and Proceedings, *supra* note 56, at col. 639 (C. A. Rodney). Rodney had raised a pointed question. Granted that Chase had, in common with other citizens, the privilege of advocating such political principles as he believed best for the country, "does this justify him as a judge in his judicial character, and from the judgment seat, to preach political sermons, and impose his private dogmas on the people, under the garb of administering the laws?" This issue was not met, probably because there was general agreement that the political charge had outlived its usefulness.

75 Charge to Grand Jury, 30 Fed. Cas. 998, at 999, Case No. 18,257 (1836) (Taney, C.J.).

II. The Judiciary and "Republican Virtue"

Members of the pre-Marshall Supreme Court while on circuit may fairly be called "teachers to the citizenry." In this phase of its role as republican schoolmaster, the Supreme Court seized upon the expedient of the grand jury charge, but with this it had uneven success. A series of bitter partisan conflicts—centering on the Neutrality Proclamation, the Alien and Sedition Acts, and the overthrow of Federalist hegemony—contributed to the disappearance of the political charge. The unfashionable became repulsive, finally foolhardy. Chase's impeachment only ratified that result. Nonetheless, the fact remains that the first Justices of the Supreme Court—among them, men such as Jay, Wilson, and Ellsworth, who had been singularly important in the drafting and defense of the Constitution and of the Judiciary Act of 1789—adopted this mode of political education as fitting, even necessary. I would now look beyond the sermon-charge (a passing phase), beyond the circuit-riding (only one aspect of the judicial role), to the larger problem subsuming all these, and more. The temporary and particular draw our attention to the fundamental reasoning for an institution designed to play a broad and permanent part in the life of the nation. That fundamental reasoning touches circuit duties only incidentally, and outright political preaching to the people only by remote construction. Political preaching presumes a kind of superiority in the judge. Was that superiority (as distinguished from the explicit preaching) an essential feature of the national judiciary?

The question is not so much whether the courts, and more particularly the Supreme Court, were expected to be "a bevy of Platonic Guardians,"[76] as whether the authors and defenders of the Constitution conceived of the courts, and of the Supreme Court more than any, as acting and speaking upon principles of public spiritedness and civic devotion beyond the probable range of other governmental officials, to say nothing of the ordinary citizens. To what extent did the Framers' plan of government require a body of judges disposed and able to transcend considerations of enlightened self-interest? That question, in turn, raises the larger issue: how did the Framers expect to sustain and perpetuate a republican regime? The manner in which the Federalists addressed themselves to this question leaves much to be desired. The Antifederalist complaint that there was a profound disharmony in the new system was

[76] Hand, Bill of Rights 73 (1958).

neither forced nor fatuous. The preconditions of republican virtue, as then understood, were not fulfilled in the extended republic envisaged by the apologists for the Constitution. When Federalist debaters chose to speak on this theme, they did not meet the issue in a uniformly candid or persuasive manner. In the preceding pages I have examined the connection between extraordinary qualities of leadership and the need for widespread citizen virtue by considering how judicial statesmen, through their teaching, promoted and sustained republican virtue. Here I am concerned with identifying what kind of citizen virtue and what kind of statesmanship the Federalists believed to be necessary for the perpetuation of their political institutions.

Though all—Federalists and Antifederalists—agreed that the new government, whatever form it might take, had to accord with the temper and genius of the American people, there were great differences on what that temper and genius were. Franklin could argue against paying the executive, adducing foreign examples—and that of General Washington—"to shew that the pleasure of doing good & serving their Country and the respect such conduct entitles them to, are sufficient motives with some minds to give up a great portion of their time to the Public, without the mean inducement of pecuniary satisfaction."[77] On the other hand, Noah Webster could propose improving the "system of the great Montesquieu," by striking out the word "virtue" wherever it appeared in the *Spirit of Laws* and substituting "property or lands in fee simple." "Virtue, patriotism, or love of country, never was and never will be, till mens' natures are changed, a fixed, permanent principle and support of government."[78]

In the midst of a very heated debate, Patrick Henry could see in the Constitution a dangerously delusive reliance upon the governors' "fair, disinterested patriotism" and upon good, but naturally weak, "luminous characters." "The real rock of political salvation

[77] 1 FARRAND, RECORDS OF THE FEDERAL CONVENTION OF 1787 84 (rev. ed. 1937). Madison wrote of Franklin's proposal: "It was treated with great respect, but rather for the author of it, than from any apparent conviction of its expediency or practicability." *Id.* at 85. For a discussion of payment for the performance of political duties as a distinctively democratic practice, see ARISTOTLE, POLITICS 6. 1. 1317b34–38; 4. 7. 1294a33–42.

[78] Webster, *An Examination into the Leading Principles of the Federal Constitution . . .*, in FORD, PAMPHLETS ON THE CONSTITUTION OF THE UNITED STATES . . . 1787–1788 59 (1888).

is self-love, perpetuated from age to age in every human breast, and manifested in every action."[79] To rely upon men's higher motives (and to the extent Henry saw the Constitution as doing that) was in effect to turn the government over to the watchful wicked, notwithstanding the republican virtue of the people at large. This argument—a strange marriage of ward-politics reasoning and deserted-house imaginings—was answered by two of the least starry-eyed defenders of the Constitution. According to John Marshall, Henry could search in vain for some American analogue to the British "exclusive personal stock of interest." The American way was so to blend public and private interests that all men (or most) would have a sense of their stake in society. When the American "promotes his own [interest], he promotes that of the community. When we consult the common good, we consult our own."[80] With such a population—alert, wary, and interested—one might establish a government of sufficient energy to rule an exclusive republic, relatively safe in the confidence that its abuses would be checked. Madison went even further in challenging Henry's pitting of the cunningly corrupt against the drowsily virtuous; it was neither a fair match nor a credible one:[81]

> . . . I go on this great republican principle, that the people will have virtue and intelligence to select men of virtue and wisdom. Is there no virtue among us? If there be not, we are in a wretched situation. No theoretical checks, no form of government, can render us secure. To suppose that any form of government will secure liberty or happiness without any virtue in the people, is a chimerical idea. If there be sufficient virtue and intelligence in the community, it will be exercised in the selection of these men; so that we do not depend on their virtue, or put confidence in our rulers, but in the people who are to choose them.

Words like these suggest that Madison was carried very far indeed by the mood and movement of the Virginia debate. It would be hard to find in this language a concession that there was a political task involved in sustaining the virtue of the people. Is then the people's republican virtue a "given"—enduring, available, sufficient? Not quite. Though in speaking at all to the issue, Madison differed

[79] 3 Elliott, Debates in the Several State Conventions on the Adoption of the Federal Constitution . . . 164–65 (2d ed. 1876).

[80] *Id.* at 232.

[81] *Id.* at 536–37.

from many Federalists, his discussion remains incomplete and hence problematic. The Federalists surely were aware of the insufficiency of their response to nagging Antifederalist questions about republican virtue. They may well have avoided a detailed discussion of that theme out of fear that the answer they would be obliged to give could only harm the more urgent cause of ratification. Moreover, since the main attack on the Constitution was mounted in the name of popular liberty, the Federalists were supplied with a double opportunity to thrash the Antifederalists on that issue, while eluding a confrontation on the problem of sustaining popular virtue.

What I have identified as the larger issue—how best to sustain and perpetuate the regime—is connected with the need for republican virtue, but the Federalists did not always choose to dwell on that connection. Hamilton, for example, could address himself to the need for statesmen and uncommon leaders (and did so repeatedly) without appearing to have to discuss popular virtue as a problem. Even when the attachment and confidence of the people were taken up as an explicit theme by him in the New York debates, the problem seems to turn less on the need for a certain kind of citizen than on the need for a certain kind of ruler:[82]

> All governments, even the most despotic, depend, in a great degree, on opinion. In free republics, it is most peculiarly the case. In these, the will of the people makes the essential principle of the government; and the laws which control the community receive their tone and spirit from the public wishes. It is the fortunate situation of our country, that the minds of the people are exceedingly enlightened and refined. Here, then, we may expect the laws to be proportionably agreeable to the standard of perfect policy, and the wisdom of public measures to consist with the most intimate conformity between the views of the representative and his constituent. . . .
>
> It was remarked yesterday, that a numerous representation was necessary to obtain the confidence of the people. This is not generally true. The confidence of the people will easily be gained by a good administration. This is the true touchstone. . . . The popular confidence depends on circumstances very distinct from considerations of number. Probably the public attachment is more strongly secured by a train of prosperous events, which are the result of wise deliberation and vigorous execution, and to which large bodies are much less competent than small ones.

[82] 2 *id.* at 252, 254.

The intelligence needed to produce "a chain of prosperous events" is to be found in the men whom the people have chosen. This is a subject to which Hamilton warmed and spoke at length. At a considerably lower level is the popular intelligence that sees or feels the advantages of "a chain of prosperous events" and knows enough to connect the presence or absence of such advantages with what the government does. This was not a subject requiring much elaboration.

We are left to wonder at the Federalists' discussion. When sustaining republican virtue is the theme, the treatment is muted and surprisingly incomplete. When the question is how to sustain the necessary conditions for popular government, the Federalists usually moved the emphasis away from the need for statesmanship and uncommon leadership, without quite ruling out the possibility that such leadership might be indispensable. Why they should have followed this tack is another of those problems admitting of more speculation than certainty. It may be that by arguing in a manner that neither foreclosed nor required statesmanship for the conduct of the new republic, the Federalists' thinking showed its origins and its limits. The leading Founders were not philosophers, but gentlemen. Their thinking, while precise and often acute, was not thorough; their goal was a sufficient understanding, not an elaborated theory. In this sense, what they thought and argued and built was very good indeed. They envisioned a government whose business would be conducted by men such as themselves; in such hands the public business would be well placed and diligently executed. "A Federalist gentleman differed only in his political views from a Republican gentleman."[83]

Credible as such an interpretation is, it is not altogether convincing. An analysis of the argument of the *Federalist Papers* shows that the Federalists relied upon quasi-aristocratic leaders and teachers—like the national judiciary—to sustain and guide the kind of public their regime presupposed. Why the defenders of the Constitution, in the stress of hard fights for state ratification, would prefer to emphasize those features that made it appear to be a self-sustaining system is immediately intelligible. It was, they argued, a constitution

[83] White, The Jeffersonians 550 (1965). White argues explicitly that the same social class dominated public life throughout the first forty years of the national government, and implicitly that the political differences among them were of only secondary importance. *Id.* at 547–50.

peculiarly fit for this particular people. And, in truth, the Framers, in their clear-eyed, unsentimental way, had cut the Constitution to the pattern of the ordinary American citizen (as he was or was likely to become). But aware of the extraordinary efforts they themselves had had to make in order to have a constitution to recommend, did they believe that their constitution would obviate such efforts by future generations? More narrowly, would the system "wholly popular" survive, even thrive, on talents wholly popular? A review of Publius' calculations and anticipations in *The Federalist*—and though polemical, they were no less careful—suggests that the answer is no. The founding of the American regime was an act of men whose talents were both great and not wholly popular. Those men thought the preservation of that regime under their constitution, if it did not require equally great men, at least stood in need of some men who were not wholly popular.

Publius was calm by nature, not given to exaggerated enthusiasms or fears, though not above playing upon such feelings. In judging human nature, he was inclined to be less, rather than more sanguine about its capacities and about its inclination with respect to good and bad; but in this judgment, as in so many other matters, he aimed at some kind of balance. "As there is a degree of depravity in mankind which requires a certain degree of circumspection and distrust: So there are other qualities in human nature, which justify a certain portion of esteem and confidence."[84] That portion might not be very great; neither did Publius trouble himself to name or describe those "other qualities." But it was certain that republican government, more than any other form, depended upon their existence. In all such political calculations, excess was to be avoided: "The supposition of universal venality in human nature is little less an error in political reasoning than the supposition of universal rectitude."[85] The famous and distinctive solution of *Federalist No. 51*, based on the "policy of supplying by opposite and rival interests, the defect of better motives,"[86] does not deny the existence of those motives, still less declare them superfluous. If the insufficiency of virtue and honor is repeatedly shown, if a reliance upon "superior virtue" is misplaced in republics, that does not settle the question.[87] True, the Constitution presupposes that its powers will be adminis-

---

[84] THE FEDERALIST, No. 55, p. 378.

[85] *Id.* No. 76, pp. 513–14.

[86] *Id.* No. 51, p. 349.

[87] *Id.* No. 22, p. 142.

tered with only "a common share of prudence."[88] The virtue of the citizens may be little more than this: that they "understand their rights and are disposed to defend them."[89] And yet Publius showed, again and again, that he was indifferent to neither the utility, beauty, nor necessity of higher and finer motives. He knew and admired "men, who under any circumstances will have the courage to do their duty at every hazard."[90] But he also knew that "this stern virtue is the growth of few soils."[91] Its presence, therefore, was not to be depended on, if that could be avoided. Still, Publius had no a priori way of knowing that all problems likely to arise under the new constitution would be capable of being accommodated satisfactorily by merely self-interested groups. He surely must have considered whether a nation could do without some leaders (like those in the Convention itself), who had "a deep conviction of the necessity of sacrificing private opinions and partial interests to the public good."[92] In fact, the promotion of the public happiness, indeed the republican cause, requires men who have "courage and magnanimity enough" to serve the people while risking popular displeasure. Why, we may ask, do these men act as they do—saving the people's interests from the consequences of their foolish inclinations—under a cloud of popular scorn and blame? Is it likely that the "lasting monuments of their gratitude" with which the people may ultimately reward their guardians are a sufficient inducement? And wherein lies the "magnanimity" of these guardians? Might they as easily, perhaps more easily, have set snares for the unwary, flattering their prejudices to betray their interests?[93] In these lines, I suggest, there is presupposed a sense of duty—rare, needful of institutional support, but in the last (and desperate) instant, indispensable. Hypocritical self-serving governors and a mean-spirited populace were Publius' Scylla and Charybdis. He dared not separate the case

---

[88] *Id.* No. 27, p. 175.

[89] *Id.* No. 28, p. 179.

[90] *Id.* No. 73, p. 497.

[91] *Id.* at 493.

[92] *Id.* No. 37, p. 239.

[93] *Id.* No. 71, pp. 482–83. *Cf.* Lincoln's *The Perpetuation of Our Political Institutions* (Jan. 27, 1838), for another analysis of the motivations of those leaders whose "*all* was staked" upon demonstrating in practice that the people were capable of self-government. BASLER, ABRAHAM LINCOLN: HIS SPEECHES AND WRITINGS 82 (1946). Consider, in the light of Lincoln's statement of the problem posed by ambition, Publius' exception of "a few aspiring characters," THE FEDERALIST, No. 57, p. 386, and his explicit silence about his own motives, *id.* No. 1, p. 6.

for good government from the case for popular government. He knew that severally and together those cases needed something more in both the leaders and the people than an overpowering absorption in self-interest. Uniting those cases was at once a political necessity and an act of high statesmanship.

No branch of government was more likely, as a regular matter of course, to shelter and provide a political platform for that presupposed sense of duty than the judiciary. There especially might this rare, nonpopular, and often unpopular virtue be fostered and used to best effect. Little, it had to be confessed, was to be expected of the House of Representatives in this respect. While not utterly devoid of elevation, its virtue would be its commonness, its similitude to the interests and sentiments of the great body of the people. Similitude does not mean perfect congruence. If it is true "that the people commonly *intend* the PUBLIC GOOD,"[94] the House may be said to borrow that intent, refining it a bit, but also possibly deflecting it by its own special humors. Its commonness, moreover, would best be secured by *avoiding* commonness as the proper basis of representation. Publius could defend the House against attack by showing that the interests and feelings of all classes of the people would best be expressed in that body by representatives drawn from certain particular classes.[95] "Bound to fidelity and sympathy" with the people by cords of "duty, gratitude, interest, [and] ambition itself," it was to be presumed that "in general" these men, "distinguished by the preference" of their fellows, would be "somewhat distinguished also, by those qualities which entitle them to it."[96] Somewhat more might be hoped for in the Senate: "there is reason to presume" that the state legislatures will choose "those men only who have become the most distinguished by their abilities and virtue."[97] In such a small body where each member can receive "a sensible degree"[98] of praise and blame, there is the motive to devote oneself to studying and attending to the public business. It is not altogether clear whether the Senate would have a "permanent motive"[99] to do so, and if so, what that motive would be. A properly constituted Senate should supply "the want of a due sense of national character," thus providing a remedy for the unenlightened, variable, and blundering

94 THE FEDERALIST, No. 71, p. 482.

95 *Id.* No. 35, pp. 218–22.

96 *Id.* No. 57, pp. 385, 387.

97 *Id.* No. 64, p. 433.

98 *Id.* No. 63, p. 423.

99 *Id.* No. 62, p. 419.

policies of the Confederation.[100] The special responsibility in foreign affairs with which the Senate (in association with the President) is charged gives added weight to the peculiar virtues that are needed and expected in that body. But the very motives of patriotism and national dignity that might encourage a Senate to take a strong stand for the national honor would also lead it to eschew "absolute inflexibility."[101] In resisting the will of the more popular branch, it would be "particularly sensible to every prospect of public danger, or of a dishonorable stagnation in public affairs."[102] The Senate will moderate its intransigence so as to avoid deadlock because of "the interest which [the Senators] will individually feel in whatever concerns the government."[103]

In comparison with either branch of the legislature, the President appears likely to be much better situated to give public expression to his "livelier sense of duty" and his "more exact regard to reputation."[104] Publius foresaw "a constant probability" that the Presidency would be occupied by "characters pre-eminent for ability and virtue."[105] One of the marks of the national government's superiority to that of the states is the knowledge that "other talents and a different kind of merit" would be needed to raise a man to "first honors" in the nation as a whole.[106] Yet in contemplating a President's temptations "to sacrifice his duty to his interest, which it would require superlative virtue to withstand," Publius, sensibly enough, did not make gratuitous assumptions.[107] "The history of human conduct does not warrant that exalted opinion of human virtue. . . ."[108] His discussion of the executive veto gives a fair measure of his expectations:[109]

> In the case for which it is chiefly designed, that of an immediate attack upon the constitutional rights of the executive, or in a case in which the public good was evidently and palpably sacrificed, a man of tolerable firmness would avail himself of his constitutional means of defence, and would listen to the admonitions of duty and responsibility. In the former supposition, his fortitude would be stimulated by his immediate

100 *Id.* No. 63, p. 422.

101 *Id.* No. 58, p. 395.

102 *Ibid.*

103 *Ibid.*

104 *Id.* No. 76, p. 511.

105 *Id.* No. 68, p. 461.

106 *Id.* at 460.

107 *Id.* No. 75, p. 505.

108 *Ibid.*

109 *Id.* No. 73, p. 497.

> interest in the power of his office; in the latter by the probability of the sanction of his constituents; who though they would naturally incline to the legislative body in a doubtful case, would hardly suffer their partiality to delude them in a very plain case. I speak now with an eye to a magistrate possessing only a common share of firmness. There are men, who under any circumstances will have the courage to do their duty at every hazard.

What sustains a President of tolerable, common firmness in his inclination to protect the common good? Not the certainty of popular approbation, nor any immediate self-interest. Standing alone, a President can count on only the probability of public approval; yet that approval, if it comes, is his alone. We ought not to be surprised to find the President considering himself both "under stronger obligations, and more interested" to fulfill his responsibilities.[110] But striking as the effects of executive leadership can be, especially in critical cases, the motivations to such public spirited acts are unreliable and insufficient. We have not yet before us the full union of private motives, institutional supports, and special training.

Of the judges, and only of the judges, did Publius declare that they would be "too far removed from the people to share much in their prepossessions."[111] It was precisely this dissimilarity, this nonpopular character, that would especially qualify the judiciary to be "an intermediate body between the people and the legislature."[112] The judiciary is the only branch of the government whose members require special training and competence, and one of the effects of that training is to set those men apart from the populace. The judicial function itself occupies some sort of middle ground between a technician's deductions from general rules and a legislator's pure reason prescribing such general rules. In construing the Constitution, the judge performs his political duty through the exercise of his technical duty. When Publius rejected the theory according to which each branch of government would make an authoritative construction of its powers binding upon the other branches, he at the same time candidly avowed that the courts would stand in a closer relation to the deliberate will of the people as expressed in the Constitution than would the representatives of the people. The

---

110 *Id.* No. 76, p. 511.

111 *Id.* No. 49, p. 341.

112 *Id.* No. 78, p. 525.

courts would be peculiarly fit to discover in the Constitution what the will of the people was. Even bolder was his conjuring of a situation when the judges would stand in need of "an uncommon portion of fortitude."[113] Said Publius:[114]

> Until the people have by some solemn and authoritative act annulled or changed the established form, it is binding upon themselves collectively, as well as individually; and no presumption, or *even knowledge of their sentiments*, can warrant their representatives in a departure from it, prior to such an act. But it is easy to see that it would require an uncommon portion of fortitude in the judges to do their duty as faithful guardians of the constitution, where legislative invasions of it had been instigated by the major voice of the community.

One may still speak of the sense of the people ruling, but in a manner that vividly brings to mind the "courage and magnanimity" it takes to serve the people "at the peril of their displeasure."[115] In this context it is genuinely anticlimactic for Publius to have urged "yet a further and a weighty reason" for permanent judicial tenure.[116] His reason—that too few combine "the requisite integrity with the requisite knowledge" of the law for there to be any "great option between fit characters"[117]—deserves his own understated comment. Weighty as such practical considerations might be, "it must be confessed that they are far inferior to those which present themselves under the other aspects of the subject."[118]

If it was Publius' wish to suggest that in the national courts would be found a locus of high statesmanship—cautious, politic, yet able and willing to cope with popular excesses—he did not leave it at only these indirections. His general, thematic discussion of the judiciary anticipates, and surely does not preclude, judges who would view themselves as teachers of republicanism using the text of the Constitution and the national laws, interpreted in a judicial spirit of moderation and fairness. The preliminary impression conveyed by Publius' account is that elements somewhat incompatible are being stirred together. If the judiciary was the least dangerous branch, it might well also be considered the least to be trusted.[119] To compli-

[113] *Id.* at 528.

[114] *Id.* at 527–28. (Emphasis added.)

[115] *Id.* No. 71, p. 483.

[116] *Id.* No. 78, p. 529.

[117] *Id.* at 530.

[118] *Ibid.*

[119] A fair—even inevitable—question would be: was there in fact, in 1787, any distrust of the judiciary on grounds of its "nondemocratic" character? According to

cate matters further, there was no prima facie evidence to show that it would be the least influential branch. The subject had to be treated judiciously.

Perhaps nothing illustrates this quite as well as those most famous lines:[120]

> Whoever attentively considers the different departments of power must perceive, that in a government in which they are separated from each other, the judiciary, from the nature of its functions, will always be the least dangerous to the political rights of the constitution; because it will be least in a capacity to annoy or injure them. . . . The judiciary . . . has no influence over either the sword or the purse, no direction either of the strength or of the wealth of the society, and can take no active resolution whatever. It may truly be said to have neither

---

Jackson Turner Main, "the argument which developed a hundred years later, that the [Supreme] Court was undemocratic because of its lack of responsibility, and that it was biased against changes desired by the majority, while implied by a few [Antifederalist] writers, was never clearly stated." ANTIFEDERALISTS: CRITICS OF THE CONSTITUTION, 1781–1788 156 (1964). One might also question whether there was much political sensitivity to a judiciary as independent as the one proposed by the Philadelphia Convention by recalling that, at the time, a majority of the states provided for judicial tenure during good behavior (including New York) and that all the states filled their highest courts by appointment, not election. Webster, *A Comparative Study of the State Constitutions of the American Revolution*, 9 ANNALS 401–03 (1897); SCHOULER, CONSTITUTIONAL STUDIES, STATE AND FEDERAL 64–65 (1904). But see POUND, FORMATIVE ERA OF AMERICAN LAW 91–92 (1938), on the prevailing distrust of judges. See also Brutus [Robert Yates], Letters No. XI and XV, New-York Journal, and Weekly Register (New York City), Jan. 31 and Mar. 20, 1788, reprinted in KENYON, THE ANTIFEDERALISTS 341–42, 351–52, 357 (1966); Federal Farmer [Richard Henry Lee], Letters No. III, Oct. 10, 1787, reprinted *id.* at 232, and XV, Jan. 18, 1788, reprinted in AN ADDITIONAL NUMBER OF LETTERS FROM THE FEDERAL FARMER TO THE REPUBLICAN 131–33, 138–39 (American Classics ed. 1962).

No moderately sensitive reader of THE FEDERALIST, No. 78, can overlook the defensive character of its rhetoric. Publius wrote as though prevailing opinion were hostile to (or uncertain of the wisdom of) the judicial arrangement adopted by the Constitution. What leads a partisan to anticipate and answer objections the opposition has not yet raised? (1) To provide as thorough a defense as he can for what is to him a supremely important cause; (2) to avoid having to dwell on other objections, more, equally, or less important; (3) to defend a position clearly seen by him as vulnerable because of his expectations (in this instance, of the political role of the Supreme Court), though not yet recognized as such by the opposition. All three motives may well be present here. I incline to the opinion that the tone and mode of argument of No. 78 are sufficiently understood by holding that Hamilton's hopes and fears took in a longer futurity than did his foes'.

120 THE FEDERALIST, No. 78, pp. 522–23.

> Force nor Will, but merely judgment; and must ultimately depend upon the aid of the executive arm even for the efficacy of its judgments.

One doubts whether we smile much more at this comparison between a maidenly innocent judiciary and the other branches than did Publius. His very next sentence begins with the words: "This simple view of the matter. . . ." Although the argument is offered in a spirit that does not disgrace the cause of truth, this view is indeed simple even considered on the premises of Publius' psychology; the view is kept simple because of the demands of Publius' rhetoric. The too sharp distinction between will and judgment defied, then as now, the good sense of any discerning man. Madison could speak in the Constitutional Convention of the analogy between the executive and judiciary, while stressing that one of the differences was that "in the administration of the [executive] much greater latitude is left to opinion and discretion than in the administration of the [judiciary]."[121] There is no suggestion here that the judicial function was free of every influence of opinion and discretion. Nor was Publius one to mistake names for things; he knew better:[122]

> The faculties of the mind itself have never yet been distinguished and defined, with satisfactory precision, by all the efforts of the most acute and metaphysical Philosophers. Sense, perception, *judgment*, desire, *volition*, memory, imagination, are found to be separated by such delicate shades, and minute gradations, that their boundaries have eluded the most subtle investigations, and remain a pregnant source of ingenious disquisition and controversy.

It is unreasonable, then, to assume that Publius thought of judicial decision-making as a thin-blooded exercise in deduction, in which discretion and will had no place or effect. He chose to speak in this manner, rather, in order to strengthen the impression that the judiciary could safely be accorded special, extraordinary supports and defenses. And, let it be added, he could speak in this manner because what he said was essentially, though not simply, true. That

121 2 Farrand, *supra* note 77, at 34.

122 The Federalist, No. 37, p. 235. (Emphasis added.) Publius was not of two minds on this matter; the author of No. 78 could say in No. 79, p. 533: "The mensuration of the faculties of the mind has, I believe, no place in the catalogue of known arts." In Federalist No. 51, pp. 348–49, there is a discussion of the will (and, for that matter, the ambition and interest) of the several departments of government without any exemption of the judiciary.

very statement characterizing the judiciary as "least dangerous" does not assert that it is weak. The Supreme Court will be innocuous: "the political rights of the constitution," "the general liberty of the people" will not be threatened by an independent and separate judiciary.[123] But the Supreme Court will not be weak or ineffectual, save in the most extreme political controversies where its will (for we must call it that) is pitted against the constitutional will of the representatives of the people. The provisions of the Constitution and the prudence of the judges will warn off the courts from most such confrontations. But within the large domain remaining the judiciary will hardly be unnoticed. Leaving aside the problem of judicial review of national legislation, the judiciary will serve as an instrument of national supremacy. Publius never suggested any weakness in the Supreme Court's carrying the authority of the Constitution and the laws to the people and in its facing local injustice and plain localism backed by popular feelings. In its capacity for harming individuals and even large numbers of individuals the judiciary is, as Montesquieu said, terrible.[124] But the judiciary cannot (or is not likely to) take over the government the way the other branches of government can, and in that specifically political sense it is "next to nothing."[125] The full force of the words is to be accorded Publius' statement of why the Supreme Court was not united with the Senate to form a court of impeachments: "I forbear to remark upon the additional pretext for clamour, against the Judiciary, which so considerable an augmentation of its authority would have afforded." There already were pretexts enough.[126]

Publius' case for an independent judiciary is inseparable from,

---

[123] THE FEDERALIST, No. 78, pp. 522, 523.

[124] See *id.* at 523, where Publius did say that the "simple view of the matter . . . proves incontestibly that the judiciary is beyond comparison the weakest of the three departments of power." He supported this with a near-quotation from the "celebrated Montesquieu" (the suppressed words being bracketed here): "of the three powers above mentioned, the JUDICIARY is [in some measure] next to nothing." The weakness of the judiciary was the unqualified last word of neither Montesquieu nor Publius. The very chapter of the *Spirit of Laws* (Bk. XI, chap. 6) from which Publius quoted also contains Montesquieu's characterization: "the judicial power, so terrible to mankind." But for the purpose of No. 78, it was useful to emphasize one aspect of the judiciary. For other purposes in other places, it was useful to emphasize the "terrible" features, and this Publius did. THE FEDERALIST, No. 16, pp. 102–03; No. 17, p. 107; consider also No. 27, p. 173.

[125] THE FEDERALIST, No. 78, p. 523; consider also No. 81, p. 545.

[126] *Id.* No. 65, pp. 443, 441.

even as it goes beyond, his case for the separation of powers. By "contriving the interior structure of the government" in the proper way, it is possible to achieve that measure of a separation of powers which is "admitted on all hands to be essential to the preservation of liberty."[127] The basis of that separation is, more fundamentally, the desired independence of each of the branches of government. By being in a position and of a mind to resist the encroachments of the others, each branch will be able to perform its distinctive function and also serve as an effective element in the system of checks and balances. A prerequisite, then, to the separation of powers is that each branch "should have a will of its own"; and that in turn requires, strictly speaking, that all appointments to the three branches "be drawn from the same fountain of authority, the people, through channels, having no communication whatever with one another."[128] The separation of powers presupposes separate derivations from the people, if only to prevent any one branch from pre-empting the right to speak in the name of the people. In a government wholly popular, the independence of the branches of government vis-à-vis one another rests on the separate dependence of each upon the sovereign people.[129] It is, however, a separate but unequal dependence.

Although each branch of government has its connection with the people, each also has a certain measure of distance or separation from them. It is "*the total exclusion of the people in their collective capacity* from any share" in the American republics that forms the "true distinction" between them and the ancient republics.[130] Decisive as this difference may be, there are further distinctions to be drawn, no less interesting, within the structure of the American republic. Nowhere is the separation from the people more complete and more necessary than in the judicial branch:[131]

> Perhaps such a plan of constructing the several departments [by drawing all appointments from the people, through channels having no communication with one another] would be less difficult in practice than it may in contemplation appear. Some difficulties however, and some additional expence, would attend the execution of it. Some deviations *therefore* from the principle must be admitted. In the constitution of the judiciary department in particular, it might be inexpedient to insist rig-

---

127 *Id.* No. 51, pp. 347–48.

128 *Id.* at 348.

129 *Id.* at 348–49.

130 *Id.* No. 63, p. 428.

131 *Id.* No. 51, p. 348. (Emphasis added.)

> orously on the principle; first, because peculiar qualifications being essential in the members, the primary consideration ought to be to select that mode of choice, which best secures these qualifications; secondly, because the permanent tenure by which the appointments are held in that department, must soon destroy all sense of dependence on the authority conferring them.

If there is to be a judiciary equal to its tasks and adequate for the preservation of liberty, there must be some relaxation of the principle of unmediated derivations from the people. That this relaxation is politically safe is suggested by two considerations. The peculiar qualifications and qualities of the judges remind us that we are discussing the "least dangerous" branch and hence the one in least need of direct popular control. Then, too, the permanent tenure with which judges hold office entails the least risk that their will may be hostage of the appointing power. There must, moreover, be a departure from "the characteristic policy of republican government" (popular election of rulers) and from the "most effectual" means of maintaining "a proper responsibility to the people" (limited terms of appointment).[132] The cause of free government requires a qualification of popular government.

To adhere to the republican principle, to the spirit of a government wholly popular, in no way entails "an unqualified complaisance to every sudden breeze of passion, or to every transient impulse which the people may receive from the arts of men, who flatter their prejudices to betray their interests."[133] Publius, like Rousseau, knew that while "the people commonly intend the PUBLIC GOOD," they do not always "*reason right* about the *means* of promoting it."[134] Indeed, we may say that the deepest justification of a separate and independent judiciary is the expectation that, more often than is politically safe, "the interests of the people are at variance with their inclinations."[135] If the "republican principle demands, that the deliberate sense of the community should govern the conduct of those to whom they entrust the management of their affairs,"[136] it also imposes a "duty" upon "the guardians of those interests" to call the people to their senses or at least to give the

[132] *Id.* No. 57, p. 384.

[133] *Id.* No. 71, p. 482.

[134] *Ibid.* See ROUSSEAU, SOCIAL CONTRACT, Bk. II, chap. 3.

[135] THE FEDERALIST, No. 71, p. 482.

[136] *Ibid.*

people the chance to come to their senses.[137] A government ought to have an unlimited range of powers, adequate to its objects and "free from every other control, but a regard to the public good and to the sense of the people."[138] A free government is one in which the sense of the people or the sense of the majority is controlling. But to secure the public good, in a manner compatible with the republican principle, requires that the deliberate sense of the community prevail. And that sense is not taken simply or unqualifiedly from what the people or a majority say to their legislative representatives at any given moment. The "deliberate sense" is found in a blend of voices, from the people and their representatives, direct and remote, present and past.[139] But in the extreme, critical, and interesting case, that sense may be taken from what "men, who had courage and magnanimity enough to serve them at the peril of their displeasure" declare to be in the people's interest.[140] Insofar as these forms of resistance to temporary passions refer to the protection of minorities, it may be said that securing the rights of all has a democratic source. Thus the popular credentials of the American regime are in no way impugned by asserting "that the whole power of the proposed government is to be in the hands of the representatives of the people" rather than in the hands of the people themselves.[141] More than this was neither necessary nor safe, in Publius' eyes. Ultimately, the people's "cool and deliberate sense" prevails over the views of their rulers; but at any given moment, their freely chosen rulers act "to suspend the blow meditated by the people against themselves."[142]

It is in such a context that Publius could look forward to the judiciary's "faithful performance of so arduous a duty"[143] as guarding the Constitution against legislative encroachments, and to the thwarting of certain popular "ill humours" by the judges.[144] When the separate judicial establishment performs its distinct function and when it serves as a complicating element in the system of checks and

---

[137] *Id.* at 482–83.

[138] *Id.* No. 31, p. 195.

[139] *Id.* No. 22, p. 139; No. 58, p. 397; No. 71, p. 482.

[140] *Id.* No. 71, p. 483.

[141] *Id.* No. 28, p. 178; *cf.* No. 21, p. 131.

[142] *Id.* No. 63, p. 425. Publius had no difficulty in speaking of "the sense of the people" being operative where that sense is determined by a select body popularly chosen. See the discussion of the Electoral College in No. 68, p. 458.

[143] *Id.* No. 78, p. 527.

[144] *Id.* at 528.

balances, the judiciary is but one of the three branches of the government and as such unexceptionable. But at still another level—transcending its other functions, and implied in the technical knowledge needed by this branch of government alone—the judiciary acts as special guardian of the principles of the Constitution. In this role it is no longer merely one of three, and no longer weak. To the extent that it can remove itself from its popular source of power, the judiciary is able to display and act in its unique character. In the last analysis, the judges ought to hold their office with permanent tenure in order to sustain their "necessary independence" of the executive and the legislature and the people.[145] If such tenure did not in fact "soon destroy all sense of dependence," if fear and a concern for popularity were to affect the quality of justice, the complications and safeguards of the Constitution would be a hollow joke.[146] Uniquely situated and uniquely protected, the judges were not expected to behave like ordinary men.

For Publius it was sufficient to remind "considerate men of every description" of the larger political benefits to be derived from a judiciary whose temper was marked by "integrity and moderation."[147] The tone and quality of the highest national court would prove decisive for the entire administration of justice, since:[148]

> [T]he national and state systems are to be regarded as ONE WHOLE. The courts of the latter will of course be natural auxiliaries to the execution of the laws of the union, and an appeal from them will as naturally lie to that tribunal, which is destined to unite and assimilate the principles of national justice and the rules of national decisions.

Such a tribunal, so placed, could display political wisdom as well as legal craftsmanship. Its opportunities and risks would be correlative. Publius could safely have adopted as his own, Aratus' understanding of the political position of the North Carolina courts: "The *Judicial* of our democracy runs an equal pace with a monarchical judiciary, but steps forward to an almost undetermined distance—not only

---

145 *Id.* at 529. 146 *Id.* No. 51, p. 348. 147 *Id.* No. 78, p. 528.

148 *Id.* No. 82, p. 556. The entire paragraph from No. 82, of which a few lines are quoted here, is reprinted in Marshall's opinion in *Cohens v. Virginia*, 6 Wheat. 264, 419 (1821), verbatim, except that "natural justice" is in the place of "national justice." It is not clear whether this error or substitution is the work of the Chief Justice, the reporter, or the typesetter. At any rate it appears in the first edition of Wheaton's *Reports* and in the subsequent reprintings of his text.

acting in all law occurrences . . . as the monarchical judiciary; but from the nature of our government, as may be easily deduced from the constitution itself, *pro salutate reipublicae*, it advances higher, and becomes the *equilibrium* or *pendulum* thereof."[149]

It was expected that the national judiciary—independent, public-spirited, and impelled by a pride in its special competence—would serve as an instrument and symbol of the power of "a more perfect Union." Such an understanding was clear and widespread.[150] But it was debatable whether more should be expected of the Justices, that is, whether their political counsel should be sought and indeed required for making public policy. The Philadelphia Convention repeatedly discussed a Council of Revision (first proposed by Governor Randolph in his presentation of the "Virginia Plan" and presumably modeled after the New York arrangement); these discussions revealed quite differing views about the province and function of judicial power. According to the Virginia Plan, a Council of Revision, composed of the national executive and "a convenient number" of the national judiciary, would possess a qualified veto over every act of the national legislature, including the latter's act of negativing any state law "contravening in the opinion of the National Legislature the articles of Union."[151] The involvement of the judiciary in this automatic review of all national legislative authority was the occasion of repeated debate. Madison saw in this involvement an apt way of bolstering an executive who was all too likely to be in need of whatever support he could get and perhaps also in need of being reminded of his duty:[152]

---

149 Aratus, Letter No. III, in State Gazette of North-Carolina (Edenton), June 4, 1789, p. 1, col. 1.

150 See Brutus [Robert Yates], Letter No. XI, New York Journal, and Weekly Register (New York City), Jan. 31, 1788, reprinted in KENYON, *supra* note 119, at 335, 339; 4 ELLIOT, *supra* note 79, at 258 (C. Pinckney, Jan. 16, 1788); THE FEDERALIST, No. 16, p. 102; No. 22, pp. 143–44; No. 80, pp. 535, 537–38.

151 1 FARRAND, *supra* note 77, at 21.

152 *Id.* at 138. Contrast Madison's argument with Daniel D. Tompkins' retrospective explanation of why newly independent New York had vested the veto power in a council of revision: On the one hand, "a veto, even qualified in its character, placed in the hands of the executive alone," was considered "an odious relict of royalty," both dangerous and unwise. Yet, the very provision of a veto over legislative enactments "was owing principally to the peculiar state of the times, and of the country." "Our people had not yet been accustomed to self-government, and many of them retained strong predilections for the forms and checks of the government under which they had hitherto lived." Hence, the framers of the New

> In a Republic personal merit alone could be the ground of political exaltation, but it would rarely happen that this merit would be so pre-eminent as to produce universal acquiescence. The Executive Magistrate would be envied & assailed by disappointed competitors: His firmness therefore wd. need support. He would not possess those great emoluments from his station, nor that permanent stake in the public interest which wd. place him out of the reach of foreign corruption: He would stand in need therefore of being controuled as well as supported. An association of the Judges in his revisionary function wd. both double the advantage and diminish the danger.

According to this argument, the American chief executive, representing the monarchic principle (and the responsibilities and temptations of solitary rule), needed to be supported and restrained in a manner that took due account of the over-all republican setting in which he would act. "Mr. Elseworth," who was to be the principal draftsman of the Judiciary Act and its jealous manager through committee and floor debates, "approved heartily of the motion" for a Council of Revision. "The aid of the Judges will give more wisdom & firmness to the Executive."[153] Madison, early in the debates, drew attention to a power of review that was not exhausted by considerations of constitutionality. "In short, whether the object of the revisionary power was to restrain the Legislature from encroaching on the other co-ordinate Departments, or on the rights of the people at large; or from passing laws unwise in their principle, or incorrect in their form, the utility of annexing the wisdom and weight of the Judiciary to the Executive seemed incontestable."[154] This expectation that the judges would not limit themselves to judgments of constitutionality—and ought not to so limit themselves—was made even more forcefully by Wilson:[155]

> Laws may be unjust, may be unwise, may be dangerous, may be destructive; and yet not be so unconstitutional as to justify the Judges in refusing to give them effect. Let them have a

York constitution of 1777 "were apprehensive, if they departed too widely from what the people had been accustomed to, and introduced alterations and innovations very glaring, that they would alarm the jealousy and prejudices of some who were otherwise well disposed to the cause of freedom, and particularly some men of property and influence." CARTER & STONE, REPORTS OF THE PROCEEDINGS AND DEBATES OF THE [NEW YORK CONSTITUTIONAL] CONVENTION OF 1821 . . . 79 (1821).

153 2 FARRAND, *supra* note 77, at 73–74.

154 1 *id.* at 139.

155 2 *id.* at 73.

> share in the Revisionary power, and they will have an opportunity of taking notice of these characters of a law, and of counteracting, by the weight of their opinions the improper views of the Legislature.

These arguments, however, were unavailing. The notion that judges ought to be charged explicitly with the delicate task of assessing the wisdom of proposed legislation was attacked, successfully, on grounds of competence and propriety. Gorham doubted whether as judges they were "to be presumed to possess any peculiar knowledge of the mere policy of public measures."[156] Gerry saw in the proposal "an improper coalition": "It was making Statesmen of the Judges; and setting them up as the guardians of the Rights of the people."[157] So far was this trust mistaken, that he feared that the executive could rather "be covered by the sanction & seduced by the sophistry of the Judges."[158] Although the Council of Revision lacked nothing in the way of able and persistent advocates, it was decisively rejected. In a final effort to extend the formal influence of the judiciary in the new government, Gouverneur Morris proposed a Council of State to assist and advise the President. Heading the list of cabinet officers was to be the "Chief Justice of the Supreme Court, who shall from time to time recommend such alterations of and additions to the laws of the U.S. as may in his opinion be necessary to the due administration of Justice, and such as may promote useful learning and inculcate sound morality throughout the Union."[159] Having once been referred to the Committee of Detail, this proposal never emerged again. Faced with clearly stated alternatives, the majority of the Convention appear to have been of the mind that "[i]t is impossible to keep the Judges too distinct from every other avocation than that of expounding the laws."[160]

We are left with an equivocal conclusion: while some of the leading Framers proposed making explicit provision for use of the political wisdom of the judges—and indeed indicated in so recommending that the judges would not otherwise have these broader duties or opportunities, the majority of the Constitutional Convention (and even the leading defenders of its work) emphatically rejected such a plan on the grounds that judges ought to be kept "judicial." The attack on the revisionary power, then, was mounted mainly for the sake of securing the proper separation of powers,

---

156 *Ibid.*

157 2 *id.* at 75.

158 1 *id.* at 139.

159 2 *id.* at 342.

160 THE FEDERALIST, No. 73, p. 499.

that is, for the sake of an effective check on the other branches of government. But the ground of that attack was the notion that judges should do—and only do—what they are trained for. Yet that technical competence points to another, higher judicial function: safeguarding the legal and political principles of the regime. Indeed, those very characteristics of the judiciary so well set forth in *Federalist No. 78* make it more likely that the purposes envisioned for the Council of Revision are better served under the present arrangement. The judiciary can better perform its higher function indirectly, through its more "technical" acts, than directly. The judges—and the judges alone, of all government officials—had to be men of special training and character in order to do their job at all. Set apart from most men by temperament, education, acquired tastes, and responsibilities, the judges (at their best) could make the most of such opportunities as came their way to act as faithful sustainers and guardians of the regime. The political grand jury charge was one response to that challenge, but not the last.

III. The Lesson of History?

An examination of the Supreme Court's work during its first decade of circuit-riding discloses that the judges were self-consciously concerned to educate their audience politically. Less conclusively, my effort to reconstruct early intentions and expectations for the national judiciary has pointed to a conception of the political role of the courts. This conception starts from the premise that "[g]overnment must be framed for man as he is, and not for man as he would be if he were free from vice."[161] It is not embarrassed when discussing the likelihood that "the faithful discharge" of the judicial power will not win the general acclaim and support of a people no longer virtuous.[162] Rather, this conception of judicial power flatly accepts the great probability of some significant political tension when the court acts as an equilibrium *pro salutate reipublicae:* "We are well aware this doctrine will sound ruffly in the ears of many of our demagogues of power."[163]

---

[161] 1 Kent, Commentaries on American Law, Part II, Lect. XIV, at 292 (5th ed. 1844).

[162] *Id.* at 291. See also Jefferson's *Notes on the State of Virginia,* Queries 13 and 17, in Koch & Peden, *supra* note 29, at 238, 277.

[163] Aratus, Letter No. III, in State Gazette of North-Carolina (Edenton), June 4, 1789, p. 1, col. 1.

Recognizing the near-certainty of heated confrontations, the early Justices took it upon themselves to mold public sentiment inasmuch as it lay in their power to do so. Teaching a people how to be good republicans would mean more than making judicial power secure. It would have the far greater effect of making the republicans safe for the republic. The Justices, in short, acted on the understanding that "[i]n this and like communities, public sentiment is everything."[164] Recognizing this underpinning of the law, the Justices acted as best they could to mold and educate that public. This action presupposed an educable people, and it presupposed the political indispensability of a population that are emphatically citizens. This is the lesson to be drawn from that early generation's deeds:[165]

> This was the platform upon which the Constitution of the United States had been erected. Its VIRTUES, its republican character, consisted in its conformity to the principles proclaimed in the Declaration of Independence, and as its administration must necessarily be always pliable to the fluctuating varieties of public opinion; its stability and duration by a like overruling and irresistible necessity, was to depend upon the stability and duration in the hearts and minds of the people of that *virtue*, or in other words, of those principles proclaimed in the Declaration of Independence, and embodied in the Constitution of the United States.

The first Justices of the Supreme Court acted in such a way as to counter the habit of mind that insisted that "there is no right principle of action but *self-interest*"[166] and to inculcate civic virtue. More, perhaps, than any other branch of the government, they were in a position and of a character to do so.

Subsequent changes in the organization of the courts and in the style of political discourse led the Supreme Court to give up the political charge. Yet in so doing, the Justices merely replaced one mode of shaping public beliefs and opinions with another mode—one that could be equally, probably more, effective. Much of Chief Justice Marshall's greatness lies in his success in, so to speak, putting

---

[164] Lincoln, *Reply to Douglas,* Ottawa, Ill. (Aug. 21, 1858), in BASLER, *supra* note 93, at 458.

[165] J. Q. ADAMS, JUBILEE OF THE CONSTITUTION 54 (1839).

[166] See Lincoln, *The Repeal of the Missouri Compromise* (Oct. 16, 1854), in BASLER, *supra* note 93, at 291.

the Supreme Court as a whole on circuit. By explicitly taking the higher role of guardian of the principles of the regime and by speaking with one voice through opinions of the Court, the Supreme Court, under Marshall's politic and artful guidance, was able to survive and even prevail in ways not easily foreseeable in 1801. Today the Supreme Court is, in some respects, more evidently and continuously on circuit and its work more often before the public eye than the warmest supporters of circuit-riding could have hoped.

One of the reasons Congress persisted in requiring members of the Supreme Court to ride circuit in the nineteenth century was a fear of the political consequences of isolating the Court from its public. The argument that was made pointed perhaps as much to judges learning as to judges teaching. It is precisely because judges have "political functions to discharge" that they should be attentive to their political support; "they should be conversant with public opinion, and imbibe the spirit of the times."[167] But it is not alone important that the judges have a clear and vivid sense of being "tethered . . . but not shackled" to public opinion.[168] It is perhaps even more important, in the long run, that the people at large have a clear and vivid sense that there is "a harmony of opinion and of action" between the Supreme Court and the inferior courts, and between the judiciary and the people for whom it is meant to establish justice.[169] "In a Government founded on opinion, it is necessary that the People should be satisfied with judicial decisions."[170]

In requiring circuit duty, Congress acted as though it believed that this harmony could be fostered by the confrontation of judges with a larger public of lawyers, court officials, litigants, and bystanders. In that encounter, the political charge after the Chase impeachment was neither appropriate nor significant; but the judges could resort to another way of teaching, more politic and effective because more obviously "judicial," and hence less visible.

---

[167] 2 Register of Debates in Congress, 19th Cong., 1st Sess., Pt. I, col. 554 (Apr. 14, 1826) (Sen. Harper).

[168] I have adapted the language of Lord Devlin: "A judge is tethered to the positive law but not shackled to it," as conveying quite precisely the kind of relation between judge and public opinion that the early Congress envisioned. Devlin, Enforcement of Morals 94 (1965).

[169] 2 Register of Debates in Congress, 19th Cong., 1st Sess., Part I, col. 878 (Jan. 4, 1826) (Rep. Webster).

[170] 2 *id.* at col. 1100 (Jan. 24, 1826) (Rep. Kerr).

Then, as now, the judges had the option of teaching by cases. By their decisions—and especially through a coherent explanation of the grounds of their decisions—the judges could partially introduce the language of the law into the vulgar tongue. What is more important, they could transfer to the minds of the citizens the modes of thought lying behind legal language and the notions of right fundamental to the regime.[171] The political sophistication needed, then and now, for conveying these lessons is surpassed only by the sense of political responsibility that continues to set judges the task of being republican schoolmasters.

I have maintained that the modern Supreme Court Justice is on public display as much as, probably more than, the itinerant Justices of the 1790's. His confrontation with a large nonprofessional public is as little subject to his discretion as was his predecessors'. But how he then conducts himself and how he fashions his speech with an eye to that public are very much within his control. When a judge publicly denies or minimizes the broad political effectiveness of judicial reasoning he is engaging in a kind of judicial teaching or preaching. He has not removed himself from the camp of Jay or Wilson, however much his teaching differs from theirs. Whether the Justice should teach the public is not and cannot be in question since teaching is inseparable from judging in a democratic regime. But whether the Justice has taught well—need one say it in these pages?—is highly debatable. In reaching a judgment of how well a Justice has taught, we have to assess both his legal craftsmanship and his political skill and understanding. The experience recounted here of that earliest generation of the national judiciary reminds us how difficult and at once how necessary it is for the Justices to know how "to confront those obstacles that can be overcome, and to steer out of the current when the tide threatens to carry them away, and with them the sovereignty of the Union and obedience to its laws."[172]

---

[171] See notes 2 and 6 *supra*.

[172] See note 1 *supra*.

WILLIAM E. LEUCHTENBURG

THE ORIGINS OF FRANKLIN D. ROOSEVELT'S "COURT-PACKING" PLAN

No event of twentieth-century American constitutional history is better remembered than Franklin D. Roosevelt's ill-fated "Court-packing" scheme of 1937; yet the origins of the plan remain obscure and often misstated. The proposal has been variously attributed to Felix Frankfurter, who abhorred it; to Benjamin Cohen and Thomas Corcoran, who favored a different remedy and had no hand in shaping this one; and to Samuel I. Rosenman, who played only a minor role after the decision had already been made.[1] Among those who have been said to have helped frame the plan were James M. Landis, who had heard only rumors of it before it was announced, and Robert H. Jackson, who first learned of the President's plan when he read about it in a Philadelphia newspaper.[2]

William E. Leuchtenburg is Professor of History, Columbia University.

1 Mallon, *Purely Confidential*, Detroit News, Feb. 8, Apr. 2, May 21, 1937; MASON, BRANDEIS: A FREE MAN'S LIFE 625 (1946); MOLEY, AFTER SEVEN YEARS 357–59 (1939) (hereinafter MOLEY); Raymond Clapper MS Diary, Feb. 8, 1937, Clapper MSS, Library of Congress (hereinafter LC); 7 Frances Perkins, Columbia Oral History Collection 128 (hereinafter COHC); Washington Post, Feb. 13, 1937. Of Frankfurter, James M. Landis recalled that he "caught hell from him" for supporting the plan. Landis, COHC 49, 302. See, too, Clapper MS Diary, Sept. 28, 1938; Frank Buxton to William Allen White, June 2, 1937, White MSS, LC, Box 189.

2 Mallon, *Purely Confidential*, Detroit News, Apr. 2, 1937; Landis, COHC 44–45; MICHELSON, THE GHOST TALKS 169–70 (1944); GERHART, AMERICA'S ADVOCATE: ROBERT H. JACKSON 105 (1958).

The project has been described either as an impulsive act born of the *hubris* created by FDR's landslide victory in 1936 or as a calculated plot hatched many months before in angry resentment at the *Schechter* verdict. Roosevelt himself never did anything to clear up the confusion. Three weeks after the President launched the proposal, Senator Hiram Johnson of California wrote a friend: "He has been beaten from pillar to post upon when he conceived the brilliant idea, and how he conceived it."[3]

I. Prologue

The constitutional crisis of 1937 had been brewing for a long time. Franklin Roosevelt began his political career at the time that his distant cousin Theodore was assaulting the sanctity of the courts and the air was loud with cries for the recall of judges and judicial decisions. In the 1920's there was mounting progressive animus toward the Taft Court manifested in such forms as the La Follette platform of 1924, which called for empowering Congress to override the Supreme Court. In the Hoover years, progressives had waged fierce contests against the confirmations of John J. Parker and Charles Evans Hughes. Increasingly, liberal critics of the Court believed that a majority of the Justices spoke for the interests of the rich and well-born.[4]

Even before Roosevelt took office, he had aroused speculation over whether his presidency would result in a confrontation with the Supreme Court. In a campaign speech in Baltimore on October 5, 1932, Roosevelt blurted out: "After March 4, 1929, the Republican party was in complete control of all branches of the government—the Legislature, with the Senate and Congress; and the executive departments; and I may add, for full measure, to make it complete, the United States Supreme Court as well."[5] This statement had been interpolated in the original text of the address, but the next day, Roosevelt told Senator James F. Byrnes: "What I said last night about the judiciary is true, and whatever is in a man's

[3] Johnson to John Francis Neylan, Feb. 26, 1937, Johnson MSS, Bancroft Library, University of California, Berkeley.

[4] St. Louis Star, June 23, 1930, clipping, Pierce Butler MSS, Minnesota Historical Society, St. Paul; 2 Pusey, Charles Evans Hughes 655–62 (1951).

[5] 1 Franklin D. Roosevelt, Public Papers and Addresses 837 (1938) (hereinafter Public Papers).

heart is apt to come to his tongue—I shall not make any explanations or apology for it!"[6] Republicans hopped on Roosevelt's statement as a warning that, if elected President, he might, in Herbert Hoover's words, "reduce the tribunal to an instrument of party policy."[7]

Roosevelt, who was right in thinking that the composition of the federal courts was heavily Republican,[8] found an even greater source of concern in the doctrines pronounced by the Court in such recent decisions as that in the *Oklahoma Ice* case.[9] The New Dealers recognized that much that they proposed to do would be invalidated by the Court if it followed the line of reasoning adopted by the Taft Court, but they hoped that the Court would recognize the depression to be an emergency justifying unprecedented government action. In his inaugural address on March 4, 1933, the new president stated: "Our Constitution is so simple and practical that it is possible always to meet extraordinary needs by changes in emphasis and arrangement without loss of essential form."[10]

Yet Roosevelt was wary of relying on the tolerance of the Court for New Deal experiments. The Administration deliberately postponed tests of the constitutionality of the legislation of the Hundred Days as long as possible; the Supreme Court did not have the opportunity to rule on a New Deal statute until 1935. Meanwhile, the New Dealers were heartened by two 1934 opinions which appeared to recognize that the emergency might be the occasion for governmental restrictions on property rights.[11] Especially encouraging was Justice Roberts' statement in the *Nebbia* case: "[T]his court from the early days affirmed that the power to promote the general welfare is inherent in government."[12]

---

[6] BYRNES, ALL IN ONE LIFETIME 65 (1958).

[7] N.Y. Times, Feb. 11, 1937.

[8] In the autumn of 1933, Roosevelt's Attorney General sent him a memorandum noting that of the 266 judges in the federal courts, only 28 per cent were Democrats. Homer Cummings to FDR, Nov. 8, 1933, Franklin D. Roosevelt Library, Hyde Park, N.Y. (henceforth cited as FDRL) OF 41, Box 114.

[9] New State Ice Co. v. Liebmann, 285 U.S. 262 (1932).

[10] 2 PUBLIC PAPERS 14–15.

[11] Home Building & Loan Ass'n v. Blaisdell, 290 U.S. 398 (1934); Nebbia v. New York, 291 U.S. 502 (1934).

[12] 291 U.S. at 524.

Such pronouncements served, for the moment, to dispel the conviction that a collision between Roosevelt and the Supreme Court was inevitable and that steps should be taken to reconstitute the Court, ideas that emerged remarkably early in the Roosevelt administration. Almost two years before the Court had invalidated the first New Deal law, an Illinois man wrote the President: "Sometimes I get thinking about the many millions who are unemployed, and I wonder if we really can get them back to work, and retain our social order. . . . If the Supreme Court's membership could be increased to twelve, without too much trouble, perhaps the Constitution would be found to be quite elastic."[13]

As early as January, 1934, the *Literary Digest* reported: "In the intimate Presidential circle the idea of reconstituting the Supreme Court has been considered. . . . In the conversation within the Roosevelt circle, a court of fifteen, instead of the present nine, has been mentioned."[14] The *Digest* added that the *Blaisdell* opinion, which appeared to indicate a liberal majority on the Court, had caused such talk among the New Dealers to subside. Yet conservatives remained uneasy. The following month, Henry Prather Fletcher, soon to be chosen Republican national chairman, wrote the columnist Mark Sullivan: "You seem to rely on the Courts for relief in the last analysis. Let us hope the Supreme Court will not bend before the storm—but even if it does not, it is the weakest of the three coordinate branches of the Government and an administration as fully in control as this one is can pack it as easily as an English Government can pack the House of Lords."[15]

II. Gold Clauses and Railroad Pensions

Early in 1935 the period of nervous calm was abruptly shattered. On January 7, 1935, in its first ruling on a New Deal law, the Court invalidated the "hot oil" provisions of the National Industrial Recovery Act.[16] The Republican New York *Herald-Tribune* commented:[17]

---

[13] John P. Byrne to FDR, Apr. 18, 1933, FDRL OF 41-A.

[14] *News and Comment from the National Capital,* 117 Literary Digest 10 (Jan. 20, 1934).

[15] Fletcher to Sullivan, Feb. 28, 1934, Fletcher MSS, LC, Box 16.

[16] Panama Refining Co. v. Ryan, 293 U.S. 388 (1935); Charles Fahy, COHC 148.

[17] *New Deal Meets Tests in Supreme Court,* 119 Literary Digest 5–6 (Jan. 19, 1935).

> In the skylarking days of 1933–34, the happy administrators of the New Deal brushed aside the Supreme Court as they brushed aside Congress and the Constitution. . . . The President paid perfunctory lip-service to the nation's charter of liberty. Behind the scene the whispers were loud enough to be beyond misunderstanding. Let the Supreme Court try to halt the march of the new order, according to F. D. R., an Act of Congress would be passed adding to its membership and packing it with enough Tugwellian jurists to overturn any conservative decision overnight.

Now, the *Tribune* exulted, the 8-to-1 decision had thrown "this revolutionary nonsense into the Potomac where it belongs."

In fact, the New Dealers took the "hot oil" decision in stride. Since the Court's objections had rested on procedural defects that could easily be corrected, the Administration was not greatly concerned by the judgment. Much more alarming were the series of tests of the constitutionality of gold legislation that were making their way relentlessly toward the Supreme Court. A ruling by the Court for the plaintiffs would deny Congress the right to regulate the currency at a time of national economic disaster and threatened financial chaos by increasing the country's debt by nearly $70 billion.[18] Washington officials, observed Arthur Krock, were more absorbed with the question of how the Court would decide than by any subject since the bank holiday of March, 1933. In contemplation of that opinion, cold shivers "chase up and down their spines when they waken in the night."[19]

At a cabinet meeting on January 11, 1935, Attorney General Homer Cummings reported on the gold clause cases, which he had just finished arguing. Secretary of the Interior Harold L. Ickes noted in his diary:[20]

> The Attorney General said that if the Court should decide against the Government in the gold certificate and Liberty Bond cases, the situation could be saved by Congress hurrying through a statute taking away from the citizens the right to sue the Government for the damages that they might claim by reason of having accepted payment in currency on bonds that, by their terms, were stated to be payable in gold. . . .
>
> The Attorney General went so far as to say that if the Court

---

18 SCHLESINGER, THE POLITICS OF UPHEAVAL 255–56 (1960) (hereinafter SCHLESINGER).

19 N.Y. Times, Jan. 15, 1935.

20 1 SECRET DIARY OF HAROLD L. ICKES 273–74 (1953) (hereinafter ICKES).

> went against the Government, the number of justices should be increased at once so as to give a favorable majority. As a matter of fact, the President suggested this possibility to me during our interview on Thursday, and I told him that that is precisely what ought to be done. It wouldn't be the first time that the Supreme Court had been increased in size to meet a temporary emergency and it certainly would be justified in this case.

Many in the Administration had an almost apocalyptic sense of inevitable conflict. After the cabinet meeting on January 11, Ickes reported:[21]

> I told the President yesterday that only a few years ago I had predicted that sooner or later the Supreme Court would become a political issue as the result of its continued blocking of the popular will through declaring acts of Congress unconstitutional. During the discussion today the Vice President said that he had read a pamphlet which had been written about a hundred years ago in which the author advanced the theory that sooner or later, through the aggrandizement of power by the Supreme Court, a political crisis of major magnitude would be precipitated in this country.

Close observers anticipated that the President would not permit the Court to disrupt his attempts to achieve recovery, even if this led to a constitutional crisis. In his Kings Feature Syndicate column, Arthur Brisbane created a stir when he questioned whether there was any constitutional authority for the practice of judicial review. Brisbane wrote:[22]

> As a matter of constitutional law, as actually written by the constitutional convention, if the Supreme Court should say to the President of the United States "We find unconstitutional, and ask you to revoke, your law abolishing the gold clause," the President might reasonably reply, "I have your message and respectfully request that you show me what part of the Constitution authorizes you to nullify a law passed by the Congress of the United States and signed by the President."
>
> If he sent that message, the Supreme Court would be puzzled, for it could show nothing in the Constitution.

Roosevelt was, in fact, ready to act much as Brisbane suggested. A month earlier, in response to an inquiry from the President, Robert Jackson, general counsel of the Bureau of Internal Revenue,

---

[21] *Id.* at 274.

[22] Brisbane to FDR, Feb. 11, 1935, FDRL OF 41-A, Box 116.

had suggested that the government might withdraw its consent to be sued.[23] Accordingly, a message to Congress was drafted recommending the withdrawal of the right to sue the United States for more than the face value of government bonds and other obligations. In the event of an adverse decision, Roosevelt was ready with a proclamation of national emergency to regulate currency transactions; for ninety days, no payment on any contract would be permitted save at the rate of $35 for an ounce of gold, the rate fixed by the President on January 31, 1934, under authority of the Gold Reserve Act.[24]

If the Supreme Court ruled against the government, Roosevelt was prepared to deliver a defiant radio address in which he would declare that the decisions, if enforced, would result in "unconscionable" profit to investors, bankruptcy for almost every railroad and for many corporations, default by state and local governments, and wholesale mortgage foreclosures on farms and in cities. It would not only increase the national debt by a staggering sum but would catapult the nation "into an infinitely more serious economic plight than we have yet experienced."[25] He did not seek a quarrel with the Supreme Court, but he did think it appropriate to quote a sentence from Lincoln's First Inaugural Address: "At the same time, the candid citizen must confess that if the policy of the government, upon vital questions affecting the whole people, is to be irrevocably fixed by decisions of the Supreme Court, the instant they are made, in ordinary litigation between parties in personal actions, the people will have ceased to be their own rulers, having to that extent practically resigned their government into the hands of that eminent tribunal."

Neither the President nor Congress, Roosevelt planned to say, could "stand idly by and . . . permit the decision of the Supreme Court to be carried through to its logical, inescapable conclusion," because this would "imperil the economic and political security of this nation." He sought only to carry out the principle that "For value received the same value should be repaid," a doctrine "in accordance with the Golden Rule, with the precepts of the Scrip-

---

23 Robert Jackson, COHC.

24 1 BLUM, FROM THE MORGENTHAU DIARIES 126–27 (1959) (hereinafter MORGENTHAU).

25 Draft of message, FDRL PSF Supreme Court.

tures, and the dictates of common sense." "In order to attain this reasonable end," the President intended to announce, "I shall immediately take such steps as may be necessary, by proclamation and by message to the Congress of the United States."

On February 18, as word reached the White House that the Court had assembled, Roosevelt took his place at the cabinet table to await word. Minutes later, the tension broke, as it became clear that in each of a series of cases, the government had won.[26] On the following day, the President sent a saucy note to Joseph P. Kennedy, chairman of the SEC:[27]

> With you I think Monday, February eighteenth, was an historic day. As a lawyer it seems to me that the Supreme Court has at last definitely put human values ahead of the "pound of flesh" called for by a contract.
>
> The Chairman of the Securities Exchange Commission turns out to be far more accurate than the Associated Press in that he reported the decisions accurately. How fortunate it is that his Exchanges will never know how close they came to being closed up by a stroke of the pen of one "J.P.K."
>
> Likewise, the Nation will never know what a great treat it missed in not hearing the marvelous radio address the "Pres" had prepared for delivery to the Nation Monday night if the cases had gone the other way.

Roosevelt could not have been pleased by the scolding he received from Chief Justice Hughes in the majority opinion, and he was aware that he had had a close call. "In spite of our rejoicing," he wrote, "I shudder at the closeness of five to four decisions in these important matters!"[28] Congressmen began to talk more seriously about the need to find some way to restrain the Court. Senator George Norris of Nebraska protested: "These five to four Supreme Court decisions on the constitutionality of congressional acts it seems to me are illogical and should not occur in a country like ours."[29] Yet, since the government had been upheld, most of the expressions of dissatisfaction came not from New Deal supporters but from the outraged conservatives, many of whom echoed

---

[26] Norman v. B. & O. R.R., 294 U.S. 240 (1935), and related cases; 1 MORGENTHAU 130.

[27] FDR to Kennedy, Feb. 19, 1935, 1 F.D.R.: HIS PERSONAL LETTERS 455 (1950) (hereinafter LETTERS).

[28] FDR to Angus MacLean, Feb. 21, 1935, FDRL OF 10-F.

[29] Norris to Layton Spicher, Mar. 29, 1935, Norris MSS, LC, Tray 27, Box 4.

Justice McReynolds' irate dissent: "Shame and humiliation are upon us now."[30]

Three months later, it was the liberals' turn to be discomforted by the Court. In another 5-to-4 decision, with Justice Roberts joining the majority, the Court invalidated the Railway Pension Act.[31] For the first time since Roosevelt took office, the Court had delivered an opinion that antagonized an important interest group who could demand restrictions on the Court's powers.[32] The president of one Railroad Brotherhood called the decision, which affected a million railroad workers, a "bitter disappointment."[33] From Wichita Falls, Texas, one man wrote Roosevelt: "I Had an idea they would turn Down that Railroad Pension. I told you the Rich Men always Run to the Supreme Court to Beat Our Laws. . . . The Supreme Court is a Public Nuisance."[34]

The implications of the rail pension decision were not limited to its effects on railroad workers. Many believed that if Justice Roberts disposed of other cases as he had this one, the pending social security legislation would also be invalidated. "Congratulations to rail carriers over pension decision yesterday," the general attorney for the Cudahy Packing Company wired a spokesman for the railroads: "That monumental decision so parallels our necessities in connection with Social Security legislation that we owe you a debt for fight now vindicating constitutional interpretation upon which all American business stands for future welfare all citizens."[35] The opinion, wrote *Business Week*, indicated that the

---

30 There is a copy of McReynolds' extemporaneous dissent, with corrections in his handwriting, in McReynolds MSS, Alderman Library, University of Virginia, Charlottesville, Va., Folder H-2. For conservative dismay, see L. E. Armstrong to Willis Van Devanter, Feb. 26, 1935, Van Devanter MSS, LC; James Beck to J. C. McReynolds, Apr. 13, 1934, Beck MSS, Princeton University Library, Carton 2; Alfred James McClure to Homer Cummings, Feb. 19, 1935, NA Dept. of Justice 105-42-11; letters in Charles Evans Hughes MSS, LC, Box 157.

31 Retirement Board v. Alton R. Co., 295 U.S. 330 (1935).

32 The Court had, of course, angered groups like bondholders by its decisions in the gold cases, but since these elements viewed the Court as a bulwark against social change, they were unlikely to support any movement to limit the Court's powers.

33 D. B. Robertson to FDR, Jan. 22, 1936, NA Dept. of Justice 235460.

34 P. J. Hasey to FDR, May 6, 1935, NA Dept. of Justice 235460.

35 Thomas Creigh to Paul Shoup, May 7, 1935, Shoup MSS, Stanford University Library, Stanford, California, Box 1.

Court "would smash any social security legislation that may be passed by Congress."[36]

Prodded by the rail pension decision, which raised the alarming likelihood that Justice Roberts had joined the conservatives to create a permanent 5-to-4 majority against the New Deal, Cummings began to explore possibilities of counter actions. Before the week was out, Cummings sent a memorandum to Assistant Attorney General Angus MacLean:[37]

> Has any study been made in this office of the question of the right of the Congress, by legislation, to limit the terms and conditions upon which the Supreme Court can pass on constitutional questions? I have seen several memoranda from time to time spelling out a theory by which this result could be achieved without a constitutional amendment. My recollection is that our files will somewhere disclose briefs on the theory that the Supreme Court has no right to pass on constitutional questions at all. Of course, quite a learned document could be prepared dealing with the historical aspects of this matter and the way in which it has developed.
>
> I think it would be well to have this pretty thoroughly covered, but in addition to this it would be well to cover the subject I first above mentioned; namely, the question of legislation which would not cut off the right of the Supreme Court to pass on constitutional questions, but which would limit it somewhere with a view to avoid 5 to 4 decisions.

III. Black Monday, 1935 Version

On "Black Monday," May 27, 1935, in three 9-to-0 decisions, the Court invalidated the National Industrial Recovery Act and the Frazier-Lemke Act and ruled, in the *Humphrey* case, that the President could not remove members of independent regulatory commissions save as Congress provided.[38] Roosevelt was incensed by the overturning of the NRA, the keystone of his industrial recovery program.[39] The Court's language in denouncing the dele-

[36] *5 to 4 Against*, Business Week 7–8 (May 11, 1935).

[37] Cummings to MacLean, May 11, 1935, NA Dept. of Justice 235773.

[38] Schechter Corp. v. United States, 295 U.S. 495 (1935); Louisville Bank v. Radford, 295 U.S. 555 (1935); Humphrey's Executor v. United States, 295 U.S. 602 (1935).

[39] It is often said that Roosevelt was relieved by the *Schechter* decision, because the NRA had become an intolerable burden. In fact, he believed strongly in the NRA approach, and persisted in later years in trying to revive it. On Roosevelt's

gation of powers and its narrow construction of the Commerce Clause appeared to place other New Deal laws in jeopardy and to bar the way to new legislation.[40] He was even more outraged by the *Humphrey* decision, which, in view of the history of the *Myers* opinion,[41] seemed a deliberate assault by the Court on his own prerogatives.[42] The unanimity of the Court in all three cases was bewildering. "Well, where was Ben Cardozo?" he asked. "And what about old Isaiah?"[43]

For four days, while the country speculated about what he would do, the President said nothing. On May 31, reporters were summoned to the White House. As they filed in, they saw on the President's desk a copy of the *Schechter* opinion and a sheaf of telegrams. Eleanor Roosevelt, seated next to her friend Mrs. Felix Frankfurter, busied herself knitting on a blue sock. For the next hour and a half, while reporters listened intently, Roosevelt, in an unusually somber mood, discoursed on the implications of the Court's opinion. Thumbing the copy of the *Schechter* decision as he spoke, the President argued that the Court's ruling had stripped the national government of its power to cope with critical national problems. "We are facing a very, very great national non-partisan issue," he said. "We have got to decide one way or the other . . . whether in some way we are going to . . . restore to the Federal Government the powers which exist in the national Governments of every other Nation in the world."[44] Of all the words the President spoke at the extraordinary conference, newspapermen singled out one sentence which headline writers emblazoned on late afternoon newspapers: "We have been relegated to the horse-and-buggy definition of interstate commerce."[45]

---

indignation at the *Schechter* opinion, see Raymond Clapper MS Diary, Feb. 24, 1937.

40 Roosevelt wrote: "It is the 'dictum' in the Schechter case opinion that is disturbing because . . . if the 'dictum' is followed in the future the Court would probably find only ten per cent of actual transactions to be directly in interstate commerce." FDR to Henry L. Stimson, June 10, 1935, 1 LETTERS 484.

41 Myers v. United States, 272 U.S. 52 (1926).

42 Landis, COHC 39–41; GERHART, *op. cit. supra* note 2, at 99.

43 GERHART, *op. cit. supra* note 2, at 99. "Isaiah" was a familiar term for Justice Brandeis.

44 4 PUBLIC PAPERS 200–22; Washington Post, June 1, 1935.

45 SCHLESINGER 284–87.

The President's "horse-and-buggy" conference created a furor. The next day, Raymond Clapper wrote in his Scripps-Howard column:[46]

> Within an hour after President Roosevelt held his press conference yesterday, you could almost feel the electric excitement about Washington.
>
> Gossip travels with lightning speed through the National Capital. . . . Long before the first newspapers reached the street corners . . . , the whole city knew that something of unusual importance had occurred.

Most commentators upbraided the President severely. The Washington *Post* typified much of the newspaper response with an editorial bluntly titled, "A President Leaves His Party." Henry Stimson wrote Roosevelt a long letter in which he protested that the "horse-and-buggy" observation "was a wrong statement, an unfair statement and, if it had not been so extreme as to be recognizable as hyperbole, a rather dangerous and inflammatory statement."[47] Senator Arthur Vandenberg, Michigan Republican, declared: "I don't think the President has any thought of emulating Mussolini, Hitler or Stalin, but his utterance as I have heard it is exactly what these men would say."[48]

Nor were all liberals pleased with Roosevelt's remarks. The Tennessee editor George Fort Milton wrote the President that his target should be not the Court but the Constitution. After all, Milton pointed out, men like Cardozo, Stone, Hughes, and the Brandeis of the *Oklahoma Ice* dissent had joined in the *Schechter* judgment; given our Constitution, they had had no other choice. Milton counseled:[49]

> Take the lead in a great program of constitutional reform. That is what we need to have done. Let the Constitution be amended so that the Congress will be given power to control indirect as well as direct effects of Interstate Commerce. Let the Constitution be amended to provide for an intelligent measure of delegation. I believe that you will get a very important and effective support from progressives all over the coun-

[46] Washington Post, June 1, 1935.

[47] Stimson to FDR, June 10, 1935, FDRL PPF 20.

[48] Washington Post, June 1, 1935; cf. Ralph Hayes to Newton Baker, June 8, 1935, Baker MSS, LC, Box 117.

[49] Milton to FDR, June 4, 1935, Milton MSS, LC, Box 18.

> try on a program such as this. But I do not believe that there would be nearly so much support and strength for a program bottomed on a criticism of the Court itself.

Despite his lengthy press conference, Roosevelt never stated directly what he proposed to do. When reporters asked him in what manner the question might be resolved, he replied: "We haven't got to that yet." Nor did he suggest immediate action: "I don't mean this summer or winter or next fall, but over a period, perhaps of five or ten years."[50]

From both within and outside the Administration, Roosevelt was urged to act immediately. In the confusion after the horse-and-buggy conference, Raymond Moley, one of the original members of the Brain Trust, called Vice President John N. Garner and Senators Byrnes and Robert M. La Follette, Jr., together and found that they, like he, favored a constitutional amendment. Encouraged by the meeting, Moley wrote an editorial for *Today* advocating this course, and Byrnes spoke in support of the idea in Charleston, South Carolina. In Congress, the demand for action produced a freshet of new proposals. Some wanted to make constitutional grants of power to Congress more explicit; others, like Senator Norris, wished to require at least a 7-to-2 vote by the Supreme Court to invalidate legislation.[51]

In the nation there was growing anti-Court sentiment, which those who wished to act right away might tap. To the forces arrayed against the Court by the rail pension opinion, the *Schechter* decision had added both those groups which had benefited from the NRA and people who resented any setback to Roosevelt and the New Deal. A Memphis man advised the President to balk the Court by declaring martial law,[52] and a Kentucky attorney wrote: "I should think that you and Congress were as tired of the Supreme Court stunts as the people are."[53]

But Roosevelt decided against immediate action. For a moment, Moley recalls, the President showed a "flicker of enthusiasm," but

---

50 4 Public Papers 222.

51 Moley 307; Schlesinger 288; H.R. No. 7997, Robert Ramsay MSS, University of West Virginia, Morgantown, W.Va.; Washington Post, May 29–June 1, 1935.

52 Edward J. Brown to FDR, June 7, 1935, FDRL OF 41-A, Box 116.

53 H. M. Stanley to FDR, July 2, 1935, FDRL OF 41-A, Box 116.

this soon dwindled.[54] Roosevelt sensed that the time was not yet ripe. The NRA had its supporters, but its detractors were more numerous; he could not go to the country with that kind of an appeal. The clamor raised by the horse-and-buggy conference indicated that the Court would have to antagonize a much larger portion of the nation before it would be politically safe to challenge it.[55] The difficulties in the way of winning approval for a constitutional amendment were inhibiting. Norris conceded: "It looks now as though it would be an absolute impossibility to pass it through the Senate or the House by the necessary two-thirds majority in order to submit it to the states."[56] Nor had the explorations in the Department of Justice proceeded far enough so that Roosevelt was ready with a specific proposal.

For the next year Roosevelt bided his time. He made no public reference to the Supreme Court even when additional adverse decisions appeared to require some sort of response. He left the impression that he was accepting the Court's verdicts without complaint and that, after having had his knuckles rapped for his horse-and-buggy remarks, he proposed neither to say nor to do anything further. In fact, as Tugwell has written, "If open battle was not at once joined, a kind of twilight war did begin."[57]

In June, 1935, the American ambassador to Italy, Breckinridge Long, returned for a brief visit to the United States; he found "one thing . . . uppermost on the minds of political America": the *Schechter* decision. At lunch alone with Long on the White House porch, Roosevelt spoke freely about the course he planned to pursue. He would move other cases up to the Supreme Court to give it an opportunity to modify its interpretation of the Commerce Clause. If the Court did not do so, then it might be necessary to

[54] MOLEY 307.

[55] TUGWELL, THE DEMOCRATIC ROOSEVELT 385 (1957).

[56] George W. Norris to William A. Ahern, July 10, 1935, Norris MSS, Tray 27, Box 4.

[57] TUGWELL, *op. cit. supra* note 55, at 385. For Roosevelt's continued concern, see FDR to Armstead Brown, July 6, 1935, FDRL PPF 2669. In a letter marked "Personal," he told the judge of the Supreme Court of Florida: "I am not worrying in any way about 1936, but I am, of course, concerned about future Supreme Court decisions. After all, we do not want to take away State's rights but, at the same time, there are a good many problems which, under modern conditions, can be solved only by Federal action."

propose an amendment. Long noted in his diary: "The amendments are not yet in specific or concrete form but might be broached under three headings: first, to define Inter-State Commerce with authority to Congress to legislate on the subject; second, to define certain phases of Inter-State Commerce; and third, taking a page from Lloyd George, to give authority to the Congress to pass over the veto of the Supreme Court legislation which the Court held unconstitutional."[58]

If and when the time came to act, the amendment route seemed the most promising path, although not everyone agreed about this. Some thought that the problem lay not in the Constitution but the Court; hence, they reasoned either that the composition of the Court must be altered or that the Court must, and perhaps could, be persuaded to change its views. The Felix Frankfurter cadre, which had always disliked the NRA anyway, opposed the amendment approach. From a different standpoint, Homer Cummings, angered by the *Schechter* decision, fumed: "I tell you, Mr. President, they mean to destroy us. . . . We will have to find a way to get rid of the present membership of the Supreme Court."[59] Yet the unanimity of the Court made it seem unlikely that the New Deal could win a majority, and it argued against solving the problem by appointing a few additional judges. After the *Schechter* opinion was handed down, Raymond Clapper wrote: "Talk of blackjacking the court by enlarging its membership collapsed when all nine justices joined in the decision. That subterfuge of packing the court, a weak and uncertain one at best, becomes ridiculous to think of now."[60]

Both Roosevelt and Cummings agreed that the Justice Department should continue to seek out solutions for the impasse. A week after the horse-and-buggy conference, Alexander Holtzoff, who was to be a central figure in the search for a plan, sent Cummings a memorandum responding to the suggestion that the Court might be stripped of most or all of its appellate jurisdiction. When Holtzoff explained that such a proposal would encounter too much

[58] Breckinridge Long MS Diary, LC, June 12, June 17, 1935. That same month, the President's son James Roosevelt, in a speech in Missouri, called for "an earlier determination of the constitutionality of the acts of the Legislature." Carlisle Bargeron, *Along the Potomac*, Washington Post, June 13, 1935, clipping in John Taber MSS, Cornell University Collection of Regional History, Ithaca, N.Y., Box 62.

[59] Schlesinger, 282, 288–89.

[60] Washington Post, May 29, 1935.

opposition and still would not eliminate all the problems confronting the Administration, Cummings was unsatisfied and told him to develop his point "a little more fully." On June 22 Holtzoff sent another five-page memorandum on the question, but the matter did not end there. On August 15, W. W. Gardner prepared a fourteen-page study for the Solicitor General in which he, too, looked into whether "the power of the Supreme Court to pass upon the constitutional validity of congressional legislation might be abolished or restricted by an Act of Congress." But he also found objections to the proposal, and the search for a satisfactory plan continued.[61]

The President displayed a lively interest in these inquiries. In July, for example, he sent Cummings a memorandum calling to his attention "two extremely interesting articles by Harold Laski" in the Manchester *Guardian*.[62] Roosevelt also corresponded with critics of the Court outside the government. In August, 1935, Charlton Ogburn, counsel for the American Federation of Labor, informed the President that he had submitted a proposed constitutional amendment to the executive council of the Federation for approval.[63] That same month, Roosevelt told Charles E. Wyzanski, Jr., solicitor of the Department of Labor: "Of course, if the Supreme Court should knock out the AAA, then the constitutional amendment would be the real issue. It probably will be anyway, and there will be less difficulty in phrasing it than many people think."[64]

Finding a satisfactory plan was only one part of Roosevelt's strategy; another part was building popular support for such a move. The horse-and-buggy conference had been one move toward that end. In August the President took another step when he met at the White House with George Creel. In collaboration with Creel, a veteran of reform wars, Roosevelt sometimes used the pages of *Collier's* to launch trial balloons. For an article entitled "Looking Ahead with Roosevelt," the President now dictated to Creel:[65]

---

[61] Holtzoff, Memorandum for the Attorney General, June 6, 1935; Cummings, Memorandum for Mr. Holtzoff, June 13, 1935; Holtzoff, Memorandum for the Attorney General, June 22, 1935; W. W. Gardner, Memorandum for the Solicitor General, Aug. 15, 1935, NA Dept. of Justice 235773.

[62] FDR to Cummings, July 5, 1935, FDRL OF 142.

[63] Charlton Ogburn to FDR, Aug. 7, 20, 1935, FDRL OF 142.

[64] 3 Schlesinger 453. See, too, Rev. Francis Haas to FDR, Oct. 25, 1935, Haas MSS, Catholic University of America, Washington, D.C.

[65] Creel, Rebel at Large 291–92 (1935).

> In the next few months, the Supreme Court will hand down fresh pronouncements with respect to New Deal laws, and it is possible the President will get another "licking." If so, much will depend on the language of the licking. In event that unconstitutionality is found, perhaps the decisions will point the way to statutory amendments. If, however, the Constitution is construed technically; if it is held that one hundred and fifty years have no bearing on the case, and that the present generation is powerless to meet social and economic problems that were not within the knowledge of the founding fathers, and therefore not made the subject of their specific consideration, then the President will have no other alternative than to go to the country with a Constitutional amendment that will lift the Dead Hand, giving the people of today the right to deal with today's vital issues.

He told Creel grimly: "Fire that as an opening gun."[66]

Contrary to Roosevelt's expectation, the trial balloon attracted almost no notice. Most of the nation in 1935 was still either indifferent to the Court question or outrightly opposed to tethering the Court. To the query: "As a general principle, would you favor limiting the power of the Supreme Court to declare acts of Congress unconstitutional?" the Gallup Poll in the autumn of 1935 received the following replies: yes, 31 per cent; no, 53 per cent; no opinion, 16 per cent. The most articulate anti-Court feeling came from those who felt they had been hurt by specific decisions. A Virginian objected: "The Supreme Court turned down my railroad pension." But many more thought the Justices wise, the system of checks and balances sacred, and Congress mercurial, even if their conception of these institutions was sometimes primitive. Asked his view of the Court, an Illinois man replied: "It's permanent. Congress is just the whims and fancies of the people." An Ohio reliefer said: "If they didn't know more than the other courts, they wouldn't be called the Supreme Court."[67]

Despite this discouraging response, the President pushed ahead quietly with his plans. At a long lunch at the White House on November 12, 1935, Ickes and Roosevelt fell to talking about the Court. The President remarked that he did not think that any Justices would retire and permit him to make new appointments. "Then," Ickes noted, "he said that while the matter could not be talked about now, he believed that the way to mend the situation was to adopt a constitutional amendment which would give

---

[66] *Id.* at 292.

[67] N.Y. Herald-Tribune, Nov. 3, 1935.

the Attorney General the right, if he has any doubt of the constitutionality of a legislative act, to apply to the Supreme Court for a ruling, that ruling to state specifically in which respects the act is unconstitutional. Then, if the next succeeding Congress, with this opinion of the Supreme Court before it, should re-enact that statute, it would, by that fact, be purged of its unconstitutionality and become the law of the land."[68]

During their conversation, the President made use of an analogy that was to crop up frequently in succeeding months in discussions of the judiciary crisis. Ickes wrote in his diary:[69]

> The President's mind went back to the difficulty in England, where the House of Lords repeatedly refused to adopt legislation sent up from the House of Commons. He recalled that when Lloyd George came into power some years ago under Edward VII, he went to the King and asked his consent to announce that if the Lords refused again to accept the bill for Irish autonomy, which had been pressed upon them several times since the days of Gladstone, he would create several hundred new peers, enough to outvote the existing House of Lords. With this threat confronting them, the bill passed the Lords.

Roosevelt's recollection was faulty—the episode actually concerned Asquith and the attempt to reform the House of Lords—but the British analogy was clearly important for him, because he recurred to it once more on December 27 at a cabinet meeting at which the Supreme Court question was again reviewed at length.[70] This time he referred not only to the Irish Home Rule Bill, but to Lloyd George's success in pushing through a social security act by the threat to create three hundred new peers.[71]

After the cabinet meeting, Ickes made a new entry in his diary:[72]

> Clearly, it is running in the President's mind that substantially all of the New Deal bills will be declared unconstitutional by the Supreme Court. This will mean that everything that this Administration has done of any moment will be nullified. The President pointed out that there were three ways of meeting such a situation: (1) by packing the Supreme Court, which

---

68 1 ICKES 467–68.

69 *Ibid.*

70 *Id.* at 494–95. The Asquith precedent was to be mentioned often during the Court fight. See, for example, Martin J. Lide to Kenneth McKellar, Feb. 16, 1937, McKellar MSS, Memphis Public Library, Memphis, Tenn., Box 229.

71 1 ICKES 495.

72 *Ibid.*

> was a distasteful idea; (2) by trying to put through a number of amendments to the Constitution to meet the various situations; and (3) by a method that he asked us to consider very carefully.
>
> The third method is, in substance, this: an amendment to the Constitution conferring explicit power on the Supreme Court to declare acts of Congress unconstitutional, a power which is not given anywhere in the Constitution as it stands. The amendment would also give the Supreme Court original jurisdiction on constitutional questions affecting statutes. If the Supreme Court should declare an act of Congress to be unconstitutional, then—a congressional election having intervened—if Congress should repass the law so declared to be unconstitutional, the taint of unconstitutionality would be removed and the law would be a valid one. By this method there would be in effect a referendum to the country, although an indirect one. At the intervening congressional election the question of the constitutionality or unconstitutionality of the law would undoubtedly be an issue.

In essence, the President's strategy was to leave the power of decision to the Supreme Court. If the Court upheld New Deal legislation, the issue would fade away. But if all the legislation were thrown out, Roosevelt warned, there would be "marching farmers and marching miners and marching workingmen throughout the land." For almost half a year, while the Court was recessed, the conflict between the President and the Court had simmered on a low flame. But during those months, as Roosevelt was keenly aware, such significant questions as the AAA processing tax had been making their way through the lower courts; the Supreme Court could be expected to render decisions on such matters early in 1936. "If the Court does send the AAA flying like the NRA," the President had told Wyzanski, "there might even be a revolution."[73]

IV. The Court Nullifies the New Deal

On January 6, 1936, the Supreme Court handed down its long-awaited decision on the AAA processing tax.[74] Divided 6 to 3, the Court ruled the tax unconstitutional, thus overturning the second of the two most important New Deal recovery programs. In an opinion that earned him scorching comments from the law journals, Justice Roberts held the levy to be an illegitimate use of the

---

[73] 3 Schlesinger 453.

[74] United States v. Butler, 297 U.S. 1 (1936).

taxing power, "the expropriation of money from one group for the benefit of another."[75]

The *Butler* decision aroused acrimonious criticism of the Court. Coming on top of the 1935 opinions, the *Butler* verdict appeared to indicate a determination by the Court to wipe out all of the New Deal. "Is Poe's Raven who croaked 'Never More' their model?" asked one man. An Oklahoman penciled a letter to the Attorney General stating that he wanted to impeach every judge who had declared the AAA invalid, and another man wrote the President: "I'm in favor of doing away with the Constitution if it's going to interfere with the general welfare of the people." The head of a Chicago advertising agency asked: "Are you aware that the people at large are getting damned tired of the United States Supreme Court, and that, if left to a popular vote, it would be kicked out?"[76]

A nation of tinkerers, the country flooded Washington with home-made inventions to improve the government machinery. Many of the contrivances stressed either the age of the Justices or the device of packing the Court, or both. A South Carolina attorney wrote: "We are hoping and believing that you and the Congress of the United States will not allow six old men to destroy this Country." A Minnesota lawyer urged compulsory retirement at 65 or 70, "whichever would retire the majority of the present members of the Court." A Los Angeles man questioned the fitness of "that body of nine old hasbeens, half-deaf, half-blind, full-of-palsy men. . . . That they are behind the times is very plain—all you have to do is to look at Charles Hughes' whiskers."[77]

---

[75] *Id.* at 61.

[76] Maurice Daley to Homer Cummings, Jan. 13, 1936, NA Dept. of Justice 5-36-346; George Thomason to Cummings, NA Dept. of Justice 235773; John W. White to FDR, Jan. 7, 1936, NA Dept. of Justice 5-36-346; W. K. Cochrane to Stephen Early, Jan. 25, 1936, FDRL OF 41-A, Box 120. Governor George Earle of Pennsylvania denounced the Court as "a political body" with "six members committed to the politics of the Liberty League." Address of George H. Earle, Jan. 18, 1935, Earle MSS, Bryn Mawr, Pa., privately held, Speech and News File No. 73. Some of the indignation was aroused by the "windfall" millers anticipated as a consequence of the decision. Clifford Hope to Chester Stevens, Apr. 21, 1936, Hope MSS, Kansas State Historical Society, Topeka, Kans., Tax (Legis.) folder, Legislative Correspondence, 1935–36.

[77] Joe P. Lane to FDR, Jan. 7, 1936, FDRL OF 274, Box 3; S. C. Odenborg to FDR, Feb. 3, 1936, NA Dept. of Justice 235241; John B. Muller to FDR, Jan. 9, 1936, FDRL OF 1-K, Misc. 1936.

From different parts of the nation came calls for additional Justices "with younger minds." Some wanted four more Justices, like the Memphis businessman who pointed out: "Business does not accept an applicant with twelve gray hairs on his head." Others thought six new Justices would have to be added to "reverse this infamy." An Arizona attorney recommended: "In order to avoid the impending seizure of this government by the special interests it is incumbent on you to increase the membership of the Supreme Court to fifteen; and appoint the new membership from the Frankfurters, Olsons, and other men who place human rights above the rights of predatory wealth." From Richmond, Virginia, came a demand for a Court of "at least twenty or more members. Nine OLD MEN, whose total age amounts to about 650 years, should have additional help." A member of the Kansas House of Representatives had an even more radical suggestion: add sixteen new members, "the new members to be not over thirty-five years of age, and retired at forty. This would put men on the court that are in step with TO-DAY."[78]

A number of correspondents seemed to believe that Roosevelt was unaware of the Court's infamy or that he needed to be stiffened to oppose the Court. A Seattle woman wrote:[79]

> I have just this minute heard the decision of the U.S. Supreme Court on the A.A.A.
>
> Mr. Roosevelt, are you going to sit back and let these few men, controlled by the selfish elements of our country, control the destinies of intelligent, thinking and country-loving people, who really make this great country of ours?

A Kansan asserted: "One who is really a man will resist to the end being governed by men who lived one hundred and fifty years ago." A Miami attorney assured the President: "If you, as the Executive, and Congress will make the Supreme Court an issue in this country it will not fail. Jackson did not fail, Grant did not fail, and the Dred-Scott decision was treated with contempt."[80]

---

[78] W. J. Young to FDR, Jan. 7, 1936, NA Dept. of Justice 5-36-346; W. B. Mills to FDR, Jan. 13, 1936; Thomas Duncan to FDR, Jan. 7, 1936; Elmer Graham to FDR, Jan. 7, 1936, NA Dept. of Justice 235773; W. F. Betts to FDR, Jan. 6, 1936, FDRL OF 1-K Misc. 1936; W. H. (Bill) Reed to FDR, Jan. 21, 1936, NA Dept. of Justice 235868.

[79] Auzias de Turenne to FDR, Jan. 6, 1936, FDRL OF 1-K Misc. 1936.

[80] R. W. Sholders to FDR, Jan. 6, 1936, NA Dept. of Justice 5-36-246; Rudolph Isom to FDR, Jan. 13, 1936, FDRL OF 41-A, Box 120.

A Mississippi editor wired Roosevelt:[81]

> On behalf of farmers and workers urge that you set aside Supreme Court decision and destroy their assumed right to declare laws of Congress unconstitutional. . . . President Andrew Jackson, our greatest Democrat, defied Supreme Court on this very point. Hope you will do the same. Sincerely believe that future of Democratic government hinges on whether you will take the bull by the horns. Drastic action is imperative. America is depending on you. Perhaps civilization and its perpetuity is involved in your acts. God grant that you have the courage to do right.

Roosevelt's strategy of "watchful waiting" seemed to be paying off. The Court, which had antagonized groups like railway employees in 1935, had now angered farmers who would be denied more than two billion dollars in AAA benefit checks in the next year. Edward A. O'Neal, president of the American Farm Bureau Federation, warned: "Those who believe the American farmer will stand idly by and watch his program for economic justice fall without a fight are badly mistaken. The fight is on—and this time it will be with the gloves off."[82] O'Neal planned to meet with the A. F. of L.'s general counsel, Charlton Ogburn, to lay plans for a farmer-labor alliance to achieve common objectives.

Yet none of this agitation moved Roosevelt to act. Despite constant prodding, he refused even to comment on the *Butler* decision. He believed that the time had not yet come. An election year was not the propitious moment to give the opposition, which was bereft of issues, an opportunity to stand by the flag. Nor had the coalition against the Court yet reached full strength. If O'Neal denounced the *Butler* opinion, other farm leaders approved it, and a Gallup Poll, which appeared the day before the decision was rendered, showed a majority of the country opposed to the AAA.[83] Nor had opponents of the Court yet reached agreement on a proposal. Ogburn, for one, thought that nothing should be done at present save to make the amending process easier.[84]

Moreover, the Administration was not yet ready for a fight on the Court issue, because it had not yet come up with a satisfactory

---

[81] H. B. Sanders to FDR, Jan. 7, 1936, NA Dept. of Justice 5-36-346.

[82] Washington Post, Jan. 7, 1936. [83] Washington Post, Jan. 8, 1936.

[84] Charlton Ogburn to FDR, Jan. 9, 1936, FDRL OF 274.

plan. Shortly after the *Butler* verdict was rendered, Assistant Attorney General John Dickinson wrote:[85]

> The way in which the high command has apparently decided to treat the AAA decision has been to smother its effect as much as possible. I am not at all sure that this is a wise strategy, but apparently the feeling is that there is a widespread readiness, throughout the country, to blaze up against the Supreme Court and that this state of mind must be wet-blanketed, for fear that otherwise it would drive the Administration into the position of either attacking the Court, or calling for an amendment, which they are not yet prepared to do.

While maintaining public silence, Roosevelt indicated privately that he was preparing for a showdown with the Court. At the cabinet meeting on January 24, 1936, Ickes recorded:[86]

> The President said that word is coming to him from widely separated parts of the country that people are beginning to show a great deal of interest in the constitutional questions that have been raised by recent Supreme Court decisions. . . . The President made the point, based upon some statement by Harold J. Laski, that the Supreme Court, in its decisions on New Deal legislation, was dictating what it believed should be the social philosophy of the nation, without reference to the law or the Constitution. . . . It is plain to see, from what the President said today and has said on other occasions, that he is not at all averse to the Supreme Court declaring one New Deal statute after another unconstitutional. I think he believes that the Court will find itself pretty far out on a limb before it is through with it and that a real issue will be joined on which we can go to the country.
>
> For my part, I hope so. Here is an issue that must be faced by the country sooner or later, unless we are prepared to submit to the arbitrary and final dictates of a group of men who are not elected by the people and who are not responsible to the people: in short, a judicial tyranny imposed by men appointed for life and who cannot be reached except by the slow and cumbersome process of impeachment.

That same day, Roosevelt prepared a memorandum for the files, with a copy to Moley, stating:[87]

> It has been well said by a prominent historian that fifty years from now the Supreme Court's AAA decision will, in all probability, be described somewhat as follows:

---

85 Dickinson to George Fort Milton, Jan. 13, 1936, Milton MSS, Box 19.

86 1 Ickes 524.

87 Memorandum, Jan. 24, 1936, FDRL OF 1-K.

(1) The decision virtually prohibits the President and Congress from the right, under modern conditions, to intervene reasonably in the regulation of nation-wide commerce and nation-wide agriculture.

(2) The Supreme Court arrived at this result by selecting from several possible techniques of constitutional interpretation a special technique. The objective of the Court's purpose was to make reasonableness in passing legislation a matter to be settled not by the views of the elected Senate and House of Representatives and not by the views of an elected President but rather by the private, social philosophy of a majority of nine appointed members of the Supreme Court itself.

Roosevelt continued to move ahead on the study of plans to curb the Court. A week after the *Butler* decision, he wrote Cummings: "What was the McArdle case . . .? I am told that the Congress withdrew some act from the jurisdiction of the Supreme Court."[88] The Attorney General replied: "The case of ex parte McCardle . . . to which you refer . . . is one of the classic cases to which we refer when considering the possibility of limiting the jurisdiction of Federal Courts. This whole matter has been the subject of considerable study in this Department, and, in view of recent developments, is apt to be increasingly important."

The exchange between the President and the Attorney General suggests the crucial development in the early weeks of 1936: loss of faith in the amendment solution and rising belief that the Court could be curbed by an act of Congress. Perhaps the most important influence on this change of plans was the division of the Court in the *Butler* case and Justice Harlan Stone's ringing dissent, less because the minority voted to sustain the processing tax than because of Stone's vigorous assault on judicial usurpation. Cummings wrote Stone:[89]

Your dissenting opinion is on a high plane—sound, constructive and human.

It may not be the law *now*—but it will be the law later, un-

---

[88] FDR to Cummings, Jan. 14, 1936; Cummings to FDR, Jan. 16, 1936, FDRL PSF Supreme Court.

[89] Cummings to Stone, Jan. 8, 1936, FDRL PSF Justice. Stone responded: "Thank you for your generous note. When one finds himself outvoted two to one he should be humble and perhaps skeptical of his own judgment. But I have a sincere faith that history and long time perspective will see the function of our court in a different light from that in which it is viewed at the moment." For Stone's views, see Mason, Harlan Fiske Stone 417 (1956).

less governmental functions are to be permanently frozen in an unescapable mold.

You spoke at a great moment and in a great way. Congratulations.

The split in the Court confirmed those who had been arguing that the problem lay not in the Constitution but in the composition of this particular Court, and Justice Stone's dissent made it easier to argue that Congress must act to regain powers which the Court had usurped. The amendment route was not abandoned, but the search for a suitable amendment now concentrated for the first time on compelling the retirement of Justices at 70, thus altering the makeup of the Court. In addition, increasing attention was given to finding a way to meet the difficulty by statute.[90]

On January 29, 1936, after talking over the Court issue at lunch with Senator Norris, the President continued the same discussion with Ickes. He told Ickes that he had reached the conclusion that he could achieve Court reform without resort to an amendment; he had also confided this to Norris. Roosevelt favored an act of Congress which would strip the lower courts of the power to pass upon the constitutionality of statutes and would confer this power on the Supreme Court as a matter of original jurisdiction. The Supreme Court would be required to give an advisory opinion on the constitutionality of a bill before it was enacted. Congress could then alter the bill to conform with the advice of the Court or it could pass it once more in its original form, and it would then become the law of the land. Ickes noted:[91]

> I made the obvious remark that the Supreme Court would declare unconstitutional such an act as the President had in mind and he said that of course it would. To meet that situation his plan would be somewhat as follows: Congress would pass a law, the Supreme Court would declare it unconstitutional, the President would then go to Congress and ask it to instruct him whether he was to follow the mandate of Congress or the mandate of the Court. If the Congress should declare

---

90 3 SCHLESINGER 493–94; FDR Memorandum to Homer Cummings, Feb. 24, 1936; FDR Memorandum for Chairman Hatton Sumners, FDRL OF 41, Box 114. During the 1936 campaign, one correspondent wrote the President: "Why not make a campaign on the opinions of Justice Stone? By taking the words of a member of the court itself there can be no justifiable charge of usurpation." Paul Webb to FDR, June 4, 1936, FDRL OF 41-A, Box 116.

91 1 ICKES 529–30.

that its own mandate was to be followed, the President would carry out the will of Congress through the offices of the United States Marshals and ignore the Court.

After their talk, Ickes reflected:[92]

There isn't any doubt at all that the President is really hoping that the Supreme Court will continue to make a clean sweep of all New Deal legislation, throwing out the TVA Act, the Securities Act, the Railroad Retirement Act, the Social Security Act, the Guffey Coal Act, and others. He thinks the country is beginning to sense this issue but that enough people have not yet been affected by adverse decisions so as to make a sufficient feeling on a Supreme Court issue.

I told the President that I hoped this would be the issue in the next campaign. I believe it will have to be fought out sooner or later, and I remarked to him that the President who faced this issue and drastically curbed the usurped power of the Supreme Court would go down through all the ages of history as one of the great Presidents.

Two days later, at a cabinet meeting, Cummings raised the question whether the government should appeal a lower court decision denying the federal government the right to condemn property for a low-cost housing project. Tom Corcoran and Ben Cohen were but two of the President's advisers who thought the government should drop the case, in part because they feared an adverse opinion from the Supreme Court that might wipe out the Public Works Administration. Ickes noted:[93]

The President was firmly of the opinion that we ought to go ahead with the case. He scouted the idea that anyone could draw an act which would pass the scrutiny of the Supreme Court in its present outlook on New Deal legislation. He thought that if all PWA projects should be suspended as the result of an adverse decision by the Supreme Court, it would be all to the good. . . . There doesn't seem to me to be any doubt that he is entirely willing to have the Supreme Court knock out every New Deal law. It is clear that he is willing to go to the country on this issue but he wants the issue to be as strong and clear as possible, which means that he hopes the

---

[92] *Id.* at 530.

[93] *Id.* at 531–32. Ickes added: "It happens that I am fully in accord with the President's view on this matter. I believe that this issue will have to be fought out sooner or later and no more important issue has arisen since the Civil War. Naturally, I would like to be in this fight and be a member of the Administration that is carrying it on."

> Supreme Court will declare unconstitutional every New Deal case that comes before it.

Yet, while blithely accepting this prospect of a constitutional Armageddon, the President continued to say nothing publicly. Early in February, George Fort Milton confided:[94]

> I thought a month ago that the Court and the Constitution were very definitely going to be in this year's presidential debate. But everything in Washington is of the hush, hush attitude. . . . What I am feeling is that maybe he is depending too much on his resourcefulness and that he could do some thinking on what would be the usefulness of being re-elected if he was going to have to go into a second term denied the essential powers of nationality. Wouldn't he be all dressed up and have nowhere to go?

Roosevelt's silence, which some interpreted as acquiescence in the Court's decisions, left the initiative for public action to Congress. In the 1936 session, congressmen introduced more than a hundred proposals to restrict the federal courts. Some measures, such as the "Human Rights Amendment," aimed to expand the powers of Congress to enact social legislation. Others, like the Cross bill, sought to strip the courts of the prerogative of judicial review. Still others resorted to enlarging the bench. In January, 1936, Representative Ernest Lundeen of Minnesota filed a bill to increase the Supreme Court by two Justices so that the Court could handle more work and because "new blood will mean a more liberal outlook on constitutional questions." Lundeen pointed out that when his bill had been adopted, and when Justice Willis Van Devanter carried out his purported plan to retire, the President would be able to name three new Justices and thus assure a liberal majority. A week earlier, Representative James L. Quinn had gone even further; he had introduced a measure to expand the Court to fifteen Justices.[95]

On February 12, 1936, George Norris delivered a major address on the floor of the Senate. He denounced the Supreme Court as a "continuous constitutional convention." To the contention that the processing tax was invalid because agricultural production was not mentioned in the Constitution, Norris retorted: "Nowhere in

---

94 Milton to George Foster Peabody, Feb. 10, 1936, Milton MSS, Box 19.

95 Thomas R. Amlie to W. Jett Lauck, Mar. 6, 1937, Amlie MSS, State Historical Society of Wisconsin, Madison, Wisc., Box 6; O. H. Cross to Stanley Reed, Jan. 17, 1936, NA Dept. of Justice 235868.

that great document is there a syllable, a word, or a sentence giving to any court the right to declare an act of Congress unconstitutional." Norris expostulated: "The members of the Supreme Court are not elected by anybody. They are responsible to nobody. Yet they hold dominion over everybody."[96] Rejecting the amendment procedure he had once favored as "impracticable," Norris asked Congress to have the "courage" to enact legislation requiring a unanimous decision to invalidate an act of Congress.

The columnist Robert S. Allen wrote Norris:[97]

> I have been wondering for weeks what the hell this session was for. Your matchless speech on the Supreme Court this afternoon cleared up the mystery. The session was solely so you could deliver this superb exposition—so it could go into the Record for all history to read—so you could say what everybody was thinking, but no other leader had the guts to say out loud.
>
> It was a grand and unequaled job, Senator. And what was no less significant was the tremendous response it is being accorded. It is really amazing the extraordinary press coverage it has received. Even the filthy Hearst jackals carried almost a column of your remarks. It was also amazing to me how deeply moved the press gallery was. Reactionary old bastards who haven't had an intelligent idea in decades spoke respectfully of your views.

Norris' concern over the Court question was long-standing, but it was heightened during these weeks by anxiety over the fate of the Tennessee Valley Authority, of which he was acknowledged to be the "father." In January, Norris had written: "Up to the time this decision was rendered in the AAA case, I had no doubt whatsoever that the Supreme Court would sustain the TVA Act. . . . Since the AAA decision, however, I would not be surprised if the Court would hold the TVA Act unconstitutional."[98] On February 17, the Court, by a surprising 8-to-1 vote, diminished these

[96] "Legislation by the Judiciary," Copy in the George Norris MSS. See, too, Norris to Francis Heney, Apr. 25, 1936, Heney MSS, Bancroft Library, University of California, Berkeley, Calif. The Norris idea was a familiar one. In January, a Tacoma assessor had written the President: "The extreme penalty is not exacted from the vilest culprit, save on a unanimous verdict. Why should the will of the people be crucified for less?" Fred A. Smith to FDR, Jan. 9, 1936, NA Dept. of Justice 235773.

[97] Allen to George W. Norris, Feb. 12, 1936, Norris MSS, Tray 27, Box 4.

[98] George W. Norris to Irving Brant, Jan. 11, 1936, Norris MSS, Tray 27, Box 5.

anxieties by upholding the power of the TVA to dispose of power generated at Wilson Dam.[99]

Although some critics pointed out that the Court still had not rendered a decisive judgment on the constitutionality of the TVA, friends of public power were delighted by the opinion. "I had completely resigned myself to a bad decision, only holding out hope that we would have some crumb of comfort in that unlike AAA and NRA we would not be swept completely out to sea, bag and baggage," wrote David Lilienthal.[100] "The decision, clearing away so many of the clouds hanging over us, makes me feel very humble. We are given an almost incredible grant of power."[101] The opinion served, for the moment, to quiet demands for reform of the judiciary.[102] By showing the fairness of the Court, the decision, observed the Washington *Post*, "should do more than anything else to end the campaign for limitation of the Court's authority."[103] From Chattanooga, George Fort Milton wrote gleefully:[104]

> Well, after TVA, I think we ought to start talking about "one old man and the eight young men." . . .
>
> I suspect that some of the members of the Court set themselves forward deliberately to show that they could render other than a Tory decision. Would you call this modernizing Mr. Dooley, so that the Supreme Court precedes the election returns?

The respite provided by the TVA decision proved short-lived. Six weeks later, the Court rebuked the Securities and Exchange Commission,[105] and on May 18, 1936, it went out of its way in the *Carter* case[106] to strike down the Guffey Coal Act in an opinion that appeared to doom not only the Wagner Labor Relations Act

[99] Ashwander v. T.V.A., 297 U.S. 288 (1936).

[100] 1 Journals of David E. Lilienthal 59 (1964).

[101] Lilienthal to Felix Frankfurter, Feb. 17, 1936, Lilienthal MSS, Princeton University Library.

[102] Knoxville News-Sentinel, Feb. 18–20, 1936, clippings, David Lilienthal Scrapbooks, Lilienthal MSS, Princeton University Library.

[103] Knoxville News-Sentinel, Feb. 18, 1936.

[104] George Fort Milton to Francis Coker, Feb. 18, 1936, Milton MSS, Box 19. *Cf.* Newton Baker to James M. Beck, Mar. 19, 1936, Beck MSS.

[105] Jones v. S.E.C., 298 U.S. 1 (1936).

[106] Carter v. Carter Coal Co., 298 U.S. 238 (1936).

but any attempt by act of Congress to control wages and hours. The *Carter* decision started a new wave of condemnations of the Court and demands for restrictions. Once more, the age of the Justices and the possibilities offered by "packing" were pointed out. "We permit old men 90, probably as childish as boys of 9, to sit on the Supreme Court bench and in case of a 5 to 4 vote one old man controls the affairs of the nation," one critic wrote the President. "In reviewing the Constitution of the United States," noted a Pennsylvania man, "it comes to my attention the fact that there is no limit to the Personell of the Supreme Court." A Los Angeles man urged the President to name four more Justices. He added helpfully: "For these four positions I nominate Senator Hiram Johnson of California and Senator Geo. W. Norris of Nebraska. Now you name two." Yet Roosevelt not only would not heed such advice but when newsmen pressed him for a statement on the *Carter* decision he brusquely closed off that line of questioning.[107]

The *Carter* decision turned out to be only the first in a series of rapid-fire blows the Court delivered at the New Deal. On successive Mondays in the spring of 1936, the Court handed down the *Carter* opinion, overturned the Municipal Bankruptcy Act,[108] and, in the most momentous ruling of all, invalidated the New York state minimum-wage law in the *Tipaldo* case.[109] Each decision came from a divided court.

For critics of the Court, the *Tipaldo* opinion was the last straw. Before that decision, even some New Dealers hoped to avoid a direct confrontation with the Court. After it, Tugwell has written, liberals agreed that "something must be done."[110] Not since the *Dred Scott* disaster had the Court inflicted on itself so deep a wound. As Alpheus T. Mason has observed: "At any time up to June 1, 1936, the Court might have retreated and thus avoided a showdown. The New York Minimum Wage opinion, handed down

---

107 Wendell Berge to E. L. Woodcos, May 20, 1936, Berge MSS, LC, Box 10; L. C. Weiss to FDR, May 20, 1936; H. C. Holland to FDR, May 23, 1936; Jan Byrd to FDR, May 20, 1936, NA Dept. of Justice 235773; Washington Post, May 20, 1936; John D. Miller to the New York Times, May 19, 1936, Miller MSS, Cornell University Collection of Regional History.

108 St. Joseph Stockyards Co. v. United States, 298 U.S. 38 (1936).

109 Morehead v. New York *ex rel.* Tipaldo, 298 U.S. 587 (1936).

110 TUGWELL, *op. cit. supra* note 55, at 391.

that day, convinced even the most reverent that five stubborn old men had planted themselves squarely in the path of progress.[111]

The *Tipaldo* decision produced a national outcry against the Court. Ickes noted angrily: "The sacred right of liberty of contract again—the right of an immature child or a helpless woman to drive a bargain with a great corporation. If this decision does not outrage the moral sense of the country, then nothing will."[112] But it was not only New Dealers who objected to the opinion. The Court had embarrassed Administration critics who had argued that protection of the rights of labor should be left to state action. "Hereafter," wrote Franklyn Waltman in the Washington *Post*, "whenever New Dealers are taunted with trying to break down the rights of the States to manage their own affairs, the taunters will have this decision tossed in their faces."[113] The *Post* labeled the opinion "An Unfortunate Decision," and Herbert Hoover called for an amendment to restore to the states "the power they thought they already had."[114]

Once more, Roosevelt was pressed to act. From California, the head of the Stockton Democratic Club wrote the President: "By another 4 to 5 decision on the part of JUDOCRACY, *one man* has been able . . . to nullify the progress of half a century along humanitarian lines, exposing the Motherhood of America to further exploitation on the part of unscrupulous employers. If this be Democracy—may God save the mark!" A telegram from Brooklyn urged: "Increase number of justices in Supreme Court with men in their fifties." The head of a New York printing firm warned the President that it would be "useless" for him to pursue his program unless he pushed through an amendment. "You can't side-step the issue," he scolded. "The people who will re-elect you will expect you to have something to say about this matter."[115]

At a press conference on June 2, 1936, Roosevelt broke his silence. For the first time since the "horse-and-buggy" meeting,

---

111 MASON, *op. cit. supra* note 89, at 438.

112 1 ICKES 614.

113 Washington Post, June 2, 1936.

114 N.Y. Times, June 7, 1936.

115 James A. Metcalf to FDR, June 3, 1936, NA Dept. of Justice 224196; E. Larkin to FDR, June 4, 1936, FDRL OF 41-A, Box 116; Earl Salley to FDR, June 5, 1936, FDRL OF 274, Box 3.

he commented on a decision of the Court. Of the *Tipaldo* opinion, he said:[116]

> It seems to be fairly clear, as a result of this decision and former decisions, using this question of minimum wage as an example, that the "no-man's-land" where no Government—State or Federal—can function is being more clearly defined. A State cannot do it, and the Federal Government cannot do it.

But when a reporter asked, "How can you meet that situation?" the President replied, "I think that is about all there is to say on it."

Roosevelt was no less circumspect about drafting the 1936 Democratic platform. Both the President and Senator Robert Wagner of New York, chairman of the Resolutions Committee, were urged to incorporate in the platform commitments to specific proposals, such as requiring a 7-to-2 majority to invalidate a law, or amending the Constitution to empower Congress and the states to enact minimum-wage laws.[117] But the Administration was determined to keep the platform ambiguous, not only because it wanted to remove the Court issue from the campaign, but because it had not yet decided on any particular plan.

In drafting their platform, the Democrats had to cope with the fact that the Republicans had already committed themselves to an amendment to overcome the *Tipaldo* decision. As Cummings warned the President, if the Democrats sought to outbid the Republicans they ran the risk of going so far as to shift the whole emphasis of the campaign to the constitutional question. Cummings hoped to avoid any specific plank, but if one were necessary he favored one so vaguely worded that it should leave the door open "to the thought that perhaps, after all, an amendment may not be necessary." Four days earlier, Donald Richberg, who had been a prominent labor attorney and chairman of the National Industrial Recovery Board, had also submitted a draft which was adroitly phrased to escape any definite commitment.[118]

On the Sunday before the 1936 Democratic convention, Roosevelt, Wagner, and several others met after dinner in the White

[116] 5 Public Papers 191–92.

[117] Louis Boehm to Robert Wagner, June 6, 1936; Clarence V. Tiers to Stephen Early, June 24, 1936, FDRL OF 1871-A.

[118] Detroit News, June 25, 1936, clipping, Blair Moody Scrapbooks, Moody MSS, Michigan Historical Collections of the University of Michigan, Ann Arbor, Mich.; Cummings to FDR, June 20, 1936, FDRL PSF Justice; Richberg to FDR, June 16, 1936, FDRL PSF Supreme Court.

House to draft the platform. When they encountered difficulties, it was decided to ask two of the participants, Samuel I. Rosenman, another member of the original Brain Trust, and Stanley High, a skillful phrase-maker, to try their hands after the meeting broke up. They worked all night at a typewriter, and by morning the President had their draft on his breakfast tray. Certain parts, including a Supreme Court plank, were still missing. After breakfast, Rosenman and High went into the President's bedroom, where they found Donald Richberg.

Recognizing that more aid might be required, the President had summoned Richberg to the White House. Richberg, who guessed why he had been called, turned up shortly after breakfast with a carbon of his proposed plank in his pocket. When Roosevelt told him that Wagner needed help, Richberg handed him the draft to read. After going over it, the President whistled softly and said, "I think this is it." The others gathered in the President's bedroom agreed, and, with minor changes, Richberg's plank was incorporated in the platform. Purposely vague, it proposed an attempt to achieve a "clarifying amendment" only "if these problems cannot be effectively solved by legislation."[119]

In the 1936 campaign, Roosevelt maintained a studied silence on the Court question despite counsel from different sides that he urge action to alter the Court or that he assure the country that he would not pack the Court. The President wanted the campaign to center not on the Constitution but on the concrete achievements of the New Deal and the past iniquities of Herbert Hoover. Within the Roosevelt circle, Felix Frankfurter and Frances Perkins opposed making an issue of the Court's rulings, and even Ickes conceded that the groundwork for it had not been laid.[120] One correspondent urged the President to leave the Court matter "till after the campaign, so as not to supply ammunition to the 'constitution cryers.' When the campaign is over, Congress could proceed in a calm mood and adopt certain changes. . . . Congress could suggest to the President to add to the present Tribunal two, four or six justices to make the number 11, 13, or 15."[121]

Nonetheless, the constitutional issue surfaced in different parts

119 Richberg, My Hero 204–05 (1954); Rosenman, Working with Roosevelt 100–03 (1953); Moley 346–47.

120 1 Ickes 524, 531, 602.

121 Jacob Hayman to FDR, Feb. 24, 1936, FDRL OF 41-A, Box 116.

of the country where conservatives warned that a Roosevelt victory would menace the Court. They were unpersuaded by New Deal avowals of reverence for the Constitution. Rexford Tugwell's theology was acceptable, noted one writer, but his actions were unorthodox, "like a Renaissance cardinal with children." Conceivably, a few votes may have been swung by the Court question. One man wrote: "In my opinion any man who sneered at the United States Supreme Court like he did in May 1935, when they ruled against N.R.A., is not worthy of my vote though I have been voting the Democratic Ticket since 1884." Yet Roosevelt's studied silence made it possible for Stephen Duggan, director of the Institute of International Education, to write a long letter, which the *New York Times* published, urging support of the President, who "has given no evidence that he wants to 'pack' the court," and for a conservative senator like Josiah Bailey of North Carolina to defend Roosevelt on the Court question. Enlarging the Supreme Court, wrote Frederick Lewis Allen shortly before the election, "need hardly be regarded as a serious possibility in the immediate future: it would be too obviously a cowardly move."[122]

V. Election Landslide

In November, 1936, Franklin Roosevelt rolled up the greatest landslide victory in the history of two-party competition by capturing the electoral votes of all but two of the forty-eight states. His political opponents routed, his policies vindicated, he could now give full attention to the challenge posed by the Supreme Court. Time was short. In just two more months the Court would reconvene; awaiting it were tests of the validity of the Social Security Act, the Wagner Labor Relations Act, the Railway Labor

[122] Sternsher, Rexford Tugwell and the New Deal 349 (1964); Raymond Clapper MS Diary, Aug. 24, 1937; S. H. Boddinghouse to Daniel Roper, Nov. 6, 1936, FDRL OF 41-A, Box 116; Henry Teigan to C. Schoening, Feb. 16, 1937, Teigan MSS, Minnesota Historical Society, Box 14; Chicago Tribune, July 24, 1936, clipping, Frank Murphy Collection, University of Michigan Law School; Frank Gannett to Alexander Falck, Mar. 7, 1936, Gannett MSS, Cornell University Collection of Regional History, Box 16; James H. Winston to FDR, Aug. 1, 1936, FDRL PPF 1786; J. A. Mulhern to Newton Baker, Oct. 22, 1936, Baker MSS, Box 52; Stephen Duggan to FDR, Nov. 13, 1936, FDRL OF 274; John Robert Moore, "Josiah William Bailey: A Political Biography," unpublished Ph.D. dissertation, Duke University, 1965; James Hamilton Lewis to Arthur Vandenberg, Sept. 18, 1936, Lewis MSS, LC; Allen, *Behind the Campaign*, 173 Harper's 476 (Oct., 1936).

Act, the Commodity Exchange Act, state minimum-wage and unemployment compensation laws, and of the powers of the PWA, the SEC, and the Federal Communications Commission. Even the gold clause resolution faced another contest.

In view of this prospect, what was Roosevelt to do? He might just wait for vacancies to develop. The laws of nature were on his side, for never in our history had a Court been composed of so elderly a group. Moreover, Justices Van Devanter and Sutherland had talked of retiring. Yet Roosevelt had seen nearly four years go by without one opportunity to make an appointment, an experience that had occurred in no other full presidential term save for the special instance of Andrew Johnson's tenure. Anyone familiar with the conversation of Justices knew enough to place a high discount on talk of retiring, and these particular Justices seemed determined to stay on the bench so long as Roosevelt was in the White House. At the first cabinet meeting after the election, the President, in a spirit of gallows humor, said that Justice McReynolds would still be on the tribunal when he was 105.[123]

Still, Roosevelt might wait to see whether the Court would follow the election returns. The switch of even one Justice could be decisive. It might be anticipated that the emphatic outcome of the election would surprise some Justices who had believed that they were speaking for a nation outraged by the New Deal. (It is clear from Van Devanter's correspondence that he thought the election would be close.)[124] Nor, it has been argued, was Justice Roberts as set against the New Deal as he appeared to be.

Yet there were risks in waiting. The Court had behaved so arrogantly in the spring of 1936 that the prospects for a change of views seemed slim. Not only did the Court's line of reasoning in its last Term leave little reason to suppose that the Court would

---

123 John H. Clarke to Newton Baker, Apr. 6, 1934, Jan. 3, 1936, Baker MSS, Box 60; Detroit News, June 2, 1937; Willis Van Devanter to Mrs. John Lacey, Jan. 11, 1933, Van Devanter MSS, Vol. 46; 1 Ickes 705.

It is not clear why the Administration did not move more forcefully to expedite the Sumners bill to make retirement more attractive. On the early history of this bill, see James M. Landis to Donald R. Richberg, Richberg MSS, LC, Box 1; Alexander Holtzoff to the Attorney General, Mar. 5, 1935, NA Dept. of Justice 235241. For post-election response, see Cummings to FDR, Dec. 29, 1936, FDRL PSF Supreme Court.

124 Van Devanter to Dennis Flynn, Oct. 19, 1936; Van Devanter to Mrs. John W. Lacey, Nov. 2, 1936, Van Devanter MSS, Vol. 52.

not strike down such landmarks as the Wagner Act and the Social Security law, but it barred the way to new legislation. Returned to office with a tremendous grant of power, Roosevelt might be denied by the Court the opportunity to use that power. If he waited to see what the Court did, he might find himself with his past achievements obliterated and the momentum for future change lost.

Roosevelt had a strong sense of his own place in history. He would not countenance being written off in the history books as a man who had been frustrated in his attempts to lead the country out of the depression and to create a more humane social order. "When I retire to private life on January 20, 1941," he remarked, "I do not want to leave the country in the condition Buchanan left it to Lincoln."[125] Nor did he wish to be known as a President who had permitted judicial usurpers to impair the office of the Executive. Finally, it should be noted, the Court, by such decisions as that in the *Humphrey* case, had wounded his self-esteem, and, by other acts, had convinced Roosevelt that it was personally hostile to him.[126] He now sought a way not merely to liberalize the Court but to chastise the Justices for their past behavior.

Six days after the election, Roosevelt returned to Washington from Hyde Park; on his very first night in the capital, he summoned Cummings to the White House to report to him on what progress had been made at the Justice Department. Cummings told him that, over the summer, work had intensified as men like Edward S. Corwin, professor of jurisprudence at Princeton University, and William Draper Lewis of the American Law Institute had been asked for advice. Within the department, under the direction of Cummings and Solicitor General Stanley Reed, arguments were being assembled for and against specific proposals.

Both Roosevelt and Cummings had a tacit understanding that at some point action would have to be taken, and they now agreed that the Court was unlikely to be changed in its ways by the election returns. Yet the President still did not indicate that the time to act had come. He treated the meeting as yet another occasion on which the Attorney General had been asked for a progress

---

[125] 29 TIME 13 (Mar. 8, 1937).

[126] For Roosevelt's belief that he had been snubbed by the Justices in 1936, see the penciled memorandum, "Court story," Harry Hopkins MSS, FDRL, Box 325. The account in SHERWOOD, ROOSEVELT AND HOPKINS 94 (1948) is slightly inaccurate.

report, and told him to come back as soon as he had something new to recommend. Meanwhile he was to maintain the closest secrecy on his research.[127]

Cummings, who may have sensed that Roosevelt was more disposed to act than he indicated, sped back to the Justice Department to order his research aides to devote full time, and overtime, to preparing reports and digests of reports for the President. Speed was important, because Roosevelt was to leave on a South American cruise on November 18. For the next nine days, messengers carried memorandums from the Justice Department to the White House and the President's comments back in the other direction. Almost every day, the Attorney General, arriving secretly through a private entrance, conferred at the White House with the President.[128]

Day after day they went over the great variety of recommendations that had come to them in the past two years. The uninvited counsel the President had received in the aftermath of the election indicated that opinion was still unsettled and that no one solution had emerged as the inevitable answer. Some urged pressing for an amendment. A Philadelphia attorney wrote, "We hope . . . you will recommend an amendment clearly adequate in scope, not only for today but for tomorrow also, when even broader needs will arise but may be met by stronger reactionary barriers." Similarly, a group of five Utah labor organizations wanted their legislature to memorialize Congress for an amendment to give Congress the power to regulate the hours of labor.[129] But other letters recommended packing the Court and emphasized the old-age theme. A Baltimore lawyer wanted "a law to be enacted at once that the personnel of the Supreme Court be increased to not less than two more judges," and a Memphis man wrote: "I think you the grandest President we have ever had, and I think God will give you a hand. . . . Mr. President, the labor people want you and Congress

---

127 ALSOP & CATLEDGE, THE 168 DAYS 20, 23–24 (1938) (hereinafter ALSOP); N.Y. Times, Feb. 12, 1937; Raymond Clapper MS Diary, Feb. 8, 1937.

128 ALSOP 27.

129 L. Stauffer Oliver to FDR, Nov. 12, 1936; George C. Christiansen *et al.* to C. W. Spence, Dec. 12, 1936, FDRL OF 274, Box 4. See, too, Virgil V. Johnson to FDR, Nov. 13, 1936, FDRL PPF 200, Reelect Cong–J.

to curb the Supreme Court. You all know just 9 old men should not rule this grand country."[130]

Roosevelt dismissed the amendment route as unacceptable for a number of reasons. In the first place, he thought an amendment would be difficult to frame. Two years of study in the Justice Department had not yet yielded a satisfactory draft, and liberals outside the government were far from a consensus. When the National Consumers' League, which had spearheaded the drive for minimum-wage legislation, polled national legal experts after the *Tipaldo* decision on whether a campaign for an amendment should be launched, the results were discouraging. Half of those polled—including Felix Frankfurter—opposed agitation for an amendment, and the other half were so far apart on what kind of an amendment should be sought that the League decided against any action at all.[131]

Even if an amendment could be framed, and approved by two-thirds of each house of Congress, it would have to run the gantlet of ratification by three-fourths of the states. If ratification was by state legislatures, as seemed most likely, it would require an adverse vote by only one house in thirteen legislatures to defeat an amendment, and the state legislatures were known to overrepresent conservative interests. Nor did Roosevelt have much faith in the probity of these assemblies. As he wrote a prominent New York lawyer three months later: "If you were not as scrupulous and ethical as you happen to be, you could make five million dollars as easy as rolling off a log by undertaking a campaign to prevent the ratification by one house of the Legislature, or even the summoning of a constitutional convention in thirteen states for the next four years. Easy money."[132] In a conversation with Ickes, Tom Corcoran had no trouble in ticking off the thirteen states "that would naturally be against a broadening amendment or in which money could be used to defeat it."[133]

---

[130] John B. McGraw to Stephen Early, Dec. 8, 1936, FDRL OF 274, Box 4; L. L. Wilson to FDR, Dec. 3, 1936, NA Dept. of Justice 235773. See, too, B. F. Welty to FDR, Dec. 29, 1936, FDRL OF 41, Box 114.

[131] Report of the Committee of Inquiry to the Board, Nov. 5, 1936, Mary Dewson MSS, FDRL, Box 6. The Dewson Papers also contain the original replies.

[132] FDR to Charles C. Burlingham, Feb. 23, 1937, 1 Letters 662.

[133] 2 Ickes 33–34.

At best, ratification would take a long time, and time was invaluable. Conscious of the brief span allotted to reform movements, Roosevelt wanted to exploit his landslide victory to drive through legislation such as a wages and hours bill while Congress still felt the full force of his popular indorsement. To be sure, the Norris lame-duck amendment had been adopted quickly, but that, he thought, was because it had not been opposed by any strongly entrenched interest. A constitutional amendment affecting the courts would not only be rejected by business interests but would encounter state legislatures largely composed of lawyers, who would be likely to be more disapproving of tinkering with the courts than would other groups.[134]

Roosevelt was especially influenced by the long, unsuccessful experience with attempting to win ratification for the child-labor amendment, a struggle then in its thirteenth year. As LaRue Brown, formerly Assistant Attorney General under Wilson, told the National Consumers' League:[135]

> My personal experience with the Child Labor Amendment leads me to view with great dubiety the prospect of ratification of an amendment increasing federal power. Our side is at so tremendous a disadvantage as to resources and so many truly liberal folk are so questioning as to the ultimate intendments of increasing the federal authority that I fear we should simply wear our hearts out in another hopeless fight.

Subsequently, Stephen Early, Roosevelt's press secretary, summed up the objections for Raymond Clapper. Clapper set down in his diary:[136]

> Steve said that the president had given him sidelight this morning on court proposal that he thought he would pass on to me to use or not as I saw fit. It was this—that people who talked about an amendment either didn't realize difficulties in that method or else did realize them and for that reason advocated this course. Steve said that to seek an amendment meant

134 Mallon, *Purely Confidential*, Detroit News, Feb. 13, 1937; N.Y. Times, Feb. 12, 1937.

135 Brown to Lucy R. Mason, Sept. 9, 1936, Mary Dewson MSS, Box 6. See, too, Donald Richberg to Raymond Clapper, Feb. 26, 1937, Richberg MSS, Box 2. Advocates of amendments pointed out that the child-labor amendment had been improperly drafted, and that the ratification process could involve conventions rather than legislatures.

136 Raymond Clapper MS Diary, Feb. 8, 1937.

> getting two-thirds of both houses and then submitting it to states where ¾ needed. He said suppose 13 governors refused to submit amendment. It dead then. He said all of us who ever been around legislatures know how easy be for moneyed interests to buy up enough legislatures to prevent action. Said this not like prohibition—here are vast and powerful groups determined to prevent action. Said another reason would be that to follow amendment course would make this an issue in 1938 campaign and might lose a number of "our congressmen." Might cost them their seats.

Even if all these objections were overcome and an amendment went through, any legislation enacted under authorization of such an amendment would still be subject to review in the courts, unless such an amendment was purely procedural. "In view of what Mr. Justice Roberts did to a clause as broad and sweeping as 'the general welfare,' " wrote Charles A. Beard, "I can see other justices of his mental outlook macerating almost any clarifying amendment less generous in its terms. If there is any phrase wider than providing for the general welfare, I am unable to conjure it up in my mind."[137] Besides, if the President should sponsor an amendment enlarging federal powers, it might seem tantamount to conceding that he had been wrong and the Supreme Court right in their dispute over the constitutionality of New Deal measures, and this Roosevelt, especially after his bracing election triumph, was less willing than ever to do.[138]

After eliminating amendment proposals, Roosevelt and Cummings next looked into various suggestions that would require only an act of Congress. First, they considered a bill stipulating more than a majority of Justices to invalidate a law; they dismissed this, because they feared that the Court would void such a statute. As Richberg later explained: "A mere statute to this effect would either be disregarded by the court, or have the result that Justices anxious to preserve the prestige of the court would join unwillingly with the majority so as to make a decision of the court effective." Moreover, such a law would limit the Court's role as a protector of civil liberties. They then examined a bill to withdraw appellate

---

137 Beard, *Rendezvous with the Supreme Court*, 88 NEW REPUBLIC 93 (Sept. 2, 1936); Beard to Nicholas Kelley, Aug. 8, 1936, Mary Dewson MSS, Box 6.

138 Washington Herald, Mar. 14, 1937, clipping, Frank Murphy Collection, University of Michigan Law School.

jurisdiction, but they were troubled by the recognition that the Court would still have original jurisdiction, especially in cases involving conflicts among states, and that the lower courts would retain their powers. By the end of the nine days, both men were leaning toward court-packing as the only feasible solution, but they were not yet committed to it, nor had they decided on the form it should take.[139]

Just before departing for South America, Roosevelt met once more with Cummings in the President's office. This time the President told an elated Cummings that he had made his decision; he would present a Court bill to Congress as soon as one was ready. Cummings gave him two stout volumes of proposed amendments and bills to take aboard ship to study, and they agreed that if any new ideas were developed they would be dispatched to the President at his ports of call. Roosevelt also took with him two lengthy memorandums from Donald Richberg, which stated that he "should not simply *defend* reasonable exercises of legislative power, but should aggressively *attack* the unconstitutional exercise of judicial power." On November 18, the President set sail for southern waters, after charging Cummings to have a plan ready for him on his return.[140]

VI. McReynolds' Petard

During the four weeks the President was touring South America, Cummings and his aides worked prodigiously at canvassing the possibilities for judicial reform. But when Roosevelt returned on December 15, they still had not found a solution. The main result of their labors was an exhaustive 65-page report which W. W. Gardner submitted to Reed, and the Solicitor General forwarded to Cummings. ("This matter has been handled confidentially," Reed assured him, "and I have my copy of the memorandum under lock.") Scholarly, shrewd, carefully written, the report was more valuable for warning of the pitfalls in various proposals than in pointing out what should be done.[141]

---

139 Alsop 28–30; N.Y. Times, Feb. 12, 1937; Washington Post, Feb. 13, 1937; Richberg to Clapper, Feb. 26, 1937, Richberg MSS, Box 2.

140 Alsop 30–31; Richberg to FDR, Nov. 16, 1936, FDRL PPF 2418.

141 Raymond Clapper MS Diary, Feb. 8, 1937; Reed, Memorandum for the Attorney General from the Solicitor General, Dec. 19, 1936, NA Dept. of Justice 235773.

Meanwhile, a much more fruitful exchange was being carried on between Cummings and Professor Corwin. The author of numerous articles and books excoriating the infringement by the Court on the prerogatives of other branches of government, Corwin had developed a close relationship with the Justice Department. Like other constitutional authorities, he had oscillated between different answers to the conflict between the President and the Court—from believing the Court should correct its own errors to favoring amendments, especially one to require more than a simple majority to invalidate laws.[142] His thinking may have been turned in a new direction by a letter he received early in September from Charles E. Clark, dean of the Yale Law School: "I do think that the possibility of increasing the size of the Court ought to be more considered in Congress than apparently it has."[143]

After the election, Corwin wrote a series of newspaper articles on the Court question. On December 3, Cummings wrote the President, who was still in South America:[144]

> Professor Corwin, of Princeton, has prepared a series of articles dealing with some of our Constitutional difficulties. These articles will shortly be published in the Philadelphia Record. They are especially pertinent to the last discussion I had with you on this subject. I have just received from Doctor Corwin the proof sheets of the articles, which I enclose herewith. I am very sure that you will find them well worth reading.

Corwin's series was a curious performance. With corrosive wit, he derided the record of the Court during the New Deal. In exposing the inadequacies of the panaceas that had been offered, he wrote brilliantly. But his own remedies were murky and even contradictory. After showing with devastating clarity why the Administration should not resort to amendments, he stated that some amendments might be needed. He called for the Court to reform itself, yet conceded that this particular Court could not be expected to do so. But one sentence in the final article emerged boldly: "No reform could be better adopted than the requirement, to be laid

142 Corwin had helped prepare the Government's brief in the *Carter* case. CORWIN, THE COMMERCE POWER VS. STATES RIGHTS 263–67 (1936); Corwin to Lucy R. Mason, Sept. 24, 1936, Mary Dewson MSS, Box 6; John Dickinson to Corwin, June 15, 1936.

143 Clark to Corwin, Sept. 3, 1936, Corwin MSS, Princeton University Library.

144 Cummings to FDR, Dec. 3, 1936, FDRL OF 41-A, Box 116; Cummings to Corwin, Dec. 3, 1936, Corwin MSS.

down by an act of Congress, or, if necessary, by constitutional amendment, that no Judge may hold office under the United States beyond his seventieth birthday."[145]

In the series, Corwin appeared to be trimming some of his beliefs in order to avoid exciting unnecessary quarrels. In particular, his deference to the amendment approach seemed less than heartfelt. On December 16, he wrote Cummings:[146]

> It is probably utopian to hope that the Court will supply the needed remedy for a situation which it has itself created. Hence we must turn either to constitutional amendment or Congressional action.
>
> As to the latter, I did not care to go on record as favoring a *tour de force;* yet it is essential to face the fact that Congressional action may be necessary.

Nor, he added, had his articles exhausted the possibilities of action. Corwin continued:

> A friend of mine has made this ingenious suggestion: that the President be authorized, whenever a majority of the Justices, or half of the Justices, are seventy or more years old, to nominate enough new Justices of less than that age to make a majority. This, too, would require only an act of Congress, and something of a legislative precedent for such a measure is furnished by § 375 of title 28, of the U.S. Code.
>
> Mr. Reed appears to think that I put too much emphasis on my age-limit proposal, but I'm not so sure. A 70-year age-limit would secure more rapid replacement of justices. Furthermore, it might serve to draw the attention of the appointing power more frequently to the faculties of our great Law-schools where superior talent emerges at an earlier age than in practice at the Bar.

---

145 The proofs are in FDRL OF 41-A, Box 116. Clark argued that Corwin had underestimated the possibilities of the amendment process. Clark to Corwin, Dec. 11, 1936, and Corwin's reply, Dec. 16, 1936. See, too, Clark to Corwin, Aug. 18, 1936, Corwin MSS.

146 The penciled draft of this letter in the Corwin Papers is undated. The letter could have been sent at any time between December 4 and 16, but December 16 seems highly probable. That same day, Corwin wrote Reed: "I was glad to get your comments on those articles—I believe that my age limit proposal, if adopted, may have considerable effect. It might not get more liberal judges, but it would assure a more rapid replacement of the Bench. Today Jefferson's complaint is well justified: 'Few die and none resign.'—indeed the statement might be made stronger. . . . I believe it could be validly accomplished by an act of Congress." Corwin to Reed, Dec. 16, 1936, NA Dept. of Justice 235868. Reed appears to have been unenthusiastic about the plan both at this point and when it finally emerged.

Since Corwin had pointed out in his series the folly of enlarging the Court, this suggestion marked an important new departure. For the first time, compulsory retirement at 70 was linked to the appointment of new Justices. On the very next day, Cummings replied to Corwin:[147]

> Of course, I realize that there is a good deal of prejudice against "packing the Court." I have been wondering to what extent we have been frightened by the phrase.
>
> Quite apart from immediate consideration, and as a mere matter of general policy, I have often thought that much was to be said for a constitutional amendment requiring retirements when the age of 70 is reached. I am wondering if there would be much opposition to such an amendment if it were so framed as not to affect the present judiciary by making it apply to future appointments only.

Corwin's contribution reached Cummings at a propitious moment. Both the Attorney General and the President had been attracted to "court-packing" for some weeks, but they recognized that the proposition violated taboos and that some principle would have to be found to justify it. Corwin offered such a formula by relating new appointments to the ages of Justices. If Corwin's suggestion (or that of Corwin's "friend") was adopted, Cummings could exploit growing popular resentment at the age of the bench.

By now, it had become commonplace to refer to the Justices as the "nine old men." A. A. Berle had used the term in passing in 1933,[148] and a column in a Kentucky newspaper reflected a popular notion when it referred to the Court as "nine old back-number owls (appointed by by-gone Presidents) who sit on the leafless, fruitless limb of an old dead tree." But it was the publication on October 26, 1936 of *The Nine Old Men* by Drew Pearson and Robert S. Allen which made the phrase a household word. The book quickly climbed onto the best-seller lists, and it was serialized in newspapers across the country. Even critics of the Justices were disturbed by the book's tone and by its inaccuracies, but this exposé helped concentrate popular attention on both the age and the viewpoint of the Court as a more sober account might not have done. Representative Thomas Amlie of Wisconsin, while regretting the book's innuendos, thought "that Pearson and Allen have done a particu-

147 Cummings to Corwin, Dec. 17, 1936, Corwin MSS.

148 Berle, *Law and the Social Revolution*, 22 Survey Graphic 594 (Dec., 1933).

larly good job on the Constitutional law angle," and Senator Joseph Guffey of Pennsylvania called for a Senate investigation of the allegations made in the book. Guffey called the volume "the most disturbing—I would say shocking book on public officials I have ever read. Its purported disclosures are sensational."[149]

After receiving Corwin's letter, Cummings was close to the end of the trail. Yet Corwin still had not shown him the precise route the Attorney General was seeking, and Cummings' reply suggests that he was still thinking that an amendment might be required, and that the present Justices might be exempted. However, once Corwin had blazed the path this far, it did not take Cummings long to discover the rest of the way.

At some point in the next five days, Cummings found his answer. While carrying on his other duties, the Attorney General had also been writing a history of his department, in collaboration with his aide, Carl McFarland. One passage in *Federal Justice*, which was about to be published, now stood out from the pages as it had not before, a recommendation that Justice McReynolds, when serving as Wilson's Attorney General, had made in 1913.

McReynolds' recommendation stated:[150]

> Judges of the United States Courts, at the age of 70, after having served 10 years, may retire upon full pay. In the past, many judges have availed themselves of this privilege. Some, however, have remained upon the bench long beyond the time that they are able to adequately discharge their duties, and in consequence the administration of justice has suffered. . . . I suggest an act providing that when any judge of a Federal court below the Supreme Court fails to avail himself of the privilege of retiring now granted by law, that the President be required, with the advice and consent of the Senate, to appoint another judge, who would preside over the affairs of the court and have precedence over the older one. This will insure at all times the presence of a judge sufficiently active to discharge promptly and adequately the duties of the court.

---

149 Charles N. Crewdson to Louis Howe, Jan. 7, 1936, FDRL OF 41-A, Box 116; Thomas Reed Powell to William O. Douglas, n.d., Douglas MSS, LC, Box 20; Herbert Hoover to Charles Evans Hughes, Feb. 19, 1937, Hughes MSS, Box 6; James A. Stone to William T. Evjue, Mar. 17, 1937, Stone MSS, Minnesota Historical Society, Box 28; Thomas R. Amlie to Donald A. Butchart, Mar. 6, 1937, Amlie MSS, Box 36; N.Y. Times, Jan. 27, 1937.

150 Report of the Attorney General for the Fiscal Year Ending June 30, 1913 5, Cummings & McFarland, Federal Justice (1937).

Cummings now reasoned that McReynolds' prescription, which had been limited to the lower courts, might also be applied to the Supreme Court. Once the principle of retirement was adopted, any age might be stipulated, but 70 seemed especially compelling. It had been the age that, on different occasions, McReynolds, Cummings, and Corwin had all hit upon, and it had the not inconsiderable advantage of having biblical sanction. That summer, an Oklahoma newspaper had proposed to retire Supreme Court Justices at seventy, "as set out in Holy Writ as the reasonable span of human life."[151] With the retirement age fixed at 70, Roosevelt would be able to name six new Justices, thus practically assuring a bench that would approve New Deal legislation.

Before presenting the plan to Roosevelt, Cummings directed his assistants in the Justice Department to prepare a series of reports. He deliberately parceled out work so that the scheme would be kept a secret even from his own aides. Except for Cummings and Reed, no one in the department save for Holtzoff and McFarland appears to have known the full scope of the proposal until it was announced. When his assistants reported back to Cummings, each gave a favorable reply. One report approved the plan's constitutionality. Another turned up historical precedent in an 1869 bill that had passed the House of Representatives. A third pulled together statistics to show that the formula would also supply enough new judges for the lower courts.[152]

Cummings' search had ended. On December 22, he sent a penciled note to the President: "I am 'bursting' with ideas anent our constitutional problems; and have a plan (of substance & approach) I would like to talk over with you when you have the time."[153] By this point, Roosevelt was already determined to "pack" the Court, but he did not yet know how, and he still thought of the idea as a birch rod to be taken out of the closet only if the Court did not mend its ways in the new Term.

He now summoned George Creel to the White House once more to prepare an article, this one to be called "Roosevelt's Plans and Purposes." During the afternoon and evening they worked to-

151 *The Federal Constitution*, Shawnee (Okla.) County Democrat, Aug. 7, 1936, clipping, FDRL OF 274, Box 4.

152 Alsop 34; Raymond Clapper MS Diary, June 12, 1938.

153 Cummings to FDR, Dec. 22, 1936, FDRL PSF Supreme Court.

gether, Creel was struck by the fact that the President, understandably, viewed the election as a purely personal victory. He told Creel that the social objectives he cherished would all have to run the gantlet of the Supreme Court. But his face brightened as he said: "I've thought of a better way than a constitutional amendment stripping the Court of its power to nullify acts of Congress. The time element makes that method useless. Granted that Congress could agree on such an amendment for submission to the several states, it would be two, three, or four years before the legislatures could or would act. What do you think of this?"[154] From a drawer in his desk, he extracted a heavily marked copy of the Constitution and riffled the pages as he read off passages and commented on the powers of Congress to act for the general welfare.

After reading Article III, § 1, he asked: "Where is there anything in that which gives the Supreme Court the right to override the legislative branch?" As the President talked, Creel wrote afterward, "I was amazed by his reading on the subject and by the grip of his mind on what he conceived to be essential facts. For example, he quoted at length from Madison's *Journal* and Elliot's *Debates*, citing them as his authority for the statement that the framers of the Constitution had voted on four separate occasions against giving judges the power to pass upon the constitutionality of acts of Congress."[155]

If Congress was to reclaim the powers that had been usurped from it, Roosevelt reasoned, it should add a rider to each bill at the next session charging the Supreme Court to remember that the Constitution vested all legislative power in Congress and authorized it to provide for the general welfare. Suppose this proved ineffective? Creel related: " 'Then,' said the President, his face like a fist, 'Congress can *enlarge* the Supreme Court, increasing the number of justices so as to permit the appointment of men in tune with the spirit of the age.' " When *Collier's* published this article on December 26, with three columns discussing the Supreme Court, Creel expected an explosion in Congress and the press. Yet, once again, the President's explicit words were ignored.[156]

On the same day that Creel's article appeared, Cummings went

---

[154] CREEL, *op. cit. supra* note 65, at 292–94; Richberg to FDR, Nov. 16, 1936, FDRL PPF 2418.

[155] CREEL, *op. cit. supra* note 65, at 293–94. [156] *Ibid.*

to the White House to report to Roosevelt. According to one account, not altogether probable, the Attorney General handed the President a packet of plans with the new scheme on the bottom. He then watched agitatedly while Roosevelt turned over each in turn until he came to Cummings' favorite; to the Attorney General's immense pleasure, Roosevelt was delighted. However it happened, it is clear that the President gave his approval that day. He was gratified that the proposal was unquestionably constitutional, and he took a mischievous pleasure in the fact that it could be attributed to McReynolds.[157]

Buoyed by the President's approval, Cummings now turned his hand to sketching the remaining details of the plan. He wanted not only to liberalize the Court but to reform the entire judiciary. By presenting "court-packing" in the guise of judicial reform, he would make the plan more palatable. Yet Cummings' interest in reform was not just expedient. He had long cherished the aim of overhauling the structure of the courts, and Roosevelt shared some of his ardor. Once they launched what they knew would be a historic fight, they wanted it to be remembered for improving the judicial system as well as for overcoming the intransigence of the Supreme Court.

For two years, William Denman, Judge of the Ninth Circuit Court of Appeals, had been bombarding Roosevelt with pleas for more lower-court judges in order to relieve congestion in the courts and prevent miscarriages of justice. Denman also argued that the lower-court system was illogically organized, and, he proposed, among other suggestions, the appointment of a proctor of the Supreme Court to supervise lower courts and the creation of "roving judges" to clear up congestion. The Judicial Conference had also, more than once, pointed out the need for additional district judges. Cummings now decided to tie all these ideas together into a single package, but to relate the call for more lower-court judges to the principle of age.[158]

---

157 ALSOP 34–35; Raymond Clapper MS Diary, June 12, 1938. Rexford Tugwell has written: "Of all the ways open to him Franklin does seem to have chosen the one most upsetting to judicial dignity." TUGWELL, *op. cit. supra* note 55, at 392.

158 Raymond Clapper MS Diary, Feb. 8, 1937; Denman to Cummings, Mar. 19, 1936; Denman to FDR, Mar. 20, 1936, FDRL OF 209-I; Memorandum for the Attorney General, Apr. 29, 1936; Denman to M. H. McIntyre, Mar. 17, 1936, FDRL PPF 336; Denman to FDR, Sept. 5, 1936, FDRL OF 41, Box 114; Charles Evans Hughes

By the end of the year, the Justice Department had prepared the first draft of the bill. In all, it went through twelve full drafts and numerous minor revisions. The measure embraced four proposals: (1) that when a judge of a federal court who had served ten years did not resign or retire within six months after his seventieth birthday, the President might name another judge as coadjutor; (2) that the Supreme Court should not have more than six added Justices, nor any lower-court bench more than two, nor the total federal judiciary more than fifty; (3) that lower-court judges might be assigned to exceptionally busy courts; and (4) that the lower courts should be supervised by the Supreme Court through a proctor.[159]

Roosevelt and Cummings decided it would be helpful to accompany the bill with both a message from the President and a letter from the Attorney General. Instead of concentrating on the desirability of a more liberal court, both documents would stress the incapacity of aged judges and the need for additional appointments to get the Court abreast of its work. By emphasizing the theme of greater efficiency, they hoped the whole plan would be accepted as a project for judicial reform rather than a stratagem to pack the Court. Once again, Cummings parceled out assignments within the department so that men were called on to supply statistics on denial of certiorari or the ages of judges without ever being told why this information was wanted or being given enough to do to be able to piece together what was happening.

When all three documents were taken to the White House, the President offered little comment on the bill, but he gave the letter, to which Holtzoff had made important contributions, a thorough going-over, and Cummings had to revise it before Roosevelt would give his approval. Even more care was lavished on the President's message, which Roosevelt recognized would be an important state paper. In the third week in January, Donald Richberg was called in to polish the draft, and on the night of January 30, when Judge Rosenman arrived at the White House for the President's birthday party, he was asked to contribute his talents. It was the first he had

---

to FDR, May 30, 1934, FDRL OF 41-A; Mallon, *Purely Confidential*, Detroit News, Apr. 2, 1937; ALSOP 31–35.

159 By January 5, the bill had reached a fifth draft. "Draft No. 5, January 5, 1937," FDRL PSF Supreme Court.

heard of the plan, even though he had helped write both the State-of-the-Union message and the Inaugural Address that month. When Rosenman told Corcoran, who had also been kept in the dark, what was happening, the President agreed that Corcoran, too, should be asked to go over the final draft of the message. But he instructed Rosenman not to let Cummings know that Corcoran was involved.[160]

The President's insistence on secrecy combined fear of premature disclosure that might promote bickering with his love of the dramatic. Save for Cummings, no one in the cabinet, not even the ubiquitous Ickes, knew of the plan. Indeed, Roosevelt, at one cabinet meeting in January, deliberately misrepresented what was going on. Nor was any member of Congress told. Some of the men who would soon bear the burden of defending it were busy drafting quite different proposals, and Henry Fountain Ashurst, who would shortly be called on to move the President's proposal through the Senate Judiciary Committee, was publicly denouncing court-packing as "the prelude to tyranny."[161]

Through all of this, the President gave almost no indication of the surprise he was about to spring. As Moley later wrote: "Roosevelt's pronouncements in the course of his good-will trip to South America would not have frightened the birds of St. Francis."[162] Despite some shafts aimed at the Supreme Court, Roosevelt's State-of-the-Union message was praised for its good-tempered restraint, and he made no mention at all of the Court in his Inaugural Address. Informed observers predicted that the President would wait to see

---

160 ALSOP 43–47; RICHBERG, *op. cit. supra* note 119, at 221–22; Raymond Clapper MS Diary, Jan. 14, 1938; ROSENMAN, *op. cit. supra* note 119, at 145–50. Two drafts of the message have been retained in the Samuel I. Rosenman MSS, FDRL, "Message to Congress on the Judiciary" folder.

161 Washington Post, Feb. 13, 1937; 2 ICKES 31; Henry Morgenthau, Jr., MS Diary, FDRL, Feb. 6, 1937; Raymond Clapper MS Diary, Feb. 5, 1937; Edward Rees to William Allen White, n.d., White MSS, Box 186; CONG. REC., 75th Cong., 1st Sess., 562. After the plan was announced, Clapper reported on an interview with the President's press secretary, Stephen Early: "Steve says that only five people were told of plan by President. He said president wouldn't want him to reveal names but he thought I knew them. Said none was in Congress. . . . Steve said reason Rvt didn't talk it over with more people was that he was afraid of a leak which would tip off opposition and enable them to start hostile build up before he got his plan out." Clapper MS Diary, Feb. 8, 1937.

162 MOLEY 356.

how the Court disposed of the Wagner cases before taking any action. On January 24, Dean Dinwoodey, editor of *United States Law Week*, wrote that "last week it was made plain that he does not at the present time have in mind any legislation directed at the Court."[163]

VII. Roosevelt Entertains the Court

By the beginning of February, the bill, the letter, and the message had all been drafted, except for a few final details. All that remained was to decide when to launch the plan. It is conceivable that Roosevelt might have waited until the Wagner cases had been decided, although this seems unlikely, but if he had any such intention, he felt compelled to abandon it. The situation in Congress, where more and more members were committing themselves publicly to divergent proposals, was getting out of hand. Outside the government, progressives had called a national conference to reach agreement on an amendment. Most important, word of Roosevelt's own plan had begun to leak out, and speculation about what the President intended was getting closer and closer to the mark.[164]

Not everyone had thought that Roosevelt's State-of-the-Union address signaled inaction. Breckinridge Long noted in his diary:[165]

> After I heard the speech I went home and read the printed speech twice. It is rather mysterious in that it is enshrouded somewhat in mystery in that he makes no intimation of his specific plan, but it is very plain that he has something definitely in mind. I say it is very plain, but I mean that it is very plain to those who read with a discriminating eye the words of his message and use as a background his whole history in connection with the Supreme Court.

The conservative Republican congressman from Minnesota, Harold Knutson, also found the address unsettling. He wrote: "I rather

163 29 Time 13–14 (Jan. 18, 1937); N.Y. Times, Jan. 5, 7, 10, 24, 1937.

164 Mallon, *Purely Confidential*, Detroit News, Feb. 13, 1937; Mary Dewson to Stanley Reed, Dec. 10, 1936; Dewson to Mrs. Armstrong, n.d.; Elmer F. Andrews to Members of the New York State Minimum Wage Conference, Jan. 26, 1937; Mrs. J. C. Pryer to Mary Dewson, Jan. 11, 1937, Dewson MSS; Alfred M. Bingham to Thomas R. Amlie, Jan. 5, 1937, Amlie MSS, Box 35. Subsequently, Clapper summed up what Cummings had told him: "Didn't know until last minute whether Rvt would go through with it or not." Clapper MS Diary, Feb. 8, 1937.

165 Breckinridge Long MS Diary, Jan. 6, 1937.

thought the President's message contained one or two disquieting features and the question that is bothering me is, will he attempt to 'pack' the Supreme Court. There is no limit on the number of judges that may be appointed to the Supreme Court and by adding two or three he could easily secure control of the judiciary. Will he go that far?"[166]

In divining the President's intentions, Long had an advantage. On the same day that Roosevelt gave his address, Long had lunched with Cummings. Afterward, he set down in his diary:[167]

> Homer has devised a means and has a specific draft to carry out the provisions intimated. It contemplates a large treatment for the whole judicial system and is not confined to the Supreme Court alone. He thinks the President has the matter definitely in mind. Procedure along that line would permit the drafting of a bill to disqualify members of the judiciary over the age of 70 years, if they have not retired voluntarily within six months after they have passed that age, and the appointment of a successor. More than that, it makes various changes in the structure of the judiciary and mobilizes the framework of the system. Whether anything will come of it is to be determined only in the future, but in the light of the President's Annual Message to the Congress it seems to my mind clearly that he has some definite proposal in mind, and after my conversation today I am of the opinion that it is this proposal.

Roosevelt's speech-writers were no more discreet than his Attorney General. Over cocktails on January 20, Donald Richberg let slip what was going on. Ray Clapper noted in his diary:[168]

> Richberg says Rvt has a number of bombshells ready to shoot which will astound country—says Rvt is in audacious mood and is even thinking of proposing to pack Supreme Court by enlarging it. R seems favor instead compulsory retirement. He says Rvt is determined to curb the court and put it in its place, and will go ahead even if many people think it unwise.

Before the month was out, the Senate began to sense what was happening. On January 24, Irving Brant, who as editor of the editorial page of the St. Louis *Star-Times* had often written on constitutional subjects, wrote the President: "Several senators have

[166] Knutson to Elmer E. Adams, Jan. 11, 1937, Adams MSS, Minnesota Historical Society, Box 42. See, too, Ray Lyman Wilbur to Dr. Arthur H. Daniels, Jan. 8, 1937, Wilbur MSS, Stanford University Library.

[167] Breckinridge Long MS Diary, Jan. 6, 1937.

[168] Raymond Clapper MS Diary, Jan. 20, 1937.

told me that you expect to make a statement about the Supreme Court within a few days."[169] On February 2, in a speech that seemed to imply more than it said, Senator William Borah of Idaho deprecated the "purloining" of state powers by the federal government and lauded the Supreme Court as the shield of individual liberties.[170] Alert Washington columnists knew that something was in the wind, but they had not yet discovered what it was. "Strange things are being said in Congress," Paul Mallon noted in his column of February 4. First there had been a speech by Ashurst, then one by Congressman Samuel Pettengill, now Borah. But what were they aiming at? Borah, he pointed out, "left the definite impression he was attacking something Mr. Roosevelt was going to propose, but he did not say what."[171]

Roosevelt could wait no longer. Since the Court was scheduled to begin hearings on the constitutionality of the Wagner Act on Monday, February 8, he wanted to submit the message before then so that it would not be interpreted as a threat to the Court. On February 2, he was scheduled to entertain the judiciary at dinner at the White House; so he could not very well present the plan before then.[172] Richberg later recalled that the President had said impishly that "his choice should be whether to take only one cocktail before dinner and have it a very amiable affair, or to have a mimeographed copy of the program laid beside the plate of each justice and then take three cocktails to fortify himself against their reactions."[173] The President was thus limited to the interval between February 3 and February 6. On February 3, the Senate recessed until February 5; so Friday, February 5, became the day the President chose to act.

The real ending of the odyssey of the search for the Court plan came not on February 5 but three days earlier when the guests assembled in the East Room of the White House for the judiciary dinner. It was a gala evening. Among the ninety guests were most of the Supreme Court Justices, Mrs. Woodrow Wilson, Senator Borah, and the Gene Tunneys. In the room sat men like Reed, whom the Justices did not suspect might soon be their colleague,

---

[169] Brant to FDR, Jan. 24, 1937, FDRL PPF 2293; Washington Post, Feb. 13, 1937.

[170] N.Y. Times, Feb. 2, 1937; Detroit News, Feb. 2, 1937.

[171] Mallon, *Purely Confidential*, Detroit News, Feb. 4, 1937.

[172] Washington Post, Feb. 13, 1937; Raymond Clapper MS Diary, Feb. 8, 1937.

[173] RICHBERG, *op. cit. supra* note 119, at 222.

and Cummings, who was told by Rosenman that he had the lean and hungry look proper to a conspirator.[174] Two of those present, Senator Ashurst and Representative Hatton Sumners, chairmen of the Senate and House Judiciary Committees, would in three more days be handed a bill to curb the power of the honored guests of the evening. As the guests filed out of the dining room, Roosevelt, in high spirits, remained seated talking to Justices Hughes and Van Devanter. Borah, seeing them together, remarked: "That reminds me of the Roman Emperor who looked around his dinner table and began to laugh when he thought how many of those heads would be rolling on the morrow."[175]

VIII. The Reality and the Myth

To put together the complete puzzle of the origins of the Court plan, one still needs a few pieces. The opening of the Homer Cummings papers, now privately held, and of the Stanley Reed memoir in the Columbia Oral History Collection, now closed, should be instructive. But most of the pieces are now available. It is clear that many of the men alleged to have been authors of the plan either knew nothing of it or played quite minor roles. The main operation, from beginning to end, involved a very few men, all of them concentrated in the Justice Department. Of those who exerted influence from outside the department, Corwin, a department consultant, was more important than such putative architects as Corcoran.

Of the plan itself, few have found much good to say. Much of this criticism is surely justified. Yet the presentation of the plan was not a capricious act but the result of a long period of gestation. During this time, other alternatives were carefully examined, favored for a while, and then discarded on not unreasonable grounds. Throughout this same period, Roosevelt was called on repeatedly to take action, and it appeared, in particular, that he would have a sizable following for a recommendation which would justify the appointment of additional Justices by stressing the infirmity of the Hughes Court. That Roosevelt misjudged the state of opinion seems probable in retrospect, but, at the time, the plan seemed to have an inherent logic and even inevitability.

---

174 Rosenman, *op. cit. supra* note 119, at 153–54.

175 Richberg, *op. cit. supra* note 119, at 222; 29 Time 15 (Feb. 15, 1937); *id.* at 13 (Mar. 1, 1937).

VIRGINIA LAW REVIEW

VOLUME 55 APRIL 1969 NUMBER 3

JUDICIAL ACTIVISM: OLD AND NEW

*Alpheus Thomas Mason**

DE TOCQUEVILLE noted in the 1830's what certain judges and commentators still refuse to recognize, or acknowledge only with apologies: the judicial function is unavoidably political. "Scarcely any *political question* arises in the United States," the French nobleman commented, "that is not resolved, sooner or later, into a *judicial question*." [1] As a result the Supreme Court has been and is a storm center. It is now, as always, under fire.

Differences concerning substantive issues are overshadowed by opposing views concerning the Court's function in a free society. Should the Court share with the political organs of government an active and creative role? Or should it stand aloof, exercise self-restraint, defer to legislature and executive, leave policy-making to the initiative of others? Speaking at Princeton in November 1967, Justice Harlan put the current controversy in the context of history:

> From the beginning . . . two views as to the proper role of the Supreme Court in our governmental system have existed. . . .
>
> The one [view] is that the Court should stand ready to bring about needed basic changes in our society which for one reason or another have failed or lagged in their accomplishment by other means.
>
> The other [view] is that such changes are best left to the political process and should not be undertaken by judges who, as they should

* Doherty Professor of Government and Law, University of Virginia. A.B., 1920, Dickinson College; A.M., 1921, Ph.D., 1923, Princeton University.
 This Article is the outgrowth of seminar discussions at the University of Virginia, 1968-69. I am especially indebted to Craig Norville and Richard Bonnie for skillful editorial surgery.

1 A. DE TOCQUEVILLE, DEMOCRACY IN AMERICA 280 (P. Bradley ed. 1945) (emphasis added).

be because of their office, are beyond the reach of political considerations....

"There can be little doubt," the Justice concluded somewhat sadly, "but that the former, broader role of the Supreme Court is the one currently in vogue, and that it is resulting in the accomplishment of basic changes in governmental relationships." [2]

Some observers would have us believe that the participation of judges in politics began after the constitutional revolution of 1937. A *Wall Street Journal* writer declares: "Judicial activism had its genesis in the Supreme Court about twenty-five years ago." [3] Professor Bickel of the Yale Law School, unearthing de Tocqueville's ages-old discovery, tells us that the Warren Court is "wrongly political," bringing its "power actively and imaginatively to bear on numerous vital issues of the day." "It has been political," Bickel observes, "after the fashion of a legislature or executive rather than a court." [4]

All inferences to the contrary notwithstanding, the judiciary has always been an instrument of government, actively involved in politics, not "a unique body of impervious legal technicians above and beyond the political struggle." [5] "Courts ought not to enter [the] political thicket," [6] Justice Frankfurter implored in 1946. The warning came too late, for the Justices had been firmly entrenched since *Marbury v. Madison*.[7] Separation of powers, the main doctrinal support for judicial review, is infinitely and even paradoxically complex. Chief Justice Marshall invoked it in support of the Court's power to set aside acts of Congress repugnant to the Constitution. Pennsylvania's Judge Gibson used the same principle to refute judicial review, arguing that "every power by which one organ of government is enabled to control the other" [8] is inescapably political. For Gibson the line between judicial *review* and judicial *supremacy* is too fine to be identified or scrupulously observed. To lessen the risk that judicial review may be-

[2] U. S. News & World Report, Dec. 18, 1967, at 36.

[3] Cummerford, *Judicial Jumble: Activism as Threat to 'Government of Laws and Not of Men,'* Wall Street Journal, April 22, 1968, at 18, col. 4.

[4] Bickel, *Is the Warren Court Too 'Political'?* N.Y. Times, Sept. 25, 1966, § 6 (Magazine) at 130.

[5] M. Shapiro, Law and Politics in the Supreme Court 15 (1964).

[6] Colgrove v. Green, 328 U.S. 549 (1946).

[7] 5 U.S. (1 Cranch) 137 (1803).

[8] Eakin v. Raub, 12 S. & R. 330, 348 (Pa. 1825) (Gibson, J., dissenting).

come a "proud pre-eminence" (Gibson's expression), the Court has proclaimed certain ground rules designed to keep it within bounds.[9]

For Chief Justice Marshall judicial review carried both positive and negative connotations. He did not want to be remembered either for having sought "to enlarge the judicial power beyond its proper bounds," *or* for having "*feared to carry it to the fullest extent duty required.*" [10] During a period of agrarianism he established enduring foundations of national power, and therefore deserves to be celebrated as much, if not more, for *McCulloch v. Maryland*[11] as for *Marbury v. Madison.* The Chief Justice felt compelled by duty and by solemn obligation to enforce Article I, Section 10 strictly. He called it a "bill of rights for the people of each state." [12]

Judicial activism continued after Marshall's passing. Whether or not it helped to precipitate the Civil War, the Taney Court's decision in *Dred Scott*[13] is the prototype of the transformation of a hotly debated political issue into a constitutional question for resolution by the judiciary. In 1896 seven Supreme Court Justices put "separate but equal" [14] into the Constitution. In 1954 nine Justices took it out.[15] Each of these decisions illustrates a form of judicial activism—one negative, restricting human freedom; the other positive, enlarging it.

Now as in the past, critics of activism do not come solely from without the councils of the judiciary. The Justices themselves feed the fires of controversy. Justice Harlan denounced the Court's "one man, one vote" command as "a piece of political ideology," "an experiment in venturesome constitutionalism," "profoundly ill-advised and constitutionally impermissible." [16] Justice Byron White deplored the 1966 decision laying down restrictive rules governing police in questioning a suspect in custody, and predicted that "[i]n some unknown number of cases the Court's [new rules] will return a killer, a rapist or other criminal to the streets . . . to repeat his crime." [17]

---

9 Justice Brandeis, concurring in Ashwander v. TVA, 297 U.S. 288, 346 (1936), listed certain "cautionary considerations."

10 Letter from Marshall to Story, October 12, 1831, *quoted in* 4 A. Beveridge, The Life of John Marshall 522 (1919) (emphasis added).

11 17 U.S. (4 Wheat.) 316 (1819).

12 Fletcher v. Peck, 10 U.S. (6 Cranch) 87, 138 (1810).

13 Scott v. Sandford, 60 U.S. (19 How.) 393 (1857).

14 Plessy v. Ferguson, 163 U.S. 537 (1896).

15 Brown v. Board of Educ., 347 U.S. 483 (1954).

16 Reynolds v. Sims, 377 U.S. 533, 590, 625, 624 (1964) (Harlan, J., dissenting).

17 Miranda v. Arizona, 384 U.S. 436, 542 (1966) (White, J., dissenting).

Nor do harsh indictments stem solely from so-called judicial neutralists—from Justices dedicated to judicial self-restraint. In several major decisions of recent years Justice Black, after spending most of his twenty-five years on the bench as an activist, has parted company with superactivist Justice William O. Douglas. Justice Black has not become an avowed exponent of the judicial self-restraint gospel in a full-blown Frankfurterian sense; in other words, he is no particular advocate of the Court's imposition of institutional restraints upon the reaching of constitutional issues.[18] But as the tone of his dissent in *Tinker v. Des Moines School District*[19] indicates, Justice Black has reacted vigorously—some might say almost violently—to assertions that the Court should extend positive constitutional protection to certain types of activity. Thus, although Black himself has been at pains to explain his alleged about-face,[20] certain commentators have moved the aging New Deal Justice from the liberal to the conservative column.[21]

---

[18] "I cannot myself subscribe to the view that judges should always and invariably avoid a determination of constitutional questions if it is in any way possible to dispose of a particular case on a nonconstitutional ground." H. Black, A Constitutional Faith 15 (1968). Noteworthy is his vote with the majority in Flast v. Cohen, 392 U.S. 83 (1968), where the Court, over Justice Harlan's lone dissent, held that a federal taxpayer had standing to challenge a statute on the ground that it violated the establishment clause of the first amendment despite the long-standing rule in Frothingham v. Mellon, 262 U.S. 447 (1923), that a federal taxpayer is without standing to challenge a federal statute.

[19] 89 S. Ct. 733, 741 (1969). The *Tinker* majority held a public high school's ban on its students' wearing of black armbands, in protest against the Vietnam war, violative of the first amendment's freedom of expression guarantee as applied to the states through the fourteenth amendment. Justice Black felt the holding either a judicial usurpation of the power to control pupils, *id.* at 742, or a "surrender" of "control of the American public school system to . . . students." *Id.* at 746. He viewed the majority opinion as based upon a "reasonableness" concept which "prevailed in this Court for a season"—the pre-1937 period of negative economic activism. *Id.* at 743. The wearing of the armbands and "comments, warnings by other students, the poking of fun at them, and a warning by an older football player that other, non-protesting students had better let them alone. . . ." *id.* at 742, were apparently equated by Justice Black with "break-ins, sit-ins, lie-ins, and smash-ins. . . ." *Id.* at 746.

[20] As to the timing of his Carpentier lectures, Justice Black remarked:

> As things have turned out, I think perhaps it is fortunate that I gave the lectures in 1968 in light of current comments that I have changed my views, with the implication that I am now deciding constitutional issues differently from the way I would have several years ago.

H. Black, *supra* note 18, at xiv.

The burden of Black's lectures is to demonstrate that the Court, not he, has changed. For a perceptive appraisal, see Howard, *Mr. Justice Black: The Negro Protest Movement and the Rule of Law*, 53 Va. L. Rev. 1030 (1967).

[21] Commission on Law and Social Action of the Am. Jewish Cong., Civil Rights

Such cleavages are not new. Black's charges against judicial activism, new style, echo the criticism Justices Holmes, Brandeis and Stone hurled against an earlier brand of judicial politics. Then as now, dissenters accused the majority of reading their predilections into the Constitution. There is a difference, however—an important one. Prior to 1937, the Justices fashioned around the "due process" clauses and other constitutional provisions a penumbra of *economic* theory to defeat regulation of the economy. Chief Justice Warren's Court has embellished the Constitution, particularly the Bill of Rights and the fourteenth amendment, with *political* theory—the doctrine of egalitarianism—to protect and promote civil liberties.

Negative Activism

Judicial activism can be and indeed has been negative, defeating the governing process, as well as positive and creative. The greatest period of judicial pre-eminence in the Court's history occurred during the years 1890-1937. In 1893 Justice David J. Brewer doffed judicial robes for an address[22] before the New York Bar Association. Various populist movements were then on the march. Justice Brewer cited "the Black flag of anarchism, flaunting destruction of property," and the "red flag of socialism, inviting a redistribution of property." "Power," the Justice commented soberly, "always chafes at but needs restraint." Individual liberty was endangered by "the mere weight of numbers," by the "so-called demand of the majority." The awful truth Edmund Burke voiced in 1790—"liberty, when men act in bodies, is power" [23]—was alarmingly evident both in labor organizations and legislatures.

"Here there is no monarch threatening to trespass upon the individual," Brewer observed. "The danger is from the multitude—the majority, with whom is the power." Labor organizations were destroying "the freedom of the laborer," and controlling "the use of capital." Legislatures were regulating charges for the use of property, thus destroying its value. Taking into account the move afoot "to minimize the power of Courts" and block "judicial interference," the Justice asked, "What should be done?" "My reply is," he retorted emphatically, "strengthen the judiciary"—that is, judicial activism.

---

and Civil Liberties Decisions of the United States Supreme Court for the 1967-1968 Term at 3 (October, 1968).

22 Brewer, *The Nation's Safeguard*, 16 Report of the New York State Bar Ass'n 37-47 (1893). In this connection, see B. Twiss, Lawyers and the Constitution (1942).

23 E. Burke, Reflections on the Revolution in France 9 (1790).

"The argument is," Brewer explained, "that judges are not adapted by their education and training" to settle complex social and economic issues. "The great body of judges," he insisted, are "well versed in the affairs of life." They must determine "what is *right* and *wrong* between employer and employees." They must decide whether "proposed rates of freight and fare are reasonable as between the public and the owners." "While as for speed," Brewer remarked, accurately foreshadowing a favorite judicial device for "settling" labor disputes, "is there anything quicker than a writ of injunction?"

No untoward consequences could be expected to follow from the Court's assumption of a policy-determining function, Brewer reassured, since the people are unaware that courts possess such power. Judges are, in any event, relatively immune to popular pressure. "Somehow or other men always link the idea of justice with that of the judge." Other governmental agencies "more readily and more freely yield to the pressure of numbers, that so-called demand of the majority." Not so the judge. He, knowing that "nothing can disturb his position, does not hesitate promptly to 'lay judgment to the line and righteous to the plummet.' "

Unless majorities in the legislature and at the ballot box were thus restrained, Justice Brewer foresaw "the departure from this western continent of government of the people, by the people and for the people." For Brewer, ironically, the organ of government closest to the legitimate will of the people was the body furthest removed, in an electoral capacity, from them—the United States Supreme Court. Even as he urged the Court to expand the range of its authority, Brewer insisted: "There is nothing in this power of the Judiciary detracting in the least from the idea of government of and by the people. The Courts hold neither purse nor sword; they cannot corrupt nor arbitrarily control. They make no laws, they establish no policy, they never enter into the domain of popular action. They do not govern. Their functions in relation to the States are limited to seeing that popular action does not trespass upon right and justice as it exists in written constitutions and natural law."

At the same time that Justice Brewer was exhorting judges to enter "the political thicket" lest republican government vanish from the earth, James Bradley Thayer was urging them to stay out, arguing that judicial self-restraint would leave "to our courts a great and stately jurisdiction." "It will only imperil the whole of it," he warned, "if it is sought to give them more." Amid clamor for judicial activism this advice was ignored. Nearly fifty years later Thayer's prophecy was all but realized.

Inspired by Brewer's plea for judicial intervention, and in the face of the informed judgment of eminent lawyers and judges urging judicial self-restraint, the Court slowed the march of social democracy. Though there were sporadic attempts to curb the judiciary, inspired by Teddy Roosevelt and Robert M. LaFollette, judicial usurpation was not seriously challenged until 1937. Even then, for reasons Brewer explored, its popular prestige remained high. Having ignored Flaubert's subtle warning—*il ne faut pas toucher aux idoles; la dorure en reste aux mains*—F. D. R. and his Court-packing proposal ran into heavy opposition. Overnight Supreme Court Justices were pictured as demigods high above the sweaty crowd, objectively weighing public policy on the delicate scales of law. The same lawmakers who, prior to Roosevelt's assault, demanded the scalps of reactionary Justices turned angrily against the President. Closing ranks with bar associations, the press lined up against Court-packing.

In the nineteen thirties, the Court precipitated a crisis by *negative* action which defeated the power to govern at all levels. Chief Justice Hughes had predicted a stepping up of the Court's activist role. "We have entered," he wrote in 1928, "upon an era of regulation with a great variety of legislative proposals, constantly multiplying governmental contacts with the activities of industry and trade. These proposals raise more frequently than in the past questions of National, as opposed to State power. If our dual system with its recognition of local authority in local concerns is worth maintaining, judicial review is likely to be of increasing value." [24] The Chief Justice had conjured up the lethal weapon of "dual federalism." In a single term (1935-36) his Court set aside eleven congressional acts, stalling government action amid economic crisis "more serious than war."

The 1950's and '60's have witnessed another period of judicial activism and evoked another drive against judicial "usurpation." Though its avowed objective is to strengthen democracy and promote human dignity, the Court's popularity is perhaps at its lowest ebb. In June 1968, 53 percent of those questioned by the Gallup Poll were unfavorably disposed toward the Court.[25] "One wonders," Archibald Cox suggests, "whether the gulf between the Supreme Court and the Congress is not

---

[24] C. Hughes, The Supreme Court of the United States 96 (1928).

[25] Commission on Law and Social Action, *supra* note 21, at 1.

partly a reflection of the closer kinship the Justices have with the intellectual community." [26]

The Warren Court is under attack for *positive* assertion of power and responsibility, for *creative* action on behalf of both civil liberties and the political process itself. Emerging from this new dispensation of judicial activism is a more sophisticated theory of the judicial function.

Judicial Review in Transition

In the minds of most Americans, judicial review is essentially negative and limiting.[27] Whenever government enters a new field the natural question is whether the action taken is constitutional, suggesting that the brakes of our constitutional machinery are more important than the ignition system, more essential than the freedom-generating functions of government. Writing in 1921, at a time when Brewer's image of a "strengthened judiciary" was almost fully realized, Judge Benjamin Cardozo stressed the positive aspect of constitutional interpretation:

> The restraining power of the judiciary does not manifest its chief worth in the few cases in which the legislature has gone beyond the lines that mark the limits of discretion. Rather shall we find its chief worth in making vocal and audible the ideals that might otherwise be silenced, in giving them continuity of life and of expression, in guiding and directing choice within the limits where choice ranges.[28]

Judicial review conceived of primarily as a barrier against governing is a comparative newcomer. Dating only from the 1890's, it reached a high point in the 1930's. The 1937 impasse between Court and legislature, "tying Uncle Sam up in a hard knot," [29] as Justice Harlan Fiske Stone put it, provoked President Roosevelt's disingenuous proposal.

---

26 A. Cox, The Warren Court: Constitutional Decision as an Instrument of Reform 14 (1968).

27 Deploring this emphasis, Justice Frankfurter observed:

> Preoccupation by our people with the constitutionality, instead of with the wisdom, of legislation or of executive action is preoccupation with a false value . . . . Focusing attention on constitutionality tends to make constitutionality synonymous with wisdom.

Dennis v. United States, 341 U.S. 494, 555-56 (1951) (Frankfurter, J., concurring). Frankfurter had voiced these sentiments in 1925. New Republic, June 17, 1925, *reprinted in* Law and Politics 197 (A. MacLeish & E. F. Pritchard ed. 1939).

28 B. Cardozo, The Nature of the Judicial Process 94 (1921).

29 *Quoted in* A. Mason, The Supreme Court from Taft to Warren 99 (1968).

Under F.D.R.'s lash the Justices lifted the blockade they had themselves imposed. On the altar of "judicial self-restraint" the peculiarly American principle of constitutional limitations apparently crumbled. The new dissenting Justices, deposed from their high perch, were in a gloomy mood. "The Constitution is gone,"[30] Justice McReynolds exploded. "If the provisions of the Constitution be not upheld when they pinch as well as when they comfort," Justice Sutherland implored fatalistically, "they may as well be abandoned."[31] The Constitution of McReynolds and Sutherland was indeed gone—the Constitution of 1890-1937 that pinched, the Constitution that prevented government from governing. Judicial activism, old style, was dead.

"It is no exaggeration to say," Frank J. Hogan of New York wrote in 1939, "that . . . what were frankly termed 'important shifts in constitutional doctrines' were in fact the most devastating destruction of constitutional limitations." In a reverential mood, Hogan prayed that the "ringing dissents" of McReynolds, Butler and Sutherland would again become rules of decision.[32] Mr. Hogan's prayers have gone unanswered. Instead the Court now safeguards values other than property, enforces other constitutional limitations, embraces a new brand of judicial activism.

These dismal prognosticators misinterpreted the events of 1937, misrepresented the Supreme Court's role in American politics, and misunderstood its authority to invalidate or to legitimize. In *The Federalist* No. 51, Madison declared:

> In framing a government which is to be administered by men over men, the great difficulty lies in this: you must first enable the government to control the governed; and in the next place oblige it to control itself. *A dependence on the people is, no doubt, the primary control on the government; but experience has taught mankind the necessity of auxiliary precautions.*[33]

By 1937, the Court had become what the Founding Fathers never intended it to be—the primary rather than an "auxiliary" check. Under

---

[30] Sherbrooke Daily Record, Feb. 20, 1935, at 4.

[31] Home Bldg. & Loan Ass'n v. Blaisdell, 290 U.S. 398, 483 (1934) (Sutherland, J., dissenting).

[32] Hogan, *Important Shifts in Constitutional Doctrines*, 25 A.B.A.J. 630 (1939).

[33] The Federalist No. 51 (Madison), *quoted in* A. Mason, Free Government in the Making 306 (3d ed. 1965) (emphasis added).

F.D.R.'s attack the judiciary relinquished what it had usurped. The Court did not abdicate from a rightfully acquired throne.

The New Activism

After 1937, the Supreme Court's position was not unlike that of an opposition political party that finally wins an election. Erstwhile dissenting Justices, advocates of judicial self-restraint, were now in the majority, but they had yet to formulate a program. Professor Corwin of Princeton suggested a new kind of judicial surveillance. Having abandoned guardianship of property, Corwin speculated, the Court would thereafter "be free, as it has not in many years, to support the humane values of free thought, free utterance and fair play." [34] Corwin predicted that the Court's surrender of its self-acquired role as protector of economic privilege would allow the Justices "to give voice to the conscience of the country." [35]

One can almost see Justice Harlan Fiske Stone, leader of the drive for judicial self-restraint before 1937, sitting down in 1938 with his law clerk, Louis Lusky, now Professor of Law at Columbia, pondering the new directions in which the Court should move. If the baby was not to be thrown out with the bath, the Court should become concerned with other values. The upshot of such cogitation was the three-paragraphed *Carolene Products* footnote of 1938.[36] In it Justice Stone suggested special judicial scrutiny—in other words, judicial activism—in three important areas: encroachments on first amendment freedoms; government action impeding or corrupting the political process; and acts affecting adversely the rights of racial, religious or national minorities. The limits of judicial self-restraint are reached when first amendment freedoms are encroached upon, when the rights of minorities are infringed, when the political process itself is thwarted.

One of the ironies of recent judicial history is that the activists of the 1950's and '60's—Warren, Brennan, Douglas, and Fortas—are the spiritual successors of avid pre-1937 supporters of self-restraint—Holmes, Brandeis and Stone. It seems ironical that Justice Stone, an eloquent exponent of judicial self-restraint in the late 1920's and early 1930's, should have formulated in a footnote the theoretical foundations of today's judicial activism.

---

[34] Corwin, *Statesmanship on the Supreme Court*, 9 Am. Scholar 159, 163 (1940).
[35] E. Corwin, Constitutional Revolution, Ltd. 112 (1941).
[36] United States v. Carolene Prods. Co., 304 U.S. 144, 152-53 n.4 (1938).

With banners reversed, a veritable war goes on within the councils of the judiciary. Upholding the constitutional jurisprudence identified with the late Justice Frankfurter, Justice Harlan deplores the majority's mad rush to expand the Bill of Rights, to bring an ever-increasing number of its provisions under the due process clause of the fourteenth amendment and to apply the equal protection clause in ways never envisioned for it—all at the expense, he says, of federalism and separation of powers. For Justice Harlan the reapportionment decisions "cut deeply into the fabric of our federalism." [37] Extending to accused persons in state courts the safeguards available to them in federal jurisdiction is denounced as "historically and constitutionally unsound and incompatible with the maintenance of our federal system . . . ." [38] Judicial censorship of obscene and indecent literature encroaches, Harlan complains, on the "prerogative of the States to differ on their ideas of morality," denying both nation and states the advantage of having fifty laboratories of experimentation for trying out "different attitudes toward the same work of literature." [39]

Harlan's primary target is Chief Justice Warren himself, who holds with Jefferson that the Bill of Rights is "the heart of any constitution." [40] "We are accustomed," Justice Harlan observes, "to speak of the Bill of Rights and the Fourteenth Amendment as the principal guarantees of personal liberty. Yet it would surely be shallow not to recognize that the structure of our political system accounts no less for the free society we have." The Founding Fathers "staked their faith that liberty would prosper in the new nation not primarily upon declarations of

---

37 Reynolds v. Sims, 377 U.S. 533, 624 (1964) (Harlan, J., dissenting).

38 Pointer v. Texas, 380 U.S. 400, 409 (1965) (Harlan, J., concurring).

39 Roth v. United States, 354 U.S. 476, 505-06 (1956) (Harlan, J., dissenting). "I am not bothered," Justice Black writes, "by the argument that applying the Bill of Rights to the states interferes with our concept of federalism in that it may prevent states from trying novel social and economic experiments. I have never believed that under the guise of federalism the states should be able to experiment with the protections afforded our citizens through the Bill of Rights." BLACK, *supra* note 18, at 40.

In Pointer v. Texas, 380 U.S. 400, 414 (1965), Justice Goldberg, concurring, said:

> To deny to the States the power to impair a fundamental constitutional right is not to increase federal power, but, rather, to limit the power of both federal and state governments in favor of safeguarding the fundamental rights and liberties of the individual. In my view this promotes rather than undermines the basic policy of avoiding excess concentration of power in government, federal or state, which underlies our concepts of federalism.

40 E. WARREN, *Address to the Legislative Joint Interior Committee on Constitutional Revision and its Advisory Committee*, in THE PUBLIC PAPERS OF CHIEF JUSTICE EARL WARREN 7 (H. Christman ed. 1959).

individual rights but upon the kind of government the Union was to have." "No view of the Bill of Rights or interpretation of any of its provisions," the Justice warns, "which fails to take due account of [federalism and separation of powers] can be considered constitutionally sound." [41]

In his persistent campaign to stem the rising tide of judicial activism under the Bill of Rights, Justice Harlan has won qualified support from Justice Black. The famous anti-contraceptive case, *Griswold v. Connecticut*,[42] revealed a certain kinship between the two Justices, although Harlan voted with the majority. Outlawing the statute, the Court's spokesman, Justice Douglas, invoked Amendments 1, 3, 4, 5, 6, 9, and 14. In none was there a specific bar against the Connecticut law; Douglas found the constitutional killer in the "right of privacy, in penumbras, formed by emanations from those guarantees that give them life and substance." "We do not sit," he observed, "as a super-legislature to determine the wisdom, need, and propriety of laws that touch economic problems, business affairs, or social conditions. This law, however, operates directly on an intimate relation of husband and wife and their physician's role in one aspect of that relation." [43] The implication was that the Court *does sit* as a super-legislature in safeguarding the penumbral right of privacy.

In dissent Justice Black denied that the Founding Fathers intended the Court to have "such awesome powers"; he condemned as shocking any doctrine that would "make of this Court's members a day-to-day constitutional convention." "I like my privacy as well as the next one," the eighty-two-year-old Justice commented feelingly, "but I am nevertheless compelled to admit that government has a right to invade it unless prohibited by some specific constitutional provision." [44]

Linked by this conceptual chain of substantive restraint, the two Justices joined in a series of "sit-in" and "stand-in" cases. In conflict were values enjoying high priority—the rights of property and freedom of speech. Dissenting against the Court's reversal of Louisiana's conviction of five young black men involved in a "stand-in" protest in a public library, Black, joined by Clark, Harlan and Stewart, vigorously objected

---

41 Address by John M. Harlan at the Dedication of the Bill of Rights Room, New York City, Aug. 9, 1964.

42 381 U.S. 479 (1965).

43 *Id.* at 482.

44 *Id.* at 510 (Black, J., dissenting).

both to the dimensions Justice Fortas accorded the right of protest and to the equation of that right with freedom of speech:

> It is high time to challenge the assumption in which too many people have too long acquiesced, that groups that think they have been mistreated or that have actually been mistreated have a constitutional right to use the public's streets, buildings, and property to protest whatever, wherever, whenever they want, without regard to whom such conduct may disturb.[45]

Harlan and Black joined again in dissenting from the 1966 decision outlawing Virginia's poll tax under the equal protection clause. "[W]hen a 'political theory' embodied in our Constitution becomes outdated," Justice Black challenged, "it seems to me that a majority of the nine members of this Court are not only without constitutional power but are far less qualified to choose a new constitutional political theory than the people of this country proceeding in the manner provided in Article V [for amending the Constitution]." [46] Also in dissent, Justices Harlan and Stewart implicitly equated the majority's decision with the usurpations of the pre-1937 Court:

> [I]t is all wrong . . . for the Court to adopt the political doctrine popularly accepted at a particular moment of our history and to declare all others to be irrational and invidious . . . . It was not too long ago that Mr. Justice Holmes felt impelled to remind the Court that the Due Process Clause of the Fourteenth Amendment does not enact the *laissez-faire* theory of society . . . . The times have changed, and perhaps it is appropriate to observe that neither does the Equal Protection Clause of that Amendment rigidly impose upon America an ideology of unrestrained egalitarianism.[47]

One hears such sweeping indictments on all sides. The Justices are accused of being "result-oriented" and of substituting their view of the good society for that of Congress. They are charged with destroying the federal system and writing political and sociological rather than legal opinions. They have been called everything from coddlers of criminals to poor judicial craftsmen.

---

45 Brown v. Louisiana, 383 U.S. 131, 162 (1966) (Black, J., dissenting).

46 Harper v. Virginia Bd. of Elections, 383 U.S. 663, 678 (1965) (Black, J., dissenting).

47 *Id.* at 686 (Harlan, J., dissenting).

Evaluating the New Activism

In an imprecise sense, judicial history is repeating itself. The Warren Court's dramatic intervention into the governing process echoes the boldness of the 1890-1937 Court. The articulate trio of Holmes, Brandeis and Stone dissented vigorously then; there are equally vigorous dissenters now. But here the parallel ends, for the goals of the two activisms are markedly different. The interests protected between 1890 and 1937 were primarily property and contract rights. Though not so labeled, these were the preferred freedoms. The Warren Court's activism concerns another category of preferred freedoms—human rights and human dignity. This distinction raises hard questions:

1. Can a rationale be fashioned for greater judicial alertness to restrictions on the political process, including speech, press, assembly and the right to vote, than to legislation regulating the economy?

2. Is it reasonable to censure judicial activism on behalf of economic interests and applaud more searching scrutiny of encroachments on first amendment and other Bill of Rights freedoms?

3. Does our political heritage accord weightier sanction to the part the Warren Court has played in fostering a revolution designed to promote human equality than to the 1890-1937 Court's activist role in halting a revolution that sought to make government an instrument of reform?

4. Can the Supreme Court, a politically non-responsible body, block the will of the majority in the name of minorities and still be considered a democratic institution?

It is hard to believe that anyone today could convincingly defend the judicial activism which resulted in 1937's self-defeating impasse between Court, Congress and President. The Hughes Court's approach was negative and restrictive rather than positive and creative. With a limited vision of things to come, Old Deal Justices impeded rather than facilitated the governing process. But the question remains whether the type of judicial activism fostered under Chief Justice Warren's leadership is any more defensible.

Tenets and Title Deeds

After 1937, political control—the ballot box—became the primary check on government. For the correction of abuse of power under laws touching economic relations, business affairs or social conditions, complainants were asked to appeal to the polls, not to the courts. In 1963, Justice Black noted that

> The doctrine that prevailed in *Lochner*, *Coppage*, *Adkins*, *Burns*, and like cases—that due process authorizes courts to hold laws unconstitutional when they believe the legislature has acted unwisely—has long since been discarded. We have returned to the original constitutional proposition that courts do not substitute their social and economic beliefs for the judgment of legislative bodies, who are elected to pass laws.[48]

Meanwhile, government intervention in our economic life mounted, making the equitable and unimpeded functioning of the political process more crucial than ever before. Therefore judicial self-restraint would have been peculiarly inappropriate in the re-apportionment cases. "[T]he case for self-restraint rests," Professor Auerback observes, "on the assumption that the Court is reviewing the legislative acts of representatives who are put in office and can be turned out of office by a majority of the people. Since the malapportionment destroys this assumption, judicial intervention to remove this obstacle to majority rule may be less intolerable than the self-perpetuation of minority rule." [49]

Even if true majority rule exists, informed political correctives are impossible in a climate of opinion which discourages free exchange of ideas. Americans were determined to decide political questions for themselves. "Instead of looking on discussion as a stumbling-block in the way of action," they, like the Athenians, considered it "an indispensable preliminary to any wise action at all." [50] Voting is patently basic, but without equal opportunity to utilize the crucial preliminaries to constituent choice—speech, press, assembly, petition and right of association—government by consent becomes an empty declamation. Where these basic rights are involved, judicial self-restraint is defensible only if one assumes the reliability, rationality and availability of the

---

48 Ferguson v. Skrupa, 372 U.S. 726, 730 (1963).

49 Auerbach, *The Reapportionment Cases: One Person, One Vote—One Vote, One Value*, 1964 Sup. Ct. Rev. 1, 2, *quoted in* Wright, *The Role of the Supreme Court in a Democratic Society—Judicial Activism or Restraint?*, 54 Corn. L. Rev. 1, 20 (1968).

50 Pericles, *Funeral Oration*, in Thucydides, The Peloponnesian War (R. Crawley transl. 1910). *Compare* Wilkinson v. United States, 365 U.S. 399, 422 (1961) (Black, J., dissenting); Beauharnais v. Illinois, 343 U.S. 250, 287 (1952) (Douglas, J., dissenting); Dennis v. United States, 341 U.S. 494, 585-86 (1951) (Douglas, J., dissenting); Whitney v. California, 274 U.S. 357, 372-80 (1927) (Brandeis, J., concurring).

political process as a recourse against abuse of power. In the eyes of those who framed the Constitution this was not a reasonable expectation. "Recognizing the occasional tyrannies of governing majorities," Brandeis observed, "[the framers] amended the Constitution so that free speech and assembly should be guaranteed." [51]

"The very purpose of a Bill of Rights," Justice Jackson commented, "was to withdraw certain subjects from the vicissitudes of political controversy, to place them beyond the reach of majorities and officials and to establish them as legal principles to be applied by Courts." [52] Jackson's words underscore the inexorable connection between government by popular choice and the vigorous protection of the rights of all the people to place their arguments before their fellow constituents. Free election between different points of view obviously cannot exist if those who hold to one side and who obtain power through the elective process control the only avenues through which dissidents can express themselves. Thus for Jackson the unelected, independent judiciary is the body to enforce the Constitution's safeguards.

The special responsibility Justices Brandeis and Jackson claimed for the judiciary in the enforcement of the Bill of Rights finds ample support in what was said and done during the formative years of our history. When anti-federalists urged adoption of a bill of rights during the debates on ratification of the Constitution, Jefferson was the proposal's leading advocate. Jefferson never endorsed James Wilson's and Alexander Hamilton's view that "a bill of rights was not necessary because all is reserved in the case of the general government which is not given . . . ." On the contrary, Jefferson held that "a bill of rights is what the people are entitled to against every government on earth, general or particular, and what no just government should refuse, or rest on inference." [53]

Initially, Madison had not considered "omission [of a bill of rights]

---

[51] Whitney v. California, 274 U.S. 357, 376 (1927) (Brandeis, J., concurring).

[52] West Virginia Bd. of Educ. v. Barnette, 319 U.S. 624, 638 (1942). *Compare* Letter from Madison to E. Randolph, May 31, 1789, 5 The Writings of James Madison 381 (G. Hunt ed. 1904). Madison stated:

> [T]he great object in view is to limit and qualify the powers of Government, by excepting out of the grant of power those cases in which the Government ought not to act, or to act only in a particular mode. They point these exceptions sometimes against the abuse of the Executive power, sometimes against the Legislative, and, in some cases, against the community itself; or, in other words, against the majority in favor of the minority.

[53] Letter from Jefferson to Madison, Dec. 20, 1787, in 12 The Papers of Thomas Jefferson 440 (J. Boyd ed. 1955).

a material defect, nor been anxious to supply it even by subsequent amendment, for any other reason than that it is anxiously desired by others." [54] By 1789, Madison had become Jefferson's convert. In voicing his "great satisfaction," Jefferson observed: "In the arguments in favor of a declaration of rights, you omit one which has great weight with me, the legal check which it puts into the hands of the judiciary." [55]

Presenting the amendments, known as the Bill of Rights, Madison adopted as his own the argument Jefferson singled out for special emphasis:

> We ought . . . to . . . declare the great rights of mankind secured under this Constitution . . . .
>
> If they are incorporated into the Constitution, independent tribunals of justice will consider themselves in a peculiar manner the guardian of those rights; they will be an impenetrable bulwark against every assumption of power in the Legislative or Executive; they will be naturally led to resist every encroachment upon rights expressly stipulated for in the Constitution by the declaration of rights.[56]

In asserting special responsibility toward the Bill of Rights, the Warren Court plays the activist role Jefferson and Madison envisioned in 1789.

Creative constitutional interpretation has been hindered by two erroneous propositions. Besides the unrealistic notion that Supreme Court judges must not decide political questions, judicial review itself is sometimes considered an alien appendage. Justice Frankfurter became entangled in both these snares. For him the Supreme Court is "nondemocratic" and "inherently oligarchic." [57] Alexander Bickel calls it a "deviant institution in American democracy." [58] Such views should be appraised in the context of our history.

By 1787, the "turbulence and follies of democracy" and unrestrained majority rule had become matters of grave concern. "Excess of democracy" [59] was a major complaint. Immediately preceding the Phila-

[54] Letter from Madison to Jefferson, Oct. 17, 1788, in 14 Papers, *supra* note 53, at 18.

[55] Letter from Jefferson to Madison, Mar. 15, 1789, in Papers, *supra* note 53, at 659.

[56] 1 Annals of Cong. 432, 439 (1834) [1789-90].

[57] AFL v. American Sash & Door Co., 335 U.S. 538, 555 (1949) (Frankfurter, J., concurring).

[58] A. Bickel, The Least Dangerous Branch 18 (1962).

[59] 1 Records of the Federal Convention 48 (rev. ed. 1937). See A. Bickel, *supra* note 58, at 26-27, 31, 48, 51, 205, 512.

delphia Convention, unjust state legislation, in particular, brought into question "the fundamental principle of republican Government, that the majority who rule in such governments are the safest Guardians both of public Good and private rights. . . ." [60] Jefferson observed that "[o]ne hundred and seventy-three despots would surely be as oppressive as one." [61] And in his First Inaugural he commented:

> All, too, will bear in mind this sacred principle, that though the will of the majority is in all cases to prevail, that will to be rightful must be reasonable; that the minority possess their equal rights, which equal law must protect, and to violate would be oppression.[62]

"[A] fear of popular majorities," Professor Corwin wrote, "lies at the very basis of the whole system of judicial review, and indeed our entire constitutional system." [63] To regard judicial review as an interloper is to disregard Madison's famous formulation of the problem of government in *The Federalist* No. 51, and to misrepresent the Court's unique role in its solution. The Constitution establishes free government. Its framers sought "to temper together these opposite elements of liberty and restraint in one consistent work . . . ." [64] Judicial review is but the most conspicuous among several precautionary devices deemed essential to the functioning of the American system of free government. As Justice Jackson said, there is a "basic inconsistency between popular government and judicial *supremacy*." [65] But in the American system of free government, judicial *review* is not a deviant institution. It is an essential adjunct of our free government, "an attempt," Professor Corwin commented pithily, "by the American Democracy to cover its bet." [66]

For the late Justice Frankfurter, an Anglophile obsessed with the virtues of the British system, judicial review was at odds with popular government. It is, of course, but one must remember that the Constitution did not adopt the unchecked legislative supremacy of English par-

---

60 *Observations by James Madison*, in 2 THE WRITINGS OF JAMES MADISON 361, 366 (G. Hunt ed. 1901).

61 *Notes on Virginia*, 2 THE WRITINGS OF THOMAS JEFFERSON 163 (Memorial ed. 1903).

62 Jefferson, *First Inaugural Address*, in 1 MESSAGES AND PAPERS OF THE PRESIDENTS 322 (Richardson ed. 1900).

63 Corwin, *The Supreme Court and the Fourteenth Amendment*, 7 MICH. L. REV. 643, 670 (1909).

64 E. BURKE, *supra* note 23, at 353.

65 R. JACKSON, THE STRUGGLE FOR JUDICIAL SUPREMACY vii (1941).

66 Corwin, *Book Review*, 56 HARV. L. REV. 484, 487 (1942).

liamentarianism.[67] Its goal was not only the preservation of the democratic processes but also the protection of certain freedoms from the majority's will.[68] Success in establishing the second goal is necessary to full achievement of the first. The new activism, according preferred status to certain civil liberties and closer scrutiny of actions impinging upon them, is conceptually and historically sound.[69]

Disavowing originality, Justice Stone found doctrinal support for judicial activism, new style, in the opinions of Marshall, Holmes, Brandeis and Hughes. Popular consent being the foundation of free government, Marshall held that when correction of governmental abuses is not forthcoming from the political process, a heightened responsibility rests on the judiciary.[70] Justice Holmes, expressing the convic-

---

67 In Perez v. Brownell, 356 U.S. 44 (1958) (majority opinion by Frankfurter held the Nationality Act of 1940 constitutional), Justice Douglas, one of four dissenters, gave Justice Frankfurter this stern reminder:

> The philosophy of the opinion that sustains this statute is foreign to our constitutional system. It gives supremacy to the Legislature in a way that is incompatible with the scheme of our written Constitution. A decision such as this could be expected in England where there is no written constitution, and where the House of Commons has the final say. But with all deference, this philosophy has no place here. By proclaiming it we forsake much of our constitutional heritage and move closer to the British scheme. That may be better than ours or it may be worse. Certainly it is not ours.

Id. at 79. Justice Douglas repeated his lecture to Frankfurter on the nature and requirements of the American system of free government in Kingsley Pictures Corp. v. Regents, 360 U.S. 684, 698-99 (1960) (Douglas, J., concurring).

68 *See* Minersville School Dist. v. Gobitis, 310 U.S. 586, 606-07 (1940) (Stone, J., dissenting):

> The Constitution expresses more than the conviction of the people that democratic processes must be preserved at all costs. It is also an expression of faith and a command that freedom of mind and spirit must be preserved, which government must obey, if it is to adhere to that justice and moderation without which no *free government* can exist.

69 In 1941, after transition to the order of judicial activism had been well launched, Robert Jackson, soon to join the Court, reflected:

> There is nothing covert or conflicting in recent judgments of the Court on social legislation and on legislative repressions of civil rights. The presumption of validity which attaches in general to legislative acts is frankly reversed in the case of interferences with free speech and free assembly, and for a perfectly cogent reason. Ordinarily, legislation whose basis in economic wisdom is uncertain can be redressed by the processes of the ballot box or the pressures of opinion. But when the channels of opinion and of peaceful persuasion are corrupted or clogged, these political correctives can no longer be relied on, and the democratic system is threatened at its most vital point. In that event the Court, by intervening, restores the processes of democratic government; it does not disrupt them.

R. Jackson, *supra* note 65, at 284-85.

70 Especially influential on Stone's thinking was the doctrine of political restraints

tion that "the ultimate good desired is better reached by free trade in ideas," called this "the theory of our Constitution." [71] Stone recalled that Justice Holmes believed that judges "should not be too rigidly bound by the tenet of judicial self-restraint in cases involving civil liberties." [72] Justice Brandeis cited "a fundamental principle of American Government" to justify the wide range accorded "freedom to think as you will and to speak as you think," tracing this priority to those "who won our independence," to men who "were not cowards," and "did not fear political change." [73] Finally, Chief Justice Hughes referred to the Bill of Rights as a barrier against "gusts of passion and prejudice which in misguided zeal would destroy the basic interests of democracy. We protect the fundamental rights of minorities, in order to save democratic government from destroying itself by the excesses of its own power." [74]

As Chief Justice, Hughes led a Court which acted on his belief that

---

which Chief Justice Marshall adumbrated in McCulloch v. Maryland, 17 U.S. (4 Wheat.) 316 (1819). Denying the suggestion that every argument which would sustain the right of the general government to tax banks chartered by the states would equally sustain state taxation of national instrumentalities, the Chief Justice explained, *id.* at 435:

> The people of all the States, and the States themselves, are represented in Congress, and, by their representatives, exercise this power. When they tax the chartered institutions of the States, they tax their constituents . . . . But, when a State taxes the operations of the government of the United States, it acts upon institutions created, not by their own constituents, but by people over whom they claim no control.

In other words, where political restraints are not available, as in the case of state taxation of the instrumentalities of the general government, judicial responsibility for providing a corrective is correspondingly heightened.

For illustrations of Justice Stone's use of Marshall's doctrine of political restraints, see Graves v. New York *ex rel.* O'Keefe, 306 U.S. 466 (1939); Helvering v. Gerhardt, 304 U.S. 405, 416 (1938); South Carolina Highway Dept. v. Barnwell Bros., 303 U.S. 177, 184-85 n.2 (1938).

71 Abrams v. United States, 250 U.S. 616, 630 (1919) (Holmes, J., dissenting).

72 Letter from Harlan Fiske Stone to Clinton L. Rossiter, April 12, 1941, *quoted in* A. Mason, Harlan Fiske Stone: Pillar of the Law 516 (1956). Professor Frankfurter noted that Holmes

> attributed very different legal significance to those liberties of the individual which history has attested as the indispensable conditions of a free society from that which he attached to liberties which derived merely from shifting economic arrangements. . . . Because these civil liberties were explicitly safeguarded in the Constitution, or conceived to be basic to any notion of the liberty guaranteed by the Fourteenth Amendment, Mr. Justice Holmes was far more ready to find legislative invasion in this field than in the area of debatable economic reform.

F. Frankfurter, Mr. Justice Holmes and the Supreme Court 51 (1938).

73 Whitney v. California, 274 U.S. 357, 375 (1927) (Brandeis, J., concurring).

74 Proceedings in Commemoration of the 150th Anniversary of the First Congress, H.R. Doc. No. 212, 76th Cong., 1st Sess. 32 (1939).

certain rights, notably speech and press, must be preserved "in order to maintain the opportunity for free political discussion, to the end that government may be responsive to the will of the people and that changes, if desired, may be obtained by peaceful means." "Therein," the Chief Justice declared emphatically, "lies the security of the Republic, the very foundation of constitutional government."[75]

Judge Learned Hand was an ardent exponent of judicial self-restraint. But in 1958, when his name was invoked in support of a bill which sought to deprive the Supreme Court of its appellate jurisdiction in a sizeable group of civil rights cases, Judge Hand wrote Senator Thomas C. Hennings, Jr., Chairman of the Senate Judiciary Committee on Constitutional Rights, that the proposed bill would be "detrimental to the best interests of the United States":

> It seems to me desirable that the Court should have the last word on questions of the character involved. Of course, there is always the chance of abuse of power wherever it is lodged, but at long last the least contentious organ of government generally is the Court. I do not, of course, mean I think it is always right, but some final authority is better than unsettled conflict.[76]

The New Activism Under Fire

As indicated above, the Warren Court's brand of judicial activism has impressive title deeds. Nevertheless, a highly articulate minority, led by Justices Harlan and Black, is convinced that the majority is headed toward the same precipice from which the Hughes Court, under pressure from Congress, the President and the country, narrowly saved itself in 1937.[77]

The current attack indeed recalls F.D.R.'s bombardment. But surely the interests and values involved and the Court's responsibility toward them differ significantly. In 1935-36 a narrow, headstrong majority,

---

[75] DeJonge v. Oregon, 299 U.S. 353, 365 (1937).

[76] L. Hand, The Spirit of Liberty, 300 (3d ed. 1960).

[77] In his dissent in the *Tinker* case, *discussed in* note 19 *supra*, Justice Black stated:

> There was at one time a line of cases holding "reasonableness" as the court saw it to be the test of a "due process" violation. Two cases upon which the Court today heavily relies for striking down these school orders used this test of reasonableness, *Meyers* [sic] *v. Nebraska*, 262 U.S. 390 (1923) and *Bartells v. Iowa*, 262 U.S. 404 (1923). . . . This constitutional test of reasonableness prevailed in this Court for a season. It was this test that brought on President Franklin Roosevelt's well-known Court fight.

Tinker v. Des Moines School Dist., 89 S. Ct. 733, 743 (1969) (Black, J., dissenting).

flounting persistent pleas for judicial self-restraint voiced by a highly esteemed minority, blocked government regulation of the economy. In the hands of an obtuse majority, the Constitution became a strait-jacket rather than what Woodrow Wilson said it should be—"a vehicle of the nation's life." The Warren Court, on the other hand, is expanding the limits of freedom, buttressing the moral foundations of society, keeping open peaceful alternatives to violent change.

Reflecting on the judicial activism of the 1920's, Professor Frankfurter noted:

> That a majority of the Court which frequently disallowed restraints upon economic power should so consistently have sanctioned restraints of the mind is perhaps only a surface paradox. There is an underlying unity between fear of ample experimentation in economics and fear of expression of heretical ideas.[78]

It seems odd that this remarkable insight into the subtleties of judicial activism should not have always enlightened Justice Frankfurter's opinions.

Thanks to the Warren Court the plea implicit in Frankfurter's words has been answered. Ideas, good, bad and indifferent, have a chance to make their influence felt. The Supreme Court provides disgruntled individuals and minorities a peaceful forum in which to air their grievances and perhaps win vindication. Madison and Hamilton did not deny the moral right of revolution, but they argued strenuously that under the proposed constitution the occasions for resort to violence would be reduced to a minimum.[79] John F. Kennedy sensed the Framers' underlying thought: "[T]hose who make peaceful revolution impossible will make violent revolution inevitable."[80]

---

78 F. Frankfurter, *supra* note 72, at 62.

79 *See* A. Mason, The Supreme Court: Palladium of Freedom 41-45 (1962).

80 *Quoted in* T. Sorensen, Kennedy 535 (1965). In his separate opinion in Bell v. Maryland, 378 U.S. 226, 242-45 (1964), Justice Douglas put the late President's thought in a judicial context:

> The people should know that when filibusters occupy other forums, when oppressions are great, when the clash of authority between the individual and the State is severe, they can still get justice in the courts. When we default, as we do today, the prestige of the law in the life of the Nation is weakened.

The increase, especially during the 1967-68 term, of cases in which the Court has refused to face up to the problems of cities, race, poverty and Vietnam, appears strange in an activist Court. See Henkin, *Foreword: The Supreme Court, 1967 Term,* 82 Harv. L. Rev. 63, 88-89 (1968) for a list of cases relating to Vietnam. In the most notable instance, Mora v. McNamara, 389 U.S. 934 (1967), Justices Douglas and Stewart protested

Through judicial review, "revolution" has, in some measure, been domesticated.[81] Change can be and indeed has been accomplished within the four corners of the Constitution. Adolf Berle calls his book on the Warren Court "a report on a revolution." "The unique fact is," Berle writes, "that the revolutionary committee is the Supreme Court of the United States." Far from condemning the Court's exercise of "senior legislative power . . . particularly in the field of education and local government," he believes "it could not have acted otherwise," and maintains that history will probably record that "the Supreme Court's action saved the country from a far more dangerous and disorderly change."[82]

In a free society, majorities—and this is the key point of democratic theory—are in flux. Tomorrow's majority may have a different composition as well as different goals. Defense of the political rights of minorities thus becomes not the antithesis of majority rule but its very foundation. The majority must leave open the political channels by which it can be replaced when it is no longer able to command popular support. The alternative is violent overthrow—revolution. By protecting the integrity and unimpeded operation of the entire process by which majorities are formed, "a bevy of Platonic Guardians"[83] becomes a surrogate for revolution, contributing positively to the preservation of a free society.

New-style judicial activism casts doubt on the accuracy of Justice Frankfurter's dictum that courts are not "a good reflex of a democratic society." More sensitive to recognized wrongs than either the executive or legislative branches of government, the Warren Court "has spear-

---

the majority's denial of certiorari in a case that would have tested the President's power to wage an undeclared war. Three soldiers had rejected duty in Vietnam, contending that the war was illegal and immoral. Said Justice Stewart:

> These are large and deeply troubling questions. . . . We cannot make these problems go away simply by refusing to hear the case of three obscure Army privates. I intimate not even tentative views upon any of these matters, but I think the Court should squarely face them by granting certiorari and setting this case for oral argument.

Id. at 935; *compare* BLACK, *supra* note 18, at 16.

81 Jefferson, in later years a bitter critic of the Court, advocated "[binding] up the several branches of government by certain laws, which, when they transgress, their acts become nullities . . . ." Such a system, he suggested, would "render unnecessary an appeal to the people, or in other words a rebellion, on every infraction of their rights . . . ." *Notes on Virginia*, 2 THE WRITINGS OF THOMAS JEFFERSON 178 (Memorial ed. 1903) (Jefferson was speaking of the government of Virginia).

82 A. BERLE, THE THREE FACES OF POWER vii, viii (1967).

83 L. HAND, THE BILL OF RIGHTS 73 (1958).

headed the progress in civil rights, administration of criminal justice, protection of individual liberty, and the strengthening and extension of political democracy."[84] In the abstract, it would have been better if encroachments on individual freedom such as Connecticut's anti-contraceptive statute, Virginia's poll tax and the police-state methods used in law enforcement, could have been remedied by the state legislatures. But remedies had not been forthcoming and the prospects for their appearance were dim. As in the areas of school desegregation, reapportionment and administration of criminal justice, failure of the states to protect individual liberties or undertake corrective measures drove the Court, sometimes in the face of delimiting precedents, into untrodden fields.

In 1776 Jefferson boldly embraced the faith that society can safely rest on reason and consent, rather than on coercion and force. But while reason and consent are the essential instruments of free government, they do not always suffice. As Archibald Cox writes:

> Social protest and even civil disobedience serve the law's need for growth. Ideally, reform would come according to reason and justice without self-help and disturbing, almost violent, forms of protest. Resort to such pressures is hardly consistent with the ideals of reason and civility. . . . No little cause will justify their action. Still, candor compels one . . . to acknowledge the gap between the ideal and the reality. Short of the millennium, sharp changes in the law depend partly upon the stimulus of protest.[85]

In the 1830's, de Tocqueville identified two possible pitfalls endangering the success of Democracy in America: ignorant change, the unreasoned and unreasonable drive of reformers, radicals and revolutionaries (Justice Holmes called them "upward and onward fellows"); and ignorant opposition to change, refusal on the part of beneficiaries of the status quo "to move altogether for fear of being moved too far."[86] In an earlier age of revolution (1640), George Herbert, recognizing valid claims on both sides, observed: "Reason lies between the spurre

---

84 A. Cox, *supra* note 26, at 4.

85 Cox, *Direct Action, Civil Disobedience, and the Constitution*, in Civil Rights, the Constitution, and the Court 22-23 (1967).

86 *Quoted in* H. S. Commager, *Democracy in America: One Hundred Years After*, N.Y. Times, December 15, 1935, (Magazine), at 15.

and the bridle." [87] In these words, Herbert went to the core of the problem of free government and of constitutional adjudication.

After two generations of debate, civil war settled the nature of the union. Industrial strikes and strife in the early 1900's and riots in the 1960's changed the existing order. "It would be impossible," Brooks Adams observed, "even were it desirable, to bind the country by unaltering laws a century old. It is of little moment whether the meaning of our great charter is slowly construed away by the ingenuity of lawyers, or whether it is roughly thrust aside by force: its fate is sealed; it must yield where it obstructs . . . ." [88]

This inevitable "yielding" is fraught with danger. Our commitment to reason and consent as the legitimate foundation of government was, as Jefferson recalled, a "bold and doubtful election." [89] He had reiterated his confidence in 1801 when the population numbered less than four million. Still at the mercy of foreign powers, America was, Jefferson said, "engaged in commerce with nations who feel power and forget right." [90] We were clearly no match for any nation that might mount an attack. Our strength lay in our "undeviating moral commitment to the idea of a free society." [91] Throwing down the challenge that is still to be tested, Jefferson observed: "If there be any among us who would wish to dissolve this Union or to change its republican form, let them stand undisturbed as monuments of the safety with which error of opinion may be tolerated where reason is left free to combat it." [92]

Thus the issue becomes whether modern America is willing to run the risks to which the Constitution's Framers committed us—dangers inescapable in a free society. Are Americans willing to take the risk that in enforcing the precautions set out in the Bill of Rights to prevent

---

87 THE WORKS OF GEORGE HERBERT, OUTLANDISH PROVERBS (F.E. Hutchinson ed. 1941), *quoted in* Boyd, *Between the Spur and the Bridle*, VA. Q. REV. 191 (Spring 1969).

88 Adams, *The Consolidation of the Colonies*, 55 ATLANTIC MONTHLY 302, 307-08 (1885).

89 Letter from Jefferson to R. Weightman, *quoted in* A. MASON, FREE GOVERNMENT IN THE MAKING 371 (3d ed. 1965).

90 *Quoted in* Boyd, *The Fear of Ideas*, 21 AM. SCHOLAR 413, 417 (1952).

91 *Quoted in* Boyd, *A Perspective View From Monticello*, SWEET BRIAR COLLEGE BULL. 14 (April 1961).

92 Jefferson, *First Inaugural Address*, *quoted in* A. MASON, *supra* note 89, at 379. Dissenting in Gitlow v. New York, 268 U.S. 652, 673 (1925), Justice Holmes echoed Jefferson's faith in a twentieth-century context:

> If in the long run the beliefs expressed in proletarian dictatorship are destined to be accepted by the dominant forces of the community, the only meaning of free speech is that they should be given their chance and have their way.

punishment of the innocent, some criminals will escape?[93] Are we willing to take the chance that dissenters will exceed the bounds of reason? Are we willing, in short, to risk radical change in the organization and structure of government itself? In a simpler agrarian age, Jefferson was willing to take that chance.

Free government's inexorable demands are measured by the periodic departures from it, by the temptation, not always resisted, to adopt the adversary's way as our own. America is now an unmatched military power. Yet the only organ of government articulating a faith commensurate with Jefferson's is the United States Supreme Court under the leadership of Earl Warren. In 1967 Chief Justice Warren declared unconstitutional a section of the Subversive Activities Control Act of 1950 which prohibits any member of a Communist-action organization under a final order to register from engaging in any employment in a defense facility. Speaking for a majority of 6, the Chief Justice observed:

> Implicit in the term "national defense" is the notion of defending those values and ideals which set this Nation apart. . . . It would indeed be ironic if, in the name of national defense, we would sanction the subversion of one of those liberties—the freedom of association—which makes the defense of the Nation worth while.[94]

In the face of this background, certain commentators and Supreme Court Justices resist the positive, creative approach. Carl Swisher insists that "[l]eadership in constitutional development must come through the legislative and executive branches." [95] For him the judicial duty is merely to "refine, restrain, and harmonize . . . . [The Court] cannot safely take over the task of leadership without threat of disaster both for itself and for the country . . . ." [96] Justice Frankfurter declared that the Judiciary is not the place for " 'originators of transforming thought'. . . ." [97] His ideological successor, Justice Harlan, mirrored this declaration in his recent expression of shock at the Court's application

[93] During his CBS television interview, December 3, 1968, Justice Black was asked whether recent Supreme Court decisions had made it more difficult for police to combat crime. "Certainly," the Justice replied firmly. "Why shouldn't they? That is what the Bill of Rights was intended to do." N.Y. Times, Dec. 4, 1968, at 30, col. 3.

[94] United States v. Robel, 389 U.S. 258, 264 (1967).

[95] Swisher, *Dred Scott One Hundred Years After*, 19 Journal of Politics 167, 183 (1957).

[96] *Id.*

[97] Frankfurter, *John Marshall and the Judicial Function*, in Of Law and Men 6 (P. Elman ed. 1956).

of the "one man, one vote" principle to malapportioned local governments:

> I am frankly astonished at the ease with which the Court has proceeded to fasten upon the entire country at its lowest political levels the strong arm of the federal judiciary, let alone a particular political ideology which has been the subject of wide debate and differences from the beginnings of our Nation.[98]

THE PARADOX OF ACTIVISM

Whatever the values involved, judicial activism results in a paradox at the heart of constitutional interpretation. While wearing the magical habiliments of the law, the Justices take sides on controversial issues. The Court must face up to the political implications of judicial review and at the same time keep alive the mystery that it is merely declaring the law.

The occult and power aspects of governing are both essential,[99] but mingling them leads to confusing complexities. The Court is both temple and forum, both symbol and instrument of government. The High Bench is the American counterpart of the British Crown, but unlike a queen on the throne, the court has real power. It can bring Congress, President, state governors and legislators to heel.

To render more palatable this oligarchic, occult element in our politics, Supreme Court Justices, including John Marshall, fostered the notion that judges exercise only judgment, not will. "The thrill is irresistible," Judge Cardozo, tongue-in-cheek, commented on Marshall's famous rationalization; "[w]e feel the mystery and awe of inspired revelation." [100] So the mystery was born and consecrated. It has been

---

98 Avery v. Midland County, 390 U.S. 474, 490 (1968) (Harlan, J., dissenting).

99 Walter Bagehot classifies the institutions of the British government as "efficient" and "dignified," the former being the Cabinet and Parliament, the latter the King or Queen. Those elements in the governing process which "excite most easy reverence," Bagehot writes, "[are] the *theatrical* elements . . . [t]hat which is mystic in its claims; that which is occult in its mode of action." W. BAGEHOT, THE ENGLISH CONSTITUTION 76 (rev. ed. 1872). To regard the Court merely as an instrument of power might limit its effectiveness. "Without a constant and sincere pursuit of the shining but never completely attainable ideal of the rule of law above men," Thurman Arnold writes, "we would not have a civilized government. If that ideal be an illusion, to dispel it would cause men to lose themselves in an even greater illusion, the illusion that personal power can be benevolently exercised." Arnold, *Professor Hart's Theology*, 73 HARV. L. REV. 1298, 1311 (1960).

100 B. CARDOZO, LAW AND LITERATURE 11 (1931). Cardozo's remark was in reaction to

exposed again and again by the Court's own actions, and yet it survives.

The dilemma judicial activism poses bothers lawyers more than it does political scientists.[101] It has been suggested that Herbert Wechsler's famous lecture, *Toward Neutral Principles of Constitutional Law*,[102] reflects the lawyer's nostalgia for legalism, underscores his reluctance to recognize the political nature of the Court's function. "The dilemma is insoluble," Archibald Cox observes. It may be eased, Cox suggests, "by preserving the power of judge-made law to command consent while at the same time changing it to serve the new and newly felt needs of the community and the demands of individual justice." [103]

The difficulty of fusing myth and reality in Supreme Court decisions is measured by the fact that for ammunition against judicial activism, whatever its orientation, the most resourceful arsenal is the dissenting opinion. "Every Justice," the late Justice Jackson observed, "has been accused of legislating and every one has joined in that accusation of others. . . ." [104] In 1937, F.D.R. drew his most telling weapons from the opinions of Brandeis and Stone. And in the 1960's one need not descend to the blunderbuss of George Wallace or Strom Thurmond for criticism of the Court; one need only read the dissenting opinions, particularly those of Justices Black and Harlan.

However, not all the dissenters from the Court's activist opinions are cut from the same mold. The process of constitutional adjudication is a continuous search for the appropriate balance between "reason" and "fiat," between the oft-conflicting imperatives of deciding "according to law" and of acknowledging compelling social needs. The two activist majorities have struck the balance in certain identifiable ways. But the dissenters, past and present, although objecting with equal vigor to what they deemed majorities functioning as naked power organs, have not advocated the same alternatives. The grounds of dissent—by Holmes, Brandeis and Stone on the one hand, and by Black and Harlan on the

---

Marshall's incredible observation: "Judicial power is never exercised for the purpose of giving effect to the will of the Judge; always for the purpose of giving effect to the will of the . . . law." Osborn v. Bank of the United States, 22 U.S. (9 Wheat.) 738, 866 (1824).

101 M. Shapiro, *supra* note 5, at 14. *See* Mason, *Myth and Reality in Supreme Court Decisions*, 48 Va. L. Rev. 1385 (1962); Deutsch, *Neutrality, Legitimacy and the Supreme Court: Some Interactions between Law and Political Science*, 20 Stan. L. Rev. 169 (1968).

102 73 Harv. L. Rev. 1 (1959).

103 A. Cox, *supra* note 26, at 22-23.

104 R. Jackson, The Supreme Court in the American System of Government 80 (Harper Torchbook ed. 1963).

other—offer yet another distinction between judicial activism, old and new.

After the constitutional revolution of the 1890's, the Supreme Court became the arbiter "between the voters on the one hand and the property owners on the other. . . ." [105] As a primary rather than an auxiliary control, the Justices functioned as a third chamber of the legislature. On the basis of vague constitutional imperatives, the Court passed on the wisdom of social and economic policy. It was trying to find a measure for the immeasurable. Justice Holmes, often in dissent, warned judges against stepping into the shoes of lawmakers. For him, as for Chief Justice Waite, "if a state of facts could exist that would justify . . . legislation, it actually did exist when the statute . . . under consideration was passed." [106]

On the other hand, consider Justice Peckham's approach in *Lochner v. New York*.[107] Declaring that "to the common understanding the trade of a baker has never been regarded as an unhealthy one," he denounced regulations as "mere meddlesome interferences." [108] Noting that such legislation was "on the increase," he used the judicial veto to stop it. Many years later, Professor Frankfurter queried Holmes about Justice Peckham's measure of "due process." "You asked me about Peckham," Holmes replied. "I used to say his major premise was God damn it. Meaning thereby that emotional predilections somewhat governed him on social themes." [109]

Peckham's search for a standard stopped at the simplicity of his own convictions; it did not proceed to the complexities of the real world. Louis D. Brandeis, the lawyer and later Supreme Court Justice, had another view of the judicial process. "In our judgment," Peckham had observed in *Lochner*, "it is not possible in fact to discover the connection between the number of hours a baker may work in the bakery

---

105 Hadley, *The Constitutional Position of Property in America*, 64 THE INDEPENDENT 834, 837 (1908).

106 Munn v. Illinois, 94 U.S. 113, 132 (1877). *Compare* Holmes' dissent in Tyson v. Banton, 273 U.S. 418, 446 (1927):

> I think the proper course is to recognize that a state legislature can do whatever it sees fit to do unless it is restrained by some express prohibition in the Constitution of the United States or of the State, and that Courts should be careful not to extend such prohibitions beyond their obvious meaning by reading into them conceptions of public policy that the particular Court may happen to entertain.

107 198 U.S. 45 (1905).

108 *Id.* at 59, 61.

109 Letter from Holmes to Frankfurter, March 28, 1922, *quoted in* A. BICKEL, THE UNPUBLISHED OPINIONS OF MR. JUSTICE BRANDEIS 164 (1957).

and the healthful quality of the bread made by the workman." [110] Three years later Brandeis, appearing as counsel in support of an Oregon hours-of-labor law for women, met Peckham's challenge, proving by recourse to "facts" a relationship between an hours-of-labor statute and the health of women and the human race. Brandeis agreed with Justice Peckham that "no law limiting the liberty of contract ought go beyond necessity." He diverged, however, in his next step. To determine "necessity," logic is not enough. "There is no logic that is properly applicable to the laws except the logic of facts." [111] All the facts, not merely those of common knowledge, are needed.

To be sure, Brandeis placed important limits on the inquiry he advocated. In the decision-making process social data were only one among several factors requiring consideration, and original fact-finding was not a judicial function.[112] But for Brandeis "[k]nowledge is essential to understanding; and understanding should precede judging." [113] It was the duty of counsel to provide such knowledge and that of the Court to regard it as relevant. Furthermore, in the role of dissenter, as in that of counsel, Brandeis would open the "priestly ears" to the call of extra-legal voices. Without exception the opinions he reinforced with social facts and statistics are in dissent.

The essential difference between Brandeis and Peckham is that the former presumed constitutionality, the latter unconstitutionality. However, Brandeis' deference to the legislature must be placed in the context of his times. It should not be taken as proof that social concerns were not relevant to the judicial function. On the contrary, when the Court, in defiance of the presumption of constitutionality or on the basis of its own "facts," interposed its awesome veto, Brandeis admonished: "To stay experimentation in things social and economic is a grave responsi-

---

110 Lochner v. New York, 198 U.S. 45, 62 (1905).

111 5 Hearings of the New York State Factory Investigating Comm'n 2893 (Jan. 22, 1915).

112 Dissenting in Jay Burns Baking Co. v. Bryan, 264 U.S. 504, 534 (1924), Brandeis stated:

> Put at its highest, our function is to determine, in the light of all facts which may enrich our knowledge and enlarge our understanding, whether the measure, enacted in the exercise of an unquestioned police power and of a character inherently unobjectionable, transcends the bounds of reason . . . .
>
> To decide, as [an original] fact, [without the aid of legislature or counsel] that [no reasonable relation exists between the regulation and the end sought] is, in my opinion, an exercise of the powers of a super-legislature—not the performance of the constitutional function of judicial review.

113 Jay Burns Baking Co. v. Bryan, 264 U.S. 504, 520 (1924).

bility. . . . If we would guide by the light of reason, we must let our minds be bold." [114]

Neither did presuming constitutionality mean to Brandeis that the Court was completely removed from the political process. His prodding of the Court to an awareness of the multiple factors governing political decisions indicates the opposite. "Government is not," he said, "an exact science." Therefore when the validity of its use as an instrument of social improvement was in issue, public opinion concerning the evil and the remedy was "among the factors deserving consideration." [115] Brandeis recognized the imprecision inherent in an approach of such depth. "Mr. Brandeis," a friend once asked, "how can you be so sure of your course of action?" "When you are 51 per cent sure," the Justice replied, "then go ahead." [116]

Like his colleague in dissent, Justice Holmes recognized that the judicial function is inescapably political and believed that judges had failed adequately to accept their duty of weighing considerations of social advantage:

> The duty is inevitable, and the result of the often proclaimed judicial aversion to deal with such considerations is simply to leave the very ground and foundation of judgments inarticulate, and often unconscious.[117]

Reflecting on the motivations influencing judicial activism, old style,

---

114 New State Ice Co. v. Liebmann, 285 U.S. 262, 311 (1932).

115 Mason, *The Case of the Overworked Laundress*, in QUARRELS THAT HAVE SHAPED THE CONSTITUTION 190 (J. Garraty ed. 1962).

116 *Id.*

117 O. HOLMES, COLLECTED LEGAL PAPERS 184 (1920). In a similar vein Judge Learned Hand wrote in 1958:

> [J]udges are seldom content merely to annul the particular solution before them; they do not, indeed they may not, say that taking all things into consideration, the legislators' solution is too strong for the judicial stomach. On the contrary they wrap up their veto in a protective veil of adjectives such as "arbitrary," "artificial," "normal," "reasonable," "inherent," "fundamental," or "essential," whose office usually, though quite innocently, is to disguise what they are doing and impute to it a derivation far more impressive than their personal preferences, which are all that in fact lie behind the decision. If we do need a third chamber it should appear for what it is, and not as the interpreter of inscrutable principles.

L. HAND, THE BILL OF RIGHTS 70 (1958). *See also* Powell, *Logic and Rhetoric of Constitutional Law*, in R. MCCLOSKEY, ESSAYS IN CONSTITUTIONAL LAW 89 (1957):

> Judges have preferences for social policies, as you and I. They form their judgments after the varying fashions in which you and I form ours. They have hands, organs, dimensions, senses, affections, passions. They are warmed and cooled by the same winter and summer and by the same ideas as a layman is.

Holmes noted that "[w]hen socialism first began to be talked about, the comfortable classes of the community were a good deal frightened. I suspect that this fear has influenced judicial action . . . ." In other words, fear had prompted judicial activism, leading "people who no longer hope to control the legislatures to look to the courts":

> I cannot but believe that if the training of lawyers led them habitually to consider more definitely and explicitly the social advantage on which the rule they lay down must be justified, they sometimes would hesitate where now they are confident, and see that really they were taking sides upon debatable and often burning questions.[118]

Holmes thought judges needed "education in the obvious—to learn to transcend our own convictions and to leave room for much that we hold dear to be done away with short of revolution by the orderly change of law." [119]

A Plea for Judicial Self-Awareness

In a period of unbridled activism Holmes and Brandeis advocated judicial self-restraint. It is well to remember, however, that their advocacy was based upon well-articulated reasons. The judiciary was busily invalidating progressive economic legislation on excessively visceral grounds. Holmes and Brandeis felt compelled to reply to such action. They suggested that the Court should recognize its role as a partner in the political process[120] and consequently take notice of the social factors necessitating government action. Judicial evaluation of legislation is complex and imprecise; overly simple standards lead to error and self-delusion.

Any statement that Holmes and Brandeis would object to positive

---

118 O. Holmes, *supra* note 117, at 184.

119 *Id.* at 295.

120 The notion that when judges upset "desirable" legislation, the blame rests squarely on the Constitution of 1789, not upon the Justices who at the moment are its interpreters, still has respectable adherents. On this patent self-deception Cardozo commented:

> Judges march at times to pitiless conclusions under the prod of a remorseless logic which is supposed to leave them no alternative. They deplore the sacrificial rite. They perform it, none the less, with averted gaze, convinced as they plunge the knife that they obey the bidding of their office.

B. Cardozo, The Growth of the Law 66 (1924). Before he was himself anointed, Felix Frankfurter was similarly realistic. "[C]onstitutional law," he declared, "is not at all a science, but applied politics." Frankfurter, *The Zeitgeist and the Judiciary*, in Law and Politics 6 (1939).

judicial action in all seasons is therefore incorrect. It is noteworthy, for example, that citations from their opinions are prominent in Justice Stone's assertion that the Court is obligated to exercise more exacting scrutiny in reviewing statutes affecting human rights than in examining economic legislation.[121] Holmes, Brandeis, Stone and Hand urged judicial self-restraint not because they believed that a judge's preference should not enter law, but because it inevitably did. The sharp barbs of their thought, Justice Stone's in particular, were intended for the flesh of judges, Right and Left, who without taking the trouble to weigh social values, *prematurely* enforced personal conviction as law. Awareness of the subjective element, inescapable in the judging process, must end in curbing it. Preference and prejudice can be tamed but not eliminated. Awareness of self is the first step toward proper exercise of the judicial role.

Such a description of Holmes' constitutional jurisprudence belies placing it in the tradition of James Bradley Thayer, whose 1893 essay[122] was for Justice Frankfurter the most important single piece of writing on American constitutional law. Thayer's essay appeared at the beginning of a period of unparalleled judicial activism in defense of property and contract rights. Judges were determined, he observed, to enlarge their part "in the political conduct of government." [123] In opposition, Thayer argued that judges "can only disregard [an act] when those who have the right to make laws have not merely made a mistake, but have made a very clear one—so clear that it is not open to rational question. . . . [W]hatever [legislative] choice is rational, is constitutional." [124] One might refuse to endorse a proposed bill on constitutional grounds as a legislator but be compelled to uphold the same measure as a judge. Thayer concluded:

> If what I have been saying is true, the safe and permanent road towards reform is that of impressing upon our people a far stronger sense than they have of the great range of possible harm and evil that our system leaves open, and must leave open, to the legislatures, and of the clear

121 In United States v. Carolene Prods., 304 U.S. 144, 152-53 (1938), Stone cited the following opinions by Holmes or Brandeis: Nixon v. Herndon, 273 U.S. 536 (1927) (Holmes); Whitney v. California, 274 U.S. 357, 372 (1927) (Brandeis, J., concurring); Gitlow v. New York, 268 U.S. 652, 672 (1925) (Holmes, J., dissenting).

122 Thayer, *The Origin and Scope of the American Doctrine of Constitutional Law*, 7 HARV. L. REV. 129 (1893).

123 *Id.* at 152.

124 *Id.* at 144.

> limits of judicial power; so that responsibility may be brought sharply home where it belongs. The checking and cutting down of legislative power, by numerous detailed prohibitions in the constitution, cannot be accomplished without making the government petty and incompetent. This process has already been carried much too far in some of our States. Under no system can the power of courts go far to save a people from ruin; our chief protection lies elsewhere.[125]

To Thayer the tendency of judicial activism was to dwarf the political capacity of the people, and to deaden its sense of moral responsibility.[126] But the political process on which his remedy presumably depends may itself become impeded and corrupted, delaying or defeating the relief he assumed would be forthcoming. Similarly, Justice Frankfurter's cure for the inequities of representation was an "informed, civically militant electorate." [127] Like Thayer, he had lost sight of "the auxiliary precautions" which, on the basis of "experience," the Founding Fathers had felt duty bound to provide.

Tensions over the nature of the Court's function are largely the product of the search for a standard suitable for constitutional adjudication. In the pre-1937 era, Peckham and Thayer, at opposite poles, evolved tests of equivalent simpilicity. On the other hand, Holmes, Brandeis and Stone recognized the complex nature of the Court's role and accordingly developed an approach of less precision but more insight. But when the Court substituted guardianship of civil liberties for protection of property and contract rights, it ran into a difficulty not unlike that experienced before 1937: the problem of finding a measure for the vague clauses of the Constitution.

The elder Justice Harlan had sought to give precision to the accordion-like provisions of the fourteenth amendment by bringing within its ambit the more precise imperatives of the Bill of Rights.[128] Harlan's so-called incorporation theory was rejected. Adopted instead was Justice Cardozo's formula of selective incorporation. Under this theory, the four-

---

125 *Id.* at 155-56. Other lawyers, contemporaries of Thayer, took up the cudgels in support of judicial self-restraint during this crucial period. *See, e.g.*, McMurtrie, *The Jurisdiction to Declare Void Acts of Legislation—When Is It Legitimate and When Mere Usurpation of Sovereignty*?, 32 AM. L. REG. 1093 (1893); Reno, *Arbitration and the Wage Contract*, 26 AM. L. REV. 837 (1892). *See generally* A. PAUL, CONSERVATIVE CRISIS AND THE RULE OF LAW (1960).

126 *See* Thayer, *supra* note 122, at 156 n.1.

127 Baker v. Carr, 369 U.S. 186, 270 (1962) (Frankfurter, J., dissenting).

128 Hurtado v. California, 110 U.S. 516, 538 (1884) (Harlan, J., dissenting); Civil Rights Cases, 109 U.S. 3, 26 (1883) (Harlan, J., dissenting).

teenth amendment incorporates only those provisions of the Bill of Rights which constitute "the matrix, the indispensable condition, of nearly every other form of freedom." The question in each case is whether the statute or action violates those " 'fundamental principles of liberty and justice which lie at the base of all our civil and political institutions.' "[129]

Nearly all the provisions of the Bill of Rights have now been brought under the broad umbrella of the fourteenth amendment. Meanwhile, Justice Black, following the path cut by the elder Justice Harlan, has been waging a persistent campaign for full incorporation. Success has rewarded his effort, not under his theory, but under Justice Cardozo's selective formula. Black is pleased, and understandably so; to him the piecemeal, one-at-a-time process of adoption is better than nothing:

> If the choice must be between the selective process of the *Palko* decision applying some of the Bill of Rights to the States, or the *Twining* rule applying none of them, I would choose the *Palko* selective process.[130]

But when certain Justices have gone beyond Black's full incorporation theory to bring within the Court's protection rights not specifically mentioned in the Constitution, such as the Right of Privacy, his pleasure has ceased. "Incorporation-plus" has evoked from Justice Black protests reminiscent of the scorn Holmes, Brandeis and Stone heaped on their colleagues in an earlier period of judicial aggrandizement. Perhaps even more significant is his inability to comprehend the need for a creative, socially aware approach under the extremely broad language of the equal protection clause.[131] Black's reaction has not yet been couched in the robust attitude Holmes credited to Peckham, but he objects with feeling:

> [T]here is a tendency now among some to look to the judiciary to make all the major policy decisions of our society under the guise of determining constitutionality. The belief is that the Supreme Court will reach a faster and more desirable resolution of our problems than the legislative or executive branches of the government. To the people

[129] Palko v. Connecticut, 302 U.S. 319, 327, 328 (1937).

[130] Adamson v. California, 332 U.S. 46, 89 (1947) (Black, J., dissenting).

[131] *Compare* Harper v. Virginia Bd. of Elections, 383 U.S. 663, 678 (1966) (Black, J., dissenting), *with* Black's silent concurrence in Reynolds v. Sims, 377 U.S. 533 (1964).

> who have such faith in our nine justices, I say that I have known a different Court from the one today. What has occurred may occur again. I would much prefer to put my faith in the people and their elected representatives to choose the proper policies for our government to follow, leaving to the courts questions of constitutional interpretation and enforcement.[132]

Apparently proceeding under the comfortable illusion that the provisions of the Bill of Rights are mathematically precise, Black would narrow the range of judicial discretion by extending "to all the people of the nation the complete protection of the Bill of Rights."[133] Black's faith recalls Justices Sutherland and Roberts, who likened the judicial function to that of the grocer weighing coffee or the dry goods clerk measuring calico. Constitutional interpretation, they argued, involves judgment, not will or power. It is a squaring operation—that of deciding whether the statute challenged conforms to the constitutional mandate.[134] Black states his position with conviction:

> [T]o pass upon the constitutionality of statutes by looking to the *particular standards* enumerated in the Bill of Rights and other parts of the Constitution is one thing; to invalidate statutes because of application of natural law deemed to be above and undefined by the Consti-

---

132 H. Black, *supra* note 18, at 11, 24.

133 Adamson v. California, 332 U.S. 46, 89 (1947) (Black, J., dissenting).

134 *See* United States v. Butler, 297 U.S. 1, 53 (1936) (Roberts, J.); West Coast Hotel Co. v. Parrish, 300 U.S. 400 (1937) (Sutherland, J., dissenting); Home Building & Loan Ass'n v. Blaisdell, 290 U.S. 398, 448 (1934) (Sutherland, J., dissenting).

In Katz v. United States, 389 U.S. 347, 352-53 (1967), the Court overturned Olmstead v. United States, 277 U.S. 438 (1928), which had evoked Justice Brandeis' classic dissent:

> [T]his Court has repeatedly sustained the exercise of power by Congress, under various clauses of that instrument [the Constitution] over objects of which the Fathers could not have dreamed. . . . We have likewise held that general limitation on the powers of Government, like those embodied in the due process clauses of the Fifth and Fourteenth Amendments, do not forbid the United States or the States from meeting modern conditions by regulations which 'a century ago, or even half a century ago, probably would have been rejected as arbitrary and oppressive. . . .' Clauses guaranteeing to the individual protection against specific abuses of power, must have a similar capacity of adaptation to a changing world.

Id. at 472. When Brandeis' dissenting views of 1928 triumphed in 1967, Justice Black refused to go along. In the spirit of Justice Sutherland in the *Minnesota Moratorium* case, Black explained: "I simply could not find that the words of the Fourth Amendment prohibiting unreasonable searches and seizures also prohibit eavesdropping." H. Black, *supra* note 18, at 9-10.

> tution is another. In the one instance, Courts *proceeding within clearly marked constitutional boundaries* seek to execute policies written into the Constitution; in the other, they roam at will in the limitless areas of their own beliefs as to reasonableness and actually select policies, a responsibility which the Constitution entrusts to the legislative representatives of the people.[135]

But in the operation of a political system based on a written Constitution, differences of interpretation are inevitable. "Poverty of language" conspires with human frailty to create divergence of opinion. "Experience has instructed us," Madison wrote in *The Federalist* No 47, "that no skill in the science of government has yet been able to discriminate and define, with sufficient certainty, its three great provinces." Obscurity arises from the "complexity of objects," imperfection of the organ of perception, and "inadequacy of the vehicle of ideas." Rousseau begged readers not to be "in a hurry to charge me with contradicting myself." Considering the "poverty of language," [136] it was unavoidable. Justice Black, sensitive to similar complaints, offers an explanation strangely at odds with Rousseau's.

Creative Activism Fulfilled

"The judge," Benjamin Cardozo wrote, "interprets the social conscience, and gives effect to it in law, but in so doing he helps to form and modify the conscience he interprets. Discovery and creation react upon each other." [137] In such areas as desegregation, reapportionment and the right to counsel, the Warren Court has not only interpreted and enforced the social conscience, it has quickened it. The Court is articulating ideals that might otherwise be silenced, upholding those ingredients of national power that make ours "the strongest Government on earth." [138]

Of the revolutionary changes accomplished during Chief Justice Warren's tenure there is no disagreement. Certain critics, otherwise at odds, may agree that the ends served are desirable. But there is wide divergence among commentators of impressive credentials concerning the legiti-

---

[135] H. BLACK, *supra* note 18, at 9-10.

[136] J. ROUSSEAU, SOCIAL CONTRACT 27 (Everyman ed. 1941).

[137] B. CARDOZO, THE GROWTH OF THE LAW 96-97 (1924).

[138] Jefferson, *First Inaugural Address, quoted in* A. MASON, FREE GOVERNMENT IN THE MAKING 379 (3d ed. 1965).

macy of the new activism. In an article teeming with sarcastic disapproval, Philip Kurland, former law clerk of Justice Frankfurter, notes that the Warren Court has "wrought more fundamental changes in the political and legal structure of the United States than during any similar span of time since the Marshall Court had the unique opportunity to express itself . . ."[139] free from encumbering precedents. Though

---

[139] Kurland, *Foreword* to *The Supreme Court, 1963 Term,* 78 HARV. L. REV. 143 (1964). One measure of the Warren Court's effectiveness as a "revolutionary committee" is that scarcely a major opinion of Justice Frankfurter now represents the law of the land. Consider the following table:

OUTRIGHT REVERSALS OF FRANKFURTER OPINIONS

Flag Salute:	Minersville School Dist. v. Gobitis, 310 U.S. 586 (1940), overruled in West Virginia Bd. of Educ. v. Barnette, 319 U.S. 624 (1943) (Jackson, J.).
Self-Incrimination:	Feldman v. United States, 322 U.S. 487 (1944), overruled in Murphy v. Waterfront Comm'n, 378 U.S. 52 (1964) (Goldberg, J.).
Use of Illegal Evidence:	Wolf v. Colorado, 338 U.S. 25 (1949), overruled in Mapp v. Ohio, 367 U.S. 643 (1961) (Clark, J.).
Alien Status and Subversive Status:	Perez v. Brownell, 356 U.S. 44 (1958), overruled in Afroyim v. Rusk, 387 U.S. 253 (1967) (Black, J.).
Search of Premises:	Frank v. Maryland, 359 U.S. 360 (1959), overruled in Camara v. Municipal Court, 387 U.S. 523 (1967) (White, J.).
Re-Apportionment:	Colegrove v. Green, 328 U.S. 549 (1946), overruled in Baker v. Carr, 369 U.S. 186 (1962). *Baker* did not in so many words reverse *Colegrove,* but the opinion by Justice Brennan was first of a series that did discard *Colegrove.* In his *Baker* dissent Justice Frankfurter begins: "The Court today reverses a uniform course of decision established by a dozen cases . . . ." *Id.* at 266.
Communist Registration:	Communist Party v. Subversive Activities Control Bd., 367 U.S. 1 (1961), overruled in Albertson v. Subversive Activities Control Bd., 382 U.S. 70 (1965) (Brennan, J.). Justice Frankfurter's opinion was not expressly reversed, but *Albertson* left nothing of the first decision except Frankfurter's 111 pages in the U.S. reports.
Right to Counsel:	Foster v. Illinois, 332 U.S. 134 (1947), overruled in Gideon v. Wainwright, 372 U.S. 335 (1963) (Black, J.) Gideon expressly reversed Justice Roberts in *Betts v. Brady,* 316 U.S. 455 (1942). The majority

recognizing, as one must, that the changes are revolutionary, Archibald Cox's appraisal is more realistic. For him the judicial function is properly creative:

> In times of economic, social, and even moral upheaval the danger of exaggerating the importance of certainty and stability as elements of law is probably greater than the risk of valuing it too lightly. There is also the danger that fascination with the lawyer's art may divert us from the human goals of the enterprise. Legal logic has no value for its own sake. Law is a human instrument designed to meet men's needs. . . .
>
> The judiciary, it is often said, should concern itself with law and leave policy to the legislatures. Such a course has much to commend it, but surely rigid adherence to this formula implies too narrow a view of both the function of law and the role of the Court. Constitutional law must grow and change in response to the needs of the community.[140]

Under Chief Justice Warren's leadership, the Supreme Court presents a remarkable paradox. In structure and organization the Court is the most oligarchical branch of our government, yet the Justices, by precept and example, provide the primary impetus in bringing us closer to the ideals embodied in the Declaration of Independence. While maintaining the golden mean Chief Justice Marshall thought he had attained,[141] the Supreme Court has become a major creative force in American life.

---

opinion in *Foster* was a child of *Betts,* in which Frankfurter had joined.

Right of Privacy: Poe v. Ullman, 367 U.S. 497 (1961), overruled in Griswold v. Connecticut, 381 U.S. 479 (1965).

I am indebted to Mr. Irving Dilliard for the material contained in this note. Mr. Dilliard began exploring Justice Frankfurter's constitutional jurisprudence in 14 FRONTIER, Dec. 1962, at 9-12. His book, THE CASE OF MR. JUSTICE FRANKFURTER, is in preparation.

140 A. Cox, *supra* note 26, at 22, 39-40.

141 In his appraisal Archibald Cox writes:

> [T]here will be few who, if they could relive recent history, would choose to exchange closer attention to conventional legal doctrines for the great strides taken under the leadership of the Warren Court in civil rights, the strengthening of democratic self-government, and the administration of criminal justice.

Id. at 23. "I am confident," Cox concludes, "that historians will write that the trend of decisions during the 1950's and 1960's was in keeping with the mainstream of American his-

If judicial self-restaint is the measure of statesmanship, Earl Warren's place in the roster of Chief Justices is not high. If, on the other hand, a more positive conception of the Court's role is recognized and accepted, he may rank with John Marshall. In a personal letter of January 22, 1967, the distinguished U.S. District Court Judge Charles E. Wyzanski, Jr., wrote:

> I have thought for some years that Chief Justice Warren will go down in history second only to Chief Justice Marshall. I am not referring to Chief Justice Warren's intellect, legal acumen, style, or personal ascendency, but to his insight as to the central purposes and potentialities of the society in which he functioned, and to his capacity to make the judicial power a chief instrument for their realization.

The striking similarity between Marshall and Warren is that for both the judicial function is positive and creative; for both the Court is not only a mystically passive weigher of "the law," but also a participant, along with other agencies of government, in the practical process of realizing the objectives set out in the Constitution's preamble.

The New Activism's Uncertain Future

The current activism of the Warren Court is not, however, the end of the story. In certain of the most crucial civil liberties cases, the Justices have been split five to four or six to three. The conviction and vehemence of present-day dissenters, led by Justice Harlan, to say nothing of political and public clamor, give one pause.[142]

Justice Black's apparent defection is also sobering. One recalls Justice Stone's doleful reflections the year before his death in 1946. Stone had been a staunch exponent of judicial self-restraint before 1937. Thereafter he laid previously discussed foundations for the Warren Court's activism in support of civil liberties. Justice Black himself had joined in

---

tory—a bit progressive but also moderate, a bit humane but not sentimental, a bit idealistic but seldom doctrinaire, and in the long run essentially pragmatic—in short, in keeping with the true genius of our institutions." *Id.* at 133-34.

142 Criticism has recently been given significant respectability by Judge Henry Friendly's proposal of a constitutional amendment to curb certain liberal trends. "The time has come," Judge Friendly observes, "when the nation should face up to the hard task of considering an amendment to the self-incrimination clause that will preserve all the framers said and some of the Court's extensions, modify others, expunge some altogether and guard against accretions quite obviously in the making." N.Y. Times, Nov. 10, 1968, § 1, at 73, col. 1.

this effort. Yet in recent years one notes a metamorphosis in Black's constitutional jurisprudence similar to that Stone's underwent in 1945. Said Stone:

> My more conservative brethren in the old days enacted their own economic prejudice into law. What they did placed in jeopardy a great and useful institution of government. The pendulum has now swung to the other extreme, and history is repeating itself. The Court is now in as much danger of becoming a legislative Constitution-making body, enacting into law its own predilections, as it was then . . . .[143]

The sentiments Justice Black embodied in his Virginia poll tax dissent[144] are but a single example of his similar and growing disenchantment with new-style judicial activism.

Those who feel that the day of reckoning is overdue may find comfort in the knowledge that our system provides various corrective devices against judicial usurpation. Some are available to the President and the Congress, as was recently illustrated when a Senate filibuster induced President Johnson to withdraw his nomination of Abe Fortas to be Chief Justice. In addition, Supreme Court Justices respond to circumstances not recorded in counsel's briefs, including Mr. Dooley's "iliction returns." Justice Stone's dictum of 1936 that the "only check upon our own exercise of power is our own sense of self-restraint" [145] has been falsified time and time again. For a generation Holmes, Brandeis and Stone, deploring judicial usurpation, argued in vain. Nothing but history was on their side. Justice Harlan believes that history will again supply a corrective for what he considers judicial usurpation. In his *Miranda* dissent the Justice remarked hopefully: "This Court is forever adding new stories to the temples of constitutional law, and the temples have a way of collapsing when one story too many is added." [146] "[A]ll constitutional questions," Justice Douglas

[143] Letter from H. Stone to Irving Brant, Aug. 25, 1945, *quoted in* A. MASON, THE SUPREME COURT FROM TAFT TO WARREN 168 (rev. ed. 1968).

[144] See text at note 46 *supra*. Shortly before his death in 1952, Justice Jackson also experienced disenchantment with the judicial activism he had helped to foster. R. JACKSON, THE SUPREME COURT IN THE AMERICAN SYSTEM OF GOVERNMENT 57-58, 80-82 (1955).

[145] United States v. Butler, 297 U.S. 1, 79 (1936) (Stone, J., dissenting).

[146] Miranda v. Arizona, 384 U.S. 436, 526 (1966) (Harlan, J., dissenting), *quoting* Douglas v. Jeanette, 319 U.S. 157, 181 (1943) (separate opinion of Jackson, J.).

observed, "are always open." [147] With refreshing candor, Justice Jackson commented: "We are not final because we are infallible, but we are infallible only because we are final." [148]

As criticism mounts in Court, Congress and country, with the appointment of new Supreme Court Justices, including a Chief Justice, in the offing, one recalls Justice Henry Baldwin's prophetic words of 1837, on the eve of Chief Justice Taney's transforming regime:

> The history and spirit of the times, past and present, admonish us that new versions of the Constitution will be promulgated to meet the varying course of political events or aspirations of power: and that if we suffer our judgments to be influenced by what has been pressed upon us as authority for present adjudication, we must pay the same respect to the same kind of authority, when future opinions shall be formed, and new expositions be announced.[149]

Dissenters and malcontents alert us, as always, to free government's most distinctive features—debate, conflict, opposition. Consensus would not be desirable even if it were possible. The end of opposition marks the end of free government. The Supreme Court is our final arbiter only in a particular case. Its decision must remain, as Lincoln said, in never-ending dialogue. We are not under absolute rule from Mount Sinai; we are dedicated to free government.

---

147 Gideon v. Wainwright, 372 U.S. 335, 346 (1963).

148 Brown v. Allen, 344 U.S. 443, 540 (1953) (Jackson, J., concurring).

149 H. Baldwin, A General View of the Origin and Nature of the Constitution and Government of the United States 3 (1837).

VOLUME 103 MAY 1990 NUMBER 7

HARVARD LAW REVIEW

THE ORIGINS AND HISTORICAL UNDERSTANDING OF FREE EXERCISE OF RELIGION

Michael W. McConnell

TABLE OF CONTENTS

ARTICLE

THE ORIGINS AND HISTORICAL UNDERSTANDING OF FREE EXERCISE OF RELIGION

*Michael W. McConnell**

The question whether the free exercise clause requires the granting of religious exemptions from generally applicable laws with secular purposes has generated lively debate. Beyond a few narrow circumstances, the Supreme Court and legal commentators have rejected claims to free exercise exemptions. In this Article, Professor McConnell argues that this debate has largely proceeded in an ahistorical fashion and has ignored the unique American conception of religious freedom from which the free exercise clause emerged. Professor McConnell discusses the approaches to church-state relations in the American colonies and traces the development of free exercise provisions in both the colonies and the post-independence states. Contrary to modern perceptions, he argues, the impetus for free exercise provisions came from the evangelical religious movements of the period, movements that espoused the primacy of religious conscience over secular laws and that viewed the constitutional guarantee of free exercise as protecting the right actively to fulfill religious duties without state interference. He contends, moreover, that the framers adopted the terminology "free exercise of religion" in place of the alternative, "rights of conscience," to ensure protection for religiously motivated conduct and to make clear that protection would not extend to secular claims of conscience. After discussing early nineteenth-century judicial interpretations, Professor McConnell concludes that an interpretation of the free exercise clause that mandates religious exemptions was both within the contemplation of the framers and consonant with popular notions of religious liberty and limited government that existed at the time of the framing.

IN the winter of 1812–1813, Daniel Philips entered the confessional of his parish church, St. Peters in New York City, to confess to God that he had knowingly received stolen goods. Under the tenets of his Roman Catholic faith, Philips had to make oral confession of his sins and perform appropriate penance before he could partake of holy communion. Under centuries-old church doctrines, he could be confident that his confession would remain between him and God —

---

* Professor of Law, University of Chicago. The author gratefully acknowledges financial support during the preparation of this paper from the Lynde and Harry Bradley Foundation, the helpful comments of Albert Alschuler, Akhil Amar, Jay Bybee, Gerhard Casper, Thomas J. Curry, Richard Fallon, Edward Gaffney, Richard Helmholz, Stephen Holmes, Douglas Laycock, Ira Lupu, Martin Marty, Henry Monaghan, Michael Paulsen, Richard Posner, Frederick Schauer, Cass Sunstein, and Mark Tushnet, and the research assistance of George Sanders and Adam Wolfson.

that the priest would not reveal to anyone what he had to say. After Philips confessed his crime, the priest, Father Kohlmann, insisted that he return the goods to their rightful owner. Under cover of confidentiality of the confessional, Philips brought the goods to Father Kohlmann, who delivered them to the owner, James Keating. Keating informed the authorities of these events, who in turn subpoenaed Father Kohlmann to appear before the grand jury to identify those responsible for the crime. The priest appeared before the court but pleaded in these words to be excused from testifying:

> [I]f called upon to testify in quality of a minister of a sacrament, in which my God himself has enjoined on me a perpetual and inviolable secrecy, I must declare to this honorable Court, that I cannot, I must not answer any question that has a bearing upon the restitution in question; and that it would be my duty to prefer instantaneous death or any temporal misfortune, rather than disclose the name of the penitent in question. For, were I to act otherwise, I should become a traitor to my church, to my sacred ministry and to my God. In fine, I should render myself guilty of eternal damnation.[1]

To this, the district attorney responded:

> [T]he constitution has granted religious "profession and worship" to all denominations, "without discrimination or preferance": but it has not granted exemption from previous legal duties. It has expelled the demon of persecution from our land: but it has not weakened the arm of public justice. Its equal and steady impartiality has soothed all the contending sects into the most harmonious equality, but to none of them has it yielded any of the rights of a well organized government.[2]

Thus was posed an issue that continues to divide and trouble the legal system: does the freedom of religious exercise guaranteed by the constitutions of the states and United States require the government, in the absence of a sufficiently compelling need, to grant exemptions from legal duties that conflict with religious obligations? Or does this freedom guarantee only that religious believers will be governed by equal laws, without discrimination or preference?

The New York court in *People v. Philips* ruled that an exemption was constitutionally required.[3] Although the government had a legit-

---

1 This speech and all the other details of the case are taken from a report of the trial published as W. SAMPSON, THE CATHOLIC QUESTION IN AMERICA 8–9 (1813 and photo. reprint 1974). The decision of the court is excerpted in *Privileged Communications to Clergymen*, 1 CATH. LAW. 199, 199–209 (1955).

2 W. SAMPSON, *supra* note 1, at 51 (emphasis omitted and punctuation altered). The internal quotations are from N.Y. CONST. of 1777, art. XXXVIII, *reprinted in* 2 FEDERAL AND STATE CONSTITUTIONS, COLONIAL CHARTERS, AND OTHER ORGANIC LAWS OF THE UNITED STATES 1328, 1338 (B. Poore 2d ed. 1878) [hereinafter FEDERAL AND STATE CONSTITUTIONS].

3 *See* W. SAMPSON, *supra* note 1, at 112–14.

imate need and the authority to compel testimony, that need did not outweigh the interference with the relationship between priests and penitents in the Roman Catholic Church. This resolution of the conflict between generally applicable law and religious conscience had deep roots in the practices of the American states both before and after independence. But it was not until the full flowering of the Warren Court that the United States Supreme Court so interpreted the free exercise clause of the first amendment. In the meantime, the Court had upheld enforcement of anti-polygamy laws against Mormons,[4] of child labor laws against a minor who wished to distribute religious tracts in the company of her aunt,[5] of a public university's suspension of students who refused on account of their religious convictions against war to participate in ROTC,[6] and of Sunday closing laws against Orthodox Jews who observed the Sabbath on Saturday rather than Sunday.[7]

In *Sherbert v. Verner*,[8] the first and leading case in the Supreme Court's modern free exercise jurisprudence, the Court held that a Seventh-Day Adventist need not agree to work on Saturday in order to be eligible for unemployment compensation. Although a state has a legitimate need and the authority to limit unemployment benefits to those who make themselves available for work, it may not enforce the limitation when it conflicts with sincere religious practices. The state is "constitutionally compelled to *carve out an exception* — and to provide benefits — for those whose unavailability is due to their religious convictions," as Justice Harlan disapprovingly put the point in dissent.[9] The *Sherbert* decision thus created the potential for challenges by religious groups and individual believers to a wide range of laws that conflict with the tenets of their faiths, because such laws impose penalties either for engaging in religiously motivated conduct or for refusing to engage in religiously prohibited conduct. For example, in the same year that the Court decided *Sherbert*, it remanded for reconsideration in light of *Sherbert* the contempt conviction of a religious objector who refused jury service.[10] A decade later, the

[4] *See* Reynolds v. United States, 98 U.S. 145 (1879) (upholding the criminal conviction of a Mormon leader for the crime of polygamy under territorial law); *see also* Cleveland v. United States, 329 U.S. 14 (1946) (upholding the conviction of a "fundamentalist" Mormon polygamist under a federal statute prohibiting the transportation of a woman across state lines for immoral purposes); Davis v. Beason, 133 U.S. 333 (1890) (upholding the requirement that voters take an oath that they are not members of an organization that teaches polygamy); *cf.* The Late Corp. of the Church of Jesus Christ of Latter-Day Saints v. United States, 136 U.S. 1 (1890) (upholding a statute revoking the charter of the Mormon Church and confiscating its property).

[5] *See* Prince v. Massachusetts, 321 U.S. 158 (1944).

[6] *See* Hamilton v. Regents of the Univ. of Cal., 293 U.S. 245 (1934).

[7] *See* Braunfeld v. Brown, 366 U.S. 599 (1961).

[8] 374 U.S. 398 (1963).

[9] *Id.* at 420 (Harlan, J., dissenting) (emphasis in original).

[10] *See In re* Jenison, 375 U.S. 14 (per curiam), *vacating and remanding In re* Jenison

Court exempted members of the Old Order Amish and the Conservative Amish Mennonite churches from compulsory education of children beyond the age of sixteen.[11] Free exercise litigation since *Sherbert* has consisted almost entirely of requests for exemption rather than for general invalidation of restrictive laws.[12]

The Court made no effort in *Sherbert* or subsequent cases to support its holdings through evidence of the historical understanding of "free exercise of religion" at the time of the framing and ratification of the first amendment. This evident lack of historical support has made the decisions vulnerable to attack. Critics have not hesitated to call the decisions "a palpable and unprecedented misconstruction of the Constitution," at variance with the Lockean liberal principles of the Founding.[13]

While in retrospect the Court's inattention to original meaning may seem characteristic of this period of constitutional jurisprudence, it was anything but characteristic of the Court's treatment of the establishment clause. For example, in the *School Prayer Cases* decided in the same Term as *Sherbert*, the author of the *Sherbert* opinion, Justice Brennan, undertook a lengthy historical analysis of school prayer and public education. He commented that "the line we must draw between the permissible and the impermissible is one which accords with history and faithfully reflects the understanding of the Founding Fathers."[14] Interpretations of the establishment clause, then as well as now, are replete with extensive analyses of the historical context and meaning. Indeed, it has been said that "[n]o provision of the Constitution is more closely tied to or given content by its generating history than the religious clause of the First Amendment."[15] Yet neither *Sherbert* nor any other Supreme Court opinion — majority, concurring, or dissenting — has ever grounded the interpretation of the free exercise clause in its historical meaning.

Academic commentary has followed a similarly ahistorical approach. While scores of law review articles and a number of scholarly

---

Contempt Proceedings, 265 Minn. 96, 120 N.W.2d 515 (1963). On remand, the Supreme Court of Minnesota reversed the conviction. *See In re* Jenison Contempt Proceedings, 267 Minn. 136, 125 N.W.2d 588 (1963).

[11] *See* Wisconsin v. Yoder, 406 U.S. 205 (1972).

[12] The only clear exception among Supreme Court free exercise cases is McDaniel v. Paty, 435 U.S. 618 (1978), which struck down a state law prohibiting ministers from serving as delegates to a constitutional convention. *Cf.* Widmar v. Vincent, 454 U.S. 263 (1981) (striking down under the free speech clause the exclusion of a student religious group from public university facilities).

[13] W. Berns, The First Amendment and the Future of American Democracy 38, 43–44 (1985).

[14] School Dist. v. Schempp, 374 U.S. 203, 294 (1963) (Brennan, J., concurring).

[15] Everson v. Board of Educ., 330 U.S. 1, 33 (1947) (Rutledge, J., dissenting); *accord* McGowan v. Maryland, 366 U.S. 420, 437–42 (1961).

books have been devoted to the historical background of the establishment clause,[16] little or no scholarly work has been devoted primarily to the history of the concept of "free exercise of religion."[17] The history of the free exercise principle is usually seen as too meager, or too inconclusive, to be of much help.[18] The few serious efforts to examine the history have concluded that the principle of constitutionally compelled free exercise exemptions from generally applicable laws is historically unsupportable.[19]

This Article analyzes the major philosophical, legal, and historical sources that preceded the free exercise clause of the first amendment to determine the probable understanding of those who drafted and

---

[16] *See, e.g.*, C. ANTIEAU, A. DOWNEY & E. ROBERTS, FREEDOM FROM FEDERAL ESTABLISHMENT (1964); G. BRADLEY, CHURCH-STATE RELATIONSHIPS IN AMERICA (1987); R. CORD, SEPARATION OF CHURCH AND STATE: HISTORICAL FACT AND CURRENT FICTION (1982); L. LEVY, THE ESTABLISHMENT CLAUSE (1986); Laycock, *"Nonpreferential" Aid to Religion: A False Claim About Original Intent*, 27 WM. & MARY L. REV. 875 (1986); Smith, *Getting Off on the Wrong Foot and Back On Again: A Reexamination of the History of the Framing of the Religion Clauses of the First Amendment and a Critique of the* Reynolds *and* Everson *Decisions*, 20 WAKE FOREST L. REV. 569 (1984); Smith, *Separation and the "Secular": Reconstructing the Disestablishment Decision*, 67 TEX. L. REV. 955 (1989) [hereinafter Smith, *Separation and the "Secular"*].

[17] The most comprehensive studies of the history of religious freedom in the United States to the time of the Constitution have been S. COBB, THE RISE OF RELIGIOUS LIBERTY IN AMERICA (1902); and T. CURRY, THE FIRST FREEDOMS: CHURCH AND STATE IN AMERICA TO THE PASSAGE OF THE FIRST AMENDMENT (1986). This Article makes liberal use of material from Curry and Cobb. Other useful recent general historical studies include W. MILLER, THE FIRST LIBERTY (1986); Adams & Emmerich, *A Heritage of Religious Liberty*, 137 U. PA. L. REV. 1559 (1989); and Kurland, *The Origins of the Religion Clauses of the Constitution*, 27 WM. & MARY L. REV. 839 (1986). None of these histories provides a clear doctrinal analysis of the free exercise clause or focuses on free exercise exemptions.

The best historical examination of free exercise exemptions is a little-noticed report to the Attorney General. *See* OFFICE OF LEGAL POLICY, DEP'T OF JUSTICE, REPORT TO THE ATTORNEY GENERAL: RELIGIOUS LIBERTY UNDER THE FREE EXERCISE CLAUSE (1986) [hereinafter REPORT TO THE ATTORNEY GENERAL]. The report relies on a much narrower range of sources than are relied upon in this Article. Moreover, although it reaches conclusions on some issues parallel to those reached here, the report reaches contrary conclusions on other, quite important questions of interpretation. Other significant historical examinations of the exemptions issue include W. BERNS, *supra* note 13; M. MALBIN, RELIGION AND POLITICS: THE INTENTIONS OF THE AUTHORS OF THE FIRST AMENDMENT (1978); and Marshall, The Case Against the Constitutionally Compelled Free Exercise Exemption (1989) (unpublished manuscript) (on file at the Harvard Law Library) (forthcoming in 40 CASE W. RES. L. REV. 357 (1989-1990)). These works reach conclusions at odds with those of this Article and will be discussed throughout at appropriate points.

[18] *See, e.g.*, Choper, *The Religious Clauses of the First Amendment: Reconciling the Conflict*, 41 U. PITT. L. REV. 673, 676 (1980); Pepper, Reynolds, Yoder, *and Beyond: Alternatives for the Free Exercise Clause*, 1981 UTAH L. REV. 309, 315; Marshall, *supra* note 17.

[19] *See* W. BERNS, *supra* note 13; M. MALBIN, *supra* note 17; Marshall, *supra* note 17; *see also* REPORT TO THE ATTORNEY GENERAL, *supra* note 17 (arguing that free exercise exemptions are limited to prohibitory law).

ratified it. The focus is on exemptions from generally applicable laws, since this has posed the most important interpretive issue. The conclusions of this analysis are (1) that exemptions were seen as a constitutionally permissible means for protecting religious freedom, (2) that constitutionally compelled exemptions were within the contemplation of the framers and ratifiers as a possible interpretation of the free exercise clause, and (3) that exemptions were consonant with the popular American understanding of the interrelation between the claims of a limited government and a sovereign God. While the historical evidence may not be unequivocal (it seldom is), it does, on balance, support *Sherbert*'s interpretation of the free exercise clause.[20]

For purposes of this Article, there is no need to presuppose agreement about an "originalist" (or any other) theory of constitutional interpretation. Even opponents of originalism generally agree that the historical understanding is relevant, even if not dispositive. Much of the criticism of the *Sherbert* doctrine is based on the supposed weakness of its historical roots.[21] Thus, even if the original understanding of the free exercise clause is not considered dispositive, a fresh look at the historical record can correct misconceptions that have arisen from the ahistorical manner in which free exercise exemptions have been created and defended.

After a brief description of the state of modern free exercise doctrine in Part I, the Article proceeds chronologically. Part II canvasses the preconstitutional history of free exercise of religion in the American colonies and states by analyzing protections found in charters, constitutions, and statutes. This Part also discusses the works of the main philosophical, political, and religious figures of the time and examines actual controversies over free exercise exemptions. Part III discusses the framing of the free exercise clause of the first amendment, as well as early interpretations of free exercise clauses in both federal and state constitutions. Part IV, the conclusion, describes the relation between religion and government that best reflects the original conception of free exercise of religion.

While much of the analysis focuses on the specific doctrinal question of free exercise exemptions, this discussion has implications for the broader controversy involving the proper relationship between law

---

20 This does not mean that the principle was necessarily correctly applied to the facts of *Sherbert*. For an analysis of whether there was a burden on free exercise in *Sherbert*, see McConnell & Posner, *An Economic Approach to Issues of Religious Freedom*, 56 U. CHI. L. REV. 1, 40–41 (1989).

21 *See, e.g.*, W. BERNS, *supra* note 13; M. MALBIN, *supra* note 17; Bork, *The Supreme Court and the Religion Clauses*, in "TURNING THE RELIGION CLAUSES ON THEIR HEADS": PROCEEDINGS OF THE NATIONAL RELIGIOUS FREEDOM CONFERENCE OF THE CATHOLIC LEAGUE FOR RELIGIOUS AND CIVIL RIGHTS 83, 85–86 (1988).

and religious obligation in a liberal republic.[22] On many levels, the legal recognition of religion as a counter-authority to law is anomalous. Religious freedom claims present paradoxical combinations of duty and liberty, neutrality and special accommodation. The characteristic tendency of the modern legal system has been to assimilate the freedom of religion into the more familiar framework of Lockean liberal individualism. This denies the singularity of religion in life and, more particularly, in political life. Under this view the religion clauses of the first amendment become an instrument of secularism to be interpreted in secular terms.[23] An understanding of the historical roots of free exercise exemptions casts doubt on this interpretation. It suggests instead a peculiarly American conception of the relation between religion and government — one that emphasizes the integrity and diversity of religious life rather than the secularism of the state.

A robust principle of liberty of conscience also conflicts with the alternative, nonliberal understanding of the governmental role, known as republicanism, under which the state has a responsibility to promote civic virtue among its citizens. The principle of free exercise of religion effectively removes government from the development and transmission of virtue at its most fundamental level — thus devolving upon voluntary religious societies (including those of atheists or agnostics) the central function thought by "republicans" to be vested in the state. The free exercise principle therefore suggests that modern attempts to understand the Founding as a clash between "liberal" and "republican" elements are radically incomplete. It points instead toward a social order that is neither strictly individualistic nor statist in its understanding of the good.

I. Free Exercise Doctrine Today

The basic framework of the free exercise exemptions doctrine is easily stated. If the plaintiff can show that a law or governmental practice inhibits the exercise of his religious beliefs,[24] the burden shifts to the government to demonstrate that the law or practice is necessary to the accomplishment of some important (or "compelling") secular objective and that it is the least restrictive means of achieving that

---

[22] The Article is mostly confined to issues of individual conscience. This is not to disparage the importance of the institutional or corporate aspects of religious exercise — the independence of religious bodies from government control. But the theoretical and historical background for those issues is sufficiently distinct that to combine them would add too much both to pages and to confusion.

[23] *See* Smith, *Separation and the "Secular"*, *supra* note 16, at 975–1015.

[24] For analysis of the requisite "burden" on free exercise, see Lupu, *Where Rights Begin: The Problem of Burdens on the Free Exercise of Religion*, 102 HARV. L. REV. 933 (1989); and McConnell & Posner, cited above in note 20, at 38–45.

objective.[25] If the plaintiff meets his burden and the government does not, the plaintiff is entitled to exemption from the law or practice at issue. In order to be protected, the claimant's beliefs must be "sincere," but they need not necessarily be consistent, coherent, clearly articulated, or congruent with those of the claimant's religious denomination.[26] "Only beliefs rooted in religion are protected by the Free Exercise Clause";[27] secular beliefs, however sincere and conscientious, do not suffice.[28]

Some twenty-five years after *Sherbert*, the legitimacy of this doctrine has increasingly come under attack, and the survival of the principle of free exercise exemptions is very much in doubt. Since 1972, the Court has rejected every claim for a free exercise exemption to come before it,[29] outside the narrow context of unemployment benefits governed strictly by *Sherbert*.[30] What once appeared to be a jurisprudence highly sympathetic to religious claims now appears virtually closed to them. Chief Justice Rehnquist and Justice Stevens have openly declared their opposition to the doctrine. Chief Justice Rehnquist has contended that when "a State has enacted a general statute, the purpose and effect of which is to advance the State's

---

[25] For analysis of the "compelling governmental interest," see Gottlieb, *Compelling Governmental Interests: An Essential but Unanalyzed Term in Constitutional Adjudication*, 68 B.U.L. REV. 917 (1988); and McConnell & Posner, cited above in note 20, at 45–54.

[26] *See* Frazee v. Illinois Dep't of Employment Sec., 109 S. Ct. 1514, 1517–18 (1989); Thomas v. Review Bd., 450 U.S. 707, 715–16 (1981). For critical appraisals of the sincerity requirement, see Noonan, *How Sincere Do You Have To Be To Be Religious?*, 1988 U. ILL. L. REV. 713; and Marshall, *supra* note 17, at 27–30.

[27] *Frazee*, 109 S. Ct. at 1517 (quoting Thomas v. Review Bd., 450 U.S. at 713); *see also* Wisconsin v. Yoder, 406 U.S. 205, 215–16 (1972) (exempting Amish children beyond the age of 16 from compulsory public school attendance on account of religious beliefs).

[28] *See, e.g.*, Africa v. Pennsylvania, 662 F.2d 1025 (3d Cir. 1981) (upholding a prison's refusal to provide a prisoner with a special diet on the ground that his belief system was not a religion); United States v. Kuch, 288 F. Supp. 439 (D.D.C. 1968) (rejecting a free exercise claim for exemption from a prohibition on marijuana use on the ground that the defendant did not demonstrate that her beliefs supporting drug use were religious). The historical basis for this limitation is discussed at pp. 1488–1500 below.

[29] *See, e.g.*, O'Lone v. Estate of Shabazz, 482 U.S. 342 (1987) (rejecting the claim of Muslim prisoners seeking a change in work schedule to accommodate Friday worship services); Goldman v. Weinberger, 475 U.S. 503 (1986) (rejecting the claim of an Orthodox Jewish Air Force officer forbidden to wear a yarmulke while on duty and in uniform); Tony & Susan Alamo Found. v. Secretary of Labor, 471 U.S. 290 (1985) (requiring members of a religious organization opposed to receiving cash wages to submit to minimum wage regulation); Bob Jones Univ. v. United States, 461 U.S. 574 (1983) (upholding a denial of religious school tax exempt status because of the university's religiously based rule against interracial dating and marriage); United States v. Lee, 455 U.S. 252 (1982) (requiring members of a self-supporting religious group to contribute to Social Security in violation of their religious tenets).

[30] The narrow holding of *Sherbert*, as it applies to unemployment benefits, has been repeatedly reaffirmed, most recently in the unanimous *Frazee* decision. In Hobbie v. Unemployment Compensation Appeals Commission, 480 U.S. 136 (1987), and Thomas v. Review Board, 450 U.S. 707 (1981), then-Justice Rehnquist was the sole dissenter.

secular goals, the Free Exercise Clause does not . . . require the State to conform that statute to the dictates of religious conscience of any group."[31] Justice Stevens has stated that there is "virtually no room for a 'constitutionally required exemption' on religious grounds from a valid . . . law that is entirely neutral in its general application."[32] Several leading scholars in the field have espoused a similar position.[33]

The debate over free exercise exemptions hinges on two different conceptions of the threat government poses to religious liberty. Under the no-exemptions view, the free exercise clause exists solely to prevent the government from singling out religious practice for peculiar disability. The evil to be prevented is, in Judge Bork's words, "laws that directly and intentionally penalize religious observance."[34] The remedy is to strike down the offending legislation and to treat religious institutions and practices the same way that comparable nonreligious institutions and practices are treated. Under the exemptions view, on the other hand, the free exercise clause protects religious practices against even the incidental or unintended effects of government action. The evil includes not only active hostility, but also majoritarian presuppositions, ignorance, and indifference. The remedy generally is to leave the government policy in place, but to carve out an exemption when the application of the policy impinges on religious practices without adequate justification.

Under both conceptions, it is unconstitutional for the government to inflict penalties on religious practices as such. For example, zoning ordinances disallowing churches while allowing meeting halls and other uses with comparable effects are unconstitutional,[35] as are "anti-cult" legislation,[36] laws barring clergy from public office,[37] and charitable solicitation regulations crafted to disadvantage a particular religious sect.[38] Under the no-exemptions view, however, religious believers and institutions cannot challenge facially neutral legislation, no matter what effect it may have on their ability or freedom to practice

---

31 Thomas v. Review Bd., 450 U.S. at 723 (Rehnquist, J., dissenting).

32 United States v. Lee, 455 U.S. at 263 (Stevens, J., concurring).

33 In addition to the sources cited in note 17 above, see P. KURLAND, RELIGION AND THE LAW (1962); Kurland, *The Irrelevance of the Constitution: The Religion Clauses of the First Amendment and the Supreme Court*, 24 VILL. L. REV. 3 (1978); and Tushnet, *"Of Church and State and the Supreme Court": Kurland Revisited*, 1989 SUP. CT. REV. 373.

34 Bork, *supra* note 21, at 84.

35 *See* Hollingsworth v. State, 37 Tenn. 518 (1858); *cf.* Catholic Bishop v. Kingery, 371 Ill. 257, 20 N.E.2d 583 (1939) (holding that a city may not zone out religious schools if it allows public schools).

36 *See* Aronin, *Cults, Deprogramming, and Guardianship: A Model Legislative Proposal*, 17 COLUM. J.L. & SOC. PROBS. 163, 201 n.258 (1982).

37 *See* McDaniel v. Paty, 435 U.S. 618 (1978).

38 *See* Larson v. Valente, 456 U.S. 228 (1982) (disallowing solicitation regulations under the establishment clause rather than the free exercise clause).

their religious faith. Thus, a requirement that all witnesses must testify to facts within their knowledge bearing on a criminal prosecution — the requirement at issue in *Philips* — if applied without exception, could abrogate the confidentiality of the confessional. Similarly, a general prohibition of alcohol consumption could make the Christian sacrament of communion illegal, uniform regulation of meat preparation could put kosher slaughterhouses out of business, and prohibitions of discrimination on the basis of sex or marital status could end the male celibate priesthood.

Both the exemption and no-exemption views can be expressed in terms of "neutrality" toward religion, but the way in which the two views define "neutrality" differs.[39] Under the no-exemption position, a law or government practice is "neutral" if it makes no reference to religion and has a secular justification unrelated to the suppression of religion. Under the exemption position, a law or governmental practice is not "neutral" if it embodies the majority's view on a contested question of religious significance to the minority, even if that question is of no religious significance to the majority.[40] For example, from the majority's perspective, a requirement that those seeking unemployment benefits be willing to work on Saturday seems secular and neutral. Only from the perspective of a sabbatarian do Saturday work environments have a religious dimension. Both the exemption and no-exemption views thus insist on neutral, "secular" laws and governmental practices, but the no-exemption view makes that judgment exclusively according to the perspective of the government, while the exemption view takes the perspective of the religious claimant, as well as the countervailing interests of the government, into account.

Likewise, these two interpretations agree that laws and governmental practices must be neutral *among* religions, but they differ about how this is to be accomplished. Under the no-exemption position, the best way to ensure equal treatment of all religions is to deny exemptions to all. The proponents of exemption, by contrast, observe that powerful and influential religions will usually receive adequate protection in the political arena.[41] One rarely sees laws that force main-

---

[39] *See* Laycock, *Formal, Substantive, and Disaggregated Neutrality Toward Religion*, 39 DE PAUL L. REV. (forthcoming 1990).

[40] Here the term "majority" is used not in the technical sense of comprising over 50% of the population, but in the sense of prevailing in the political process, and the term "minority," in the sense of losing in the political process. Obviously, "majorities" in the technical sense sometimes lose, and "minorities" sometimes win.

[41] *See, e.g.*, Volstead Act, 41 Stat. 305, 308–39 (1919), *repealed by* U.S. CONST. amend. 21 (1933) (exempting sacramental wine from prohibition); Civil Rights Restoration Act, 20 U.S.C. § 1681(3) (1988) (exempting religious institutions); Nation's Capital Religious Liberty and Academic Freedom Act (Armstrong Amendment), Pub. L. No. 100-462, § 145, 102 Stat. 2269 (1988)

stream Protestants to violate their consciences. Judicially enforceable exemptions under the free exercise clause are therefore needed to ensure that unpopular or unfamiliar faiths will receive the same consideration afforded mainstream or generally respected religions by the representative branches.

Opposition to free exercise exemptions arises from two jurisprudentially distinct positions. The first looks to the constitutionally required separation of powers and is grounded in a philosophy of judicial restraint. This objection holds that courts are not the proper institutions to craft exemptions from generally applicable statutes that have a secular purpose and lack an intent to suppress religious freedom. Any exemptions must be made by the legislature or by executive officials acting within their delegated authority. The opinions of Chief Justice Rehnquist exemplify this position on the modern Court. The second objection, most forcefully articulated on the modern Court by Justice Stevens, argues that whether made by courts or legislatures, exemptions directed to religion alone are generally unwarranted because determining the "sincerity" of religious claimants is dangerously intrusive, because granting exemptions for religious beliefs discriminates against secular beliefs, and because "special treatment" may give the appearance of aid to and endorsement of religion. While these two positions lead to virtually identical results in free exercise cases, they lead to opposite results in many cases involving the establishment clause, in which legislative exemptions and accommodations are at issue.[42]

As this Article went to press, a five-Justice majority abandoned the free exercise exemptions doctrine except in cases involving a free exercise claim "in conjunction with other constitutional protections."[43] The historical record casts doubt on this interpretation of the free exercise clause.

(exempting Georgetown University from a Washington D.C. law prohibiting discrimination on the basis of sexual preference).

[42] *See, e.g.*, Texas Monthly, Inc. v. Bullock, 109 S. Ct. 890 (1989) (striking down a statute exempting religious magazines from sales tax) (Stevens, J., in the majority and Rehnquist, C.J., dissenting); Estate of Thornton v. Caldor, Inc., 472 U.S. 703 (1985) (striking down a statute providing Sabbath observers the right not to work on their chosen Sabbath in the private workplace) (Stevens, J., in the majority and Rehnquist, J., dissenting). Even Justice Stevens sometimes votes to uphold a legislative accommodation specifically tailored to religion. *See, e.g.*, Corporation of the Presiding Bishop of the Church of Jesus Christ of Latter-Day Saints v. Amos, 483 U.S. 327 (1987) (upholding a statutory exemption for religious organizations from the prohibition of employment discrimination on the basis of religion).

[43] Employment Div. v. Smith, No. 88-1213, slip op. at 8 (U.S. Apr. 17, 1990) (1990 U.S. LEXIS 2021, *16).

II. Free Exercise Before the Constitution

Although the free exercise and establishment clauses were proposed in 1789 and ratified in 1791, the American states had already experienced 150 years of a higher degree of religious diversity than had existed anywhere else in the world. They had, moreover, seen the results of religious conflict in England and of a variety of approaches to church-state relations in the colonies, ranging from near-theocracy to religious pluralism to state domination of the church. If the states can serve as "laboratories of democracy,"[44] the American colonies surely served as laboratories for the exploration of different approaches to religion and government. The free exercise clause cannot be understood or appreciated without knowing what happened before.

A. Four Approaches to Church-State Relations in the Colonies

The English legacy was not a happy one. During the early settlement of the colonies in the seventeenth century, England suffered from chronic religious strife and intolerance.[45] The Church of England was the established church of the realm, and both Roman Catholicism and extreme Protestantism (of which Puritanism was the most prominent element) were suppressed. After the deposition of Charles I in the English Civil War, the Protestant dissenters assumed power, and Parliament took it upon itself to rewrite the prayer book and confession of faith, dissolve the episcopal structure of the Church, and confiscate the property of the bishoprics. Parliament ostensibly guaranteed free exercise of religion to most Protestants but denied religious freedom to "papists, the adherents of prelacy and the advocates of 'blasphemous, licentious or profane' doctrines."[46] Baptist leaders were imprisoned, and ministers who insisted on frequent use of the prayer book were ejected from clerical office.[47]

Upon restoration of the monarchy in 1660, Parliament reconstituted the Church of England. Suspected of conspiring with France or Spain to the detriment of England's Protestant rulers, Catholics continued to be targets for hostile legislation, as much for political as for religious reasons. But Protestant dissenters' rights were limited as well. The Test Act of 1672,[48] for example, restricted public and military office to Anglicans. The Act also required officeholders to

---

[44] New State Ice Co. v. Liebmann, 285 U.S. 262, 311 (1932) (Brandeis, J., dissenting).

[45] For a discussion of religious strife in England during this period, see F. Makower, The Constitutional History and Constitution of the Church of England 68–95 (1895 and photo. reprint 1972).

[46] *Id.* at 86.

[47] *See id.* at 85–86.

[48] 1672, 25 Car. 2, ch. 2.

swear an oath in court denying transubstantiation and acknowledging the King's supremacy over the Church and to present proof that they had taken communion within the preceding year in accordance with the rites of the Church of England.[49] The Toleration Act of 1688[50] ended official persecution of Protestant dissenters but left the favored position of Anglicans unchanged. The anti-Catholic elements of the Test Act persisted throughout the eighteenth century.

The English religious policy did not automatically extend to the colonies, where four different approaches to church-state relations developed. The settlers of New England (outside of Rhode Island) were predominantly English Calvinists called "Puritans" or "Congregationalists." They moved to the wilderness of the New World in order to establish a Christian commonwealth where, for the first time in history, society would be directed by the revealed word of God. Both civil and church governance were established in accordance with their "congregational" understanding of church polity, under which each town would constitute a congregation and would select its own minister (within certain standards of education set by the General Court) and would maintain a minister and church through compulsory taxes. Authority in the system was decentralized and genuinely democratic, but the results were foreordained. The local churches were invariably of the Congregationalist persuasion. Nonetheless, ministers in the system were accorded a high degree of autonomy from civil control, and indeed frequently lectured colonial authorities on their civic and spiritual derelictions.[51]

Having carved their communities out of the rocky wilderness of a distant land, the Puritans of New England saw no reason to allow ungodly individuals to spoil their vision of a Christian commonwealth. This vision allowed no room for religious pluralism or even for toleration. "Polipiety [a variety of sects] is the greatest impiety in the world," according to a well-known tract by Nathaniel Ward.[52] The great preacher John Cotton declared that "it was Toleration that made the world anti-Christian."[53] Cotton reasoned:

> Fundamentals are so cleare, that a man cannot but be convinced in Conscience of the Truth of them after two or three Admonitions: and that therefore such a Person as still continues obstinate, is condemned of himselfe: and if he then be punished, He is not punished for his Conscience, but for sinning against his owne Conscience.[54]

---

[49] *See id.*

[50] 1 W. & M., ch. 18.

[51] For a general discussion of church-state relations in New England during this period, see 1 W. McLoughlin, New England Dissent: 1630-1833, at 3–110 (1971).

[52] S. Cobb, *supra* note 17, at 68 (quoting N. Ward, The Simple Cobler of Aggawam in America (4th ed. 1647 and photo. reprint 1905)).

[53] *Id.*

[54] J. Cotton, The Bloudy Tenent Washed 9 (London 1647 & photo. reprint 1972).

Massachusetts, the most rigorous of the New England Congregationalist establishments, actively persecuted dissenters. Baptists were banished from the colony by statute in 1644,[55] and four Quakers, who insisted on returning after being expelled, were hanged.[56] Other dissenters were horsewhipped or jailed. By the 1680's, these violent measures came to an end, although the established church and the hostility to religious diversity continued in New England well into the nineteenth century.[57]

By contrast, in Virginia the Church of England was established by order of the Crown and maintained, in large part, as an instrument of social control by the governing authorities and the local gentry. The government financed and tightly controlled the Church. Although Virginia and New England both maintained religious establishments, the two systems were in a more profound sense opposites. The New England establishments arose from a grassroots movement born of the conviction that religious truth should control all of society, while the Virginia establishment was imposed from above and dedicated to governmental control over religion.

For the first century of its existence, the Virginia establishment required little overt coercion, for few dissenters ventured into the colony. Even so, ministers sent to serve the small Puritan community in Virginia were expelled, as was the Catholic Lord Baltimore.[58] As in Massachusetts, harsh measures, including banishment, were authorized against Quakers, but there is little evidence that they were put into effect.[59] In the eighteenth century, waves of newcomers, first Presbyterians but later Baptists and a few Quakers, entered the colony. The authorities blocked the Presbyterians' ability to preach at every turn, and the Baptists were "reviled" and "met with violence."[60] Baptists continued to be horsewhipped and jailed for their preaching until the Revolution. In the eighteenth century, Virginia was the most intolerant of the colonies.[61]

Cotton's position had roots in both the Catholic and Reformed traditions and can be traced to St. Augustine. *See, e.g.*, Letter from Augustine to Boniface, *The Correction of the Donatists* (A.D. 417), *excerpted in* J. NOONAN, THE BELIEVER AND THE POWERS THAT ARE 19 (1987) (embracing the use of coercion against heretics and schismatics); *see also* D. RICHARDS, TOLERATION AND THE CONSTITUTION 87–88 (1986) (discussing St. Augustine's views regarding schismatic Christians and heretics).

55 *See* T. CURRY, *supra* note 17, at 12–13.

56 *See id.* at 22.

57 *See id.* at 88.

58 *See* S. COBB, *supra* note 17, at 82, 84–87.

59 *See id.* at 89–90. *But cf. id.* at 91 (noting that some Quakers were arraigned and fined under Governor Berkeley).

60 J. LEWIS, THE PURSUIT OF HAPPINESS: FAMILY AND VALUES IN JEFFERSON'S VIRGINIA 49 (1987). For a discussion of Presbyterian difficulties, see T. CURRY, *supra* note 17, at 99; for a discussion of Virginia's persecution of Baptists, see text accompanying note 152 below.

61 *See* S. COBB, *supra* note 17, at 93, 111–14; T. CURRY, *supra* note 17, at 134–35; R. ISAAC,

In time, the Virginia system spread to Maryland and throughout the South, though with less violence toward dissenters. Georgia, the last colony to be settled, represents an interesting variation. The Trustees of the Georgia colony firmly supported the established Church of England. With the assistance of the Anglican-based Society for the Propagation of the Gospel, they financed and supervised ministers, built churches, and encouraged attendance and support for religion.[62] Unlike the Virginians, the Georgia Trustees demonstrated remarkable tolerance toward Protestant dissenters and even toward Jews. (Savannah contained a substantial Jewish community, which was allowed to worship in peace and participate in public affairs.) Catholics, however, were detested and excluded from the colony.[63]

The third approach to religious liberty might be described as benign neglect. In New York and New Jersey, a policy of de facto religious toleration evolved, largely due to the extraordinary religious diversity of the area. Although the four counties of metropolitan New York had a formally established church, and although there were periodic episodes when the royal governor attempted to enforce conformity to the Anglican Church, for the most part Protestants remained free to live and worship in these colonies as they chose, and Quakers and Jews were generally unmolested.[64]

The fourth approach to religious freedom in seventeenth-century America arose in those colonies that were established explicitly as havens for religious dissenters. There were four such foundings, each with a different religious cast. Maryland, the first haven for dissenters, was founded by a Catholic proprietor, George Calvert (the first Lord Baltimore), and his son, Cecil Calvert, to provide a place for English Catholics to escape the persecution they suffered in the mother country.[65] After 1689, however, the proprietor was removed and the Protestant majority in Maryland established the Church of England and initiated a program of discrimination and intolerance toward dissenters, particularly Roman Catholics. In the eighteenth century, Maryland rivaled Virginia for the narrowness and intolerance of its laws. Roger Williams, an extreme Protestant dissenter, founded Rhode Island as a refuge for those who could not endure the Massa-

---

THE TRANSFORMATION OF VIRGINIA 148–54, 162–63, 175–77, 192–94, 198–203 (1982); H. McILWAINE, THE STRUGGLE OF PROTESTANT DISSENTERS FOR RELIGIOUS TOLERATION IN VIRGINIA (Johns Hopkins Univ. Studies in Hist. and Pol. Sci., 12th Series, No. 4 April, 1894).

[62] *See* R. STRICKLAND, RELIGION AND STATE IN GEORGIA IN THE EIGHTEENTH CENTURY 44–92 (1939).

[63] *See id.* at 79–83.

[64] *See* S. COBB, *supra* note 17, at 301–62, 399–418; T. CURRY, *supra* note 17, at 62–73.

[65] *See* W. RUSSELL, MARYLAND: THE LAND OF SANCTUARY (2d ed. 1908); Lasson, *Free Exercise in the Free State: Maryland's Role in Religious Liberty and the First Amendment*, 31 J. CHURCH & ST. 419 (1989).

chusetts establishment.[66] William Penn founded Pennsylvania and Delaware as sanctuaries for Quakers.[67] Although each of these colonies was established for the benefit of a particular religious sect, all extended freedom of religion to groups beyond their own. Finally, Carolina was founded by a group of proprietors, with the assistance of John Locke, who followed Enlightenment principles of toleration.[68] Early in the eighteenth century, North and South Carolina abandoned these principles and instituted a rigid establishment of the Church of England along lines parallel to Virginia's.[69] It was in these colonies — Maryland, Rhode Island, Pennsylvania, Delaware, and Carolina — that the free exercise of religion emerged as an articulated legal principle.

The term "free exercise" first appeared in an American legal document in 1648, when Lord Baltimore required his new Protestant governor and councilors in Maryland to promise not to disturb Christians ("and in particular no Roman Catholic") in the "free exercise" of their religion.[70] The proprietor had previously attempted to attract settlers from Boston by a promise of "free liberty of religion," to which offer Massachusetts Governor John Winthrop responded that none "of our people . . . [had a] temptation that way."[71] In 1649, the Maryland Assembly passed a statute containing the first "free exercise" clause on the continent: "noe person . . . professing to beleive in Jesus Christ, shall from henceforth bee any waies troubled . . . for . . . his or her religion nor in the free exercise thereof . . . nor any way [be] compelled to the beliefe or exercise of any other Religion against his or her consent."[72]

Rhode Island's Charter of 1663[73] was the first to use the formulation "liberty of conscience." The founder, Roger Williams, was a man of extreme and idiosyncratic religious views who was banished from Puritan Massachusetts. Williams wrote frequently, eloquently, and vituperatively in defense of freedom of conscience.[74] With a few glaring exceptions (Rhode Island barred Jews from citizenship, a provision that was not abandoned until 1842,[75] and barred Catholics

---

[66] *See* S. COBB, *supra* note 17, at 422–23.

[67] *See id.* at 440–41.

[68] *See id.* at 115–19.

[69] *See id.* at 124–26.

[70] W. RUSSELL, *supra* note 65, at 130.

[71] 2 J. WINTHROP, THE HISTORY OF NEW ENGLAND FROM 1630–1649, at 149 (1825 and photo. reprint 1972).

[72] Act Concerning Religion of 1649, *reprinted in* 5 THE FOUNDERS' CONSTITUTION 49, 50 (P. Kurland & R. Lerner eds. 1987).

[73] R.I. CHARTER of 1663, *reprinted in* 2 FEDERAL AND STATE CONSTITUTIONS, *supra* note 2, at 1595, 1596.

[74] His most prominent work, written in 1644, was R. WILLIAMS, THE BLOUDY TENENT OF PERSECUTION, in 3 THE COMPLETE WRITINGS OF ROGER WILLIAMS 1 (S. Caldwell ed. 1963).

[75] *See* M. BORDEN, JEWS, TURKS, AND INFIDELS 13 (1984).

from public office[76]), the colony lived up to its royal Charter of 1663 as a "livelie experiment . . . with a full libertie in religious concernements."[77] In 1641, the legislature ordered that "none be accounted a delinquent for doctrine, provided that it be not directly repugnant to the government or laws established."[78] This tends to support historian Thomas Curry's statement that "[t]he Rhode Island towns carefully reiterated that liberty of conscience did not exempt one from the civil law."[79] Later, the royal Charter of 1663 protected residents of the colony from being "in any wise molested, punished, disquieted, or called into question, for any differences in opinione in matters of religion, and doe not actually disturb the civill peace of our sayd colony,"[80] and stated that they may "freelye and fullye have and enjoye his and theire owne judgments and consciences, in matters of religious concernments . . . ; they behaving themselves peaceblie and quietlie and not useing this libertie to lycentiousnesse and profanenesse, nor to the civill injurye or outward disturbeance of others."[81] In comparison with the earlier language, this provision implies that believers were not required to obey *all* "laws established," but only those directed to maintaining the "civill peace" and preventing licentiousness and profaneness, or the injury of others.

It is tempting to assume that other American colonies observed and eventually imitated the vision of Roger Williams and the Rhode Island "experiment," for the depth and breadth of the Rhode Island commitment to religious freedom were unparalleled until after the American Revolution.[82] The truth, however, is that Williams' writings were lost and forgotten until Massachusetts Baptist apologist and historian Isaac Backus rediscovered them in 1773.[83] In fact, far from being a positive example, Rhode Island was the pariah among the colonies, with a reputation for disorder and instability: "During and after the colonial period, Rhode Island, 'the licentious Republic' and

---

[76] *See* T. CURRY, *supra* note 17, at 90.

[77] R.I. CHARTER of 1663, *reprinted in* 2 FEDERAL AND STATE CONSTITUTIONS, *supra* note 2, at 1595, 1596.

[78] S. COBB, *supra* note 17, at 430.

[79] T. CURRY, *supra* note 17, at 20.

[80] R.I. CHARTER of 1663, *reprinted in* 2 FEDERAL AND STATE CONSTITUTIONS, *supra* note 2, at 1595, 1596.

[81] *Id.*, *reprinted in* 2 FEDERAL AND STATE CONSTITUTIONS, *supra* note 2, at 1597.

[82] For scholarly works taking this approach, see M. HOWE, THE GARDEN AND THE WILDERNESS (1965); P. MILLER, ROGER WILLIAMS: HIS CONTRIBUTION TO THE AMERICAN TRADITION (1953); W. MILLER, cited above in note 17; and L. TRIBE, AMERICAN CONSTITUTIONAL LAW § 14-3, at 1158–59 (2d ed. 1988).

[83] *See* T. CURRY, *supra* note 17, at 91; *see also* 1 W. MCLOUGHLIN, *supra* note 51, at 8 ("[A]lmost no one in colonial New England ever praised his experiment, sought his advice, quoted his books, or tried to imitate his practices.").

'sinke hole of New England,' was an example to be shunned."[84] It is unlikely that the Rhode Island provisions had much direct influence on subsequent developments of the free exercise principle.

The language of the Rhode Island Charter of 1663, however, had a second and third life elsewhere in the colonies. In 1664, the proprietors of Carolina issued an "Agreement" with prospective settlers, using words almost identical to the Rhode Island charter of the previous year,[85] and two of the Carolina proprietors also obtained the grant of New Jersey, where they promulgated an almost identical provision.[86] The language of the Rhode Island, Carolina, and New Jersey provisions represented the most common form of protection for religious freedom in the early colonies, although the provisions in other colonies were less expansive. The language did not survive in North Carolina, South Carolina, or New Jersey, as it was superseded by later (and more limited) religious freedom provisions. But the substance of these early provisions later re-emerged as the most common pattern in the constitutions adopted by the states after the Revolution.[87]

Three features of these early provisions warrant attention. First, the free exercise provisions expressly overrode any "Law, Statute or clause, usage or custom of this realm of England to the contrary."[88] Second, they extended to all "judgments and contiences in matters of religion";[89] they were not limited to opinion, speech and profession, or acts of worship. Third, they limited the free exercise of religion only as necessary for the prevention of "Lycentiousnesse" or the injury or "outward disturbance of others,"[90] rather than by reference to all generally applicable laws. As discussed more fully below, these fea-

---

[84] 1 W. McLoughlin, *supra* note 51, at 8. This illuminates the irony in the remark by Benjamin Huntington, Representative from Connecticut, during the debate over the religion clauses of the first amendment that "[b]y the charter of Rhode Island, no religion could be established by law; he could give a history of the effects of such a regulation; indeed the people were now enjoying the blessed fruits of it." 1 Annals of Cong. 758 (J. Gales ed. 1834) (Aug. 15, 1789). Huntington opposed the amendment.

Two printings exist of the first two volumes of the *Annals of Congress*. They contain different pagination, running heads, and back titles. The printing with the running head "History of Congress" conforms to the remaining volumes of the series, while the printing with the running head "Gales & Seaton's history of debates in Congress" is unique. *See* Checklist of United States Public Documents 1789–1909, at 1463 (3d ed. 1911). All page citations herein are to the latter printing. Readers with the "History of Congress" printing can most easily find parallel citations by referring to the date.

[85] *See* S. Cobb, *supra* note 17, at 117.

[86] *See id.* at 400.

[87] For a discussion of the later constitutions, see pp. 1456–57 & note 242 below.

[88] S. Cobb, *supra* note 17, at 117.

[89] *Id.*

[90] *Id.*

tures are consistent with the idea of free exercise exemptions and indicate the lengthy pedigree of modern exemptions under the free exercise clause of the United States Constitution.[91]

Under the second Charter of Carolina, issued in 1665,[92] the availability of free exercise exemptions was made yet more explicit. Recognizing that "it may happen that some of the people and inhabitants of the said province cannot, in their private opinions, conform" to the Church of England,[93] the charter authorized the proprietors "to give and grant unto such person and persons . . . such indulgences and dispensations, in that behalf" as they "shall, in their discretion, think fit and reasonable."[94] "Indulgences" and "dispensations" are technical legal terms, referring to the King's asserted power to exempt citizens from the enforcement of a law enacted by Parliament. Charles II and James II used these powers frequently to exempt Roman Catholics (and sometimes Protestant dissenters) from oppressive laws.[95] The proprietors used this authority, among other things, to exempt Quakers from the colony's oath requirements and to allow settlements made up of non-Anglicans to choose their own ministers.[96]

In 1669, the proprietors issued the Fundamental Constitutions,[97] though it was never fully put into effect.[98] The Fundamental Constitutions is of particular interest because John Locke, as principal adviser and assistant to Lord Ashley, the most active and influential of the Carolina colony proprietors, helped to draft it. Indeed, the published text was first printed from a copy in Locke's own handwriting and bears an obvious resemblance to Locke's theories of religious toleration.[99] The Fundamental Constitutions established the Church of England as "the only true and orthodox" church.[100] Nonetheless, persons of "different opinions concerning matters of religion," other than atheists, were welcomed into the colony.[101] In a remark-

---

[91] *See infra* pp. 1461–64.

[92] *See* CAROLINA CHARTER of 1665, *reprinted in* 2 FEDERAL AND STATE CONSTITUTIONS, *supra* note 2, at 1390.

[93] *Id.*, *reprinted in* 2 FEDERAL AND STATE CONSTITUTIONS, *supra* note 2, at 1397.

[94] *Id.*, *reprinted in* 2 FEDERAL AND STATE CONSTITUTIONS, *supra* note 2, at 1397.

[95] *See* J. KENYON, THE STUART CONSTITUTION: DOCUMENTS AND COMMENTARY 401–13 (1966); F. MAITLAND, THE CONSTITUTIONAL HISTORY OF ENGLAND 302–06 (1968); 2 W. STUBBS, THE CONSTITUTIONAL HISTORY OF ENGLAND 581–84 (3d ed. 1887 & photo. reprint 1987). The English Bill of Rights of 1689 curtailed the royal power of dispensation. *See* Bill of Rights, 1689, 1 W. & M., ch. 2, *reprinted in* 5 THE FOUNDERS' CONSTITUTION, *supra* note 72, at 1.

[96] *See* T. CURRY, *supra* note 17, at 56.

[97] *See* FUNDAMENTAL CONSTITUTIONS of 1669, *reprinted in* 2 FEDERAL AND STATE CONSTITUTIONS, *supra* note 2, at 1397.

[98] *See* H. BOURNE, THE LIFE OF JOHN LOCKE 243–44 (1876 and photo. reprint 1969).

[99] *See id.* at 239 & n.1.

[100] FUNDAMENTAL CONSTITUTIONS of 1669, § 96, *reprinted in* 2 FEDERAL AND STATE CONSTITUTIONS, *supra* note 2, at 1397, 1406.

[101] *Id.* § 97, *reprinted in* 2 FEDERAL AND STATE CONSTITUTIONS, *supra* note 2, at 1406.

able display of broadmindedness for its day, the document specifically extended protection to "Jews, heathens, and other dissenters from the purity of Christian religion," as well as to the "natives of that place."[102] Even slaves were free to select "what church or profession any of them shall think best, and, therefore, be as fully members as any freeman."[103]

While the Fundamental Constitutions provided exceptionally broad freedom to choose among religions, there was no freedom of non-religion or of individualistic, non-institutionalized belief. Atheists were banned from the colony, and every person was required to be enrolled as a member of one (and only one) church. "[A]ny seven or more persons agreeing in any religion, shall constitute a church or profession"[104] and could worship without molestation, provided they adhered to three tenets:

> Ist. "That there is a God."
> II. "That God is publicly to be worshipped."
> III. "That it is lawful and the duty of every man, being thereunto called by those that govern, to bear witness to truth; and that every church or profession shall, in their terms of communion, set down the external way whereby they witness a truth as in the presence of God . . . ."[105]

Under this system, churches were required to register their membership with the authorities, and any religious assemblies that did not register would "not be esteemed as churches, but unlawful meetings, and be punished as other riots."[106] This system suggested a respect for the role of religion in supporting social stability, coupled with an indifference to the choice of religion that is made and a fear of secret religion and private faith. It had the strange effect of simultaneously denying ultimate authority over religious matters to the state, the church, and the individual. This corresponds to no popular conception of church-state relations and perhaps accounts for the system's failure of implementation.

In actual practice, the most influential examples of religious pluralism were the middle colonies, where no church was established (except in the four counties of metropolitan New York) and the widest

---

[102] *Id.* § 97, *reprinted in* 2 FEDERAL AND STATE CONSTITUTIONS, *supra* note 2, at 1406–07.

[103] *Id.* § 107, *reprinted in* 2 FEDERAL AND STATE CONSTITUTIONS, *supra* note 2, at 1407.

[104] *Id.* § 97, *reprinted in* 2 FEDERAL AND STATE CONSTITUTIONS, *supra* note 2, at 1406–07.

[105] *Id.* § 100, *reprinted in* 2 FEDERAL AND STATE CONSTITUTIONS, *supra* note 2, at 1407.

[106] *Id.* § 108, *reprinted in* 2 FEDERAL AND STATE CONSTITUTIONS, *supra* note 2, at 1407.

range of religious persuasions lived in relative harmony. William Penn's colonies were particularly associated with religious freedom and harmony because of Penn's widely read work, *The Great Case of Liberty of Conscience*, published in 1670.[107] Under his 1701 Charters of Privileges,[108] Pennsylvania and Delaware protected the religious profession of all theists (but confined public office to Christians). This example caught the eye of statesmen in other colonies, for Pennsylvania's promise of toleration contributed to the highest level of immigration of any of the colonies, and with immigration, prosperity. Madison later contrasted the religious repression of Virginia, which turned away useful settlers, with "[t]he allurements presented by other situations,"[109] probably referring to Pennsylvania.

B. Locke and Theories of Religious Toleration

These variations in the scope of free exercise in pre-revolutionary America paralleled an intense and controversial theoretical debate on the other side of the Atlantic regarding the proper relation between religion and the state. Most of the great political thinkers of the period — among them Hobbes, Bodin, Spinoza, Locke, Hume, Bayle, Voltaire, Montesquieu, Montaigne, Smith, and Burke — contributed to the subject and in some manner, however indirect, influenced the American solution to the problem.

This section concentrates on the thought of John Locke, both because his discussion of the religion question was most extensive and because his influence on the Americans and the first amendment was most direct. Jefferson carefully read and made notes on Locke's *The Reasonableness of Christianity*[110] and his *Letters on Religious Toleration*.[111] Major portions of Jefferson's Bill for Establishing Religious

---

[107] *See* W. PENN, *The Great Case of Liberty of Conscience*, in 1 A COLLECTION OF THE WORKS OF WILLIAM PENN 443 (London 1726 and photo. reprint 1974).

[108] *See* DEL. CHARTER of 1701, *reprinted in* 1 FEDERAL AND STATE CONSTITUTIONS, *supra* note 2, at 270; PA. CHARTER OF PRIVILEGES of 1701, *reprinted in* 2 FEDERAL AND STATE CONSTITUTIONS, *supra* note 2, at 1536; *see also* S. COBB, *supra* note 17, at 440–53 (discussing the religious histories of colonial Pennsylvania and Delaware); T. CURRY, *supra* note 17, at 72–77, 159–62 (same); Gaustad, *Colonial Religion and Liberty of Conscience*, in THE VIRGINIA STATUTE FOR RELIGIOUS FREEDOM: ITS EVOLUTION AND CONSEQUENCES IN AMERICAN HISTORY 35 (M. Peterson & R. Vaughan eds. 1988) [hereinafter VIRGINIA STATUTE FOR RELIGIOUS FREEDOM] (same).

[109] J. MADISON, *Memorial and Remonstrance Against Religious Assessments*, in 2 THE WRITINGS OF JAMES MADISON 183, 188 (G. Hunt ed. 1901) [hereinafter J. MADISON, *Memorial and Remonstrance*]. *Memorial and Remonstrance* is also reprinted as an appendix to Justice Rutledge's dissenting opinion in Everson v. Board of Education, 330 U.S. 1, 28 app. at 63 (1947) (Rutledge, J., dissenting).

[110] J. LOCKE, THE REASONABLENESS OF CHRISTIANITY (I. Ramsey ed. 1958) (1st ed. 1695).

[111] The *Letters* are reprinted in 6 J. LOCKE, THE WORKS OF JOHN LOCKE (London 1823 and 1963 photo. reprint) [hereinafter WORKS OF LOCKE]. Jefferson's notes appear in T. JEFFERSON, *Notes on Locke and Shaftesbury*, in 1 THE PAPERS OF THOMAS JEFFERSON 544, 544–48, 549–51 (J. Boyd ed. 1950) [hereinafter PAPERS OF JEFFERSON].

Freedom[112] derived from passages in Locke's first *Letter Concerning Toleration.*[113] Jefferson's bill, in turn, was one of the major precursors of the religion clauses of the first amendment.[114] Four of the five states used language from Jefferson's bill in their proposals for a religion amendment.[115] Moreover, James Madison served as floor leader in the Virginia assembly in support of Jefferson's bill; only three years later, he would serve as draftsman and floor leader in the House of Representatives in support of the Bill of Rights. Locke's ideas also entered the American debate (though more selectively) through the writings of Massachusetts Baptist apologist Isaac Backus.[116] Locke's ideas, then, are an indispensable part of the intellectual backdrop for the framing of the free exercise clause.[117] The ways in which American advocates of religious freedom departed from Locke, however, are as significant as the ways in which they followed him.

John Locke was one of the earliest, and certainly one of the most influential, advocates of religious freedom on a theoretical ground. Writing in the aftermath of religious turmoil in England and throughout Europe, he viewed religious rivalry and intolerance as among the most important of political problems. Religious intolerance was inconsistent both with public peace and with good government. Locke's resolution of the problem involved two elements: a modification of the nature and claims of religion and an abandonment of the government's role in upholding religious truth. His teachings on religion, most prominently in *The Reasonableness of Christianity*, urged that Christianity be made more rational and tolerant but less engaged in questions of earthly significance. Thus, the dissension among Christian

---

[112] Jefferson, *A Bill for Establishing Religious Freedom* (June 12, 1779), *reprinted in* 5 THE FOUNDERS' CONSTITUTION, *supra* note 72, at 77.

[113] *See* J. LOCKE, *A Letter Concerning Toleration*, in 6 WORKS OF LOCKE, *supra* note 111, at 1 [hereinafter J. LOCKE, *A Letter Concerning Toleration*]; Sandler, *Lockean Ideas in Thomas Jefferson's* Bill for Establishing Religious Freedom, 21 J. HIST. IDEAS 100 (1960); *see also* W. BERNS, *supra* note 13, at 18–24 (tracing the Lockean roots of Jefferson's insistence that principles of consent and free opinion require religious freedom); M. MALBIN, *supra* note 17, at 29 (noting and summarizing Jefferson's reliance upon the first *Letter Concerning Toleration* in drafting the Bill for Establishing Religious Freedom); Kessler, *Locke's Influence on Jefferson's "Bill for Establishing Religious Freedom,"* 25 J. CHURCH & ST. 231 (1983) (cataloging the similarities between Locke's *Letters* and Jefferson's bill).

[114] *See* Marty, *The Virginia Statute Two Hundred Years Later*, in VIRGINIA STATUTE FOR RELIGIOUS FREEDOM, *supra* note 108, at 1, 10–11. *But cf.* C. ANTIEAU, A. DOWNEY & E. ROBERTS, *supra* note 16 (explaining the varieties of religious establishment and toleration in the colonies and illustrating the wide range of opinion and practice that lies behind the adoption of the religion clauses); P. KAUPER, RELIGION AND THE CONSTITUTION 48–50 (1964) (warning against too heavy a reliance on the views of Madison and Jefferson for interpretation of the first amendment).

[115] *See infra* TAN 359–362.

[116] *See* McLoughlin, *Introduction*, in I. BACKUS, ISAAC BACKUS ON CHURCH, STATE, AND CALVINISM 1, 40–44 (W. McLoughlin ed. 1968) [hereinafter CHURCH, STATE, AND CALVINISM].

[117] *See* D. RICHARDS, *supra* note 54, at 105–10.

denominations would be softened and would be less likely to create political problems.

Although his little-known earlier works, *Two Tracts on Government*,[118] advocated that government reduce religious turmoil by enforcing religious unity,[119] by 1689 Locke had concluded that such attempts were the source of the problem: "It is not the diversity of opinions, which cannot be avoided; but the refusal of toleration to those that are of different opinions, which might have been granted, that has produced all the bustles and wars, that have been in the Christian world, upon account of religion."[120] Accordingly, Locke became an advocate of a sweeping toleration toward religious dissenters, with the exceptions of Catholics (because of their allegiance to a foreign prince), atheists (because they cannot be trusted to carry out their promises and oaths), and those who refuse to support tolerance for others.[121] "Nobody . . . [has] any just title to invade the civil rights and worldly goods of [another], upon pretence of religion," Locke stated. "Those that are of another opinion, would do well to consider with themselves how pernicious a seed of discord and war, how powerful a provocation to endless hatreds, rapines, and slaughters, they thereby furnish unto mankind."[122]

In Locke's view, religious strife stems from the tendency of both religious and governmental leaders to overstep their bounds and intermeddle in the others' province: "I esteem it above all things necessary to distinguish exactly the business of civil government from that of religion, and to settle the just bounds that lie between the one and the other."[123] The proper division between the realms of government and religion comes down to this: "all the power of civil government relates only to men's civil interests, is confined to the care of the things of this world, and hath nothing to do with the world to come,"[124] while "churches have [no] jurisdiction in worldly mat-

---

118 J. LOCKE, TWO TRACTS ON GOVERNMENT (P. Abrams ed. 1967). Not to be confused with his TWO TREATISES OF GOVERNMENT (P. Laslett rev. ed. 1963) (3d ed. 1698), these essays were written by Locke in 1660, at the age of 30, but he did not publish them. Both *Tracts* are devoted to defending the power of the magistrate over religion.

119 Locke's *Two Tracts on Government* resembled Thomas Hobbes' teaching that civil government should have complete authority over religion, extending not just to conduct but to religious profession and worship as well. *See* T. HOBBES, LEVIATHAN, pt. III, ch. 43, at 355 (M. Oakeshott ed. 1957) (1st ed. 1651). Hobbes denied any right to exemption from civil law on account of religious scruple, both because it would engender "confusion and civil war," *id.*, and because true Christianity required only two "virtues" for salvation: "*faith in Christ*, and *obedience to Laws*." *Id.* at 385 (emphasis in original).

120 J. LOCKE, *A Letter Concerning Toleration*, *supra* note 113, at 53.

121 *See id.* at 46–47.

122 *Id.* at 20.

123 *Id.* at 9.

124 *Id.* at 12–13.

ters."[125] Thus, Locke was concerned not only with limiting the powers of government, but also with limiting the purview of religion. "The end of a religious society," he wrote, "is the public worship of God, and by means thereof the acquisition of eternal life. All discipline ought therefore to tend to that end, and all ecclesiastical laws to be thereunto confined."[126]

To be sure, Locke's ideal of separation was less than complete, for he was willing to countenance governmental encouragement of the state religion. "[T]he magistrate may make use of arguments," wrote Locke, "and thereby draw the heterodox into the way of truth, and procure their salvation . . . . But it is one thing to persuade, another to command; one thing to press with arguments, another with penalties."[127] He also accepted government financial support of state religion and never condemned the English system of supporting the church with taxes; indeed, he served as secretary to the Lord Chancellor for the presentation of benefices — that is, the dispensing of religious patronage.[128] While Locke opposed what would be called interference with free exercise, he thus approved of what would be called an establishment under modern constitutional doctrine.

For the purposes of this Article, two aspects of Locke's teaching are particularly significant: his advocacy of legislative supremacy with respect to conflicts between public power and individual conscience and his rejection of religious exemptions. Although Locke's prescription for religious harmony depends upon the division between the religious and the secular jurisdictions, he anticipated that some matters, such as "[m]oral actions," belong "to the jurisdiction both of the . . . magistrate and conscience."[129] He recognized that this creates "great danger, lest one of these jurisdictions intrench upon the other."[130] As a practical matter, the possible overlap in jurisdiction did not greatly concern Locke, for "if government be faithfully administered, and the counsels of the magistrate be indeed directed to

---

[125] *Id.* at 19.

[126] *Id.* at 15–16. This understanding has its modern echo in the claim that religion is a strictly "private" matter, which ought not be allowed to influence public decisions. An example of this position, though not using precisely the words in text, is Justice Stevens' opinion in Webster v. Reproductive Health Services, 109 S. Ct. 3040 (1989), in which he argues that religiously based premises about the value of life form an illegitimate basis for legislation. *See id.* at 3082–85 (Stevens, J., concurring in part and dissenting in part). For a critique of this position, see K. GREENAWALT, RELIGIOUS CONVICTIONS AND POLITICAL CHOICE 12 (1988), which concludes that it is appropriate for citizens and legislators to rely upon their religious convictions when "shared premises of justice and criteria for determining truth cannot resolve critical questions of fact"; and *Religion and the State*, 27 WM. & MARY L. REV. 833, 1011–1109 (1986).

[127] J. LOCKE, *A Letter Concerning Toleration*, *supra* note 113, at 11.

[128] *See* 1 P. KING, THE LIFE OF JOHN LOCKE 62 (London 1830).

[129] J. LOCKE, *A Letter Concerning Toleration*, *supra* note 113, at 41.

[130] *Id.*

the public good," it will "seldom happen" that the magistrate enjoins "'any thing by his authority, that appears unlawful to the conscience of a private person.'"[131] In theory, however, such clashes might occur; Locke proposed that under these circumstances the individual should disobey the law and accept punishment from the state. "[T]he private judgment of any person concerning a law enacted in political matters, for the public good, does not take away the obligation of that law, nor deserve a dispensation."[132]

Locke gave a modicum of rhetorical support to the individual, exempting from this requirement of obedience those laws "not within the verge of the magistrate's authority."[133] But when the magistrate believes that a law is within his authority, and the individual believes the contrary, the magistrate prevails: "Who shall be judge between them? I answer, God alone; for there is no judge upon earth between the supreme magistrate and the people. . . . You will say then the magistrate being the stronger will have his will, and carry his point. Without doubt."[134] In other words, the *government's perception* of public need defines the boundaries of freedom of conscience. As Professor Walter Berns puts the point: "according to liberalism — one renders unto Caesar whatever Caesar demands and to God whatever

---

[131] *Id.* at 43.

[132] *Id.*

[133] *Id.*

[134] *Id.* at 44–45. This passage is similar to Locke's treatment of the wider theme of constitutional limits on government in *The Second Treatise of Government*. There, he posited that "the body of the people" are the "proper umpire" in cases of controversy over the powers of the government. *See* J. LOCKE, *The Second Treatise of Government* § 242, in TWO TREATISES OF GOVERNMENT, *supra* note 118, at 307, 476–77. But there is no lawful institution for vindication of the people's judgment. If the government does not honor the determination of the people on a contested point, "the appeal then lies nowhere but to heaven." *Id.* By this Locke meant revolution — a "state of war" between government and the people. The "supreme power" reverts to the people, who then have authority to "continue the legislative in themselves, or erect a new form, or under the old form place it in new hands, as they think good." *Id.* § 243, at 139. At a verbal level this "appeal to heaven" is the same remedy prescribed in *A Letter Concerning Toleration* for a violation of religious freedom, but with an important difference. In the case of religious freedom, Locke did not claim that the "body of the people" — or anyone else on earth — can serve as judge between the believer and the government. Perhaps this is because duties to God (unlike other constitutional limits) are not defined or governed by the social contract. Perhaps it is also because, as Madison perceived, the "body of the people" are as likely to violate the conscience of a religious minority as is the government. For this reason, the "appeal to heaven" is unlikely to take the form of revolution unless the believers whose rights are violated constitute a majority, or at least a powerful minority. In the context of religious freedom, therefore, Locke pointed to the otherworldly consequences of the appeal to heaven: "God, I say, is the only judge in this case, who will retribute unto every one at the last day according to his deserts . . . ." J. LOCKE, *A Letter Concerning Toleration*, *supra* note 113, at 44. No political institution, nor even the remedy of revolution available under Locke's political theories, can be expected to vindicate these rights if the magistrate chooses not to do so. Locke's language thus subtly suggests that religious freedom is fundamentally more vulnerable than other rights.

Caesar permits."[135] When individual conscience conflicts with the governmental policy, the government will always prevail and the individual will always be forced to submit or suffer the punishment.

This understanding of religious toleration expressly precludes free exercise exemptions. The rights of religious exercise, according to Locke, are simply rights of nondiscrimination. "Whatsoever is lawful in the commonwealth, cannot be prohibited by the magistrate in the church. Whatsoever is permitted unto any of his subjects for their ordinary use, neither can nor ought to be forbidden by him to any sect of people for their religious uses."[136] Locke gave the example of a sect that wishes to sacrifice a calf. "I deny that that ought to be prohibited by a law," he said.[137] Since individuals can lawfully kill a calf at home, and burn any part they see fit, they may do the same thing in a religious meeting.[138] They are not entitled, however, to dispensations or exceptions:

> [T]hose things that are prejudicial to the commonweal of a people in their ordinary use, and are therefore forbidden by laws, those things ought not to be permitted to churches in their sacred rites. Only the magistrate ought always to be very careful that he do not misuse his authority, to the oppression of any church, under pretence of public good.[139]

Accordingly, if the "interest of the commonwealth required all slaughter of beasts should be forborn for some while," the ritual slaughter of a calf for religious purposes may be forbidden as well.[140]

Locke's assertion of legislative supremacy and his opposition to special religious exemptions from generally applicable laws are consonant with arguments against free exercise exemptions. Unless there is reason to believe that the understanding of the free exercise clause held by the framers and ratifiers differed markedly from that of their intellectual forebear, Locke, *Sherbert* is historically unsupportable.[141] As the next section demonstrates, however, the movement towards a more expansive notion of religious liberty would gain momentum in the wake of the American Revolution and shape the framing of both state and federal constitutions.

---

135 W. BERNS, *supra* note 13, at 44.

136 J. LOCKE, *A Letter Concerning Toleration*, *supra* note 113, at 34.

137 *Id.*

138 *See id.*

139 *Id.* at 34-35.

140 *Id.* at 34.

141 The arguments against free exercise exemptions offered by Berns and Michael Malbin are based almost exclusively on Locke and his Enlightenment counterparts in America. *See* W. BERNS, *supra* note 13; M. MALBIN, *supra* note 17.

C. *Development of the Expansive Conception of Religious Freedom*

1. Disestablishment in the States. — The American Revolution immediately disrupted the relationship between religion and government in those states with an Anglican establishment. The Church of England was discredited during the Revolution by its connection to the Crown and the loyalist sympathies of most of its clergy. Accordingly, the Georgia Constitution of 1777, the South Carolina Constitution of 1778, the North Carolina Constitution of 1776, and the New York Constitution of 1777 (with reference to the four metropolitan counties that had an Anglican establishment) eliminated the special preferences and state support that had been given to the Church of England. South Carolina "established" the Protestant religion but gave it no governmental support, while Georgia authorized the imposition of a tax for the support of the taxpayer's "own profession." New York and North Carolina joined the ranks of states (Pennsylvania, New Jersey, Delaware, and Rhode Island) with no establishment.[142]

Virginia and Maryland were slower to adjust. Virginia adopted a free exercise provision in its Bill of Rights of 1776[143] and exempted dissenters from payment of tithes to the Anglican Church; shortly thereafter, it temporarily suspended mandatory tithes for everyone. The Church was formally disestablished in 1785, after a major popular and legislative battle in which James Madison played the leading role.[144] The Maryland Declaration of Rights of 1776 authorized the legislature to "lay a general and equal tax, for the support of the Christian religion,"[145] but during a protracted dispute in the Assembly in the 1780's, supporters of an assessment were never able to prevail.[146] Nonetheless, the Maryland legislature exercised continuing control over church affairs. So subservient was the established Church that in 1783 its clergy asked the legislature for permission to make changes in the prayer book.[147] Accordingly, the Episcopal

---

[142] *See* GA. CONST. of 1777, art. LVI, *reprinted in* 1 FEDERAL AND STATE CONSTITUTIONS, *supra* note 2, at 377, 383; N.Y. CONST of 1777, art. XXXV, *reprinted in* 2 FEDERAL AND STATE CONSTITUTIONS, *supra* note 2, at 1328, 1338; N.C. CONST. of 1776, art. XXXIV, *reprinted in* 2 FEDERAL AND STATE CONSTITUTIONS, *supra* note 2, at 1409, 1413–14; S.C. CONST. of 1778, art. XXXVIII, *reprinted in* 2 FEDERAL AND STATE CONSTITUTIONS, *supra* note 2, at 1620, 1626–27.

[143] *See* Va. Bill of Rights of 1776, *reprinted in* 2 FEDERAL AND STATE CONSTITUTIONS, *supra* note 2, at 1908.

[144] *See* T. BUCKLEY, CHURCH AND STATE IN REVOLUTIONARY VIRGINIA, 1776–1787, at 155–64 (1977).

[145] Md. Declaration of Rights of 1776, art. XXXIII, *reprinted in* 1 FEDERAL AND STATE CONSTITUTIONS, *supra* note 2, at 817, 819.

[146] *See* T. CURRY, *supra* note 17, at 154.

[147] *See id.* at 154–55.

Church of Maryland got the bitter of state meddling in church affairs without the sweet of regular state financial support.

The Congregational establishments of Connecticut, Massachusetts, New Hampshire, and Vermont were more firmly entrenched and emerged from the Revolution strengthened by their association with the patriot cause. In reference to the Massachusetts Congregationalists, John Adams observed that "[w]e might as soon expect a change in the solar system, as to expect that they would give up their establishment."[148] And indeed, by 1789 only these states maintained actual legal and financial support for the church. Outside of New England, only Maryland, South Carolina, and Georgia retained constitutional provisions permitting some form of establishment, and in none of these states did actual financial or other material support go into effect.

By 1834, no state in the Union would have an established church, and the tradition of separation between church and state would seem an ingrained and vital part of our constitutional system. But as the delegates gathered at the Constitutional Convention in Philadelphia in 1787 and at the meeting of the First Congress in New York in 1789, some form of establishment still held sway in most of New England, and the resolution of disestablishment controversies elsewhere could not be seen as assured.

2. The Evangelical Impetus Toward Religious Freedom. — The movement for freedom of religion in the 1780's was part of a broad reaction against the dominant but uninspired religious cultures represented by the Congregationalists of New England and the Anglicans of the South. It is a mistake to read the religion clauses under the now prevalent assumption that "the governing intellectual climate of the late eighteenth century was that of deism (or natural law)."[149] America was in the wake of a great religious revival. Historian Henry May has commented that the Enlightenment world view "excludes many, probably most, people who lived in America in the eighteenth and nineteenth centuries."[150] To determine the meaning of the religion clauses, it is necessary to see them through the eyes of their proponents, most of whom were members of the most fervent and evangelical denominations in the nation.[151]

One historian's portrait of Madison's neighbors, the Virginia Baptists, in the 1760's may help recreate the actual intellectual — more

---

148 1 W. McLoughlin, *supra* note 51, at 560 (quoting Isaac Backus' account of his confrontation with the Massachusetts delegation).

149 Marshall, *supra* note 17, at 18; *see also* W. Berns, *supra* note 13, at 1–2, 15–32 (same).

150 H. May, The Enlightenment in America at xiv (1976).

151 This point was first brought to the attention of legal scholars by M. Howe, cited above in note 82.

precisely, spiritual — climate among the proponents of religious freedom:

> Perhaps because they were at first largely lower class; perhaps because their worship sometimes caused their members to cry, bark like dogs, tremble, jerk, and fall to the ground; perhaps because they openly disdained the established religion and gentry mores; and perhaps because, as one Virginian charged, "they cannot meet a man on the road but they must ram a text of Scripture down his throat," the Baptists were reviled. They were seen as troublesome, and they were met with violence.[152]

It must have been particularly irksome to the gentry that the Baptists converted slaves in large numbers[153] and included them "as 'brothers' and 'sisters' in their close communities."[154] Even the Presbyterians, now pillars of mainstream Protestantism, were considered dangerously "enthusiastic" (meaning fanatical) by the authorities. Itinerant Presbyterian preachers in Virginia were said to "screw up the People to the greatest heights of religious Phrenzy, and then leave them in that wild state."[155]

The drive for religious freedom was part of this evangelistic movement. It is anachronistic to assume, based on modern patterns, that governmental aid to religion and suppression of heterodoxy were opposed by the more rationalistic and supported by the more intense religious believers of that era. The most intense religious sects opposed establishment on the ground that it injured religion and subjected it to the control of civil authorities. Guaranteed state support was thought to stifle religious enthusiasm and initiative. As Madison noted, the use of compulsory state taxes to support ministers would produce "pride and indolence in the Clergy; ignorance and servility in the laity."[156] Moreover, establishment served as an instrument for state control over religion. This was particularly true in the states of the Anglican establishment, including Virginia, where the governor, legislature, and gentry exercised direct authority over the established church and the power of licensing over preachers of dissenting denominations.[157] The establishment was localized and more democratic in

---

[152] J. LEWIS, *supra* note 60, at 49. A similar, though more sympathetic, portrayal is found in R. ISAAC, cited above in note 61, at 164–68.

[153] *See* R. ISAAC, *supra* note 61, at 165–66.

[154] *Id.* at 171–72.

[155] *Id.* at 150; *see also* D. BOORSTIN, THE AMERICANS: THE COLONIAL EXPERIENCE 135–36 (1958) (providing an unflattering portrayal of the "Enthusiastick Preachers" of New Light Presbyterianism).

[156] J. MADISON, *Memorial and Remonstrance*, *supra* note 109, at 187. This argument is elaborated by Adam Smith in A. SMITH, THE WEALTH OF NATIONS, bk. 5, ch. 1, pt. 3, art. 3, at 740–66 (E. Cannan ed. 1937) (5th ed. 1789).

[157] *See, e.g.*, D. BOORSTIN, *supra* note 155, at 126–27, 129 (describing how, in the absence

New England, but even there, the government set standards for licensing ministers and regulated ministerial tenure (hence ministerial independence) and itinerancy.[158]

State financial support was inevitably linked to control. The Baptists' declaration against the Virginia assessment proposal observed:

> If, therefore, the State provide a Support for Preachers of the Gospel, and they receive it in Consideration of their Services, they must certainly when they Preach act as Officers of the State, and ought to be Accountable thereto for their Conduct, not only as Members of civil Society, but also *as Preachers*. The Consequence of this is, that those whom the State employs in its Service, it has a Right to *regulate* and *dictate to*; it may judge and determine *who* shall preach; *when* and *where* they shall preach; and *what* they must preach.[159]

The newer, more enthusiastic sects had the most to gain from breaking the monopoly of the old established church. This would allow new, often uneducated and itinerant preachers to conduct worship services and revival meetings and would make the financial support of a preacher dependent on the enthusiasm he generated among his adherents. The greatest support for disestablishment and free exercise therefore came from evangelical Protestant denominations, especially Baptists and Quakers, but also Presbyterians, Lutherans, and others.[160] The decisive political event in the Virginia disestablishment struggle was the decision of the Presbyterians to

---

of a bishop in Virginia, the Anglican church was governed in temporal matters by the House of Burgesses and in other respects by the local gentry); S. COBB, *supra* note 17, at 97–98, 351–53 (giving examples of restrictive licensing of ministers in Virginia and New York); *id.* at 107 (recounting instances of investiture and defrocking of ministers by Virginia's governor); *id.* at 126 (discussing governmental control over ministers under North Carolina law); *id.* at 393–94 (illustrating control by the proprietor over investiture in Maryland); T. CURRY, *supra* note 17, at 99 (describing Virginia's prohibition of itinerant preaching); R. ISAAC, *supra* note 61, at 148–54 (recounting the struggle by Presbyterians in Virginia for permission to hold religious meetings); R. STRICKLAND, *supra* note 62, at 70, 83–87 (describing control by trustees over both the Church of England and Presbyterian ministries in Georgia).

[158] *See, e.g.*, S. COBB, *supra* note 17, at 174, 202–03 (providing examples of the Massachusetts General Court's power to regulate doctrinal purity and the qualifications of preachers); *id.* at 272–73 (recounting the adoption of laws against itinerant preaching in Connecticut); T. CURRY, *supra* note 17, at 99, 118 (discussing Connecticut laws against itinerant preaching); *id.* at 171 (discussing a Massachusetts law requiring ministers to possess degrees).

[159] Declaration of the Virginia Association of Baptists (Dec. 25, 1776), in 1 PAPERS OF JEFFERSON, *supra* note 111, at 660, 661 (emphasis in original).

[160] The small Jewish population of Philadelphia made its contribution to the struggle for free exercise with petitions against religious tests for office in Pennsylvania and at the federal level. *See, e.g.*, Petition of the Philadelphia Synagogue to Council of Censors of Pennsylvania (Dec. 23, 1783), *reprinted in* 4 THE FOUNDERS' CONSTITUTION, *supra* note 72, at 635; Letter from Jonas Phillips to the President and Members of the Convention (Sept. 7, 1787), *reprinted in* 3 THE RECORDS OF THE FEDERAL CONVENTION OF 1787, at 78, 78–79 (M. Farrand ed. 1911 and photo. reprint 1966) [hereinafter FARRAND RECORDS].

desert the assessment cause and join the opposition.[161] Madison's *Memorial and Remonstrance Against Religious Assessments*, with its mixed religious and secular arguments against the relatively liberal form of establishment proposed for Virginia in 1785, garnered thousands of supportive signatures. Over twice as many Virginians, however, subscribed to petitions arguing against the assessment in frankly religious terms — stating, among other things, that the bill violated "the Spirit of the Gospel."[162]

Religious rationalists, who are often credited with the leading intellectual role in the movement for religious freedom, were far more likely than the enthusiastic believers to side with the established church (with notable exceptions such as Jefferson).[163] Ironically, it was the Unitarian wing of the Standing Order, Jefferson's favored theological position, that led the fight against disestablishment in Massachusetts,[164] while the "enthusiastic" Baptists sought to cast down all vestiges of the establishment. The established religions — the Congregational churches of New England and the Anglican churches of the South — tended to be far more intellectual, uninspired, and agreeable to rationalist sensibilities, in contrast to the disturbing enthusiasm of the upstart denominations.

The religious supporters of disestablishment and free exercise in the various states also supported adoption of constitutional protections at the federal level, for essentially the same reasons. They were joined in the latter cause by a heterogeneous coalition called the Antifederalists, who used the absence of a bill of rights as an argument against ratification of the Constitution. This was little more than a marriage

---

[161] As the established church of Scotland, the Presbyterians had no doctrinal tradition of opposition to establishment. Their principal concern with the proposed assessment bill was that its provision for support of the clergy would undermine the control of the elders over the minister and the church. *See* T. BUCKLEY, *supra* note 144, at 92–96, 137–139. Shortly after the assessment controversy, the Presbyterians in the United States formally amended their Confession of Faith to renounce their prior support for establishment. *See* PRESBYTERIAN CHURCH (U.S.A.), "GOD ALONE IS LORD OF THE CONSCIENCE": POLICY STATEMENT AND RECOMMENDATIONS REGARDING RELIGIOUS LIBERTY 7, 69–70 (1988) [hereinafter PRESBYTERIAN POLICY STATEMENT].

[162] *See* T. BUCKLEY, *supra* note 144, at 148–50; T. CURRY, *supra* note 17, at 143–44.

[163] *See* T. CURRY, *supra* note 17, at 171 ("Religious rationalists in Massachusetts, such as Samuel West, Charles Chauncey, and other ministers who benefited from the state-supported religious system, remained its devoted upholders and insisted on its fairness."); *see also* D. BOORSTIN, *supra* note 155, at 132–39 (describing the undogmatic character of the Anglican Church of Virginia); R. ISAAC, *supra* note 61, at 120–21 (same); *id.* at 153 (reporting a sermon by an Anglican minister to the Virginia House of Burgesses that advocated "rational" religion and denounced the New Light evangelical movement); R. STRICKLAND, *supra* note 62, at 65 (describing a "typical eighteenth century Church of England man" in Georgia as "decrying Calvinism, 'enthusiasm' and the doctrines of regeneration").

[164] *See* McLoughlin, *Editor's Introduction* to I. BACKUS, *Government and Liberty Described*, in CHURCH, STATE, AND CALVINISM, *supra* note 116, at 345, 346.

of political convenience, for the advocates of religious freedom had little in common with the political principles of most Antifederalists. The Baptists of Virginia must have found it awkward to join forces with Patrick Henry, Virginia's leading Antifederalist, who had so recently championed the movement for religious assessments. Yet in the ratification convention in Virginia it was Henry who took up the issue of religious freedom and the absence of a Bill of Rights,[165] while Madison, the erstwhile supporter of religious freedom, urged ratification of the Constitution without amendment.[166]

The political theory of the advocates of free exercise sharply conflicted with the "republican" ideology that prevailed among most Antifederalists (as well as many Federalists).[167] The central preoccupation of republican political theory was the necessity of public "virtue." In its religious manifestation, this meant that government should support and encourage religion in order to promote public morality.[168] The Massachusetts Constitution of 1780, for example, justified its ministerial taxes on the ground that "the happiness of a people and the good order and preservation of civil government essentially depend on piety, religion, and morality."[169] The Virginia assessment proposal was defended on the same ground. A petition by citizens of Isle of Wight County, for example, stated: "being thoroughly convinced that the prosperity and happiness of this country essentially depends on the progress of religion, they . . . [pray] that an act may pass to compel every one to contribute something, in proportion to his property, to the support of religion."[170] The most famous statement of this sort was Washington's farewell address, in which he stated that "[o]f all the dispositions and habits which lead to political prosperity, religion and morality are indispensable supports. . . . And let us with caution indulge the supposition that morality can be maintained without religion."[171]

---

165 *See* 3 THE DEBATES IN THE SEVERAL STATE CONVENTIONS ON THE ADOPTION OF THE FEDERAL CONSTITUTION 317–18 (J. Elliott 2d ed. 1836) [hereinafter ELLIOT'S DEBATES] (June 12, 1788).

166 *See id.* at 330.

167 For recent analyses of republican ideology, see M. TUSHNET, RED, WHITE, AND BLUE: A CRITICAL ANALYSIS OF CONSTITUTIONAL LAW 4–14 (1988); Michelman, *The Supreme Court, 1985 Term — Foreword: Traces of Self Government*, 100 HARV. L. REV. 4 (1986); and Sunstein, *Beyond the Republican Revival*, 97 YALE L. J. 1539 (1988).

168 *See* G. WOOD, THE CREATION OF THE AMERICAN REPUBLIC 1776-1787, at 426–29 (1969).

169 Mass. Declaration of Rights of 1780, art. III, in 1 FEDERAL AND STATE CONSTITUTIONS, *supra* note 2, at 957.

170 Petition for General Assessment (Nov. 4, 1784), *reprinted in* C. JAMES, DOCUMENTARY HISTORY OF THE STRUGGLE FOR RELIGIOUS LIBERTY IN VIRGINIA 125, 125 (1900 and photo. reprint 1971).

171 Washington, *Farewell Address* (Sept. 17, 1796), *reprinted in* 1 DOCUMENTS OF AMERICAN HISTORY 169, 173 (H. Commager 9th ed. 1973).

These arguments ran directly contrary to the position of the evangelical advocates of the religion clauses. To be sure, these advocates did not deny that religion is necessary to civil society. Isaac Backus, for example, affirmed that "religion is as necessary for the well-being of human society as salt is to preserve from putrefaction or as light is to direct our way and to guard against enemies, confusion, and misery."[172] But they did deny that governmental support is necessary, or even useful, to religion.[173] According to Elder John Leland, leader of the Virginia Baptists, "[i]t is error alone, that stands in need of government to support it; truth can and will do better without . . . it."[174] Moreover, the evangelicals found this very mode of argument objectionable, because it implied that religion was to be used as an instrument of statecraft, thus implicitly subordinating religion to the goal of "political prosperity." As Backus caustically observed of the Massachusetts establishment, "a little while ago" the establishment was "for religion," but now it is said to be "for the good of *civil society*."[175]

The paradox of the religious freedom debates of the late eighteenth century is that one side employed essentially secular arguments based on the needs of civil society for the support of religion, while the other side employed essentially religious arguments based on the primacy of duties to God over duties to the state in support of disestablishment and free exercise. It was Baptist preacher John Leland who first stated that "[t]he notion of a Christian commonwealth, should be exploded forever."[176]

Although the secular strain of republicanism was less an object of the evangelicals' polemics, it was no less inconsistent with their understanding of the proper role of the state. Civic republicanism sought to inculcate public virtue through various devices, including sumptuary laws, education, and participatory politics. To the evangelical advocates of religious freedom, this too was a vain extension of the governmental sphere; virtue is either impossible or incoherent when divorced from duty to God. Their position places the state in the precarious posture of depending upon autonomous institutions to preserve the moral conditions necessary to the survival of republican government.

Thus, the evangelical position ultimately coalesced with the secular liberal position, as against the dying tradition of civic republicanism.

---

[172] I. BACKUS, *Policy, as Well as Honesty, Forbids the Use of Secular Force in Religious Affairs*, in CHURCH, STATE, AND CALVINISM, *supra* note 116, at 367, 371.

[173] *See supra* pp. 1438–40.

[174] J. LELAND, *The Virginia Chronicle*, in THE WRITINGS OF THE LATE ELDER JOHN LELAND 91, 118 (L. Greene ed. 1845) [hereinafter LELAND WRITINGS].

[175] I. BACKUS, *An Appeal to the Public for Religious Liberty*, in CHURCH, STATE, AND CALVINISM, *supra* note 116, at 303, 324 (emphasis in original).

[176] J. LELAND, *supra* note 174, at 107.

This explains why the more fervent evangelicals, including the Baptists, tended to become Jeffersonians, notwithstanding the deism of Jefferson and the piety of his opponents. Religion, the evangelicals believed, is vital to civic harmony. But voluntary religious societies — not the state — are the best and only legitimate institutions for the transmission of religious faith and, with it, virtue. The only support that churches can legitimately expect from the government, apart from equal participation in the benefits of civil society, is protection and noninterference.[177]

3. Advances Beyond Locke in the Popular Understanding of Religious Freedom. — The same evangelical forces converged in support of protections for religious liberty through free exercise provisions in state constitutions. It is no accident that Locke's vocabulary ("toleration of religion") was rejected in favor of more sweeping terms — not just the "exercise," but the "free exercise" of religion, or "full and equal rights of conscience." When George Mason proposed the term "toleration" for the religious liberty clause of the Virginia Bill of Rights,[178] Madison objected on the ground that the word "toleration" implies an act of legislative grace, which in Locke's understanding it was. Madison proposed, and the Virginia assembly adopted, the broader phrase: "the full and free exercise of [religion]."[179]

Madison was far from alone in his rejection of the concept of "toleration." Tench Coxe, a prominent essayist, stated that "[m]ere toleration is a doctrine exploded by our general constitution."[180] He said that the Americans had "substituted an unqualified admission and assertion, that their own modes of worship and of faith equally belong to all the worshippers of God, of whatever church, sect, or denomination."[181] George Washington, in his famous address to the Hebrew

---

[177] *See* J. LELAND, *The Rights of Conscience Inalienable*, in LELAND WRITINGS, *supra* note 174, at 179, 184. Leland wrote:

> Let every man speak freely without fear, maintain the principles that he believes, worship according to his own faith, either one God, three Gods, no God, or twenty Gods; and let government protect him in so doing, i.e., see that he meets with no personal abuse, or loss of property, for his religious opinions.

Id. The Presbyterian Church formally adopted a similar position at its first General Assembly in 1788: "'We do not even wish to see any religious constitution aided by the civil power, further than may be necessary for protection and security, at the same time be equal and common to all others.'" PRESBYTERIAN POLICY STATEMENT, *supra* note 161, at 7 (quoting the Presbyterian Principles of Church Order).

[178] *See* Hunt, *James Madison and Religious Liberty*, 1 ANN. REP. AM. HIST. A. 163, 166 (1901). Mason's proposal read in relevant part: "'that all men should enjoy the fullest toleration in the exercise of religion, according to the dictates of conscience, unpunished and unrestrained by the magistrate, unless under color of religion any man disturb the peace, the happiness, or safety of society.'" *Id.*

[179] *Id.*

[180] Kurland, *supra* note 17, at 857 (quoting T. COXE, A VIEW OF THE UNITED STATES OF AMERICA 103–04 (Philadelphia 1794)).

[181] *Id.*

Congregation of Newport, Rhode Island, stated: "It is now no more that toleration is spoken of, as if it was by the indulgence of one class of people, that another enjoyed the exercise of their inherent natural rights."[182] More pungently, Thomas Paine commented: "Toleration is not the *opposite* of intolerance, but is the *counterfeit* of it. Both are despotisms. The one assumes to itself the right of withholding liberty of conscience, and the other of granting it."[183] The United States, several millions of dissenters and a century of pluralism ahead of Locke's England, had advanced beyond mere toleration of religion.

There are two primary reasons to believe that the popular conception of free exercise on this side of the Atlantic was more expansive than Locke's doctrine of religious toleration: the advent of judicial review, and a difference in conception of the nature and role of religion.

(a) Judicial Review. — One reason that Locke's doctrines may have seemed so limited from an American perspective is that he did not envision an authority within the law that was capable of limiting the sovereign power of the "magistrate" (by which he meant the government, the King, and Parliament). "[T]here is no judge upon earth between the supreme magistrate and the people."[184] While Locke recognized the moral imperative to obey God instead of civil rulers,[185] his conception of political institutions did not include a mediator who could transform this moral, prepolitical right into positive law. In the absence of such a mediator, individual conscience could be compelled to yield to government in the event of a conflict. For Locke, the field left to untrammeled conscience could only extend to that in which the civil magistrate had no particular interest — principally, to things pertaining to the world to come. Religious liberty could only be defined negatively; any broader definition would be pointless, since the magistrate would be judge of his own powers.

Locke's key assumption of legislative supremacy no longer holds under a written constitution with judicial review. The revolutionary American contribution to political theory was that the people themselves are sovereign and therefore possess inherent power to limit the power of the magistrate, through a written constitution enforced by judges independent of the legislature and executive. As Madison would predict during deliberation over the Bill of Rights:

> If [the provisions of the Bill of Rights] are incorporated into the constitution, independent tribunals of justice will consider themselves

---

[182] 31 G. Washington, The Writings of George Washington 93 n.65 (J. Fitzpatrick ed. 1939).

[183] T. Paine, *The Rights of Man*, pt. 1, in 1 The Complete Writings of Thomas Paine 243, 291 (P. Foner ed. 1945) (emphasis in original).

[184] J. Locke, *A Letter Concerning Toleration*, *supra* note 113, at 44.

[185] *See id.* at 43–45.

> in a peculiar manner the guardians of those rights; they will be an impenetrable bulwark against every assumption of power in the legislative or executive; they will be naturally led to resist every encroachment upon rights expressly stipulated for in the constitution by the declaration of rights.[186]

Once the courts are vested with the power to determine the proper boundary between individual conscience and the magistrate's authority, based on the words of a written charter derived from the people, fuller protection for conscience becomes conceivable. An independent judiciary could define religious liberty affirmatively, in terms of what religious liberty requires, and not merely what the legislature concedes. The modern "judicial restraint" position, that legislatures are entitled to make free exercise exemptions but courts are not, is a relic of Lockean legislative supremacy. Once the people empowered the courts to enforce the boundary between individual rights and the magistrate's power, they entrusted the courts with a responsibility that prior to 1789 had been exercised only by the legislature.

(b) The Nature and Role of Religion. — Those most engaged in the struggle for religious freedom guarantees in the United States also departed from Locke's understanding of the role of religion and the utility of religious liberty. While they put Locke's arguments to good effect in legitimating their position, the free exercise apologists used Locke opportunistically, ignoring implications of his argument that were inconvenient to their case. To Locke, religious divisions and discord presented a political problem; the solution was to keep the peace by making religion irrelevant to the things of this world — other than a reasonable, uncontroversial advocacy of good morals, which would be fully consistent with the public good, publicly defined.

This was not the religious enthusiasts' idea of religion and not their idea of religious liberty. To them, the church-state problem was principally a religious problem: the state too frequently used its power to prevent the practice and spread of the gospel. The Baptists languishing in the Culpepper jail and the Presbyterians fighting legislative interference with their form of church governance were not fearful of religion. They were fearful of government. To the evangelical spirit of the minority Protestant sects in America, Locke's conception of the separation between the secular and the religious would have seemed absurd. Does not the will of God govern all of life? Is He not sovereign over all? To the preachers who only recently had been among the leading advocates of revolution against the King, Locke's

---

186 1 ANNALS OF CONG. 457 (J. Gales ed. 1834) (June 8, 1789). The evidence is overwhelming that the framers and ratifiers understood and intended the courts to engage in constitutional judicial review. For a brief summary, see D. CURRIE, THE CONSTITUTION IN THE SUPREME COURT: THE FIRST HUNDRED YEARS 1789-1888, at 69–70 (1985).

claim that they should be "forbidden meddling with making or executing laws in their preaching"[187] must have seemed quaint, as well as presumptuous. If Locke and Jefferson wished to promote a peaceable, rational religion that minds its own business, is tolerant of others, and does not meddle in affairs of state,[188] their aspirations were diametrically opposed to those whose political efforts produced the first amendment.

These differing conceptions of the purposes of religious freedom have clear implications for the question of free exercise exemptions. From the religious perspective, the scope of free exercise cannot be defined, in the first instance, by asking what matters the public is rightly concerned about. Religion involves itself in many matters of importance to the public. Free exercise must be defined, in the first instance, by what matters God is concerned about, according to the conscientious belief of the individual.

In this respect, Madison's argument in the *Memorial and Remonstrance* echoed evangelical convictions about the roles of religion and civil government. His position that duty to God precedes the claims of civil society[189] strongly resembles the teachings of John Witherspoon, the nation's leading Presbyterian clergyman and President of the College of New Jersey (Princeton) while Madison was a student. In an address that Madison might have heard, Witherspoon observed:

> Another reason why the servants of God are represented as troublesome is, because they will not, and dare not comply with the sinful commandments of men. In matters merely civil, good men are the most regular citizens and the most obedient subjects. But, as they have a Master in heaven, no earthly power can constrain them to deny his name or desert his cause.[190]

The demands of civil society must be judged against the demands of God. That is why the "servants of God" seem "troublesome" and why a society that determines to respect the claims of conscience must recognize exemptions from its laws.

---

[187] J. LOCKE, ESSAYS ON THE LAW OF NATURE 275 (W. von Leyden ed. 1954) (ca. 1660).

[188] Compare Jefferson's praise for the Virginia Methodists with his criticism of the Presbyterian clergy: "The Methodists are republican mostly, satisfied with their governmt. [,] medling with nothing but the concerns of their own calling and opposing nothing"; the Presbyterian clergy "are violent, ambitious of power, and intolerant in politics as in religion and want nothing but license from the laws to kindle again the fires of their leader John Knox, and to give us a 2d blast from his trumpet." Letter from Thomas Jefferson to Dr. Thomas Cooper (March 13, 1820), in THE LIFE AND SELECTED WRITINGS OF THOMAS JEFFERSON 697, 697 (A. Koch & W. Peden eds. 1944) [hereinafter SELECTED WRITINGS OF JEFFERSON].

[189] See *infra* text accompanying notes 229–230.

[190] J. WITHERSPOON, *The Charge of Sedition and Faction Against Good Men, Especially Faithful Ministers, Considered and Accounted for*, in 2 THE WORKS OF THE REV. JOHN WITHERSPOON 415, 427 (Philadelphia 1802).

While the argument for exemptions tended to be oblique and by implication, opponents of free exercise automatically assumed that liberty of conscience must entail exemptions, and thus claimed that free exercise was tantamount to anarchy. Proponents of exemptions could have responded by denying any claim to exemptions and confining their opposition to discriminatory treatment. But this was not their approach. Proponents did attempt to minimize the practical consequences of the exemptions position by stoutly declaring their fealty to almost all of the laws. But they cleverly used ambiguous language to leave open the theoretical possibility that conscience would prevail over wrongful legislation.

The question of exemptions arose for the first time in the disputation between John Cotton and Roger Williams in the 1640's and 1650's.[191] Williams argued that the government has no authority to enforce the so-called "First Table" (the first four commandments, which deal with religious worship).[192] Cotton responded that this undermined the government's authority to enforce the "Second Table" (murder, theft, perjury, etc.), as well.[193] As Thomas Curry, author of the of the leading history of church-state conflicts in preconstitutional America, observes:

> This rebuttal to Williams derived its strength from its solid foundation in a very real problem, which Williams was unable to tackle and which still has not been solved: how to distinguish between those areas that belong only to religion or conscience and those that belong to the law. In other words, to what extent does a claim to the free exercise of religion exempt one from the laws of the land?[194]

If conscience must be respected, and if conscience can be defined in no way other than by the individual believer, then doesn't liberty of conscience give believers a license to violate laws vital to social order?

Williams never provided a direct response to this question. William Penn did. In *The Great Case of Liberty of Conscience*, Penn posed and answered a number of "objections" made by opponents of religious freedom. To objection number three, "[b]ut at this Rate ye may pretend to Cut our Throats, and do all Manner of Savage Acts,"[195] Penn responded:

> Though the Objection be frequent, yet it is as foully ridiculous[.] We are pleading only for such a *Liberty of Conscience*, as preserves the Nation in Peace, Trade, and Commerce; and would not exempt any

191 The exchange is summarized in T. CURRY, cited above in note 17, at 18.

192 *See id.*

193 *See id.*

194 *Id.*

195 W. PENN, *supra* note 107, at 457.

Man, or Party of Men, from not keeping those excellent Laws, that tend to Sober, Just, and Industrious Living.[196]

This endorsement of certain "excellent laws" falls conspicuously short of a denial of exemption from *any* laws. Penn went on to deny that the Quakers had violated any laws, properly so called, even though "[i]f the enacting *any Thing* can make it lawful," it was true that the Quakers had violated the "law" against unlawful assemblies.[197] His position was that "law" in the true sense was confined to limited purposes, which could not conflict with Quaker practices. He argued that "the Words *Lawful* or *Unlawful*" must "bear their Signification from the Nature of the Things they stand for" rather than from mere enactment into statutes.[198]

A century later, John Leland, the leader of the Baptists in Virginia during the assessment controversy and the enactment of the first amendment, addressed the same question. Like Penn, he condemned in the strongest language the notion that liberty of conscience would justify crimes such as murder or tax evasion:

> Should a man refuse to pay his tribute for the support of government, or any wise disturb the peace and good order of the civil police, he should be punished according to his crime, let his religion be what it will; but when a man is a peacable subject of state, he should be protected in worshipping the Deity according to the dictates of his own conscience.[199]

But also like Penn, Leland made clear that this did not mean that believers could be required to obey *all* laws. "It is often the case," he wrote, "that laws are made which prevent the liberty of conscience; and because men cannot stretch their consciences like a nose of wax, these non-conformists are punished as vagrants that disturb the peace."[200] Unfortunately, Leland supplied no clear basis for distinguishing between the cases. "Let any man read the laws," he said, "and see who were the aggressors."[201] Instead, he seems to have assumed that the distinction would be readily apparent. When a believer's "practice is opposed to good law, he is to be punished,"[202] but when the law has invaded the province of conscience, punishment would be an aggression.

---

196 *Id.*

197 *Id.* at 458.

198 *Id.*

199 J. LELAND, *The Yankee Spy*, in LELAND WRITINGS, *supra* note 174, at 213, 228.

200 *Id.*

201 *Id.*

202 *Id.*; *see also* I. BACKUS, *supra* note 175, at 317 ("We view it to be our incumbent duty to render unto Caesar the things that are his but also that it is of as much importance not to render unto him anything that belongs only to God, who is to be obeyed rather than any man.").

Locke's position of no exemptions would have been an easier one to maintain, especially for the Baptists, whose religious practices did not conflict with any generally applicable secular laws. But the Baptists and other proponents of religious freedom in America did not adopt Locke's position, presumably because they insisted on defining liberty of conscience as adherence to the demands of God. This, then, is the key difference between the Lockean view and the popular American view: the former takes the perspective of government and the latter the perspective of the believer. It remains to be seen which of these perspectives dominated the legal arrangements for religious liberty in the years leading up to 1789.

4. The Views of the Framers. — The growing popular support for broad religious freedom within the newly formed American states helped to shape the views of the framers of the Constitution and the free exercise clause. Of particular interest are the contrasting positions of Jefferson and Madison regarding the religion issue, not only because they played the key roles in formulating the free exercise clauses of Virginia and the federal Constitution, but also because their differences illuminate the American evolution away from the narrower conception of religious liberty championed by Locke.

Like Locke, Jefferson favored a mild, tolerant, and rationalistic brand of religion.[203] Professor Sanford Kessler points out that "Jefferson's debt to Locke in theological matters was so great that in some instances he accepted Locke's interpretation of the gospels over what he believed to be the doctrines of Jesus himself."[204] As Locke advocated a watered-down and de-politicized Christianity in his *Reasonableness of Christianity*, so Jefferson took the more radical step of composing his own version of the gospels, excluding everything at variance with his understanding of science and natural morality.[205] Jefferson far surpassed Locke in his hostility to orthodox Christianity. Jefferson called Athanasius and Calvin — the pillars of Catholic and Reformed theology — "impious dogmatists" and "mere usurpers of the Christian name, teaching a counter-religion made up of the *deliria* of crazy imaginations."[206] He denied the divinity of Christ and the

---

[203] *See* Kessler, *Jefferson's Rational Religion*, in THE CONSTITUTIONAL POLITY: ESSAYS ON THE FOUNDING PRINCIPLES OF AMERICAN POLITICS 58 (S. Pearson ed. 1983); Kessler, *supra* note 113; Little, *Thomas Jefferson's Religious Views and Their Influence on the Supreme Court's Interpretation of the First Amendment*, 26 CATH. U.L. REV. 57, 58–64 (1976).

[204] Kessler, *supra* note 113, at 247–48 (footnotes omitted).

[205] *See* T. JEFFERSON, THE LIFE AND MORALS OF JESUS OF NAZARETH (Philadelphia 1804 and photo. reprint 1904). For example, Jefferson deleted from his narrative all of the miracles of Jesus reported in the New Testament.

[206] Letter from Thomas Jefferson to Dr. Benjamin Waterhouse (June 26, 1822), in 12 THE WORKS OF THOMAS JEFFERSON 241, 242 (P. Ford ed. 1905) [hereinafter WORKS OF JEFFERSON] (emphasis in original); *see also* Letter from Thomas Jefferson to John Adams (April 11, 1823), in SELECTED WRITINGS OF JEFFERSON, *supra* note 188, at 705–06 (calling Calvin "an atheist, . . . or rather his religion was daemonism").

authority of scripture,[207] condemned the Protestant doctrine that forgiveness of sins is achieved through repentance as opposed to good works,[208] and ridiculed Presbyterians, among others, for "fanaticism" in matters of religion.[209] He was equally contemptuous of Judaism, whose theology he called "degrading and injurious" and whose ethics he called "repulsive."[210]

Jefferson advocated religious freedom, in large part, as a means of combatting religious enthusiasm and advancing the day when all would become adherents of Unitarianism, his idea of a rational and sensible religion:

> I rejoice that in this blessed country of free inquiry and belief, which has surrendered its creed and conscience to neither kings nor priests, the genuine doctrine of one only God is reviving, and I trust that there is not a *young man* now living in the United States who will not die an Unitarian.[211]

This Lockean-Jeffersonian preference for rational over traditional religion continues to characterize one strain, perhaps the dominant strain, of American liberalism.[212]

In many respects, Jefferson advocated a fuller freedom of religion than Locke. Whereas Locke favored a single established church, Jefferson opposed any form of state-established church, even the broad multiple establishment proposed for Virginia. Unlike Locke, Jefferson

---

[207] *See* Letter from Thomas Jefferson to Peter Carr (Aug. 10, 1787), in SELECTED WRITINGS OF JEFFERSON, *supra* note 188, at 429, 431–33; Letter from Thomas Jefferson to William Short (Aug. 4, 1820), in 15 THE WRITINGS OF THOMAS JEFFERSON 257, 261–62 (A. Lipscomb ed. 1903) [hereinafter WRITINGS OF JEFFERSON].

[208] *See* Letter from Thomas Jefferson to William Short (April 13, 1820), in 15 WRITINGS OF JEFFERSON, *supra* note 207, at 243, 244.

[209] Letter from Thomas Jefferson to Dr. Thomas Cooper (Nov. 2, 1822), in THOMAS JEFFERSON: WRITINGS 1463, 1464 (M. Peterson ed. 1984). Jefferson once wrote to John Adams: "If, by *religion*, we are to understand *Sectarian dogmas*, in which no two of them agree, then your exclamation on that hypothesis is just, 'that this would be the best of all possible worlds, if there were no religion in it.'" Letter from Thomas Jefferson to John Adams (May 5, 1817), in 2 THE ADAMS-JEFFERSON LETTERS 512, 512 (L. Cappon ed. 1959) (emphasis in original).

[210] *See* Letter from Thomas Jefferson to Dr. Benjamin Rush (April 21, 1803), in SELECTED WRITINGS OF JEFFERSON, *supra* note 188, at 566, 569 (enclosing Jefferson's Syllabus of an Estimate of the Merit of the Doctrines of Jesus, Compared with Those of Others); *see also* Letter from Thomas Jefferson to John Adams (Oct. 12, 1813), in 2 THE ADAMS-JEFFERSON LETTERS, *supra* note 209, at 383, 383–84 (commenting on the "wretched depravity of sentiment and manners" which prevailed among the Jews, and which Jesus undertook to reform).

[211] Letter from Thomas Jefferson to Dr. Benjamin Waterhouse (June 26, 1822), *supra* note 206, at 243 (emphasis in original). To similar effect, see Letter from Thomas Jefferson to James Smith (Dec. 8, 1822), in SELECTED WRITINGS OF JEFFERSON, cited above in note 188, at 703; *cf.* Letter from Thomas Jefferson to John Adams (April 11, 1823), in 2 THE ADAMS-JEFFERSON LETTERS, *supra* note 209, at 591, 593–94 (rejecting the doctrine of a Holy Spirit separate from God).

[212] *See, e.g.*, J. DEWEY, A COMMON FAITH (1934).

would extend toleration to atheists and Catholics, though he appeared to agree that toleration should be denied those who would not tolerate others.[213] Unlike Locke, Jefferson would deny all power to the government to provide financial support for religious teaching, arguing that "to compel a man to furnish contributions of money for the propagation of opinions which he disbelieves and abhors, is sinful and tyrannical."[214] Finally, Jefferson departed from Locke's views by denying the authority of governmental officials to promote or encourage religion, even through persuasion.[215]

Jefferson's understanding of the scope and rationale of free exercise rights, however, was more limited even than Locke's. Like Locke, he based his advocacy of freedom of religion on the judgment that religion, properly confined, can do no harm: "The legitimate powers of government extend to such acts only as are injurious to others. But it does me no injury for my neighbour to say there are twenty gods, or no god. It neither picks my pocket nor breaks my leg."[216] On this rationale, Jefferson espoused a strict distinction between belief, which should be protected from governmental control, and conduct, which should not. As he wrote in his famous "wall of separation" letter to the Danbury Baptist Association, "the legislative powers of government reach actions only, and not opinions . . . . [M]an . . . has no natural right in opposition to his social duties."[217] It was in reliance on Jefferson that the Supreme Court later held that there can be no free exercise right to exemption from a generally applicable law when such laws are directed at actions and not opinions.[218]

Jefferson's advocacy of a belief-action distinction placed him at least a century behind the argument for full freedom of religious exercise in America. William Penn wrote in 1670 that "by *Liberty of Conscience*, we understand not only a meer *Liberty of the Mind*, in believing or disbelieving . . . *but the exercise of ourselves in a visible way of worship*."[219] Historian Thomas Curry recounts the 1651 flogging of Obediah Holmes, a Baptist, for holding a religious meeting in Lynn, Massachusetts: "To the familiar argument that he was sentenced not for conscience but for practice, Clark replied that there could be

---

[213] *See* T. JEFFERSON, *supra* note 111, at 550 n.2.

[214] Jefferson, *A Bill for Establishing Religious Freedom* (June 12, 1779), *reprinted in* 5 THE FOUNDERS' CONSTITUTION, *supra* note 72, at 77, 77.

[215] *See* Letter from Thomas Jefferson to the Rev. Samuel Miller (Jan. 23, 1808), in 11 WORKS OF JEFFERSON, *supra* note 206, at 7 (explaining his refusal to issue a presidential proclamation of a day of fasting and prayer).

[216] T. JEFFERSON, NOTES ON THE STATE OF VIRGINIA 159 (W. Peden ed. 1955) (1st ed. 1787).

[217] Letter from Thomas Jefferson to a Committee of the Danbury Baptist Association (Jan. 1, 1820), in 16 WRITINGS OF JEFFERSON, *supra* note 207, at 281, 281–82.

[218] *See* Reynolds v. United States, 98 U.S. 145, 164 (1878).

[219] W. PENN, *supra* note 107, at 447 (emphasis in original).

no such thing as freedom of conscience without freedom to act."[220] It is unlikely that many Americans would have disputed that position by 1789. St. George Tucker, no radical, wrote in 1803 that "[l]iberty of conscience in matters of religion consists in the absolute and unrestrained exercise of our religious opinions, *and duties*, in that mode which our own reason and conviction dictate."[221] Thus, while Jefferson was one of the most advanced advocates of disestablishment, his position on free exercise was extraordinarily restrictive for his day.[222]

Although often linked with Jefferson's "Enlightenment-deist-rationalist" stance toward religious freedom,[223] Madison's views on the religion-state question should be distinguished from those of his fellow Virginian, and hence from Locke.[224] To begin with, Madison possessed a far more sympathetic attitude toward religion than did Jefferson.[225] While Madison's religious convictions as an adult are unknown, as a young man he attended a Presbyterian college in New Jersey (Princeton) instead of pursuing the more natural course of study at the Anglican college, William and Mary, in his own state. Madison's correspondence with his close friend, William Bradford, suggests that the more evangelical Presbyterian teachings took hold, at least for a time; he urged Bradford to become a "fervent Advocate[] in the cause of Christ."[226] None of Madison's writings displayed the disdain Jefferson expressed for the more intense manifestations of religious spirit. Indeed, the sight of "5 or 6 well meaning men" — Baptist preachers imprisoned in Culpepper, Virginia "for publishing their religious Sentiments which in the main are very orthodox" — sparked his concern for religious freedom. The usually soft-spoken Madison described such persecution as a "diabolical Hell conceived principle,"

---

220 T. CURRY, *supra* note 17, at 15.

221 ST. GEORGE TUCKER, 1 BLACKSTONE'S COMMENTARIES, *reprinted in* 5 THE FOUNDERS' CONSTITUTION, *supra* note 72, at 96, 97 (emphasis added).

222 For this reason, Michael Malbin's argument against free exercise exemptions must be rejected. After noting that Jefferson opposed free exercise exemptions, Malbin contends that "whatever protection the free exercise clause might have meant to give to religion, it was not likely to have been greater than the protection Jefferson thought religion should be given." M. MALBIN, *supra* note 17, at 36.

223 *See* D. RICHARDS, *supra* note 54, at 111–21, 147–48; Pepper, *supra* note 18, at 314. The Supreme Court has repeatedly linked Jefferson and Madison as if their thought were identical. *See, e.g.*, School Dist. v. Schempp, 374 U.S. 203, 214 (1963); McGowan v. Maryland, 366 U.S. 420, 465 (1961) (Frankfurter, J. concurring); Everson v. Board of Educ., 330 U.S. 1, 40 (1947) (Rutledge, J. dissenting); Reynolds v. United States, 98 U.S. 145, 163–64 (1878).

224 *See* Pepper, *supra* note 18, at 320–21. For a discussion of differences between Madison and Jefferson in other areas, see A. KOCH, JEFFERSON AND MADISON: THE GREAT COLLABORATION 43–46 (1950).

225 *See* Ketcham, *James Madison and Religion: A New Hypothesis*, in JAMES MADISON ON RELIGIOUS LIBERTY 175 (R. Alley ed. 1985).

226 Letter from James Madison to William Bradford (Sept. 25, 1773), in 1 THE PAPERS OF JAMES MADISON 95, 96 (R. Rutland & C. Hobson eds. 1977) [hereinafter MADISON PAPERS].

and stated that it "vexes me the most of any thing whatsoever."[227] He recounted that he had "squabbled and scolded abused and ridiculed so long about it, [to so lit]tle purpose that I am without common patience."[228] This formative experience exemplifies the marked difference between Madison and Jefferson in their attitudes towards religious liberty. In all Jefferson's writings about liberty of conscience, he never once showed concern for those who wish to practice an active faith; to Jefferson, unlike Madison, liberty of conscience meant largely freedom from sectarian religion, rather than freedom to practice religion in whatever form one chooses.

Consistent with this more affirmative stance toward religion, Madison advocated a jurisdictional division between religion and government based on the demands of religion rather than solely on the interests of society. In his *Memorial and Remonstrance*, he wrote:

> The Religion then of every man must be left to the conviction and conscience of every man; and it is the right of every man to exercise it as these may dictate. . . . It is the duty of every man to render to the Creator such homage, and such only, as he believes to be acceptable to him.[229]

Moreover, Madison claimed that this duty to the Creator is "precedent both in order of time and degree of obligation, to the claims of Civil Society," and "therefore that in matters of Religion, no man's right is abridged by the institution of Civil Society."[230]

This striking passage illuminates the radical foundations of Madison's writings on religious liberty. While it does not prove that Madison supported free exercise exemptions, it suggests an approach toward religious liberty consonant with them. If the scope of religious liberty is defined by religious duty (man must render to God "such homage . . . as he believes to be acceptable to him"), and if the claims of civil society are subordinate to the claims of religious freedom, it would seem to follow that the dictates of religious faith must take precedence over the laws of the state, even if they are secular and generally applicable. This is the central point on which Madison differs from Locke, Jefferson, and other Enlightenment advocates of religious freedom.[231]

---

[227] Letter from James Madison to William Bradford (Jan. 24, 1774), in 1 MADISON PAPERS, *supra* note 226, at 104, 106.

[228] *Id.*

[229] J. MADISON, *Memorial and Remonstrance*, *supra* note 109, at 183, 184.

[230] *Id.* at 184–85.

[231] Walter Berns, an astute scholar of Locke and the liberal Enlightenment, argues against free exercise exemptions on Lockean grounds: "Congress does not have to grant an exemption to someone who follows the command of God rather than the command of the law because the Congress established by the Constitution denies . . . *that God issues any such commands.*" W. BERNS, *supra* note 13, at 48 (emphasis in original). "Liberalism," Professor Berns goes on to

Additional evidence supports the conclusion that Madison believed freedom of religion to include exemption from generally applicable laws in some circumstances. As discussed more fully below,[232] Madison supported a formulation of the Virginia Bill of Rights that allowed generous scope for free exercise exemptions and proposed an express religious exemption from military conscription for inclusion in the Bill of Rights.[233] These positions tend to confirm the "pro-exemptions" reading of the *Memorial and Remonstrance*.

Another passage in the *Memorial and Remonstrance* arguably contradicts such a reading. Virginia's proposed assessment bill made special provision for "Quakers and Menonists," who could use the funds appropriated from their members "in a manner which they shall think best calculated to promote their particular mode of worship," rather than being required, like other denominations, to use the money exclusively "for a Minister or Teacher of the Gospel of their denomination, or the providing places of divine worship."[234] In response to this special provision, Madison commented:

> As the Bill violates equality by subjecting some to peculiar burdens; so it violates the same principle, by granting to others peculiar exemptions. Are the Quakers and Menonists the only sects who think a compulsive support of their religions unnecessary and unwarantable? Can their piety alone be intrusted with the care of public worship? Ought their Religions to be endowed above all others, with extraordinary privileges, by which proselytes may be enticed from all others?[235]

This passage provides some support for the no-exemptions view, since it describes the "peculiar exemptions" in the bill as "extraordinary privileges" that violate the principle of religious equality. However, the meaning of the passage is ambiguous and must be weighed against evidence that Madison departed from the Lockean objection to exemptions. Instead of indicating a general objection to exemptions, the passage can be read as objecting only to the fact that the bill singled out two sects by name, giving them a preference over others that might have similar scruples. Alternatively, the quoted passage may

---

say, "began in the effort to subordinate religious opinion to the law." *Id.* at 50. Professor Berns has no doubt correctly summarized Locke's position — and Jefferson's as well — but this position is at odds with Madison's. According to Madison, it is precisely because God *does* issue commands (though there will be disagreement over what they are) that the state must respect religious liberty, as a subordinate must respect the commands of a superior power.

232 *See infra* pp. 1462–63.

233 *See infra* text accompanying note 466.

234 Va. House of Delegates, A Bill Establishing a Provision for Teachers of the Christian Religion (December 24, 1784), *reprinted in* Everson v. Board of Educ., 330 U.S. 1, 28 app. at 72 (1947) (Rutledge, J., dissenting).

235 J. MADISON, *Memorial and Remonstrance*, *supra* note 109, at 186.

mean no more than that one reason to reject establishments is that they generate a need for otherwise unnecessary exemptions. The passage therefore does not tell us whether Madison would oppose exemptions from legitimate secular legislation that create unavoidable conflicts with conscience.

No other political figure played so large a role in the enactment of the religion clauses as Jefferson and Madison.[236] To a large extent, Jefferson reflected the rationalist premises of Locke, and it is these premises that the modern courts and commentators have relied upon in arguing for a no-exemption interpretation of the free exercise clause. The evidence indicates, however, that Madison, with his more generous vision of religious liberty, more faithfully reflected the popular understanding of the free exercise provision that was to emerge both in state constitutions and the Bill of Rights.

D. *Legal Protections After Independence*

The Revolution inspired a wave of constitution-writing in the new states. Eleven of the thirteen states (plus Vermont) adopted new constitutions between 1776 and 1780. Of those eleven, six (plus Vermont) included an explicit bill of rights; three more states adopted a bill of rights between 1781 and 1790. With the exception of Connecticut, every state, with or without an establishment, had a constitutional provision protecting religious freedom by 1789, although two states confined their protections to Christians and five other states confined their protections to theists.[237] There was no discernible difference between the free exercise provisions adopted by the states with an establishment and those without. The free exercise clauses of Massachusetts and New Hampshire were almost identical to those of

---

[236] Fisher Ames of Massachusetts drafted the last version of the amendment to pass the House; his version was quite similar to the amendment that was ultimately ratified. His views, therefore, could be relevant. But Ames, who wrote numerous letters and essays on various issues of public importance, never made any reference in them to free exercise or to religious freedom. *See* F. AMES, WORKS OF FISHER AMES (S. Ames ed. 1854). His biographer does not even mention his authorship of the free exercise clause. *See* W. BERNHARD, FISHER AMES: FEDERALIST AND STATESMAN: 1758–1808 (1965). Nor do his opinions regarding religion seem noteworthy. He was a member of the majority denomination in his state, the Congregational Church, and left late in life to join the Episcopal Church, apparently because of political differences with the pastor. *See* W. BERNHARD, *supra*, at 330–31. Evidently, his role in drafting the free exercise clause was one of political peacemaker, rather than exponent of a particular vision of religious freedom.

[237] Maryland and Delaware explicitly limited their free exercise protections to Christians, although a related provision of the Delaware Declaration of Rights contains language that is not so confined. New Hampshire, Massachusetts, New Jersey, North Carolina, and Pennsylvania limited their free exercise protections to believers in God. New York, Georgia, Rhode Island, and South Carolina extended their protections to all religions. Virginia's Bill of Rights is ambiguous; it contains a theistic definition of religion but also contains language that may be broader in application. *See infra* pp. 1456–57 & note 242.

New Jersey, Pennsylvania, and Delaware. Freedom of religion was universally said to be an unalienable right; the status of other rights commonly found in state bills of rights, such as property or trial by jury, was more disputed and often considered derivative of civil society.[238]

These state constitutions provide the most direct evidence of the original understanding, for it is reasonable to infer that those who drafted and adopted the first amendment assumed the term "free exercise of religion" meant what it had meant in their states. The wording of the state provisions thus casts light on the meaning of the first amendment.

New York's 1777 Constitution was typical:

> [T]he free exercise and enjoyment of religious profession and worship, without discrimination or preference, shall forever hereafter be allowed, within this State, to all mankind: *Provided*, That the liberty of conscience, hereby granted, shall not be so construed as to excuse acts of licentiousness, or justify practices inconsistent with the peace or safety of this State.[239]

Likewise, New Hampshire's provision stated:

> Every individual has a natural and unalienable right to worship GOD according to the dictates of his own conscience, and reason; and no subject shall be hurt, molested, or restrained in his person, liberty or estate for worshipping GOD, in the manner and season most agreeable to the dictates of his own conscience, . . . provided he doth not disturb the public peace, or disturb others, in their religious worship.[240]

---

[238] The New Hampshire Constitution of 1784 declared: "Among the natural rights, some are in their very nature unalienable, because no equivalent can be given or received for them. Of this kind are the RIGHTS OF CONSCIENCE." N.H. CONST. of 1784, pt. I, art. IV, *reprinted in* 2 FEDERAL AND STATE CONSTITUTIONS, *supra* note 2, at 1280, 1280–81. The Pennsylvania Constitution of 1790 listed both liberty of conscience and the rights of property and reputation as among the "inherent and indefeasible rights." PA. CONST. of 1790, art. IX, §§ 1, 3, *reprinted in* 2 FEDERAL AND STATE CONSTITUTIONS, *supra* note 2, at 1548, 1554; *see also* 1 ANNALS OF CONG. 454 (J. Gales ed. 1834) (speech by James Madison, June 8, 1789) ("Trial by jury cannot be considered as a natural right, but a right resulting from a social compact which regulates the action of the community, but is as essential to secure the liberty of the people as any one of the pre-existent rights of nature."); Madison, *Property*, National Gazette, Mar. 29, 1792, *reprinted in* 6 THE WRITINGS OF JAMES MADISON, *supra* note 109, at 101, 101–03 (treating property as a right "dependent on positive law"). *See generally* M. WHITE, THE PHILOSOPHY OF THE AMERICAN REVOLUTION 195–228 (1978) (discussing the distinction between unalienable and alienable rights, placing "the right to worship" in the former category, and recounting Jefferson's view that "property," an example from the latter category, should not be enumerated in the Declaration of Independence).

[239] N.Y. CONST. of 1777, art. XXXVIII, *reprinted in* 2 FEDERAL AND STATE CONSTITUTIONS, *supra* note 2, at 1328, 1338.

[240] N.H. CONST. of 1784, pt. I, art. V, *reprinted in* 2 FEDERAL AND STATE CONSTITUTIONS, *supra* note 2, at 1280, 1281.

As a final example, Georgia's religious liberty clause read: "All persons whatever shall have the free exercise of their religion; provided it be not repugnant to the peace and safety of the State."[241] Other state provisions were similar.[242] In addition to these state provisions, article

---

[241] GA. CONST. of 1777, art. LVI, *reprinted in* 1 FEDERAL AND STATE CONSTITUTIONS, *supra* note 2, at 377, 383.

[242] Together with the provisions quoted in the text, the following is a complete collection of state free exercise provisions at the time of the adoption of the first amendment.

The Delaware Declaration of Rights and Fundamental Rules of 1776 provided:

> 2. That all Men have a natural and unalienable Right to worship Almighty God according to the Dictates of their own Consciences and Understandings; that no Man ought or of Right can be compelled to attend any religious Worship or maintain any Ministry contrary to or against his own free Will and Consent, and that no Authority can or ought to be vested in, or assumed by any Power whatever that shall in any Case interfere with, or in any Manner controul the Right of Conscience in the Free Exercise of Religious Worship.
>
> 3. That all Persons professing the Christian Religion ought forever to enjoy equal Rights and Privileges in this State, unless, under Colour of Religion, any Man disturb the Peace, the Happiness or Safety of Society.

Del. Declaration of Rights and Fundamental Rules of 1776, §§ 2, 3, *reprinted in* 5 THE FOUNDERS' CONSTITUTION, *supra* note 72, at 70.

The Maryland Declaration of Rights of 1776 provided:

> That, as it is the duty of every man to worship God in such manner as he thinks most acceptable to him; all persons, professing the Christian religion, are equally entitled to protection in their religious liberty; wherefore no person ought by any law to be molested in his person or estate on account of his religious persuasion or profession, or for his religious practice; unless, under colour of religion, any man shall disturb the good order, peace or safety of the State, or shall infringe the laws of morality, or injure others, in their natural, civil, or religious rights . . . .

Md. Declaration of Rights of 1776, art. XXXIII, *reprinted in* 1 FEDERAL AND STATE CONSTITUTIONS, *supra* note 2, at 817, 819.

The Massachusetts Constitution of 1780 provided:

> It is the right as well as the duty of all men in society, publicly and at stated seasons, to worship the Supreme Being, the great Creator and Preserver of the universe. And no subject shall be hurt, molested, or restrained, in his person, liberty, or estate, for worshipping God in the manner and season most agreeable to the dictates of his own conscience, or for his religious profession or sentiments, provided he doth not disturb the public peace or obstruct others in their religious worship.

MASS. CONST. of 1780, art. II, *reprinted in* 1 FEDERAL AND STATE CONSTITUTIONS, *supra* note 2, at 956, 957.

The New Jersey Constitution of 1776 provided: "That no person shall ever, within this Colony, be deprived of the inestimable privilege of worshipping Almighty God in a manner agreeable to the dictates of his own conscience; nor, under any pretence whatever, be compelled to attend any place of worship, contrary to his own faith and judgment . . . ." N.J. CONST. of 1776, art. XVIII, *reprinted in* 2 FEDERAL AND STATE CONSTITUTIONS, *supra* note 2, at 1310, 1313.

The North Carolina Constitution of 1776 provided: "That all men have a natural and unalienable right to worship Almighty God according to the dictates of their own consciences." N.C. CONST. of 1776, art. XIX, *reprinted in* 2 FEDERAL AND STATE CONSTITUTIONS, *supra* note 2, at 1409, 1410.

The Pennsylvania Constitution of 1776 provided:

> That all men have a natural and unalienable right to worship Almighty God according to the dictates of their own consciences and understanding: And that no man ought or of right can be compelled to attend any religious worship, or erect or support any place of worship, or maintain any ministry, contrary to, or against, his own free will and

I of the Northwest Ordinance of 1787, enacted contemporaneously with the drafting of the Constitution and re-enacted by the First Congress, provided: "No person, demeaning himself in a peaceable and orderly manner, shall ever be molested on account of his mode of worship, or religious sentiments, in the said territory."[243]

While differing in their particulars, these constitutional provisions followed the model set by the early Rhode Island, Carolina, and New Jersey charters, both in the scope of the liberty and in its limitations. Each of these elements warrants attention.

1. Scope of the Liberty. — Each of the state constitutions first defined the scope of the free exercise right in terms of the conscience

---

> consent: Nor can any man, who acknowledges the being of a God, be justly deprived or abridged of any civil right as a citizen, on account of his religious sentiments or peculiar mode of religious worship: And that no authority can or ought to be vested in, or assumed by any power whatever, that shall in any case interfere with, or in any manner controul, the right of conscience in the free exercise of religious worship.

PA. CONST. of 1776, art. II, *reprinted in* 2 FEDERAL AND STATE CONSTITUTIONS, *supra* note 2, at 1540, 1541.

The Charter of Rhode Island and Providence Plantations of 1663 provided:

> [N]oe person within the sayd colonye, at any tyme hereafter, shall bee any wise molested, punished, disquieted, or called in question, for any differences in opinione in matters of religion, and doe not actually disturb the civill peace of our sayd colony; but that all and everye person and persons may, from tyme to tyme, and at all tymes hereafter, freelye and fullye have and enjoye his and theire owne judgments and consciences, in matters of religious concernments, throughout the tract of lande hereafter mentioned; they behaving themselves peaceblie and quietlie, and not useing this libertie to lycentiousnesse and profanenesse, nor to the civill injurye or outward disturbeance of others; any lawe, statute, or clause, therein contayned, or to bee contayned, usage or custome of this realme, to the contrary hereof, in any wise, notwithstanding.

R.I. CHARTER of 1663, *reprinted in* 2 FEDERAL AND STATE CONSTITUTIONS, *supra* note 2, at 1595, 1596–97.

The South Carolina Constitution of 1790 provided:

> The free exercise and enjoyment of religious profession and worship, without discrimination or preference, shall forever hereafter be allowed within this State to all mankind: *Provided*, That the liberty of conscience thereby declared shall not be so construed as to excuse acts of licentiousness, or justify practices inconsistent with the peace or safety of this State.

S.C. CONST. of 1790, art. VIII, § 1, *reprinted in* 2 FEDFRAL AND STATE CONSTITUTIONS, *supra* note 2, at 1628, 1632–33 (emphasis in original). The South Carolina Constitution of 1778 contained a much more limited religious freedom clause, similar to the Fundamental Constitutions of 1669. *See* S.C. CONST. of 1778, art. XXXVIII, *reprinted in* 2 FEDERAL AND STATE CONSTITUTIONS, *supra* note 2, at 1620, 1626–27. References in text are to the 1790 constitution unless otherwise specified.

The Virginia Bill of Rights of 1776 provided:

> That religion, or the duty which we owe to our Creator, and the manner of discharging it, can be directed only by reason and conviction, not by force or violence; and therefore all men are equally entitled to the free exercise of religion, according to the dictates of conscience; and that it is the mutual duty of all to practise Christian forbearance, love, and charity towards each other.

Va. Bill of Rights of 1776, § 16, *reprinted in* 2 FEDERAL AND STATE CONSTITUTIONS, *supra* note 2, at 1908, 1909.

[243] Northwest Territorial Ordinance of 1787, art. I, *reprinted in* 1 FEDERAL AND STATE CONSTITUTIONS, *supra* note 2, at 429, 431.

of the individual believer and the actions that flow from that conscience. None of the provisions confined the protection to beliefs and opinions, as did Jefferson, nor to expression of beliefs and opinions, as some recent scholars have suggested.[244] Indeed, the language appears to have been drafted precisely to refute those interpretations. Maryland, for example, prohibited punishment of any person "on account of his religious persuasion *or* profession, *or* for his religious practice."[245] Opinion, expression of opinion, and practice were all expressly protected. The key word "exercise," found in six of the constitutions, was defined in dictionaries of the day to mean "action."[246] Two of the other constitutions used terms as broad or broader — Maryland referred to religious "practice," Rhode Island to matters of "religious concernment."[247]

Nor did these constitutions follow Locke in defining the scope of free exercise negatively, as a sphere of otherworldly concern that does not affect the public interest. The free exercise provisions defined the free exercise right affirmatively, based on the scope of duties to God perceived by the believer. The New Hampshire formulation defined the believer's right by "the dictates of *his own* conscience, and reason";[248] it extended to all "matters of religious concernment," according to Rhode Island. These could, and often would, include matters of concern to the public. This is consistent with the proposition, reflected in Madison's *Memorial and Remonstrance*, that the right of free exercise precedes and is superior to the social contract.[249]

Although the free exercise right plainly extends to some forms of conduct, the scope of protected conduct in these clauses is less clear. The provisions fall into two categories. Four states — Virginia, Georgia, Maryland, and Rhode Island — protected all actions stemming from religious conviction, subject to certain limitations.[250] The Virginia Bill of Rights, the model for three of the state proposals for the first amendment and presumably the greatest influence on Madison, is especially clear on this point. It provides that "all men are equally entitled to the free exercise of religion, according to the dictates of conscience" and defines "religion" as "the duty which we owe to our

---

[244] *See* Marshall, *Solving the Free Exercise Dilemma: Free Exercise as Expression*, 67 MINN. L. REV. 545 (1983).

[245] Md. Declaration of Rights of 1776, art. XXXIII, *reprinted in* 1 FEDERAL AND STATE CONSTITUTIONS, *supra* note 2, at 817, 819 (emphasis added).

[246] *See infra* text accompanying notes 407–409.

[247] *See* Md. Declaration of Rights of 1776, art. XXXIII, *reprinted in* 1 FEDERAL AND STATE CONSTITUTIONS, *supra* note 2, at 817, 819; R.I. CHARTER of 1663, in 2 FEDERAL AND STATE CONSTITUTIONS, *supra* note 2, at 1595, 1596.

[248] N.H. CONST. of 1784, art. V, *reprinted in* 2 FEDERAL AND STATE CONSTITUTIONS, *supra* note 2, at 1280, 1281 (emphasis added).

[249] *See supra* text accompanying notes 229–230.

[250] *See supra* text accompanying note 241 & note 242.

Creator, and the manner of discharging it."[251] In the biblical tradition, "duties" to God included actions, perhaps all of life, and not just speech and opinion. So according to Virginia, the right of free exercise extended to all of a believer's duties to God and included a choice of means as well as ends.

By contrast, eight states — New York, New Hampshire, Delaware, Massachusetts, New Jersey, North Carolina, Pennsylvania, and South Carolina — plus the Northwest Ordinance, confined their protection of conduct to acts of "worship." The word "worship" usually signifies the rituals or ceremonial acts of religion, such as the administration of sacraments or the singing of hymns, and thus would indicate a more restrictive scope for the free exercise provisions.[252]

The limitation to "worship" was not carried over into the federal free exercise clause, which in this respect most closely resembles the Georgia provision.[253] No direct evidence suggests whether the adoption of the broader formulation was deliberate, but this seems consistent with the general theological currents of Protestant America, which were "low church" and anti-ritualistic. One of the main elements of the Great Awakening was the insistence that duties to God extend beyond the four walls of the church and the partaking of the sacraments. From the evangelical Protestant perspective, "worship" would not have been sharply distinguished from "the duty we owe to our Creator."[254] The ready availability of narrow models in the recently enacted Northwest Ordinance and the constitution of final drafter Fisher Ames' home state of Massachusetts makes it likely that the choice of broader language was deliberate. The federal free exercise

---

[251] Va. Bill of Rights of 1776, § 16, *reprinted in* 2 FEDERAL AND STATE CONSTITUTIONS, *supra* note 2, at 1908, 1909. The definition of "religion" resembles the one provided by James Buchanan in 1757: "Piety, godliness, the worship of God, and the practice of any duty in obedience to his commands." J. BUCHANAN, LINGUAE BRITANNICAE VERA PRONUNCIATIO (R. Alston ed. 1967) (London 1757). Under this definition, the exercise of "religion" would include both "worship" and "the practice of any duty" to God.

[252] Samuel Johnson's A DICTIONARY OF THE ENGLISH LANGUAGE (Philadelphia 1805) defines the verb "worship" as "[t]o adore; to honour or venerate with religious rites." *Id.* Other dictionaries of the day are less specific in the connection to religious ritual. *See* J. BUCHANAN, *supra* note 251 (defining "worship" as "[t]o adore or praise the Almighty"); N. WEBSTER, A DICTIONARY OF THE ENGLISH LANGUAGE 301 (New Haven 1807) (defining "worship" as "to adore, perform adoration"). The latter two definitions make no direct reference to religious ceremonials. Modern definitions, like Johnson's, are more specific. *Webster's Third New International Dictionary* defines "worship" as "the reverence or veneration tendered a divine being or supernatural power; *also*: an act, process, or instance of expressing such veneration by performing or taking part in religious exercises or ritual." WEBSTER'S THIRD NEW INTERNATIONAL DICTIONARY OF THE ENGLISH LANGUAGE 2637 (P. Gove ed. 1986) (emphasis in original).

[253] *See supra* text accompanying note 241.

[254] R. MEHL, THE SOCIOLOGY OF PROTESTANTISM 107–08 (J. Farley trans. 1970) (explaining that "worship" is understood as "[a]ll that one calls 'the Christian life,' with all its ethical components").

clause seems in every respect to have followed the most expansive models among the states.

Indeed, even in the states that apparently limited free exercise to acts of "worship," it is not clear that the limitation had any actual effect. In none of the state free exercise cases in the early years of the Republic did the lawyers argue or the courts hold that religiously motivated conduct was unprotected because it was not "worship." Since the scope and nature of religious duty was itself a contested issue among religions, it seems unlikely that the state provisions intended to interject a judicial discrimination among forms of religious practice, and especially unlikely that this interjection would favor ritual over pious conduct. Interestingly, Pennsylvania (a state whose substantial Quaker population had an interest in exemptions) revised its constitutional protection for liberty of conscience in 1790, removing the language that had limited it to acts of worship.[255] Kentucky borrowed this broader language for its first constitution in 1792.[256] This may suggest a movement toward broader protections, simultaneous with the ratification of the first amendment.

In any event, it would be difficult on this evidence to conclude that the framers of the free exercise clause intended it to be confined to acts of "worship." That would require the assumption that Fisher Ames and the First Congress accidentally failed to use familiar language that would have precisely expressed their meaning and adopted instead new language that went beyond their intentions. Either the broader meaning was intended, or no thought was given to the matter at all.

2. *Limits on the Liberty.* — The second common element in state free exercise provisions is that the provisions limit the right by particular, defined state interests. Nine of the states limited the free exercise right to actions that were "peaceable" or that would not disturb the "peace" or "safety" of the state.[257] Four of these also expressly disallowed acts of licentiousness or immorality;[258] two for-

---

[255] The 1776 Declaration of Rights of the Inhabitants of the State of Pennsylvania states that "no authority can or ought to be vested in, or assumed by any power whatever, that shall in any case interfere with, or in any manner controul, the right of conscience in the free exercise of religious worship." A Declaration of Rights of the Inhabitants of the State of Pennsylvania of 1776, *reprinted in* 2 FEDERAL AND STATE CONSTITUTIONS, *supra* note 2, at 1541, 1541. The 1790 Pennsylvania Constitution states that "no human authority can, in any case whatever, control or interfere with the rights of conscience." PA. CONST. of 1790, art. IX, § 3, *reprinted in* 2 FEDERAL AND STATE CONSTITUTIONS, *supra* note 2, at 1548, 1554.

[256] *See* KY. CONST. of 1792, art. XII, *reprinted in* 1 FEDERAL AND STATE CONSTITUTIONS, *supra* note 2, at 647, 654.

[257] The nine states are New York, New Hampshire, Georgia, Delaware, Maryland, Massachusetts, New Jersey, Rhode Island, and South Carolina. *See supra* p. 1456 & note 242.

[258] The four states are New York, Maryland, Rhode Island, and South Carolina. *See supra* text accompanying note 239 & note 242.

bade acts that would interfere with the religious practices of others;[259] one forbade the "civil injury or outward disturbance of others";[260] one added acts contrary to "good order";[261] and one disallowed acts contrary to the "happiness," as well as the peace and safety, of society.[262]

These provisos are the most revealing and important feature of the state constitutions. They further confirm that the free exercise right was not understood to be confined to beliefs. Beliefs without more do not have the capacity to disturb the public peace and safety. As Virginia's Bill for Establishing Religious Freedom, drafted by Jefferson, stated, "it is time enough for the rightful purposes of civil government for its officers to interfere when principles break out into overt acts against peace and good order."[263] If the basic right did not extend to "overt acts," the provisos would be unnecessary.

Moreover, the state provisions make sense only if free exercise envisions religiously compelled exemptions from at least some generally applicable laws. Since even according to the Lockean no-exemptions view, religious persons cannot be prohibited from engaging in otherwise legal activities, the provisos would only have effect if religiously motivated conduct violated the general laws in some way. The "peace and safety" clauses identify a narrower subcategory of the general laws; the free exercise provisions would exempt religiously motivated conduct from these laws up to the point that such conduct breached public peace or safety.

The language of these provisos cannot be dismissed as boilerplate, synonymous with "an assertion of interest on the part of the public." The debates surrounding the drafting of these provisos suggest that they served as independent criteria for evaluating assertions of legislative power. The debate over the free exercise provision of the Virginia Bill of Rights of 1776 most clearly demonstrates the understanding of the states that passed these provisos. George Mason, chief architect of the religious liberty clause of the Declaration, proposed "that all men should enjoy the fullest toleration in the exercise of religion, according to the dictates of conscience, unpunished and unrestrained by the magistrate, unless under color of religion any man disturb the peace, the happiness, or safety of society."[264] Madison objected to the proposal on two grounds. First, he criticized the use of the word "toleration" for reasons already discussed.[265] He offered

---

[259] The two states are New Hampshire and Massachusetts. *See supra* text accompanying note 240 & note 242.

[260] The state is Rhode Island. *See supra* note 242.

[261] The state is Maryland. *See id.*

[262] The state is Delaware. *See id.*

[263] Jefferson, *A Bill for Establishing Religious Freedom* (June 12, 1779), *reprinted in* 5 THE FOUNDERS' CONSTITUTION, *supra* note 72, at 77.

[264] S. COBB, *supra* note 17, at 491.

[265] *See id.* at 492.

a substitute that read that "all men are equally entitled to the full and free exercise of religion according to the dictates of conscience."[266] This change was accepted, with minor alteration. Second, Madison criticized the breadth of Mason's proposed state interest limitation. Madison proposed instead that free exercise be protected "unless under color of religion the preservation of equal liberty and the existence of the State are manifestly endangered."[267] This is obviously a much narrower state interest exception than Mason's. While "peace" and "safety" refer to the fundamental peacekeeping functions of government, "happiness" is a term as compendious as all of public policy.[268] The "peace, happiness, or safety of society" is therefore a standard that would encompass virtually all legitimate forms of legislation. The "preservation of equal liberty" and "manifest endangerment of the existence of the State," on the other hand, is a standard that only the most critical acts of government can satisfy.

The Virginia legislature ultimately passed a religious liberty guarantee that did not spell out the nature of the state interest that could outweigh a free exercise claim. Apparently, the legislature could not decide between the Mason and Madison formulations and compromised through silence. It is fair to assume, however, that the state's interest must fall somewhere between "the peace, the happiness, or safety of society" — Mason's broad formulation — and "manifest danger" to the "preservation of equal liberty, and existence of the State" — Madison's more limited formulation. If so, Virginia was typical of its sister states. While none adopted a proviso as restrictive as Madison's, only one (Delaware) adopted a proviso as broad as Mason's. Almost all opted for the terms "peace" or "safety," presumably on the ground that "happiness" was too broad. In any event, the dispute between Madison and Mason would not have mattered if the proviso were of no legal significance, and the proviso would have been of no legal significance if the "full and free exercise of religion" did not include the right of exemption from generally applicable laws that conflict with religious conscience.

---

[266] *Id.*

[267] *Id.* In a private letter many years later, Madison endorsed a different formulation under which religion is immune from governmental authority "in every case where it does not trespass on private rights or the public peace." Letter from James Madison to Edward Livingston (July 10, 1822), in 9 THE WRITINGS OF JAMES MADISON, *supra* note 109, at 98, 100.

[268] Samuel Johnson's two-volume A DICTIONARY OF THE ENGLISH LANGUAGE (London 1755), chooses two of five exemplars of the use of the word "happiness" from political sources. It quotes Richard Hooker to the effect that: "*Happiness* is that estate whereby we attain, so far as possibly may be attained, the full possession of that which simply for itself is to be desired, and containeth in it after an eminent sort, the contentation of our desires, the highest degree of all our perfection." *Id.* It also quotes John Locke: "The various and contrary choices that men make in the world, argue that the same thing is not good to every man alike: this variety of pursuits shews, that every one does not place his *happiness* in the same thing." *Id.* (emphasis in original).

The wording of the state constitutions also provides some guidance regarding when the government's interest is sufficiently strong to override an admitted free exercise claim. The modern Supreme Court has stated only that the government's interest must be "compelling," "of the highest order," "overriding," or "unusually important."[269] These formulations are unnecessarily open-ended, leading to grudging and inconsistent results. The historical sources suggest that the government's interest can be more precisely delimited in a few specific areas, although other cases will remain difficult to resolve.[270]

The most common feature of the state provisions was the government's right to protect public peace and safety. As Madison expressed it late in life, the free exercise right should prevail "in every case where it does not trespass on private rights or the public peace."[271] This indicates that a believer has no license to invade the private rights of others or to disturb public peace and order, no matter how conscientious the belief or how trivial the private right on the other side. There is no free exercise right to kidnap another person for the purposes of proselytizing, or to trespass on private property — whether it be an abortion clinic or a defense contracting plant — to protest immoral activity. Conduct on public property must be peaceable and orderly, so that the rights of others are not disturbed.

Where the rights of others are not involved, however, the free exercise right prevails. The state constitutional provisions give no warrant to paternalistic legislation touching on religious concerns. They protect the "public" peace and safety but respect the right of the believer to weigh spiritual costs without governmental interference. Thus, some modern free exercise controversies, such as the refusal by Jehovah's Witnesses to receive blood transfusions[272] or the enforcement of minimum wage laws in a religious community,[273] should be easy to resolve and require no subjective judicial judgments about the importance of public policy. Moreover, the early free exercise clauses seem to allow churches and other religious institutions to define their own doctrine, membership, organization, and internal requirements

---

269 Goldman v. Weinberger, 475 U.S. 503, 529–30 (1986) (O'Connor, J., dissenting) (summarizing free exercise tests from earlier cases).

270 For another discussion of governmental interest in light of the early state constitutions, see REPORT TO THE ATTORNEY GENERAL, cited above in note 17, at 61–68.

271 Letter from James Madison to Edward Livingston (July 10, 1822), in 9 THE WRITINGS OF JAMES MADISON, *supra* note 109, at 98, 100.

272 *But see In re* President and Directors of Georgetown College, 331 F.2d 1000 (D.C. Cir.), *cert. denied*, 377 U.S. 978 (1964); John F. Kennedy Memorial Hosp. v. Heston, 58 N.J. 576, 279 A.2d 670 (1971).

273 *But see* Tony and Susan Alamo Found. v. Secretary of Labor, 471 U.S. 290 (1985). The author of this Article was the principal author of the Secretary's brief in that case but believes the position was wrong.

without state interference. As Jefferson wrote to the Reverend Samuel Miller, "the government of the United States [is] interdicted by the Constitution from intermeddling with religious institutions, their doctrines, discipline, or exercises."[274] That their internal practices may seem unjust or repugnant to the majority should be of no moment.[275] Only a handful of states allowed laws against "licentiousness" or immorality to override free exercise claims, and those provisions may well have referred to public displays of immoral behavior.

Obvious connections exist between the scope of the free exercise right defined by these provisions and the wider liberal political theory of which they are an expression. The central conception of liberalism, as summarized in the Declaration of Independence, is that government is instituted by the people in order to secure their rights to life, liberty, and the pursuit of happiness. Governmental powers are limited to those needed to secure these legitimate ends. In contrast to both ancient and modern non-liberal regimes, government is not charged with promotion of the good life for its citizens. Except as needed for mutual protection and a limited class of common interests, government must leave the definition of the good life to private institutions, of which family and church are the most conspicuous. Even in the absence of a free exercise clause, liberal theory would find the assertion of governmental power over religion illegitimate, except to the extent necessary for the protection of others.

To eighteenth-century evangelicals, this issue was posed in theological terms but the answer was much the same. God instituted government for the punishment of wrongdoing,[276] which they interpreted to mean injury to others.[277] While the evangelicals could not accede to the Lockean proposition that the reach of governmental authority is defined by the judgments of civil authorities, they found the liberal theory of government a way to reconcile their insistence on the primacy of conscience with their equal insistence on the divinely ordained authority of government. Thus, when describing the legiti-

---

[274] Letter from Thomas Jefferson to the Rev. Samuel Miller (Jan. 23, 1808), in 11 WORKS OF JEFFERSON, *supra* note 206, at 7, 7.

[275] *But cf.* Bob Jones Univ. v. United States, 461 U.S. 574 (1983) (finding no violation of the free exercise clause when the IRS refused to grant charitable status to a religious school due to its proscription of interracial dating).

[276] "Let every soul be subject unto the higher powers. For there is no power but of God: the powers that be are ordained of God. Whosoever therefore resisteth the power, resisteth the ordinance of God: and they that resist shall receive to themselves damnation." *Romans* 13:1–2.

[277] *See, e.g.*, J. LELAND, *supra* note 174, at 118 ("The legitimate powers of government extend only to punish men for working ill to their neighbors . . . ."); I. BACKUS, *supra* note 175, at 313–14 (interpreting *Romans* 13:1–10 as "clearly show[ing] that the crimes which fall within magistrates' jurisdiction to punish are only such as work ill to our neighbors," while "church government respects our behavior toward God as well as man").

mate reach of government, the evangelical writers sounded little different from the American followers of Locke.[278]

The "peace and safety" limitations of the state constitutions are therefore neither simple restatements of unbridled governmental supremacy in a clash with religious precepts, nor mere expedient exceptions to what would otherwise be unlimited rights of religiously motivated conduct. Both the affirmative free exercise protections and the peace and safety limitations follow logically from the liberal and evangelical theories of government, which reached similar conclusions from different premises about the origin and scope of legitimate government.

E. Actual Free Exercise Controversies

An examination of actual free exercise controversies in the preconstitutional period bears out these conclusions. To be sure, the issue of exemptions did not often arise.[279] The American colonies were peopled almost entirely by adherents of various strains of Protestant Christianity.[280] The Protestant moral code and mode of worship was, for the most part, harmonious with the mores of the larger society. Even denominations like the Quakers, whose theology and religious practice differed sharply from the others, entertained similar beliefs about public decorum.[281] Moreover, the governments of that era were far less intrusive than the governments of today. Thus, the occasions when religious conscience came into conflict with generally applicable secular legislation were few.

Nonetheless, the issue of exemptions did arise, primarily centered around three issues: oath requirements, military conscription, and religious assessments. The resolution of these conflicts suggests that exemptions were seen as a natural and legitimate response to the tension between law and religious convictions.

---

[278] For example, compare the passages quoted in note 277 above with Jefferson's statement that "[t]he legitimate powers of government extend to such acts only as are injurious to others." T. JEFFERSON, NOTES ON THE STATE OF VIRGINIA, *supra* note 216, at 159.

[279] Professor Marshall relies heavily on this point in his attack on free exercise exemptions. *See* Marshall, *supra* note 17, at 19–20. But of course, few instances are not the same as no instances.

[280] For a discussion of the number of churches of each denomination at the end of the colonial period, see 1 A. STOKES, CHURCH AND STATE IN THE UNITED STATES 273 & n.50 (1950). The largest groups, in order, were Congregationalists, Presbyterians, Baptists, and Anglicans. Out of 3,005 congregations, only 50 were Roman Catholic. *See id.* There were fewer than 2,000 Jews, concentrated in five cities — New York, Philadelphia, Newport, Charleston, and Savannah. *See* M. BORDEN, *supra* note 75, at 6.

[281] *See* T. CURRY, *supra* note 17, at 81. In the early days of the American colonies, the Quakers' behavior had been more unconventional. *See* W. RUSSELL, *supra* note 65, at 3 n.1 (describing offensive Quaker practices, including interrupting others' worship services and going naked in public in protest against cruelty and sinfulness).

1. Oaths. — By far the most common source of friction was the issue of oaths. The oath requirement was the principal means of ensuring honest testimony and of solemnizing obligations. At a time when perjury prosecutions were unusual, extratemporal sanctions for telling falsehoods or reneging on commitments were thought indispensable to civil society. Quakers and certain other Protestant sects, however, conscientiously refused to take oaths,[282] producing more serious consequences than it might at first seem. A regime requiring oaths prior to court testimony effectively precluded these groups from using the court system to protect themselves and left them vulnerable to their adversaries, "who could sue them for property and never doubt the result."[283] There are three possible responses. First, the government could eliminate the oath-taking requirement for everyone, making oath-taking purely voluntary. Second, the government could continue to insist on the oath requirement, making it impossible for dissenters to give evidence in court or participate in any civic activity involving an oath. Third, the government could continue the oath requirement for the majority, allowing those with religious scruples to comply by an alternative procedure. According to the no-exemption view, only the first two possibilities are available. But the first possibility is disruptive of the entire judicial system and the second is unnecessarily harsh to the dissenters.

The third alternative — to create a religious exception to the oath requirement — was in fact adopted in most of the colonies. As early as the seventeenth century the proprietors of the Carolina colony permitted Quakers to enter pledges in a book in lieu of swearing an oath. Similarly, New York passed a law in 1691 permitting Quakers to testify by affirmation in civil cases,[284] and in 1734 passed a law permitting Quakers to qualify for the vote by affirmation instead of oath.[285] Jews in Georgia received dispensation to omit the words "on the faith of a Christian" from the naturalization oath required in 1740.[286] In 1743, Massachusetts, one of the states with a strong established church tradition, substituted an affirmation requirement for "'Quakers [who] profess to be in their consciences scrupulous of

---

[282] Their refusal to take oaths was based on *Matthew* 5:33–37:

> Again, ye have heard that it hath been said by them of old time, Thou shalt not forswear thyself, but shalt perform unto the Lord thine oaths: But I say unto you, swear not at all; neither by heaven; for it is God's throne: Nor by the earth; for it is his footstool: neither by Jerusalem; for it is the city of the great King. Neither shalt thou swear by thy head, because thou canst not make one hair white or black. But let your communication be, Yea, yea; Nay, nay; for whatsoever is more than these cometh of evil.

Id.

[283] R. BRUGGER, MARYLAND: A MIDDLE TEMPERAMENT 30 (1988).

[284] *See* T. CURRY, *supra* note 17, at 64.

[285] *See id.* at 71.

[286] *See* R. STRICKLAND, *supra* note 62, at 29.

taking oaths.'"[287] By 1789, virtually all of the states had enacted oath exemptions.[288]

2. Military Conscription. — The exemption issue also arose in connection with military conscription. Exemption from conscription provides a particularly telling example due to the entirely secular nature of conscription, its importance to preservation of the state in times of war, and the high costs the granting of exemptions imposes on others. Several denominations in colonial America, most prominently the Quakers and Mennonites, refused on religious grounds to bear arms. As early as 1670–80, Quakers in several states asserted that liberty of conscience exempted them from bearing arms. Rhode Island,[289] North Carolina,[290] and Maryland[291] granted the exemptions; New York refused.[292] It is presumably not coincidental that Rhode Island, North Carolina, and Maryland had explicit free exercise or liberty of conscience clauses in the seventeenth century, while New York did not.

In Georgia, the Moravians claimed a right to be exempt from military service during the troubles with Spanish Florida, and when they were denied, the entire Moravian community departed Georgia between 1737 and 1740 and moved to Pennsylvania.[293] Pennsylvania, where Quakers were most numerous and influential, went without a militia until 1755, when one was organized on a voluntary basis.[294] The issue arose in New York again in 1734, and again the Quakers were denied exemption from penalties imposed for refusal to train for military service.[295] The colony finally relented in 1755, provided the objector would pay a commutation fee or send a substitute.[296] Massachusetts and Virginia soon adopted similar policies.[297] New Hampshire exempted Quakers from conscription in 1759.[298] Later, the Continental Congress was to grant exemptions in these words:

---

[287] T. CURRY, *supra* note 17, at 90 (citing 1 MASSACHUSETTS ACTS AND RESOLVES 305; and 2 *id.* at 494–95).

[288] *See* Adams & Emmerich, *supra* note 17, at 1631–32.

[289] *See* Russell, *Development of Conscientious Objector Recognition in the United States*, 20 GEO. WASH. L. REV. 409, 412–13 (1952). Roger Williams opposed militia exemptions. *See* Adams & Emmerich, *supra* note 17, at 1624, 1630.

[290] *See* T. CURRY, *supra* note 17, at 56.

[291] S. COBB, *supra* note 17, at 380 & n.2.

[292] *See* T. CURRY, *supra* note 17, at 63.

[293] *See* R. STRICKLAND, *supra* note 62, at 76–78.

[294] *See* Russell, *supra* note 289, at 413.

[295] *See* S. COBB, *supra* note 17, at 356.

[296] *See* Act of Feb. 19, 1755, *reprinted in* U.S. SELECTIVE SERVICE SYSTEM, 2 BACKGROUNDS OF SELECTIVE SERVICE: MILITARY OBLIGATION pt. 9, at 186, 203–04 (A. Vollmer ed. 1947) [hereinafter SELECTIVE SERVICE].

[297] *See* Act of Nov. 31, 1757, *reprinted in* SELECTIVE SERVICE, *supra* note 296, pt. 6, at 195, 195–97 (Massachusetts); Act of Nov. 1776, *reprinted in* SELECTIVE SERVICE, *supra* note 296, pt. 14, at 249, 249–53 (Virginia).

[298] An Act for the More Speedy Levying One Thousand or at Least Eight Hundred Men

> As there are some people, who, from religious principles, cannot bear arms in any case, this Congress intend no violence to their consciences, but earnestly recommend it to them, to contribute liberally in this time of universal calamity, to the relief of their distressed brethren in the several colonies, and to do all other services to their oppressed Country, which they can consistently with their religious principles.[299]

The language as well as the substance of this policy is particularly significant, since it recognizes the superior claim of religious "conscience" over civil obligation, even at a time of "universal calamity," and leaves the appropriate accommodation to the judgment of the religious objectors.

3. Religious Assessments. — A third example of a religious exception recognized under the preconstitutional free exercise provisions is found only in states with established churches. Such states often required the citizens to make payments for the support of ministers either of the established church or of their own denomination. Not uncommonly, however, these states accommodated the objection of members of sects conscientiously opposed to compelled tithes. For example, from 1727 on, Massachusetts and Connecticut exempted Baptists and Quakers from ministerial taxes. This exception was expressly, if grudgingly, made in recognition of the "alleged scruple of conscience" of these sects.[300] From 1692 on, New Hampshire exempted anyone who could prove in a contested proceeding that he was "conscientiously" of "a different persuasion," attended services of his own faith regularly ("constantly," in the words of the statute), and made financial contributions toward its support.[301] New Hampshire also exempted Quakers who served as constables from the duty of collecting the assessments from others.[302] Virginia exempted Huguenots in 1700, German Lutherans in 1730, and all dissenters from the Anglican Church in 1776.[303]

Inclusive of Officers to be Employd in His Majestys Service in the Current Year, 32 Geo. 2. Orig. Acts, vol. 4, p. 55; recorded Acts, vol. 2, p. 412; N.H. Province Laws 196, 198 (enacted Mar. 9, 1759).

299 *See* Resolution of July 18, 1775, *reprinted in* 2 JOURNALS OF THE CONTINENTAL CONGRESS, 1774–1789, at 187, 189 (W. Ford ed. 1905 & photo. reprint 1968).

300 *See* T. CURRY, *supra* note 17, at 89–90 (quoting 1 MASSACHUSETTS ACTS AND RESOLVES 305; 2 JOURNALS OF THE CONTINENTAL CONGRESS, 1774–1789, *supra* note 299, at 494–95). Cobb's account is slightly different from Curry's. *See* S. COBB, *supra* note 17, at 234–35. Cobb reports that in 1727, Massachusetts passed a law similar to one already existing in Connecticut, allowing Episcopalians to pay tithes to their own churches (instead of to the prevailing Congregational churches) and that Massachusetts extended this treatment to Quakers and Baptists in 1728. Massachusetts exempted Quakers from any religious assessment whatsoever in 1731, and "Anabaptists" in 1734. *See id.*

301 *See* S. COBB, *supra* note 17, at 298–99.

302 *See* An Act to Exempt Those People Called Quakers From Gathering the Rates for the Ministers of Other Perswations Within the Province of New Hampshire, 4 Geo. 2. Orig. Acts, vol. 2, p. 50; recorded Acts, vol. 1, p. 329; N.H. Province Laws 530 (enacted May 10, 1731).

303 *See* S. COBB, *supra* note 17, at 98, 492.

Exemptions were a far from perfect solution to the assessment problem. Having obtained inclusion in the certificate system, the Baptists of Massachusetts eventually concluded that the system would not work. In 1773, the association of Baptist churches voted to urge their members to refuse to provide the certificates required for legal exemption.[304] Through civil disobedience, the Baptists resolved to pressure the legislature to abolish mandatory tithes altogether.

The Baptists' objections arose from both practice and principle. Administration of the certificate system was in the hands of local officials and local courts, who gave vent to the general hostility against the Baptists. Certificates were sometimes ignored[305] and more often rejected on technicalities.[306] In addition, popular opposition (amounting in some instances to violence) made the certificate system unworkable.[307] It became evident that exemptions would not be administered evenhandedly. Moreover, the Baptists objected to the requirement of certifying which "members" (itself a theologically loaded term) were "conscientiously" of the Baptist persuasion, a judgment they believed could only be made by God.[308] These objections foreshadow two critiques of modern free exercise exemptions: that their administration is implicitly biased in favor of familiar religions,[309] and that the "sincerity" requirement is an inappropriate governmental inquiry.[310] But in the case of religious assessments, these problems could be resolved by abolishing the system of ministerial taxes — a solution not always available for secular interferences with conscience.

It might be objected that the example of exemptions from religious assessments is inapt, because the generally applicable law is itself religious, not secular, and would be unconstitutional under the establishment clause today. This is a valid point, even though the assessment laws were most frequently defended in terms of the secular need to promote morality.[311] The decisive question, however, is whether the people at the time of adoption of the first amendment would likely have considered exemptions, whether legislative or judicial, an appropriate remedy when law and conscience conflict. Those states with

---

304 *See* 1 W. McLOUGHLIN, *supra* note 51, at 550–54.

305 *See id.* at 548.

306 *See id.* at 549 (describing a certificate deemed invalid because it was signed by two persons plus the Elder, rather than three); *id.* at 549–50 (discussing a certificate rejected because it did not state that the persons listed "belonged to" the church); *id.* at 547–48 (discussing a certificate rejected because "it did not state that the persons listed were 'conscientiously' of the Baptist persuasion").

307 *See id.* at 550 (describing instances of mob action).

308 *See* I. BACKUS, *supra* note 175, at 333.

309 *See, e.g.*, Tushnet, *supra* note 33, at 381–83. The greater the variance between religious practices and the prevailing social norm, the greater will be the difficulty of accommodation.

310 *See, e.g.*, Noonan, *supra* note 26, at 718–20.

311 *See* T. CURRY, *supra* note 17, at 139–41.

established churches had free exercise provisions which were almost identical to the provisions in states without establishment; and the establishment states understood the principle of free exercise to entail exemption from religious assessments, solely for the benefit of those with religious scruples. If exemptions were a recognized form of free exercise protection in establishment states, they likely would also have been recognized in the others (although the occasions for exemptions would be less frequent). The fact that exemptions were also made available from military conscription laws (plainly secular) and from oath requirements (largely secular), as well as from other secular laws, supports the broader principle.

4. Other Religious Exemptions. — Other colonies and states responded to particular conflicts between religious convictions and generally applicable laws by exempting those faced with the conflict. The Trustees of Georgia, for example, allowed certain groups of Protestant refugees from the European Continent virtual rights of self-government, a form of wholesale exemption that enabled these dissenters from the Church of England to organize themselves in accordance with their own faith.[312] A group from Salzburg formed the town of Ebenezer, described by one historian as "a state within a state, a sort of theocracy under the direction of their ministers with daily conferences of the entire congregation in which God's guidance was invoked at the beginning and end."[313] In 1764, the colonial legislature of Rhode Island passed a statute waiving the laws governing marriage ceremonies for "any persons possessing [professing] the Jewish religion who may be joined in marriage, according to their own usages and rites."[314] In 1798, the state legislature exempted Jewish residents from the operation of state incest law, "within the degrees of affinity or consanguinity allowed by their religion."[315] This was important because Jewish law was understood to encourage the marriage between uncle and niece, a relationship illegal under Rhode Island law.

Similarly, both North Carolina[316] and Maryland[317] exempted Quakers from the requirement of removing their hats in court, which

---

[312] *See* R. STRICKLAND, *supra* note 62, at 21–22, 71–76, 87. These groups were required to obey the colonial laws regarding military service, "property, place and good government," but were otherwise free to govern themselves. *Id.* at 72.

[313] *Id.*

[314] Hartogensis, *Rhode Island and Consanguineous Jewish Marriages*, 20 PUBLICATION AM. JEWISH HIST. SOC'Y 137, 144 (1911).

[315] An Act Regulating Marriage and Divorce, 1798 R.I. Pub. Laws § 7; *see also* Hartogensis, *supra* note 314, at 139–40 (discussing the Rhode Island law as an early example of religious exemptions in family law); Weisbrod, *Family, Church and State: An Essay on Constitutionalism and Religious Authority*, 26 J. FAM. L. 741, 744 n.6 (1988) (same).

[316] *See* An Act to prescribe the affirmation of allegiance and fidelity to this state to be taken by the people called quakers, and for granting them certain indulgences therein mentioned, 1784 N.C. Laws ch. 209, at 488.

[317] *See* R. BRUGGER, *supra* note 283, at 29–30.

they considered a form of obeisance to secular authority forbidden by their religion. This exemption may seem trivial today,[318] but it was an issue of historical and emotional importance to the Quakers of that day. One of the most notorious courtroom cases of religious intolerance in England involved William Penn's refusal to remove his hat when he appeared in court to face an indictment for speaking to an unlawful assembly. Penn came to court bareheaded, but knowing his religious scruple, the judge ordered a court official to place a hat on his head. Penn then refused to remove the hat in respect to the court. Although acquitted on the charge on which he was tried, Penn was held in contempt and imprisoned for refusing to doff his hat.[319] This case became a *cause célèbre* in America, and the North Carolina and Maryland exemptions were no doubt passed as a result.[320]

The history of oath requirements, military conscription, religious assessments, and other sources of conflict between religious convictions and general legislation demonstrates that religion-specific exemptions were familiar and accepted means of accommodating these conflicts. Rather than make oaths, military service, and tithes voluntary for everyone, which would undercut important public programs and objectives, and rather than coerce the consciences of otherwise loyal and law-abiding citizens who were bound by religious duty not to comply, the colonies and states wrote special exemptions into their laws. Lest the exemptions be extended too broadly, they confined the exemptions to denominations or categories known or proven to be "conscientiously" opposed. This aspect of the historical practice parallels in its purposes the requirement of "sincerity" under current law,[321] although

---

[318] Interestingly, the right to wear a hat has featured prominently in modern free exercise litigation. *See, e.g.*, Goldman v. Weinberger, 475 U.S. 503 (1986) (denying an Orthodox Jewish officer the right to wear a yarmulke with his military uniform); Cooper v. Eugene School Dist., 301 Or. 358, 723 P.2d 298 (1986) (upholding a revocation of tenure and teaching certificate when a Sikh teacher violated the dress statute by wearing a turban while teaching), *appeal dismissed*, 480 U.S. 942 (1987) (Brennan, Marshall, and O'Connor, JJ., dissenting).

[319] An excellent summary of the case may be found in I. BRANT, THE BILL OF RIGHTS 62–67 (1965).

[320] It is interesting that this subject came up for oblique discussion in the First Congress, during the debate over the Bill of Rights. Theodore Sedgwick of Massachusetts had ridiculed the Select Committee's list of freedoms to be protected, saying that "they might have declared that a man should have a right to wear his hat if he pleased; that he might get up when he pleased, and go to bed when he thought proper; but he would ask the gentleman whether he thought it necessary to enter these trifles in a declaration of rights." 1 ANNALS OF CONG. 759–60 (J. Gales ed. 1834) (Aug. 15, 1789). John Page of Virginia responded:

> The gentleman from Massachusetts . . . objects to the clause, because the right is of so trivial a nature. He supposes it no more essential than whether a man has a right to wear his hat or not; but let me observe to him that such rights have been opposed, and a man has been obliged to pull off his hat when he appeared before the face of authority; people have also been prevented from assembling together on their lawful occasions.

Id. at 760. This was an evident reference to Penn's case. *See* I. BRANT, *supra* note 319, at 53–55.

[321] *See supra* text accompanying notes 26–28.

the tendency to recognize only those beliefs that are a formal part of the religious dogma of the claimant's denomination has been superseded by a more individualistic view of religious conscience.[322]

An obvious objection to all these examples would be that they were initiated by the legislature. While these examples may refute the absolute no-exemption position, they are not inconsistent with the "judicial restraint" position. If, however, as seems to be the case, the exemptions were granted because legislatures believed the free exercise principle required them, it is reasonable to suppose that framers of constitutional free exercise provisions understood that similar applications of the principle would be made by the courts, once courts were entrusted with the responsibility of enforcing the mandates of free exercise.

III. The Federal Free Exercise Clause

A. The Constitution of 1787

The original Constitution drafted by the Convention in 1787 and ratified by the states in 1788 contained no provision protecting the general freedom of religion. It was not, however, entirely silent about religion. Two provisions of the Constitution reflect a spirit and purpose similar to that of the free exercise clause: the prohibition on religious tests for office in article VI,[323] and the allowance of affirmations in lieu of oaths in articles I, II, and VI.[324] Both provisions

---

[322] *See, e.g.*, Frazee v. Illinois Dep't of Employment Sec., 109 S. Ct. 1514 (1989).

[323] Article VI provides: "no religious Test shall ever be required as a Qualification to any Office or public Trust under the United States." U.S. Const. art. VI, § 3. This provision was first proposed by Charles Pinckney of South Carolina as a freestanding amendment, *see* 2 1787: Drafting the U.S. Constitution 1487 (W. Benton ed. 1986) [hereinafter Drafting the Constitution], and 10 days later, as an amendment to the article on the oath of office, *see id.* at 1488. Debate was brief. Roger Sherman of Connecticut "thought it unnecessary, the prevailing liberality being a sufficient security against such tests," but Gouverneur Morris of Pennsylvania and Pinckney's second cousin, General Charles Cotesworth Pinckney, supported the motion, which passed unanimously. *See id.* at 1488–89; 2 Farrand Records, *supra* note 160, at 457, 460–61 (Journal, Aug. 30, 1787); *id.* at 461, 468 (Madison's notes, Aug. 30, 1787). Later, during the ratification debates, the provision generated some opposition from those who believed that atheists, "heathens," non-Christians, "Papists," or "Mahometans" should be excluded from office. *See, e.g.*, 2 Elliot's Debates, *supra* note 165, at 119 (noting Col. Jones' opposition to the provision during the Massachusetts convention); 4 *id.* at 199 (noting Caldwell's argument against the provision during the North Carolina convention); *id.* at 215 (noting W. Lancaster's opposition during the North Carolina convention). On the importance of this provision, see C. Antieau, A. Downey & E. Roberts, cited above in note 16, at 92–110; and Bradley, *The No Religious Test Clause and the Constitution of Religious Liberty: A Machine That Has Gone of Itself*, 37 Case W. Res. L. Rev. 674 (1987).

[324] Article I requires that the Senate "shall be on Oath or Affirmation" when sitting for the trial of impeachments. U.S. Const. art. I, § 3, cl. 6. As originally proposed by Gouverneur Morris and as reported by the Committee on Style, this provision required an oath. *See* 1

were designed to prevent restrictions hostile to particular religions and thus to make the government of the United States more religiously inclusive. Neither provision, however, used the device of a religion-specific exemption.

The framers' decision to ban religious tests was a dramatic departure from the prevailing practice in the states, eleven of which then banned non-Christians and at least four of which banned non-Protestants from office.[325] While innovative in practice, however, the provision was unexceptional in theory. From the outset, the prevention of persecution, penalties, or incapacities on account of religion has served as a common ground among all the various interpretations of religious liberty. Religious tests for office are classic examples of laws that single out particular religious beliefs for peculiar disability, and they would be unconstitutional under any intelligible construction of the religion clauses.[326] As Oliver Ellsworth of Connecticut, later Chief Justice of the United States, wrote during the ratification campaign:

> [T]he sole purpose and effect of [the ban on religious tests for office] is to exclude persecution, and to secure to you the important right of religious liberty . . . . In our country every man has a right to worship God in that way which is most agreeable to his own conscience. If he be a good and peaceable citizen, he is liable to no penalties or incapacities on account of his religious sentiments; or in other words, he is not subject to persecution.[327]

DRAFTING THE CONSTITUTION, *supra* note 323, at 640, 641. The words "or affirmation" were added on September 14, 1787, by unanimous vote of the Convention. *See id.* at 641.

Article II provides:

> Before he enter on the Execution of his Office, [the President] shall take the following Oath or Affirmation: "I do solemnly swear (or affirm) that I will faithfully execute the Office of President of the United States, and will to the best of my Ability, preserve, protect, and defend the Constitution of the United States."

U.S. CONST. art. II, § 1, cl. 8. The allowance of an affirmation in lieu of an oath was part of the original provision as drafted by the Committee of Detail. *See* 2 DRAFTING THE CONSTITUTION, *supra* note 323, at 1488.

Article VI provides: "The Senators and Representatives before mentioned, and the Members of the several State Legislatures, and all executive and judicial Officers . . . shall be bound by Oath or Affirmation, to support this Constitution." U.S. CONST. art. VI, cl. 3. As originally proposed by the Committee of Detail, this provision required an oath. This appears to have been an oversight; the words "or affirmation" were added, apparently on the floor of the Convention, without separate vote. *See* 2 DRAFTING THE CONSTITUTION, *supra* note 323, at 1488.

[325] *See* Bradley, *supra* note 323, at 681–83. By this time, Virginia had eliminated religious tests. New York allowed Jews but banned Catholics; Maryland banned Jews but allowed Catholics. *See* M. BORDEN, *supra* note 75, at 13–14.

[326] *See* Torcaso v. Watkins, 367 U.S. 488 (1961) (striking down Maryland's religious test under the first amendment). *But cf.* Davis v. Beason, 133 U.S. 333 (1890) (upholding an anti-Mormon oath requirement for voting).

[327] Ellsworth, *A Landholder VII*, in 14 THE DOCUMENTARY HISTORY OF THE RATIFICATION OF THE CONSTITUTION 448, 449 (J. Kaminski & G. Saladino eds. 1983) (originally published

The significance of the "oath or affirmation" provisions is more subtle. Oaths of office were serious matters, so serious that the President's oath of office is spelled out in the otherwise spare text of article II. Moreover, the 1787 Constitution requires that *state* as well as federal officers be "bound by Oath or Affirmation, to support this Constitution" — one of the few provisions of the Constitution directed at state officers. Yet the framers of the Constitution realized that several small religious sects, including the influential Quakers, refused to swear oaths, on authority of *Matthew* 5:33–37. Lest members of these sects be excluded from office, it was necessary to provide alternatives.

As has already been noted, this problem had arisen in most of the states in connection with the oaths required of witnesses in court, as well as with oaths of office.[328] The usual solution was to create an exemption only for those with the religious objection and to require all others to take the oath. The framers of the federal Constitution, however, did not follow this model; they allowed any person, whether "conscientiously scrupulous" or not, to promise by affirmation instead of oath. Perhaps this was an act of verbal economy. Perhaps it reflected a principled objection to exemptions limited to those of particular beliefs. In any event, the framers solved the oath problem without the need for a free exercise exemption.

The new Constitution made no other provision for religious differences. Indeed, it appears the subject did not come up, though Luther Martin (not always the most reliable of sources) stated that he was "positive" that "[a]n honorable member from South Carolina" made an "attempt to have a stipulation in favour of liberty of conscience, but in vain."[329] The prevailing view among the Federalists, the supporters of the new Constitution, was that additional guarantees of individual liberty were unnecessary. Explicit guarantees might even be counterproductive, since the express mention of some liberties might be taken to disparage the existence of other rights, which were

---

in the *Connecticut Courant*, Dec. 17, 1787). Oddly, Ellsworth supported a strict religious test for office in his own state. *See* M. BORDEN, *supra* note 75, at 18.

[328] *See supra* pp. 1467–68.

[329] Martin, *Reply to The Landholder* (Mar. 19, 1788), *reprinted in* 3 FARRAND RECORDS, *supra* note 160, at 286, 290. Martin was probably recalling Charles Pinckney's several efforts to ban religious tests for office. A less likely possibility is that Martin recalled Pinckney's original draft of a constitution, which may have provided: "The Legislature of the United States shall pass no Law on the subject of Religion." *The Pinckney Plan, reprinted in* 3 FARRAND RECORDS, *supra* note 160, at 595, 599. This draft (if it existed) was never debated, and the Committee of Detail included no such provision in the drafts it presented to the Convention. *See* 3 FARRAND RECORDS, *supra* note 160, at 595. According to Farrand, "it is established beyond all doubt" that the draft containing this language was not at all similar to the original Pinckney plan. *See id.* at 603; Jameson, *Studies in the History of the Federal Convention of 1787*, 1 ANN. REP. AM. HIST. A. 89, 111–32 (1902).

adequately secured through the careful enumeration and delimitation of federal powers.[330]

Other participants in the debate were less trustful of the novel and distant federal government. Patrick Henry complained that a too-powerful federal government could override religious freedoms that had been hard won at the state level.[331] "Philadelphiensis," a Pennsylvania pamphleteer, objected to the transfer of control over military service to the federal government for fear that the Quakers would lose the exemptions from compulsory service they had won at the state level: "Their influence in the state of Pennsylvania is fully sufficient to save them from suffering very materially on this account; but in the great vortex of the whole continent it can have no weight."[332] The leader of the Virginia Baptists, John Leland, opposed ratification on the ground that religious freedom was "not sufficiently secured."[333] "[I]f Oppression dose not ensue," he wrote, "it will be owing to the Mildness of administration & not to any Constitutional defence."[334] In the Rhode Island town meetings of 1788–89, citizens spoke out against the lack of protection for liberty of conscience "and other fundamental liberties," and the state refused to ratify the Constitution until after the Bill of Rights had been proposed.[335] Others, perhaps more numerous, supported ratification but demanded amendments incorporating a bill of rights. These advocates were sufficiently persuasive (or sufficiently numerous) to extract the promise of a Bill of Rights as the price for ratification of the rest of the Constitution.

Perhaps the most significant political battleground for future development of a strong protection for religious freedom was in the foothills of Virginia, where the young James Madison, recently returned from the Constitutional Convention, was seeking a seat in the first House of Representatives. Like other proponents of the Consti-

---

[330] *See, e.g.*, 1 ANNALS OF CONG. 456 (J. Gales ed. 1834) (statement of James Madison, June 8, 1789); THE FEDERALIST No. 84, at 510 (A. Hamilton) (C. Rossiter ed. 1961).

[331] *See* 3 ELLIOT'S DEBATES, *supra* note 165, at 317–18 (June 12, 1788).

[332] 3 THE COMPLETE ANTI-FEDERALIST § 3.9.12, at 107 (H. Storing ed. 1981). A similar argument was made by another pamphleteer nicknamed "An Old Whig." *See id.* § 3.3.29, at 36.

[333] 4 DOCUMENTARY HISTORY OF THE CONSTITUTION OF THE UNITED STATES OF AMERICA 528 (U.S. Dep't of State ed. 1905) [hereinafter DOCUMENTARY HISTORY OF THE CONSTITUTION]. The Virginia Baptist Association voted unanimously to oppose ratification, a fact that several men quickly communicated to Madison, with the request that he take steps to mollify them. *See* R. SEMPLE, A HISTORY OF THE RISE AND PROGRESS OF THE BAPTISTS IN VIRGINIA 99 (Richmond 1810); Letter from James Madison, Sr., to James Madison (Jan. 30, 1788), in 5 THE WRITINGS OF JAMES MADISON, *supra* note 109, at 105 n.1; Letter from Joseph Spencer to James Madison (Feb. 28, 1788), in 4 DOCUMENTARY HISTORY OF THE CONSTITUTION, *supra*, at 525.

[334] 4 DOCUMENTARY HISTORY OF THE CONSTITUTION, *supra* note 333, at 528.

[335] *See* C. ANTIEAU, A. DOWNEY & E. ROBERTS, *supra* note 16, at 152–53; F. BATES, RHODE ISLAND AND THE FORMATION OF THE UNION 165–76 (1898).

tution of 1787, Madison initially lacked enthusiasm for adding a Bill of Rights, though he came to recognize the need for one to assuage the demands of the Antifederalist opposition. In a letter to Washington, he called "several of" Virginia's proposed amendments "highly objectionable."[336] But when he initiated his candidacy for Congress, he discovered that his Baptist constituents were prepared to throw their support to his opponent, James Monroe. On advice of his political adviser, George Nicholas,[337] Madison contacted Baptist leaders and proclaimed his support for "the most satisfactory provisions for all essential rights, particularly the rights of Conscience in the fullest latitude."[338] He then championed a constitutional provision for religious liberty as a campaign issue.[339] The Baptist leaders responded by giving him their electoral support, which contributed to his narrow margin of victory. A letter to Madison contains an interesting eyewitness account of a gathering at the Blue Run Baptist Church, at which the minister, the Reverend George Eve, "took a very Spirited and decided Part in your favour" and "Spoke Long" on the subject of Madison's contributions to religious freedom.[340]

There were two strands to the Federalist argument against a free exercise amendment. First, under the Constitution, the new federal government was not given any powers to pass laws affecting religion. As Madison told the Virginia ratifying convention, "There is not a shadow of right in the general government to intermeddle with religion. Its least interference with it would be a most flagrant usurpation."[341] Proponents of a free exercise amendment understandably

---

336 *See* Letter from James Madison to George Washington (June 27, 1788), in 11 MADISON PAPERS, *supra* note 226, at 182; *see also* Letter from James Madison to Thomas Jefferson (Oct. 17, 1788), in 5 THE WRITINGS OF JAMES MADISON, *supra* note 109, at 271 (stating that Madison had never viewed the Bill of Rights "in an important light").

337 *See* Letter from George Nicholas to James Madison (Jan. 2, 1789), in 11 MADISON PAPERS, *supra* note 226, at 406.

338 Letter from James Madison to the Rev. George Eve (Jan. 2, 1789), in 11 MADISON PAPERS, *supra* note 226, at 404, 405; *see also* Letter from James Madison to Thomas M. Randolph (Jan. 13, 1789), in 11 MADISON PAPERS, *supra* note 226, at 415, 416.

339 *See* Letter from James Madison published in the Fredricksburg (Va.) Herald (Jan. 29, 1789), in 11 MADISON PAPERS, *supra* note 226, at 428 (promising to sponsor a constitutional amendment); Letter from James Madison to George Washington (Jan. 14, 1789), in 11 MADISON PAPERS, *supra* note 226, at 417 (describing his speeches and newspaper campaign to dispel a report that he opposed constitutional amendments); *see also* Letter from David Jameson, Jr., to James Madison, in 11 MADISON PAPERS, *supra* note 226, at 419 (Jan. 14, 1789) (thanking Madison for making an address in Culpepper County on the issue of amendments).

340 Letter from Benjamin Johnson to James Madison (Jan. 19, 1789), in 11 MADISON PAPERS, *supra* note 226, at 423, 424.

341 3 ELLIOT'S DEBATES, *supra* note 165, at 330 (June 12, 1788). James Iredell made a similar argument in the North Carolina ratifying convention. *See* 4 *id.* at 194 (July 30, 1788). Roger Sherman of Connecticut continued to make the argument in the First Congress in

rejected this argument. The federal government would exercise plenary regulatory authority in the territories,[342] the District of Columbia,[343] and the military.[344] Its powers of taxation,[345] spending,[346] immigration and naturalization,[347] copyright,[348] international trade,[349] bankruptcy,[350] and relations with Indian tribes[351] and foreign governments[352] could, with little imagination, be expected to affect the exercise of religion. The potential of the necessary and proper clause might be viewed — and was viewed, according to Madison — as the most threatening of all.[353] Thus, a federal government bent

---

opposition to enactment of the religion clauses. *See* 1 ANNALS OF CONG. 757 (J. Gales ed. 1834) (statement of Roger Sherman, Aug. 15, 1789).

342 *See* Reynolds v. United States, 98 U.S. 145 (1878) (upholding the petitioner's conviction under territorial legislation outlawing the Mormon practice of polygamy).

343 *See* H. Rep., Returned Bill 21 (Feb. 23, 1811), *reprinted in* 5 THE FOUNDERS' CONSTITUTION, *supra* note 72, at 99 (recording President Madison's veto of "An Act incorporating the Protestant Episcopal Church in the town of Alexandria, in the District of Columbia," on the ground that Congress' authority over the District of Columbia should not be used to define the functions and governance of a church).

344 *See* Goldman v. Weinberger, 475 U.S. 503 (1986) (upholding an Air Force uniform regulation prohibiting the wearing of a yarmulke).

345 *See* Hernandez v. Commissioner, 109 S. Ct. 2136 (1989) (rejecting a claim that disallowance of claimed charitable contributions violated the religion clauses).

346 *See* Flast v. Cohen, 392 U.S. 83 (1968) (holding that federal taxpayers who alleged that the appropriation of federal funds to religious schools violated the establishment and free exercise clauses had standing to sue).

347 *See* Girouard v. United States, 328 U.S. 61 (1946) (holding that the Nationality Act did not require Seventh-day Adventist aliens to swear to bear arms in defense of the country); United States v. Aguilar, 871 F.2d 1436 (9th Cir. 1989) (sustaining the conviction of defendants engaged in a sanctuary movement who challenged enforcement of immigration laws as violative of their free exercise rights).

348 *See* United Christian Scientists v. Christian Science Bd. of Directors, 829 F.2d 1152 (D.C. Cir. 1987) (holding that congressional extension of the Christian Science Church's copyright on all Christian Science scripture unconstitutionally contravened the first amendment rights of a dissident group that wished to publish a variant).

349 *See* 19 U.S.C. § 1202, sch. 8, pt. 4, ¶ 850 (1988) (exempting certain religious artifacts from import duties).

350 *See In re* Reynolds, 83 Bankr. 684 (W.D. Mo. 1988) (regulating the religious contributions of a debtor in bankruptcy).

351 *See* Quick Bear v. Leupp, 210 U.S. 50 (1908) (maintaining that prohibiting the exercise of Indian treaty power to appropriate tribal and trust funds for sectarian education would deny an Indian's free exercise of religion).

352 *See* Americans United for Separation of Church & State v. Reagan, 786 F.2d 194 (3d Cir.) (upholding denial of standing to a group raising an establishment clause challenge to the appointment of an ambassador to the Vatican), *cert. denied*, 479 U.S. 914 (1986).

353 *See* 1 ANNALS OF CONG. 758 (J. Gales ed. 1834) (speech by James Madison, Aug. 15, 1789). Madison observed:

> [S]ome of the State Conventions . . . seemed to entertain an opinion that under the clause of the constitution, which gave power to Congress to make all laws necessary and proper to carry into execution the constitution, and the laws made under it, enabled them to make laws of such a nature as might infringe the rights of conscience, and establish a national religion.

Id.

on religious oppression could accomplish such oppression under pretext of one of the enumerated powers. Moreover, the argument that the lack of enumerated power could serve as a sufficient assurance of religious liberty offered no comfort to those who understood free exercise of religion to entail exemption from otherwise legitimate general legislation. Such legislation is by definition within the enumerated powers of the federal government.

The second strand of the Federalist argument was more persuasive. The Federalists argued that the structure of government, combined with the multiplicity of religious sects, would provide an effective guarantee against religious oppression. Madison's defense of the Constitution in the Virginia convention typified this position:

> Religion is not guarded; there is no bill of rights declaring that religion should be secure . . . . Happily for the states, they enjoy the utmost freedom of religion. This freedom arises from that multiplicity of sects which pervades America, and which is the best and only security for religious liberty in any society; for where there is such a variety of sects, there cannot be a majority of any one sect to oppress and persecute the rest.[354]

This argument exactly parallels Madison's famous defense of the Constitutional structure in *Federalist* No. 51. There he says that the "security for civil rights must be the same as that for religious rights. It consists in the one case in the multiplicity of interests, and in the other in the multiplicity of sects."[355] The best cure for factional oppression is a large republic with many conflicting factions and a representative government with checks and balances.[356]

---

[354] 3 ELLIOT'S DEBATES, *supra* note 165, at 330 (June 12, 1788).

[355] THE FEDERALIST No. 51, at 324 (J. Madison) (C. Rossiter ed. 1961). *See also id.* No. 10, at 79 (J. Madison) (citing "[a] zeal for different opinions concerning religion" as his first example of a "faction").

[356] Madison's theory of religious faction was no doubt a product of his experiences during the assessment controversy in Virginia, where the two largest denominations — Anglican and Presbyterian — were played off against one another. It also had roots in European thought. Madison was fond of quoting Voltaire that "'[i]f one religion only were allowed in England, . . . the government would possibly become arbitrary; if there were but two, the people would cut each other's throats; but, as there are such a multitude, they all live happy and in peace.'" W. RIVES, 2 HISTORY OF THE LIFE AND TIMES OF JAMES MADISON 220 n.1 (1866) (quoting F. VOLTAIRE, LETTRES SUR LES ANGLAIS). Similarly, Adam Smith, in *The Wealth of Nations*, observed:

> The interested and active zeal of religious teachers can be dangerous and troublesome only where there is, either but one sect tolerated in the society, or where the whole of a large society is divided into two or three great sects; the teachers of each acting by concert, and under a regular discipline and subordination. But that zeal must be altogether innocent where the society is divided into two or three hundred, or perhaps into as many thousand small sects, of which no one could be considerable enough to disturb the public tranquillity.

A. SMITH, *supra* note 156, bk. 5, ch. 1, pt. 3, art. 3, at 745.

If the principal danger to religious liberty was the deliberate oppression of religious minorities by the majority, then the Madisonian vision offered a more powerful answer to those demanding a free exercise clause. In a nation of many different religious groups, each jealous of the others, it would be difficult if not impossible for any group to impose its beliefs on the others. Yet Madison's argument did not carry the day. Perhaps the reason is that his argument did not satisfy the concerns of those, like the Quakers addressed by "Philadelphiensis," who feared not deliberate oppression, but the unintended effects of legislation passed without regard to the religious scruples of small minorities. The multiplicity of sects provides no protection against ignorance or indifference. Indeed, the position of religious minorities might be made much worse. Because settlements of minorities tend to be concentrated in particular regions, most sects had greater influence at the state level than in "the great vortex of the whole continent."[357] The same extended Union that protected minority faiths against oppression would make them more vulnerable to thoughtless general legislation.

Federalist assurances thus failed to assuage the concerns of America's religious sects, including many of Madison's own constituents. Only a bill of rights would do.

B. Framing and Ratifying the Free Exercise Clause

1. Debates in the First Congress. — Madison admitted that the lack of a provision protecting the rights of conscience had "alarmed many respectable Citizens," and he pledged to work for "the most satisfactory provisions for all essential rights, particularly the rights of Conscience in the fullest latitude, the freedom of the press, trials by jury, security against general warrants &c."[358] Lawmakers in other states responded to the same popular pressure. Seven states drafted proposals for amendments, and five of them (plus the minority report in Pennsylvania) urged protection for religious freedom. New York, for example, ratified the Constitution but proposed a bill of rights including the following provision: "That the people have an equal, natural, and unalienable right freely and peaceably to exercise their religion, according to the dictates of conscience . . . ."[359] Virginia proposed a similar provision, using the phrase "free exercise of reli-

---

[357] 3 THE COMPLETE ANTI-FEDERALIST, *supra* note 332, § 3.9.12, at 107.

[358] Letter from James Madison to the Rev. George Eve (Jan. 2, 1789), in 11 MADISON PAPERS, *supra* note 226, at 404, 404–05. Madison subsequently published this promise in the Fredericksburg Herald. *See* Letter from James Madison published in the Fredericksburg (Va.) Herald (Jan. 29, 1789), in 11 MADISON PAPERS, *supra* note 226, at 428.

[359] 1 ELLIOT'S DEBATES, *supra* note 165, at 327 (July 26, 1788).

gion";[360] Rhode Island[361] and North Carolina[362] made proposals virtually identical to Virginia's.

Only New Hampshire, of the states that proposed a federal bill of rights, used a markedly different formulation: "Congress shall make no laws touching religion, or to infringe the rights of conscience."[363] The wording of this proposal tends to support the exemptions view, since the second clause would have little, if any, application unless secular, generally applicable laws (laws not "touching religion") could violate the rights of conscience. This proposal was considered on the floor of the House of Representatives, briefly adopted, and then rejected in favor of a formulation similar to today's free exercise clause.[364]

The recorded debates in the House over these proposals cast little light on the meaning of the free exercise clause. Indeed, the main controversy during these debates centered on establishment. The key changes in free exercise language ("free exercise of religion" in place of "equal rights of conscience," and "prohibiting" in place of "infring[ing]") took place after the recorded debate. Thus, we must rely primarily on the successive drafts of the clause during its passage through the First Congress.

Madison undertook an initial draft of the Bill of Rights, to be proposed to the House of Representatives. His draft free exercise clause did not follow the language of the state proposals. Rather, he suggested the following formulation: "The civil rights of none shall be abridged on account of religious belief or worship, [n]or shall any national religion be established, nor shall the full and equal rights of conscience be in any manner, nor on any pretext, infringed."[365] Three aspects of the Madison proposal are suggestive. First, the formulation "full and equal rights of conscience" implies that the liberty has both a substantive and an equality component: the rights must be both "full" and "equal." Hence, the liberty of conscience is entitled not only to equal protection, but also to some absolute measure of protection apart from mere governmental neutrality.

---

360 The Virginia proposal read:

> That religion, or the duty which we owe to our Creator, and the manner of discharging it, can be directed only by reason and conviction, not by force or violence; and therefore all men have an equal, natural, and unalienable right to the free exercise of religion, according to the dictates of conscience . . . .

3 *id.* at 659 (June 27, 1788). The Virginia proposal was taken almost verbatim from the Virginia Bill of Rights of 1776. *See supra* text accompanying note 251.

361 *See* 1 ELLIOT'S DEBATES, *supra* note 165, at 334 (May 29, 1790).

362 *See* 4 *id.* at 244 (Aug. 1, 1788).

363 1 *id.* at 326 (June 21, 1788).

364 *See* 1 ANNALS OF CONG. 757–59 (J. Gales ed. 1834) (Aug. 15, 1789), 796 (Aug. 20, 1789).

365 *Id.* at 451 (proposal of James Madison, June 8, 1789).

Second, the formulation that the rights in question shall not "in any manner nor on any pretext" be infringed suggests protection from infringements in any form, even those not expressly directed at religious practice. This proposal recognized that infringements on rights of conscience could result from Congress' exercise of its enumerated powers even when the legislation made no direct reference to religion. For the most part these infringements would be indirect — secular laws that invaded religious freedom as applied, rather than acts directed toward religious practice or belief as such.

Third, Madison favored the formulation "rights of conscience" over the formulation "free exercise of religion," which was found both in his own state's laws and in three of the five state proposals. This choice of language was ultimately reversed after deliberation by the House and the Senate; its meaning is considered below.[366]

Rather than debating Madison's proposal, the Select Committee proposed a much shorter version: "no religion shall be established by law, nor shall the equal rights of conscience be infringed."[367] The Committee deleted Madison's reference to "Civil Rights," probably because it was redundant, and shortened his "full and equal rights of conscience" to "equal rights of conscience." If this change was more than stylistic, which seems doubtful, it might suggest a move toward a no-exemptions view of free exercise, since it emphasizes equal treatment rather than full substantive protection.

The Select Committee language ran into trouble in the House, largely because of concerns that its establishment provision might interfere with the ability of the states to support religion — an issue especially important to those states with established churches. After a brief flirtation with the New Hampshire language, previously discussed,[368] the House adopted a formulation proposed by Fisher Ames of Massachusetts: "Congress shall make no law establishing religion, or to prevent the free exercise thereof, or to infringe the rights of conscience."[369] This version omitted the modifiers "full" and "equal" from the phrase "rights of conscience." This suggests that the deletion of "full" by the Committee was no more than stylistic and that the word "equal" was deleted so as not to create a negative inference.

More strikingly, the Ames version introduced a new term into the debate: "free exercise of religion." "Free exercise" had been part of most of the state proposals but had not appeared in the Madison, Select Committee, or New Hampshire proposals previously debated in the House, all of which had used the alternative formulation "rights of conscience." In many contexts, the phrases "rights of conscience"

---

366 *See infra* pp. 1488–1500.

367 1 ANNALS OF CONG. 757 (J. Gales ed. 1834) (Aug. 15, 1789).

368 *See supra* text accompanying notes 363–364.

369 1 ANNALS OF CONG. 796 (J. Gales ed. 1834) (proposal of Fisher Ames, Aug. 20, 1789).

and "free exercise of religion" seem to have been used interchangeably. But here, Ames, a notoriously careful draftsman and meticulous lawyer, thought it necessary to use both terms. The significance of this change will be considered below.[370]

The House of Representatives approved the amendment as proposed by Ames without recorded debate or discussion. Both the House and the Senate journals record that the House passed and sent to the Senate a proposed amendment slightly different from the Ames proposal: "Congress shall make no law establishing Religion, or prohibiting the free exercise thereof, nor shall the rights of conscience be infringed."[371] The difference between these two versions is a shift in verbs from "prevent" to "prohibit" and a shift in grammatical form from infinitives to gerunds. Whether these changes result from an unrecorded amendment or from mistranscription in either the *Annals* or the final copy of the engrossed bill is unknown.[372]

Whatever the precise chain of events, the language considered by the Senate and ultimately employed in the first amendment was "prohibiting the free exercise [of religion]." This wording has proven significant to the Supreme Court's interpretation of the free exercise clause and is discussed in detail below.[373]

In the Senate, the debate was not recorded, but various versions of the religion clauses were adopted and rejected in succession. The versions adopted, in order, were as follows:

> (1) "Congress shall make no law establishing one religious sect or society in preference to others, nor shall the rights of conscience be infringed."[374]
>
> (2) "Congress shall make no law establishing religion, or prohibiting the free exercise thereof."[375]

---

[370] *See infra* pp. 1488–1500.

[371] 1 DOCUMENTARY HISTORY OF THE FIRST FEDERAL CONGRESS OF THE UNITED STATES OF AMERICA 136 (L. De Pauw ed. 1972) (Senate Journal); 3 *id.* at 159 (House Journal) [hereinafter DOCUMENTARY HISTORY].

[372] *See* Laycock, *supra* note 16, at 879 n.27. The *Annals* is not entirely reliable. *See id.* at 885. For a glaring example, see 1 ANNALS OF CONG. 948 (J. Gales ed. 1834) (Sept. 24, 1789) (transcribing the final version of the free exercise clause adopted by both Houses as ". . . or prohibiting *a* free exercise thereof" (emphasis added)). Madison wrote that the reporter's notes, later printed in the *Annals*, showed "'the strongest evidences of mutilation & perversion, and of the illiteracy of the Editor.'" Tinling, *Thomas Lloyd's Reports of the First Federal Congress*, 18 WM. & MARY Q. 519, 532–33 (3d ser. 1961) (quoting PAPERS OF JAMES MADISON XI, No. 58, Lib. Congress). *See generally* Hutson, *The Creation of the Constitution: The Integrity of the Documentary Record*, 65 TEX. L. REV. 1 (1986) (arguing that most records of the drafting and ratification of the Constitution may be seriously unreliable).

[373] *See infra* pp. 1486–88.

[374] 1 DOCUMENTARY HISTORY, *supra* note 371, at 151 (Senate Journal).

[375] *Id.*

> (3) "Congress shall make no law establishing articles of faith or a mode of worship, or prohibiting the free exercise of religion . . . ."[376]

Note that each of these versions used either the phrase "rights of conscience" or the phrase "free exercise of religion." No version used the phrases in conjunction, as had the Ames proposal.

The third version passed the Senate and was transmitted to the House, which rejected it, presumably because of its narrow provision on establishment. A Conference Committee, on which Madison served, proposed the version of the religion clauses that was ultimately ratified.[377] The free exercise clause itself was unchanged from the final Senate bill.

One final point about the debate in the First Congress deserves mention. In addition to the provision already discussed, which applied only to the federal government, Madison proposed an amendment that would have been applicable to the states. It read: "[N]o State shall infringe the equal rights of conscience, nor the freedom of speech or of the press, nor of the right of trial by jury in criminal cases."[378] Madison said that he conceived this to be "the most valuable amendment in the whole list. If there were any reason to restrain the Government of the United States from infringing upon these essential rights, it was equally necessary that they should be secured against the State Governments."[379] Significantly, Madison did not propose that the establishment clause be made applicable to the states; this reflects the prevailing view at the time that states should be permitted to set their own course with respect to establishment, but that liberty of conscience was an unalienable right. With minor editorial change, the House adopted Madison's proposal.[380] Later the Senate rejected the proposal, presumably in deference to states' rights.[381] This left the provisions of the Bill of Rights solely as limitations against the federal government,[382] as they were to remain

---

[376] *Id.* at 166 (Senate Journal).

[377] *See* 3 *id.* at 228 (House Journal).

[378] 1 ANNALS OF CONG. 783 (J. Gales 1834) (Aug. 17, 1789).

[379] *Id.*

[380] *See id.* at 784.

[381] No less a Federalist than James Iredell had commented in his state's ratifying convention:

> It has been asked . . . why a *guaranty* of religious freedom was not included. . . . Had Congress undertaken to guaranty religious freedom, or any particular species of it, they would then have had a pretence to interfere in a subject they have nothing to do with. Each state, so far as the [republican form of government clause] does not interfere, must be left to the operation of its own principles.

4 ELLIOT'S DEBATES, *supra* note 165, at 194–95 (July 30, 1788) (emphasis in original).

[382] *See* Permoli v. Municipality No. 1, 44 U.S. (3 How.) 588, 609 (1845) ("The Constitution makes no provision for protecting the citizens of the respective States in their religious liberties; this is left to the State constitutions and laws.").

until the Supreme Court held that they had been selectively "incorporated" pursuant to the fourteenth amendment.[383]

Any interpretation of the religion clauses as applying to the states is thus somewhat anachronistic. Because the free exercise clause at the federal level was itself modeled on free exercise provisions in the various state constitutions, however, no structural distortions arise from assuming that, for modern purposes (after "incorporation"), the free exercise clause means the same thing for states that it has always meant for the federal government.[384]

2. Ratification. — The ratification debates in the state legislatures were unilluminating. Most states ratified the proposed amendments quickly, with little debate or controversy. Three states — Georgia, Massachusetts, and Connecticut — failed to ratify, but the refusal seems to have been unrelated to questions of religious freedom. Only in Virginia is there record of opposition to the religion clauses as proposed by Congress. In Virginia, the Senate delayed ratification of the first amendment, partly on the ground that it "does not prohibit the rights of conscience from being violated or infringed."[385] The reasons for this are difficult to fathom, since neither Virginia's own Bill of Rights nor the amendment on religious freedom the state proposed to the Congress contained a separate "rights of conscience" clause, and in the only legal document in which the "rights of conscience" and the "exercise of religion" were differentiated — the Georgia Charter of 1732[386] — free exercise was broader than the rights of conscience.[387] Historian Leonard Levy attributes the delay to Antifederalist political maneuvering rather than to serious substantive opposition to the language of the first amendment.[388] After two years, the first amendment was ratified without additional comment.

3. Two Issues of Interpretation. — As has been noted,[389] two key modifications in the language that ultimately became the free exercise clause were made after the close of recorded debate. In the House, the verb "prohibit" was substituted for the broader term "infringe."

---

383 *See* Cantwell v. Connecticut, 310 U.S. 296, 303 (1940) (applying the free exercise clause to the states for the first time through the fourteenth amendment).

384 Incorporation of the establishment clause presents far more serious interpretive difficulties, since there existed no national consensus on the question of governmental aid to religion, other than to leave the question to the states; in addition, the ramifications of establishment are different for small than for large units of government.

385 C. ANTIEAU, A. DOWNEY & E. ROBERTS, *supra* note 16, at 145 (quoting JOURNAL OF THE SENATE OF VIRGINIA FOR 1789, at 51 (available at Virginia State Library, Richmond)).

386 *See* GA. CHARTER of 1732, *reprinted in* 1 FEDERAL AND STATE CONSTITUTIONS, *supra* note 2, at 369.

387 *See infra* pp. 1489–90.

388 *See* L. LEVY, *supra* note 16, at 86–89.

389 *See supra* p. 1481.

In the Senate, the term "free exercise of religion" was adopted and the term "rights of conscience" was deleted. Both changes could have important implications for the meaning of the free exercise clause. But since there was no recorded debate or discussion of these later versions, we can only rely on context, contemporary diction, and other indirect evidence of meaning.

(a) The Meaning of "Prohibiting." — The prior drafts considered by the House used the verbs "infringing" or "preventing" to describe the forbidden effect on the rights of conscience. Moreover, in parallel clauses of the first amendment, the framers used the verb "abridging" to protect the freedoms of speech, assembly, and petition. The Supreme Court later relied on this choice of words to support a restrictive reading of the free exercise clause. In *Lyng v. Northwest Indian Cemetery Protective Association*,[390] the Court reasoned: "The crucial word in the constitutional text is 'prohibit'"; therefore, the free exercise clause does not require the government "to bring forward a compelling justification" for actions "which may make it more difficult to practice certain religions but which have no tendency to coerce individuals into acting contrary to their religious beliefs."[391] This textual argument is further developed in the Department of Justice study of the origins of the free exercise clause: "'[P]rohibiting' and 'abridging' are denotatively and connotatively distinct. 'Prohibiting' means to forbid or prevent, while 'abridging' means to reduce or limit. Thus, 'prohibiting' connotes a finality, certitude, or damning not present in 'abridging,' which connotes limitations falling short of the finality of prohibition or prevention."[392] On the strength of this textual evidence alone, the report concludes that laws that discourage or inhibit religious exercise by denying government benefits (even those enacted in "purposeful discrimination" against a religion) do not violate the free exercise clause.[393] Only laws that make a religious practice unlawful or impossible are forbidden.

While contemporaneous definitions of "prohibit" indicate that it was a stronger and narrower term than "abridge" or "infringe," the distinction is probably overdrawn in the context of the free exercise debate in 1789. Among the synonyms for "prohibit" listed in Samuel Johnson's 1755 edition is "to hinder,"[394] which seems weaker and broader than "abridge" or "infringe." Since the verb form used for the establishment clause ("respecting") was different from the verb form used for the free speech clause ("abridging"), it seems more likely

[390] 485 U.S. 439 (1988).

[391] *Id.* at 451.

[392] REPORT TO THE ATTORNEY GENERAL, *supra* note 17, at 17 (citing various dictionaries, including a 1755 edition of Samuel Johnson's and an 1828 edition of Noah Webster's).

[393] *See id.* at 47 n.84.

[394] 2 S. JOHNSON, A DICTIONARY OF THE ENGLISH LANGUAGE, *supra* note 268.

that the drafters found it less awkward or more euphonious to use yet a third verb form ("prohibiting") for the free exercise clause.[395] No one in the debate, in or out of Congress, expressed the view that infringements that are not final, certain, or "damning"[396] should be allowed. Madison had promised to support "the most satisfactory provisions for all essential rights, particularly the rights of Conscience in the fullest latitude,"[397] and Daniel Carroll, a Roman Catholic from Maryland, had stated that the "rights of conscience . . . will little bear the gentlest touch of governmental hand" and that "many sects have concurred in opinion that they are not well secured under the present constitution."[398] If the final version had been understood to allow infringements short of outright prohibition, one of these gentlemen would surely have spoken up. But both seemed satisfied with the bill's language, as did their constituents. A Baptist leader wrote Madison to tell him "that the amendments had entirely satisfied the disaffected of his Sect."[399]

Ten years after the House debate, Madison commented on the difference in verbs in the three portions of the first amendment (laws *respecting* Establishment, laws *prohibiting* free exercise, and laws *abridging* the freedom of speech, press, or assembly). The argument had been made (by no less a figure than John Marshall) that Congress had greater power over the press than over the establishment of religion, because the term "abridging" was less encompassing than the term "respecting."[400] Madison, in response, stated that "the liberty of conscience and the freedom of the press were *equally* and *completely*

---

[395] The word choice may therefore reflect what is called "elegant variation," disapproved of by modern authorities. *See* H. FOWLER, A DICTIONARY OF MODERN ENGLISH USAGE 130–33 (1927).

[396] *See* REPORT TO THE ATTORNEY GENERAL, *supra* 17, at 17.

[397] Letter from James Madison to the Rev. George Eve (Jan. 2, 1789), in 11 MADISON PAPERS, *supra* note 226, at 404, 405.

[398] 1 ANNALS OF CONG. 757–58 (J. Gales ed. 1834) (Aug. 15, 1789).

[399] Letter from James Madison to George Washington (Nov. 20, 1789), in 5 THE WRITINGS OF JAMES MADISON, *supra* note 109, at 429.

[400] *See* Marshall, *Report of the Minority on the Virginia Resolutions* (Jan. 22, 1799), *reprinted in* 5 THE FOUNDERS' CONSTITUTION, *supra* note 72, at 136, 138. Marshall's argument, in full, was as follows:

> In a solemn instrument, as is a constitution, words are well weighed and considered before they are adopted. A remarkable diversity of expression is not used, unless it be designed to manifest a difference of intention. Congress is prohibited from making any law RESPECTING a religious establishment, but not from making any law RESPECTING the press. When the power of Congress relative to the press is to be limited, the word RESPECTING is dropt, and Congress is only restrained from the passing any law ABRIDGING its liberty. This difference of expression with respect to religion and the press, manifests a difference of intention with respect to the power of the national legislature over those subjects, both in the person who drew, and in those who adopted this amendment.

Id.

exempted from all authority whatever of the United States."[401] He went on to argue:

> [I]f Congress may regulate the freedom of the press, provided they do not abridge it, because it is said only "they shall not abridge it," and is not said "they shall make no law respecting it," the analogy of reasoning is conclusive that Congress may *regulate* and even *abridge* the free exercise of religion, provided they do not *prohibit* it; because it is said only "they shall not prohibit it," and is *not* said "they shall make no law *respecting*, or no law *abridging* it."[402]

Madison found this interpretation of the free exercise clause so absurd that to state it was to refute it. Despite its plausibility as a textual matter, the narrow interpretation of "prohibiting" should therefore be rejected, and the term should be read as meaning approximately the same as "infringing" or "abridging."

(b) The Substitution of "Free Exercise of Religion" for the "Rights of Conscience." — As noted above,[403] the states requesting constitutional protection for religious freedom, with one exception, employed the language free "exercise" of "religion," borrowing from the Virginia Bill of Rights. Madison, for reasons that remain mysterious, did not follow this lead in his draft, using instead the term "rights of conscience," a term also used by the Select Committee and New Hampshire drafts debated on the floor of the House of Representatives. The term "free exercise of religion" reappeared after the close of recorded debate, in the Ames version, which protected *both* "free exercise of religion" *and* the "rights of conscience," and which passed the House. The Senate first voted to protect "rights of conscience" and then settled upon protecting the "free exercise of religion" alone, a formulation that ultimately carried the day. It is possible that these changes in language were without substantive meaning, for in many of the debates in the preconstitutional period, the concepts of "liberty of conscience" and "free exercise of religion" were used interchangeably. There are, nonetheless, three principal differences between the terms that may have significance for interpretation.

The least ambiguous difference is that the term "free exercise" makes clear that the clause protects religiously motivated conduct as well as belief. This point merits emphasis, because in 1879 the Supreme Court, relying on Jefferson, explicitly rejected this reading.[404] Only in 1940 did the Court begin to include religiously motivated conduct within the ambit of the free exercise clause, and even then,

---

[401] Madison, *Report on the Virginia Resolutions* (Jan. 18, 1800), *reprinted in* 5 THE FOUNDERS' CONSTITUTION, *supra* note 72, at 141, 146 (emphasis in original).

[402] *Id.*

[403] *See supra* pp. 1481–82.

[404] *See* Reynolds v. United States, 98 U.S. 145, 164 (1879).

only to a limited degree.[405] The belief-action distinction is often used to suggest that protection for religiously motivated conduct is far weaker than that accorded to free speech or other, seemingly "absolute" freedoms.[406]

The choice of the words "free exercise of religion" in lieu of "rights of conscience" is therefore of utmost importance. As defined by dictionaries at the time of the framing, the word "exercise" strongly connoted action. The American edition of Samuel Johnson's *Dictionary of the English Language*, published in Philadelphia in 1805, used the following terms to define "exercise": "Labour of the body," "Use; actual application of any thing," "Task; that which one is appointed to perform," and "Act of divine worship, whether public or private."[407] Noah Webster's American dictionary defined "exercise" as "employment."[408] James Buchanan's 1757 dictionary defined "exercise" as "[t]o use or practice."[409] "Conscience" was more likely to have been understood as opinion or belief. Johnson equated "conscience" with the terms "knowledge," "Real sentiment; veracity; private thoughts," "Scruple; difficulty," and "reason; reasonableness."[410] Webster defined it as "natural knowledge, or the faculty that decides on the right or wrong of actions."[411] Buchanan defined it as the "testimony of one's own mind."[412]

The Georgia Charter of 1732 is the only legal document of the period to make a distinction between the two phrases. It provided "that there shall be a liberty of conscience allowed in the worship of God, to all persons inhabiting, or which shall inhabit or be resident within our said province, and that all such persons, except papists, shall have a free exercise of religion."[413] Since Roman Catholics were

---

405 *See* Cantwell v. Connecticut, 310 U.S. 296, 303–04 (1940).

406 *See, e.g.*, McDaniel v. Paty, 435 U.S. 618, 626–27 (1978) (plurality opinion); Braunfeld v. Brown, 366 U.S. 599, 603–07 (1961); Walker v. Superior Court, 47 Cal. 3d 112, 139, 763 P.2d 852, 869, 253 Cal. Rptr. 1, 18 (1988) (holding that the prosecution for manslaughter of a mother who refused any medical treatment except prayer for her son was not prohibited by the free exercise clause); Molko v. Holy Spirit Ass'n for the Unification of World Christianity, 46 Cal. 3d 1092, 1112, 762 P.2d 46, 56, 252 Cal. Rptr. 122, 132 (1988) (holding that the free exercise clause does not bar an action for fraud against a religious organization when that action implicates conduct, not belief); Madsen v. Erwin, 395 Mass. 715, 727–27, 481 N.E.2d 1160, 1167 (1985) (holding that the free exercise clause would not prevent the consideration of tort claims arising out of the termination of a Christian Science Monitor employee who refused to seek healing through the church for her sexual preference).

407 S. Johnson, *supra* note 252.

408 N. Webster, A Compendious Dictionary of the English Language (New Haven 1806).

409 J. Buchanan, *supra* note 251.

410 S. Johnson, *supra* note 252.

411 N. Webster, *supra* note 252.

412 J. Buchanan, *supra* note 251.

413 Ga. Charter of 1732, *reprinted in* 1 Federal and State Constitutions, *supra* note 2, at 369, 375.

guaranteed liberty of conscience but not the free exercise of religion, this suggests that the former was understood to be narrower than the latter.[414] The most plausible reading of the provision is that it permitted Catholics to believe what they wished (and possibly to worship as they liked, though that is more doubtful), but did not permit them to put their faith into action. Such a policy would be consistent with the fears of the papacy that existed at the time.

By using the term "free exercise," the first amendment extended the broader freedom of action to all believers. As noted, the freedom of religion was almost universally understood (with Jefferson being the prominent exception) to include conduct as well as belief.[415] Accordingly, free exercise is more likely than mere liberty of conscience to generate conflicts with, and claims for exemption from, general laws and social mores.

A second important difference between the terms "conscience" and "religion" is that "conscience" emphasizes individual judgment,[416] while "religion" also encompasses the corporate or institutional aspects of religious belief. In the great battle cry of the Protestant Reformation — "God alone is Lord of the conscience"[417] — the individual conscience was used in contradistinction to the teaching of the institutional church. "Religion," by contrast, connotes a community of believers. The most widely accepted derivation of the word "religion" is from the Latin "religare" — to bind.[418] Religion binds believers together; conscience refers to the inner faculty of judgment. Thus, the "free exercise of religion" suggests that the government may not interfere with the activities of religious bodies, even when the interference has no direct relation to a claim of conscience.[419] This inter-

---

[414] It is not apparent what "liberty of conscience" included as applied to Catholics, or if the charter provision was enforced at all. During this period, Catholics were excluded from the colony, and those who entered were not permitted to receive land grants, inherit property, or hold public office. *See* R. STRICKLAND, *supra* note 62, at 80–81. Later, when governance of the colony was transfered from the Trustees to the Crown, the instructions to the royal governor denied even the liberty of conscience to Catholics and omitted any reference to "free exercise." *See id.* at 120.

[415] For a discussion of the belief-action distinction prior to the framing, see pp. 1451–52 above.

[416] *See supra* p. 1489 (quoting contemporaneous dictionary definitions of "conscience").

[417] This statement was formally adopted as part of their creed by the Calvinists of Great Britain in 1647. *See The Westminster Confession of Faith*, in 3 THE CREEDS OF CHRISTENDOM 600 (P. Schaft 4th ed. 1919). It presumably derived from John Calvin's *Reply to Cardinal Sadolet*, published in 1539, which stated: "There is nothing of Christ, then, in him who does not hold the elementary principle, that it is God alone who enlightens our minds to perceive his truth, who by his Spirit seals it on our hearts, and by his sure attestation to it confirms our conscience." J. CALVIN, *Reply to Letter by Cardinal Sadolet to the Senate and People of Geneva*, in JOHN CALVIN: SELECTIONS FROM HIS WRITINGS 81, 105 (J. Dillenberger ed. 1971).

[418] *See* RANDOM HOUSE DICTIONARY OF THE ENGLISH LANGUAGE 1628 (2d ed. 1987).

[419] An example would be the application of a nondiscrimination law to the employment of

pretation is also consistent with the distinction drawn in the Georgia Charter, since the private devotions of individual Catholics would be of less concern to the state than the operations of an institutional Church with supposed connections to foreign powers.

The third, and most controversial, difference between the "free exercise of religion" and the "rights of conscience" is that the latter might seem to extend to claims of conscience based on something other than religion — to belief systems based on science, history, economics, political ideology, or secular moral philosophy. By deleting references to "conscience," the final version of the first amendment singles out religion for special treatment. And so the Supreme Court has held: "A way of life, however virtuous and admirable, may not be interposed as a barrier to reasonable state regulation . . . if it is based on purely secular considerations; to have the protection of the Religion Clauses, the claims must be rooted in religious belief."[420]

This distinction between religion and other belief systems has come under substantial attack in academic circles.[421] Religion is understood

---

a minister. *See, e.g.*, Rayburn v. General Conference of Seventh-Day Adventists, 772 F.2d 1164 (4th Cir. 1985), *cert. denied*, 478 U.S. 1020 (1986). Under the view of free exercise espoused in the text, such a law would be an unconstitutional interference in a religious function even if the religious group in question had no doctrinal tenet requiring or allowing discrimination.

[420] Wisconsin v. Yoder, 406 U.S. 205, 215–16 (1972). This position was unanimously reaffirmed in Frazee v. Illinois Dep't of Employment Sec., 109 S. Ct. 1514, 1517 (1989); *see also* Texas Monthly, Inc. v. Bullock, 109 S. Ct. 890, 901 n.8 (1989) (plurality opinion) (Brennan, J.) (noting that exemptions conferred exclusively on religious groups or individuals on account of their religious convictions do not violate the establishment clause if they are "designed to alleviate government intrusions that might significantly deter adherents of a particular faith from conduct protected by the Free Exercise Clause"); Marsh v. Chambers, 463 U.S. 783, 812 (1983) (Brennan, J., dissenting) ("[I]n one important respect, the Constitution is *not* neutral on the subject of religion: Under the Free Exercise Clause, religiously motivated claims of conscience may give rise to constitutional rights that other strongly held beliefs do not." (emphasis in original)) .

The draft cases of the Vietnam War era marked the only instance in the Court's history that it extended religious exemptions to persons with essentially secular claims of conscience. *See* Welsh v. United States, 398 U.S. 333 (1970). Four members of the Court in *Welsh* rested their decision on (not very persuasive) statutory construction grounds. One member of the Court — Justice Harlan — joined the majority on the ground that a distinction between religious and secular claims of conscience would be unconstitutional. *See id.* at 356 (Harlan, J., concurring).

Although the Supreme Court has consistently confined the constitutional protections of the free exercise clause to religion, it sometimes takes the opposite position with regard to accommodations not required under the free exercise clause. *Compare* Estate of Thornton v. Caldor, Inc., 472 U.S. 703, 711 (1985) (O'Connor, J., concurring) (finding a statute unconstitutional because it "singles out Sabbath observers for special . . . protection without according similar accommodation to ethical and religious beliefs and practices of other private employees") *and* *Caldor*, 472 U.S. at 710 n. 9 (same) *with* Corporation of the Presiding Bishop of the Church of Jesus Christ of Latter-Day Saints v. Amos, 483 U.S. 327, 338 (1987) ("Where . . . government acts with the proper purpose of lifting a regulation that burdens the exercise of religion, we see no reason to require that the exemption come packaged with benefits to secular entities.").

[421] *See, e.g.*, R. DWORKIN, TAKING RIGHTS SERIOUSLY 200–01 (1977); M. KONVITZ, RELIGIOUS LIBERTY AND CONSCIENCE 73–106 (1968); D. RICHARDS, *supra* note 54, at 136–46; Gamwell, *Religion and Reason in American Politics*, 2 J.L. & RELIGION 325, 325–27 (1984).

to be a product of individual choice, and protected as such. It is said to be arbitrary (and even unconstitutional) to differentiate between belief systems, all of which are the product of individual judgment, on the ground that some are "religious" and some are not.

David A.J. Richards has presented the most sustained and thoughtful exposition of this position.[422] Professor Richards' conception of free exercise is rooted in liberal individualism. He views religious freedom as an aspect of the "equal respect" that must be shown "for the capacity to exercise our twin moral powers of rationality and reasonableness."[423] It is ultimately based on "respect for the person as an independent source of value."[424] A definition of "conscience" sufficiently broad to encompass all that "neutrality requires" would "include[] everything and anything, including purely scientific beliefs about the causal structure of the world integrated into some larger rational and reasonable conception of one's ends."[425] If the science of the origin and structure of the universe is included, so presumably must be the soft sciences of economics, politics, history, psychology, and the like. Richards thus contends that "the motivation for universal toleration must encompass all belief systems, religious and nonreligious, expressive of our moral powers of rationality and reasonableness."[426]

Under this view, religious claims have no higher status than nonreligious claims — and maybe even lower status, to the extent that modern moral philosophy elevates "rationality and reasonableness" over the characteristic religious claims of revelation, tradition, and spirit-filled inspiration. And if the distinction between religious and nonreligious conscience is arbitrary, then it amounts to an indefensible preference — an establishment of religion — to accommodate religious and not nonreligious claims of comparable magnitude.

The question is therefore whether the principle of free exercise, as enacted by the framers and ratifiers of the first amendment, was a specific instantiation of a wider liberty of conscience encompassing individual moral judgments rooted in nonreligious as well as religious sources, or whether religious conscience is different in some fundamental respect from other forms of individual judgment, in which case the free exercise clause would provide no warrant for protecting a broader class of claims.[427] The question is all the more significant

---

[422] *See* D. RICHARDS, *supra* note 54, at 136–46.

[423] *Id.* at 136.

[424] *Id.* at 142.

[425] *Id.* at 141–42.

[426] *Id.* at 138.

[427] Professor Richards agrees that this issue must be resolved by reference to the "history and practice of religion clause jurisprudence," *id.* at 141, but he devotes no attention to the actual history of the free exercise clause bearing on the specific point (nor to its "practice"). *See*

for the practical reason that if the exercise of religion extends to "everything and anything,"[428] the interference with ordinary operations of government would be so extreme that the free exercise clause would fall of its own weight. To protect everything is to protect nothing.

The historical materials uniformly equate "religion" with belief in God or in gods,[429] though this can be extended without distortion to transcendent extrapersonal authorities not envisioned in traditionally theistic terms.[430] By contrast, Noah Webster's *Dictionary of the English Language*, the first comprehensive American dictionary (published in 1807), defined "conscience" as: "natural knowledge, or the faculty that decides on the right or wrong of actions in regard to one's self."[431] Similarly, James' Buchanan's 1757 dictionary, *Linguae Britannicae Vera Pronunciatio*, defined "conscience" as "[t]he testimony of one's own mind."[432] And Samuel Johnson's great *Dictionary of the English Language* gave as the first definition: "The knowledge or faculty by which we judge of the goodness or wickedness of ourselves."[433] In none of these definitions was there specific reference to religion, although about half of the literary examples Johnson gave in the four volume edition had a religious context.[434]

On the other hand, outside of dictionaries, the vast preponderance of references to "liberty of conscience" in America were either expressly or impliedly limited to religious conscience.[435] A few examples suffice to make the point; dozens of others would do as well. St. George

---

id. Significantly, Richards uses a vocabulary that was deliberately rejected by the framers. He talks of "toleration," although the framers condemned the concept of toleration. *See supra* pp. 1443–49. And he speaks of "conscience," when the framers considered drafts employing the term and chose to use the term "religion" instead.

[428] D. RICHARDS, *supra* note 54, at 141.

[429] *See* Freeman, *The Misguided Search for the Constitutional Definition of "Religion,"* 71 GEO. L.J. 1519, 1520 (1983). For example, the Virginia Bill of Rights defined "religion" as "the duty which we owe to our Creator, and the manner of discharging it." Virginia Bill of Rights of 1776, § 16, *reprinted in* 2 FEDERAL AND STATE CONSTITUTIONS, *supra* note 2, at 1908, 1909.

[430] Madison, for example, deliberately chose terms other than "God" to refer to the object of religious homage, including "Creator," "Governor of the Universe," and "Universal Sovereign." J. MADISON, *Memorial and Remonstrance*, *supra* note 109, at 184–85. This suggests an attempt at a definition more compendious than the familiar Judeo-Christian God, but it retains the distinction between transcendent authority and personal judgment. *See* Freeman *supra* note 429, at 1521–23; Ingber, *supra* note 429, at 251. The literature on the meaning of "religion" under the first amendment is vast. *See id.* at 233 n.3.

[431] N. WEBSTER, *supra* note 252.

[432] J. BUCHANAN, *supra* note 251.

[433] S. JOHNSON, *supra* note 252.

[434] *See id.*

[435] *See* 1 A. STOKES, *supra* note 280, at 16–17; Adams & Emmerich, *supra* note 17, at 1599 n. 174.

Tucker's 1803 commentary on American constitutional law divided "[t]he right of personal opinion" into two subcategories: "liberty of conscience in all matters relative to religion" and "liberty of speech and of discussion in all speculative matters, whether religious, philosophical, or political."[436] Madison himself used the terms "free exercise of religion" and "liberty of conscience" interchangeably when explaining the meaning of the first amendment.[437] The laws of at least ten of the states expressly linked "liberty of conscience" to religion. The Massachusetts Charter of 1691 provided that "a liberty of Conscience [be] allowed in the Worshipp of God to all Christians (Except Papists),"[438] and the Connecticut legislature passed a similar measure in 1784, entitled "An Act for securing the Rights of Conscience in Matters of Religion, to Christians of every Denomination."[439] The Carolina proprietors' Agreement with proposed settlers granted "liberty of conscience in all religious and spiritual things."[440] Maryland's Toleration Act of 1649 declared "the enforcing of the conscience in matters of Religion . . . to be of dangerous consequence."[441]

Religious and popular writings also linked conscience and religion. Elisha Williams, sometime president of Yale, wrote a pamphlet in 1744 called *The essential Rights and Liberties of Protestants. A seasonable Plea for the Liberty of Conscience, and The Right of private Judgment in Matters of Religion without any Control from Human Authority*.[442] Virginia Baptist leader John Leland's pamphlet, *The Rights of Conscience Inalienable*, focused on attacking religious establishments and state-supported religion.[443] There was no recorded controversy in preconstitutional America in which the right of "conscience" was invoked on behalf of beliefs of a political, social, philosophical, economic, or secular moral origin.

In any event, the final version of the amendment adopted by Congress and ratified by the states omitted any reference to "rights of conscience" and protected the "free exercise of religion" instead. There

---

436 ST. GEORGE TUCKER, BLACKSTONE'S COMMENTARIES, *reprinted in* 5 THE FOUNDERS' CONSTITUTION, *supra* note 72, at 96–97.

437 *See e.g.*, Madison, *Report on the Virginia Resolutions* (Jan. 18, 1800), *reprinted in* 5 THE FOUNDERS' CONSTITUTION *supra* note 72, at 141.

438 MASS. BAY CHARTER of 1691, *reprinted in* 1 FEDERAL AND STATE CONSTITUTIONS, *supra* note 2, at 942, 950.

439 T. CURRY, *supra* note 17, at 180 (quoting ACTS AND LAWS OF THE STATE OF CONNECTICUT 21–22).

440 S. COBB, *supra* note 17, at 116.

441 *Id.* at 376; *see also id.* at 293–94 (New Hampshire); *id.* at 303–04, 308, 323–54 (New York); *id.* at 401–02 (New Jersey); *id.* at 419 (Georgia); *id.* at 431 (Rhode Island).

442 *See* T. CURRY, *supra* note 17, at 97–98 & n.59 (citing E. WILLIAMS, THE ESSENTIAL RIGHTS AND LIBERTIES OF PROTESTANTS (Boston 1744)).

443 *See* J. LELAND, *supra* note 174, at 179–92.

are two possible explanations for this. The reference to conscience could have been dropped because it was redundant, or it could have been dropped because the framers chose to confine the protections of the free exercise clause to religion.

The "redundancy" explanation can be supported by the absence of any recorded speech or discussion of differences between the terms.[444] The drafters alternated between the two formulations without apparent pattern,[445] and participants in the debate later referred to the free exercise clause as a "liberty of conscience" provision without apparent awareness of the difference in denotation.

Still, the theory that the phrase "free exercise of religion" was deliberately used in order to exclude nonreligious conscience seems more likely, since the different drafts called attention to the question. If no distinction was intended, it would have been more natural to stick with a single formulation and to concentrate on the wording of the contested establishment clause. This theory also derives support from Samuel Huntington's comment that he hoped "the amendment would be made in such a way as to secure the rights of conscience, and a free exercise of the rights of religion, but not to patronize those who professed no religion at all."[446]

It derives further support from the debate over a proposed constitutional exception for those "religiously scrupulous of bearing arms."[447] Representative Thomas Scott of Pennsylvania opposed the clause, stating:

> There are many sects I know, who are religiously scrupulous in this respect; I do not mean to deprive them of any indulgence the law affords; my design is to guard against those who are of no religion. It has been urged that religion is on the decline; if so, the argument is more strong in my favor, for when the time comes that religion shall be discarded, the generality of persons will have recourse to these pretexts to get excused from bearing arms.[448]

---

[444] The sole exception is the objection posed by the Virginia State Senate to the first amendment, discussed above at text accompanying note 385, which can be read as distinguishing between the terms.

[445] The Senate adopted three different versions of the religion clauses in turn, which included three different formulations of the establishment provision, each of which was coupled with either a "free exercise of religion" clause or a "rights of conscience" clause. See *supra* pp. 1483–84. There is no apparent pattern that might connect the free exercise/liberty of conscience terminology with the establishment formulations. The term "free exercise" seems to be associated with both the broadest and the narrowest conceptions of disestablishment, and "rights of conscience" associated with the intermediate establishment provision. It is difficult to harmonize this with an understanding of religious liberty.

[446] 1 ANNALS OF CONG. 758 (J. Gales ed. 1834) (Aug. 15, 1789).

[447] *See infra* pp. 1500–03.

[448] 1 ANNALS OF CONG. 796 (J. Gales ed. 1834) (Aug. 20, 1789).

Why the proposed language ("religiously scrupulous") was not adequate for Scott's purposes is hard to say, but his underlying view of the proper scope of free exercise exemptions is clear: they should be reserved for cases of conflict with actual religious beliefs. Elbridge Gerry expressed a similar view.[449]

In any event, it does not matter which explanation — redundancy or intentionality — is correct, for under either explanation, nonreligious "conscience" is not included within the free exercise clause. If "the rights of conscience" were dropped because they were redundant, "conscience" must have been used in its narrow, religious, sense. If the omission was a substantive change, then the framers deliberately confined the clause to religious claims. Neither explanation supports the view that free exercise exemptions must be extended to secular moral conflicts.

The textual insistence on the special status of "religion" is, moreover, rooted in the prevailing understandings, both religious and philosophical, of the difference between religious faith and other forms of human judgment. Not until the second third of the nineteenth century did the notion that the opinions of individuals have precedence over the decisions of civil society gain currency in American thought. In 1789, most would have agreed with Locke that "the private judgment of any person concerning a law enacted in political matters, for the public good, does not take away the obligation of that law, nor deserve a dispensation."[450]

Religious convictions were of a different order. Conflicts arising from religious convictions were conceived not as a clash between the judgment of the individual and of the state, but as a conflict between earthly and spiritual sovereigns. The believer was not seen as the instigator of the conflict; the believer was simply caught between the inconsistent demands of two rightful authorities, through no fault of his own. This understanding was grounded in the Protestant doctrine of "two kingdoms," taught by both Calvin and Luther,[451] and had still older roots in Augustinian thought.[452]

---

[449] 1 ANNALS OF CONG. 779 (J. Gales ed. 1834) (Aug. 17, 1789) (reporting that Gerry "wished the words to be altered so as to be confined to persons belonging to a religious sect scrupulous of bearing arms").

[450] J. LOCKE, *A Letter Concerning Toleration*, *supra* note 113, at 43. Locke wrote:

> [E]very man, by consenting with others to make one Body Politic under one Government, puts himself under an Obligation to every one of that Society to submit to the determination of the *majority*, and to be concluded by it; or else this *original Compact* . . . would signifie nothing, and be no Compact . . . .

J. LOCKE, *The Second Treatise of Government*, *supra* note 134, § 97, at 376 (emphasis in original).

[451] *See* 2 J. CALVIN, INSTITUTES OF THE CHRISTIAN RELIGION 1485 (J. McNeill ed. 1960); M. LUTHER, *Temporal Authority: To What Extent It Should Be Obeyed*, in 45 LUTHER'S WORKS 81, 89–129 (W. Brandt ed. 1962).

[452] *See* ST. AUGUSTINE, THE CITY OF GOD 376–77 (M. Dods ed. 1950). For a brief discussion of "two kingdoms" doctrine and its relation to religious liberty, see Adams & Em-

Not only were the spiritual and earthly authorities envisioned as independent, but in the nature of things the spiritual authorities had a superior claim. "[O]bedience is due in the first place to God, and afterwards to the laws," according to Locke.[453] The American conception of religious liberty was accordingly defended in those terms. The key passage in Madison's *Memorial and Remonstrance* reads as follows:

> Before any man can be considered as a member of Civil Society, he must be considered as a subject of the Governor of the Universe: And if a member of Civil Society, who enters into any subordinate Association, must always do it with a reservation of his duty to the general authority; much more must every man who becomes a member of any particular Civil Society, do it with a saving of his allegiance to the Universal Sovereign.[454]

Far from being based on the "respect for the person as an independent source of value,"[455] the free exercise of religion is set apart from mere exercise of human judgment by the fact that the "source of value" is prior and superior to both the individual and the civil society. The freedom of religion is unalienable because it is a duty to God and not a privilege of the individual. The free exercise clause accords a special, protected status to religious conscience not because religious judgments are better, truer, or more likely to be moral than nonreligious judgments, but because the obligations entailed by religion transcend the individual and are outside the individual's control.

It is important to remember that the framers and ratifiers of the first amendment found it conceivable that a God — that is, a universal and transcendent authority beyond human judgment — might exist. If God might exist, then it is not arbitrary to hold that His will is superior to the judgments of individuals or of civil society. Much of the criticism of a special deference to sincere religious convictions arises from the assumption that such convictions are *necessarily* mere subcategories of personal moral judgments.[456] This amounts to a denial of the possibility of a God (or at least of a God whose will is made manifest to humans). But while this skeptical position is tenable

merich, cited above in note 17, at 1623–24; *see also* Cover, *Obligation: A Jewish Jurisprudence of the Social Order*, 5 J.L. & RELIGION 65 (1987) (contrasting the Jewish jurisprudence of obligation with the liberal jurisprudence of rights); Garvey, *Free Exercise and the Values of Religious Liberty*, 18 CONN. L. REV. 779, 798–801 (1986) (drawing an analogy between religion and insanity to assert that "religious claimants [are] different from other people, and therefore deserving of special constitutional protection"); Note, *Religious Exemptions Under the Free Exercise Clause: A Model of Competing Authorities*, 90 YALE L.J. 350 (1980) (advocating a "model of competing authorities" to replace current exemption doctrine).

[453] J. LOCKE, *A Letter Concerning Toleration*, *supra* note 113, at 43.

[454] J. MADISON, *Memorial and Remonstrance*, *supra* note 109, at 185.

[455] D. RICHARDS, *supra* note 54, at 142.

[456] *See, e.g.*, R. DWORKIN, *supra* note 421, at 200–01.

as a theoretical or philosophical proposition, it is a peculiar belief to project upon the framers and ratifiers of the first amendment, for whom belief in the existence of God was natural and nearly universal. It is an anachronism, therefore, to view the free exercise clause as a product of modern secular individualism. From the perspective of the advocates of religious freedom in 1789, the protection of private judgment (secular "conscience") fundamentally differs from the protection of free exercise of religion.

The religious distinction between the City of God and the City of Man had its counterpart in secular Enlightenment thought. Religious belief, as Locke argued in his *Third Letter for Toleration*, "is not capable of demonstration"; it is not, therefore, "capable to produce knowledge, how well grounded and great soever the assurance of faith may be wherewith it is received; but faith it is still, and not knowledge; persuasion, and not certainty."[457] Natural law and morality, on the other hand, are subjects for rational inquiry and knowledge. That is the epistemological premise of Locke's scientific investigations into psychology and politics.

The "magistrates of the world" thus have no authority to coerce individuals on account of religious opinion, for in this sphere they can have no basis for action other than "their own belief, their own persuasion,"[458] which is as likely to support the false as the true religion. As Madison observed, "that the Civil Magistrate is a competent Judge of Religious truth . . . is an arrogant pretension."[459] By contrast, the very purpose of civil society is to grant the magistrate authority to coerce all members of society to comply with the rational principles that order human affairs.[460] When individuals err (however conscientiously) in their judgments about earthly things — politics, economics, natural morals — the magistrate is, and must be, empowered to correct them. It is no usurpation of authority for the government to use its power in these cases. Only when the individual's judgment is grounded in beliefs outside the ken of government is the government required to defer.

A distinction between religious and secular conscience is, therefore, consistent both with the religious and the Enlightenment perspective on free exercise. From the religious point of view, the difference

---

[457] J. LOCKE, *A Third Letter for Toleration*, in 6 WORKS OF LOCKE, *supra* note 111, at 139, 144 [hereinafter J. LOCKE, *Third Letter for Toleration*]; *cf.* T. HOBBES, *supra* note 119, at 242 (contrasting the "principles of nature," which our "experience has found true," with matters that depend on the "supernatural revelations of the will of God"). This casts doubt on Professor Richards' assumption that religious judgment is an exercise of Kantian practical reason. *See* D. RICHARDS, *supra* note 54, at 136.

[458] J. LOCKE, *Third Letter for Toleration*, *supra* note 457, at 143.

[459] J. MADISON, *Memorial and Remonstrance*, *supra* note 109, at 187.

[460] *See* J. LOCKE, *The Second Treatise of Government*, *supra* note 134, §§ 87–89, at 366–69.

between religious and secular forms of conscience is that the former represent an obligation to an authority higher than the individual, while the latter are manifestations of mere individual will or judgment. From the Enlightenment point of view, the difference is that the government has no basis for evaluating the truth of religious claims, while it inevitably must evaluate claims based on rational inquiry and knowledge. The religious view emphasizes the importance of the individual; the Enlightenment, the incapacity of the government. Madison combined these points in his *Memorial and Remonstrance*.[461] Both perspectives lead to the same conclusion: it is sensible to restrict the power of government to influence or coerce religious conscience, even when government has the power to influence or coerce judgments based on science, history, political ideology, economics, moral philosophy, or other secular sources.

This raises the question whether the free exercise clause protects atheists or other unbelievers. As previously noted, Locke excluded atheists from his proposed system of religious toleration, while Jefferson departed from Locke in this respect.[462] Six of the state constitutions as of 1789 confined free exercise protections to theists, two (Virginia and Delaware) were ambiguous, and four extended protection to all religious beliefs without limitation. Since the free exercise clause of the federal Constitution contained no limitation, it is most plausible to assume that, in this as in other respects, it was imitating the more expansive of the state provisions. But this begs the question of what free exercise protection might mean for a person who does not recognize any form of transcendent, extrapersonal authority — to a person who does not "exercise" a "religion."

For the most part, the prohibition on an establishment of religion should suffice to protect unbelievers from discrimination, ill-treatment, or coercion (from test oaths, for example).[463] There should be no doubt that government action that abridges the unbeliever's right not to engage in or support a religious practice is unconstitutional. By 1789, it was generally agreed that compelled homage is of no value to God or to man. In Madison's words, "[i]t is the duty of every man to render to the Creator such homage, and such only, as he believes to be acceptable to him."[464]

As a practical matter, the question whether the free exercise clause protects atheists arises only with reference to claims for exemption.

---

[461] *See* J. MADISON, *Memorial and Remonstrance*, *supra* note 109, at 184–85.

[462] *See supra* text accompanying notes 121 & 213.

[463] *See* Torcaso v. Watkins, 367 U.S. 488 (1961). In *Torcaso*, the Court did not specify which of the two religion clauses the test oath violated. Under the analysis here, a test oath is an establishment of religion under any circumstances, since it coerces an affirmation of a religious belief. However, a test oath is a violation of the free exercise rights only of those whose religions forbids taking the oath.

[464] J. MADISON, *Memorial and Remonstrance*, *supra* note 109, at 184.

If it is true that the right to exemption from generally applicable laws on ground of conflict with religious doctrine is confined to those who have duties arising from their religious beliefs, then it has no application to unbelievers. Unbelievers undoubtedly make judgments of right and wrong that sometimes conflict with generally applicable law. But if these do not stem from obedience to a transcendent authority prior to and beyond the authority of civil government, they do not receive exemption under the free exercise clause. To subject an atheist to civil disabilities would be a violation of free exercise; but to require an atheist who objects to war on secular grounds to go to war would not, since his conduct is not (and by definition could not be) motivated by his religious belief.

4. The Militia Exemption Clause. — Although the debates in the First Congress over the free exercise clause itself did not explicitly raise the question of exemptions, the question arose during the debate over what would become the second amendment, in connection with service in the state militias. Three states (North Carolina, Virginia, and Rhode Island) had proposed that "any person religiously scrupulous of bearing arms ought to be exempted, upon payment of an equivalent to employ another to bear arms in his stead."[465] Madison's draft bill of rights contained a similar proposal, appended to what is now the second amendment, although Madison left the requirement of a substitute to legislative discretion.[466] The Select Committee proposed and the House of Representatives debated a more generous exemption: "no person religiously scrupulous shall be compelled to bear arms."[467] The proposal was quite controversial; it passed the House by a mere 24–22 vote and was rejected by the Senate. Since this is the only discussion in the First Congress specifically bearing on religious exemptions from generally applicable legal duties, it warrants detailed consideration.

The most eloquent defender of the proposal, Representative Elias Boudinot of New Jersey, Presbyterian and later President of the American Bible Society, hoped "that in establishing this Government, we may show the world that proper care is taken that the Government may not interfere with the religious sentiments of any person."[468] He argued that it would be both pointless and unjust to compel "men who are conscientious in this respect . . . to bear arms, when, according to their religious principles, they would rather die than use them."[469]

---

465 1 ELLIOT'S DEBATES, *supra* note 165, at 335 (quoting from the Rhode Island ratification of the Constitution, May 29, 1790).

466 "[N]o person religiously scrupulous of bearing arms shall be compelled to render military service in person." 1 ANNALS OF CONG. 451 (J. Gales ed. 1834) (June 8, 1789).

467 *Id.* at 778 (Aug. 17, 1789).

468 *Id.* at 796 (Aug. 20, 1789).

469 *Id.*

One may wonder why, if this is so, objectors were not protected under the free exercise clause without need for a separate provision.[470] There are at least three possible answers. First, the militias are arms of the state governments except when in actual service; thus, the free exercise clause probably did not apply to them. Second, it does not necessarily follow from the fact of free exercise exemptions that the particular case of military service will be held protected. That determination will depend, in part, on the judiciary's assessment of the governmental interest in conscription. Thus, even if Boudinot expected conscientious objection from military service to be protected under the free exercise clause, it was prudent to spell it out. Third, as Boudinot pointed out, if Congress struck out the militia exemption clause, this would create an inference that there is an intention in the general government to compel all its citizens to bear arms. Indeed, some scholars have cited Congress' rejection of the militia exemption clause as conclusive evidence that there is no constitutional right to conscientious objection from military service.[471]

The significance of Boudinot's position for present purposes is that he, with a majority of the House, considered exemption from a generally applicable legal duty to be "necessary" to protect religious freedom. Whether or not the particular application of this principle to bearing arms would be accepted by the Senate (it was not)[472] or the courts (it was not),[473] it strongly suggests that the general idea of free exercise exemptions was part of the legal culture.

Opposition to the militia exemption clause arose on two grounds. First, James Jackson, Revolutionary War hero and representative from Georgia, commented that it would be "unjust" to require "one part" of the nation "to defend the other in case of invasion."[474] If he had left it at that, this argument would resemble the modern anti-exemptions view that to exempt some citizens from legal obligations on religious grounds constitutes an unconstitutional preference for religion.[475] Jackson went on to propose, however, that the militia exemption clause be amended by inserting at the end of it, "upon paying an equivalent, to be established by law."[476] This demonstrates that Jackson's objection was not to the *principle* of exemption, but to the extent of the accommodation in this particular case. Taken as a

---

[470] *See* Marshall, *supra* note 17, at 76 ("[T]he fact that a conscientious objection amendment was proposed suggests that the free exercise clause was not thought, by itself, to provide for religious exemptions from neutral laws.").

[471] *See* W. BERNS, *supra* note 13, at 54–55; M. MALBIN, *supra* note 17, at 39–40 & n.4.

[472] *See* 1 ANNALS OF CONG. 779 (J. Gales ed. 1834) (remark of Rep. Jackson, Aug. 17, 1789).

[473] *See, e.g.*, United States v. MacIntosh, 283 U.S. 605, 623–25 (1931).

[474] 1 ANNALS OF CONG. 779 (J. Gales ed. 1834) (remark of Rep. Jackson, Aug. 17, 1789).

[475] *See* Marshall, *supra* note 17, at 30–35.

[476] 1 ANNALS OF CONG. 779 (J. Gales ed. 1834) (remark of Rep. Jackson, Aug. 17, 1789).

whole, Jackson's position must be counted as favoring exemptions for religious conscience, but balancing the interests of believers and nonbelievers somewhat differently.

The most cogent argument against the militia exemption clause came from Egbert Benson of New York. Benson argued that "[n]o man can claim this indulgence of right. It may be a religious persuasion, but it is no natural right, and therefore ought to be left to the discretion of the Government."[477] Benson did not oppose religious exemptions in principle, however. On the contrary, he had "no reason to believe but the Legislature will always possess humanity enough to indulge this class of citizens in a matter they are so desirous of; but they ought to be left to their discretion."[478] Though he considered religious exemption from military service "humane" and "benevolent," he did not think it fell within the class of natural rights. Accordingly, he could not support its inclusion in the Bill of Rights.

Benson's position is a sophisticated version of the "judicial restraint" or "separation of powers" argument against recognizing exemptions under the free exercise clause. He distinguished between the functions of the legislature and the judiciary, confining the latter to enforcing natural law positively enacted in the Constitution. There is no doubt that Benson, like the other participants in the debate, understood that by constitutionalizing the principle of militia exemptions they were transferring decisionmaking authority from the legislature to the courts. Benson felt that "[i]f it stands part of the constitution, it will be a question before the Judiciary on every regulation you make with respect to the organization of the militia."[479] No one challenged this assumption. *Marbury v. Madison*[480] was thirteen years in the future, but Benson and the others clearly anticipated that governmental action would be judicially reviewable under the Bill of Rights.

Nonetheless, Benson's position was ambiguous on the key question of interest here. Did he believe there is no natural right to exemption from militia service because there is no natural right to exemption from any generally applicable law? Or did he believe there is no natural right to exemption from militia service because the government's interest is potentially compelling, and the degree of necessity for universal military service must be left to legislative discretion? The latter seems slightly more probable. Benson stated he "would

---

[477] *Id.* at 780 (motion of Rep. Benson, Aug. 17, 1789).

[478] *Id.* This point was echoed by Thomas Scott of Pennsylvania, who said that he conceived exemption from militia service "to be a legislative right altogether." *Id.* at 796 (objection of Rep. Scott, Aug. 20, 1789). His main "design," though, was to ensure that exemptions were not extended to the nonreligious. *See id.*

[479] 1 ANNALS OF CONG. 780 (J. Gales ed. 1834) (Aug. 17, 1789).

[480] 5 U.S. (1 Cranch) 137 (1803).

always leave it to the benevolence of the Legislature, for, modify it as you please, it will be impossible to express it in such a manner as to clear it from ambiguity."[481] Although this statement is far from conclusive, it suggests that Benson's opposition to the exemptions was based on the impossibility of capturing in language the great variety of circumstances that would influence the grant or denial of exemptions in any particular case in the future. If so, it does not necessarily imply that he would disagree with the modern construction of the free exercise clause.

C. Early Judicial Interpretation

The religion clauses of the federal and state constitutions did not engender many lawsuits in the early years of the Republic, and fewer still raised the question of free exercise exemptions. The largest volume of litigation was over the competency to testify in court of those, like Universalists, who did not believe in a future state of rewards and punishments. There were also a number of blasphemy prosecutions that raised issues under the religion clauses. Since both of these categories of cases involved laws specifically directed at religion, they did not raise the exemption question.

The free exercise clause of the federal Constitution generated no reported decisions at all until 1845. *Permoli v. Municipality No. 1*,[482] the Supreme Court's first free exercise case, involved a municipal ordinance prohibiting open-casket funerals by Catholic priests except when performed at a single city-approved obituary chapel. In substance (though not in form), this was a generally applicable regulation, since the Protestants conducted services for the dead at graveside, leaving Catholics the only denomination performing open-casket funerals in the area to which the prohibition applied. Justice Catron's opinion for a unanimous Court is uninformative about the meaning of the free exercise clause. It holds only that "[t]he Constitution makes no provision for protecting the citizens of the respective states in their religious liberties; this is left to the state constitutions and laws."[483] But it is suggestive that counsel for the city felt it necessary to defend the ordinance under the "law of necessity" in light of its purpose to prevent the spread of yellow fever.[484] This may indicate that the legal profession believed that interference with religious activities required compelling justification.

---

[481] 1 ANNALS OF CONG. 779–80 (J. Gales ed. 1834) (statement of Rep. Benson, Aug. 17, 1789).

[482] 44 U.S. (3 How.) 588 (1845).

[483] *Id.* at 609.

[484] *See id.* at 601 (argument of counsel).

In the state courts, there was only one reported case involving a religious exemption claim during the twenty years following ratification of the first amendment. Unfortunately, it is nothing more than a cryptic paragraph in Dallas' reports from the Supreme Court of Pennsylvania.[485] The reporter's summary of the case states the holding as follows: "A Jew refusing to be sworn as a witness, because it was Saturday, his Sabbath, the Court fined him £ 10."[486]

The earliest state court decision expressly addressing the exemption question was the case with which this Article began, *People v. Philips*.[487] It involved the exemption of a Catholic priest from compliance with a subpoena requiring him to testify to matters he heard in the confessional. Noting that "this is a great constitutional question, which must not be solely decided by the maxims of the common law, but by the principles of our government,"[488] the court (through the Honorable DeWitt Clinton, then mayor, later governor, and candidate for President against Madison in 1812) construed the New York Constitution to hold that the priest must be exempted from the subpoena requirement. "It is essential to the free exercise of a religion, that its ordinances should be administered — that its ceremonies as well as its essentials should be protected," the court noted. "To decide that the minister shall promulgate what he receives in confession, is to declare that there shall be no penance; and this important branch of the Roman Catholic religion would be thus annihilated."[489] The court thought it so obvious that "[e]very man who hears me will answer in the affirmative" that a law of the state that prevented administration of one of the Protestant sacraments would be unconstitutional. The same right belongs to the Catholics.[490]

The court's argument bears on the issue of neutrality among religious beliefs. The court did not believe it was granting Catholics a benefit to which persons of other beliefs are not entitled. Rather, it saw the exemption as necessary to ensure that Catholics are treated no worse than Protestants would be treated under comparable circumstances. Since it was inconceivable that the Protestant majority of New York would so seriously interfere with the administration of

---

[485] *See* Stansbury v. Marks, 2 Dall. 213 (Pa. 1793).

[486] 2 Dall. at xv. The full case description suggests, however, that the actual outcome was less repressive than the holding. It recounts that the witness was fined for his refusal to testify, but that the defendant waived the benefit of his testimony, whereupon the fine was discharged. *See* Stansbury v. Marks, 2 Dall. at 213.

[487] Court of General Sessions, City of New York (June 14, 1813). This case was not officially reported, but a full record of the arguments and opinion are found in W. SAMPSON, *supra* note 1, at 9, *excerpted in Privileged Communications to Clergymen*, *supra* note 1, at 199.

[488] *Privileged Communications to Clergymen*, *supra* note 1, at 206.

[489] *Id.* at 207.

[490] *Id.*

Protestant sacraments, the court had the responsibility of extending the same right to the Roman Catholic minority.

The court responded in two ways to the prosecutor's argument that "the peace or safety of the state"[491] requires enforcement of the subpoena. First, it noted that as a functional matter priest-penitent confidentiality often served as an "instrument of great good":[492] "The sinner may be admonished and converted from the evil of his ways: Whereas if his offence was locked up in his own bosom, there would be no friendly voice to recall him from his sins . . . ."[493] The question is not whether concealment of information is a public injury in any particular case, but whether "the natural tendency of it is to produce practices inconsistent with the public safety or tranquility."[494] Second, the court argued that the proviso applies to "acts committed, not to acts omitted."[495] The state may override free exercise claims when the claimant's actions would injure the public, but it may not do so to compel affirmative public benefits.

The very fact that the court evaluated the strength of the government's interest in enforcing a subpoena under the "peace or safety" standard confirms that such state provisos were understood to limit legislative authority from encroaching on religious liberty even through generally applicable laws. The court concluded as follows:

> Although we differ from the witness and his brethren, in our religious creed, yet we have no reason to question the purity of their motives, or to impeach their good conduct as citizens. They are protected by the laws and constitution of this country, in the full and free exercise of their religion, and this court can never countenance or authorize the application of insult to their faith, or of torture to their consciences.[496]

Four years after this decision, another New York municipal court distinguished the *Philips* decision and denied the motion of a defendant in a murder trial to bar testimony of a Protestant clergyman to whom he had confessed while in prison.[497] The clergyman informed the court that he had no objection to testifying, whereupon the court ruled "that the testimony was admissible, and took distinction between auricular confessions made to a priest in the course of discipline, according to the canons of the Church, and those made to a minister

---

491 *Id.* at 207–08.

492 *Id.* at 208.

493 *Id.*

494 *Id.*

495 *Id.*

496 *Id.* at 209. By "country," the court presumably meant New York.

497 *See* People v. Smith, 2 City Hall Recorder (Rogers) 77 (N.Y. 1817), *reprinted in Privileged Communications to Clergymen*, *supra* note 1, at 209.

of the gospel in confidence, merely as a friend or adviser."[498] The logic appears to be that no violation of religious tenets was involved. In response to this decision, the New York legislature passed a statute forbidding any minister or priest "of any denomination whatsoever" from disclosing "any confessions made to him in his professional character."[499]

Similarly, the Supreme Judicial Court of Massachusetts refused, without explanation, to overturn a criminal conviction based on a confession made by a man to the members of his church.[500] The defendant had contended that it would be "in some shape an infringement of the rights of conscience, to make use of confessions, made under these circumstances . . . [where] in a theological view, he is obliged in conscience to perform it."[501] Counsel for the prosecution argued that the defendant's confession was "purely voluntary" and was not "required by any known ecclesiastical rule"[502] but did not contest the validity of the defendant's interpretation of freedom of conscience.[503] It is, of course, impossible to tell whether the Supreme Judicial Court accepted the defendant's legal theory, since it stated no reasons for its decision. But it is noteworthy that the prosecution confined its argument to the facts and did not contest the defendant's interpretation of constitutional principles.

The most interesting line of cases arose in the Supreme Court of Pennsylvania. The first, *Commonwealth v. Wolf*,[504] involved a challenge by a Jewish merchant, Abraham Wolf, to Pennsylvania's Sunday closing law, on the ground that as applied to one who observed Saturday as his day of rest and worship, it conflicted with the commonwealth's constitutional protection of the rights of conscience. The challenge was rejected, but on grounds that would admit the principle of free exercise exemptions. The dispositive question as the court posed the case was not whether the state constitution required exemptions, but whether the law conflicted with Wolf's religious conscience. Wolf's attorney conceded that Jewish doctrine does not "immediately" require work on Sunday; it is possible for a Jewish merchant to comply with the Sunday closing law without violating religious duty. But the attorney attempted an ingenious argument that enforcement of the Sunday closing laws, in conjunction with the

---

498 *Privileged Communications to Clergymen*, *supra* note 1, at 211.

499 N.Y. REV. STAT. 1828, pt. 3, ch. 7, tit. 3, § 72.

500 Commonwealth v. Drake, 15 Mass. 161 (1818).

501 *Id.* at 161.

502 *Id.* at 161–62.

503 There was no doubt that the defendant's claim was understood to be based in part on the Massachusetts Constitution. Counsel for the prosecution referred to the claim as a "legal or constitutional principle." *Id.* at 161.

504 3 Serg. & Rawle 48 (Pa. 1817).

Jewish law forbidding work on Saturday, would force the plaintiff to violate the fourth commandment: "six days shalt thou labour, and do all that thou hast to do."[505] The court rejected this argument not in theory, but on the facts: "the Jewish Talmud, containing the traditions of that people, and the Rabbinical constitutions and explications of their law, asserts no such doctrine."[506] If there were no such doctrine, there would be no burden on Wolf's liberty of conscience and hence no ground for granting an exemption. The unstated assumption was that if the law had required Wolf to violate his conscience, he might have had a claim.[507]

The next two Pennsylvania cases, *Commonwealth v. Lesher*[508] and *Simon's Executors v. Gratz*,[509] both contain opinions by Chief Justice John Bannister Gibson, a highly regarded jurist who is best known today for his dissenting opinion in *Eakin v. Raub*,[510] in which he rebutted Chief Justice Marshall's position in *Marbury* that the judiciary has authority to declare void unconstitutional acts of the legislature.[511] Gibson also was the foremost judicial opponent of free exercise exemptions in the nineteenth century. His decision in *Simon's Executors* was the leading precedent in the thirteen original states prior to the Civil War for the proposition that free exercise does not include the right of exemption from generally applicable law. An examination of Gibson's opinions in *Lesher* and *Simon's Executors* shows that his rejection of constitutional judicial review and his position on free exercise exemptions were closely related.

In *Lesher*, a prospective juror had been excluded for cause from jury service in a capital case, on the basis of his religious objection to capital punishment.[512] The defendant was convicted and appealed on the ground that the juror's exclusion had been unlawful.[513] On appeal, the majority affirmed the conviction on the basis of the state's interest in obtaining a trial in which the jurors complied with the law, without finding it necessary to address the religion clauses of the state constitution.[514] Gibson dissented on the ground that religious scruples

---

505 *Id.* at 50.

506 *Id.*

507 The case was a precursor to Braunfeld v. Brown, 366 U.S. 599 (1961), in which the United States Supreme Court rejected a similar challenge to a Sunday closing law by a Jewish merchant. Whether such a challenge should succeed under the modern doctrine of free exercise exemptions is a close question. *See* McConnell & Posner, *supra* note 20, at 41–42.

508 17 Serg. & Rawle 155 (Pa. 1828).

509 2 Pen. & W. 412 (Pa. 1831).

510 12 Serg. & Rawle 330 (Pa. 1825).

511 *See id.* at 356 (Gibson, C.J., dissenting). Gibson added one caveat: the judiciary could declare state laws that violate the federal Constitution void, there being an express grant of such power under the supremacy clause. *See id.* at 356–57.

512 *See Lesher*, 17 Serg. & Rawle at 155.

513 *See id.*

514 *See id.* at 156–60.

cannot be a basis for exemption from a civic duty, such as jury service.[515]

Gibson's *Lesher* dissent formed the basis for a majority holding in *Simon's Executors*. In that case, a contract action had been set for trial on a Saturday and the plaintiff, Levi Philips, who was Jewish, moved for a continuance on the ground that "he had scruples of conscience against appearing in court to-day, and attending to any secular business; and that he believes his presence and aid will be material in the progress of the cause."[516] The motion was denied; Philips' counsel took a nonsuit and appealed on the basis of the liberty of conscience clause of the Pennsylvania Constitution.[517] The decision was affirmed, in another opinion by Gibson.[518]

In his *Simon's Executors* opinion, Gibson expressly disapproved the New York precedent of *People v. Philips*,[519] which had been cited by counsel for the defendant:

> No one is more sensible than I, of the benefit derived by society from the offices of the Catholic clergy, or of the policy of protecting the secrets of auricular confession. But considerations of policy address themselves with propriety to the legislature, and not to a magistrate whose course is prescribed not by discretion, but rules already established.[520]

In his *Lesher* dissent, Gibson defined the "rights of conscience" as follows:

> Simply a right to worship the Supreme Being according to the dictates of the heart; to adopt any creed or hold any opinion whatever on the subject of religion; and to do, or forbear to do, any act for conscience sake, the doing or forbearing of which, *is not prejudicial to the public weal*.[521]

Relying on the authority of Jefferson (about whom he said "a more resolute champion of toleration perhaps never lived"[522]), Gibson argued that "were the laws dispensed with, wherever they happen to be in collision with some supposed religious obligation, government would be perpetually falling short of the exigence."[523] Since jury

---

[515] *See id.* at 160–61 (Gibson, C.J., dissenting).

[516] Simon's Executors v. Gratz, 2 Pen. & W. 412, 412 (Pa. 1831) (quoting the deposition of Levi Philips). Presumably, this was an attempt to relitigate Stansbury v. Marks, 2 Dall. 213 (Pa. 1793), *see supra* p. 1504, by a relative of the original party.

[517] *See Simon's Executors*, 2 Pen. & W. at 414.

[518] *See id.* at 416–18.

[519] *See supra* pp. 1504–05.

[520] *See Simon's Executors*, 2 Pen. & W. at 414.

[521] Commonwealth v. Lesher, 17 Serg. & Rawle 155, 160 (Pa. 1828) (Gibson C.J., dissenting) (emphasis in original).

[522] *Id.*

[523] *Id.* at 161.

service is a general obligation on all citizens, and the legislature had enacted no exemption, there was no legal basis for excusing the juror. Gibson did not engage in any analysis of whether an exemption in the case would in fact be "prejudicial to the public weal,"[524] apparently considering existence of the law conclusive as to its necessity. Indeed, he went out of his way to opine that the effect of refusing to exclude a juror with religious scruples against capital punishment was to grant the accused an "unreasonable advantage[]."[525] "No one," he said, "is more thoroughly convinced of the . . . abstract propriety of the objection to the juror here,"[526] but for Gibson the remedy lay with the legislature.[527]

In *Simon's Executors*, Gibson explained the theoretical basis for his position. "Rightly considered," he said, "there are no duties half so sacred as those which the citizen owes to the laws."[528] "That every other obligation shall yield to that of the laws, as to a superior moral force," he wrote, "is a tacit condition of membership in every society, whether lay or secular, temporal or spiritual, because no citizen can lawfully hold communion with those who have associated on any other terms."[529] Gibson's statement may be contrasted with Madison's position in the *Memorial and Remonstrance*. Madison contended that religious duty "is precedent both in order of time and degree of obligation, to the claims of Civil Society."[530] Gibson held that a person entering into civil society must assume the obligation of yielding to all the laws, because no other form of association is possible. Madison held that "every man" who becomes a member of a civil society "*must* always do it with a reservation . . . of his allegiance to the Universal Sovereign."[531] What Gibson said is impossible, Madison said is necessary. Gibson's view of the nature of religious freedom thus conflicts directly with that of one of the leading framers of the federal free exercise clause.

Gibson's rejection of the principle of judicial review, as explained in *Eakin v. Raub*,[532] provides further reason to doubt that he represented the prevailing view on the interpretation of free exercise. Like Locke, Gibson believed in legislative supremacy. In *Lesher*, he attributed his conclusion to his "horror of judicial legislation"[533] and said

---

[524] *Id.* at 160 (emphasis omitted).

[525] *Id.* at 164.

[526] *Id.*

[527] *See id.*

[528] Simon's Executors v. Graz, 2 Pen. & W. 412, 417 (Pa. 1831).

[529] *Id.*

[530] J. MADISON, *Memorial and Remonstrance*, *supra* note 109, at 184–85.

[531] *Id.* (emphasis added).

[532] *See* Eakin v. Raub, 12 Serg. & Rawle 330, 344–58 (Pa. 1825) (Gibson, J., dissenting).

[533] Commonwealth v. Lesher, 17 Serg. & Rawle 155, 164 (Pa. 1828) (Gibson, C.J., dissenting).

that he "would suffer any extremity of inconvenience, rather than step beyond the legitimate province of the court."[534] As discussed above, the advent of judicial review had transformed a principle of free exercise previously enforced solely through legislative action into one enforceable through the courts.[535] Since virtually all of the framers and ratifiers of the first amendment expected and intended their work to be judicially enforceable, Gibson's contrary position was almost surely idiosyncratic.

Seventeen years after *Simon's Executors*, the Pennsylvania Supreme Court had its next free exercise exemptions case, *Specht v. Commonwealth*.[536] Like *Wolf*, it involved a challenge to enforcement of the Sunday closing law by a sabbatarian, in this case a member of the Seventh Day Baptist Congregation. Also as in *Wolf*, the challenge was rejected. Toward the beginning of the opinion, the court stated that "conscientious doctrines and practices can claim no immunity from the operation of general laws made for the government and to promote the welfare of the whole people,"[537] citing Gibson's opinions in *Lesher* and *Simon's Executors*. Toward the end of the opinion, however, the court appeared to reject the claim on the facts, much as it had in *Wolf*. The court described the effect of the Sunday closing law on sabbatarians as "an incidental worldly disadvantage, temporarily injurious"[538] and stated that if a person were under a religious duty both to observe Saturday as a sabbath and to work six days out of the week, "the law which compels him to inaction upon one of the six, might well be regarded as an invasion of his conscientious conviction."[539] Thus, having restated the no-exemptions precedent, the court narrowed its holding to the facts of the case, leaving open the possibility that an exemption might be granted when an actual conflict arose.

The only other religious exemption decision located from this period is *State v. Willson*,[540] an 1823 decision by the Constitutional Court of South Carolina. In that case, a member of "the sect of christians usually called Covenanters" refused on ground of religious conscience to serve as a grand juror and prosecuted an appeal as a test case.[541] The court unanimously rejected the claim that "a fixed & scrupulous moral objection to the discharge of a duty required by law, which springs conscientiously from the religious tenets of a man,

---

534 *Id.*

535 *See supra* pp. 1444–45.

536 8 Pa. 312 (1848).

537 *Id.* at 322.

538 *Id.* at 325.

539 *Id.* at 326.

540 13 S.C.L. (2 McCord) 393 (1823).

541 *Id.* at 394.

amounts to a justification for refusing to perform the duty so required."[542] The court observed that all religions required "a ready obedience to the laws of the country" and urged the Covenanter to "'obey the powers that be.'"[543] In addition, the court expressed concern that if the sincere objections of believers were indulged, it would open the gates to the "hipocritical" and the "deceitful."[544] Oddly, the court neither quoted nor cited the free exercise provision of the South Carolina Constitution.

The court's first argument in *Willson* proves either too much or too little. On the one hand, it suggests that there can be no religious limitation on the powers of the government, since obedience to all laws is a sacred obligation of the citizen. On the other hand, it disregards the possibility that free exercise limitations are themselves a part of the law, and that to rely on constitutional protections does not constitute disobedience to the law. The court's second argument resembles criticism of the "sincerity" requirement under modern free exercise doctrine[545] and contains an implicit bias in favor of familiar religious practices and against religious practices that are not widely held and hence suspect.

It is surprising that cases involving jury service did not arise more often, since Quakers as well as Covenanters refused jury service and were not shy about pressing their claims in court. The explanation is probably that trial judges were vested with broad discretion to excuse jurors and usually did so in cases of religious objection. Indeed, such a de facto exemption had occurred in *Lesher*, and the court in *Willson* noted that it often occurred in South Carolina, as well.[546] The *Willson* case itself was taken to the constitutional court simply to "settle a principle."[547] This strongly suggests that the actual practice favored exemptions, even though the appellate decisions went the other way.

D. Summary of the Evidence

While the historical evidence is limited and on some points mixed, the record shows that exemptions on account of religious scruple should have been familiar to the framers and ratifiers of the free exercise clause. There is no substantial evidence that such exemptions were considered constitutionally questionable, whether as a form of establishment or as an invasion of liberty of conscience. Even opponents of exemptions did not make that claim. The modern argument

---

542 *Id.*

543 *Id.* at 396.

544 *Id.* at 394.

545 *See* Marshall, *supra* note 17, at 27–30.

546 *See Willson*, 13 S.C.L. (2 McCord) at 395–96.

547 *Id.* at 394.

against religious exemptions, based on the establishment clause, is thus historically unsupportable. Likewise unsupportable are suggestions that free exercise of religion is limited to opinions or to profession of religious opinions, as opposed to conduct.

It is more difficult to claim, on this evidence, that the framers and ratifiers specifically understood or expected that the free exercise clause would vest the courts with authority to create exceptions from generally applicable laws on account of religious conscience. Exemptions were not common enough to compel the inference that the term "free exercise of religion" necessarily included an enforceable right to exemption, and there was little direct discussion of the issue. Without overstating the force of the evidence, however, it is possible to say that the modern doctrine of free exercise exemptions is more consistent with the original understanding than is a position that leads only to the facial neutrality of legislation.

Indeed, the evidence suggests that the theoretical underpinning of the free exercise clause, best reflected in Madison's writings, is that the claims of the "universal sovereign" precede the claims of civil society, both in time and in authority, and that when the people vested power in the government over civil affairs, they necessarily reserved their unalienable right to the free exercise of religion, in accordance with the dictates of conscience. Under this understanding, the right of free exercise is defined in the first instance not by the nature and scope of the laws, but by the nature and scope of religious duty. A religious duty does not cease to be a religious duty merely because the legislature has passed a generally applicable law making compliance difficult or impossible.

The language of the free exercise and liberty of conscience clauses of the state constitutions, from the early Rhode Island, Carolina, and New Jersey charters to the new constitutions passed after 1776, strongly supports this hypothesis. These constitutions curtailed free exercise rights when they would conflict with the peace and safety of society. These "peace and safety" provisos would not be necessary if the concept of free exercise had been understood as nothing more than a requirement of nondiscrimination against religion.

Moreover, in the actual free exercise controversies in the colonies and states prior to passage of the first amendment, the rights of conscience were invoked in favor of exemptions from such generally applicable laws as oath requirements, military conscription, and ministerial support. Many of the framers, including Madison, a majority of the House of Representatives in the First Congress, and the members of the Continental Congress of 1775, believed that a failure to exempt Quakers and others from conscription would violate freedom of conscience. These experiences, while not so frequent or notorious as to warrant firm conclusions, nonetheless suggest that exemptions were part of the legal landscape. They are sufficient to shift the burden of persuasion to those who contend that the free exercise clause precludes exemptions.

The history subsequent to adoption of the first amendment is inconclusive but tends to point against exemptions. One lower court in New York squarely adopted the exemptions interpretation, and the supreme courts of Pennsylvania and South Carolina rejected it. None of these decisions was handed down within twenty years of the first amendment, and they are therefore weak indicators of the original understanding. The Pennsylvania holding is entitled to especially little weight since it was connected to a rejection of constitutional judicial review in general. Indeed, the contrast between the rationale of Chief Justice Gibson for the Pennsylvania court and the rationales offered by Madison for religious liberty tends, if anything, to reinforce the conclusion that Madison's position requires exemptions.

IV. Conclusion: The New American Philosophy of Religious Pluralism

The free exercise clause may well be the most philosophically interesting and distinctive feature of the American Constitution. Viewed in its true historical light, as the product of religious pluralism and intense religious sectarianism in the American states and colonies, with limited influence from the rationalistic Enlightenment, the free exercise clause represents a new and unprecedented conception of government and its relation to claims of higher truth and authority.

Until the Protestant Reformation, the separation of church and state was the product not of theory or design but of geopolitical reality. It was graphically illustrated by the throne of St. Peter in Rome and the throne of the king in each of the nation-states of Christendom. At times, the church was under the domination of the state; at times, though more rarely, the state was under the domination of the church. More often, the church and the state were independent powers, supported by different claims of authority, acting in varying degrees antagonistically or cooperatively one with the other. This separation, a product of a "catholic" church in a post-imperial world, was instrumental in staving off incipient despotism. Mankind's two great loyalties, to God and to country, were of necessity divided; claims of ultimate right were pitted against the power of the state. "'To that conflict of four hundred years,'" according to Lord Acton, "'we owe the rise of civil liberty.'"[548]

The Reformation introduced religious factions to Western Europe, and with them, two novel dangers to public peace and freedom. First,

548 B. Tierney, *Medieval Canon Law and Western Constitutionalism*, in Church Law and Constitutional Thought in the Middle Ages, pt. XV, at 8 (1979).

the rivalry among religious sects broke out into bloody warfare, both between countries, as in the Thirty Years War, and within countries, as in the English Civil War and the Huguenot wars in France. Second, as the universal church was sundered, it became possible to form national churches, such as the Church of England, which could be more easily dominated by the government.[549] Thus, a complete and enduring fusion of earthly and spiritual authority became a serious possibility for the first time since the fall of Rome.

The Enlightenment writers on the subject tended to concentrate on the danger of religious rivalry. Sectarian intolerance and struggle for hegemony was a major cause of unrest, violence, rebellion, and persecution. There were two promising ways to ameliorate and, if possible, eliminate such violence and persecution, and both had proponents among the thinkers of the Enlightenment. One solution was to suppress religious differences by establishing a national church and supporting it with public funds. This solution was proposed by Hobbes,[550] the youthful Locke,[551] and Hume,[552] among others. It would have two advantages: by unifying religion, it would reduce religious factionalism, and by guaranteeing financial support to the clergy, it would cause them to become indolent and subservient. The difficulty with this solution was that it would enrage dissenters from the established church (or at least the most intense among them) and might well exacerbate religious unrest. For this reason, the mature Locke proposed the second approach: to extend toleration to all (except Catholics and atheists), on condition that each religion adopt toleration as one of the tenets of its faith. Toleration, it was hoped, would calm the fevers of religious dissension. To the Enlightenment skeptic, convinced of the absurdity of the more intense varieties of religious expression and likewise convinced of the power of reason, this approach seemed to offer the additional advantage that reason, and with it rational religion, would prevail over the sectarians. Hence Jeffer-

---

549 *See* F. MAKOWER, *supra* note 45, at 97 ("In the sixteenth century the reformation robbed the church almost wholly of its independence.").

550 *See* T. HOBBES, *supra* note 119, pt. III, ch. 42, at 293–95; *see id.* at 293 ("[T]he Right of Judging what Doctrines are fit for Peace, and to be taught the Subjects, is in all Commonwealths inseparably annexed . . . to the Soveraign Power Civill.").

551 *See* J. LOCKE, TWO TRACTS ON GOVERNMENT, *supra* note 118, at 124–27.

552 Hume wrote:

> [E]cclesiatical establishments, though commonly they arose at first from religious view, prove in the end advantageous to the political interests of society . . . . [T]he civil magistrate [should] bribe their [the clergy's] indolence, by assigning stated salaries to their profession, and rendering it superfluous for them to be farther active, than merely to prevent their flock from straying in quest of new pastures.

1 D. HUME, HISTORY OF ENGLAND, ch. 29, at 552–553 (1851); *see also* D. HUME, *Idea of a Perfect Commonwealth*, in ESSAYS: MORAL, POLITICAL, AND LITERARY 512, 520 (E. Miller ed. 1985).

son's hope that with religious freedom in America, all would become Unitarians.[553]

An aggressive interpretation of the free exercise clause would be incompatible with the Enlightenment theory of toleration. Free exercise exemptions are likely to encourage dissident sects to maintain practices at variance with the mores of society, and thus perpetuate the very religious factionalism that is the root of the problem. While deliberate oppression of minority religious groups is counterproductive, indirect measures that increase the cost and inconvenience of exotic religious practices likely will dampen the enthusiasm for religious differentiation and thereby reduce religious strife.

As with the establishment solution, however, the toleration solution seemed less than realistic from the American side of the Atlantic. Too many Americans had come to these shores precisely because they could not practice their faith in the controlled environs of Europe. Too many sectarians were spreading their views, and religious factionalism was already too deeply ingrained. Dissenters were a vexatious minority in Britain; in America they were (in the aggregate) a large majority, divided into many sects. And experience had shown that Americans were attracted — not repulsed — by the "irrational" surges of enthusiastic religion that peaked in the Great Awakening.

Madison, for one, grasped that the United States was not amenable to the Enlightenment solutions.[554] In a letter to Jefferson, he stated that "[h]owever erroneous or ridiculous these grounds of dissention and faction may appear to the enlightened Statesman or the benevolent philosopher, the bulk of mankind, who are neither Statesman nor philosophers, will continue to view them in a different light."[555] Religious sectarianism will not go away. Universal Unitarianism, even if desirable, is not going to come about. The Madisonian contribution, familiar to us from *The Federalist* Nos. 10 and 51, is to understand factions, including religious factions, as a source of peace and stability. If there are enough factions, they will check and balance one another and frustrate attempts to monopolize or oppress, no matter how intolerant or fanatical any particular sect may be.

This point of view is consistent with an aggressive interpretation of the free exercise clause, which protects the interests of religious minorities in conflict with the wider society and thereby encourages the proliferation of religious factions. To increase the number of religious sects and the vigor of the small ones will not, as Locke

---

553 *See supra* text accompanying note 211.

554 On the difference between American styles of thinking and the ideas of the European Enlightenment in other contexts, see D. BOORSTIN, cited above in note 155, at 149–52.

555 Letter from James Madison to Thomas Jefferson (Oct. 24, 1787), *reprinted in* 5 THE WRITINGS OF JAMES MADISON, *supra* note 109, at 17, 29.

appeared to believe, exacerbate the problem of religious turmoil. More likely, it will make religious oppression all the more impossible and therefore all the more unprofitable to attempt. Rather than try to foster an ecumenical spirit, the state allows each sect to promote its own cause with zeal. The Madisonian perspective points toward pluralism, rather than assimilation, ecumenism, or secularism, as the organizing principle of church-state relations. Under this view, the Supreme Court errs if it attempts to calm or suppress religious fervor by confining it to the margins of public life. It should welcome religious participation in all its diversity and dissension. The Court should not ask, "Will this advance religion?," but rather, "Will this advance religious pluralism?" The Court should not ask, "Will this be religiously divisive?," but rather, "Will this tend to suppress expression of religious differences?" Most of all, the Court should extend its protection to religious groups that, because of their inability to win accommodation in the political process, are in danger of forced assimilation into our secularized Protestant culture. The happy result of the Madisonian solution is to achieve *both* the unrestrained practice of religion in accordance with conscience (the desire of the religious "sects") *and* the control of religious warfare and oppression (the goal of the Enlightenment).

So understood, the free exercise clause also makes an important statement about the limited nature of governmental authority. While the government is powerless and incompetent to determine what particular conception of the divine is authoritative, the free exercise clause stands as a recognition that such divine authority may exist and, if it exists, has a rightful claim on the allegiance of believers who happen to be American citizens. The actual occasions for free exercise exemptions may be rare now, as in our early history; but the importance of the principle outstrips its practical consequences. If government admits that God (whomever that may be) is sovereign, then it also admits that its claims on the loyalty and obedience of the citizens is partial and instrumental. Even the mighty democratic will of the people is, in principle, subordinate to the commands of God, as heard and understood in the individual conscience. In such a nation, with such a commitment, totalitarian tyranny is a philosophical impossibility.

Dissenting in *West Virginia Board of Education v. Barnette*,[556] Justice Felix Frankfurter wrote:

> The constitutional protection of religious freedom terminated disabilities, it did not create new privileges. It gave religious equality, not civil immunity. Its essence is freedom from conformity to religious dogma, not freedom from conformity to law because of religious

[556] 319 U.S. 624 (1943).

> dogma. . . . Otherwise each individual could set up his own censor against obedience to laws conscientiously deemed for the public good by those whose business it is to make laws.[557]

So saying, Justice Frankfurter overlooked the unique American contribution to church-state relations and embraced instead the Enlightenment ideal of Locke and Jefferson. Locke and Jefferson may well have been animated, in Justice Frankfurter's words, by the "freedom from conformity to religious dogma." But that is not what the Baptists, Quakers, Lutherans, and Presbyterians who provided the political muscle for religious freedom in America had in mind. To them, the freedom to follow religious dogma was one of this nation's foremost blessings, and the willingness of the nation to respect the claims of a higher authority than "those whose business it is to make laws" was one of the surest signs of its liberality.

---

[557] *Id.* at 653 (Frankfurter, J., dissenting).

SUPREME COURT SUPERSTARS: THE TEN GREATEST JUSTICES

Bernard Schwartz†

I. Introduction

"The human animal differs from the lesser primates in his passion for lists of Ten Best."[1] To be sure, any such ranking — whether of all-star athletes or the greatest Supreme Court Justices — is a personal matter, bound to be based upon the lister's own subjective evaluation. After all, as Justice Frankfurter points out, "Greatness in the law is

† Bernard Schwartz is the Chapman Distinguished Professor of Law at the University of Tulsa College of Law, Tulsa, Oklahoma.

1. David Wallechinsky et al., The Book of Lists at xvii (1977).

not a standardized quality, nor are the elements that combine to attain it."[2] There are no "objective" standards of comparison between the Justices — no batting averages like those which distinguish the Ty Cobbses or Ted Williamses from their lesser counterparts.

Perhaps the most that can be done here is to apply Justice Stewart's celebrated aphorism to Supreme Court greatness: "I could never succeed in [defining it]. But I know it when I see it . . . ."[3] It may be impossible to say exactly what makes a great Justice. But I know greatness when I see it. These are the ten whom *I know* as the ten greatest in Supreme Court History:

1. John Marshall (1755-1835), Chief Justice of the United States, 1801- 1835
2. Joseph Story (1779-1845), Justice, United States Supreme Court, 1811-1845
3. Roger Brooke Taney (1777-1864), Chief Justice of the United States, 1836-1864
4. Stephen J. Field (1816-1899), Justice, United States Supreme Court, 1863-1897
5. Oliver Wendell Holmes (1841-1935), Justice, United States Supreme Court, 1902-1932
6. Louis Dembitz Brandeis (1856-1941), Justice, United States Supreme Court, 1916-1939
7. Charles Evans Hughes (1862-1948), Justice, United States Supreme Court, 1910-1916, Chief Justice of the United States, 1930-1941
8. Hugo Lafayette Black (1886-1971), Justice, United States Supreme Court, 1937-1971
9. Earl Warren (1891-1974), Chief Justice of the United States, 1953-1969
10. William J. Brennan, Jr. (1906-), Justice, United States Supreme Court, 1956-1990

II. The Justices[4]

A. *The Ten Greatest*

1. John Marshall

"[I]f American law," says Justice Holmes, "were to be represented by a single figure, sceptic [sic] and worshipper alike would

2. William D. Pederson & Norman W. Provizer, Great Justices of the U.S. Supreme Court 3 (1993) (*quoting* Felix Frankfurter, *The Supreme Court in the Mirror of Justices*, 105 U. Pa. L. Rev. 781, 784 (1957)).

3. Jacobellis v. Ohio, 378 U.S. 184, 197 (1964) (Stewart, J., concurring).

4. Portions of this section of the text are derived from Bernard Schwartz, A History of the Supreme Court (1993).

agree without dispute that the figure could be one alone, and that one, John Marshall."[5] Certainly, more so than any other justice, Marshall has been the subject of inquiry. His role in constructing the keystone of the constitutional-law arch was crucial. "[T]he extraordinary judgments of Mr. Chief Justice Marshall upon constitutional law"[6] have been confirmed over the ages by the continuing imprimatur of the highest Court. Ever since his day, the Court's governing approach has been associated with Marshall, has never been successfully challenged as sound constitutional principle, and has remained the keystone of our constitutional edifice.

Marshall's task was to translate the constitutional framework into the reality of decided cases. He was not merely the expounder of our constitutional law; he was its author, its creator. "'Marshall found the Constitution paper; and he made it power,' said James A. Garfield. 'He found a skeleton, and he clothed it with flesh and blood.'"[7]

The roster of Marshall's principal decisions is a list of leading American constitutional law principles. His most important opinions were summarized by Beveridge in the following manner:

> In *Marbury vs. Madison*[8] [Marshall] established that fundamental principal of liberty that a permanent written constitution controls a temporary Congress; . . . in *M'Culloch vs. Maryland*[9] and *Cohens vs. Virginia*[10] he made the Government of the American people a living thing; but in *Gibbons vs. Ogden*,[11] he welded that people into a unit by the force of their mutual interests.[12]

A major part of our constitutional law has been merely gloss upon these key Marshall opinions. Without the principles established by these opinions, the American constitutional system would be entirely different.

For Marshall, the law was essentially a social instrument — with the Constitution itself to be shaped to special and particular ends. The Constitution was not to be applied formalistically; it must be applied in light of its purpose. To Marshall, there was no doubt that the

5. THE MIND AND FAITH OF JUSTICE HOLMES 385 (Max Lerner ed., 1943).

6. 1 JOSEPH STORY, COMMENTARIES ON THE CONSTITUTION OF THE UNITED STATES at ix (Melville M. Bigelow ed., 1905) (5th ed. 1891).

7. CHARLES WARREN, A HISTORY OF THE AMERICAN BAR 402 (Howard Fertig, Inc. ed., Little, Brown, and Co. 1966) (1911).

8. 5 U.S. (1 Cranch) 137 (1803).

9. 17 U.S. (4 Wheat.) 316 (1819).

10. 19 U.S. (6 Wheat.) 264 (1821).

11. 22 U.S. (9 Wheat.) 1 (1824).

12. 4 ALBERT J. BEVERIDGE, THE LIFE OF JOHN MARSHALL 430 (1919).

organic instrument's overriding purpose was to establish a nation endowed with all necessary governmental powers. At the Chief Justice's death, John Quincy Adams wrote that Marshall "settled many great constitutional questions favorably to the continuance of the Union. [He] has cemented the Union. . . ."[13]

The key to Marshall's conception is his seminal dictum: "[W]e must never forget, that it is *a constitution* that we are expounding."[14] Justice Frankfurter once described this as the "most important, single sentence in American Constitutional Law."[15] It set the theme for constitutional construction — the Constitution should not be read as "an insurance clause in small type, but [as] a scheme of government . . . intended for the undefined and unlimited future."[16]

Marshall interpreted the Constitution to lay the legal foundation of an effective nation. He consistently aimed to use the Supreme Court for that purpose. During his tenure, instrumentalist jurisprudence reached its climax. More so than any other jurist, Marshall employed the law as a means to attain the political and economic ends that he favored. In this sense, he was the very paradigm, during our law's formative era, of the result-oriented judge. Moreover, the law which he used was, in major part, molded by him as well. Marshall's ability to both shape and use the law is evident in his public-law decisions: "[H]e hit the Constitution much as the Lord hit the chaos, at a time when everything needed creating."[17] The constitutional principles which Marshall proclaimed in his cathedral tones were, in large part, principles of his own creation.

Marshall was undoubtedly one of the greatest legal reasoners.[18] But his ability to reason effectively only masked the fact that he authored as well as expounded his legal doctrines. His public-law opinions were based on supposedly timeless basic principles which, once accepted, led by unassailable logic to the conclusions that he favored. In Marshall's seminal opinions "[t]he movement from premise to conclusion is put before the observer as something more impersonal than the working of the individual mind. It is the inevitable progress of an

13. Diary of John Quincy Adams (July 10, 1835) *in* WARREN, *supra* note 7, at 421.

14. McCulloch v. Maryland, 17 U.S (4 Wheat.) 316, 407 (1819).

15. FELIX FRANKFURTER REMINISCES 166 (Harlan B. Phillips ed., 1960) (emphasis omitted).

16. *Id.*

17. JOHN P. FRANK, MARBLE PALACE 62 (1972).

18. G. EDWARD WHITE, THE MARSHALL COURT AND CULTURAL CHANGE 373 (1988).

inexorable force."[19] Even Marshall's strongest critics were affected by the illusion. "All wrong, all wrong," we are told was the despairing comment of one critic, "but no man in the United States can tell why or wherein."[20]

Marshall was once described by a contemporary as "too much disposed to govern the world according to rules of logic."[21] Marshall the logician is, of course, best seen in his magisterial opinions, which, to an age still under the sway of the syllogism, built up in broad strokes a body so logical that it baffled his critical contemporaries.[22] To Marshall, however, logic, like law, was only a tool. Indeed, the great Chief Justice's opinions taken together are a prime judicial example of the famous Holmes aphorism: "The life of the law has not been logic: it has been experience."[23] Marshall, more than any other early judge, molded his decisions to accord with "[t]he felt necessities of the time."[24] If this was often intuitive rather than conscious on his part, his intuitions certainly furthered his notion of the public interest.

For Marshall, then, the constitution was a tool, and the same was true of the common law. Both public law and private law were employed to lay the doctrinal foundations of the polity and economy which served his nationalistic vision of the new nation. Compared to Jefferson's, Marshall's vision may have been conservative. However, though their visions may not have been the same, both the great Chief Justice and his lifelong antagonist looked at the law from an instrumentalist point of view.

Jefferson wrote of "the rancorous hatred which Marshall bears to the government of his country."[25] However, both men simply had different conceptions of what the American polity should become. Marshall himself saw all too acutely that the Jeffersonian theme was sweeping all before it. "In democracies," he noted in 1815, "which all the world confirms to be the most perfect work of political wisdom, equality is the pivot on which the grand machine turns."[26] As he grew older, Marshall fought the spread of the equality principle, notably in

19. SELECTED WRITINGS OF BENJAMIN NATHAN CARDOZO 342-43 (Margaret E. Hall ed., 1947).

20. EDWARD S. CORWIN, JOHN MARSHALL AND THE CONSTITUTION 124 (1919).

21. 2 BEVERIDGE, *supra* note 12, at 437.

22. CORWIN, *supra* note 20, at 123-24.

23. OLIVER W. HOLMES, THE COMMON LAW 1 (Boston, Little Brown, and Co. 1881).

24. *Id.*

25. 9 THE WRITINGS OF THOMAS JEFFERSON 275 (Paul L. Ford ed., 1898).

26. John Marshall to Richard Peters, July 21, 1815, Marshall Papers, Library of Congress, *quoted in* SCHWARTZ, *supra* note 4, at 68.

the Virginia Convention of 1829-1830. As he saw it, "equality demands that he who has a surplus of anything in general demand should parcel it out among his needy fellow citizens."[27]

However, though Marshall's last effort against the triumph of Jacksonian democracy was doomed to failure, the broader battle for acceptance of his conception of law was triumphantly vindicated. Even those persons least conversant with our public law know that Marshall's conception of the Constitution has dominated Supreme Court jurisprudence, particularly during the present century. But the same has also been true of Marshall's concept of private law. The Marshall Court decisions which adapt the common law to the needs of the expanding market economy led the way to the remaking of private law in the entrepreneurial image. Free individual action and decision became the ultimate end of law, as well as that of society itself. Law became a prime instrument for the continent's conquest and for the opening of the economy to men of all social strata. Paradoxically perhaps, it was Marshall, opponent of Jefferson-Jackson democracy though he was, whose conception of law laid the constitutional cornerstone for a legal system furthering opportunity and equality in the marketplace to an extent never before imagined.

2. Joseph Story

Joseph Story was the youngest Justice ever appointed, as well as the most learned scholar ever to sit on the Supreme Court. On the Marshall Court, Story supplied the one thing the great Chief Justice lacked — legal scholarship. "Now, Story," Marshall once said to his colleague, "that is the law; you find the precedents for it."[28] Story's scholarship was, indeed, prodigious. "Brother Story here . . . can give us the cases from the Twelve Tables down to the latest reports,"[29] Marshall said on another occasion. If Marshall disliked the labor of investigating legal authorities to support his decisions, Story reveled in it. His opinions were usually long and learned and relied heavily on prior cases and writers.

Moreover, Story himself was also a leading writer upon whom American judges relied during the last century. Indeed, when discussing the legal sources used for his study of the American democracy, de

---

27. *Id.*

28. CORWIN, *supra* note 20, at 116.

29. WILLIAM PLUMER, JR., LIFE OF WILLIAM PLUMER 205-206 (1857), *quoted in* GERALD T. DUNNE, JUSTICE JOSEPH STORY AND THE RISE OF THE SUPREME COURT 91 (1970).

Tocqueville wrote, "I have consulted the three most respected commentaries: the *Federalist*, . . . Kent's *Commentaries*, and those of Justice Story."[30] Kent and Story were the two great commentators on the developing law; there appeared for the first time in their works systematic expositions of early American law.

Kent was author of the American *Blackstone* — the first general survey of the law in this country[31] — although it was Story who published the first great specialized treatises on American law. "I have now published seven volumes," he wrote in 1836, "and, in five or six more, I can accomplish all I propose."[32] By the end of his career he had published nine treatises (in thirteen volumes) on subjects ranging from constitutional to commercial law. Story's treatises confirmed the victory of the common law in the United States and presented judges with authoritative guides.

Story's best-known work — his three-volume *Commentaries on the Constitution*[33] — was really just a restatement of the Marshall constitutional doctrines in textual form. Accepted as a classic as soon as it appeared, the Story volumes confirmed the Marshall construction as accepted law. They showed, through virtual clause-by-clause analysis, that the Marshall-Story jurisprudence was the "correct" constitutional doctrine. With Story's work, the nationalistic view of governmental power was firmly established, at least legally. Marshall's view could finally serve as the basis for the harmonization of law with the country's newly-emerging economic forces.

Justice Story soon became the principal supporter of the Marshall constitutional doctrines on the bench as well. Story's opinion in *Martin v. Hunter's Lessee*[34] contributed as much as any the Chief Justice delivered to laying the jurisprudential foundation of a strong nation. Indeed, the opinion was one that, save for some turgidity of language, the Chief Justice could have written. Without doubt, its impact was as great as any Marshall opinion. After Story delivered his *Martin* opinion, there was no disputing the appellate power of the U.S. Supreme Court over state court decisions. He demonstrated conclusively that the Union itself could not continue if state courts were able to defy it.

30. ANDRE JARDIN, TOCQUEVILLE 201 (1988).
31. JAMES KENT, COMMENTARIES ON AMERICAN LAW (New York, O. Halsted 1826-30).
32. 2 LIFE AND LETTERS OF JOSEPH STORY 240 (William W. Story ed., Books for Libraries Press 1971) (1851).
33. JOSEPH STORY, COMMENTARIES ON THE CONSTITUTION OF THE UNITED STATES (Boston, Little, Brown, and Company 1833).
34. 14 U.S. (1 Wheat.) 304 (1816).

But Story was not simply a junior Marshall. Much as Marshall was the prime molder of early American public law, Story left his imprint on American private law. Early American commercial and admiralty law were largely Story's creation. His opinions strikingly exemplified the common law's capacity to reshape itself to meet the changing needs of the new industrial order. Story's important decisions blended the law of trusts with the rudimentary law of corporations to produce the modern business corporation, a hybrid creature with organizational and managerial functions divorced from the control of capital, but with the ability to conduct its own affairs like a natural person.

Bank of the United States v. Dandridge[35] played a key role in the development of corporations. That case saw Chief Justice Marshall taking an unusual narrow view, and refusing to allow corporations to show approval of their agents acts by presumptive testimony, but only by written record and vote. Marshall's approach would have required corporate contracts to be cast in the elaborate forms of English law, with a record and vote required for each contract. That holding would have substantially hindered the growth of the business corporation in this country.

In *Dandridge*, however, Story, not Marshall, spoke for the Court. Story held that approval could be shown by presumptive evidence. He stated specifically that the English common law governing corporations was irrelevant to an American corporation created by statute. Instead, corporations were to be treated like natural persons: "[T]he acts of artificial persons afford the same presumptions as the acts of natural persons."[36]

Dandridge played a vital part in the development of the business corporation, which (as Kent noted) was beginning to "increase in a rapid manner and to a most astonishing extent."[37] By permitting corporations to operate as freely as individuals, Story played a crucial role in accommodating the corporate form to the demands of an expanding American economy. The ability of the American courts to adapt the common law to the new nation's requirements is nowhere better seen than in *Dandridge*.

Writing to a British judge, Story noted the predicament in which American law had found itself. "We had not the benefit of a long-

35. 25 U.S. (12 Wheat.) 64 (1827).
36. *Id.* at 70.
37. 1 CHARLES WARREN, THE SUPREME COURT IN UNITED STATES HISTORY 697 (1922).

established and well-settled jurisdiction, and of an ancient customary law. . . . The . . . Law was in a great measure a new system to us; and we had to grope our way as well as we could . . . ."[38] Story's great work was to restate common law and equity in American form. The result justified Story's "hope that a foundation has now been laid, upon which my successors in America may be able to build with more ease and security than fell to my lot."[39]

Story was well aware of the need to modify common-law doctrines to make them suitable for the republican institutions and burgeoning economy on this side of the Atlantic. In *Van Ness v. Pacard*,[40] he consciously altered the common-law rule on fixtures to make it serve the needs of the mobile business economy and, in *Dandridge*,[41] he permitted the corporate person to operate as freely as individuals.[42] In his writings, Story also sought to build an *American* system upon the common-law foundation and to state its principles in a manner that would further the polity and economy that he favored. In this sense, he was as much an instrumentalist as Marshall or, indeed, any jurist of his time.

Above all others, Story laid the foundations of modern financial law. Though a Republican when appointed, Story had none of the Jeffersonian hostility toward business. Instead, he espoused the new gospel of capitalism. Commerce, he declared, "imparts life and intelligence to the body politic, increases the comforts and enjoyments," and "liberalizes and expands the mind, as well as fosters the best interests of humanity."[43] To this end, progress in the field depended upon the creation of a *uniform* commercial law upon which businessmen could rely. Uniform commercial law, made by the federal judges without the interference of juries (merchants, as Story noted, "are not fond of juries")[44] and according to accepted mercantile custom and convenience, was what the commercial community wanted.[45] Some of

38. 1 STORY, *supra* note 32, at 318.

39. *Id.* at 319.

40. 27 U.S. (2 Pet.) 52 (1829).

41. 25 U.S. (12 Wheat.) 64 (1827).

42. In a letter to Kent, Story wrote, "I . . . rejoice, that the Supreme Court has at last come to the conclusion, that a corporation is a citizen, an artificial citizen, I agree, but still a citizen." 2 STORY, *supra* note 32, at 469.

43. THE MISCELLANEOUS WRITINGS OF JOSEPH STORY 93-94 (William W. Story ed., Da Capo Press 1972) (1852).

44. 1 STORY, *supra* note 32, at 270.

45. R. KENT NEWMYER, SUPREME COURT JUSTICE JOSEPH STORY 124-25 (1985).

the most important Story opinions contributed to the establishment of such a law.[46]

To jurists such as Story, the instrumentalist conception of law was implicit in all their legal works. "It is obvious," Story wrote in an 1825 article, "that the law must fashion itself to the wants, and in some sort to the spirit of the age."[47] In that article Story spoke of the growth of commercial law — the field where Story's emphasis was most clearly placed on the ends to be served by the developing law. Commercial law, above all other law, "must . . . expand with the exigencies of society."[48] The old legal landmarks "no longer indicate the travelled road, or mark the busy, shifting channels of commerce."[49] Here, "[a]s new cases arise, they must be governed by new principles . . . ."[50] Above all, the law should "favor every attempt to build up commercial doctrines upon the most liberal foundation."[51]

Despite his Republican (Jeffersonian) origins, Story is usually considered a paradigm of the conservative judge. But his approach to private law — particularly as it relates to commercial development — was transforming. Story, more than any other Justice, helped ensure that our private law would have a common-law foundation that would be adaptable to the conditions of the new nation. Story, as well as Kent, restated the common law in American form. Their work so clearly presented American common law that the courts' energies could be devoted to applying the new principles to concrete cases.

3. Roger Brooke Taney

How can Taney, the Chief Justice who presided over the most discredited decision in Supreme Court history, be placed on a list of the ten greatest Justices? However great his one judicial blunder, the answer remains that Taney's monumental mistake in *Dred Scott*[52] should not overshadow his numerous accomplishments on the Court. Taney was second only to Marshall in laying the foundation of our constitutional law.[53]

---

46. *E.g.*, Swift v. Tyson, 41 U.S. (16 Pet.) 1 (1842); De Lovio v. Boit, 7 F. Cas. 418 (C.C.D. Mass. 1815).

47. THE MISCELLANEOUS WRITINGS OF JOSEPH STORY, *supra* note 43, at 279.

48. *Id.*

49. *Id.*

50. *Id.*

51. *Id.* at 287.

52. Scott v. Sandford, 60 U.S. (19 How.) 393 (1856).

53. FRANKFURTER, THE COMMERCE CLAUSE UNDER MARSHALL, TANEY AND WAITE 73 (1964).

Taney was the first Chief Justice to wear trousers; his predecessors had always given judgment in knee breeches.[54] There was something of portent in his wearing democratic garb beneath judicial robes;[55] under Taney and the new majority appointed by President Andrew Jackson, the Supreme Court for the first time mirrored the Jacksonian emphasis upon public power as a counterweight to the property rights stressed by the Federalists and the Whigs.

Taney was one of the foremost exponents of Jacksonian democracy; some scholars say that the Jacksonian political theory is more completely developed and more logically stated in Taney's writings than anywhere else.[56] This assertion may be extreme, but it cannot be denied that Taney's years on the Court marked a growing judicial concern for safeguarding the rights of the community — a burgeoning emphasis on public, not private, welfare. "We believe property should be held subordinate to man, and not man to property," declared a leading Jacksonian editor, "and therefore that it is always lawful to make such modifications of its constitution as the good of Humanity requires."[57] Under Chief Justice Taney, the Court elevated this concept to the constitutional plane.

The most significant development under the Taney Court was the seminal concept of the police power — the most important constitutional instrument by which property rights may be limited. It was the Taney Court which first gave to the notion of police power something like its modern connotation. "But what," Taney asked in the 1847 *License Cases*,

> are the police powers of a State? They are nothing more or less than the powers of government inherent in every sovereignty to the extent of its dominions. And whether a State passes a quarantine law, or a law to punish offenses, or to establish courts of justice, or requiring certain instruments to be recorded, or to regulate commerce within its own limits, in every case it exercises the same power; that is to say, the power of sovereignty, the power to govern men and things within the limits of its dominion.[58]

Of course, such a broad conception of state power over internal government may be inconsistent with the fullest exertion of individual rights. Taney saw this inconsistency as inherent in the very nature of

54. Carl B. Swisher, Roger B. Taney 359 (1935).
55. *Id.*
56. Charles W. Smith, Roger B. Taney 3 (1936).
57. Orestes Brownson, "Laboring Classes," Boston Quarterly Review 481 (October 1840), *quoted in* Arthur M. Schlesinger, The Age of Jackson 312 (1945).
58. 46 U.S. (5 How.) 504, 583 (1847).

the police power. Indeed, his chief contribution was to recognize and articulate the superior claim, in appropriate cases, of public over private rights. The Taney Court developed the police power as the basic instrument through which property might be controlled in the public interest. Community rights were thus ruled "paramount to all private rights . . . , and these last are, by necessary implication, held in subordination to this power, and must yield in every instance to its proper exercise."[59]

It was Taney's opinion in the *License Cases* which gave currency to the "police power" concept as a necessary complement to the expansion of governmental power, an outstanding feature of the Jacksonian period. During that period "the demand went forth for a large governmental programme: for the public construction of canals and railroads, for free schools, for laws regulating the professions, for antiliquor legislation . . . ."[60] In the police power concept, the law developed the constitutional theory needed to enable the states to meet the public demand. The Taney Court could thus clothe the states with the authority to enact social legislation for the welfare of their citizens. Government was given the "power of accomplishing the end for which it was created."[61] Through the police power a state might, "for the safety or convenience of trade, or for the protection of the health of its citizens,"[62] regulate the rights of property and person. Thenceforth, a principal task of the Supreme Court was to be determination of the proper balance between individual rights and the police power.

Edward S. Corwin compares what he calls the "constitutional revolution" reported in "Volume 301 of the *United States Supreme Court Reports* [to] a single counterpart in the Court's annals. I mean Volume 11 of Peters's *Reports*, wherein is recorded the somewhat lesser revolution in our constitutional law precisely 100 years earlier, which followed upon Taney's succession to Marshall."[63]

It is customary to point to the drastic change that occurred in constitutional jurisprudence when Taney succeeded Marshall. The traditional historical view was summarized over a generation ago by Justice Frankfurter:

---

59. West River Bridge v. Dix, 47 U.S. (6 How.) 507, 532 (1848).

60. Edward S. Corwin, *The Doctrine of Due Process of Law before the Civil War*, 24 HARV. L. REV. 460, 461 (1911).

61. Charles River Bridge v. Warren Bridge, 36 U.S (11 Pet.) 420, 547 (1837).

62. License Cases, 46 U.S. (5 How.) 504, 579 (1847).

63. EDWARD S. CORWIN, CONSTITUTIONAL REVOLUTION, LTD. 65 (1941).

> [E]ven the most sober historians have conveyed Taney as the leader of a band of militant 'agrarian,' 'localist,' 'pro-slavery' judges, in a strategy of reaction against Marshall's doctrines. They stage a dramatic conflict between Darkness and Light: Marshall, the architect of a nation; Taney, the bigoted provincial and protector of slavery.[64]

Such an approach is incorrect. "It is not true that Taney accomplished a wholesale reversal of Marshall's doctrines."[65] To be sure, the Justices appointed by President Jackson and his successors inevitably had a different outlook than their predecessors, products of an earlier day. As already emphasized, Taney and his colleagues shared the Jacksonian belief that property rights must be subject to control by the community.

But the Taney Court did not translate wholesale the principles of Jacksonian democracy into constitutional law. Instead, paradoxical though it may seem, the erstwhile Jacksonian politicians did as much as Marshall and his colleagues to promote economic development and the concentrations of wealth and financial power that were its inevitable concomitants.

Chief Justice Taney may have had the strong Jacksonian bias against what Jackson called "the multitude of corporations with exclusive privileges which [the moneyed interests] have succeeded in obtaining in the different States,"[66] but it was the Taney opinions in cases like *Charles River Bridge v. Warren Bridge*[67] and *Bank of Augusta v. Earle*[68] which opened the door to the greatest period of corporate expansion in our history. The statistics underline the stimulus given to corporate expansion by the decisions favorable to corporate personality rendered by the Taney Court. In the 1830s and 1840s there was a sharp increase in the number of corporations, particularly those engaged in manufacturing.[69] Before Taney, only $50 million was invested in manufacturing; that figure had grown to $1 billion by 1860.[70]

Perhaps the major change in the jurisprudence of the Taney Court arose from its tendency, in doubtful cases, to give the benefit of the doubt to the existence of state power far more than had been the case in Marshall's day; but this is far from saying that Taney and his

---

64. Frankfurter, *supra* note 53, at 48.
65. *Id.* at 49.
66. 3 James D. Richardson, A Compilation of the Messages and Papers of the Presidents 306 (Washington, Government Printing Office 1896).
67. 36 U.S. (11 Pet.) 420 (1837).
68. 38 U.S. (13 Pet.) 519 (1839).
69. George H. Evans, Jr., Business Incorporations in the United States 13 (1948).
70. Harold V. Faulkner, American Economic History 243 (8th ed. 1960).

confreres were ready to overturn the edifice of effective national authority constructed so carefully by their predecessors. On the contrary, like Jackson himself, they were strong believers in national supremacy where there was a clear conflict between federal and state power. When state authorities acted to interfere with federal power, Chief Justice Taney and his colleagues were firm in upholding federal supremacy. Hence, despite its greater willingness to sustain state authority, it is unfair to characterize the Taney Court as concerned only with states' rights.

When the occasion demanded, Taney could assert federal power in terms characterized by Chief Justice Hughes as "even more 'national' than Marshall himself."[71] This is shown dramatically by *The Genesee Chief v. Fitzhugh*,[72] which arose out of a collision between two ships on Lake Ontario. A damage suit was brought in a federal court under an 1845 statute extending federal admiralty jurisdiction to the Great Lakes and connecting navigable waters. The constitutionality of this law was upheld in *The Genesee Chief.* An earlier case[73] had confined the territorial extent of federal admiralty jurisdiction to that followed under English doctrine, namely, to the high seas and to rivers only as far as the ebb and flow of the tide extended. In a small island like Britain, where practically all streams are tidal, such a limitation might be adequate, but it hardly proved so in a country of continental extent.

The Taney opinion in *The Genesee Chief* well illustrates the manner in which the law changes to meet changed external conditions. When the Constitution went into operation, the English "tidal flow" test of admiralty jurisdiction may well have sufficed. In the original thirteen states, as in England, almost all navigable waters were tidewaters. With the movement of the nation west and the consequent growth of commerce on the inland waterways, the English test became inadequate. "It is evident," says the Taney opinion,

> that a definition that would at this day limit public rivers in this country to tide-water rivers is utterly inadmissible. We have thousands of miles of public navigable water, including lakes and rivers in which there is no tide. And certainly there can be no reason for admiralty power over a public tide-water, which does not

71. Charles E. Hughes, *Roger Brooke Taney*, 17 A.B.A. J. 785, 787 (1931).
72. 53 U.S. (12 How.) 443 (1852).
73. The Thomas Jefferson, 23 U.S. (10 Wheat.) 428 (1825).

apply with equal force to any other public water used for commercial purposes . . . .[74]

An inexorable advocate of states' rights would scarcely have written *The Genesee Chief* opinion. In fact, the extreme Jacksonian on the Court, Justice Daniel, flatly refused to countenance the "revolutionary"[75] enlargement of federal jurisdiction approved by the decision and delivered a stinging dissent. But Daniel's opinion was (as he himself conceded) "contracted and antiquated, unsuited to the day in which we live."[76] The Taney opinion was dictated by sound common sense; it was a legitimate nationalizing decision brought on by the changed conditions resulting from the geographic growth of the nation. As Ralph Waldo Emerson put it, in commenting on the case, "The commerce of rivers, the commerce of railroads, and who knows but the commerce of air balloons, must add an American extension to the pondhole of admiralty."[77]

A decision like *The Genesee Chief* shows how difficult it is to pigeonhole Justices like Taney. His states'-rights heritage did not blind him to the need for effective federal governmental power. His distrust of corporations did not make him disregard the practical possibilities of the corporate device and its utility in an expanding economy. Indeed, it was Taney, Justice Frankfurter tells us, "who adapted the Constitution to the emerging forces of modern economic society."[78] Jacksonianism was, at bottom, only an ethical conception of the social responsibilities of private property.[79] To translate that conception into decisions like that in the *Charles River Bridge* case was the great constitutional contribution of the Taney Court.

Henry Clay, who had led the fight against Taney's confirmation, was later to tell the Chief Justice that "no man in the United States could have been selected, more abundantly able to wear the ermine which Chief Justice Marshall honored."[80] The judgment of history has confirmed the Clay estimate. The pendulum has shifted from the post-*Dred Scott* censures by men like Charles Sumner to the more sober estimate of those who sat with Taney on the bench or argued

---

74. 53 U.S. (12 How.) at 457.
75. The term used in 2 WARREN, *supra* note 37, at 239.
76. 53 U.S. (12 How.) at 465.
77. *Quoted in* BERNARD C. STEINER, LIFE OF ROGER BROOKE TANEY 292 n.48 (1922).
78. FELIX FRANKFURTER ON THE SUPREME COURT 462 (Philip B. Kurland ed., 1970).
79. FRANKFURTER, *supra* note 53, at 71.
80. 2 WARREN, *supra* note 37, at 16.

before him at the Bar. According to a vituperative denunciation published at his death, Taney "was, next to Pontius Pilate, perhaps the worst that ever occupied the seat of judgment."[81] Today we reject such partisan bias and agree with the estimate of Justice Frankfurter:

> The devastation of the Civil War for a long time obliterated the truth about Taney. And the blaze of Marshall's glory will permanently overshadow him. But the intellectual power of his opinions and their enduring contribution to a workable adjustment of the theoretical distribution of authority between two governments for a single people, place Taney second only to Marshall in the constitutional history of our country.[82]

4. Stephen J. Field

If influence upon the law is a criterion of judicial greatness, there were few Justices who deserve inclusion in my list more than Stephen J. Field. For it was he who elevated the laissez-faire conception of law to the level of accepted doctrine. That occurred toward the end of the nineteenth century when, as Justice Frankfurter tells us, the Justices "wrote Mr. Justice Field's dissents into the opinions of the Court."[83] It was Justice Stephen J. Field who was largely responsible for the expansion of substantive due process that became the major theme of constitutional jurisprudence during the Gilded Age.

Field himself was one of the most colorful men ever to sit on the highest Court. He was the brother of David Dudley Field (himself one of the great names in American legal history), studied law in his brother's New York office, and began his legal career there as a partner in 1841. A few years later, he was, as he put it, "swept away by the current which set, in 1849, for the Eldorado of the West."[84] He joined the gold rush to California, becoming a frontier lawyer and carrying a pistol and bowie knife. He became involved in a quarrel with a judge, during which he was disbarred, sent to jail, fined, and embroiled in a duel.[85] His lengthy feud with another judge, David Terry (Chief Justice of the California Supreme Court when Field won election to that body in 1857), led Terry to threaten to shoot Field. Years later, in

81. WALKER LEWIS, WITHOUT FEAR OR FAVOR 477 (1965).
82. FRANKFURTER, *supra* note 53, at 72-73.
83. Felix Frankfurter, *Mr. Justice Holmes and the Constitution*, 41 HARV. L. REV. 121, 141-42 (1927).
84. Stephen J. Field, *The Centenary of the Supreme Court of the United States*, 24 AM. L. REV. 351 (1890).
85. Field himself wrote about his California experience in STEPHEN J. FIELD, PERSONAL REMINISCENCES OF EARLY DAYS IN CALIFORNIA (1893).

1889, when Field had long been a Justice of the United States Supreme Court, Terry assaulted him in a restaurant and was shot by a federal marshal assigned to guard Field. The marshal was indicted for murder, but the Supreme Court held the killing justified.[86]

Field was appointed to the Supreme Court by President Lincoln in 1863. His years on the Court saw the law responding to the demands of the burgeoning capitalism of the post-Civil War period by insulating business from governmental interference. Field was the leader in inducing the Court to employ the Due Process Clause to protect property rights. He served in an influential capacity on the Court for over thirty-four years — the longest tenure save that of Justice William O. Douglas. While on the Court, Field wrote 620 opinions, then a record for any Justice.

Justice Field's most important opinions were dissents, but as the Frankfurter quote above tells us, they were ultimately written into Supreme Court jurisprudence. Indeed, it was Field who first showed the potential of the dissenting opinion as what Chief Justice Hughes was to call "an appeal to the brooding spirit of the law, to the intelligence of a future day, when a later decision may possibly correct the error into which the dissenting judge believes the court to have been betrayed."[87] Field's appeals for the constitutionalization of laissez faire may not at first have swayed a majority of his colleagues; but it took only a quarter century for "the rejected dissents of Mr. Justice Field [to have] gradually established themselves as the views of the Court."[88]

The starting point for this development was the *Slaughter-House Cases*.[89] That decision set the early theme for interpretation of the recently adopted Fourteenth Amendment — a restrictive approach which adopted the limited view that the amendment was intended only to protect the Negro in his newly acquired freedom. Under that view, the Due Process Clause could not be used to strike down state restrictions on property rights. For over a decade after it was decided, *Slaughter-House* sharply confined the reach of the Fourteenth Amendment and its Due Process Clause.[90]

86. *In re* Neagle, 135 U.S. 1 (1890).

87. Charles E. Hughes, The Supreme Court of the United States 68 (192[illegible]).

88. Frankfurter, *supra* note 83, at 141.

89. 83 U.S. (16 Wall.) 36 (1873).

90. Charles M. Hough, *Due Process of Law — Today*, 32 Harv. L. Rev. 218, 224, 226 (1919).

The law at issue in *Slaughter-House* gave one company the exclusive right to slaughter livestock in New Orleans. This law, voted amid charges of widespread bribery, put one thousand butchers out of business. But it was held constitutional despite the Fourteenth Amendment. Four Justices, however, strongly disputed the Court's "casual dismissal" of the Due Process Clause.[91] As summarized by Justice Frankfurter, "four dissenting Justices, under the lead of Mr. Justice Field, sought to encrust upon the undefined language of the due process clause the eighteenth century 'law-of-nature' doctrines."[92]

To Justice Field, the Fourteenth Amendment was not limited to protection of the emancipated race. Instead, "It is general and universal in its application" and "was intended to give practical effect to the declaration of 1776 of inalienable rights, rights which are the gift of the Creator, which the law does not confer, but only recognizes."[93]

Moving from the rights guaranteed in the Declaration of Independence to substantive due process was a natural transition for the *Slaughter-House* dissenters. As they saw it, "Rights to life, liberty, and the pursuit of happiness are equivalent to the rights of life, liberty, and property. These are the fundamental rights which can only be taken away by due process of law . . . ."[94] A law like that at issue in *Slaughter-House*, in the dissenting view, did violate due process: "[A] law which prohibits a large class of citizens from adopting a lawful employment, or from following a lawful employment previously adopted, does deprive them of liberty as well as property, without due process of law."[95]

Much of the substance of public law history in the next quarter century involved the elevation of the *Slaughter-House* dissents into the law of the land. The judicial development starts with cases involving railroad regulation. In the *Granger Cases*,[96] the Court followed the strict *Slaughter-House* approach, ruling that the Due Process Clause did not subject the legislative judgment in fixing rates to judicial review: "For protection against abuses by legislatures the people must resort to the polls, not to the courts."[97]

---

91. The term used in EDWARD S. CORWIN, LIBERTY AGAINST GOVERNMENT 122 (1948).
92. Frankfurter, *supra* note 83.
93. 83 U.S. (16 Wall.) at 90, 105.
94. *Id.* at 116.
95. *Id.* at 122.
96. 94 U.S. 113 (1876).
97. *Id.* at 134.

Justice Field wrote a dissent that was a strong protest against the *Granger* decision. If, he asserted, the majority position

> be sound law, if there be no protection, either in the principles upon which our republican government is founded, or in the prohibitions of the Constitution against such invasion of private rights, all property and all business in the State are held at the mercy of a majority of its legislature.[98]

The Due Process Clause, Field went on, "has a much more extended operation than [the] court . . . has given to it."[99] The clause, he stressed, protects "liberty" and "property." For Field, "liberty" meant

> freedom to go where one may choose, and to act in such manner, not inconsistent with the equal rights of others, as his judgment may dictate for the promotion of his happiness; that is, to pursue such callings and avocations as may be most suitable to develop his capacities, and give to them their highest enjoyment.[100]

According to one commentator, this statement illustrates "Field's conviction that the word secures the beneficent state of economic affairs which is the first condition of social justice. . . . It is economic liberty he is talking about; it is Sumnerism he is preaching."[101] More specifically, the Field statement defines liberty in terms of Herbert Spencer's first principle[102] and is, like it, based upon hostility toward governmental interferences with economic liberty.

Field goes on in his *Granger* dissent to say that the "same liberal construction . . . should be applied to the protection of private property"[103] in the Due Process Clause, which "places property under the same protection as life and liberty."[104] "Of what avail," Field asked in one of the *Granger Cases*, "is the constitutional provision that no State shall deprive any person of his property except by due process of law, if the State can, by fixing the compensation which he may receive for its use, take from him all that is valuable in the property?"[105]

Field's dissents fell on anything but deaf ears. The extreme *Granger* approach was itself abandoned during the next decade. The

98. *Id.* at 140.
99. *Id.* at 141.
100. *Id.* at 142.
101. Robert G. McCloskey, American Conservatism in the Era of Enterprise 81 (1964).
102. "Every man has freedom to do all that he wills, provided he infringes not the equal freedom of any other man." Herbert Spencer, Social Statics 55 (D. Appleton and Company 1896) (1850).
103. *Granger*, 94 U.S. at 142.
104. *Id.* at 141.
105. Stone v. Wisconsin, 94 U.S. 181, 186 (1876).

Court soon held that the power to regulate was not the power to confiscate;[106] whether rates fixed were unreasonable "is eminently a question for judicial investigation, requiring due process of law."[107] The rule laid down was that the Due Process Clause permits the courts to review the substance of rate fixing legislation — at least to determine whether particular rates are so low as to be confiscatory.[108]

The judicial balance definitely shifted toward Justice Field's due process approach during the 1880s and 1890s. This was true not only in the Supreme Court, but also in the state courts. "With Field as their chief authority, the state courts in decision after decision made it clear that liberty, property, and due process of law were not to be narrowly construed."[109] The New York court, which had first given due process its substantive gloss in the pre-Civil War period,[110] again led the way. Anticipating the language of the Supreme Court in cases such as *Allgeyer v. Louisiana*[111] and *Lochner v. New York*,[112] the New York court declared in 1885 that the "liberty" protected by due process meant one's right to live and work where and how he will;[113] laws that limit one's choice or place of work "are infringements upon his fundamental rights of liberty, which are under constitutional protection."[114] Other state courts followed a similar due process approach during the next few years; particularly the courts in Illinois and Pennsylvania.[115] The state decisions had a direct influence on the Supreme Court's adoption of the substantive due process concept: "All that happened was that the Supreme Court joined hands with most of the appellate tribunals of the older states."[116]

The joining of hands occurred in *Allgeyer v. Louisiana*,[117] a decision which, according to Justice Frankfurter, "wrote Mr. Justice Field's dissents into the opinions of the Court."[118] In *Allgeyer*, for the first time, a state law was set aside on the ground that it infringed upon the

---

106. Railroad Commission Cases, 116 U.S. 307, 331 (1886).
107. Chicago, M, & St. P. Ry. v. Minnesota, 134 U.S. 418, 458 (1890).
108. *See* Smyth v. Ames, 169 U.S. 466, 526 (1898) (holding that state deprivation of private property without compensation violates due process).
109. SIDNEY FINE, LAISSEZ FAIRE AND THE GENERAL WELFARE STATE 150 (1964).
110. Wynehamer v. People, 13 N.Y. 378 (1856).
111. 165 U.S. 578 (1897).
112. 198 U.S. 45 (1905).
113. Application of Jacobs, 98 N.Y. 98, 105 (1897).
114. *Id.* at 107.
115. Frorer v. People, 31 N.E. 395 (Ill. 1892); Godcharles v. Wigeman, 6 A. 354 (Pa. 1886).
116. Hough, *supra* note 90, at 228.
117. 165 U.S. 578 (1897).
118. Frankfurter, *supra* note 83, at 141-42.

"liberty" guaranteed by due process. The statute in question prohibited an individual from contracting with an out-of-state insurance company for a policy covering property within the state. Such a law, it was held, "deprives the defendants of their liberty without due process of law."[119] The "liberty" referred to in the Due Process Clause, said the opinion, embraces property rights, including that to pursue any lawful calling: "In the privilege of pursuing an ordinary calling or trade and of acquiring, holding and selling property, must be embraced the right to make all proper contracts in relation thereto . . . ."[120] A state law that takes from its citizens the right to contract outside the state for insurance on their property deprives them of their "liberty" without due process.

Between the dictum of the *Granger Cases*, that for protection against legislative abuse "the people must resort to the polls, not to the courts," and *Allgeyer v. Louisiana* and its progeny "lies the history of the emergence of modern large-scale industry, of the consequent public control of business, and of judicial review of such regulation."[121] Thenceforth, all governmental action — whether federal or state — would have to run the gauntlet of substantive due process. The substantive as well as the procedural aspect of such action would be subject to the scrutiny of the highest Court: "The legislatures had not only domestic censors, but another far away in Washington, to pass on their handiwork."[122]

For Justice Field and the Court that adopted his approach, substantive due process was not utilized merely to control governmental action in the abstract. Court control was directed to a particular purpose, namely, the invalidation of state legislation that conflicted with the doctrine of laissez faire that dominated thinking at the turn of the century.[123] What Justice Frankfurter termed "the shibboleths of a pre-machine age . . . were reflected in juridical assumptions that survived the facts on which they were based. . . . Basic human rights expressed by the constitutional conception of 'liberty' were equated with theories of *laissez faire*."[124] The result was that due process "became the rallying point for judicial resistance to the efforts of the

---

119. *Allgeyer*, 165 U.S. at 591.
120. *Id.* at 591.
121. *Compare* Frankfurter, *supra* note 83, at 142 (discussing the propriety of judicial review of commerce regulation).
122. Hough, *supra* note 90, at 228.
123. *See* Hume v. Moore-McCormack Lines, 121 F.2d 336, 339-40 (2d Cir. 1942) (discussing the Court's willingness to strike down "legislative interference" with freedom of contract).
124. American Fed. of Labor v. American Sash and Door Co., 335 U.S. 538, 543 (1949).

states to control the excesses and relieve the oppressions of the rising industrial economy."[125]

To Justice Field, the law had become a negative concept to be used to implement a laissez-faire policy. He dissented in the *Granger Cases* because the law "sanctions intermeddling with all business and pursuits in property in the community."[126] In an important opinion, Field quoted Adam Smith on the worker's property interest in his labor: "To hinder his employing this strength and dexterity in what manner he thinks proper" is "a manifest encroachment upon the just liberty both of the workman" and his employer.[127] Among the "inalienable rights" protected by due process is "the right to pursue any lawful business or vocation . . . without let or hindrance."[128] By this he meant the right to engage in economic activity "in any manner not inconsistent with the equal rights of others"[129] — still another version of Herbert Spencer's first principle.[130]

Upon his retirement in 1897, Field delivered a valedictory which stated that the law was "[t]he safeguard that keeps the whole mighty fabric of government from rushing to destruction. This negative power, the power of resistance, is the only safety."[131] The role of the jurist was not to create new rules and doctrines that would further societal development but to follow a nonintervention policy while such development proceeded unimpaired. Jurists were needed who would ensure that economic forces could assert themselves freely.

To us, a century later, Field's laissez-faire approach appears an extreme shifting of the balance in favor of property rights. However, it set the tone for constitutional law for half a century. That Justice Field's own views were, indeed, extreme is shown by his opinion in the *Income Tax Case*.[132] The Court there ruled invalid the federal income tax law of 1894, even though a similar statute had previously been upheld. The decision can be explained less in legal terms than in terms of the personal antipathies of the Justices. Opposing the statute, Joseph H. Choate depicted the income tax as "a doctrine worthy of a Jacobin Club,"[133] the "new doctrine of this army of 60,000,000 —

125. Robert H. Jackson, The Struggle for Judicial Supremacy 48 (1941).
126. Stone v. Wisconsin, 94 U.S. 181, 186-87 (1876) (Field, J., dissenting).
127. Butchers' Union v. Crescent City, 111 U.S. 746, 757 (1884) (Field, J. concurring).
128. *Id.*
129. *Id.*
130. Spencer, *supra* note 102.
131. Field, *supra* note 84, at 366-67.
132. 157 U.S. 429 (1895).
133. *Id.* at 549.

this triumphant and tyrannical majority — who want to punish men who are rich and confiscate their property."[134]

Such an attack upon the income tax (though, technically speaking, irrelevant) found a receptive ear. "The present assault upon capital," declared Justice Field, "is but the beginning. It will be but the stepping-stone to others, larger and more sweeping, till our political contests will become a war of the poor against the rich; a war constantly growing in intensity and bitterness." If the Court were to sanction the income tax law, "it will mark the hour when the sure decadence of our present government will commence."[135]

The judge who felt this way about a tax of 2 percent on annual incomes above $4,000 was the same Justice who furnished the newly fashioned tool of substantive due process, by which the law was made into an instrument for the judicial protection of private enterprise.

5. Oliver Wendell Holmes

Oliver Wendell Holmes is usually considered the most influential Associate Justice ever to sit on the Supreme Court. I have already quoted Holmes' statement that if American law were to be represented by a single figure, all would agree that the figure would be John Marshall. It is also true that if our law were to be represented by a second figure, most jurists would say that it should be Holmes himself. It was Holmes, more than any other legal thinker, who set the agenda for modern American jurisprudence. In doing so, he became as much a part of American legend as law: the Yankee from Olympus — the patrician from Boston who made his mark on his own age and on ages still unborn as few men have done. To summarize Holmes's work is to trace the development of law from the nineteenth-century to the present day. Indeed, a major part of twentieth-century Supreme Court doctrine is a product of Holmes' handiwork.

The great Holmes theme was stated at the very outset of his career, in *The Common Law*:

> The life of the law has not been logic: it has been experience. The felt necessities of the time, the prevalent moral and political theories, intuitions of public policy, avowed or unconscious, even the prejudices which judges share with their fellow-men, have had a

134. The Income Tax Case, 39 L. Ed. 759, 807 (1895).
135. *Id.* at 607.

> good deal more to do than the syllogism in determining the rules by which men should be governed.[136]

When Holmes wrote these words, he was pointing the way to a new era of jurisprudence that would, in Francis Biddle's words, "break down the walls of formalism and empty traditionalism which had grown up around the inner life of the law in America."[137] The courts, Holmes urged, should recognize that they must perform a legislative function, in its deeper sense. "[T]he secret root from which the law draws" its life is "consideration of what is expedient for the community . . . ."[138] "The felt necessities of the time," intuitions of what best serve the public interest, "even the prejudices which judges share with their fellowmen" — all have much more to do with determining the legal rules which govern the society than does logic.[139] The formalistic jurisprudence that judges professed to be applying early in this century was actually the result of their view of public policy, perhaps "the unconscious result of instinctive preferences and inarticulate convictions, but none the less traceable to views of public policy in the last analysis."[140]

On the Supreme Court itself, Holmes' two great contributions were recently summarized by Judge Posner:

> 1. In the *Lochner* dissent and other famous opinions opposing the use of the due process clause of the Fourteenth Amendment to prevent social and economic experimentation by the states, Holmes created the . . . theory of judicial self-restraint. . . .
> 2. In his opinions in *Schenck*, *Abrams*, and *Gitlow*, which launched the "clear and present danger" test and the "marketplace of ideas" conception of free speech, Holmes laid the foundations not only for the expansive modern American view of free speech but also for the double standard in constitutional adjudication that is so conspicuous a feature of modern constitutional law: laws restricting economic freedom are scrutinized much less stringently than those restricting speech and other noneconomic freedoms.[141]

The theme of judicial self-restraint was repeated many times in Holmes opinions. Its most famous expression was in *Lochner v. New York*[142] — aptly characterized by Chief Justice Rehnquist as "one of

136. HOLMES, *supra* note 23.
137. FRANCIS BIDDLE, MR. JUSTICE HOLMES 61 (1942 ed.).
138. HOLMES, *supra* note 23, at 35.
139. *Id.* at 1.
140. *Id.* at 36.
141. Richard A. Posner, *Introduction* to THE ESSENTIAL HOLMES at xii (Richard A. Posner ed., 1992).
142. 198 U.S. 45 (1905).

the most ill-starred decisions that [the Court] ever rendered."[143] The *Lochner* statute prescribed the maximum hours bakers could work in a week. In holding the law invalid, the majority substituted its independent judgment for that of the legislature and decided for itself that the statute was not reasonably related to any of the ends for which governmental power might validly be exercised.[144] The *Lochner* Court struck down the statute as unreasonable because a majority of the Justices disagreed with the economic theory on which the state legislature had acted.

Justice Holmes consistently rejected such an approach. "[A] constitution," he urged, "is not intended to embody a particular economic theory, whether of paternalism . . . or of *laissez faire*."[145] Holmes continually reiterated that, "as a judge he was not concerned with the wisdom of the social policy involved" in a challenged legislative act.[146] The responsibility for determining what measures were necessary to deal with economic and other problems lay with the people and their elected representatives, not judges. In Holmes' view, the test to be applied was whether a reasonable legislator — the legislative version of the "reasonable man" — could have adopted a law like that at issue. Was the statute as applied so clearly arbitrary that "legislators acting reasonably could not have believed it to be necessary or appropriate" for public health, safety, morals, or welfare?[147]

In the individual case, to be sure, the legislative judgment might well be debatable. But that was the whole point about Holmes' approach. Under it, opposed views of public policy, respecting business, economic, and social affairs, were considerations for the legislative choice[148] to which the courts must defer unless it was demonstrably arbitrary and irrational.[149] "In short, the judiciary may not sit as a superlegislature to judge the wisdom or desirability of legislative policy determinations . . . in the local economic sphere, it is only the . . . wholly arbitrary act, which cannot stand . . . ."[150]

But, the theme of judicial restraint was overridden by another Holmes theme in cases involving the freedom of expression guaranteed by the First Amendment. The governing criterion here was the

143. WILLIAM REHNQUIST, THE SUPREME COURT: HOW IT WAS, HOW IT IS 205 (1987).
144. *Lochner*, 198 U.S. at 64.
145. *Id.* at 75 (Holmes, J., dissenting).
146. MAX LERNER, THE MIND AND FAITH OF JUSTICE HOLMES 92 (1943).
147. Burns Baking Co. v. Bryan, 264 U.S. 504, 534 (1924).
148. North Dakota Bd. of Pharmacy v. Snyder's Drug Stores, 414 U.S. 156, 167 (1973).
149. Duke Power Co. v. Carolina Envtl. Study Group, Inc., 438 U.S. 59, 84 (1978).
150. New Orleans v. Dukes, 427 U.S. 297, 303-04 (1976) (per curiam).

Clear and Present Danger Test which Holmes developed just after World War I. Under this test, even speech advocating unlawful action was not to be restricted unless "the words used are used in such circumstances and are of such a nature as to create a clear and present danger that they will bring about the substantive evils that Congress has a right to prevent."[151] Speech may be restricted only if there is a real threat — a danger, both clear and present, that the speech will lead to an evil that the legislature has the power to prevent.

Although the Clear and Present Danger Test has been criticized by some as too restrictive, it represented a real step forward in favor of free speech. As characterized by Justice Brandeis, Holmes' test "is a rule of reason. Correctly applied, it will preserve the right of free speech both from suppression by tyrannous, well-meaning majorities and from abuse by irresponsible, fanatical minorities."[152]

Holmes' contribution was, however, greater than the constitutional doctrines just discussed. Holmes, more than any other Justice, pointed the way to a whole new era of jurisprudence. Holmes' concept of law was essentially positivist. Hence, he once wrote, "I don't care a damn if twenty professors tell me that a decision is not law if I know that the courts will enforce it."[153]

Holmes' positivist approach was, however, different in important respects from that followed by other jurists at the time. In the first place, he rejected the mechanical formalism that characterized the law of the period. From his early days, he deprecated "the notion that the only force at work in the development of the law is logic."[154] At the beginning of *The Common Law*, he specifically denied that the law could be dealt with as if it were contained in a book of mathematics.[155] The legal process is not the same as doing one's sums right.

Of course, formal logic is the method of jurisprudence; the language of law is mainly the language of logic. "And the logical method and form flatter that longing for certainty and for repose which is in every human mind." But the longing can never be satisfied: "[C]ertainty generally is illusion, and repose is not the destiny of man." To be sure, "You can give any conclusion a logical form. You

151. Schenck v. United States, 249 U.S. 47, 52 (1919).
152. Schaefer v. United States, 251 U.S. 466, 482 (1920) (Brandeis, J., concurring).
153. 1 HOLMES-LASKI LETTERS 115 (Mark D. Howe ed., 1953).
154. OLIVER W. HOLMES, COLLECTED LEGAL PAPERS 180 (1920).
155. HOLMES, *supra* note 23.

always can imply a condition in a contract. But why do you imply it?"[156]

Holmes answers "[you imply i]t . . . because of some belief as to the practice of the community or of a class, or because of some opinion as to policy."[157] Here we have the principal difference between Holmes' conception of law and that of the dominant jurisprudence of the day. For Holmes, the law was consciously made to give effect to the policies that would promote the needs of the society. Neither logic nor "*elegantia juris*" was the life of the law; the life of the law was the work of the courts based on "considerations of what is expedient for the community concerned."[158] The key to Holmes' conception lies in what he wrote of Chief Justice Lemuel Shaw: "[F]ew have lived who were his equals in their understanding of the grounds of public policy to which all laws must ultimately be referred."[159] At the time, the law was looked upon as something developed through gradual accretion — found through discovering and applying principles that were "the necessary product of the life of society, and therefore incapable of being made at all . . . ."[160] Jurisprudence was based upon the assumption that the law was a closed, logical system. "Judges do not make law: they merely declare the law which, in some Platonic sense, already exists."[161] The judicial function was limited to the discovery of the true rules of law and had nothing to do with adapting them to changing needs.

Holmes' concept of law was, on the contrary, based upon "conscious recognition of the legislative function of the courts."[162] In a 1909 opinion, Holmes wrote, "Law is a statement of the circumstances in which the public force will be brought to bear upon men through the courts."[163] The judges may have professed to deduce their rules from a priori postulates, but they were "able and experienced men, who know too much to sacrifice good sense to a syllogism."[164] In a deeper sense, Holmes declared, the work of the courts is legislative:

> It is legislative in its grounds. The very considerations which judges most rarely mention, and always with an apology, are the secret root

156. HOLMES, *supra* note 154, at 181.
157. *Id.*
158. HOLMES, *supra* note 23, at 35.
159. *Id.* at 106.
160. JAMES C. CARTER, LAW: ITS ORIGIN, GROWTH, AND FUNCTION 182 (1907).
161. GRANT GILMORE, THE AGES OF AMERICAN LAW 62 (1977).
162. HOLMES, *supra* note 23, at 36.
163. American Banana Co. v. United Fruit Co., 213 U.S. 347, 356 (1909).
164. HOLMES, *supra* note 23, at 36.

> from which the law draws all the juices of life. I mean, of course, considerations of what is expedient for the community concerned. Every important [legal] principle . . . is in fact and at bottom the result of more or less definitely understood views of public policy.[165]

Hence, "every rule [a body of law] contains is referred articulately and definitely to an end which it subserves. . . ."[166]

Holmes not only showed that the law was made in accordance with policy considerations, he also believed that it should consciously be so made. Instead of a system based upon logical deduction from a priori principles, the Holmes concept was one of law fashioned to meet the needs of the community. Law was once again to be a "utilitarian instrument" for the satisfaction of social needs.[167] Legal principles were to be derived from "accurately measured social desires" and, for these, "[w]hat proximate test . . . can be found except . . . conformity to the wishes of the dominant power . . . in the community?"[168]

The law was to be judged, not by "the simple tool of logic,"[169] but by "its effects and results."[170] More than that, the law could be molded to yield the results best suited to the particular society. A famous Holmes statement speaks of "[l]aw, wherein, as in a magic mirror, we see reflected, not only our own lives, but the lives of all men that have been!"[171] To Holmes, however, the law was more than a reflection of society. It also served the society which it reflected and could be shaped to further the goals sought by the community. Holmes would have none of the negative approach to conscious law-making followed by the dominant jurisprudence. James C. Carter, the leading legal philosopher of the day, had declared, "The *Written* Law is victorious upon paper and powerless elsewhere."[172] To Holmes this was — to use one of his favorite epithets — "humbug."[173]

Yet, if Holmes opened the door to the twentieth-century conception of law, he himself did not enter fully into the legal edifice that lay beyond. Holmes anticipated the later approach to law as consisting of

---

165. *Id.* at 35.
166. HOLMES, *supra* note 154, at 186.
167. Thomas C. Grey, *Holmes and Legal Pragmatism*, 41 STAN. L. REV. 787, 788 (1989).
168. HOLMES, *supra* note 154, at 226, 258.
169. *Id.* at 239.
170. 1 HOLMES-LASKI LETTERS, *supra* note 153, at 20.
171. HOLMES, *supra* note 154, at 26.
172. CARTER, *supra* note 160, at 213.
173. EDWARD J. BANDER, JUSTICE HOLMES EX CATHEDRA 453 (1966).

patterns of judicial conduct. He showed that law should be defined, not in terms of rules derived from a priori immutable postulates, but in terms of the way judges act. In addition, he stressed that "the judges themselves [had] their duty of weighing considerations of social advantage."[174] Not logic, but "the felt necessities of the time"[175] are the primary forces at work in the development of the law.[176] Once again, the law was seen to be a means to an end — the instrument by which the society secures "the ends which the several rules seek to accomplish."[177]

Still, though Holmes' jurisprudence was to return American law to an instrumentalist conception, it was, in Holmes himself, largely a value-free instrumentalism. For Holmes "the proper attitude is that we know nothing of . . . values and bow our heads — seeing reason enough for doing all we can and not demanding the plan of campaign of the General — or even asking whether there is any general or any plan."[178] The law was to serve social ends, but it was not for the jurist to determine those ends. Instead, he should give effect to "the existing notions of public policy."[179] When it came to "the development of a *corpus juris* the ultimate question is what do the dominant forces of the community want and do they want it hard enough . . . ."[180]

It so happened that the Holmes concept of law led to his doctrine of judicial restraint. That, in turn, led to his reluctance to invalidate regulatory legislation.[181] Thus, he came to be lionized as the great "liberal" on the bench. Yet the whole point about Holmes' jurisprudence was that his personal views ("he was 'liberal' only in the nineteenth-century sense of that term,"[182] basically "uncritical about the orthodox economic axioms on which he had been brought up")[183] were irrelevant to his legal work.

What is plain, however, is that it was Holmes who set legal thought on its coming course. When Holmes asserted in *The Common Law* that, "[t]he life of the law has not been logic: it has been

174. HOLMES, *supra* note 154, at 184.
175. HOLMES, *supra* note 23.
176. *See* HOLMES, *supra* note 154, at 180 ("The fallacy . . . is the notion that . . . the force at work in the development of law is logic.").
177. *Id.* at 198.
178. 2 HOLMES-POLLOCK LETTERS 163 (1991).
179. JUSTICE HOLMES TO DOCTOR WU 1921-1932, at 38 (Central Book Co. n.d.).
180. *Id.* at 37.
181. William P. LaPiana, *Victorian from Beacon Hill: Oliver Wendell Holmes's Early Legal Scholarship*, 90 COLUM. L. REV. 809, 832 (1990).
182. *Id.*
183. BIDDLE, *supra* note 137, at 88.

experience," and that the law finds its philosophy in "considerations of what is expedient for the community concerned,"[184] he was sounding the clarion of twentieth-century jurisprudence. If the law reflected the "felt necessities of the time,"[185] then those needs rather than theory should determine what the law should be. These were not, to be sure, the views followed by American judges and lawyers at the beginning of this century — or even by the majority of the Supreme Court during Holmes' tenure on that tribunal. But the good that men do also lives after them. If the nineteenth century was dominated by the passive jurisprudence of men like James C. Carter, the twentieth was, ultimately, to be that of Mr. Justice Holmes.

6. Louis D. Brandeis

Louis D. Brandeis was another Justice who added a new dimension to legal thought — one that emphasized the facts to which the law applied. "In the past," Brandeis tells us, "the courts have reached their conclusions largely deductively from preconceived notions and precedents. The method I have tried to employ in arguing cases before them has been inductive, reasoning from the facts."[186]

The Brandeis method was inaugurated by the brief submitted by him in *Muller v. Oregon*[187] — a new form of legal argument, ever since referred to as the Brandeis Brief. To persuade the Court to uphold an Oregon law prohibiting women from working in factories more than ten hours a day, Brandeis marshaled an impressive mass of statistics to demonstrate "that there is reasonable ground for holding that to permit women in Oregon to work . . . more than ten hours in one day is dangerous to the public health, safety, morals or welfare."[188] The Brandeis Brief and argument in *Muller* were devoted almost entirely to the facts — and to facts not in the record, but which the Court was asked to accept as "facts of common knowledge."[189] The *Muller* brief contains 113 pages; only two of them are devoted to argument on the law.

The *Muller* Court upheld the Oregon law and did so by relying upon the Brandeis approach, expressly noting in its opinion how the

184. Holmes, *supra* note 23, at 1, 35.
185. *Id.* at 1.
186. The Words of Justice Brandeis 78 (Solomom Goldman ed. 1953).
187. 208 U.S. 412 (1908).
188. *Id.* at 416.
189. Brief for Defendant in Error, *id.*, *reprinted in* Louis D. Brandeis and Josephine Goldmark, Women in Industry 10 (1969).

Brandeis Brief had supplied the factual basis for its decision. *Muller* thus was, as Justice Frankfurter termed it, "'epoch making,' . . . because of the authoritative recognition by the Supreme Court that the way in which Mr. Brandeis presented the case — the support of legislation by an array of facts which established the *reasonableness* of the legislative action, however it may be with its wisdom — laid down a new technique for counsel."[190] The Brandeis Brief still remains the model for constitutional cases.

With the Brandeis Brief, the courts were brought down to the solid earth of facts. Interventions in the economy were to be judged, not by whether they were logically consistent with an a priori principle of absolute liberty of contract, but by whether they were justified by the factual background that had led to their enactment. According to a critic of the prior prevailing jurisprudence, "For one who really understands the facts and forces involved, it is mere juggling with words and empty legal phrases."[191] The Brandeis Brief ensured that the judges would begin to understand the "facts and forces involved."

For Brandeis, his *Muller* brief marked the culmination of his career before his Supreme Court appointment. He grew up in Louisville, attended Harvard Law School (where he compiled an academic record still unequaled), and went into practice in Boston in 1879, where he formed a partnership with his fellow Harvard classmate, Samuel D. Warren. The firm prospered, and its success gave Brandeis the financial independence to devote an increasing amount of time to work, often without pay, on behalf of unions, consumers, and small stockholders. He came to be known as the "People's Attorney" for his dedication "with a monastic fervor to what he conceived to be the service of the public."[192]

Brandeis was appointed to the Supreme Court in 1916 and was confirmed over bitter opposition, both by business interests and the organized Bar (Brandeis himself wrote that "[t]he dominant reasons for the opposition . . . are that he is considered a radical and is a Jew.")[193] On the bench, Justice Brandeis continued to use the new technique he had developed in his *Muller* brief — emphasizing the

190. Felix Frankfurter, *Hours of Labor and Realism in Constitutional Law*, 29 HARV. L. REV. 353, 365 (1916).

191. Roscoe Pound, *Liberty of Contract*, 18 YALE L.J. 454 n.3 (1909) (quoting RICHARD T. ELY, ECONOMIC THEORY AND LABOR LEGISLATION 18 (n.d.)).

192. Max Lerner, *The Social Thought of Mr. Justice Brandeis*, *in* MR. JUSTICE BRANDEIS 14 (Felix Frankfurter ed., 1932).

193. PHILIPPA STRUM, LOUIS D. BRANDEIS: JUSTICE FOR THE PEOPLE 293 (1984).

facts in the resolution of legal issues, particularly "the facts of modern industry which provoke regulatory legislation."[194]

Brandeis on the bench was only a more exalted version of Brandeis in the forum. If the Brandeis Brief replaced the "black-letter" judge with "the man of statistics and the master of economics,"[195] Justice Brandeis himself was the prime exemplar of the new jurist in action. Above all, as in his brief, the Justice was a master of the facts in his opinions. For him the search of the legal authorities was the beginning, not the end, of research. He saw that the issues which came to the Court were framed by social and economic conditions unimagined even a generation before. Hence, "the judicial weighing of the interests involved should, he believed, be made in the light of facts, sociologically determined and more contemporary than those which underlay the judicial approach to labor questions at the time."[196]

Detailed knowledge of the facts was the foundation of the Brandeis process of decision. Justice Holmes recalled that his colleague "had an insatiable appetite for facts."[197] Once, after Brandeis had marshaled his usual mass of facts in one of his opinions, Holmes characterized a Justice who had written the other way, "I should think [he] would feel as if a steam roller had gone over him."[198]

The Brandeis emphasis upon facts, both at the Bar and on the high bench, created what Justice Frankfurter calls "a new technique" in jurisprudence.[199] Until Brandeis, says Frankfurter, "social legislation was supported before the courts largely *in vacuo* — as an abstract dialectic between 'liberty' and 'police power,' unrelated to a world of trusts and unions, of large-scale industry and all its implications."[200] With Brandeis, all this changed. In his briefs and opinions, "the facts of modern industry which provoke regulatory legislation were, for the first time, adequately marshaled before the Court."[201]

---

194. Felix Frankfurter, *Mr. Justice Brandeis and the Constitution*, *in* MR. JUSTICE BRANDEIS 52 (Felix Frankfurter ed., 1932).

195. HOLMES, *supra* note 154, at 187.

196. DEAN ACHESON, MORNING AND NOON 82 (1965).

197. 2 HOLMES-LASKI, *supra* note 153, at 28.

198. *Id.* at 209.

199. Frankfurter, *supra* note 194, at 52.

200. *Id.*

201. *Id.*

Brandeis' fact-centered style may have "rarely sparkled," but the Justice's "purpose was education and persuasion" rather than attainment of the Holmes-like epigrammatic immortality.[202] A Brandeis opinion referred to

> [t]he change in the law by which strikes once illegal and even criminal are now recognized as lawful. . . . This reversal of a common-law rule was not due to the rejection by the courts of one principle and the adoption in its stead of another, but to a better realization of the facts of industrial life.[203]

Brandeis himself was the means by which this realization was achieved.[204]

The Brandeis method was used for a particular purpose. The Justice completely rejected the prevailing notion that the law was to be "equated with theories of *laissez faire*."[205] Brandeis firmly believed that "[r]egulation . . . is necessary to the preservation and best development of liberty. We have long curbed the physically strong, to protect those physically weaker. More recently we have extended such prohibitions to business. . . . The right to competition must be limited in order to preserve it."[206]

If twentieth-century law has enabled the society to move from laissez faire to the Welfare State, that has been true in large part because it has accepted the Brandeis approach. Emphasis upon the facts has led to increasing understanding of the reality that called for interventions in the economy. "The small man," said Brandeis, "needs the protection of the law," but, under the laissez-faire conception, "the law becomes the instrument by which he is destroyed."[207] If the law simply allows the market to operate, "you have necessarily a condition of inequality between the two contending forces."[208]

To prevent that result, "business must yield to the paramount interests of the community."[209] The social and economic perils of the industrial age require interventions in the economy that business considers arbitrary and oppressive.[210] The Brandeis jurisprudence was a

202. ACHESON, *supra* note 196, at 83.
203. Duplex Printing Co. v. Deering, 254 U.S. 443, 481 (1921) (Brandeis, J., dissenting).
204. Acheson, *supra* note 196, at 84.
205. American Fed'n of Labor v. American Sash and Door Co., 335 U.S. 538, 543 (1949) (Frankfurter, J., concurring).
206. THE WORDS OF JUSTICE BRANDEIS, *supra* note 186, at 154.
207. *Id.* at 148.
208. *Id.* at 135.
209. Louis K. Liggett Co. v. Lee, 288 U.S. 517, 574 (1933) (Brandeis, J., dissenting).
210. Olmstead v. United States, 277 U.S. 438, 472 (1928) (Brandeis, J., dissenting).

major factor in leading the law to adopt a more benign attitude to economic regulation. "Nobody," Brandeis once wrote, "can form a judgment that is worth having without a fairly detailed and intimate knowledge of the facts."[211] The Brandeis technique helped persuade jurists that the legal conception of "liberty" should no longer be "synonymous with the laissez faire of Herbert Spencer."[212] Instead, jurists have come to believe with Brandeis that "[r]egulation . . . is necessary to the preservation and best development of liberty."[213] That in turn has led to acceptance of the Brandeis rejection of laissez faire as the foundation of our jurisprudence.

7. Charles Evans Hughes

When Chief Justice Taft resigned, President Hoover nominated Charles Evans Hughes to succeed him. Hoover later wrote, "It was the obvious appointment."[214] Despite Hughes' eminent qualifications, his nomination led to the bitterest confirmation fight over a Chief Justice since Chief Justice Taney was named a century earlier. Hughes' chief opponent was Senator George Norris, who asserted, "No man in public life so exemplifies the influence of powerful combinations in the political and financial world as does Mr. Hughes."[215] Despite the opposition, Hughes was confirmed by a vote of fifty-two to twenty-six.

Chief Justice Hughes was sixty-eight when he was appointed — the oldest man chosen to head the Court. However, he undertook his new duties with the vigor of a much younger person. In addition, his more than distinguished career endowed him with prestige which few in the highest judicial office had had. "He took his seat at the center of the Court," Justice Frankfurter was to write, "with a mastery, I suspect, unparalleled in the history of the court . . . ."[216]

"Central casting," Chief Justice Rehnquist tells us, "could not have produced a better image of a chief justice, and his presence matched his appearance."[217] As a leader of the Court, Hughes must be ranked with Marshall and Taney. Whatever the test of leadership,

211. The Words of Justice Brandeis, *supra* note 186, at 134.
212. Alpheus T. Mason, Brandeis: A Free Man's Life 581 (1956).
213. The Words of Justice Brandeis, *supra* note 186, at 154.
214. 2 Merlo J. Pusey, Charles Evans Hughes 651 (1963).
215. 3 Leon Friedman & Fred L. Israel, The Justices of the United States Supreme Court 1903 (1969).
216. Frankfurter, *supra* note 78, at 491.
217. Rehnquist, *supra* note 143, at 222.

in Frankfurter's words, "Chief Justice Hughes possessed it to a conspicuous degree. In open court he exerted this authority by the mastery and distinction with which he presided. He radiated this authority in the conference room."[218] The Hughes manner of conducting the Court's business has been described by Frankfurter, who had served as a Justice under him:

> In Court and in conference he struck the pitch, as it were, for the orchestra. He guided discussion by opening up the lines for it to travel, focusing on essentials, evoking candid exchange on subtle and complex issues, and avoiding redundant talk. He never checked free debate, but the atmosphere which he created, the moral authority which he exerted, inhibited irrelevance, repetition, and fruitless discussion.[219]

The Hughes conferences were military-like models of efficiency. According to Justice Brandeis these "lasted for six hours and the Chief Justice did virtually all the speaking."[220] This was an exaggeration, but Hughes is still noted for his tight control over the conference discussion. "Rarely did anyone speak out of turn," and Hughes made sure that the discussion did not stray from the issues he had stated in his incisive presentation.[221] As Chief Justice Rehnquist puts it, "you did not speak up in that conference unless you were very certain that you knew what you were talking about. Discipline and restraint was the order of the day."[222] Seeing Hughes preside, Justice Frankfurter concludes, "was exciting, quietly exciting, just as every member of the orchestra, I'm sure was taut when Koussevitsky conducted and Toscanini conducted."[223]

The new Chief Justice's leadership abilities were precisely what the Court needed to enable it to confront its most serious crisis in almost a century. Some years earlier, Justice Holmes had written that, while things at the Court were quiet then, it was really only "the quiet of a storm centre."[224] The same could be said of the Court when Hughes took its center chair.

---

218. Felix Frankfurter, Of Law and Men 149 (Philip Elman ed., 1956).
219. *Id.* at 141.
220. Paul A. Freund, Book Review, 65 Harv. L. Rev. 370 (1951).
221. Rehnquist, *supra* note 143, at 292.
222. *Id.*
223. Frankfurter, *supra* note 15, at 268.
224. Holmes, *supra* note 154, at 292.

From outward appearances, the Hughes Court also seemed quiet — ready to continue along the conservative path taken by its predecessors. Yet from almost the beginning of the new Chief Justice's tenure, it was "enclosed in a tumultuous privacy of storm."[225] In decisions like that in the *Adkins* case,[226] the Court's conservative core had carried their laissez-faire interpretation of the Constitution to the point where there was, in the famous Holmes phrase, "hardly any limit but the sky to the invalidating of [laws] if they happen to strike a majority of this Court as for any reason undesirable."[227] In *Planned Parenthood v. Casey*,[228] the 1992 abortion case, the Court itself stated that the pre-Hughes decisions were "exemplified by" the 1923 decision in "*Adkins v. Children's Hospital* . . . in which this Court held it to be an infringement of constitutionally protected liberty of contract to require the employers of adult women to satisfy minimum wage standards."[229]

By the time of the Hughes Court, the *Planned Parenthood* opinion tells us, "the Depression had come and, with it, the lesson that seemed unmistakable to most people by 1937, that the interpretation of contractual freedom protected in *Adkins* rested on fundamentally false factual assumptions about the capacity of a relatively unregulated market to satisfy minimal levels of human welfare."[230] When Chief Justice Hughes ascended the bench early in 1930, the country was already deep in the most serious economic crisis in our history. The crisis only became worse as the Hughes term went on — putting the entire leadership of the country, and not least the Court itself, to perhaps its most severe test.

The new Chief Justice had to meet the test with a Court composed almost entirely of Justices who had served under his predecessor. Four of the five Justices who had made up the *Adkins* majority (Van Devanter, McReynolds, Sutherland, and Butler) were still on the bench, serving as the nucleus for decisions extending the Taft Court's jurisprudence. Despite this, the new Chief Justice was able to persuade a bare majority that the Constitution should no longer be treated as a legal sanction for laissez faire. Writing in 1941, Justice Jackson asserted, "The older world of *laissez faire* was recognized

225. Ralph Waldo Emerson, The Snow-Storm.
226. Adkins v. Children's Hospital, 261 U.S. 525 (1923).
227. Baldwin v. Missouri, 281 U.S. 586, 595 (1930) (Holmes, J., dissenting).
228. 112 S. Ct. 2791 (1992).
229. *Id.* at 2812.
230. *Id.*

everywhere outside the Court to be dead."[231] It was Chief Justice Hughes who ensured that the same recognition penetrated the Marble Palace.

It is true that Chief Justice Hughes, like other Court heads who ultimately led important changes in Court jurisprudence (Chief Justice Warren, in particular, comes to mind), proceeded slowly during his first years in the Court's center chair. In 1937, however, he was able to lead the Court to what amounted to a veritable revolution in the Court's jurisprudence, which one commentator characterized as "Constitutional Revolution, Ltd."[232]

Justice Frankfurter once said that Chief Justice Hughes "was, in fact, the head of two courts, so different . . . was the supreme bench in the two periods of the decade during which Hughes presided over it."[233] The first Hughes Court sat from the Chief Justice's appointment in 1930 until 1937. This period was dominated by decisions which both nullified the most important New Deal legislation and restricted state regulatory power. In both respects, the Court confirmed the laissez-faire jurisprudence of its predecessors.

The grim economic background behind the New Deal measures, however, indicated how totally unrealistic was reliance on laissez faire. Giant industries prostrate, nationwide crises in production and consumption, the economy in a state of virtual collapse — if ever there was a need for exertion of federal power, it was after 1929. The market and the states found the crisis beyond their competence. The choice was between federal action and chaos. A system of constitutional law that required the latter could hardly endure. The New Deal decisions, the Supreme Court was later to concede, "produced a series of consequences for the exercise of national power over industry conducted on a national scale which the evolving nature of our industrialism foredoomed to reversal."[234]

The national economy could be resuscitated only by extended federal intervention. For the Government in Washington to be able to exercise regulatory authority upon the necessary national scale, it was essential that the Supreme Court liberalize its construction of the Constitution. To quote Justice Roberts:

231. JACKSON, *supra* note 125, at 85.
232. CORWIN, *supra* note 63.
233. FRANKFURTER, *supra* note 218, at 148.
234. Mandeville Island Farms v. American Coastal Sugar Co., 334 U.S. 219, 230 (1948).

> An insistence by the court on holding federal power to what seemed its appropriate orbit when the Constitution was adopted might have resulted in even more radical changes in our dual structure than those which have been gradually accomplished through the extension of the limited jurisdiction conferred on the federal government.[235]

In the 1992 *Planned Parenthood* case, the Court itself referred to "the terrible price that would have been paid if the Court had not overruled as it did."[236]

It was Chief Justice Hughes who was responsible for the reversal in jurisprudence that occurred in 1937 — a reversal so great that its effects justify the characterization of "constitutional revolution."[237] On March 29, 1937, Chief Justice Hughes announced a decision upholding a minimum wage law, basically similar to the one the *Adkins* Court had held to be beyond governmental power.[238] There is no doubt that it was the Chief Justice himself who led the Court to repudiate cases such as *Adkins*. The Court to which Hughes came contained, we saw, four of the conservative Justices who had made up the *Adkins* majority. It also contained three liberal Justices (Brandeis, Stone, and Cardozo), who were strongly in favor of overruling the *Adkins* line of cases. The remaining members were the Chief Justice and Justice Roberts, who had taken his seat at the same time as Hughes.

Roberts himself was far from an outstanding Justice. "Who am I," he wrote after leaving the bench, "to revile the good God that he did not make me a Marshall, a Taney, a Bradley, a Holmes, a Brandeis or a Cardozo."[239] He was nevertheless to play a crucial role as the "swing man" in the Hughes Court. It had been his key vote that enabled the conservative bloc to prevail in the decisions striking down the important New Deal measures during the first part of Chief Justice Hughes' tenure. It was Justice Roberts' vote as well that enabled the Chief Justice to bring about the great jurisprudential reversal that took place in 1937.

It was Chief Justice Hughes who persuaded Justice Roberts to vote with the new majority in the minimum wage case. The success of

---

235. Owen J. Roberts, The Court and the Constitution 62 (1951).
236. 112 S. Ct. 2791, 2814 (1992).
237. Corwin, *supra* note 63.
238. West Coast Hotel Co. v. Parrish, 300 U.S. 379 (1937).
239. Frankfurter, *supra* note 78, at 517.

his efforts was, of course, crucial to the Court's acceptance of increased governmental power as the foundation of the new constitutional jurisprudence. Hughes himself fully realized the critical importance of Roberts' vote. He later told how, when the Justice told him that he would vote to sustain the minimum-wage law, he almost hugged him[240] — which, coming from one with so great a reputation for icy demeanor, says a great deal.

It was because of Hughes' lead and his successful persuasion of Justice Roberts that the Chief Justice was able to announce the decision upholding the minimum wage law and overruling *Adkins*. And it was Hughes who wrote the landmark opinion in *National Labor Relations Board v. Jones & Laughlin Steel Corp.*[241] — the seminal decision of the 1937 constitutional revolution. In it, the constitutionality of the National Labor Relations Act of 1935 was upheld.[242] Justice Jackson termed the decision there the most far-reaching victory ever won on behalf of labor in the Supreme Court.[243] This was no overstatement, for the 1935 Act was the Magna Carta of the American labor movement. It guaranteed the right of employees to organize collectively in unions and made it an unfair labor practice prohibited by law for employers to interfere with that right or to refuse to bargain collectively with the representatives chosen by their employees.[244]

The Labor Act was intended to apply to industries throughout the Nation, to those engaged in production and manufacture as well as to those engaged in commerce, literally speaking. But this appeared to bring the Act directly in conflict with prior decisions drastically limiting the scope of the Federal Government's authority over interstate commerce, including some of the decisions of the 1934-1936 period on which the ink was scarcely dry. In the *Jones & Laughlin* case, these precedents were not followed. "These cases," laconically stated Chief Justice Hughes for the Court, "are not controlling here."[245] Instead, the Hughes opinion gave the federal power over interstate commerce its maximum sweep. Mines, mills and factories, whose activities had formerly been decided to be "local," and hence immune from federal regulation, were now held to affect interstate commerce directly enough to justify Congressional control.

240. 2 PUSEY, *supra* note 214, at 757.
241. 301 U.S. 1 (1937).
242. *Id.* at 49.
243. JACKSON, *supra* note 125, at 214.
244. *Jones & Laughlin*, 301 U.S. at 23-24.
245. 301 U.S. at 41.

Once again, there is no doubt that the Chief Justice himself was primarily responsible for the *Jones & Laughlin* decision. In his Hughes biography, Merlo J. Pusey emphasizes the vigor and thoroughness with which the Chief Justice presented *Jones & Laughlin* at the conference. He also states that Hughes told him that he had not "pleaded with Roberts to save the NLRB."[246] The Hughes disclaimer should be taken with a grain of salt. Strong Chief Justices, such as Hughes and Earl Warren, are noted for their success in persuading their colleagues to follow their views. Hughes never denied publicly that he had influenced Justice Roberts' vote. All he states in his *Autobiographical Notes* is, "I am able to say with definiteness that [Roberts'] view in favor of [*Jones & Laughlin*] would have been the same if the President's [Court-packing] bill had never been proposed."[247] Of course, it would have, since it was the Chief Justice's persuasion, not the President's threat, that led to the Roberts vote.

8. Hugo Lafayette Black

During the second third of this century, two members of the highest Court were the paradigms of the new constitutional jurisprudence: Hugo Lafayette Black and Earl Warren. Neither had a defined philosophy of law; neither was a founder, a leader, or even a follower of any school of jurisprudence. Yet each had an influence upon twentieth-century legal thought greater than almost all of the acknowledged molders of jurisprudence. Their forte was one peculiar to the demands of the emerging twentieth-century society — not so much adaptation of the law to deal with changing conditions as a virtual transformation of the law to meet a quantum acceleration in the pace of societal change.

Chief Justice Rehnquist calls Justice Black the "most influential of the many strong figures who have sat during . . . his Justiceship."[248] During much of the Black tenure, he and Justice Felix Frankfurter were polar opposites on the Court. A recent book about the two is titled *The Antagonists*.[249] Yet the issue between them was more basic than the differences engendered by personal antipathies. At the core, there was a fundamental disagreement over the proper role of the law

246. 2 Pusey, *supra* note 214, at 768.
247. The Autobiographical Notes of Charles Evans Hughes 313 (Daniel J. Danelski & Joseph J. Tulchin eds., 1973).
248. Rehnquist, *supra* note 143, at 73.
249. James F. Simon, The Antagonists: Hugo Black, Felix Frankfurter and Civil Liberties in Modern America (1989).

in a period of unprecedented development. Frankfurter on the Court remained true to the Holmes rule of restraint. For him, it was not for the jurist to mold the course of societal change, but only to defer to the course decreed by the political branches, who alone were given the function of deciding these issues in a representative democracy.

Justice Black considered the Frankfurter restraint approach a repudiation of the duty delegated to the judge. As Black saw it, abnegation in the end came down to abdication by the Court of its essential role. "If, as I think," he wrote in a 1962 letter, "the judiciary is vested with the supreme constitutional power and responsibility to pass on the validity of legislation, then I think it cannot 'defer' to the legislative judgment 'without abdicating its own responsibility . . . .'"[250] The decision had to be made on the judge's independent judgment; to "defer" to others meant a passing of the buck that had been placed squarely on the judge. To Black the judicial function meant that the judge was to remain true to his own conception of law however much it differed from that of the legislature or the prior law on the matter.

In a 1942 article, Justice Black characterized the changing jurisprudence: "[L]egal realism replaces legal fictionalism."[251] Black himself was the prime example of the new approach in operation. The law, said the Realists, is what the judges do in fact.[252] Black carried this one step further — what the judge does should be based upon his own conception, without deference to the view of others or even the fact that there is established law the other way.

Black's approach in this respect was the basis for the two positions he most forcefully advocated on the Court: (1) the absolutist view of the First Amendment, and (2) the incorporation of the Bill of Rights in the Due Process Clause of the Fourteenth Amendment.

Without a doubt, in the popular mind Justice Black stands primarily for the absolutist literal interpretation of the First Amendment. The Black position meant, "without deviation, without exception, without any ifs, buts, or whereases, that freedom of speech" was protected from *any and all* governmental infringements.[253] When the amendment says that no laws abridging speech or press shall be made,

250. Hugo Black to Fred Rodell, Sept. 5, 1962, Black Papers, Library of Congress, *quoted in* Bernard Schwartz, Super Chief: Earl Warren and his Supreme Court 41 (1983).

251. Gerald T. Dunne, Hugo Black and the Judicial Revolution 184 (1977).

252. *See* Jerome Frank, Law and the Modern Mind 125-137 (1930) (stating that the law is made by judicial decisions).

253. Edmond Cahn, *Justice Black and First Amendment "Absolutes": A Public Interview*, 37 N.Y.U. L. Rev. 549, 559 (1962).

it means flatly that *no* such laws shall, under any circumstances, be made.

Justice Black's absolutist view has never been accepted by the Court. Countless cases hold that, while speech is protected by the First Amendment, that does not necessarily mean that it is wholly immune from governmental regulation. Such rulings did not, however, deter Black from following the view of law that he deemed correct. The same was true of the Black assertion that the framers of the Fourteenth Amendment sought to overrule the decision in *Barron v. Mayor of Baltimore*,[254] which limited application of the Federal Bill of Rights to federal action. The Bill of Rights, Black urged, was incorporated in the Due Process Clause of the Fourteenth Amendment.[255] This meant that all the Bill of Rights guarantees were binding upon the states as well as the Federal Government.

Once again, the established law was clearly the other way. Since 1884,[256] the Court had rejected the view that the Fourteenth Amendment absorbed all the provisions of the Bill of Rights and hence placed upon the states the limitations which the specific articles of the first eight amendments had theretofore placed upon the Federal Government. Against the more than half century of uniform precedents, Justice Black set only his own view of what the law should be, based upon *his* reading of the relevant constitutional provision, that led him to reject all the weighty precedents the other way and take issue with what seemed so settled in Supreme Court doctrine.[257]

As a Justice, Black used the law to reach the results that he believed would best serve the interests of the American society that he saw developing. He had been a populist Senator and now he employed judicial power to make social policy that would favor the individual and protect him against the governmental and corporate interests that the law had fostered. From this point of view, Justice Frankfurter's satiric portrayal of Justice Black acting as though he were "back in the Senate"[258] contained some truth. Black, however, did not have any overriding social vision. His jurisprudence was instead, like that of many of his judicial confreres, illustrative of the pragmatic instrumentalism that had come to be dominant in American law.

---

254. 32 U.S. (7 Pet.) 243 (1833).
255. Adamson v. California, 332 U.S. 46, 68 (1947).
256. Hurtado v. California, 110 U.S. 516 (1884).
257. *See Adamson*, 332 U.S. at 71-72 (Black, J., dissenting).
258. *See* SCHWARTZ, *supra* note 250, at 45-46.

In the end, however, it was Justice Black, not his great rival, who ranks as a prime molder of twentieth-century legal thought. Black, more than Frankfurter, was more in tune with contemporary constitutional needs. History has vindicated the Black approach, for it has helped protect personal liberties in an era of encroaching public power.

That Black's absolutist advocacy was a prime mover in the First Amendment jurisprudence of the past half century cannot be denied. The absolutist view may not have been accepted, but the "firstness" of the first Amendment has been firmly established. If, as he stated in an opinion, "[f]reedom to speak and write about public questions . . . is the heart"[259] of today's constitutional scheme, it is in large part due to Black's consistent evangelism on the matter.

Similarly, Justice Black's position on incorporation may never have been able to command a Court majority. However, under Black's prodding, the Justices increasingly expanded the scope of the Fourteenth Amendment's Due Process Clause. Though the Court continued to hold that only those rights deemed "fundamental" are included in due process, the meaning of "fundamental" became flexible enough to accomplish virtually the result Black had urged. One by one almost all the individual guarantees of the Bill of Rights were absorbed into the Due Process Clause.[260] By the end of Black's judicial tenure, the rights which had been held binding on the states under the Fourteenth Amendment included all the rights guaranteed by the Bill of Rights except the right to a grand jury indictment and that to a jury trial in civil cases involving over twenty dollars.[261] Justice Black may have appeared to lose the Bill of Rights incorporation battle, but he won the due process war.

Justice Black, as much as anyone, changed the very way we think about public law. If the focus of juristic inquiry has shifted from duties to rights and personal rights have been elevated to the preferred plane — it has in large part been the result of Black's jurisprudence. If impact on legal thought is a hallmark of the outstanding judge, few occupants of the bench have been more outstanding than Black. Justice Black led the Court to tilt the law in favor of individual rights and

259. Drivers Union v. Meadowmoor Co., 312 U.S. 287, 301-02 (1941) (Black, J., dissenting).

260. Williams v. Florida, 399 U.S. 78, 130-32 (1970).

261. BERNARD SCHWARTZ, THE GREAT RIGHTS OF MANKIND 217-21 (Madison House, expanded ed. 1992) (1977). *See, e.g.*, Mapp v. Ohio, 367 U.S. 643 (1961); Gideon v. Wainwright, 372 U.S. 335 (1963); Benton v. Maryland, 395 U.S. 784 (1969); Malloy v. Hogan, 378 U.S. 1 (1964).

liberties and was, before Chief Justice Warren, the intellectual leader in what Justice Abe Fortas once termed "the most profound and pervasive revolution ever achieved by substantially peaceful means."[262] Even where Black's views have not been adopted literally, they have tended to prevail in a more general, modified form. Nor has his impact been limited to his positions which the Court has accepted. It is found in the totality of today's judicial awareness of the Bill of Rights and the law's new-found sensitivity to liberty and equality.

9. Earl Warren

The period during which Earl Warren served as Chief Justice was, in many ways, a second formative era in our legal history, a period in which the law underwent changes as profound as those occurring in the nation at large. The Warren Court led the movement to remake the law in the image of the evolving society. Such change required the Justices to perform the originative role that the jurist is not normally called upon to exercise in more stable times — a role usually considered more appropriate for the legislator than for the judge. In terms of creative impact on the law, the Warren tenure can be compared only with that of Marshall himself.

Even today, many assume that Warren was only the titular chief of his Court — that while Warren may have been the nominal head of the Court that bears his name, other Justices furnished the actual leadership. My own biography of Warren, on the contrary, portrays him as a strong Chief Justice whose leadership of the Court is best characterized by the book's title, *Super Chief* — the title used by Justice Brennan after Warren's retirement and adopted by members of the Court who looked back upon the Warren years with nostalgia.[263]

Warren's leadership abilities and skill as a statesman enabled him to be one of the most effective Chief Justices. Those Justices who served with Warren stressed his leadership abilities, particularly his skill in conducting the conference. At conference, Warren may have stated the issues in a deceptively simple way; but he had the knack of reaching the heart of the matter while stripping it of legal technicalities. As a newspaper noted, "Warren helped to steer cases from the

262. THE FOURTEENTH AMENDMENT CENTENNIAL VOLUME 34 (Bernard Schwartz ed., 1970).

263. SCHWARTZ, *supra* note 250, at 771.

moment they were first discussed simply by the way he framed the issues."[264]

In his first conference on *Brown v. Board of Education*,[265] Warren presented the question before the Court in terms of racial inferiority. He told the Justices that segregation could be justified only by belief in the inherent inferiority of blacks and, if *Plessy v. Ferguson*[266] (which upheld segregation) was followed, it would have to be upon that basis. A scholar such as Justice Frankfurter would certainly not have presented the case that way. But Warren's "simplistic" words went straight to the ultimate human values involved. In the face of such an approach, arguments based on legal scholarship would have seemed inappropriate, almost pettifoggery.

Warren, like Marshall, had primarily a political, rather than a legal background. In 1920, shortly after he had obtained his law degree, Warren began his legal career in the office of the District Attorney of Alameda County, across the Bay from San Francisco. He was elected District Attorney five years later and served in that position until 1938.[267] Raymond Moley, who conducted a 1931 survey of American district attorneys, declared without hesitation that Warren was "the best district attorney in the United States."[268]

In 1938, Warren was elected Attorney General of California, and in 1942, Governor. Warren proved an able administrator and was the only Governor of his state to be elected to three terms. President Eisenhower appointed Warren to head the Supreme Court, and Warren resigned as Governor so that he could take up his new duties as Chief Justice.[269]

There is an antinomy inherent in every system of law: "[T]he law must be stable and yet it cannot stand still."[270] It is the task of the judge to reconcile these two conflicting elements. In doing so, jurists tend to stress one principle over the other. Stability and change may be the twin sisters of the law, but few judges can keep an equipoise between the two. Chief Justice Warren never pretended to try to maintain a balance.

---

264. Fred Barbash, *New Book Offers Inside Look at Earl Warren's Supreme Court*, WASH. POST, June 15, 1983, at A16.
265. 347 U.S. 483 (1954).
266. 163 U.S. 537 (1896).
267. SCHWARTZ, *supra* note 250, at 9.
268. RAYMOND MOLEY, 27 MASTERS OF POLITICS — IN A PERSONAL PERSPECTIVE 89 (1949), *quoted in* LEO KATCHER, EARL WARREN: A POLITICAL BIOGRAPHY 63 (1967).
269. SCHWARTZ, *supra* note 250, at 7.
270. ROSCOE POUND, INTERPRETATIONS OF LEGAL HISTORY 1 (1923).

He came down firmly on the side of change, leading the effort to enable the law to cope with a rapidly changing society. Warren rejected the philosophy of judicial restraint because he believed that it thwarted effective performance of the Court's constitutional role. Judicial restraint, in the Chief Justice's view, all too often meant judicial abdication of the duty to enforce constitutional guarantees. Judicial restraint meant that, "for a long, long time we have been sweeping under the rug a great many problems basic to American life. We have failed to face them squarely, and they have piled up on us, and now they are causing a great deal of dissension and controversy of all kinds."[271] To Warren, it was the Court's job "to remedy those things eventually," regardless of the controversy involved.[272]

The Warren approach, like that of Justice Black, never considered cases in light of any desired deference to the legislature. Instead, Warren relied upon his own independent judgment, normally giving little weight to the fact that a reasonable legislator might have voted for the challenged law.

To Chief Justice Warren, the Court functioned to ensure fairness and equity, particularly in cases where other governmental processes had not secured such results. When a constitutional requirement remained unenforced due to governmental default, the Court had to act. The alternative, as Warren saw it, was an empty Constitution, with essential provisions rendered nugatory because they could not be enforced.

Legislative inaction in enforcing legal rights led to the most important Warren decisions. The Chief Justice felt that he had to intervene when the political branches had not acted to vindicate certain rights and governmental correction seemed unlikely. From this point of view, Warren and his Court acted not so much out of an activist desire to remake the law and society, but rather out of the need to remedy the effects of governmental paralysis. The principal decisions of the Warren Court, including *Brown v. Board of Education*,[273] the Warren Court's most important decision and in many ways the watershed case of the century, sustain this thesis.

The *Brown* decision striking down school segregation and signaling the beginning of effective civil-rights enforcement in American

271. *Earl Warren Talks about the Warren Court*, U.S. NEWS & WORLD REP., July 15, 1968, at 64.

272. *Id.*

273. 347 U.S. 483 (1954).

law, was a direct consequence of the political processes' failure to enforce the Fourteenth Amendment's guaranty of racial equality. Before *Brown*, it had become a constitutional cliché that the amendment had not succeeded in securing equality for blacks; that situation largely resulted from governmental default. Government had not acted to eliminate the almost patent violation of equal protection; instead, both state and federal laws perpetuated the segregation that existed in much of the country, including the nation's capital.

For Chief Justice Warren, the years of legislative inaction, coupled with the unlikelihood that Congress would correct the situation in the foreseeable future, made it imperative for the Court to intervene. The alternative would leave untouched a practice that flagrantly violated both the Constitution and the ultimate human values involved. The Chief Justice found that alternative unpalatable. Since the other branches had defaulted in their responsibility, the Court had to ensure enforcement of the prohibition against racial discrimination.

Second only to *Brown*, the most significant Warren Court case was *Baker v. Carr*.[274] The decision there led to a drastic shift in political power throughout the nation. Through *Baker v. Carr* and its progeny, the Warren Court ultimately worked an electoral reform comparable to that achieved by the British Parliament when it incorporated the program of the English Reform Movement into the statute book.

Even more than *Brown*, *Baker v. Carr* may be explained as a judicial response to the default of the political branches. By the time of the case, the 1901 statute that apportioned seats in the state legislature was completely out of line with the state's population distribution.[275] To correct this situation by a nonjudicial remedy, the very legislature whose existence depended upon the malapportionment under the 1901 statute would have had to pass a new reapportionment law. To expect such an action would have been quixotic.

To remedy this problem, the Supreme Court finally had "to enter this political thicket."[276] The lack of any other remedy was the key factor behind the Court's decision. As Justice Clark put it in a note jotted down while he was considering the case, "Here a minority by [sic] representatives ignores the needs and desires of the majority — and for their own selfish purpose hamper and oppress them — debar

274. 369 U.S. 186 (1962).
275. *Id.* at 187-89.
276. Colegrove v. Green, 328 U.S. 549, 556 (1946).

them from equal privileges and equal rights — that means the failure of our constitutional system"[277] The Chief Justice and his colleagues decided that only a judicial remedy could redress that failure. Warren's own extrajudicial statement regarding his Court's reapportionment decisions bears quoting: "Most of these problems could have been solved through the political processes rather than through the courts. But as it was, the Court had to decide."[278] The decision in *Baker v. Carr* was made because "the political processes" had failed to remedy the constitutional violation that deprived Baker of an equal vote.

The bases of the landmark Warren decisions were fairness and equality. For the Chief Justice, the technical issues traditionally fought over in constitutional cases always seemed to merge into the larger question of fairness.[279] His great concern was expressed in the question he so often asked at argument: "But was it fair?"[280] His conception of fairness was the key to most of the Warren Court's criminal-law decisions. When government lawyers tried to justify decisions below by traditional legal arguments, Warren would interject, "Why did you treat him this way?"[281] When the Chief Justice concluded that an individual had been treated in an unfair manner, he would not let legal rules or precedents stand in the way of his effort to remedy the situation.

Even more important than fairness was the notion of equality in the Warren jurisprudence. The Warren concept of law was one that applied equally to all components of an increasingly pluralistic society. It is true that, ever since de Tocqueville, observers have emphasized equality as the overriding American passion.[282] But it was not until the decisions of the Warren Court that our law really developed the concept of equality. If one great theme recurred in Warren's jurisprudence, it was that of equality before the law — equality of races, of citizens, of rich and poor, of prosecutor and defendant. The result was that seeming oxymoron: A revolution made by judges. Without the

277. SCHWARTZ, *supra* note 250, at 422.

278. JACK W. POLLACK, EARL WARREN: THE JUDGE WHO CHANGED AMERICA 209 (1979).

279. 4 FRIEDMAN & ISRAEL, *supra* note 215, at 2725.

280. *Id.*

281. *Id.*

282. *See* 2 ALEXIS DE TOCQUEVILLE, DEMOCRACY IN AMERICA 94 (Phillips Bradley ed. & Henry Reeve trans., 1956) ("The first and foremost intense passion that is produced by equality of condition is, I need hardly say, the love of that equality.").

Warren Court decisions giving ever-wider effect to the right to equality before the law, most of the movements for equality that have permeated American society might never have started.

Equality was the great Warren theme in the *Brown* school segregation case, as well as the decisions enshrining the "one person, one vote" principle in the law. In addition to racial and political equality, Chief Justice Warren moved to ensure equality in criminal justice. The landmark case was *Griffin v. Illinois*.[283] Griffin had been convicted of armed robbery in a state court. He filed a motion requesting a free transcript of the trial record, alleging that he was indigent and could not get adequate appellate review without the transcript. The motion was denied. In the *Griffin* conference, Warren pointed out that the state had provided for full appellate review in such cases. A defendant who could pay for a transcript should not be given an advantage over one who could not. "We cannot," declared the Chief Justice, "have one rule for the rich and one for the poor."[284] Hence, he would require the state to furnish the transcript. The Court followed the Warren lead and held that it violates the Constitution for a state to deny free transcripts of trial proceedings to defendants alleging poverty.

As it turned out, *Griffin* was a watershed in Warren's jurisprudence. In it the Court made its first broad pronouncement of equality in the criminal process. After *Griffin*, Warren and his colleagues appeared to agree with Bernard Shaw that "the worst of crimes is poverty,"[285] as they tried to equalize criminal law between those possessed of means and the less affluent.

Perhaps Warren as a judge will never rank with the consummate legal craftsmen who have fashioned the structure of Anglo-American law over the generations — "each professing to be a pupil, yet each a builder who has contributed his few bricks."[286] But Warren was never content to deem himself a mere vicar of the common-law tradition. Instead, he was the epitome of the "result-oriented" judge, who used his power to secure the result he deemed right. Employing the authority of the ermine to the utmost, he never hesitated to do whatever he thought necessary to translate his conceptions of fairness and justice into the law of the land.

283. 351 U.S. 12 (1956).

284. Harold H. Burton Papers, Library of Congress, *quoted in* SCHWARTZ, *supra* note 250, at 193.

285. George B. Shaw, *Preface* of MAJOR BARBARA (1905).

286. Learned Hand, *Mr. Justice Cardozo*, 52 HARV. L. REV. 361 (1939).

In reaching what he considered the just result, the Chief Justice was not deterred by the demands of stare decisis. For Warren, principle was more compelling than precedent. The key decisions of the Warren Court overruled decisions of earlier Courts. Those precedents had left the enforcement of constitutional rights to the political branches. Yet, the latter had failed to act. In Warren's view, this situation left the Court with the choice either to follow the precedent or to vindicate the right. For the Chief Justice, there was never any question as to which was the correct alternative.

Warren can neither be deemed a great technical jurist, nor one noted for his mastery of the common law. But he never pretended to be a legal scholar or professed interest in legal philosophy or reasoning. To him, the outcome of a case mattered more than the reasoning behind the decision.

When all is said and done, Warren's place in the legal pantheon rests, not upon his opinions, but upon his decisions. In terms of impact on the law, few occupants of the bench have been more outstanding than Earl Warren. In this respect, indeed, he must be placed second only to Marshall in the list of outstanding Chief Justices.

Justice Fortas once told me that in conference presentations, Chief Justice Warren normally went straight to the ultimate moral values involved — just as he did in his first *Brown* conference. Faced with that approach, traditional legal arguments seemed inappropriate. As Fortas put it, "opposition based on the hemstitching and embroidery of the law appeared petty in terms of Warren's basic value approach."[287] The same appears true when we consider Warren's performance as a judge. To criticize him for his lack of scholarship or judicial craftsmanship seems petty when we weigh these deficiencies against the contributions he made as leader in the greatest judicial transformation of the law since the days of John Marshall.

10. William J. Brennan, Jr.

If we look at Justices in terms of their role in the decision process, William J. Brennan, Jr., was actually the most influential Associate Justice in Supreme Court history:[288] "[M]ore than any justice in

287. SCHWARTZ, *supra* note 250, at 87.

288. Oliver Wendell Holmes is usually considered the most influential Associate Justice ever to sit on the Supreme Court. It was Holmes, more than any other legal thinker, who set the agenda for modern constitutional jurisprudence. Nevertheless, as Judge Posner points out, "the primary vehicles of Holmes's innovations were dissenting opinions that, often after his death, became and have remained the majority position." Posner, *supra* note 141, at xiii. At the time

United States history Brennan would change the way Americans live."[289] Justice Brennan served as the catalyst for some of the most significant decisions during his tenure. He was the leader of the Court's liberal wing under Chief Justices Warren, Burger, and Rehnquist. More important, the Brennan jurisprudence set the pattern for much of American legal thought toward the end of this century. So pervasive was the Brennan influence that the English periodical *The Economist* headed its story on his retirement, *A Lawgiver Goes*.[290]

The Economist characterization is not an exaggeration. So consequential was the Brennan role, in fact, that Dennis J. Hutchinson, an editor of the *Supreme Court Review* declared that to call it the "Warren Court" is a misnomer: "it was 'the Brennan Court.'"[291] As shown by my analysis of Chief Justice Warren, this assertion unduly denigrates Warren's leadership. Still, it is hard to argue with Hutchinson's conclusion, in another portion of his review: "When the public record is added to Schwartz's numerous behind-the-scenes examples, . . . Brennan emerges clearly as the single most important justice of the period."[292] If the Warren Court era saw the most important period of constitutional development since Chief Justice Marshall's day, with so much of the corpus of our public law remade in the process, Justice Brennan was a leader in this development.

It is true that, after Chief Justice Warren's retirement, Justice Brennan was no longer the trusted insider. Yet, even under Chief Justice Burger, Brennan was able to secure the votes for his position in many important cases. In his last years on the bench, the Court, under Chief Justice Rehnquist, moved more toward the right and Brennan spoke increasingly in dissent. Nevertheless, in the Rehnquist Court, too, Justice Brennan secured notable victories, particularly in the areas of abortion, separation of church and state, freedom of expression, and affirmative action. He was primarily responsible for the decisions

---

they were delivered, Holmes' dissents spoke only for their author's conception of the proper legal doctrine. While Justice Holmes was on the Court, its jurisprudence remained dominated by the concepts that he was ultimately to relegate to legal limbo. The Justice's dissents may have sounded the clarion of the coming constitutional era. But they did not greatly influence our law until after his death. However crucial may have been the role that Holmes played in American jurisprudence, it cannot be said that, as a Justice, he played a dominant part in the Supreme Court decision process.

289. Kim I. Eisler, A Justice for All: William J. Brennan, Jr., and the Decisions that Transformed America 13 (1993).

290. *A Lawgiver Goes*, The Economist, July 28, 1990, at 20. *Compare* Eisler, *supra* note 289 ("Brennan [was] the most influential justice of the twentieth century.").

291. Dennis J. Hutchinson, *Hail to the Chief: Earl Warren and the Supreme Court*, 81 Mich. L. Rev. 922, 923 (1983).

292. *Id.* at 929.

toward the end of his tenure that the First Amendment protected flag burning[293] and that broad Congressional authority in the field of affirmative action ought to be upheld.[294]

Before his 1956 appointment by President Eisenhower, Brennan served as a judge in New Jersey for seven years, rising from the state trial court to its highest bench. "One of the things," Justice Felix Frankfurter once wrote, "that laymen, even lawyers, do not always understand is indicated by the question you hear so often: 'Does a man become any different when he puts on a gown?' I say, 'If he is any good, he does.'"[295] Certainly Justice Brennan on the highest bench proved a complete surprise to those who saw him as a middle-of-the-road moderate. He quickly became a firm adherent of the activist philosophy and a principal architect of the Warren Court's jurisprudence. Brennan had been Frankfurter's student at Harvard Law School; yet if Frankfurter expected the new Justice to continue his pupilage, he was soon disillusioned. After Brennan had joined the Warren Court's activist wing, Frankfurter supposedly quipped, "that while he had always encouraged his students to think for themselves, Brennan goes too far"[296]

A judge's decisions and opinions reveal his jurisprudence. Brennan's concept of law can be derived from his important opinions. These will be summarized here.

Chief Justice Warren wrote in his *Memoirs* that *Baker v. Carr*[297] "was the most important case of my tenure on the Court."[298] It ruled the federal courts competent to entertain an action challenging legislative apportionments as contrary to equal protection. Before *Baker*, the Court had held that legislative apportionment presented a "political question" beyond judicial competence.[299] In *Baker*, the Brennan opinion overruled the earlier cases and held that attacks on legislative apportionments could be heard and decided by the federal courts.

The *Baker* opinion was the foundation for the principle that the Constitution lays down an "equal population" principle for legislative

293. Texas v. Johnson, 491 U.S. 397 (1989).

294. Metro Broadcasting v. FCC, 497 U.S. 547 (1990).

295. FRANKFURTER, *supra* note 218, at 133.

296. William J. Brennan, Jr., *The Warren Court: A Personal Remembrance,* SUP. CT. HIST. SOC'Y Q., Vol. XV, No. 4, 1994, at 6.

297. 369 U.S. 186 (1962).

298. EARL WARREN, THE MEMOIRS OF EARL WARREN 306 (1977).

299. Colegrove v. Green, 328 U.S. 549 (1946).

apportionment. Under this principle, substantially equal representation is demanded for all citizens. Just as important is the *Baker* illustration of the Brennan juristic approach. Justice Frankfurter, Brennan's old teacher, had warned against courts entering "this political thicket."[300] Brennan replied, "The mere fact that a suit seeks protection of a political right does not mean that it presents a political question."[301] That, says an English commentator, was the Brennan watchword.[302]

In *New York Times Co. v. Sullivan*,[303] Justice Brennan gave a new perspective to freedom of expression by ruling that governmental power to fix the bounds of libelous speech is confined by the Constitution. A public official had recovered substantial libel damages against a newspaper. The Brennan opinion reversed, holding that the newspaper publication was protected by the First Amendment, which required, "a federal rule that prohibits a public official from recovering damages for a defamatory falsehood relating to his official conduct unless he proves that the statement was made with 'actual malice' — that is, with knowledge that it was false or reckless disregard of whether it was false or not."[304]

Justice Brennan's opinion was based upon "[t]he general proposition that freedom of expression upon public questions is secured by the First Amendment."[305] It gave effect, Brennan said, to the "profound national commitment to the principle that debate on public issues should be uninhibited, robust, and wide-open, and that it may well include vehement, caustic, and sometimes unpleasantly sharp attacks on government and public officials."[306]

In terms of legal impact, no Brennan opinion was more far-reaching than *Shapiro v. Thompson*.[307] The Justices originally voted to uphold a state law requiring a year's residence for welfare assistance on the ground that it had a rational basis in the state's desire to use its resources for its own residents. Justice Brennan persuaded a majority to reject this approach and strike down the residence requirement.

300. *Id.* at 556.
301. 369 U.S. at 209.
302. *A Lawgiver Goes*, *supra* note 290, at 20.
303. 376 U.S. 254 (1964).
304. *Id.* at 279-80.
305. *Id.* at 269.
306. *Id.* at 270.
307. 394 U.S. 618 (1969).

Brennan's opinion ruled that since the requirement restricted the fundamental right to travel, it had to be supported by a *compelling* governmental interest and none was present.[308]

Under Justice Brennan's *Shapiro* opinion, the test of mere rationality gives way, in cases involving fundamental rights, to one of strict scrutiny under which a challenged law will be ruled invalid unless justified by a "compelling" government interest. Since *Shapiro*, judicial review has taken place within a two-tier framework, with two principal modes of analysis: strict scrutiny and mere rationality. The tier in which legislation is placed all but determines the outcome of constitutional challenges. Legislation is virtually always upheld under the rationality test, since a law is almost never passed without any rational basis. The converse is true under the compelling-interest test; if a statute is subject to strict scrutiny, it is nearly always struck down.[309]

Justice Brennan's *Shapiro* approach has become established doctrine. It has been applied to a wide range of rights deemed fundamental: the rights guaranteed by the First Amendment,[310] the right to vote,[311] the right to marry,[312] and the right of women to control their own bodies, including the right to terminate pregnancies.[313]

Roe v. Wade,[314] which upheld the last of these rights, was based directly upon Brennan's *Shapiro* approach. In striking down state abortion laws, the Court applied the compelling-interest test. "Where certain 'fundamental rights' are involved . . .," states the *Roe* opinion, "regulation limiting these rights may be justified only by a 'compelling state interest.'"[315] The state's determination to recognize prenatal life was held not to constitute a compelling state interest, at least during the first trimester of pregnancy.

One may doubt that *Roe v. Wade* would have been decided this way if the Brennan *Shapiro* opinion had not laid the doctrinal foundation. Had *Shapiro* confirmed the rational-basis test as the review standard even in cases involving fundamental rights, *Roe v. Wade* would have been deprived of its juristic base. One of the most controversial Court decisions might never have been made.

308. *Id.* at 634.
309. *See* Massachusetts Board of Retirement v. Murgia, 427 U.S. 307, 319 (1976).
310. *See* Buckley v. Valeo, 424 U.S. 1, 93-94 (1976).
311. Bullock v. Carter, 405 U.S. 134 (1972).
312. Zablocki v. Redhail, 434 U.S. 374 (1978).
313. Roe v. Wade, 410 U.S. 113 (1973).
314. *Id.*
315. *Id.* at 155 (citations omitted).

One has only to list Justice Brennan's other important opinions[316] to realize his crucial role in recent constitutional jurisprudence. But the Brennan influence on our constitutional corpus extends far beyond his own opinions. His forte was leading the Justices to the decisions he favored, even at the cost of compromising his own position, as in the adoption of the intermediate-review standard in sex discrimination cases.[317] More than any Justice, Brennan was the strategist behind Supreme Court jurisprudence — the most active lobbyist (in the nonpejorative sense) in the Court, always willing to take the lead in trying to mold a majority for the decisions that he favored. "In case after case," Hutchinson writes about my Warren biography, "Schwartz documents . . . how Brennan would accommodate his own drafts and views in order to preserve an opinion of the Court that was tumbling toward a plurality or worse."[318]

In particular, Hutchinson cites Justice Brennan's behind-the-scenes influence in securing constitutional recognition for the right of privacy in *Griswold v. Connecticut*:[319] "The most startling fact about the genesis of opinions that Schwartz catalogues is that Brennan, not Douglas, designed the spectral theory of *Griswold*, which Douglas, in a first draft, had tried to dispose of on the basis of freedom of association under the first amendment . . . ."[320] Brennan wrote to Justice Douglas suggesting the privacy rationale, urging that a right of privacy would be inferred from the Bill of Rights' specific guarantees. Douglas followed the Brennan suggestion and the final *Griswold* opinion ruled that there is a constitutionally protected right of privacy.[321] Justice Brennan was also responsible for upholding affirmative-action programs in *Regents v. Bakke*,[322] the leading case on the subject. Justice Powell, whose vote provided the 5-4 majority, had decided to vote against affirmative-action programs. However, Brennan persuaded him to rule in his crucial opinion that, although the quota provisions in

316. *See generally* Jencks v. United States, 353 U.S. 657 (1957); Cooper v. Aaron, 358 U.S. 1 (1958); Fay v. Noia, 371 U.S. 391 (1963); Sherbert v. Verner, 374 U.S. 398 (1963); Katzenbach v. Morgan, 384 U.S. 641 (1966); Green v. County Sch. Bd., 391 U.S. 430 (1968); Frontiero v. Richardson, 411 U.S. 677 (1973); Keyes v. Denver Sch. Dist., 413 U.S. 189 (1973); Craig v. Boren, 429 U.S. 190 (1976); Michelin Tire Corp. v. Wages, 423 U.S. 276 (1976); Hughes v. Oklahoma, 441 U.S. 322 (1979).

317. Craig v. Boren, 429 U.S. 190 (1976). *See* BERNARD SCHWARTZ, THE UNPUBLISHED OPINIONS OF THE BURGER COURT 67 (1988).

318. Hutchinson, *supra* note 291, at 929.

319. 381 U.S. 479 (1965).

320. Hutchinson, *supra* note 291, at 929.

321. *See* BERNARD SCHWARTZ, THE UNPUBLISHED OPINIONS OF THE WARREN COURT 237-38 (1985).

322. 458 U.S. 265 (1978).

the medical school admissions program before the Court were invalid, race could be considered as a factor in determining which students to admit.[323] That ruling has enabled almost all affirmative-action programs to continue in operation.

Brennan's approach to law has been pervasively influential during the latter part of this century. Indeed, Brennan's jurisprudence helped make activism the dominant legal approach — both in the forum and the academy — during his judicial tenure. With Chief Justice Warren's retirement, many expected the Court to tilt away from its activist posture. If the Warren Court had made a legal revolution, a counter-revolution was seemingly at hand. It did not, however, turn out that way. If anything, the intended counter-revolution served only as a confirmation of most of the Warren Court jurisprudence.[324] As one commentator puts it, "[T]he entire record of the [post-Warren] Court . . . is one of activism."[325] The Warren concept of the Court as Platonic philosopher-king continued unabated under Brennan's leadership. Indeed, as Anthony Lewis summed it up, "We are all activists now."[326]

In the end, of course, the underlying question in jurisprudence comes down to how we resolve the antinomy in the already-stated aphorism: "[L]aw must be stable and yet it cannot stand still."[327]

During his confirmation hearings, Chief Justice Rehnquist was asked, "how can you not acknowledge that the Constitution is a living, breathing document?"[328] Some years earlier, then-Justice Rehnquist delivered a lecture entitled *The Notion of a Living Constitution.*[329] In it he indicated that the question of "whether he believed in a living Constitution" was similar to asking whether he was in favor of any

---

323. BERNARD SCHWARTZ, BEHIND BAKKE: AFFIRMATIVE ACTION AND THE SUPREME COURT 96 (1988).

324. *See* BERNARD SCHWARTZ, THE ASCENT OF PRAGMATISM: THE BURGER COURT IN ACTION 401-04 (1990).

325. HERMAN SCHWARTZ, *Introduction* to THE BURGER YEARS: RIGHTS AND WRONGS IN THE SUPREME COURT 1969-1986, at xx (H. Schwartz ed., 1987).

326. Anthony Lewis, *Foreward* to THE BURGER COURT: THE COUNTER-REVOLUTION THAT WASN'T at ix (Vincent Blasi ed. 1983).

327. POUND, *supra* note 270.

328. *Nomination of Justice William H. Rehnquist to be Chief Justice of the United States: Report from the Committee on the Judiciary, United States Senate,* 99th Cong., 2d Sess. 354 (1986).

329. William J. Rehnquist, *The Notion of a Living Constitution*, 54 TEX. L. REV. 693 (1976) ("[R]evised text of the ninth annual Will E. Orgain Lecture, delivered at the University of Texas School of Law on March 12, 1976.").

other desirable thing. "At first blush," Rehnquist said, "it seems certain that a *living* Constitution is better than what must be its counterpart, a *dead* Constitution. It would seem that only a necrophile could disagree."[330]

Despite his flippant response, the question put to Rehnquist is a crucial one. Justice Brennan never had any doubt about the proper answer. A legal system created in an age of knee breeches and three-cornered hats can serve the needs of an entirely different day only because our law has recognized that it could not endure through the ages if its provisions were fixed as irrevocably as the laws of the Medes and Persians. The constantly evolving nature of constitutional jurisprudence has alone enabled our system to make the transition from the eighteenth to the twentieth century.

Justice Brennan is the outstanding example of a judge who has not taken stability alone as his legal polestar. Thus, he has been the leading opponent of the view that constitutional construction must be governed only by the original intention of the Framers. As explained by Brennan himself, "this view demands that Justices discern exactly what the Framers thought about the question under consideration and simply follow their intention in resolving the case before them."[331] Throughout his tenure, Brennan rejected this "original intention" jurisprudence; to him, the meaning of the Constitution is to be found in today's needs, not in a search for what was intended by its eighteenth-century draftsmen.

To Justice Brennan, then, the outstanding feature of the Constitution is its plastic nature. The same is true of his general conception of law. Its rules and doctrines are also malleable and must be construed to meet the changing needs of different periods. The opinions already discussed show that he has succeeded in elevating his view to the level of accepted doctrine. They bear ample witness to his success in giving effect to the concept of a flexible law which is constantly being adapted to meet contemporary needs. Above all, the Brennan jurisprudence was based upon what he termed "the constitutional ideal of human dignity."[332] This ideal led him to his constant battle against the death penalty, which he considered a violation of the ban against cruel and unusual punishment. His battle to outlaw capital punishment was

330. *Id.*

331. William J. Brennan, Jr., *in* The Great Debate: Interpreting Our Written Constitution 14 (1986).

332. *Id.* at 25.

a losing one for Brennan but it was the only major battle he lost in his effort to ensure what he said was "the ceaseless pursuit of the constitutional ideal."[333] The ultimate Brennan legacy was that no important decision of the Warren Court was overruled while the Justice sat on the Burger and Rehnquist Courts.

B. *The Also-Rans — Justices on Other Lists*

I am, of course, not alone in my attempt to draw up a list of the greatest Justices. The most recent effort of this type is contained in *Great Justices of the U.S. Supreme Court*, published in 1993 by two political scientists.[334] Their work was based upon a survey sent to scholars, lawyers, judges, and students. The list of great Justices, according to a combined list of all the respondents surveyed, contains four names not included in my list: Benjamin N. Cardozo, Felix Frankfurter, William O. Douglas, and William H. Rehnquist.[335]

Why were these four not included in my list of Supreme Court all-stars?

1. Benjamin N. Cardozo

Cardozo was on my earlier list of the ten greatest American judges and well deserved his place there.[336] Indeed, Cardozo's is one of the truly great names in our law. He was the outstanding common-law jurist of the twentieth century; according to Arthur Goodhart, he will always "be regarded as the great interpreter of the common law."[337] Cardozo led the way in adapting the common law to the requirements of the post-industrial society. Cardozo showed how the common law could be freed to serve present needs — how the judge could be truly innovative while remaining true to the experience of the past. By doing so, he moved the law closer to the goal of making the law an effective instrument of social welfare.

---

333. *Id.*

334. PEDERSON & PROVIZER, *supra* note 2.

335. *Id.* at 18. For an earlier list based upon a poll of professors, see ALBERT P. BLAUSTEIN & ROY M. MERSKY, THE FIRST ONE HUNDRED JUSTICES 37 (1978). Professor Mersky has brought this list up to date with a more recent poll. His new list of Supreme Court greats: John Marshall; Oliver W. Holmes; Louis D. Brandeis; Joseph Story; Earl Warren; Hugo L. Black; William J. Brennan; John M. Harlan I; Charles E. Hughes. Letter from Roy M. Mersky to author, April 20, 1995 (with enclosed list).

336. Bernard Schwartz, *The Judicial Ten: America's Greatest Judges*, 1979 S. ILL. U. L.J. 405, 407 (1979).

337. ARTHUR L. GOODHART, FIVE JEWISH LAWYERS OF THE COMMON LAW 55 (1949).

All the same, the Cardozo place in American jurisprudence is not based upon his service on the Supreme Court. Cardozo's judicial contribution was made on the New York court, where he spent fifteen years, most of his judicial career. During the Cardozo years, that court was recognized as the strongest in the country, and its judgments had a decisive influence on American law. Cardozo was then, as Laski wrote to Holmes, "quite *hors concours* among state judges — the best, I should guess since you were on the Massachusetts Court."[338] Cardozo, however, was able to serve on the U.S. Supreme Court only six years — scarcely long enough for him to make the substantial contribution to its jurisprudence that his judicial ability warranted.

2. Felix Frankfurter

Few members of the Supreme Court have been of greater interest both to the public and to Court specialists than Felix Frankfurter. In large measure, that has been true because his career has posed something of a puzzle. Before his appointment to the bench, he was known for his interest in libertarian causes and it was generally expected that, once on the Court, he would continue along a liberal path. Yet, if one thing is certain, it is that it is risky to try to predict how new appointees will behave after they don the robe. Frankfurter seemed an altogether different man as a Justice than he had been before taking his seat on the bench. From academic eminence behind the New Deal to leader of the conservative Court cabal — that was the way press and public tended to tag Justice Frankfurter.

News of the Frankfurter Court appointment led to a champagne celebration in Harold Ickes' Department of the Interior office, attended by leading New Deal liberals. "We were all very happy," Ickes wrote, "there will be on the bench of the Supreme Court a group of liberals under aggressive, forthright, and intelligent leadership."[339]

It did not turn out that way. There would be a cohesive liberal majority on the Court, but it would not be led by Justice Frankfurter.[340] Instead, Frankfurter's judicial rivals, Justice Black and later Chief Justice Warren, assumed the liberal leadership. Frankfurter became the leader of the Court's conservative core, particularly during the Vinson and early Warren years.

338. 2 Holmes-Laski Letters, *supra* note 153, at 1202-03.
339. Simon, *supra* note 249, at 64.
340. *Id.* at 64-65.

On the Court, Justice Frankfurter's unfailing adherence to judicial restraint appeared increasingly anomalous. In an era of encroaching public power, the deference doctrine did not provide enough protection for personal liberties. What George Orwell called the "[m]achine, the genie that man has thoughtlessly let out of its bottle and cannot put back again,"[341] had created new concentrations of power, particularly in government, which dwarfed the individual and threatened individuality as never before. Judicial restraint no longer appeared adequate to ensure the "Blessings of Liberty" in a world that had seen so clearly the consequences of their denial. It had become a brake upon the judicial ability to protect personal rights.

No matter how Justice Frankfurter tried to clothe his opinions with the Holmes mantle, there was an element of shabbiness in his results in too many cases. For example, after Frankfurter delivered his opinion upholding a compulsory flag salute,[342] he was talking about the opinion over cocktails at the Roosevelt home in Hyde Park. In her impulsive way, Mrs. Eleanor Roosevelt declared that, notwithstanding the Justice's learning and legal skills, there was "something wrong with an opinion . . . that forced little children to salute a flag when such a ceremony was repugnant to their conscience."[343] To critics, there was only hypocrisy in Frankfurter's constant insistence that he could not reach judgments on the bench which he would readily have favored as a private citizen.

With all his intellect and legal talents, Frankfurter's judicial career remained a lost opportunity. As far as the law was concerned, he may well have had more influence as a professor than as a Supreme Court Justice.[344] There is no doubt that Frankfurter expected to be the intellectual leader of the Court, as he had been of the Harvard law faculty. As it happened, that leadership role was performed first by Justice Black, and then by Chief Justice Warren.

---

341. THE COLLECTED ESSAYS, JOURNALISM AND LETTERS OF GEORGE ORWELL 75 (1968).

342. Minersville Sch. Dist. v. Gobitis, 310 U.S. 586 (1940), *rev'd*, West Virginia State Bd. of Educ. v. Barnette, 319 U.S. 624 (1943).

343. MAX FREEDMAN, ROOSEVELT AND FRANKFURTER: THEIR CORRESPONDENCE 1928-1945, at 701 (1967).

344. *See* JOSEPH P. LASH, FROM THE DIARIES OF FELIX FRANKFURTER 87 (1975) ("[T]here are Frankfurter admirers who believe that Frankfurter's influence on constitutional law was greater before he went onto the bench than after . . . .").

3. William O. Douglas

Justice Douglas' place on other lists is a reflection less of his contribution as a member of the Court than of his public image as a potential President and world traveler. To outside observers, Douglas seemed to personify the last frontier — the down-to-earth Westerner whose granite-hewed physique always seemed out of place in Parnassus. Moreover, Douglas was the Court's Horatio Alger, whose early life was a struggle against polio and poverty. Told that he would never walk, he became a noted sportsman. After riding east on a freight car to enroll at Columbia Law School, with six cents in his pocket, he became an eminent law professor, chairman of the Securities and Exchange Commission, and at the age of forty a Supreme Court Justice.[345]

However, the real Douglas was different from his public image. Douglas was the quintessential loner, and he personified the lover of humanity who did not like people. Throughout his tenure on the Supreme Court, no one among the Justices or the law clerks was really close to the strapping Westerner. On the bench, as in his personal life, Justice Douglas was a maverick, who went his own way regardless of how others felt. Douglas would stick to his own views, quick to state his own way of deciding in concurrence or dissent. It made little difference whether he carried a majority or stood alone. He would rarely stoop to lobbying for his position and seemed more interested in making his own stand public than in working to get it accepted. As one law clerk put it, "Douglas was just as happy signing a one-man dissent as picking up four more votes."[346]

There is no doubt that Justice Douglas had a brilliant mind, but he was erratic. He could whip up opinions faster than any of the others. In fact, he wrote both the majority and dissenting opinions in one case. (Justice Whittaker, who had been assigned the Court opinion, was unable to write it; Douglas sent him a draft within an hour after learning this).[347] But his opinions were too often unpolished, as though he lacked interest in the sustained work required to transform first drafts into finished products. Lack of interest in the Court's work was, indeed, apparent in Douglas' very attitude as a judge. Though

---

345. For a detailed biography of Justice Douglas, see generally JAMES F. SIMON, INDEPENDENT JOURNEY (1980).

346. SCHWARTZ, *supra* note 250, at 51.

347. WILLIAM O. DOUGLAS, THE COURT YEARS 1939-1975, at 173-74 (1980). The case was Meyer v. United States, 364 U.S. 410 (1960).

Chief Justice Warren came to appreciate Douglas' supporting votes for his own positions, he always felt that the peripatetic Justice spent too much time writing books and doing other things that were unrelated to his Court duties.

As it turned out, one commentator concludes, "Douglas's many publicized outside activities . . . overshadowed his judicial work."[348] His most important opinions followed Justice Black's lead.[349] With all his potential, he made little significant contribution to jurisprudence; in Supreme Court history, he is now remembered primarily as the Black auxiliary among the Justices.

4. William H. Rehnquist

As mentioned above, Chief Justice Rehnquist also appears on the Pederson and Provizer list of great Justices that was created by combining the 1990 survey results from all four groups of participants. In addition, he is included in the lists compiled from the responses of the attorneys and students surveyed.[350] The "inclusion of Chief Justice Rehnquist," says the introductory commentary of the 1993 book in which the list is published, "marks the first appearance of one of the current members of the Supreme Court on a list of great justices."[351]

It is true that Chief Justice Rehnquist has been a more effective Court head than his predecessor. Nevertheless, elevation of the present Chief Justice to the list of Supreme Court greats appears unwarranted. That is true not because of disagreement with his extreme conservative posture (after all, Justice Field's even more conservative views did not bar him), but because the Rehnquist contribution to constitutional jurisprudence does not begin to bear comparison with those of the Justices on my list.

To be sure, Chief Justice Rehnquist has led the Court's recent tilt toward the right. He has not, all the same, been able to carry out the goals he had at the time of his appointment. There is no doubt that Rehnquist came to the Court with an agenda that included some dismantling of the jurisprudential structure erected by the Warren Court. Justice Rehnquist took his seat with a "desire to correct some of the 'excesses' of the . . . Warren Court"[352] — to see, as he put it, that the

348. SIMON, *supra* note 249, at 191.
349. *Id.*
350. PEDERSON & PROVIZER, *supra* note 2, at 16-17.
351. *Id.* at 17.
352. Stuart Taylor, Jr., *A Pair of Rehnquist Opinions Set Legal Experts Buzzing*, N.Y. TIMES, Feb. 28, 1988, §4, at 1.

"Court has called a halt to a number of the sweeping rulings that were made in the days of the Warren Court."[353]

Rehnquist's agenda was not carried out either in the Burger or Rehnquist years. Instead, the intended counter-revolution served only as a confirmation of most of the Warren Court jurisprudence. Indeed, as already noted, no important Warren Court decision was overruled during the Burger and Rehnquist tenures.

We can see this even in the field of criminal justice, where Rehnquist was most eager to disown the Warren heritage — in Rehnquist's phrase, to make "the law dealing with the constitutional rights of accused criminal defendants . . . more even-handed now than it was when I came on the Court."[354] The celebrated Warren trilogy — *Gideon, Mapp,* and *Miranda*[355] — has been consistently followed by both the Burger and Rehnquist Courts.

When he was elevated to the Court's center chair, Chief Justice Rehnquist indicated that he had even more ambitious goals. As a law clerk, Rehnquist had written a memo on the *Brown* case[356] urging that the separate-but-equal doctrine was "right and should be affirmed."[357] Just before he became Court head, Justice Rehnquist stated in a *New York Times* interview that his views had changed and that he accepted *Brown* as the law of the land.[358] His votes in cases involving civil rights, however, clearly place him in the right wing of the Court on civil rights issues.

What is not known generally outside the Marble Palace is that Chief Justice Rehnquist has urged even more extreme views on civil rights than have appeared in his published opinions. In *Patterson v. McLean Credit Union*,[359] the Court heard argument on "[w]hether or not the interpretation of 42 U.S.C § 1981 adopted by this Court in *Runyon v. McCrary*[360] . . . should be reconsidered."[361] At the post-argument conference, Chief Justice Rehnquist declared that *Runyon*

353. John A. Jenkins, *The Partisan*, N.Y. TIMES, March 3, 1985, §6 (magazine), at 28, 35.

354. *Id.* at 34, 35.

355. Gideon v. Wainwright, 372 U.S. 335 (1963); Mapp v. Ohio, 367 U.S. 643 (1961); Miranda v. Arizona, 384 U.S. 436 (1966).

356. Brown v. Board of Educ., 347 U.S. 483 (1954).

357. SCHWARTZ, *supra* note 321, at 29.

358. Jenkins, *supra* note 353, at 32.

359. 491 U.S. 164 (1989).

360. 427 U.S. 160 (1976).

361. *Patterson*, 491 U.S. at 171 (*quoting* Patterson v. McLean Credit Union, 485 U.S. 617 (1988)).

was wrong and that Justice White was correct in his dissent in that case. Therefore, he urged, the Court should overrule *Runyon.*

The Chief Justice did not, however, stop with his recommendation to overrule *Runyon.* He also told the *Patterson* conference that the Court should overrule *Jones v. Alfred H. Mayer Co.*[362] as well.[363] Rehnquist's position in this respect was not a new one, though it was unknown outside the Court. The Chief Justice had written an April 7, 1987, letter to Justice White on a 1987 case involving section 1981 in which he stated, "I once again question the soundness of our opinion in *Jones v. Alfred H. Mayer Co.*, . . . which held that this class was protected not merely against state action but against action by other private individuals."[364]

The Rehnquist attempt to overrule the two leading civil-rights decisions failed. *Jones v. Alfred H. Mayer Co.* was not questioned in any published opinion and, in *Patterson v. McLean Credit Union*, the Court expressly refused to overrule *Runyon v. McCrary.* In *Patterson*, even the Justices who agreed with Rehnquist's view that *Runyon* had been wrongly decided refused to go along with the Chief Justice and overrule that case.

Another Rehnquist *bête noire* has been *Roe v. Wade*,[365] where he was one of the two dissenters. In *Webster v. Reproductive Health Services*,[366] the Chief Justice actually circulated a draft opinion of the Court that would have relegated *Roe* to virtual constitutional limbo.[367] However, the Rehnquist *Webster* opinion lost its majority when Justice O'Connor refused to join and the Chief Justice had to issue it only as a plurality opinion. Since then, though the Chief Justice has dissented in cases following *Roe*, he has not succeeded in securing a Court to follow him in overruling *Roe.* At present writing, indeed, that case remains as secure in Supreme Court jurisprudence as it has ever been.

A Chief Justice who cannot persuade a Court to give effect to his judicial agenda can scarcely be considered a great Chief Justice. For, as we shall now see, influence upon the law is perhaps the primary criterion that elevates a Justice to the judicial pantheon.

---

362. 392 U.S. 409 (1968).

363. BERNARD SCHWARTZ, THE UNPUBLISHED OPINIONS OF THE REHNQUIST COURT 198 (1996).

364. Letter from Chief Justice William H. Rehnquist to Justice Byron White, United States Supreme Court (Apr. 7, 1987) (on file with the *Tulsa Law Journal*).

365. 410 U.S. 113 (1973).

366. 492 U.S. 490 (1989).

367. *Reprinted in* SCHWARTZ, *supra* note 363, at 266-88.

III. Greatness and Influence

The Pederson and Provizer survey of Great Justices also lists the criteria used by those responding to the survey to establish a Justice as "great." These are summarized as follows:

> While writing and intellectual ability seem to be common criteria for the different groups, protection of individual rights is a criterion used frequently by only two of the groups, attorneys and students. Similarly, leadership appears to be a concern for two of the groups, judges and scholars, while not getting much attention from either attorneys or students.[368]

To me, however, Supreme Court greatness is virtually synonymous with influence on the law. This results in the virtual elimination of Justices, outstanding though they may have been as judges, who did not serve long enough on the Court to have a substantial impact on its jurisprudence. I have already given the example of Justice Cardozo, who was one of the greatest judges in our history, but whose high-bench tenure was too brief for him to make the contribution on the Court that his ability warranted.

An equally pertinent example is to be found in Justice Benjamin R. Curtis' Court career. Curtis served only six years as a Justice; yet, even in that brief period, he made major contributions to both the law and the country. It was Justice Curtis who wrote the now-classic dissent in the *Dred Scott* case,[369] showing definitively the errors in that baneful decision. To the Court specialist, the Curtis opinion in the *Cooley* case[370] was just as important. It not only resolved one of the most important issues presented to the early Court (that of the proper scope of concurrent state power over commerce); it also first stated a new balancing approach that foreshadowed modern constitutional jurisprudence. "No one," says Justice Frankfurter, "can have seriously studied the United States Reports and not have felt the impact of Curtis' qualities — short as was the term of his office."[371] Yet the fact remains that Curtis' tenure was too brief to enable him to realize his full potential as an outstanding Supreme Court Justice.

All the Justices on my list served on the Court long enough to enable them to make their major contributions. The shortest term among them was that of Chief Justice Hughes. Yet even he served for

368. Pederson & Provizer, *supra* note 2, at 22.
369. Scott v. Sandford, 60 U.S. (19 How.) 393 (1857).
370. Cooley v. Board of Wardens, 53 U.S. (12 How.) 299 (1851).
371. 2 Friedman & Israel, *supra* note 215, at 905.

eleven years (almost twice the tenures of Justices Curtis and Cardozo) and, more important, he led the Court during the crucial 1937 revolution in constitutional law.

There is truth in Holmes' observation that Marshall's "greatness consists in his being there"[372] — that he sat in the Court's center chair when our public law was being formed. Certainly, Chief Justice Hughes, too, was *there* at a crucial juncture in Supreme Court history. But the greatness of a Chief Justice such as Hughes consists in more than his being *there*. If Chief Justice Taft, Hughes' predecessor, had continued to preside over the Court, it is doubtful that the 1937 constitutional revolution would have occurred. Hughes was not only *there*, but he also seized the opportunity to lead the Court to its recognition that the pre-1937 jurisprudence "rested on fundamentally false . . . assumptions" and that that recognition "warranted the repudiation of the old law."[373]

The same is true of Chief Justice Warren's great accomplishment in securing the *Brown* decision. Chief Justice Vinson, Warren's predecessor, was also *there* for *Brown*,[374] for he was the Court head when *Brown* came to the Court. However, had he been able to preside during the entire *Brown* decision process, the result would have been a fragmented decision and one that might well have reaffirmed *Plessy v. Ferguson*.[375] It was Chief Justice Warren's leadership that produced the unanimous decision striking down segregation. And it was also Warren who was the catalyst for this century's second revolution in constitutional jurisprudence. If Vinson or one of the other candidates considered by President Eisenhower had headed the Court during the Warren years, that person would have been *there*, but the constitutional corpus would have been very different from that produced during Warren's tenure.

In my view, then, it all comes down to influence upon the law. The Justices on my list are there because each changed the course of Supreme Court jurisprudence. Marshall laid the foundation for both our public law and the Supreme Court's role as the fulcrum of the constitutional system. Story led the early movement to adjust the common law to the needs of the new nation. Taney led his Court in molding the Marshall constitutional edifice to recognize both public

372. LERNER, *supra* note 146, at 385.
373. Planned Parenthood v. Casey, 112 S.Ct. 2791, 2812 (1992).
374. Brown v. Board of Educ., 347 U.S. 483 (1954).
375. Plessy v. Ferguson, 163 U.S. 537 (1896).

power and burgeoning corporate expansion. Field shifted the emphasis to private rights and in the process shielded business from regulatory power. Holmes set the theme for twentieth-century law and recognized the need to adapt it to the "felt necessities of the time."[376] Brandeis laid the juristic foundation for the Welfare State and in the process developed a new method for deciding cases. Hughes led the Court in repudiating Field's jurisprudence and upholding broad governmental power. Black tilted the constitutional balance toward protection of personal rights. Warren led a new activism that has made the Court the vital center of the constitutional system. Finally, Brennan ensured that "[w]e are all activists now"[377] and that his concept of a "living Constitution" would dominate contemporary jurisprudence.

No other Justices in Court history have had an influence upon the law comparable to these ten. All of them employed their authority to mold constitutional jurisprudence to meet what they deemed the needs of the nation during their judicial tenure. All were activists who did not hesitate to use the power of the highest bench to adapt the law to the time's necessities. Not all of them were masters of the common law or consummate judicial craftsmen. But all employed the authority of the ermine to the utmost. This, in the end, is what made them great. More than any other Justices, they seized the occasion to alter constitutional jurisprudence with their transforming touch.

376. HOLMES, *supra* note 23.
377. Lewis, *supra* note 326, at ix.

WAYNE LAW REVIEW

VOLUME 4 | SPRING, 1958 | NUMBER 2

"STATES' RIGHTS" AND THE ORIGIN OF THE SUPREME COURT'S POWER AS ARBITER IN FEDERAL-STATE RELATIONS

John R. Schmidhauser†

The ideological content of states' rights doctrine has, over the past century and one half, undergone so fundamental a transformation[1] that a resurrected John Taylor of Caroline probably would cheerfully embrace the nationalistic welfare state. For the modern states' rights philosophy, with its primary objective the protection of vested interests, could hardly be acceptable to a political theorist who sought to defend the rights of the many against political and economic power in the hands of the few.

Despite the remarkable changes affecting the purposes of states' rights doctrine in American history, the methods of achieving these purposes have remained essentially the same. Political argument based upon alleged constitutional scruples has been for over sixteen decades the big gun in the states' rights polemical arsenal.

One of the most important of the states' rights constitutional arguments concerns the legitimacy of the Supreme Court's power to render definitive decisions in conflicts between the federal government and the states, or between individuals and states which denied them rights guaranteed by the Federal Constitution. Whether the decisions were those in the notable *M'Culloch* or *Cohens*[2] cases in the early nineteenth century or those of the "Tidelands Oil" or racial segregation cases[3] in the middle of the twentieth century, the consistent states' rights reaction has been to deny that the Supreme Court had constitutional authority to render such decisions.[4] The continued vitality of this old constitutional argument was strikingly illustrated on March 12, 1956, when Senator Walter George introduced a manifesto signed by nineteen Senators and seventy-seven Representatives from the Southern states.[5] The manifesto referred to the Supreme Court's decision in *Brown v. Board of Education*[6] as "judicial usurpation," a substitution of "naked power for

† Assistant Professor, Department of Political Science, State University of Iowa.

1. Harris, States' Rights and Vested Interests, 15 J. of Politics 457-71 (1953).
2. M'Culloch v. Maryland, 17 U.S. (4 Wheat.) 415 (1819), and Cohens v. Virginia, 19 U.S. (6 Wheat.) 264 (1821), respectively.
3. United States v. Louisiana, 339 U.S. 699 (1950), and Brown v. Bd. of Educ., 347 U.S. 483 (1955), respectively.
4. 1 Warren, The Supreme Court in United States History 487-88, 495 (1937); Dodd, Chief Justice Marshall and Virginia, 1813-1821, 12 Am. Hist. Rev. 782-85 (1907).
5. 102 Cong. Rec. 3948 (1956).
6. 347 U.S. 483 (1955).

established law" and an "unwarranted exercise of power . . . contrary to the Constitution."[7]

Although the supporters of this manifesto made no attempt to formulate serious theoretical or historical arguments to buttress their charge of judicial usurpation, they may properly be considered the intellectual heirs of the constitutional argument of John C. Calhoun. For in advocating the repeal of the twenty-fifth section of the Judiciary Act of 1789, Calhoun unequivocally denied that the framers of the Constitution had chosen the Supreme Court as federal umpire.[8]

The challenges of judicial usurpation of the power to arbitrate in federal-state relations, whether made by a Calhoun or one of his modern successors such as Byrnes or Talmadge, are susceptible to historical examination. The record of history unequivocally demolishes these challenges.

The conception of a powerful judicial body maintaining a division of powers between a government of a whole nation and governments of its parts or sections did not appear miraculously to the Justices of the Supreme Court after the adoption of the Constitution. It was clearly understood and partially applied during the period when America was a colony of Great Britain and under the old Articles of Confederation.

The British Empire maintained the fiction that it was a unitary system until after the American Revolution, but the Empire's relationships with the thirteen colonies had, in reality, become essentially federal. The government of the whole Empire, that of Great Britain, had been forced by the pressure of European wars and great distances to leave most problems of domestic legislation and administration to the governments of the "parts" of the Empire, notably the American colonial governments. Naturally enough, the development of local autonomy in the colonies led to conflicts of authority between the mother country and the colonies as well as among the colonies themselves. It was a quasi-judicial institution of the British Empire, the Committee on Trade and Plantations of the British Privy Council, which resolved such conflicts.[9]

After the American colonies broke with Great Britain, a new problem arose, that of balancing the powers of the states and the new central government in North America. A temporary solution was found in the creation of a confederate system. The old Articles of Confederation established a very limited form of judicial arbitration in two narrow fields, the settlement of disputes between the states and the settlement of disputes between the Confederation Congress and the states concerning cases of capture at sea.

The first category of disputes was to be settled in accordance with

7. 102 Cong. Rec. 3948 (1956).

8. Discourse on the Constitution and Government of the United States, 1 Works of John C. Calhoun 238 (Cralle ed. 1851).

9. The Committee later became the Board of Trade. Dickerson, American Colonial Government, 1695-1765, at 225 (1912); McLaughlin, The Background of American Federalism, 12 Am. Pol. Sci. Rev. (May 1918).

the ninth article of the Articles of Confederation. This provided that "the united states in Congress assembled shall also be the last resort on appeal in all disputes and differences now subsisting or that hereafter may arise between two or more states concerning boundary, jurisdiction or any other cause whatever. . . ." The parties to a dispute could be directed by Congress "to appoint by joint consent, commissioners or judges to constitute a court for hearing and determining the matter in question." Or if the disputing parties could not agree, Congress could itself make the appointments. The article further provided that "the judgment and sentence of the court . . . shall be final and conclusive. . . ."[10] A serious land dispute was peacefully resolved under this article in 1782.[11] Yet such a court of arbitration lacked permanence. Consequently, it was probably the second judicial institution created under the Confederation which was more influential in the evolution of the judicial arbiter concept in American federalism. For the Court of Appeals in cases of capture was a permanent judicial body which heard 118 cases before the Articles of Confederation were replaced by the new Federal Constitution. A member of this court, Judge John Lowell, made the experiences of this judicial body available to the constitutional framers in 1787 and to the Senate in 1789, sketching a plan for a federal judiciary in a letter to some of the framers and later, in 1789, giving his counsel and advice to the Senate Judiciary Committee.[12]

During the waning years of the Confederation itself, serious attention was given to various proposals to establish a more powerful central judiciary capable of putting an end to state encroachments on or defiance of the authority of the Confederation government. Although these proposals never were adopted by the Confederation, they do provide unmistakable evidence that political leaders of this era were fully aware of the potentialities of a judicial arbiter in confederate or federal governmental systems. A confederation congress committee report, submitted in 1786 by Charles Pinckney, contained, in essence, a complete arrangement for creation of a federal court capable of umpiring federal-state disputes. Pinckney's committee suggested that the Confederation Congress be authorized:

> . . . to institute a federal judicial court for trying and punishing all officers appointed by congress for all crimes, offenses, and misbehavior in their offices, and to which court an appeal shall be allowed from the judicial courts of the several states in all causes wherein any question shall arise on the meaning and construction of treaties entered into by the United States with any foreign power, or on any law of nations, or wherein any question shall arise respecting any regulations that may hereafter be made by congress

10. Documents of American History 113 (Commager ed. 1934).
11. Jensen, The New Nation: A History of the United States During the Federation, 1781-1789, at 335-37 (1950).
12. Jameson, The Predecessor of the Supreme Court, in Essays in the Constitutional History of the United States in the Formative Period, 1775-1789, at 3-44 (1889).

> relative to trade and commerce, or the collection of federal revenues pursuant to powers that shall be vested in that body, or wherein questions of importance may arise, and the United States shall be a party. . . .[13]

Similar ideas for strengthening the confederation government through creation of some sort of federal judicial arbiter were formulated or discussed by Rufus King,[14] James Madison,[15] and Nathan Dane.[16] Just prior to the Philadelphia Convention of 1787, however, a significantly different argument was discussed widely. Instead of viewing a federal judicial arbiter as primarily a defender of the central government, a broadly circulated pamphlet proposed that:

> In order to prevent an oppressive exercise of powers deposited with Congress, a jurisdiction should be established to interpose and determine between the individual States and the Federal body upon all disputed points, and being stiled The Equalizing Court, should be constituted and conducted in the following manner. . . .

This proposal appeared in the *Pennsylvania Gazette* in Philadelphia on June 6, 1787 and was republished in the leading newspapers during the early days of the Convention.[17] Thus, while supporters of the idea of a strong national government had begun to favor the judicial arbiter concept as a means of restraining the states, those who feared the encroachments of a strong national government had begun to look upon a strong judicial system as a protector of individual and states rights. Recognition of this development makes more understandable the absence of states' rights or anti-Federalist opposition to most of the proposals made in the Convention which strengthened the federal judiciary.

One of the major reasons for holding the Philadelphia Convention had been the necessity to find a remedy for the evils arising from state legislation which hurt or interfered with the interests of other states, infringed treaties made by the Confederation Congress, oppressed individuals, or invaded the sphere of authority of the confederation government. The convention delegates were faced with the task of finding suitable means of restraining such state legislation or action. Despite the fact that the idea of a judicial arbiter was understood and widely discussed before the opening of the Convention, the creation of a high federal court to solve this problem was by no means a foregone conclusion. Years after the close of the Convention, James Madison referred

---

13. Quoted in 2 Bancroft, History of the Formation of the Constitution, 376-77 (1903).

14. Letter to Jonathan Jackson, September 3, 1786, as quoted by Warren, op. cit. supra note 4, at 5.

15. Letter to George Washington, April 16, 1787, as quoted by Carson, The History of the Supreme Court 88 (1891). Madison deemed the judicial arbiter of secondary importance to a congressional negative of state laws; however, see Rufus King's letter referred to in note 14 supra.

16. Published in the Independent Gazetter, November 30, 1786, as quoted by Warren, The Making of the Constitution 319 (1929).

17. Id. at 169.

to the situation in the following manner: " . . . [T]he obvious necessity of a control on the laws of the States so far as they might violate the Constitution and laws of the United States left no option, but as to mode . . . ," noting as the three possible choices "a veto [executive] on the passage of the State laws, a Congressional repeal of them, a judicial annulment of them."[18]

Analysis of the record of the Philadelphia Convention underscores the fact that the granting of power to the Federal Supreme Court to arbitrate finally in federal-state relations came about through a complex series of developments. Basically they represented a compromise between the strong nationalists who originally wanted a veto over the states vested in the new national legislature or executive and the states' righters who either opposed such supervision of the states or preferred that such power be vested, in what they considered, a weaker and more impartial agency, notably the supreme federal court suggested in the original Paterson Plan.

Among the more important of these developments were (a) the repudiation of coercion of the states by force and the adoption of coercion of individuals by law, (b) the readiness of every major bloc in the Convention to set up a federal judiciary, (c) the demands of one powerful group for a system of inferior federal tribunals, (d) the defeat of the congressional negative proposals and the substitution by Luther Martin of a supremacy clause, and (e) the tendency to look upon a federal judiciary as a protector of individual and states rights which was reflected in the proposals for a Council of Revision. Very often these developments seemed totally unrelated, but their cumulative effect was the granting of final interpretive powers in federal-state relations to a supreme federal tribunal.

A provision for a congressional veto of state laws was prominent among the resolutions for the Union presented by Edmund Randolph at the opening session of the Convention. It provided "That the national legislature ought to be empowered . . . to negative all laws, passed by the several States, contravening, in the opinion of the national legislature, the articles of union." Later, on May 31, the Convention, in committee of the whole house, amended it by addition of the phrase "or any treaties subsisting under the authority of the Union." The entire resolution was agreed to by the committee without debate or dissent.[19] However, when this resolution was reported from the committee to the Convention on July 17, it met with violent opposition. Gouverneur Morris thought such power "likely to be terrible to the States"; Luther Martin considered it improper; and Sherman believed that since the state courts would hold invalid any laws contravening the authority of the Union, such a veto would be unnecessary. Madison and Charles Pinckney did not share Sherman's confidence in the state courts, however, and held

18. Letter to Nicholas P. Trist, 1831, as quoted by id. at 318.
19. 1 Records of the Federal Convention 54 (Farrand ed. 1911).

that the congressional negative was necessary as, in the words of Madison, "the most mild and certain means of preserving the harmony of the system." In spite of Madison's appeal, the Convention defeated the proposal for a congressional negative on state laws by a vote of seven to three.[20]

Even before the rejection of the congressional negative by the Convention on July 17, there was clear-cut evidence that the advocates of a strong central government were prepared to limit the congressional negative by providing for final appeal to a national judiciary. As early as July 10, Randolph had sent Madison a list of concessions to be used "as an accommodating proposition to small states" which then were bitterly opposed to the principle of representation based upon population.[21] In terms of the judicial arbiter concept, the fourth and fifth of Randolph's proposals were particularly significant, because they clearly anticipated the Supreme Court's modern role as both a federal umpire and as a defender of individual rights against state infringement. His suggestions provided:

> IV. That although every negative given to the law of a particular state shall prevent its operation, any state may appeal to the national judiciary against a negative, and that such negative if adjudged to be contrary to the powers granted by the articles of the Union, shall be void.
>
> V. That any individual, conceiving himself injured or oppressed by the partiality or injustice of a law of any particular state, may resort to the national judiciary, who may adjudge such a law to be void, if found contrary to the principles of equity and justice.[22]

Randolph was prepared to offer these conciliatory proposals to the Convention on July 16, but did not do so because of the victory of the small states, on that day, in securing equal voting rights in the Senate.[23]

Throughout the course of the Philadelphia Convention the major discussions of the federal judicial arbiter were generally related to the nationalists' attempts to gain approval for the congressional negative of state laws. However, other discussions in the Convention also contributed to the evolution of the supreme federal tribunal. The proposals for a council of revision, composed of the chief executive and judges of the highest national court, while eventually defeated, stimulated discussion of the power of judicial review.[24] Rejection by the Convention of

---

20. 2 id. at 27-28.

21. 3 id. at 55; see also Brant, James Madison, Father of the Constitution, 1781-1800, at 63-100 (1950).

22. Published in 5 Elliot, Debates of the State Ratifying Conventions 579-80 (1901).

23. 2 Farrand, op. cit. supra note 19, at 17-18.

24. During these debates, Mercer of Maryland unequivocally opposed "the Doctrine that the judges as expositors of the Constitution should have authority to declare a law void." 2 id. at 298-99. Mercer's stand represents the only instance within the Convention of direct opposition to the granting of power to judges (but not a council of revision composed of the judges and the executive) to negative unconstitutional laws. 1 id. at 93-94, 96-97, 138-40 and 2 id. at 73, 76, 298-99.

the proposals to coerce the states by force, contained in both the Randolph and Paterson Plans, were followed by adoption of the principle of direct coercion of individuals by the national government itself. This solution reflected the recognition by Convention leaders of the need to discover a peaceful mode of limiting state interference with national authority.[25] The initiative in finding such a solution was now taken by the leaders of the small states bloc in the Convention, many of whom were of states' rights persuasion.

Using as their starting point a clause from the Paterson Plan guaranteeing the supremacy of the national government within the sphere of its legitimate authority, states' rights supporters attempted to placate the nationalists who were bitterly disappointed by the defeat of the congressional negative proposal on July 17. Luther Martin submitted what he undoubtedly considered a mild substitute for such a negative.[26] His original proposal stated:

> . . . [T]hat the Legislative acts of the United States made by virtue and in pursuance of the Articles of Union, and all treaties made and ratified under the authority of the United States shall be the supreme law of the respective States, as far as those acts or treaties shall relate to the said states, or their citizens and inhabitants—and that the Judiciaries of the several States shall be bound thereby in their decision, anything in the respective laws of the individual States to the contrary notwithstanding.[27]

Later, the nationalists in the Convention changed this relatively mild resolution in several important respects. These amendments were made in the closing days of the Convention in August and September. On August 5, 1787, the Convention's committee on detail had compressed Martin's resolution and made two significant changes—federal laws were declared supreme over state constitutions as well as state laws, and the duty to uphold the supreme law was imposed on "the Judges in the several States" instead of on "the Judiciaries of the respective states." On August 23, John Rutledge proposed the following important addition: "This Constitution and the laws of the United States made in pursuance thereof . . . shall be the supreme law of the several states."

25. 1 id. at 21, 34, 54, 165, 245, 256, 320, 339-40.

26. Later, in his "Reply to the Landholder," March 18, 1788, Martin pointed out, bitterly, that, "When this clause was introduced, it was not established that inferior continental courts should be appointed for trial of all questions arising on treaties and on the laws of the general government, and it was my wish and hope that every question of that kind would have been determined in the first instance in the courts of the respective states; had this been the case, the propriety and the necessity that treaties duly made and ratified, and the laws of the general government, should be binding on the state judiciaries which were to decide upon them, must be evident to every capacity, while at the same time, if such treaties or laws were inconsistent with our [i.e. the state] constitution and bill of rights, the judiciaries of this state would be bound to respect the first and abide by the last, since in the form I introduçed the clause, notwithstanding treaties and laws of the general government were intended to be superior to the laws of our state government, were [sic] they should be opposed to each other, yet that they were not proposed nor meant to be superior to our constitution and bill of rights. It was afterwards altered and amended to the form in which it stands in the system now published . . . ." 3 id. at 287.

27. 2 id. at 28-29.

Thus the Constitution was made judicially enforceable law. The Convention adopted his proposal without debate.[28] Finally, on September 12, the committee on style completed the final draft of the Constitution. Luther Martin's resolution had become a part of Article VI. From the point of view of federal-state relations this was the crucial provision in the fundamental document. Section three of that article read:

> This Constitution, and the laws of the United States which shall be made in pursuance thereof; and all treaties made, or which shall be made, under the authority of the United States, shall be the supreme law of the land; and the judges in every state shall be bound thereby, anything in the Constitution or laws or any state to the contrary notwithstanding.

Defeat of the congressional negative plan left the Convention with two institutional alternatives for the enforcement of national supremacy. The first was an ultra-nationalistic suggestion put forth by Alexander Hamilton in his plan for union. Section ten of the plan provided that "all laws of the particular States contrary to the Constitution or laws of the United States to be utterly void; and the better to prevent such laws being passed, the Governour or president of each state shall be appointed by the General Government and shall have a negative upon the laws about to be passed in the state of which he is Governour or President."[29] Hamilton's alternative was not even seriously considered by the Convention. The second was the judicial arbiter which had been an integral part of the original Paterson Plan. Section five had provided "that a federal judiciary be established to consist of a supreme tribunal the judges of which to be appointed by the Executive. . . ." Section two of the same plan proposed that violations of acts of the federal congress be tried in the first instance in "the superior Common Law Judiciary" of the state concerned, "subject . . . for the correction of all errors, both in law and fact . . . , to an appeal to the Judiciary of the United States."[30]

Actually, every major plan for union—Randolph's, Hamilton's and Paterson's—had provided for a national judicial system. The essential difference between the nationalistic plans of Randolph and Hamilton and the states' rights plan of Paterson is that the latter failed to provide a system of inferior federal courts.[31] The nationalists did not actually oppose the adoption of a judicial arbiter, but merely felt, as James Wilson later indicated, that a judicial check on the states would not be sufficient to maintain a strong central government. On August 10, 1787, Charles Pinckney grudgingly admitted that the federal judges "will even be the Umpires between the United States and individual states as well as between one State and another."[32] However, a few days later, on August 23, he tenaciously sought to reinstate the congressional negative, but was

28. 2 id. at 389.
29. 1 id. at 293.
30. 1 id. at 243-44.
31. 1 id. at 21, 243-44, 292.
32. 2 id. at 248.

defeated by a six to five vote. In urging support for Pinckney's motion, Wilson recognized impliedly that in the absence of a congressional negative, the national judiciary would seek to maintain the supremacy of the national government. This he felt was not enough because "the firmness of Judges is not of itself sufficient. Something further is requisite—it will be better to prevent the passage of an improper law, than to declare it void when passed."[33]

A letter exchange between Thomas Jefferson and James Madison concerning the relative merits of the congressional negative and the judicial arbiter illustrates clearly the contrasting positions of the states' righters and the nationalists. Although he did not attend the Convention, Jefferson was representative of those who, while they feared establishment of a national government in which all authority would be centralized, realized quite clearly that some degree of centralized control was necessary to bring stability to the then chaotic thirteen states. In his reply to Madison's inquiry concerning a congressional negative on state laws, Jefferson presented a viewpoint which might be taken as indicative of the attitude of other advocates of strictly limited government. He wrote:

> The negative proposed to be given them on all the acts of the several Legislatures is now for the first time suggested to my mind. Prima Facie I do not like it. It fails in an essential character, that the hole and the patch should be commensurate; but this proposes to mend a small hole by covering the whole garment. . . . Would not an appeal from the state judicatures to a federal court in all cases where the act of Confederation controlled the question, be as effectual a remedy, and exactly commensurate to the defect?[34]

On the other hand, the advocates of a strong central government, while favoring the granting of broad judicial powers, had realized that judicial nullification of state laws was possible only when federal questions arose in bona fide cases before the new Supreme Court. Madison's letter to Jefferson after the close of the Convention indicated that the lack of assurance he shared with other strong government advocates. He wrote:

> It may be said that the Judicial authority under our new system will keep the states within their proper limits and supply the place of a negative on their laws. The answer is that it is more convenient to prevent the passage of a law than to declare it void, after it is passed; that this will be particularly the case, where the law aggrieves individuals who may be unable to support an appeal against a state to the Supreme Judiciary, that a state which would violate the legislative rights of the Union would not be very ready to obey a Judicial decree in support of them, and that a recurrence to force, which in the event of disobedience would be necessary, is an evil which the new Constitution meant to exclude as far as possible.

33. 2 id. at 390-91.
34. To Madison, June 20, 1787, as quoted by Warren, op. cit. supra note 16, at 168-69.

> A Constitutional negative on the laws of the states seems equally necessary to secure individuals against encroachments on their rights. The mutability of the laws of the States is found to be a serious evil.[35]

After the final defeat of the congressional negative in the Convention on August 23, the nationalists determined to make the best of an unhappy situation by strengthening the federal arbiter by means of grants of broad constitutional jurisdiction and through institution of a complete system of inferior federal courts. The extension of the Supreme Court's jurisdiction to all cases, state and federal, arising under the Constitution was made without states' rights argument. But the attempt at creation of a system of inferior federal courts aroused such fierce opposition that the nationalists were compelled to accept a compromise by which the establishment of such courts was left to the discretion of the new Congress.[36]

Nationalist bitterness at the substitution of a judicial arbiter for their cherished congressional negative persisted to the end of the Convention. For example, on September 12, James Madison supported a motion by Mason which provided that the clause relating to export duties be amended to allow the states to lay such duties for "the sole purpose of defraying the charges of inspecting, packing, storing and indemnifying the losses in keeping the commodities in the care of public officers before exportation." Gorham and Langdon had asked: "How was redress to be obtained in case duties should be laid beyond the purpose expressed?" Madison coldly replied that "[t]here will be the same security as in other cases—The jurisdiction of the Supreme Court must be the source of redress. So far only had provision been made by the plan against injurious acts of the States. His own opinion was, that this was insufficient,—A negative on the State laws alone could meet all the shapes which these could assume. But this had been overruled."[37]

The Philadelphia Convention record indicates unmistakably that the new Supreme Court had been clearly designated the final judicial arbiter in federal-state relations and that it was primarily the states' righters in the Convention who had brought this to pass. The nationalists had not opposed the creation of the judicial arbiter, but had felt strongly that a national judiciary would not, by itself, be strong enough to cope with state encroachments on national authority.

In spite of their misgivings, the advocates of strong central government did not let lack of confidence in a federal judiciary weaken their efforts to secure ratification of the Constitution. Two of the contributions to the *Federalist* by Madison and Hamilton were devoted to an examination of the proposed judicial arbiter, its purposes and its impartial character.[38] Within the state ratifying conventions, the national-

35. To Jefferson, October 24, 1787, as quoted by id. at 324.
36. Id. at 326, 334-38.
37. 2 Farrand, op. cit. supra note 19, at 588-89.
38. The Federalist No.'s 39 & 80, at 238, 494-95 (Lodge ed. 1904).

ists frequently found themselves the staunchest defenders of the same judicial arbiter for which they had indicated only luke-warm enthusiasm during the Philadelphia Convention; for serious states' rights objections were raised to certain provisions of the judicial clauses in the new Constitution, notably those concerning the possible establishment of a system of inferior federal courts and those extending federal jurisdiction to suits between a state and individuals.[39] In five of the more important of the state ratifying conventions—Connecticut,[40] North Carolina,[41] Virginia,[42] Pennsylvania,[43] and South Carolina[44]—the new Supreme Court's function of resolving state and federal conflicts was discussed clearly and ultimately was accepted. In virtually all of the ratifying conventions some jurisdictional grants to the new federal court system were subjected to severe criticism. Out-and-out opponents of the Constitution, such as Robert Yates of New York, recognized the scope of the Supreme Court's power and made the judicial grants a major point for attack on the proposed new system of government. Under the pseudonym of "Brutus," Yates wrote that "the opinions of the Supreme Court . . . will have the force of law; because there is no power provided in the Constitution that can correct their errors or control their jurisdiction. From this court there is no appeal."[45] But in the end, the nationalists managed to secure early ratification in all of the most important states.

These facts stand out as a result of this analysis of the Philadelphia Convention and the state ratifying conventions. Both the nationalists and the states' righters were in substantial agreement on the need for a supreme judicial arbiter in federal-state relations. By 1789 it was clearly understood that the Supreme Court of the United States was to fulfill that role. Naturally enough, the nationalists tended to emphasize the aspect of judicial arbitership concerned with the protection of national supremacy against state encroachments. However, both nationalists and states' righters explicitly recognized that the Supreme Court's role was that of an *impartial* arbiter. Thus, it was also anticipated that federal laws violative of states' rights were to be declared unconstitutional. The prevailing contemporary conception of the new Supreme Court's role is best illustrated by Oliver Ellsworth's description in the Connecticut Ratifying Convention of January, 1788:

> This Constitution defines the extent of the powers of the general government. If the general legislature should at any time overleap their limits, the judicial department is a constitutional check. If the United States go beyond their powers, if they make a law which the Constitution does not authorize, it is void; and the

39. Willoughby, The Supreme Court 20-21 (1890).
40. 2 Elliot, op. cit. supra note 22, at 196.
41. 4 id. at 155.
42. 3 id. at 532.
43. 2 id. at 408-09, 439-40, 445-46, 468-69, 478, 480-81.
44. 4 id. at 257-58.
45. As quoted by Davis, Annulment of Legislation by the Supreme Court, 7 Am. Pol. Sci. Rev. 577 (Nov. 1913).

judicial power, the national judges, who, to secure their impartiality, are to be made independent, will declare it to be void. On the other hand, if the states go beyond their limits, if they make a law which is a usurpation upon the general government, the law is void; and upright, independent judges will declare it so.[46]

On March 4, 1789, the wheels of the new central government began to turn; but for eleven months after the United States came into existence, it lacked a judicial branch of government. Although the first judiciary bill was introduced the very next day after the new Senate was organized, it was six months before the bill became law and before President Washington could appoint members to the first Supreme Court.[47]

While the constitutional framers had drawn the broad outlines of the judicial power, they had left to congressional discretion the composition of the federal courts, the extent of the appellate jurisdiction of the Supreme Court, the existence or nonexistence of any inferior federal courts and the extent of their jurisdiction. Consequently, the manner in which the first Congress dealt with these problems in the Judiciary Act of September 24, 1789, set the pattern for subsequent development of the federal judicial system. This act was especially important because without broad grants of appellate jurisdiction to the Supreme Court by Congress, the entire judicial arbiter plan would have fallen into abeyance for lack of implementation.

The first judiciary act was largely the product of the Senate Judiciary Committee, and within the committee, Oliver Ellsworth and William Paterson took leading roles in drafting the bill. In the early stages of this drafting, Ellsworth sought to establish a complete network of inferior federal courts and to extend their jurisdiction to the limits set by the Constitution. However, to secure the concurrence of Richard Henry Lee, Ellsworth apparently had to accept a more limited inferior federal court system. This setback was mitigated by inclusion of a provision which allowed a defendant sued in a state court in a case involving a federal question to remove the case to a federal circuit court, or to appeal to the Supreme Court, by writ of error, after trial in the highest court of law or equity in a state in which a decision in the suit could be had.[48]

When debate on the draft bill began in the Senate in committee of the whole, on June 22, the issue centered around the question whether there should be any district courts at all or whether the functions of executing federal laws should be left in the first instance to the state courts. Ellsworth had been opposed to giving the state courts such power on the grounds discussed in a letter he wrote later on the subject. He felt that "to annex to State Courts jurisdiction which they had not before, as of admiralty cases, and perhaps, of offenses against the

46. 2 Elliot, op. cit. supra note 22, at 196.

47. Warren, The First Decade of the Supreme Court of the United States, 7 U. Chi. L. Rev. 631 (1940).

48. Warren, New Light on the History of the Federal Judiciary Act of 1789, 37 Harv. L. Rev. 49 (1923).

United States, would be constituting the Judges of them, *pro tanto*, Federal Judges, and of course they would continue such during good behavior, and on fixed salaries, which in many cases, would illy comport with their present tenure of office. Besides, if the State Courts, as such, could take cognizance of those offenses, it might not be safe for the General Government to put the trial and punishment of them entirely out of its own hands."[49]

Debate over the various proposals in the bill raged for three months in the Senate and the House. The crucial issues were whether there should be any inferior federal courts, and, if there were to be any such courts, whether the Constitution required that they be vested with the full jurisdiction which the Constitution permitted. In its final form the bill was a compromise. The nationalists were forced to abandon their contention that the federal courts be granted the broadest jurisdiction possible under the Constitution, while the states' righters were unable to confine federal cases to state courts, subject only to final appeal to the new federal Supreme Court. Section twenty-five, which became the very cornerstone of federal judicial supremacy, established the appellate jurisdiction of the Supreme Court over state courts where such courts decided against a claimed federal right. Significantly, the states' righters in Congress actually advocated this crucial grant of jurisdiction in 1789.[50]

In sum, the modern states' rights charges of federal "judicial usurpation" of power to arbitrate in federal-state relations may be viewed as a particularly persistent bit of political mythology. For examination of the Philadelphia Convention, the state ratifying conventions, and the legislative history of the first judiciary act indicates unmistakably that the framers clearly intended that the Supreme Court be given responsibility for umpiring the federal system,[51] that the federal judicial arbiter was

49. To Law, August 4, 1789 as quoted by Warren, id. at 66.

50. Id. at 102-05.

51. For arguments in opposition to this interpretation see Harris, Judicial Review in the United States of America, 56 Dick. L. Rev. 177 (1952), and 2 Crosskey, Politics and the Constitution, at 1008-1046 (1953). Harris alleged that the constitutional framers denied to the Supreme Court the power of judicial review. His account of the Philadelphia Convention is, however, inaccurate because it overlooks a great deal of evidence contradicting his thesis and misinterprets major developments in rather startling fashion. Professor Crosskey's position may be summed up as follows: With a single exception, "Our *entire* record of what was said on the subject of judicial review, in the Federal Convention, consists of parts of James Madison's notes . . . since the man in question was not . . . a very credible witness on this particular subject, the possibility that his testimony may have been, not inadvertently, but deliberately, false and misleading . . . is one that cannot lightly be passed over . . . ." Later Crosskey asserted that "apart from Madison's own notes, [there is] virtually no known evidence relating to the Convention which even vaguely suggests" the view that the Supreme Court was granted power to act as an "ultimate guardian" between the nation and the states. (2 Politics and the Constitution at 1009-10.)

Madison's reliability as a recorder of the proceedings of the Philadelphia Convention remains unshaken by Crosskey's attack at least with regard to his notes relating to the judicial powers. For even if one were to disregard Madison's notes on the evolution of the judicial arbiter in federal-state relations, the letters and public statements of opponents (such as Luther Martin and Robert Yates), and supporters (such as Charles Pinckney, James Wilson, Alexander Hamilton, William Davie and Oliver Ellsworth) indicated unmistakably a conception of the judicial arbiter similar to Madison's. (See notes 26, 40-44

understood and accepted by the more important of the state ratifying conventions, and that appellate jurisdiction necessary for the fulfillment of its responsibilities was granted the Supreme Court by the first Congress.

Ironically, it was the states' righters of that era—the anti-Federalists—who were largely responsible for the acceptance of the judicial arbiter in the Philadelphia Convention. Similarly, they strongly supported its implementation in the first Congress. Later their basic assumption, gloomily shared by many nationalists, that the federal judicial arbiter would be a rather mild check on state authority proved to be false. And later, the confidence of the states' righters in the impartiality of the Supreme Court was shaken, particularly during the tenure of Chief Justice John Marshall. But during the formative period, 1786-1789, both the states' righters and the nationalists, the former with confidence, the latter with grave misgivings, had accepted the new Supreme Court as the arbiter in federal-state relations.

---

supra.) Significantly, all of these individuals were, like Madison, members of the Philadelphia Convention.

RACIST SPEECH, DEMOCRACY, AND THE FIRST AMENDMENT

ROBERT C. POST*

The curse of racism continues to haunt the Nation. Everywhere we face its devastation, the bitter legacy of, in William Lloyd Garrison's prophetic words, our "covenant with death and . . . agreement with Hell."[1] This is the living consequence of the history that has produced us. We cannot overcome that history without changing ourselves and therefore also our legal order. Since *Brown v. Board of Education*[2] vast stretches of our law have passed through the flame of this challenge.[3] The question is always what to preserve, what to alter.

Now it is the turn of the first amendment. Largely inspired by Richard Delgado's article, *Words That Wound*,[4] the past few years have witnessed an extraordinary spate of articles analyzing the constitutionality of restrictions on racist speech.[5] This anal-

---

* Professor of Law, School of Law (Boalt Hall), University of California at Berkeley. B.A., Harvard College, 1969; J.D., Yale University, 1977; Ph.D., Harvard University, 1980.
I am deeply indebted to the many friends and colleagues who read the manuscript of this essay: Alexander Aleinikoff, Richard Delgado, Melvin Eisenberg, Cynthia Fuchs Epstein, Bryan Ford, Angela Harris, Sanford Kadish, Kenneth Karst, Mari Matsuda, Frank Michelman, Martha Minow, Paul Mishkin, Rachel Moran, John Powell, Terrance Sandalow, Joseph Sax, Philip Selznick, Reva Siegel, Jerome Skolnick, Jan Vetter, James Weinstein, and Franklin Zimring.

1. D. DUMOND, ANTISLAVERY: THE CRUSADE FOR FREEDOM IN AMERICA 273 (1961) (quoting William Lloyd Garrison).

2. 347 U.S. 483 (1954).

3. For a representative discussion, see Fiss, *Foreword: The Forms of Justice*, 93 HARV. L. REV. 1 (1979).

4. Delgado, *Words That Wound: A Tort Action for Racial Insults, Epithets, and Name-Calling*, 17 HARV. C.R.-C.L. L. REV. 133 (1982) [hereinafter Delgado, *Words That Wound*]; *see* Heins, *Banning Words: A Comment on "Words That Wound,"* 18 HARV. C.R.-C.L. L. REV. 585 (1983); Delgado, *Professor Delgado Replies*, 18 HARV. C.R.-C.L. L. REV. 593 (1983).

5. Delgado, *Campus Antiracism Rules: Constitutional Narratives in Collision*, 85 NW. U.L. REV. 343 (1990); Gale, *On Curbing Racial Speech*, RESPONSIVE COMMUNITY, Winter 1990-91, at 47; Glass, *Anti-Racism and Unlimited Freedom of Speech: An Untenable Dualism*, 8 CAN. J. PHIL. 559 (1978); Grano, *Free Speech v. the University of Michigan*, ACADEMIC QUESTIONS, Spring 1990, at 7; Greenawalt, *Insults and Epithets: Are They Protected Speech?*, 42 RUTGERS L. REV. 287 (1991); Grey, *Civil Rights vs. Civil Liberties: The Case of Discriminatory Verbal Harassment*, SOC. PHIL. & POL'Y, Spring 1991, at 81; Hughes, *Prohibiting Incitement to Racial Discrimination*, 16 U. TORONTO L.J. 361 (1966); Jones, *Article 4 of the International Convention on the Elimination of All Forms of Racial Discrimination and the First Amendment*, 23 HOW. L.J. 429 (1980); Kretzmer, *Freedom of Speech and Racism*, 8 CARDOZO L. REV. 445 (1987); *Language as Violence v. Freedom of Expression: Canadian and American Perspectives on Group Defamation*, 37 BUFFALO L.

ysis is not merely academic. Motivated by an alarming increase in racist incidents,[6] universities throughout the Nation have turned toward the task of restraining racist expression.[7] The justification for these restraints, and their relationship to first amendment values, has become a matter of intense controversy.[8]

One approach has been to attempt to use legal regulation to eradicate all visible signs of that "racist sentiment" which, in the view of some, our history has caused to "pervade[ ] the life of virtually all white Americans."[9] The rules of the University of

REV. 337 (1989) [hereinafter *Language as Violence*]; Lasson, *Racial Defamation as Free Speech: Abusing the First Amendment*, 17 COLUM. HUM. RTS. L. REV. 11 (1985) [hereinafter Lasson, *Racial Defamation*]; Lasson, *Group Libel Versus Free Speech: When Big Brother* Should *Butt In*, 23 DUQ. L. REV. 77 (1984) [hereinafter Lasson, *Group Libel*]; Lawrence, *If He Hollers Let Him Go: Regulating Racist Speech on Campus*, 1990 DUKE L.J. 431; Love, *Discriminatory Speech and the Tort of Intentional Infliction of Emotional Distress*, 47 WASH. & LEE L. REV. 123 (1990); Matsuda, *Public Response to Racist Speech: Considering the Victim's Story*, 87 MICH. L. REV. 2320 (1989); Minow, *On Neutrality, Equality, & Tolerance: New Norms for a Decade of Distinction*, CHANGE, Jan.-Feb. 1990, at 17; Partlett, *From Red Lion Square to Skokie to the Fatal Shore: Racial Defamation and Freedom of Speech*, 22 VAND. J. TRANSNAT'L L. 431 (1989); Richardson, *Racism: A Tort of Outrage*, 61 OR. L. REV. 267 (1982); Smolla, *Rethinking First Amendment Assumptions About Racist and Sexist Speech*, 47 WASH. & LEE L. REV. 171 (1990); Strossen, *Regulating Racist Speech on Campus: A Modest Proposal*, 1990 DUKE L.J. 484; Wedgwood, *Freedom of Expression and Racial Speech*, 8 TEL AVIV U. STUD. L. 325 (1988); Wright, *Racist Speech and the First Amendment*, 9 MISS. C. L. REV. 1 (1988); Note, *A Communitarian Defense of Group Libel Laws*, 101 HARV. L. REV. 682 (1988); Note, *The University of California Hate Speech Policy: A Good Heart in Ill-Fitting Garb*, 12 J. COMM. & ENT. L. 593 (1990); Comment, *Freedom From Fear*, 15 LINCOLN L. REV. 45 (1984) (authored by Kammy Au); Edelman, *Punishing Perpetrators of Racist Speech*, Legal Times, May 15, 1989, at 20.

6. *See, e.g.*, H. EHRLICH, CAMPUS ETHNOVIOLENCE AND THE POLICY OPTIONS 41-72 (1990); Gibbs, *Bigots in the Ivory Tower: An Alarming Rise in Hatred Roils U.S. Campuses*, TIME, May 7, 1990, at 104.

7. David Rieff writes that 137 American universities "have in the past two years passed proscriptions on hate speech." Rieff, *The Case Against Sensitivity*, 114 ESQUIRE 120, 124 (1990). *See Lessons From Bigotry 101*, NEWSWEEK, Sept. 25, 1989, at 48; Wilson, *Colleges' Anti-Harassment Policies Bring Controversy Over Free-Speech Issues*, Chronicle of Higher Educ., Oct. 4, 1989, at A1; Fields, *Colleges Advised to Develop Strong Procedures to Deal With Incidents of Racial Harassment*, Chronicle of Higher Educ., July 20, 1988, at A11.

8. For a chronicle of the effect of this controversy on the American Civil Liberties Union (ACLU), see Hentoff, *The Colleges: Fear, Loathing, and Suppression*, Village Voice, May 8, 1990, at 20; Hentoff, *What's Happening to the ACLU?*, Village Voice, May 15, 1990, at 20; Hentoff, *Putting the First Amendment on Trial*, Village Voice, May 22, 1990, at 24; Hentoff, *A Dissonant First Amendment Fugue*, Village Voice, June 5, 1990, at 16; Hentoff, *An Endangered Species: A First Amendment Absolutist*, Village Voice, June 12, 1990, at 24; Hentoff, *The Civil Liberties Shootout*, Village Voice, June 19, 1990, at 26; *Policy Concerning Racist and Other Group-Based Harassment on College Campuses*, ACLU NEWSL., Aug.-Sept. 1990, at 2.

9. J. KOVEL, WHITE RACISM: A PSYCHOHISTORY 34 (1970); *see* Lawrence, *The Id, the Ego, and Equal Protection: Reckoning with Unconscious Racism*, 39 STAN. L. REV. 317, 321-26 (1987).

Connecticut, for example, plainly evince this remarkable ambition. These rules prohibit "[b]ehavior that denigrates others because of their race [or] ethnicity."[10] They provide that the "use of derogatory names, inappropriately directed laughter, inconsiderate jokes, anonymous notes or phone calls, and conspicuous exclusion from conversations and/or classroom discussions are examples of harassing behaviors that are prohibited."[11] The rules list the "signs" of proscribed "Harassment, Discrimination and Intolerance," some of which are

> Stereotyping the experiences, background, and skills of individuals
> Treating people differently solely because they are in some way different from the majority
> Responding to behaviors or situations negatively because of the background of the participants . . .
> Imitating stereotypes in speech or mannerisms . . .
> Attributing objections to any of the above actions to "hypersensitivity" of the targeted individual or group.[12]

These rules are plainly not designed to regulate specific forms of behavior or expression, but rather to encompass and to forbid all exterior "signs" of an interior frame of mind. One can readily understand the logic of this purpose. If our "common historical and cultural heritage" has made us "all racists,"[13] then racism must be seen as an unredeemed form of identity, whose every manifestation ought to be challenged and sanctioned. Punitive legal regulations are thus faced with the task of attempting to imagine and specify every possible indication of racism. But because the racist personality can express itself in an infinite

---

10. Department of Student Affairs, University of Connecticut, Protect Campus Pluralism (available from the Dean of Students Office, University of Connecticut). The regulations provide that "[e]very member of the University is obligated to refrain from actions that intimidate, humiliate, or demean persons or groups or that undermine their security or self-esteem." They define "harassment" as "abusive behavior directed toward an individual or group because of race, ethnicity, ancestry, national origin, religion, gender, sexual preference, age, physical or mental disabilities," and they prohibit "harassment that has the effect of interfering with an individual's performance or creating an intimidating, hostile or offensive environment." *Id.*

11. *Id.* The regulations continue: "All members of the University community are responsible for the maintenance of a positive environment in which everyone feels comfortable working and learning." *Id.*

12. *Id.* The regulations instruct a student to inform the "Discrimination and Intolerance Response Network" if "[y]ou have experienced or witnessed any of the signs" and to "[k]now that the University will not tolerate such behavior." *Id.*

13. Lawrence, *supra* note 9, at 322.

variety of ways, the task is intrinsically elusive. The University of Connecticut rules are clearly caught up in the frustrating spiral of this logic, a logic that, when carried to its conclusion, can end only in the complete legal subjugation of the individual.[14]

The incompatibility of this logic with even the most elementary standards of freedom of speech is obvious. Any communication can potentially express the racist self, and thus no communication can ever be safe from legal sanction. It is therefore no surprise that the University of Connecticut was forced to withdraw its regulations, although apparently with reluctance and distress, because of a threatened lawsuit.[15] If the ambition of legal regulation is to suppress manifestations of racist personality, the necessary consequence will be the wholesale abandonment of all principles of freedom of expression.

To the extent that we care about first amendment values, therefore, we must make do with more modest aspirations.[16] The possibility of effecting a reconciliation between principles of freedom of expression and restraints on racist speech depends upon deflecting our focus away from its spontaneous target, which is the racism of our cultural inheritance, and toward the redress of particular and distinct harms caused by racist expression. The specification of these harms will lead to the definition of discrete forms of speech, the legal regulation of which can then be assessed in light of relevant first amendment values.

---

14. One is reminded of the escalating efforts of the Inquisition in sixteenth-century Spain to discover and punish all external signs of inward backsliding on the part of Moors and Jews who had outwardly converted to Catholicism in order to avoid expulsion. These efforts eventually led the Inquisition to conclude that eating couscous or disliking pork were themselves punishable as heresy. *See* Root, *Speaking Christian: Orthodoxy and Difference in Sixteenth-Century Spain*, REPRESENTATIONS, Summer 1988, at 118, 126, 129.

15. Ravo, *Campus Slur Alters a Code Against Bias*, N.Y. Times, Dec. 11, 1989, at B1, B3.

16. Modest aspirations, however, will not be easy in the highly charged atmosphere of many universities. *See* Detlefsen, *White Like Me*, NEW REPUB., Apr. 10, 1989, at 18. The University of Connecticut is hardly unique in its use of punitive legal regulation to block all manifestations of racism. The Board of Regents of Higher Education of the Commonwealth of Massachusetts, for example, adopted on June 13, 1989 a "Policy Against Racism" that "prohibits all forms of racism." Board of Regents of Higher Education, Commonwealth of Massachusetts, Policy Against Racism and Guidelines for Campus Policies Against Racism 1 (June 13, 1989). This prohibition includes:

> all conditions and all actions or omissions including all acts of verbal harassment or abuse which deny or have the effect of denying to anyone his or her rights to equality, dignity, and security on the basis of his or her race, color, ethnicity, culture, or religion. . . .
>
> Racism in any form, expressed or implied, intentional or inadvertent, individual or institutional, constitutes an egregious offense to the tenets of human dignity and to the accords of civility guaranteed by law.

Id. at 2.

Such, in any event, will be the strategy of this essay. Its ambition is to be illustrative rather than comprehensive: the general issue of racist speech simply has too many facets to be encompassed by the small scope of this study. Although Part I attempts to isolate and describe five specific kinds of harm said to be caused by racist speech, Part II offers an account of only one of several possible relevant and important first amendment values, that of democratic self-governance. In my view this value is primarily responsible for the constitutional safeguards that currently protect public discourse. The major part of this essay, Part III, therefore addresses the narrow issue of the constitutionality of regulating public discourse to ameliorate specific harms caused by racist speech. Part IV then briefly compares the quite different constitutional issues posed by the regulation of racist speech within public institutions of higher learning.

One significant drawback of this analytic structure is that it renders the term "racist speech" into something of a cipher. As the University of Connecticut regulations illustrate, the term is inherently labile and ambiguous. It probably has as many different definitions as there are commentators, and it would be pointless to pursue its endlessly variegated shades of meaning. I have decided, therefore, to focus instead on the constitutional implications of specific justifications for restraining racist expression, and to let the term "racist speech" absorb the content implied by these various justifications.

I should add that writing this essay has been difficult and painful. I am committed both to principles of freedom of expression and to the fight against racism. The topic under consideration has forced me to set one aspiration against the other, which I can do only with reluctance and a heavy heart.

I. The Harms of Racist Speech

Even a brief survey of the contemporary debate reveals it to be rich with textured and complex characterizations of the harms of racist expression. It would be impossible within the limited scope of this essay to disentangle and evaluate each of the many harms suggested in this literature. It will therefore be necessary to group these harms into five rough categories that represent the most prominent lines of analysis and that are at the same time convenient for first amendment analysis.[17]

17. These categories by no means exhaust the field. The European literature, for

A. *The Intrinsic Harm of Racist Speech*

A recurring theme in the contemporary literature is that racist expression ought to be regulated because it creates what has been termed "deontic" harm.[18] The basic point is that there is an "elemental wrongness"[19] to racist expression, regardless of the presence or absence of particular empirical consequences such as "grievous, severe psychological injury."[20] It is argued that toleration for racist expression is inconsistent with respect for "the principle of equality"[21] that is at the heart of the fourteenth amendment.[22]

> The thrust of this argument is that a society committed to ideals of social and political equality cannot remain passive: it must issue unequivocal expressions of solidarity with vulnerable minority groups and make positive statements affirming its commitment to those ideals. Laws prohibiting racist speech must be regarded as important components of such expressions and statements.[23]

If the basic harm of racist expression lies in its intrinsic and symbolic incompatibility with egalitarian ideals, then the distinct class of communications subject to legal regulation will be defined by reference to those ideals. If the fourteenth amendment is thought to enshrine an antidiscrimination principle, then "any speech (in its widest sense) which supports racial prejudice or discrimination"[24] ought to be subject to regulation. If the relevant ideals are thought to embody substantive racial equality, then the relevant class of communications should be defined as speech containing a "message . . . of racial inferiority."[25]

---

example, contains a well-developed jurisprudence of regulating racist speech based upon the harm of potential violence. *See* Cotterrell, *Prosecuting Incitement to Racial Hatred*, 1982 PUB. L. 378; Kretzmer, *supra* note 5, at 456; Leopold, *Incitement to Hatred—The History of a Controversial Criminal Offense*, 1977 PUB. L. 389, 391-93. I do not discuss this category of harm because it is relatively unimportant in the American setting. I suspect that this is largely because of the accepted dominion of the *Brandenburg* version of the clear and present danger test. *See* Brandenburg v. Ohio, 395 U.S. 444, 447-49 (1969).

18. Wright, *supra* note 5, at 14-22.
19. *Id.* at 10.
20. *Id.* at 9.
21. Hughes, *supra* note 5, at 364.
22. Lawrence, *supra* note 5, at 438-49.
23. Kretzmer, *supra* note 5, at 456.
24. *Id.* at 454.
25. Matsuda, *supra* note 5, at 2357.

B. Harm to Identifiable Groups

A second theme in the current debate is that racist expression ought to be regulated because it harms those groups that are the target. There are two basic variations on this theme. One draws its inspiration from the tradition of group libel[26] and the decision of the Supreme Court in *Beauharnais v. Illinois.*[27] On this view speech likely to cast contempt or ridicule on identifiable groups ought to be regulated to prevent injury to the status and prospects of the members of those groups. A second variation derives from the more contemporary understanding of racism as "the structural subordination of a group based on an idea of racial inferiority."[28] Racist expression is viewed as especially unacceptable because it locks in the oppression of already marginalized groups: "Racist speech is particularly harmful because it is a mechanism of subordination, reinforcing a historical vertical relationship."[29]

If the prevention of group harm is the basis for the regulation of communication, the definition of legally proscribed speech will depend upon one's understanding of the nature of the group harm at issue and the way in which communication is seen as causing that harm. Regulation that derives from a theory of group defamation, for example, would tend to safeguard all groups,[30] whereas regulation that derives from a theory of subordinate groups would sanction only speech "directed against a historically oppressed group."[31]

C. Harm to Individuals

A third prominent theme in the contemporary literature is that racist expression harms individuals. This theme essentially analogizes racist expression to forms of communication that are regulated by the dignitary torts of defamation, invasion of privacy, and intentional infliction of emotional distress. The law

26. Riesman, *Democracy and Defamation: Control of Group Libel*, 42 COLUM. L. REV. 727 (1942).

27. 343 U.S. 250 (1952). For work in this vein, see Lasson, *Group Libel*, *supra* note 5; Lasson, *Racial Defamation*, *supra* note 5; Note, *Group Vilification Reconsidered*, 89 YALE L.J. 308 (1979).

28. Matsuda, *supra* note 5, at 2358.

29. *Id.*

30. *See, e.g.*, Lasson, *Racial Defamation*, *supra* note 5, at 48.

31. Matsuda, *supra* note 5, at 2357.

compensates persons for dignitary and emotional injuries caused by such communication, and it is argued that racist expression ought to be subject to regulation because it causes similar injuries. These injuries include "feelings of humiliation, isolation, and self-hatred,"[32] as well as "dignitary affront."[33] The injuries are particularly powerful because "racial insults . . . conjure up the entire history of racial discrimination in this country."[34] In Patricia Williams' striking phrase, racist expression is a form of "spirit-murder."[35]

Regulating racist expression because of its negative impact on particular persons would suggest that the class of communications subject to legal sanction be narrowed to those that are addressed to specific individuals or that in some other way can be demonstrated to have adversely affected specific individuals. The nature of that class would vary, however, depending upon the particular kind of harm sought to be redressed. If the focus is on preventing "dignitary harm,"[36] the injury might be understood to inhere in the very utterance of certain kinds of racist communications;[37] if the focus is instead on emotional damage, independent proof of distress might be required to sustain recovery.[38] Regulation will also vary depending upon whether harm to individuals is understood to flow from the ideational content of racist expression, or instead from its abusive nature.[39]

---

32. Delgado, *Words That Wound*, *supra* note 4, at 137.

33. *Id.* at 143.

34. *Id.* at 157.

35. Williams, *Spirit-Murdering the Messenger: The Discourse of Fingerpointing as the Law's Response to Racism*, 42 U. MIAMI L. REV. 127, 151 (1987).

36. Love, *supra* note 5, at 158.

37. Richard Delgado, for example, proposes that courts create a tort for racial insult whenever a plaintiff can prove that "[l]anguage was addressed to him or her by the defendant that was intended to demean through reference to race; that the plaintiff understood as intended to demean through reference to race; and that a reasonable person would recognize as a racial insult." Delgado, *Words That Wound*, *supra* note 4, at 179.

38. See, for example, the proposed regulation of The University of Texas at Austin, which prohibits racial harassment and which defines racial harassment "as extreme or outrageous acts or communications that are intended to harass, intimidate or humiliate a student or students on account of race, color, or national origin and that reasonably cause them to suffer severe emotional distress." President's Ad Hoc Committee on Racial Harassment, The University of Texas at Austin, Report of President's Ad Hoc Committee on Racial Harassment 4-5 (Nov. 27, 1989). The drafters of the proposed regulation state that it is "much preferable for a racial harassment policy to focus on the real injury of severe emotional distress." *Id.* at 20.

39. Compare, for example, the regulations of the University of Wisconsin, which reach "racist or discriminatory comments, epithets or other expressive behavior directed at an

D. Harm to the Marketplace of Ideas

A fourth theme in the current debate is that racist expression harms the very marketplace of ideas that the first amendment is designed to foster. A variety of different arguments have been brought forward to support this position. It is argued that racist expression ought to be "proscribed . . . as a form of assault, as conduct" inconsistent with the conditions of respect and noncoercion prerequisite to rational deliberation.[40] It is argued that racist expression is inconsistent with rational deliberation because it "infects, skews, and disables the operation of the market . . . . Racism is irrational and often unconscious."[41] Finally, it is argued that racism "systematically" silences "whole segments of the population,"[42] either through the "visceral" shock and "preemptive effect on further speech" of racist words,[43] or through the distortion of "the marketplace of ideas by muting or devaluing the speech of blacks and other non-whites."[44]

The class of communications subject to legal sanction would depend upon which of these various arguments is accepted. Depending upon exactly how racist expression is understood to damage the marketplace of ideas, the class might be confined to communication experienced as coercive and shocking, or it might be expanded to include communication perceived as unconsciously and irrationally racist, or it might be expanded still further to encompass speech explicitly devaluing and stigmatizing victim groups.

E. Harm to Educational Environment

Each of the four categories of harm so far discussed can be caused by racist expression within public discourse. There is,

individual," Board of Regents of the University of Wisconsin System, Wis. Admin. Code UWS § 17.06(2)(a) (Aug. 1989) (currently being challenged as a violation of the first amendment in UWM Post, Inc. v. Board of the Univ. of Wis. Sys., No. 90-C-0328 (E.D. Wis. filed Mar. 29, 1990)), with that of Stanford University, which reaches only racist speech that is "addressed directly to the individual or individuals whom it insults or stigmatizes" and that consists of "insulting or 'fighting' words." Stanford University, Fundamental Standard Interpretation: Free Expression and Discriminatory Harassment 2 (draft, Mar. 15, 1990).

40. Lasson, *Group Libel*, *supra* note 5, at 123. "The speech clause protects the marketplace of ideas, not the battleground." *Id.*

41. Lawrence, *supra* note 5, at 468.

42. *Id.* at 447 n.66 (quoting MacKinnon, *Not a Moral Issue*, 2 YALE L. & POL'Y REV. 321, 340 (1984)).

43. *Id.* at 452.

44. *Id.* at 470.

however, yet a fifth kind of harm which is quite important to the contemporary controversy, but which is relevant only to the specific educational environment of institutions of higher learning. This is the harm that racist expression is understood to cause to the educational mission of universities or colleges. The prevention of this harm is central to the definition of a great number of campus regulations.

Universities and colleges characteristically seek to regulate racist communications that "directly create a substantial and immediate interference with the educational processes of the University," without articulating exactly how racist expression can cause that interference.[45] Some campus regulations are more specific, focusing on the damage that racist expression is understood to cause to particular individuals or groups. For example, some regulations only proscribe racist expression that "will interfere with the victim's ability to pursue effectively his or her education or otherwise to participate fully in University programs and activities."[46] Presumably this interference will occur for reasons similar to those that we have already canvassed.

In a number of instances, however, college or university regulations enunciate special educational goals that are understood to be inherently incompatible with racist expression. For example, Mount Holyoke seeks to inculcate the value of diversity, which it views as plainly inconsistent with racist expression. Accordingly Mount Holyoke's regulations provide:

---

45. Office of Student Life Policy and Service, Rutgers University at New Brunswick, University Student Life Policy Against Insult, Defamation, and Harassment 1 (May 31, 1989) (revised); *see also* Doe v. University of Mich., 721 F. Supp. 852, 856 (E.D. Mich. 1989); Oberlin College, Policy on Race Relations and Informal Procedures for Racial Grievances; Office of the Dean for Student Affairs and the Special Assistants to the President, Massachusetts Institute of Technology, Information on Harassment (Sept. 1989); State University of New York College at Brockport, Discriminatory Harassment § 285.02; University of Pennsylvania, Harassment Policy (Almanac Supp., Sept. 29, 1987) (as published originally in the Almanac of June 2, 1987).

46. University of California, Universitywide Student Conduct: Harassment Policy (Sept. 21, 1989) (available from Office of the President). For an example of a regulation based upon group harm, see Clark University's Code of General Conduct: "Harassment includes any verbal or physical conduct which has the intent or effect of unreasonably interfering with any individual's or group's work or study, or creating an intimidating, hostile, or offensive environment." Clark University, Code of General Conduct and University Judicial Procedures 1 (Fall Semester 1988). For other examples of similar kinds of regulations, see Emory University, Policy Statement on Discriminatory Harassment; Marquette University, Racial Abuse and Harassment Policy (May 5, 1989); Office of University News and Information of Kent State University, Policy to Combat Harassment, For the Record, Vol. 5, No. 5 (Feb. 6, 1989).

> To enter Mount Holyoke College is to become a member of a community. . . .
>
> . . . .
>
> Our community is committed to maintaining an environment in which diversity is not only tolerated, but is celebrated. Towards this end, each member of the Mount Holyoke community is expected to treat all individuals with a common standard of decency.[47]

Marquette University defines itself "as a Christian and Catholic institution . . . dedicated to the proposition that all human beings possess an inherent dignity in the eyes of their Creator and equality as children of God."[48] Accordingly Marquette's regulations seek to maintain "an environment in which the dignity and worth of each member of its community is respected" and in which "racial abuse or harassment . . . will not be tolerated."[49] Mary Washington College sets forth what appears to be a secular version of this same educational mission; its regulations provide that the "goal of the College is to help all students achieve academic success in an environment that nurtures, encourages growth, and develops sensitivity and appreciation for all people."[50] Accordingly "any activity or conduct that detracts from this goal—such as racial or sexual harassment—is inconsistent with the purposes of the college community."[51]

In such instances, racist expression interferes with education not merely because of general harms that it may inflict on groups or individuals or the marketplace of ideas,[52] but also, and more intrinsically, because racist expression exemplifies conduct that is contrary to the particular educational values that specific colleges or universities seek to instill.[53]

---

47. Mount Holyoke College, The Honor Code: Academic and Community Responsibility § III, Community Responsibility, Introduction (reprinted from the Student Handbook).

48. Marquette University, Racial Abuse and Harassment Policy 1 (May 5, 1989).

49. *Id.*

50. Mary Washington College, Mary Washington College Student Handbook 20 (1990-91) (available from Office of the Dean of Students).

51. *Id.*

52. "If the university stands for anything, it stands for freedom in the search for truth. . . . [But] [c]an truth have its day in court when the courtroom is made into a mud-wrestling pit where vicious epithets are flung?" Laney, *Why Tolerate Campus Bigots?*, N.Y. Times, Apr. 6, 1990, at A35.

53. Thus James T. Laney, the President of Emory University, stated:

> Educators are by definition professors of value. Through education we pass on to the next generation not merely information but the habits and manners of our civil society. The university differs from society at large in its insistence on not only free expression but also an environment conducive to mutual engagement.

Id.

II. The Values of the First Amendment

As any constitutional lawyer knows, first amendment doctrine is neither clear nor logical. It is a vast Sargasso Sea of drifting and entangled values, theories, rules, exceptions, predilections. It requires determined interpretive effort to derive a useful set of constitutional principles by which to evaluate regulations of expression. In recent years there has been an unfortunate tendency, by no means limited to the controversy surrounding racist speech, to avoid this difficult work by relying instead on formulaic invocations of first amendment "interests" which can be captured in such conclusory labels as "individual self-fulfillment," "truth," "democracy," and so forth.[54] These formulas cast an illusion of stability and order over first amendment jurisprudence, an illusion that can turn dangerous when it substitutes for serious engagement with the question of why we really care about protecting freedom of expression.

What is most disappointing about the expanding literature proposing restrictions on racist speech is the palpable absence of that engagement. The most original and significant articles in the genre concentrate on uncovering and displaying the manifold harms of racist communications; the harms of regulating expression are on the whole perfunctorily dismissed. Of course this emphasis is readily understandable. It is a formidable task to attempt to carve out a new exception to the general protection of speech afforded by the armor of first amendment doctrine. Even so staunch a defender of minority rights as Justice William Brennan might seem unsympathetic, given his recent observation in *United States v. Eichman*[55] that "virulent ethnic and religious epithets"[56] ought to receive constitutional protection because of the "'bedrock principle underlying the First Amendment . . . that the Government may not prohibit the expression of an idea simply because society finds the idea itself offensive or disagreeable.'"[57] In the face of such daunting obstacles, it is natural for

54. *See, e.g.*, Delgado, *Words That Wound*, *supra* note 4, at 175-79; Note, *A First Amendment Justification for Regulating Racist Speech on Campus*, 40 CASE W. RES. 733 (1989-90).

55. 110 S. Ct. 2404 (1990).

56. *Id.* at 2410.

57. *Id.* (quoting Texas v. Johnson, 109 S. Ct. 2533, 2544 (1989)). See Brennan's remark in *Texas v. Johnson* to the same effect: "The First Amendment does not guarantee that . . . concepts virtually sacred to our Nation as a whole—such as the principle that discrimination on the basis of race is odious and destructive—will go unquestioned in the

proponents of restraints on racist speech to emphasize their affirmative case and to minimize countervailing considerations.

I agree, of course, that the question of regulating racist speech ought not to be settled simply by reference to present doctrine. But it is equally important that the question ought not to be settled without serious engagement with the values embodied in that doctrine. Regulations like those promulgated by the University of Connecticut and many other universities suggest that this lack of engagement is a real and practical problem.[58] Although earnest inquiry into the first amendment values involved in the restraint of racist speech cannot by itself definitively solve the difficult constitutional issues we face, it can at least illuminate what is most deeply at stake for us in this controversy, and to that extent clarify the choices we must make.

A. *Democracy, Public Discourse, and the First Amendment*

This essay concentrates on the relevance for the regulation of racist speech of only one strand of first amendment values. It is, however, an extraordinarily important strand, one which in my view accounts for a good deal of the shape of contemporary first amendment doctrine. It concerns the relationship between freedom of expression and democratic self-governance. Its basic thrust is to provide certain kinds of protection to communication deemed necessary for the processes of democracy, communication that the Court has labelled "public discourse."[59]

In protecting public discourse the first amendment serves the purposes of democracy, and the question at hand is what we believe those purposes to be. This is not a simple question. Even so powerful a first amendment theorist as Frederick Schauer can argue that "[a]ny distinct restraint on majority power, such as a

---

marketplace of ideas." *Johnson*, 109 S. Ct. at 2546. Brennan supported this remark by citing Brandenburg v. Ohio, 395 U.S. 444 (1969), in which the Court extended first amendment protection to a Ku Klux Klan rally featuring such revolting comments as: "Bury the n— —s"; "A dirty n— —r"; and "Send the Jews back to Israel." *Id.* at 446 n.1.

58. Charles Lawrence, for example, writes that the University of Michigan regulations recently invalidated by a federal court, see *supra* note 45, were so patently unconstitutional that "it is difficult to believe that anyone at the University of Michigan Law School was consulted" in their drafting. Lawrence, *supra* note 5, at 477 n.161. "It is almost as if the university purposefully wrote an unconstitutional regulation so that they could say to the black students, 'We tried to help but the courts just won't let us do it.'" *Id.* A great many contemporary university regulations are similar to those of the University of Michigan.

59. Hustler Magazine v. Falwell, 485 U.S. 46, 54 (1988).

principle of freedom of speech, is by its nature anti-democratic, anti-majoritarian."[60] If democracy means no more to us than that in each instance the majority ought to have its way, then of course Schauer is quite correct that speech comprising public discourse ought not for that reason to have any special exemption from majoritarian regulation.[61] But the underlying equation of democracy with the simple exercise of majority will is radically inadequate not only as an explanation of contours of contemporary doctrine, but also as an account of the normative attraction of democracy.[62]

A far more persuasive account is one that begins with

> the distinction between autonomy and heteronomy: democratic forms of government are those in which the laws are made by the same people to whom they apply (and for that reason they are autonomous norms), while in autocratic forms of government the law-makers are different from those to whom the laws are addressed (and are therefore heteronomous norms).[63]

This distinction between autonomy and heteronomy formed the basis of Hans Kelsen's definition of "democracy," which he viewed as a form of government resting on "the principle of self-determination."[64] The distinction is manifestly at the root of the Court's repudiation of seditious libel in *New York Times Co. v. Sullivan*,[65] which turned on Madison's differentiation of American and English forms of government: in England "the Crown was sovereign and the people were subjects," whereas in America "'[t]he people,

60. F. SCHAUER, FREE SPEECH: A PHILOSOPHICAL ENQUIRY 40 (1982). On the equation of democracy with majoritarianism, see A. DE TOCQUEVILLE, DEMOCRACY IN AMERICA 254 (F. Bowen trans. 1945): "The very essence of democratic government consists in the absolute sovereignty of the majority. . . ."

61. Schauer writes:

> The more we accept the premise of the argument from democracy, the less can we impinge on the right of self-government by restricting the power of the majority. If the argument from democracy would allow to be said things that the "people" do not want to hear, it is not so much an argument based on popular will as it is an argument against it.

F. SCHAUER, *supra* note 60, at 41.

62. The equation is nevertheless quite commonplace. *See, e.g.*, Partlett, *supra* note 5, at 458 (footnote omitted) ("I take it that a central tenet of democracy is majority rule. If the majority decides to suppress free speech, how can it be defended upon democratic lines?").

63. N. BOBBIO, DEMOCRACY AND DICTATORSHIP 137 (P. Kennealy trans. 1989).

64. H. KELSEN, GENERAL THEORY OF LAW AND STATE 284-86 (A. Wedberg trans. 1961).

65. 376 U.S. 254 (1964).

not the government, possess absolute sovereignty.'"[66] For this reason in America "'the censorial power is in the people over the Government, and not in the Government over the people.'"[67]

If democracy as a form of government is important to us because it embodies the value of self-determination, we must ask what it means for a collection of persons to decide governmental policy in a way that facilitates that value.[68] Kelsen answers the question in a way that begins with Rousseau's formulation in *The Social Contract*,[69] but that moves rapidly to a distinctively modern perspective:

> A subject is politically free insofar as his individual will is in harmony with the "collective" (or "general") will expressed in the social order. Such harmony of the "collective" and the individual will is guaranteed only if the social order is created by the individuals whose behavior it regulates. Social order means determination of the will of the individual. Political freedom, that is, freedom under social order, is self-determination of the individual by participating in the creation of the social order.[70]

Because it is unconvincing to imagine that the will of individuals can be "in harmony" with the general will in all matters of political moment, Kelsen ultimately locates the value of self-determination in the ability of persons to participate in the process by which the social order is created. He conceives that process as preeminently one of communication:

> The will of the community, in a democracy, is always created through a running discussion between majority and minority, through free consideration of arguments for and against a certain regulation of a subject matter. This discussion takes place not only in parliament, but also, and foremost, at political meetings, in newspapers, books, and other vehicles of public opinion. A democracy without public opinion is a contradiction in terms.[71]

---

66. *Id.* at 274 (quoting 4 ELLIOT'S DEBATES 569 (1876)) (citation omitted in original).
67. *Id.* at 275 (quoting 4 ANNALS OF CONGRESS 934 (1794)).
68. This is the central problematic of Alexander Meiklejohn's work. A. MEIKLEJOHN, POLITICAL FREEDOM: THE CONSTITUTIONAL POWERS OF THE PEOPLE 11 (1948). Meiklejohn was concerned to analyze "the difference between a political system in which men do govern themselves and a political system in which men, without their consent, are governed by others." *Id.*
69. J. ROUSSEAU, THE SOCIAL CONTRACT (C. Frankel trans. 1947).
70. H. KELSEN, *supra* note 64, at 285.
71. *Id.* at 287-88.

For Kelsen, then, democracy serves the principle of self-determination because it subjects the political and social order to public opinion, which is the product of a dialogic communicative exchange open to all. The normative essence of democracy is thus located in the communicative processes necessary to instill a sense of self-determination,[72] and in the subordination of political decisionmaking to those processes.

This logic is widely shared. It leads Benjamin Barber, for example, to conclude that "there can be no strong democratic legitimacy without ongoing talk."[73] It leads John Dewey to remark that "[d]emocracy begins in conversation."[74] It leads Durkheim to observe that "[t]he more that deliberation and reflection and a critical spirit play a considerable part in the course of public affairs, the more democratic the nation."[75] It leads Claude Lefort to claim that

> modern democracy invites us to replace the notion of a regime governed by laws, of a legitimate power, by the notion of a regime founded upon *the legitimacy of a debate as to what is legitimate and what is illegitimate*—a debate which is necessarily without any guarantor and without any end.[76]

In fact the notion that self-determination requires the maintenance of a structure of communication open to all commands a wide consensus. Jürgen Habermas characterizes that structure as determined by the effort to attain "a common will, communicatively shaped and discursively clarified in the political public sphere."[77] John Rawls views it as a process of "reconciliation through public reason."[78] Frank Michelman regards it as the practice of "jurisgenerative politics" through the "dialogic 'modulation' of participants' pre-political understandings."[79] For all three thinkers the goal of the structure is to facilitate the

---

72. For a good discussion of this point, see Freeman, *Reason and Agreement in Social Contract Views*, 19 PHIL. & PUB. AFF. 122, 154-57 (1990).

73. B. BARBER, STRONG DEMOCRACY: PARTICIPATORY POLITICS FOR A NEW AGE 136 (1984); *see* Pitkin & Shumer, *On Participation*, DEMOCRACY, Fall 1982, at 43, 43-54.

74. DIALOGUE ON JOHN DEWEY 58 (C. Lamont ed. 1959).

75. E. DURKHEIM, PROFESSIONAL ETHICS AND CIVIC MORALS 89 (C. Brookfield trans. 1958).

76. C. LEFORT, DEMOCRACY AND POLITICAL THEORY 39 (D. Macey trans. 1988).

77. 2 J. HABERMAS, THE THEORY OF COMMUNICATIVE ACTION 81 (T. McCarthy trans. 1987).

78. Rawls, *Justice as Fairness: Political not Metaphysical*, 14 PHIL. & PUB. AFF. 223, 230 (1985).

79. Michelman, *Law's Republic*, 97 YALE L.J. 1493, 1526-27 (1988).

attainment of "agreement" that is "uncoerced, and reached by citizens in ways consistent with their being viewed as free and equal persons."[80]

Coercion is precluded from public debate because the very purpose of that debate is the practice of self-determination. The goal is "agreement" (or the attainment of "a common will") because in such circumstances the individual will is by hypothesis completely reconciled with the general will. It is important to understand, however, that this goal is purely aspirational. In fact, it is precisely because absolute agreement can never actually be reached that the debate which constitutes democracy is necessarily "without any end," and hence must be independently maintained as an ongoing structure of communication.

Without this structure, the simple kind of majoritarian rule Schauer equates with democracy loses its grounding in the principle of self-determination and merely represents the heteronomous submission of a minority to the forceful command of a majority. With such a structure in place, on the other hand, both majority and minority can each be understood to have had the opportunity freely to participate within a "system"[81] of communication upon which the legitimacy of all political arrangements depends. Whether that opportunity will actually establish the value of autonomous self-determination for both majority and minority is a complex and contingent question, dependent upon specific historical circumstances. But, in the absence of that opportunity, realization of the value of autonomous self-determination will be precluded under conditions characteristic of the modern state.[82]

The first amendment principles that this essay considers are those that function to safeguard from majoritarian interference this structure of public discourse, so that our democracy will be able to serve the end of collective self-determination. Four aspects of that structure require emphasis, for they will be of importance when we subsequently examine in detail the regulation of racist speech.

---

80. Rawls, *supra* note 78, at 229-30; *see* 1 J. HABERMAS, THE THEORY OF COMMUNICATIVE ACTION 25-26 (T. McCarthy trans. 1984); Michelman, *supra* note 79, at 1526-27.

81. Fiss, *supra* note 3, at 38.

82. I do not mean to foreclose the possibility that, under special conditions of charismatic leadership or identification with traditional authority, the value of self-determination can be achieved in the absence of a communicative structure of public discourse. I mean only to imply that such conditions will not ordinarily obtain in the modern rational and bureaucratic state.

First, the function of public discourse is to reconcile, to the extent possible, the will of individuals with the general will. Public discourse is thus ultimately grounded upon a respect for individuals seen as "free and equal persons."[83] In the words of Jean Piaget,

> The essence of democracy resides in its attitude towards law as a product of the collective will, and not as something emanating from a transcendent will or from the authority established by divine right. It is therefore the essence of democracy to replace the unilateral respect of authority by the mutual respect of autonomous wills.[84]

The individualism so characteristic of first amendment doctrine[85] thus flows directly from the central project of democracy.[86]

Second, some form of public/private distinction is necessarily implied by democracy understood as a project of self-determination. This is because the state undermines the *raison d'être* of its own enterprise to the extent that it itself coercively forms the "autonomous wills" that democracy seeks to reconcile into public opinion.[87] If the adjective "private" is understood to designate that which is beyond the coercive formation of the state, public discourse must be conceptualized as a process through which "private" perspectives are transformed into public power.

Third, democracy is on this account inherently incomplete. This is because the "autonomous wills" postulated by democratic the-

---

83. Rawls, *supra* note 78, at 230.

84. J. PIAGET, THE MORAL JUDGMENT OF THE CHILD 366 (M. Gabain trans. 1948).

85. *See* Post, *Cultural Heterogeneity and Law: Pornography, Blasphemy, and the First Amendment*, 76 CALIF. L. REV. 297, 314-24 (1988).

86. See, for example, Kateb, *Democratic Individuality and the Claims of Politics*, 12 POL. THEORY 331, 332 (1984):

> To speak, therefore, of individualism is to speak of the most characteristically democratic political and moral commitment. It would be a sign of defection from modern democracy to posit some other entity as the necessary or desirable center of life. There is therefore nothing special (much less, arbitrary) in assuming that the doctrine of the individual has the preeminent place in the theory of democracy.

87. *See, e.g.*, Bowers v. Hardwick, 478 U.S. 186, 205-06 (1986) (Blackmun, J., dissenting). Such a public/private distinction must, of course, be understood as inherently unstable and problematic, for all government regulation influences, to one degree or another, the formation of individual identity. *See, e.g.*, Sunstein, *Legal Interference with Private Preferences*, 53 U. CHI. L. REV. 1129, 1138-39 (1986). For this reason, the distinction should be regarded as a pragmatic instrument for distinguishing those aspects of the self considered indispensable for the exercise of political and moral autonomy, and hence as beyond the coercive formation of the state.

ory do not and cannot appear *ex nihilo*. The only reason that a person possesses a personality capable of autonomous choice is because the person has internalized "the institutions of [the] community into his own conduct."[88] This process of socialization, which is prerequisite for personal identity, is not itself a matter of independent election, but rather is attributable to accidents of birth and acculturation. Democracy thus necessarily presupposes important (not to say foundational) aspects of the social world organized along nondemocratic lines. For this reason public discourse must always exist in tension with other forms of communication ("nonpublic speech").

Fourth, democracy, like all forms of government, must ultimately be capable of accomplishing the tasks of governance. As Alexander Meiklejohn notes, "Self-government is nonsense unless the 'self' which governs is able and determined to make its will effective."[89] Democratic governments must therefore have the power to regulate behavior. But because public discourse is understood as the communicative medium through which the democratic "self" is itself constituted, public discourse must in important respects remain exempt from democratic regulation. We use the speech/action distinction to mark the boundaries of this exemption. Because all "[w]ords are deeds,"[90] this distinction is purely pragmatic. We designate the communicative processes necessary to sustain the principle of collective self-determination "speech" and thus insulate it from majoritarian interference.

B. Community, Civility Rules, and Public Discourse

Restraints on racist speech characteristically involve certain general first amendment issues that I briefly review in this Section in light of the functional concerns of public discourse. In so doing I confine myself to summarizing conclusions, the detailed arguments for which I have developed elsewhere.[91]

If democratic self-governance presupposes a social world in which "autonomous wills" are to be coordinated and reconciled,

---

88. G. MEAD, MIND, SELF & SOCIETY 162 (C. Morris ed. 1934).

89. A. MEIKLEJOHN, *supra* note 68, at 14.

90. L. WITTGENSTEIN, CULTURE AND VALUE 46e (P. Winch trans. 1980).

91. *See generally* Post, *The Constitutional Concept of Public Discourse: Outrageous Opinion, Democratic Deliberation, and* Hustler Magazine v. Falwell, 103 HARV. L. REV. 601 (1990) [hereinafter Post, *The Constitutional Concept*]; Post, *The Social Foundations of Defamation Law: Reputation and the Constitution*, 74 CALIF. L. REV. 691 (1986) [hereinafter Post, *Defamation Law*]; Post, *The Social Foundations of Privacy: Community and Self in the Common Law Tort*, 77 CALIF. L. REV. 957 (1989) [hereinafter Post, *Privacy*].

there is an important form of social organization, which I call "community," that rests on exactly the opposite presupposition. Building on the work of Michael Sandel,[92] I define a "community" as a social formation that inculcates norms into the very identities of its members. So far from being considered autonomous, persons within a community are understood to depend, for the very integrity and dignity of their personalities, upon the observance of these norms.

For hundreds of years an important function of the common law has been to safeguard the most important of these norms, which I call "civility rules." These rules apply to communication as well as to action, and their enforcement lies at the foundation of such communicative torts as defamation,[93] invasion of privacy,[94] and intentional infliction of emotional distress.[95] Through these torts the common law not only protects the integrity of the personality of individual community members, but it also serves authoritatively to articulate a community's norms and hence to define a community's identity.

There is an obvious tension between community and democracy. Public discourse within a democracy is legally conceived as the communicative medium through which individuals choose the forms of their communal life; public discourse within a community is legally conceived as a medium through which the values of a particular life are displayed and enacted.[96] Democracy seeks to open the space of public discourse for collective self-constitution; community seeks to bound that space through the enforcement of civility rules. In the inevitable negotiation between democracy and community, the first amendment has, since the 1940's, generally served the purposes of democracy by suspending the enforcement of civility rules in such landmark cases as *Cantwell v. Connecticut*,[97] *New York Times Co. v. Sullivan*,[98] *Cohen v. California*,[99] and *Hustler Magazine v. Falwell*.[100]

---

92. *See* M. SANDEL, LIBERALISM AND THE LIMITS OF JUSTICE (1982).

93. *See* Post, *Defamation Law*, *supra* note 91, at 699-719.

94. *See* Post, *Privacy*, *supra* note 91, at 959-87.

95. *See* Post, *The Constitutional Concept*, *supra* note 91, at 616-46.

96. *See, e.g.*, *id.* at 627-33.

97. 310 U.S. 296 (1940).

98. 376 U.S. 254 (1964).

99. 403 U.S. 15 (1971).

100. 485 U.S. 46 (1988). The American first amendment is unique in thus separating democracy from community. I suspect that the origins of this separation lie both in our tradition of individualism and in the fact of our cultural diversity. For instructive

There is, however, a complex and reciprocal relationship between democracy and community. Democracy necessarily presupposes some form of social institution, like community, through which the concrete identities of "autonomous" democratic citizens can be defined and instantiated. The paradigmatic examples of such institutions are the family and the elementary school. In these settings a child's identity is created in the first instance through decidedly undemocratic means; it "comes to be by way of the internalization of sanctions that are de facto threatened and carried out."[101]

This fact has important consequences for the practice of public discourse. The specific purpose of that discourse is the achievement of some form of "reconciliation through public reason,"[102] yet because the identity of democratic citizens will have been formed by reference to community norms, speech in violation of civility rules will characteristically be perceived as both irrational and coercive.[103] This creates what I have elsewhere termed the "paradox of public discourse": the first amendment, in the name of democracy, suspends legal enforcement of the very civility rules that make rational deliberation possible.[104] The upshot of the paradox is that the separation of public discourse from community depends in some measure upon the spontaneous persistence of civility. In the absence of such persistence, the use of legal regulation to enforce community standards of civility may be required as an unfortunate but necessary option of last resort. A paradigmatic example of this use may be found in the "fighting words" doctrine of *Chaplinsky v. New Hampshire*.[105]

If community norms thus infiltrate and make possible the practice of democracy, so the ethical imperatives of democracy can be expected to reshape the terms of community life. A stable and successful democratic state will regulate the lives of its citizens in ways consistent with the underlying principle of "their being viewed as free and equal persons."[106] Such regulation will influence community institutions, moving them closer toward the

---

contrasts, see Jacobsohn, *Alternative Pluralisms: Israeli and American Constitutionalism in Comparative Perspective*, REV. POL., Spring 1989, at 159; Kommers, *The Jurisprudence of Free Speech in the United States and the Federal Republic of Germany*, 53 S. CAL. L. REV. 657 (1980).

101. 2 J. HABERMAS, *supra* note 77, at 38.

102. Rawls, *supra* note 78, at 230.

103. Post, *The Constitutional Concept*, *supra* note 91, at 641-44.

104. *Id.*

105. 315 U.S. 568 (1942).

106. Rawls, *supra* note 78, at 230.

realization of specifically democratic principles. The only intrinsic limitation on the ability of the democratic state to regulate community institutions in this manner is the public/private distinction, which requires that at some point the coercive formation of the identity of individuals remain beyond the purview of the state.

C. The Domain of Public Discourse

This essay primarily concerns the regulation of racist expression within public discourse. "Public discourse" may be defined as encompassing the communicative processes necessary for the formation of public opinion, whether or not that opinion is directed toward specific government personnel, decisions, or policies. Democratic self-governance requires that public opinion be broadly conceived as a process of "collective self-definition"[107] that will necessarily precede and inform any specific government action or inaction. Public discourse cannot encompass all communication within a democracy, however, because both the public/private distinction and the paradox of public discourse imply that the processes of democratic self-governance depend upon the persistence of other nondemocratic forms of social organization, such as community.

Because the first amendment extends extraordinary protection to public discourse, it is important to demarcate the boundary between such discourse and other speech. I have discussed this issue in detail elsewhere[108] and will not repeat that analysis here. Suffice it to say that the boundary is inherently uncertain and subject to perennial reevaluation. Factors that the Supreme Court has used to delineate the boundary include the content of speech and the manner of its dissemination.[109] Speech that can be said to be about matters of "public concern" is ordinarily classified as public discourse,[110] as is speech that is widely distributed to the public at large through the mass media. There are exceptions, however, like commercial speech, which flow from the influence of traditional conventions that define for us a recognizable "genre" of public speech.[111]

107. Pitkin, *Justice: On Relating Private and Public*, 9 POL. THEORY 327, 346 (1981).
108. *See* Post, *The Constitutional Concept*, *supra* note 91, at 667-84.
109. *Id.* at 667.
110. *Id.*
111. *Id.* at 680.

It is difficult to discuss profitably the abstract question of setting the boundaries of public discourse. At the most general level, these boundaries mark the point at which our commitment to the dialogue of autonomous self-governing citizens shifts to other values, as for example to that of the socially implicated self characteristic of community. The particular points at which our commitments alter is a highly specific and contextual inquiry requiring case-by-case assessment.

I confine myself, therefore, to two preliminary observations. First, the constitutional protections extended to public discourse differ importantly from those extended to nonpublic speech. Thus even if the first amendment were to immunize from legal regulation the circulation of certain racist ideas in newspapers, it would not follow that the expression of those same ideas could not be restrained by the government within the workplace, where an image of dialogue among autonomous self-governing citizens would be patently out of place.[112] The first amendment values at stake in the regulation of nonpublic speech are complex and diverse,[113] and I will not be able to review them within the limited span of this essay.

Second, the category of racist expression cannot be excluded as such from the domain of public discourse. The racist content of a particular communication is only one of many factors relevant to the determination of whether the communication lies within or without of that domain. Thus the leaflet at issue in *Beauharnais v. Illinois*,[114] which was an effort "to petition the mayor and council of Chicago to pass laws for segregation,"[115] was plainly

---

112. *See, e.g.*, Rogers v. EEOC, 454 F.2d 234, 237-38 (5th Cir. 1971), *cert. denied*, 406 U.S. 957 (1972); EEOC v. Murphy Motor Freight Lines, 488 F. Supp. 381, 385 (D. Minn. 1980); *cf.* Meritor Sav. Bank v. Vinson, 477 U.S. 57, 65-66 (1986) (holding that speech that constitutes sexual harassment may be regulated). I do not mean to imply, however, that *all* speech within the workplace is excluded from public discourse. *See, e.g.*, Connick v. Myers, 461 U.S. 138, 149 (1983); Givhan v. Western Line Consol. School Dist., 439 U.S. 410, 415-16 (1979).

113. It should be emphasized that in text I am using the adjective "public" in a discrete and stipulative sense to refer to that speech necessary for democratic self-governance. Thus I do not mean to imply that speech within the workplace is "nonpublic" in the sense that it is unimportant, or that it is "private" in the sense of being intrinsically insulated from governmental control or regulation. *See* Karst, *Private Discrimination and Public Responsibility: Patterson in Context*, 1989 SUP. CT. REV. 1, 10-11; *supra* text accompanying notes 106-11. My point is instead that if the regulation of nonpublic speech is in fact protected by the first amendment, it will be on the basis of constitutional values other than democratic self-governance.

114. 343 U.S. 250 (1952). The leaflet is reproduced in Justice Black's dissenting opinion. *Id.* at 276 (Black, J., dissenting).

115. *Id.* at 267 (Black, J., dissenting).

an effort to engage in public discourse, despite its overt and virulent racism. Similarly, the infamous Nazi march in Skokie was also an attempt to participate in public discourse, notwithstanding its repulsive political symbolism.[116] In both cases racists used well-recognized media for the communication of ideas in order to address and affect public opinion.[117]

III. Racist Speech and Public Discourse

We are now in a position to assess the justifications for the regulation of racist expression in light of the first amendment values associated with public discourse. In some cases this assessment allows us to reach definite conclusions; in others it simply helps to clarify the issues raised by particular forms of regulation. In each case I use the term "racist speech" to encompass the class of communications that would have to be regulated in order to ameliorate the specific harm under consideration.

A. Public Discourse and the Intrinsic Harm of Racist Ideas

It is of course a commonplace of first amendment jurisprudence "that the government must remain neutral in the marketplace of ideas."[118] The justification for this principle as applied to public discourse is straightforward. Democracy serves the value of self-determination by establishing a communicative structure within which the varying perspectives of individuals can be reconciled through reason. If the state were to forbid the expression of a particular idea, the government would become, with respect to individuals holding that idea, heteronomous and nondemocratic. This is incompatible with a form of government predicated upon treating its citizens "in ways consistent with their being viewed as free and equal persons."[119]

For this reason the value of self-determination requires that public discourse be open to the opinions of all. "[S]ilence coerced by law—the argument of force in its worst form"[120] is constitu-

---

116. *See* Collin v. Smith, 447 F. Supp. 676 (N.D. Ill.), *aff'd*, 578 F.2d 1197 (7th Cir.), *cert. denied*, 439 U.S. 916 (1978).

117. To exclude from public discourse the category of racist speech as such would be equivalent to establishing a per se exclusion of racist ideas from public discourse, a form of regulation whose constitutionality is assessed in Section III(A), *infra*.

118. Hustler Magazine v. Falwell, 485 U.S. 46, 56 (1988) (quoting FCC v. Pacifica Found., 438 U.S. 726, 745-46 (1978)).

119. Rawls, *supra* note 78, at 230.

120. Whitney v. California, 274 U.S. 357, 375-76 (1927) (Brandeis, J., concurring).

tionally forbidden. In a democracy, as Piaget notes, "there are no more crimes of opinion, but only breaches of procedure. All opinions are tolerated so long as their protagonists urge their acceptance by legal methods."[121] The notion that racist ideas ought to be forbidden within public discourse because of their "elemental wrongness"[122] is thus fundamentally irreconcilable with the rationale for first amendment freedoms.

The contemporary debate nevertheless contains three distinct arguments that racist ideas ought to be proscribed because of their "deontic" harm. The first is that the idea of racism is "*sui generis*" because it is "universally condemned."[123] The same authors who make this claim, however, also stress "the structural reality of racism in America," a reality manifested not merely in an "epidemic of racist incidents," but also in the widespread racist beliefs characteristic of "upper-class whites" and important social "institutions."[124] In fact it is probably fair to characterize these authors as proponents of regulating racist speech precisely because of their urgent sense of the *prevalence* of racist practices. Although the nightmare of these practices ought to occasion strong public response, their prevalence substantially undermines the conclusion that racism is "universally condemned"[125] in any sense relevant for first amendment analysis. Such practices can be understood only as manifestations of strongly held but otherwise unarticulated racist ideas.[126]

A second argument is that the failure to regulate racist ideas amounts to a symbolic endorsement of racist speech, which is intolerable in "a society committed to ideals of social and political equality."[127] In essence this argument rejects the public/private

---

121. J. PIAGET, *supra* note 84, at 57; *see id.* at 63.

122. Wright, *supra* note 5, at 10.

123. Matsuda, *supra* note 5, at 2359; *see* Kretzmer, *supra* note 5, at 458.

124. Matsuda, *supra* note 5, at 2332-34. "Racist hate messages are rapidly increasing and are widely distributed in this country using a variety of low and high technologies." *Id.* at 2336. Kretzmer is also concerned with the potential spread of racist ideas. *See* Kretzmer, *supra* note 5, at 464-65.

125. *See supra* note 123 and accompanying text.

126. I thus do not reach the theoretically more fundamental question of why it should make a constitutional difference that racist ideas are "universally condemned." See, for example, the Court's rejection in United States v. Eichman, 110 S. Ct. 2404, 2409 (1990), of the Solicitor General's invitation to overrule Texas v. Johnson, 109 S. Ct. 2533 (1989), on the grounds of "Congress' recent recognition of a purported 'national consensus' favoring a prohibition on flag-burning. . . . Even assuming such a consensus exists, any suggestion that the Government's interest in suppressing speech becomes more weighty as popular opposition to that speech grows is foreign to the First Amendment." *Eichman*, 110 S. Ct. at 2409.

127. Kretzmer, *supra* note 5, at 456; *see* Matsuda, *supra* note 5, at 2338:

distinction required by democratic self-governance.[128] But if responsibility for ideas advanced by individuals in public discourse were to be attributed to government, the government could not then also be deemed *responsive* to those ideas in the way required by the principle of self-determination. Just as a library could not function if it were understood as endorsing the views of the authors whose books it collects and displays, so also in a democracy the government could not serve the value of autonomy if it were understood as endorsing the ideas expressed by private persons in public discourse.[129]

A third argument is that the free expression of racist ideas is inconsistent with our commitment to the egalitarian ideals of the fourteenth amendment. At root this argument rejects autonomy as the principal value of democracy and substitutes instead what Kenneth Karst has eloquently argued is "the substantive center of the fourteenth amendment: the principle of equal citizenship."[130] Although some political theorists have endorsed this position,[131] it runs against the overwhelming American commitment to the importance of "self-rule," to the fundamental belief "that the American people are politically free insomuch as they are governed by themselves collectively."[132]

Of course the principle of self-rule contains its own commitment to the value of equal citizenship, to the notion that, as a formal matter, citizens must be "viewed as free and equal persons."[133] But the meaning of this commitment is measured by the purpose of enabling the processes of self-determination. The appeal to the fourteenth amendment, on the other hand, is meant to signify

---

> However irrational racist speech may be, it hits right at the emotional place where we feel the most pain. The aloneness comes not only from the hate message itself, but also from the government response of tolerance. When hundreds of police officers are called out to protect racist marchers, when the courts refuse redress for racial insult, . . . the victim becomes a stateless person. Target-group members can either identify with a community that promotes racist speech, or they can admit that the community does not include them.

128. Matsuda, *supra* note 5, at 2378.

129. *See* Greenawalt, *supra* note 5, at 304-05.

130. Karst, *Citizenship, Race, and Marginality*, 30 WM. & MARY L. REV. 1, 1 (1988).

131. *See, e.g.*, N. BOBBIO, *supra* note 63, at 157-58; C. GOULD, RETHINKING DEMOCRACY: FREEDOM AND COOPERATION IN POLITICS, ECONOMY, AND SOCIETY 90 (1988); J. PENNOCK, DEMOCRATIC POLITICAL THEORY 3-161 (1979).

132. Michelman, *supra* note 79, at 1500-01. Michelman notes that "no earnest, nondisruptive participant in American constitutional debate is quite free to reject" this "belief." *Id.* at 1500.

133. Rawls, *supra* note 78, at 230.

commitment to a substantive value of equality that is not defined by reference to this purpose, so that the implementation of the value may adversely affect processes of self-determination.[134] The argument thus envisions the possibility of "balancing" fourteenth amendment values against first amendment principles.

In balancing the value of equal citizenship against the principle of self-determination, however, we must ask who is empowered to interpret the meaning of the highly contestable value of equal citizenship. To the extent that the value of equal citizenship is used to justify limiting public discourse, the interpreter of the value cannot be the people, because the very function of the appeal to the fourteenth amendment is to truncate the communicative processes by which the people clarify their collective will.[135] In such circumstances the Ultimate Interpreter, whoever or whatever it may finally turn out to be, must impose its will without popular accountability. Our government currently contains no such Interpreter, not even the Supreme Court, whose constitutional decisions are always shadowed by the potential of constitutional amendment or political reconstruction through subsequent appointments. The impossibility of locating such an Interpreter suggests the difficulties that attend the argument from the fourteenth amendment.[136]

B. *Public Discourse and Harm to Identifiable Groups*

The purpose of public discourse is to reconcile through reason the differences occasioned by a collection of "autonomous wills." Groups neither reason nor have an autonomous will; only persons do. This is the source of the profound individualism that characterizes first amendment doctrine. The question is whether that

---

134. See, for example, *Language as Violence*, *supra* note 5, at 360 (remarks of Mari Matsuda):

> I use the principle of equality as a starting point. . . . [I]f I were to give primacy to any one right, and if I were to create a hierarchy, I would put equality first, because the right of speech is meaningless to people who do not have equality. I mean substantive as well as procedural equality.

135. That members of minority groups are now embraced within the circle of the people and afforded the formal equality required by first amendment processes of self-determination is not, of course, due to any principle of the first amendment, but rather to the principle of equal citizenship embodied in the fourteenth amendment. In this fundamental sense, therefore, no hierarchical relationship between the first and fourteenth amendments can exist.

136. For fuller consideration of a sophisticated argument for "balancing" the values of the fourteenth amendment against those of the first, see *infra* text accompanying notes 210-19.

individualism is compatible with the regulation of public discourse in order to prevent harm to groups.

It is rather common for the laws of other countries to restrain speech deemed harmful to groups, speech that, in the words of the Illinois statute at issue in *Beauharnais*, casts "contempt, derision, or obloquy" on a particular group.[137] Such laws subordinate individual expression to the protection of group status and dignity, typically on the theory that group membership is an essential ingredient of personal identity. Hence, as Gary Jacobsohn notes in his description of Israeli law, groups are seen "as units whose corporate identity carries with it . . . claim[s] upon the state for specific entitlement."[138] Thus the law will in certain situations give "greater priority to fraternal and communal attachments over the subjective choices of individuals."[139]

In American law, by contrast, there is a tendency to view groups as mere "collections of individuals,"[140] whose claims are no greater than those of their constituent members.[141] This tendency is virtually fixed by the individualist presuppositions of public discourse. Thus in *Cantwell v. Connecticut*[142] the Court extended first amendment protection to an anti-Catholic diatribe so violent that it "would offend not only persons of that persuasion, but all others who respect the honestly held religious faith of their fellows."[143] The Court reasoned that this constitutional immunity was necessary so that "many types of life, character, opinion and belief can develop unmolested and unobstructed."[144] This reasoning presupposes that groups evolve through the informed choices of individuals.[145] The Court subordinated the sen-

---

137. Beauharnais v. Illinois, 343 U.S. 250, 251 (1952) (citing ILL. REV. STAT. ch. 38, ¶ 471 (1949)). Antiblasphemy regulations are a common example of such laws. *See* Post, *supra* note 85, at 305-17; THE LAW COMMISSION, OFFENCES AGAINST RELIGION AND PUBLIC WORSHIP 39-53 (Working Paper No. 79, 1981). Many countries also have laws prohibiting group defamation. *See, e.g.*, E. BARENDT, FREEDOM OF SPEECH 161-67 (1985); Lasson, *Group Libel*, *supra* note 5, at 88-89; Matsuda, *supra* note 5, at 2341-48.

138. Jacobsohn, *supra* note 100, at 175.

139. *Id.* at 170.

140. *Id.* at 175.

141. *See, e.g.*, City of Richmond v. J.A. Croson Co., 488 U.S. 469 (1989).

142. 310 U.S. 296 (1940).

143. *Id.* at 309.

144. *Id.* at 310.

145. For an excellent study of the efforts of contemporary Americans to forge new communities, like the Castro district in San Francisco, and hence to "reinvent themselves" by constructing "new lives, new families, even new societies," see F. FITZGERALD, CITIES ON A HILL: A JOURNAL THROUGH CONTEMPORARY AMERICAN CULTURES 23 (1986). FitzGerald views such efforts as "quintessentially American"; try to imagine, she suggests, "Parisians

sibilities of members of established groups, such as Catholics, to the communicative structure necessary for these choices.[146] It thus refused to allow unattractive and highly offensive representations of the Church to be excluded from public discourse.

Cantwell makes special sense because American religious groups have since the nineteenth century been organized on the principle of "voluntarism,"[147] on the notion that "religion is . . . a matter of individual choice."[148] It might be argued, however, that race is quite another matter, one in which a certain kind of group identity is inescapably imposed upon a person by accident of birth. For this reason group identity might be seen as primary with respect to race, and the individualist foundations of public discourse—the assumption that racial groups are determined by processes of individual decisionmaking—repudiated as unrealistic.

This argument is powerful and requires close attention. In analyzing it, we can draw on the distinction that has emerged in feminist writings between "sex," which refers to biological facts, and "gender," which refers to socially constructed roles.[149] To confuse the two, to predicate the social content of gender upon the biological fact of sex, is to fall into "the determinist or essentialist trap."[150] The political point of the distinction is to keep perpetually open for discussion and analysis the social meaning of being born female and included within the group "women."[151] Even if one is not free to opt out of the group, the possibility ought nevertheless to be preserved that the identity of the group be ultimately determined, in the language of Nancy Fraser, "through dialogue and collective struggle."[152] Fraser writes that "[i]n a society as complex as ours, it does not seem to me wise or even possible to extrapolate" the outcome of that dialogue

---

creating a gay colony or a town for grandparents." *Id.* If in Europe or Canada group identity precedes the attempt to ask "the essential questions of who we . . . are, and how we ought to live," *id.* at 20, 389-90, FitzGerald's work illustrates the extent to which group identity in America tends to follow on that attempt, and hence ultimately to rest on individualist premises.

146. For a more detailed discussion, see Post, *supra* note 85, at 319-35.

147. *See* P. Miller, The Life of the Mind in America 40-43 (1965).

148. R. Bellah, R. Madsen, W. Sullivan, A. Swidler, & S. Tipton, Habits of the Heart: Individualism and Commitment in American Life 225 (1985).

149. *See, e.g.*, D. Rhode, Justice and Gender 5 (1989); Marcus, *Reflections on the Significance of the Sex/Gender System: Divorce Law Reform in New York*, 42 U. Miami L. Rev. 55, 55-63 (1987).

150. Marcus, *supra* note 149, at 61; *see* Harris, *Race and Essentialism in Feminist Legal Theory*, 42 Stan. L. Rev. 581 (1990).

151. *See* Harris, *supra* note 150, at 615-16.

152. Fraser, *Toward a Discourse Ethic of Solidarity*, 5 Praxis Int'l 425, 429 (1986).

"from the current, prepoliticized experiences and idiolects of women, especially since it is likely, in my view, that these will turn out to be the current prepoliticized experiences and idiolects only of *some* women."[153]

Fraser's point is that regardless of the biological basis of sex, the social meaning of gender is a political issue whose outcome, like that of all political issues, must be regarded as indeterminate. She thus applies the structure of democratic self-determination to the constitution of group identity. The individualist assumptions of that structure create a form of communication in which political indeterminacy is preserved; they guarantee that the dialogue envisioned by Fraser will remain open to the perspectives of *all* women. If the identity of the group "women" were understood to have a content determinate enough to employ the force of law to silence dissenting views, the law would hegemonically impose the perspective of only *some* women.

The same logic, I believe, holds true for racial groups. We must distinguish race as a biological category from race as a social category. Even if unfortunately "the attempt to establish a *biological* basis of race has not been swept into the dustbin of history,"[154] it would nevertheless be deplorable to construct first amendment principles on the basis of a biological view of race. What is most saliently at issue is rather "race as a social concept": "The effort must be made to understand race as *an unstable and 'decentered' complex of social meanings constantly being transformed by political struggle.*"[155] To the extent that the social meaning of race is thus profoundly controversial[156]—and it is controversial not merely for members of minority groups but also for the entire Nation[157]—the individualist premises of public

---

153. *Id.*

154. M. OMI & H. WINANT, RACIAL FORMATION IN THE UNITED STATES: FROM THE 1960s TO THE 1980s 59 (1986). For an example of the persistence of a biological model of race, see Herrnstein, *Still an American Dilemma*, PUB. INTEREST, Winter 1990, at 3.

155. M. OMI & H. WINANT, *supra* note 154, at 60, 68. Omi and Winant write of the "continuous temptation to think of race as an *essence*, as something fixed, concrete and objective." *Id.* at 68; *see* Appiah, *The Uncompleted Argument: Du Bois and the Illusion of Race*, in H. GATES, "RACE," WRITING AND DIFFERENCE 36 (1986): "Talk of 'race' is particularly distressing for those of us who take culture seriously. . . . What exists 'out there' in the world—communities of meaning, shading variously into each other in the rich structure of the social world—is the province not of biology but of hermeneutic understanding."

156. For a good example, see Scales-Trent, *Black Women and the Constitution: Finding Our Place, Asserting Our Rights*, 24 HARV. C.R.-C.L. L. REV. 9 (1989).

157. For a brief history of the interdependence of understandings of national identity

discourse will ensure that it remains open to democratic constitution.

This lack of closure may of course be threatening, for it casts the creation of group identity upon the uncertain currents of public discourse. The safe harbor of legal regulation may, by contrast, appear to promise members of minority groups more secure control over the meaning of their social experience. But that promise is illusory, for it is profoundly inconsistent with the analysis of racism prevalent in the contemporary literature. To the extent that racism is viewed as pervasive among whites, and to the extent that whites, as a dominant group, can be expected to hold the levers of legal power, there would seem little reason to trust the law to establish socially acceptable meanings for race. Such meanings cannot be determined by reference to easy or bright-line distinctions, as for example those between positive or negative ascriptions of group identity. The work of figures as diverse as William Julius Wilson,[158] Shelby Steele,[159] and Louis Farrakhan[160] illustrates how highly critical characterizations of racial groups can nevertheless serve constructive social purposes. To vest in an essentially white legal establishment the power to discriminate authoritatively among such characterizations and purposes would seem certain to be disempowering.[161]

---

and understandings of race, see Gleason, *American Identity and Americanization*, in W. Petersen, M. Novak, & P. Gleason, Concepts of Ethnicity 57 (1982). A small but I suspect paradigmatic example of this interdependence may be found in the following passage from a student letter to *The Daily Californian*:

> Advertising, television, schools and government are areas of society where racism is largely promoted. Its existence is not easily eradicated. Phrases like "blackmail," "black ball" and "black mood" are common ways "blackness" is communicated in negative terms. . . . One of my professors frequently employs terms like "black lie" to mean the worst of all lies. It takes a conscious effort to disregard these statements and prevent such negative influence on one's psyche. But we must understand that daily use of this terminology reinforces the attack on African-American identity and value.

Broughton, *Promote Afro-American Culture*, The Daily Californian, Sept. 12, 1989, at 4. The writer's point is relevant to the perspectives of members of *both* minority and majority groups; in fact the point effectively demonstrates the essential reciprocity of these perspectives.

158. Wilson, *Social Research and the Underclass Debate*, Bull. Am. Acad. Arts & Sci., Nov. 1989, at 30.

159. S. Steele, The Content of Our Character: A New Vision of Race in America (1990).

160. See *Black Power, Foul and Fragrant*, Economist, Oct. 12, 1985, at 25, for a summary of Farrakhan's critical assessment of the condition of many African-Americans.

161. Note, in this regard, Nadine Strossen's evidence that regulations of racist speech have historically proved to be "particularly threatening to the speech of racial and political minorities." Strossen, *supra* note 5, at 556-59.

The conclusion that group harm ought not to justify legal regulation is reflected in technical first amendment doctrine in the fact that virtually all communications likely to provoke a claim of group harm will be privileged as assertions of evaluative opinion.[162] The following language, for example, gave rise to legal liability in *Beauharnais*: "If persuasion and the need to prevent the white race from becoming mongrelized by the negro will not unite us, then the aggressions . . . rapes, robberies, knives, guns and marijuana of the negro, SURELY WILL."[163] Justice Frankfurter interpreted this language as a false factual assertion: "No one will gainsay that it is libelous falsely to charge another with being a rapist, robber, carrier of knives and guns, and user of marijuana."[164] This interpretation, however, seems plainly incorrect. To accuse an individual of using marijuana is to assert that she has committed certain specific acts, but to accuse the group "blacks" of using marijuana is not to make an analogous assertion. Some blacks will have used marijuana, and most will not have. The question is thus not the existence of certain specific acts, but rather whether those acts can appropriately be used to characterize the group. The fundamental issue is the nature of the group's identity, an issue that almost certainly ought to be characterized as one of evaluative opinion.

Because the social meaning of race is inherently controversial, most statements likely to give rise to actions for group harm will be negative assessments of the identity of racial groups, and hence statements of evaluative opinion. No serious commentator would advocate a trial to determine the truth or falsity of such statements; the point is rather that such statements should not be made at all because of the deep injury they cause. But in a context in which group identity is a matter for determination through political struggle and disagreement, the hypostatized injury of a group cannot, consistent with the processes that instantiate the principle of self-determination, be grounds to legally silence characterizations of group identity within public discourse.

---

162. Or, in the language that the Court recently proposed in Milkovich v. Lorain Journal Co., 110 S. Ct. 2695 (1990), claims of group harm will most likely be privileged as nonfactual assertions of "ideas." For a discussion of the first amendment distinction between fact and ideas, see Post, *The Constitutional Concept*, *supra* note 91, at 649-61. For a discussion of the close relationship between group defamation and nonfactual ideas, see D. RICHARDS, TOLERATION AND THE CONSTITUTION 190-93 (1986); Greenawalt, *supra* note 5, at 305-06.

163. Beauharnais v. Illinois, 343 U.S. 250, 276 (1952) (ellipsis in original).

164. *Id.* at 257-58.

Commentators who stress the theme of group harm vigorously emphasize the fact that racist speech does not injure random groups; it damages precisely those groups who have historically suffered egregious oppression and subordination.[165] But although the tragedy of this fact is obvious, its constitutional implications are not. Our history certainly warrants the assumption that racist speech will inflict terrible injuries on victim groups. But the question is whether these injuries are so unspeakable as to justify suspending the democratic constitution of group identities. One approach might be to avoid this tension by characterizing the injuries of racist speech in such a way that their legal redress would actually be required by the principles of public discourse. Thus it can be argued that the stigmatizing and disabling effects of racist speech effectively exclude its victims from participation in public discourse. This approach suggests an important line of analysis, but I wish to defer consideration of it until Section III(D), *infra*, when it can be placed in the context of other justifications for restraints on racist speech that turn on harms to the marketplace of ideas.

Another method of avoiding the tension between group harm and democratic principles would be to claim that racist speech ought to be characterized as a "mechanism of subordination" within a larger system of suppression, rather than as a form of communication.[166] This claim requires us to determine the criteria by which speech can be designated as action and hence excluded from public discourse. The standard implicitly advanced by the claim is that if communication is intimately connected to larger social relationships that are deeply undesirable, the communication can for that reason be characterized as action.

The difficulty with this standard is that all communication grows out of and embodies social relationships; for this reason all communication is both speech and action. The function of public discourse is to create a protected space within which communication, even if embodying social relationships, can be protected as speech if formulated and disseminated in ways relevant for democratic self-governance. Such a space opens up the possibility of subjecting social relationships to rational reflection, dialogue, and (hence) *self*-control. It thus enables "self-rule" to be reconciled with rule "by laws."[167] If communication

---

165. *See, e.g.*, Matsuda, *supra* note 5, at 2358.
166. *Id.*
167. Michelman, *supra* note 79, at 1501.

could be excluded from this space because it embodies social relations of which we disapprove, public discourse could no longer perform this function. There is no difference between excluding speech from public discourse because we condemn the social relationships it embodies and excluding speech from public discourse because we condemn the ideas by which those social relationships are embodied. In the end, therefore, the argument that racist speech is a form of action reduces to the claim, which we have already considered, that racist speech ought to be restrained because of its inconsistency with the egalitarian ideals of the fourteenth amendment.

C. *Public Discourse and Harm to Individuals*

There appear at first blush to be important differences between claims of group harm and claims of individual harm. To the extent group identity is understood to be a matter of political struggle (and hence dialogic interaction), speech containing negative ascriptions of that identity cannot be censored without undermining the democratic nature of that struggle. But individual identity does not seem to rest on political struggle and dialogue in this way. Indeed, one's spontaneous image is of fully formed individuals entering the realm of public discourse to reach agreement on issues that concern their collective, rather than personal, lives. Speech damaging personal life can thus be restricted without undercutting the very purposes of public discourse.

This perspective, however, rests on a rather sharp distinction between individual and collective identity, a distinction that simply cannot be maintained. The very reason that racist speech harms individual persons is because it so violently ruptures the forms of social respect that are necessary for the maintenance of individual personality. These forms of respect, when taken together, constitute a collective, community identity. Hence the state can prevent the individual harm caused by racist speech only by enforcing pertinent standards of community identity. The interdependence of individual and collective identity is thus presupposed in the very concept of individual harm.

This interdependence lies behind well-established constitutional prohibitions on restricting public discourse because it is "offensive"[168] or "outrageous,"[169] or because it affronts "dignity"

168. Cohen v. California, 403 U.S. 15, 16 (1971).
169. Hustler Magazine v. Falwell, 485 U.S. 46, 52 (1988).

or is "insulting" or causes "public odium" or "public disrepute."[170] Such speech causes intense individual suffering because it violates community norms, yet the Court has required its toleration in order to prevent the state from using the authority of law to enforce particular conceptions of collective life.[171]

Questions of personal identity are in fact always at stake in discussions of collective self-definition. For this reason effective political dialogue requires that participants be constantly willing to be transformed. As Frank Michelman points out, public discourse is impossible so long as "the participants' pre-political self-understandings and social perspectives must axiomatically be regarded as completely impervious to the persuasion of the process itself."[172] As our collective aspirations change, so will our respective personal identities. Thus restrictions on public discourse designed to protect those identities from harm will necessarily also restrict self-determination as to our collective life. If group harm is an inevitable price of the political constitution of group identity, individual injury is an unavoidable cost of the political constitution of community identity.

It is important to emphasize the narrowness of this conclusion. In recent years an important theme of our national life has been the opposition to racism. We have enacted that opposition by legally regulating racist behavior like discrimination. Because action both creates and manifests identity, this regulation inhibits the formation and expression of racist identities. So also does regulation prohibiting certain kinds of racist speech in nonpublic speech, as for example in the workplace.[173] In effect we have determined to use government force to reshape community institutions in order to combat racism. This is an appropriate and laudable use of democratic power.[174] But it is legitimate precisely

---

170. Boos v. Barry, 485 U.S. 312, 316, 322 (1988). "[I]n public debate our own citizens must tolerate insulting, and even outrageous, speech in order to provide 'adequate breathing space to the freedoms protected by the First Amendment.' " *Id.* at 322 (quoting *Hustler Magazine*, 485 U.S. at 56); *see* Texas v. Johnson, 109 S. Ct. 2533, 2543-47 (1989).

171. I elaborate on this argument in Post, *The Constitutional Concept*, *supra* note 91, at 626-46. The cases cited in notes 168-70 *supra* thus stand foursquare against the application to public discourse of the tort of racial insult as proposed by Delgado, *supra* note 4, Love, *supra* note 5, and Wright, *supra* note 5.

172. Michelman, *supra* note 79, at 1526; *see* F. CUNNINGHAM, DEMOCRATIC THEORY AND SOCIALISM 188-91 (1987).

173. *See supra* notes 112-13 and accompanying text.

174. It should be noted, however, that the public/private distinction necessary for democratic governance will require that at some point limitations be placed on the ability of the state coercively to form citizens with nonracist identities. *See supra* note 87.

because we have adopted it in a manner consistent with the principle of self-determination; it reflects a national identity that we have freely chosen.

This legitimacy is possible because of public discourse, which serves the value of self-determination because it is so structured that every call for national identity has the opportunity to make its case. There is a significant difference, therefore, between proscribing racial insults directed toward individuals in the workplace[175] and proscribing them in a political discussion or debate.[176] The harm to the individual victim may be the same, but for public discourse to enable *self*-government, racist speech within that discourse must be repudiated on the merits, rather than be silenced by force of law.

D. Public Discourse and Harm to the Marketplace of Ideas

The most effective arguments for regulating racist speech are those that double back on the concept of public discourse itself and contend that such regulation is necessary for public discourse truly to instantiate the principle of self-determination. On the surface there appear to be two distinct lines of analysis. The first stresses the irrational and coercive qualities of racist speech; the second the untoward effects of racist speech in silencing victim groups. In the end these lines of argumentation cross and depend upon each other.

1. Racist Speech as Irrational and Coercive

Public discourse must be more than simply a register of private preferences in order to serve as a medium for the enactment of collective autonomy. If persons communicated in public discourse merely through polling organizations to make known their "votes" on public issues, democracy would degenerate into the heteronomous system of majoritarian rule described by Schauer. The purposes of collective self-determination require instead that public action be founded upon a public opinion formed through open and interactive processes of rational deliberation. The argument that racist speech is irrational and coercive, that it is

---

175. *See, e.g.*, Contreras v. Crown Zellerbach Corp., 88 Wash. 2d 735, 565 P.2d 1173 (1977); Alcorn v. Anbro Eng'g, 2 Cal. 3d 493, 468 P.2d 216, 86 Cal. Rptr. 88 (1970); Love, *supra* note 5, at 128-33.

176. *Cf.* Dominguez v. Stone, 97 N.M. 211, 638 P.2d 423 (1981) (penalizing racist speech in political speech).

nothing more than a kind of "linguistic abuse (verbal abuse on an unwilling target),"[177] thus cuts to the very root of public discourse.

The argument, however, points to a more general problem, for all communication that violates civility rules is perceived as both irrational and coercive.[178] Because civility rules embody the norms of respect and reason we are accustomed to receive from members of our community, communication inconsistent with those rules is experienced as an instrument "of aggression and personal assault."[179] The argument from coercion and irrationality thus poses a generic dilemma for first amendment doctrine. If the state were permitted to enforce civility rules, it would in effect exclude from public discourse those whose speech advocated and exemplified unfamiliar and marginalized forms of life. But if the state were to suspend the enforcement of civility rules, it would endanger the possibility of rational deliberation by permitting the dissemination of abusive and coercive speech. This tension between the requirement that self-government respect all of its citizens "as free and equal persons," and the requirement that self-government proceed through processes of rational deliberation, creates the paradox of public discourse.[180]

It might be thought that the specific case of racist speech dissolves this paradox, for such speech by hypothesis violates norms of both equality and civility and hence appears to be suppressible without harm to public discourse. But this conclusion is not accurate. The principle of equality at issue in the paradox of public discourse is purely formal; its extension to all persons

---

177. Lasson, *Group Libel*, *supra* note 5, at 122.

178. Thus "fighting words" are understood to be those that "by their very utterance inflict injury." Chaplinsky v. New Hampshire, 315 U.S. 568, 572 (1942). Outrageous words intentionally inflicting emotional distress are "nothing more than a surrogate" for a "punch or kick." Wright, Hustler Magazine v. Falwell *and the Role of the First Amendment*, 19 CUMB. L. REV. 19, 23 (1988). "Ridicule" is experienced as a form of "intimidation." Dewey, *Creative Democracy—The Task Before Us*, in CLASSIC AMERICAN PHILOSOPHERS 389, 393 (M. Fisch ed. 1951). Pornography is received not as "expression depicting the subordination of women, but [as] the *practice of subordination* itself." Brest & Vandenberg, *Politics, Feminism, and the Constitution: The Anti-Pornography Movement in Minneapolis*, 39 STAN. L. REV. 607, 659 (1987). And blasphemous communications are nothing more than a form of "brawls." F. HOLT, THE LAW OF LIBEL 70-71 (1816).

179. Time, Inc. v. Hill, 385 U.S. 374, 412 (1967) (Fortas, J., dissenting). Alexander Bickel once remarked that such communication "amounts to almost physical aggression." A. BICKEL, THE MORALITY OF CONSENT 72 (1975); *see also* Cohen v. California, 403 U.S. 15, 27 (1971) (Blackmun, J., dissenting) (characterizing Cohen's actions as being more like conduct than speech).

180. *See supra* text accompanying notes 91-105.

is the fundamental precondition of the possibility of self-government. To the extent that the principle is circumscribed, so also is the reach of self-determination. The norm of equality violated by racist speech, on the other hand, is substantive; it reflects a particular understanding of how we ought to live. It is the kind of norm that ought to emerge from processes of public deliberation. Although the censorship of racist speech is consistent with this substantive norm of equality, it is inconsistent with the formal principle of equality, because such censorship would exclude from the medium of public discourse those who disagree with a particular substantive norm of equality. Such persons would thus be cut off from participation in the processes of collective self-determination.

First amendment doctrine has tended to resolve the paradox of public discourse in favor of the principle of formal equality, largely because violations of that principle limit pro tanto the domain of self-government, whereas protecting uncivil speech does not automatically destroy the possibility of rational deliberation. The visceral shock of uncivil speech can sometimes actually serve constructive purposes, as when it causes individuals to question the community standards into which they have been socialized and hence enables them, perhaps for the first time, to acknowledge the claims of others from radically different cultural backgrounds.[181] There is in fact a long tradition of oppressed and marginalized groups using uncivil speech to force recognition of the intensity and urgency of their needs.[182]

Tolerating uncivil speech, moreover, does not necessarily undermine the process of rational deliberation, so long as the extent of such speech is confined and does not infect the process as a

181. Thus in *Terminiello v. Chicago*:

> [A] function of free speech under our system of government is to invite dispute. It may indeed best serve its high purpose when it induces a condition of unrest, creates dissatisfaction with conditions as they are, or even stirs people to anger. Speech is often provocative and challenging. It may strike at prejudices and preconceptions and have profound unsettling effects as it presses for acceptance of an idea. That is why freedom of speech, though not absolute . . . is nevertheless protected against censorship or punishment, unless shown likely to produce a clear and present danger of a serious substantive evil that rises far above public inconvenience, annoyance, or unrest. . . . There is no room under our Constitution for a more restrictive view. For the alternative would lead to standardization of ideas either by legislatures, courts, or dominant political or community groups.

337 U.S. 1, 4-5 (1949) (citations omitted).

182. For an excellent discussion, see Karst, *Boundaries and Reasons: Freedom of Expression and the Subordination of Groups*, 1990 U. ILL. L. REV. 95.

whole. The judgment that rational deliberation can continue in spite of the presence of uncivil speech is exactly the point of Harlan's opinion in *Cohen v. California*,[183] in which the Court refused to permit the state to use the force of law "to maintain . . . a suitable level of discourse within the body politic":[184]

> The constitutional right of free expression is powerful medicine in a society as diverse and populous as ours. It is designed and intended to remove governmental restraints from the arena of public discussion, putting the decision as to what views shall be voiced largely into the hands of each of us, in the hope that use of such freedom will ultimately produce a more capable citizenry and more perfect polity and in the belief that no other approach would comport with the premise of individual dignity and choice upon which our political system rests. . . .
>
> To many, the immediate consequence of this freedom may often appear to be only verbal tumult, discord, and even offensive utterance. These are, however, within established limits, in truth necessary side effects of the broader enduring values which the process of open debate permits us to achieve. That the air may at times seem filled with verbal cacophony is, in this sense not a sign of weakness but of strength.[185]

It is of course a matter of judgment whether "open debate" within "the arena of public discussion" is indeed achieving "broader enduring values." How one makes that judgment will depend very much on one's circumstances. The call in recent literature to attend more carefully to "the victim's perspective"[186] is well taken in this regard. Members of dominant groups may be satisfied with the overall quality of public deliberation, but members of victim groups, at whom racist speech is systematically targeted, may feel quite otherwise.

It is at this point that the line of analysis stressing the irrational, coercive quality of racist speech crosses and depends upon the line of analysis stressing the silencing of victim groups. For when pressed the point is not that public discourse is pervasively disabled by racist speech, but rather that the concentrated effect of such speech on members of victim groups is to foreclose public discourse as an effective avenue of collective

183. 403 U.S. 15.
184. *Id.* at 23.
185. *Id.* at 24-25.
186. Matsuda, *supra* note 5, at 2340; *see* Lawrence, *supra* note 5, at 436.

self-determination. In the contemporary debate this effect has been addressed under the rubric of "silencing."

2. Racist Speech as Silencing Minority Groups

The literature on silencing has burgeoned. So far as I can make out the literature presents three distinct arguments to support the concept of silencing:[187] victim groups are silenced because their perspectives are systematically excluded from the dominant discourse;[188] victim groups are silenced because the pervasive stigma of racism systematically undermines and devalues their speech; and victim groups are silenced because the visceral "fear, rage, [and] shock" of racist speech systematically preempts response.[189] This Section analyzes each of these arguments separately; the following Section weaves them together into a more complex indictment of racist speech.

The first argument, more developed in the context of recent feminist literature than in that of racist speech, is that the language of public discourse, although seemingly neutral and objective, has a built-in bias that prevents the articulation of minority positions.[190] Thus racism in the dominant discourse is compressed into "the neutralized word 'discrimination,' " in which "the role of power, domination, and oppression as the source of the evil" is effaced, and "[m]uch of the political, historical, and moral content of 'equality' has been dropped."[191] Similarly, the understanding of whites that racism is an "intentional belief in white supremacy"—the perpetrators' perspective—has been folded into the very language of public debate, whereas the understanding of minorities that racism " 'refers *solely* to minority subordination' "—the victims' perspective—is banished from the language.[192]

Although the premise of this argument seems to me true, it does not by itself support the conclusion that racist speech ought

---

187. I omit discussion of speech that silences through outright intimidation and threats. The regulation of such speech is not problematic under any theory.

188. For a good introduction to the concept of "discourse," see Bové, *Discourse*, in CRITICAL TERMS FOR LITERARY STUDY 50 (F. Lentricchia & T. McLaughlin eds. 1990).

189. Lawrence, *supra* note 5, at 452.

190. *Id.* at 474-75; *see* Crenshaw, *Race, Reform, and Retrenchment: Transformation and Legitimation in Antidiscrimination Law*, 101 HARV. L. REV. 1331, 1370-81 (1988).

191. Finley, *Breaking Women's Silence in Law: The Dilemma of the Gendered Nature of Legal Reasoning*, 64 NOTRE DAME L. REV. 886, 889 (1989).

192. Note, *Racism and Race Relations in the University*, 76 VA. L. REV. 295, 304 n.32 (1990) (quoting Brooks, *Anti-Minority Mindset in the Law School Personnel Process: Toward an Understanding of Racial Mindsets*, 5 J.L. & INEQUALITY 1, 8-11 (1987)).

to be regulated. All communication rests on foundations of unarticulated assumptions. The very function of dialogue is often to move toward enlightenment by uncovering and exposing these assumptions. Enlightenment can be gradual and progressive, or it can result from the shock of intense political struggle. That our language always encompasses both more and less than our intentions is thus not an argument for the suppression of racist speech, but rather for the encouragement of further public debate.

The point might be made, however, that public debate fails to achieve such enlightenment because the pervasive racism of American society devalues and stigmatizes minority contributions to this debate. The voice of the victims goes unheard. There is thus a call for an "outsider jurisprudence"[193] which will legitimate that voice and enable "[l]egal insiders . . . [to] imagine a life disabled in a significant way by hate propaganda."[194]

Once again, the premise of this argument appears sound, but its conclusion does not. Audiences always evaluate communication on the basis of their understanding of its social context.[195] This is not a deformity of public discourse, but one of its generic characteristics.[196] It poses the question of how an audience's prepolitical understanding of social context may be altered, a question that confronts all participants in public dialogue. The urgency of the question does not justify restricting public discourse; it is rather a call for more articulate and persuasive speech, for more intense and effective political engagement.

Taken together, the argument from the inherent bias of accepted discourse and the argument from the stigmatic devaluation of minority speech fuse into a single indictment of public discourse as irrational. The systematic derogation of the specific perspectives of victim groups is said to be caused by the Nation's particular history of racial oppression, rather than by concerns that would properly affect a legitimately rational public dialogue. Both arguments thus ultimately appeal to the concept of false consciousness,[197] to the notion that there is an ideal vantage from

---

193. Matsuda, *supra* note 5, at 2323-26.

194. *Id.* at 2375; *see* Lawrence, *supra* note 5, at 458-61.

195. Riesman, *Democracy and Defamation: Fair Game and Fair Comment II*, 42 COLUM. L. REV. 1282, 1306-07 (1942).

196. *See* P. CHEVIGNY, MORE SPEECH: DIALOGUE RIGHTS AND MODERN LIBERTY 53-72 (1988); Michelman, *Conceptions of Democracy in American Constitutional Argument: The Case of Pornography Regulation*, 56 TENN. L. REV. 291, 313 (1989).

197. For a general discussion of the concept of "false consciousness," see R. GEUSS, THE IDEA OF A CRITICAL THEORY: HABERMAS AND THE FRANKFURT SCHOOL (1981).

which the rationality of discourse can be "objectively" assessed.

But it is one thing to use the idea of false consciousness as a weapon *within* public discourse to convince others of the need to break with the prejudices of the past, and it is quite another to use the idea as a justification to limit public discourse itself. The first is a familiar rhetorical strategy. It is consistent with the processes of public discourse because its effectiveness ultimately depends upon its persuasive power. The second, however, presupposes an intimacy with truth so vital as to foreclose opposing positions. The very point of using the idea of false consciousness to limit public discourse is to justify legally disregarding certain perspectives, on the grounds that these perspectives could not possibly be respected as true expressions of autonomous individuality. Circumscribing public discourse to ameliorate false consciousness thus does not protect public discourse from harm, but rather contradicts its very purpose of providing a medium for the reconciliation of autonomous wills.

The third argument for restraining racist speech does not turn on the characterization of public discourse as irrational, but rather as coercive. Recent literature contains searing documentation of the profound personal injury of racist speech, and this injury may in particular circumstances be so shocking as to literally preempt responsive speech. Although the analogous harm of uncivil speech is randomly scattered throughout the population, the disabilities attendant upon racist speech are concentrated upon members of victim groups. Hence, where members of dominant groups perceive "isolated incidents,"[198] members of victim groups perceive instead a suffocating and inescapable "racism that is a persistent and constituent part of the social order, woven into the fabric of society and everyday life."[199]

Under such conditions it is to be expected that members of dominant and victim groups may well come to conflicting judgments about whether racist speech shocks significant segments of victim group population into silence. The recent literature proposing restraints on racist speech is eloquent on the need to "listen[ ] to the real victims" of such speech and to display "empathy or understanding for their injury."[200] And of course any fair and just determination about the regulation of public discourse would require exactly this kind of sensitivity. But there

198. Matsuda, *supra* note 5, at 2331.
199. Note, *supra* note 192, at 295.
200. Lawrence, *supra* note 5, at 436.

is also a tendency in recent literature to move from the proposition that a fair determination cannot be made unless "the victims of racist speech are heard,"[201] to the very different proposition that such a determination ought to use "the experience of victim-group members [as] a guide."[202] The latter proposition seems to me plainly false.

The issue on the table is whether irrationality and coercion have so tainted the medium of public discourse as to require shrinking the scope of self-government. That issue significantly affects every citizen, and its resolution therefore cannot be ceded to the control of any particular group. In fact I do not see how the issue can be adequately resolved at all unless some notion of civic membership is invoked that transcends mere group identification. Unless we can strive to deliberate together as citizens, distancing ourselves from (but not abandoning) our specific cultural backgrounds, the issue can be resolved only through the exercise of naked group power, a solution not at all advantageous to the marginalized and oppressed.[203]

Paradoxically, therefore, the question of whether public discourse is irretrievably damaged by racist speech must itself ultimately be addressed through the medium of public discourse. Because those participating in public discourse will not themselves have been silenced (almost by definition), a heavy, frus-

---

201. *Id.* at 481.

202. Matsuda, *supra* note 5, at 2369. This tendency is explicitly thematized in Iris Marion Young's artless proposal that "a democratic public" should cede to "constituent groups that are oppressed or disadvantaged" a "veto power regarding specific policies that affect a group directly." Young, *Polity and Group Difference*, 99 ETHICS 250, 261-62 (1989).

203. The "grand tradition" of republican participation, the notion that "we can lift our public life above the fallen and compromised realm of factional politics," thus does not seem to me so easily abandoned as would appear from recent literature stressing fidelity to the particular cultural "tradition" of minority groups. *See* Lopez, *The Idea of a Constitution in the Chicano Tradition*, 37 J. LEGAL EDUC. 162, 163-64 (1987). Even Young notes that a "heterogeneous public . . . is a *public*, where participants discuss together the issues before them and are supposed to come to a decision that they determine as best or most just." Young, *supra* note 202, at 267.

> It is possible for persons to maintain their group identity and to be influenced by their perceptions of social events derived from their group-specific experience, and at the same time to be public spirited, in the sense of being open to listening to the claims of others and not being concerned for their own gain alone. It is possible and necessary for people to take a critical distance from their own immediate desires and gut reactions in order to discuss public proposals. Doing so, however, cannot require that citizens abandon their particular affiliations, experiences, and social location.

Id. at 257-58.

trating burden is de facto placed on those who would truncate public discourse in order to save it. They must represent themselves as "speaking for" those who have been deprived of their voice. But the negative space of that silence reigns inscrutable, neither confirming nor denying this claim. And the more eloquent the appeal, the less compelling the claim, for the more accessible public discourse will then appear to exactly the perspectives racist speech is said to repress.

Even if this burden is lifted, however, and it is simply accepted that members of victim groups are intimidated into silence, it would still not follow that restraints on racist speech within public discourse are justified. One might believe, for example, that such silencing occurs chiefly through the structural conditions of racism, rather than specifically through the shock of racist speech. "The problem," as the Chairman of the Black Studies Department of New York's City College recently remarked apropos of the racist comments of an academic colleague, does not lie with specific communicative acts, but rather with "racism" itself, "insidious in our society and built into our culture."[204] If that were true, restraints on racist speech would impair public discourse without at the same time repairing the silence of victim groups.

Alternatively, one might believe that racist speech silences victim groups primarily because of its "ideas," because of its messages of racial inferiority, rather than because of its incivility. The distinction is important for the following reason: although it is consistent with the internal logic of public discourse to excise in extreme circumstances certain kinds of uncivil speech that are experienced as coercive,[205] it is fundamentally incompatible with public discourse to excise specific ideas because they are "analogously" deemed to be coercive. Public discourse is the medium within which our society assesses the democratic acceptability of ideas; to exclude certain ideas as prima facie "coercive" and hence destructive of public discourse is to contradict precisely this function. Therefore "harm" to public discourse cannot justify restraints on racist ideas on the grounds that such ideas are perceived to be threatening or coercive.[206]

---

204. Berger, *Professors' Theories on Race Stir Turmoil at City College*, N.Y. Times, Apr. 20, 1990, at B1, col. 2.

205. *See supra* text accompanying notes 178-80.

206. Note that the argument in text does not hold against the contention that certain ideas should be excluded from public discourse because they cause extensive harm to

There are also other possibilities. One might believe, for example, that because it is difficult to distinguish ideas from incivility, and because it is vitally important to collective self-determination to protect all ideas, the law will as a practical matter be able to restrain only a small category of blatant racist epithets, which, although deeply offensive and lacking in ideational content, have relatively little to do with the more widespread phenomenon of silencing. Or one might believe that racist speech silences primarily when shocking racist epithets are used in the face-to-face confrontations characteristic of the "fighting words" doctrine of *Chaplinsky*,[207] so that the essential insight of the argument from silencing is already reflected within first amendment doctrine.

My own conclusion, in light of these alternative considerations, is that the case has not yet been made for circumscribing public discourse to prevent the kind of preemptive silencing that occurs when members of victim groups experience "fear, rage, [and] shock." I say this with some hesitation, and with considerable ambivalence. But even if the empirical claim of systematic preemptive silencing were accepted (and I am not sure that I do accept it), it is in my view most directly the result of the social and structural conditions of racism, rather than specifically of racist speech. Because the logic of the argument from preemptive silencing does not impeach the necessity of preserving the free expression of ideas,[208] public discourse could at most be regulated in a largely symbolic manner so as to purge it of outrageous racist epithets and names. It seems to me highly implausible to claim that such symbolic regulation will eliminate the preemptive silencing that is said to justify restraints on public discourse.

---

individuals or victim groups. Such harm is extrinsic to the function of public discourse. To evaluate the contention that public discourse ought to be limited because of harm to individuals or groups, therefore, we must assess the importance of democratic self-governance in light of our commitment to protecting stable personal and group identities. *See supra* Sections III(B) & (C).

The argument considered in text that certain ideas ought to be excluded from public discourse because they are intrinsically coercive, on the other hand, turns upon harm to the function of public discourse itself. The argument is unsatisfactory because the concept of "coercion" must itself be defined by reference to a "moral baseline" determined by the practice in question. *See* A. WERTHEIMER, COERCION 217 (1987). Within the practice of public discourse, no idea can be deemed intrinsically coercive because the very function of public discourse presupposes a formal equality of persons and hence of ideas.

207. Chaplinsky v. New Hampshire, 315 U.S. 568 (1942).

208. *See supra* note 206.

3. Racist Speech as Symbolic Cultural Oppression

When distinguished and parsed in this analytic manner, therefore, the various arguments for restraining racist speech in order to preserve the integrity of public discourse do not in my judgment support their desired conclusion. But the arguments can be braided together to fund an accusation more powerful than its separate strands.

In ordinary life, members of victim groups do not experience a string of distinct disadvantages. Rather, if representations in the current literature are accepted as true, these groups confront in public discourse an undifferentiated complex of circumstances in which they are systematically demeaned, stigmatized, ignored; in which the very language of debate resists the articulation of their claims; in which they are harassed, abused, intimidated, and systematically and egregiously injured both individually and collectively. The question is not whether these liabilities, when taken individually and singly, justify restraining racist speech within public discourse, but rather whether, when taken together as a complex whole, they render public discourse unfit as an instrument of collective self-determination for members of victim groups, and whether this unacceptable situation would be cured by restraints on racist speech.

What makes this question so very formidable is that it turns on the nexus between public discourse and the value of collective self-determination. Although the formal preconditions of that nexus can be described, its actual substantive realization must remain contingent upon conditions of history, culture, and social structure. Thus when members of victim groups claim that public discourse no longer serves for them the value of self-government, it is no answer to reply that they have been embraced within its formal preconditions. If members of victim groups in fact perceive themselves to be systematically excluded from public dialogue, that dialogue can scarcely achieve for them those "broader enduring values" that are its democratic justification. The very legitimacy of democratic self-governance is thus called into question.

The dependence of the value of public discourse upon matters of social perception poses complex and delicate questions, but the difficulty of these questions is profoundly magnified in the context of the controversy over racist speech. First, the truth of the claim that members of victim groups are cut off from meaningful participation within public discourse cannot be directly experienced and hence evaluated by members of dominant groups. Its resolution must therefore depend, to one degree or another, upon acceptance of the representations of members of victim groups. As a practical political matter, therefore, what is called into question is not merely the truth of these representations, but also the trust and respect with which they are received by members of dominant groups.[209] Second, the focus on trust and respect is reinforced by the remedial claim that racist speech ought to be censored so as to open up public discourse to victim groups. Essentially this claim requires that self-determination be denied to some so that it may be made available to others. Thus society's willingness to circumscribe public discourse is transformed into a touchstone of the esteem with which it regards victim groups.

In fact it is this transformation that most precisely supports the argument. The argument turns on the interpretive meaning that members of victim groups ascribe to their place in American life; the contention is that this meaning is one of exclusion. Such an interpretation cannot be reduced to any specific empirical claims or conditions. Instead the need of those who feel alienated is most exactly met by a gesture of social esteem. By conveying in the strongest possible terms messages of respect and welcome, the censorship of racist speech might go a long way toward allowing members of victim groups to reinterpret their experience as one of inclusion within the dialogue of public discourse. The objection we noted earlier, that the regulation of racist speech within public discourse could at most restrict the publication of highly offensive racist epithets and names, and that such regulation could only serve symbolic purposes, is thus no longer pertinent. For the argument now turns squarely on the politics of cultural symbolism.

The most salient characteristic of such politics is that the particular content of government regulation is less important than its perceived meaning. We have already noted how claims like those of individual injury or preemptive silencing define concrete classes of communications that are said empirically to cause a particular harm. But the claim of cultural exclusion is fundamentally different, for it implies no such specific referent.

---

209. *See* Lawrence, *supra* note 5, at 474-75. That this is a general characteristic of group claims can be seen by the development of an analogous dynamic among those who support the regulation of pornography. *See, e.g.*, C. MacKinnon, *On Collaboration*, in Feminism Unmodified: Discourses on Life and Law 198 (1987).

The claim, when pressed, is not that any specific class of communications actually causes members of victim groups to feel excluded, but rather that a particular regulatory gesture will be the occasion for members of victim groups to feel included.[210]

This suggests, however, that restraints on public discourse are only one of a wide variety of strategies that government can pursue to ameliorate the sense of cultural exclusion experienced by victim groups. Other alternatives might include antidiscrimination laws, affirmative action programs, redistribution of economic resources, restraints on racist forms of nonpublic speech, and so forth. All these modifications of community life could be interpreted as significant gestures of respect and inclusion. It is a matter of political choice and characterization to reject these alternatives as insufficient and to deem the limitation of public discourse as necessary to overcome the alienation of victim groups.

At root, therefore, the argument from cultural exclusion seeks to subordinate public discourse, whose very purpose is to serve as the framework for all possible forms of politics, to a particular political perspective. The argument begins with the sound premise that a cultural sense of participation is necessary for public discourse to serve the value of collective self-determination. But instead of conceiving public discourse as a means of rousing the Nation's political will to actions designed to facilitate that sense of participation, the argument instead turns on public discourse itself, and, as a matter of political perception and assertion, deems the limitation of that discourse to be prerequisite for the elimination of disabling alienation. The argument therefore does not ultimately rest on the importance of protecting public discourse from harm, but rather on the need to sacrifice public discourse in order to recuperate profound social dislocations.

Bluntly expressed, the argument requires us to balance the integrity of public discourse as a general structure of communication against the importance of enhancing the experience of political participation by members of victim groups. The argument thus reiterates the position that public discourse ought to be subordinated to the egalitarian ideals of the fourteenth amend-

---

210. The success or failure of the gesture will depend entirely on the perception of members of victim groups. There is thus no guarantee that any particular regulatory scheme will in fact actually cause members of victim groups to reinterpret their position within public discourse. This inherent gap between regulatory design and the achievement of regulatory purpose, coupled with the fact that only members of victim groups can experience and evaluate the claim of cultural exclusion, creates disturbing possibilities for strategic manipulation.

ment. It adopts a sophisticated version of that position, however, for it is able to contend that public discourse need be impaired in only slight and symbolic ways. Even so minimal a gesture as purging outrageous and shocking racist epithets could be sufficient to make members of victim groups feel welcome within the arena of public discourse, and thus to enable public discourse to serve for them the value of self-determination.[211] In this form the argument is analogous to that advanced in the controversy over prohibiting flag burning, in which it is also urged that public discourse ought to be minimally impaired for highly important symbolic reasons.[212] Just as it has been contended that any idea can be expressed without burning a flag,[213] so it can be asserted that any idea can be expressed without recourse to vile racist epithets.[214] In both cases, therefore, it can be argued that the de minimis effects on public discourse are outweighed by the significance of the interests at stake.[215]

I believe, however, that this invitation to balance ought to be declined. This is not because balancing can be ruled out in advance by some "absolutist" algorithm; the attraction of a purely formal democracy may itself in extreme circumstances no longer command limitless conviction. It is rather because, in the American context, the temptation to balance rests on what might be termed the fallacy of immaculate isolation.[216] The effect on public

---

211. Of course so minimal a gesture might not be sufficient to achieve this purpose. The intrinsically speculative quality of the argument must be taken into account in its evaluation.

212. According to the Solicitor General, the state's interest in prohibiting flag burning turns on the importance of "safeguard[ing] the flag's identity 'as the unique and unalloyed symbol of the Nation.'" United States v. Eichman, 110 S. Ct. 2404, 2408 (1990) (quoting Brief for United States at 28, 29).

213. Texas v. Johnson, 109 S. Ct. 2533, 2553-54 (1989) (Rehnquist, C.J., dissenting).

214. I should be plain that I myself reject the premise of this argument and do not believe that the rhetorical meaning of speech can be disentangled from the manner of its presentation. Style and substance are always interdependent, for, in the words of Georg Lukács, "[c]ontent determines form." G. LUKÁCS, REALISM IN OUR TIME: LITERATURE AND THE CLASS STRUGGLE 19 (J. & N. Mander trans. 1962). For a discussion, see Post, *The Constitutional Concept*, *supra* note 91, at 663 n.314. I therefore do not think that the impact on public discourse of prohibiting certain kinds of words can ever properly be said to be de minimis. I nevertheless want to evaluate the case for balancing on the strong assumption of this kind of de minimis impact.

215. For a discussion of this argument in the context of flag burning, see *Eichman*, 110 S. Ct. at 2410-12 (Stevens, J., dissenting).

216. In evaluating this balance, I do not mean to call into question the holding of *Chaplinsky*, which in my view attempts to distinguish private fracases from political debate. *See* Post, *The Constitutional Concept*, *supra* note 91, at 679-81. It is clear enough that racial epithets, when uttered in certain face-to-face situations, would constitute

discourse is acceptable only if it is de minimis, and it is arguably de minimis only when a specific claim is evaluated in isolation from other, similar claims. But no claim is in practice immaculately isolated in this manner. As the flag burning example suggests, there is no shortage of powerful groups contending that uncivil speech within public discourse ought to be "minimally" regulated for highly pressing symbolic reasons.[217]

This is evident even if the focus of analysis is narrowly limited to the structure of the claim at issue in the debate over racist speech. In a large heterogeneous country populated by assertive and conflicting groups, the logic of circumscribing public discourse to reduce political estrangement is virtually unstoppable. The Nation is filled with those who feel displaced and who would feel less so if given the chance symbolically to truncate public discourse. This is already plain in the regulations that have proliferated on college campuses, which commonly proscribe not merely speech that degrades persons on the basis of their race, but also, to pick a typical list, speech that demeans persons on the basis of their "color, national origin, religion, sex, sexual orientation, age, handicap, or veteran's status."[218] The claim of de minimis impact loses credibility as the list of claimants to special protection grows longer.

"fighting words" and hence not form part of public discourse. *See* Greenawalt, *supra* note 5, at 306. The point of the argument in text, however, is to evaluate restraints on racist epithets in what would otherwise clearly be deemed public discourse, as for example in political debates, newspapers, pamphlets, magazines, novels, movies, records, and so forth.

217. Anyone inclined to doubt this proposition should review again the current controversy over funding for the National Endowment for the Arts, or the recent prosecutions occasioned by the Mapplethorpe exhibition or the recordings of 2 Live Crew. *See Rap Band Members Found Not Guilty in Obscenity Trial*, N.Y. Times, Oct. 21, 1990, § 1, at 1, col. 1 (discussing 2 Live Crew's acquittal after being charged with giving obscene performance and record store owner's conviction after being charged with selling obscene 2 Live Crew album); *Cincinnati Jury Acquits Museum in* Mapplethorpe *Obscenity Case*, N.Y. Times, Oct. 6, 1990, § 1, at 1, col. 1; *Reverend Wildman's War on the Arts*, N.Y. Times, Sept. 2, 1990, § 6 (Magazine), at 22, col. 1.

218. Emory University, Policy Statement on Discriminatory Harassment (1988); *see* Doe v. University of Mich., 721 F. Supp. 852, 856 (E.D. Mich. 1989) (concerning sanctions for speech victimizing an individual "on the basis of race, ethnicity, religion, sex, sexual orientation, creed, national origin, ancestry, age, marital status, handicap or Vietnam-era veteran status"). The regulations of Michigan State University include the prohibited category of "political persuasion." Michigan State University, Your Ticket to an Adventure in Understanding (1988) (available from University Housing Programs). The regulations of West Chester University include the category of "lifestyle." West Chester University, Ram's Eye View: Every Student's Guide to West Chester University 61 (1990) (available from Student Development Office). The regulations of Hampshire College include that of "socio-economic class." Hampshire College, College Policies: Updates and Revisions (1988-89).

The point I want to press does not depend upon the intellectual difficulty of drawing lines to separate similar claims. It is rather that the remedial and political logic of equal participation applies with analogous force to a broad and growing spectrum of group claims. One might, of course, devise arguments, perhaps based on the specific history of the fourteenth amendment, to distinguish racial epithets from blasphemous imprecations, or from degrading and pornographic characterizations of women, or from vicious antigay slurs, or from gross ethnic insults. But the question is whether such arguments can withstand the compelling egalitarian logic that unites these various situations. My strong intuition is that they cannot, and hence that the claim of de minimis impact on public discourse is implausible.[219]

In the specific context of the argument from cultural exclusion, moreover, a refusal to balance is far less harsh than it might superficially appear. The fundamental challenge is to enable members of victim groups to reinterpret their experience within the American political and cultural order as one of genuine participation. There are a host of ways to address this challenge short of truncating public discourse. The most obvious and potentially effective strategy would be to dismantle systematically and forcefully the structural conditions of racism. If we were so blessed as to be able to accomplish that feat—if we were truly able to eliminate such conditions as chronic unemployment, inadequate health care, segregated housing, or disproportionately low incomes—then we would no doubt also have succeeded in ameliorating the experience of cultural exclusion.

IV. The First Amendment and Harm to the Educational Environment

If public discourse is bounded on one side by the necessary structures of community life, it is bounded on the other by the need of the state to create organizations to achieve explicit public objectives. These organizations, which are nonpublic forums, regulate speech in ways that are fundamentally incompatible with the requirements of public discourse.[220] Public discourse is the

---

219. This claim is also implausible, as I noted earlier, because of its vulnerable assumption that style can be sharply distinguished from substance. *See supra* note 214.

220. The argument in this and the following two paragraphs is developed in detail in Post, *Between Governance and Management: The History and Theory of the Public Forum*, 34 UCLA L. Rev. 1713 (1987) [hereinafter Post, *Between Governance*]. *See also* Post, *The Constitutional Concept*, *supra* note 91, at 684-85.

medium through which our democracy determines its purposes, and for this reason the legal structure of public discourse requires that all such purposes be kept open to question and reevaluation. Within nonpublic forums, on the other hand, government objectives are taken as established, and communication is regulated as necessary to achieve those objectives.

Although the Supreme Court has often held that "the First Amendment rights of speech and association extend to the campuses of state universities," and even that "the campus of a public university, at least for its students, possesses many of the characteristics of a public forum,"[221] in fact state institutions of higher learning are public organizations established for the express purpose of education. The Court has always held that "a university's mission is education" and has never construed the first amendment to deny a university's "authority to impose reasonable regulations compatible with that mission upon the use of its campus and facilities."[222] The Court has explicitly recognized "a university's right to exclude . . . First Amendment activities that . . . substantially interfere with the opportunity of other students to obtain an education."[223] Thus student speech incompatible with classroom processes may be censored; faculty publications inconsistent with academic standards may be evaluated and judged; and so forth.

The regulation of racist speech within public institutions of higher learning, therefore, does not turn on the value of democratic self-governance and its realization in public discourse. Instead the constitutionality of such regulation depends upon the logic of instrumental rationality, and specifically upon three factors: (1) the nature of the educational mission of the university; (2) the instrumental connection of the regulation to the attainment of that mission; and (3) the deference that courts ought to display toward the instrumental judgment of institutional authorities.[224] The current controversy regarding the constitutionality of regulating racist speech on university and college campuses may most helpfully be interpreted as a debate about the first of these factors, the constitutionally permissible educational objectives of public institutions of higher learning.[225]

---

221. Widmar v. Vincent, 454 U.S. 263, 267 n.5, 268-69 (1981).

222. *Id.* at 268 n.5.

223. *Id.* at 277 (citing Healy v. James, 408 U.S. 169, 189 (1972)).

224. Judicial application of these factors in nonpublic fora like universities is discussed in greater detail in Post, *Between Governance*, *supra* note 220, at 1765-1824.

225. This short discussion considers only issues pertaining to the *constitutionality* of

Courts have advanced at least three different concepts of those objectives. The most traditional concept, which I refer to as "civic education," views public education as an instrument of community life, and holds "that respect for constituted authority and obedience thereto is an essential lesson to qualify one for the duties of citizenship, and that the schoolroom is an appropriate place to teach that lesson."[226] Civic education conceptualizes instruction as a process of cultural reproduction, whereby community values are authoritatively handed down to the young. The validity of those values is largely taken for granted, and there is a strong tendency to use them as a basis for the regulation of speech in the manner of the traditional common law.

The concept of civic education held sway in the years before the Warren Court and has recently been forcefully resurrected with regard to the regulation of speech within high schools. Thus in *Bethel School District No. 403 v. Fraser*[227] the Court upheld the punishment of a high school student for having delivered an "offensive" and "indecent" student-government speech.[228] The Court reasoned that "the objectives of public education" included "the 'inculcat[ion of] fundamental values necessary to the maintenance of a democratic political system.' "[229] Among these values were "the habits and manners of civility as . . . indispensable to the practice of self-government."[230]

> The undoubted freedom to advocate unpopular and controversial views in schools and classrooms must be balanced against the society's countervailing interest in teaching students the boundaries of socially appropriate behavior. . . .
>
> . . . .
>
> . . . [S]chools must teach by example the shared values of a civilized social order. . . . The schools, as instruments of the state, may determine that the essential lessons of civil, mature conduct cannot be conveyed in a school that tolerates lewd, indecent, or offensive speech and conduct such as that indulged in by this confused boy.[231]

---

the regulation of racist speech. It does not consider the *educational* issues raised by such regulation. These issues are, however, profound and revolve around the question of whether legal restraint is the heuristically most effective response to racist speech.

226. Pugsley v. Sellmeyer, 158 Ark. 247, 253, 250 S.W. 538, 539 (1923).

227. 478 U.S. 675 (1986).

228. *Id.* at 678.

229. *Id.* at 681 (quoting Ambach v. Norwick, 441 U.S. 68, 77 (1979)).

230. *Id.* (quoting C. BEARD & M. BEARD, NEW BASIC HISTORY OF THE UNITED STATES 228 (1968)).

231. *Id.* at 681, 683. For a more recent example of the same kind of reasoning, see Hazelwood School Dist. v. Kuhlmeier, 484 U.S. 260, 271-72 (1988).

That the concept of civic education would lead to similar conclusions if applied to institutions of higher learning is evidenced by Chief Justice Burger's 1973 dissent in *Papish v. University of Missouri Curators*:[232]

> In theory, at least, a university is not merely an arena for the discussion of ideas by students and faculty; it is also an institution where individuals learn to express themselves in acceptable, civil terms. We provide that environment to the end that students may learn the self-restraint necessary to the functioning of a civilized society and understand the need for those external restraints to which we must all submit if group existence is to be tolerable.[233]

Because racist speech is both deeply uncivil and contrary to "the shared values of [our] civilized social order,"[234] its restraint would be relatively unproblematic if civic education were understood to constitute a constitutionally acceptable purpose of public institutions of higher learning.[235] A number of public universities have fashioned their regulations on exactly this understanding. For example, the Policy Against Racism of the Board of Regents of Higher Education of the Commonwealth of Massachusetts argues that "institutions must vigorously strive to achieve diversity in race, ethnicity, and culture sufficiently reflective of our society. However, diversity alone will not suffice":

> There must be a unity and cohesion in the diversity which we seek to achieve, thereby creating an environment of pluralism. Racism in any form, expressed or implied, intentional or inadvertent, individual or institutional, constitutes an egregious offense to the tenets of human dignity and to the accords of civility guaranteed by law. Consequently, racism undermines the establishment of a social and academic environment of genuine racial pluralism.[236]

The policy clearly postulates the fundamental task of the university to be the inculcation of the value of "genuine racial plural-

232. 410 U.S. 667 (1973).

233. *Id.* at 672 (Burger, C.J., dissenting).

234. Bethel v. School Dist. No. 403 v. Frazer, 478 U.S. 675, 681 (1986).

235. For the development of this logic at the pre-university level, see, for example, Clarke v. Board of Educ., 215 Neb. 250, 338 N.W.2d 272 (1983).

236. Commonwealth of Massachusetts Board of Regents of Higher Education, Policy Against Racism and Guidelines for Campus Policies Against Racism 2 (June 13, 1989).

ism," and it proscribes racist speech because of its incompatibility with that value.

A second concept of the mission of public education, which I refer to as "democratic education," begins with the very different premise that the "public school" is "in most respects the cradle of our democracy,"[237] and it therefore understands the purpose of public education to be the creation of autonomous citizens, capable of fully participating in the rough and tumble world of public discourse.[238] Democratic education strives to introduce that world into the generically more sheltered environment of the school.

The concept of democratic education was most fully expressed during the era of the Warren Court in *Tinker v. Des Moines School District*,[239] in which the Court held that the purpose of public education is to prepare students for the "sort of hazardous freedom . . . that is the basis of our national strength and of the independence and vigor of Americans who grow up and live in this relatively permissive, often disputatious, society."[240] The majority in *Tinker* explicitly rejected the premise of civic education that the purpose of public schooling is the transmission of canonical values. It concluded instead that "[i]n our system, state-operated schools may not be enclaves of totalitarianism. . . . [S]tudents may not be regarded as closed-circuit recipients of only that which the [s]tate chooses to communicate. They may not be confined to the expression of those sentiments that are officially approved."[241] According to *Tinker* the object of public education is to lead students to think for themselves.

The chief characteristic of democratic education is its tendency to assimilate speech within public educational institutions to a model of public discourse. Recognizing that this ambition is "not without its costs in terms of the risk to the maintenance of civility and an ordered society," the Court nevertheless strongly advanced the concept of democratic education during the late

---

237. Adler v. Board of Educ., 342 U.S. 485, 508 (1952) (Douglas, J., dissenting). For a fully developed statement of this position, see Abington School Dist. v. Schempp, 374 U.S. 203, 241-42 (1963) (Brennan, J., concurring).

238. The tension between the concepts of democratic and civic education closely recapitulates the informative debate between Piaget and Durkheim over the question of how to teach moral values. Durkheim stressed the importance of discipline, authority, and constraint, whereas Piaget emphasized cooperation, agreement, and autonomy. *See* J. PIAGET, *supra* note 84, at 341-71.

239. 393 U.S. 503 (1969).

240. *Id.* at 508-09.

241. *Id.* at 511.

1960's and early 1970's, in part because it believed the concept essential to the maintenance of "our vigorous and free society."[242] If, as I have argued, racist speech is and ought to be immune from regulation within public discourse, we can expect courts guided by the concept of democratic education to be quite hostile to the regulation of racist speech within universities, preferring instead to see students realistically prepared for participation in the harsh but inevitable world of public discourse.

There is yet a third concept of public education, one most often specifically associated with institutions of higher learning. This concept, which I refer to as "critical education," views the university as an institution whose distinctive "primary function" is "to discover and disseminate knowledge by means of research and teaching."[243] Critical education locates the principal prerequisite for university life in "the need for unfettered freedom, the right to think the unthinkable, discuss the unmentionable, and challenge the unchallengeable."[244]

> [I]f a university is a place for knowledge, it is also a special kind of small society. Yet it is not primarily a fellowship, a club, a circle of friends, a replica of the civil society outside it. Without sacrificing its central purpose, it cannot make its primary and dominant value the fostering of friendship, solidarity, harmony, civility, or mutual respect. To be sure, these are important values; other institutions may properly assign them the highest, and not merely a subordinate priority; and a good university will seek and in some significant measure attain these ends. But it will never let these values, important as they are, override its central purpose. We value freedom of expression precisely because it provides a forum for the new, the provocative, the disturbing, and the unorthodox. Free speech is a barrier to the tyranny of authoritarian or even majority opinion as to the rightness or wrongness of particular doctrines or thoughts.[245]

The university as the purveyor of critical education serves important social purposes. These include not only the disciplined

242. Healy v. James, 408 U.S. 169, 194 (1972).

243. *Report of the Committee on Freedom of Expression at Yale*, 4 HUM. RTS. 357, 357 (1975) [hereinafter *Report of the Committee*]. This function is not one that we ordinarily attribute to high schools, much less elementary schools.

244. *Id.*

245. *Id.* at 357-58; *see* Schmidt, *Freedom of Thought: A Principle in Peril?*, YALE ALUMNI MAG., Oct. 1989, at 65, 65-66.

pursuit of truth, but also the exemplary enactment of a "model of expression that is meaningful as well as free, coherent yet diverse, critical and inspirational."[246] The concept of critical education has strong affinities to the traditional "marketplace of ideas" theory of the first amendment, and it is not uncommon for courts who use the concept to speak of the "classroom" as "peculiarly the 'marketplace of ideas,'" deserving of protection because the "Nation's future depends upon leaders trained through wide exposure to that robust exchange of ideas which discovers truth 'out of a multitude of tongues, [rather] than through any kind of authoritative selection.'"[247]

The concept of critical education differs significantly from both civic and democratic education. In contrast to civic education, it rejects the notion of canonical values that are to be reproduced in the young. Hence public universities committed to critical education are not free to posit certain values (apart from the value of critical education itself) and to punish those who disagree. The logic of critical education would constitutionally require that a public university "not restrict speech . . . simply because it finds the views expressed by any group to be abhorrent."[248] This stands in stark contrast to the educational project of institutions like the University of Massachusetts, Mount Holyoke, Marquette, or Mary Washington,[249] which are committed to the mission of civic education.

The concept of critical education would also sharply limit the ability of universities to censor uncivil speech. Speech can be uncivil for many reasons, including the assertion of ideas that are perceived to be offensive, revolting, demeaning, and stigmatizing. Critical education, however, would require the toleration

---

246. Byrne, *Academic Freedom: A "Special Concern of the First Amendment,"* 99 YALE L.J. 251, 261 (1989). The presence of such a model

> contributes profoundly to society at large. We employ the expositors of academic speech to train nearly everyone who exercises leadership within our society. Beyond whatever specialized learning our graduates assimilate, they ought to be persuaded that careful, honest expression demands an answer in kind. The experience of academic freedom helps secure broader, positive liberties of expression.

Id.

247. Keyishian v. Board of Regents, 385 U.S. 589, 603 (1967) (quoting United States v. Associated Press, 52 F. Supp. 362, 372 (S.D.N.Y. 1943)); *see* Healy v. James, 408 U.S. 169, 180-81 (1972).

248. *Healy*, 408 U.S. at 187-88.

249. *See supra* notes 47-51 and accompanying text.

of all ideas, however uncivil.[250] This toleration would be consistent with the Court's 1973 holding that "the mere dissemination of ideas—no matter how offensive to good taste—on a state university campus may not be shut off in the name alone of 'conventions of decency.' "[251]

Critical education also differs in important respects from democratic education. The telos of critical education lies in the pursuit of truth, rather than in the instantiation of the responsible autonomy of the citizen. The pursuit of truth requires not only an unfettered freedom of ideas, but also honesty, fidelity to reason, and respect for method and procedures. Reason, as we have seen, carries its own special requirements of civility, which preclude coercion and abuse.[252] Although enforcement of these requirements and values would be inconsistent with democratic education, it may well be required by critical education. Moreover critical education requires freedom of ideas only with respect to that speech which forms part of the truth-seeking dialogue of the university. Thus, for example, nothing in the concept of critical education would prevent a university from penalizing malicious racist speech communicated *solely for the purpose* of harassing, humiliating, or degrading a victim.[253] The trick, of course, would be to distinguish such speech in a manner that does not chill communication intended to form part of a truth-seeking exchange.[254] This represents a formidable technical challenge, for it is all too easy to permit revulsion with the content of speech to infect regulation ostensibly justified by other reasons.[255]

Although there is not space in this short essay to engage in a full-scale exploration of the purposes of higher education, some conclusions are clear enough. The Constitution would not permit a public university, in the name of civic education, to prohibit

250. "If the university's overriding commitment to free expression is to be sustained, secondary social and ethical responsibilities must be left to the informal processes of suasion, example, and argument." *Report of the Committee*, *supra* note 243, at 360.

251. Papish v. University of Mo. Curators, 410 U.S. 667, 670 (1973).

252. *See supra* Section III(D)(1).

253. As a matter of policy, however, it is always dangerous to make the legality of speech depend primarily upon an assessment of a speaker's intent, for there is a powerful tendency to attribute bad motives to those with whom we fundamentally disagree.

254. The inability to make this distinction contributed to a court's recent decision to strike down as unconstitutional the regulations of the University of Michigan. *See* Doe v. University of Mich., 721 F. Supp. 852 (E.D. Mich. 1989); Grano, *supra* note 5, at 7.

255. For an admirable attempt to meet this challenge, see Grey, *supra* note 5, and the regulations that Professor Grey drafted for Stanford University.

the teaching of communism because of its conflict with community values. Nor would the Constitution, in the name of democratic education, preclude a public university from enforcing regulations against highly offensive racial epithets within a classroom.

Examples like these incline me toward the concept of critical education, yet the extent to which state universities ought constitutionally to be *required* to pursue one or the other of these educational missions does not seem to me without difficulties.[256] The analysis is complicated by the possibility that public universities may have various educational functions with constitutionally distinct characteristics. Thus it is conceivable that public universities may be permitted to pursue the mission of civic education within their dormitories, but be required to follow the requirements of democratic education with regard to their open spaces.[257] These are matters that require further and careful consideration.

I conclude, therefore, by stressing two brief points. First, the constitutionality of restraints on racist speech within public universities does not depend upon the constitutionality of such regulation within public discourse. Second, the constitutionality of restraints on racist speech within public universities will depend to a very great extent upon the educational purposes that we constitutionally attribute to public institutions of higher learning, and upon the various modalities through which such institutions are understood to pursue those purposes. We ought to see debate turn toward the achievement of a fuller and more reflective comprehension of these questions.

V. Conclusion: The Question of Formal Democracy

This account of the constitutionality of university restrictions on racist speech suggests that a principal flaw of the contemporary debate has been its pervasive assumption that the relationship of racist speech to the first amendment can be assessed

256. Cases like *Tinker* and *Healy* make clear, however, that the Supreme Court's first amendment jurisprudence has rested on the assumption that there are constitutional limits to the freedom of public educational institutions to define their own educational mission.

257. Some universities have regulated racist speech in ways that turn on similar functional and geographic considerations. *See Doe*, 721 F. Supp. at 856; *Tufts Restores Free Speech After T-Shirt Confrontation*, San Francisco Chron., Dec. 9, 1989, at B6, col. 1; Wilson, *Colleges Take 2 Basic Approaches in Adopting Anti-Harassment Plans*, Chron. Higher Educ., Oct. 4, 1989, at A38, col. 1; Russo, *Free Speech at Tufts: Zoned Out*, N.Y. Times, Sept. 27, 1989, at A29.

independently of social context. Communication, however, does not form a constitutionally undifferentiated terrain. The standards of first amendment protection afforded to public discourse will not be the same as those applied to nonpublic speech, and these in turn will differ from those that govern the regulation of speech within instrumental governmental institutions like universities. The concrete circumstances of racist speech thus figure prominently in the constitutional equation.

Public discourse is the realm of communication we deem necessary to facilitate the process of self-determination. As that process is open-ended, reflecting the boundless possibility of social self-constitution, so we fashion public discourse to be as free from legal constraint as is feasible to sustain. But as self-determination requires the antecedent formation of a "self" through socialization into the particularity of a given community life, so public discourse must at some point be bounded by nonpublic speech, in which community values are embodied and enforced. And as the decisions of a self-determining democracy require actual implementation, so public discourse must at some other point be bounded by the instrumentally regulated speech of the nonpublic forum.

I have attempted to explain the unique protections that American first amendment jurisprudence affords to public discourse through a self-consciously formal analysis; that is, I have attempted to uncover the formal prerequisites for the instantiation of the value of democracy as self-determination. Although this kind of formal analysis has the advantage of forcing us to clearly articulate the values in whose name we purport to act, it has the disadvantage of obscuring the messy complications of the world. Formal analysis is always subject to the critique that actual, substantive conditions have undermined its very point and meaning.

From a formal perspective, democracy fulfills the purposes of autonomous self-government because we accept an image of independent citizens deliberating together to form public opinion. We therefore structure constitutional policy according to the requirements of that image. But it is an image blatantly vulnerable to the most forceful empirical attack.[258] Citizens are not autonomous; they are manipulated by the media, coerced by private corporations, immured in the toils of racism. Citizens do

258. *See, e.g.*, E. PURCELL, THE CRISIS OF DEMOCRATIC THEORY: SCIENTIFIC NATURALISM AND THE PROBLEM OF VALUE (1973).

not communicate together; they are passive, irrational, and voiceless. Deliberation is impossible because of the technical and economic structure of the mass media; public opinion is therefore imposed upon citizens rather than spontaneously arising from them. The very aspiration to self-determination reinforces preexisting inequalities by empowering those with the resources and competence to take advantage of democratic processes; it systematically handicaps socially marginalized groups who lack this easy and familiar access to the media of democratic deliberation. And so forth: the litany is by now depressingly familiar.

Of course these criticisms, and others like them, contain important elements of truth. They therefore force us to choose: either we decide to retain the ideal of democracy as deliberative self-determination and work to minimize the debilitating consequences of these criticisms, or we decide that these criticisms have so undermined the ideal of deliberative self-determination that it must be abandoned and a different value for democracy embraced. If we choose the second alternative, we have the responsibility of articulating and defending a new vision of democracy. But if we choose the first, we have the responsibility of working to foster the constitutional values upon which we rely. We have the obligation of doing so, however, in ways that do not themselves contravene the necessary preconditions of the ideal of deliberative self-determination.[259] The function of formal analysis is to make clear the content of that obligation.

The strict implication of this essay, then, is not that racist speech ought not to be regulated in public discourse, but rather that those who advocate its regulation in ways incompatible with the value of deliberative self-governance carry the burden of moving us to a different and more attractive vision of democracy. Or, in the alternative, they carry the burden of justifying suspensions of our fundamental democratic commitments. Neither burden is light.

---

259. For a striking illustration of the untoward (and in retrospect horrifying) consequences of repudiating that obligation, see Marcuse, *Repressive Tolerance*, in R. WOLFF, B. MOORE, & H. MARCUSE, A CRITIQUE OF PURE TOLERANCE 81 (1965).

THE BIRTH ORDER ODDITY IN SUPREME COURT APPOINTMENTS

by
PAUL J. WEBER
Associate Professor of Political Science
University of Louisville

The concept of birth order has intrigued members of the scholarly community ever since 1874 when Sir Francis Galton noted that a disproportionate number of eminent scientists were first born or only sons.[1] With the development of sophisticated research techniques (and a rapidly expanding number of researchers, no doubt) the past two decades have witnessed over four hundred articles and dissertations on birth order.[2] Yet few studies have focused on birth orders of politicans.[3]

This article considers the birth order factor in presidential selection of Supreme Court Justices. It studies the birth orders of all one hundred two appointments and notes several significant differences, namely, that there is a disproportionate number of first borns on the high bench, that Republicans are far more likely to appoint first borns than are Democrats, that some Presidents had definite preferences, and that the appointments of Chief Justices follow a curious, if not statistically significant pattern. On the other hand, it also notes that contrary to several birth order hypotheses, attempts to translate birth order differences into quantifiable behaviorial patterns have not succeeded. The birth order oddity remains a mystery to be solved.

The Birth Order Hypothesis

The basic birth order hypothesis is that the order in which one is born into a family has a major impact on one's social and personality development. Corollary hypotheses are that birth order will influence one's choice of vocation, choice of marriage partner and level of achievement. The most important categories are only child, first born, middle born and last born. In general, those who stress the important of birth order also caution that ". . . birth order is only one of many environmental factors important in developing and maintaining life roles . . . (and) it is not the position of birth that is important but rather your experiences with other members of your family as a result of being the oldest, middle, youngest or only child."[4]

Birth order is only important because, the theory holds, differences in order lead to differences in behavior.[5] Only children are more likely to be self-confident, prefer to work in solitude, without developing high affiliative needs as adults. They are likely to be quite verbal, perfectionists and high achievers. First borns have many of the same characteristics as only children. They tend to imbibe parental norms to a greater extent than later children, are conscientious, anxious to please authority, ambitious, and high achievers. They have a preference for high status professions and tend to work hard. They fear failure and will go to great lengths to achieve success. As a result they rise to the top of their chosen professions in disproportionate numbers. They also seem to prefer working with ideas, have a high degree of self discipline and either prefer and/or have a high tolerance for tightly structured situations. A more controversial hypothesis is that first borns are more authoritarian and conservative.[6] It has also been contended that they generally do not emphathize with disadvantaged people.[7]

Middle borns have always been forced to compete with one or more older siblings and learn early that direct confrontations and head to head power struggles are not the only way to achieve results. Negotiation and diplomacy are middle born traits. Parents are apparently more relaxed and at ease with later children and middle borns tend to be friendlier and more easy going about rules, regulations and societal norms than are first borns. They do not have the same high achievement needs as first and only children and therefore are not as likely to rise to the tops of their professions. A more controversial claim is that "A middle son tends to be mentally flexible, with tolerance for novelty and variation, but once a notion is set he tends to be dogmatic."[8]

Last borns are by definition "the baby of the family." Like only children they have never had to cope with displacement by younger siblings, but unlike only and first borns they have other less authority-figure models as they grow up. Last borns tend to be playful and lighthearted. They soon become accustomed to attention and affection, and work hard to be liked. They tend to be highly social and affiliative, but they are not highly achievement-oriented. One study concludes that last born children were most often selected by others in their classes as playmates. But when it came to achieving an objective, first born children were more often selected."[9] Curiously, if from poor or deprived families, last borns often show very high achievement needs.

Judicial Appointments

We can be quite certain that in selecting Justices from among potential candidates Presidents have never seriously considered just where they fit in their family constellations. Yet the differences are significant. If one considers all 102 appointments to the Supreme Court, 56 (55%) have been first or only sons, 27 (26%) were middle born and 19 (19%) were last born and one daughter.

The exact significance of this distribution is difficult to state without further data on birth rates during the 18th and 19th centuries. Such data is crude and unreliable. Census data is not useful since it did not collect this type of information until 1940.[10] One early study estimated that the average 18th-century American family included eight children.[11] Another study estimated that the average free woman bore about seven children in her lifetime.[12] If these figures are accurate, the expected frequency for Justices born in the 18th century would be First Borns 25%, Middle Borns 50%, Last Borns 25%.

Table 1

Birth Order Distribution on the Supreme Court

	First/Only	Middle	Last
Actual	56 (55%)	27 (26%)	19 (19%)
Anticipated	38 (37%)	26 (26%)	38 (37%)
			N = 102

Kolmogorov - Smirnov Test
D = .36**
** significant at .01 level.

A later study of birth orders of lawyers born between 1913–1942 used a weighted average to determine the expected frequency of first borns in the general population.[13] The expected frequency was 37.2%.

As Table I illustrates, even using this latter, probably much too conservative a basis for determining a normal birth order distribution, the differences in judicial appointments are significant at the .01 level, and support the birth order hypothesis that first borns tend to achieve at a disproportionate rate. Middle borns are represented as expected, and last borns are notably underrepresented.

A more puzzling finding is the substantial differences between the Presidents of different parties in their penchant for appointing to the court persons of different birth orders. As Table II shows, the Democratic-Republican, Democrat Presidents had 42 opportunities to make appointments, while Federalist-Whig-Republicans had 62. Yet the former chose first borns only 40% of the time and the latter 66%. If one looks at appointees only since the Republican and Democratic Parties were established, i.e., from Lincoln to Reagan, the difference is even more dramatic. Democrat Presidents chose first borns 36% of the time and Republican Presidents 73%.

Just as intriguing is Federalist-Whig-Republican dislike for last borns. While Democratic Presidents appointed last borns, 33% of the time, Republicans did so only 8% of the time.

So far I have not found a satisfactory explanation for this phenomenon.[14] One is tempted to attribute the difference to the variant socio-economic status between Democrats and Republicans. An examination of the relative SES of individual ap-

Table 2

Judicial Appointments by Birth Order and Party of the President

Actual	First & Only	Middle	Last	N
Democratic-Republican, Democrat	17	11	14	42
Federalist, Whig Republican	41	16	5	62
N	58	27	19	

Kolmogorov - Smirnov Two Sample Test
Dmax = .274
x^2 = 7.509
Sig. at .01 level
N = 104 (Justices Edward White and Charles Hughes were each appointed to Chief Justice position by a different President than made the initial appointment.)

pointees did not reveal a positive correlation. A more likely explanation is the conservative-liberal tendencies of Presidents in the two-party traditions. Republican Presidents are more likely to choose more conservative persons for the court, Democratic Presidents more liberal. While Supreme Court appointees do not always turn out as Presidents desire,[15] if the birth order hypothesis is correct, first borns are more likely to be conservative and Presidential instincts would be quite correct. To test this hypothesis on recent judicial appointments Professor Tate's article ranking 25 Justices (Hugo Black through John Paul Stevens) on liberalism in civil rights and economic issues was utilized.[16] Correlating this data with the Justice's birth orders, and using Kendall's tau-b, adjusted for ties, a high negative number would indicate if a relationship existed between birth order and conservatism. Unfortunately as Table III shows there is a value of only –.1764 on civil liberties cases and –.1354 for economics cases.

There may be other tests to run but so far it seems we are simply left without an explanation why Republican Presidents are far more likely to appoint first borns than are Democrats, and far less likely to appoint last borns. One conclusion is certain: there is no significant correlation between being a first born and being a conservative on the Supreme Court.

Table 3

Birth Order and Liberalism of Supreme Court Justices

Justice	Birth Order	Rank-C.L.	Rank-Econ
Rehnquist	1st	25	25
Reed	1st	24	14
Minton	1st	23	12
Clark	1st	18	10
Blackmun	1st	17	18
Powell	1st	15	16
Jackson	1st	14	24
Stewart	1st	12	17
Frankfurter	1st	11	21
Stevens	1st	10	13
Warren	1st	8	5
Rutledge	1st	7	1
Berger	Mid	22	22
Harlan	Mid	19	20
Whittaker	Mid	16	23
Brennan	Mid	6	6
Douglas	Mid	2	4
Murphy	Mid	1	2
Vinson	Last	21	15
Burton	Last	20	19
White	Last	13	11
Black	Last	9	3
Marshall	Last	5	8
Fortas	Last	4	7
Goldberg	Last	3	9
		r = −0.1764	r = −0.1354

Kendall's tau-b

Presidential Preferences

No one President made enough appointments to the Supreme Court to provide statistically significant numbers. Yet is is clear that some Presidents were more likely to prefer one birth order over another. Table IV shows the Justices in the order in which they were appointed, their birth orders, and the appointing Presidents. Presidents Grant and Theodore Roosevelt used their four and three appointments respectively to choose first borns exclusively. Taft chose five first borns for six openings and both Benjamin Harrison and Richard Nixon chose three of four. On the other end, Kennedy and Johnson used their four opportunities exclusively for last borns. Wilson chose two of three last borns and Truman split his appointments between two first borns and two last borns. Eisenhower was the only President with multiple ap-

Table 4

Judicial Appointments

Justice	Appointment	Years	Birth Order	Appointed By	Party
*1. John Jay	1789	5	Middle	Washington	Federalist
2. John Rutledge	1789	1	First	"	
3. William Cushing	1789	20	First	"	
4. James Wilson	1790	8	Middle	"	
5. John Blair	1789	6	Middle	"	
6. James Iredell	1790	9	First	"	
7. Thomas Johnson	1791	1	Middle	"	
8. William Paterson	1793	13	Middle	"	
9. Samuel Chase	1796	15	Only	"	
*10. Oliver Ellsworth	1796	4	Last	"	
11. Bushrod Washington	1798	31	Middle	Adams	Federalist
12. Alfred Moore	1799	4	Only	"	
*13. John Marshall	1801	34	First	"	
14. William Johnson	1804	30	First	Jefferson "	Democratic-Republican
15. Brockholst Livingston	1806	16	Middle	"	
16. Thomas Todd	1807	18	Last	"	
17. Gabriel Duvall	1812	22	Middle	Madison "	Democratic-Republican
18. Joseph Story	1811	33	First	"	
19. Smith Thompson	1823	20	Middle	Monroe	Democratic-Republican
20. Robert Trimble	.1826	2	First	J. Q. Adams	Dem.-Rep.
21. John McLean	1829	32	First	Jackson	Democrat
22. Henry Baldwin	1830	14	Last	"	
23. James M. Wayne	1835	32	Middle	"	
*24. Roger B. Taney	1836	28	Middle	"	
25. Philip P. Barbour	1836	5	Last	"	
26. John Catron	1837	28	First	Jackson	
27. John McKinley	1837	15	Only	Van Buren	Democrat
28. Peter Daniel	1841	19	Middle	"	
29. Samuel Nelson	1845	27	Middle	Tyler	Whig
30. Levi Woodbury	1845	5	Middle	Polk	Democrat
31. Robert Grier	1846	23	First	"	
32. Benjamin Curtis	1851	6	First	Fillmore	Whig
33. John Campbell	1853	8	First	Pierce	Democrat
34. Nathan Clifford	1851	23	First	Buchanan	Democrat
35. Noah Swayne	1862	18	Last	Lincoln	Republican
36. Samuel F. Miller	1862	28	First	"	
37. David Davis	1862	14	First	"	
38. Stephen J. Field	1863	34	Middle	"	
*39. Salmon P. Chase	1864	8	Middle	"	
40. William Strong	1870	10	First	Grant	Republican
41. Joseph P. Bradley	1870	21	First	"	
42. Ward Hunt	1873	9	First	"	
*43. Morrison R. Waite	1874	14	First	"	
44. John M. Harlan	1877	34	Last	Hayes	Republican
45. William B. Woods	1881	6	First	"	
46. Stanley Matthews	1881	7	First	Garfield	Republican
47. Horace Gray	1882	20	First	Arthur	Republican
48. Samuel Blatchford	1882	11	Only	"	
49. Lucius Q. C. Lamar	1888	5	Middle	Cleveland	Democrat
*50. Melville W. Fuller	1888	21	Middle	"	
51. David J. Brewer	1890	20	Last	Harrison	Republican

Table 4 (cont.)

Justice	Appointment	Years	Birth Order	Appointed By	Party
52. Henry B. Brown	1891	15	First	"	
53. George Shiras, Jr.	1893	10	First	"	
54. Howell E. Jackson	1893	2	First	"	
*55. Edward D. White	1894	16	First	Cleveland	Democrat
	(1910)	11		(Taft - R)	
56. Rufus W. Peckham	1896	13	Last	Cleveland	Democrat
57. Joseph McKenna	1898	26	First	McKinley	Republican
58. Oliver W. Holmes	1902	29	First	T. Roosevelt	Republican
59. William R. Day	1903	19	Only	"	
60. William H. Moody	1906	3	First	"	
61. Horace H. Lurton	1910	4	Only	Taft	Republican
*62. Charles E. Hughes	1910	6	Only	"	
	1930	11		(Hoover - R)	
63. Willis Van Devanter	1911	26	First	Taft	Republican
64. Joseph R. Lamar	1911	5	First	"	
65. Mahlon Pitney	1912	10	Middle	"	
66. James McReynolds	1914	26	First	Wilson	Democrat
67. Louis D. Brandeis	1915	22	Last	"	
68. John H. Clarke	1916	5	Last	"	
*69. William H. Taft	1921	8	Middle	Harding	Republican
70. George Sutherland	1922	15	First	"	
71. Pierce Butler	1922	16	Middle	"	
72. Edward T. Sanford	1923	7	First	"	
*73. Harlan F. Stone	1925	15	First	Coolidge	Republican
	1941	5		(F.D. Roosevelt - D)	
74. Owen J. Roberts	1930	15	First	Hoover	Republican
75. Benjamin Cardozo	1932	6	Last	"	
76. Hugo L. Black	1937	34	Last	F. D. Roosevelt	Democrat
77. Stanley F. Reed	1938	19	Only	"	
78. Felix Frankfurter	1939	23	First	"	
79. William O. Douglas	1939	36	Middle	"	
80. Frank Murphy	1940	9	Middle	"	
81. James F. Byrnes	1941	1	Last	"	
82. Robert H. Jackson	1941	13	First	"	
83. Wiley B. Rutledge	1943	6	First	"	
84. Harold H. Burton	1945	13	Last	Truman	Democrat
*85. Fred M. Vinson	1946	7	Last	"	
86. Tom C. Clark	1949	18	First	"	
87. Sherman Minton	1949	7	First	"	
*88. Earl Warren	1953	16	First	Eisenhower	Republican
89. John M. Harlan	1955	16	Middle	"	
90. William Brennan	1956		Middle	"	
91. Charles Whittaker	1957	5	Middle	"	
92. Potter Stewart	1958	23	First	"	
93. Byron R. White	1962		Last	Kennedy	Democrat
94. Arthur Goldberg	1962	3	Last	"	
95. Abe Fortas	1965	4	Last	Johnson	Democrat
96. Thurgood Marshall	1967		Last	"	
*97. Warren E. Burger	1969		Middle	Nixon	Republican
98. Harry Blackman	1970		First	"	
99. Lewis Powell, Jr.	1971		First	"	
100. William Rehnquist	1971		First	"	
101. John Paul Stevens	1975		First	Ford	Republican
102. Sandra Day O'Connor	1981		First	Reagan	Republican

* Chief Justices

pointments to chose a majority of middle borns.

Selection of Chief Justices

In 1970 the American Psychological Association published a short report on the birth order of the Presidents.[17] According to that report,

> There is a significant degree of clustering in the birth ranks of first and third child and first and third son. Most striking is the distribution of sons; in 68% of the elections, the President has been a first or third son (if only children and only sons are included, this increases to 85%.[18]

More interesting still is the fact that "during every war but one (the Spanish-American War) the President has been a first born or only son." Is there any similar pattern among Chief Justices? Indeed, there seems to be, both for the 19th century and for the history of the Court as a whole.

Exactly how one best divides the court history is not always beyond dispute, but if one looks for those periods in which the Court showed great initiative, expanded its power, faced a major crisis, or established a new direction for judicial policy-making as opposed to those periods of court history in which the Court saw fit to hold the line, consolidate past gains and reestablish the prestige and perceived legitimacy of the court, a birth order pattern emerges. As Table V illustrates the aggressive, initiating court was led by a first born Chief Justice. A consolidating or passive court was led by a middle or last born Chief Justice.

The pattern of Judicial Leadership is quite clear, although the meaning of that pattern is considerably less so. In every instance in which the Court became an aggressive, effective actor in the political arena, whenever it established a new direction for judicial decision-making, it was led by a first born. Each such period was followed by a time of consolidation, holding the line and a rebuilding of the court's prestige and legitimacy. In each such period the Court was headed by a middle born.

Whether one can argue the other way, namely that "first born leadership makes things happen" on the Court is more of a problem. Chief Justice Rutledge can be dismissed from consideration since he served as Chief Justice for only one August term of the Court as a recess appointee. His nomination was then rejected by the Senate. The other two first born Chief Justices who did not preside over a vigorous Court were White and Stone, both of whom served during wartime – never a good time for new court initiatives.

The data on birth order and court leader-

Table 5

Chief Justices and Judicial Leadership

Chief Justice	Birth Order	Status of the Court
John Jay	Middle	Weak, passive court
John Rutledge	First	Weak, passive court
Oliver Ellsworth	Last	Weak, passive court
John Marshall	First	Expansion of judicial and national power
Roger Taney	Middle	Consolidation of gains, holding the line
Salmon Chase	Middle	Rebuilding the court's prestige, legitimacy
Morrison Waite	First	New direction for ct.-Protect Economic Freedom
Melville Fuller	Middle	Consolidation of gains, holding the line
Edward White	First	Period of World War I
William Taft	Middle	Consolidation of gains
Charles Hughes	Only	Strong court: aggressive defense of old order followed by new direction-support govt. contr.
Harlan Stone	First	Period of World War II
Fred Vinson	Last	Consolidation of gains, holding the line
Earl Warren	First	Strong court-new direction: protect civil liberties
Warren Burger	Middle	Consolidation of gains, holding the line

ship is interesting, but its significance remains to be established. According to the birth order hypothesis first borns tend to be leaders and initiators. Middle borns are negotiators and diplomats with less of a need to achieve than their older siblings. They are also more likely to compromise and seek reconciliation among competing interests. To some extent, then, the pattern of leadership on the Court would seem to validate the birth order hypothesis.

The one major exception in the 19th century may actually be seen to support this point, *Dred Scott v Sandford* came to the court in 1856. In an earlier case, *Strader v Graham* (1851) the question of whether slaves became free when they entered free territory had been skirted by the Taney Court when it held that "the status of the Negroes in question depended on the laws of the state where they now lived—Kentucky."[19] The court was inclined to take the same non-confrontive position in *Dred Scott*. A majority, led by middle born Justices Nelson and Taney was inclined to take this position. The threat by Justice McLean, a first born, to dissent and raise the crucial issue of Congress' power to enact the Missouri Compromise, caused the collapse of the fragile majority. Taney has gone down in history as the author of the most infamous of the Court's opinion. In reality his is only one of eight opinions in the case, and represents more the collapse of his own attempt to *avoid* a conflict than his attempt to establish public policy. The main point here is not Taney's personal views on the slavery issue, but his willingness to forego stating his views to avoid taking sides and splitting the court. The fact that he wrote an opinion at all in *Dred Scott* was out of character for Taney and he lived to regret that he did not follow his own first instincts for compromise and reconciliation. If the middle borns had had their way, there would have been no Dred Scott decision at all!

With the single exception of *Dred Scott v Sandford* the leadership pattern on the Supreme Court has reflected that which would be expected in the birth order hypothesis. But we are still left with the troubling question of significance. The number of Chief Justices is so small and the change that took place in the directions of the Court so gradual that one cannot dismiss the possibility that chance alone accounts for the pattern of first born-middle born leadership.

Summary and Conclusion

This paper ends as it began, on a note of curious skepticism. There is some merit to the birth order hypothesis as applied to Supreme Court appointments. The Justices who have served on the Court have been disproportionately first born sons. The explanation for this is by no means clear. One plausible explanation is that Justices tend to be drawn from families in a high socio-economic status, and such families tend to have fewer children, increasing the chance of being a first born son. An attempt to rank birth order with the socio-economic status of the family of origin, however, showed no significant correlations. Middle and last born Justices were just as likely to come from well-to-do families as were first borns. A second explanation may be that law, like engineering and science, tends to be a field to which first borns are drawn. Since Justices are drawn from among lawyers, perhaps the dominance of first borns reflects a general vocational choice.

Equally remarkable is the fact that Republicans and Democrats, as well as their respective predecessors differ markedly in their preference for first borns in judicial selection. Republicans chose first borns about 73% of the time, and Democrats about 36%. The significance of this increases if one accepts the proposition that the legal profession is dominated by first borns.

The leadership patterns of Chief Justices is intriguing. First borns have presided whenever the Court dramatically increased its power or set out in a new direction. Middle borns (or in the case of Vinson, a last born) presided when the Court was more passive or consolidating the previous gains. Exactly what predictive value this might have remains unsettled.

There are other interesting phenomena not discussed in this paper, for example, the fact that four of the five Jewish Justices have been last born sons. (The only religious correlation that was discovered.) One must ask in conclusion whether there are enough indications of birth order significance to warrant a more comprehensive study. So far we are left with a birth order oddity in search of explanation.

Notes

1. Sir Francis Galton, *English Men of Science* (London, MacMillan and Co., 1874).
2. Lucille K. Forer, "Bibliography of Birth Order Literature in the 70's," *Journal of Individual Psychology*, Vol. 38, May, 1977.
3. The preeminent articles to date have been Louis Stewart, "The Politics of Birth Order," *Proceedings, 79th Annual Convention of the American Psychological Association*, Vol. 5, 1970, p. 365; Gordon B. Forbes, "Birth Order and Political Success: A Study of the 1970 Illinois General Election," *Psychological Reports* Vol. 29, 1971, p. 1239; R. L. Zweigenhaft, "Birth Order, Approval-Seeking and Membership in Congress," *Journal of Individual Psychology* Vol. 31, 1975, p. 205.
4. Lucille K. Forer, *The Birth Order Factor*, (New York, D. McKay Company, 1976), p. 6.
5. In general, no one position is considered superior to others. Each has its strengths and weaknesses, its advantages and disadvantages. Also since the impact on personal development is a result of socialization, there may be a number of intervening variables which moderate or even outweigh birth order in individual cases. Major variables are sex differences, family size and spacing, infant mortality rate, influence of half brothers and sisters, illness and socio-economic status. For the purposes of this study I have not attempted to account for the variables as they have affected individual Justices.
6. R. Boshier and F. H. Walker, "Birth Order and Conservatism: An Adlerian Myth?" *Psychological Report*, Vol. 29, 1971, p. 392.
7. Forer, *Birth Order Factor*, p. 43.
8. Ibid., p. 49.
9. "What Research Shows About Birth Order, Personality and I.Q.," Report of the National Institute of Mental Health, as reported in *The New York Times* Feb. 6, 1976, p. C-1.
10. Indeed, throughout the 19th and early 20th century the word "family" in census data stood for any person or group of persons who occupied a dwelling place or part of a dwelling place. This included persons living alone in cabins, tents or stables as well as occupants of hotels and boarding houses. Average family size in the census data, is a totally misleading concept.
11. Cited by George J. Engleman, 'Education Not the Cause of Race Decline,' *Popular Science Monthly* Vol. 69 (June, 1903), p. 177.
12. Cited by Donald J. Bogue, *Principle of Demography*, (New York, John Wiley, 1969), p. 662.
13. P. S. Very and R. W. Prull, "Birth Order, Personality Development, and The Choice of Law as a Profession," *The Journal of Genetic Psychology* Vol. 116 (1970) p. 220.
14. One of my more conservative colleagues suggested that Republican Presidents choose first borns because they want strong, principled leadership, and Democratic Presidents appoint their cronies!
15. Philip B. Kurland, "The Appointment and Disappointment of Supreme Court Justices," *Law and Social Order*, Vol. 1972, p. 183.
16. C. Neal Tate, "Personality Attribute Models of the Voting Behavior of U.S. Supreme Court Justices: Liberalism in Civil Liberties and Economic Decisions, 1946–1978," *The American Political Science Review*, 75 June, 1981, p. 355.
17. Louis Stewart, "The Politics of Birth Order," *The Proceedings* 78th Annual Convention, APA, 1970, pp. 365–366.
18. Ibid.
19. R. G. McCloskey, *The American Supreme Court*, (Chicago, University of Chicago Press 1960), p. 92.

HOFSTRA LAW REVIEW

Volume 10, No. 3 Spring 1982

THE INTEGRITY OF HOLMES' JURISPRUDENCE

*G. Edward White**

Writing about Oliver Wendell Holmes can be likened to playing Hamlet in the theatre: It is a kind of appreticeship that legal scholars undertake as a way of measuring their fitness to endure the academic travails ahead. Holmes himself engaged in a similar rite de passage when he wrote an essay on Plato as a Harvard undergraduate. Plato's thought, Holmes claimed, "needed a complete remodeling"; Holmes' generation "start[ed] far beyond the place where Plato rested."[1] Ralph Waldo Emerson, to whom Holmes showed a draft of his essay, suggested that "[w]hen you strike at a king, you must *kill* him."[2] The urge to strike at Holmes has been recurrent, and the man, as a jurist, is far from dead.

Ten years ago I suggested that Holmes' reputation was on the decline, and complained about his "articulated refusal to take pride in being human."[3] In an intellectual culture dominated by liberal humanism, I surmised, Holmes would not be likely to fare well: He

* Professor of Law, University of Virginia School of Law. B.A., 1963, Amherst College; M.A., 1964; Ph.D., 1967, Yale University; J.D., 1970, Harvard University. My thanks to Jeffrey O'Connell for his comments on an earlier draft of this essay.

1. Holmes, *Plato,* 2 U.Q. 205, 206 (1860).
2. Letter from Oliver Wendell Holmes to Elizabeth Shepley Sergeant (Dec. 7, 1926), *quoted in* 1 M. Howe, Justice Oliver Wendell Holmes 54 (1957) (emphasis in original).
3. White, *The Rise and Fall of Justice Holmes,* 39 U. Chi. L. Rev. 51, 77 (1971).

was not much of a liberal and certainly not a humanist. Once again Holmes seems to have triumphed over his critics. His thought has had a capacity to contain insights sufficiently diverse and contradictory to appeal to someone regardless of prevailing intellectual fashions. And the gap between Holmes and prevailing opinion has narrowed rather than widened in the 1970's. The "disturbing dissonance" I found between Holmes' "very conspicuous social and professional success" and his "gloomy musings that . . . man has no more cosmic significance than a baboon or a grain of sand"[4] presupposed an obligation in those whom life has favored to believe in the optimistic possibilities of living. Optimism is harder to come by these days; what I called a "cranky negativism"[5] in Holmes now seems more like sensible resignation. At any rate, interest in Holmes has dramatically revived,[6] and I should not like to be thought of as having given up on him too soon.

My concern in this essay is with a feature of Holmes that, for all that has been written on him, scholars are just beginning to address. The feature involves an apparent discontinuity between Holmes' theory of judging in the private law and public law spheres. Holmes' famous book, *The Common Law,*[7] reads like a credo for activist judging in pursuit of broad general principles of law; judges are to help arrange legal subjects in what Holmes called a philosophically continuous series.[8] His constitutional opinions on the Supreme Court, by contrast, extol the virtues of judicial deference. How is Holmes simultaneously the reformer of private law and the passive public law judge? How could the same judge who wanted to take all grade crossing cases away from juries[9] feel comfortable allowing legislatures to make all sorts of discriminatory classifications, so long as they were arguably rational?[10] Are these tendencies another example of the internal contradictions in Holmes' thought, which have been

---

4. *Id.* at 76.
5. *Id.* at 77.
6. In the past two academic years, Harvard Law School, Northwestern University School of Law, the University of Illinois School of Law, and the American Society for Legal History have devoted lectures or symposia to Holmes' work, and Professors Patrick Atiyah, Robert Cover, Grant Gilmore, Robert Gordon, Morton Horwitz, Saul Touster, and Jan Vedder, as well as Judge Benjamin Kaplan, have delivered papers on various features of Holmes' career.
7. O. W. HOLMES, THE COMMON LAW (1881).
8. O. W. HOLMES, *The Soldier's Faith*, in OCCASIONAL SPEECHES 73, 78-79 (M. Howe ed. 1962).
9. *See infra* text accompanying notes 171-178.
10. *See infra* text accompanying notes 161-166.

so regularly pointed out? Or is there a basic, if latent, integrity to Holmes' jurisprudence?

The reason this inquiry may be put as a fresh proposition so late in the history of scholarship on Holmes is that scholars have thus far given only limited attention to his experience as a judge on the Supreme Judicial Court of Massachusetts. Although Holmes was sixty-one when appointed to the Supreme Court of the United States, he remained a Justice for over twenty-nine years and made his public reputation as a Justice. Early scholarship on Holmes paid almost no attention to his years as a Massachusetts judge, and although a major biography, that of Mark DeWolfe Howe,[11] was begun in the 1950's, Howe died before he had addressed the Massachusetts cases. Howe's last volume on Holmes appeared in 1963;[12] there was a gap of nearly fifteen years before any detailed treatment of Holmes' Massachusetts years appeared.[13]

The explanation for this neglect of Holmes' state court opinions is obvious. Scholarship in American legal history that emphasized private law subjects languished in the 1950's and 1960's; there was little interest in the opinions of any state court judges. Further, there was so much else in Holmes' career of interest—his early scholarship, his Supreme Court opinions, his engaging correspondence—that scholars could justify neglecting what seemed to be a collection of boring, insignificant Massachusetts cases.

Holmes himself, as we will see, found his state cases relatively trivial and dull exercises. His opinions are not particularly pathbreaking, rarely detailed, and not even the rich source of aphorisms and epigrams that his Supreme Court opinions are.[14] But the experience of being a state court judge, when taken in connection with the other two major roles of Holmes' career—scholar and Supreme Court Justice—was a vital link in the forging of Holmes' jurisprudence. The experience of a Massachusetts judgeship transformed Holmes' thought from its expansive, conceptualistic, reformist early form to its cryptic, skeptical later variety. It was on the Massachu-

11. M. Howe, Justice Oliver Wendell Holmes (vol. 1, 1957; vol. 2, 1963).

12. 2 *id.*

13. *See* Tushnet, *The Logic of Experience: Oliver Wendell Holmes on the Supreme Judicial Court*, 63 Va. L. Rev. 975 (1977).

14. There are a few exceptions. *See, e.g.*, Crocker v. Cotting, 170 Mass. 68, 71, 48 N.E. 1023, 1024 (1898) ("The jurisdiction is not affected by a defendant's recalcitrance"); Laplante v. Warren Cotton Mills, 165 Mass. 487, 489, 43 N.E. 294, 295 (1896) ("A boy who is dull at fifteen probably was dull at fourteen"); Lincoln v. Commonwealth, 164 Mass. 368, 378, 41 N.E. 489, 491 (1895) ("All values are anticipations of the future").

setts bench that Holmes came to adopt his familiar posture of resignation, a posture he had never expected to adopt as a judge.

This article traces the evolution of Holmes' jurisprudence in the three major phases of his career. The first section discusses Holmes' early scholarship, which culminated in *The Common Law* in 1881, and the theory of judging that Holmes held at the time of *The Common Law's* publication. Section II examines the process by which Holmes' ideas about judging private law cases became modified with his experiences as a Massachusetts judge, and contrasts the scholarship he produced between 1882 and 1902 with his earlier efforts. Section III discusses the relationship of Holmes' revised theory of judging, which had been developed in a private law setting, to his approach to public law cases as a Supreme Court justice. The fourth section assesses some of the implications of Holmes' jurisprudence for contemporary judging.

I. The Early Scholarship: Order and Activism

Holmes' early life, as a practitioner in a Boston firm, a lecturer and professor at Harvard, and an editor of the *American Law Review*, has been one of the most fully examined phases of his career.[15] We know that by the 1870's Holmes had become attracted to the idea of "analys[ing] what seem to me the fundamental notions and principles of our substantive law [and] putting them in an order."[16] Beginning in 1870 he published a series of unsigned articles and book reviews, primarily in the *American Law Review*, in which he argued that the purpose of legal scholarship should be "classification," by which he meant the organization of a subject "from the most general conception to the most specific proposition or exception in the order of logical subordination."[17]

We know, as well, that Holmes found the subject of Torts a particularly fruitful one to examine in this fashion. After an original judgment that Torts was "not a proper subject for a law book,"[18] Holmes, by 1873, had concluded that "there is no fault to be found with the contents of [Torts] text-books."[19] Torts appealed to Holmes

15. *See, e.g.*, 1 M. Howe, *supra* note 11, at 245-86 (Boston law practice); 2 *id.* at 26-95, 253-83 (Harvard years); *id.* at 1-95 (editor experience).

16. Letter from Oliver Wendell Holmes to James Bryce (Aug. 17, 1879), *quoted in* 2 M. Howe, *supra* note 11, at 25.

17. *The Arrangement of the Law—Privity*, 7 Am. L. Rev. 46, 47 n.2 (1872).

18. Book Notices, 5 Am. L. Rev. 341 (1870).

19. *The Theory of Torts*, 7 Am. L. Rev. 652, 659-60 (1873).

because it seemed to be a subject ripe for classification. While earlier Torts treatises had attempted to associate concepts, like trespass, evidence, and defamation, that bore no "cohesion or legal relationship" to one another, Holmes became convinced that some fundamental notions and principles could be derived.[20] He claimed that "an enumeration of the [tort] actions which have been successful, and of those which have failed, define[d] the extent of the primary duties imposed by the law."[21] This was in keeping with his belief that "form[s] of action" could be made "to correspond to every substantial duty," and thereby "embod[y] in a practical shape a classification of the law."[22] Holmes discovered that the tort writs could be divided into three groups, one requiring culpability as a prerequisite for liability, another indifferent to culpability, and a third determining culpability from "motives of policy . . . kept purposely indefinite."[23]

The last category of wrongs introduced for Holmes the standard of modern negligence, which he seized upon as a clarifying principle for tort law. Eight years after his preliminary survey of tort writs he was prepared to argue, in *The Common Law,* that the negligence principle had increasingly dominated tort law.[24] And that shift from analytic classification to philosophical synthesis was characteristic of his scholarship in the late 1870's. In five articles in the *American Law Review*[25] between 1876 and 1880 Holmes revealed a new style of scholarship. His subjects and his explorations were primarily historical; his purpose, however, was not merely to clarify the historical origins of doctrine, but to claim that doctrine could not be understood apart from its historical origins. A historical exploration of a legal subject, for Holmes, revealed its essentials: its standards of liability, its core elements, its character. History, he later said, was "the first step . . . towards a deliberate reconsideration of the worth of those rules."[26] "History sets us free and enables us to make up our minds dispassionately whether the survival which we are enforcing answers any new purpose when it has ceased to answer the old."[27]

---

20. Book Notices, *supra* note 18, at 341.
21. *The Theory of Torts, supra* note 19, at 659-60.
22. Book Notices, 5 AM. L. REV. 359 (1871).
23. *The Theory of Torts, supra* note 19, at 659.
24. O. W. HOLMES, *supra* note 7, at 89.
25. *See* 2 M. HOWE, *supra* note 11, at 136.
26. O. W. HOLMES, *The Path of the Law,* in COLLECTED LEGAL PAPERS 167, 186-87 (1920).
27. O. W. HOLMES, *Law in Science and Science in Law,* in COLLECTED LEGAL PAPERS

The pattern of scholarship first introduced in Holmes' articles on tort law thus continued through other subjects to culminate in *The Common Law*. As Mark Howe has shown,[28] *The Common Law* was a reformist work in two senses of the word. In his efforts to show that all the common law fields—criminal law, property, torts, and contracts—had arguably been governed by shifting external standards of liability throughout their history, Holmes was attempting to reform jurisprudence by emphasizing the derivation of general principles rather than the pleading of specific writs. Uncertainty would be reduced in the law if common law subjects were arranged according to general principles and lawyers recognized that those principles were simply manifestations of current community preferences. The study of law was thus to proceed from the individual case through history to the derivation of general principles. This would require, among other things, a basic change in the way law was taught and practiced.

Holmes was also advocating another kind of reform in *The Common Law*. Since certainty and predictability were desirable goals for the legal profession, those institutions in the legal system that fostered certainty should be rewarded at the expense of those that appeared to hinder its pursuit. In his 1873 essay on torts Holmes expressed what he took to be the view of "many whose opinion is entitled to respect" that "negligence [was] always and in the nature of things a question for the jury."[29] This echoed a position he had taken two years earlier, when he said that "we suppose it is wholly for the jury to say whether the party has used such care as a reasonable and prudent man would have used under the circumstances of the particular case."[30] But by 1880 Holmes had changed his mind about the efficacy of allowing legal standards to be formulated by juries. In *The Common Law* he complained about "leav[ing] all our rights and duties throughout a great part of the law to the necessarily more or less accidental feelings of a jury," arguing that "the sphere in which [a judge] is able to rule without taking [jury] opinion at all should be continually growing."[31] This was in keeping with his belief that "the tendency of the law must

---

210, 225 (1920).

28. 2 M. Howe, *supra* note 11, at 196-97.

29. *The Theory of Torts*, *supra* note 19, at 658.

30. Book Notices, 5 Am. L. Rev. 536 (1870).

31. O. W. Holmes, *supra* note 7, at 124-26.

always be to narrow the field of uncertainty."[32]

Holmes' early scholarship, in its final phases, thus envisaged a "creative epoch"[33] in late nineteenth-century American private law in which a philosophically oriented class of scholars would join with a class of judges who had acquired "a fund of experience"[34] to develop broad, predictable rules. The pursuit of order in American jurisprudence would be fostered by judicial activism. Given Holmes' confidence in the techniques of analysis he had used in *The Common Law* and in the principles he had derived as a result of their use, it was hard for him to imagine that others could not do likewise. But those others would have to be persons capable of understanding the law and its history, and dedicated to the goals of certainty, predictability, and coherence. Judges were such persons.

One of the curiosities of Holmes' early life is why, after finding his scholarly labors finally coming to fruition as he approached forty, he did not regard a life of future scholarship with more enthusiasm. After severely pressing himself to secure some scholarly achievement by his fortieth birthday—the result of which was some petty competitiveness with other scholars, a neglect of his home life, and a "fearful grip upon his work" that made him "a melancholy sight" to one observer[35]—Holmes, who had written *The Common Law* while in active law practice, was then given an opportunity to continue a life of scholarship. By November, 1881, he had been offered a position on the Harvard Law School faculty, subject to the contingency of funds being raised to endow a new professorship, and had indicated his readiness to accept. In his letter of acceptance, however, Holmes reserved the right "not . . . to feel bound in honor not to consider" a judgeship should one subsequently be offered him.[36]

Less than a year later, after finally accepting Harvard's offer of a professorship in jurisprudence, Holmes resigned to go on the Supreme Judicial Court. The circumstances of his resignation—he consulted no one on the Harvard faculty and accepted the judgeship three hours after it was offered—produced a good deal of bitterness at Harvard. James Bradley Thayer, who had helped raise funds for

32. *Id.* at 127.

33. *Id.* at 89.

34. *Id.* at 124.

35. Letter from Mrs. Henry James to Henry James, Jr., *quoted in* 1 R. PERRY, THE THOUGHT AND CHARACTER OF WILLIAM JAMES 519 (1935).

36. Letter from Oliver Wendell Holmes to Charles W. Eliot (Nov. 1, 1881), *quoted in* 2 M. HOWE, *supra* note 11, at 261.

the professorship that brought Holmes to Harvard, poured out his resentment in a diary. "[W]ith all his attractive qualities and his solid merits," Thayer concluded, Holmes was "wanting sadly in the noblest region of human character,—selfish, vain, throughtless of others."[37] Much later, when Felix Frankfurter was considering joining the Harvard faculty, Holmes wrote him that "academic life is but half life—it is withdrawal from the fight in order to utter smart things that cost you nothing except the thinking them from a cloister." He also said, in the same letter, "My wife thinks I unconsciously began to grow sober with an inarticulate sense of limitation in the few months of my stay in Cambridge."[38]

Apparently Holmes was unsure where a scholarly life would take him. He wrote James Bryce shortly after his decision to take the judgeship that he "had already realized at Cambridge that the field for generalization inside the body of the law was small and that the day would soon come when one felt that the only remaining problems were of detail."[39] The choice, he later wrote to Harold Laski, "seemed to be between applying one's theories to practice and details or going into another field."[40] Judging appeared to provide "an all round experience," and a "share in the practical struggle of life."[41] It "hardens the fibre," Holmes later said, and "is more likely to make more of a man of one who turns it to success."[42] Had he stayed at Harvard he would have felt that he "had chosen the less manly course."[43]

The striking feature of Holmes' conception of the academic and judicial worlds at this point in his career is not his sense that academic life was more cloistered or less "manly" than a judgeship. It is rather his feeling that "the field for generalization inside the body of the law was small" and that "as a philosopher" Holmes needed to

---

37. Thayer, Memorandum (Dec. 22, 1882), *quoted in* 2 M. HOWE, *supra* note 11, at 268.

38. Letter from Oliver Wendell Holmes to Felix Frankfurter (July 15, 1913), *quoted in* 2 M. HOWE, *supra* note 11, at 282.

39. Letter from Oliver Wendell Holmes to James Bryce (Dec. 31, 1882), *quoted in* 2 M. HOWE, *supra* note 11, at 280.

40. Letter from Oliver Wendell Holmes to Harold Laski (Nov. 17, 1920), *quoted in* 2 M. HOWE, *supra* note 11, at 281.

41. Letter from Oliver Wendell Holmes to James Bryce (Dec. 31, 1882), *quoted in* 2 M. HOWE, *supra* note 11, at 280-81.

42. Letter from Oliver Wendell Holmes to Felix Frankfurter (July 15, 1913), *quoted in* 2 M. HOWE, *supra* note 11, at 282.

43. Letter from Oliver Wendell Holmes to James Bryce (Dec. 31, 1882), *quoted in* 2 M. HOWE, *supra* note 11, at 281.

"extend his range."[44] Holmes apparently believed that his labors on *The Common Law* had resulted in a comprehensive theory of jurisprudence, that he was not likely to modify that theory, and that the remainder of academic life, if he stayed in the law, would be filling in the details.[45] This was not as limited a conception of scholarship as it might first appear. Holmes was reluctant to abandon an insight once he had formulated it; nearly forty years after publishing *The Common Law* he defended its findings against critics.[46] Moreover, the seminal work of many scholars is done early in their careers, and there are temptations to rest on one's reputation and "fill in the details." Holmes may have understood that there was not much more he could do, at least in the private law subjects that held his greatest interest, after he had plumbed their depths in *The Common Law*.

But if Holmes was interested in "generalization" and the pursuit of "tempting [philosophical] themes,"[47] why did he choose to become a judge? He never made the reasons for his choice explicit, but he appears to have thought that if he were going to "apply one's theories to practice and details," performing their function in "the practical struggle for life," rather than in a "cloister," would be more satisfying. Academic detail was just nit-picking; judicial detail was "the gradual weaving of one's contribution into the practical system of the law."[48] Judging was to provide a means by which the theories of *The Common Law* were to have an impact on "business in the world."[49]

One cannot review Holmes' choice to forego academic life for a judgeship without sensing that he was proceeding under the assumption that judging would give him an opportunity to put his theories into practice. He had spent too much time deriving his views on contracts, the criminal law, property and torts to regard them merely as "smart things"; his jurisprudence was the jurisprudence of reform. Here was an opportunity to put his reforms into action, to rewrite the corpus of Massachusetts jurisprudence. Here was an opportunity

---

44. *Id.* at 280.

45. *Id.*

46. Letter from Oliver Wendell Holmes to Harold Laski (Feb. 1, 1919), *quoted in* 2 M. HOWE, *supra* note 11, at 137.

47. Letter from Oliver Wendell Holmes to Harold Laski, (Nov. 17, 1920), *quoted in* 2 M. HOWE, *supra* note 11, at 281.

48. Letter from Oliver Wendell Holmes to Lady Castletown (Mar. 5, 1897), *quoted in* 2 M. HOWE, *supra* note 11, at 282.

49. Letter from Oliver Wendell Holmes to Felix Frankfurter (July 15, 1913), *quoted in* 2 M. HOWE, *supra* note 11, at 282.

to be an activist judge creating an orderly, predictable system of laws.

II. The Supreme Judicial Court: Deflated Expectations

In 1900, after nearly twenty years as a judge, Holmes asked himself "what is there to show for this half lifetime that has passed?"[50] He had considered "[a] thousand cases, many of them upon trifling or transitory matters." He "would have liked to study to the bottom and to say his say on every question which the law has ever presented." He would have liked to "invent new problems which should be the test of doctrine, and then to generalize it all and write it in continuous, logical, philosophic exposition, setting forth the whole corpus with its roots in history and its justifications of expedience." Instead he had decided a great many dull cases. That was "life," he felt; "we cannot live our dreams."[51]

The experience of judging had not conformed to Holmes' expectations. He had contemplated being able to study cases "to the bottom," to "say his say" fully on matters of common law doctrine, to use existing cases as a means of anticipating "new problems," and perhaps even to "generalize it all." For the most part he had not been able to do these things. There was not enough time to study cases in depth. Saying one's say fully ran the risk of offending one's colleagues: Opinions were joint projects. Lawyers, litigants, and even judges were not so interested in a case as an index of future doctrinal development; practical issues were at stake, results had to be reached and decisions made. And the common law, as it evolved in the Massachusetts Supreme Judicial Court, was hardly a "continuous, logical, philosophic" system. It was better described as a series of largely dilatory cases that were decided without much attention to the "whole corpus."[52]

Decisionmaking on the Massachusetts court was best captured by the old metaphor that Holmes had first written in his 1873 essay, *The Theory of Torts*,[53] where he had speculated on the development of the law:

> Two widely different cases suggest a general distinction, which is a clear one when stated broadly. But as new cases cluster around the

50. O. W. Holmes, *Speech at Bar Dinner*, in Occasional Speeches 122, 123 (M. Howe ed. 1962).

51. *Id.*

52. *Id.*

53. *The Theory of Torts*, *supra* note 19.

> opposite poles, and begin to approach each other, the distinction becomes more difficult to trace; the determinations are made one way or the other on a very slight predominance of feeling, rather than articulate reason; and at last a mathematical line is arrived at by the contact of contrary decisions, which is so far arbitrary that it might equally well have been drawn a little further to the one side or to the other.[54]

Rather than studying cases to their bottom, appellate courts made determinations on a "predominance of feeling." The "mathematical lines" drawn by courts were "arbitrary." Clear distinctions evolved into intuitive preferences.

A random survey[55] of Holmes' torts opinions on the Massachusetts court provides an entry to his work as a state judge. Torts had been the private law field in which Holmes had arguably made his greatest scholarly contributions. It is possible to claim that in essays such as *The Theory of Torts* and *Trespass and Negligence,*[56] and in *The Common Law,* Holmes had supplied a principle for late nineteenth-century tort law—the modern negligence principle—that allowed torts to develop its identity as a discrete branch of law. Holmes' achievement had been to see that it was possible to speak of the myriad tort writs as manifestiations of a general civil duty owed by everyone not to carelessly injure others. The concept of this duty of very great generality and the limitation of the duty through the fault principle—reasonable conduct under the circumstances—were major catalysts to the growth of modern tort law. Almost all the leading torts theorists of the late nineteenth century—Thomas Cooley,[57] Melville Bigelow,[58] John Wigmore,[59] Jeremiah Smith[60]—owed their conception of the subject as dealing with universally imposed civil duties to Holmes.[61]

---

54. *Id.* at 654.

55. Even the term "random survey" may impart too much rigor. I have examined Holmes' torts opinions in three time periods from 1881 to 1902. Adjustments were made if the number of opinions in a given year seemed too low to be revealing. I was interested in the significance or insignificance of the case, as suggested by Holmes' opinion and subsequent treatment of the opinion, and in comparisons between Holmes' jurisprudential perspective in one time frame and another.

56. Holmes, *Trespass and Negligence,* 14 AM. L. REV. 1 (1880).

57. *See* T. COOLEY, A TREATISE ON THE LAW OF TORTS 628-58 (1880).

58. *See* M. BIGELOW, THE LAW OF TORTS 106-16 (8th ed. 1907).

59. *See* 1 J. WIGMORE, SELECT CASES ON THE LAW OF TORTS 7-8 (1912).

60. *See* Smith, *Tort and Absolute Liability—Suggested Changes in Classfication,* in SELECTED ESSAYS ON THE LAW OF TORTS 176, 189-90 (1924).

61. *See* G. WHITE, TORT LAW IN AMERICA 6-62 (1980).

What were the tort cases that Holmes, with this rich scholarly background, considered on the Massachusetts court? Holmes wrote over 400 torts opinions, the most he wrote on any legal subject and nearly one-third of his entire output. Of these only three were dissents.[62] One would have thought that with this amount of cases, the very high percentage of majority opinions, and Holmes' understanding of the intellectual foundations of tort law, he would have had ample opportunity to put his scholarly theories into practice. Instead his torts opinions were exceptionally routine. Two opinions in the 1883 term merely disposed of evidentiary exceptions taken by the defendant at trial.[63] A third was a conventional assumption-of-risk case that was decided on its facts.[64]

Only in *Cowley v. Pulsifer,*[65] a case testing the limits of the record libel privilege, did Holmes attempt an elaborate discussion. The case involved publication in a newspaper of the contents of a petition to remove an attorney from the bar. Before the petition had been presented to the court or entered on the docket, it appeared in the paper. Holmes stated that "no binding authority has been called to our attention which precisely determines this case, and we must be governed in our conclusion mainly by a consideration of the reasons upon which admitted principles have been established."[66] He then grounded the decision on a distinction between proceedings in open court, which could be recorded without subjecting the recorder to a libel suit, and "preliminary written statement[s] of a claim or charge."[67] The record libel privilege did not extend to the latter.

Trivial torts cases again outnumbered significant ones in the 1884 term. Of the seven cases in which Holmes wrote opinions, two simply disposed of exceptions,[68] one held that the technical requirements for a libel had been made out,[69] one allowed an action for

---

62. May v. Wood, 172 Mass. 11, 14, 51 N.E. 191, 192 (1898) (Holmes, J., dissenting); Nash v. Minnesota Title Ins. & Trust Co., 163 Mass. 574, 586, 40 N.E. 1039, 1042 (1895) (Holmes, J., dissenting); Hanson v. Globe Newspaper Co., 159 Mass. 293, 299, 34 N.E. 462, 464 (1893) (Holmes, J., dissenting).

63. McMahon v. O'Connor, 137 Mass. 216 (1884); McAvoy v. Wright, 137 Mass. 207 (1884).

64. Williams v. Churchill, 137 Mass. 243 (1884).

65. 137 Mass. 392 (1884).

66. *Id.* at 393.

67. *Id.* at 394.

68. New Salem v. Eagle Mill Co., 138 Mass. 8 (1884); Purple v. Greenfield, 138 Mass. 1 (1884).

69. Hurley v. Fall River Daily Herald Pub. Co., 138 Mass. 334 (1885).

diverting water to be maintained by a citizen of another state,[70] one refused to find contributory negligence as a matter of law where an officer in the act of arresting a person stepped into a partly covered well in the darkness,[71] and one labeled the actions of a deputy sheriff misrepresentations of fact.[72] Only in *Dietrich v. Northampton*[73] did Holmes find a case on which he could ruminate. There a pregnant woman slipped on a defective highway constructed by the town of Northampton and suffered a miscarriage. She recovered for her physical injuries, and the deceased child's administrator sought to recover for the child's death. The case raised a number of issues, including whether infants could maintain actions for injuries suffered before birth, whether an injured fetus was a "person" entitled to legal redress, and whether the common law of negligence had a different standard of liability from that imposed on towns for failure to maintain highways in proper repair. For Holmes the case turned on the proposition that "no case, so far as we know, has ever decided that, if the infant survived, it could maintain an action for injuries received by it while in its mother's womb."[74] That dictum was to survive in tort law for seventy-five years.[75]

The 1890 Term contained more cases that approximated the typical late nineteenth-century tort action: the industrial accident leading to a suit in negligence. None of the negligence cases, however, involved more than a simple application of reasonable conduct standards to their facts. An employee assumed the risk when he passed closely to a band saw, slipped, and put his hand on it.[76] A conductor of a street car was not contributorially negligent when knocked off the car by a protruding post from an excavation barrier.[77] A husband and wife injured at a grade crossing where the gates were up and no whistle or bell was sounded by the approaching train were entitled to have the question of their contributory negligence decided by a jury.[78] A commuter who, ignoring closed gates,

70. Mannville v. Worcester, 138 Mass. 89 (1884).

71. Learoyd v. Godfrey, 138 Mass. 315 (1885).

72. Burns v. Lane, 138 Mass. 350 (1885).

73. 138 Mass. 14 (1884).

74. *Id.* at 15.

75. The first case to extend a right of action for prenatal injuries was Verkennes v. Cornifa, 229 Minn. 365, 38 N.W.2d 838 (1949). Dietrich v. Northampton, 138 Mass. 14 (1884), was not limited until Keyes v. Construction Serv., Inc., 340 Mass. 633, 165 N.E.2d 912 (1960).

76. May v. Whittier Mach. Co., 154 Mass. 29, 27 N.E. 768 (1891).

77. Powers v. Boston, 154 Mass. 60, 27 N.E. 995 (1891).

78. Merrigan v. Boston & A. R.R., 154 Mass. 189, 28 N.E. 149 (1891).

walked behind one train and was hit by another train on a neighboring track was grossly negligent as a matter of law.[79] A town had a responsibility to repair a mudhole in a road that caused the driver of a wagon to injure himself when he drove off the road to avoid it.[80] An unauthorized person using a water closet in a railroad station was owed no duty of care by the railroad, and no liability ensued when he was killed by a train that ran off its track.[81] The maintenance of a heavy steam hammer by a car wheel company was not a nuisance.[82]

Only one case in the Term, ***Burt v. Advertiser Newspaper Co.***,[83] presented Holmes with an opportunity to clarify legal doctrine. ***Burt*** was a libel action against the ***Boston Daily Advertiser*** for a series of articles on fraud in the New York customs house. Two brothers, James and Silas Burt, were mentioned in the articles; James Burt, a broker, was accused of "outrageous sugar frauds"[84] and Silas Burt, a naval officer, of having a "long-time connection with some of the most disreputable elements in the New York custom-house."[85] In response to a letter of protest the ***Advertiser***, while conceding that Silas Burt had not been accused of any wrongdoing, said that James Burt's practices "hold the New York custom-house up as a national disgrace."[86] The question raised by the ***Burt*** case was the scope of the *Advertiser's* privilege of "fair criticism upon matters of public interest."[87] That privilege, Holmes held, did not extend to the publication of false facts. It was the criticism—the opinions of the critics—that was privileged. Holmes distinguished between "private inquiries . . . about a private person,"[88] such as "answers to inquiries about the character of a servant"[89] and comment on public matters. The *Advertiser's* reasonable belief that its allegations about James Burt were true did not constitute a defense, Holmes noted: "A person publishes libelous matter at his peril."[90] The ***Burt*** case furnishes a good example of nineteenth-century common law attitudes toward

---

79. Debbons v. Old Colony R.R., 154 Mass. 402, 28 N.E. 274 (1891).
80. Pomeroy v. Westfield, 154 Mass. 462, 28 N.E. 899 (1891).
81. Dillon v. Connecticut River R.R., 154 Mass. 478, 28 N.E. 899 (1891).
82. Wesson v. Washburn Car Wheel Co., 154 Mass. 514, 28 N.E. 679 (1891).
83. 154 Mass. 238, 28 N.E. 1 (1891).
84. *Id.* at 241, 28 N.E. at 3.
85. *Id.* at 239, 28 N.E. at 2.
86. *Id.* at 241, 28 N.E. at 3.
87. *Id.* at 242, 28 N.E. at 4.
88. *Id.* at 243, 28 N.E. at 4.
89. *Id.* at 242, 28 N.E. at 4.
90. *Id.* at 245, 28 N.E. at 5 (citations omitted).

freedom of the press in defamation cases. Not even a showing that a reasonable editor would have believed the false facts about James Burt to be true would have helped the *Advertiser*: Strict liability was the standard in defamation cases.

The 1891 Term produced no significant torts cases. The city of New Bedford was exonerated from liability for nuisance when a homeowner who connected his drain with a sewer, which concededly had a narrow outlet, had his basement filled during a heavy rainstorm with water and sewage.[91] A person who fell down unlighted cellar stairs in the course of delivering wood was held to assume the risk of an open cellar being near the house.[92] A case where a woman fell down a lighted flight of stairs was not sufficient for res ipsa loquitur, and could be taken from the jury since its elements were "permanent, few, and simple."[93] A workman who set on fire a shafting box soaked with oil, thereby damaging the owner's premises, was negligent as a matter of law.[94] And a traveler who picked up a loose telephone wire in a road, and was injured from electric current, was considered to be owed a duty by the city of Cambridge, which had negligently allowed the wire to fall into the road.[95] In none of the above cases did Holmes' opinions extend beyond a few paragraphs.

By the 1901 Term Holmes had become Chief Justice, and his workload had increased. He wrote Sir Frederick Pollock in 1899 that he "had more to do than ever," and that he had been taking on himself "perhaps rather a lion's share."[96] But the torts cases were no more significant than they had been in the 1880's or 1890's. Holmes found no contributory negligence in a parent whose child had been run over by a wagon in a quiet road,[97] but did find it where another child was run over by an electric car in a "teeming" city street.[98] He upheld a jury's verdict that a street railway car had negligently run into a baker's wagon that had been lawfully driving on the streetcar tracks,[99] construed a dram shop act to impose liability on the owner of a bar who illegally sold liquor to a person who while intoxicated

91. Buckley v. New Bedford, 155 Mass. 64, 29 N.E. 201 (1891).

92. Walker v. Winstanley, 155 Mass. 301, 29 N.E. 518 (1892).

93. Pinney v. Hall, 156 Mass. 225, 226, 30 N.E. 1016 (1892).

94. Perry v. Smith, 156 Mass. 340, 31 N.E. 9 (1892).

95. Bourget v. Cambridge, 156 Mass. 391, 31 N.E. 390 (1892).

96. Letter from Oliver Wendell Holmes to Frederick Pollock (Dec. 1, 1899), in 1 HOLMES-POLLOCK LETTERS 98 (M. Howe ed. 1941).

97. Walsh v. Loorem, 180 Mass. 18, 61 N.E. 222 (1901).

98. Cotter v. Lynn & B.R.R., 180 Mass. 145, 61 N.E. 818 (1901).

99. Vincent v. Norton & Taunton St. Ry., 180 Mass. 104, 61 N.E. 822 (1901).

stumbled into the path of a train,[100] and refused to impute to a passenger the alleged contributory negligence of a driver of a coal wagon.[101] He found a spout that spilled water on a sidewalk, causing ice to form, to be a nuisance, and its owner strictly liable for the injuries of a pedestrian who slipped on the ice.[102] He held that proof that a woman had committed adultery was not a defense against calling her a dirty old whore.[103] He allowed recovery from emotional distress when accompanied by a slight physical injury.[104] He found a gateman who inexplicably stood between the tracks of a railroad and was killed by a freight train in the process of coupling and uncoupling cars to be contributorially negligent.[105] And he denied recovery to a postal clerk who had sued the railroad owning the train on which he was unloading mail for injuries suffered when a car from another railroad negligently hit that train.[106]

In only one torts case that Term was there a glimpse of the kind of role Holmes might have expected himself to play as a judge. In *Patnoude v. New York, New Haven, and Hartford Railway*[107] a street railway company and the New York, New Haven and Hartford Railroad had agreed to unload a streetcar at a point on the railroad's tracks near the streetcar company's barn. The unloading process required the temporary dismantling of a fence that shielded the tracks from an adjoining highway. While the fence was dismantled and the streetcar, covered with a white canvas, was resting on a flat car of the railroad, a rider drove by on the adjacent highway and his horse, startled by the sight of the streetcar, reared and threw him. The question was whether the railroad was liable in nuisance or in negligence.

"As in many cases," Holmes said in his opinion finding for the railroad, "two principles or social desiderata present themselves, each of which it would be desirable to carry out but for the other, but which at this point come into conflict." It was "desirable that as far as possible people should be able to drive in the streets without their horses being frightened, [and it was also] desirable that the owners of land should be free to make profitable and otherwise inno-

100. McNary v. Blackburn, 180 Mass. 141, 61 N.E. 885 (1901).
101. Murray v. Boston Ice Co., 180 Mass. 165, 61 N.E. 1001 (1901).
102. Davis v. Rich, 180 Mass. 235, 62 N.E. 375 (1902).
103. Rutherford v. Paddock, 180 Mass. 289, 62 N.E. 381 (1902).
104. Homans v. Boston Elev. Ry., 180 Mass. 456, 62 N.E. 737 (1902).
105. Tirrell v. New York, N.H. & H.R.R., 180 Mass. 490, 62 N.E. 745 (1902).
106. Stoddard v. New York, N.H. & H.R.R., 181 Mass. 422, 63 N.E 927 (1902).
107. 180 Mass. 119, 61 N.E. 813 (1901).

cent use of it." A "line has to be drawn to separate the domains of the irreconciliable desires, [but] such a line [could] not be drawn in general terms."[108] In the *Patnoude* case, however, the condition of the railroad's car and fence was transitory, and its potential for frightening horses did not necessarily mean that it was unlawful.[109] Torts cases involved drawing lines, balancing irreconciliable desires, and giving common sense interpretations to facts. General propositions were not much help in deciding them.

With *Patnoude* one can see how far Holmes' conception of judging had evolved from the one he held when first appointed to the Massachusetts court.[110] While he had enjoyed getting to the bottom of things and formulating generalizations as a scholar, such activities were not easily related to appellate judging. The facts of individual cases were so diverse, and the competing principles so generally worthy, that arbitrary line-drawing was the inevitable result. Such line-drawing could not be generalized. Setting forth "the whole corpus" of law, or "writ[ing] it in continuous, logical, philosophic exposition"[111] were tasks beyond the reach of judges, who had to decide difficult, limited, and largely trivial cases.

Holmes had learned two lessons from his experience on the Supreme Judicial Court of Massachusetts. The first lesson was that cases inevitably presented conflicts between desirable social principles, and judges simply had to choose. That choice was an act of policymaking, not an inevitable unfolding of common law principles. The second lesson was that since such choices were arbitrary, and since the process of line-drawing could not be generalized, judging was a far more modest and less creative activity than Holmes had expected. These lessons fostered two judicial habits in Holmes: the habit of deferring especially arbitrary policy choices to some other body, such as a legislature or a jury, that arguably reflected community sentiment; and the habit of not agonizing over the reasoning that justified an arbitrary choice. By the time Holmes left the Massachusetts court in 1902 his opinions were already notable for their brevity, their assertiveness, and their cryptic language. It was as if Holmes recognized that his decisionmaking process was largely arbitrary and decided to get on with it.

The Massachusetts years were also notable for a significant

---

108. *Id.* at 120-21, 61 N.E. at 814.
109. *Id.*
110. *See supra* text accompanying notes 50-61.
111. O. W. HOLMES, *supra* note 50, at 123.

change in the attitudes expressed in Holmes' scholarship. *The Common Law,* I have argued,[112] had been a reformist tract, seeking to show by example that a thorough canvass of private law subjects could yield some clarifying and organizing principles. One message of *The Common Law* was that such principles were there to be extracted and applied to real life situations by judges. The meaning of a private law subject, Holmes seemed to be saying, could be found in this body of intelligible principles.

By 1897, when he delivered his address, *The Path of the Law,*[113] Holmes was offering a very different definition of the meaning of law. Notwithstanding the claims of "some text writers," that law was "a system of reason" or "a deduction from principles of ethics or admitted axioms," law could be most accurately described as "prophecies of what the courts will do in fact."[114] While the "language of judicial decision" was "mainly the language of logic," behind the "logical form" lay "a judgment as to the relative worth and importance of competing legislative grounds." Judicial decisions were "opinion[s] as to policy" that merely "embod[ied] the preference of a given body in a given time and place."[115] The "duty" of judges was to weigh "considerations of social advantage."[116]

The Path of the Law had stressed lesson one of Holmes' experience as a judge: While judges may attempt to cloak their decisions in logic, the decisions were instinctive policy preferences. *Law in Science and Science in Law,*[117] delivered two years later, stressed lesson two. Holmes had some faith in science as a vehicle for measuring the social desires that he saw competing in a case.[118] He conceded that an "absolutely final and quantitative determination" could only occasionally be reached "because the worth of the competing social ends which respectively solicit a judgment for the plaintiff or the defendant cannot be reduced to number and accurately fixed."[119] Since policy grounds lay behind the use of legal rules, a "quantitative comparison" of the competing social desiderata seemed desirable. Such a comparison led Holmes back to a variant on his original

112. *See supra* text accompanying notes 28-32.
113. O. W. HOLMES, *supra* note 26, at 167.
114. *Id.* at 172-73.
115. *Id.* at 181.
116. *Id.* at 184.
117. O. W. HOLMES, *supra* note 27, at 210.
118. *Id.* at 226.
119. *Id.* at 231.

passage from *The Theory of Torts.*[120]

> In our approach towards exactness we constantly tend to work out definite lines or equators to mark distinctions which we first notice as a difference of poles. . . . When [we] ha[ve] discovered that a difference is a difference of degree, that distinguished extremes have between them a penumbra in which one gradually shades into the other, . . . [we realize that we have] to draw the line, and an advocate of more experience will show the arbitrariness of the line proposed by putting cases very near to it on one side or the other. But the theory of the law is that such lines exist . . . . We like to disguise the arbitrariness, we like to save ourselves the trouble of nice and doubtful discriminations.[121]

Thus Holmes concluded that judging ended up being the arbitrary resolution of "a conflict between two social desires, each of which seeks to extend its dominion over the case, and which cannot both have their way." In making that resolution judges were "exercis[ing] the sovereign prerogative of choice."[122] They were "weigh[ing] the reasons for the particular right claimed and those for the competing right." Their solutions could not be in general terms, because "generalities [were] worse then useless."[123] Their solutions were bound to rest on "general grounds of policy blindly felt."[124]

Such were the lessons of twenty years on the Massachusetts bench. And there were two curious, and potentially contradictory, corollaries to those lessons. Since legal decisions were at bottom choices between competing social policies, it was essential that such choices reflect the wishes and feelings of the community, so that the law might keep pace with current thought.[125] Judge-made law had a tendency to prefer the logical form to the candid policy statement, and consequently sometimes became ridden with anachronistic rules and outmoded propositions. Especially in doubtful cases, then, Holmes thought that the practice of deferring policy choices to the jury was a good one: Juries were apt to "introduce into their verdict a certain amount . . . of popular prejudice."[126] In a case like

120. For the original passage from *The Theory of Torts*, see *supra* text accompanying note 54.

121. O. W. HOLMES, *supra* note 27, at 232-33.

122. *Id.* at 239.

123. *Id.* at 242.

124. *Id.* at 232.

125. *Id.* at 238.

126. *Id.* at 237-38.

Patnoude, where a right to ride without fear of injury conflicted with a right to use property in a profitable manner, one could label as a question of fact whether the use that invaded the right was negligent, and let a jury decide which social desideratum it preferred. A sense of the arbitrariness of judicial decisionmaking, then, led to a desire to defer, in close cases, to a more community-minded tribunal.

At the same time, however, that sense of arbitrariness led to a desire to exercise the sovereign prerogative of choice. Holmes had no particular confidence that juries "could see further into things or form a saner judgment than a sensible and well trained judge."[127] He thought that a well-trained judge could "follow the existing body of dogma into its highest generalizations," then "discover from history how it has come to be what it is," and finally "consider the ends which the several rules seek to accomplish"[128] and make a choice. Indeed, he thought that a judge need not do all those things; he might have liked to have done them, but he had not done them often in his opinions. What he had done was to see the internal conflict presented by a case, measure the competing social desires in his mind, and make an arbitrary choice. Having done that, he had made use of logic and his own command of language, and had produced an opinion. Judging in that manner was not difficult, so long as one recognized what one was doing.

In these two peculiarly divergent corollaries lay the seeds of Holmes' constitutional jurisprudence. Holmes' opinions on the Supreme Court were of two very different types. The first type, which brought him public acclaim,[129] emphasized the unsoundness of judges substituting their judgment on social issues for that of legislatures. Legislatures, like juries, were repositories of contemporary prejudices; there was something to be said for letting them decide difficult policy questions. In this deferential stance Holmes appeared as a judge aware of his own limitations, an appearance that was deceptive. The second type of opinion that Holmes produced on the Court resembled many of his private law opinions in Massachusetts: It was a brief, cursory, and cryptic determination of a difficult and complex issue. In the first type of opinion Holmes seemed chastened

---

127. *Id.* at 237.

128. O. W. Holmes, *supra* note 26, at 198.

129. *See, e.g.*, Dewey, *Justice Holmes and the Liberal Mind,* 53 New Republic 210, 211 (1928); Frankfurter, *The Constitutional Opinions of Justice Holmes,* 29 Harv. L. Rev. 683, 691-94 (1916); Pound, *Judge Holmes' Contributions to the Science of Law,* 34 Harv. L. Rev. 449, 450 (1921).

by the recognition of his arbitrary power; in the second he seemed to revel in it.

III. The Supreme Court: A "Job" Mentality

After being appointed to the Supreme Court in 1902 Holmes wrote Pollock of his delight with his new position. "I am . . . more absorbed, interested and impressed than ever I had dreamed I might be," he said. "The variety and novelty to me of the questions, the remote spaces from which they come, the amount of work they require, all help the effect."[130] But before long Holmes began to see recurrent themes. Most questions before the Court were questions of degree; beneath "the lion's hide" of a case was "the same old donkey of a question of law."[131] Holmes could write two opinions a week, finishing the first one assigned to him at a Saturday conference by Tuesday and the second by Saturday. In listening to counsel argue before the Court he could summarize an argument before the lawyer had finished making it. His law clerks, whom he hired from 1905 on at the suggestion of John Chipman Gray, Ezra Thayer, or Felix Frankfurter, had very little legal research to do: Holmes wrote his own opinions, asking only for an occasional citation. The clerks paid his bills, answered routine correspondence, read to him in his last years, and above all were sounding boards on contemporary issues. When another justice needed research help, Holmes lent them out.[132]

Despite the "burning themes" that appeared in constitutional cases and despite the great public attention that his opinions, especially his dissents, received, Holmes primarily thought of his work on the Supreme Court as a "job." In 1928 Holmes wrote Lewis Einstein that "when I am on my job I don't care a damn what you want or what [a President] wants."[133] Yosal Rogat once likened Holmes' attitude toward his work on the Supreme Court to that of a pony express rider who "had to undertake a dangerous and exhausting series of rides in order to insure the survival of the city." While Holmes may have ridden hard, he "was not motivated by the city's survival . . . . Rather, he executed the assignment simply because he had

---

130. Letter from Oliver Wendell Holmes to Frederick Pollock (Dec. 28, 1902), in 1 Holmes-Pollock Letters, *supra* note 96, at 109.

131. Letter from Oliver Wendell Holmes to Frederick Pollock (Dec. 11, 1909), in 1 Holmes-Pollock Letters, *supra* note 96, at 156.

132. For the reminiscences of one of Holmes' law clerks on these matters, see Derby, *Recollections of Mr. Justice Holmes*, 12 N.Y.U. L. Rev. 345, 349-50 (1935).

133. Letter from Oliver Wendell Holmes to Lewis Einstein (Apr. 1, 1928), in Holmes-Einstein Letters 279 (1964).

undertaken it and . . . to bring back a map of the terrain."[134] Repeatedly in his Supreme Court opinions Holmes conveyed this sense of detachment. He once said in a dissent that "[t]here is nothing that I more deprecate than the use of the Fourteenth Amendment . . . to prevent the making of social experiments . . . in the insulated chambers afforded by the several States, even though the experiments may seem futile or even noxious to me."[135]

Detachment seems the most accurate term to characterize Holmes' stance on the Supreme Court. He was not merely skeptical; his emotions were for the most part not engaged. To put it more precisely, his emotions were stimulated by the professional features of his work but not by its substance. Few judges could pack more emotion into an opinion, but the emotion was not often generated from compassion for the litigants or concern for the seriousness of the issue at stake. It was the emotion of a literary talent, a person who liked the sound of memorable phrases. Holmes' aphorisms were original and incisive; they were also repeated often.

One can see Holmes' stance of detachment as a culmination of his intellectual history. By all accounts he was not only serious about philosophy and jurisprudence as a young man; he was in dead earnest. He clung to his manuscript on Kent, taking it with him to meals; he taught himself German so as to be able to read the contribution of German jurists in the original; he worked nights on the lectures that became *The Common Law;* he apparently married Fanny Dixwell, whom he had known most of his life, only when someone else mentioned that she was pining away out of love for him.[136] From the 1870's, when he first began to think and write about jurisprudence, to the time he went on the Supreme Judicial Court of Massachusetts, he was a passionate and zealous legal reformer, eager "to say his say on every question which the law has ever presented." And then, as we have seen, the futility of his grand design revealed itself: Cases were not vehicles for propounding a grand theory, but merely clusterings around poles; judging was not writing law "in continuous, logical, philosophic exposition" but an exercise in the arbitrary drawing of lines. One could not live one's dreams: "We are lucky enough if we can give a sample of our best . . . ."[137]

134. Rogat, *The Judge as Spectator,* 31 U. Chi. L. Rev. 213, 244 (1964).
135. Truax v. Corrigan, 257 U.S. 312, 344 (1921) (Holmes, J., dissenting).
136. *See* C. Bowen, Yankee From Olympus 259-61, 270-74 (1945).
137. O. W. Holmes, *supra* note 50, at 123-24.

Holmes' sense of his professional role thus radically contracted over time, and his reduced expectations combined with traits of personality to produce detachment. Acquaintances of Holmes had from his early years noted his apparent indifference to others. His father thought he "look[ed] at life as at a solemn show where he is only a spectator;"[138] William James called him "a powerful battery, formed like a planing machine to gouge a deep self-beneficial groove through life;"[139] James Bradley Thayer, embittered over Holmes' leaving Harvard for the Massachusetts court, had said that he was selfish, vain and thoughtless.[140] Holmes did not read a newspaper, paid little attention to contemporary affairs, had most of his intimate friendships with persons from whom he was physically separated, and once said that he was glad that he had no children.[141] The themes that engaged him, such as intellectual effort and war, were related to central personal experiences. Beyond that he seemed content to "do my job in the station in which we were born."[142]

Holmes' job at the Supreme Court consisted of, in many instances, reviewing the constitutionality of actions of a legislature. In such cases Holmes forged his famous attitude of deference, which was seen as humility and "self-restraint" by admirers and had the added advantage of sustaining "progressive" legislation about which a number of early 20th-century intellectuals were enthusiastic.[143] Deference to legislative policymaking was consistent with the views Holmes had developed on the Massachusetts court. In twenty years on that court he had held unconstitutional only one Massachusetts statute.[144] His general attitude was expressed in an advisory opinion on the constitutionality of the legislature's authorizing towns to buy coal and wood and sell them to their inhabitants as fuel.[145] "[W]hen money is taken to enable a public body to offer to the public . . . an article of general necessity," Holmes wrote, "the purpose is no less public when that article is wood or coal than when it is water or gas

---

138. O.W. Holmes, Sr., 3 The Complete Writings of Oliver Wendell Holmes 142 (1900).

139. Letter from William James to Henry James (July 5, 1876), *quoted in* 1 R. Perry, *supra* note 35, at 371.

140. Thayer, *supra* note 37.

141. *See* 1 M. Howe, *supra* note 11, at 8.

142. *Holmes-Cohen Correspondence*, 9 J. Hist. Ideas 10 (1948).

143. *See* White, *supra* note 3, at 56-61.

144. Lorden v. Coffey, 178 Mass. 489, 60 N.E. 124 (1901).

145. Opinion of the Justices, 155 Mass. 598, 607, 30 N.E. 1142, 1146 (1892) (opinion of Holmes, J.).

or electricity or education, to say nothing of cases like the support of paupers, or the taking of land for railroads."[146] Holmes was unconcerned with "the need or expediency of such legislation;" he could simply "see no ground for denying the power of the legislature."[147]

Deference, of course, was consistent with Holmes' belief that judging was an arbitrary exercise in policy choices, and, that being so, some policy choices were better made by more "representative" bodies of government. He may have been motivated to express his views more openly, however, by the clumsy policymaking of his contemporaries on the Supreme Court. In the first years of the twentieth century the constitutionality of a number of pieces of "welfare" legislation was tested by the Court. The legislation sought to regulate the working hours of certain occupations or persons, to insure minimum wage standards, to eliminate child labor, and other such "reforms." Holmes was not personally sympathetic to most of the legislation, but he was even less sympathetic to the treatment of it by majorities on his Court. Those majorities had invalidated the legislation by the use of the "liberty of contract" doctrine, which Holmes later called a "dogma."[148] Liberty of contract was objectionable to Holmes in that it attempted to decide "concrete cases" on the basis of a "general proposition" that was suspect as a matter of textual interpretation and debatable as a matter of economic theory.[149] The Court had sustained many legislative acts that interfered with freedom of contract, and the Constitution was "not intended to embody a particular economic theory."[150] To transform the fourteenth amendment into an ideological creed was to "pervert" it.[151]

It is instructive to dwell on what Holmes thought was wrong with the majority's decisions in such liberty of contract cases as *Lochner v. New York*,[152] *Adair v. United States*,[153] and *Adkins v. Children's Hospital*.[154] He did not object to the substance of the doctrine itself; he would have "to study it further and long" before

146. *Id.*
147. *Id.*
148. Adkins v. Children's Hosp., 261 U.S. 525, 568 (1923) (Holmes, J., dissenting) (overruled in West Coast Hotel Co. v. Parrish, 300 U.S. 379 (1937)); *see* G. White, The American Judicial Tradition 164-67 (1976).
149. Lochner v. New York, 198 U.S. 45, 76 (1905) (Holmes, J., dissenting).
150. *Id.* at 75 (Holmes, J., dissenting).
151. *Id.* at 76 (Holmes, J., dissenting).
152. 198 U.S. 45 (1905).
153. 208 U.S. 161 (1908).
154. 261 U.S. 525 (1923) (overruled in West Coast Hotel Co. v. Parrish, 300 U.S. 379 (1937)).

endorsing it or rejecting it.[155] Nor did he necessarily object, at least as a general proposition, to the Court's substitution of its judgment for that of a legislature. What he objected to was the clumsy use of a "dogma" to decide questions that ought to have been decided by a consideration of the ends that rules seek to accomplish, the reasons those ends are desired, what is given up to gain them, and whether they are worth the price.[156] Such a consideration was presumptively suited to a legislative judgment, and if the Court were to distrust that judgment it ought to do so in a manner that did not so transparently expose the "convictions or prejudices" of its members.[157]

In deferring, Holmes thus neither espoused the worth of legislation nor expressed concern that judges ought to leave policy decisions to someone else. He merely felt that if judges were going to make arbitrary choices, they ought not to base those choices on vulnerable dogmas. Thus the principal problem with decisions like *Lochner* was not that the Court based its judgments on an economic theory, although Holmes said that a constitution was not made to embody economic theories,[158] but that it based its judgments on a theory that "a large part of the country does not entertain."[159] While a constitution was "made for people of fundamentally differing views," the views that counted were those of the majority.[160] Policymaking in America was largely a majoritarian activity; where minorities, such as the courts, made policy, they had better keep their "theories" in line with popular sentiment.

Holmes' deference thus sustained repressive legislation as much as benevolent legislation. The Pennsylvania legislature could, under a wild game protection act, keep aliens from owning firearms because its members believed that aliens were more prone to violence in this area than native citizens.[161] The Virginia legislature could sterilize persons thought to be feebleminded because it assumed that imbecility bred imbecility and that imbeciles were a burden on the state.[162] The Iowa legislature could forbid the teaching of all languages except English in public schools because it believed that in this fashion

155. 198 U.S. at 75 (Holmes, J., dissenting).
156. *See, e.g., Adkins*, 261 U.S. at 568 (Holmes, J., dissenting).
157. *Lochner*, 198 U.S. at 75 (Holmes, J., dissenting).
158. *Id.* (Holmes, J., dissenting).
159. *Id.* (Holmes, J., dissenting).
160. *Id.* at 76 (Holmes, J., dissenting).
161. Patsone v. Pennsylvania, 232 U.S. 138 (1914).
162. Buck v. Bell, 274 U.S. 200 (1927).

German culture and influence within the state would be reduced.[163] Congress could restrict speech so long as the words created "a clear and present danger that they will bring about the substantive evils that Congress has a right to prevent,"[164] and those evils might be defined by mass prejudice. The most one could expect of legislation, Holmes had written very early in his career, was that it "modify itself in accordance with the will of the de facto supreme power in the community."[165] Keeping "the sacrifice of minorities to a minimum" was dependent on "the spread of an educated sympathy."[166]

Students of Holmes have found his posture of deference so fascinating that they have defined his entire career on the Court in terms of it.[167] But the bulk of Holmes' Supreme Court opinions were cases in which he did not defer to a legislative policy judgment, but rather made one himself, and made it, as he had on the Massachusetts court, with relatively little attention to exposition. Three cases are representative: *Baltimore and Ohio Railroad v. Goodman,*[168] *United Zinc & Chemical Co. v. Britt,*[169] and *Pennsylvania Coal Co. v. Mahon.*[170]

In *The Common Law* Holmes, in the course of arguing that courts would increasingly take negligence cases away from juries, supported his argument with some observations about grade-crossing accidents. "If the whole evidence," he wrote, "was that a party . . . stood on a railway track, looking at an approaching engine until it ran him down, no judge would leave it to a jury."[171] On the other hand: "If the whole evidence was that he attempted to cross a level track, which was visible for half a mile each way, and on which no engine was in sight, no court would allow a jury to find negligence."[172] These examples suggested to Holmes that "the limit of safety" in grade crossing cases "could be determined almost to a foot by mathematical calculation."[173] *Goodman* was a grade crossing

163. Bartels v. Iowa, 262 U.S. 404, 412 (1923) (Holmes and Sutherland, JJ., dissenting).

164. Schenck v. United States, 249 U.S. 47, 52 (1919).

165. *Summary of Events, The Gas-Stokers' Strike,* 7 Am. L. Rev. 582, 583 (1873).

166. *Id.*

167. *See, e.g.,* F. Frankfurter, Mr. Justice Holmes and the Supreme Court 36-45 (1938).

168. 275 U.S. 66 (1927).

169. 258 U.S. 268 (1922).

170. 260 U.S. 393 (1922).

171. O. W. Holmes, *supra* note 7, at 128-29.

172. *Id.* at 129.

173. *Id.*

case in which Holmes attempted to prove that point. Nathan Goodman, the driver of a truck, was approaching a grade crossing at the speed of about five to six miles an hour. The crossing was over a level section of track, but Goodman's view on one side was obscured by a section house, so that he could not see anything until he was about twenty feet from the first train rail, and "then the engine was still obscured by the section house."[174] Goodman continued to cross the tracks, was hit by a train going at least sixty miles an hour, and was killed.

After stating the facts Holmes announced that "it appears to us plain that nothing is suggested by the evidence to relieve Goodman from responsibility for his own death."[175] He then overturned a jury verdict for the driver, holding that Goodman was contributorially negligent as a matter of law. He declared that "if a driver cannot be sure otherwise whether a train is dangerously near he must stop and get out of his vehicle, although obviously he will not often be required to do more than to stop and look."[176] This was a clear standard of conduct and was to be "laid down once for all by the Courts," although "the question of due care very generally is left to the jury."[177]

Goodman seems to have been a case in which Holmes had forgotten the lessons of his Massachusetts experience. He may have continued to believe in 1927 that "the limit of safety" in grade crossing cases "could be determined almost to a foot," and he may have been correct that under the circumstances Goodman was negligent. But "mathematical calculation" or Holmes' "stop, look and listen" exercise was not going to fix the limits of safety in grade crossing cases. Some drivers might follow Holmes' standard, get back in their cars, and then get hit by a train that was plainly obvious from a considerable distance. Were they to be exonerated? Others might decide not to get out of their cars because of the dangers of approaching traffic. Were they necessarily negligent? Holmes' formula ended up being a good argument for retaining jury discretion in grade crossing cases, and seven years later the Supreme Court, with Justice Cardozo treading carefully, abandoned the formula.[178]

Goodman shows Holmes anxious not only to make a judgment

---

174. 275 U.S. at 69.
175. *Id.*
176. *Id.* at 70.
177. *Id.*
178. Pokora v. Wabash Ry., 292 U.S. 98, 106 (1934).

himself but to deprive juries of the opportunity to make that judgment in subsequent cases. The case was striking in that it lent itself to Holmes' "competing desiderata" analysis. A policy of allowing drivers to drive on the streets without being injured competed with a policy of allowing railroads to use their property in profitable ways. In *Patnoude* Holmes had said that the line that "had to be drawn to separate the domains of the irreconcilable desires" could not be "drawn in general terms."[179] In *Goodman* he had attempted to do so. One could hardly call his posture deferential.

Holmes' decision in *Britt* was somewhat less ambitious. He sought to ascertain the limits of the "child trespasser" doctrine, by which landowners were deemed to owe a duty of care to children trespassing on their premises if the children could be said to have been attracted onto the premises by something on the land. Examples were railroad turntables, ponds, and excavations. In the *Britt* case two boys were camping near land where the United Zinc & Chemical Company had formerly operated a sulphuric acid plant. The company had abandoned the plant but left its foundations, in which residue from sulphuric acid and zinc sulphate remained. Water had accumulated over the foundations, giving the area the appearance of a pond, but the water, although clear, had been poisoned by the residue. The two boys investigated the site, a little over 100 feet from a dirt road, were poisoned, and died.

Holmes distinguished previous child trespasser cases on the grounds that the United Zinc & Chemical Company did not know that children had been in the habit of visiting the site and had not maintained the site adjacent to the road. "[I]t is at least doubtful," he wrote, "whether the water could be seen from any place where the children lawfully were." There had been no inducements, Holmes felt; there was no evidence that the water had "led [the boys] to enter the land." There was no pattern of children trespassing on the land that might have informed the United Zinc & Chemical Company of potential dangers. Even the presence of roads close to the site were not invitations: "[A] road is not an invitation to leave it elsewhere than at its end."[180]

Britt seems to have been a case ideally suited to leave to a jury, and as such raises the question why Holmes did not adopt that course of action. Child trespasser cases inevitably turn on their facts:

---

179. *See supra* text accompanying notes 108-109.
180. 258 U.S. at 276.

how much of an "inducement" the dangerous substance was, how much awareness the landowner had of trespassers, how easy the dangerous substance was to reach, etc. Given the fact that landowners had long been held to owe no duty to trespassers, the child trespasser doctrine seemed designed for those circumstances where a landowner knew that he was maintaining a dangerous substance on his land and knew or should have known that it would be attractive to children. If the railroad turntable was a paradigmatic attractive nuisance, since it was adjacent to a roadway and since it was the kind of substance that would appeal to children as a place to play, a pond near an abandoned building was not far from that paradigm. The only complicating factors in the *Britt* case were that the company apparently had no experience with trespassers on the site and that the site was not adjacent to the road. But those were surely not conclusive on the question of liability, given the very dangerous condition of the pond. The case seemed designed to be decided by the "common sense" of a jury.

It appears that some of the same tendencies that motivated Holmes to lay down the "stop, look and listen" standard in *Goodman* were at work in *Britt*. In his early career Holmes had been dismayed at the unpredictability and uncertainty of jury-made rules: If the child trespasser doctrine was to be invoked or not invoked depending on the sympathies of a jury, it was not a doctrine whose existence helped landowners (or potential trespassers) plan their affairs. Holmes seems to have wanted to use the *Britt* case as a means of confining the doctrine to those cases where a landowner had notice of children trespassing near a dangerous substance on his property. So formulated, the doctrine's impact would be greatly reduced, since it could never be invoked against a landowner in a "first accident" case. Once two boys had died as a result of coming into contact with a zinc company's dangerous abandoned plant it is unlikely that the company would permit the plant to remain in that condition; at a minimum it would post conspicuous warnings. Only if the company did nothing and a second accident involving children occurred would the child trespasser doctrine come into play. That was a predictable state of affairs; it was also unlikely to happen.

Goodman and *Britt* may suggest that Holmes' "activist" decisions on the Supreme Court were confined to those instances where he had engaged himself as a scholar. But many of Holmes' most famous opinions came in areas, such as the first amendment, that he had not addressed in his early career, and in some of these opinions he dropped his usual pose of deference to legislatures. The line of first amendment cases, stretching from *Abrams v. United States*[181] through *Gitlow v. New York,*[182] *Whitney v. California,*[183] and *United States v. Schwimmer*[184] to *Near v. Minnesota,*[185] was one set of examples: Holmes attempted to fix the outer limits of legislative regulation of speech. *Nixon v. Herndon,*[186] a case invalidating a Texas primary system that excluded blacks from participation, was another. Holmes said for the Court: "States may do a good deal of classifying that it is difficult to believe rational, but there are limits . . . ."[187] *Olmstead v. United States*[188] was yet another: There Holmes read the fourth and fifth amendments to prohibit the use of illegally seized evidence in a criminal prosecution. The case invoked "two objects of desire, both of which we cannot have," Holmes said; "we must . . . make up our minds which to choose."[189] He was unwilling in that instance to let a legislature make the choice.

Nor was Holmes willing to defer to a legislative judgment in *Mahon.*[190] There the Pennsylvania legislature had passed a statute that forbade the mining of anthracite coal on land in such a way as to endanger structures erected on the surface of the land in question. A landowner sought to apply the statute to prevent the Pennsylvania Coal Company from mining on land he had bought from the company. The company had expressly reserved sub-surface rights to the land and had also retained the right to remove coal from beneath the surface. Since the contract between the coal company and the land-

---

181. 250 U.S. 616, 628-31 (1919) (Holmes, J., dissenting) (stating that defendant had right to publish leaflets supporting Russian revolution and attacking United States policy).

182. 268 U.S. 652, 672-73 (1925) (Holmes and Brandeis, JJ., dissenting) (stating that Socialist Party member should not have been convicted of criminal anarchy merely because he advocated a proletarian dictatorship).

183. 274 U.S. 357, 379 (1927) (Brandeis and Holmes, JJ., concurring) (overruled in Brandenburg v. Ohio, 395 U.S. 444 (1969) (per curiam)) (stating that mere advocacy of the desirability of proletarian revolution is protected speech but intent to commit serious present crimes is not protected).

184. 279 U.S. 644, 653-55 (1929) (Holmes, J., dissenting) (stating that a Quaker should not be denied United States citizenship because of her pacifist views).

185. 283 U.S. 697 (1931) (Minnesota statute authorizing "previous restraints" of periodicals that publish defamatory or malicious articles held unconstitutional infringement of freedom of press).

186. 273 U.S. 536 (1927).

187. *Id.* at 541.

188. 277 U.S. 438, 469 (1928) (Holmes, J., dissenting) (overruled in Katz v. United States, 389 U.S. 347 (1967)).

189. *Id.* at 470 (Holmes, J., dissenting).

190. 260 U.S. 393 (1922).

owner had been made prior to the passage of the statute, the question was whether the statute was an unconstitutional deprivation of existing property and contract rights.

Holmes, for a majority of the Court, held that it was. "The general rule," he announced, "is, that while property may be regulated to a certain extent, if regulation goes too far it will be recognized as taking." Here the Pennsylvania legislature had provided no compensation for the mining companies, and thus had infringed their rights. "We are in danger of forgetting," Holmes noted, "that a strong public desire to improve the public condition is not enough to warrant achieving the desire by a shorter cut than the constitutional way of paying for the change." Even if the statute had been passed "upon the conviction that an exigency existed," the "question at bottom [was] upon whom the loss of the changes desired should fall."[191]

Compensation cases such as *Mahon* involved "question[s] of degree," Holmes said, and "therefore [could] not be disposed of by general propositions." That being said, he did not defer to legislative balancing. The Pennsylvania statute went "beyond any of the [compensation] cases decided by this Court." A strong public desire for property did not itself justify a taking without compensation; otherwise the legislature could invoke its police power "more and more until at last private property disappears."[192]

Mahon was not different for Holmes from the speech cases or from *Nixon v. Herndon*: There were limits to what states could do under their discretionary authority. Commentators have reacted differently to *Mahon* because Holmes protected property rights rather than personhood rights, but Holmes made no such jurisprudential distinctions. When he invoked the Constitution to invalidate a legislative restriction on rights, that was because the legislature had gone "too far." What was "too far" was a "question of degree," but sometimes the answer was obvious. When it was, Holmes saw no reason—"exigencies" notwithstanding—to defer to legislative judgments.[193]

Neither conventional political labels nor common terms from jurisprudence help clarify Holmes' stance on the Supreme Court. Several commentators have shown that his opinions are imperfectly described as "liberal" or "conservative."[194] This article suggests that

191. *Id.* at 412-16.

192. *Id.* at 415-16.

193. *See, e.g., id.*

194. For a recent collection of such efforts, see D. BURTON, WHAT MANNER OF LIB-

they are no more satisfactorily described as "activist" or deferential. When Holmes' tenure on the Supreme Court is subjected to detailed analysis, two striking and hitherto largely unremarked features appear. First, Holmes was nowhere near as activist in private law cases as his early scholarship suggested he might have been, but he was more activist, if anything, than he had been on the Supreme Judicial Court of Massachusetts. The *Goodman* and *Britt* opinions were in some sense throwbacks to his earlier theory, formulated as a scholar, of how negligence cases ought to be decided. Holmes retained on the Supreme Court the idea that most cases presented policy choices between competing "social desiderata," and while this led him toward deference to legislatures in many cases, it did not prevent him from making choices in others. He believed the choices to be arbitrary, but he made them anyway. Calling Holmes an advocate of self-restraint on the Court does not fully capture him.

Second, while Holmes saw that at the bottom of nearly every Supreme Court case was a choice between competing public policies, he was not deterred by that realization from making a prompt decision. If he chose to defer to a legislature, he spent very little time justifying the legislature's actions: The simplest bow to minimal rationality generally sufficed. Sometimes, in cases like *Patsone v. Pennsylvania,*[195] Holmes did not even seem to be lingering over the question of legislative rationality. In that case he blithely accepted the legislature's premise that aliens were more dangerous to wild life than citizens. Nor was Holmes any less peremptory when he chose to upset a legislative judgment. That the Texas legislature had gone too far in *Nixon v. Herndon* was "too clear for extended argument."[196] That the Pennsylvania statute in *Mahon* went "beyond any of the cases decided by this Court" needed only to be stated.[197]

The overwhelming impression of Holmes' performance on the Supreme Court, then, is the same impression one gets of his performance in Massachusetts: Here was a judge whose principal interest seems to have been in having cases decided, written up, and disposed of. The vivid sentence with which Holmes ended his opinion in *Britt,* "a road is not an invitation to leave it elsewhere than at its end,"[198] captures the mood in which Holmes appears to have written

---

ERAL? 155-56 (1979).

195. 232 U.S. 138 (1914).

196. 273 U.S. at 541.

197. 260 U.S. at 416.

198. 258 U.S. at 276.

most of his opinions. The sentence is striking, but it is not much help, either as a general statement or as an explanation of the case. Travelers leave roads at a variety of places—indeed almost no one who travels on a road leaves it at its end. A road, in fact, is not an "invitation" to leave it at all; if anything, it is an invitation to take it somewhere, as being an easier place on which to travel than a field or a stream. But the sentence is designed to dismiss the argument that the presence of the road in *Britt* may have been an enticement to travel near the poisoned site. The sentence does "dismiss" that argument, but only through a largely erroneous statement that captures our attention. It is as if having turned a phrase Holmes decided that he had said enough, and could get on to something else. Holmes makes cases seem like toys scattered in a child's room: The idea is to pick them up and put them in place, not to linger over the differences among them nor to give some more special meaning than others. When the job is over, the room is clean; the toys are "put away."

IV. Remembering Holmes: What Does He Leave Us?

However much Holmes is written about or ignored, his reputation seems secure. I have suggested that his reputation may contain some erroneous components, such as the idea that he was consistently an apostle of judicial self-restraint, but that is not to suggest that it will not endure. Three of Holmes' contributions seem so significant as to resist even the most aggressive form of historical debunking. First, he identified judging as an exercise in intuitive policy choices at a time when few other judges or jurists were prepared to concede that judging was anything other than finding and applying preexistent legal principles. For Holmes to see that cases were repositories of clashing policies was a keen enough insight; for him to come upon that insight in the midst of a jurisprudential climate that denied any policymaking component to judging was remarkable.

Second, Holmes helped develop a significant corollary to his insight that judges were policymakers. The corollary was his theory of deference, and while he did not originate the theory nor practice it exclusively, several of his opinions were powerful arguments for its use. This was particularly true in the public law area, and most particularly true in Supreme Court cases, where Holmes' version of good sense was juxtaposed against tortured judicial efforts to preserve "dogma" at all costs. The accident of Holmes' being on the Supreme Court at a time when legislatures had become more active, and the Court had not developed a theory of responding to that activism, made him one of the original spokesmen on the Court for a theory of constitutional adjudication that was to have great influence in the twentieth century. While Holmes was never as zealous a proponent of self-restraint as some of his disciples, his opinion in *Lochner* gave deference intellectual respectability.

Third, as the last sentence from *Britt* illustrates, Holmes had a distinctively arresting style. No Supreme Court Justice matched Holmes in this regard; only Robert Jackson occasionally came close. The holdings of Holmes' opinions may be forgotten, but the epigrams remain. "A word is . . . the skin of a living thought;"[199] "[g]reat cases like hard cases make bad law;"[200] "[t]he Fourteenth Amendment does not enact Mr. Herbert Spencer's *Social Statics*;"[201] "the best test of truth is the power of the thought to get itself accepted in the competition of the market;"[202] "[t]hree generations of imbeciles are enough."[203] Not one of these sentences was necessary to the decision in the case in which it appeared; all contain overstatements or ambiguities. Each, however, helps to universalize the act of opinion writing, to make it a process of communicating at the deepest levels of human experience. When a judge can write in that fashion subsequent generations will be gripped by his style. No notes of dissatisfaction with his opinions as guidelines for future conduct will fully detract from his appeal. Holmes wrote lines that spanned time.

But can one remember Holmes as more than the author of arresting epigrams? Does his jurisprudence leave us a foundation for thinking about judging? Here it seems that on some issues Holmes seems so overwhelmingly right that one wonders how a contrary position was ever seriously maintained, and on other issues Holmes seems so disinclined to explore questions once he has raised them that one is tempted to conclude that an important function of his jurisprudence is to cut off thinking at preliminary stages.

Holmes may have thought, when he was at the fever pitch of his scholarly efforts in the 1870's, that, while absolute certainty might be unattainable, fields of private law could be made more certain, in

199. Towne v. Eisner, 245 U.S. 418, 425 (1918).

200. Northern Securities Co. v. United States, 193 U.S. 197, 400 (1904) (Holmes, J., dissenting).

201. Lochner v. New York, 198 U.S. 45, 75 (1905) (Holmes, J., dissenting).

202. Abrams v. United States, 250 U.S. 616, 630 (1919) (Holmes, J., dissenting).

203. Buck v. Bell, 274 U.S. 200, 207 (1927).

the sense of being more regularized and predictable. The impulse toward certainty is a strong one in legal scholarship: Recently we have seen the "laws" of welfare economics offered as yet another source of regularizing the common law. But we should have learned the lesson Holmes had learned after sixteen years as a judge: "[C]ertainty generally is illusion, and repose is not the destiny of man."[204] Too many variables exist for certainty in the law to be realizable: the discrete personalities and idiosyncracies of judges and other lawmakers; the changing intellectual climates in which research is conducted, which affect the normative dimensions of research and thereby insure that scholarly contributions will never be timeless; the fortuitious allocation of talent and incentives among counsel for one side or another; the strange ways in which the facts of a case compel a rule, which then evaporates when the facts fade into memory. Holmes may have been sensible, as a young scholar, to search for certainty; had he not thought it attainable he might not have tried to study private law subjects to their bottom. But he was even more sensible to abandon certainty as a judge. His metaphor of "growth" in the law, a series of decisions clustering around two poles and finally being separable only by an arbitrary line, rings truer than all the pronouncements that law can be made "scientific." I would not call Holmes' metaphorical description a process of growth, merely one of change, but I think as a description it is uncontroverted.

Does it follow, then, that since certainty in jurisprudence is elusive, humility and deference are the only appropriate lawmaking postures? Here I think Holmes' own indifference and the misguided labors of his disciples have contributed to lend prominence to a theory of judging that possesses serious limitations. During Holmes' tenure judicial deference resulted in legislation that helped alleviate some of the inequalities of rampant industrialism; in the 1950's and 1960's a similar version of deference would have perpetuated malapportioned legislatures, racially segregated facilities, the absence of legal representation for impoverished persons, and restrictions on the use and dispensation of birth control devices. The simple truth that law cases in America serve as a forum for testing conflicting ideas about public policy does not suggest that all such decisions should be made by "representative" or "community-minded" bodies, such as legislatures or juries. Sometimes the choices of the public are benighted or hasty

204. O. W. HOLMES, *supra* note 26, at 181.

or prejudiced; sometimes the majority oppresses those who differ with it. If Holmes taught us that judges, if unchecked, will make justice synonymous with their own prejudices, the Warren Court taught us that legislatures will do the same.

Deference or activism is thus a function of time and place and of the seriousness of the issues at stake. Sometimes a court does well to defer: The issues are volatile, the public divided, the principles hard to grasp. At other times a court seemingly has an obligation not to defer: A more representative body has forgotten elementary principles of justice and needs to be admonished by an institution whose popularity is not so dependent on majoritarian whim. It stretches Holmes beyond recognition to make him a Warren Court Justice, but he had his own areas, ranging from speech to sub-surface mining, where he found majoritarian solutions defective. Still, while one would like to blame Holmes' disciples for the agonized state in which self-restraint theory found itself after World War II, Holmes set it on that path.[205] He found legislative rationality in too many mere pretexts, he tolerated repression in the name of democracy too often. Before long judges who considered themselves intellectuals and "liberals" in the tradition of Holmes were allowing legislatures to compel school children to salute the flag and to require that college professors go on record as opposing Communism.[206] Holmes' theory of deference had led them there; his having scrapped the theory when it suited him did not excuse his putting it on the market for others to misuse.

Linked to Holmes' beliefs that certainty was an illusion and that deference was often a sensible judicial posture was his conviction that judicial decisons were at bottom arbitrary exercises. As we have seen, the discovery of arbitrariness led Holmes in two directions, toward deference and also toward a "job mentality" that emphasized deciding cases so that they could be decided. Arbitrariness raises two separate issues: Are we resigned to its presence, and, if so, what can we do about it? As to the first, to sense that human decisionmaking is arbitrary seems to me the beginning of wisdom about the way persons conduct their affairs. All of us have our memories of a nakedly arbitrary decision, ranging from a situation when two devotees of one side of an issue forgot the date of a meeting, and the

---

205. *See* White, *supra* note 3, at 65-71.

206. For an example of one justice's agonized attempts to adopt Holmes' theory of deference to mid-20th-century cases, see H. HIRSCH, THE ENIGMA OF FELIX FRANKFURTER (1981).

other side won by a single vote, to a situation where a committee was deeply divided on the resolution of an academic matter, and finally decided in accordance with the views of the sole member who prepared written comments. Beyond those examples, all of us sense that many decisions are made that would have been made differently had different personnel been involved, had the timing of events been different, or had the issue been presented in different form. Holmes was right to see arbitrariness built into every discretionary decision; he was also right not to be afraid of it.

But does arbitrariness provide a justification for the kind of limited explanations for decisions that Holmes so regularly produced? Here it seems to me that one can advance two interpretations of the purpose of a judicial decision, and the explanations that one produces for one's results will be affected by the interpretation one chooses. One can see the decisions of cases as single existential phenomena: They occur, they dispose of a controversy, they cease to have an existence. Or one can see such decisions as communications beyond the immediate controversy, directed, potentially, at future litigants, future judges, commentators, the general public. If one holds to the first view there is not much point in advancing extensive justifications of one's results. New cases will necessarily be different; a whole host of variables will serve to distinguish them from the past, and prior explanations will not prove much use. I think that in many instances Holmes adopted this view, or at least was sufficiently skeptical of the utility of extensive explanations and sufficiently motivated to get on with the job that he acted as if he adopted it. On other occasions, of course, Holmes regarded a decision as a means of communicating more extensively; he did not dissent just to see how many memorable phrases he could turn.

The idea that judicial opinions communicate to audiences beyond the immediate parties in the dispute is one that once led me to characterize constitutional adjudication as a dialectical process.[207] The dialectical theory holds that judicial decisions, at least when they interpret the Constitution, are in a kind of provisional state of acceptance: They possess the authority of the court that delivers them but their eventual acceptance—their legitimacy—has not been achieved. The process of legitimation involves a testing, over time, of the justifications advanced for the given interpretation. Of course the

207. White, *The Evolution of Reasoned Elaboration: Jurisprudential Criticism and Social Change*, 59 VA. L. REV. 279, 296-98 (1973).

interpretation yields a definite result, and the controversial nature of the result will play a part in how swiftly or how searchingly the interpretation is tested. But the process occurs to some extent in all decisions.

When a decision is being "tested," the pressure points of its explanatory apparatus may make a difference in how fully it becomes legitimated. To take a contemporary example, an opinion that seems not yet to have reached the status of being legitimated is *Roe v. Wade*,[208] which is eight years old at this writing. *Roe v. Wade*'s indeterminate status is partially a function of the controversial nature of the issue it purports to resolve: Abortion is not an issue easily "settled" in one fashion or another. The decision's indeterminate status seems also linked, however, to its explanatory strategy, which chose to emphasize the state of medical knowledge about when a life is "in being" as a crucial determinant for when an abortion is permissible. Such an emphasis, of course, renders the decision vulnerable to changes in the state of medical knowledge. If the time a life is said to come into being were to recede, in the view of a dominant number of qualified medical practitioners, until a point so close to conception that any abortion would be a termination of "life," *Roe v. Wade*'s guidelines for abortion, which allow a mother unrestricted autonomy to terminate a pregnancy in the first trimester, might be threatened. In that instance *Roe v. Wade* could be taken as a communication into the future that was eventually found lacking in persuasive power due to the outmoded assumptions on which it rested.

Such seems to be the fate of many constitutional opinions. But one might argue that this form of communication, regardless of its vulnerability, is preferable to the cryptic, assertive form adopted by Holmes in many of his opinions. An explanation like that advanced in *Roe v. Wade* seems to be saying: "Here are my choices, between life and the autonomy of personhood; my decision to choose one over the other is necessarily arbitrary, but is influenced by some assumptions about the medical nature of 'life'; if those assumptions are subsequently called into question, another arbitrary choice may result." Holmes' explanations rarely sought to communicate in so extended a fashion. Indeed when Holmes retreats to the kind of language he used to explain his results in such cases as *Patsone*—a reasonable man might well think aliens are dangerous to wildlife[209]—one gets

208. 410 U.S. 113 (1973).

209. *See supra* note 161 and accompanying text.

the impression that his tongue is in his cheek; that he is using the convention of deference to *cut off* communication rather than to open it up.

Here, finally, I come back to Holmes' job mentality. There are many cases, he seems to be saying, where the choices are between generally desirable policies that happen to conflict; we must prefer one or the other; we will surely not invariably prefer that one on every occasion; we have a case to decide; let's get on with it. But that method tells us precious little about why one policy should prevail over another even in this case. It seems to tell us, in fact, only that the judge made a choice; another judge might have decided differently. That message leads us to *The Path of the Law* and the "prophecies of what the courts will do in fact,"[210] to the idea that law is synonymous with the arbitrary fiats of officials, and to related cynical revelations. If we end up endorsing such cynicism, Holmes can take some of the credit.

But I think Holmes intended to convey something more in his cryptic explanations. I think he was attempting to show that in a truly "hard" case, if you force an extended explanation, that explanation will crumble to pieces on reflection. And as one explanation after another crumbles, one is left with the fact of judicial power, the force of judicial intuition, and the way the law has of correcting itself over time. After a while, Holmes seems to say, it is not the explanations that count—they all crumble, eventually—but the decisions. One's job as a judge becomes to *decide*—that is what people count on one to do; that is what judges have the power to do where ordinary people do not—and not to agonize about why. Cryptic explanations, then, are intended to cut off thinking about issues that are sufficiently complicated and difficult to benumb one's mind. At some point one has to stop thinking and choose. It may be that Holmes' view of judging makes sense—and if it does, the concept of a dialectic of constitutional adjudication seems so much academic gossamer—but even if it cuts off thought and explanation too soon, it may not be the easy way out. The easy way out may be to pretend that sooner or later some disinterested, reasoned justification will emerge mysteriously out of one's ruminations as one tries to decide a case. Holmes looked to the bottom of cases and saw only his own reflection. Should we probe so far, we might conclude that reasoning in epigrams was preferable to more extended ratiocinations. Length is not the equivalent of depth.

---

210. *See supra* note 114 and accompanying text.

VIRGINIA LAW REVIEW

VOLUME 61 JUNE 1975 NUMBER 5

THE SUPREME COURT, THE EQUAL PROTECTION CLAUSE, AND THE THREE FACES OF CONSTITUTIONAL EQUALITY

*J. Harvie Wilkinson III**

All shall equal be.
The Earl, the Marquis, and the Dook,
The Groom, the Butler, and the Cook,
The Aristocrat who banks with Coutts,
The Aristocrat who cleans the boots.

From Gilbert and Sullivan's *The Gondoliers*

I. INTRODUCTION†

Equality, as a constitutional value, has had to wait its turn. For years, it was distrusted as a threat to privilege and property, next permitted or endured as an exercise of legislative sovereignty, and only finally actively promoted by the Supreme Court. Not until the last decade of the Warren Court did the equal protection clause evolve from a largely moribund constitutional provision to a potent egalitarian instrument. Yet when its hour did come, there was no mistaking it. Professor Bickel concluded that "a broadly-conceived egalitarianism was the main theme in the music to which the Warren Court marched."[1] Archibald Cox, a friend of that Court, regarded "egalitarianism" as one of the powerful factors "shaping

* Assistant Professor of Law, University of Virginia. B.A. 1967, Yale University; J.D. 1972, University of Virginia.

† I wish to thank my colleagues, Professors Richard Bonnie and Ernest Gellhorn for detailed and valuable criticism. Michael Wells of the Virginia Law Review contributed many helpful editorial suggestions, and my student assistant, Zack Clement, gave most generously of his time and thought. They are not, of course, responsible for any errors that may remain.

[1] A. BICKEL, THE SUPREME COURT AND THE IDEA OF PROGRESS 103 (1970).

current constitutional decisions."[2] The Court's arch-critic, Philip Kurland, agreed: "To the extent that the Warren Court has opened new frontiers, it has been in the development of the concept of equality as a constitutional standard."[3]

The Court's new trademark of equality was, of course, as evident to dissenting Justices as to sideline critics. "It was not too long ago," wrote Justice Harlan in protest to the Court's abolition of state poll-taxes,

> that Mr. Justice Holmes felt impelled to remind the Court that the Due Process Clause of the Fourteenth Amendment does not enact the *laissez-faire* theory of society, *Lochner* v. *New York*, 198 U.S. 45, 75-76. The times have changed, and perhaps it is appropriate to observe that neither does the Equal Protection Clause of that Amendment rigidly impose upon America an ideology of unrestrained egalitarianism.

Despite the talk about constitutional equality, it remains to date a formless concept. Yet this need not be the case. The equal protection clause may be profitably approached through the meaning of equality itself. The first and basic step in equal protection analysis must consist of asking just what kind of equality has been denied. The general notion of constitutional equality subdivides into three categories: (1) political equality, (2) equality of opportunity, and (3) economic equality. This article argues that the Court has a strong commitment in the first area, a qualified duty in the second, and an obligation generally to refrain from acting in the third.

This Equality Analysis appears preferable to present equal protection analysis in two respects. Unlike the Court's approach, which depends too largely on the ad hoc elevation of rights and values, equality analysis develops chiefly from a broad and coherent look at the doctrine of separation of powers and the role that courts might legitimately play in support of equal treatment and human dignity. Secondly, an equality focus will replace with a natural and straightforward approach the often strained and contradictory adjudications under the Court's models. Subsequent analysis will demonstrate the vulnerabilities of the Court's present equal protection doctrines; hopefully, a primary focus on equality may help guide

---

[2] A. Cox, The Warren Court 6 (1968).

[3] P. Kurland, Politics, The Constitution and the Warren Court 98 (1970).

[4] Harper v. Virginia Bd. of Elections, 383 U.S. 663, 686 (1966) (Harlan, J., dissenting).

equal protection law yet further away from its present preoccupation with two tiers of scrutiny to an approach rooted firmly to the judiciary's proper role in a democratic society.

A. *The Recent Emergence of Constitutional Equality*

Some early stirrings of the equal protection clause did take place before Chief Justice Warren's arrival. Previous Courts, under Chief Justices Hughes and Vinson took the first tentative steps in desegregating higher education,[5] and the Vinson Court forbade enforcement of racially restrictive covenants.[6] But such stirrings, and the related steps under the 15th Amendment to outlaw the white primary,[7] were largely confined to remedying racial inequality[8] and, even in this area, the Vinson Court paled in comparison to the efforts of its successor.

Indeed the Warren Court's promotion of equality is often thought synonomous with its efforts for blacks. Yet for all the Warren Court did to champion racial justice, its most significant imprint may lie elsewhere. It may lie in the Court's widening the constitutional arc of equality *beyond* mere race, in its halting and uneven recognition of a broader standard of equality as a constitutionally attainable goal. In the 1960's the equal protection clause was expanded to protect, for example, indigent criminal suspects,[9] illegitimate children,[10] disenfranchised[11] or underenfranchised[12] groups, and newly resident applicants for state welfare.[13] The expansion enabled

---

[5] *See* McLaurin v. Oklahoma State Regents, 339 U.S. 637 (1950); Sweatt v. Painter, 339 U.S. 629 (1950); Sipuel v. Bd. of Regents, 332 U.S. 631 (1948); Missouri *ex rel.* Gaines v. Canada, 305 U.S. 337 (1938).

[6] Shelley v. Kraemer, 334 U.S. 1 (1948).

[7] Terry v. Adams 345 U.S. 461 (1953), *following* Smith v. Allwright, 321 U.S. 649 (1944), decided during Chief Justice Stone's tenure.

[8] The Vinson Court did use the equal protection clause for the benefit of Japanese aliens residing in the United States, Takahashi v. Fish & Game Comm'n, 334 U.S. 410 (1948); Oyama v. California, 332 U.S. 633 (1948).

[9] Douglas v. California, 372 U.S. 353 (1963), entitled indigent state defendants to counsel in their first appeals as of right. Griffin v. Illinois, 351 U.S. 12 (1956), awarded indigent petitioners free transcripts of trial proceedings claimed necessary for state appellate review of alleged non-federal errors in their convictions.

[10] Levy v. Louisiana, 391 U.S. 68 (1968).

[11] Kramer v. Union Free School Dist., 395 U.S. 621 (1969); Carrington v. Rash, 380 U.S. 89 (1965).

[12] Avery v. Midland County , 390 U.S. 474 (1968); Reynolds v. Sims, 377 U.S. 533 (1964); Baker v. Carr, 369 U.S. 186 (1962).

[13] Shapiro v. Thompson, 394 U.S. 618 (1969).

Justice Thurgood Marshall to remark, with justification, that "[i]t is far too late in the day to contend that the Fourteenth Amendment prohibits only racial discrimination. . . ."[14]

It is the more remarkable that this broadened view of equality emerged within the framework of a rigid and generally deferential equal protection test that still reflected a revulsion to the Court's earlier substantive due process period.[15] "Legislatures," the Court might lamely declare as late as 1969, "are presumed to have acted constitutionally . . . and their statutory classifications will be set aside only if no grounds can be conceived to justify them."[16] Perhaps because of this framework, the Court's first steps to a broadened view of equality were bound to be uncomfortable. It fell to Justice Douglas to author, in cryptically unorthodox fashion, many of the groundbreaking opinions[17] whose methodology even the Court's supporters felt obliged to criticize.[18] But with Warren's retirement, the first, painful steps had been taken, and the beginnings of a broader, more active judicial role in behalf of equality had been established.

The fears of some[19] that the Burger Court would abruptly halt and even repeal the Warren Court's innovations seem, in general, overdrawn. At least the broadened idea of equality left by the Warren

---

[14] James v. Valtierra, 402 U.S. 137, 145 (1971) (Marshall, J., dissenting).

[15] The prevalent two-tiered analysis has been well explained elsewhere, *Developments in the Law—Equal Protection*, 82 Harv. L. Rev. 1065, 1076-1132 (1969). This analysis is deferential because the lenient "rational basis" scrutiny applied to most statutes almost never results in voidance of the legislation, though the heightened "compelling state interest" scrutiny almost invariably will. It is rigid because in theory it permits only two widely variant levels of scrutiny with no gradations for rights of intermediate importance. It is deficient because, as Professor Freund once remarked, the world does not move on a "binary principle."

[16] McDonald v. Bd. of Election Comm'rs, 394 U.S. 802, 809 (1969). The Court was, of course, articulating the so-called rational basis standard of review of statutes that did not impinge upon fundamental rights or disadvantage a suspect class.

[17] *See, e.g.*, Levy v. Louisiana, 391 U.S. 68 , (1968); Harper v. Virginia Bd. of Elections, 383 U.S. 663 (1966); Douglas v. California, 372 U.S. 353 (1963).

[18] With regard to *Harper, see* Cox, *supra* note 2, at 125-26. Professor Karst in an illuminating view of Justice Douglas' equal protection contributions conceded the major Douglas opinions are "long on conclusory statements and short on the kind of painstaking analysis that one might expect from a lawyer of Justice Douglas' intellectual attainments." Professor Karst, however, sees benefit in the opinions providing "the only glimpse of the world that exists outside the walls of doctrine. . . . Having said that, I have to confess that I still yearn for a little more explanation." Karst, *Invidious Discrimination: Justice Douglas and the Return of the "Natural-Law-Due-Process Formula,"* 16 U.C.L.A. L. Rev. 716, 749 (1969).

[19] *See* Gunther, *The Supreme Court, 1971 Term—Foreword: In Search of Evolving Doctrine on a Changing Court: A Model for a Newer Equal Protection*, 86 Harv. L. Rev. 1, 2 n.5 (1972) for a listing of the fearful.

Court now appears secure. There have been, to be sure, decisions that constitute major setbacks to constitutional egalitarianism. The new Court has bluntly refused to treat equal protection claims to public welfare assistance,[20] a decent shelter,[21] or education[22] with much more solicitude than a corporation's plea to be free of restrictive legislation.[23] And at least one member of the Court, Justice Rehnquist, would again confine active equal protection scrutiny to matters of race.[24]

There is, however, little chance of any such development. The Burger Court, with the new Nixon appointees writing and joining many of the opinions, has extended the equal protection clause to protect from discrimination the rights of women[25] (though perhaps not of men),[26] and of resident aliens to a greater extent than heretofore.[27] It has solidified and in some cases expanded the Warren Court's special solicitude for illegitimate children,[28] indigent[29] and incompetent[30] criminal defendants, and the needs of new state residents for basic necessities.[31] And the new Court has, on occasion, given vigorous protection to the right to vote.[32] Thus, it now is not

[20] *See* Jefferson v. Hackney, 406 U.S. 535 (1972); Richardson v. Belcher, 404 U.S. 78 (1971); Dandridge v. Williams, 397 U.S. 471 (1970). *But cf.* United States Dep't. of Agriculture v. Moreno, 413 U.S. 528 (1973).

[21] *See* Lindsey v. Normet, 405 U.S. 56 (1972). ,

[22] *See* San Antonio Indep. School Dist. v. Rodriguez, 411 U.S. 1 (1973).

[23] In Dandridge v. Williams, 397 U.S. 471, 485 (1972), the Court stated as much.

[24] *See* Sugarman v. Dougall, 413 U.S. 634, 649 (1973) (Rehnquist, J., dissenting); Weber v. Aetna Cas. & Sur. Co., 406 U.S. 164, 177 (1972) (Rehnquist, J., dissenting).

[25] Weinberger v. Wiesenfeld, 95 S. Ct. 1225 (1975); Frontiero v. Richardson, 411 U.S. 677 (1973); Reed v. Reed, 404 U.S. 71 (1971). *Cf.* Taylor v. Louisiana, 419 U.S. 522 (1975).

[26] *See* Schlesinger v. Ballard, 419 U.S. 498 (1975); Kahn v. Shevin, 416 U.S. 351 (1974). *But see* Stanley v. Illinois, 405 U.S. 645 (1972), and Weinberger v. Wiesenfeld, 95 S. Ct. 1225 (1975), involving, in addition to discrimination against female wage earners, prejudice to surviving fathers who wished to remain home and care for a minor child.

[27] *See In re* Griffiths, 413 U.S. 717 (1973); Sugarman v. Dougall, 413 U.S. 634 (1973); Graham v. Richardson, 403 U.S. 365 (1971).

[28] Weber v. Aetna Cas. & Sur. Co., 406 U.S. 164 (1972).

[29] *See* James v. Strange, 407 U.S. 128 (1972); Mayer v. City of Chicago, 404 U.S. 189 (1971); Tate v. Short, 401 U.S. 395 (1971); Williams v. Illinois, 399 U.S. 235 (1970). *But cf.* Ross v. Moffitt, 417 U.S. 600 (1974); Fuller v. Oregon, 417 U.S. 40 (1974).

[30] *See* Jackson v. Indiana, 406 U.S. 715 (1972).

[31] Memorial Hospital v. Maricopa County, 415 U.S. 250 (1974). At issue here was the validity of an Arizona one-year county durational residency requirement necessary for indigents to qualify for free non-emergency hospital or medical care. The Court held the statute violated the equal protection clause by impinging on the right to interstate travel.

[32] *See, e.g.*, Lubin v. Panish, 415 U.S. 709 (1974); O'Brien v. Skinner, 414 U.S. 524 (1974);

only apparent that the Warren Court's amplifications of equality have managed to survive. In the hands of a more cautious Supreme Court, the constitutional meanings of equality have, if anything, slowly multiplied.

B. *The Standards of Equal Protection Review*

That analysis of equal protection law should commence with the concept of equality itself might seem a self-evident proposition. Recent commentary, however, has not always proceeded in such fashion. Much of it has focused not so much on various dimensions of the concept of equality[33] as on the levels of scrutiny the Court has applied to equal protection claims.[34] The most thoughtful of the articles, Professor Gerald Gunther's Foreword to the Harvard Law Review's survey of the 1971 Supreme Court term, suggested a model of "means scrutiny" whereby the Court should seek to ensure that the means chosen by the legislature substantially further some articulated, rather than any judicially imagined, state purpose.[35] Gunther hoped the new model would, among other things, remove the Court's automatic and "toothless" deference to most legislative enactments and simultaneously avoid the subjective and disordered application of strict judicial review.[36] The question when Gunther wrote was whether the Court's recent equal protection decisions were indeed trending toward such a model or whether they merely evidenced a sense of drift, a possibility Gunther himself recognized.[37]

Recent equal protection decisions, most of them since Gunther's

Kusper v. Pontikes, 414 U.S. 51 (1973) (infringement on voting mobility in party primaries, voided not on equal protection grounds but on first amendment grounds of free political association); Dunn v. Blumstein, 405 U.S. 330 (1972); Bullock v. Carter, 405 U.S. 134 (1972). *But cf.* Richardson v. Ramirez, 418 U.S. 24 (1974) (decided under section two of the fourteenth amendment). Storer v. Brown, 415 U.S. 724 (1974); Rosario v. Rockefeller, 410 U.S. 752 (1973).

[33] Two notable exceptions are Michelman, *The Supreme Court, 1968 Term—Foreword: On Protecting the Poor Through the Fourteenth Amendment*, 83 HARV. L. REV. 7 (1969) and Winter, *Poverty, Economic Equality and the Equal Protection Clause*, 1972 SUPREME COURT REV. 41, discussed in part IV *infra*.

[34] *See, e.g.*, Note, *Legislative Purpose, Rationality, and Equal Protection*, 82 YALE L.J. 123 (1972); Comment, *Fundamental Personal Rights: Another Approach to Equal Protection*, 40 U. CHI. L. REV. 802 (1973).

[35] *See* Gunther, *supra* note 19, at 20-48.

[36] *Id.* at 18, 19, 21.

[37] *Id.* at 1, 30.

article, have accentuated the sense of drift. Nominally, the Court continues to adhere to the two-tiered system of equal protection review. It will look at most statutory classifications to determine only whether the classification bears "a rational relationship to a [permissible] state objective."[38] The Court scrutinizes more intently classifications impinging on so-called fundamental rights, namely the right to vote,[39] the right to interstate travel,[40] the right to freedom of association,[41] and perhaps the right to a criminal appeal,[42] to determine whether such classifications advance a compelling state interest. Statutory classifications based on race,[43] alienage,[44] or national origin[45] are formally suspect and must likewise satisfy a compelling state interest. Sex,[46] illegitimacy,[47] and indigency[48] hover on the perimeter of the suspect category and appear to require some unspecified level of heightened review.

Beyond this, however, little is clear. The Court's application of its own standards has been erratic, particularly in those difficult cases where an egalitarian result seems desirable, but without far-reaching doctrinal consequences.[49] On occasion, the Court has appeared uncertain even as to the overall framework of equal protection review. In *Weber v. Aetna Casualty & Surety Co.*, the Court

---

[38] Village of Belle Terre v. Boraas, 416 U.S. 1, 8 (1974), *quoting* Reed v. Reed, 404 U.S. 71, 76 (1971).

[39] *E.g.*, Dunn v. Blumstein, 405 U.S. 330 (1972).

[40] *E.g.*, Memorial Hospital v. Maricopa County, 415 U.S. 250 (1974); Dunn v. Blumstein, 405 U.S. 330 (1972); Shapiro v. Thompson, 394 U.S. 618 (1969). *But see* Sosna v. Iowa, 419 U.S. 393 (1975).

[41] *E.g.*, Douglas v. California, 372 U.S. 353 (1963). *But cf.* Ross v. Moffitt, 417 U.S. 600 (1974).

[42] *E.g.* Kusper v. Pontikes, 414 U.S. 51 (1973). Although the criminal appeals and freedom of association cases often do not contain precise "compelling state interest" language, the ingredients of analysis are much the same as in the more orthodox voting and right to travel opinions. Though *Kusper*, for example, purports to be based solely on first amendment grounds, its analysis and citation of precedent closely align it with strict scrutiny equal protection.

[43] *E.g.*, Loving v. Virginia, 388 U.S. 1 (1967).

[44] *E.g.*, Graham v. Richardson, 403 U.S. 365 (1971).

[45] *Id.*

[46] In Frontiero v. Richardson, 411 U.S. 677 (1973), four Justices (Brennan, Douglas, Marshall, and White) voted to make sex a suspect classification. All members of the Court, save Justice Rehnquist, were willing to void the sex-based statutory classification.

[47] *E.g.*, Weber v. Aetna Cas. & Sur. Co., 406 U.S. 164 (1972).

[48] *E.g.*, Douglas v. California, 372 U.S. 353 (1963).

[49] *See* Cleveland Bd. of Educ. v. LaFleur, 414 U.S. 632 (1974); James v. Strange, 407 U.S. 128 (1972); Weber v. Aetna Cas. & Sur. Co., 406 U.S. 164 (1972); Reed v. Reed, 404 U.S. 71 (1971).

articulated something close to an equal protection balancing test of state interests against important personal rights.[50] In *San Antonio Independent School District v. Rodriguez*, the majority rejected any inference of balancing and reverted, quite explicitly, to the traditional two-tiered system of review.[51] But the rigidity of the two-tiered system continues to cause uneasiness, and more and more the Court has simply refused, sometimes over strenuous dissent, even to identify which level of scrutiny it employed.[52]

Where the standard has been identified, it has been unevenly applied. In *Rodriguez*, only rights "explicitly or implicitly protected by the Constitution" were to be subject to strict scrutiny,[53] even though the various suspect classes or the right to a criminal appeal find slender support in constitutional text.[54] Rational basis scrutiny likewise has yielded to various formulations and applications. The *McGowan* and *McDonald* tests of ultimate deference to legislative enactments continue to be cited.[55] But other formulations of rational basis review are also used, ones that require the challenged statutory distinction rationally to further some "legitimate, articulated state purpose"[56] or the statutory class to bear a relationship of "some rationality" to legislative aims.[57] Rational basis scrutiny also

---

[50] The Court expressed the test thusly: "The essential inquiry . . . is . . . inevitably a dual one: What legitimate state interest does the classification promote? What fundamental personal rights might the classification endanger?" 406 U.S. 164, 173 (1971).

[51]
> We must decide, first, whether the Texas system of financing public education operates to the disadvantage of some suspect class or impinges upon a fundamental right explicitly or implicitly protected by the Constitution, thereby requiring strict judicial scrutiny. If so, the judgment of the District Court should be affirmed. If not, the Texas scheme must still be examined to determine whether it rationally furthers some legitimate, articulated state purpose and therefore does not constitute an invidious discrimination in violation of the Equal Protection Clause of the Fourteenth Amendment.

411 U.S. 1, 17 (1973).

[52] *See, e.g.*, Lubin v. Panish, 415 U.S. 709 (1970); Rosario v. Rockefeller, 410 U.S. 752 (1973).

[53] 411 U.S. at 17.

[54] *See* Justice Marshall's dissent in *Rodriguez*, 411 U.S. at 100.

[55] For the *McDonald* test, *see* note 16 *supra* and accompanying text. McGowan v. Maryland, 366 U.S. 420, 426 (1961), states the question as whether "any state of facts reasonably may be conceived to justify" the statutory discrimination. Examples of recent cases relying on one or both of these tests are Lindsey v. Normet, 405 U.S. 56, 70 (1972); Schilb v. Kuebel, 404 U.S. 357, 364 (1971); Dandridge v. Williams, 397 U.S. 471, 485 (1970).

[56] This formulation has so far appeared in two of Justice Powell's opinions for the Court, San Antonio Indep. School Dist. v. Rodriguez, 411 U.S. 1, 17 (1973), and McGinnis v. Royster, 410 U.S. 263, 270 (1973).

[57] Fuller v. Oregon, 417 U.S. 40 (1974); James v. Strange, 407 U.S. 128, 140 (1972); Rinaldi

may result, somewhat haphazardly and mysteriously, in the voidance of classifications that appear quite rationally supportable.[58] For some claims, whose flavor has been distinctly one of equal protection, yet whose resolution posed severe doctrinal difficulties, the Court managed to jettison equal protection altogether and hold the statutory classifications irrebutable presumptions in violation of the due process clause.[59] One plausible inference from all of this is, that despite lip service to a two-tiered test, certain classifications call, sub-silentio, for some intermediate level of review.[60]

The Court's varying approaches to the equal protection clause are not, of course, without explanation. Equal protection law has been a fluid and fast-developing area from which coherent doctrine will not likely spring full-blown. The Court's membership has also changed rapidly: development of a philosophy of equal protection takes time and, perhaps, several false starts. Then, too, each Justice in a majority opinion may understandably try to tilt the Court toward his distinctive equal protection approach. Even so, the extent of fluctuation must dishearten those who had hoped, if not for a neutral and consistent set of equal protection principles, at least for some candid explanation of the reasons for inconsistency. What instead has developed is not, as some would fear, an ultra-

---

v. Yeager, 384 U.S. 305, 308-09 (1966).

[58] *See, e.g.*, Eisenstadt v. Baird, 405 U.S. 438 (1972). A more startling case is United States Dept. of Agriculture v. Moreno, 413 U.S. 528 (1973), where the Court held "wholly without any rational basis" a 1971 Amendment to the federal Food Stamp Act limiting eligibility for assistance to "households." The definition of "household" was in turn limited largely to groups of *related* persons and excluded from the program groups of unrelated individuals under age sixty. The exclusion was, surprisingly, held irrational by a vote of 7-2 despite the Government assertions that it helped prevent fraud and abuse of the food stamp program. The justifications were no weaker than many previously sustained; as the Harvard Law Review noted:

> the Court could have accepted the Government's reasonable, if less than powerful, argument that unrelated households are especially likely to contain abusers, and that such abusers are difficult to detect.

Supreme Court, 1972 Term, 87 HARV. L. REV. 1, 130 (1973).

[59] Cleveland Bd. of Educ. v. LaFleur, 414 U.S. 632 (1974); Vlandis v. Kline, 412 U.S. 441 (1973). *See* Bezanson, *Some Thoughts on the Emerging Irrebuttable Presumption Doctrine*, 7 IND. L. REV. 644 (1974).

[60] Classifications based on sex and illegitimacy seem to belong to this category. *See, e.g.*, Jimenez v. Weinberger, 417 U.S. 628 (1974); Reed v. Reed, 404 U.S. 71 (1971). For some thoughts on the emergence of an intermediate standard, see Gunther, *supra* note 19; Goodpaster, *The Constitution and Fundamental Rights*, 15 ARIZ. L. REV. 479, 503 (1973); Nowak, *Realigning the Standards of Review Under the Equal Protection Guarantee—Prohibited, Neutral, and Permissive Classifications*, 62 GEO. L.J. 1071 (1974).

conservative equal protection outlook but an accumulation of ad hoc doctrines flexible enough to accommodate a cautious Court's preferences for mildly progressive results.

Again, these comments are not wholly by way of criticism. There is, as we must remind ourselves, much more to law than method and technique. The Burger Court's approach to equal protection may represent an admirably cautious and sober enlargement of the principle of constitutional equality. But the meaning of the evolution is *not* to be found in identifying tiers or standards of review or by measuring the Court's performance against some hopefully neutral model of adjudication. Coherence in equal protection law must be found rather in the meanings of equality itself and by assessing the legitimacy of the Court's efforts against the kinds of equality it is attempting to achieve.

C. The Three Faces of Constitutional Equality

Despite the consensus that egalitarianism is a new constitutional force of major importance, there has been scant attention paid, either by the Court or its critics, to exactly what kinds of equality the Court has been promoting. To date, in fact, constitutional egalitarianism has not been much more than an aimless and ill-defined impulse. Decisions have been rendered with little consideration of what part they will play in the advancement of overall notions of constitutional equality. A coherent look at the different dimensions of this equality seems both desirable and overdue. To this end, equality may usefully be viewed as a divisible concept; whether the Court is justified in promoting equality depends considerably on just what species of equality one happens to mean.

Species of equality are apparently inexhaustible. Recent commentators have spoken of "accidental equality," "intrinsic equality,"[61] "equality in religious freedom," "racial equality,"[62] the Liberal, Conservative, and Socialist concepts of equality,[63] and "numerical" and "proportional" equality.[64] It is not the purpose of this article to attempt any metaphysical dissection of the word. This much, however, is clear: many, perhaps most, kinds of inequality remain beyond the capacity of the judiciary, or indeed of govern-

[61] J. Wilson, Equality 81, 89 (1966).
[62] A. Grimes, Equality in America 18, 41 (1964).
[63] S. Lakoff, Equality in Political Philosophy 1-11 (1964).
[64] *Developments*, *supra* note 15, at 1165-66.

ment generally, to alter. Inequalities of social status, for example, would elude the reach of the judiciary except when those inequalities rest upon public laws that discriminate in ways that imply inferiority. The causes of poverty are too pervasive, resistant, and complex for the judiciary to uproot, though courts may and indeed have alleviated some of its effects. Native disparities between individuals in intellect and motivation remain basically unchangeable; courts at most can create fairer opportunities for innate abilities to emerge and operate. Thus inequalities, both man-made and natural, remain so deeply layered that the most egalitarian judiciary can make only the most limited headway in removing them. Viewed from this perspective, the Supreme Court's efforts seem as notable for the domains of inequality left untouched as for those more limited manifestations of inequality it has managed to remove.

To say this is not to disparage the effort but to recognize its inevitably circumscribed character. The arenas of equality into which the Supreme Court has so far ventured have been three. The Court has sought to promote, in a limited manner, equality of participation within the political process. Secondly, it has advanced, in incipient fashion, an equality of competitive opportunity. Thirdly, it has addressed economic and material inequality to the extent of relieving a few of poverty's harsher consequences.

There is, of course, no bright line separating these three faces of constitutional equality. Several of the Court's own landmark cases fall into more than one category. *Harper v. Virginia Board of Elections*, where the Court abolished state poll taxes under the equal protection clause,[65] is simultaneously a case that promotes political equality and relieves a burden on the less well-off. More recently, *San Antonio Independent School District v. Rodriguez* may be seen as failing to relieve a consequence of poverty and as a failure to provide more equal competitive opportunities for children of property-poor school districts.[66] The Court's promotion of racial justice might validly be regarded as a venture into all three areas of equality. The Court's object was to secure for blacks participation in the political process[67] and a stronger position of competitive op-

---

[65] 383 U.S. 663 (1966).

[66] 411 U.S. 1 (1973). In *Rodriguez*, the Court upheld the Texas system of public school financing that relied heavily on local property taxes and consequently produced substantial disparities among the state's school districts in per pupil expenditures.

[67] *See, e.g.*, Harper v. Virginia Bd. of Elections, 383 U.S. 663 (1950).

portunity[68] through racially integrated education. Finally, the Court's efforts to ameliorate the burdens of poverty were simultaneously efforts to remove a condition that weighed disproportionately on blacks.

Granting some intermingling and overlap, these three dimensions of equality still provide the best means of analyzing what the Court has done and where it is going in the equal protection area. This article will attempt to define what the Court has accomplished in each of the three different areas of equality. An attempt will be made to analyze egalitarianism from a conviction that the persuasiveness of the arguments for judicial intervention varies considerably depending on the kind of equality at issue. The discussion will no doubt be fragmentary and incomplete. But decisions on equal protection cannot help but profit when analysis fastens first on the crucial element of equality itself and on just what pattern of equality a given decision falls within.

II. Political Equality

I will first examine the realm of equality in which judicial intervention is most desirable and justifiable: that of political equality. Before the Warren Court, state election laws generally enjoyed the immunity accorded political questions. The Court for the most part heeded the flat admonition of Justice Frankfurter that "[i]t is hostile to a democratic system to involve the judiciary in the politics of the people."[69] By the end of the Warren era, however, this maxim had been largely overturned. The Court had undertaken to supervise broadly the ground rules under which elective combat was conducted and to order state election laws to equalize each man's input into the process of democratic decision.

This pattern of intervention was established beyond the point of retreat, even had the post-Warren Supreme Court desired to do so. Instead, the Burger Court has made some important additional contributions to the idea of political equality.[70] It has recognized the

[68] *See, e.g.*, Swann v. Charlotte-Mecklenburg Bd. of Educ. 402 U.S. 1 (1971); Green v. County School Bd., 391 U.S. 430 (1968); Brown v. Bd. of Educ., 347 U.S. 483 (1954).

[69] Colegrove v. Green, 328 U.S. 549, 553-54 (1946).

[70] *See* Lubin v. Panish, 415 U.S. 709 (1974), voiding state filing fees for candidate access to primary ballots and Bullock v. Carter, 405 U.S. 134 (1972). Dunn v. Blumstein, 405 U.S. 330 (1972), which invalidated by a 6-1 vote Tennessee's durational residency requirements for voters, is an important post-Warren Court decision promoting political equality, but it is doubtful that it belongs to the Burger Court. Chief Justice Burger dissented in the case;

obligation to oversee state election laws, even while it has intervened less daringly than its predecessor. Justice White, writing for the Court in *Storer v. Brown*, expressed the new mood: more cautious certainly, but still firm in its recognition that for better or worse the Supreme Court had become an arbiter of political fair play:

> [T]he rule fashioned by the Court to pass on constitutional challenges to specific provisions of election laws provides no litmus-paper test for separating those restrictions that are valid from those that are invidious under the Equal Protection Clause. The rule is not self-executing and is no substitute for the hard judgments that must be made. Decision in this context, as in others, is very much a "matter of degree" . . . What the result of this process will be in any specific case may be very difficult to predict with great assurance.[71]

A. *The Principles of Political Equality*

The grand themes of Supreme Court intervention into the political process have not been difficult to discern. The Court has been convinced, firstly, that as many people as possible should be allowed to vote. Secondly, it has insisted that each man's vote count equally. With *Williams v. Rhodes*,[72] yet a third principle of political equality emerged: that for the vote to be meaningful, the ballot must reflect a sufficiently representative choice of parties or candidates. In all cases, the handle for judicial intervention has invariably been protection of the right to vote or, rather, the right of both voter and candidate to ballot access.

One hardly need mention that the Court's current efforts have not brought about a world of equal political influence. Some natural inequalities will always remain: individuals differ sharply in their political talents and motivations. More pertinently, the heavy reliance of American politics on private financing "requires private wealth to play the leading role in the gate-keeping and handicapping of political campaigns."[73] The Court has not yet addressed

---

Justice Blackmun concurred only in the result, and Justices Powell and Rehnquist were not on the Court.

The Burger Court has, of course, also decided against the concept of political equality. *See, e.g.*, Richardson v. Ramirez, 418 U.S. 24 (1974); Rosario v. Rockefeller, 410 U.S. 752 (1973).

[71] 415 U.S. 724, 730 (1974).

[72] 393 U.S. 23 (1968).

[73] Fleishman, *Public Financing of Election Campaigns: Constitutional Constraints on Steps Toward Equality of Political Influence of Citizens*, 52 N. CAR. L. REV. 349, 350 (1973).

seriously the question put by some commentators:[74] whether there exists an affirmative constitutional obligation to remove the distortions that natural inequalities of means bring to democratic elections. Instead the Court has followed the more modest course of scrutinizing only those state-created restrictions on the right to vote.

The first principle of political equality—that the franchise should be broadly available—was implemented by the Court's stripping away, one by one, state-erected barriers to the ballot. The Supreme Court has, in recent terms, voided poll taxes,[75] military status,[76] property ownership,[77] durational residency,[78] and prior party affiliation[79] as conditions to exercise of the franchise. Implicit in the notion of the franchise as a right available to all was the rejection of an inegalitarian theory of an earlier day. The earlier theory regarded the vote as a privilege to be exercised only upon some demonstration of civic responsibility—whether of interest in public affairs by paying a poll tax, of a stake in political life stemming from ownership of property, or of a familiarity with and commitment to state politics resulting from living within the state's boundaries a respectable period. The new move toward political equality swept this theory away[80] because, complained Justice Harlan, it was "not in accord with current egalitarian notions of how a modern democracy should be organized."[81]

---

[74] *See* Fleishman, *supra* note 73; Nicholson, *Campaign Financing and Equal Protection*, 26 STAN. L. REV. 815 (1974). Many of the arguments made for political equality in this section would also appear to support some form of public financing of political campaigns. Yet the question is of a much different magnitude from the cases so far coming before the Court. The loosening of the state action concept, the problems of framing a remedy and of judicially mandating significant legislative expenditures, and the objections raised against public financing under the first amendment are but a few of the difficulties that place the question of a constitutional attack on present campaign financing practices beyond the immediate scope of this article.

[75] Harper v. Virginia Bd. of Elections, 383 U.S. 663 (1966).

[76] Carrington v. Rash, 380 U.S. 89 (1965).

[77] Cipriano v. City of Houma, 395 U.S. 701 (1969); Kramer v. Union Free School Dist., 395 U.S. 621 (1969).

[78] Dunn v. Blumstein, 405 U.S. 330 (1972).

[79] Kusper v. Pontikes, 414 U.S. 51 (1973). *But cf.* Rosario v. Rockefeller, 410 U.S. 752 (1973). Restrictions on candidacy because of prior affiliation with another party are apparently more permissible than such restrictions on voting. *See* Storer v. Brown, 415 U.S. 724 (1974); Lippitt v. Cipollone, 404 U.S. 1032 (1972).

[80] See the arguments rejected, either directly or implicitly, in Dunn v. Blumstein, 405 U.S. 330 (1972); Kramer v. Union Free School Dist., 395 U.S. 621 (1969); Harper v. Virginia Bd. of Elections, 383 U.S. 663 (1966).

[81] Harper v. Virginia Bd. of Elections, 383 U.S. 663, 686 (Harlan, J., dissenting).

The second strand of political equality—that each vote count equally[82]—paraded under the slogans of majoritarianism and "one-man, one-vote." The Court has applied this slogan extensively: to congressional districts,[83] state legislatures,[84] local governments,[85] nominating petitions,[86] elected junior college trustees,[87] to most elective governmental bodies, except, for example, the directors of a water storage district.[88] Like the previous ideal of a universally available franchise, the theme of one-man, one-vote also toppled pre-existing political theory. The theory was one of interest representation and held that the goal of a reapportionment plan was to reflect a state's or county's distinctive interest groupings, which might be regionally, historically, or occupationally based. But the Court decreed otherwise; henceforth representation would follow a formula of pure population, with its dangers, in Madison's words, of "the superior force of an interested and overbearing majority."[89]

The third principle of political equality, first set forth in *Williams v. Rhodes*,[90] insisted not only that the franchise be available, but that its exercise be meaningful. Among "our most precious freedoms," stated the Court, was "the right of qualified voters, regardless of their political persuasion, to cast their votes effectively."[91] An effective vote meant a ballot listing a sufficient number of parties or candidates to reflect, within reason, the voter's preference. The thrust of *Williams* was to permit greater ballot access for minority

---

[82] The word "equal" may overstate what the Warren Court actually did. *See* note 139 *infra*.

[83] *See* Wesberry v. Sanders, 376 U.S. 1 (1964).

[84] *See* Reynolds v. Sims, 377 U.S. 533 (1964).

[85] *See* Avery v. Midland County, 390 U.S. 474 (1968).

[86] *See* Moore v. Ogilvie, 394 U.S. 814 (1969).

[87] *See* Hadley v. Junior College Dist. of Metropolitan Kansas City, 397 U.S. 50 (1970).

[88] Salyer Land Co. v. Tulane Lake Basin Water Stor. Dist., 410 U.S. 719 (1973). There have been other limitations as well on the application of one-man, one-vote to state elections. In Wells v. Edwards, 409 U.S. 1095 (1973), the Court somewhat mysteriously rejected in a summary affirmance the application of one-man, one-vote to the election of state Supreme Court Justices. Contradictory signals have emerged from the Court on the application of one-man, one-vote to the election of Georgia statewide officials. In Gray v. Sanders, 372 U.S. 368 (1963), the Court invalidated the Georgia county unit system as a violation of majoritarianism only to later affirm the election by the state legislature of a Georgia governor with the lesser number of popular votes. Fortson v. Morris, 385 U.S. 231 (1966).

Of course, the explicit commands of article II, section 1 and article I, section 3 concerning election to the United States Senate and the Presidency override the more nebulous requirements of the fifth amendment due process clause with regard to election of those officials.

[89] THE FEDERALIST, No. 10, at 130 (B. Wright ed. 1961) (J. Madison).

[90] 393 U.S. 23 (1968).

[91] *Id.* at 30.

parties and independent candidates, though subsequent to that decision the Court has generally upheld state election laws regulating such access.[92] A more important egalitarian consequence of the decision lies in the support *Williams* has provided to the Court's attack on state filing fees. In *Bullock v. Carter*, the Court made the critical connection established in *Williams*—that restrictions on candidates or parties affect voters as well.[93] In *Lubin v. Panish*, where the Court voided California's filing fees for indigent candidates, the influence of *Williams* was also quite apparent. "It is to be expected," noted the Court, "that a voter hopes to find on the ballot a candidate who comes near to reflecting his policy preferences on contemporary issues."[94]

As with the Court's promotion of a broadly available and an equally weighted franchise, the theory of political equality in *Williams v. Rhodes* challenged prevailing political wisdom. This time the wisdom was not Madisonian in its origins but derived from the Progressive era at the turn of the century. Reformers of that era hoped to limit the size of the ballot so as to reduce voter confusion and to enhance voter discernment.[95] *Williams v. Rhodes*, of course, represented the opposing trend of greater political opportunity for greater numbers of candidates and parties. In the *Williams* line of cases, however, the older political theory was not so completely discarded as the pre-existing theories were by *Harper* and *Reynolds*. Unlike the reapportionment cases, where interest group representation was abruptly and explicitly dismissed, "the State's interest in keeping its ballots within manageable, understandable limits is of the highest order."[96] What developed was not a displacement of earlier theory but rather an accommodation between the Progressive precepts and those of the modern era, in which the Court would not void all burdens on ballot access for candidates and parties but only those that "*severely* burdened the right to associate for political purposes and the right to vote effectively . . . ."[97] The more compromising approach in the *Williams* progeny may reflect the fact that the core constitutional right to

[92] American Party of Texas v. White, 415 U.S. 767 (1974); Storer v. Brown, 415 U.S. 724 (1974); Jenness v. Fortson, 403 U.S. 431 (1971).
[93] 405 U.S. 134, 142-44 (1972).
[94] 415 U.S. 709, 716 (1974).
[95] *See* H. Croly, Progressive Democracy 289 (1914).
[96] Lubin v. Panish, 415 U.S. 709, 715 (1974).
[97] Storer v. Brown, 415 U.S. 724, 729 (1974) (emphasis added).

vote is less directly implicated in such cases,[98] or simply the more cautious course of the Burger Court.

B. The Case for Judicial Promotion of Political Equality

These, then, are the themes of political equality the Supreme Court has advanced through intervention into state election laws.[99] The Supreme Court acts most justifiably when it ensures that state political systems encourage broadened and more equal political participation and that they embody, to put it bluntly, some basic sense of political fair play. Judicial intervention into state political processes should not proceed lightly, but there exist important considerations that make the Court's promotion of political equality both a legitimate and necessary exercise of judicial power.

Political equality is uniquely important. The state enjoys an ultimate monopoly on coercive power which allows it—to take two elemental examples—to declare war and to collect taxes. Such an important and coercive monopoly as public power must provide access to and involvement within itself if it is to represent fairly the human forces over which it presides. It is hardly enough for the Court, under the equal protection clause, simply to police the most flagrant abuses of public power *after* they occur. It is necessary to require an open and equal access to the wielding of power to help ensure that its application, if not always wise, is at least representative.

To begin with, the Court's obligations to political equality bear close connection to its mandate to ensure freedom of expression, especially expression of political dissent. Though the Constitution provides free speech more explicit textual support, the purposes of the Court's promotion of free speech under the first amendment and political equality under the equal protection clause are much the same. In both cases the aim is to preserve "the potential fluidity of American political life"[100] and to prevent those presently in power

---

[98] One is not barred from voting, only from having listed on the ballot the candidate of his first choice.

[99] One may question my decision to limit the major principles of political equality to three. One might say, for example, that the poll tax (*Harper*) and filing fees cases (*Bullock* and *Lubin*) evidence yet a fourth theme of political equality—that of minimizing the influence of wealth in public elections. The poll tax and filing fee cases, however, seemed more appropriately grouped under one of the three major principles discussed in the preceding section. Without one of those three major principles at issue, the Court might well have proceeded differently.

[100] Jenness v. Fortson, 403 U.S. 431, 439 (1971).

from passing laws designed to shackle opposition to their positions and policies. One chief purpose of the first amendment is to preserve a vocal opposition to incumbent political interests; a central goal of the Court's search for political equality is to preserve a viable political opposition to those same interests, free from threats of dilution or destruction of its voting strength. The constitutional concepts of free speech and political equality must thus be recognized as partners in the maintenance of an open political society.

A doctrinal convergence of first amendment rights with those of political equality has been obvious in many cases before the Court. The inquiry as to voting rights and the first amendment right of freedom of association has very often been identical. The Court asks whether the right to vote or the freedom to associate is substantially burdened. If it is, the offending law must satisfy a compelling state interest. If it does not, the inquiry becomes how the state's legitimate but less than compelling interests may be advanced by less drastic means. Often the same law offends both voting and first amendment rights, as in *Williams v. Rhodes*[101] where laws burdening ballot access of minority parties were found to impinge both on the right to vote effectively and on the right of individuals to associate with political parties for advancement of their political beliefs. In *Kusper v. Pontikes*,[102] the Court invalidated an Illinois law which prohibited a person from voting in a primary election of a political party if he had voted in another party's primary within the past twenty-three months. The law was held to violate the first amendment right to freedom of association, but the Court could as easily have used traditional equal protection analysis to reach the same result.[103]

If the Court will not allow a legislature to still the speech of its opponents, it should not grant a legislature any greater leeway to smother opposition by manipulating the ground rules of election. Oppresive election laws are surely as damaging to a democratic system as those restricting freedom of expression. Examples abound. The poll tax was often not so much a device to promote civic responsibility as a strategem by vested political interests to

[101] 393 U.S. 23 (1968).

[102] 414 U.S. 51 (1973).

[103] The question of why it did not is an intriguing one. It may indicate Justice Stewart's general restiveness with "compelling state interest" formulations outside the area of racial classifications. *Cf.* Cleveland Bd. of Educ. v. LaFleur, 414 U.S. 632 (1974); Vlandis v. Kline, 412 U.S. 441 (1973); Rosario v. Rockefeller, 410 U.S. 752 (1973).

maintain a small, manageable and predictable electorate and to disenfranchise those on the lower end of the economic spectrum.[104] The refusal to reapportion allowed entrenched rural officeholders to retain strangleholds on state legislatures, despite shifts of population and resources to urban and suburban centers. Filing fees as exorbitant as those in *Bullock v. Carter* effectively discouraged a broad segment of potential opposition.[105] The obstacles to third-party ballot listing in *Williams v. Rhodes* had, as Justice Black recognized, given "the two old, established parties a decided advantage over any new parties struggling for existence. . . ."[106]

In many of these instances, the hope for political self-correction seemed dim. Those who stood to benefit most from reform were often effectively shut off from the means of bringing it about.[107] Incumbent interests benefited too much from established practices to seek their dissolution. When restrictive election practices were on the wane, as was the poll tax in most states at the time of *Harper*, dissenting Justices argued that the final demise ought to be left to "the affected States" and to the "federal political process."[108] But patience with the self-corrective promise of politics seems no more warranted in these instances than a patient hope an aberrant legislature might repeal a law requiring the burning of books written by suspected subversives.

Probably the chief obstacle to the Court's promotion of political equality is the value of experimental federalism. The value is that of a pluralistic society, the conviction that worthwhile reform will more likely take place when individual states are allowed to experiment with different systems than when the Supreme Court binds them to national standards of its own making. This view constitutes the cutting edge of the major dissents to political equality, as, for example, in Justice Harlan's celebrated listing in *Reynolds v. Sims* of ten factors states were precluded from using as the basis for legislative districting[109] and Justice Stewart's plea that "a system of

---

[104] *See* V. Key, Jr., Southern Politics in State and Nation 578-618 (1949).

[105] The fees challenged in *Bullock* were $1424.60 for County Commissioner, $6,300 for County Judge, and $1,000 for Commissioner of General Land Office.

[106] 393 U.S. at 31.

[107] Those wanting a more equitable apportionment scheme, for example, could hardly achieve adequate legislative representation under the existing districts to bring it about. Many of those most desirous of poll tax repeal were unable to vote their convictions because they had not paid their poll taxes.

[108] Harper v. Virginia Bd. of Elections, 383 U.S. 663, 680 (1966) (Harlan, J., dissenting).

[109] Reynolds v. Sims, 377 U.S. 533, 622-23 (1964). (Harlan, J., dissenting). *See* Wilkinson,

legislative apportionment which might be best for South Dakota, might be unwise for Hawaii with its many islands, or Michigan with its Northern Peninsula."[110]

Such arguments can be answered, though not simply by reiterating that "[l]egislators represent people, not trees or acres."[111] Every constitutional provision implies some impairment of state power to experiment and, inevitably, some preference for a national ideal over the values of pluralism. Moreover, the value in having states experiment varies broadly with the setting. State experimentation with substantive laws for the common benefit is a wholly different matter from experimentation with the structure of government and the procedure of coming elections.[112] The judgment of a state legislature on appropriations for mental hospitals, for example, must be presumed in the general welfare, an exercise of the core power and essential duty for which the legislature was elected. Judgment on election law merits no such reflexive deference. Election law by its very nature excites the basic instinct for self-perpetuation and a desire, often not to experiment, but to preserve the status quo which led to power. The basic fact of our political system is that incumbents exercise near-exclusive control over rules under which they themselves seek reelection.[113] The minority party and the non-incumbent candidate have relatively little say.

The above arguments speak primarily to the need snd propriety of some judicial intervention into state election law. They do not address the question whether judicial intervention, once it occurs, need come with all the egalitarian force of the Warren Court. Justice

---

Justice John M. Harlan and the Values of Federalism, 57 VA. L. REV. 1185, 1192-99 (1971).

[110] Lucas v. Colorado Gen. Assembly, 377 U.S. 713, 749 (1964) (Stewart, J., dissenting).

[111] Reynolds v. Sims, 377 U.S. 533, 562 (1964).

[112] The distinction between procedure and substance is, of course, one that is often made in justifying an active judicial role under the First Amendment:

> In other words, the judicial institutions are here [in First Amendment cases] dealing with the methods of conducting the democratic process, not with the substantive results of that process. In this differentiation of function lies a generic distinction between the role of the judiciary and the role of the legislature.

T. EMERSON, THE SYSTEM OF FREEDOM OF EXPRESSION 13 (1970).

[113] Much of this, of course, may be unavoidable. If law of any sort is to be made, elected incumbents must be the ones to make it. Yet courts can properly be more skeptical toward the passage of laws under which the lawmakers themselves seek to be returned to office. The presence of an opposition party in the legislature and the possibility of denouncing unfair election laws before the electorate may provide some safeguards to the passage of arbitrary election law, but it is hardly so complete a safeguard as to eliminate the need for a judicial role.

Stewart, who joined the Court in *Baker v. Carr*[114] but dissented in *Lucas v. Colorado General Assembly*,[115] proposed a more moderate ground in the reapportionment cases:

> [S]o long as a State's apportionment plan reasonably achieves, in the light of the State's own characteristics, effective and balanced representation of all substantial interests, without sacrificing the principle of effective majority rule, that plan cannot be considered irrational.[116]

Professor Bickel sounded a similar theme, more specifically:

> The Court might have been inclined to stop shortly after its initial venture into the field, and to be content with striking down obsolete apportionments, with requiring legislatures to act after each census, and with formulating otherwise only the rule that at least one institution of a state government, commonly the executive, must be purely majoritarian.[117]

These tests, of course, meet initial difficulty in determining what in fact are "obsolete apportionments" and just what constitutes a state plan achieving "effective and balanced representations of all substantial interests." To what minority interest would we permit majoritarianism to be sacrificed? The question is baffling. Even more fundamentally, the Stewart-Bickel position misconceives the essential purpose of judicial intervention into the political process. Judicial protection of political equality vindicates individual rights fully as much as judicial protection of, for example, the right to counsel and the privilege against self-incrimination. One may, to be sure, characterize judicial intervention into state elections as Justice Stewart once did: an attempt which "forever freezes one theory of political thought into our Constitution."[118] In the same breath, one may depict *Gideon v. Wainwright*[119] or *Miranda v. Arizona*[120] as attempts to freeze in the Constitution a particular theory of criminal justice. But it is not so much the preference for one form of

---

[114] 369 U.S. 186 (1962).

[115] 377 U.S. 713, 744-65 (1964). This is a companion case to Reynolds v. Sims, 377 U.S. 533 (1964), where Justice Stewart, in effect, concurred in the result. *See id.* at 588.

[116] 377 U.S. at 751.

[117] BICKEL, *supra* note 1, at 174.

[118] Lucas v. Colorado Gen. Assembly, 377 U.S. 713, 748 (1964) (Stewart, J., dissenting).

[119] 372 U.S. 335 (1963).

[120] 384 U.S. 436 (1966).

political theory or one form of criminal process over another that the Court is trying to achieve as an insistence that some basic protection of individual rights undergird whatever theory of political organization or of criminal justice is subsequently adopted. If providing this basic protection limits the state's options, this is the necessary price for enforcement of any constitutional rights.

The Stewart-Bickel position falls short in this respect. It is difficult to see how political rights can be meaningfully vindicated in a democracy short of the right to an equal, meaningful, and broadly available vote. Government affects each man's life in its most intimate aspects. Government may tax him, draft him, or send him to jail. The roads on which he drives, the safety of what he buys, the privacy he knows, the school to which his child will go, the health care he receives, the very air he breathes are all quite significantly the products of public acts or omissions. Since government so intimately affects him, courts cannot lightly sanction the dilution of his capacity, in turn, to affect his government.

One may contend, of course, that government affects us unequally, that air pollution and urban renewal legislation affect urban residents more than rural, for example, just as a farm-to-market road-building program more closely affects the latter.[121] Yet calculating different governmental effects on different population segments as a basis for different weights of votes would be a hopeless undertaking. It literally would be impossible to aggregate the numerous effects, both obvious and subtle, that a government of general powers exercises on the different groups within its jurisdiction. One cannot easily measure all the effects of any single public action on citizens, much less balance the impact of public acts on one group of citizens in the field of education, for example, against the impact on others of road-building, public health, crime prevention, or low-cost housing programs. The only feasible solution, reflecting the pervasiveness with which government affects us all, is that of an equal, effective, and broadly available vote.[122]

---

[121] Even this proposition is debatable. Urban residents, for example, help pay through taxes for the building of secondary, farm-to-market roads. The price and freshness of food reaching urban markets may in turn reflect the quality of farm-to-market transportation.

[122] This rationale becomes somewhat less forceful in the case of special or single purpose governing bodies. With special purpose government, an inequality of impact on citizens becomes easier to trace. The Warren Court minimized this problem in Kramer v. Union Free School Dist., 395 U.S. 621 (1969), which overturned a New York statute providing that residents of school districts could vote in school trustee elections only if they owned or leased

The advocacy of political equality thus recognizes the equal and pervasive impact government has on all the governed, or, more accurately, the impossibility of calculating the inequalities. The federal judiciary is the best body to ensure such equality, detached as it is from motives of partisan self-preservation engendered by the hazards of periodic reelection.[123] At the same time, the judiciary might be more restrained in reviewing substantive legislation if confident the process of enactment had itself been fair.[124]

These arguments seek only to justify a basic judicial role in ensuring that state election law fairly protects political equality. None of this, however, justifies promiscuous judicial intervention without close examination of the practical pitfalls and difficulties involved in implementing particular decisions. Some of these will be the subject of the following section.

C. *Implementation of the Principles of Political Equality*

The Supreme Court's dramatic quest for political equality should

---

taxable real property within the district or were parents or guardians of children enrolled in the local public schools. The Court's rejection of these restrictions left it somewhat vulnerable to Professor Bickel's broadside:

> [T]he New York statute excluded boarders and lodgers without school-age children . . . and tax-free parents whose children went to private school. It defies comprehension how these excluded groups could be deemed not to be "in fact substantially less interested or affected," unless the Court was telling us, without quite saying so, that the law may recognize no gradation of interest in public education, because the schools serve above all else the general interest of the society at large, and may not be confided to the care of the discrete communities that support them, or which they immediately serve . . . .

BICKEL, *supra* note 1, at 164.

The Burger Court reverted somewhat to Professor Bickel's conception in upholding a system of franchise restrictions and weighted voting in the election of directors of a California water storage district. *See* Salyer Land Co. v. Tulane Water Dist., 410 U.S. 719 (1973). Only landowners were permitted to vote, and votes were apportioned according to the assessed valuation of the land. The voting scheme in *Salyer Land*, however, more so than in *Kramer*, smacked additionally of wealth discrimination. Small landholdings may be as valuable and important to the small landholder as large landholdings are to the large one, and resident nonlandowners, wholly excluded from the franchise, could nonetheless be deeply affected by the district's decisions.

[123] One might attempt to achieve a similar neutrality through the public appointment of an Elections Board. Nevertheless, it is hard to conceive of the process of appointment being less political than that of judges, and the special sensitivity of the judiciary to basic constitutional requirements would be lost if members of Elections Boards made these decisions.

[124] It would, however, be naive to assume that even an environment of complete political equality, something that is still remote, would eliminate the need for judicial review of substantive legislation. Constitutional rights of various unpopular minorities, for example, would continue to require judicial protection.

not obscure the still considerable authority that states retain over elections held within their borders. The Burger Court has, in fact, begun to reject occasional equal protection challenges to state election laws, most notably laws regulating the ballot access of small parties and independent candidates[125] and those setting lengthy registration deadlines for voting in party primaries.[126] More important is that large body of state election law that remains unchallenged and probably unchallengeable. States and localities still designate, for example, the years and the frequency with which state officials are elected, their order of appearance on the ballot, the kinds of questions to be submitted to referenda, the dates of party primaries, the location and number of polling places, and the availability and location of voting registration. It is conceivable that any or all of these functions may burden the right to vote. The burden may be substantial if, for example, the state somehow made registering to vote unduly inconvenient. Yet the liklihood of a successful constitutional challenge to the above areas of state political discretion appears dim. Federal courts would not happily assume what are essentially ministerial functions of state legislatures and Boards of Elections. Even more importantly, challenges to these areas of state election law would in many cases add to political contests no real measure of equality.

Beyond this, however, the question of Supreme Court intervention into state election law becomes more complex. Even in those instances where intervention may enhance political equality, its desirability depends partly on practical considerations. The chief such consideration is whether a constitutional ideal may, in the words of *Baker v. Carr*, be embodied in "judicially discoverable and manageable standards."[127] Put slightly differently, the Supreme Court must communicate with precision to the political branches just what election laws and practices are constitutionally permissible. It must hold to a minimum the need for repeated clarifying litigation on a problem in the lower federal courts or at the Supreme Court itself. Few things rub political nerves so raw as the unsettled status of laws under which candidates compete. Few frustrate a

---

[125] American Party of Texas v. White, 415 U.S. 767 (1974); Storer v. Brown, 415 U.S. 724 (1974); Jenness v. Fortson, 403 U.S. 431 (1971).

[126] Rosario v. Rockefeller, 410 U.S. 752 (1973). *But cf.* Kusper v. Pontikes, 414 U.S. 51 (1973).

[127] 369 U.S. 186, 217 (1962).

coordinate branch quite so much as judicial discarding of election districts in which candidates have laid plans to run. Uncertainty and litigation can be kept to a minimum only if the Court lines brightly the bounds of constitutionality.

In some cases, clear communication from the Court to political institutions poses little difficulty. The political process was not left greatly in doubt by such decisions as *Harper*,[128] *Carrington v. Rash*,[129] and *Kramer v. Union Free School District*.[130] Those cases, to be sure, afforded powerful doctrinal tools for future assaults on other state election laws, but the resolution of the immediate problem with which they dealt was clear. Poll taxes, military status, property ownership, and parentage were henceforth invalid as barriers to the ballot.[131] The remedy was simply the repeal of the statute ruled unconstitutional. No substitute enactments were necessary.

A more difficult problem of communication attends decisions such as *Reynolds v. Sims*[132] and *Dunn v. Blumstein*.[133] Whereas states can dispense altogether with a poll tax or property qualifications to a ballot, some residency requirement for new voters and some plan of legislative apportionment will be necessary. In the case of durational residency, the Court stated initially that thirty[134] and later that fifty days "approaches the outer constitutional limits in this area."[135] The Court's relative clarity on the issue of durational residency contrasted with its prolonged waffling on constitutional limits in reapportionments. Absolute mathematical equality in the population of districts was unachievable, so the question became

[128] 383 U.S. 663 (1966).

[129] 380 U.S. 89 (1965).

[130] 395 U.S. 621 (1969).

[131] *Kramer* concerned property and parentage restrictions on the franchise in school board elections. *Kramer* arguably did leave some questions as to the validity of such restrictions in other limited purpose elections, but the invalidity of such restrictions not only in school board elections but in general governmental elections was made plain.

[132] 377 U.S. 533 (1964).

[133] 405 U.S. 330 (1972). The Court here invalidated Tennessee's durational residency requirement for voters. Tennessee had required residence of one year in the state and three months in the county in order to vote.

[134] *Id.* at 360.

[135] Burns v. Fortson, 410 U.S. 686, 687 (1973); Marston v. Lewis, 410 U.S. 679 (1973). The rationale of Justice Blackmun's concurrence in the result in the *Burns* case would have left the area in continued confusion: "I am not prepared to intimate at this point that a period of time in excess of 50 days cannot be sustained, no matter how supportive the record may be . . . . I feel that each case in this area should be decided on its own record unrestricted by an arbitrary number-of-days figure." 410 U.S. at 687-88.

how much deviation would be tolerated.

The Court's haphazard ventures into reapportionment after *Reynolds* left no clear idea of the answer. Working largely on an ad hoc basis, the Court voided populational disparities of over 30% in the Florida legislature,[136] upheld a disparity of 11.9% in the legislature of Rockland County, New York,[137] and struck down a 5.97% disparity among congressional districts in Missouri.[138] Not until 1973, almost a decade after *Reynolds*, did the Court finally state that a variation of 10% in the population of state legislative districts required no justification, thus freeing the political process to operate within precisely marked constitutional guideposts.[139] Figures such as 50 days and 10% are surely arbitrary, but they performed the indispensible tasks of preserving the essence of constitutional ideals while keeping the operations of courts and the political process at arms length.

A single, magic figure of 50 days or 10% is not always feasible. Laws burdening access of minority parties and independent candidates to the ballot stand or fall constitutionally on multiple factors. The first temptation in such cases is to fasten on the number or percentage of actual or registered voters whose signatures the minority party must collect for a place on the ballot. But other factors are just as important: the filing deadline for the petition, the length of time permitted to collect the signatures, the pool from which signatures may be drawn, including the eligibility to sign of those who voted in a major party primary or convention.[140] The factors deter-

---

[136] Swann v. Adams, 385 U.S. 440 (1967).

[137] Abate v. Mundt, 403 U.S. 182 (1971).

[138] Kirkpatrick v. Preisler, 394 U.S. 526 (1969).

[139] White v. Regester, 412 U.S. 755 (1973). Even with *White v. Regester*, the limits of constitutionality in reapportionment are not finally clear. In Mahan v. Howell, 410 U.S. 315 (1973), the Court held a 16.4% deviation in the lower house of the Virginia legislature to be justified by "the State's policy of maintaining the integrity of political subdivision lines." 410 U.S. at 325. The question after *Mahan* and *Regester* is, of course, what state policies permit more than a 10% deviation and just how much more a deviation do they permit. The Court has also intimated that greater population deviation is apparently permissible in state-initiated than in court-ordered plans, though how much greater is again not clear. *See* Chapman v. Meier, 420 U.S. 1 (1975).

In congressional districting, even population variances of less than 10% still require justification, White v. Weiser, 412 U.S. 783 (1973), though just how small a deviation will suffice is not yet known.

[140] The Court's decisions have generally taken this broader view. *See* American Party of Texas v. White, 415 U.S. 767 (1974); Storer v. Brown, 415 U.S. 724 (1973); Jenness v. Fortson, 403 U.S. 431 (1971); Williams v. Rhodes 393 U.S. 23 (1968). ,

mining constitutionality are all, fortunately, numerical and objective, but their multiplicity makes the problem of communicating and standards in this area a more difficult one.

Occasionally, the difficulty of communication becomes so great as to preclude intervention altogether. Such undoubtedly underlies the reluctance of the Court to scrutinize gerrymanders.[141] The most frequently mentioned corrective for gerrymandering is, of course, some requirement that districts be compact and contiguous. Not only is any requirement of compactness hopelessly less definite than a figure of 50 days or 10% deviations; its main virtue may be little more than a pleasing appearance on a legislative districting map. An even more fundamental difficulty lies in defining a "gerrymander." Every drawing of districts, even compact ones, places some voting groups and interests in a minority position and some candidates in unfriendly territory. When such placement constitutes a permissible exercise of legislative power would be a formidable, if not impossible, task for the judiciary to undertake.[142] At the very least,

---

[141] *See* Gaffney v. Cummings, 412 U.S. 735 (1973).

[142] The commentators have not, however, been similarly deterred. *See, e.g.*, Note, *Political Gerrymandering: A Statutory Compactness Standard as an Antidote for Judicial Impotence*, 41 U. CHI. L. REV. 398 (1974); Clinton, *Further Explorations in the Political Thicket: The Gerrymander and the Constitution*, 59 IOWA L. REV. 1 (1973); Edwards, *Gerrymander and "One Man, One Vote,"* 46 N.Y.U.L. REV. 879 (1971).

Much the same reasons underlie the Court's hesitancy to overturn multi-member districts in state apportionment plans, *see* Whitcomb v. Chavis, 403 U.S. 124 (1971); Kilgarlin v. Hill, 386 U.S. 120 (1967); Burns v. Richardson, 384 U.S. 73 (1966); Fortson v. Dorsey, 379 U.S. 433 (1965). The dissent in *Chavis*, in fact, contended that the problem of multi-member districts was nothing more than "whether a gerrymander can be 'constitutionally impermissible.' " 403 U.S. at 176. Where, however, the Court has found clear evidence that gerrymanders and multi-member districts have cancelled out or minimized "the voting strength of racial groups ," it has found such practices invalid. White v. Regester, 412 U.S. 755 (1973); Gomillion v. Lightfoot, 364 U.S. 339 (1960) (the disposition of *Gomillion* coming under the fifteenth amendment). The Court has further made plain that absent "particularly pressing" reasons a United States District Court should refrain from imposing multi-member districts upon a state, Chapman v. Meier, 420 U.S. 1 (1975); Connor v. Johnson, 402 U.S. 690 (1971).

The spectre of the discriminatory gerrymander may have been somewhat overdramatized. The claim of discrimination assumes what over time may prove less true: that individuals vote their racial or ethnic identity. More crucially, once an equal vote, as per *Reynolds*, has been guaranteed, it becomes more difficult for the legislature to discriminate. One must ask how significant a difference it really makes whether an ethnic vote is 60% in one district or 30% in two or whether the black vote is exercised in a single all-black district or in a member district in an at-large election. In both instances, there is the chance of political influence either as the possible majority interest in one district or as a block and possibly swing minority influence over several. Counter-balanced against such arguments, of course, is the understandable tendency of minorities to want representatives of their own races, a possibility the legislature may indeed make less likely with at-large elections.

frequent and unsettling judicial incursions into the process of politics would become necessary.

A commitment to political equality does not, therefore, presuppose indiscriminate judicial intervention into state election practice, especially where sharply etched definitions of constitutionality may be hard to come by. The old warning of the "political thicket" retains, at least in such areas as gerrymandering, some potency. Even where clarity is possible, the Court may well refrain from extreme extensions of the principles of political equality. The Court, in fact, has so far given the principle of majoritarianism, or one-man, one-vote, a circumscribed application. Limitless extension of that principle might require that states hold all legislative and congressional elections at large,[143] but no one has, as yet, seriously suggested that the states forsake, in the name of majoritarianism, the benefits of district representation.

Where, however, the Court finds that state election laws or practices seriously prejudice political equality, they should be presumptively invalid. In some instances, the results of this focus on political equality may be no different from those reached under the fundamental right—compelling state interest test, but the analytical method will be less strained. Present equal protection analysis asks whether a particular state law burdens the right to vote, in which case a compelling state interest is necessary to support it. The difficulty with so wooden a question is that virtually all of state election law, including age qualifications, location of polling places, and registration deadlines, may somehow burden the right to vote. Rather than incantation of the fundamental right—compelling state interest formula when it wishes to void state election practices, and artful avoidance of that formula when it wishes to uphold them, the Court should begin by stating its basic obligation to ensure political equality and then undertake a particularized analysis of the threat to that equality and its own competence to respond to that threat.

An instructive example of the Court's failure to approach a case with the presumption of protecting political equality may be found in *Gordon v. Lance*. That case involved a West Virginia

[143] Where legislators represent districts, the will of the minority might theoretically win out. Where a bill is defeated 51-49 in a state legislature, for example, it is entirely possible the 49 legislators collectively amassed a greater popular vote total than the 51 in the majority. Such possibilities, however, do not constitute a serious argument for at-large elections.

constitutional provision that political subdivisions "may not incur bonded indebtedness or increase tax rates beyond those established by the Constitution without the approval of 60% of the voters in a referendum election."[144] In upholding the requirement, the Court reversed the state's own supreme court, which had reasoned that

> the right to protection against the dilution or debasement of the weight or force of an individual's vote, is fully as sound, sacred and important when he is voting on issues involving taxation, public revenue and the promotion of an adequate public school system, as when he is voting for the nomination or election of a constable, a state senator, a governor or any other public official to represent the voter in government.[145]

Even more distressing than the result reached by the United States Supreme Court was its reasoning. Chief Justice Burger's brief opinion avoided the rigid fundamental right—compelling state interest formula, but its analogies were haphazard and undiscerning and illustrate well how the Court's obligation toward political equality can be evaded or overlooked:

> The Federal Constitution itself provides that a simple majority vote is insufficient on some issues; the provisions on impeachment and ratification of treaties are but two examples. Moreover, the Bill of Rights removes entire areas of legislation from the concept of majoritarian supremacy. The constitution of many States prohibit or severely limit the power of the legislature to levy new taxes or to create or increase bonded indebtedness, thereby insulating entire areas from majority control. Whether these matters of finance and taxation are to be considered as less "important" than matters of treaties, foreign policy, or impeachment of public officers is more properly left to the determination by the States and the people than to the courts operating under the broad mandate of the Fourteenth Amendment.[146]

It is true, as the Court implies, that supermajority requirements abound in American politics. There are supermajority requirements in the federal and many state constitutions to override a presidential[147] or gubernatorial veto, to impeach a President[148] or Governor,

---

[144] 403 U.S. 1, 2 (1971).
[145] Lance v. Bd. of Educ., 153 W. Va. 559, 572, 170 S.E.2d 783, 790-91 (1969).
[146] 403 U.S. at 6.
[147] U.S. CONST. art. I, § 7.
[148] *Id.* § 3.

to ratify a treaty,[149] to propose and ratify constitutional amendments,[150] to pass certain forms of substantive legislation,[151] and in the case of the United States Senate's well-known cloture rule, to bring an end to debate. But the Court's opinion lumps them together, implying that because some supermajorities are time-honored and quite legitimate, all must be.

Such is not the case. Ironically, some supermajority requirements may even protect the principle of majoritarianism, not undermine it as the West Virginia provisions in *Gordon v. Lance* clearly did. A Governor or President, elected as he is by the entire state or the nation, is the very embodiment of majoritarianism, a larger and more commanding majoritarian figure than any single legislator or even the will of the legislative majority.[152] Supermajority impeachment and veto provisions may only protect his position.

Supermajority requirements on matters of impeachment, executive veto, constitutional amendments, and cloture are also very different in kind from the provision challenged in *Gordon v. Lance*. The former are neutral modes of procedure which may at different times serve different interests and political viewpoints. Depending on the legislation at issue, it may be labor or management, consumer or producer who benefits from requiring a two-thirds vote to override an executive veto. The supermajority requirement in *Gordon v. Lance*, however, predictably and repeatedly benefits one side of a political issue. It invariably dilutes the votes of those supporting capital improvements in public services, be they schools, sewers, or highways, and invariably magnifies the votes of those opposing the higher taxes and bonded indebtedness necessary to pay for them.

Finally, the Court's analogy of the West Virginia provision to the Bill of Rights seems far afield, for the basic liberties of individual citizens in the Bill of Rights and the West Virginia tax and spending provisions are strikingly different. The former are thought endangered in the hands of the majority, while the latter are the very type of policy question the majority should decide. Moreover, the

---

[149] *Id.* art. II, § 2.
[150] *Id.* art. V.
[151] These requirements exist only in state constitutions.
[152] As stated in note 143 *supra*, a minority of state legislators on any issue may represent a larger popular vote than those in the majority.

On the federal level, the President embodies the principle of majoritarianism to a greater extent than the United States Senate.

decision had been made in West Virginia actually to submit the question of bonded indebtedness to an elective referendum, something that has hardly been contemplated for the Bill of Rights. The question is whether once the issue has been committed to a political forum it can be resolved in such anti-majoritarian fashion.

Perhaps these distinctions did not persuade the Court, but it was at the very least obliged to consider them.[153] It would be foolish to contend that constitutional principles of political equality require an end to all state supermajority laws. But here there existed a denial of political equality to voters supporting capital improvements in public services, something the Court in hazy analogy to the Bill of Rights and the impeachment process chose not to detect.

Approaching questions of state election law from the broader vantagepoint of political equality has distinct advantages over the present operation of strict scrutiny in the political realm. The question of state durational residency requirements for gubernatorial candidates may help illustrate. The Supreme Court only recently summarily affirmed lower court rulings upholding a seven year durational residency provision for gubernatorial candidates in New Hampshire[154] and a similar five year requirement in South Carolina.[155] It is difficult to speculate as to the basis of any summary affirmance, but the Court may have felt, using the two-tier model, that the fundamental right to vote was implicated in these cases only in the indirect sense that restrictions on candidates likewise affect voters,[156] or that the state's interest in assuring candidate familiarity with state problems was a "compelling" one.

The medium of the "fundamental" right to vote offers, however, too narrow a perspective from which to view this problem. What is really at stake from the broader vantagepoint of political equality is the equal right of citizens in a state to run for office, surely a basic political freedom and arguably a more important one than the right to vote.[157] As with the right to vote, some restrictions on office

[153] For two political scientists' critique of the *Gordon* decision, see Lacy & Martin, *The Extraordinary Majority: The Supreme Court's Retreat from Voting Equity*, 10 CALIF. WESTERN L. REV. 551 (1974).

[154] Chimento v. Stark . 353 F. Supp. 1211 (D.N.H.), *aff'd without opinion*, 414 U.S. 802 (1973).

[155] Kanapaux v. Ellisor, 419 U.S. 891 (1974).

[156] Certainly the fundamental right to vote was less directly implicated than in Dunn v. Blumstein, 405 U.S. 330 (1972), where the Court voided lengthy durational residency requirements as to *voters* themselves.

[157] Candidacy obviously offers the chance for far more direct and significant political action

seeking may and probably should exist,[158] but requiring seven years residency before giving someone an equal opportunity to offer his views and program by seeking high elective office seems unduly restrictive. This coupled with the inherent tendency of candidates and officeholders with longer residence to want to restrict new ones, presents a classic denial of political equality.[159] The state's interest in assuring candidate familiarity with state problems sounds legitimate enough, but it is anti-democratic. One's election opponent will most assuredly level a carpetbagger charge against too new a resident, to which the voters themselves are perfectly capable of responding.

In sum, the Court's current approach to political equality—that of applying strict scrutiny to the fundamental right to vote—seems too narrow and rigid a method of analysis. One must confess to some mystification as to why such scrutiny is applied in some cases and withheld in others, when the burden on voting rights seems much the same.[160] Further, under present equal protection analysis, voting rights are, in theory, accorded no higher constitutional preference than the fundamental right to interstate travel and the various suspect classes. But the guardianship of political equality should be the threshold equal protection obligation, for courts have few greater duties in a democracy than to ensure an equal chance to influence government to those whose lives government so intimately affects. The Court may thus begin analysis of state election law by asking, simply and straightforwardly, whether a significant measure of political equality has been denied. If it has, the practical inquiry must be whether judicial standards of sufficient coherence and specificity exist to remedy the problem.

III. Equality of Opportunity

A judicial role should exist in behalf of equality of opportunity, stronger than that for economic equality but not so affirmative as in the area of political equality. With the single exception of race, the Court's efforts on behalf of equality of opportunity have been

---

than does mere voting.

[158] Some minimum age level and some demonstration of minimum support through petition signatures are two obviously desirable restrictions.

[159] *See* p.963 *supra*.

[160] Why for example, applied in *Dunn v. Blumstein*, *supra*, and withheld in *Rosario v. Rockefeller*, *supra?*

most noted for their modesty. Opportunity in America has historically meant education, and in this regard, the present Court's sympathies may only be stiffening. *Brown v. Board of Education* is popularly remembered as a race case, but it also had important things to say about education generally:

> Today, education is perhaps the most important function of state and local governments. . . . In these days, it is doubtful that any child may reasonably be expected to suceed in life if he is denied the opportunity of an education. Such an opportunity, where the state has undertaken to provide it, is a right which must be made available to all on equal terms.[161]

Almost twenty years after *Brown*, the Court was asked to clothe this rhetoric with constitutional significance. It declined, and the chief opportunity right of education remains constitutionally a non-fundamental one.[162]

Recognition of the constitutional fundamentality of education would be the boldest step toward equality of opportunity the Court might now take. But there are other, admittedly more cautious, ways of promoting equality of opportunity, ones that the Justices have pursued. The Court has moved against state and federal laws that explicitly denied women the opportunities of men,[163] blacks the opportunities of whites,[164] illegitimate children the chances of those

---

[161] The paragraph is worth quoting in full:

> Today, education is perhaps the most important function of state and local governments. Compulsory school attendance laws and the great expenditures for education both demonstrate our recognition of the importance of education to our democratic society. It is required in the performance of our most basic public responsibilities, even service in the armed forces. It is the very foundation of good citizenship. Today it is a principal instrument in awakening the child to cultural values, in preparing him for later professional training, and in helping him to adjust normally to his environment. In these days, it is doubtful that any child may reasonably be expected to succeed in life if he is denied the opportunity of an education. Such an opportunity, where the state has undertaken to provide it, is a right which must be made available to all on equal terms.

347 U.S. at 493.

[162] San Antonio Indep. School Dist. v. Rodriguez, 411 U.S. 1 (1973). In Goss v. Lopez, 419 U.S. 565 (1975), the Court accorded a student's interest in education procedural due process protection, underscoring once again the different treatment accorded rights under the equal protection and due process clauses. *Compare, e.g.*, Dandridge v. Williams, 397 U.S. 471 (1970), *with* Goldberg v. Kelley, 397 U.S. 254 (1970) (welfare benefits).

[163] *See, e.g.*, Weinberger v. Wiesenfeld, 95 S. Ct. 1225 (1975); Frontiero v. Richardson, 411 U.S. 677 (1973); Reed v. Reed, 404 U.S. 71 (1971).

[164] *See, e.g.*, Lee v. Washington, 390 U.S. 333 (1968); Schiro v. Bynum, 375 U.S. 395 (1964);

legitimately born,[165] and aliens the opportunites of American citizens.[166] Even in this limited area, the Court's caution has been apparent. A majority of the Court has so far declined to make discrimination against women and illegitimate children, for example, fully suspect.[167] And outside of race, the Court has insisted that the challenged discrimination be a bald one. When California excluded pregnancy from disability insurance coverage, the Court found sex discrimination not involved. The fact that only women became pregnant did not matter; a finding of sex discrimination required, in the Court's view, an illness to which both sexes were subject and for which only one received coverage.[168]

A. *The Principles of Equality of Opportunity: The Suspect Class*

The Court's primary vehicle for ensuring equality of opportunity has been the suspect classification. As with the principles of political equality, the very concept of the suspect classification challenged the prevailing faith and order of the American past. Traditionally, the place of preeminence in society belonged to the wealthy, white, Anglo-American male. His preeminence was reflected in laws that designated aliens or native ethnics, illegitimates, women, or blacks as a separate and less privileged caste. The suspect classification disputed this preeminence. Henceforth, it implied, the opportunities and eventually the rewards of society must become available more on the basis of personal merit, and less on class identification.

Yet if the impulse behind the suspect classification is clear enough, the law of suspect classes is largely one of latent confusion. In the hierarchy of suspect and potentially suspect classes, there are angels and archangels, but for no readily discernable or articulated reason. Race, presumbly because of the historical purposes of the fourteenth amendment, is a super-suspect classification, even to the

Johnson v. Virginia, 373 U.S. 61 (1963); State Atheletic Comm'n v. Dorsey, 359 U.S. 533 (1959); Gayle v. Browder, 352 U.S. 903 (1956); Holmes v. City of Atlanta, 350 U.S. 879 (1955); Mayor & City Council of Baltimore v. Dawson, 350 U.S. 877 (1955); Muir v. Louisville Park Theatrical Ass'n, 347 U.S. 971 (1954); Brown v. Bd. of Educ., 347 U.S. 483 (1954). The cases after *Brown* are per curiam orders extending Brown's prohibition of racial segregation from schools to other public facilities.

[165] *See, e.g.*, Gomez v. Perez, 409 U.S. 535 (1973); Weber v. Aetna Cas. & Sur. Co., 406 U.S. 164 (1972); Levy v. Louisiana, 391 U.S. 68 (1968).

[166] *See, e.g., In re* Griffiths, 413 U.S. 717 (1973); Sugarman v. Dougall, 413 U.S. 634 (1973).

[167] *See, e.g.*, Jimenez v. Weinberger, 417 U.S. 628 (1974); Frontiero v. Richardson, 411 U.S. 677 (1973).

[168] Geduldig v. Aiello, 417 U.S. 484 (1974).

point of requiring publicly distasteful steps to redress past discrimination.[169] Alienage also has been formally ordained suspect,[170] though unlike race, one can imagine contexts in which the Court would uphold such discrimination.[171] But there are other near suspect classes that leave one in doubt as to just how heightened a level of equal protection scrutiny the Court will apply. Sex has so far been accorded much more than rational basis scrutiny[172] but denied full suspect status, perhaps because of the Court's misgivings about preempting the political struggle over the equal rights amendment.[173] And the Court, on at least four occasions, has eluded the question of the suspectness of illegitimacy,[174] perhaps because state interests in proof of paternity would be a legitimate but less than compelling interest the Court might wish to uphold. Indigency is "at least in some settings" called suspect,[175] though neither the setting nor the nature of the indigency classification has been systematically defined.[176]

The cure for such uncertainties is not a wooden approach that would treat all the various suspect classes alike. But it is ironic that the jurisprudence of suspect classes has become so finely graded in the hands of a Court that still adheres formally to no more than two levels of scrutiny.

Worse still, the Court has not defined satisfactorily the elements of a suspect class. The classic definition, first enunciated in *United States v. Carolene Products Co.* and often relied upon, is that a

---

169 *See* Swann v. Charlotte-Mecklenburg Bd. of Educ., 402 U.S. 1 (1971).

170 Graham v. Richardson, 403 U.S. 365, 372 (1971).

171 Citizenship, unlike race, would be a permissible criterion for limiting the right to vote or to hold high public office, Sugarman v. Dougall, 413 U.S. 634, 647 (1973). Citizenship would presumably be a permissible criterion of classification were a government to demonstrate, more convincingly than in *Sugarman*, that its basic security interests were at stake. On the other hand, laws limiting the right of noncitizens to use a state's natural resources, to inherit, and otherwise to acquire real property may no longer be permissible, Graham v. Richardson, 403 U.S. 365, 373-74 (1971), despite prior decisions upholding such enactments.

172 In Reed v. Reed, 404 U.S. 71, 76 (1971), for example, despite the Court's outward application of rational basis scrutiny, the state's rational interest of reducing the workload on probate courts and avoiding intrafamily controversy were rejected. *See* Gunther, *supra* note 19, at 34.

173 Frontiero v. Richardson, 411 U.S. 677, 692 (1973) (Powell, J., concurring). The opinion was joined by Chief Justice Burger and Justice Blackmun.

174 Jimenez v. Weinberger, 417 U.S. 628 (1974); Gomez v. Perez, 409 U.S. 535 (1973); Weber v. Aetna Cas. & Sur. Co., 406 U.S. 164 (1972); Levy v. Louisiana, 391 U.S. 68 (1968).

175 San Antonio Indep. School Dist. v. Rodriguez, 411 U.S. 1, 61 (1973), (Stewart, J., concurring).

176 *See* section IV *infra*.

suspect class must be a "discrete and insular minorit[y]."[177] To this classic and wholly enigmatic description, Justice Brennan's plurality opinion in *Frontiero v. Richardson*[178] suggested three further relevant factors: (1) that suspect classes suffer from "an immutable characteristic determined solely by the accident of birth," which "bears no relation to ability to perform or contribute to society;"[179] (2) that suspect classes have suffered historical vilification, as illustrated by Justice Brennan's assertion that the 19th century "position of women in our society was, in many respects, comparable to that of blacks under the pre-Civil War slave codes";[180] and (3) that the suspect class, largely because of past discrimination, lacks effective political power and redress.[181]

Superficially, these characteristics of suspectness appear helpful. In reality, however, they only disqualify some of those groups to which the Court has already accorded some measure of heightened scrutiny under the equal protection clause. Take the "immutable characteristic" criterion as an example. Blacks and women have indeed suffered discrimination stemming from their sex and skin color over which they obviously lacked control. Illegitimate children also could not help being born such, though the stigma may in some cases be cured by acknowledgment. That indigency is immutable, however, is doubtful.[182] And what of alienage? Resident aliens, of course, cannot control their country of birth, but they did voluntarily journey to the United States, and many have for some time been eligible to shed their alienage and become American citizens.

---

[177] 304 U.S. 144, 153 n.4 (1938).

[178] 411 U.S. 677 (1973). Justice Brennan sought to make sex a suspect classification in the opinion.

[179] *Id.* at 686.

[180] *Id.* at 685.

[181] The presence of this criterion is implied by footnote 17 of the opinion:

> It is true, of course, that when viewed in the abstract, women do not constitute a small and powerless minority. Nevertheless, in part because of past discrimination, women are vastly underrepresented in this Nation's decisionmaking councils. There has never been a female President, nor a female member of this Court. Not a single woman presently sits in the United States Senate, and only 14 women hold seats in the House of Representatives. And, as appellants point out, this underrepresentation is present throughout all levels of our State and Federal Government.

Id. at 686 n.17.

[182] The ultimate imponderable in the equation is, of course, whether the disadvantages of the income class into which one is born may be overcome. Even if one decides that for *most* persons they may not be, the question remains whether the immutable characteristic must obtain, as with race and sex, for every member of the class or simply for a substantial majority.

Similar questions and inconsistencies attend the other elements of suspectness. Blacks, aliens, perhaps illegitimates, may conceivably qualify as "discrete and insular minorities," if a generous connotation is given to those words. But the very designation of groups as "discrete and insular minorities" has so far been more a matter of "feel" on the part of the Court than of any rationally justifiable process.[183] The label is more emotive than analytical. Justice Rehnquist has observed that our

> society, consisting of over 200 million individuals of multitudinous origins, customs, tongues, beliefs, and cultures is, to say the least, diverse. It would hardly take extraordinary ingenuity for a lawyer to find 'insular and discrete' minorities at every turn in the road.[184]

Even this open-ended nature of the term, however, may not support the inclusion of several groups whom the Court has found suspect or near-suspect. Indigency, for example, seems too diffuse to be discrete and insular, and the female sex is not only not insular but a majority as well.

As to the criteria of historic abuse and a lack of political redress on the part of suspect classes, the Court has been less than precise. It has not, for example, defined what quantum, kind, or how recent past discrimination is required.[185] Likewise, the Court has failed to make clear what political impotence means. The right to vote apparently does not cure a condition of political powerlessness, for blacks, women, indigents, and illegitimates may all vote and yet all remain suspect or candidates for suspect status. If suspect classes are politically powerless because they lack the money to influence campaigns and elections, the Court has not intimated it, nor could it easily do so.[186] Justice Brennan in *Frontiero* impliedly equated political frailty with under-representation in public office,[187] but the

---

[183] In Graham v. Richardson, 403 U.S. 365, 372 (1971), the Court simply labelled without explanation aliens "a prime example" of the discrete and insular minority contemplated in *Carolene Products*.

[184] Sugarman v. Dougall, 413 U.S. 634, 657 (1973) (Rehnquist, J., dissenting).

[185] One wonders, for example, what, if any, historic discrimination against indigents the Court has in mind or what difference, if any , it makes that discrimination against women has been less severe than that against blacks, or that discrimination against aliens in our country has been cyclical and sporadic alternating with periods , of openness and receptivity. *See* J. HIGHAM, STRANGERS IN THE LAND (2d ed. 1965).

[186] Though indigents, for example, lack the means to influence candidates and elections, it is not clear that women and illegitimates do so.

[187] *See* note 181 *supra*.

Court has expressly rejected in another context any idea that lack of representation in public office in proportion to one's population may alone afford minorities the basis for a claim of unconstitutional discrimination.[188]

If one accepts the above criteria as determinative of suspectness, the Court must also be questioned for its sins of omission. Arguments will be made that homosexuals are, for example, a minority and quite an ingrown and insular one at that.[189] Homosexuality is a stubborn and, by much medical testimony, an immutable condition. Nor is it difficult to understand the impediments to a political solution of the problem of discrimination against homosexuals. And homosexuals are but one group seemingly encompassed by the criteria of suspectness but which the Court has thus far failed to recognize. The stated criteria of suspectness apply not implausibly to the aged, ex-felons, and the mentally ill.[190]

Even where the Court agrees that a certain group should be accorded suspect status, the analytical problems may be legion. Conferring the label "suspect" on a group may only enlarge rather than resolve the difficulties. Four Justices—Brennan, Douglas, Marshall, and White—agreed in *Frontiero v. Richardson*[191] that sex was suspect. Yet one term later, in the case of *Kahn v. Shevin*,[192] even this apparent consensus flew apart. The question in *Kahn* ostensibly was one of benign discrimination: whether Florida could provide widows but not widowers an annual $500 tax exemption. And on this, the *Frontiero* plurality splintered hopelessly. For Justice Douglas, who wrote the Court's opinion upholding the Florida law, the suspectness of sex apparently included women but not men. Justice Brennan, joined by Justice Marshall, found that *all* gender-based classifications were suspect, that the Florida classification was supported by the compelling state interest of "providing special benefits for a needy segment of society long the victim of purposeful discrimination and neglect," but that the state's compelling interest could be

---

[188] Whitcomb v. Chavis, 403 U.S. 124 (1971) rejected a claim that multi-member districts in the state legislature underrepresented minorities "because the proportion of legislators with residences in the ghetto elected from 1960 to 1968 was less than the ghetto's proportion of the population, . . . and less than the ghetto would likely have elected had the county consisted of single-member districts." *Id.* at 148.

[189] *See* Chaitlin & Lefcourt, *Is Gay Suspect?* 8 LINCOLN L. REV. 24 (1973).

[190] *See, e.g.*, Note, *Mental Illness: A Suspect Classification?* 83 YALE L.J. 1237 (1974).

[191] 411 U.S. 677 (1973).

[192] 416 U.S. 351 (1974).

served more precisely by a statute excluding from tax benefits those widows of "substantial economic means."[193] The fourth member of the *Frontiero* plurality, Justice White, took yet a different position. Like Brennan, White found the classification suspect, but unlike Brennan, thought the proper remedy to be a statutory scheme that focused on the individual needs of widow and widower alike.

The disarray in *Kahn* of the *Frontiero* plurality resulted from a factor no one bothered to address: some of the very criteria urged in *Frontiero* to make sex, or rather the female sex, suspect excluded males from similar protection. Though masculinity and feminity are both immutable characteristics, men, unlike women, had not suffered a history of discrimination, and men, unlike women, are politically well represented.[194] Whether men, or perhaps more pertinently widowers, are a discrete and insular minority is the kind of nebulous and argumentative inquiry that ends nowhere. While Justice Brennan ignored these differences in finding all "gender-based" classifications suspect, Justice Douglas apparently acknowledged them sub silentio, because the supine rational basis scrutiny employed in *Kahn* does not at all resemble the vigorous, though still nominally rational, scrutiny in *Reed v. Reed*. The overlooking in *Kahn* of the *Frontiero* criteria was unfortunate, but even a searching focus on the criteria of suspectness provides, as the next section will illustrate, a most limited perspective on the basic problem in *Kahn*, that of benign discrimination.

The suspect class is thus an unruly horse which the Court refuses to tame. The law of suspect classes has developed fine gradations on a Court which adheres, at least formally, to a two-tiered test. The criteria of suspectness have not been thoughtfully defined or consistently applied. Even as to formally suspect classes, quite divergent analysis remains possible. Chief Justice Burger has aptly captured the problem. The "code phrase" of "suspect classification," he complained, has tended "to stop analysis while appearing to suggest an analytical process."[195]

---

[193] *Id.* at 358-60.

[194] A lurking question which the Court has not addressed, is how many of the *Carolene Products* and *Frontiero* elements of suspectness must conjoin for a group to qualify for suspect status.

[195] *In re* Griffiths, 413 U.S. 717, 730 (1973) (Burger, C.J., dissenting).

B. *Justifications and Drawbacks to Judicial Promotion of Equality of Opportunity*

The presently muddled state of the law of suspect classes does not in the least argue the abandonment of greater equality of opportunity as a judicial goal. Rather, an approach must develop to equality of opportunity more sensitive and searching than the "suspect class." *Reynolds v. Sims*[196] and *Dandridge v. Williams*[197] may have, in broad brush, guided the Court to an acceptable view of political and economic inequality, but the same cannot be said of the concept of suspect classes and inequality of opportunity. This is because judicial promotion of equality of opportunity is a more subtle exercise than judicial activity in the two other areas. Voting as a fundamental right may reflect the Court's paramount obligation to support political equality and the non-fundamental status of welfare a wise reluctance to intervene in the economic arena. But inequality of opportunity simply does not fit neatly on either the higher or lower level of the two-tiered test, as the suspect class—compelling state interest formula might imply.

Equality of opportunity must first be defined. A pure equality of opportunity would place, in the words of the ancient metaphor, the runners of life at the same starting line. It seeks, to put it bluntly, conditions where native talent and industry can win out. John Rawls has fittingly described the concept:

> [W]e might say that those with similar abilities and skills should have similar life chances. . . . In all sectors of society there should be roughly equal prospects of culture and achievement for everyone similarly motivated and endowed.[198]

This is hardly a concept of equality universally accepted, nor, as Rawls himself would argue, is it even the most just one.[199] But it is the basic view of opportunity equality the Supreme Court has encouraged[200] as well as a concept with deep roots in the American

---

[196] 377 U.S. 533 (1964).

[197] 397 U.S. 471 (1970).

[198] J. Rawls, A Theory of Justice 73 (1971).

[199] "There is no more reason to permit the distribution of income and wealth to be settled by the distribution of natural assets than by historical and social fortune." *Id.* at 74.

[200] Note, for example, the opening of Justice Marshall's dissent in *Rodriguez*, 411 U.S. at 70-71: "[t]he majority's holding can only be seen as a retreat from our historic commitment to equality of educational opportunity . . . . In my judgment, the right of every American

past. It finds expression in such diverse American phenomena as Jefferson's notion of a natural aristocracy,[201] our tradition of free public education and the salutation on the Statue of Liberty. America—Land of Opportunity—beckons he who, by dint of native skill and determination, can duly struggle and succeed.

Such swollen rhetoric, however, does not begin to define the judicial role in this area or indeed whether there ought to be a judicial role in behalf of equal opportunity at all. For years, the question of equal opportunity in America was left largely to politics and, in one case, to the outcome of war. Yet modern constitutionalism now dictates a substantial judicial role in preserving equal opportunities, and the reasons for that role lie both in the Supreme Court's recent history and in the basic premises of constitutional theory.

To take the theoretical reason first: Few things are more dear to us than the opportunity to use our natural endowments and to realize our personal aspirations. These innate talents and aspirations are so much the essence of ourselves that limitations must exist on the power of government to stunt or restrict them. Opportunity rights thus protect each individual's interest in reaching his or her personal potential. Seen in this light, opportunity rights derive from the high value our society places on the individual himself. The importance of this value has led the Court to protect it through the right to privacy, for example, even when no explicit provisions of the constitution seem to protect the particular interest asserted.

Thus, using the right to privacy as its justification, the Supreme Court has protected such individual interests as the right of married couples to use contraceptives,[202] of a woman to abort her pregnancy,[203] and of an individual to possess obscene literature in his home.[204] Concern for the right to privacy has also influenced decisions such as those protecting the rights of unhappy couples to obtain divorces,[205] of unwed persons to purchase contraceptives,[206]

to an equal start in life . . . is far too vital to permit state discrimination on grounds as tenuous as those presented by this record."

[201] "There is a natural aristocracy among men. The grounds of this are virtue and talents. . . . There is, also, an artificial aristocracy, founded on wealth and birth without either virtue or talents: for with these it would belong to the first class. The natural aristocracy I consider as the most precious gift of nature for the instruction, the trusts, and government of society." 1 THE JEFFERSONIAN CYCLOPEDIA 48 (J. Foley, ed. 1967).

[202] *See* Griswold v. Connecticut, 381 U.S. 479, 484-85 (1965).

[203] *See* Roe v. Wade, 410 U.S. 113, 152-54 (1973).

[204] *See* Stanley v. Georgia, 394 U.S. 557, 564 (1969).

[205] *See* Boddie v. Connecticut, 401 U.S. 371, 374 (1971).

[206] *See* Eisenstadt v. Baird, 405 U.S. 438, 453-54 (1972).

and of convicts not to be sterilized.[207] In all of these cases, the state's interest in, for example, upholding moral standards, has fallen before the interests of the individual in living as he pleases.

While the right to privacy responds to the individual's interest in making what he wants of his life, opportunity rights respond to his interest in making the most of that life. The two are complementary aspects of self-realization. Indeed, it would be anomalous for the Court to recognize the constitutional nature of the individual's interest in flouting community regulation of properly private behavior, but to acquiesce when the state attempts to unfairly deny him opportunities, granted others, to make full use of his talents. If anything, the latter set of rights seems more compelling than the former.

Nor can it be argued that, given the importance of these rights, they are adequately protected through the political process once political equality is guaranteed. The most dangerous notion of judicial abdication would be that a guarantee of equal political rights somehow justifies abandoning opportunity rights completely to the political process, there to sink or swim. The desire for self protection from competitive pressure or simple prejudice and caste stereotyping too often tempts political majorities to restrict the right of select members of society to make fair use of their personal potential, as the sad histories of racial and sexual discrimination illustrate.

The rights that lie closest to our opportunity to take best advantage of our personal potential are education, whose function it is to develop our natural gifts and interests, and the right to seek a career commensurate with our abilities and desires.[208] While educational

---

[207] *See* Skinner v. Oklahoma *ex rel.* Williamson, 316 U.S. 535, 541-42 (1942).

[208] In the following section (IV), I argue that the Court generally ought to refrain from redressing inequalities of means and classifications that arise in the distribution of public funds. Yet it is surely true that economic deprivation may also hamper individual self-realization in a basic way. For example, a child's nutritional level may be so low as to badly handicap his educational performance. The state may not be obliged, given the state action requirement of the fourteenth amendment, to provide affirmatively for the needs of such a child, but where a state nutritional program did exist, its discriminatory application might be seen to deeply impair the ability of some non-recipients even to function in school. This kind of clearly discernible effect may present an inviduous discrimination calling for judicial intervention. *See* p. 1015 *infra*.

But the need for great caution in such intervention is apparent. *See* section IV *infra*. The relationship that efforts to redress relative economic disadvantage bear to the process of personal self-realization, whether in an educational, career, or any other sense, is often a subtle and an unfathomable one. Welfare benefits, for example, may in certain instances spark individual incentives but in other instances depress it. The effect of cumulative redistri-

and career aspirations are the most important opportunity rights, infringement on them does not exhaust the state's capacity to deny equal opportunity. Individuals may claim some right in not being unequally denied the opportunity to inherit, to recreate or, to take a mundane but important function, to drive an automobile or to use a subway.[209]

Of course, the government is not obligated to let innate potential run riot. If our natural talents and aspirations extend to a career in crime, the government is justified in obstructing them, especially since the obstruction, in the form of a criminal law, would normally fall equally on all members of society. If, however, government were to define as criminal for one group of persons a career permissible for another, an important denial of equal opportunity would be established.

If sound theoretical reasons thus exist for judicial protection of equal opportunity, certain of the Court's recent decisions further support such a role. The most striking, of course, is *Brown v. Board of Education*.[210] As *Brown* is perhaps the Court's best known and widely applauded twentieth century judicial venture, its symbolic importance cannot be overstated. The symbolism must not be trimmed solely to the question of race,[211] for *Brown* represents something far more: the beginnings of a broader American and judicial goal of personal opportunity. As the Court's creation of newer suspect classes has proceeded largely by analogy of the newer suspect classes to the disadvantages faced by blacks,[212] this broader meaning

butions of income on incentives throughout society is neither easy to predict nor easy to discern. Furthermore, as argued more fully in section IV, no judicial attempt to redress economic inequality can be launched without serious intrusion upon the fundamental mission of the legislative branch to collect and disburse public funds. Vindication of important opportunity rights, however, often can and should be accomplished short of direct interference with so important a political prerogative.

[209] This assumes that placing a reasonable fee or fare on subway service, a driver's license, or use of a public park, etc. does not create an unfair denial of opportunity. *See* section IV *infra*.

[210] 347 U.S. 483 (1954).

[211] *See* note 161 *supra*.

[212] *See* Graham v. Richardson, 403 U.S. 365, 371-72 (1971). The most explicit analogy to race came in Justice Brennan's plurality opinion in *Frontiero*: "[O]ur statute books gradually became laden with gross, stereotyped distinctions between the sexes and, indeed, throughout much of the 19th century the position of women in our society was, in many respects, comparable to that of blacks under the pre-Civil War slave codes," 411 U.S. at 685, and "sex, like race and national origin, is an immutable characteristic determined solely by the accident of birth . . . ." 411 U.S. at 686.

of *Brown* as a guarantor of equal opportunity has become gradually more apparent.

The Court thus inescapably confronts an obligation to protect equality of opportunity, but it is far from clear just how extensive the obligation ought to be. America may indeed be a land of opportunity, but it, along with every other society, is hardly a land of equal opportunity, and cumulative inequalities stretch far beyond the capacity of the judicial branch or of government generally to erase. The income and social class into which we are born and the influence of the family predetermine to a large extent our chances for personal development. Yet these and other so-called "natural" inequalities in our condition are only marginally thought the province of any branch of government, much less the judiciary, to alter.[213]

Even where inequalities of opportunity are clearly state-created,[214] courts often ought to refrain from redressing them. Many public denials of personal opportunity are not only necessary but quite fair and beneficial. This can be illustrated by a very simple example. Suppose a state has a statute that one must be sixteen years of age to acquire a driver's license. The law obviously operates to deny all those under sixteen years of age an important opportunity: that of driving a car. Further, the class denied this opportunity may contain a good many talented and capable fifteen and fourteen year old drivers. Yet the denial should easily withstand constitutional objection. To begin with, it is a temporary one, and those most disadvantaged—the capable fifteen and fourteen year olds—will escape it within a year or two. Further, the state is well justified in sparing itself the administrative inconvenience of driver-testing large numbers of fifteen and fourteen year olds to winnow out a smaller percentage of capable drivers than would be present within the sixteen year old age group. Finally, though the state might test a driver's technical competence with some accuracy,

213 The word "natural" here distinguishes these inequalities from the blatantly state-created denials of opportunity present in cases such as *Brown*. Even "natural" inequalities are not wholly beyond the capacity of government to redress, as the present graduated structure of federal income and estate taxes helps to demonstrate. But the extent to which the Court ought to use the equal protection clause to overcome natural disabilities which lead to differences in opportunities is beyond the scope of this article.

214 Often, of course, the line between "natural" and "state-created" disability is a blurred one. *See* Cox, *Foreword: Constitutional Adjudication and the Promotion of Human Rights*, 80 Harv. L. Rev. 91, 92-93 (1966).

measuring his maturity in handling a car is a more subjective and controversial step, but one without which the state might risk an unacceptable addition to the number of dangerous motorists on the road. Thus this statute and many other denials of equal opportunity pose no serious constitutional question.

Public denials of personal opportunities thus range in degree from the invidiousness of that in *Brown* to the harmless and indeed beneficial denial of opportunity to our would-be fifteen year old driver. Given the judicial obligation to equal opportunity that clearly exists, and the differences in kind and importance of different denials of opportunity, a more sensitive device than the suspect classification is needed to distinguish the permissible denials of opportunity from those that are not.

I recommend that a balancing approach be used. A balancing test has, of course, achieved greatest acceptance in first amendment free speech cases where, as here, individual interests directly confront governmental ones. The chief advantage of such an approach is its flexibility in recognizing differences in the strengths of governmental and individual interests flowing from the factual contexts of particular cases.[215] One can, for example, distinguish two claims, both asserting freedom of speech, on the ground that one involves the freedom to libel a public official while the other involves libel of a private citizen.[216] Or one can distinguish a state interest in maintaining order, as expressed through a ban on "fighting words," from that same state interest expressed through a prohibition on words which are not so "inherently inflammatory."[217]

Such an approach is less helpful in a context such as political equality, where the interest in equality is presumptively stronger than state interests asserted to deny it, and the important task is therefore to set forth rules by which judicial power should be exercised. But balancing seems ideally suited to the opportunity equality area, with its many distinctions among opportunity rights and state interests encountered in particular cases.

Though several Justices have flirted openly with balancing or sliding scale techniques in equal protection cases, the flirtation has

---

[215] Insights on the advantages of interest balancing as a tool of constitutional adjudication may be found in Gunther, *In Search of Judicial Quality on a Changing Court: The Case of Justice Powell*, 24 STAN. L. REV. 1001 (1972).

[216] *See* Rosenbloom v. Metromedia, 403 U.S. 29, 70 (1971) (Harlan, J., dissenting).

[217] *See* Street v. New York, 394 U.S. 576, 592 (1969).

been either short-lived or in a non-opportunity context. In his important *Dandridge v. Williams* dissent,[218] Justice Marshall articulated a balancing or sliding-scale equal protection approach:

> In my view, equal protection analysis of this case is not appreciably advanced by the *a priori* definition of a "right," fundamental or otherwise. Rather, concentration must be placed upon the character of the classification in question, the relative importance to individuals in the class discriminated against of the governmental benefits that they do not receive, and the asserted state interests in support of the classification.[219]

The idea of sliding scales is not per se a bad one. The deficiency of Justice Marshall's approach in *Dandridge*, an economic equality case, stemmed primarily from the context in which he propounded it. What would be appropriate where public denial of a basic personal opportunity is at stake may be wholly inapposite where the challenge is to the asserted denial of economic equality.[220] Indeed Justice Marshall, only shortly after *Dandridge* in his *Rodriquez* dissent, intimated not only the constitutional primacy of a denial of the opportunity right of education over alleged discrimination in public welfare and housing benefits, but also the closer relationship of education to the high constitutional priority given political equality.[221]

---

[218] 397 U.S. 471, 508 (1970). The Court in *Dandridge* rejected equal protection challenges to Maryland's distribution of AFDC welfare benefits.

[219] 397 U.S. 471, 520-21 (1970) (Marshall, J., dissenting).

[220] The differences and the interrelationships in these two situations are developed more fully in section IV. *See also* note 208 *supra*.

[221] 411 U.S. at 109, 110, 116 (Marshall, J., dissenting).

> I believe that the close nexus between education and our established constitutional values with respect to freedom of speech and participation in the political process makes this a different case from our prior decisions concerning discrimination affecting public welfare or housing. There can be no question that, as the majority suggests, constitutional rights may be less meaningful for someone without enough to eat or without decent housing. But the crucial difference lies in the closeness of the relationship. Whatever the severity of the impact of insufficient food or inadequate housing on a person's life, they have never been considered to bear the same direct and immediate relationship to constitutional concerns for free speech and for our political processes as education has long been recognized to bear. Perhaps, the best evidence of this fact is the unique status which has been accorded public education as the single public service nearly unanimously guaranteed in the constitutions of our States. Education, in terms of constitutional values, is much more analogous, in my judgment, to the right to vote in state elections than to public welfare or public housing. Indeed, it is not without significance that we have long recognized education as an essential step in

An overt sliding scale approach enjoyed a fleeting period of favor on the Court in *Weber v. Aetna Casualty & Surety Co.*[222] And the sliding scale formulation this time at least arguably emerged in the context of an opportunity right. In upholding the right of illegitimate children to recover workmen's compensation benefits on an equal footing with legitimate offspring,[223] the Court framed the common inquiry in all equal protection cases as "inevitably a dual one: What legitimate state interest does the classification promote? What fundamental personal rights might the classification endanger?"[224] One term later, however, the *Weber* test was jettisoned by the very Justice who had earlier propounded it. In *San Antonio Independent School District v. Rodriguez*,[225] Justice Powell, for the Court, reaffirmed two-tiered equal protection to uphold Texas' system of public school financing with its heavy reliance upon local property taxes. Yet *Rodriguez* posed precisely that denial of a basic personal opportunity in which a more sensitive constitutional inquiry was necessary.

The constitutional inquiry to test governmental denials of equal opportunity ought to weigh and to balance carefully the following elements. (1) the importance of the opportunity being unequally burdened or denied; (2) the strength of the state interest served in denying it; and (3) the character of the groups whose opportunities are denied.[226] The test is very different from the present suspect classification inquiry which focuses almost exclusively on the third element, purportedly ignores the first altogether if no suspect class is involved, and scrutinizes state interests only in two widely variant categories of rational and compelling.

The three-pronged inquiry to test denials of equal opportunity thus achieves a broader and more sensible look at all the competing

---

providing the disadvantaged with the tools necessary to achieve economic self-sufficiency.

Id. at 115 n.74.

[222] 406 U.S. 164 (1972).

[223] In one sense, of course, recovery of workmen's compensation benefits, wrongful death damages, and inheritance through intestate succession are economic in character. But they differ from the class of rights discussed in section IV *infra*, where the claim is for some direct public monetary benefit, not, as here, for recovery of funds from a private party.

[224] 406 U.S. at 173.

[225] 411 U.S. 1 (1973).

[226] In other words, the sliding scale test in Justice Marshall's *Dandridge* dissent may profitably be applied to test denials of equality of opportunity as opposed to denials of economic equality. (As to the latter, see section IV).

interests involved than an inquiry limited primarily to the suspectness of the class—surely only one element in the total problem. The crucial question, which the suspect classification inquiry ignores, is why courts should reflexively tolerate public denial to individuals of their most basic opportunity rights simply because they do not happen to comprise a suspect class. This is precisely what happened in *Rodriguez*. The Court first found no suspect class involved in the lack of equal public funding of Texas school districts. Next, it found education not to be a fundamental equal protection right on the novel theory that the Constitution had not *explicitly* guaranteed it. Rather than embracing this previously overlooked theory of constitutional explicitness,[227] the Court ought at least to have addressed the real nature of the deprivation in question. Challenged in *Rodriguez* was a system which allegedly operated to deny, on a basis unrelated to ability, vast numbers of persons the basic opportunity right to an equal education—the right most intimately related to personal potential and development. This, as we have seen, is precisely the kind of political discrimination against individuals the courts must be most alert to protect, and it was the logical point for constitutional analysis to begin.

Beginning the inquiry of *Rodriguez* with an examination of the importance of the opportunity being denied does not, however, assure a result different from that actually reached by the Court. One must still consider under element two of the test the state interests served by the Texas financing scheme and under element three the character of the group whose opportunities are being unequally burdened. One of the interests at stake in *Rodriguez* was the right of Texas to tax and spend without judicial interference, a particularly strong state interest.[228] Another closely related problem was the difficulty of judicially devising a satisfactory constitutional standard with which to supplant state and local discretion in school financing.[229] Under the third element of the test, a denial of the most basic

[227] *See* 411 U.S. at 99, 109, 110 (Marshall, J., dissenting). For a sharply critical view of the decision, *see* Richards, *Equal Opportunity and School Financing: Toward a Moral Theory of Constitutional Adjudication*, 41 U. Chi. L. Rev. 32 (1973).

[228] *See* section IV *infra*.

[229] For an example of how court interference in school financing can badly disrupt the administration of local schools, see Hamilton, School Order Brings Inequity, Washington Post, Feb. 9, 1975, at Al, col. 6. That article describes the chaos created in the Washington, D.C. public school system by a court order that, as a way of ending discrimination against poor and black children, required the school system to spend the same amount of money for

opportunity right to the poor would seem especially harsh. It is not at all clear, however, that the poor is the group whose equal educational rights suffer from school district financing relying heavily on property taxation. It is even questionable, as the Court recognized,[230] whether poor families are clustered in property-poor districts, and, in the larger sense, whether any requirement of equal funding for all school districts might not operate to deprive at least some of the poor of the level of funding they now receive. Thus, while not guaranteeing a different result in *Rodriguez*, the test in this section can at least provide a less awkward framework than two-tiered scrutiny for assessing the relevant issues.

Cleveland Board of Education v. LaFleur[231] further illustrates the potential value of the three-pronged test focusing, in part, on what kind of equal opportunity is being denied. The Court in *LaFleur* upheld the challenge of female public school teachers to mandatory maternity leave rules which required a teacher to quit her job five months before the expected birth of her child. The problem in *LaFleur* was not the result, but the Court's contortions in achieving it. Desiring to invalidate the regulations, but still unwilling to accept the consequences of declaring sex a suspect class, the Court retreated to the due process clause and the open-ended notion of irrebuttable presumptions, to the consternation of commentators[232] and Justice Rehnquist's telling dissent.[233] Justice Powell, concurring in the result, sought a different, though equally unsupportable, way out of the dilemma. He declared the maternity leave rules "invalid under rational basis standards of equal protection review,"[234] even though it is surely rational for the school board to assume a teacher

teachers' salaries for every elementary school student in the city. Both the school administration and the plaintiff in the original action are now, after innumerable difficulties and dislocations, requesting that the order be revised. Anticipating many of these problems is Kurland, *Equal Educational Opportunity: The Limits of Constitutional Jurisprudence Undefined*, 35 U. CHI. L. REV. 583 (1968).

[230] 411 U.S. at 23.

[231] 414 U.S. 632 (1974).

[232] *See* Bezanson, *Some Thoughts on the Emerging Irrebutable Presumption Doctrine*, 7 IND. L. REV. 644 (1974); Note, *The Irrebutable Presumption Doctrine in the Supreme Court*, 87 HARV. L. REV. 1534 (1974); Note, *Conclusive Presumption Doctrine: Equal Process or Due Protection?* 72 MICH. L. REV. 800 (1974).

[233] "The Court's disenchantment with 'irrebuttable presumptions' and its preference for 'individualized determination,' is in the last analysis nothing less than an attack upon the very notion of lawmaking itself." 414 U.S. at 660 (Rehnquist, J., dissenting).

[234] 414 U.S. at 653.

in the fourth or fifth month of pregnancy is more likely to have classroom performance impaired than one without child.[235]

The point is that the Court's result should have been reached comfortably under the rubric of the equal protection clause. The Court should first have focused on the kind of equal opportunity denied. The regulation burdened the opportunity of women to hold teaching jobs in public schools by requiring an extended and uncompensated leave during pregnancy and an unnecessary uncertainty of regaining employment afterwards.[236] The opportunity deprivation—affecting a woman's self-fulfillment in a career—is thus a severe one.[237] The Court would be further justified, of course, in observing that the impact of the rule falls exclusively upon a group, the female sex, that has historically lacked political representation and has been historically disadvantaged in terms of career opportunities.[238] Moreover, the rule works in a way that may bear no relationship to the fitness of an individual female teacher to perform her job. Against this, the state's primary interest—that of keeping unfit teachers out of the classroom[239]—hardly seems sufficient to salvage the regulation, especially since the interest may be served by a shorter time period or a more individualized determination of teacher fitness.[240] Much the same analysis would support the results reached by the Court in other recent career opportunity cases—*Reed v. Reed*,[241] *Frontiero v. Richardson*,[242] *In Re Griffiths*,[243]

---

[235] Justice Rehnquist, in challenging the majority opinion, implicitly replied to Justice Powell as well. "But, so far as I am aware, the medical evidence also suggests that in some cases there may be physical impairment at the stage of pregnancy fastened on by the regulations in question and that the probability of physical impairment increases as the pregnancy advances." 414 U.S. at 660.

[236] This equal protection focus on unequal burdens on employment thus differs somewhat from the Court's due process focus on freedom of personal choice in matters of marriage and family life.

[237] This, of course, is the inquiry required by element one of the test on p. 991 *supra*.

[238] Element three of the test on p. 991 *supra*, would require such an acknowledgment.

[239] The Court effectively dismisses the relevance of the state's other proffered interest—that of maintaining continuity of classroom instruction. 414 U.S. at 641-43.

[240] The interest is thus at bottom, one of administrative convenience.

[241] 404 U.S. 71 (1971). Here women were denied an equal opportunity with men to administer decedent's estates.

[242] 411 U.S. 677 (1973). Here servicewomen were not given the same chance as servicemen to claim a spouse as a dependent for the purpose of obtaining increased quarters allowances and medical benefits. Discrimination in job compensation, while not an outright denial of career opportunity, so obviously and heavily burdens that opportunity to be cognizable as such.

[243] 413 U.S. 717 (1973). Here resident aliens were prevented from practicing law.

and *Sugarman v. Dougall*[244] but without the awkward burdens of seeming compliance with two-tiered scrutiny.[245]

Not every denial of even a career opportunity would be constitutionally impermissible. State occupational licensing, whether of lawyers or candlestick makers, would normally be valid, where the licensing or examining procedure aided in ensuring honest and competent service to the public. But occupational licensing is not invariably above reproach, especially where vested interests within a profession seek to maintain a lockhold. *Kotch v. Board of River Port Pilot Commissioners*[246] is a suitable benchmark. In that case, the only persons certified to be river pilots in Louisiana were relatives and friends of the incumbents. And Justice Black, for the Court, found that "the benefits to morale and esprit de corps which family and neighborly tradition might contribute" were sufficient to uphold the "closely knit pilotage system" of Louisiana.[247]

A contemporary equal protection challenge to the system might well fail, because the rejected pilots are not members of any suspect class, nor has the Court been so bold as to resurrect a fundamental right of employment.[248] But that result hardly seem supportable. In contrast, the analysis advocated in this section would not countenance such a denial of crucial opportunity rights to poorly connected aspirants on a basis wholly unrelated to merit, and on the speculative state assertion that ingrown systems promote morale.[249]

---

[244] 413 U.S. 634 (1973). Here resident aliens were denied permanent positions in the state civil service.

[245] The three-pronged test advocated in this section offers a less forced analysis. All four cases involved the common and discredited element of a public denial of equal career and job opportunity, and to historically and politically disadvantaged groups. The varying levels of state-interests—ranging from administrative convenience in *Frontiero* to assuring loyalty within the civil service and professionalism within the bar in *Sugarman* and *Griffiths*—either lack relevance to the discrimination or sufficient strength to uphold it.

[246] 330 U.S. 552 (1947).

[247] *Id.* at 563.

[248] The right to pursue a lawful calling having been first articulated as a substantive due process right in Allgeyer v. Louisiana, 165 U.S. 578 (1897) and Lochner v. New York, 198 U.S. 45 (1905).

[249] One may speculate whether the Court's overreaction to the *Lochner* era did not bring about a significant shortchanging of the old right to pursue a lawful calling. Williamson v. Lee Optical Co., 348 U.S. 483 (1955), ought to be considered in addition to the *Kotch* case mentioned above. One central question in the case was whether opticians could fit old glasses into new frames without a prescription, something the three-judge court below had found a mechanical and nonprescriptive task. The harm to opticians of putting prospective customers to the expense of a prescription was obvious. Yet the Court upheld the statute, incanting that laws "regulatory of business and industrial conditions" were ones for the political process to

The three-pronged balancing test thus grants more flexibility to the Court than suspect classification analysis with its severe compelling state interest requirement. The balancing test, with its partial focus on equality of opportunity, may, on occasion, uphold public practices of sex differentiation where no real denial of equal opportunity is present. The simple and frequently mentioned matter of male and female restrooms may help illustrate. There may be sex discrimination or rather differentiation in separate restrooms, but, focusing on element one of the test, there is no real denial of equal opportunity, so long as the restrooms for each sex are more or less equally functional and convenient. Weightier examples likewise exist. Suppose on the campus of a public coeducational university, a new sorority or fraternity seeks the use of university space for an organizational meeting. Sororities and fraternities are, by definition, sexually discriminatory, and their use of public space might, if sex were suspect, be held to violate equal protection of the laws. The three-pronged balancing test would uphold the use of such space, however, so long as no real denial of equal opportunity were present, that is, so long as the university demonstrated equal willingness to donote space both to fraternities and sororities for their meetings.[250]

Finally, the three-pronged balancing test deals less artificially with the problem of discrimination in favor of a group, such as blacks or women, that has itself received constitutional protection from the Court. This so-called "benign" discrimination is troublesome for traditional suspect classification analysis. The very notion that the constitutional objection to a statute lies in the method, such as gender or race, by which it classifies seems to imply that it makes no difference who benefits from the classification. But if, say, the criteria used by the *Frontiero* plurality were applied to males, they would surely be excluded from the protection given women by that opinion.[251]

---

decide. Application of the test advocated by this section would, given the importance of the opportunity right being equally burdened and the apparent lack of a persuasive public health interest, have produced a different result.

[250] This in no way suggests that a regime of separate but equal will routinely pass constitutional challenge. The implications of "separate but equal" classrooms for men and women in a state-supported university are far more ominous than donating university space equally for social functions. Though separate restrooms for men and women would be permissible, racially segregated restrooms very clearly would not.

[251] *See* pp. 981-82 *supra*.

Faced in *Kahn v. Shevin*[252] with this conflict between its criteria for finding suspect classes and the seeming focus of equal protection review upon the mode of classification, both the majority and the dissent stumbled badly. The majority cited and relied upon *Reed v. Reed*, only to assume, without explanation, a deference wholly different from that of the *Reed* opinion. And Justice Brennan's dissent simply labelled "suspect" all "gender-based" classifications without addressing the distinction between male and female that the *Frontiero* criteria themselves suggested.[253]

The Court might, of course, avoid such confusion by stating that the focus of its inquiry is on the class disadvantaged and not the mode of classification employed.[254] But perhaps because it wishes to preserve the politically attractive argument that equal protection is less intrusive on the political process than the now largely discredited substantive due process, the Court has not yet adopted this method of handling benign discrimination. For the argument that equal protection is less intrusive loses credibility if it is admitted that the group favored by a method of classification determines whether the classification stands.

The three-pronged test focuses more realistically and flexibly on the problem of benign discrimination. Element three—the characteristics of the group discriminated against—allows the Court to acknowledge openly the difference in the historical disadvantages and present political posture of men and women. But such factors, though relevant, do not alone resolve the problem. Element one—the importance of the opportunity denied—tends toward disallowing denial of equal opportunities to any segment of society, whether or not the Court formally labels the group suspect. And under element two, the strength of the state's own interest in a benign discrimination must be suitably weighed. Though not

---

252 416 U.S. 351 (1974).

253 *See* pp. 981-82 *supra*.

254 *See* Ely, *The Constitutionality of Reverse Discrimination*, 41 U. Chi. L. Rev. 723 (1974). Others argue that the compelling interest test should be met no matter which group is discriminated against in a racial context, but that the state can demonstrate a compelling state interest in overcoming the disadvantages faced by blacks. *See* O'Neil, *Racial Preference and Higher Education: The Larger Context*, 60 Va. L. Rev. 925 (1974). This approach may be satisfactory in the racial context, but it is too inflexible to deal adequately with cases involving, say, discrimination in favor of women, where the state interest might not be compelling but may nevertheless be strong enough to outweigh the male's interest in equal opportunity.

ensuring a universally agreeable result, the three-pronged test, unlike current suspect class analysis, helps ensure a focus on the relevant issues.

The Court's problem in the field of equal opportunity stems from the basic defect of an equal protection analysis which fails to focus on and develop from the notion of equality itself. Traditional two-tiered analysis has failed sadly in shaping and defining a judicial role with respect to equality of opportunity. That analysis has not even addressed the central question of why and when equal opportunity must be given judicial protection. It has ignored distinctions among opportunity rights, including the special obligation of the judiciary to protect equal educational and career opportunities that are a part of each man's basic right in society to individual self-realization.[255] Finally, the Court has developed in the suspect classification a concept both highly arbitrary and badly confused. Granting that the judicial relationship to equal opportunity is a subtle and a complex matter, the analysis suggested here would at least aid substantially in assessing the relevant factors.

IV. Economic Equality

Equal protection as an antidote to economic inequality implies differing steps of varying magnitude. It may be thought to require states to distribute available welfare benefits more evenhandedly among the poor,[256] to relieve the poor from payment of selected

---

[255] One may legitimately ask whether the formulation of opportunity rights in this section, particularly career rights, do not return the Court too nearly to Justice Peckham's words in Lochner v. New York, 198 U.S. 45 (1905), where the Court struck down a New York labor law prohibiting employment in bakeries for more than 60 hours a week or 10 hours a day:

> Is this a fair, reasonable, and appropriate exercise of the police power of the State, or is it an unreasonable interference with the right of the individual to his personal liberty or to enter into those contracts in relations to labor which may seem to him appropriate or necessary for the support of himself and his family?

Id. at 56.

The differences between *Lochner* and the present analysis are important. To begin with, cases would not be approached through the medium of liberty of contract which often ended in vindicating the employer's interests, even in such contexts as minimum wage laws, where the employer's right to a particular career (as opposed to his liberty of contract) was not primarily involved. Secondly, the denials of career opportunities before the modern Court most often demonstrate discrimination against politically disadvantaged groups which the group itself has reason to deplore. Finally, such important public interests as protection of the health of bakers, as in *Lochner*, or of women, as in *Adkins*, would be accorded substantial weight under the balancing analysis proposed in this section, not readily dismissed.

[256] Shapiro v. Thompson, 394 U.S. 618 (1969).

public fees or for selected services,[257] or, in its more advanced stages, to undertake some affirmative steps to satisfy the indigent's "just wants" or most basic needs.[258] Such different constitutional obligations are often overlooked in discussions of economic inequality,[259] and the Court itself has been wavering and unclear on the potential of our Constitution to relieve poverty. The confusion, however unsatisfying analytically, has had at least the virtue of caution. A headlong charge by the Court at economic inequality would be the least defensible use of the equal protection clause.

A. *The Principles of Economic Equality*

The principles of economic equality have been slow developing. In the 1950's and 1960's, a triumvirate of cases appeared whose extravagant rhetoric appeared to herald some broad constitutional advance against inequalities of means. The first of those cases, *Griffin v. Illinois*, announced that "there can be no equal justice where the kind of trial a man gets depends on the amount of money he has,"[260] and held that states must provide indigents with a free transcript of trial proceedings, where necessary for adequate appellate review. In 1963, *Douglas v. California*[261] borrowed the *Griffin* rationale and language in requiring the appointment of counsel for indigents on their first appeal of right. The final case of the triumvirate, *Harper v. Virginia Board of Elections*, declared that "lines drawn on the basis of wealth or property, like those of race, are traditionally disfavored,"[262] and ruled state poll taxes unconstitutional.

These cases tantalized the hopes of commentators,[263] and indeed

---

[257] Boddie v. Connecticut, 401 U.S. 371 (1971).

[258] Douglas v. California, 372 U.S. 353 (1963).

[259] *See* Michelman, *Foreword: On Protecting the Poor Through the Fourteenth Amendment*, 83 HARV. L. REV. 7 (1969).

[260] 351 U.S. 12, 19 (1956). There was no majority opinion in *Griffin*. Justice Black wrote for four members of the Court, and Justice Frankfurter concurred in the judgment.

[261] 372 U.S. 353 (1963).

[262] 383 U.S. 663, 668 (1966).

[263] "The principle of [Griffin v. Illinois] . . . . will constitute a new charter of freedom for the poor." Willcox and Bloustein, *The Griffin Case—Poverty and the Fourteenth Amendment*, 43 CORNELL L.Q. 1, 26 (1957).

"The principles developed in *Griffin, Douglas,* and *Harper* have implications far beyond their narrow fact situations. The most obvious applications are within the criminal law area, but the principles might also be extended to civil litigation, education, medical care, or any area in which there is important state involvement." Note, *Discrimination Against the Poor and the Fourteenth Amendment*, 81 HARV. L. REV. 435, 446 (1967).

their principles were, in the hands of a receptive Court, capable of quite far-flung application. The Court in *Griffin-Douglas-Harper* had not moved in the manner of *Brown* against explicit de jure discrimination but against state practices whose major vice was that of treating unequals equally. Thus in *Griffin* and *Harper*, for example, the constitutional deficiency was not singling out the poor for more severe and burdensome treatment, but rather requiring poor and rich alike to pay the poll tax or purchase a trial transcript. A second stated infirmity was that "the ability to pay [transcript] costs in advance bears no rational relationship to a defendant's guilt or innocence . . . ."[264] Quite similar deficiencies may inhere, of course, in any flat public charge, whether a licensing fee, school tuition, freeway toll, criminal fine, or gasoline and sales taxes.

The constitutional shadow of *Griffin* and *Douglas* did not stop at public fees. Justice Harlan, in a well-known dissent, saw in *Douglas* an affirmative duty on the part of the State "to lift the handicap flowing from differences in economic circumstances. . . ."[265] The *Griffin-Douglas* affirmative duty to provide counsel or a transcript[266] might indeed eventuate in a public obligation to relieve through cash or the provision of services the harsher edges of poverty. It might also consign the nettlesome limitation of state action to the graveheap of outmoded doctrine.[267]

The affirmative duty overtones of *Griffin* and *Douglas* were not present in *Harper*, but something almost as far-reaching was. *Griffin* and *Douglas*, innovative as they were, still confined themselves to the circumstance of indigency. The Court gave no indication that counsel must be appointed or a free transcript provided to those who could afford them. In *Harper*, however, the poll tax was suddenly and without explanation eliminated for everyone. On the question of relative wealth as opposed to indigency classifications,

---

[264] 351 U.S. at 17-18.

[265] 372 U.S. at 362. Justice Harlan went on to argue that "[t]he state may have a moral obligation to eliminate the evils of poverty, but it is not required by the Equal Protection Clause to give to some what others can afford." *Id.* The Harlan dissent may have been somewhat overdrawn. There was at least state action in *Douglas* to the extent of compelling the defendant to go to court.

[266] The affirmative duty here differs from the use of affirmative duty in the school desegregation cases as a remedy for some past constitutional violation, *i.e.* de jure segregation.

[267] *See, e.g.*, Van Alstyne and Karst, *State Action*, 14 STAN. L. REV. 3 (1961); Silard, *A Constitutional Forecast: Demise of the State Action Limit on the Equal Protection Guarantee*, 66 COLUM. L. REV. 855 (1966); Black, *Foreword "State Action" Equal Protection, and California's Proposition* 14, 81 HARV. L. REV. 69 (1967).

as on virtually everything else, *Harper* was unclear. Did the Court mean to proclaim certain rights and services so sacred that their exercise may not be made to depend upon any monetary exaction, or that those relatively less well off could constitutionally challenge, alongside indigents, charges of particular onerousness? Or did the Court, as well as the dissents, simply overlook the significance of the step it had taken?

By the end of Chief Justice Warren's tenure, *Griffin-Douglas-Harper* had opened a plethora of unsolved constitutional questions in the area of economic inequality. By 1975, however, the questions no longer seemed quite so open-ended. The Burger Court has not occasioned outright rejection of the *Griffin-Douglas-Harper* trilogy[268] so much as the deflation of its more speculative applications. The rhetoric of those opinions now appears more the product of the generous impulses of the opinion writers than the beginnings of any broad-based assault on economic inequality.

The deflation can be briefly traced. In invalidating for indigents a sixty dollar fee necessary to bring an action for divorce, *Boddie v. Connecticut*[269] appeared to revive for a time the trilogy's skepticism toward public financial exactions, especially on court access, which indigents could not easily satisfy. Though the question was resolved in terms of Justice Harlan's favorite of due process, the language and flavor of the case was very much that of *Griffin.*[270] *Boddie,* however, was abruptly limited two years later, perhaps to divorce alone, when the Court upheld a federal $50 filing fee in voluntary bankruptcy proceedings[271] and Oregon's $25 filing fee for judicial review of administrative rulings on welfare benefits.[272]

The other burgeoning principles of economic equality in the *Griffin-Douglas-Harper* trilogy have fared little better. In finding no suspect class of indigents disadvantaged by Texas' system of public school financing, the Court in *Rodriguez* surveyed the precedents and found that the persons "discriminated against in our prior cases shared two distinguishing characteristics: *because of their impecunity they were completely unable to pay for some desired benefit*, and

---

[268] *See*, in the area of criminal procedure, Tate v. Short, 401 U.S. 395 (1971), and Williams v. Illinois, 399 U.S. 255 (1970).

[269] 401 U.S. 371 (1971).

[270] Note for example, Justice Harlan's statement that there is "no necessary connection between a litigant's assets and the seriousness of his motives in bringing suit." *Id.* at 381.

[271] United States v. Kras, 409 U.S. 434 (1973).

[272] Ortwein v. Schwab, 410 U.S. 656 (1973).

as a consequence, they sustained an absolute deprivation of a meaningful opportunity to enjoy that benefit."[273] The relative wealth aspect of *Harper* was thus disowned seven years later by a Court determined to make it, as Justice Frankfurter once said, "an isolated deviation . . . a derelict on the waters of the law."[274]

Finally, the hopes released by *Griffin* and *Douglas* for imposing on states an affirmative obligation to redress the basic needs of the poor have been dampened in the very setting in which the affirmative duty doctrine originated: that of the criminal appeal. In *Ross v. Moffitt*,[275] the Court held that *Douglas* required appointment of counsel only on the first appeal as of right and did not extend to discretionary state appeals and applications for Supreme Court review.

An even more crucial blow to affirmative duty doctrine may have come in *Dandridge v. Williams*[276] where the Court held that welfare was not a fundamental right. Ostensibly, the affirmative duty doctrine was not principally involved in *Dandridge*.[277] That case involved a challenge to a statutory scheme under which large families received less per child than small families. Whether welfare was a fundamental right in the *Dandridge* context may therefore have meant not an inherent substantive right to an adequate welfare income but only the right of children of large families to a more equitable share of what finite funds were available. Had welfare been ruled constitutionally fundamental, however, it is not difficult to foresee the right expanding from that of a more equitable share of available funds, to that of a minimally adequate and guaranteed income. At the very least, one can envision the pressures in that direction.

The deflation of the *Griffin-Douglas-Harper* trilogy is not the only evidence that the present Court's enthusiasm for a constitutional attack on economic inequalities is waning. Once plausible assertions that indigency was a suspect class or that the needs of the poor were constitutionally deserving must now be viewed more skeptically. It is true, of course, that the pleas of the poor carry great human appeal which the Court continues to emphasize in its opinions.

[273] 411 U.S. at 20. (emphasis added).
[274] Lambert v. California, 355 U.S. 225, 232 (1957) (dissenting opinion).
[275] 417 U.S. 600 (1974).
[276] 397 U.S. 471 (1970).
[277] The point is explored at greater length at pp. 1005-07 *infra*.

Shapiro v. Thompson[278] and *Memorial Hospital v. Maricopa County*,[279] for example, may seem less intent on vindicating the right to travel than on meeting the needs "necessary to basic sustenance" of a particular class of indigents.[280] But if indigency remains something of a catalyst to judicial action, it also remains less than suspect. The Court has been careful not to uphold claims of economic injustice, unless coupled with some element independently meriting heightened constitutional solicitude. Economic equality, unlike political equality, for example, does not stand on its own bottom.

Often the element coupled with the economic claim had only recently been found or reaffirmed by the Court to be of fundamental importance. Such was clearly the case in *Harper*, where the wealth classification impinged upon the right to vote, something the Court had characterized as constitutionally fundamental only two years before in *Reynolds v. Sims*. *Shapiro* and *Maricopa County*, which vindicated the claims of newly resident indigents to welfare and non-emergency hospital care, rested constitutionally on the fundamental right to travel, a right whose constitutional importance the Court had reaffirmed shortly before in *United States v. Guest*,[281] though admittedly in a different setting. *Douglas* and *Griffin* both arose in the context of the criminal appeal, something delegated to the special care and province of the Court by the spirit, if not the precise language, of the fourth, fifth, and sixth amendments.[282] *Douglas*, in fact, was announced the same day as *Gideon v. Wainwright*,[283] which afforded a sixth amendment right to counsel to indigents accused of felonies in state court.

Other successful claims of economic injustice bear only a slightly more attenuated connection to subjects independently qualifying for special judicial scrutiny. In *Department of Agriculture v. Moreno*,[284] the Court voided a congressional limitation of the food stamp program to households of related persons. The Court, per-

[278] 394 U.S. 618 (1969).

[279] 415 U.S. 250 (1974).

[280] *Id.* at 259.

[281] 383 U.S. 745 (1966). There had been, to be sure, cases long before *Guest* and *Reynolds* which had recognized the importance of voting and interstate travel rights. *See, e.g.*, Yick Wo v. Hopkins, 118 U.S. 356 (1886) (voting) and Crandall v. Nevada, 73 U.S. (6 Wall.) 35 (1867) (travel).

[282] Unlike voting and the right to travel, the right to a criminal appeal has not been explicitly desginated fundamental, though it is hard to avoid the suspicion that the Warren Court so viewed it. As for the Burger Court, see Ross v. Moffitt, 417 U.S. 600 (1974).

[283] 372 U.S. 335 (1963).

[284] 413 U.S. 528 (1973).

haps obliquely,[285] and Justice Douglas, quite overtly,[286] found the first amendment right of free association also at issue. In *Boddie v. Connecticut*,[287] as in *Griffin*, the question was access of indigents to the courts. *Boddie* was, of course, a civil divorce action, not a criminal appeal, but Justice Harlan's opinion clearly articulated the importance of the individual's interest in living his private life as he chose. Hence, the case may rest generally on the right to privacy and more specifically on the right to marry[288] and to dissolve marriage.

Where the claim of economic deprivation, however poignant, stands unsupported by some other constitutionally significant interest, the Court has found it wanting, regardless of whether the claim allegedly fell within the fundamental right or suspect classification branch of strict scrutiny. The economic rights of welfare[289] or housing,[290] the Court has stated flatly, are not, standing alone, constitutionally fundamental. The answer is little different with respect to indigency as a suspect class, though some members of the Court are not so ready to acknowledge it.[291] In *James v. Valtierra*,[292] for example, the Court upheld a California constitutional provision prohibiting the public development of low-rent housing projects unless approved by a majority of voters in a local referendum. The case could be seen as testing either the fundamentality of housing[293] or the suspectness of poverty, but the Court's opinion appeared to deal primarily with the latter. On the non-suspectness of indigency, the Court leaves little doubt.[294] Or at least Justice Marshall's dissent so implies:

---

[285] "[T]he 1971 amendment excludes from participation in the food stamp program . . . *only* those persons who are so desparately in need of aid that they cannot even afford to alter their living arrangements so as to retain their eligibility." 413 U.S. at 538. *See also id.* at 530-31 n.3.

[286] *Id.* at 541 (Douglas, J., concurring). Justice Marshall, building upon Justice Douglas' concurrence in *Moreno*, makes a similar first amendment argument in Village of Belle Terre v. Boraas, 416 U.S. 1, 17-18 (1974) (Marshall, J., dissenting).

[287] 401 U.S. 371 (1971).

[288] *See also* Loving v. Virginia, 388 U.S. 1 (1967), where the Court articulated the importance of the right to marry in invalidating a Virginia anti-miscegenation statute.

[289] Jefferson v. Hackney, 406 U.S. 535 (1972); Richardson v. Belcher, 404 U.S. 78 (1971); Dandridge v. Williams, 397 U.S. 471 (1970).

[290] Lindsey v. Normet, 405 U.S. 56 (1972).

[291] *See, e.g.*, Justice Stewart's concurrence in *Rodriguez* terming indigency suspect "at least in some settings." 411 U.S. at 61.

[292] 402 U.S. 137 (1971).

[293] It was decided before Lindsey v. Normet, 405 U.S. 56 (1972), which denied housing the status of a fundamental constitutional right.

[294] *See* 402 U.S. at 140-41.

> It [the California provision] is rather an explicit classification on the basis of poverty—a suspect classification which demands exacting judicial scrutiny . . .
>
> The Court, however, chooses to subject the article to no scrutiny whatever and treats the provision as if it contained a totally benign, technical economic classification. . . . [S]ingling out the poor to bear a burden not placed on any other class of citizen tramples the values that the Fourteenth Amendment was designed to protect . . . .[295]

The Burger Court has dealt the constitutional push for economic equality a heavy blow. But it is not dead. There is enough loose dicta, especially in the early cases, for a future Court to build upon. And there is enough ambiguity even in the Burger Court's work for economic equality still to be a live issue. The refusal of *Dandridge*, for example, to accord special constitutional status to necessities is contrary to many other phases of the Court's work in the welfare area. The due process decisions regard the denial of economic necessities and welfare of sufficient importance to require a hearing;[296] the Court has upheld AFDC welfare litigants on a wide variety of statutory claims,[297] not to mention the right to travel decisions and the *Moreno* case in which necessitous litigants have prevailed. The fact that some future Court may rekindle the embers of economic equality does not, however, make it right to do so. In fact, few things would prove more distressing.

B. *The Case Against Judicial Promotion of Economic Equality*

The argument here is not that greater equality of wealth is somehow undesirable or even unachievable, but that it is not the place of the judiciary to attempt it. As mentioned at the outset of this

[295] 402 U.S. at 144-45. This case may better be viewed as an example of a denial of political equality. The votes of most citizens for representatives entitle them to a voice in the legislature to express all their interests, while under this statute the poor must resort to the referendum process for vindication of some of their interests. They are thus denied the benefits minority interests gain from the legislative process, where votes can be traded and swapped, and are relegated to referendums in local subdivisions where none of the poor may even live.

[296] Goldberg v. Kelly, 397 U.S. 254 (1970); Sniadach v. Family Finance Corp., 395 U.S. 337 (1968).

[297] *See, e.g.*, Carleson v. Remillard, 406 U.S. 598 (1972); Townsend v. Swank, 404 U.S. 282 (1971); King v. Smith, 392 U.S. 309 (1968). *But cf.* New York State Dept. of Social Serv. v. Dublino, 413 U.S. 405 (1973); Jefferson v. Hackney, 406 U.S. 535 (1972). The statutory claims in these cases have, to say the least, afforded the Court a great latitude in interpretation.

section, the judiciary can proceed to the relief of poverty in one of three ways: by voiding public fees on the exercise of critical rights, by a more evenhanded distribution of available welfare benefits among differing groups of the poor, and, lastly, by requiring the political branch to affirmatively satisfy the basic needs of the most inpecunious.

It is largely on the latter proposition that the most provocative scholarly confrontation—that between Professors Michelman and Winter—has taken place.[298] It is not at all clear, however, that the above three methods of attacking poverty ought to be viewed any differently for purposes of the equality analysis advocated here. Some decisions seem to invoke more than one method: for example, *Griffin* illustrates both an affirmative duty to provide a transcript and the public fee principle. Further, all three prongs of the attack are income redistributive,[299] though the affirmative duty doctrine is most obviously and significantly so. Finally, it is not easy to see how the positions of the *Shapiro* majority and the *Dandridge* dissent, both of which ostensibly speak to inequalities *among* the poor in welfare distribution, can logically be prevented from encompassing an affirmative duty to provide at least minimum subsistence. If the right to travel is really at issue in *Shapiro*, can a state then be permitted to provide a general level of benefits so low as to discourage all in-migration of the poor? And do the *Dandridge* dissenters really contemplate that compliance with their position might come merely through the state's downward adjustment of a previously determined standard of need, to provide equality between large and small families, while simultaneously saving resources? Or would the state soon be under an affirmative obligation to achieve the equality by providing all children, regardless of family size, with the basic standard of need deemed necessary to subsistence?[300]

---

[298] *See* note 33 *supra*. For a recent reply to Professor Winter, see Wheeler, *In Defense of Economic Equal Protection*, 22 KAN. L. REV. 1 (1973). The most caustic view of the Burger Court's motives and reasoning in the area of economic equality is to be found in Tushnet, ". . . *And Only Wealth Will Buy You Justice"—Some Notes on the Supreme Court. 1972 Term*, 1974 WIS. L. REV. 177.

[299] This is not hard to see. After *Griffin, Douglas*, and *Boddie*, others must be taxed to support the services provided free to indigents. And the provision of free service is itself an enhancement of the recipient's income.

The principle of reallocating available benefits among the poor is by definition redistributive, not to mention the redistributive impact of providing the poor their basic needs from public revenues.

[300] Professor Winter hints strongly at the latter view. Winter, *supra* note 33, at 57.

It is just such troubling interrelationships between the three methods of attacking inequalities of means that lead to the following proposition: whenever a claim of economic inequality is principally at issue—and where there is no significant denial of political equality as in *Harper* or opportunity equality as in *Rodriguez*—the Court should reject it. Where some truly base or "invidious" discrimination is present—and most de jure discrimination against the poor, women, and blacks would fall into this category—a different result is mandated.[301] But other claims of economic injustice ought, for the good health both of the judiciary and the Republic, to be generally resisted.

Public acceptance of any significant judicial effort at reducing poverty would not, to say the least, come easy. It is hard enough for a great many Americans to accept legislative redistribution of income, not to mention one judicially engineered. One would be deaf not to hear the grumbling over "high taxes for handouts" that persists throughout much of the country. The tendency of some to disparage this attitude as mean and uncharitable will not make it disappear. While public acceptance certainly is not a predicate to judicial action, the Court can spend its good will on causes constitutionally more legitimate.

It is not enough, citing the *Slaughterhouse Cases*,[302] to argue that elimination of poverty bears precious little relevance to the historic concern of the fourteenth amendment with race discrimination. A purely historical approach to the fourteenth amendment ignores too much of the Court's own history, both recent[303] and more ancient.[304] Then, too, the arguments made previously in behalf of political

---

[301] Any invidious discrimination will be most likely to arise in the context of a plea to equalize benefits among the poor in an existing public program and almost never under the public fee or affirmative duty principle, the latter presenting a case where the legislature has not even acted, much less invidiously.

As my colleague, Professor Jerry L. Mashaw, reminds, "The history of social benefit programs reveals a consistent and highly visible tendency to stigmatize which might provide a significant basis for judicial concern." *See, e.g.*, United States Dept. of Agriculture v. Moreno, 413 U.S. 528 (1973), where the legislative history suggested a purpose to exclude "hippie communes" from the food stamp program.

[302] 83 U.S. (16 Wall.) 36 (1872).

[303] This would include at least every case, most of them Warren Court precedents, creating non-racial suspect classifications or fundamental rights. *See* section I *supra*.

[304] The more ancient history would include, of course, the substantive due process cases beginning perhaps with Lochner v. New York, 198 U.S. 45 (1905), and continuing through what some have called *Lochner*'s modern offspring, Roe v. Wade, 410 U.S. 113 (1973), and Griswold v. Connecticut, 381 U.S. 479 (1965).

equality and equality of opportunity are essentially non-historical. What can be said is that the political climate at the time of the fourteenth amendment's adoption was actually antithetical to the present constitutional brand of economic equality, and that against the backdrop of social Darwinism and laissez-faire,[305] the fourteenth amendment framers did not contemplate a judicial effort at income redistribution. There is a difference between not slavishly following an amendment's history and openly flouting it, the course that advocates of a constitutional attack on economic inequalities are obliged to take.

A different historical point—one relating to the Court's own past rather than to the history of the amendment's enactment—must also be raised against contemporary constitutional efforts in behalf of economic equality. It has been argued by commentators too numerous to mention that fundamental rights under the equal protection clause are not noticeably more neutral than, say, the old substantive due process right to contract. But the substantive due process era ought to operate as more of a caution to contemporary economic equality than to judicial protection of political equality or equality of opportunity. It was, after all, economic intervention that characterized the old *Lochner* era. Thus, present judicial efforts in behalf of *economic* equality may seem and be even more clearly a reincarnation of the *Lochner* regime than, for example, creation under the equal protection clause of a fundamental right to vote.

But, we are told in the *Dandridge* dissent, the "Court's earlier excesses" involved

> using the Constitution to protect interests that have more than enough power to protect themselves in the legislative halls. This case, involving the literally vital interests of a powerless minority—poor families without breadwinners—is far removed from the area of business regulation, as the Court concedes.[306]

The image Justice Marshall invokes—of business interests able to muscle their way through legislative halls whose doors are shut to the poor—is an appealing one. Whether it is accurate, however, is an altogether different question. *Lochner* and cases like it arose precisely because business was not getting its way, because what

[305] A good popular portrait of the period is B. Schwartz, The Law in America 117-91 (1974). *See also* Winter, *supra* note 32, at 46.

[306] Dandridge v. Williams, 397 U.S. 471, 520 (1970) (Marshall, J., dissenting).

were then thought traditional employer prerogatives were succumbing to a rising tide of social and regulatory legislation. Conversely, it may not be accurate to picture the poor as politically powerless. The legislative trend even since the New Deal has been running more and more toward social welfare programs—Social Security, Medicare, unemployment and disability compensation, AFDC benefits, food stamps, rent subsidies, to name a few ready examples—whose stated purpose is to help the poor and less well off. Indiscriminate application of Justice Marshall's *Dandridge* position, therefore, would invite the thought that the major change since *Lochner* is that the Court has switched political sides.

The point of this argument is not that the Court in interpreting the fourteenth amendment must altogether avoid judicially crafted values. In a century of Supreme Court interpretation that has already spanned *Lochner* to *Roe v. Wade*,[307] that argument probably can no longer be made with a straight face. The inquiry still relevant, however, is rather in what areas judicially fashioned values are permissible and in what areas they are not. A central understanding of Supreme Court jurisprudence, most crudely and oversimply put, is that the libertarian dimension of our society—certain precious and stated personal liberties—have been confided a more permanent identity and consigned to constitutional safekeeping, but that the character of our economic system is to be alterable by the *political* will. This seems a permissible inference from the *Carolene Products* footnote[308] as well as from those numerous statements in the Court's withdrawal period from *Lochner* that "debatable issues as respects business, economic, and social affairs" would be left "to legislative decision."[309] It is a line which *Griswold v. Connecticut* and *Roe v. Wade*, for all their vulnerability,[310] did not traverse.[311] The protection of political and opportunity equality also keeps the

---

[307] 410 U.S. 113 (1973).

[308] 304 U.S. 144, 152-53 n.4 (1938).

[309] Day-Brite Lighting, Inc. v. Missouri, 342 U.S. 421, 425 (1952). While many *Lochner*-withdrawal cases speak in terms of the regulation of business and industrial conditions as being primarily within the province of the legislature, they contain little suggestion that the constitutional calculus was to change when economic regulation affected the poor. *See, e.g.*, Williamson v. Lee Optical Co., 348 U.S. 483 (1955); Lincoln Federal Labor Union v. Northwestern Iron & Metal Co., 335 U.S. 525 (1949).

[310] *See generally* Kauper, *Penumbras, Peripheries, and Emanations, Things Fundamental and Things Forgotten: The Griswold Case*, 64 MICH. L. REV. 235 (1965), and Ely, *The Wages of Crying Wolf: A Comment on* Roe v. Wade, 82 YALE L.J. 920 (1973).

[311] Privacy, after all, is not "economic."

Court on the proper side of this understanding in a way that an attack on economic inequalities does not.

This last statement is open to legitimate challenge. One may be willing to concede that fundamental personal liberties are at stake in the right to equal political participation and in the right to self-realization through an opportunity to pursue an appropriate job and education. And I have earlier argued that career and educational opportunities involve personal rights of such importance that the Court should scrutinize their unfair denial, even though the legislation denying them may conceivably be labelled social or economic.[312] Why, then, do not modern claims of economic equality raise issues of the same character. For there must come a point at which economic equality and equality of opportunity intersect. Take the *Dandridge* case as an example. May not the denial of adequate AFDC benefits to children of large families potentially affect not only their health, but their performance in school, their fair chance for employment, and even the articulateness and persuasiveness of their political participation—the very rights protected under the previous sections?

The answer is, of course, that a denial of welfare benefits may have such effects. And where discrimination in existing public benefit programs leads most clearly to such effects, the classification may be seen as so invidious as to call for judicial intervention. But the dangers of intervention are apparent. One is that, in voiding public welfare classifications, courts engage in what is indisputably the most basic of all legislative functions—from whom and to whom to raise and distribute revenue. For the very essence of politics is often simply a matter of who gets and who pays.

Any constitutional decision, of course, may require public spending as a byproduct of compliance. The reapportionment decisions undoubtedly recalled many legislatures into special session with an attendant drain on public funds. The *LaFleur* case, by invalidating certain automatic maternity leaves for public school teachers, placed upon schools the cost of hearing claims of fitness to teach in the middle months of pregnancy. *Brown* and its progeny have entailed significant costs for public school districts in the course of converting to a unitary system. But decisions upholding claims of

[312] Examples of cases meriting such scrutiny are Cleveland Bd. of Educ. v. LaFleur, 414 U.S. 632 (1974); *In Re* Griffiths, 413 U.S. 717 (1973) and Kotch v. Bd. of River Port Pilot Comm'rs, 330 U.S. 552 (1947), all discussed in section III *supra*.

economic inequality constitute a far more exact and direct interference with the taxing and appropriations process: for example, *Shapiro* required legislatures to grant welfare to the newly resident poor precisely equal to that given long-time citizen; *Boddie* commanded complete exemption of a certain class of citizens from an otherwise generally applicable tax or fee.[313] And Professor Michelman's theory would entail a judicial directive to legislatures to appropriate sufficient funds to satisfy the "just wants" of impecunious citizens. When extended sufficiently, judicial reduction of economic disparities reduces politics almost to a nullity. It is difficult to see how one's vote means anything if it is not a broad entrustment to legislatures of the power to raise and disburse, according to the wisdom of their own priorities, the public funds.

Here, the equality focus advocated runs some risk of inconsistency. While a great many opportunity rights can be constitutionally vindicated without direct interference in the legislature's financing prerogatives,[314] I have earlier argued that education is a premier opportunity right requiring some judicial protection. Yet any protection of educational rights in the context of *Rodriguez*, for example, would entail direct judicial interference with the raising and spending of revenue and the rechanneling of public funds under judicial mandate to property-poor districts. This, of course, is the very interference in revenue distribution just condemned.

The intuitive response must be that education bears more certainly than welfare levels and adequacy of housing on the realization of one's innate gifts and potential.[315] The relationship between relative economic disadvantage and personal self-realization is extremely difficult to detect. One can appreciate this position from a utilitarian as well as an individual point of view. In protecting against unfair denial of educational opportunity as well as against unfair denial of opportunity generally, the courts can assist each individual to rise to a competitive level commensurate with his innate ability and motivation.[316] Presumably overall economic

---

[313] The consequence of the exemption being that the legislature may well have less to spend on other needs.

[314] Cleveland Bd. of Educ. v. LaFleur, 414 U.S. 632 (1974); *In Re* Griffiths, 413 U.S. 717 (1973), and Reed v. Reed, 404 U.S. 71 (1971), are excellent examples of opportunity rights being vindicated without such direct interference.

[315] This is not to say, of course, that welfare and housing have no bearing. *See* p. 1010 *supra*.

[316] Surely this is one result of In Re *Griffiths*, where the Court allowed qualified aliens to become lawyers, and in *Brown v. Bd. of Educ.* where greater educational opportunity opened

productivity will increase if individuals are not arbitrarily denied basic career or educational opportunities which on merit they can fill. With welfare, however, one cannot be so sure. It may indeed be that adequate welfare or housing assistance will also help release individual incentive, but the risk of unacceptable disincentives seems far higher than in a more purely opportunity realm. Courts simply have no reliable way to calculate whether welfare benefits ultimately encourage or diminish effort on the part of a recipient, or how much higher welfare levels and broader eligibility standards depress the incentives of other relatively disadvantaged persons to find jobs and seek training, or whether and when cumulative redistributive effects lessen the productivity of those in professional and business leadership upon whose drive and creativity the jobs and well-being of many others may depend,[317] or, finally, to what extent a general leveling of income distorts preferences toward more pleasant, but less productive jobs. Professor Winter posed the risks of judicial intervention well in pointing out that

> the elimination of poverty seems generally to have been the result, not of governmental action, but of individual members of the society making themselves more productive. It would be tragic irony to retard this successful war on poverty.[318]

Put simply, the reduction of economic inequality, by whatever means, is terribly complicated business. I profess to no more than a dim awareness of a few of the most commonly stated difficulties. They include not only an assessment of the disincentive effects, but some knowledge as to the costs of transfer of resources between rich and poor, both the bureaucratic costs and the expenses of litigation needed to make good on a claim. Added difficulties are whether redistribution might come in kind or in cash, the former presumably requiring on the part of the distributing authority some dictation as to the preferred lifestyle and spending patterns of the poor, the latter risking expenditures by indigents for "useless" ends.[319]

---

for qualified blacks.

317 Even the more ardent redistributors, Professors Rawles and Michelman, would retain those "inequalities of wealth and income . . . necessary to a system which assures to those who turn out to occupy society's least advantageous positions a better situation than they could reasonably expect under a system which distributed the net social product in equal shares." Michelman, *supra* note 33, at 15.

318 Winter, *supra* note 33, at 82.

319 "Useless," of course, only from the donor's point of view.

Unforeseen collateral consequences may attend the redistributive process, in the form of generally increased consumer demand in the case of cash redistribution, and, with redistribution in kind, accelerated demand and thus higher prices for basic commodities in the specific area of the social program.[320] Capping off this complexity is the frustration of knowing that the most benevolently intentioned programs may not work out that way.[321]

Justices and the judicial process seem manifestly unsuited to grappling with such complexities. It implies no disrespect to say that judges are not trained or very knowledgeable in the techniques of modern economics, neither are their law clerk staffs. The lawyers who argue before them are hardly dependable agents for bringing to the judge the empirical data and professional insight needed to fully understand the problems. Moreover, constitutional adjudication with its imprimatur of permanence seems a poor technique with which to approach the redress of economic inequality, where knowledge is in such a developing and conflicting state. The argument is not, however, that the political branch has mastered the intricacies of income distribution, but rather that it has more experience in the area,[322] better access to expert opinion, greater staff assistance, a broader range of relevant testimony, and, presumably, a better overview of the public finances involved and what both the economy and the public are likely to tolerate. The presumption has been, since the New Deal, that a dialogue between executive and legislature was the best way to set policies pertinent to the economy and marketplace. A subject so intricately woven as the redress of economic inequality seems the poorest possible place to reverse it. With courts we are much too likely to find, as Justice Harlan once put it, that "newly contrived constitutional rights have been established without any apparent concern for the empirical process that goes with legislative reform."[323]

---

[320] In cataloguing the difficulties of redistribution, I am much indebted to Professor Winter's admittedly "elementary" but quite useful summary on pp. 61-85 of his article. Winter, *supra* note 33, at 61-85.

[321] One might investigate at length the inhumane consequences of humanely inspired programs. The results of welfare spending on the very poor may not pinch the rich so much as the marginally poor; minimum wage laws may shut the poor, black, and young from the job market, and disincentive effects may make everyone, including the poor, worse off in an absolute sense. The remedy need not be abandonment of humane inspiration, but reform attended by caution and much hard thought.

[322] It was Congress, after all, that initiated the graduated income tax as long ago as 1913.

[323] Berger v. New York, 388 U.S. 41, 89 (1967) (Harlan, J., dissenting).

As demonstrated earlier, when dealing with the problems of political equality, courts must embody constitutional ideals in communicable form, so as not to leave the political branches wondering what was required.[324] The need would be no less in correcting economic inequality. If the redress of political inequality involves courts in the sensitive matter of election ground rules, economic equality involves the spectre of judicial interference in the equally central matter of taxing and spending.

The abrasion of relitigating legislative appropriations should surely, by any view, be minimized. Yet how could courts communicate to the legislature the bounds of constitutionality in welfare appropriations, had *Dandridge*, for example, gone the other way? Justice Marshall's dissent in the end may give little more guidance to legislatures than to make the distinctions among welfare recipients a little fairer. But with limited welfare resources and limitless needs, the fairness of the legislative classification must always be open to question. Innumerable statutory lines must perforce be drawn both as to eligibility and to levels of funding, in an effort simply to conserve meager resources and to match them to the most acute needs. Many of the lines will inevitably appear arbitrary and unkind both to those not benefited and to the courts before whom their plaintive circumstances are brought. The outlook would be for judicial supervision both endless and formless.

There is, conceivably, one way for the Court ultimately to cure the uncertainties: to fix a magic line in the welfare area of a minimum guaranteed income. This figure presumably would be the counterpart of one-man, one-vote in the reapportionment area. But the minimum income figure, no less than the pronouncement of one-man, one-vote, would not bring an end to litigation.[325] The figure would need to be revised upward from time to time with inflation and varied from place to place with the cost of living. Questions would arise as to who qualified for the subsidy and for how much, and as to why the guaranteed figure itself could not be adjusted on the basis of dependency, disability, and other needs. Presumably courts might then allow legislatures the latitude to cope with some of these problems through a variation of 10 to 20% in the magic figure, something akin to *White v. Register*[326] in the reapportionment area. Just such a scenario is not inconceivably at the end of

---

[324] *See* pp. 969-71 *supra*.

[325] *See* pp. 69-70.

[326] 412 U.S. 755 (1973).

the road of the *Dandridge* dissent, and with it a rather extraordinary displacement of democratic power with judicial.

Finally, I must caution that equality analysis may not require the rejection of claims of economic equality in cases where interests of a higher constitutional order, such as political equality in *Harper* and educational opportunity in *Rodriguez* are also present. One must be quite wary, however, of redressing opportunity rights, especially those less crucial than education, in those instances where legislative funding priorities are directly and intimately involved.[327] Take *Shapiro v. Thompson* as an example. One might analyze this case, which involved denial of welfare benefits to new state residents, in terms of an unequal denial of the opportunity right to travel and apply to the denial the balancing test suggested for opportunity rights in section III assessing in turn the importance of the right to travel the extent to which it is burdened, the fact that a segment of the poor constitute the group unequally denied the right, balanced against the state's interest in preserving a more adequate level of benefits for longtime residents. Such an analysis should, however, accord a most substantial weight to the legislative determination to concentrate its resources on improving the condition of longtime residents while achieving administrative simplicity in the distribution of welfare benefits. For discretion in the disbursing process, upon which *Shapiro* intrudes, is one of the foremost things equality analysis seeks to leave in legislative hands.[328]

---

[327] There are, to repeat, many instances of opportunity denials where funding priorities are not directly in issue. *See* notes 312-13 *supra* and accompanying text.

[328] *Shapiro* and *Maricopa County, supra*, both are suspect decisions on grounds of impermissible interference with the legislative prerogative to disburse public welfare and services, *Maricopa* would have been more justifiable had emergency as opposed to non-emergency medical care been withheld since withholding of emergency care rises close to the level of invidiousness. Ironically, Sosna v. Iowa, 419 U.S. 393 (1975), which upheld Iowa's one-year durational residency requirement for divorce, presents a better case for overturning a state durational residency test. For unlike *Shapiro* and *Maricopa County*, no direct interference with legislative distribution of public monetary benefits was involved in *Sosna* (Iowa may still require Ms. Sosna to pay her court costs); and important personal opportunity—that of readjusting the "fundamental human relationship," Boddie v. Connecticut, 401 U.S. 371, 374 (1971), was being unequally denied new residents; and the state's most telling interest, that of protecting its divorce decrees from collateral attack in a sister state, can be sufficiently protected through a good-faith determination by Iowa courts of the applicant's domicile. *See* 419 U.S. 393 at 419-20 (Marshall, J., dissenting).

Finally, Dunn v. Blumstein, 405 U.S. 330 (1972), which struck Tennessee's durational residency requirement for voting, is a most defensible decision, redressing, as it does, a serious denial of political equality.

Boddie v. Connecticut might also temptingly be viewed in the context of a denial of a basic opportunity right: that of the "adjustment of the fundamental human relationship" through divorce.[329] But the dangers of intervention suggested by equality analysis should be readily apparent. *Boddie*, unlike *Shapiro*, involved at most implicit, de facto discrimination, the voidance of which cast a constitutional shadow over pay-as-you-go financing of public services, at least those involving indigent court access. The subsequent *Kras*[330] and *Ortwein*[331] decisions, involving challenges to fees in bankruptcy proceedings and judicial review of administrative welfare rulings, illustrated fully the difficulty of applying any principled limitation to the *Boddie* doctrine.[332] Yet the absence of limitations results in a broad judicial directive to the legislature to enhance the income of one group in our society (*e.g.* indigents seeking divorce) through the provision of a free public service which others, not themselves all well off, must be taxed to provide.[333] *Boddie's* claim, carrying genuine humanitarian appeal, is nonetheless precisely the kind the judiciary must resist if it is to accord meaningful scope to the exercise of political authority.

Thus opportunity rights must on occasion be denied in the name of preserving what seems central in the exercise of political authority. If the line just drawn seems somehow harsh or arbitrary, I can do no better than to quote Professor Bork's reminder:

> Not too much should be made of the undeniable fact that there will be hard cases. . . . The question is whether the general location of the cut is justified. The existence of close cases is not a reason to refuse to draw a line and so deny majorities the power to govern in areas where their power is legitimate.[334]

That inequalities of means remain a matter of legislative wisdom is deeply argued. America has long looked most ambivalently at the

[329] 401 U.S. 371, 383 (1971).

[330] 409 U.S. 134 (1973).

[331] 410 U.S. 656 (1973).

[332] Both were 5-4 decisions with Justices Brennan, Douglas, Marshall, and Stewart dissenting, largely on the strength of the *Boddie* rationale.

[333] A similar pitfall did not lurk in *Sosna v. Iowa*, 419 U.S. 393 (1975), where the Court faced no challenge to Iowa's capacity to charge Ms. Sosna court costs.

[334] Bork, *Neutral Principles and Some First Amendment Problems*, 47 Ind. L.J. 1, 28 (1971). The quotation is not meant to imply agreement with Professor Bork's conclusions on the First Amendment.

status of poverty. Is it a state of helplessness before crushing obstacles or rather a condition escapable under the discipline of self-betterment? Does it represent indolence, disability, or a string of irreversible past hard knocks and circumstances? Is assistance "used" or squandered? Does aid promote or undermine an effort at personal improvement? Are the claims of the poor on public funds their just due or a taking of others' efforts? What, one may ask to sum it up, gives one an innate claim to public funds? The anguished and elemental philosophical difficulty of this question parallels the ambiguities in the state of poverty itself, simultaneously calling for sympathy and realism. For the judiciary to pre-empt such legitimate debate with judgment on one side—albeit the allegedly compassionate one—is to replace with self-righteous fiat an ancient dilemma that should be thought and argued out among the people themselves.

V. Conclusion

The most bewildering chapter in the recent history of the Supreme Court has been its handling of equal protection of the laws. Commentators demonstrate a growing sensitivity to flaws in two-tiered scrutiny as well as suspicion that the Court adheres to that model more in name than in fact.[335] Two-tiered scrutiny was regrettably often inflexible in its all-or-nothing approach, in its examination of only certain elements of a problem, and in its seemingly ad hoc elevation of fundamental rights and values. As equal protection doctrine, it was better suited to the impulses of a withdrawal from earlier excesses than to a period, such as the present, when the Court recognizes a multifarious duty under the equal protection clause.

Surely, then, the Supreme Court must square its results with the stated premises for achieving them. No less importantly, the Court must articulate equal protection principles more responsive to the question of its proper role in government as well as to the broader range of values present in any given case.

The Equality Analysis advocated here is rooted in the question of what courts ought and ought not to be attempting in a democratic

[335] *See, e.g.*, Gunther, *supra* note 19; Nowak, *supra* note 60; Gellhorn & Hornby, *Constitutional Limitations on Admissions Procedures and Standards—Beyond Affirmative Action*, 60 Va. L. Rev. 975 (1974).

society. The analysis draws on a search for those values which can validly be said to be protectable by the judiciary, most especially the Supreme Court. For many tough questions ahead, these thoughts are surely no more than a beginning. But the conviction is clear. An initial focus on the three dimensions of equality at issue provides the most coherent anchoring principle for a much tossed and buffeted provision of our Constitution.

A Theory of U.S. Constitutional History

CHRISTOPHER WOLFE

CONSTITUTIONAL INTERPRETATION and the role of the judiciary in American politics are often discussed as if the nature of judicial review has been fundamentally constant throughout our history. The basic thesis of this paper is that there have been two fundamentally different kinds of judicial review in American history: the first or "traditional" form, which predominated during the founding and through the Civil War period, and the second or "modern" form, which has been dominant on the Supreme Court level since 1937. (The time in between was a transitional era possessing characteristics of each.) To use the term "judicial review" without understanding that it is quite a different power in different contexts is to misunderstand American political life.

There are elements of this thesis which are very well known, by lawyers, judges and educated laymen. Thus it would come as no surprise to most political scientists that contemporary justices have a much broader leeway than earlier justices to make law.

On the whole, though, this thesis tends to run contrary to important elements of the broad prevailing views of constitutional history, which have been strongly shaped by legal realism. The Court is typically divided into eras (e.g., Marshall, Taney, post-Civil War, laissez-faire, Roosevelt, Warren, and Burger) and each era is defined in terms of the particular political bent of Court decisions vis-a-vis the salient issues of the day.

While there is much that is informative in such a view, there are certain limits to it, the most important of which is its concern only for the content of the decisions, their political causes and effects, and the political strategy involved. Such an approach assumes that the nature of judicial review is constant and that differences arise primarily from the different political purposes for which it is employed. Thus the essential change in the nature of judicial review which has occurred in American history cannot appear with any clarity in this conventional framework: neither *that* it has occurred nor *what* precisely it is.

The deficiencies of this view are in part a result of its being rooted in one of the two fundamental approaches (the modern one) and its interpreting all of U.S. constitutional history in the light of that approach. Closer attention to the approach of the founding is necessary to re-discover *its* understanding of constitutional interpretation and judicial review and to reveal that the modern approach is an *alternative* to that previous understanding.

A more accurate understanding of the nature of judicial review in U.S. constitutional history, apart from being desirable simply for its own sake, will help to put discussions of judicial review (historical, theoretical, and practical) in a much clearer perspective. For instance, it would be possible to discuss contemporary judicial review without making the mistake of thinking that it is based on Marshall's reasoning in *Marbury v. Madison*, thus forcing a clearer public elaboration of an alternative basis. Given the increased power of the judiciary in modern American political life, and given the apparently never ending debate about the proper extent of that power, such a contribution would be a valuable one for political scientists and citizens alike.

The First Approach: the Traditional View

From the founding until the later part of the nineteenth century, the Supreme Court generally operated under views of the Constitution, constitutional interpretation, and judicial review which might be called the "traditional" view. The greatest representative of this position was John Marshall, understood not as he is often portrayed in modern discussions but as he understood himself.[1] The fundamental underlying principle of this approach to the Constitution,

[1] That is, Marshall understands himself to be, not the molder of a malleable document, but the faithful interpreter of a permanent, enduring document. See my article, "John Marshall and Constitutional Law," in Sidney Pearson, ed. *The Constitutional Polity* (unpublished manuscript).

constitutional interpretation, and judicial review is fidelity to an intelligible, broad, and substantive Constitution.

Constitutional Interpretation

The kind of constitutional interpretation which dominated this period is summarized and described in Justice Joseph Story's *Commentaries on the Constitution of the United States.*[2] One chapter is particularly useful: Book III, chapter V, "Rules for interpreting the Constitution of the United States." Drawing on the *Federalist* and the great constitutional opinions of Marshall, Story elaborates a set of rules for constitutional interpretation. The 19 rules given by Story can be combined and summarized in four basic rules. First, the interpreter should start with the plain and common meaning of words, which are the best expression of the lawgiver's intention, in this case, the intention of the people, who adopted the Constitution on a "just survey" of its text. Yet words may be ambiguous, or of doubtful meaning and so recourse must be had to other rules. Thus, the second rule is that doubtful words may be clarified best by looking to the nature and design, the scope and objects of the instrument. These will be ascertained first, from the structure of the whole, and its component parts, including the "spirit" of the instrument, as collected chiefly from its letter; second, from the circumstances in which it was adopted, which were the "subject-matter" and the "causes" with a view to which it was formed; and third, from contemporary exposition, although with considerable reserve and qualification (due to the intrinsic uncertainty of the degree to which particular expositions represented the intention of the whole people), and especially from the practice of the departments of government.

The third rule, which helps to explain the second, is that the nature of the Constitution is a frame or fundamental law of government, which requires a reasonable interpretation giving to the government efficacy and force, with respect to its apparent objects. The powers of the government are to be neither narrowed, because of probable conjectures about their impropriety, or fear of abuse, nor enlarged beyond their limitations because of fear that these limitations are impolitic. The fourth and final rule is that rules of verbal criticism and particular maxims arising from the use of words

[2] Boston: Hilliard, Grey, & Co., 1833 (especially 134-162).

in practical life, shall be used to assist the interpretation of the instrument, insofar as their use stands well with the context and subject matter.[3]

Judicial Review

The conception of judicial review with which these rules of interpretation were allied is that of *Federalist* No. 78 and *Marbury v. Madison*. In the *Federalist*, Hamilton provides the framework for his discussion by comparing the three branches of government. The legislature "commands the purse (and) prescribes the rules by which the duties and rights of every citizen are to be regulated"—it is society's *will*. The executive "dispenses the honors (and) holds the sword of the community"—it is society's *force*. The judiciary has "neither FORCE nor WILL, but merely judgment." He assumes that the judiciary is the weakest of the three, ". . . so long as the judiciary remains truly distinct from both the legislature and the executive." Thus, judicial independence is necessary to support the exercise of judicial review, i.e., the duty of the courts "to declare all acts contrary to the manifest tenor of the Constitution void." Judges can determine constitutionality because "the interpretation of the laws is the proper and peculiar province of the courts" and "a constitution is, in fact, and must be regarded by the judge, as a fundamental law." Since judicial review involves only enforcement of the Constitution, it does not "suppose a superiority of the judicial to the legislative power. It only supposes that the power of the people is superior to both."[4]

An essential feature of this form of judicial review is its limited character. Judging is "truly distinct" from legislating and consists of judgment, not will. Judicial review is to declare void "all acts contrary to the *manifest* tenor of the Constitution." (emphasis added)

That judicial review was originally limited in character is difficult to believe for many today who do not have an accurate understanding of Hamilton and Marshall. The classic description and defense

[3] This section summarizes a lengthier analysis contained in my unpublished doctoral dissertation, "Constitutional Interpretation in the American Founding," (Boston College, 1978), chapter 5.

[4] See Cooke, ed. *The Federalist* (Middletown, Connecticut: Wesleyan University Press, 1961) No. 78, 522-525; *Marbury v. Madison* 1 Cranch 137 (1803).

of this form of judicial review is "The Origin and Scope of the American Doctrine of Constitutional Law" by James Bradley Thayer. In the third section, in particular, Thayer describes a "rule of administration" which has guided the exercise of judicial review: laws will not be declared void "unless the violation of the constitution is so manifest as to leave no room for reasonable doubt." He collects numerous texts from the early history of judicial review which indicate the prevailing view that it ought to be exercised only when there is a "clear" or "plain" breach of the Constitution.[5]

The limited character of traditional judicial review is clear also from the original understanding of most Americans regarding enforcement of the Bill of Rights. While modern Americans assume that the chief defense of constitutional rights is judicial power, the traditional view, e.g., during the Founding, was quite different. The primary vindicator of rights was thought to be an "aroused popular conscience" acting through elections – judicial enforcement was thought of as a less frequent and more secondary enforcement. This view is true of both Hamilton, who argued against a Bill of Rights in the *Federalist* on the grounds that security of rights "must altogether depend on public opinion," and of Jefferson, who (in a letter denying judicial supremacy) stated that he knew "no safe depository of the ultimate powers of the society but the people themselves . . . this is the true corrective of abuses of Constitutional power."[6]

I find support for this perhaps controversial conclusion in the following facts: first, the rarity of judicial review on the state level 1776-87 (no authority contends that such a power was exercised more than about a dozen times); second, the arguments of Hamilton in *Federalist* No. 84, where he says (of liberty of the press) ". . . that its security, whatever fine declarations may be inserted in any constitution respecting it, must altogether depend on public opinion, and on the general spirit of the people and the government."

Third, the failure of Madison *even to mention* the judiciary in his

[5] *Harvard Law Review* 129 (1893). I concede, however, that Thayer sometimes puts this too strongly. See, for instance, Marshall's comment in *Ogden v. Saunders*: "The plainness of the repugnancy does not change the question. That may be very clear to one intellect which is far from being so to another." 12 Wheaton 213, 339.

[6] "Aroused popular conscience" is from Justice Felix Frankfurter's dissent in *Baker v. Carr* 369 U.S. 186, 270 (1962); *Federalist* No. 84, 580; Bergh, ed. *The Writings of Thomas Jefferson* (Washington, DC: Thomas Jefferson Memorial Association, 1903) XV, 278 (Letter to Jarvis; September 28, 1820).

arguments for a bill of rights, in his letter to Jefferson of October 17, 1788, which could hardly have occurred if the primary use of the bill of rights was thought to be the judicial check it made possible; fourth, Marshall's comment in the Virginia State ratifying convention that bills of right were only "recommendatory" in relation to the legislative power.[7]

Distinguishing Features

Some of the distinguishing features of this traditional position on constitutional interpretation and judicial review are its emphasis on rules of interpretation, its search for "intelligible" standards, and the relative infrequency of judicial review.

Emphasis on Rules of Interpretation. The classic pre-Civil War cases of the Supreme Court contain frequent discussions of rules of interpretation and therefore emphasis on the meanings of words. Marshall's great constitutional decisions in particular are attentive to this task.

> It is essential to just construction, that many words which import something excessive, should be understood in a more mitigated sense—in that sense which common usage justifies. . . . This word, then, like others, is used in various senses; and, in its construction, the subject, the context, the intention of the person using them, are all to be taken into view. *(McCulloch v. Maryland)*
>
> To say that the intention of the instrument must prevail; that this intention must be collected from its words; that its words are to be understood in that sense in which they are generally used by those for whom the instrument was intended; that its provisions are neither to be restricted into insignificance, nor extended to objects not comprehended by them, nor contemplated by its framers; is to repeat what has been already said more at large, and is all that can be necessary. *(Ogden v. Saunders)*[8]

This citation could be continued at much greater length in order to show how consistently Marshall referred to rules of interpretation in his cases, a fact which must raise serious questions about the prevailing view of Marshall as fundamentally a policy-maker, unless his constitutional arguments are merely cynical after-the-fact rationalizations. The consistent appeal to rules of interpretation in

[7] On judicial review 1776-1787 see Levy, "Judicial Review, History, and Democracy," Levy, ed. *Judicial Review and the Supreme Court* (New York: Harper, 1967); *Federalist* No. 84, 580; Hunt, ed. *The Writings of James Madison* (New York: G. P. Putnam's Sons, 1904) V, 269; Marshall, comment cited by Corwin *Liberty Against Government* (Baton Rouge: LSU Press, 1948), 59.

[8] 4 Wheaton 316, 414-415 (1819); 12 Wheaton 213, 332 (1827); see "John Marshall and Constitutional Law" (fn. 1) for more extensive citations.

constitutional debates, as well as in Supreme Court cases, is testimony to the serious regard for this question in the first part of American history.[9]

It is important to note that this concern for rules of interpretation was not a narrow minded literalism, or what later came to be called "mechanical jurisprudence." The rules cited above are not those of a verbal formalism—rather they allow for broad interpretation in light of the nature of a constitution and of political affairs generally. There is a balance between emphasis on the words and emphasis on the overall subject-matter, context, and intention which avoids the naivete of interpretation by mere linguistic nicety, yet does so without permitting interpretation to lose its essential rooting in the document itself. (This is the substance of what I call "fidelity to the Constitution.")

Intelligible Standards. A second distinguishing feature of the traditional position is the search for "intelligible" standards. This idea appears in *McCulloch v. Maryland*, when Marshall says that measuring the state's power of taxation by the extent of its sovereignty provides us with "an intelligible standard, applicable to every case to which the power may be applied . . . we are not driven to the perplexing inquiry, so unfit for the judicial department, what degree of taxation is the legitimate use, and what degree may amount to abuse of the power."[10]

This marked preference for standards based on considerations of *kind* rather than *degree* is rooted in the desire for fidelity to the Constitution. Since questions of degree necessarily turn on factual, circumstantial determinations beyond the purview of the Constitution, the Constitution cannot provide guidance to the judiciary in such a form of interpretation. The Constitution *can* prescribe broad categories or *kinds* of powers (and of limits on power), leaving questions of degree to the prudential determination of the political branches which exercise a given power. So, for example, Marshall might argue that "seditious speech" as a category was suppressible—limiting judicial review to the questions, "Does a given law, as formulated, go beyond this category in its suppression?" and, "Does the utterance at issue in the case constitute seditious speech?" The questions of the circumstances of the speech and its likely ef-

[9] See "Constitutional Interpretation in the American Founding" (fn. 3), chapter 3, for a number of these non-judicial constitutional debates.

[10] 4 Wheaton 316, 429-430 (1819).

fects—which would be essential in determining the *degree* of harm caused by the speech—would be the proper province of the political branches. (Thus Marshall could uphold the *constitutionality* of the Alien & Sedition Acts, while voting in Congress for their *repeal* as unwise.)[11]

Infrequency of Judicial Review. A third distinguishing feature of the traditional view is the relative infrequency of judicial review in early American history. From 1789 until the Civil War, only two Congressional acts were struck down (in *Marbury* and *Dred Scott)* and about 36 state acts. While this observation may partly be explained by the fact that society was smaller and less complex in certain ways (technology and economics, for instance) and the fact that the 14th Amendment's extension of judicial power over state acts still lay in the future, the character of judicial review is at least an important factor. An important piece of evidence for this is the extremely limited federal case law in the area of due process, a clause which has proved enormously fruitful in producing cases in later eras.[12]

Thus, the early period of American history saw the dominance of a view of constitutional interpretation rather deeply anchored in the document itself, and a notion of judicial review which gave it a very important, but also a quite limited, place in our politics.

The Second Approach: the Modern View

The major alternative to the traditional approach to constitutional interpretation and judicial review is the modern view which had its origins in late nineteenth century developments and established itself as the dominant view on the Supreme Court in 1937. Like the traditional approach, the modern view has its own

[11] For Marshall's view see Roche, ed., *John Marshall: Major Opinions and Other Writings* (Indianapolis: Bobbs-Merrill, 1967) 29-48; for the alternative modern approach see Brandeis' concurrence elaborating the clear and present danger test (stated earlier by Holmes) in *Whitney v. California* 274 U.S. 357, 372 (1927); for a modern view in some ways closer to Marshall's see Learned Hand's opinion in *Masses Publishing Co. v. Patten* 244 Fed. 535 (1917).

[12] *Marbury v. Madison* 1 Cranch 137 (1803) and *Scott v. Sanford* 19 Howard 393 (1856); on state acts struck down, see *The Constitution* (Washington, D.C.: Legislative Reference Service, 1964), Appendix B; due process case law was more developed on the state level, but the first major due process case on the federal level was *Murray v. Hoboken Land Improvement Co.* 18 Howard 272 (1856).

characteristic understandings of constitutional interpretation and judicial review.

Constitutional Interpretation

Modern constitutional interpretation may be described as the specification of vague constitutional generalities. ("Specification" is used here in the sense of "making specific," i.e., giving a specific content to what otherwise is merely an abstract and ambiguous principle). The essential purpose of this specification of generalities is the adaptation of the Constitution to new and changing circumstances in the life of the nation. Perhaps the best statement of this approach to constitutional interpretation is found in the writings of Justices Oliver Wendell Holmes, Jr. and Benjamin Cardozo.

Holmes' classic statement on constitutional interpretation is found in *Missouri v. Holland*:

> When we are dealing with words that also are a constituent act, like the Constitution of the United States, we must realize that they have called into life a being the development of which could not have been foreseen completely by the most gifted of the begetters. . . . (Thus) the case before us must be considered in the light of our whole natural experience and not merely in the light of what was said a hundred years ago. The treaty in question does not contravene any prohibitory words in the Constitution. The only question is whether it is forbidden by some invisible radiation from the general terms of the Tenth Amendment. We must consider what this country has become in deciding what the Amendment has reserved.[13]

The emphasis in this conception of interpretation is on change (development, becoming), not "merely" what was said in the past, and it suggests the need for an interpreter who will adapt the Constitution to the new circumstances which its framers could not have completely foreseen. Holmes stresses less the adequacy of the Constitution than the need to adapt it. This idea of the need for change and development is very characteristic of Holmes and the modern approach.

The emphasis on adaptation is even clearer in Holmes' disciple, Benjamin Cardozo. In *The Nature of the Judicial Process*, generally regarded as a small classic, Cardozo describes the European school of free legal decision, with its emphasis on the discretionary power of the interpreter to seek justice and argues that

> . . . the method of free decision has become, I think, the dominant one today. The

[13] 252 U.S. 416, 433-434 (1929).

great generalities of the constitution have a content and significance that vary from age to age. The method of free decision sees through the transitory particulars and reaches what is permanent behind them. Interpretation, thus enlarged, becomes more than the ascertainment of the meaning and intent of lawmakers whose collective will has been declared. It supplements the declaration, and fills the vacant spaces, by the same processes and methods that have built up the customary law.[14]

This passage is informative because it suggests that modern adaptation of the Constitution is much broader than a more traditional idea of the Constitution's adaptability. The more traditional notion of the Constitution's adaptability is quite simple: it is that the meanings of words and the concepts they represent remain the same, but that new particulars arise which fall into the established categories. For example, the Constitution gave Congress the power to regulate certain forms of commerce and, although the "most gifted" of the framers could not have "foreseen completely" the development of trains and planes, "commerce" is a word which, without any stretching, provides a basis for regulation of trains and planes.

Moreover, Congress is given certain limited powers, but it is also given a general power "to pass all necessary and proper laws for carrying into execution" those enumerated powers. Thus, the power to raise an army is not hampered by changing technology because Congress can use modern weapons for a modern army: it can "adapt" its means to its ends.

It is in this sense that Marshall speaks in his classic, and often misunderstood, statement that the Constitution was ". . . intended to endure for ages to come, and consequently, to be adapted to the various crises of human affairs."[15] The adaptation of which he spoke was a result of the breadth or generality of the language of the Constitution and the ability of the legislature to adapt appropriate means to achieve its legitimate ends. This adaptability is intrinsic to the Constitution: it is adaptation *within* the Constitution rather than adaptation *of* the Constitution.

Now the modern notion of adaptation, as Cardozo describes it, goes beyond this more traditional formulation of "adaptability." The new understanding of adaptation is that the interpreter "sup-

[14] Cardozo, *The Nature of the Judicial Process* (Yale University Press: New Haven, 1921), 17; I use this book as a statement of the principles underlying modern judicial review because it has been so highly regarded. See, for example, Abraham, *The Judicial Process*, 3rd ed. (New York: Oxford University Press, 1975), where the author of this leading text uses Cardozo as the representative defender of judicial review, using extracts from this book.

[15] *McCulloch v. Maryland* 4 Wheaton 316, 415 (1819).

plements" the Constitution's provisions, and fills in its "vacant spaces" by the same processes and methods that have built up the "customary law" (i.e., common law, or "judge-made" law). "Supplement" suggests that there is an addition of something that was lacking and "vacant spaces" suggests an absence of substantive content, neither of which seems consistent with the traditional notion of adaptability.

Yet modern adaptation is not typically described as an effort to *change* the Constitution. It is defended as a process of giving content to certain "great generalities." Chief among these generalities are the due process clauses and (since the Warren Court) the equal protection clause. The character of these clauses is important to note, since it is connected with the changed understanding of adaptation. If "commerce" is general, nonetheless, it is a fairly limited or defined concept. The modern interpretation of the due process clause is that a person is guaranteed a reasonable degree of liberty from arbitrary government action, and likewise the equal protection clause guarantees a reasonable degree of equality of treatment.[16] "Liberty" and "equality" are much vaguer terms than "commerce" – virtually *any* law can be understood in terms of its effect on liberty and equality.

Thus it becomes possible to defend judicial review as no more than enforcement of Constitutional commands, while at the same time providing for a quite "malleable document": a container into which the desired content may be poured. The appearance of continuity can be maintained without denying judges the ability to apply modern notions of liberty and equality by filling in the content of allegedly vague generalities. Judicial review can be given a substantially new character without the necessity of what one noted commentator called "atavistic regressions to the simplicities of *Marbury v. Madison.*"[17]

Sometimes the Court is more explicit about the "adaptive" character of its decisions in civil liberties. For example, when dealing with "cruel and unusual punishment," Chief Justice Warren remarked, "The Amendment must draw its meaning from the evolv-

[16] This is shorthand for a very complex and very large body of case law on due process and equal protection, but it is an accurate expression of the basic interpretation of these clauses, however much subsequent analysis might refine notions of what is reasonable or arbitrary.

[17] "Malleable" is Cardozo's word, 170; Alexander Bickel, *The Least Dangerous Branch* (Indianapolis: Bobbs-Merrill Co., 1958), 74.

ing standards of decency that mark the progress of a maturing society." And in deciding *Brown v. Board of Education* Warren again argued, "In approaching this problem, we cannot turn the clock back to 1868, when the Amendment was adopted. . . ."[18]

Judicial Review

The adaptive character of modern constitutional interpretation points clearly to the modern character of judicial review, i.e., its *legislative* character. Holmes as usual, has ". . . summed it up in one of his flashing epigrams: 'I recognize without hesitation that judges must and do legislate, but they do so 'only interstitially.' " This view had been so well established by the time of Cardozo's classic (1921) that he could state simply at the start of his lectures, as an assumption, "I take judge-made law as one of the existing realities of life."[19]

Lest this statement be interpreted as a reference only to common law, Cardozo shortly after argues, "The work of a judge in interpreting and developing 'constitution and statute' has indeed its problems and its difficulties, but they are . . . not different in kind or measure from those besetting him in other fields." He notes that the process of filling in the gaps is "legislation" and that the yet wider freedom of adaptation in the continental school of "free legal decision" is the dominant method in constitutional law today.[20]

Thus, the judge's role is legislative not only in cases where the legislature has not acted and where past judges have made law, but also in cases where judges are overruling legislatures which have acted. The distinction is important because "judicial legislation"

[18] *Trop v. Dulles* 356 U.S. 86, 101 (1958); *Brown v. Board of Education* 347 U.S. 483, 492 (1954); moreover an examination of the original intent of the 1st Amendment [regarding which the modern Court consistently quotes the minority view of Jefferson and Madison—see e.g., Levy *Legacy of Suppression* (New York: Harper, 1963)] and of such provisions as the right to counsel [where the Court ignored almost 150 years of precedent in expanding it to a right to appointed counsel in *Johnson v. Zerbst* 304 U.S. 458 (1938)] shows clearly the "adaptive" activity of the modern Court.

For an example of the development and underpinnings of the modern view, see my "Woodrow Wilson: Interpreting the Constitution," 41 *Review of Politics* 121 (1979). A fine analysis of the modern approach from a somewhat different perspective may be found in Jacobsohn, *Pragmatism, Statesmanship, and the Supreme Court* (Ithaca: Cornell University Press, 1977).

[19] Cardozo, 69, 10.

[20] Cardozo, 18, 16-17.

which has the effect of overturning only prior judicial legislation would not modify the democratic principle of majority rule to the same extent as judicial legislation which overrules the action of democratically elected legislatures.

The legislative character of judicial review in the modern era is not defended only in terms of the relatively vague principle of adaptation. Rather the adaptation is understood in terms of particular goals which are meant to defend the democratic *bona fides* of judicial review. Judicial review is said to be useful for the protection of the integrity of the political process and the rights of minorities, and, by protecting or furthering *liberty* and *equality* in particular, it is democratic in its *purpose* or effect.

A classic expression of this argument is Eugene Rostow's "The Democratic Character of Judicial Review," which argues that the Court has properly withdrawn itself from the area of economic regulation, but that it should remain very active in protecting constitutional rights which, as Justice Jackson argued in *West Virginia v. Barnette,* depend on the outcome of no election: the right to life, liberty, property, freedoms of speech and press and of religion, etc. By protecting these important liberties from overbearing majorities the judiciary helps our political system to achieve some of its essential democratic purposes.[21]

Distinguishing Features

Some of the distinguishing features of the modern approach to constitutional interpretation and judicial review include its deemphasis on rules of interpretation, the predominance of questions of degree, and the very extensive use of judicial review.

De-emphasis on Rules of Interpretation. With respect to rules of interpretation, the most notable and revealing fact is the extremely infrequent concern for them. It is rather like Sherlock Holmes' observation to Watson in one case that he was struck by the way the dog had acted the night of the crime. To Watson's comment that the dog had done nothing, Holmes replied that *that* was the in-

[21] 66 *Harvard Law Review* 193 (1952). Recent, thoughtful attempts to elaborate a more limited basis for judicial review (but still within the framework of the modern approach) include Ely, *Democracy and Distrust: A Theory of Judicial Review* (Cambridge: Harvard University Press, 1980), and Choper, *The Supreme Court and the Political Branches: Judicial Review in the National Political Process* (Chicago: University of Chicago Press, 1980).

teresting fact! The distinctive aspect of modern discussions of rules of interpretation is . . . that they hardly exist. The underlying reason for this omission is that modern interpretation can be called interpretation only in a very weak sense of the word. If the whole purpose of interpretation and judicial review is to *adapt* a constitution to keep it from becoming outmoded and to *give content to* otherwise vague and general provisions, then such is not interpretation in the normal sense of the term. (Perhaps one could say that it is interpretation in much the same sense that a Rohrschach test would be!) Interpretation involves the ascertainment and expression of the intelligible content of some speech or writing: if there is no real content, there can be no strict interpretation.

Moreover, the absence of discussion of rules of interpretation is not, on the whole, accidental. To have a set of rules of interpretation would be to put an excessive limit on the capacity of the judiciary to *adapt* the Constitution. This is clearly deducible from the fact that some of the most important "interpretations" of the modern era are very difficult to explain as interpretations of the document.

For example, cases involving the application of the 1st Amendment to the states, many of the recent "privacy" right cases, and desegregation of D.C. schools rest on the doctrine of "substantive due process."[22] But the way to get from a provision that on its face seems to deal with procedural rights to an interpretation which outlaws "arbitrary" restraints on liberty generally is obscure, to say the very least. On a few occasions modern judges have hinted at this obscurity, although without suggesting any changes in the present status of the doctrine.[23]

Substantive due process may be defended, of course, in terms of its policy consequences (i.e., practically speaking, as a judicial constitutional amendment, and often in conjunction with an argument from "tacit consent"), or as a matter of precedent. It is difficult to defend as an interpretation of the words of the due process clause, although the most interesting fact is that apparently no one feels the need to *try* to defend it that way!

[22] *Gitlow v. New York* 268 U.S. 652 (1975); *Roe v. Wade* 410 U.S. 113 (1973); *Bolling v. Sharpe* 347 U.S. 497 (1954).

[23] Brandeis in *Whitney v. California* 274 U.S. 359, 373 (1927); Harlan in *Poe v. Ullman* 367 U.S. 497, 540 (1951); White in *Moore v. City of East Cleveland* 431 U.S. 494, 543, 544 (1977).

Even if one agreed to accept substantive due process as given, how would one explain the interpretive basis for a second doctrine, namely the "double standard" which the Court applies today, accepting review of civil liberties cases but rejecting review of economic regulation cases (or, more precisely, economic liberty cases)? McCloskey has shown brilliantly that there is no principled interpretive basis for the distinction, and little non-interpretive basis.[24]

These different Court positions are mentioned here not to oppose or favor them, but simply to point out that the main defense of them will likely be a defense based not on interpretation of the words of the Constitution, but rather on broad political grounds.[25]

The conclusion to be derived from this is that, as Thomas Grey and others have noted, judicial review is not to be understood now as "interpretive" judicial review—it is something quite different, i.e., legislation. Constitutional interpretation is not interpretation in the strict sense of the term, but rather a way of *adapting* (i.e., modifying, changing, or extending) the Constitution.

Questions of Degree. What is meant by "interpretation" in the modern sense becomes clear in the second distinguishing feature of the modern approach: the predominance of questions of *degree.* Rather than determining *kinds* or classes of government power or limits on power, modern interpretation starts with a principle which can be characterized as a general *presumption* in favor of something and leaves the application of this presumption to circumstances in the hands of the "interpreter." For instance, in the area of the First Amendment, freedom of speech is a favored, but not absolute, principle. The application of this presumption to particular circumstances is (usually) a function of the judicial application of the clear and present danger test, which requires a case by case judicial examination of the particular circumstances of a particular utter-

[24] McCloskey, "Economic Due Process: An Exhumation and Reburial," in 1962 *Supreme Court Review* 34 (note that the exhumation is articulated much more clearly than the reburial!).

[25] These observations on the non-interpretive character of judicial review in the twentieth century have also been made by some who favor the more legislative role of modern judicial review. See, for example, Thomas Grey, "Do We Have An Unwritten Constitution," 27 *Stanford Law Review* 703 (1975). Grey differs with me insofar as he contends that this form of non-interpretive judicial review has *always* been characteristic of the Supreme Court's activity. A similar analysis is contained in Chapter One of Ely's *Democracy and Distrust.*

ance. "The question," as Holmes says, "is one of proximity and degree."[26] How clear is the danger arising from this particular act? How serious? How imminent?

Perhaps the most typical form of modern interpretation and judicial review is the "balancing test," broadly understood as any weighing of conflicting interests in order to decide how to strike a balance between them.[27] Such a test requires the determination of how important the alleged government interests are; how important the individual rights impinged upon are; and the *relative* importance of these vis-a-vis each other (as well, often, as questions regarding alternative means to achieve the same ends). For example, in *Roe v. Wade* the Court balanced the right of privacy (which is said to include the mother's right to choose to have an abortion) against asserted state interests of protecting maternal health and "potential" human life and, in effect, wrote a statute based on its weighing of those factors.[28]

What guides the judge in these determinations? Whatever the guide, it cannot be the Constitution, which is held only to state a general, but not absolute, presumption. If the guide is not the Constitution, it must be the judge's own view of the interests and rights involved or, what amounts to much the same thing, some other nonconstitutional guide selected by the judge. The judge may choose to rely on precedent, perhaps even to a considerable extent, but in the final analysis adherence to precedent itself is determined by the judge's sense of whether this would further the final end of "social welfare."[29]

Frequency of Judicial Review. The third distinguishing factor is the frequent use of the power of judicial review. This point needs no proof—the frequency of judicial review in the modern era is obvious. (This is especially true of review of state acts, but it holds regarding congressional or presidential acts as well.) This is not to

[26] *Schenck v. U.S.* 249 U.S. 47, 52 (1919).

[27] This would include all varieties of compelling state interest and substantial interest tests. (It is not merely the narrower Frankfurtian balancing which *opposed* more restrictive tests, where from the start the balance was shifted toward individual rights and away from government power.) This includes not only the modern court tests in civil liberties and equality questions, but also its tests in areas such as the commerce clause (regarding state regulation) e.g., *Southern Pacific v. Arizona* 325 U.S. 761 (1945), and even the contract clause, e.g., *U.S. Trust v. New Jersey* 431 U.S. 1 (1977).

[28] *Roe v. Wade* 410 U.S. 113 (1973).

[29] See Cardozo, 150.

say that it could not have been exercised more, as some have argued that it should have been; it is only to point out that there is no comparison between the relatively infrequent exercise of the power before the Civil War and the relatively frequent exercise of the power since the late nineteenth century. While growth of population, technology, etc. explain this to some extent, one can hardly view the much expanded notion of judicial review as merely "coincidental."

The theory of U.S. constitutional history implicit in this analysis does not assume a rigid line between the eras and a monolithic character within each era. There are examples of constitutional interpretation and judicial review in the traditional era that seem more "modern" in character and examples in some areas or cases of modern constitutional law that seem more "traditional."[30]

There are also significant differences between leading figures of a given era.[31] The important point is that there is a predominant thrust of the theory and practice of an era which can be observed and described and which can be regarded as setting the tone of the era. It is this predominant thrust that is the basis for characterizing the different approaches to constitutional interpretation and judicial review in U.S. constitutional history.[32]

[30] An example of "modern" interpretation in the traditional era was the partial reliance on "principles of natural justice" apart from the Constitution as a basis for judicial review in a few cases, e.g., *Fletcher v. Peck*, 6 Cranch 87 (1810) and *Terrett v. Taylor*, 9 Cranch 45 (1815). As Thayer noted, however (fn. 5) no holding relied exclusively on this basis; moreover, the number of such cases is quite limited. An example of what looks like a more "traditional" approach in the modern era is the apparent "interpretivism" of Justice Hugo Black, e.g., *Griswold v. Connecticut* 381 U.S. 479, 522 (1965). But see my analysis of Black in a review of Dunne's *Hugo Black and the Judicial Revolution* in *The Alternative: An American Spectator* October, 1977.

[31] The differences between Marshall and Jefferson, for instance are discussed in "Constitutional Interpretation in the American Founding," (fn. 3) Chapter Three; differences between leading modern justices such as Frankfurter and Black (and others) can be seen in, e.g., *Adamson v. California* 332 U.S. 46 (1947), and in *Griswold* (preceding fn.).

[32] Space limitations preclude a discussion of the transition from the traditional to the modern form of judicial review, which is found essentially in the doctrine of economic substantive due process. The judges who used the due process clause to strike down economic regulation *understood themselves* to be simply enforcing the command of the Constitution and rejected the notion of judicial review as adapting the Constitution. See, for example, Sutherland in *Home Building and Loan v. Blaisdell* 290 U.S. 398 (1934). Yet economic substantive due process was in fact a distinctly modern form of judicial review, since it employed an allegedly vague constitutional guarantee in order to support broad judicial policy-making.

Problem Areas

It will be difficult for many to take the thesis of this paper seriously unless a few words are said to counter what will strike them as a huge hole in the hypothesis through which one might drive a judicial tank. The objection is this: the whole thesis assumes a distinction between judicial review which is faithful to the Constitution and judicial review which seeks to adapt the Constitution. But what if the due process clause, and especially the Fourteenth Amendment, do *justify* broad modern interpretation and judicial power—wouldn't that be fidelity to the Constitution?

The answer to this objection is that it reverses the true causal relationship: it argues that a changed Constitution results in changed constitutional interpretation and judicial review, whereas, in fact, it was the changed constitutional interpretation and judicial review that resulted in a changed Constitution. The assumption implicit in my argument is that the actual or original constitutional meanings of the Due Process Clause and Fourteenth Amendment are narrower than their modern interpretations. In the context of this article, I can only make a few observations to defend this assumption.

Due Process

I think that overwhelming evidence suggests that the due process clause is much narrower than its modern interpretation, and that substantial evidence suggests that its intended interpretation was quite narrow. First, the *words* of the clause seem to suggest a *procedural* content to the clause. Certainly, if the framers intended to embody in the clause a general prohibition of arbitrary legislation, they chose a rather obscure—or rather simply inappropriate—clause to do it. "No one shall be deprived of life, liberty, or property without due process of law" implies that *with* due process of law, life, liberty, and property may be taken. How can one extract a general prohibition of "arbitrary legislation" from the phrase "due process of law?" Second, the placement of the clause in the Fifth Amendment strongly suggests a narrower meaning. Is it likely that the framers intended to bury a general prohibition of arbitrary legislation in the second half of the third of four clauses of the Fifth Amendment? Even if one assumes (what I think ought to be denied) that the authors were simply inattentive to phraseology and positioning, it would be hard to imagine them being *that* inattentive! Third, the historical evidence supporting the notion of substantive due process is very weak, although not utterly nonexistent. The negative evidence is most impressive: the due process clause went through congressional approval of the Bill of Rights virtually without discussion. In an age in which judicial review was still a very controversial topic, it is unlikely that the judiciary would have been entrusted with a virtual blank check to strike down arbitrary legislation—and that the bestowing of such a trust would have gone by without objection.

While much more should be said on this topic to treat it comprehensively, these observations are reasonable grounds, I think, on which to reject the notion that the due process clause was intended to be a general prohibition of arbitrary legislation.

What does the due process clause mean then? The wording assumes that *with* due process of law, life, liberty, and property may be taken, and thus suggests that the limit is less on the legislature than on the other possible subject of its terms: the executive and the judiciary, who are responsible for enforcing the law. What the clause means is that in addition to the other specific, procedural guarantees of the Bill of Rights there is a general guarantee that each person shall have the benefit of those procedural guarantees provided for by law. This interpretation fits in well with the clause's historical antecedents (*Magna Carta*—directed against the King and his agents),[33] its wording and placement, and the limited notion of judicial review which prevailed in the founding period.

While there are suggestions before the Civil War of a broader interpretation,[34] the due process clause did not become a frequent basis of judicial review on the federal level until the very end of the nineteenth century. On the whole, then, it seems rather likely that the modern development of due process is not a development of a principle latent in the founding, but rather a fundamental modification of original constitutional principles.

The Fourteenth Amendment

The Fourteenth Amendment is a more difficult problem to deal

[33] On due process' historical meaning see Miller, "The Forest of Due Process of Law: The American Constitutional Tradition," in *Due Process*, ed. Pennock and Chapman (New York: NYU Press, 1977).

[34] *Bank of Columbia v. Okeley* 4 Wheaton 235, 244 (1819), *Scott v. Sanford* 19 Howard 393, 450 (1856), *Murray v. Hoboken Land Improvement Corporation* 18 Howard 272 (1856).

with, especially briefly. I will confine myself here to observations which suggest that a fair reading of the Fourteenth Amendment does not necessarily result in greatly expanded forms of constitutional interpretation and judicial review (which itself suggests that the principles of post-traditional eras are responsible for the choice to give it a very broad interpretation).

The essential problem of the Fourteenth Amendment is that it is a poorly written amendment, by traditional standards and by the expressed intentions of the framers of the Fourteenth Amendment themselves. Marshall's rules of interpretation assume that generally the framers of the Constitution were skilled enough to embody their intent in the language (and structure) of the Constitution with a fair degree of clarity (i.e., as much as the nature of a Constitution—intended to establish broad outlines—allows). An examination of the debates surrounding the adoption of the Fourteenth Amendment makes it fairly clear, on the other hand, that its framers were not so skilled (especially regarding section one, which is the part most relevant to our discussion).[35] Even an examination of the language itself suggests serious difficulties. Normally, draftsmen try to avoid redundancy and imprecision, but section one is clearly full of redundancy and imprecision.

With regard to historical intent, the overwhelming problem is that there were a number of "intents" to the Fourteenth Amendment, which cannot be fully reconciled with each other and the language of the Amendment. It is clear that the intent of the Fourteenth Amendment was to deal with post-Civil War problems, above all ". . . the protection of the newly-made freeman and citizen from the oppressions of those who had formerly exercised unlimited dominion over him" (*Slaughterhouse Cases*). The language is broader (i.e., does not specifically refer to blacks) because there might be some whites, allies of the new freedmen, subject to oppression on fundamentally racial grounds, and also needing protection. The breadth of provisions also is a result of the fact that the author of section one wanted primarily a constitutional provision which would provide an incontrovertible basis for the constitutionality of a congressional Civil Rights Act intended to help blacks in the South.[36]

[35] See for example Fairman, "Does the Fourteenth Amendment Incorporate the Bill of Rights?" *Stanford Law Review* 1 (1949), 30-31, 53-54, 66, 138; and Berger, *Government By Judiciary* (Cambridge: Harvard University Press, 1977), 145.

[36] *Slaughterhouse Cases* 16 Wall 36, 71 (1873); see Fairman, 138 (on "privileges and immunities," but it applies to the entire section 1 of the Fourteenth Amendment, I

The understanding of the Congress which passed the Fourteenth Amendment was that the impact of the Amendment would be almost entirely on the South. On many occasions defenders of the Amendment denied the repeated charges of their opponents that the Amendment would bring about a fundamental change in the nature of American federalism. The debate in both Congress and the state legislatures which ratified the Amendment focused almost entirely on its effect in the South.[37]

These intents are not fully compatible with each other and with the words. The words of section one are very broad, although the other sections of the Amendment (two, three and four) put them in a post-Civil War context. The focus on helping blacks (and whites sympathetic to blacks) in the South suggests a narrower overall intent (although it may suggest broad power in that limited, racial context), and this is confirmed by denials that the Amendment will bring about fundamental changes in federalism.

What is one to do with such a confused set of intents? Miller, in the *Slaughterhouse Cases* came to the conclusion that the Amendment ought to be construed in such a way as to avoid a revolution in American constitutional principles, given the absence of any clear indication that this revolution was intended. On the whole, this position seems to be the best available interpretation, provided that a corollary to it be that cases involving *racial* discrimination (the clearest intent of the Amendment) employ a somewhat broader understanding of the Amendment. This position is elaborated by Justice Rehnquist (in the context of a discussion of the equal protection clause) in his dissent in *Trimble v. Gordon*: employ strict scrutiny for those cases involving racial discrimination, and a generally deferential standard of review in other cases.[38]

The Supreme Court adopted this narrowing line in the *Slaughterhouse Cases,* and other immediately post-14th Amendment ratification cases. *Davidson v. New Orleans* in particular condemns the "strange misconception" whereby the 14th Amendment ". . . is looked upon as a means of bringing to the test of the decision of this court the abstract opinions of every unsuccessful

believe): "If one seeks some inclusive and exclusive definition, such that one could say, this is precisely what they had in mind – pretty clearly there never was any such clear conception."

[37] Fairman, 28, 32, 63, 84; Berger, 17-18.

[38] *Trimble v. Gordon* (Rehnquist dissent) 430 U.S. 762, 777 (1977).

litigant in a State court of the justice of the decision against him, and of the merits of the legislation on which such a decision may be founded."[39]

Besides the unintended consequence of radically altering the nature of American federalism, another constitutional revolution inadvertently arose from the failure to draft the 14th Amendment precisely. This radical change was the role of the judiciary in American politics which has been the subject of this essay. The phrasing of section one in terms of general principle rather than as a power of Congress (dealt with separately by section five) made it possible for judges to assert their power as guarantors of those rights, understood as they understood them, and thus provided a necessary (though not sufficient) condition for the radical expansion of judicial power discussed at length by Raoul Berger's *Government by Judiciary: The Transformation of the Fourteenth Amendment.*[40]

Justifying "accidental" constitutional revolutions on the basis of generally democratic principles is problematic, unless one employs a doctrine of judicial amendment (united perhaps with the doctrine of tacit consent). But this is precisely the rationale for modern constitutional "interpretation" and judicial review. The line of causation is not from the Fourteenth Amendment (cause) to modern judicial review (effect), but rather from the principles of modern judicial review (cause) to the expanded notion of the Fourteenth Amendment (effect).

Implications

The analysis of judicial review in U.S. constitutional history elaborated in this paper has some important implications for our understanding of constitutional interpretation and judicial review. First, it suggests that the normal distinction between narrow or strict construction and broad or loose construction may be somewhat inaccurate. The distinction should be three-fold: narrow, broad, and loose construction. Narrow construction would be the term aptly describing the approach to constitutional interpretation adopted by Jefferson in the founding period; he argued (in a

[39] 96 U.S. 97, 104 (1878).

[40] While Berger's analysis is often revealing and would support certain parts of the theory of constitutional history elaborated in this article, there are serious differences as well. See for instance the review by John Burleigh in *The Public Interest* No. 50 (Winter, 1978).

controversy over the Treaty power): "In every event I would rather construe so narrowly as to oblige the nation to amend; and thus declare what powers they would agree to yield, than too broadly and indeed so broadly as to enable the Executive and Senate to do things which the Constitution forbids."[41] When in doubt Jefferson chose the "safe" construction, by which he meant the construction that narrowed the powers of government rather than interpreting them broadly.[42]

"Broad" construction would be the approach advocated by Marshall, which was the most influential view during the traditional era of constitutional interpretation. This broad construction was, in fact, viewed by its advocates as strict construction, i.e., the approach to interpretation which most faithfully attended to the meaning and implications of the document and its intent. Marshall's indirect references to Jefferson, Spencer Roane, and others' narrow interpretation are critical of them on the ground that such interpretation results in destroying the Constitution, making it useless, by imposing on it views which are not compatible with it.[43]

"Loose" construction would seem to be a term more accurately describing the modern approach to interpretation, since it implies that strict adherence to the document is not the fundamental aim. It emphasizes the "play in the joints" which allows for legislation by judges in the "interstices" of the law (though the word "interstices" does not properly indicate the *magnitude* of such judicial power in the area of constitutional interpretation). Because the provisions of the Constitution are "great generalities" which need to be given specific content by judicial interpretation, the link between the Constitution and the opinion need not be as close—the tie can be much more "loose."[44]

The essential point in this three-fold categorization of construction or interpretation is that between narrow construction on the one hand and loose construction on the other, there is a category which is both broad and at the same time "strict," i.e., concerned primarily with fidelity to a document which is intelligible and substantive.

[41] Jefferson, *Writings* I, 408; the reasoning of the quote is circular, it should be noted.

[42] Ibid. at X, 418-419.

[43] See especially the reference in *Gibbons v. Ogden* 9 Wheaton 1, 222 (1825).

[44] "Play in the joints" is from Holmes' opinion in *Bain Peanut Co. v. Pinson* 282 U.S. 499, 501 (1930); "interstices" is used by Holmes and especially by Cardozo, 69, 103, 114; "great generalities" is from Cardozo, 17.

A second implication is that there are two essentially different kinds of judicial self-restraint. One is a notion that the judges are limited by the *Constitution*: the only legitimate basis for judicial review is a violation of the Constitution, because judicial review is understood as a resolution of the conflict between an ordinary act and an extraordinary act, between a legislative statute or executive act and a "supreme law." The traditional approach exemplifies this form of self-restraint, which is really a judicial recognition of restraints implicit in the Constitution itself.

The more modern form of self-restraint is essentially a *discretionary* act. Judges *could* act, because judicial review has a much broader foundation: judges can strike down any arbitrary deprivations of liberty and equality under the due process or equal protection clauses, and this power makes it possible (*in principle*) to find objections to almost any law (since virtually all laws can be classified in some way as a restraint on liberty or a denial of equality). Self-restraint in this context is the exercise of a discretionary power not to strike down an act. The law could be upheld or struck down, but the judge determines that—according to prudence, not the Constitution—it should be upheld. (Probably the best statement of this position is contained in Alexander M. Bickel's discussion of the "passive virtues.")[45] Thus, a simple reference to judicial self-restraint is not enough to indicate what is intended—it is still necessary to know what *kind* of self-restraint is involved.

Other implications have been developed in early parts of the paper. For example, there are different notions of "adaptation" proper to the traditional and modern positions: the traditional idea being the adaptability permitted *within* the Constitution, the modern idea being essentially that of adapting (i.e., changing) the Constitution itself.

There is no space in this article to consider the relative merits of the two positions. That question turns on the broader questions of whether the Constitution as interpreted "traditionally" is an adequate basis for modern government and, if not, whether the judiciary should exercise the broad legislative power of balancing fundamental societal principles, given the normal capacities of

[45] 75 *Harvard Law Review* 40 (1961). Another somewhat different example of modern self-restraint is Wechsler's "Toward Neutral Principles of Constitutional Law," 73 *Harvard Law Review* 1 (1959). *Neutral* principles are not necessarily *Constitutional* principles.

judges and the efficacy of those limits on their power which prevent abuses of it.

Let me only suggest, for the moment, that contemporary commentary on the Court (from all parts of the political spectrum) seems increasingly to be concerned with the possibility that the present exercise of judicial review lacks the uniformity and clarity of principle demanded by those who prefer government by law to government by men.[46] Perhaps then the modern form of judicial review, despite the good it may accomplish by furthering liberty and equality in some particular cases, is too much like a "will independent of society" (at least for long periods of time), which, as Madison suggested in *Federalist* No. 51, is "but a precarious security." If such is the case, then at least a serious examination of the traditional view might be in order.

[46] See for example Leonard Levy, *Against the Law: The Nixon Court and Criminal Justice* (New York: Harper and Row, 1974) and Raoul Berger's trenchant critique of Levy in Chapter 18 of *Government By Judiciary*.

Acknowledgments

Abraham, Henry. "'A Bench Happily Filled': Some Historical Reflections on the Supreme Court Appointment Process," *Judicature* 66 (1983): 282–95. Reprinted with the permission of the American Judicature Society.

Benedict, Michael Les. "Preserving Federalism: Reconstruction and the Waite Court," *Supreme Court Review* (1978): 39–79. Reprinted with the permission of the University of Chicago Press, publisher. Copyright 1978 by the University of Chicago Press.

Beth, Loren P. "Civil Liberties and the American Supreme Court," *Political Studies* 6 (1958): 134–46. Reprinted with the permission of Blackwell Publishers.

Choper, Jesse H. "On the Warren Court and Judicial Review," *Catholic University Law Review* 17 (1967-68): 20-43. Reprinted with the permission of the *Catholic University Law Review*.

Cox, Archibald. "The Role of the Supreme Court in American Society," *Marquette Law Review* 1 (1967): 575–93. Reprinted with the permission of the *Marquette Law Review*.

Dahl, Robert A. "Decision-Making in a Democracy: The Supreme Court as a National Policy-Maker," *Journal of Public Law* 6 (1957): 279–95. Reprinted with the permission of the *Journal of Public Law*.

Ely, John Hart. "The Wages of Crying Wolf: a Comment on *Roe* v. *Wade*," *Yale Law Journal* 823 (1973): 920–49. Reprinted by permission of The Yale Law Journal Company and Fred B. Rothman and Company.

Kennedy, Randall L. "*McCleskey* v. *Kemp*: Race, Capital Punishment, and the Supreme Court," *Harvard Law Review* 101 (1988): 1388–1443. Copyright 1988 by the Harvard Law Review Association.

Lasser, William. "The Supreme Court in Periods of Critical Realignment," *Journal of Politics* 47 (1985): 1174–87. Reprinted with the permission of Blackwell Publishers.

Lerner, Ralph. "The Supreme Court as Republican Schoolmaster," *Supreme Court Review* (1967): 127–80. Reprinted with the permission of the University of Chicago Press, publisher. Copyright 1967 by the University of Chicago Press.

Leuchtenburg, William E. "The Origins of Franklin D. Roosevelt's "Court-Packing" Plan," *Supreme Court Review* (1966): 347–400. Reprinted with the permission of the University of Chicago Press, publisher. Copyright 1966 by the University of Chicago Press.

Mason, Alpheus Thomas. "Judicial Activism: Old and New," *Virginia Law Review* 55 (1969): 385–426. Reprinted with the permission of the University of Virginia, School of Law.

McConnell, Michael W. "The Origins and Historical Understanding of Free Exercise of Religion," *Harvard Law Review* 103 (1990): 1409–1517. Copyright 1990 by the Harvard Law Review Association.

Schwartz, Bernard. "Supreme Court Superstars: The Ten Greatest Justices," *Tulsa Law Journal* 31 (1995): 93–159. Reprinted with the permission of the *Tulsa Law Journal.*

Schmidhauser, John R. "'States' Rights' and the Origins of the Supreme Court's Power as Arbiter in Federal-State Relations," *Wayne Law Review* 4 (1958): 101–14. Reprinted by permission of the *Wayne Law Review.*

Post, Robert C. "Racist Speech, Democracy, and the First Amendment," *William and Mary Law Review* 32 (1991): 267–327. Reprinted with the permission of the College of William and Mary.

Weber, Paul J. "The Birth Order Oddity in Supreme Court Appointments," *Presidential Studies Quarterly* 14 (1984): 561–68. Reprinted with the permission of Sage Publications Inc.

White, G. Edward. "The Integrity of Holmes' Jurisprudence," *Hofstra Law Review* 10 (1982): 633–71. Reprinted with the permission of the Hofstra Law Review Association.

Wilkinson, J. Harvie, III. "The Supreme Court, the Equal Protection Clause, and the Three Faces of Constitutional Equality," *Virginia Law Review* 61 (1975): 945–1018. Reprinted with the permission of the University of Virginia, School of Law.

Wolfe, Christopher. "A Theory of U.S. Constitutional History," *Journal of Politics* 43 (1981): 292–316. Reprinted with the permission of Blackwell Publishers.